at 86

THE
DECLINE AND FALL
OF THE ROMAN EMPIRE

★

AN ABRIDGMENT

THE
DECLINE AND FALL
OF THE
ROMAN EMPIRE

BY

EDWARD GIBBON

—•◦◉◦•—

An Abridgment by

D. M. LOW

BONANZA BOOKS
New York

This 1985 edition is published by Bonanza Books,
distributed by Crown Publishers, Inc., by arrangement with
Harcourt Brace Jovanovich, Inc.

Printed and Bound in the United States of America

Library of Congress Cataloging in Publication Data

Gibbon, Edward, 1737-1794
  The decline and fall of the Roman Empire.
  Originally published under title: History of
the decline and fall of the Roman Empire.
  Bibliography; p.
  Includes index.
  1. Rome—History—Empire, 30 B.C.-476 A.D.
2. Byzantine Empire—History, I. Low, D M.
(David Morrice), 1890— . II. Title.
DG311.G54 1985   937'.06   85-16627
ISBN: 0-517-467887
h g f e d c b a

Contents

THE DECLINE OF THE EMPIRE
IN THE EAST

THE CRUSADES

THE END OF THE ROMAN EMPIRE

CONTENTS

THE EPILOGUE: MEDIEVAL ROME AND THE DAWN
OF THE RENAISSANCE

Introduction

THIS abridgement of *The History of The Decline and Fall of the Roman Empire* has been made in the hope of winning new readers and of providing something compendious to those more familiar with a work which can seldom be obtained in less than six volumes and often runs to more.

The Roman Empire and its decline and fall remains to this day the dominant historical event of Europe and the Near East, and nowhere is the march of those events better narrated than in Gibbon's work. It is a commonplace that his book is a fusion of erudition, rarely equalled, and of incomparable literary skill. It is less often recognised how far these qualities are mutually supporting. Although Gibbon's work was written a long time ago, and much has been discovered and written since, there is general agreement that it holds its place, and is all the more readable for its artistic excellence. If *The Decline and Fall* had lost its historical value, it would be vain to hope that it would be read much for its style alone except by a few literary anatomists. A selection therefore should aim at exhibiting both these qualities. Any method of making snippets and piecing them together for their mere factual value would do this great work an injury and conceal its true excellence from the reader. The work has to be viewed as a whole and consideration given to the problem of reducing its bulk, so far as possible, without impairing the impression that it gives of an organic entity.

It was Madame Necker who first described *The Decline and Fall* as a bridge that carried one from the ancient world to the modern. Gibbon himself claimed to have narrated the triumph of barbarism and of religion. Whatever may be one's view or belief, this dictum can hardly be disputed. At the ancient end of his bridge Gibbon very carefully set the scene and announced his themes in three masterly chapters of survey. These have been included with few omissions, since Gibbon's intentions and conclusions cannot be understood without them. Examples of omissions are passages on the Roman provinces and the armed forces, specialised interests which can be better approached in modern works. The scene having been set, the narrative is followed through the main fluctuations and developments of the imperial government down to the final dissolution of the Roman Empire in the West about 476. In the course of this some whole chapters have been omitted, and passages of particularly tangled narrative have been replaced by brief summaries.

In the second half of the work the story is told of nearly a thousand years in contrast to the much shorter period between A.D. 180 and 476. Gibbon's narrative is inevitably swift and often summary, and the limitations of his knowledge and estimate of Byzantine history have long been exposed. Notwithstanding this, it must not be forgotten that much of his most brilliant writing lies in this second half, and his marshalling of the central theme leading to the fall of Constantinople remains unrivalled. The abridgement has adhered to this central theme with some sacrifice of the tributary topics. The essentials even of these have been retained. The rise of Islam, for instance, has been included, but not the extension of Arabian conquest and civilisation as far west as Spain, which by that time lay outside the confines of the Empire. Similarly, the accounts of the development of the modern European nations and of the progress of the Holy Roman Empire have been either omitted or curtailed. On the other hand, the chief invasions of Italy and sacks of Rome that came after the fall of the Empire in the West have been retained with some fulness. Rome could never cease entirely to be an imperial city, and her troubles were never long absent from Gibbon's thoughts.

This sense of Rome's immanence is one of Gibbon's abiding merits as an historian. He perceived the single entity of the Roman Empire with a sureness which has not been bestowed on every later writer. Even when the imperial territories were divided between the Western and Eastern governments, yet there were not two empires, but one empire, and although the use of Latin died out in Constantinople, the Greek citizens regarded themselves, rightly, as Romans, and they called their language "Romaic" even as modern Greek is so called colloquially to this day. When therefore in 1453 the conqueror Mahomet II rode into Constantinople not merely had that city fallen; the Roman Empire, which may be conveniently dated from 27 B.C., had at last come to total extinction. Gibbon's story nevertheless does not end there.

He has told us in a famous passage of his moment of inspiration to write *The Decline and Fall*. He recorded also that his original plan was "circumscribed to the decay of the city rather than of the empire." It was some time before the plan which he eventually achieved was elaborated. This first inspiration was never forgotten. Throughout the work he recurs from time to time to describe the City's progressive decay, and when the final crash of New Rome had been narrated with moving pomp he put the final touch on his masterpiece by adding a tranquil epilogue in which is described the state of medieval and sixteenth-century Rome, which in its general appearance differed but little from the scene which he had himself so minutely examined in the course of his single visit. His thoughts surely reverted to those early days as he wrote these elegiac chapters while at the same time readers are carried back to the opening chapters in which the scene and theme had been so carefully set. *The Decline and Fall* indeed is like some great and brooding symphony in which the *motifs* announced at the beginning are taken up and resolved in a final meditation upon the awful downfall which had ensued, over which nevertheless were already spreading some rays from the dawn of the Renaissance and of that modern world in which the historian was to live and work. So intimately are the life and work of this man intertwined.

Since not every reader who has begun *The Decline and Fall* has finished it, and so may have failed to recognise its consummate planning, it is hoped that it will prove to be one of the merits of this abridgement that the beginning and the end are here brought together under one cover.[1]

The famous 15th and 16th chapters, which describe the rise of Christianity, have been included in their entirety. It was felt that excisions here might give the impression in some way that the editor was putting his own judgment between Gibbon and the reader in this vital narrative. From the publication in 1776 of the first quarto volume of which these chapters were the artfully designed climax, they have remained the most notorious part of Gibbon's handling of Christianity, and for many people indeed the only familiar part. This has been unfortunate. Therefore large portions of the later chapters dealing with theological and ecclesiastical developments have been included. The history of the barbarian invasions and the internal history of the empire in the East cannot be understood without reference to the progress of Arianism, of the doctrines of the Trinity, and of the Incarnation. It is timely here to recall that Cardinal Newman ruefully observed that Gibbon was our only ecclesiastical historian. Time and industry have remedied that. Nevertheless, the most valued historians of the Churches are really at one with Gibbon in denouncing uncritical credulity, idle superstition, and deliberate deception, and in deploring that falling off from primitive ideals towards worldly ambitions which enters into so much of all religious history. Gibbon was the first to make the history of religion a secular study. His successors have for the most part only differed in their approach and tone. Something must here be said on that topic. It is a facile mode among some writers to speak of Gibbon's antipathy to Christianity. It is true that he wrote with levity of things such as Gilbert Murray in our own day dismissed as "pernicious rubbish." But Gibbon never attacks "the pure and simple precepts of the Gospel." He never challenges Christian morality as some later agnostics have done. He always respects sincerity and brave attachment to ideals. Consider his treatment of Cyprian, Athanasius, and John Chrysostom. Consider also the irony which he could apply impartially to Julian the Apostate's religious views and practices. It would, all the same, be idle to pretend that Gibbon had much special sympathy with the spiritual life. His mind had been matured among the *philosophes* of the Continent of whom Lytton Strachey wrote in his essay on Mme du

---

[1] The Editor is, of course, aware that when the opening chapters were written, Gibbon had not decided to carry his history as far as 1453. This consideration need not detract from the conscious perfection of the design as its author finally arranged it.

Deffand, "the scepticism of that generation was the most uncompromising that the world has known; for it did not even trouble to deny; it simply ignored. It presented a blank wall of perfect indifference alike to the mysteries of the universe and to the solutions of them." If in the long run Gibbon's sustained use of "the grave and temperate irony" which he learned from Pascal becomes a trifle wearisome, we should remember, with J. B. Bury, that an oblique approach was a necessary precaution in the eighteenth century when the Church might have stirred in its "fat slumbers" and launched a prosecution for blasphemy.

The ecclesiastics of his day and still more some laymen did not and could not understand what Gibbon was doing. They did not try. They were unnerved by what they saw as an attack on an institution which was bound up with the established order of things. For want of a better case they followed the classic method of abusing the plaintiff's attorney. The target at first sight was an easy one. Gibbon was corpulent and a fop— a combination which the English mind not easily forgives. For a century it was the habit to follow up ridicule of his person with persistent denigration of his character. Since then more sober evaluations of his qualities have demonstrated to those who will take the trouble to listen that while we may still laugh at the man's oddities—it would be priggish not to do so—we must assert that Gibbon was a man of moral as well as intellectual integrity. He was a man of warm humanity as was recognised by his intimate friends, and these qualities pervade his history.

It is natural to make comparisons between the course of the Roman Empire and that of modern European history. In the complacency of sixty years ago Lord Bryce drew an interesting parallel between the Empire of the Augustan Settlement and the British Empire. Today those who feel they are living in a crumbling civilisation may find much to compare in the story of the Roman Empire's decline. Readers may be left to do this for themselves. One or two comments on Gibbon's attitude to his chosen subject may, however, not be out of place.

Gibbon began his work after a youth and early manhood devoted to ancient literature, especially that of the Latin writers, and his outlook is conditioned by the standards which he found in them. He writes almost throughout his work as though he were a cultivated senator of the better days of the empire. His conception of decline and fall would be a natural one for such a senator on the assumption that the age of the Antonines was truly golden, and the assumption would not be weakened by the fact that, as later research has shown, the economic serenity was specious. Having committed himself to this theory of decline not only from prosperity but from the classic literary and philosophic standards, Gibbon pursues his story at least as far as the fall of the empire in the West without glaring inconsistency. His conventional laments over the loss of political freedom do not prevent him from recording with great discernment much political and administrative invention from the principate of Augustus to the organisations of Diocletian and Constantine. Incidentally, his antipathy to court ceremonial, which originating in Asia was adopted by Diocletian and his successors and later spread through all Europe, is not less marked than his indifference to religion.

Gibbon in his senatorial or Roman attitude naturally sees in the barbarian invasions little but waves of destruction. From a different stance, such as Bury took, it can be realised that the invaders were not always seeking to destroy, but to incorporate themselves in the fair domains of ancient civilisation. This difference of viewpoint must vary one's judgment, for instance, on the settlement of Germanic peoples within the imperial frontiers. Moreover, these people brought with them many devices, which have added to the amenities of European life, such as the Græco-Roman world had never discovered.

But most of all the theory of decline to which Gibbon had committed himself leads him astray on the history of the Byzantine civilisation. Modern authors must be sought as antidotes here. The reader may be left with one question. How is it that in one sentence Constantinople is said to be in a state of continuous decay and yet survived as a bulwark of Europe for over a thousand years?

Yet the fact remains that the Empire in the West and in the East came to an end. Later historians have rather busied themselves in discovering the causes of this fall than in plainly narrating it. There is no certain agreement among these investigators. One may turn to Gibbon's cool observations on the extinction of the Empire in the West. There we find him not so much looking for the causes of the fall as expressing wonder that such a complicated organisation could have cohered for so many centuries. We who have seen what were held to be stronger imperial systems disintegrate in a matter of years may applaud Gibbon's wisdom and share his wonder.

When all is allowed for, it is indeed a merit and not a defect that Gibbon took up his stance in the Roman world to tell his story. It takes us into the heart of that world and gives us a single-minded narrative from the light of the ancient authorities and with a fullness of detail from them such as cannot be found in any other modern work. Ultimately Gibbon's work transcends the details of the Roman Empire. It is a prose epic, as has been widely recognised, in which all historical experience is reviewed on an universal scale, and if he saw history as but "the register of the crimes and follies and misfortunes of mankind," his vision in its breadth and compassion places him only lower than the great poets.

With one notable exception the abridgement follows the order of Gibbon's text. The exception is the opening passage headed *Prologue*. This, as noted, is taken from the end of Chapter 3. It seemed to make a better opening than the beginning of Chapter 1, and space precluded the selection of both pieces. So without presuming to rise superior to the author's own judgment it was decided to make this solitary exception to the order of the text. Since each chapter is a carefully conceived and executed piece—a movement as it were in what has been described above as a great symphony, and since these movements come as a rule to a definite and impressive close—it has been the aim as far as possible to include whole chapters. The consequent compensation has to be found in omitting whole chapters. The chapters included bear the numbers assigned to them in the whole work. The reader can then easily refer to the complete chapters. The numbers of the omitted chapters have been noted. When whole chapters have been included no further indication has seemed necessary. The ideal, however, of including whole chapters has necessarily been considerably modified. Where portions have been omitted two means of indication have been employed. If the passages so omitted are relatively unimportant to the continuity of the narrative, a line of asterisks has been used. Over wider gaps a brief summary has been interpolated in italic type. These summaries have been made as succinct as is compatible with supplying the necessary information. Owing to the various cuts in the text, it has not been possible to retain the original chapter headings. Others have been substituted. Typographical economy has also caused the disappearance of Gibbon's marginal headings from paragraph to paragraph. In their place to a limited extent cross-headings have been inserted in the text to break up passages of undue length and to guide the reader. In many cases these are the same or nearly the same as the original paragraph headings.

Interference with what Gibbon wrote has stopped at these external phrases. In no place has the main text been altered or manipulated in order to piece extracts together. The aim has been to print exactly what Gibbon wrote, apart from the modernisation of his spelling which has been generally practised for a long time. The present text has been taken from Dr. William Smith's issue of Dean Milman's edition which first appeared in 1854–55. It is believed to be on the whole the soundest text. Obvious errors of the press appeared in editions published in Gibbon's lifetime. Some of these have been perpetuated in modern editions and, in some, fresh variations have been added. It is improbable that a really accurate text of *The Decline and Fall* exists in any edition.[1] In the present text a few certain corrections have been silently incorporated and one is suggested in a footnote. Modernisation of spelling had been carried a stage further; but a few obsolete forms that carry an eighteenth century flavour have not been sacrificed to an ideal consistency.

[1] For more information on textual points see Miss J. E. Norton's *A Bibliography of the Works of Edward Gibbon* (Oxford, 1940), p. 40. J. B. Bury's great edition unfortunately perpetuated some sixty-eight long-standing errors. One modern reprint contains serious corruptions of its own creating.

There have been previous abridgements and selections of *The Decline and Fall*. None of these has included the footnotes or at least such a generous selection of them as is found here. Only those have been included which are of general interest and are, for the most part, unencumbered with Latin and Greek quotations. They are as Gibbon wrote them with the exception that references to his authorities, which are, naturally, quoted from obsolete editions or works no longer easily accessible, have been deleted. These notes not only illuminate the text. They reflect every aspect of the author's character and might be collected as his table-talk. They have informed, amused, and occasionally, so one hears, shocked generations of readers. The impress of personality with which *The Decline and Fall* as a whole is sealed would have been impaired in some way without an adequate accompaniment of the footnotes.

D. M. Low

Acknowledgments

Many friends have advised me freely on this abridgement, and the zeal with which they urged me on has been unflagging. Had all their suggestions been accepted we should have had nearly a complete text of *The Decline and Fall*. Mr. Frank V. Morley has a pre-eminent claim to my gratitude not only for his discerning encouragement but also for the readiness and unrelenting vigilance with which he performed the big task of reading the proofs. My wife's assistance in the same work has also been invaluable. I most gladly acknowledge the enthusiasm and acumen which Mr. Colin Haycraft brought to the final revision of the selections and the preparation of them for the press. He has also had a corrective hand in the intermediate summaries and the headings. Without his help the work might well have proved too heavy. Finally, to members of Messrs. Chatto and Windus Ltd. in this work, as in others for many years past, I owe my warmest thanks for their interest and consideration at every stage of preparing a much complicated piece of editing.

D. M. L.

THE
DECLINE AND FALL
OF THE
ROMAN EMPIRE

THE GOLDEN AGE OF THE ANTONINES

Prologue

(*Extract from Chapter 3*)

IF a man were called to fix the period in the history of the world during which the condition of the human race was most happy and prosperous, he would, without hesitation, name that which elapsed from the death of Domitian to the accession of Commodus. The vast extent of the Roman empire was governed by absolute power, under the guidance of virtue and wisdom. The armies were restrained by the firm but gentle hand of four successive emperors whose characters and authority commanded involuntary respect. The forms of the civil administration were carefully preserved by Nerva, Trajan, Hadrian, and the Antonines, who delighted in the image of liberty, and were pleased with considering themselves as the accountable ministers of the laws. Such princes deserved the honour of restoring the republic, had the Romans of their days been capable of enjoying a rational freedom.

The labours of these monarchs were overpaid by the immense reward that inseparably waited on their success; by the honest pride of virtue, and by the exquisite delight of beholding the general happiness of which they were the authors. A just but melancholy reflection embittered, however, the noblest of human enjoyments. They must often have recollected the instability of a happiness which depended on the character of a single man. The fatal moment was perhaps approaching, when some licentious youth, or some jealous tyrant, would abuse, to the destruction, that absolute power which they had exerted for the benefit, of their people. The ideal restraints of the senate and the laws might serve to display the virtues, but could never correct the vices, of the emperor. The military force was a blind and irresistible instrument of oppression; and the corruption of Roman manners would always supply flatterers eager to applaud, and ministers prepared to serve, the fear or the avarice, the lust or the cruelty, of their masters.

These gloomy apprehensions had been already justified by the experience of the Romans. The annals of the emperors exhibit a strong and various picture of human nature, which we should vainly seek among the mixed and doubtful characters of modern history. In the conduct of those monarchs we may trace the utmost lines of vice and virtue; the most exalted perfection and the meanest degeneracy of our own species. The golden age of Trajan and the Antonines had been preceded by an age of iron. It is almost superfluous to enumerate the unworthy successors of Augustus. Their unparalleled vices, and the splendid theatre on which they were acted, have saved them from oblivion. The dark unrelenting Tiberius, the furious Caligula, the feeble Claudius, the profligate and cruel Nero, the beastly Vitellius, and the timid inhuman Domitian, are condemned to everlasting infamy. During fourscore years (excepting only the short and doubtful respite of Vespasian's reign) Rome groaned beneath an unremitting tyranny, which exterminated the ancient families of the republic, and was fatal to almost every virtue and every talent that arose in that unhappy period.

Under the reign of these monsters the slavery of the Romans was accompanied with two peculiar circumstances, the one occasioned by their former liberty, the other by their extensive conquests, which rendered their condition more completely wretched than that of the victims of tyranny in any other age or country. From these causes were derived, 1. The exquisite sensibility of the sufferers; and 2. The impossibility of escaping from the hand of the oppressor.

I. When Persia was governed by the descendants of Sefi, a race of princes whose wanton cruelty often stained their divan, their table, and their bed with the blood of their favourites, there is a saying recorded of a young nobleman, That he never departed from the sultan's presence without satisfying himself whether his head was still on his shoulders. The experience of every day might almost justify the scepticism of Rustan. Yet the fatal sword, suspended above him by a single thread, seems not to have disturbed the slumbers, or interrupted the tranquillity, of the Persian. The monarch's frown, he well knew, could level him with the dust; but the stroke of lightning or apoplexy might be equally fatal; and it was the part of a wise man to forget the inevitable calamities of human life in the enjoyment of the fleeting hour. He was dignified with the appellation of the king's slave; had, perhaps, been purchased from obscure parents, in a country which he had never known; and was trained up from his infancy in the severe discipline of the seraglio. His name, his wealth, his honours, were the gift of a master, who might, without injustice, resume what he had bestowed. Rustan's knowledge, if he possessed any, could only serve to confirm his habits by prejudices. His language afforded not words for any form of government, except absolute monarchy. The history of the East informed him that such had ever been the condition of mankind.[1] The Koran, and the interpreters of that divine book, inculcated to him that the sultan was the descendant of the prophet, and the vicegerent of heaven; that patience was the first virtue of a Mussulman, and unlimited obedience the great duty of a subject.

[1] Chardin says that European travellers have diffused among the Persians some ideas of the freedom and mildness of our governments. They have done them a very ill office.

The minds of the Romans were very differently prepared for slavery. Oppressed beneath the weight of their own corruption and of military violence, they for a long while preserved the sentiments, or at least the ideas, of their freeborn ancestors. The education of Helvidius and Thrasea, of Tacitus and Pliny, was the same as that of Cato and Cicero. From Grecian philosophy they had imbibed the justest and most liberal notions of the dignity of human nature and the origin of civil society. The history of their own country had taught them to revere a free, a virtuous, and a victorious commonwealth; to abhor the successful crimes of Cæsar and Augustus; and inwardly to despise those tyrants whom they adored with the most abject flattery. As magistrates and senators they were admitted into the great council which had once dictated laws to the earth, whose name still gave a sanction to the acts of the monarch, and whose authority was so often prostituted to the vilest purposes of tyranny. Tiberius, and those emperors who adopted his maxims, attempted to disguise their murders by the formalities of justice, and perhaps enjoyed a secret pleasure in rendering the senate their accomplice as well as their victim. By this assembly the last of the Romans were condemned for imaginary crimes and real virtues. Their infamous accusers assumed the language of independent patriots, who arraigned a dangerous citizen before the tribunal of his country; and the public service was rewarded by riches and honours. The servile judges professed to assert the majesty of the commonwealth, violated in the person of its first magistrate, whose clemency they most applauded when they trembled the most at his inexorable and impending cruelty. The tyrant beheld their baseness with just contempt, and encountered their secret sentiments of detestation with sincere and avowed hatred for the whole body of the senate.

II. The division of Europe into a number of independent states, connected, however, with each other by the general resemblance of religion, language, and manners, is productive of the most beneficial consequences to the liberty of mankind. A modern tyrant, who should find no resistance either in his own breast or in his people, would soon experience a gentle restraint from the example of his equals, the dread of present censure, the advice of his allies, and the apprehension of his enemies. The object of his displeasure, escaping from the narrow limits of his dominions, would easily obtain, in a happier climate, a secure refuge, a new fortune adequate to his merit, the freedom of complaint, and perhaps the means of revenge. But the empire of the Romans filled the world, and, when that empire fell into the hands of a single person, the world became a safe and dreary prison for his enemies. The slave of Imperial despotism, whether he was condemned to drag his gilded chain in Rome and the senate, or to wear out a life of exile on the barren rock of Seriphus, or the frozen banks of the Danube, expected his fate in silent despair.[1] To resist was fatal, and it was impossible to fly. On every side he was encompassed with a vast extent of sea and land, which he could never hope to traverse without being discovered, seized, and restored to his irritated master. Beyond the frontiers his anxious view could discover nothing, except the ocean, inhospitable deserts, hostile tribes of barbarians, of fierce manners and unknown language, or dependent kings, who would gladly purchase the emperor's protection by the sacrifice of an obnoxious fugitive.[2] "Wherever you are," said Cicero to the exiled Marcellus, "remember that you are equally within the power of the conqueror."

[1] Seriphus was a small rocky island in the Ægean Sea, the inhabitants of which were despised for their ignorance and obscurity. The place of Ovid's exile is well known by his just but unmanly lamentations. It should seem that he only received an order to leave Rome in so many days, and to transport himself to Tomi. Guards and gaolers were unnecessary.

[2] Under Tiberius, a Roman knight attempted to fly to the Parthians. He was stopped in the straits of Sicily; but so little danger did there appear in the example, that the most jealous of tyrants disdained to punish it.

Chapter 1

THE EXTENT AND GENERAL IDEA OF THE ROMAN EMPIRE

*   *   *   *   *

THE principal conquests of the Romans were achieved under the republic; and the emperors, for the most part, were satisfied with preserving those dominions which had been acquired by the policy of the senate, the active emulation of the consuls, and the martial enthusiasm of the people. The seven first centuries were filled with a rapid succession of triumphs; but it was reserved for Augustus to relinquish the ambitious design of subduing the whole earth, and to introduce a spirit of moderation into the public councils. Inclined to peace by his temper and situation, it was easy for him to discover that Rome, in her present exalted situation, had much less to hope than to fear from the chance of arms; and that, in the prosecution of remote wars, the undertaking became every day more difficult, the event more doubtful, and the possession more precarious and less beneficial. The experience of Augustus added weight to these salutary reflections, and effectually convinced him that, by the prudent vigour of his counsels, it would be easy to secure every concession which the safety or the dignity of Rome might require from the most formidable barbarians. Instead of exposing his person and his legions to the arrows of the Parthians, he obtained, by an honourable treaty, the restitution of the standards and prisoners which had been taken in the defeat of Crassus.

His generals, in the early part of his reign, attempted the reduction of Ethiopia and Arabia Felix. They marched near a thousand miles to the south of the tropic; but the heat of the climate soon repelled the invaders, and protected the unwarlike natives of those sequestered regions. The northern countries of Europe scarcely deserved the expense and labour of conquest. The forests and morasses of Germany were filled with a hardy race of barbarians, who despised life when it was separated from freedom; and though, on the first attack, they seemed to yield to the weight of the Roman power, they soon, by a signal act of despair, regained their independence, and reminded Augustus of the vicissitude of fortune. On the death of that emperor, his testament was publicly read in the senate. He bequeathed, as a valuable legacy to his successors, the advice of confining the empire within those limits which nature seemed to have placed as its permanent bulwarks and boundaries: on the west the Atlantic Ocean; the Rhine and Danube on the north;

5

the Euphrates on the east; and towards the south the sandy deserts of Arabia and Africa.

Happily for the repose of mankind, the moderate system recommended by the wisdom of Augustus was adopted by the fears and vices of his immediate successors. Engaged in the pursuit of pleasure, or in the exercise of tyranny, the first Cæsars seldom shewed themselves to the armies, or to the provinces; nor were they disposed to suffer that those triumphs which *their* indolence neglected should be usurped by the conduct and valour of their lieutenants. The military fame of a subject was considered as an insolent invasion of the Imperial prerogative; and it became the duty, as well as interest, of every Roman general, to guard the frontiers intrusted to his care, without aspiring to conquests which might have proved no less fatal to himself than to the vanquished barbarians.

The only accession which the Roman empire received during the first century of the Christian Era was the province of Britain. In this single instance the successors of Cæsar and Augustus were persuaded to follow the example of the former, rather than the precept of the latter. The proximity of its situation to the coast of Gaul seemed to invite their arms; the pleasing, though doubtful, intelligence of a pearl fishery attracted their avarice; and as Britain was viewed in the light of a distinct and insulated world, the conquest scarcely formed any exception to the general system of continental measures. After a war of about forty years, undertaken by the most stupid, maintained by the most dissolute, and terminated by the most timid of all the emperors, the far greater part of the island submitted to the Roman yoke. The various tribes of Britons possessed valour without conduct, and the love of freedom without the spirit of union. They took up arms with savage fierceness; they laid them down, or turned them against each other, with wild inconstancy; and while they fought singly, they were successively subdued. Neither the fortitude of Caractacus, nor the despair of Boadicea, nor the fanaticism of the Druids, could avert the slavery of their country, or resist the steady progress of the Imperial generals, who maintained the national glory, when the throne was disgraced by the weakest or the most vicious of mankind. At the very time when Domitian, confined to his palace, felt the terrors which he inspired, his legions, under the command of the virtuous Agricola, defeated the collected force of the Caledonians at the foot of the Grampian hills; and his fleets, venturing to explore an unknown and dangerous navigation, displayed the Roman arms round every part of the island. The conquest of Britain was considered as already achieved; and it was the design of Agricola to complete and ensure his success by the easy reduction of Ireland, for which, in his opinion, one legion and a few auxiliaries were sufficient. The western isle might be improved into a valuable possession, and the Britons would wear their chains with the less reluctance, if the prospect and example of freedom was on every side removed from before their eyes.

But the superior merit of Agricola soon occasioned his removal from the government of Britain; and for ever disappointed this rational, though extensive, scheme of conquest. Before his departure the prudent general had provided for security as well as for dominion. He had observed that the island is almost divided into two unequal parts by the opposite gulfs, or, as they are now called, the Friths of Scotland. Across the narrow interval of about forty miles he had drawn a line of military stations, which was afterwards fortified, in the reign of Antoninus Pius, by a turf rampart, erected on foundations of stone. This wall of Antoninus, at a small distance beyond the modern cities of Edinburgh and Glasgow, was fixed as the limit of the Roman province. The native Caledonians preserved, in the northern extremity of the island, their wild independence, for which they were not less indebted to their poverty than to their valour. Their incursions were frequently repelled and chastised, but their country was never subdued. The masters of the fairest and most wealthy climates of the globe turned with contempt from gloomy hills assailed by the winter tempest, from lakes concealed in a blue mist, and from cold and lonely heaths, over which the deer of the forest were chased by a troop of naked barbarians.

Such was the state of the Roman frontiers, and such the maxims of Imperial policy, from the death of Augustus to the accession of Trajan. That virtuous and active prince had received the education of a soldier, and possessed the talents of a general. The peaceful system of his predecessors was interrupted by scenes of war and conquest; and the legions, after a long interval, beheld a military emperor at their head. The first exploits of Trajan were against the Dacians, the most warlike of men, who dwelt beyond the Danube, and who, during the reign of Domitian, had insulted, with impunity, the majesty of Rome. To the strength and fierceness of barbarians they added a contempt for life, which was derived from a warm persuasion of the immortality and transmigration of the soul. Decebalus, the Dacian king, approved himself a rival not unworthy of Trajan; nor did he despair of his own and the public fortune, till, by the confession of his enemies, he had exhausted every resource both of valour and policy. This memorable war, with a very short suspension of hostilities, lasted five years; and as the emperor could exert, without control, the whole force of the state, it was terminated by an absolute submission of the barbarians. The new province of Dacia, which formed a second exception to the precept of Augustus, was about thirteen hundred miles in circumference. Its natural boundaries were the Dniester, the Theiss or Tibiscus, the Lower Danube, and the Euxine Sea. The vestiges of a military road may still be traced from the banks of the Danube to the neighbourhood of Bender, a place famous in modern history, and the actual frontier of the Turkish and Russian empires.

Trajan was ambitious of fame; and as long as mankind shall continue to bestow more liberal applause on their destroyers than on their benefactors, the thirst of military glory will ever be the vice of the most exalted characters. The praises of Alexander, transmitted by a succession of poets and historians, had kindled a dangerous emulation in the mind of Trajan. Like him, the Roman emperor undertook an expedition against the nations of the East; but he lamented with a sigh that his advanced age scarcely left him any hopes of equalling the renown of the son of Philip. Yet the success of Trajan, however transient, was rapid and specious. The degenerate Parthians, broken by intestine discord, fled before his arms. He descended the river Tigris in triumph, from the mountains of Armenia to the Persian gulf. He enjoyed the honour of being the first, as he was the last, of the Roman generals who ever navigated that remote sea. His fleets ravaged the coasts of Arabia; and Trajan vainly flattered himself that he was approaching towards the confines of India. Every day the astonished senate received the intelligence of new names and new nations that acknowledged his sway. They were informed that the kings of Bosphorus, Colchis, Iberia, Albania, Osrhoëne, and even the Parthian monarch himself, had accepted their diadems from the hands of the emperor; that the independent tribes of the Median and Carduchian hills had implored his protection; and that the rich countries of Armenia, Mesopotamia, and Assyria, were reduced into the state of provinces. But the death of Trajan soon clouded the splendid prospect; and it was justly to be dreaded that so many distant nations would throw off the unaccustomed yoke, when they were no longer restrained by the powerful hand which had imposed it.

It was an ancient tradition that, when the Capitol was founded by one of the Roman kings, the god Terminus (who presided over boundaries, and was represented according to the fashion of that age by a large stone) alone, among all the inferior deities, refused to yield his place to Jupiter himself. A favourable inference was drawn from his obstinacy, which was interpreted by the augurs as a sure presage that the boundaries of the Roman power would never recede. During many ages the prediction, as it is usual, contributed to its own accomplishment. But though Terminus had resisted the majesty of Jupiter, he submitted to the authority of the emperor Hadrian. The resignation of all the eastern conquests of Trajan was the first measure of his reign. He restored to the Parthians the election of an independent sovereign; withdrew the Roman garrisons from the provinces of Armenia, Mesopotamia, and Assyria; and, in compliance with the precept of Augustus, once more established the Euphrates as the frontier of the empire. Censure, which arraigns the public actions and the private motives of princes, has ascribed to envy a conduct which might be attributed to the prudence and moderation of Hadrian. The various character of that emperor, capable, by turns of the meanest and the most generous sentiments, may afford some colour to the suspicion. It was, however, scarcely in his power to place the superiority of his predecessor in a more conspicuous light than by thus confessing himself unequal to the task of defending the conquests of Trajan.

The martial and ambitious spirit of Trajan formed a very singular contrast with the moderation of his successor. The restless activity of Hadrian was not less remarkable when compared with the gentle repose of Antoninus Pius. The life of the former was almost a perpetual journey; and as he possessed the various talents of the soldier, the statesman, and the scholar, he gratified his curiosity in the discharge of his duty. Careless of the difference of seasons and of climates, he marched on foot, and bareheaded, over the snows of Caledonia, and the sultry plains of the Upper Egypt; nor was there a province of the empire which, in the course of his reign, was not honoured with the presence of the monarch. But the tranquil life of Antoninus Pius was spent in the bosom of Italy; and, during the twenty-three years that he directed the public administration, the longest journeys of that amiable prince extended no farther than from his palace in Rome to the retirement of his Lanuvian villa.

Notwithstanding this difference in their personal conduct, the general system of Augustus was equally adopted and uniformly pursued by Hadrian and by the two Antonines. They persisted in the design of maintaining the dignity of the empire, without attempting to enlarge its limits. By every honourable expedient they invited the friendship of the barbarians; and endeavoured to convince mankind that the Roman power, raised above the temptation of conquest, was actuated only by the love of order and justice. During a long period of forty-three years their virtuous labours were crowned with success; and, if we except a few slight hostilities that served to exercise the legions of the frontier, the reigns of Hadrian and Antoninus Pius offer the fair prospect of universal peace. The Roman name was revered among the most remote nations of the earth. The fiercest barbarians frequently submitted their differences to the arbitration of the emperor; and we are informed by a contemporary historian that he had seen ambassadors who were refused the honour which they came to solicit, of being admitted into the rank of subjects.

A survey of the armed forces and of the provinces has been omitted here.

GENERAL IDEA OF THE ROMAN EMPIRE

This long enumeration of provinces, whose broken fragments have formed so many powerful kingdoms, might almost induce us to forgive the vanity or ignorance of the ancients. Dazzled with the extensive sway, the irresistible strength, and the real or affected moderation of the emperors, they permitted themselves to despise, and sometimes to forget, the outlying countries which had been left in the enjoyment of a barbarous independence; and they gradually usurped the licence of confounding the Roman monarchy with the globe of the earth. But the temper, as well as knowledge, of a modern historian require a more sober and accurate language. He may impress a juster image of the greatness of Rome by observing that the empire was above two thousand miles in breadth, from the wall of Antoninus and the northern limits of Dacia to Mount Atlas and the tropic of Cancer; that it extended in length more than three thousand miles, from the Western Ocean to the Euphrates; that it was situated in the finest part of the Temperate Zone, between the twenty-fourth and fifty-sixth degrees of northern latitude; and that it was supposed to contain above sixteen hundred thousand square miles, for the most part of fertile and well-cultivated land.

Chapter 2

THE UNION AND INTERNAL PROSPERITY OF THE ROMAN EMPIRE. THE PROVINCES AND MONUMENTS. IMPROVEMENT OF AGRICULTURE

IT is not alone by the rapidity or extent of conquest that we should estimate the greatness of Rome. The sovereign of the Russian deserts commands a larger portion of the globe. In the seventh summer after his passage of the Hellespont, Alexander erected the Macedonian trophies on the banks of the Hyphasis. Within less than a century, the irresistible Zingis, and the Mogul princes of his race, spread their cruel devastations and transient empire from the sea of China to the confines of Egypt and Germany. But the firm edifice of Roman power was raised and preserved by the wisdom of ages. The obedient provinces of Trajan and the Antonines were united by laws and adorned by arts. They might occasionally suffer from the partial abuse of delegated authority; but the general principle of government was wise, simple, and beneficent. They enjoyed the religion of their ancestors, whilst in civil honours and advantages they were exalted, by just degrees, to an equality with their conquerors.

I. The policy of the emperors and the senate, as far as it concerned religion, was happily seconded by the reflections of the enlightened, and by the habits of the superstitious, part of their subjects. The various modes of worship which prevailed in the Roman world were all considered by the people as equally true; by the philosopher as equally false; and by the magistrate as equally useful. And thus toleration produced not only mutual indulgence, but even religious concord.

The superstition of the people was not embittered by any mixture of theological rancour; nor was it confined by the chains of any speculative system. The devout polytheist, though fondly attached to his national rites, admitted with implicit faith the different religions of the earth. Fear, gratitude, and curiosity, a dream or an omen, a singular disorder or a distant journey, perpetually disposed him to multiply the articles of his belief, and to enlarge the list of his protectors. The thin texture of the Pagan mythology was interwoven with various, but not discordant materials. As soon as it was allowed that sages and heroes, who had lived or who had died for the benefit of their country, were exalted to a state of power and immortality, it was universally confessed that they deserved, if not the adoration, at least the reverence of all mankind. The deities of a thousand groves and a thousand streams possessed,

11

in peace, their local and respective influence; nor could the Roman who deprecated the wrath of the Tiber deride the Egyptian who presented his offering to the beneficent genius of the Nile. The visible powers of Nature, the planets, and the elements, were the same throughout the universe. The invisible governors of the moral world were inevitably cast in a similar mould of fiction and allegory. Every virtue, and even vice, acquired its divine representative; every art and profession its patron, whose attributes, in the most distant ages and countries, were uniformly derived from the character of their peculiar votaries. A republic of gods of such opposite tempers and interests required, in every system, the moderating hand of a supreme magistrate, who, by the progress of knowledge and flattery, was gradually invested with the sublime perfections of an Eternal Parent and an Omnipotent Monarch. Such was the mild spirit of antiquity, that the nations were less attentive to the difference, than to the resemblance of their religious worship. The Greek, the Roman, and the Barbarian, as they met before their respective altars, easily persuaded themselves that, under various names and with various ceremonies, they adored the same deities. The elegant mythology of Homer gave a beautiful, and almost a regular form to the polytheism of the ancient world.

The philosophers of Greece deduced their morals from the nature of man, rather than from that of God. They meditated, however, on the Divine Nature as a very curious and important speculation; and in the profound inquiry they displayed the strength and weakness of the human understanding. Of the four most celebrated schools, the Stoics and the Platonists endeavoured to reconcile the jarring interests of reason and piety. They have left us the most sublime proofs of the existence and perfections of the first cause; but, as it was impossible for them to conceive the creation of matter, the workman in the Stoic philosophy was not sufficiently distinguished from the work; whilst, on the contrary, the Spiritual God of Plato and his disciples resembled an idea rather than a substance. The opinions of the Academics and Epicureans were of a less religious cast; but whilst the modest science of the former induced them to doubt, the positive ignorance of the latter urged them to deny, the providence of a Supreme Ruler. The spirit of inquiry, prompted by emulation and supported by freedom, had divided the public teachers of philosophy into a variety of contending sects; but the ingenuous youth, who, from every part, resorted to Athens and the other seats of learning in the Roman empire, were alike instructed in every school to reject and to despise the religion of the multitude. How, indeed, was it possible that a philosopher should accept as divine truths the idle tales of the poets, and the incoherent traditions of antiquity; or that he should adore as gods those imperfect beings whom he must have despised as men? Against such unworthy adversaries Cicero condescended to employ the arms of reason and eloquence; but the satire of Lucian was a much more adequate, as well as more efficacious weapon. We may be well assured that a writer conversant with the world would never have ventured to expose the gods of his country to public ridicule, had they not already been the objects of secret contempt among the polished and enlightened orders of society.

Notwithstanding the fashionable irreligion which prevailed in the age of the Antonines, both the interest of the priests and the credulity of the people were sufficiently respected. In their writings and conversation the philosophers of antiquity asserted the independent dignity of reason; but they resigned their actions to the commands of law and of custom. Viewing with a smile of pity and indulgence the various errors of the vulgar, they diligently practised the ceremonies of their fathers, devoutly frequented the temples of the gods, and, sometimes condescending to act a part on the theatre of superstition, they concealed the sentiments of an Atheist under the sacerdotal robes. Reasoners of such a temper were scarcely inclined to wrangle about their respective modes of faith or of worship. It was indifferent to them what shape the folly of the multitude might choose to assume; and they approached, with the same inward contempt and the same external reverence, the altars of the Libyan, the Olympian, or the Capitoline Jupiter.

It is not easy to conceive from what motives a spirit of persecution could introduce itself into the Roman councils. The magistrates could not be actuated by a blind though honest bigotry, since the magistrates were themselves philosophers; and the schools of Athens had given laws to the senate. They could not be impelled by ambition or avarice, as the temporal and ecclesiastical powers were united in the same hands. The pontiffs were chosen among the most illustrious of the senators; and the office of Supreme Pontiff was constantly exercised by the emperors themselves. They knew and valued the advantages of religion, as it is connected with civil government. They encouraged the public festivals which humanize the manners of the people. They managed the arts of divination as a convenient instrument of policy; and they respected, as the firmest bond of society, the useful persuasion that, either in this or in a future life, the crime of perjury is most assuredly punished by the avenging gods. But, whilst they acknowledged the general advantages of religion, they were convinced that the various modes of worship contributed alike to the same salutary purposes; and that, in every country, the form of superstition which had received the sanction of time and experience was the best adapted to the climate and to its inhabitants. Avarice and taste very frequently despoiled the vanquished nations of the elegant statues of their gods and the rich ornaments of their temples; but, in the exercise of the religion which they derived from their ancestors, they uniformly experienced the indulgence, and even protection, of the Roman conquerors. The province of Gaul seems, and indeed only seems, an exception to this universal toleration.

Under the specious pretext of abolishing human sacrifices, the emperors Tiberius and Claudius suppressed the dangerous power of the Druids: but the priests themselves, their gods, and their altars, subsisted in peaceful obscurity till the final destruction of Paganism.

Rome, the capital of a great monarchy, was incessantly filled with subjects and strangers from every part of the world, who all introduced and enjoyed the favourite superstitions of their native country. Every city in the empire was justified in maintaining the purity of its ancient ceremonies; and the Roman senate, using the common privilege, sometimes interposed to check this inundation of foreign rites. The Egyptian superstition, of all the most contemptible and abject, was frequently prohibited; the temples of Serapis and Isis demolished, and their worshippers banished from Rome and Italy. But the zeal of fanaticism prevailed over the cold and feeble efforts of policy. The exiles returned, the proselytes multiplied, the temples were restored with increasing splendour, and Isis and Serapis at length assumed their place among the Roman deities. Nor was this indulgence a departure from the old maxims of government. In the purest ages of the commonwealth, Cybele and Æsculapius had been invited by solemn embassies; and it was customary to tempt the protectors of besieged cities by the promise of more distinguished honours than they possessed in their native country. Rome gradually became the common temple of her subjects; and the freedom of the city was bestowed on all the gods of mankind.

II. The narrow policy of preserving, without any foreign mixture, the pure blood of the ancient citizens, had checked the fortune and hastened the ruin of Athens and Sparta. The aspiring genius of Rome sacrificed vanity to ambition, and deemed it more prudent, as well as honourable, to adopt virtue and merit for her own wheresoever they were found, among slaves or strangers, enemies or barbarians. During the most flourishing era of the Athenian commonwealth the number of citizens gradually decreased from about thirty to twenty-one thousand. If, on the contrary, we study the growth of the Roman republic, we may discover that, notwithstanding the incessant demands of wars and colonies, the citizens, who, in the first census of Servius Tullius, amounted to no more than eighty-three thousand, were multiplied, before the commencement of the Social War, to the number of four hundred and sixty-three thousand men able to bear arms in the service of their country. When the allies of Rome claimed an equal share of honours and privileges, the senate indeed preferred the chance of arms to an ignominious concession. The Samnites and the Lucanians paid the severe penalty of their rashness; but the rest of the Italian states, as they successively returned to their duty, were admitted into the bosom of the republic, and soon contributed to the ruin of public freedom. Under a democratical government the citizens exercise the powers of sovereignty; and those powers will be first abused, and afterwards lost, if they are committed to an unwieldy multitude. But when the popular assemblies had been suppressed by the administration of the emperors, the conquerors were distinguished from the vanquished nations only as the first and most honourable order of subjects; and their increase, however rapid, was no longer exposed to the same dangers. Yet the wisest princes, who adopted the maxims of Augustus, guarded with the strictest care the dignity of the Roman name, and diffused the freedom of the city with a prudent liberality.

Till the privileges of Romans had been progressively extended to all the inhabitants of the empire, an important distinction was preserved between Italy and the provinces. The former was esteemed the centre of public unity, and the firm basis of the constitution. Italy claimed the birth, or at least the residence, of the emperors and the senate. The estates of the Italians were exempt from taxes, their persons from the arbitrary jurisdiction of governors. Their municipal corporations, formed after the perfect model of the capital, were intrusted, under the immediate eye of the supreme power, with the execution of the laws. From the foot of the Alps to the extremity of Calabria all the natives of Italy were born citizens of Rome. Their partial distinctions were obliterated, and they insensibly coalesced into one great nation, united by language, manners, and civil institutions, and equal to the weight of a powerful empire. The republic gloried in her generous policy, and was frequently rewarded by the merit and services of her adopted sons. Had she always confined the distinction of Romans to the ancient families within the walls of the city, that immortal name would have been deprived of some of its noblest ornaments. Virgil was a native of Mantua; Horace was inclined to doubt whether he should call himself an Apulian or a Lucanian: it was in Padua that an historian was found worthy to record the majestic series of Roman victories. The patriot family of the Catos emerged from Tusculum; and the little town of Arpinum claimed the double honour of producing Marius and Cicero, the former of whom deserved, after Romulus and Camillus, to be styled the Third Founder of Rome; and the latter, after saving his country from the designs of Catiline, enabled her to contend with Athens for the palm of eloquence.

THE PROVINCES

The provinces of the empire (as they have been described in the preceding chapter) were destitute of any public force or constitutional freedom. In Etruria, in Greece, and in Gaul, it was the first care of the senate to dissolve those dangerous confederacies which taught mankind that, as the Roman arms prevailed by division, they might be resisted by union. Those princes, whom the ostentation of gratitude or generosity permitted for a while to hold a precarious sceptre, were dismissed from their thrones as soon as they had performed their appointed task of fashioning to the yoke the vanquished nations. The free states and cities which had embraced the cause of Rome were rewarded with a nominal alliance, and insensibly sunk into real servitude. The public authority was everywhere exercised by the ministers of the senate and of the emperors, and that authority was absolute and without control. But the same salutary maxims of government, which had secured the peace and obedience of Italy, were extended to the most distant conquests. A nation of Romans was gradually formed in the provinces, by the double expedient of introducing colonies, and of admitting the most faithful and deserving of the provincials to the freedom of Rome.

"Wheresoever the Roman conquers, he inhabits," is a very just observation of Seneca, confirmed by history and experience. The natives of Italy, allured by pleasure or by interest, hastened to enjoy the advantages of victory; and we may remark, that, about forty years after the reduction of Asia, eighty thousand Romans were massacred in one day by the cruel orders of Mithridates. These voluntary exiles were engaged, for the most part, in the occupations of commerce, agriculture, and the farm of the revenue. But after the legions were rendered permanent by the emperors, the provinces were peopled by a race of soldiers; and the veterans, whether they received the reward of their service in land or in money, usually settled with their families in the country where they had honourably spent their youth. Throughout the empire, but more particularly in the western parts, the most fertile districts, and the most convenient situations, were reserved for the establishment of colonies; some of which were of a civil, and others of a military nature. In their manners and internal policy the colonies formed a perfect representation of their great parent; and as they were soon endeared to the natives by the ties of friendship and alliance, they effectually diffused a reverence for the Roman name, and a desire, which was seldom disappointed, of sharing, in due time, its honours and advantages. The municipal cities insensibly equalled the rank and splendour of the colonies; and in the reign of Hadrian it was disputed which was the preferable condition, of those societies which had issued from, or those which had been received into, the bosom of Rome. The right of Latium, as it was called, conferred on the cities to which it had been granted a more partial favour. The magistrates only, at the expiration of their office, assumed the quality of Roman citizens; but as those offices were annual, in a few years they circulated round the principal families. Those of the provincials who were permitted to bear arms in the legions; those who exercised any civil employment; all, in a word, who performed any public service or displayed any personal talents, were rewarded with a present, whose value was continually diminished by the increasing liberality of the emperors. Yet even in the age of the Antonines, when the freedom of the city had been bestowed on the greater number of their subjects, it was still accompanied with very solid advantages. The bulk of the people acquired, with that title, the benefit of the Roman laws, particularly in the interesting articles of marriage, testaments, and inheritances; and the road of fortune was open to those whose pretensions were seconded by favour or merit. The grandsons of the Gauls who had besieged Julius Cæsar in Alesia commanded legions, governed provinces, and were admitted into the senate of Rome. Their ambition, instead of disturbing the tranquillity of the state, was intimately connected with its safety and greatness.

So sensible were the Romans of the influence of language over national manners, that it was their most serious care to extend, with the progress of their arms, the use of the Latin tongue. The ancient dialects of Italy, the Sabine, the Etruscan, and the Venetian, sunk into oblivion; but in the provinces, the East was less docile than the West to the voice of its victorious preceptors. This obvious difference marked the two portions of the empire with a distinction of colours, which, though it was in some degree concealed during the meridian splendour of prosperity, became gradually more visible as the shades of night descended upon the Roman world. The western countries were civilised by the same hands which subdued them. As soon as the barbarians were reconciled to obedience, their minds were opened to any new impressions of knowledge and politeness. The language of Virgil and Cicero, though with some inevitable mixture of corruption, was so universally adopted in Africa, Spain, Gaul, Britain, and Pannonia, that the faint traces of the Punic or Celtic idioms were preserved only in the mountains or among the peasants. Education and study insensibly inspired the natives of those countries with the sentiments of Romans; and Italy gave fashions, as well as laws, to her Latin provincials. They solicited with more ardour, and obtained with more facility, the freedom and honours of the state; supported the national dignity in letters and in arms; and, at length, in the person of Trajan, produced an emperor whom the Scipios would not have disowned for their countryman. The situation of the Greeks was very different from that of the barbarians. The former had been long since civilized and corrupted. They had too much taste to relinquish their language, and too much vanity to adopt any foreign institutions. Still preserving the prejudices, after they had lost the virtues, of their ancestors, they affected to despise the unpolished manners of the Roman conquerors, whilst they were compelled to respect their superior wisdom and power.[1] Nor was the influence of the Grecian language and sentiments confined to the narrow limits of that once celebrated country. Their empire, by the progress of colonies and conquest, had been diffused from the Adriatic to the Euphrates and the Nile. Asia was covered with Greek cities, and the long reign of the

[1] There is not, I believe, from Dionysius to Libanius, a single Greek critic who mentions Virgil or Horace. They seem ignorant that the Romans had any good writers.

Macedonian kings had introduced a silent revolution into Syria and Egypt. In their pompous courts those princes united the elegance of Athens with the luxury of the East, and the example of the court was imitated, at an humble distance, by the higher ranks of their subjects. Such was the general division of the Roman empire into the Latin and Greek languages. To these we may add a third distinction for the body of the natives in Syria, and especially in Egypt. The use of their ancient dialects, by secluding them from the commerce of mankind, checked the improvements of those barbarians. The slothful effeminacy of the former exposed them to the contempt, the sullen ferociousness of the latter excited the aversion, of the conquerors. Those nations had sub-mitted to the Roman power, but they seldom desired or deserved the freedom of the city: and it was remarked that more than two hundred and thirty years elapsed after the ruin of the Ptolemies, before an Egyptian was admitted into the senate of Rome.

It is a just though trite observation, that victorious Rome was herself subdued by the arts of Greece. Those immortal writers who still com-mand the admiration of modern Europe soon became the favourite object of study and imitation in Italy and the western provinces. But the elegant amusements of the Romans were not suffered to interfere with their sound maxims of policy. Whilst they acknowledged the charms of the Greek, they asserted the dignity of the Latin tongue, and the exclusive use of the latter was inflexibly maintained in the adminis-tration of civil as well as military government. The two languages exercised at the same time their separate jurisdiction throughout the empire: the former, as the natural idiom of science; the latter, as the legal dialect of public transactions. Those who united letters with business were equally conversant with both; and it was almost im-possible, in any province, to find a Roman subject, of a liberal educa-tion, who was at once a stranger to the Greek and to the Latin language.

It was by such institutions that the nations of the empire insensibly melted away into the Roman name and people. But there still remained, in the centre of every province and of every family, an unhappy condi-tion of men who endured the weight, without sharing the benefits, of society. In the free states of antiquity the domestic slaves were exposed to the wanton rigour of despotism. The perfect settlement of the Ro-man empire was preceded by ages of violence and rapine. The slaves consisted, for the most part, of barbarian captives, taken in thousands by the chance of war, purchased at a vile price, accustomed to a life of independence, and impatient to break and to revenge their fetters. Against such internal enemies, whose desperate insurrections had more than once reduced the republic to the brink of destruction, the most severe regulations and the most cruel treatment seemed almost justified by the great law of self-preservation. But when the principal nations of Europe, Asia, and Africa were united under the laws of one sovereign, the source of foreign supplies flowed with much less abundance, and the Romans were reduced to the milder but more tedious method of propagation. In their numerous families, and particularly in their country estates, they encouraged the marriage of their slaves. The sentiments of nature, the habits of education, and the possession of a dependent species of property, contributed to alleviate the hardships of servitude. The existence of a slave became an object of greater value; and though his happiness still depended on the temper and circumstances of the master, the humanity of the latter, instead of being restrained by fear, was encouraged by the sense of his own interest. The progress of manners was accelerated by the virtue or policy of the emperors; and by the edicts of Hadrian and the Antonines the protection of the laws was extended to the most abject part of mankind. The jurisdiction of life and death over the slaves, a power long exercised and often abused, was taken out of private hands, and reserved to the magistrates alone. The subterraneous prisons were abolished; and, upon a just complaint of intolerable treatment, the injured slave obtained either his deliverance or a less cruel master.

Hope, the best comfort of our imperfect condition, was not denied to the Roman slave; and if he had any opportunity of rendering himself either useful or agreeable, he might very naturally expect that the diligence and fidelity of a few years would be rewarded with the inestimable gift of freedom. The benevolence of the master was so frequently prompted by the meaner suggestions of vanity and avarice, that the laws found it more necessary to restrain than to encourage a profuse and undistinguishing liberality, which might degenerate into a very dangerous abuse. It was a maxim of ancient jurisprudence, that a slave had not any country of his own; he acquired with his liberty an admission into the political society of which his patron was a member. The consequences of this maxim would have prostituted the privileges of the Roman city to a mean and promiscuous multitude. Some seasonable exceptions were therefore provided; and the honourable distinction was confined to such slaves only as, for just causes, and with the approbation of the magistrate, should receive a solemn and legal manumission. Even these chosen freedmen obtained no more than the private rights of citizens, and were rigorously excluded from civil or military honours. Whatever might be the merit or fortune of their sons, they likewise were esteemed unworthy of a seat in the senate, nor were the traces of a servile origin allowed to be completely obliterated till the third or fourth generation. Without destroying the distinction of ranks, a distant prospect of freedom and honours was presented, even to those whom pride and prejudice almost disdained to number among the human species.

It was once proposed to discriminate the slaves by a peculiar habit; but it was justly apprehended that there might be some danger in acquainting them with their own numbers. Without interpreting in their utmost strictness the liberal appellations of legions and myriads, we may venture to pronounce that the proportion of slaves who were valued as property was more considerable than that of servants, who can be computed only as an expense. The youths of a promising genius were instructed in the arts and sciences, and their price was ascertained by the degree of their skill and talents. Almost every profession, either liberal or mechanical, might be found in the household of an opulent senator. The ministers of pomp and sensuality were multiplied beyond the conception of modern luxury. It was more for the interest of the merchant or manufacturer to purchase than to hire his workmen; and in the country slaves were employed as the cheapest and most laborious instruments of agriculture. To confirm the general observation, and to display the multitude of slaves, we might allege a variety of particular instances. It was discovered, on a very melancholy occasion, that four hundred slaves were maintained in a single palace of Rome. The same number of four hundred belonged to an estate which an African widow, of a very private condition, resigned to her son, whilst she reserved for herself a much larger share of her property. A freedman, under the reign of Augustus, though his fortune had suffered great losses in the civil wars, left behind him three thousand six hundred yoke of oxen, two hundred and fifty thousand head of smaller cattle, and, what was almost included in the description of cattle, four thousand one hundred and sixteen slaves.

The number of subjects who acknowledged the laws of Rome, of citizens, of provincials, and of slaves, cannot now be fixed with such a degree of accuracy as the importance of the object would deserve. We are informed that, when the emperor Claudius exercised the office of censor, he took an account of six millions nine hundred and forty-five thousand Roman citizens, who, with the proportion of women and children, must have amounted to about twenty millions of souls. The multitude of subjects of an inferior rank was uncertain and fluctuating. But, after weighing with attention every circumstance which could influence the balance, it seems probable that there existed in the time of Claudius about twice as many provincials as there were citizens, of either sex and of every age; and that the slaves were at least equal in number to the free inhabitants of the Roman world. The total amount of this imperfect calculation would rise to about one hundred and twenty millions of persons: a degree of population which possibly exceeds that of modern Europe, and forms the most numerous society that has ever been united under the same system of government.

Domestic peace and union were the natural consequences of the moderate and comprehensive policy embraced by the Romans. If we turn our eyes towards the monarchies of Asia, we shall behold despotism in the centre and weakness in the extremities; the collection of the revenue, or the administration of justice, enforced by the presence of an army; hostile barbarians established in the heart of the country, hereditary satraps usurping the dominion of the provinces, and subjects inclined to rebellion, though incapable of freedom. But the obedience of the Roman world was uniform, voluntary, and permanent. The vanquished nations, blended into one great people, resigned the hope, nay even the wish, of resuming their independence, and scarcely considered their own existence as distinct from the existence of Rome. The established authority of the emperors pervaded without an effort the wide extent of their dominions, and was exercised with the same facility on the banks of the Thames, or of the Nile, as on those of the Tiber. The legions were destined to serve against the public enemy, and the civil magistrate seldom required the aid of a military force. In this state of general security, the leisure as well as opulence both of the prince and people were devoted to improve and to adorn the Roman empire.

ROMAN MONUMENTS

Among the innumerable monuments of architecture constructed by the Romans, how many have escaped the notice of history, how few have resisted the ravages of time and barbarism! And yet even the majestic ruins that are still scattered over Italy and the provinces would be sufficient to prove that those countries were once the seat of a polite and powerful empire. Their greatness alone, or their beauty, might deserve our attention: but they are rendered more interesting by two important circumstances, which connect the agreeable history of the arts with the more useful history of human manners. Many of those works were erected at private expense, and almost all were intended for public benefit.

It is natural to suppose that the greatest number, as well as the most considerable of the Roman edifices, were raised by the emperors, who possessed so unbounded a command both of men and money. Augustus was accustomed to boast that he had found his capital of brick, and that he had left it of marble. The strict economy of Vespasian was the source of his magnificence. The works of Trajan bear the stamp of his genius. The public monuments with which Hadrian adorned every province of the empire were executed not only by his orders, but under his immediate inspection. He was himself an artist; and he loved the arts, as they conduced to the glory of the monarch. They were encouraged by the Antonines, as they contributed to the happiness of the people. But if the emperors were the first, they were not the only architects of their dominions. Their example was universally imitated by their principal subjects, who were not afraid of declaring to the world that they had spirit to conceive, and wealth to accomplish, the noblest undertakings. Scarcely had the proud structure of the Coliseum been dedicated at

Rome, before edifices, of a smaller scale indeed, but of the same design and materials, were erected for the use, and at the expense, of the cities of Capua and Verona. The inscription of the stupendous bridge of Alcantara attests that it was thrown over the Tagus by the contribution of a few Lusitanian communities. When Pliny was intrusted with the government of Bithynia and Pontus, provinces by no means the richest or most considerable of the empire, he found the cities within his jurisdiction striving with each other in every useful and ornamental work that might deserve the curiosity of strangers or the gratitude of their citizens. It was the duty of the proconsul to supply their deficiencies, to direct their taste, and sometimes to moderate their emulation. The opulent senators of Rome and the provinces esteemed it an honour, and almost an obligation, to adorn the splendour of their age and country; and the influence of fashion very frequently supplied the want of taste or generosity. Among a crowd of these private benefactors, we may select Herodes Atticus, an Athenian citizen, who lived in the age of the Antonines. Whatever might be the motive of his conduct, his magnificence would have been worthy of the greatest kings.

The family of Herod, at least after it had been favoured by fortune, was lineally descended from Cimon and Miltiades, Theseus and Cecrops, Æacus and Jupiter. But the posterity of so many gods and heroes was fallen in the most abject state. His grandfather had suffered by the hands of justice, and Julius Atticus, his father, must have ended his life in poverty and contempt, had he not discovered an immense treasure buried under an old house, the last remains of his patrimony. According to the rigour of law, the emperor might have asserted his claim, and the prudent Atticus prevented, by a frank confession, the officiousness of informers. But the equitable Nerva, who then filled the throne, refused to accept any part of it, and commanded him to use, without scruple, the present of fortune. The cautious Athenian still insisted that the treasure was too considerable for a subject, and that he knew not how to *use it*. *Abuse it then*, replied the monarch, with a goodnatured peevishness; for it is your own. Many will be of opinion that Atticus literally obeyed the emperor's last instructions, since he expended the greatest part of his fortune, which was much increased by an advantageous marriage, in the service of the public. He had obtained for his son Herod the prefecture of the free cities of Asia; and the young magistrate, observing that the town of Troas was indifferently supplied with water, obtained from the munificence of Hadrian three hundred myriads of drachms (about a hundred thousand pounds) for the construction of a new aqueduct. But in the execution of the work the charge amounted to more than double the estimate, and the officers of the revenue began to murmur, till the generous Atticus silenced their complaints by requesting that he might be permitted to take upon himself the whole additional expense.

The ablest preceptors of Greece and Asia had been invited by liberal rewards to direct the education of young Herod. Their pupil soon became a celebrated orator, according to the useless rhetoric of that age, which, confining itself to the schools, disdained to visit either the Forum or the Senate. He was honoured with the consulship at Rome: but the greatest part of his life was spent in a philosophic retirement at Athens and his adjacent villas; perpetually surrounded by sophists, who acknowledged, without reluctance, the superiority of a rich and generous rival. The monuments of his genius have perished; some considerable ruins still preserve the fame of his taste and munificence: modern travellers have measured the remains of the stadium which he constructed at Athens. It was six hundred feet in length, built entirely of white marble, capable of admitting the whole body of the people, and finished in four years, whilst Herod was president of the Athenian games. To the memory of his wife Regilla he dedicated a theatre, scarcely to be paralleled in the empire: no wood except cedar, very curiously carved, was employed in any part of the building. The Odeum, designed by Pericles for musical performances and the rehearsal of new tragedies, had been a trophy of the victory of the arts over barbaric greatness; as the timbers employed in the construction consisted chiefly of the masts of the Persian vessels. Notwithstanding the repairs bestowed on that ancient edifice by a king of Cappadocia, it was again fallen to decay. Herod restored its ancient beauty and magnificence. Nor was the liberality of that illustrious citizen confined to the walls of Athens. The most splendid ornaments bestowed on the temple of Neptune in the Isthmus, a theatre at Corinth, a stadium at Delphi, a bath at Thermopylæ, and an aqueduct at Canusium in Italy, were insufficient to exhaust his treasures. The people of Epirus, Thessaly, Eubœa, Bœotia, and Peloponnesus, experienced his favours; and many inscriptions of the cities of Greece and Asia gratefully style Herodes Atticus their patron and benefactor.

In the commonwealths of Athens and Rome, the modest simplicity of private houses announced the equal condition of freedom; whilst the sovereignty of the people was represented in the majestic edifices destined to the public use; nor was this republican spirit totally extinguished by the introduction of wealth and monarchy. It was in works of national honour and benefit that the most virtuous of the emperors affected to display their magnificence. The golden palace of Nero excited a just indignation, but the vast extent of ground which had been usurped by his selfish luxury was more nobly filled under the succeeding reigns by the Coliseum, the baths of Titus, the Claudian portico, and the temples dedicated to the goddess of Peace and to the genius of Rome. These monuments of architecture, the property of the Roman people, were adorned with the most beautiful productions of Grecian painting and sculpture; and in the temple of Peace a very curious [1] library was open to the curiosity of the learned. At a small distance from thence was situated the Forum of Trajan. It was surrounded with a lofty portico in the form of a quadrangle, into which four triumphal arches opened a noble and spacious entrance: in the centre arose a column of marble, whose height, of one hundred and ten feet, denoted the elevation of the hill that had been cut away. This column, which still subsists in its ancient beauty, exhibited an exact representation of the Dacian victories of its founder. The veteran soldier contemplated the story of his own campaigns, and, by an easy illusion of national vanity, the peaceful citizen associated himself to the honours of the triumph. All the other quarters of the capital, and all the provinces of the empire, were embellished by the same liberal spirit of public magnificence, and were filled with amphitheatres, theatres, temples, porticos, triumphal arches, baths, and aqueducts, all variously conducive to the health, the devotion, and the pleasures of the meanest citizen. The last mentioned of those edifices deserve our peculiar attention. The boldness of the enterprise, the solidity of the execution, and the uses to which they were subservient, rank the aqueducts among the noblest monuments of Roman genius and power. The aqueducts of the capital claim a just pre-eminence; but the curious traveller, who, without the light of history, should examine those of Spoleto, of Metz, or of Segovia, would very naturally conclude that those provincial towns had formerly been the residence of some potent monarch. The solitudes of Asia and Africa were once covered with flourishing cities, whose populousness, and even whose existence, was derived from such artificial supplies of a perennial stream of fresh water.

We have computed the inhabitants, and contemplated the public works, of the Roman empire. The observation of the number and greatness of its cities will serve to confirm the former and to multiply the latter. It may not be unpleasing to collect a few scattered instances relative to that subject, without forgetting, however, that, from the vanity of nations and the poverty of language, the vague appellation of city has been indifferently bestowed on Rome and upon Laurentum. I. *Ancient* Italy is said to have contained eleven hundred and ninety-seven cities; and for whatsoever era of antiquity the expression might be intended, there is not any reason to believe the country less populous in the age of the Antonines than in that of Romulus. The petty states of Latium were contained within the metropolis of the empire, by whose superior influence they had been attracted. Those parts of Italy which have so long languished under the lazy tyranny of priests and viceroys had been afflicted only by the more tolerable calamities of war; and the first symptoms of decay which *they* experienced were amply compensated by the rapid improvements of the Cisalpine Gaul. The splendour of

[1] It would seem at least probable that Gibbon wrote or meant to write "copious".
—D.M.L.

Verona may be traced in its remains: yet Verona was less celebrated than Aquileia or Padua, Milan or Ravenna. II. The spirit of improvement had passed the Alps, and been felt even in the woods of Britain, which were gradually cleared away to open a free space for convenient and elegant habitations. York was the seat of government; London was already enriched by commerce; and Bath was celebrated for the salutary effects of its medicinal waters. Gaul could boast of her twelve hundred cities; and though, in the northern parts, many of them, without excepting Paris itself, were little more than the rude and imperfect townships of a rising people, the southern provinces imitated the wealth and elegance of Italy. Many were the cities of Gaul—Marseilles, Arles, Nismes, Narbonne, Toulouse, Bordeaux, Autun, Vienne, Lyons, Langres, and Trèves—whose ancient condition might sustain an equal, and perhaps advantageous comparison with their present state. With regard to Spain, that country flourished as a province, and has declined as a kingdom. Exhausted by the abuse of her strength, by America, and by superstition, her pride might possibly be confounded, if we required such a list of three hundred and sixty cities as Pliny has exhibited under the reign of Vespasian. III. Three hundred African cities had once acknowledged the authority of Carthage, nor is it likely that their numbers diminished under the administration of the emperors: Carthage itself rose with new splendour from its ashes; and that capital, as well as Capua and Corinth, soon recovered all the advantages which can be separated from independent sovereignty. IV. The provinces of the East present the contrast of Roman magnificence with Turkish barbarism. The ruins of antiquity scattered over uncultivated fields, and ascribed by ignorance to the power of magic, scarcely afford a shelter to the oppressed peasant or wandering Arab. Under the reign of the Cæsars, the proper Asia alone contained five hundred populous cities, enriched with all the gifts of nature, and adorned with all the refinements of art. Eleven cities of Asia had once disputed the honour of dedicating a temple to Tiberius, and their respective merits were examined by the senate. Four of them were immediately rejected as unequal to the burden; and among these was Laodicea, whose splendour is still displayed in its ruins. Laodicea collected a very considerable revenue from its flocks of sheep, celebrated for the fineness of their wool, and had received, a little before the contest, a legacy of above four hundred thousand pounds by the testament of a generous citizen. If such was the poverty of Laodicea, what must have been the wealth of those cities whose claim appeared preferable, and particularly of Pergamus, of Smyrna, and of Ephesus, who so long disputed with each other the titular primacy of Asia? The capitals of Syria and Egypt held a still superior rank in the empire; Antioch and Alexandria looked down with disdain on a crowd of dependent cities, and yielded with reluctance to the majesty of Rome itself.

All these cities were connected with each other, and with the capital, by the public highways, which, issuing from the Forum of Rome, traversed Italy, pervaded the provinces, and were terminated only by the frontiers of the empire. If we carefully trace the distance from the wall of Antoninus to Rome, and from thence to Jerusalem, it will be found that the great chain of communication, from the north-west to the south-east point of the empire, was drawn out to the length of four thousand and eighty Roman miles. The public roads were accurately divided by milestones, and ran in a direct line from one city to another, with very little respect for the obstacles either of nature or private property. Mountains were perforated, and bold arches thrown over the broadest and most rapid streams. The middle part of the road was raised into a terrace which commanded the adjacent country, consisted of several strata of sand, gravel, and cement, and was paved with large stones, or, in some places near the capital, with granite. Such was the solid construction of the Roman highways, whose firmness has not entirely yielded to the effort of fifteen centuries. They united the subjects of the most distant provinces by an easy and familiar intercourse; but their primary object had been to facilitate the marches of the legions; nor was any country considered as completely subdued, till it had been rendered, in all its parts, pervious to the arms and authority of the conqueror. The advantage of receiving the earliest intelligence, and of conveying their orders with celerity, induced the emperors to establish throughout their extensive dominions the regular institution of posts. Houses were everywhere erected at the distance only of five or six miles; each of them was constantly provided with forty horses, and by the help of these relays it was easy to travel an hundred miles in a day along the Roman roads. The use of the posts was allowed to those who claimed it by an Imperial mandate; but though originally intended for the public service, it was sometimes indulged to the business or conveniency of private citizens. Nor was the communication of the Roman empire less free and open by sea than it was by land. The provinces surrounded and enclosed the Mediterranean: and Italy, in the shape of an immense promontory, advanced into the midst of that great lake. The coasts of Italy are, in general, destitute of safe harbours; but human industry had corrected the deficiencies of nature; and the artificial port of Ostia, in particular, situate at the mouth of the Tiber, and formed by the emperor Claudius, was an useful monument of Roman greatness. From this port, which was only sixteen miles from the capital, a favourable breeze frequently carried vessels in seven days to the Columns of Hercules, and in nine or ten to Alexandria in Egypt.

THE IMPROVEMENT OF AGRICULTURE

Whatever evils either reason or declamation have imputed to extensive empire, the power of Rome was attended with some beneficial consequences to mankind; and the same freedom of intercourse which extended the vices, diffused likewise the improvements, of social life. In the more remote ages of antiquity the world was unequally divided. The East was in the immemorial possession of arts and luxury: whilst the West was inhabited by rude and warlike barbarians, who either disdained agriculture, or to whom it was totally unknown. Under the protection of an established government, the productions of happier climates, and the industry of more civilised nations, were gradually introduced into the western countries of Europe; and the natives were encouraged, by an open and profitable commerce, to multiply the former, as well as to improve the latter. It would be almost impossible to enumerate all the articles, either of the animal or the vegetable reign, which were successively imported into Europe from Asia and Egypt; but it will not be unworthy of the dignity, and much less of the utility, of an historical work, slightly to touch on a few of the principal heads. 1. Almost all the flowers, the herbs, and the fruits, that grow in our European gardens, are of foreign extraction, which, in many cases, is betrayed even by their names: the apple was a native of Italy; and when the Romans had tasted the richer flavour of the apricot, the peach, the pomegranate, the citron, and the orange, they contented themselves with applying to all these new fruits the common denomination of apple, discriminating them from each other by the additional epithet of their country. 2. In the time of Homer the vine grew wild in the island of Sicily, and most probably in the adjacent continent; but it was not improved by the skill, nor did it afford a liquor grateful to the taste, of the savage inhabitants. A thousand years afterwards Italy could boast that, of the fourscore most generous and celebrated wines, more than two-thirds were produced from her soil. The blessing was soon communicated to the Narbonnese province of Gaul; but so intense was the cold to the north of the Cevennes, that, in the time of Strabo, it was thought impossible to ripen the grapes in those parts of Gaul. This difficulty, however, was gradually vanquished; and there is some reason to believe that the vineyards of Burgundy are as old as the age of the Antonines. 3. The olive, in the western world, followed the progress of peace, of which it was considered as the symbol. Two centuries after the foundation of Rome, both Italy and Africa were strangers to that useful plant; it was naturalised in those countries, and at length carried into the heart of Spain and Gaul. The timid errors of the ancients, that it required a certain degree of heat, and could only flourish in the neighbourhood of the sea, were insensibly exploded by industry and experience. 4. The cultivation of flax was transported from Egypt to Gaul, and enriched the whole country, however it might impoverish the particular lands on which it was sown. 5. The use of artificial grasses became familiar to the farmers both of Italy and the provinces, particularly the lucerne, which derived its name and origin from Media. The assured supply of wholesome and plentiful food for the cattle during winter multiplied the number of the flocks and herds, which in their turn contributed to the fertility of the soil. To all these improvements may be added an assiduous attention to mines and fisheries, which, by employing a multitude of laborious hands, serve to increase the pleasures of the rich and the subsistence of the poor. The elegant treatise of Columella describes the advanced state of the Spanish husbandry under the reign of Tiberius; and it may be observed that those famines which so frequently afflicted the infant republic were seldom or never experienced by the extensive empire of Rome. The accidental scarcity, in any single province, was immediately relieved by the plenty of its more fortunate neighbours.

Agriculture is the foundation of manufactures; since the productions of nature are the materials of art. Under the Roman empire, the labour of an industrious and ingenious people was variously, but incessantly, employed in the service of the rich. In their dress, their table, their houses, and their furniture, the favourites of fortune united every refinement of conveniency, of elegance, and of splendour, whatever could soothe their pride, or gratify their sensuality. Such refinements, under the odious name of luxury, have been severely arraigned by the moralists of every age; and it might perhaps be more conducive to the virtue, as well as happiness, of mankind, if all possessed the necessaries, and none the superfluities, of life. But in the present imperfect condition of society, luxury, though it may proceed from vice or folly, seems to be the only means that can correct the unequal distribution of property. The diligent mechanic and the skilful artist, who have obtained no share in the division of the earth, receive a voluntary tax from the possessors of land; and the latter are prompted, by a sense of interest, to improve those estates, with whose produce they may purchase additional pleasures. This operation, the particular effects of which are felt in every society, acted with much more diffusive energy in the Roman world. The provinces would soon have been exhausted of their wealth, if the manufactures and commerce of luxury had not insensibly restored to the industrious subjects the sums which were exacted from them by the arms and authority of Rome. As long as the circulation was confined within the bounds of the empire, it impressed the political machine with a new degree of activity, and its consequences, sometimes beneficial, could never become pernicious.

But it is no easy task to confine luxury within the limits of an empire. The most remote countries of the ancient world were ransacked to supply the pomp and delicacy of Rome. The forest of Scythia afforded some valuable furs. Amber was brought over land from the shores of the Baltic to the Danube; and the barbarians were astonished at the price which they received in exchange for so useless a commodity. There was a considerable demand for Babylonian carpets, and other manufactures of the East; but the most important and unpopular branch of foreign trade was carried on with Arabia and India. Every year, about the time of the summer solstice, a fleet of an hundred and twenty vessels sailed from Myos-hormos, a port of Egypt, on the Red Sea. By the periodical assistance of the monsoons, they traversed the ocean in about forty days. The coast of Malabar, or the island of Ceylon, was the usual term of their navigation, and it was in those markets that the merchants from the more remote countries of Asia expected their arrival. The return of the fleet of Egypt was fixed to the months of December or January; and as soon as their rich cargo had been transported on the backs of camels from the Red Sea to the Nile, and had descended that river as far as Alexandria, it was poured, without delay, into the capital of the empire. The objects of oriental traffic were splendid and trifling; silk, a pound of which was esteemed not inferior in value to a pound of gold; precious stones, among which the pearl claimed the first rank after the diamond;[1] and a variety of aromatics, that were consumed in religious worship and the pomp of funerals. The labour and risk of the voyage was rewarded with almost incredible profit; but the profit was made upon Roman subjects, and a few individuals were enriched at the expense of the public. As the natives of Arabia and India were contented with the productions and manufactures of their own country, silver, on the side of the Romans, was the principal, if not the only, instrument of commerce. It was a complaint worthy of the gravity of the senate, that, in the purchase of female ornaments, the wealth of the state was irrecoverably given away to foreign and hostile nations. The annual loss is computed, by a writer of an inquisitive but censorious temper, at upwards of eight hundred thousand pounds sterling. Such was the style of discontent, brooding over the dark prospect of approaching poverty. And yet, if we compare the proportion between gold and silver, as it stood in the time of Pliny, and as it was fixed in the reign of Constantine, we shall discover within that period a very considerable increase. There is not the least reason to suppose that gold was become more scarce; it is therefore evident that silver was grown more common; that, whatever might be the amount of the Indian and Arabian exports, they were far from exhausting the wealth of the Roman world; and that the produce of the mines abundantly supplied the demands of commerce.

Notwithstanding the propensity of mankind to exalt the past and to depreciate the present, the tranquil and prosperous state of the empire was warmly felt and honestly confessed by the provincials as well as Romans. "They acknowledged that the true principles of social life, laws, agriculture, and science, which had been first invented by the

---

[1] The two great pearl-fisheries were the same as at present, Ormuz and Cape Comorin. As well as we can compare ancient with modern geography, Rome was supplied with diamonds from the mine of Jumelpur, in Bengal, which is described in the Voyages de Tavernier.

wisdom of Athens, were now firmly established by the power of Rome, under whose auspicious influence the fiercest barbarians were united by an equal government and common language. They affirm that, with the improvement of arts, the human species was visibly multiplied. They celebrate the increasing splendour of the cities, the beautiful face of the country, cultivated and adorned like an immense garden; and the long festival of peace, which was enjoyed by so many nations, forgetful of their ancient animosities, and delivered from the apprehension of future danger." Whatever suspicions may be suggested by the air of rhetoric and declamation which seems to prevail in these passages, the substance of them is perfectly agreeable to historic truth.

It was scarcely possible that the eyes of contemporaries should discover in the public felicity the latent causes of decay and corruption. This long peace, and the uniform government of the Romans, introduced a slow and secret poison into the vitals of the empire. The minds of men were gradually reduced to the same level, the fire of genius was extinguished, and even the military spirit evaporated. The natives of Europe were brave and robust. Spain, Gaul, Britain, and Illyricum supplied the legions with excellent soldiers, and constituted the real strength of the monarchy. Their personal valour remained, but they no longer possessed that public courage which is nourished by the love of independence, the sense of national honour, the presence of danger, and the habit of command. They received laws and governors from the will of their sovereign, and trusted for their defence to a mercenary army. The posterity of their boldest leaders was contented with the rank of citizens and subjects. The most aspiring spirits resorted to the court or standard of the emperors; and the deserted provinces, deprived of political strength or union, insensibly sunk into the languid indifference of private life.

The love of letters, almost inseparable from peace and refinement, was fashionable among the subjects of Hadrian and the Antonines, who were themselves men of learning and curiosity. It was diffused over the whole extent of their empire; the most northern tribes of Britons had acquired a taste for rhetoric; Homer as well as Virgil were transcribed and studied on the banks of the Rhine and Danube; and the most liberal rewards sought out the faintest glimmerings of literary merit. The sciences of physic and astronomy were successfully cultivated by the Greeks; the observations of Ptolemy and the writings of Galen are studied by those who have improved their discoveries and corrected their errors; but if we except the inimitable Lucian, this age of indolence passed away without having produced a single writer of original genius, or who excelled in the arts of elegant composition. The authori⁺·⁄ of Plato and Aristotle, of Zeno and Epicurus, still reigned in the schools; and their systems, transmitted with blind deference from one generation of disciples to another, precluded every generous attempt to exercise the powers, or enlarge the limits, of the human mind. The beauties of the poets and orators, instead of kindling a fire like their own, inspired only cold and servile imitations: or, if any ventured to deviate from those models, they deviated at the same time from good sense and propriety. On the revival of letters, the youthful vigour of the imagination after a long repose, national emulation, a new religion, new languages, and a new world, called forth the genius of Europe. But the provincials of Rome, trained by an uniform artificial foreign education, were engaged in a very unequal competition with those bold ancients who, by expressing their genuine feelings in their native tongue, had already occupied every place of honour. The name of Poet was almost forgotten; that of Orator was usurped by the sophists. A cloud of critics, of compilers, of commentators, darkened the face of learning, and the decline of genius was soon followed by the corruption of taste.

The sublime Longinus, who in somewhat a later period, and in the court of a Syrian queen, preserved the spirit of ancient Athens, observes and laments this degeneracy of his contemporaries, which debased their sentiments, enervated their courage, and depressed their talents. "In the same manner," says he, "as some children always remain pigmies, whose infant limbs have been too closely confined; thus our tender minds, fettered by the prejudices and habits of a just servitude, are unable to expand themselves, or to attain that well-proportioned greatness which we admire in the ancients, who, living under a popular government, wrote with the same freedom as they acted."[1] This diminutive stature of mankind, if we pursue the metaphor, was daily sinking below the old standard, and the Roman world was indeed peopled by a race of pigmies, when the fierce giants of the north broke in and mended the puny breed. They restored a manly spirit of freedom; and, after the revolution of ten centuries, freedom became the happy parent of taste and science.

---

[1] Here, too, we may say of Longinus, "his own example strengthens all his laws." Instead of proposing his sentiments with a manly boldness, he insinuates them with the most guarded caution; puts them into the mouth of a friend, and, as far as we can collect from a corrupted text, makes a show of refuting them himself.

Chapter 3

THE CONSTITUTION OF THE ROMAN EMPIRE. GENERAL IDEA OF THE IMPERIAL SYSTEM

THE obvious definition of a monarchy seems to be that of a state in which a single person, by whatsoever name he may be distinguished, is intrusted with the execution of the laws, the management of the revenue, and the command of the army. But, unless public liberty is protected by intrepid and vigilant guardians, the authority of so formidable a magistrate will soon degenerate into despotism. The influence of the clergy, in an age of superstition, might be usefully employed to assert the rights of mankind; but so intimate is the connexion between the throne and the altar, that the banner of the church has very seldom been seen on the side of the people. A martial nobility and stubborn commons, possessed of arms, tenacious of property, and collected into constitutional assemblies, form the only balance capable of preserving a free constitution against enterprises of an aspiring prince.

Every barrier of the Roman constitution had been levelled by the vast ambition of the dictator; every fence had been extirpated by the cruel hand of the triumvir. After the victory of Actium the fate of the Roman world depended on the will of Octavianus, surnamed Cæsar by his uncle's adoption, and afterwards Augustus by the flattery of the senate. The conqueror was at the head of forty-four veteran legions, conscious of their own strength and of the weakness of the constitution, habituated during twenty years' civil war to every act of blood and violence, and passionately devoted to the house of Cæsar, from whence alone they had received and expected the most lavish rewards. The provinces, long oppressed by the ministers of the republic, sighed for the government of a single person, who would be the master, not the accomplice, of those petty tyrants. The people of Rome, viewing with a secret pleasure the humiliation of the aristocracy, demanded only bread and public shows, and were supplied with both by the liberal hand of Augustus. The rich and polite Italians, who had almost universally embraced the philosophy of Epicurus, enjoyed the present blessings of ease and tranquillity, and suffered not the pleasing dream to be interrupted by the memory of their old tumultuous freedom. With its power the senate had lost its dignity; many of the most noble families were extinct. The republicans of spirit and ability had perished in the field of battle, or in the proscription. The door of the assembly had been designedly left open for a mixed multitude of more than a thousand persons, who reflected disgrace upon their rank, instead of deriving honour from it.

The reformation of the senate was one of the first steps in which Augustus laid aside the tyrant, and professed himself the father of his country. He was elected censor; and, in concert with his faithful Agrippa, he examined the list of the senators, expelled a few members whose vices or whose obstinacy required a public example, persuaded near two hundred to prevent the shame of an expulsion by a voluntary retreat, raised the qualification of a senator to about ten thousand pounds, created a sufficient number of patrician families, and accepted for himself the honourable title of Prince of the Senate, which had always been bestowed by the censors on the citizen the most eminent for his honours and services. But, whilst he thus restored the dignity, he destroyed the independence of the senate. The principles of a free constitution are irrecoverably lost when the legislative power is nominated by the executive.

Before an assembly thus modelled and prepared, Augustus pronounced a studied oration, which displayed his patriotism, and disguised his ambition. "He lamented, yet excused, his past conduct. Filial piety had required at his hands the revenge of his father's murder; the humanity of his own nature had sometimes given way to the stern laws of necessity, and to a forced connexion with two unworthy colleagues: as long as Antony lived, the republic forbad him to abandon her to a degenerate Roman and a barbarian queen. He was now at liberty to satisfy his duty and his inclination. He solemnly restored the senate and people to all their ancient rights; and wished only to mingle with the crowd of his fellow-citizens, and to share the blessings which he had obtained for his country."

It would require the pen of Tacitus (if Tacitus had assisted at this assembly) to describe the various emotions of the senate; those that were suppressed, and those that were affected. It was dangerous to trust the sincerity of Augustus; to seem to distrust it was still more dangerous. The respective advantages of monarchy and a republic have often divided speculative inquirers; the present greatness of the Roman state, the corruption of manners, and the licence of the soldiers, supplied new arguments to the advocates of monarchy; and these general views of government were again warped by the hopes and fears of each individual. Amidst this confusion of sentiments the answer of the senate was unanimous and decisive. They refused to accept the resignation of Augustus; they conjured him not to desert the republic which he had saved. After a decent resistance the crafty tyrant submitted to the orders of the senate; and consented to receive the government of the provinces, and the general command of the Roman armies, under the well-known names of PROCONSUL and IMPERATOR. But

he would receive them only for ten years. Even before the expiration of
that period he hoped that the wounds of civil discord would be completely healed; and that the republic, restored to its pristine health and
vigour, would no longer require the dangerous interposition of so
extraordinary a magistrate. The memory of this comedy, repeated
several times during the life of Augustus, was preserved to the last ages
of the empire by the peculiar pomp with which the perpetual monarchs
of Rome always solemnized the tenth years of their reign.

Without any violation of the principles of the constitution, the general
of the Roman armies might receive and exercise an authority almost
despotic over the soldiers, the enemies, and the subjects of the republic.
With regard to the soldiers, the jealousy of freedom had, even from the
earliest ages of Rome, given way to the hopes of conquest, and a just
sense of military discipline. The dictator, or consul, had a right to
command the service of the Roman youth; and to punish an obstinate
or cowardly disobedience by the most severe and ignominious penalties,
by striking the offender out of the list of citizens, by confiscating his
property, and by selling his person into slavery. The most sacred rights
of freedom, confirmed by the Porcian and Sempronian laws, were suspended by the military engagement. In his camp the general exercised an
absolute power of life and death; his jurisdiction was not confined by
any forms of trial or rules of proceeding, and the execution of the sentence was immediate and without appeal. The choice of the enemies of
Rome was regularly decided by the legislative authority. The most important resolutions of peace and war were seriously debated in the
senate, and solemnly ratified by the people. But when the arms of the
legions were carried to a great distance from Italy, the generals assumed
the liberty of directing them against whatever people, and in whatever
manner, they judged most advantageous for the public service. It was
from the success, not from the justice, of their enterprises that they
expected the honours of a triumph. In the use of victory, especially after
they were no longer controlled by the commissioners of the senate, they
exercised the most unbounded despotism. When Pompey commanded
in the East, he rewarded his soldiers and allies, dethroned princes,
divided kingdoms, founded colonies, and distributed the treasures of
Mithridates. On his return to Rome he obtained, by a single act of the
senate and people, the universal ratification of all his proceedings. Such
was the power over the soldiers, and over the enemies of Rome, which
was either granted to or assumed by the generals of the republic. They
were at the same time the governors, or rather monarchs, of the conquered provinces, united the civil with the military character, administered justice as well as the finances, and exercised both the executive and
legislative power of the state.

From what has been already observed in the first chapter of this work,
some notion may be formed of the armies and provinces thus intrusted

to the ruling hand of Augustus. But, as it was impossible that he could personally command the legions of so many distant frontiers, he was indulged by the senate, as Pompey had already been, in the permission of devolving the execution of his great office on a sufficient number of lieutenants. In rank and authority these officers seemed not inferior to the ancient proconsuls; but their station was dependent and precarious. They received and held their commissions at the will of a superior, to whose *auspicious* influence the merit of their action was legally attributed. They were the representatives of the emperor. The emperor alone was the general of the republic, and his jurisdiction, civil as well as military, extended over all the conquests of Rome. It was some satisfaction, however, to the senate that he always delegated his power to the members of their body. The imperial lieutenants were of consular or prætorian dignity; the legions were commanded by senators; and the prefecture of Egypt was the only important trust committed to a Roman knight.

Within six days after Augustus had been compelled to accept so very liberal a grant he resolved to gratify the pride of the senate by an easy sacrifice. He represented to them that they had enlarged his powers even beyond that degree which might be required by the melancholy condition of the times. They had not permitted him to refuse the laborious command of the armies and the frontiers; but he must insist on being allowed to restore the more peaceful and secure provinces to the mild administration of the civil magistrate. In the division of the provinces Augustus provided for his own power and for the dignity of the republic. The proconsuls of the senate, particularly those of Asia, Greece, and Africa, enjoyed a more honourable character than the lieutenants of the emperor, who commanded in Gaul or Syria. The former were attended by lictors, the latter by soldiers. A law was passed, that, wherever the emperor was present, his extraordinary commission should supersede the ordinary jurisdiction of the governor; a custom was introduced, that the new conquests belonged to the imperial portion; and it was soon discovered that the authority of the *Prince*, the favourite epithet of Augustus, was the same in every part of the empire.

In return for this imaginary concession, Augustus obtained an important privilege, which rendered him master of Rome and Italy. By a dangerous exception to the ancient maxims, he was authorised to preserve his military command, supported by a numerous body of guards, even in time of peace, and in the heart of the capital. His command, indeed, was confined to those citizens who were engaged in the service by the military oath; but such was the propensity of the Romans to servitude, that the oath was voluntarily taken by the magistrates, the senators, and the equestrian order, till the homage of flattery was insensibly converted into an annual and solemn protestation of fidelity.

Although Augustus considered a military force as the firmest foundation, he wisely rejected it as a very odious instrument, of government. It was more agreeable to his temper, as well as to his policy, to reign under the venerable names of ancient magistracy, and artfully to collect in his own person all the scattered rays of civil jurisdiction. With this view, he permitted the senate to confer upon him, for his life, the powers of the consular and tribunitian offices, which were, in the same manner, continued to all his successors. The consuls had succeeded to the kings of Rome, and represented the dignity of the state. They superintended the ceremonies of religion, levied and commanded the legions, gave audience to foreign ambassadors, and presided in the assemblies both of the senate and people. The general control of the finances was intrusted to their care; and though they seldom had leisure to administer justice in person, they were considered as the supreme guardians of law, equity, and the public peace. Such was their ordinary jurisdiction; but whenever the senate empowered the first magistrate to consult the safety of the commonwealth, he was raised by that decree above the laws, and exercised, in the defence of liberty, a temporary despotism. The character of the tribunes was, in every respect, different from that of the consuls. The appearance of the former was modest and humble; but their persons were sacred and inviolable. Their force was suited rather for opposition than for action. They were instituted to defend the oppressed, to pardon offences, to arraign the enemies of the people, and, when they judged it necessary, to stop, by a single word, the whole machine of government. As long as the republic subsisted, the dangerous influence which either the consul or the tribune might derive from their respective jurisdiction was diminished by several important restrictions. Their authority expired with the year in which they were elected; the former office was divided between two, the latter among ten persons; and, as both in their private and public interest they were adverse to each other, their mutual conflicts contributed, for the most part, to strengthen rather than to destroy the balance of the constitution. But when the consular and tribunitian powers were united, when they were vested for life in a single person, when the general of the army was, at the same time, the minister of the senate and the representative of the Roman people, it was impossible to resist the exercise, nor was it easy to define the limits, of his imperial prerogative.

To these accumulated honours the policy of Augustus soon added the splendid as well as important dignities of supreme pontiff and of censor. By the former he acquired the management of the religion, and by the latter a legal inspection over the manners and fortunes of the Roman people. If so many distinct and independent powers did not exactly unite with each other, the complaisance of the senate was prepared to supply every deficiency by the most ample and extraordinary concessions. The emperors, as the first ministers of the republic, were exempted from the obligation and penalty of many inconvenient laws: they were authorised to convoke the senate, to make several motions in the same day, to recommend candidates for the honours of the state, to enlarge the bounds of the city, to employ the revenue at their discretion, to declare peace and war, to ratify treaties; and by a most comprehensive clause, they were empowered to execute whatsoever they should judge advantageous to the empire, and agreeable to the majesty of things private or public, human or divine.

When all the various powers of executive government were committed to the *Imperial magistrate*, the ordinary magistrates of the commonwealth languished in obscurity, without vigour, and almost without business. The names and forms of the ancient administration were preserved by Augustus with the most anxious care. The usual number of consuls, prætors, and tribunes were annually invested with their respective ensigns of office, and continued to discharge some of their least important functions. Those honours still attracted the vain ambition of the Romans; and the emperors themselves, though invested for life with the powers of the consulship, frequently aspired to the title of that annual dignity, which they condescended to share with the most illustrious of their fellow-citizens. In the election of these magistrates, the people, during the reign of Augustus, were permitted to expose all the inconveniences of a wild democracy. That artful prince, instead of discovering the least symptom of impatience, humbly solicited their suffrages for himself or his friends, and scrupulously practised all the duties of an ordinary candidate. But we may venture to ascribe to his councils the first measure of the succeeding reign, by which the elections were transferred to the senate. The assemblies of the people were for ever abolished, and the emperors were delivered from a dangerous multitude, who, without restoring liberty, might have disturbed, and perhaps endangered, the established government.

By declaring themselves the protectors of the people, Marius and Cæsar had subverted the constitution of their country. But as soon as the senate had been humbled and disarmed, such an assembly, consisting of five or six hundred persons, was found a much more tractable and useful instrument of dominion. It was on the dignity of the senate that Augustus and his successors founded their new empire; and they affected, on every occasion, to adopt the language and principles of Patricians. In the administration of their own powers they frequently consulted the great national council, and *seemed* to refer to its decision the most important concerns of peace and war. Rome, Italy, and the internal provinces, were subject to the immediate jurisdiction of the senate. With regard to civil objects, it was the supreme court of appeal; with regard to criminal matters, a tribunal, constituted for the trial of all offences that were committed by men in any public station, or that affected the peace and majesty of the Roman people. The exercise of the judicial power became the most frequent and serious occupation of the senate; and the important causes that were pleaded before them afforded a last refuge to the spirit of ancient eloquence. As a council of state, and as a court of justice, the senate possessed very considerable prerogatives; but in its legislative capacity, in which it was supposed virtually to represent the people, the rights of sovereignty were acknowledged to reside in that assembly. Every power was derived from their authority, every law was ratified by their sanction. Their regular meetings were held on three stated days in every month, the Calends, the Nones, and the Ides. The debates were conducted with decent freedom; and the emperors themselves, who gloried in the name of senators, sat, voted, and divided with their equals.

GENERAL IDEA OF THE IMPERIAL SYSTEM

To resume, in a few words, the system of the Imperial government; as it was instituted by Augustus, and maintained by those princes who understood their own interest and that of the people, it may be defined an absolute monarchy disguised by the forms of a commonwealth. The masters of the Roman world surrounded their throne with darkness, concealed their irresistible strength, and humbly professed themselves the accountable ministers of the senate, whose supreme decrees they dictated and obeyed.

The face of the court corresponded with the forms of the administration. The emperors, if we except those tyrants whose capricious folly violated every law of nature and decency, disdained that pomp and ceremony which might offend their countrymen, but could add nothing to their real power. In all the offices of life they affected to confound themselves with their subjects, and maintained with them an equal intercourse of visits and entertainments. Their habit, their palace, their table, were suited only to the rank of an opulent senator. Their family, however numerous or splendid, was composed entirely of their domestic slaves and freedmen.[1] Augustus or Trajan would have blushed at employing the meanest of the Romans in those menial offices which, in the household and bedchamber of a limited monarch, are so eagerly solicited by the proudest nobles of Britain.

The deification of the emperors is the only instance in which they departed from their accustomed prudence and modesty. The Asiatic Greeks were the first inventors, the successors of Alexander the first objects, of this servile and impious mode of adulation. It was easily transferred from the kings to the governors of Asia; and the Roman magistrates very frequently were adored as provincial deities, with the pomp of altars and temples, of festivals and sacrifices. It was natural

[1] A weak prince will always be governed by his domestics. The power of slaves aggravated the shame of the Romans; and the senate paid court to a Pallas or a Narcissus. There is a chance that a modern favourite may be a gentleman.

that the emperors should not refuse what the proconsuls had accepted; and the divine honours which both the one and the other received from the provinces attested rather the despotism than the servitude of Rome. But the conquerors soon imitated the vanquished nations in the arts of flattery; and the imperious spirit of the first Cæsar too easily consented to assume, during his lifetime, a place among the tutelar deities of Rome. The milder temper of his successor declined so dangerous an ambition, which was never afterwards revived, except by the madness of Caligula and Domitian. Augustus permitted indeed some of the provincial cities to erect temples to his honour, on condition that they should associate the worship of Rome with that of the sovereign; he tolerated private superstition, of which he might be the object; but he contented himself with being revered by the senate and the people in his human character, and wisely left to his successor the care of his public deification. A regular custom was introduced, that, on the decease of every emperor who had neither lived nor died like a tyrant, the senate by a solemn decree should place him in the number of the gods: and the ceremonies of his apotheosis were blended with those of his funeral. This legal, and, as it should seem, injudicious profanation, so abhorrent to our stricter principles, was received with a very faint murmur by the easy nature of Polytheism; but it was received as an institution, not of religion, but of policy. We should disgrace the virtues of the Antonines by comparing them with the vices of Hercules or Jupiter. Even the characters of Cæsar or Augustus were far superior to those of the popular deities. But it was the misfortune of the former to live in an enlightened age, and their actions were too faithfully recorded to admit of such a mixture of fable and mystery as the devotion of the vulgar requires. As soon as their divinity was established by law, it sunk into oblivion, without contributing either to their own fame or to the dignity of succeeding princes.

In the consideration of the Imperial government, we have frequently mentioned the artful founder under his well-known title of Augustus, which was not however conferred upon him till the edifice was almost completed. The obscure name of Octavianus he derived from a mean family in the little town of Aricia. It was stained with the blood of the proscription; and he was desirous, had it been possible, to erase all memory of his former life. The illustrious surname of Cæsar he had assumed as the adopted son of the dictator; but he had too much good sense either to hope to be confounded, or to wish to be compared, with that extraordinary man. It was proposed in the senate to dignify their minister with a new appellation; and after a very serious discussion, that of Augustus was chosen, among several others, as being the most expressive of the character of peace and sanctity which he uniformly affected. *Augustus* was therefore a personal, *Cæsar* a family distinction. The former should naturally have expired with the prince on whom it was bestowed; and however the latter was diffused by adoption and female alliance, Nero was the last prince who could allege any hereditary claim to the honours of the Julian line. But, at the time of his death, the practice of a century had inseparably connected those appellations with the Imperial dignity, and they have been preserved by a long succession of emperors—Romans, Greeks, Franks, and Germans—from the fall of the republic to the present time. A distinction was, however, soon introduced. The sacred title of Augustus was always reserved for the monarch, whilst the name of Cæsar was more freely communicated to his relations; and, from the reign of Hadrian, at least, was appropriated to the second person in the state, who was considered as the presumptive heir of the empire.

The tender respect of Augustus for a free constitution which he had destroyed can only be explained by an attentive consideration of the character of that subtle tyrant. A cool head, an unfeeling heart, and a cowardly disposition, prompted him at the age of nineteen to assume the mask of hypocrisy, which he never afterwards laid aside. With the same hand, and probably with the same temper, he signed the pro-scription of Cicero and the pardon of Cinna. His virtues, and even his vices, were artificial; and according to the various dictates of his interest, he was at first the enemy, and at last the father, of the Roman world.[1] When he framed the artful system of the Imperial authority, his modera-tion was inspired by his fears. He wished to deceive the people by an image of civil liberty, and the armies by an image of civil government.

I. The death of Cæsar was ever before his eyes. He had lavished wealth and honours on his adherents; but the most favoured friends of his uncle were in the number of the conspirators. The fidelity of the legions might defend his authority against open rebellion; but their vigilance could not secure his person from the dagger of a determined republican; and the Romans, who revered the memory of Brutus, would applaud the imitation of his virtue. Cæsar had provoked his fate as much by the ostentation of his power as by his power itself. The con-sul or the tribune might have reigned in peace. The title of king had armed the Romans against his life. Augustus was sensible that mankind is governed by names; nor was he deceived in his expectation that the senate and people would submit to slavery, provided they were respect-fully assured that they still enjoyed their ancient freedom. A feeble senate and enervated people cheerfully acquiesced in the pleasing illu-sion, as long as it was supported by the virtue, or by even the prudence,

---

[1] As Octavianus advanced to the banquet of the Cæsars, his colour changed like that of the chameleon; pale at first, then red, afterwards black, he at last assumed the mild livery of Venus and the Graces. This image, employed by Julian in his in-genious fiction, is just and elegant; but when he considers this change of character as real, and ascribes it to the power of philosophy, he does too much honour to philo-sophy and to Octavianus. (Lucian—*Cæsars*).

of the successors of Augustus. It was a motive of self-preservation, not a principle of liberty, that animated the conspirators against Caligula, Nero, and Domitian. They attacked the person of the tyrant without aiming their blow at the authority of the emperor.

There appears, indeed, *one* memorable occasion, in which the senate, after seventy years of patience, made an ineffectual attempt to reassume its long-forgotten rights. When the throne was vacant by the murder of Caligula, the consuls convoked that assembly in the Capitol, condemned the memory of the Cæsars, gave the watch-word *liberty* to the few cohorts who faintly adhered to their standard, and during eight-and-forty hours acted as the independent chiefs of a free commonwealth. But while they deliberated, the prætorian guards had resolved. The stupid Claudius, brother of Germanicus, was already in their camp, invested with the Imperial purple, and prepared to support his election by arms. The dream of liberty was at an end; and the senate awoke to all the horrors of inevitable servitude. Deserted by the people, and threatened by a military force, that feeble assembly was compelled to ratify the choice of the prætorians, and to embrace the benefit of an amnesty, which Claudius had the prudence to offer, and the generosity to observe.

II. The insolence of the armies inspired Augustus with fears of a still more alarming nature. The despair of the citizens could only attempt, what the power of the soldiers was, at any time, able to execute. How precarious was his own authority over men whom he had taught to violate every social duty! He had heard their seditious clamours; he dreaded their calmer moments of reflection. One revolution had been purchased by immense rewards; but a second revolution might double those rewards. The troops professed the fondest attachment to the house of Cæsar; but the attachments of the multitude are capricious and inconstant. Augustus summoned to his aid whatever remained in those fierce minds of Roman prejudices; enforced the rigour of discipline by the sanction of law; and, interposing the majesty of the senate between the emperor and the army, boldly claimed their allegiance as the first magistrate of the republic.

During a long period of two hundred and twenty years from the establishment of this artful system to the death of Commodus, the dangers inherent to a military government were, in a great measure, suspended. The soldiers were seldom roused to that fatal sense of their own strength, and of the weakness of the civil authority, which was, before and afterwards, productive of such dreadful calamities. Caligula and Domitian were assassinated in their palace by their own domestics: the convulsions which agitated Rome on the death of the former were confined to the walls of the city. But Nero involved the whole empire in his ruin. In the space of eighteen months four princes perished by the sword; and the Roman world was shaken by the fury of the contending armies. Excepting only this short, though violent, eruption of military licence, the two centuries from Augustus to Commodus passed away unstained with civil blood, and undisturbed by revolutions. The emperor was elected by *the authority of the senate*, and *the consent of the soldiers*. The legions respected their oath of fidelity; and it requires a minute inspection of the Roman annals to discover three inconsiderable rebellions, which were all suppressed in a few months, and without even the hazard of a battle.

In elective monarchies the vacancy of the throne is a moment big with danger and mischief. The Roman emperors, desirous to spare the legions that interval of suspense, and the temptation of an irregular choice, invested their designed successor with so large a share of present power, as should enable him, after their decease, to assume the remainder without suffering the empire to perceive the change of masters. Thus Augustus, after all his fairer prospects had been snatched from him by untimely deaths, rested his last hopes on Tiberius, obtained for his adopted son the censorial and tribunitian powers, and dictated a law by which the future prince was invested with an authority equal to his own over the provinces and the armies. Thus Vespasian subdued the generous mind of his eldest son. Titus was adored by the eastern legions, which, under his command, had recently achieved the conquest of Judæa. His power was dreaded, and, as his virtues were clouded by the intemperance of youth, his designs were suspected. Instead of listening to such unworthy suspicions, the prudent monarch associated Titus to the full powers of the Imperial dignity; and the grateful son ever approved himself the humble and faithful minister of so indulgent a father.

The good sense of Vespasian engaged him indeed to embrace every measure that might confirm his recent and precarious elevation. The military oath, and the fidelity of the troops, had been consecrated, by the habits of an hundred years, to the name and family of the Cæsars; and although that family had been continued only by the fictitious rite of adoption, the Romans still revered, in the person of Nero, the grandson of Germanicus, and the lineal successor of Augustus. It was not without reluctance and remorse that the prætorian guards had been persuaded to abandon the cause of the tyrant. The rapid downfall of Galba, Otho, and Vitellius, taught the armies to consider the emperors as the creatures of *their* will, and the instruments of *their* licence. The birth of Vespasian was mean: his grandfather had been a private soldier, his father a petty officer of the revenue, his own merit had raised him, in an advanced age, to the empire; but his merit was rather useful than shining, and his virtues were disgraced by a strict and even sordid parsimony. Such a prince consulted his true interest by the association of a son whose more splendid and amiable character might turn the public attention from the obscure origin to the future glories of the Flavian house. Under the mild administration of Titus, the Roman world enjoyed a transient felicity, and his beloved memory served to protect, above fifteen years, the vices of his brother Domitian.

Nerva had scarcely accepted the purple from the assassins of Domitian before he discovered that his feeble age was unable to stem the torrent of public disorders which had multiplied under the long tyranny of his predecessor. His mild disposition was respected by the good; but the degenerate Romans required a more vigorous character, whose justice should strike terror into the guilty. Though he had several relations, he fixed his choice on a stranger. He adopted Trajan, then about forty years of age, and who commanded a powerful army in the Lower Germany; and immediately, by a decree of the senate, declared him his colleague and successor in the empire. It is sincerely to be lamented, that, whilst we are fatigued with the disgustful relation of Nero's crimes and follies, we are reduced to collect the actions of Trajan from the glimmerings of an abridgment, or the doubtful light of a panegyric. There remains, however, one panegyric far removed beyond the suspicion of flattery. Above two hundred and fifty years after the death of Trajan, the senate, in pouring out the customary acclamations on the accession of a new emperor, wished that he might surpass the felicity of Augustus and the virtue of Trajan.

We may readily believe that the father of his country hesitated whether he ought to intrust the various and doubtful character of his kinsman Hadrian with sovereign power. In his last moments, the arts of the empress Plotina either fixed the irresolution of Trajan, or boldly supposed a fictitious adoption; the truth of which could not be safely disputed, and Hadrian was peaceably acknowledged as his lawful successor. Under his reign, as has been already mentioned, the empire flourished in peace and prosperity. He encouraged the arts, reformed the laws, asserted military discipline, and visited all his provinces in person. His vast and active genius was equally suited to the most enlarged views and the minute details of civil policy. But the ruling passions of his soul were curiosity and vanity. As they prevailed, and as they were attracted by different objects, Hadrian was, by turns, an excellent prince, a ridiculous sophist, and a jealous tyrant. The general tenor of his conduct deserved praise for its equity and moderation. Yet in the first days of his reign he put to death four consular senators, his personal enemies, and men who had been judged worthy of empire; and the tediousness of a painful illness rendered him, at last, peevish and cruel. The senate doubted whether they should pronounce him a god or a tyrant; and the honours decreed to his memory were granted to the prayers of the pious Antoninus.

The caprice of Hadrian influenced his choice of a successor. After revolving in his mind several men of distinguished merit, whom he esteemed and hated, he adopted Ælius Verus, a gay and voluptuous nobleman, recommended by uncommon beauty to the lover of

Antinoüs. But whilst Hadrian was delighting himself with his own applause, and the acclamations of the soldiers, whose consent had been secured by an immense donative, the new Cæsar was ravished from his embraces by an untimely death. He left only one son. Hadrian commended the boy to the gratitude of the Antonines. He was adopted by Pius; and, on the accession of Marcus, was invested with an equal share of sovereign power. Among the many vices of this younger Verus, he possessed one virtue—a dutiful reverence for his wiser colleague, to whom he willingly abandoned the ruder cares of empire. The philosophic emperor dissembled his follies, lamented his early death, and cast a decent veil over his memory.

As soon as Hadrian's passion was either gratified or disappointed, he resolved to deserve the thanks of posterity by placing the most exalted merit on the Roman throne. His discerning eye easily discovered a senator about fifty years of age, blameless in all the offices of life; and a youth of about seventeen, whose riper years opened the fair prospect of every virtue: the elder of these was declared the son and successor of Hadrian, on condition, however, that he himself should immediately adopt the younger. The two Antonines (for it is of them that we are now speaking) governed the Roman world forty-two years with the same invariable spirit of wisdom and virtue. Although Pius had two sons, he preferred the welfare of Rome to the interest of his family, gave his daughter Faustina in marriage to young Marcus, obtained from the senate the tribunitian and proconsular powers, and with a noble disdain, or rather ignorance of jealousy, associated him to all the labours of government. Marcus, on the other hand, revered the character of his benefactor, loved him as a parent, obeyed him as his sovereign, and, after he was no more, regulated his own administration by the example and maxims of his predecessor. Their united reigns are possibly the only period of history in which the happiness of a great people was the sole object of government.

Titus Antoninus Pius has been justly denominated a second Numa. The same love of religion, justice, and peace, was the distinguishing characteristic of both princes. But the situation of the latter opened a much larger field for the exercise of those virtues. Numa could only prevent a few neighbouring villages from plundering each other's harvests. Antoninus diffused order and tranquillity over the greatest part of the earth. His reign is marked by the rare advantage of furnishing very few materials for history; which is, indeed, little more than the register of the crimes, follies, and misfortunes of mankind. In private life he was an amiable as well as a good man. The native simplicity of his virtue was a stranger to vanity or affectation. He enjoyed with moderation the conveniences of his fortune and the innocent pleasures of society; and the benevolence of his soul displayed itself in a cheerful serenity of temper.

The virtue of Marcus Aurelius Antoninus was of a severer and more laborious kind. It was the well-earned harvest of many a learned conference, of many a patient lecture, and many a midnight lucubration. At the age of twelve years he embraced the rigid system of the Stoics, which taught him to submit his body to his mind, his passions to his reason; to consider virtue as the only good, vice as the only evil, all things external as things indifferent. His Meditations, composed in the tumult of a camp, are still extant; and he even condescended to give lessons of philosophy, in a more public manner than was perhaps consistent with the modesty of a sage or the dignity of an emperor. But his life was the noblest commentary on the precepts of Zeno. He was severe to himself, indulgent to the imperfection of others, just and beneficent to all mankind. He regretted that Avidius Cassius, who excited a rebellion in Syria, had disappointed him, by a voluntary death, of the pleasure of converting an enemy into a friend; and he justified the sincerity of that sentiment, by moderating the zeal of the senate against the adherents of the traitor. War he detested, as the disgrace and calamity of human nature, but when the necessity of a just defence called upon him to take up arms, he readily exposed his person to eight winter campaigns on the frozen banks of the Danube, the severity of which was at last fatal to the weakness of his constitution. His memory was revered by a grateful posterity, and, above a century after his death, many persons preserved the image of Marcus Antoninus among those of their household gods.

*   *   *   *   *

THE CHALLENGE TO THE
OLD REGIME

Chapter 4

THE REIGN OF COMMODUS

THE mildness of Marcus, which the rigid discipline of the Stoics was unable to eradicate, formed, at the same time, the most amiable, and the only defective, part of his character. His excellent understanding was often deceived by the unsuspecting goodness of his heart. Artful men, who study the passions of princes and conceal their own, approached his person in the disguise of philosophic sanctity, and acquired riches and honours by affecting to despise them. His excessive indulgence to his brother, his wife, and his son, exceeded the bounds of private virtue, and became a public injury by the example and consequences of their vices.

Faustina, the daughter of Pius and the wife of Marcus, has been as much celebrated for her gallantries as for her beauty. The grave simplicity of the philosopher was ill calculated to engage her wanton levity, or to fix that unbounded passion for variety which often discovered personal merit in the meanest of mankind. The Cupid of the ancients was, in general, a very sensual deity; and the amours of an empress, as they exact on her side the plainest advances, are seldom susceptible of much sentimental delicacy. Marcus was the only man in the empire who seemed ignorant or insensible of the irregularities of Faustina; which, according to the prejudices of every age, reflected some disgrace on the injured husband. He promoted several of her lovers to posts of honour and profit, and, during a connexion of thirty years, invariably gave her proofs of the most tender confidence, and of a respect which ended not with her life. In his Meditations he thanks the gods, who had bestowed on him a wife so faithful, so gentle, and of such a wonderful simplicity of manners.[1] The obsequious senate, at his earnest request, declared her a goddess. She was represented in her temples, with the attributes of Juno, Venus, and Ceres; and it was decreed that, on the day of their nuptials, the youth of either sex should pay their vows before the altar of their chaste patroness.

The monstrous vices of the son have cast a shade on the purity of the father's virtues. It has been objected to Marcus, that he sacrificed the

---

[1] The world has laughed at the credulity of Marcus; but Madam Dacier assures us (and we may credit a lady) that the husband will always be deceived, if the wife condescends to dissemble.

happiness of millions to a fond partiality for a worthless boy; and that he chose a successor in his own family rather than in the republic. Nothing, however, was neglected by the anxious father, and by the men of virtue and learning whom he summoned to his assistance, to expand the narrow mind of young Commodus, to correct his growing vices, and to render him worthy of the throne for which he was designed. But the power of instruction is seldom of much efficacy, except in those happy dispositions where it is almost superfluous. The distasteful lesson of a grave philosopher was, in a moment, obliterated by the whisper of a profligate favourite; and Marcus himself blasted the fruits of this laboured education, by admitting his son, at the age of fourteen or fifteen, to a full participation of the Imperial power. He lived but four years afterwards: but he lived long enough to repent a rash measure, which raised the impetuous youth above the restraint of reason and authority.

Most of the crimes which disturb the internal peace of society are produced by the restraints which the necessary, but unequal, laws of property have imposed on the appetites of mankind, by confining to a few the possession of those objects that are coveted by many. Of all our passions and appetites, the love of power is of the most imperious and unsociable nature, since the pride of one man requires the submission of the multitude. In the tumult of civil discord the laws of society lose their force, and their place is seldom supplied by those of humanity. The ardour of contention, the pride of victory, the despair of success, the memory of past injuries, and the fear of future dangers, all contribute to inflame the mind, and to silence the voice of pity. From such motives almost every page of history has been stained with civil blood; but these motives will not account for the unprovoked cruelties of Commodus, who had nothing to wish, and everything to enjoy. The beloved son of Marcus succeeded to his father, amidst the acclamations of the senate and armies; and when he ascended the throne, the happy youth saw round him neither competitor to remove, nor enemies to punish. In this calm elevated station it was surely natural that he should prefer the love of mankind to their detestation, the mild glories of his five predecessors to the ignominious fate of Nero and Domitian.

Yet Commodus was not, as he has been represented, a tiger born with an insatiate thirst of human blood, and capable, from his infancy, of the most inhuman actions. Nature had formed him of a weak, rather than a wicked disposition. His simplicity and timidity rendered him the slave of his attendants, who gradually corrupted his mind. His cruelty, which at first obeyed the dictates of others, degenerated into habit, and at length became the ruling passion of his soul.

Upon the death of his father, Commodus found himself embarrassed with the command of a great army, and the conduct of a difficult war against the Quadi and Marcomanni. The servile and profligate youths whom Marcus had banished soon regained their station and influence about the new emperor. They exaggerated the hardships and dangers of a campaign in the wild countries beyond the Danube; and they assured the indolent prince that the terror of his name and the arms of his lieutenants would be sufficient to complete the conquest of the dismayed barbarians, or to impose such conditions as were more advantageous than any conquest. By a dexterous application to his sensual appetites, they compared the tranquillity, the splendour, the refined pleasures of Rome, with the tumult of a Pannonian camp, which afforded neither leisure nor materials for luxury. Commodus listened to the pleasing advice; but whilst he hesitated between his own inclination and the awe which he still retained for his father's counsellors, the summer insensibly elapsed, and his triumphal entry into the capital was deferred till the autumn. His graceful person, popular address, and imagined virtues, attracted the public favour; the honourable peace which he had recently granted to the barbarians diffused an universal joy; his impatience to revisit Rome was fondly ascribed to the love of his country; and his dissolute course of amusements was faintly condemned in a prince of nineteen years of age.

During the three first years of his reign, the forms, and even the spirit, of the old administration were maintained by those faithful counsellors to whom Marcus had recommended his son, and for whose wisdom and integrity Commodus still entertained a reluctant esteem. The young prince and his profligate favourites revelled in all the licence of sovereign power; but his hands were yet unstained with blood; and he had even displayed a generosity of sentiment, which might perhaps have ripened into solid virtue. A fatal incident decided his fluctuating character.

One evening, as the emperor was returning to the palace through a dark and narrow portico in the amphitheatre, an assassin, who waited his passage, rushed upon him with a drawn sword, loudly exclaiming "*The senate sends you this.*" The menace prevented the deed; the assassin was seized by the guards, and immediately revealed the authors of the conspiracy. It had been formed, not in the state, but within the walls of the palace. Lucilla, the emperor's sister, and widow of Lucius Verus, impatient of the second rank, and jealous of the reigning empress, had armed the murderer against her brother's life. She had not ventured to communicate the black design to her second husband, Claudius Pompeianus, a senator of distinguished merit and unshaken loyalty; but among the crowd of her lovers (for she imitated the manners of Faustina) she found men of desperate fortunes and wild ambition, who were prepared to serve her more violent, as well as her tender passions. The conspirators experienced the rigour of justice, and the abandoned princess was punished, first with exile, and afterwards with death.

But the words of the assassin sunk deep into the mind of Commodus, and left an indelible impression of fear and hatred against the whole body of the senate. Those whom he had dreaded as importunate ministers, he now suspected as secret enemies. The Delators, a race of men discouraged, and almost extinguished, under the former reigns, again became formidable as soon as they discovered that the emperor was desirous of finding disaffection and treason in the senate. That assembly, whom Marcus had ever considered as the great council of the nation, was composed of the most distinguished of the Romans; and distinction of every kind soon became criminal. The possession of wealth stimulated the diligence of the informers; rigid virtue implied a tacit censure of the irregularities of Commodus; important services implied a dangerous superiority of merit; and the friendship of the father always insured the aversion of the son. Suspicion was equivalent to proof; trial to condemnation. The execution of a considerable senator was attended with the death of all who might lament or revenge his fate; and when Commodus had once tasted human blood, he became incapable of pity or remorse.

Of these innocent victims of tyranny, none died more lamented than the two brothers of the Quintilian family, Maximus and Condianus, whose fraternal love has saved their names from oblivion, and endeared their memory to posterity. Their studies and their occupations, their pursuits and their pleasures, were still the same. In the enjoyment of a great estate, they never admitted the idea of a separate interest: some fragments are now extant of a treatise which they composed in common; and in every action of life it was observed that their two bodies were animated by one soul. The Antonines, who valued their virtues, and delighted in their union, raised them in the same year to the consulship; and Marcus afterwards intrusted to their joint care the civil administration of Greece, and a great military command, in which they obtained a signal victory over the Germans. The kind cruelty of Commodus united them in death.

The tyrant's rage, after having shed the noblest blood of the senate, at length recoiled on the principal instrument of his cruelty. Whilst Commodus was immersed in blood and luxury, he devolved the detail of the public business on Perennis; a servile and ambitious minister, who had obtained his post by the murder of his predecessor, but who possessed a considerable share of vigour and ability. By acts of extortion, and the forfeited estates of the nobles sacrificed to his avarice, he had accumulated an immense treasure. The Prætorian guards were under his immediate command; and his son, who already discovered a military genius, was at the head of the Illyrian legions. Perennis aspired to the empire; or what, in the eyes of Commodus, amounted to the same crime, he was capable of aspiring to it, had he not been prevented, surprised, and put to death. The fall of a minister is a very trifling incident in the general history of the empire; but it was hastened by an extraordinary circumstance, which proved how much the nerves of discipline were already relaxed. The legions of Britain, discontented with the administration of Perennis, formed a deputation of fifteen hundred select men, with instructions to march to Rome, and lay their complaints before the emperor. These military petitioners, by their own determined behaviour, by inflaming the divisions of the guards, by exaggerating the strength of the British army, and by alarming the fears of Commodus, exacted and obtained the minister's death, as the only redress of their grievances. This presumption of a distant army, and their discovery of the weakness of government, was a sure presage of the most dreadful convulsions.

The negligence of the public administration was betrayed soon afterwards by a new disorder, which arose from the smallest beginnings. A spirit of desertion began to prevail among the troops, and the deserters, instead of seeking their safety in flight or concealment, infested the highways. Maternus, a private soldier, of a daring boldness above his station, collected these bands of robbers into a little army, set open the prisons, invited the slaves to assert their freedom, and plundered with impunity the rich and defenceless cities of Gaul and Spain. The governors of the provinces, who had long been the spectators, and perhaps the partners, of his depredations, were at length roused from their supine indolence by the threatening commands of the emperor. Maternus found that he was encompassed, and foresaw that he must be overpowered. A great effort of despair was his last resource. He ordered his followers to disperse, to pass the Alps in small parties and various disguises, and to assemble at Rome during the licentious tumult of the festival of Cybele. To murder Commodus, and to ascend the vacant throne, was the ambition of no vulgar robber. His measures were so ably concerted that his concealed troops already filled the streets of Rome. The envy of an accomplice discovered and ruined this singular enterprise in the moment when it was ripe for execution.

Suspicious princes often promote the last of mankind, from a vain persuasion that those who have no dependence, except on their favour, will have no attachment except to the person of their benefactor. Cleander, the successor of Perennis, was a Phrygian by birth; of a nation over whose stubborn but servile temper blows only could prevail. He had been sent from his native country to Rome, in the capacity of a slave. As a slave he entered the imperial palace, rendered himself useful to his master's passions, and rapidly ascended to the most exalted station which a subject could enjoy. His influence over the mind of Commodus was much greater than that of his predecessor; for Cleander was devoid of any ability or virtue which could inspire the emperor with envy or distrust. Avarice was the reigning passion of his soul, and the great principle of his administration. The rank of consul, of patrician, of senator, was exposed to public sale; and it would have been considered as disaffection if any one had refused to purchase these empty and disgraceful honours with the greatest part of his fortune. In the lucrative provincial employments the minister shared with the governor the spoils of the people. The execution of the laws was venal and arbitrary. A wealthy criminal might obtain not only the reversal of the sentence by which he was justly condemned, but might likewise inflict whatever punishment he pleased on the accuser, the witnesses, and the judge.

By these means Cleander, in the space of three years, had accumulated more wealth than had ever yet been possessed by any freedman. Commodus was perfectly satisfied with the magnificent presents which the artful courtier laid at his feet in the most seasonable moments. To divert the public envy, Cleander, under the emperor's name, erected baths, porticos, and places of exercise, for the use of the people. He flattered himself that the Romans, dazzled and amused by this apparent liberality, would be less affected by the bloody scenes which were daily exhibited; that they would forget the death of Byrrhus, a senator to whose superior merit the late emperor had granted one of his daughters; and that they would forgive the execution of Arrius Antoninus, the last representative of the name and virtues of the Antonines. The former, with more integrity than prudence, had attempted to disclose to his brother-in-law the true character of Cleander. An equitable sentence pronounced by the latter, when proconsul of Asia, against a worthless creature of the favourite, proved fatal to him. After the fall of Perennis the terrors of Commodus had, for a short time, assumed the appearance of a return to virtue. He repealed the most odious of his acts, loaded his memory with the public execration, and ascribed to the pernicious counsels of that wicked minister all the errors of his inexperienced youth. But his repentance lasted only thirty days; and, under Cleander's tyranny, the administration of Perennis was often regretted.

Pestilence and famine contributed to fill up the measure of the calamities of Rome. The first could be only imputed to the just indignation of the gods; but a monopoly of corn, supported by the riches and power of the minister, was considered as the immediate cause of the second. The popular discontent, after it had long circulated in whispers, broke out in the assembled circus. The people quitted their favourite amusements for the more delicious pleasure of revenge, rushed in crowds towards a palace in the suburbs, one of the emperor's retirements, and demanded, with angry clamours, the head of the public enemy. Cleander, who commanded the Prætorian guards, ordered a body of cavalry to sally forth and disperse the seditious multitude. The multitude fled with precipitation towards the city; several were slain, and many more were trampled to death; but when the cavalry entered the streets their pursuit was checked by a shower of stones and darts from the roofs and windows of the houses. The footguards, who had been long jealous of the prerogatives and insolence of the Prætorian cavalry, embraced the party of the people. The tumult became a regular engagement, and threatened a general massacre. The Prætorians at length gave way, oppressed with numbers; and the tide of popular fury returned with redoubled violence against the gates of the palace, where Commodus lay dissolved in luxury, and alone unconscious of the civil war. It was death to approach his person with the unwelcome news. He would have perished in this supine security, had not two women, his eldest sister Fadilla, and Marcia the most favoured of his concubines, ventured to break into his presence. Bathed in tears, and with dishevelled hair, they threw themselves at his feet, and, with all the pressing eloquence of fear, discovered to the affrighted emperor the crimes of the minister, the rage of the people, and the impending ruin which in a few minutes would burst over his palace and person. Commodus started from his dream of pleasure, and commanded that the head of Cleander should be thrown out to the people. The desired spectacle instantly appeased the tumult; and the son of Marcus might even yet have regained the affection and confidence of his subjects.

But every sentiment of virtue and humanity was extinct in the mind of Commodus. Whilst he thus abandoned the reins of empire to these unworthy favourites, he valued nothing in sovereign power except the unbounded licence of indulging his sensual appetites. His hours were spent in a seraglio of three hundred beautiful women and as many boys, of every rank and of every province; and, wherever the arts of seduction proved ineffectual, the brutal lover had recourse to violence. The ancient historians have expatiated on these abandoned scenes of prostitution, which scorned every restraint of nature or modesty; but it would not be easy to translate their too faithful descriptions into the decency of modern language. The intervals of lust were filled up with the basest amusements. The influence of a polite age and the labour of an attentive education had never been able to infuse into his rude and brutish mind the least tincture of learning; and he was the first of the Roman emperors totally devoid of taste for the pleasures of the understanding. Nero himself excelled, or affected to excel, in the elegant arts of music and poetry; nor should we despise his pursuits, had he not converted the pleasing relaxation of a leisure hour into the serious business and ambition of his life. But Commodus, from his earliest infancy, discovered an aversion to whatever was rational or liberal, and a fond attachment to the amusements of the populace—the sports of the circus and amphitheatre, the combats of gladiators, and the hunting of wild beasts. The masters in every branch of learning, whom Marcus provided for his son, were heard with inattention and disgust; whilst the Moors and Parthians, who taught him to dart the javelin and to shoot with the bow, found a disciple who delighted in his application, and soon equalled the most skilful of his instructors in the steadiness of the eye and the dexterity of the hand.

The servile crowd, whose fortune depended on their master's vices, applauded these ignoble pursuits. The perfidious voice of flattery reminded him that, by exploits of the same nature, by the defeat of the Nemæan lion, and the slaughter of the wild boar of Erymanthus, the Grecian Hercules had acquired a place among the gods, and an immortal memory among men. They only forgot to observe that, in the first ages of society, when the fiercer animals often dispute with man the possession of an unsettled country, a successful war against those savages is one of the most innocent and beneficial labours of heroism. In the civilised state of the Roman empire the wild beasts had long since retired from the face of man and the neighbourhood of populous cities. To surprise them in their solitary haunts, and to transport them to Rome, that they might be slain in pomp by the hand of an emperor, was an enterprise equally ridiculous for the prince and oppressive for the people.[1] Ignorant of these distinctions, Commodus eagerly embraced the glorious resemblance, and styled himself (as we still read on his medals) the *Roman Hercules*. The club and the lion's hide were placed by the side of the throne amongst the ensigns of sovereignty; and statues were erected, in which Commodus was represented in the character and with the attributes of the god whose valour and dexterity he endeavoured to emulate in the daily course of his ferocious amusements.

Elated with these praises, which gradually extinguished the innate sense of shame, Commodus resolved to exhibit before the eyes of the Roman people those exercises which till then he had decently confined within the walls of his palace and to the presence of a few favourites. On the appointed day the various motives of flattery, fear, and curiosity attracted to the amphitheatre an innumerable multitude of spectators; and some degree of applause was deservedly bestowed on the uncommon skill of the imperial performer. Whether he aimed at the head or heart of the animal, the wound was alike certain and mortal. With arrows, whose point was shaped into the form of a crescent, Commodus often intercepted the rapid career and cut asunder the long bony neck of the ostrich. A panther was let loose; and the archer waited till he had leaped upon a trembling malefactor. In the same instant the shaft flew, the beast dropped dead, and the man remained unhurt. The dens of the amphitheatre disgorged at once a hundred lions: a hundred darts from the unerring hand of Commodus laid them dead as they ran raging round the *Arena*. Neither the huge bulk of the elephant nor the scaly hide of the rhinoceros could defend them from his stroke. Ethiopia and India yielded their most extraordinary productions; and several

[1] The African lions, when pressed by hunger, infested the open villages and cultivated country; and they infested them with impunity. The royal beast was reserved for the pleasures of the emperor and the capital; and the unfortunate peasant who killed one of them, though in his own defence, incurred a very heavy penalty. This extraordinary *game-law* was mitigated by Honorius, and finally repealed by Justinian.

animals were slain in the amphitheatre which had been seen only in the representations of art, or perhaps of fancy.[1] In all these exhibitions the securest precautions were used to protect the person of the Roman Hercules from the desperate spring of any savage who might possibly disregard the dignity of the emperor and the sanctity of the god.

But the meanest of the populace were affected with shame and indignation when they beheld their sovereign enter the lists as a gladiator, and glory in a profession which the laws and manners of the Romans had branded with the justest note of infamy. He chose the habit and arms of the *Secutor*, whose combat with the *Retiarius* formed one of the most lively scenes in the bloody sports of the amphitheatre. The *Secutor* was armed with an helmet, sword, and buckler; his naked antagonist had only a large net and a trident; with the one he endeavoured to entangle, with the other to despatch, his enemy. If he missed the first throw he was obliged to fly from the pursuit of the *Secutor* till he had prepared his net for a second cast. The emperor fought in this character seven hundred and thirty-five several times. These glorious achievements were carefully recorded in the public acts of the empire; and that he might omit no circumstance of infamy, he received from the common fund of gladiators a stipend so exorbitant that it became a new and most ignominious tax upon the Roman people. It may be easily supposed that in these engagements the master of the world was always successful: in the amphitheatre his victories were not often sanguinary; but when he exercised his skill in the school of gladiators, or his own palace, his wretched antagonists were frequently honoured with a mortal wound from the hand of Commodus, and obliged to seal their flattery with their blood. He now disdained the appellation of Hercules. The name of Paulus, a celebrated Secutor, was the only one which delighted his ear. It was inscribed on his colossal statues, and repeated in the redoubled acclamations of the mournful and applauding senate. Claudius Pompeianus, the virtuous husband of Lucilla, was the only senator who asserted the honour of his rank. As a father he permitted his sons to consult their safety by attending the amphitheatre. As a Roman he declared that his own life was in the emperor's hands, but that he would never behold the son of Marcus prostituting his person and dignity. Notwithstanding his manly resolution, Pompeianus escaped the resentment of the tyrant, and, with his honour, had the good fortune to preserve his life.

Commodus had now attained the summit of vice and infamy. Amidst the acclamations of a flattering court, he was unable to disguise from

---

[1] Commodus killed a camelopardalis or giraffe, the tallest, the most gentle, and the most useless of the large quadrupeds. This singular animal, a native only of the interior parts of Africa, has not been seen in Europe since the revival of letters; and though M. de Buffon (Hist. Naturelle, tom. xiii.) has endeavoured to describe, he has not ventured to delineate, the giraffe.

himself that he had deserved the contempt and hatred of every man of sense and virtue in his empire. His ferocious spirit was irritated by the consciousness of that hatred, by the envy of every kind of merit, by the just apprehension of danger, and by the habit of slaughter which he contracted in his daily amusements. History has preserved a long list of consular senators sacrificed to his wanton suspicion, which sought out, with peculiar anxiety, those unfortunate persons connected, however remotely, with the family of the Antonines, without sparing even the ministers of his crimes or pleasures. His cruelty proved at last fatal to himself. He had shed with impunity the noblest blood of Rome: he perished as soon as he was dreaded by his own domestics. Marcia, his favourite concubine, Eclectus, his chamberlain, and Lætus, his Prætorian prefect, alarmed by the fate of their companions and predecessors, resolved to prevent the destruction which every hour hung over their heads, either from the mad caprice of the tyrant, or the sudden indignation of the people. Marcia seized the occasion of presenting a draught of wine to her lover, after he had fatigued himself with hunting some wild beasts. Commodus retired to sleep; but whilst he was labouring with the effects of poison and drunkenness, a robust youth, by profession a wrestler, entered his chamber, and strangled him without resistance. The body was secretly conveyed out of the palace, before the least suspicion was entertained in the city, or even in the court, of the emperor's death. Such was the fate of the son of Marcus, and so easy was it to destroy a hated tyrant, who, by the artificial powers of government, had oppressed, during thirteen years, so many millions of subjects, each of whom was equal to their master in personal strength and personal abilities.

In his account of Commodus Gibbon relies on conservative gossip which was outraged by the emperor's behaviour. Commodus was non-Roman in outlook and challenged the traditional ideas of freedom. He began the deposition of Rome from her central pre-eminence. As Hercules Romanus and the Rising Sun he transcended and united the old national cults, and he opened the way for the House of Severus. His murderers represented reactionary forces. These conspirators offered the principate to Pertinax, an aged and conservative senator. After some attempted reforms, Pertinax was murdered by the Prætorians. His reign lasted eighty six days.

THE GROWTH OF MILITARY AUTOCRACY AND THE INFLUX OF ORIENTALISM

Chapter 5

THE SALE OF THE EMPIRE
BY THE PRÆTORIANS. THE RISE OF SEPTIMIUS SEVERUS

THE power of the sword is more sensibly felt in an extensive monarchy than in a small community. It has been calculated by the ablest politicians, that no state, without being soon exhausted, can maintain above the hundredth part of its members in arms and idleness. But although this relative proportion may be uniform, the influence of the army over the rest of the society will vary according to the degree of its positive strength. The advantages of military science and discipline cannot be exerted, unless a proper number of soldiers are united into one body, and actuated by one soul. With a handful of men, such an union would be ineffectual; with an unwieldy host it would be impracticable; and the powers of the machine would be alike destroyed by the extreme minuteness or the excessive weight of its springs. To illustrate this observation we need only reflect that there is no superiority of natural strength, artificial weapons, or acquired skill, which could enable one man to keep in constant subjection one hundred of his fellow-creatures: the tyrant of a single town, or a small district, would soon discover that an hundred armed followers were a weak defence against ten thousand peasants or citizens; but an hundred thousand well-disciplined soldiers will command, with despotic sway, ten millions of subjects; and a body of ten or fifteen thousand guards will strike terror into the most numerous populace that ever crowded the streets of an immense capital.

The Prætorian bands, whose licentious fury was the first symptom and cause of the decline of the Roman empire, scarcely amounted to the last-mentioned number. They derived their institution from Augustus. That crafty tyrant, sensible that laws might colour, but that arms alone could maintain, his usurped dominion, had gradually formed this powerful body of guards, in constant readiness to protect his person, to awe the senate, and either to prevent or to crush the first motions of rebellion. He distinguished these favoured troops by a double pay and superior privileges; but, as their formidable aspect would at once have alarmed and irritated the Roman people, three cohorts only were stationed in the capital; whilst the remainder was dispersed in the adjacent towns of Italy. But after fifty years of peace and servitude, Tiberius ventured on a decisive measure, which for ever riveted the fetters of his country. Under the fair pretences of relieving Italy from the heavy burden of military quarters, and of introducing a stricter discipline among the guards, he assembled them at Rome in a permanent camp, which was fortified with skilful care, and placed on a commanding situation.

Such formidable servants are always necessary, but often fatal, to the throne of despotism. By thus introducing the Prætorian guards as it were into the palace and the senate, the emperors taught them to perceive their own strength, and the weakness of the civil government; to view the vices of their masters with familiar contempt, and to lay aside that reverential awe which distance only and mystery can preserve towards an imaginary power. In the luxurious idleness of an opulent city, their pride was nourished by the sense of their irresistible weight; nor was it possible to conceal from them that the person of the sovereign, the authority of the senate, the public treasure, and the seat of empire, were all in their hands. To divert the Prætorian bands from these dangerous reflections, the firmest and best-established princes were obliged to mix blandishments with commands, rewards with punishments, to flatter their pride, indulge their pleasures, connive at their irregularities, and to purchase their precarious faith by a liberal donative; which, since the elevation of Claudius, was exacted as a legal claim on the accession of every new emperor.

The advocates of the guards endeavoured to justify by arguments the power which they asserted by arms; and to maintain that, according to the purest principles of the constitution, *their* consent was essentially necessary in the appointment of an emperor. The election of consuls, of generals, and of magistrates, however it had been recently usurped by the senate, was the ancient and undoubted right of the Roman people. But where was the Roman people to be found? Not surely amongst the mixed multitude of slaves and strangers that filled the streets of Rome; a servile populace, as devoid of spirit as destitute of property. The defenders of the state, selected from the flower of the Italian youth, and trained in the exercise of arms and virtue, were the genuine representatives of the people, and the best entitled to elect the military chief of the republic. These assertions, however defective in reason, became unanswerable when the fierce Prætorians increased their weight by throwing, like the barbarian conqueror of Rome, their swords into the scale.

The Prætorians had violated the sanctity of the throne by the atrocious murder of Pertinax; they dishonoured the majesty of it by their subsequent conduct. The camp was without a leader, for even the prefect Lætus, who had excited the tempest, prudently declined the public indignation. Amidst the wild disorder, Sulpicianus, the emperor's father-in-law, and governor of the city, who had been sent to the camp on the first alarm of mutiny, was endeavouring to calm the fury of the multitude, when he was silenced by the clamorous return of the murderers, bearing on a lance the head of Pertinax. Though history has accustomed us to observe every principle and every passion yielding to the imperious dictates of ambition, it is scarcely credible that, in these moments of horror, Sulpicianus should have aspired to ascend a throne polluted with the recent blood of so near a relation and so excellent a prince. He had already begun to use the only effectual argument, and to treat for the Imperial dignity; but the more prudent of the Prætorians, apprehensive that, in this private contract, they should not obtain a just price for so valuable a commodity, ran out upon the ramparts, and, with a loud voice, proclaimed that the Roman world was to be disposed of to the best bidder by public auction.

This infamous offer, the most insolent excess of military licence, diffused an universal grief, shame, and indignation throughout the city. It reached at length the ears of Didius Julianus, a wealthy senator, who, regardless of the public calamities, was indulging himself in the luxury of the table. His wife and his daughter, his freedmen and his parasites, easily convinced him that he deserved the throne, and earnestly conjured him to embrace so fortunate an opportunity. The vain old man hastened to the Prætorian camp, where Sulpicianus was still in treaty with the guards, and began to bid against him from the foot of the rampart. The unworthy negotiation was transacted by faithful emissaries, who passed alternately from one candidate to the other, and acquainted each of them with the offers of his rival. Sulpicianus had already promised a donative of five thousand drachms (above one hundred and sixty pounds) to each soldier; when Julian, eager for the prize, rose at once to the sum of six thousand two hundred and fifty drachms, or upwards of two hundred pounds sterling. The gates of the camp were instantly thrown open to the purchaser; he was declared emperor, and received an oath of allegiance from the soldiers, who retained humanity enough to stipulate that he should pardon and forget the competition of Sulpicianus.

It was now incumbent on the Prætorians to fulfil the conditions of the sale. They placed their new sovereign, whom they served and despised, in the centre of their ranks, surrounded him on every side with their shields, and conducted him in close order of battle through the deserted streets of the city. The senate was commanded to assemble; and those who had been the distinguished friends of Pertinax, or the personal enemies of Julian, found it necessary to affect a more than common share of satisfaction at this happy revolution. After Julian had filled the senate-house with armed soldiers, he expatiated on the freedom of his election, his own eminent virtues, and his full assurance of the affections of the senate. The obsequious assembly congratulated their own and the public felicity; engaged their allegiance, and conferred on him all the several branches of the Imperial power. From the senate Julian was conducted by the same military procession to take possession of the palace. The first objects that struck his eyes were the abandoned trunk of Pertinax, and the frugal entertainment prepared for his supper. The one he viewed with indifference; the other with contempt. A magnificent feast was prepared by his order, and he amused himself till a very late hour with dice and the performances of Pylades, a celebrated dancer. Yet it was observed that, after the crowd of flatterers dispersed, and left him to darkness, solitude, and terrible reflection, he passed a sleepless night; revolving most probably in his mind his own rash folly, the fate of his virtuous predecessor, and the doubtful and dangerous tenure of an empire which had not been acquired by merit, but purchased by money.

He had reason to tremble. On the throne of the world he found himself without a friend, and even without an adherent. The guards themselves were ashamed of the prince whom their avarice had persuaded them to accept; nor was there a citizen who did not consider his elevation with horror, as the last insult on the Roman name. The nobility, whose conspicuous station and ample possessions exacted the strictest caution, dissembled their sentiments, and met the affected civility of the emperor with smiles of complacency and professions of duty. But the people, secure in their numbers and obscurity, gave a free vent to their passions. The streets and public places of Rome resounded with clamours and imprecations. The enraged multitude affronted the person of Julian, rejected his liberality, and, conscious of the impotence of their own resentment, they called aloud on the legions of the frontiers to assert the violated majesty of the Roman empire.

Septimius Severus was declared emperor by the legions of Pannonia, and crossing the Alps was acknowledged by the senate. Julianus was put to death. Severus then defeated rival claimants, Pescennius Niger, governor of Syria, and Albinus, governor of Britain.

SEPTIMIUS SEVERUS

The true interest of an absolute monarch generally coincides with that of his people. Their numbers, their wealth, their order, and their security are the best and only foundations of his real greatness; and were he totally devoid of virtue, prudence might supply its place, and would dictate the same rule of conduct. Severus considered the Roman empire as his property, and had no sooner secured the possession, than he bestowed his care on the cultivation and improvement of so valuable an acquisition. Salutary laws, executed with inflexible firmness, soon corrected most of the abuses with which, since the death of Marcus, every part of the government had been infected. In the administration of justice, the judgments of the emperor were characterised by attention, discernment, and impartiality; and, whenever he deviated from the strict line of equity, it was generally in favour of the poor and oppressed; not so much indeed from any sense of humanity, as from the natural propensity of a despot to humble the pride of greatness, and to sink all his subjects to the same common level of absolute dependence. His expensive taste for building, magnificent shows, and, above all, a constant and liberal distribution of corn and provisions, were the surest means of captivating the affection of the Roman people. The misfortunes of civil discord were obliterated. The calm of peace and prosperity was once more experienced in the provinces; and many cities, restored by the munificence of Severus, assumed the title of his colonies, and attested by public monuments their gratitude and felicity. The fame of the Roman arms was revived by that warlike and successful emperor, and he boasted, with a just pride, that, having received the empire oppressed with foreign and domestic wars, he left it established in profound, universal, and honourable peace.

Although the wounds of civil war appeared completely healed, its mortal poison still lurked in the vitals of the constitution. Severus possessed a considerable share of vigour and ability; but the daring soul of the first Cæsar, or the deep policy of Augustus, were scarcely equal to the task of curbing the insolence of the victorious legions. By gratitude, by misguided policy, by seeming necessity, Severus was induced to relax the nerves of discipline. The vanity of his soldiers was flattered with the honour of wearing gold rings; their ease was indulged in the permission of living with their wives in the idleness of quarters. He increased their pay beyond the example of former times, and taught them to expect, and soon to claim, extraordinary donatives on every public occasion of danger or festivity. Elated by success, enervated by luxury, and raised above the level of subjects by their dangerous privileges, they soon became incapable of military fatigue, oppressive to the country, and impatient of a just subordination. Their officers asserted the superiority of rank by a more profuse and elegant luxury. There is still extant a letter of Severus, lamenting the licentious state of the army, and exhorting one of his generals to begin the necessary reformation from the tribunes themselves; since, as he justly observes, the officer who has forfeited the esteem, will never command the obedience, of his soldiers. Had the emperor pursued the train of reflection, he would have discovered that the primary cause of this general corruption might be ascribed, not, indeed to the example, but to the pernicious indulgence, however, of the commander-in-chief.

The Prætorians, who murdered their emperor and sold the empire, had received the just punishment of their treason; but the necessary, though dangerous, institution of guards, was soon restored on a new model by Severus, and increased to four times the ancient number. Formerly these troops had been recruited in Italy; and as the adjacent provinces gradually imbibed the softer manners of Rome, the levies were extended to Macedonia, Noricum, and Spain. In the room of these elegant troops, better adapted to the pomp of courts than to the uses of war, it was established by Severus, that from all the legions of the frontiers the soldiers most distinguished for strength, valour, and fidelity should be occasionally draughted, and promoted, as an honour and reward, into the more eligible service of the guards. By this new institution the Italian youth were diverted from the exercise of arms, and the capital was terrified by the strange aspect and manners of a multitude of barbarians. But Severus flattered himself that the legions would consider these chosen Prætorians as the representatives of the whole military order; and that the present aid of fifty thousand men, superior in arms and appointments to any force that could be brought into the field against them, would for ever crush the hopes of rebellion, and secure the empire to himself and his posterity.

The command of these favoured and formidable troops soon became the first office of the empire. As the government degenerated into military despotism, the Prætorian prefect, who in his origin had been a simple captain of the guards, was placed not only at the head of the army, but of the finances, and even of the law. In every department of administration he represented the person, and exercised the authority, of the emperor. The first prefect who enjoyed and abused this immense power was Plautianus, the favourite minister of Severus. His reign lasted above ten years, till the marriage of his daughter with the eldest son of the emperor, which seemed to assure his fortune, proved the occasion of his ruin.[1] The animosities of the palace, by irritating the ambition and alarming the fears of Plautianus, threatened to produce a revolution, and obliged the emperor, who still loved him, to consent with reluctance to his death. After the fall of Plautianus, an eminent lawyer, the celebrated Papinian, was appointed to execute the motley office of Prætorian prefect.

Till the reign of Severus the virtue, and even the good sense, of the emperors had been distinguished by their real or affected reverence for the senate, and by a tender regard to the nice frame of civil policy instituted by Augustus. But the youth of Severus had been trained in the implicit obedience of camps, and his riper years spent in the despotism of military command. His haughty and inflexible spirit could not discover, or would not acknowledge, the advantage of preserving an intermediate power, however imaginary, between the emperor and the army.

[1] One of his most daring and wanton acts of power was the castration of an hundred free Romans, some of them married men, and even fathers of families, merely that his daughter, on her marriage with the young emperor, might be attended by a train of eunuchs worthy of an eastern queen.

He disdained to profess himself the servant of an assembly that detested his person and trembled at his frown; he issued his commands where his request would have proved as effectual; assumed the conduct and style of a sovereign and a conqueror, and exercised, without disguise, the whole legislative as well as the executive power.

The victory over the senate was easy and inglorious. Every eye and every passion were directed to the supreme magistrate, who possessed the arms and treasure of the state; whilst the senate, neither elected by the people, nor guarded by military force, nor animated by public spirit, rested its declining authority on the frail and crumbling basis of ancient opinion. The fine theory of a republic insensibly vanished, and made way for the more natural and substantial feelings of monarchy. As the freedom and honours of Rome were successively communicated to the provinces, in which the old government had been either unknown or was remembered with abhorrence, the tradition of republican maxims was gradually obliterated. The Greek historians of the age of the Antonines observe, with a malicious pleasure, that, although the sovereign of Rome, in compliance with an obsolete prejudice, abstained from the name of king, he possessed the full measure of regal power. In the reign of Severus the senate was filled with polished and eloquent slaves from the eastern provinces, who justified personal flattery by speculative principles of servitude. These new advocates of prerogative were heard with pleasure by the court, and with patience by the people, when they inculcated the duty of passive obedience, and descanted on the inevitable mischiefs of freedom. The lawyers and the historians concurred in teaching that the Imperial authority was held, not by the delegated commission, but by the irrevocable resignation of the senate; that the emperor was freed from the restraint of civil laws, could command, by his arbitrary will, the lives and fortunes of his subjects, and might dispose of the empire as of his private patrimony. The most eminent of the civil lawyers, and particularly Papinian, Paulus, and Ulpian, flourished under the house of Severus; and the Roman jurisprudence, having closely united itself with the system of monarchy, was supposed to have attained its full maturity and perfection.

The contemporaries of Severus, in the enjoyment of the peace and glory of his reign, forgave the cruelties by which it had been introduced. Posterity, who experienced the fatal effects of his maxims and example, justly considered him as the principal author of the decline of the Roman empire.

Chapter 6

THE DYNASTY OF SEVERUS. CARACALLA AND GETA; ELAGABALUS; ALEXANDER SEVERUS. THE GROWTH OF FEMININE INFLUENCE AT COURT

THE ascent to greatness, however steep and dangerous, may entertain an active spirit with the consciousness and exercise of its own powers: but the possession of a throne could never yet afford a lasting satisfaction to an ambitious mind. This melancholy truth was felt and acknowledged by Severus. Fortune and merit had, from an humble station, elevated him to the first place among mankind. "He had been all things," as he said himself, "and all was of little value." Distracted with the care, not of acquiring, but of preserving an empire, oppressed with age and infirmities, careless of fame, and satiated with power, all his prospects of life were closed. The desire of perpetuating the greatness of his family was the only remaining wish of his ambition and paternal tenderness.

Like most of the Africans, Severus was passionately addicted to the vain studies of magic and divination, deeply versed in the interpretation of dreams and omens, and perfectly acquainted with the science of judicial astrology; which, in almost every age except the present, has maintained its dominion over the mind of man. He had lost his first wife whilst he was governor of the Lyonnese Gaul. In the choice of a second he sought only to connect himself with some favourite of fortune; and as soon as he had discovered that a young lady of Emesa in Syria had *a royal nativity*, he solicited and obtained her hand. Julia Domna (for that was her name) deserved all that the stars could promise her. She possessed, even in an advanced age, the attractions of beauty, and united to a lively imagination a firmness of mind and strength of judgment seldom bestowed on her sex. Her amiable qualities never made any deep impression on the dark and jealous temper of her husband; but, in her son's reign, she administered the principal affairs of the empire with a prudence that supported his authority, and with a moderation that sometimes corrected his wild extravagancies. Julia applied herself to letters and philosophy with some success and with the most splendid reputation. She was the patroness of every art, and the friend of every man of genius. The grateful flattery of the learned has celebrated her virtues; but, if we may credit the scandal of ancient history, chastity was very far from being the most conspicuous virtue of the empress Julia.

63

Two sons, Caracalla and Geta, were the fruit of this marriage, and the destined heirs of the empire. The fond hopes of the father, and of the Roman world, were soon disappointed by these vain youths, who displayed the indolent security of hereditary princes, and a presumption that fortune would supply the place of merit and application. Without any emulation of virtue or talents, they discovered, almost from their infancy, a fixed and implacable antipathy for each other.

Their aversion, confirmed by years, and fomented by the arts of their interested favourites, broke out in childish, and gradually in more serious, competitions; and at length divided the theatre, the circus, and the court into two factions, actuated by the hopes and fears of their respective leaders. The prudent emperor endeavoured, by every expedient of advice and authority, to allay this growing animosity. The unhappy discord of his sons clouded all his prospects, and threatened to overturn a throne raised with so much labour, cemented with so much blood, and guarded with every defence of arms and treasure. With an impartial hand he maintained between them an exact balance of favour, conferred on both the rank of Augustus, with the revered name of Antoninus; and for the first time the Roman world beheld three emperors. Yet even this equal conduct served only to inflame the contest, whilst the fierce Caracalla asserted the right of primogeniture, and the milder Geta courted the affections of the people and the soldiers. In the anguish of a disappointed father, Severus foretold that the weaker of his sons would fall a sacrifice to the stronger; who, in his turn, would be ruined by his own vices.

In these circumstances the intelligence of a war in Britain, and of an invasion of the province by the barbarians of the North, was received with pleasure by Severus. Though the vigilance of his lieutenants might have been sufficient to repel the distant enemy, he resolved to embrace the honourable pretext of withdrawing his sons from the luxury of Rome, which enervated their minds and irritated their passions; and of inuring their youth to the toils of war and government. Notwithstanding his advanced age (for he was above three-score), and his gout, which obliged him to be carried in a litter, he transported himself in person into that remote island, attended by his two sons, his whole court, and a formidable army. He immediately passed the walls of Hadrian and Antoninus, and entered the enemy's country with a design of completing the long attempted conquest of Britain. He penetrated to the northern extremity of the island without meeting an enemy. But the concealed ambuscades of the Caledonians, who hung unseen on the rear and flanks of his army, the coldness of the climate, and the severity of a winter march across the hills and morasses of Scotland, are reported to have cost the Romans above fifty thousand men. The Caledonians at length yielded to the powerful and obstinate attack, sued for peace, and surrendered a part of their arms and a large tract of territory. But their apparent submission lasted no longer than the present terror. As soon as the Roman legions had retired they resumed their hostile independence. Their restless spirit provoked Severus to send a new army into Caledonia, with the most bloody orders, not to subdue but to extirpate the natives. They were saved by the death of their haughty enemy.

This Caledonian war, neither marked by decisive events nor attended with any important consequences, would ill deserve our attention; but it is supposed, not without a considerable degree of probability, that the invasion of Severus is connected with the most shining period of the British history or fable. Fingal, whose fame, with that of his heroes and bards, has been revived in our language by a recent publication, is said to have commanded the Caledonians in that memorable juncture, to have eluded the power of Severus, and to have obtained a signal victory on the banks of the Carun, in which the son of *the King of the World*, Caracul, fled from his arms along the fields of his pride. Something of a doubtful mist still hangs over these Highland traditions; nor can it be entirely dispelled by the most ingenious researches of modern criticism; but, if we could with safety indulge the pleasing supposition that Fingal lived and that Ossian sung, the striking contrast of the situation and manners of the contending nations might amuse a philosophic mind. The parallel would be little to the advantage of the more civilised people, if we compared the unrelenting revenge of Severus with the generous clemency of Fingal; the timid and brutal cruelty of Caracalla with the bravery, the tenderness, the elegant genius of Ossian; the mercenary chiefs who, from motives of fear or interest, served under the Imperial standard, with the free-born warriors who started to arms at the voice of the king of Morven; if, in a word, we contemplated the untutored Caledonians glowing with the warm virtues of nature, and the degenerate Romans polluted with the mean vices of wealth and slavery.

CARACALLA AND GETA

The declining health and last illness of Severus inflamed the wild ambition and black passions of Caracalla's soul. Impatient of any delay or division of empire, he attempted, more than once, to shorten the small remainder of his father's days, and endeavoured, but without success, to excite a mutiny among the troops. The old emperor had often censured the misguided lenity of Marcus, who, by a single act of justice, might have saved the Romans from the tyranny of his worthless son. Placed in the same situation, he experienced how easily the rigour of a judge dissolves away in the tenderness of a parent. He deliberated, he threatened, but he could not punish; and this last and only instance of mercy was more fatal to the empire than a long series of cruelty. The disorder of his mind irritated the pains of his body; he wished impatiently for death, and hastened the instant of it by his impatience. He expired at York, in the sixty-fifth year of his life, and in the eighteenth of a glorious and successful reign. In his last moments he recommended concord to his sons, and his sons to the army. The salutary advice never reached the heart, or even the understanding, of the impetuous youths; but the more obedient troops, mindful of their oath of allegiance and of the authority of their deceased master, resisted the solicitations of Caracalla, and proclaimed both brothers emperors of Rome. The new princes soon left the Caledonians in peace, returned to the capital, celebrated their father's funeral with divine honours, and were cheerfully acknowledged as lawful sovereigns by the senate, the people, and the provinces. Some pre-eminence of rank seems to have been allowed to the elder brother; but they both administered the empire with equal and independent power.

Such a divided form of government would have proved a source of discord between the most affectionate brothers. It was impossible that it could long subsist between two implacable enemies, who neither desired nor could trust a reconciliation. It was visible that one only could reign, and that the other must fall; and each of them, judging of his rival's designs by his own, guarded his life with the most jealous vigilance from the repeated attacks of poison or the sword. Their rapid journey through Gaul and Italy, during which they never ate at the same table, or slept in the same house, displayed to the provinces the odious spectacle of fraternal discord. On their arrival at Rome, they immediately divided the vast extent of the imperial palace. No communication was allowed between their appartments; the doors and passages were diligently fortified, and guards posted and relieved with the same strictness as in a besieged place. The emperors met only in public, in the presence of their afflicted mother; and each surrounded by a numerous train of armed followers. Even on these occasions of ceremony, the dissimulation of courts could ill disguise the rancour of their hearts.

This latent civil war already distracted the whole government, when a scheme was suggested that seemed of mutual benefit to the hostile brothers. It was proposed, that, since it was impossible to reconcile their minds, they should separate their interest, and divide the empire between them. The conditions of the treaty were already drawn with some accuracy. It was agreed that Caracalla, as the elder brother, should remain in possession of Europe and the western Africa; and that he should relinquish the sovereignty of Asia and Egypt to Geta, who might fix his residence at Alexandria or Antioch, cities little inferior to Rome itself in wealth and greatness; that numerous armies should be constantly encamped on either side of the Thracian Bosphorus, to guard the frontiers of the rival monarchies; and that the senators of European extraction should acknowledge the sovereign of Rome, whilst the natives of Asia followed the emperor of the East. The tears of the empress Julia interrupted the negotiation, the first idea of which had filled every

Roman breast with surprise and indignation. The mighty mass of conquest was so intimately united by the hand of time and policy, that it required the most forcible violence to rend it asunder. The Romans had reason to dread that the disjointed members would soon be reduced by a civil war under the dominion of one master; but if the separation was permanent, the division of the provinces must terminate in the dissolution of an empire whose unity had hitherto remained inviolate.

Had the treaty been carried into execution, the sovereign of Europe might soon have been the conqueror of Asia; but Caracalla obtained an easier, though a more guilty, victory. He artfully listened to his mother's entreaties, and consented to meet his brother in her apartment, on terms of peace and reconciliation. In the midst of their conversation, some centurions, who had contrived to conceal themselves, rushed with drawn swords upon the unfortunate Geta. His distracted mother strove to protect him in her arms; but, in the unavailing struggle, she was wounded in the hand, and covered with the blood of her younger son, whilst she saw the elder animating and assisting the fury of the assassins. As soon as the deed was perpetrated, Caracalla, with hasty steps, and horror in his countenance, ran towards the Prætorian camp, as his only refuge, and threw himself on the ground before the statues of the tutelar deities. The soldiers attempted to raise and comfort him. In broken and disordered words he informed them of his imminent danger and fortunate escape; insinuating that he had prevented the designs of his enemy, and declared his resolution to live and die with his faithful troops. Geta had been the favourite of the soldiers; but complaint was useless, revenge was dangerous, and they still reverenced the son of Severus. Their discontent died away in idle murmurs, and Caracalla soon convinced them of the justice of his cause, by distributing in one lavish donative the accumulated treasures of his father's reign. The real *sentiments* of the soldiers alone were of importance to his power or safety. Their declaration in his favour commanded the dutiful *professions* of the senate. The obsequious assembly was always prepared to ratify the decision of fortune; but as Caracalla wished to assuage the first emotions of public indignation, the name of Geta was mentioned with decency, and he received the funeral honours of a Roman emperor. Posterity, in pity to his misfortune, has cast a veil over his vices. We consider that young prince as the innocent victim of his brother's ambition, without recollecting that he himself wanted power, rather than inclination, to consummate the same attempts of revenge and murder.

The crime went not unpunished. Neither business, nor pleasure, nor flattery, could defend Caracalla from the stings of a guilty conscience; and he confessed, in the anguish of a tortured mind, that his disordered fancy often beheld the angry forms of his father and his brother rising into life to threaten and upbraid him. The consciousness of his crime should have induced him to convince mankind, by the virtues of his reign, that the bloody deed had been the involuntary effect of fatal necessity. But the repentance of Caracalla only prompted him to remove from the world whatever could remind him of his guilt, or recall the memory of his murdered brother. On his return from the senate to the palace, he found his mother in the company of several noble matrons, weeping over the untimely fate of her younger son. The jealous emperor threatened them with instant death; the sentence was executed against Fadilla, the last remaining daughter of the emperor Marcus; and even the afflicted Julia was obliged to silence her lamentations, to suppress her sighs, and to receive the assassin with smiles of joy and approbation. It was computed that, under the vague appellation of the friends of Geta, above twenty thousand persons of both sexes suffered death. His guards and freedmen, the ministers of his serious business, and the companions of his looser hours, those who by his interest had been promoted to any commands in the army or provinces, with the long-connected chain of their dependants, were included in the proscription; which endeavoured to reach every one who had maintained the smallest correspondence with Geta, who lamented his death, or who even mentioned his name. Helvius Pertinax, son to the prince of that name, lost his life by an unseasonable witticism. It was a sufficient crime of Thrasea Priscus to be descended from a family in which the love of liberty seemed an hereditary quality. The particular causes of calumny and suspicion were at length exhausted; and when a senator was accused of being a secret enemy to the government, the emperor was satisfied with the general proof that he was a man of property and virtue. From this well-grounded principle he frequently drew the most bloody inferences.

The execution of so many innocent citizens was bewailed by the secret tears of their friends and families. The death of Papinian, the Prætorian prefect, was lamented as a public calamity. During the last seven years of Severus he had exercised the most important offices of the state, and, by his salutary influence, guided the emperor's steps in the paths of justice and moderation. In full assurance of his virtue and abilities, Severus, on his deathbed, had conjured him to watch over the prosperity and union of the Imperial family. The honest labours of Papinian served only to inflame the hatred which Caracalla had already conceived against his father's minister. After the murder of Geta, the prefect was commanded to exert the powers of his skill and eloquence in a studied apology for that atrocious deed. The philosophic Seneca had condescended to compose a similar epistle to the senate, in the name of the son and assassin of Agrippina. "That it was easier to commit than to justify a parricide," was the glorious reply of Papinian; who did not hesitate between the loss of life and that of honour. Such intrepid virtue, which had escaped pure and unsullied from the intrigues of courts, the habits of business, and the arts of his profession, reflects more lustre on the memory of Papinian than all his great employments, his numerous writings, and the superior reputation as a lawyer which he has preserved through every age of the Roman jurisprudence.

It had hitherto been the peculiar felicity of the Romans, and in the worst of times their consolation, that the virtue of the emperors was active, and their vice indolent. Augustus, Trajan, Hadrian, and Marcus visited their extensive dominions in person, and their progress was marked by acts of wisdom and beneficence. The tyranny of Tiberius, Nero, and Domitian, who resided almost constantly at Rome or in the adjacent villas, was confined to the senatorial and equestrian orders. But Caracalla was the common enemy of mankind. He left the capital (and he never returned to it) about a year after the murder of Geta. The rest of his reign was spent in the several provinces of the empire, particularly those of the East, and every province was, by turns, the scene of his rapine and cruelty. The senators, compelled by fear to attend his capricious motions, were obliged to provide daily entertainments at an immense expense, which he abandoned with contempt to his guards; and to erect in every city magnificent palaces and theatres, which he either disdained to visit, or ordered to be immediately thrown down. The most wealthy families were ruined by partial fines and confiscations, and the great body of his subjects oppressed by ingenious and aggravated taxes. In the midst of peace, and upon the slightest provocation, he issued his commands at Alexandria, in Egypt, for a general massacre. From a secure post in the temple of Serapis, he viewed and directed the slaughter of many thousand citizens, as well as strangers, without distinguishing either the number or the crime of the sufferers; since, as he coolly informed the senate, *all* the Alexandrians, those who had perished, and those who had escaped, were alike guilty.

The wise instructions of Severus never made any lasting impression on the mind of his son, who, although not destitute of imagination and eloquence, was equally devoid of judgment and humanity. One dangerous maxim, worthy of a tyrant, was remembered and abused by Caracalla—"To secure the affections of the army, and to esteem the rest of his subjects as of little moment." But the liberality of the father had been restrained by prudence, and his indulgence to the troops was tempered by firmness and authority. The careless profusion of the son was the policy of one reign, and the inevitable ruin both of the army and of the empire. The vigour of the soldiers, instead of being confirmed by the severe discipline of camps, melted away in the luxury of cities. The excessive increase of their pay and donatives exhausted the state to enrich the military order, whose modesty in peace, and service in war, is best secured by an honourable poverty. The demeanour of Caracalla was haughty and full of pride; but with the troops he forgot even the proper dignity of his rank, encouraged their insolent familiarity, and, neglecting the essential duties of a general, affected to imitate the dress and manners of a common soldier.

It was impossible that such a character and such a conduct as that of
Caracalla could inspire either love or esteem; but, as long as his vices
were beneficial to the armies, he was secure from the danger of rebellion.
A secret conspiracy, provoked by his own jealousy, was fatal to the
tyrant. The Prætorian prefecture was divided between two ministers.
The military department was intrusted to Adventus, an experienced
rather than an able soldier; and the civil affairs were transacted by
Opilius Macrinus, who, by his dexterity in business, had raised himself,
with a fair character, to that high office. But his favour varied with the
caprice of the emperor, and his life might depend on the slightest suspicion or the most casual circumstance. Malice or fanaticism had suggested to an African, deeply skilled in the knowledge of futurity, a very
dangerous prediction, that Macrinus and his son were destined to reign
over the empire. The report was soon diffused through the province;
and when the man was sent in chains to Rome, he still asserted, in the
presence of the prefect of the city, the faith of his prophecy. That
magistrate, who had received the most pressing instructions to inform
himself of the *successors* of Caracalla, immediately communicated the
examination of the African to the Imperial court, which at that time
resided in Syria. But, notwithstanding the diligence of the public
messengers, a friend of Macrinus found means to apprise him of the
approaching danger. The emperor received the letters from Rome; and,
as he was then engaged in the conduct of a chariot-race, he delivered
them unopened to the Prætorian prefect, directing him to despatch the
ordinary affairs, and to report the more important business that might
be contained in them. Macrinus read his fate and resolved to prevent it.
He inflamed the discontents of some inferior officers, and employed the
hand of Martialis, a desperate soldier, who had been refused the rank of
centurion. The devotion of Caracalla prompted him to make a pilgrimage from Edessa to the celebrated temple of the Moon at Carrhæ.
He was attended by a body of cavalry; but having stopped on the road
for some necessary occasion, his guards preserved a respectful distance,
and Martialis, approaching his person under a pretence of duty, stabbed
him with a dagger. The bold assassin was instantly killed by a Scythian
archer of the Imperial guard. Such was the end of a monster whose life
disgraced human nature, and whose reign accused the patience of the
Romans. The grateful soldiers forgot his vices, remembered only his
partial liberality, and obliged the senate to prostitute their own dignity
and that of religion by granting him a place among the gods. Whilst he
was upon earth Alexander the Great was the only hero whom this god
deemed worthy his admiration. He assumed the name and ensigns of
Alexander, formed a Macedonian phalanx of guards, persecuted the
disciples of Aristotle, and displayed, with a puerile enthusiasm, the only
sentiment by which he discovered any regard for virtue or glory. We
can easily conceive that, after the battle of Narva and the conquest of

Poland, Charles the Twelfth (though he still wanted the more elegant accomplishments of the son of Philip) might boast of having rivalled his valour and magnanimity; but in no one action of his life did Caracalla express the faintest resemblance of the Macedonian hero, except in the murder of a great number of his own and of his father's friends.

Macrinus was now elevated by the Prætorians. His attempts to reform the army made him unpopular. Julia Mæsa the sister-in-law of Septimius Severus gave out that her grandson was Caracalla's child. He was declared emperor and assumed the name of Antoninus. Macrinus was defeated and killed and Antoninus and his court set out for Rome.

ELAGABALUS

As the attention of the new emperor was diverted by the most trifling amusements, he wasted many months in his luxurious progress from Syria to Italy, passed at Nicomedia his first winter after his victory, and deferred till the ensuing summer his triumphal entry into the capital. A faithful picture, however, which preceded his arrival, and was placed by his immediate order over the altar of Victory in the senate-house, conveyed to the Romans the just but unworthy resemblance of his person and manners. He was drawn in his sacerdotal robes of silk and gold, after the loose flowing fashion of the Medes and Phœnicians; his head was covered with a lofty tiara, his numerous collars and bracelets were adorned with gems of an inestimable value. His eyebrows were tinged with black, and his cheeks painted with an artificial red and white. The grave senators confessed with a sigh, that, after having long experienced the stern tyranny of their own countrymen, Rome was at length humbled beneath the effeminate luxury of Oriental despotism.

The Sun was worshipped at Emesa, under the name of Elagabalus, and under the form of a black conical stone, which, as it was universally believed, had fallen from heaven on that sacred place. To this protecting deity, Antoninus, not without some reason, ascribed his elevation to the throne. The display of superstitious gratitude was the only serious business of his reign. The triumph of the god of Emesa over all the religions of the earth was the great object of his zeal and vanity; and the appellation of Elagabalus (for he presumed as pontiff and favourite to adopt that sacred name) was dearer to him than all the title of Imperial greatness. In a solemn procession through the streets of Rome the way was strewed with gold-dust; the black stone, set in precious gems, was placed on a chariot drawn by six milk-white horses richly caparisoned. The pious emperor held the reins, and, supported by his ministers moved slowly backwards, that he might perpetually enjoy the felicity of the divine presence. In a magnificent temple raised on the Palatine Mount, the sacrifices of the god Elagabalus were celebrated with every circumstance of cost and solemnity. The richest wines, the most extraordinary victims, and the rarest aromatics, were profusely consumed on his altar. Around the altar a chorus of Syrian damsels performed their lascivious dances to the sound of barbarian music, whilst the gravest personages of the state and army, clothed in long Phœnician tunics, officiated in the meanest functions with affected zeal and secret indignation.

To this temple, as to the common centre of religious worship, the Imperial fanatic attempted to remove the Ancilia, the Palladium, and all the sacred pledges of the faith of Numa. A crowd of inferior deities attended in various stations the majesty of the god of Emesa; but his court was still imperfect, till a female of distinguished rank was admitted to his bed. Pallas had been first chosen for his consort; but as it was dreaded lest her warlike terrors might affright the soft delicacy of a Syrian deity, the Moon, adored by the Africans under the name of Astarte, was deemed a more suitable companion for the Sun. Her image, with the rich offerings of her temple as a marriage portion, was transported with solemn pomp from Carthage to Rome, and the day of these mystic nuptials was a general festival in the capital and throughout the empire.

A rational voluptuary adheres with invariable respect to the temperate dictates of nature, and improves the gratifications of sense by social intercourse, endearing connections, and the soft colouring of taste and the imagination. But Elagabalus (I speak of the emperor of that name), corrupted by his youth, his country, and his fortune, abandoned himself to the grossest pleasures with ungoverned fury, and soon found disgust and satiety in the midst of his enjoyments. The inflammatory powers of art were summoned to his aid: the confused multitude of women, of wines, and of dishes, and the studied variety of attitudes and sauces, served to revive his languid appetites. New terms and new inventions in these sciences, the only ones cultivated and patronised by the monarch,[1] signalised his reign, and transmitted his infamy to succeeding times. A capricious prodigality supplied the want of taste and elegance; and whilst Elagabalus lavished away the treasures of his people in the wildest extravagance, his own voice and that of his flatterers applauded a spirit and magnificence unknown to the tameness of his predecessors. To confound the order of seasons and climates, to sport with the passions and prejudices of his subjects, and to subvert every law of nature and decency, were in the number of his most delicious amusements. A long train of concubines, and a rapid succession of wives, among whom was a vestal virgin, ravished by force from her sacred asylum, were insufficient to satisfy the impotence of his passions.

---

[1] The invention of a new sauce was liberally rewarded; but as it was not relished, the inventor was confined to eat of nothing else till he had discovered another more agreeable to the Imperial palate.

The master of the Roman world affected to copy the dress and manners of the female sex, preferred the distaff to the sceptre, and dishonoured the principal dignities of the empire by distributing them among his numerous lovers; one of whom was publicly invested with the title and authority of the emperor's, or, as he more properly styled himself, of the empress's husband.

It may seem probable the vices and follies of Elagabalus have been adorned by fancy and blackened by prejudice. Yet, confining ourselves to the public scenes displayed before the Roman people, and attested by grave and contemporary historians, their inexpressible infamy surpasses that of any other age or country. The licence of an eastern monarch is secluded from the eye of curiosity by the inaccessible walls of his seraglio. The sentiments of honour and gallantry have introduced a refinement of pleasure, a regard for decency, and a respect for the public opinion, into the modern courts of Europe; but the corrupt and opulent nobles of Rome gratified every vice that could be collected from the mighty conflux of nations and manners. Secure of impunity, careless of censure, they lived without restraint in the patient and humble society of their slaves and parasites. The emperor, in his turn, viewing every rank of his subjects with the same contemptuous indifference, asserted without control his sovereign privilege of lust and luxury.

The most worthless of mankind are not afraid to condemn in others the same disorders which they allow in themselves; and can readily discover some nice difference of age, character, or station, to justify the partial distinction. The licentious soldiers who had raised to the throne the dissolute son of Caracalla, blushed at their ignominious choice, and turned with disgust from that monster to contemplate with pleasure the opening virtues of his cousin Alexander, the son of Mamæa. The crafty Mæsa, sensible that her grandson Elagabalus must inevitably destroy himself by his own vices, had provided another and surer support of her family. Embracing a favourable moment of fondness and devotion, she had persuaded the young emperor to adopt Alexander and to invest him with the title of Cæsar, that his own divine occupations might be no longer interrupted by the care of the earth. In the second rank that amiable prince soon acquired the affections of the public, and excited the tyrant's jealousy, who resolved to terminate the dangerous competition, either by corrupting the manners, or by taking away the life, of his rival. His arts proved unsuccessful; his vain designs were constantly discovered by his own loquacious folly, and disappointed by those virtuous and faithful servants whom the prudence of Mamæa had placed about the person of her son. In a hasty sally of passion Elagabalus resolved to execute by force what he had been unable to compass by fraud, and by a despotic sentence degraded his cousin from the rank and honours of Cæsar. The message was received in the senate with silence, and in the camp with fury. The Prætorian guards swore to protect

Alexander, and to revenge the dishonoured majesty of the throne. The tears and promises of the trembling Elagabalus, who only begged them to spare his life and to leave him in the possession of his beloved Hierocles, diverted their just indignation; and they contented themselves with empowering their prefects to watch over the safety of Alexander and the conduct of the emperor.

It was impossible that such a reconciliation should last, or that even the mean soul of Elagabalus could hold an empire on such humiliating terms of dependence. He soon attempted, by a dangerous experiment, to try the temper of the soldiers. The report of the death of Alexander, and the natural suspicion that he had been murdered, inflamed their passions into fury, and the tempest of the camp could only be appeased by the presence and authority of the popular youth. Provoked at this new instance of their affection for his cousin, and their contempt for his person, the emperor ventured to punish some of the leaders of the mutiny. His unseasonable severity proved instantly fatal to his minions, his mother, and himself. Elagabalus was massacred by the indignant Prætorians, his mutilated corpse dragged through the streets of the city and thrown into the Tiber. His memory was branded with eternal infamy by the senate; the justice of whose decree has been ratified by posterity.

ACCESSION OF ALEXANDER SEVERUS

In the room of Elagabalus his cousin Alexander was raised to the throne by the Prætorian guards. His relation to the family of Severus, whose name he assumed, was the same as that of his predecessor; his virtue and his danger had already endeared him to the Romans, and the eager liberality of the senate conferred upon him in one day the various titles and powers of the Imperial dignity. But as Alexander was a modest and dutiful youth of only seventeen years of age, the reins of government were in the hands of two women, of his mother Mamæa, and of Mæsa his grandmother. After the death of the latter, who survived but a short time the elevation of Alexander, Mamæa remained the sole regent of her son and of the empire.

In every age and country the wiser, or at least the stronger, of the two sexes, has usurped the powers of the state, and confined the other to the cares and pleasures of domestic life. In hereditary monarchies, however, and especially in those of modern Europe, the gallant spirit of chivalry and the law of succession have accustomed us to allow a singular exception; and a woman is often acknowledged the absolute sovereign of a great kingdom, in which she would be deemed incapable of exercising the smallest employment, civil or military. But as the Roman emperors were still considered as the generals and magistrates of the republic, their wives and mothers, although distinguished by the name of Augusta, were never associated to their personal honours; and a female reign would have appeared an inexpiable prodigy in the eyes of those primitive Romans, who married without love, or loved without delicacy and respect. The haughty Agrippina aspired, indeed, to share the honours of the empire which she had conferred on her son; but her mad ambition, detested by every citizen who felt for the dignity of Rome, was disappointed by the artful firmness of Seneca and Burrhus. The good sense, or the indifference, of succeeding princes, restrained them from offending the prejudices of their subjects; and it was reserved for the profligate Elagabalus to disgrace the acts of the senate with the name of his mother Soæmias, who was placed by the side of the consuls, and subscribed, as a regular member, the decrees of the legislative assembly. Her more prudent sister, Mamæa, declined the useless and odious prerogative, and a solemn law was enacted excluding women for ever from the senate, and devoting to the infernal gods the head of the wretch by whom this sanction should be violated. The substance, not the pageantry, of power was the object of Mamæa's manly ambition. She maintained an absolute and lasting empire over the mind of her son, and in his affection the mother could not brook a rival. Alexander, with her consent, married the daughter of a patrician; but his respect for his father-in-law and love for the empress were inconsistent with the tenderness or interest of Mamæa. The patrician was executed on the ready accusation of treason, and the wife of Alexander driven with ignominy from the palace and banished into Africa.

Notwithstanding this act of jealous cruelty, as well as some instances of avarice with which Mamæa is charged, the general tenor of her administration was equally for the benefit of her son and of the empire. With the approbation of the senate she chose sixteen of the wisest and most virtuous senators as a perpetual council of state, before whom every public business of moment was debated and determined. The celebrated Ulpian, equally distinguished by his knowledge of, and his respect for, the laws of Rome, was at their head; and the prudent firmness of this aristocracy restored order and authority to the government. As soon as they had purged the city from foreign superstition and luxury, the remains of the capricious tyranny of Elagabalus, they applied themselves to remove his worthless creatures from every department of public administration, and to supply their places with men of virtue and ability. Learning, and the love of justice, became the only recommendations for civil offices; valour, and the love of discipline, the only qualifications for military employments.

But the most important care of Mamæa and her wise counsellors was to form the character of the young emperor, on whose personal qualities the happiness or misery of the Roman world must ultimately depend. The fortunate soil assisted, and even prevented, the hand of cultivation. An excellent understanding soon convinced Alexander of the advantages of virtue, the pleasure of knowledge, and the necessity of labour. A

natural mildness and moderation of temper preserved him from the
assaults of passion and the allurements of vice. His unalterable regard
for his mother, and his esteem for the wise Ulpian, guarded his unexperienced youth from the poison of flattery.

The simple journal of his ordinary occupations exhibits a pleasing
picture of an accomplished emperor, and, with some allowance for the
difference of manners, might well deserve the imitation of modern
princes. Alexander rose early; the first moments of the day were consecrated to private devotion, and his domestic chapel was filled with the
images of those heroes who, by improving or reforming human life, had
deserved the grateful reverence of posterity. But, as he deemed the
service of mankind the most acceptable worship of the gods, the greatest
part of his morning hours was employed in his council, where he discussed public affairs, and determined private causes, with a patience and
discretion above his years. The dryness of business was relieved by the
charms of literature; and a portion of time was always set apart for his
favourite studies of poetry, history, and philosophy. The works of Virgil
and Horace, the Republics of Plato and Cicero, formed his taste, enlarged his understanding, and gave him the noblest ideas of man and
government. The exercises of the body succeeded to those of the mind;
and Alexander, who was tall, active, and robust, surpassed most of his
equals in the gymnastic arts. Refreshed by the use of the bath and a
slight dinner, he resumed, with new vigour, the business of the day; and,
till the hour of supper, the principal meal of the Romans, he was attended
by his secretaries, with whom he read and answered the multitude of
letters, memorials, and petitions, that must have been addressed to the
master of the greatest part of the world. His table was served with the
most frugal simplicity; and whenever he was at liberty to consult his own
inclination, the company consisted of a few select friends, men of learning and virtue, amongst whom Ulpian was constantly invited. Their
conversation was familiar and instructive; and the pauses were occasionally enlivened by the recital of some pleasing composition, which
supplied the place of the dancers, comedians, and even gladiators, so
frequently summoned to the tables of the rich and luxurious Romans.
The dress of Alexander was plain and modest, his demeanour courteous
and affable: at the proper hours his palace was open to all his subjects,
but the voice of a crier was heard, as in the Eleusinian mysteries, pronouncing the same salutary admonition: "Let none enter those holy
walls unless he is conscious of a pure and innocent mind."

Such an uniform tenor of life, which left not a moment for vice or
folly, is a better proof of the wisdom and justice of Alexander's government than all the trifling details preserved in the compilation of Lam-
pridius. Since the accession of Commodus the Roman world had experienced, during the term of forty years, the successive and various
vices of four tyrants. From the death of Elagabalus it enjoyed an

auspicious calm of thirteen years. The provinces, relieved from the oppressive taxes invented by Caracalla and his pretended son, flourished in peace and prosperity, under the administration of magistrates who were convinced by experience that to deserve the love of the subjects was their best and only method of obtaining the favour of their sovereign. While some gentle restraints were imposed on the innocent luxury of the Roman people, the price of provisions and the interest of money were reduced by the paternal care of Alexander, whose prudent liberality, without distressing the industrious, supplied the wants and amusements of the populace. The dignity, the freedom, the authority of the senate was restored; and every virtuous senator might approach the person of the emperor without a fear and without a blush.

The name of Antoninus, ennobled by the virtues of Pius and Marcus, had been communicated by adoption to the dissolute Verus, and by descent to the cruel Commodus. It became the honourable appellation of the sons of Severus, was bestowed on young Diadumenianus, and at length prostituted to the infamy of the high priest of Emesa. Alexander, though pressed by the studied, and perhaps sincere, importunity of the senate, nobly refused the borrowed lustre of a name; whilst in his whole conduct he laboured to restore the glories and felicity of the age of the genuine Antonines.

Although the traditional portrait of Severus Alexander was idealised, as Gibbon knew, he was a temperate and conscientious ruler. His reforms made him unpopular, and with the rising threats on the Persian and German fronts he lost any ascendancy over the army. Gibbon concludes chapter 6 with a digression on the finances of the empire.

THE DISRUPTION OF THE EMPIRE

Chapter 7

BARBARIAN EMPEROR.
THE GORDIANS. PHILIP THE ARAB

OF the various forms of government which have prevailed in the world, an hereditary monarchy seems to present the fairest scope for ridicule. Is it possible to relate without an indignant smile, that, on the father's decease, the property of a nation, like that of a drove of oxen, descends to his infant son, as yet unknown to mankind and to himself, and that the bravest warriors and the wisest statesmen, relinquishing their natural right to empire, approach the royal cradle with bended knees and protestations of inviolable fidelity? Satire and declamation may paint these obvious topics in the most dazzling colours, but our more serious thoughts will respect a useful prejudice that establishes a rule of succession, independent of the passions of mankind; and we shall cheerfully acquiesce in any expedient which deprives the multitude of the dangerous, and indeed the ideal, power of giving themselves a master.

In the cool shade of retirement we may easily devise imaginary forms of government, in which the sceptre shall be constantly bestowed on the most worthy by the free and incorrupt suffrage of the whole community. Experience overturns these airy fabrics, and teaches us that in a large society the election of a monarch can never devolve to the wisest or to the most numerous part of the people. The army is the only order of men sufficiently united to concur in the same sentiments, and powerful enough to impose them on the rest of their fellow-citizens; but the temper of soldiers, habituated at once to violence and to slavery, renders them very unfit guardians of a legal or even a civil constitution. Justice, humanity, or political wisdom, are qualities they are too little acquainted with in themselves to appreciate them in others. Valour will acquire their esteem, and liberality will purchase their suffrage; but the first of these merits is often lodged in the most savage breasts; the latter can only exert itself at the expense of the public; and both may be turned against the possessor of the throne by the ambition of a daring rival.

The superior prerogative of birth, when it has obtained the sanction of time and popular opinion, is the plainest and least invidious of all distinctions among mankind. The acknowledged right extinguishes the hopes of faction, and the conscious security disarms the cruelty of the monarch. To the firm establishment of this idea we owe the peaceful succession and mild administration of European monarchies. To the defect of it we must attribute the frequent civil wars through which an Asiatic despot is obliged to cut his way to the throne of his fathers. Yet, even in the East, the sphere of contention is usually limited to the princes of the reigning house, and, as soon as the more fortunate competitor has removed his brethren by the sword and the bow-string, he no longer entertains any jealousy of his meaner subjects. But the Roman empire, after the authority of the senate had sunk into contempt, was a vast scene of confusion. The royal and even noble families of the provinces had long since been led in triumph before the car of the haughty republicans. The ancient families of Rome had successively fallen beneath the tyranny of the Cæsars; and whilst those princes were shackled by the forms of a commonwealth, and disappointed by the repeated failure of their posterity, it was impossible that any idea of hereditary succession should have taken root in the minds of their subjects. The right to the throne, which none could claim from birth, every one assumed from merit. The daring hopes of ambition were set loose from the salutary restraints of law and prejudice, and the meanest of mankind might, without folly, entertain a hope of being raised by valour and fortune to a rank in the army, in which a single crime would enable him to wrest the sceptre of the world from his feeble and unpopular master. After the murder of Alexander Severus and the elevation of Maximin, no emperor could think himself safe upon the throne, and every barbarian peasant of the frontier might aspire to that august but dangerous station.

About thirty-two years before that event, the emperor Severus, returning from an eastern expedition, halted in Thrace, to celebrate, with military games, the birthday of his younger son, Geta. The country flocked in crowds to behold their sovereign, and a young barbarian of gigantic stature earnestly solicited, in his rude dialect, that he might be allowed to contend for the prize of wrestling. As the pride of discipline would have been disgraced in the overthrow of a Roman soldier by a Thracian peasant, he was matched with the stoutest followers of the camp, sixteen of whom he successively laid on the ground. His victory was rewarded by some trifling gifts, and a permission to enlist in the troops. The next day the happy barbarian was distinguished above a crowd of recruits, dancing and exulting after the fashion of his country. As soon as he perceived that he had attracted the emperor's notice, he instantly ran up to his horse, and followed him on foot, without the least appearance of fatigue, in a long and rapid career. "Thracian," said Severus with astonishment, "art thou disposed to wrestle after thy race?" "Most willingly, Sir," replied the unwearied youth; and, almost in a breath, overthrew seven of the strongest soldiers in the army. A gold collar was the prize of his matchless vigour and activity, and he was immediately appointed to serve in the horse-guards who always attended on the person of the sovereign.

Maximin, for that was his name, though born on the territories of the empire, descended from a mixed race of barbarians. His father was a Goth, and his mother of the nation of the Alani. He displayed on every occasion a valour equal to his strength, and his native fierceness was soon tempered or disguised by the knowledge of the world. Under the reign of Severus and his son, he obtained the rank of centurion, with the favour and esteem of both those princes, the former of whom was an excellent judge of merit. Gratitude forbade Maximin to serve under the assassin of Caracalla. Honour taught him to decline the effeminate insults of Elagabalus. On the accession of Alexander he returned to court and was placed by that prince in a station useful to the service and honourable to himself. The fourth legion, to which he was appointed tribune, soon became, under his care, the best disciplined of the whole army. With the general applause of the soldiers, who bestowed on their favourite hero the names of Ajax and Hercules, he was successively promoted to the first military command; and had not he still retained too much of his savage origin, the emperor might perhaps have given his own sister in marriage to the son of Maximin.

Instead of securing his fidelity, these favours served only to inflame the ambition of the Thracian peasant, who deemed his fortune inadequate to his merit as long as he was constrained to acknowledge a superior. Though a stranger to real wisdom, he was not devoid of a selfish cunning, which showed him that the emperor had lost the affection of the army, and taught him to improve their discontent to his own advantage. It is easy for faction and calumny to shed their poison on the administration of the best of princes, and to accuse even their virtues by artfully confounding them with those vices to which they bear the nearest affinity. The troops listened with pleasure to the emissaries of Maximin. They blushed at their own ignominious patience, which, during thirteen years, had supported the vexatious discipline imposed by an effeminate Syrian, the timid slave of his mother and of the senate. It was time, they cried, to cast away that useless phantom of the civil power, and to elect for their prince and general a real soldier, educated in camps, exercised in war, who would assert the glory and distribute among his companions the treasures of the empire. A great army was at that time assembled on the banks of the Rhine, under the command of the emperor himself, who, almost immediately after his return from the Persian war, had been obliged to march against the barbarians of Germany. The important care of training and reviewing the new levies was intrusted to Maximin. One day, as he entered the field of exercise, the troops, either from a sudden impulse or a formed conspiracy, saluted him emperor, silenced by their loud acclamations his obstinate refusal, and hastened to consummate their rebellion by the murder of Alexander Severus.

The circumstances of his death are variously related. The writers who suppose that he died in ignorance of the ingratitude and ambition of Maximin affirm that, after taking a frugal repast in the sight of the army, he retired to sleep, and that about the seventh hour of the day a part of his own guards broke into the Imperial tent, and, with many wounds, assassinated their virtuous and unsuspecting prince. If we credit another, and indeed a more probable account, Maximin was invested with the purple by a numerous detachment, at the distance of several miles from the headquarters, and he trusted for success rather to the secret wishes than to the public declarations of the great army. Alexander had sufficient time to awaken a faint sense of loyalty among his troops; but their reluctant professions of fidelity quickly vanished on the appearance of Maximin, who declared himself the friend and advocate of the military order, and was unanimously acknowledged emperor of the Romans by the applauding legions. The son of Mamæa, betrayed and deserted, withdrew into his tent, desirous at least to conceal his approaching fate from the insults of the multitude. He was soon followed by a tribune and some centurions, the ministers of death; but instead of receiving with manly resolution the inevitable stroke, his unavailing cries and entreaties disgraced the last moments of his life, and converted into contempt some portion of the just pity which his innocence and misfortunes must inspire. His mother Mamæa, whose pride and avarice he loudly accused as the cause of his ruin, perished with her son. The most faithful of his friends were sacrificed to the first fury of the soldiers. Others were reserved for the more deliberate cruelty of the usurper, and those who experienced the mildest treatment were stripped of their employments and ignominiously driven from the court and army.

The former tyrants, Caligula and Nero, Commodus and Caracalla, were all dissolute and unexperienced youths, educated in the purple, and corrupted by the pride of the empire, the luxury of Rome, and the perfidious voice of flattery. The cruelty of Maximin was derived from a different source, the fear of contempt. Though he depended on the attachment of the soldiers, who loved him for virtues like their own, he was conscious that his mean and barbarian origin, the savage appearance, and his total ignorance of the arts and institutions of civil life, formed a very unfavourable contrast with the amiable manners of the unhappy Alexander. He remembered, that, in his humbler fortune, he had often waited before the door of the haughty nobles of Rome, and had been denied admittance by the insolence of their slaves. He recollected too the friendship of a few who had relieved his poverty, and assisted his rising hopes. But those who had spurned, and those who had protected the Thracian, were guilty of the same crime, the knowledge of his original obscurity. For this crime many were put to death; and by the execution of several of his benefactors, Maximin published, in characters of blood, the indelible history of his baseness and ingratitude.

The dark and sanguinary soul of the tyrant was open to every suspicion against those among his subjects who were the most distinguished by their birth or merit. Whenever he was alarmed with the sound of treason, his cruelty was unbounded and unrelenting. A conspiracy against his life was either discovered or imagined, and Magnus, a consular senator, was named as the principal author of it. Without a witness, without a trial, and without an opportunity of defence, Magnus, with four thousand of his supposed accomplices, were put to death. Italy and the whole empire were infested with innumerable spies and informers. On the slightest accusation, the first of the Roman nobles, who had governed provinces, commanded armies, and been adorned with the consular and triumphal ornaments, were chained on the public carriages, and hurried away to the emperor's presence. Confiscation, exile, or simple death, were esteemed uncommon instances of his lenity. Some of the unfortunate sufferers he ordered to be sewed up in the hides of slaughtered animals, others to be exposed to wild beasts, others again to be beaten to death with clubs. During the three years of his reign he disdained to visit either Rome or Italy. His camp, occasionally removed from the banks of the Rhine to those of the Danube, was the seat of his stern despotism, which trampled on every principle of law and justice, and was supported by the avowed power of the sword. No man of noble birth, elegant accomplishments, or knowledge of civil business, was suffered near his person; and the court of a Roman emperor revived the idea of those ancient chiefs of slaves and gladiators, whose savage power had left a deep impression of terror and detestation.

As long as the cruelty of Maximin was confined to the illustrious senators, or even to the bold adventurers who in the court or army expose themselves to the caprice of fortune, the body of the people viewed their sufferings with indifference, or perhaps with pleasure. But the tyrant's avarice, stimulated by the insatiate desires of the soldiers, at length attacked the public property. Every city of the empire was possessed of an independent revenue, destined to purchase corn for the multitude, and to supply the expenses of the games and entertainments. By a single act of authority, the whole mass of wealth was at once confiscated for the use of the Imperial treasury. The temples were stripped of their most valuable offerings of gold and silver, and the statues of gods, heroes, and emperors, were melted down and coined into money. These impious orders could not be executed without tumults and massacres, as in many places the people chose rather to die in the defence of their altars than to behold in the midst of peace their cities exposed to the rapine and cruelty of war. The soldiers themselves, among whom this sacrilegious plunder was distributed, received it with a blush; and hardened as they were in acts of violence, they dreaded the just reproaches of their friends and relations. Throughout the Roman world a general cry of indignation was heard, imploring vengeance on the common enemy of human kind; and at length, by an act of private oppression, a peaceful and unarmed province was driven into rebellion against him.

The procurator of Africa was a servant worthy of such a master, who considered the fines and confiscations of the rich as one of the most fruitful branches of the imperial revenue. An iniquitous sentence had been pronounced against some opulent youths of that country, the execution of which would have stripped them of far the greater part of their patrimony. In this extremity, a resolution that must either complete or prevent their ruin was dictated by despair. A respite of three days, obtained with difficulty from the rapacious treasurer, was employed in collecting from their estates a great number of slaves and peasants blindly devoted to the commands of their lords, and armed with the rustic weapons of clubs and axes. The leaders of the conspiracy, as they were admitted to the audience of the procurator, stabbed him with the daggers concealed under their garments, and, by the assistance of their tumultuary train, seized on the little town of Thysdrus, and erected the standard of rebellion against the sovereign of the Roman empire. They rested their hopes on the hatred of mankind against Maximin, and they judiciously resolved to oppose to that detested tyrant an emperor whose mild virtues had already acquired the love and esteem of the Romans, and whose authority over the province would give weight and stability to the enterprise. Gordianus, their proconsul, and the object of their choice, refused, with unfeigned reluctance, the dangerous honour, and begged, with tears, that they would suffer him to terminate in peace a long and innocent life, without staining his feeble age with civil blood. Their menaces compelled him to accept the Imperial purple, his only refuge indeed against the jealous cruelty of Maximin; since, according to the reasoning of tyrants, those who have been esteemed worthy of the throne deserve death, and those who deliberate have already rebelled.

THE GORDIANS

The family of Gordianus was one of the most illustrious of the Roman senate. On the father's side he was descended from the Gracchi; on his mother's, from the emperor Trajan. A great estate enabled him to support the dignity of his birth, and in the enjoyment of it he displayed an elegant taste and beneficent disposition. The palace in Rome formerly inhabited by the great Pompey had been, during several generations, in the possession of Gordian's family. It was distinguished by ancient trophies of naval victories, and decorated with the works of modern painting. His villa on the road to Præneste was celebrated for baths of singular beauty and extent, for three stately rooms of an hundred feet in length, and for a magnificent portico, supported by two hundred columns of the four most curious and costly sorts of marble. The public shows exhibited at his expense, and in which the people were entertained with many hundreds of wild beasts and gladiators, seem to surpass the fortune of a subject; and whilst the liberality of other magistrates was confined to a few solemn festivals in Rome, the magnificence of Gordian was repeated, when he was ædile, every month in the year, and extended, during his consulship, to the principal cities of Italy. He was twice elevated to the last-mentioned dignity, by Caracalla and by Alexander; for he possessed the uncommon talent of acquiring the esteem of virtuous princes, without alarming the jealousy of tyrants. His long life was innocently spent in the study of letters and the peaceful honours of Rome; and, till he was named proconsul of Africa by the voice of the senate and the approbation of Alexander, he appears prudently to have declined the command of armies and the government of provinces. As long as that emperor lived, Africa was happy under the administration of his worthy representative; after the barbarous Maximin had usurped the throne, Gordianus alleviated the miseries which he was unable to prevent. When he reluctantly accepted the purple, he was above fourscore years old; a last and valuable remains of the happy age of the Antonines, whose virtues he revived in his own conduct, and celebrated in an elegant poem of thirty books. With the venerable proconsul, his son, who had accompanied him into Africa as his lieutenant, was likewise declared emperor. His manners were less pure, but his character was equally amiable with that of his father. Twenty-two acknowledged concubines, and a library of sixty two thousand volumes, attested the variety of his inclinations; and from the productions which he left behind him, it appears that the former as well as the latter were designed for use rather than for ostentation. The Roman people acknowledged in the features of the younger Gordian the resemblance of Scipio Africanus, recollected with pleasure that his mother was the grand-daughter of Antoninus Pius, and rested the public hope on those latent virtues which had hitherto, as they fondly imagined, lain concealed in the luxurious indolence of a private life.

As soon as the Gordians had appeased the first tumult of a popular election they removed their court to Carthage. They were received with the acclamations of the Africans, who honoured their virtues, and who, since the visit of Hadrian, had never beheld the majesty of a Roman emperor. But these vain acclamations neither strengthened nor confirmed the title of the Gordians. They were induced by principle, as well as interest, to solicit the approbation of the senate; and a deputation of the noblest provincials was sent, without delay, to Rome, to relate and justify the conduct of their countrymen, who, having long suffered with patience, were at length resolved to act with vigour. The letters of the new princes were modest and respectful, excusing the necessity which had obliged them to accept the Imperial title, but submitting their election and their fate to the supreme judgment of the senate.

The inclinations of the senate were neither doubtful nor divided. The birth and noble alliances of the Gordians had intimately connected them with the most illustrious houses of Rome. Their fortune had created many dependents in that assembly, their merit had acquired many friends. Their mild administration opened the flattering prospect of the restoration, not only of the civil but even of the republican government. The terror of military violence, which had first obliged the senate to forget the murder of Alexander, and to ratify the election of a barbarian peasant, now produced a contrary effect, and provoked them to assert the injured rights of freedom and humanity. The hatred of Maximin towards the senate was declared and implacable; the tamest submission had not appeased his fury, the most cautious innocence would not remove his suspicions; and even the care of their own safety urged them to share the fortune of an enterprise, of which (if unsuccessful) they were sure to be the first victims. These considerations, and perhaps others of a more private nature, were debated in a previous conference of the consuls and the magistrates. As soon as their resolution was decided they convoked in the temple of Castor the whole body of the senate, according to an ancient form of secrecy, calculated to awaken their attention and to conceal their decrees. "Conscript fathers," said the consul Syllanus, "the two Gordians, both of consular dignity, the one your proconsul, the other your lieutenant, have been declared emperors by the general consent of Africa. Let us return thanks," he boldly continued, "to the youth of Thysdrus; let us return thanks to the faithful people of Carthage, our generous deliverers from an horrid monster—Why do you hear me thus coolly, thus timidly? Why do you cast those anxious looks on each other? why hesitate? Maximin is a public enemy! may his enmity soon expire with him, and may we long enjoy the prudence and felicity of Gordian the father, the valour and constancy of Gordian the son!" The noble ardour of the consul revived the languid spirit of the senate. By an unanimous decree the election of the Gordians was ratified; Maximin, his son, and his adherents were pronounced enemies of their country; and liberal rewards were offered to whomsoever had the courage and good fortune to destroy them.

During the emperor's absence a detachment of the Prætorian guards remained at Rome to protect, or rather to command, the capital. The prefect Vitalianus had signalised his fidelity to Maximin by the alacrity with which he had obeyed, and even prevented, the cruel mandates of the tyrant. His death alone could rescue the authority of the senate, and the lives of the senators, from a state of danger and suspense. Before their resolves had transpired, a quæstor and some tribunes were commissioned to take his devoted life. They executed the order with equal boldness and success; and, with their bloody daggers in their hands, ran through the streets, proclaiming to the people and the soldiers the news of the happy revolution. The enthusiasm of liberty was seconded by the promise of a large donative in lands and money; the statues of Maximin were thrown down; the capital of the empire acknowledged, with transport, the authority of the two Gordians and the senate, and the example of Rome was followed by the rest of Italy.

A new spirit had arisen in that assembly, whose long patience had been insulted by wanton despotism and military licence. The senate assumed the reins of government, and, with a calm intrepidity, prepared to vindicate by arms the cause of freedom. Among the consular senators, recommended by their merit and services to the favour of the emperor Alexander, it was easy to select twenty, not unequal to the command of an army and the conduct of a war. To these was the defence of Italy intrusted. Each was appointed to act in his respective department, authorised to enrol and discipline the Italian youth, and instructed to fortify the ports and highways against the impending invasion of Maximin. A number of deputies, chosen from the most illustrious of the senatorian and equestrian orders, were despatched at the same time to the governors of the several provinces, earnestly conjuring them to fly to the assistance of their country, and to remind the nations of their ancient ties of friendship with the Roman senate and people. The general respect with which these deputies were received, and the zeal of Italy and the provinces in favour of the senate, sufficiently prove that the subjects of Maximin were reduced to that uncommon distress, in which the body of the people has more to fear from oppression than from resistance. The consciousness of that melancholy truth inspires a degree of persevering fury seldom to be found in those civil wars which are artificially supported for the benefit of a few factious and designing leaders.

For, while the cause of the Gordians was embraced with such diffusive ardour, the Gordians themselves were no more. The feeble court of Carthage was alarmed with the rapid approach of Capelianus, governor of Mauritania, who, with a small band of veterans and a fierce host of barbarians, attacked a faithful but unwarlike province. The younger Gordian sallied out to meet the enemy at the head of a few guards, and a numerous undisciplined multitude, educated in the peaceful luxury of Carthage. His useless valour served only to procure him an honourable death in the field of battle. His aged father, whose reign had not exceeded thirty-six days, put an end to his life on the first news of the defeat. Carthage, destitute of defence, opened her gates to the conqueror, and Africa was exposed to the rapacious cruelty of a slave, obliged to satisfy his unrelenting master with a large account of blood and treasure.

The senate was now committed to resisting Maximin and elected two emperors jointly, Pupienus (Maximus in Gibbon's text) and Balbinus. Maximin prepared to enter Italy in a manner which gave a foretaste of the barbarian invasions.

While in Rome and Africa revolutions succeeded each other with such amazing rapidity, the mind of Maximin was agitated by the most furious passions. He is said to have received the news of the rebellion of the Gordians, and of the decree of the senate against him, not with the temper of a man, but the rage of a wild beast; which, as it could not discharge itself on the distant senate, threatened the life of his son, of his friends, and of all who ventured to approach his person. The grateful intelligence of the death of the Gordians was quickly followed by the assurance that the senate, laying aside all hopes of pardon or accommodation, had substituted in their room two emperors, with whose merit he could not be unacquainted. Revenge was the only consolation left to Maximin, and revenge could only be obtained by arms. The strength of the legions had been assembled by Alexander from all parts of the empire. Three successful campaigns against the Germans and the Sarmatians had raised their fame, confirmed their discipline, and even increased their numbers by filling the ranks with the flower of the barbarian youth. The life of Maximin had been spent in war, and the candid severity of history cannot refuse him the valour of a soldier, or even the abilities of an experienced general. It might naturally be expected that a prince of such a character, instead of suffering the rebellion to gain stability by delay, should immediately have marched from the banks of the Danube to those of the Tiber, and that his victorious army, instigated by contempt for the senate, and eager to gather the spoils of Italy, should have burned with impatience to finish the easy and lucrative conquest. Yet, as far as we can trust to the obscure chronology of that period, it appears that the operations of some foreign war deferred the Italian expedition till the ensuing spring. From the prudent conduct of Maximin we may learn that the savage features of his character have been exaggerated by the pencil of party; that his passions, however impetuous, submitted to the force of reason; and that the barbarian possessed something of the generous spirit of Sylla, who subdued the enemies of Rome before he suffered himself to revenge his private injuries.

When the troops of Maximin, advancing in excellent order, arrived at the foot of the Julian Alps, they were terrified by the silence and desolation that reigned on the frontiers of Italy. The villages and open towns had been abandoned on their approach by the inhabitants, the cattle was driven away, the provisions removed or destroyed, the bridges broke down, nor was anything left which could afford either shelter or subsistence to an invader. Such had been the wise orders of the generals

of the senate, whose design was to protract the war, to ruin the army of
Maximin by the slow operation of famine, and to consume his strength
in the sieges of the principal cities of Italy, which they had plentifully
stored with men and provisions from the deserted country. Aquileia
received and withstood the first shock of the invasion. The streams that
issue from the head of the Hadriatic gulf, swelled by the melting of the
winter snows, opposed an unexpected obstacle to the arms of Maximin.
At length, on a singular bridge, constructed, with art and difficulty, of
large hogs-heads, he transported his army to the opposite bank, rooted
up the beautiful vineyards in the neighbourhood of Aquileia, demolished
the suburbs, and employed the timber of the buildings in the engines
and towers with which on every side he attacked the city. The walls,
fallen to decay during the security of a long peace, had been hastily
repaired on this sudden emergency: but the firmest defence of Aquileia
consisted in the constancy of the citizens; all ranks of whom, instead of
being dismayed, were animated by the extreme danger, and their knowledge of the tyrant's unrelenting temper. Their courage was supported
and directed by Crispinus and Menophilus, two of the twenty lieutenants
of the senate, who, with a small body of regular troops, had thrown
themselves into the besieged place. The army of Maximin was repulsed
in repeated attacks, his machines destroyed by showers of artificial fire;
and the generous enthusiasm of the Aquileians was exalted into a confidence of success by the opinion that Belenus, their tutelar deity, combated in person in the defence of his distressed worshippers.

The emperor Maximus, who had advanced as far as Ravenna to
secure that important place and to hasten the military preparations,
beheld the event of the war in the more faithful mirror of reason and
policy. He was too sensible that a single town could not resist the persevering efforts of a ˌ ːeat army; and he dreaded lest the enemy, tired
with the obstinate resistance of Aquileia, should on a sudden relinquish
the fruitless siege and march directly towards Rome. The fate of the
empire and the cause of freedom must then be committed to the chance
of a battle; and what arms could he oppose to the veteran legions of the
Rhine and Danube? Some troops newly levied among the generous but
enervated youth of Italy, and a body of German auxiliaries, on whose
firmness, in the hour of trial, it was dangerous to depend. In the midst
of these just alarms, the stroke of domestic conspiracy punished the
crimes of Maximin and delivered Rome and the senate from the calamities that would surely have attended the victory of an enraged barbarian.

The people of Aquileia had scarcely experienced any of the common
miseries of a siege; their magazines were plentifully supplied, and
several fountains within the walls assured them of an inexhaustible
resource of fresh water. The soldiers of Maximin were, on the contrary,
exposed to the inclemency of the season, the contagion of disease, and

the horrors of famine. The open country was ruined, the rivers filled with the slain and polluted with blood. A spirit of despair and disaffection began to diffuse itself among the troops; and as they were cut off from all intelligence, they easily believed that the whole empire had embraced the cause of the senate, and that they were left as devoted victims to perish under the impregnable walls of Aquileia. The fierce temper of the tyrant was exasperated by disappointments, which he imputed to the cowardice of his army; and his wanton and ill-timed cruelty, instead of striking terror, inspired hatred and a just desire of revenge. A party of Prætorian guards, who trembled for their wives and children in the camp of Alba, near Rome, executed the sentence of the senate. Maximin, abandoned by his guards, was slain in his tent with his son (whom he had associated to the honours of the purple), Anulinus the prefect, and the principal ministers of his tyranny. The sight of their heads, borne on the point of spears, convinced the citizens of Aquileia that the siege was at an end; the gates of the city were thrown open, a liberal market was provided for the hungry troops of Maximin, and the whole army joined in solemn protestations of fidelity to the senate and the people of Rome, and to their lawful emperors Maximus and Balbinus. Such was the deserved fate of a brutal savage, destitute, as he has generally been represented, of every sentiment that distinguishes a civilised, or even a human being. The body was suited to the soul. The stature of Maximin exceeded the measure of eight feet, and circumstances almost incredible are related of his matchless strength and appetite. Had he lived in a less enlightened age, tradition and poetry might well have described him as one of those monstrous giants whose supernatural power was constantly exerted for the destruction of mankind.

It is easier to conceive than to describe the universal joy of the Roman world on the fall of the tyrant, the news of which is said to have been carried in four days from Aquileia to Rome. The return of Maximus was a triumphal procession; his colleague and young Gordian went out to meet him, and the three princes made their entry into the capital, attended by the ambassadors of almost all the cities of Italy, saluted with the splendid offerings of gratitude and superstition, and received with the unfeigned acclamations of the senate and people, who persuaded themselves that a golden age would succeed to an age of iron. The conduct of the two emperors corresponded with these expectations. They administered justice in person; and the rigour of the one was tempered by the other's clemency. The oppressive taxes with which Maximin had loaded the rights of inheritance and succession were repealed, or at least moderated. Discipline was revived, and with the advice of the senate many wise laws were enacted by their Imperial ministers, who endeavoured to restore a civil constitution on the ruins of military tyranny. "What reward may we expect for delivering Rome from a monster?" was the question asked by Maximus in a moment of freedom and confidence. Balbinus answered it without hesitation, "The love of the senate, of the people, and of all mankind." "Alas!" replied his more penetrating colleague, "Alas! I dread the hatred of the soldiers and the fatal effects of their resentment." His apprehensions were but too well justified by the event.

The death of Maximin was followed in a short time by the massacre of Pupienus and Balbinus by the Prætorians. After Gordian III's brief reign the soldiers' votes conferred the empire on Philip "an Arab by birth and consequently ... a robber by profession."

PHILIP THE ARAB

On his return from the East to Rome, Philip, desirous of obliterating the memory of his crimes, and of captivating the affections of the people, solemnised the secular games with infinite pomp and magnificence. Since their institution or revival by Augustus, they had been celebrated by Claudius, by Domitian, and by Severus, and were now renewed the fifth time, on the accomplishment of the full period of a thousand years from the foundation of Rome. Every circumstance of the secular games was skilfully adapted to inspire the superstitious mind with deep and solemn reverence. The long interval between them exceeded the term of human life; and as none of the spectators had already seen them, none could flatter themselves with the expectation of beholding them a second time. The mystic sacrifices were performed, during three nights, on the banks of the Tiber; and the Campus Martius resounded with music and dances, and was illuminated with innumerable lamps and torches. Slaves and strangers were excluded from any participation in these national ceremonies. A chorus of twenty-seven youths, and as many virgins, of noble families, and whose parents were both alive, implored the propitious gods in favour of the present, and for the hope of the rising generation; requesting, in religious hymns, that, according to the faith of their ancient oracles, they would still maintain the virtue, the felicity, and the empire of the Roman people. The magnificence of Philip's shows and entertainments dazzled the eyes of the multitude. The devout were employed in the rites of superstition, whilst the reflecting few revolved in their anxious minds the past history and the future fate of the empire.

Since Romulus, with a small band of shepherds and outlaws, fortified himself on the hills near the Tiber, ten centuries had already elapsed. During the four first ages, the Romans, in the laborious school of poverty, had acquired the virtues of war and government: by the vigorous exertion of those virtues, and by the assistance of fortune, they had obtained, in the course of the three succeeding centuries, an absolute empire over many countries of Europe, Asia, and Africa. The last three hundred years had been consumed in apparent prosperity and internal decline. The nation of soldiers, magistrates, and legislators, who composed the thirty-five tribes of the Roman people, was dissolved into the common mass of mankind, and confounded with the millions of servile provincials, who had received the name, without adopting the spirit, of Romans. A mercenary army, levied amongst the subjects and barbarians of the frontier, was the only order of men who preserved and abused their independence. By their tumultuary election, a Syrian, a Goth, or an Arab, was exalted to the throne of Rome, and invested with despotic power over the conquests and over the country of the Scipios.

The limits of the Roman empire still extended from the Western Ocean to the Tigris, and from Mount Atlas to the Rhine and the Danube. To the undiscerning eye of the vulgar, Philip appeared a monarch no less powerful than Hadrian or Augustus had formerly been. The form was still the same, but the animating health and vigour were fled. The industry of the people was discouraged and exhausted by a long series of oppression. The discipline of the legions, which alone, after the extinction of every other virtue, had propped the greatness of the state, was corrupted by the ambition, or relaxed by the weakness, of the emperors. The strength of the frontiers, which had always consisted in arms rather than in fortifications, was insensibly undermined; and the fairest provinces were left exposed to the rapaciousness or ambition of the barbarians, who soon discovered the decline of the Roman empire.

While frontier wars had long been a constant preoccupation with the imperial government, the great barbarian invasions which were now imminent were the effect of fresh causes. In the East the Arsacid power of the Parthians ended and the new threat came from Persia. On the northern frontiers the eastern German peoples hitherto unfamiliar to the Romans were now gathering. Gibbon devotes two chapters (8 and 9) to these topics.

Chapter 10

GENERAL MISFORTUNES OF THE
REIGNS OF VALERIAN AND GALLIENUS. INROADS OF THE
GOTHS. THE PERSIAN INVASION OF ARMENIA AND THE
CAPTIVITY OF VALERIAN

*Philip was murdered in 249 and succeeded by Decius, a man of
ability. He took the field against the Goths, and both he and his
son were killed in battle in the Dobrudska. There followed in quick
succession the reigns of Gallus and Æmilianus and in 253 Valerian
became Emperor and soon associated his son Gallienus. Gibbon
gives a uniformly depreciative account of Gallienus. Modern criticism has largely rehabilitated him. Nevertheless Gibbon's picture of
the disasters of the reigns of Valerian and Gallienus is just.*

VALERIAN was about sixty years of age when he was invested
with the purple, not by the caprice of the populace or the
clamours of the army, but by the unanimous voice of the
Roman world. In his gradual ascent through the honours of the state
he had deserved the favour of virtuous princes, and had declared himself
the enemy of tyrants. His noble birth, his mild but unblemished manners, his learning, prudence, and experience, were revered by the senate
and people; and, if mankind (according to the observation of an ancient
writer) had been left at liberty to choose a master, their choice would
most assuredly have fallen on Valerian. Perhaps the merit of this
emperor was inadequate to his reputation; perhaps his abilities, or at
least his spirit, were affected by the languor and coldness of old age.
The consciousness of his decline engaged him to share the throne with
a younger and more active associate: the emergency of the times
demanded a general no less than a prince; and the experience of the
Roman censor might have directed him where to bestow the Imperial
purple as the reward of military merit. But, instead of making a judicious choice, which would have confirmed his reign and endeared his
memory, Valerian, consulting only the dictates of affection or vanity,
immediately invested with the supreme honours his son Gallienus, a
youth whose effeminate vices had been hitherto concealed by the
obscurity of a private station. The joint government of the father and
the son subsisted about seven, and the sole administration of Gallienus
continued about eight years. But the whole period was one uninterrupted series of confusion and calamity. As the Roman empire was at

the same time, and on every side, attacked by the blind fury of foreign invaders and the wild ambition of domestic usurpers, we shall consult order and perspicuity by pursuing not so much the doubtful arrangement of dates as the more natural distribution of subjects. The most dangerous enemies of Rome, during the reigns of Valerian and Gallienus, were—1. The Franks; 2. The Alemanni; 3. The Goths; and 4. The Persians. Under these general appellations we may comprehend the adventures of less considerable tribes, whose obscure and uncouth names would only serve to oppress the memory and perplex the attention of the reader.

I. As the posterity of the Franks compose one of the greatest and most enlightened nations of Europe, the powers of learning and ingenuity have been exhausted in the discovery of their unlettered ancestors. To the tales of credulity have succeeded the systems of fancy. Every passage has been sifted, every spot has been surveyed, that might possibly reveal some faint traces of their origin. It has been supposed that Pannonia, that Gaul, that the northern parts of Germany, gave birth to that celebrated colony of warriors. At length the most rational critics, rejecting the fictitious emigrations of ideal conquerors, have acquiesced in a sentiment whose simplicity persuades us of its truth. They suppose that, about the year two hundred and forty, a new confederacy was formed under the name of Franks by the old inhabitants of the Lower Rhine and the Weser. The present circle of Westphalia, the Landgraviate of Hesse, and the duchies of Brunswick and Luneburg, were the ancient seat of the Chauci, who, in their inaccessible morasses, defied the Roman arms; of the Cherusci, proud of the fame of Arminius; of the Catti, formidable by their firm and intrepid infantry; and of several other tribes of inferior power and renown. The love of liberty was the ruling passion of these Germans; the enjoyment of it their best treasure; the word that expressed that enjoyment the most pleasing to their ear. They deserved, they assumed, they maintained the honourable epithet of Franks, or Freemen; which concealed, though it did not extinguish, the peculiar names of the several states of the confederacy. Tacit consent and mutual advantage dictated the first laws of the union; it was gradually cemented by habit and experience. The league of the Franks may admit of some comparison with the Helvetic body; in which every canton, retaining its independent sovereignty, consults with its brethren in the common cause, without acknowledging the authority of any supreme head or representative assembly. But the principle of the two confederacies was extremely different. A peace of two hundred years has rewarded the wise and honest policy of the Swiss. An inconstant spirit, the thirst of rapine, and a disregard to the most solemn treaties, disgraced the character of the Franks.

The Romans had long experienced the daring valour of the people of Lower Germany. The union of their strength threatened Gaul with a more formidable invasion, and required the presence of Gallienus, the heir and colleague of Imperial power. Whilst that prince and his infant son Saloninus displayed in the court of Treves the majesty of the empire, its armies were ably conducted by their general Posthumus, who, though he afterwards betrayed the family of Valerian, was ever faithful to the great interest of the monarchy. The treacherous language of panegyrics and medals darkly announces a long series of victories. Trophies and titles attest (if such evidence can attest) the fame of Posthumus, who is repeatedly styled The Conqueror of the Germans, and the Saviour of Gaul.

But a single fact, the only one indeed of which we have any distinct knowledge, erases in a great measure these monuments of vanity and adulation. The Rhine, though dignified with the title of Safeguard of the provinces, was an imperfect barrier against the daring spirit of enterprise with which the Franks were actuated. Their rapid devastations stretched from the river to the foot of the Pyrenees; nor were they stopped by those mountains. Spain, which had never dreaded, was unable to resist, the inroads of the Germans. During twelve years, the greatest part of the reign of Gallienus, that opulent country was the theatre of unequal and destructive hostilities. Tarragona, the flourishing capital of a peaceful province, was sacked and almost destroyed, and so late as the days of Orosius, who wrote in the fifth century, wretched cottages, scattered amidst the ruins of magnificent cities, still recorded the rage of the barbarians. When the exhausted country no longer supplied a variety of plunder, the Franks seized on some vessels in the ports of Spain and transported themselves into Mauritania. The distant province was astonished with the fury of these barbarians, who seemed to fall from a new world, as their name, manners, and complexion were equally unknown on the coast of Africa.

II. In that part of Upper Saxony, beyond the Elbe, which is at present called the Marquisate of Lusace, there existed in ancient times a sacred wood, the awful seat of the superstition of the Suevi. None were permitted to enter the holy precincts without confessing, by their servile bonds and suppliant posture, the immediate presence of the sovereign Deity. Patriotism contributed, as well as devotion, to consecrate the Sonnenwald, or wood of the Semnones. It was universally believed that the nation had received its first existence on that sacred spot. At stated periods the numerous tribes who gloried in the Suevic blood resorted thither by their ambassadors; and the memory of their common extraction was perpetuated by barbaric rites and human sacrifices. The wide extended name of Suevi filled the interior countries of Germany, from the banks of the Oder to those of the Danube. They were distinguished from the other Germans by their peculiar mode of dressing their long hair, which they gathered into a rude knot on the crown of the head; and they delighted in an ornament that showed their ranks more lofty and terrible in the eyes of the enemy. Jealous as the Germans were of military renown, they all confessed the superior valour of the Suevi; and the tribes of the Usipetes and Tencteri, who, with a vast army, encountered the dictator Cæsar, declared that they esteemed it not a disgrace to have fled before a people to whose arms the immortal gods themselves were unequal.

In the reign of the emperor Caracalla an innumerable swarm of Suevi appeared on the banks of the Main, and in the neighbourhood of the Roman provinces, in quest either of food, of plunder, or of glory. The hasty army of volunteers gradually coalesced into a great and permanent nation, and, as it was composed from so many different tribes, assumed the name of Alemanni, or *Allmen*, to denote at once their various lineage and their common bravery. The latter was soon felt by the Romans in many a hostile inroad. The Alemanni fought chiefly on horseback; but their cavalry was rendered still more formidable by a mixture of light infantry selected from the bravest and most active of the youth, whom frequent exercise had enured to accompany the horseman in the longest march, the most rapid charge, or the most precipitate retreat.

This warlike people of Germans had been astonished by the immense preparations of Alexander Severus; they were dismayed by the arms of his successor, a barbarian equal in valour and fierceness to themselves. But, still hovering on the frontiers of the empire, they increased the general disorder that ensued after the death of Decius. They inflicted severe wounds on the rich provinces of Gaul: they were the first who removed the veil that covered the feeble majesty of Italy. A numerous body of the Alemanni penetrated across the Danube, and through the Rhætian Alps into the plains of Lombardy, advanced as far as Ravenna, and displayed the victorious banners of barbarians almost in sight of Rome. The insult and the danger rekindled in the senate some sparks of their ancient virtue. Both the emperors were engaged in far distant wars, Valerian in the East, and Gallienus on the Rhine. All the hopes and resources of the Romans were in themselves. In this emergency the senators resumed the defence of the republic, drew out the Prætorian guards, who had been left to garrison the capital, and filled up their numbers by enlisting into the public service the stoutest and most willing of the Plebeians. The Alemanni, astonished with the sudden appearance of an army more numerous than their own, retired into Germany laden with spoil; and their retreat was esteemed as a victory by the unwarlike Romans.

When Gallienus received the intelligence that his capital was delivered from the barbarians, he was much less delighted than alarmed with the courage of the senate, since it might one day prompt them to rescue the public from domestic tyranny, as well as from foreign invasion. His timid ingratitude was published to his subjects in an edict which prohibited the senators from exercising any military employment, and even from approaching the camps of the legions. But his fears were groundless. The rich and luxurious nobles, sinking into their natural character, accepted as a favour this disgraceful exemption from military service; and as long as they were indulged in the enjoyment of their baths, their theatres, and their villas, they cheerfully resigned the more dangerous cares of empire to the rough hands of peasants and soldiers.

Another invasion of the Alemanni, of a more formidable aspect, but more glorious event, is mentioned by a writer of the Lower Empire. Three hundred thousand of that warlike people are said to have been vanquished, in a battle near Milan, by Gallienus in person, at the head of only ten thousand Romans. We may, however, with great probability, ascribe this incredible victory either to the credulity of the historian, or to some exaggerated exploits of one of the emperor's lieutenants. It was by arms of a very different nature that Gallienus endeavoured to protect Italy from the fury of the Germans. He espoused Pipa, the daughter of a king of the Marcomanni, a Suevic tribe, which was often confounded with the Alemanni in their wars and conquests. To the father, as the price of his alliance, he granted an ample settlement in Pannonia. The native charms of unpolished beauty seem to have fixed the daughter in the affections of the inconstant emperor, and the bands of policy were more firmly connected by those of love. But the haughty prejudice of Rome still refused the name of marriage to the profane mixture of a citizen and a barbarian; and has stigmatised the German princess with the opprobrious title of concubine of Gallienus.

INROADS OF THE GOTHS

III. We have already traced the emigration of the Goths from Scandinavia, or at least from Prussia, to the mouth of the Borysthenes, and have followed their victorious arms from the Borysthenes to the Danube. Under the reigns of Valerian and Gallienus, the frontier of the last-mentioned river was perpetually infested by the inroads of Germans and Sarmatians; but it was defended by the Romans with more than usual firmness and success. The provinces that were the seat of war recruited the armies of Rome with an inexhaustible supply of hardy soldiers; and more than one of these Illyrian peasants attained the station, and displayed the abilities, of a general. Though flying parties of the barbarians, who incessantly hovered on the banks of the Danube, penetrated sometimes to the confines of Italy and Macedonia, their progress was commonly checked, or their return intercepted, by the Imperial lieutenants. But the great stream of the Gothic hostilities was diverted into a very different channel. The Goths, in their new settlement of the Ukraine, soon became masters of the northern coast of the Euxine: to the south of that inland sea were situated the soft and wealthy provinces of Asia Minor, which possessed all that could attract, and nothing that could resist, a barbarian conqueror.

The banks of the Borysthenes are only sixty miles distant from the narrow entrance of the peninsula of Crim Tartary, known to the ancients under the name of Chersonesus Taurica. On that inhospitable shore Euripides, embellishing with exquisite art the tales of antiquity, has placed the scene of one of his most affecting tragedies. The bloody sacrifices of Diana, the arrival of Orestes and Pylades, and the triumph of virtue and religion over savage fierceness, serve to represent an historical truth, that the Tauri, the original inhabitants of the peninsula, were in some degree reclaimed from their brutal manners by a gradual intercourse with the Grecian colonies which settled along the maritime coast. The little kingdom of Bosphorus, whose capital was situated on the straits through which the Mæotis communicates itself to the Euxine, was composed of degenerate Greeks and half-civilised barbarians. It subsisted as an independent state from the time of the Peloponnesian war, was at last swallowed up by the ambition of Mithridates, and, with the rest of his dominions, sunk under the weight of the Roman arms. From the reign of Augustus the kings of Bosphorus were the humble, but not useless, allies of the empire. By presents, by arms, and by a slight fortification drawn across the isthmus, they effectually guarded, against the roving plunderers of Sarmatia, the access of a country which, from its peculiar situation and convenient harbours, commanded the Euxine Sea and Asia Minor. As long as the sceptre was possessed by a lineal succession of kings, they acquitted themselves of their important charge with vigilance and success. Domestic factions, and the fears or private interest of obscure usurpers who seized on the vacant throne, admitted the Goths into the heart of Bosphorus. With the acquisition of a superfluous waste of fertile soil, the conquerors obtained the command of a naval force sufficient to transport their armies to the coast of Asia. The ships used in the navigation of the Euxine were of a very singular construction. They were slight flat-bottomed barks framed of timber only, without the least mixture of iron, and occasionally covered with a shelving roof on the appearance of a tempest. In these floating houses the Goths carelessly trusted themselves to the mercy of an unknown sea, under the conduct of sailors pressed into the service, and whose skill and fidelity were equally suspicious. But the hopes of plunder had banished every idea of danger, and a natural fearlessness of temper supplied in their minds the more rational confidence which is the just result of knowledge and experience. Warriors of such a daring spirit must have often murmured against the cowardice of their guides, who required the strongest assurances of a settled calm before they would venture to embark, and would scarcely ever be tempted to lose sight of the land. Such, at least, is the practice of the modern Turks; and they are probably not inferior in the art of navigation to the ancient inhabitants of Bosphorus.

The fleet of the Goths, leaving the coast of Circassia on the left hand, first appeared before Pityus, the utmost limits of the Roman provinces; a city provided with a convenient port, and fortified with a strong wall. Here they met with a resistance more obstinate than they had reason to expect from the feeble garrison of a distant fortress. They were repulsed; and their disappointment seemed to diminish the terror of the Gothic name. As long as Successianus, an officer of superior rank and merit, defended that frontier, all their efforts were ineffectual; but as soon as he was removed by Valerian to a more honourable but less important station, they resumed the attack of Pityus; and, by the destruction of that city, obliterated the memory of their former disgrace.

Circling round the eastern extremity of the Euxine Sea, the navigation from Pityus to Trebizond is about three hundred miles. The course of the Goths carried them in sight of the country of Colchis, so famous by the expedition of the Argonauts; and they even attempted, though without success, to pillage a rich temple at the mouth of the river Phasis. Trebizond, celebrated in the retreat of the Ten Thousand as an ancient colony of Greeks, derived its wealth and splendour from the munificence of the emperor Hadrian, who had constructed an artificial port on a coast left destitute by nature of secure harbours. The city was large and populous; a double enclosure of walls seemed to defy the fury of the Goths, and the usual garrison had been strengthened by a reinforcement of ten thousand men. But there are not any advantages capable of supplying the absence of discipline and vigilance. The numerous garrison of Trebizond, dissolved in riot and luxury, disdained to guard their impregnable fortifications. The Goths soon discovered the supine negligence of the besieged, erected a lofty pile of fascines, ascended the walls in the silence of the night, and entered the defenceless city, sword in hand. A general massacre of the people ensued, whilst the affrighted soldiers escaped through the opposite gates of the town. The most holy temples, and the most splendid edifices, were involved in a common destruction. The booty that fell into the hands of the Goths was immense: the wealth of the adjacent countries had been deposited in Trebizond, as in a secure place of refuge. The number of captives was incredible as the victorious barbarians ranged without opposition through the extensive province of Pontus. The rich spoils of Trebizond filled a great fleet of ships that had been found in the port. The robust youth of the sea-coast were chained to the oar; and the Goths, satisfied with the success of their first naval expedition, returned in triumph to their new establishments in the kingdom of Bosphorus.

The second expedition of the Goths was undertaken with greater powers of men and ships; but they steered a different course, and, disdaining the exhausted provinces of Pontus, followed the western coast of the Euxine, passed before the wide mouths of the Borysthenes, the Dniester, and the Danube, and, increasing their fleet by the capture of a great number of fishing barks, they approached the narrow outlet through which the Euxine Sea pours its waters into the Mediterranean, and divides the continents of Europe and Asia. The garrison of Chalcedon was encamped near the temple of Jupiter Urius, on a promontory that commanded the entrance of the strait; and so inconsiderable were the dreaded invasions of the barbarians, that this body of troops surpassed in number the Gothic army. But it was in numbers alone that they surpassed it. They deserted with precipitation their advantageous post, and abandoned the town of Chalcedon, most plentifully stored with arms and money, to the discretion of the conquerors. Whilst they hesitated whether they should prefer the sea or land, Europe or Asia, for the scene of their hostilities, a perfidious fugitive pointed out Nicomedia, once the capital of the kings of Bithynia, as a rich and easy conquest. He guided the march, which was only sixty miles from the camp of Chalcedon, directed the resistless attack, and partook of the booty; for the Goths had learned sufficient policy to reward the traitor whom they detested. Nice, Prusa, Apamæa, Cius, cities that had sometimes rivalled or imitated the splendour of Nicomedia, were involved in the same calamity, which, in a few weeks, raged without control through the whole province of Bithynia. Three hundred years of peace, enjoyed by the soft inhabitants of Asia, had abolished the exercise of arms, and removed the apprehension of danger. The ancient walls were suffered to moulder away, and all the revenue of the most opulent cities was reserved for the construction of baths, temples, and theatres.

When the city of Cyzicus withstood the utmost effort of Mithridates, it was distinguished by wise laws, a naval power of two hundred galleys, and three arsenals—of arms, of military engines, and of corn. It was still the seat of wealth and luxury; but of its ancient strength nothing remained except the situation, in a little island of the Propontis, connected with the continent of Asia only by two bridges. From the recent sack of Prusa, the Goths advanced within eighteen miles of the city, which they had devoted to destruction; but the ruin of Cyzicus was delayed by a fortunate accident. The season was rainy, and the lake Apolloniates, the reservoir of all the springs of Mount Olympus, rose to an uncommon height. The little river of Rhyndacus, which issues from the lake, swelled into a broad and rapid stream and stopped the progress of the Goths. Their retreat to the maritime city of Heraclea, where the fleet had probably been stationed, was attended by a long train of waggons laden with the spoils of Bithynia, and was marked by the flames of Nice and Nicomedia, which they wantonly burnt. Some obscure hints are mentioned of a doubtful combat that secured their retreat. But even a complete victory would have been of little moment, as the approach of the autumnal equinox summoned them to hasten their return. To navigate the Euxine before the month of May, or after that of September, is esteemed by the modern Turks the most unquestionable instance of rashness and folly.

When we are informed that the third fleet, equipped by the Goths in the ports of Bosphorus, consisted of five hundred sail of ships, our ready imagination instantly computes and multiplies the formidable armament; but, as we are assured by the judicious Strabo that the piratical vessels used by the barbarians of Pontus and the Lesser Scythia were not capable of containing more than twenty-five or thirty men, we may safely affirm that fifteen thousand warriors at the most embarked in this great expedition. Impatient of the limits of the Euxine, they steered their destructive course from the Cimmerian to the Thracian Bosphorus. When they had almost gained the middle of the straits they were suddenly driven back to the entrance of them; till a favourable wind, springing up the next day, carried them in a few hours into the placid sea, or rather lake, of the Propontis. Their landing on the little island of Cyzicus was attended with the ruin of that ancient and noble city. From thence issuing again through the narrow passage of the Hellespont, they pursued their winding navigation amidst the numerous islands scattered over the Archipelago or the Ægean Sea. The assistance of captives and deserters must have been very necessary to pilot their vessels, and to direct their various incursions, as well on the coast of Greece as on that of Asia. At length the Gothic fleet anchored in the port of Piræus, five miles distant from Athens, which had attempted to make some preparations for a vigorous defence. Cleodamus, one of the engineers employed by the emperor's orders to fortify the maritime cities against the Goths, had already begun to repair the ancient walls fallen to decay since the time of Sylla. The efforts of his skill were ineffectual, and the barbarians became masters of the native seat of the muses and the arts. But while the conquerors abandoned themselves to the licence of plunder and intemperance, their fleet, that lay with a slender guard in the harbour of Piræus, was unexpectedly attacked by the brave Dexippus, who, flying with the engineer Cleodamus from the sack of Athens, collected a hasty band of volunteers, peasants as well as soldiers, and in some measure avenged the calamities of his country.

But this exploit, whatever lustre it might shed on the declining age of Athens, served rather to irritate than to subdue the undaunted spirit of the northern invaders. A general conflagration blazed out at the same time in every district of Greece. Thebes and Argos, Corinth and Sparta, which had formerly waged such memorable wars against each other, were now unable to bring an army into the field, or even to defend their ruined fortifications. The rage of war, both by land and by sea, spread from the eastern point of Sunium to the western coast of Epirus. The Goths had already advanced within sight of Italy, when the approach of such imminent danger awakened the indolent Gallienus from his dream of pleasure. The emperor appeared in arms; and his presence seems to have checked the ardour, and to have divided the strength, of the enemy. Naulobatus, a chief of the Heruli, accepted an honourable capitulation, entered with a large body of his countrymen into the service of Rome, and was invested with the ornaments of the consular dignity, which had never before been profaned by the hands of a barbarian. Great numbers of the Goths, disgusted with the perils and hardships of a tedious voyage, broke into Mæsia, with a design of forcing their way over the Danube to their settlements in the Ukraine. The wild attempt would have proved inevitable destruction if the discord of the Roman generals had not opened to the barbarians the means of an escape. The small remainder of this destroying host returned on board their vessels, and, measuring back their way through the Hellespont and the Bosphorus, ravaged in their passage the shores of Troy, whose fame, immortalised by Homer, will probably survive the memory of the Gothic conquests. As soon as they found themselves in safety within the bason of the Euxine they landed at Anchialus in Thrace, near the foot of Mount Hæmus, and, after all their toils, indulged themselves in the use of those pleasant and salutary hot baths. What remained of the voyage was a short and easy navigation. Such was the various fate of this third and greatest of their naval enterprises. It may seem difficult to conceive how the original body of fifteen thousand warriors could sustain the losses and divisions of so bold an adventure. But as their numbers were gradually wasted by the sword, by shipwrecks, and by the influence of a warm climate, they were perpetually renewed by troops of banditti and deserters, who flocked to the standard of plunder, and by a crowd of fugitive slaves, often of German or Sarmatian extraction, who eagerly seized the glorious opportunity of freedom and revenge. In these expeditions the Gothic nation claimed a superior share of honour and danger; but the tribes that fought under the Gothic banners are sometimes distinguished and sometimes confounded in the imperfect histories of that age; and as the barbarian fleets seemed to issue from the mouth of the Tanais, the vague but familiar appellation of Scythians was frequently bestowed on the mixed multitude.

In the general calamities of mankind, the death of an individual, however exalted, the ruin of an edifice, however famous, are passed over with careless inattention. Yet we cannot forget that the temple of Diana at Ephesus, after having risen with increasing splendour from seven repeated misfortunes, was finally burnt by the Goths in their third naval invasion. The arts of Greece and the wealth of Asia had conspired to erect that sacred and magnificent structure. It was supported by an hundred and twenty-seven marble columns of the Ionic order; they were the gifts of devout monarchs, and each was sixty feet high. The altar was adorned with the masterly sculptures of Praxiteles, who had, perhaps, selected from the favourite legends of the place the birth of the divine children of Latona, the concealment of Apollo after the slaughter of the Cyclops, and the clemency of Bacchus to the vanquished Amazons. Yet the length of the temple of Ephesus was only four hundred and twenty-five feet, about two-thirds of the measure of the church of St. Peter's at Rome. In the other dimensions it was still more inferior to that sublime production of modern architecture. The spreading arms of a Christian cross require a much greater breadth than the oblong temples of the Pagans; and the boldest artists of antiquity would have been startled at the proposal of raising in the air a dome of the size and proportions of the Pantheon. The temple of Diana was, however, admired as one of the wonders of the world. Successive empires, the Persian, the Macedonian, and the Roman, had revered its sanctity and enriched its splendour. But the rude savages of the Baltic were destitute of a taste for the elegant arts, and they despised the ideal terrors of a foreign superstition.

Another circumstance is related of these invasions, which might deserve our notice were it not justly to be suspected as the fanciful conceit of a recent sophist. We are told that in the sack of Athens the Goths had collected all the libraries, and were on the point of setting fire to this funeral pile of Grecian learning, had not one of their chiefs, of more refined policy than his brethren, dissuaded them from the design, by the profound observation, that as long as the Greeks were addicted to the study of books they would never apply themselves to the exercise of arms. The sagacious counsellor (should the truth of the fact be admitted) reasoned like an ignorant barbarian. In the most polite and powerful nations genius of every kind has displayed itself about the same period; and the age of science has generally been the age of military virtue and success.

PERSIAN INVASION OF ARMENIA: CAPTIVITY OF VALERIAN

IV. The new sovereigns of Persia, Artaxerxes and his son Sapor, had triumphed (as we have already seen) over the house of Arsaces. Of the many princes of that ancient race, Chosroes, king of Armenia, had alone preserved both his life and his independence. He defended himself by the natural strength of his country; by the perpetual resort of fugitives and malcontents; by the alliance of the Romans; and, above all, by his own courage. Invincible in arms during a thirty years' war, he was at length assassinated by the emissaries of Sapor, king of Persia. The patriotic satraps of Armenia, who asserted the freedom and dignity of the crown, implored the protection of Rome in favour of Tiridates the lawful heir. But the son of Chosroes was an infant, the allies were at a distance, and the Persian monarch advanced towards the frontier at the head of an irresistible force. Young Tiridates, the future hope of his country, was saved by the fidelity of a servant, and Armenia continued above twenty-seven years a reluctant province of the great monarchy of Persia. Elated with this easy conquest, and presuming on the distresses or the degeneracy of the Romans, Sapor obliged the strong garrisons of

Carrhæ and Nisibis to surrender, and spread devastation and terror on either side of the Euphrates.

The loss of an important frontier, the ruin of a faithful and natural ally, and the rapid success of Sapor's ambition, affected Rome with a deep sense of the insult as well as of the danger. Valerian flattered himself that the vigilance of his lieutenants would sufficiently provide for the safety of the Rhine and of the Danube; but he resolved, notwithstanding his advanced age, to march in person to the defence of the Euphrates. During his progress through Asia Minor the naval enterprises of the Goths were suspended, and the afflicted province enjoyed a transient and fallacious calm. He passed the Euphrates, encountered the Persian monarch near the walls of Edessa, was vanquished, and taken prisoner by Sapor. The particulars of this great event are darkly and imperfectly represented; yet, by the glimmering light which is afforded us, we may discover a long series of imprudence, of error, and of deserved misfortunes on the side of the Roman emperor. He reposed an implicit confidence in Macrianus, his Prætorian prefect. That worthless minister rendered his master formidable only to the oppressed subjects, and contemptible to the enemies, of Rome. By his weak or wicked counsels the Imperial army was betrayed into a situation where valour and military skill were equally unavailing. The vigorous attempt of the Romans to cut their way through the Persian host was repulsed with great slaughter; and Sapor, who encompassed the camp with superior numbers, patiently waited till the increasing rage of famine and pestilence had ensured his victory. The licentious murmurs of the legions soon accused Valerian as the cause of their calamities; their seditious clamours demanded an instant capitulation. An immense sum of gold was offered to purchase the permission of a disgraceful retreat. But the Persian, conscious of his superiority, refused the money with disdain; and, detaining the deputies, advanced in order of battle to the foot of the Roman rampart, and insisted on a personal conference with the emperor. Valerian was reduced to the necessity of intrusting his life and dignity to the faith of an enemy. The interview ended as it was natural to expect. The emperor was made a prisoner, and his astonished troops laid down their arms. In such a moment of triumph the pride and policy of Sapor prompted him to fill the vacant throne with a successor entirely dependent on his pleasure. Cyriades, an obscure fugitive of Antioch, stained with every vice, was chosen to dishonour the Roman purple; and the will of the Persian victor could not fail of being ratified by the acclamations, however reluctant, of the captive army.

The Imperial slave was eager to secure the favour of his master by an act of treason to his native country. He conducted Sapor over the Euphrates, and, by the way of Chalcis, to the metropolis of the East. So rapid were the motions of the Persian cavalry that, if we may credit a very judicious historian, the city of Antioch was surprised when the

idle multitude was fondly gazing on the amusements of the theatre.
The splendid buildings of Antioch, private as well as public, were either
pillaged or destroyed; and the numerous inhabitants were put to the
sword or led away into captivity. The tide of devastation was stopped
for a moment by the resolution of the high priest of Emesa. Arrayed
in his sacerdotal robes he appeared at the head of a great body of fanatic peasants, armed only with slings, and defended his god and his
property from the sacrilegious hands of the followers of Zoroaster. But
the ruin of Tarsus, and of many other cities, furnishes a melancholy
proof that, except in this singular instance, the conquest of Syria and
Cilicia scarcely interrupted the progress of the Persian arms. The advantages of the narrow passes of Mount Taurus were abandoned, in
which an invader whose principal force consisted in his cavalry would
have been engaged in a very unequal combat: and Sapor was permitted
to form the siege of Cæsarea, the capital of Cappadocia; a city, though
of the second rank, which was supposed to contain four hundred thousand inhabitants. Demosthenes commanded in the place, not so much
by the commission of the emperor as in the voluntary defence of his
country. For a long time he deferred its fate; and when at last Cæsarea
was betrayed by the perfidy of a physician, he cut his way through the
Persians, who had been ordered to exert their utmost diligence to take
him alive. This heroic chief escaped the power of a foe who might either
have honoured or punished his obstinate valour; but many thousands
of his fellow-citizens were involved in a general massacre, and Sapor
is accused of treating his prisoners with wanton and unrelenting cruelty.
Much should, undoubtedly, be allowed for national animosity, much
for humbled pride and impotent revenge; yet, upon the whole, it is
certain that the same prince who, in Armenia, had displayed the mild
aspect of a legislator, showed himself to the Romans under the stern
features of a conqueror. He despaired of making any permanent
establishment in the empire, and sought only to leave behind him a
wasted desert, whilst he transported into Persia the people and the
treasures of the provinces.

At the time when the East trembled at the name of Sapor, he received
a present not unworthy of the greatest kings—a long train of camels
laden with the most rare and valuable merchandises. The rich offering
was accompanied with an epistle, respectful but not servile, from Odenathus, one of the noblest and most opulent senators of Palmyra.
"Who is this Odenathus" (said the haughty victor, and he commanded
that the presents should be cast into the Euphrates), "that he thus insolently presumes to write to his lord? If he entertains a hope of mitigat-
ing his punishment, let him fall prostrate before the foot of our throne,
with his hands bound behind his back. Should he hesitate, swift
destruction shall be poured on his head, on his whole race, and on his
country." The desperate extremity to which the Palmyrenian was

reduced called into action all the latent powers of his soul. He met Sapor; but he met him in arms. Infusing his own spirit into a little army collected from the villages of Syria and the tents of the desert, he hovered round the Persian host, harassed their retreat, carried off part of the treasure, and, what was dearer than any treasure, several of the women of the Great King; who was at last obliged to repass the Euphrates with some marks of haste and confusion. By this exploit Odenathus laid the foundations of his future fame and fortunes. The majesty of Rome, oppressed by a Persian, was protected by a Syrian or Arab of Palmyra.

The voice of history, which is often little more than the organ of hatred or flattery, reproaches Sapor with a proud abuse of the rights of conquest. We are told that Valerian, in chains, but invested with the Imperial purple, was exposed to the multitude, a constant spectacle of fallen greatness; and that, whenever the Persian monarch mounted on horseback, he placed his foot on the neck of a Roman emperor. Notwithstanding all the remonstrances of his allies, who repeatedly advised him to remember the vicissitude of fortune, to dread the returning power of Rome, and to make his illustrious captive the pledge of peace, not the object of insult, Sapor still remained inflexible. When Valerian sunk under the weight of shame and grief, his skin, stuffed with straw, and formed into the likeness of a human figure, was preserved for ages in the most celebrated temple of Persia; a more real monument of triumph than the fancied trophies of brass and marble so often erected by Roman vanity. The tale is moral and pathetic, but the truth of it may very fairly be called in question. The letters still extant from the princes of the East to Sapor are manifest forgeries; nor is it natural to suppose that a jealous monarch should, even in the person of a rival, thus publicly degrade the majesty of kings. Whatever treatment the unfortunate Valerian might experience in Persia, it is at least certain that the only emperor of Rome who had ever fallen into the hands of the enemy languished away his life in hopeless captivity.

The emperor Gallienus, who had long supported with impatience the censorial severity of his father and colleague, received the intelligence of his misfortunes with secret pleasure and avowed indifference. "I knew that my father was a mortal," said he; "and, since he has acted as becomes a brave man, I am satisfied." Whilst Rome lamented the fate of her sovereign, the savage coldness of his son was extolled by the servile courtiers as the perfect firmness of a hero and stoic. It is difficult to paint the light, the various, the inconstant character of Gallienus, which he displayed without constraint as soon as he became sole possessor of the empire. In every art that he attempted his lively genius enabled him to succeed; and, as his genius was destitute of judgment, he attempted every art, except the important ones of war and government. He was a master of several curious but useless sciences, a ready orator, an elegant poet, a skilful gardener, an excellent cook, and most contemptible prince. When the great emergencies of the state required his presence and attention, he was engaged in conversation with the philosopher Plotinus, wasting his time in trifling or licentious pleasures, preparing his initiation to the Grecian mysteries, or soliciting a place in the Areopagus of Athens. His profuse magnificence insulted the general poverty; the solemn ridicule of his triumphs impressed a deeper sense of the public disgrace. The repeated intelligence of invasions, defeats, and rebellions he received with a careless smile; and singling out, with affected contempt, some particular production of the lost province, he carelessly asked whether Rome must be ruined unless it was supplied with linen from Egypt and Arras cloth from Gaul? There were, however, a few short moments in the life of Gallienus when, exasperated by some recent injury, he suddenly appeared the intrepid soldier and the cruel tyrant; till, satiated with blood or fatigued by resistance, he insensibly sunk into the natural mildness and indolence of his character.

At a time when the reins of government were held with so loose a hand, it is not surprising that a crowd of usurpers should start up in every province of the empire against the son of Valerian. It was probably some ingenious fancy, of comparing the thirty tyrants of Rome with the thirty tyrants of Athens, that induced the writers of the Augustan History to select that celebrated number, which has been gradually received into a popular appellation. But in every light the parallel is idle and defective. What resemblance can we discover between a council of thirty persons, the united oppressors of a single city, and an uncertain list of independent rivals, who rose and fell in irregular succession through the extent of a vast empire? Nor can the number of thirty be completed, unless we include in the account the women and children who were honoured with the Imperial title. The reign of Gallienus, distracted as it was, produced only nineteen pretenders to the throne: Cyriades, Macrianus, Balista, Odenathus, and Zenobia in the east; in Gaul and the western provinces, Posthumus, Lollianus, Victorinus and his mother Victoria, Marius, and Tetricus. In Illyricum and the confines of the Danube, Ingenuus, Regillianus, and Aureolus; in Pontus, Saturninus; in Isauria, Trebellianus; Piso in Thessaly; Valens in Achaia; Æmilianus in Egypt; and Celsus in Africa. To illustrate the obscure monuments of the life and death of each individual would prove a laborious task, alike barren of instruction and of amusement. We may content ourselves with investigating some general characters, that most strongly mark the condition of the times and the manners of the men, their pretensions, their motives, their fate, and the destructive consequences of their usurpation.

It is sufficiently known that the odious appellation of *Tyrant* was often employed by the ancients to express the illegal seizure of supreme power, without any reference to the abuse of it. Several of the pretenders who raised the standard of rebellion against the emperor Gallienus were shining models of virtue, and almost all possessed a considerable share of vigour and ability. Their merit had recommended them to the favour of Valerian, and gradually promoted them to the most important commands of the empire. The generals who assumed the title of Augustus were either respected by their troops for their able conduct and severe discipline, or admired for valour and success in war, or beloved for frankness and generosity. The field of victory was often the scene of their election; and even the armourer Marius, the most contemptible of all the candidates for the purple, was distinguished however by intrepid courage, matchless strength, and blunt honesty. His mean and recent trade cast, indeed, an air of ridicule on his elevation; but his birth could not be more obscure than was that of the greater part of his rivals, who were born of peasants, and enlisted in the army as private soldiers. In times of confusion every active genius finds the place assigned him by nature; in a general state of war military merit is the road to glory and to greatness. Of the nineteen tyrants Tetricus only was a senator; Piso alone was a noble. The blood of Numa, through twenty-eight successive generations, ran in the veins of Calphurnius Piso, who, by female alliances, claimed a right of exhibiting, in his house, the images of Crassus and of the great Pompey. His ancestors had been repeatedly dignified with all the honours which the commonwealth could bestow; and, of all the ancient families of Rome, the Calphurnian alone had survived the tyranny of the Cæsars. The personal qualities of Piso added new lustre to his race. The usurper Valens, by whose order he was killed, confessed, with deep remorse, that even an enemy ought to have respected the sanctity of Piso; and, although he died in arms against Gallienus, the senate, with the emperor's generous permission, decreed the triumphal ornaments to the memory of so virtuous a rebel.

The lieutenants of Valerian were grateful to the father, whom they esteemed. They disdained to serve the luxurious indolence of his unworthy son. The throne of the Roman world was unsupported by any principle of loyalty; and treason against such a prince might easily be considered as patriotism to the state. Yet if we examine with candour the conduct of these usurpers, it will appear that they were much oftener driven into rebellion by their fears than urged to it by their ambition. They dreaded the cruel suspicions of Gallienus: they equally dreaded the capricious violence of their troops. If the dangerous favour of the army had imprudently declared them deserving of the purple, they were marked for sure destruction; and even prudence would counsel them to secure a short enjoyment of empire, and rather to try the fortune of war than to expect the hand of an executioner. When the clamour of the soldiers invested the reluctant victims with the ensigns of sovereign authority, they sometimes mourned in secret their approaching fate. "You have lost," said Saturninus, on the day of his elevation, "you have lost a useful commander, and you have made a very wretched emperor."

The apprehensions of Saturninus were justified by the repeated experience of revolutions. Of the nineteen tyrants who started up under the reign of Gallienus, there was not one who enjoyed a life of peace, or a natural death. As soon as they were invested with the bloody purple, they inspired their adherents with the same fears and ambition which had occasioned their own revolt. Encompassed with domestic conspiracy, military sedition, and civil war, they trembled on the edge of precipices, in which, after a longer or shorter term of anxiety, they were inevitably lost. These precarious monarchs received, however, such honours as the flattery of their respective armies and provinces could bestow; but their claim, founded on rebellion, could never obtain the sanction of law or history. Italy, Rome, and the senate, constantly adhered to the cause of Gallienus, and he alone was considered as the sovereign of the empire. That prince condescended indeed to acknowledge the victorious arms of Odenathus, who deserved the honourable distinction by the respectful conduct which he always maintained towards the son of Valerian. With the general applause of the Romans, and the consent of Gallienus, the senate conferred the title of Augustus on the brave Palmyrenian; and seemed to intrust him with the government of the East, which he already possessed, in so independent a manner, that, like a private succession, he bequeathed it to his illustrious widow Zenobia.

The rapid and perpetual transitions from the cottage to the throne, and from the throne to the grave, might have amused an indifferent philosopher, were it possible for a philosopher to remain indifferent amidst the general calamities of human kind. The election of these precarious emperors, their power and their death, were equally destructive to their subjects and adherents. The price of their fatal elevation was instantly discharged to the troops by an immense donative drawn from the bowels of the exhausted people. However virtuous was their character, however pure their intentions, they found themselves reduced to the hard necessity of supporting their usurpation by frequent acts of rapine and cruelty. When they fell they involved armies and provinces in their fall. There is still extant a most savage mandate from Gallienus to one of his ministers, after the suppression of Ingenuus, who had assumed the purple in Illyricum. "It is not enough," says that soft but inhuman prince, "that you exterminate such as have appeared in arms: the chance of battle might have served me as effectually. The male sex of every age must be extirpated; provided that, in the execution of the children and old men, you can contrive means to save our reputation. Let every one die who has dropped an expression, who has entertained a thought against me, against *me*, the son of Valerian, the father and brother of so many princes. Remember that Ingenuus was made emperor: tear, kill, hew in pieces. I write to you with my own hand, and would inspire you with my own feelings." Whilst the public forces of the state were dissipated in private quarrels, the defenceless provinces lay exposed to every invader. The bravest usurpers were compelled, by the perplexity of their situation, to conclude ignominious treaties with the common enemy, to purchase with oppressive tributes the neutrality or services of the barbarians, and to introduce hostile and independent nations into the heart of the Roman monarchy.

Such were the barbarians, and such the tyrants, who, under the reigns of Valerian and Gallienus, dismembered the provinces, and reduced the empire to the lowest pitch of disgrace and ruin, from whence it seemed impossible that it should ever emerge. As far as the barrenness of materials would permit, we have attempted to trace, with order and perspicuity, the general events of that calamitous period. There still remain some particular facts—I. The disorders of Sicily; II. The Tumults of Alexandria; and III. The rebellion of the Isaurians—which may serve to reflect a strong light on the horrid picture.

I. Whenever numerous troops of banditti, multiplied by success and impunity, publicly defy, instead of eluding, the justice of their country, we may safely infer that the excessive weakness of the government is felt and abused by the lowest ranks of the community. The situation of Sicily preserved it from the barbarians; nor could the disarmed province have supported an usurper. The sufferings of that once flourishing and still fertile island were inflicted by baser hands. A licentious crowd of slaves and peasants reigned for a while over the plundered country, and renewed the memory of the servile wars of more ancient times. Devastations, of which the husbandman was either the victim or the accomplice, must have ruined the agriculture of Sicily; and as the principal estates were the property of the opulent senators of Rome, who often enclosed within a farm the territory of an old republic, it is not improbable that this private injury might affect the capital more deeply than all the conquests of the Goths or the Persians.

II. The foundation of Alexandria was a noble design, at once conceived and executed by the son of Philip. The beautiful and regular form of that great city, second only to Rome itself, comprehended a circumference of fifteen miles; it was peopled by three hundred thousand free inhabitants, besides at least an equal number of slaves. The lucrative trade of Arabia and India flowed through the port of Alexandria to the capital and provinces of the empire. Idleness was unknown. Some were employed in blowing of glass, others in weaving of linen, others again manufacturing the papyrus. Either sex, and every age, was engaged in the pursuits of industry, nor did even the blind or the lame want occupations suited to their condition. But the people of Alexandria, a various mixture of nations, united the vanity and inconstancy of the Greeks with the supersition and obstinacy of the Egyptians. The most trifling occasion, a transient scarcity of flesh or lentils, the neglect of an accustomed salutation, a mistake of precedency in the public baths, or even a religious dispute, were at any time sufficient to kindle a sedition among that vast multitude, whose resentments were furious and implacable. After the captivity of Valerian and the insolence of his son had relaxed the authority of the laws, the Alexandrians abandoned themselves to the ungoverned rage of their passions, and their unhappy country was the theatre of a civil war, which continued (with a few short and suspicious truces) above twelve years. All intercourse was cut off between the several quarters of the afflicted city, every street was polluted with blood, every building of strength converted into a citadel; nor did the tumults subside till a considerable part of Alexandria was irretrievably ruined. The spacious and magnificent district of Bruchion, with its palaces and museum, the residence of the kings and philosophers of Egypt, is described, above a century afterwards, as already reduced to its present state of dreary solitude.

III. The obscure rebellion of Trebellianus, who assumed the purple in Isauria, a petty province of Asia Minor, was attended with strange and memorable consequences. The pageant of royalty was soon destroyed by an officer of Gallienus; but his followers, despairing of mercy, resolved to shake off their allegiance, not only to the emperor but to the empire, and suddenly returned to the savage manners from which they had never perfectly been reclaimed. Their craggy rocks, a branch of the wide-extended Taurus, protected their inaccessible retreat. The tillage of some fertile valleys supplied them with necessaries, and a habit of rapine with the luxuries of life. In the heart of the Roman monarchy, the Isaurians long continued a nation of wild barbarians. Succeeding princes, unable to reduce them to obedience either by arms or policy, were compelled to acknowledge their weakness by surrounding the hostile and independent spot with a strong chain of fortifications, which often proved insufficient to restrain the incursions of these domestic foes. The Isaurians, gradually extending their territory to the sea-coast, subdued the western and mountainous part of Cilicia, formerly the nest of those daring pirates against whom the republic had once been obliged to exert its utmost force, under the conduct of the great Pompey.

Our habits of thinking so fondly connect the order of the universe with the fate of man, that this gloomy period of history has been decorated with inundations, earthquakes, uncommon meteors, preternatural darkness, and a crowd of prodigies fictitious or exaggerated. But a long and general famine was a calamity of a more serious kind. It was the inevitable consequence of rapine and oppression, which extirpated the produce of the present and the hope of future harvests. Famine is almost always followed by epidemical diseases, the effect of scanty and unwholesome food. Other causes must, however, have contributed to the furious plague which, from the year two hundred and fifty to the year two hundred and sixty-five, raged without interruption in every province, every city, and almost every family of the Roman empire. During some time five thousand persons died daily in Rome, and many towns that had escaped the hands of the barbarians were entirely depopulated.

We have the knowledge of a very curious circumstance, of some use perhaps in the melancholy calculation of human calamities. An exact register was kept at Alexandria of all the citizens entitled to receive the distribution of corn. It was found that the ancient number of those comprised between the ages of forty and seventy had been equal to the whole sum of claimants, from fourteen to fourscore years of age, who remained alive after the reign of Gallienus. Applying this authentic fact to the most correct tables of mortality, it evidently proves that above half the people of Alexandria had perished; and could we venture to extend the analogy to the other provinces, we might suspect that war, pestilence, and famine had consumed, in a few years, the moiety of the human species.

THE TURN OF THE TIDE

Chapter 11

ZENOBIA AND THE KINGDOM
OF PALMYRA. THE TRIUMPH AND DEATH OF AURELIAN

Gallienus was succeeded by a series of strong emperors who, in Gibbon's words, "deserved the glorious title of Restorers of the Roman world." The new emperor, Claudius, reformed the army and gained a signal victory over the Goths. Aurelian, his successor, ended the Gothic war by confining the Goths in the province of Dacia and withdrawing troops from the Dacian frontier. He then repulsed an invasion of the Alemanni and put down the usurper Tetricus, who had assumed authority over Gaul, Spain, and Britain. The defeat of Tetricus which Gibbon places in AD 271 is now held to have followed Zenobia's downfall and to have occurred in 274.

AURELIAN had no sooner secured the person and provinces of Tetricus than he turned his arms against Zenobia, the celebrated queen of Palmyra and the East. Modern Europe has produced several illustrious women who have sustained with glory the weight of empire; nor is our own age destitute of such distinguished characters. But if we except the doubtful achievements of Semiramis, Zenobia is perhaps the only female whose superior genius broke through the servile indolence imposed on her sex by the climate and manners of Asia. She claimed her descent from the Macedonian kings of Egypt, equalled in beauty her ancestor Cleopatra, and far surpassed that princess in chastity and valour. Zenobia was esteemed the most lovely as well as the most heroic of her sex. She was of a dark complexion (for in speaking of a lady these trifles become important). Her teeth were of a pearly whiteness, and her large black eyes sparkled with uncommon fire, tempered by the most attractive sweetness. Her voice was strong and harmonious. Her manly understanding was strengthened and adorned by study. She was not ignorant of the Latin tongue, but possessed in equal perfection the Greek, the Syriac, and the Egyptian languages. She had drawn up for her own use an epitome of oriental history, and familiarly compared the beauties of Homer and Plato under the tuition of the sublime Longinus.

This accomplished woman gave her hand to Odenathus, who, from a private station, raised himself to the dominion of the East. She soon became the friend and companion of a hero. In the intervals of war Odenathus passionately delighted in the exercise of hunting; he pursued with ardour the wild beasts of the desert, lions, panthers, and bears; and the ardour of Zenobia in that dangerous amusement was not inferior to his own. She had inured her constitution to fatigue, disdained the use of a covered carriage, generally appeared on horseback in a military habit, and sometimes marched several miles on foot at the head of the troops. The success of Odenathus was in a great measure ascribed to her incomparable prudence and fortitude. Their splendid victories over the Great King, whom they twice pursued as far as the gates of Ctesiphon, laid the foundations of their united fame and power. The armies which they commanded, and the provinces which they had saved, acknowledged not any other sovereigns than their invincible chiefs. The senate and people of Rome revered a stranger who had avenged their captive emperor, and even the insensible son of Valerian accepted Odenathus for his legitimate colleague.

After a successful expedition against the Gothic plunderers of Asia, the Palmyrenian prince returned to the city of Emesa in Syria. Invincible in war, he was there cut off by domestic treason, and his favourite amusement of hunting was the cause, or at least the occasion, of his death. His nephew, Mæonius, presumed to dart his javelin before that of his uncle; and, though admonished of his error, repeated the same insolence. As a monarch, and as a sportsman, Odenathus was provoked, took away his horse, a mark of ignominy among the barbarians, and chastised the rash youth by a short confinement. The offence was soon forgot, but the punishment was remembered; and Mæonius, with a few daring associates, assassinated his uncle in the midst of a great entertainment. Herod, the son of Odenathus, though not of Zenobia, a young man of a soft and effeminate temper, was killed with his father. But Mæonius obtained only the pleasure of revenge by this bloody deed. He had scarcely time to assume the title of Augustus before he was sacrificed by Zenobia to the memory of her husband.

With the assistance of her most faithful friends, she immediately filled the vacant throne, and governed with manly counsels Palmyra, Syria, and the East, above five years. By the death of Odenathus, that authority was at an end which the senate had granted him only as a personal distinction; but his martial widow, disdaining both the senate and Gallienus, obliged one of the Roman generals who was sent against her to retreat into Europe, with the loss of his army and his reputation. Instead of the little passions which so frequently perplex a female reign, the steady administration of Zenobia was guided by the most judicious maxims of policy. If it was expedient to pardon, she could calm her resentment; if it was necessary to punish, she could impose silence on the voice of pity. Her strict economy was accused of avarice; yet on every proper occasion she appeared magnificent and liberal. The neighbouring states of Arabia, Armenia, and Persia, dreaded her enmity, and solicited her alliance. To the dominions of Odenathus, which extended from the Euphrates to the frontiers of Bithynia, his widow added the inheritance of her ancestors, the populous and fertile kingdom of Egypt. The emperor Claudius acknowledged her merit, and was content that, while *he* pursued the Gothic war, *she* should assert the dignity of the empire in the East. The conduct, however, of Zenobia was attended with some ambiguity; nor is it unlikely that she had conceived the design of erecting an independent and hostile monarchy. She blended with the popular manners of Roman princes the stately pomp of the courts of Asia, and exacted from her subjects the same adoration that was paid to the successors of Cyrus. She bestowed on her three sons a Latin education, and often showed them to the troops adorned with the Imperial purple. For herself she reserved the diadem, with the splendid but doubtful title of Queen of the East.

When Aurelian passed over into Asia, against an adversary whose sex alone could render her an object of contempt, his presence restored obedience to the province of Bithynia, already shaken by the arms and intrigues of Zenobia. Advancing at the head of his legions, he accepted the submission of Ancyra, and was admitted into Tyana, after an obstinate siege, by the help of a perfidious citizen. The generous though fierce temper of Aurelian abandoned the traitor to the rage of the soldiers: a superstitious reverence induced him to treat with lenity the countrymen of Apollonius the philosopher.[1] Antioch was deserted on his approach, till the emperor, by his salutary edicts, recalled the fugitives, and granted a general pardon to all who, from necessity rather than choice, had been engaged in the service of the Palmyrenian queen. The unexpected mildness of such a conduct reconciled the minds of the Syrians, and, as far as the gates of Emesa, the wishes of the people seconded the terror of his arms.

Zenobia would have ill deserved her reputation, had she indolently permitted the emperor of the West to approach within an hundred miles of her capital. The fate of the East was decided in two great battles; so similar in almost every circumstance, that we can scarcely distinguish them from each other, except by observing that the first was fought near Antioch, and the second near Emesa. In both the queen of Palmyra animated the armies by her presence, and devolved the execution of her orders on Zabdas, who had already signalised his military talents by the conquest of Egypt. The numerous forces of Zenobia consisted for the most part of light archers, and of heavy cavalry clothed in complete steel. The Moorish and Illyrian horse of Aurelian were unable to sustain the ponderous charge of their antagonists. They fled in real or affected disorder, engaged the Palmyrenians in a laborious pursuit, harassed them by a desultory combat, and at length discomfited this im-

---

[1] Apollonius of Tyana was born about the same time as Jesus Christ. His life (that of the former) is related in so fabulous a manner by his disciples, that we are at a loss to discover whether he was a sage, an impostor, or a fanatic.

penetrable but unwieldy body of cavalry. The light infantry, in the mean time, when they had exhausted their quivers, remaining without protection against a closer onset, exposed their naked sides to the swords of the legions. Aurelian had chosen these veteran troops who were usually stationed on the Upper Danube, and whose valour had been severely tried in the Alemannic war. After the defeat of Emesa, Zenobia found it impossible to collect a third army. As far as the frontier of Egypt, the nations subject to her empire had joined the standard of the conqueror, who detached Probus, the bravest of his generals, to possess himself of the Egyptian provinces. Palmyra was the last resource of the widow of Odenathus. She retired within the walls of her capital, made every preparation for a vigorous resistance, and declared, with the intrepidity of a heroine, that the last moment of her reign and of her life should be the same.

Amid the barren deserts of Arabia a few cultivated spots rise like islands out of the sandy ocean. Even the name of Tadmor, or Palmyra, by its signification in the Syriac as well as in the Latin language, denoted the multitude of palm-trees which afforded shade and verdure to that temperate region. The air was pure, and the soil, watered by some invaluable springs, was capable of producing fruits as well as corn. A place possessed of such singular advantages, and situated at a convenient distance between the Gulf of Persia and the Mediterranean, was soon frequented by the caravans which conveyed to the nations of Europe a considerable part of the rich commodities of India. Palmyra insensibly increased into an opulent and independent city, and, connecting the Roman and the Parthian monarchies by the mutual benefits of commerce, was suffered to observe an humble neutrality, till at length, after the victories of Trajan, the little republic sunk into the bosom of Rome, and flourished more than one hundred and fifty years in the subordinate though honourable rank of a colony. It was during that peaceful period, if we may judge from a few remaining inscriptions, that the wealthy Palmyrenians constructed those temples, palaces, and porticos of Grecian architecture, whose ruins, scattered over an extent of several miles, have deserved the curiosity of our travellers. The elevation of Odenathus and Zenobia appeared to reflect new splendour on their country, and Palmyra, for a while, stood forth the rival of Rome: but the competition was fatal, and ages of prosperity were sacrificed to a moment of glory.

In his march over the sandy desert between Emesa and Palmyra, the emperor Aurelian was perpetually harassed by the Arabs; nor could he always defend his army, and especially his baggage, from those flying troops of active and daring robbers, who watched the moment of surprise, and eluded the slow pursuit of the legions. The siege of Palmyra was an object far more difficult and important, and the emperor, who, with incessant vigour, pressed the attacks in person, was himself wounded with a dart. "The Roman people," says Aurelian, in an original letter, "speak with contempt of the war which I am waging against a woman. They are ignorant both of the character and of the power of Zenobia. It is impossible to enumerate her warlike preparations, of stones, of arrows, and of every species of missile weapons. Every part of the walls is provided with two or three *balistæ*, and artificial fires are thrown from her military engines. The fear of punishment has armed her with a desperate courage. Yet still I trust in the protecting deities of Rome, who have hitherto been favourable to all my undertakings." Doubful, however, of the protection of the gods, and of the event of the siege, Aurelian judged it more prudent to offer terms of an advantageous capitulation; to the queen, a splendid retreat; to the citizens, their ancient privileges. His proposals were obstinately rejected, and the refusal was accompanied with insult.

The firmness of Zenobia was supported by the hope that in a very short time famine would compel the Roman army to repass the desert; and by the reasonable expectation that the kings of the East, and particularly the Persian monarch, would arm in the defence of their most natural ally. But fortune and the perseverance of Aurelian overcame every obstacle. The death of Sapor, which happened about this time, distracted the councils of Persia, and the inconsiderable succours that attempted to relieve Palmyra were easily intercepted either by the arms or the liberality of the emperor. From every part of Syria a regular succession of convoys safely arrived in the camp, which was increased by the return of Probus with his victorious troops from the conquest of Egypt. It was then that Zenobia resolved to fly. She mounted the fleetest of her dromedaries, and had already reached the banks of the Euphrates, about sixty miles from Palmyra, when she was overtaken by the pursuit of Aurelian's light horse, seized and brought back a captive to the feet of the emperor. Her capital soon afterwards surrendered, and was treated with unexpected lenity. The arms, horses, and camels, with an immense treasure of gold, silver, silk, and precious stones, were all delivered to the conqueror, who, leaving only a garrison of six hundred archers, returned to Emesa, and employed some time in the distribution of rewards and punishments at the end of so memorable a war, which restored to the obedience of Rome those provinces that had renounced their allegiance since the captivity of Valerian.

When the Syrian queen was brought into the presence of Aurelian, he sternly asked her, How she had presumed to rise in arms against the emperors of Rome? The answer of Zenobia was a prudent mixture of respect and firmness. "Because I disdained to consider as Roman emperors an Aureolus or a Gallienus. You alone I acknowledge as my conqueror and my sovereign." But as female fortitude is commonly artificial, so it is seldom steady or consistent. The courage of Zenobia deserted her in the hour of trial; she trembled at the angry clamours of the soldiers, who called aloud for her immediate execution, forgot the generous despair of Cleopatra, which she had proposed as her model, and ignominiously purchased life by the sacrifice of her fame and her friends. It was to their counsels, which governed the weakness of her sex, that she imputed the guilt of her obstinate resistance; it was on their heads that she directed the vengeance of the cruel Aurelian. The fame of Longinus, who was included among the numerous and perhaps innocent victims of her fear, will survive that of the queen who betrayed, or the tyrant who condemned him. Genius and learning were incapable of moving a fierce unlettered soldier, but they had served to elevate and harmonise the soul of Longinus. Without uttering a complaint, he calmly followed the executioner, pitying his unhappy mistress, and bestowing comfort on his afflicted friends.

Returning from the conquest of the East, Aurelian had already crossed the Straits which divide Europe from Asia, when he was provoked by the intelligence that the Palmyrenians had massacred the governor and garrison which he had left among them, and again erected the standard of revolt. Without a moment's deliberation, he once more turned his face towards Syria. Antioch was alarmed by his rapid approach, and the helpless city of Palmyra felt the irresistible weight of his resentment. We have a letter of Aurelian himself, in which he acknowledges that old men, women, children, and peasants, had been involved in that dreadful execution, which should have been confined to armed rebellion; and although his principal concern seems directed to the re-establishment of a temple of the Sun, he discovers some pity for the remnant of the Palmyrenians, to whom he grants the permission of rebuilding and inhabiting their city. But it is easier to destroy than to restore. The seat of commerce, of arts, and of Zenobia, gradually sunk into an obscure town, a trifling fortress, and at length a miserable village. The present citizens of Palmyra, consisting of thirty or forty families, have erected their mud-cottages within the spacious court of a magnificent temple.

Another and a last labour still awaited the indefatigable Aurelian; to suppress a dangerous though obscure rebel, who, during the revolt of Palmyra, had arisen on the banks of the Nile. Firmus, the friend and ally, as he proudly styled himself, of Odenathus and Zenobia, was no more than a wealthy merchant of Egypt. In the course of his trade to India he had formed very intimate connexions with the Saracens and the Blemmyes, whose situation, on either coast of the Red Sea, gave them an easy introduction into the Upper Egypt. The Egyptians he inflamed with the hope of freedom, and, at the head of their furious multitude, broke into the city of Alexandria, where he assumed the Imperial purple, coined money, published edicts, and raised an army, which, as he vainly boasted, he was capable of maintaining from the sole profits of his paper trade. Such troops were a feeble defence against the approach of

Aurelian; and it seems almost unnecessary to relate that Firmus was routed, taken, tortured, and put to death. Aurelian might now congratulate the senate, the people, and himself, that, in little more than three years, he had restored universal peace and order to the Roman world.

TRIUMPH AND DEATH OF AURELIAN

Since the foundation of Rome no general had more nobly deserved a triumph than Aurelian; nor was a triumph ever celebrated with superior pride and magnificence. The pomp was opened by twenty elephants, four royal tigers, and above two hundred of the most curious animals from every climate of the North, the East, and the South. They were followed by sixteen hundred gladiators, devoted to the cruel amusement of the amphitheatre. The wealth of Asia, the arms and ensigns of so many conquered nations, and the magnificent plate and wardrobe of the Syrian queen, were disposed in exact symmetry of artful disorder. The ambassadors of the most remote parts of the earth, of Ethiopia, Arabia, Persia, Bactriana, India, and China, all remarkable by their rich or singular dresses, displayed the fame and power of the Roman emperor, who exposed likewise to the public view the presents that he had received, and particularly a great number of crowns of gold, the offerings of grateful cities. The victories of Aurelian were attested by the long train of captives who reluctantly attended his triumph—Goths, Vandals, Sarmatians, Alemanni, Franks, Gauls, Syrians, and Egyptians. Each people was distinguished by its peculiar inscription, and the title of Amazons was bestowed on ten martial heroines of the Gothic nation who had been taken in arms. But every eye, disregarding the crowd of captives, was fixed on the emperor Tetricus and the queen of the East. The former, as well as his son, whom he had created Augustus, was dressed in Gallic trowsers,[1] a saffron tunic, and a robe of purple. The beauteous figure of Zenobia was confined by fetters of gold; a slave supported the gold chain which encircled her neck, and she almost fainted under the intolerable weight of jewels. She preceded on foot the magnificent chariot in which she once hoped to enter the gates of Rome. It was followed by two other chariots, still more sumptuous, of Odenathus and of the Persian monarch. The triumphal car of Aurelian (it had formerly been used by a Gothic king) was drawn, on this memorable occasion, either by four stags or by four elephants. The most illustrious of the senate, the people, and the army closed the solemn procession.

---

[1] The use of *braccæ*, breeches, or trowsers, was still considered in Italy as a Gallic and barbarian fashion. The Romans, however, had made great advances towards it. To encircle the legs and thighs with *fasciæ*, or bands, was understood, in the time of Pompey and Horace, to be a proof of ill health or effeminacy. In the age of Trajan the custom was confined to the rich and luxurious. It gradually was adopted by the meanest of the people.

Unfeigned joy, wonder, and gratitude swelled the acclamations of the multitude; but the satisfaction of the senate was clouded by the appearance of Tetricus; nor could they suppress a rising murmur that the haughty emperor should thus expose to public ignominy the person of a Roman and a magistrate.

But, however in the treatment of his unfortunate rivals Aurelian might indulge his pride, he behaved towards them with a generous clemency which was seldom exercised by the ancient conquerors. Princes who, without success, had defended their throne or freedom, were frequently strangled in prison as soon as the triumphal pomp ascended the Capitol. These usurpers, whom their defeat had convicted of the crime of treason, were permitted to spend their lives in affluence and honourable repose. The emperor presented Zenobia with an elegant villa at Tibur or Tivoli, about twenty miles from the capital; the Syrian queen insensibly sunk into a Roman matron, her daughters married into noble familes, and her race was not yet extinct in the fifth century. Tetricus and his son were reinstated in their rank and fortunes. They erected on the Cælian hill a magnificent palace, and, as soon as it was finished, invited Aurelian to supper. On his entrance he was agreeably surprised with a picture which represented their singular history. They were delineated offering to the emperor a civic crown and the sceptre of Gaul, and again receiving at his hands the ornaments of the senatorial dignity. The father was afterwards invested with the government of Lucania, and Aurelian, who soon admitted the abdicated monarch to his friendship and conversation, familiarly asked him, Whether it were not more desirable to administer a province of Italy than to reign beyond the Alps? The son long continued a respectable member of the senate; nor was there any one of the Roman nobility more esteemed by Aurelian, as well as by his successors.

So long and so various was the pomp of Aurelian's triumph, that, although it opened with the dawn of day, the slow majesty of the procession ascended not the Capital before the ninth hour; and it was already dark when the emperor returned to the palace. The festival was protracted by theatrical representations, the games of the circus, the hunting of wild beasts, combats of gladiators, and naval engagements. Liberal donatives were distributed to the army and people, and several institutions, agreeable or beneficial to the city, contributed to perpetuate the glory of Aurelian. A considerable portion of his oriental spoils was consecrated to the gods of Rome; the Capitol, and every other temple, glittered with the offerings of his ostentatious piety; and the temple of the Sun alone received above fifteen thousand pounds of gold. This last was a magnificent structure, erected by the emperor on the side of the Quirinal hill, and dedicated, soon after the triumph, to that deity whom Aurelian adored as the parent of his life and fortunes. His mother had been an inferior priestess in a chapel of the Sun; a peculiar devotion to the god of Light was a sentiment which the fortunate peasant imbibed in his infancy; and every step of his elevation, every victory of his reign, fortified superstition by gratitude.

The arms of Aurelian had vanquished the foreign and domestic foes of the republic. We are assured that, by his salutary rigour, crimes and factions, mischievous arts and pernicious connivance, the luxuriant growth of a feeble and oppressive government, were eradicated throughout the Roman world. But if we attentively reflect how much swifter is the progress of corruption than its cure, and if we remember that the years abandoned to public disorders exceeded the months allotted to the martial reign of Aurelian, we must confess that a few short intervals of peace were insufficient for the arduous work of reformation. Even his attempt to restore the integrity of the coin was opposed by a formidable insurrection. The emperor's vexation breaks out in one of his private letters: "Surely," says he, "the gods have decreed that my life should be a perpetual warfare. A sedition within the walls has just now given birth to a very serious civil war. The workmen of the mint, at the instigation of Felicissimus, a slave to whom I had intrusted an employment in the finances, have risen in rebellion. They are at length suppressed; but seven thousand of my soldiers have been slain in the contest, of those troops whose ordinary station is in Dacia and the camps along the Danube." Other writers, who confirm the same fact, add likewise, that it happened soon after Aurelian's triumph; that the decisive engagement was fought on the Cælian hill; that the workmen of the mint had adulterated the coin; and that the emperor restored the public credit, by delivering out good money in exchange for the bad, which the people was commanded to bring into the treasury.

We might content ourselves with relating this extraordinary transaction, but we cann t dissemble how much, in its present form, it appears to us inconsistent and incredible. The debasement of the coin is indeed well suited to the administration of Gallienus; nor is it unlikely that the instruments of the corruption might dread the inflexible justice of Aurelian. But the guilt, as well as the profit, must have been confined to a few; nor is it easy to conceive by what arts they could arm a people whom they had injured against a monarch whom they had betrayed. We might naturally expect that such miscreants should have shared the public detestation with the informers and the other ministers of oppression; and that the reformation of the coin should have been an action equally popular with the destruction of those obsolete accounts which, by the emperor's order, were burnt in the forum of Trajan. In an age when the principles of commerce were so imperfectly understood, the most desirable end might perhaps be effected by harsh and injudicious means; but a temporary grievance of such a nature can scarcely excite and support a serious civil war. The repetition of intolerable taxes, imposed either on the land or on the necessaries of life, may at last provoke those who will not, or who cannot, relinquish their country. But the case is far otherwise in every operation which, by whatsoever expedients, restores the just value of money. The transient evil is soon obliterated by the permanent benefit, the loss is divided among multitudes; and if a few wealthy individuals experience a sensible diminution of treasure, with their riches they at the same time lose the degree of weight and importance which they derived from the possession of them. However Aurelian might choose to disguise the real cause of the insurrection, his reformation of the coin could furnish only a faint pretence to a party already powerful and discontented. Rome, though deprived of freedom, was distracted by faction. The people, towards whom the emperor, himself a plebeian, always expressed a peculiar fondness, lived in perpetual dissension with the senate, the equestrian order, and the Prætorian guards. Nothing less than the firm though secret conspiracy of those orders, of the authority of the first, the wealth of the second, and the arms of the third, could have displayed a strength capable of contending in battle with the veteran legions of the Danube, which, under the conduct of a martial sovereign, had achieved the conquest of the West and of the East.

Whatever was the cause or the object of this rebellion, imputed with so little probability to the workmen of the mint, Aurelian used his victory with unrelenting rigour. He was naturally of a severe disposition. A peasant and a soldier, his nerves yielded not easily to the impressions of sympathy, and he could sustain without emotion the sight of tortures and death. Trained from his earliest youth in the exercise of arms, he set too small a value on the life of a citizen, chastised by military execution the slightest offences, and transferred the stern discipline of the camp into the civil administration of the laws. His love of justice often became a blind and furious passion; and, whenever he deemed his own or the public safety endangered, he disregarded the rules of evidence and the proportion of punishments. The unprovoked rebellion with which the Romans rewarded his services exasperated his haughty spirit. The noblest families of the capital were involved in the guilt or suspicion of this dark conspiracy. A hasty spirit of revenge urged the bloody prosecution, and it proved fatal to one of the nephews of the emperor. The executioners (if we may use the expression of a contemporary poet) were fatigued, the prisons were crowded, and the unhappy senate lamented the death or absence of its most illustrious members. Nor was the pride of Aurelian less offensive to that assembly than his cruelty. Ignorant or impatient of the restraints of civil institutions, he disdained to hold his power by any other title than that of the sword, and governed by right of conquest an empire which he had saved and subdued.

It was observed by one of the most sagacious of the Roman princes, that the talents of his predecessor Aurelian were better suited to the command of an army than to the government of an empire. Conscious of the character in which nature and experience had enabled him to excel, he again took the field a few months after his triumph. It was expedient to exercise the restless temper of the legions in some foreign war, and the Persian monarch, exulting in the shame of Valerian, still braved with impunity the offended majesty of Rome. At the head of an army, less formidable by its numbers than by its discipline and valour, the emperor advanced as far as the Straits which divide Europe from Asia. He there experienced that the most absolute power is a weak defence against the effects of despair. He had threatened one of his secretaries who was accused of extortion, and it was known that he seldom threatened in vain. The last hope which remained for the criminal was to involve some of the principal officers of the army in his danger, or at least in his fears. Artfully counterfeiting his master's hand, he showed them, in a long and bloody list, their own names devoted to death. Without suspecting or examining the fraud, they resolved to secure their lives by the murder of the emperor. On his march, between Byzantium and Heraclea, Aurelian was suddenly attacked by the conspirators, whose stations gave them a right to surround his person, and, after a short resistance, fell by the hand of Mucapor, a general whom he had always loved and trusted. He died regretted by the army, detested by the senate, but universally acknowledged as a warlike and fortunate prince, the useful though severe reformer of a degenerate state.

After Aurelian's death the senate exerted its authority for the last time and elected M. Claudius Tacitus. The army accepted him and he campaigned successfully against the Alans. After his murder the army elected M. Aurelius Probus. He won victories on the Rhine and Danube before his murder at Sirmium. His successor M. Aurelius Carus died mysteriously at the opening of a campaign against Persia. His sons succeeded. However, a group of officers at Chalcedon elected C. Aurelius Valerius Diocletianus. Carinus, the surviving son of Carus, ruled in the west for a while. At the battle of Margus (Moraoa) Diocletian was victorious and was now sole master of the Roman world. All this is narrated in Chapter 12, omitted here.

THE NEW IMPERIAL SYSTEM

Chapter 13

THE REIGN OF DIOCLETIAN AND HIS THREE ASSOCIATES.
HIS TRIUMPH AND NEW ORDER. THE GROWTH OF COURT
CEREMONIAL. ABDICATION AND DEATH OF DIOCLETIAN.
DECLINE OF THE ARTS

AS the reign of Diocletian was more illustrious than that of any of
his predecessors, so was his birth more abject and obscure. The
strong claims of merit and of violence had frequently superseded
the ideal prerogatives of nobility; but a distinct line of separation was
hitherto preserved between the free and the servile part of mankind.
The parents of Diocletian had been slaves in the house of Anulinus, a
Roman senator; nor was he himself distinguished by any other name
than that which he derived from a small town in Dalmatia, from whence
his mother deduced her origin. It is, however, probable that his father
obtained the freedom of the family, and that he soon acquired an office
of scribe, which was commonly exercised by persons of his condition.
Favourable oracles, or rather the consciousness of superior merit,
prompted his aspiring son to pursue the profession of arms and the
hopes of fortune; and it would be extremely curious to observe the
gradation of arts and accidents which enabled him in the end to fulfil
those oracles, and to display that merit to the world. Diocletian was
successively promoted to the government of Mæsia, the honours of the
consulship, and the important command of the guards of the palace.
He distinguished his abilities in the Persian war; and after the death of
Numerian, the slave, by the confession and judgment of his rivals, was
declared the most worthy of the Imperial throne. The malice of religious zeal, whilst it arraigns the savage fierceness of his colleague Maximian, has affected to cast suspicions on the personal courage of the
emperor Diocletian. It would not be easy to persuade us of the cowardice of a soldier of fortune who acquired and preserved the esteem of the
legions, as well as the favour of so many warlike princes. Yet even
calumny is sagacious enough to discover and to attack the most vulner-
able part. The valour of Diocletian was never found inadequate to his
duty, or to the occasion; but he appears not to have possessed the daring
and generous spirit of a hero, who courts danger and fame, disdains
artifice, and boldly challenges the allegiance of his equals. His abilities
were useful rather than splendid—a vigorous mind improved by the
experience and study of mankind; dexterity and application in business;
a judicious mixture of liberality and economy, of mildness and rigour;

profound dissimulation under the disguise of military frankness; steadiness to pursue his ends; flexibility to vary his means; and, above all, the great art of submitting his own passions, as well as those of others, to the interest of his ambition, and of colouring his ambition with the most specious pretences of justice and public utility. Like Augustus, Diocletian may be considered as the founder of a new empire. Like the adopted son of Cæsar, he was distinguished as a statesman rather than as a warrior; nor did either of those princes employ force, whenever their purpose could be effected by policy.

The victory of Diocletian was remarkable for its singular mildness. A people accustomed to applaud the clemency of the conqueror, if the usual punishments of death, exile, and confiscation were inflicted with any degree of temper and equity, beheld, with the most pleasing astonishment, a civil war, the flames of which were extinguished in the field of battle. Diocletian received into his confidence Aristobulus, the principal minister of the house of Carus, respected the lives, the fortunes, and the dignity of his adversaries, and even continued in their respective stations the greater number of the servants of Carinus. It is not improbable that motives of prudence might assist the humanity of the artful Dalmatian: of these servants, many had purchased his favour by secret treachery; in others, he esteemed their grateful fidelity to an unfortunate master. The discerning judgment of Aurelian, of Probus, and of Carus, had filled the several departments of the state and army with officers of approved merit, whose removal would have injured the public service, without promoting the interest of the successor. Such a conduct, however, displayed to the Roman world the fairest prospect of the new reign, and the emperor affected to confirm this favourable prepossession by declaring that, among all the virtues of his predecessors, he was the most ambitious of imitating the humane philosophy of Marcus Antoninus.

The first considerable action of his reign seemed to evince his sincerity as well as his moderation. After the example of Marcus, he gave himself a colleague in the person of Maximian, on whom he bestowed at first the title of Cæsar, and afterwards that of Augustus. But the motives of his conduct, as well as the object of his choice, were of a very different nature from those of his admired predecessor. By investing a luxurious youth with the honours of the purple, Marcus had discharged a debt of private gratitude, at the expense, indeed, of the happiness of the state. By associating a friend and a fellow-soldier to the labours of government, Diocletian, in a time of public danger, provided for the defence both of the East and of the West. Maximian was born a peasant, and, like Aurelian, in the territory of Sirmium. Ignorant of letters, careless of laws, the rusticity of his appearance and manners still betrayed in the most elevated fortune the meanness of his extraction. War was the only art which he professed. In a long course of service he had distinguished himself on every frontier of the empire; and though his military talents were formed to obey rather than to command, though, perhaps, he never attained the skill of a consummate general, he was capable, by his valour, constancy, and experience, of executing the most arduous undertakings. Nor were the vices of Maximian less useful to his benefactor. Insensible to pity, and fearless of consequences, he was the ready instrument of every act of cruelty which the policy of that artful prince might at once suggest and disclaim. As soon as a bloody sacrifice had been offered to prudence or to revenge, Diocletian, by his seasonable intercession, saved the remaining few whom he had never designed to punish, gently censured the severity of his stern colleague, and enjoyed the comparison of a golden and an iron age, which was universally applied to their opposite maxims of government. Notwithstanding the difference of their characters, the two emperors maintained, on the throne, that friendship which they had contracted in a private station. The haughty turbulent spirit of Maximian, so fatal afterwards to himself and to the public peace, was accustomed to respect the genius of Diocletian, and confessed the ascendant of reason over brutal violence. From a motive either of pride or superstition, the two emperors assumed the titles, the one of Jovius, the other of Herculius. Whilst the motion of the world (such was the language of their venal orators) was maintained by the all-seeing wisdom of Jupiter, the invincible arm of Hercules purged the earth from monsters and tyrants.

But even the omnipotence of Jovius and Herculius was insufficient to sustain the weight of the public administration. The prudence of Diocletian discovered that the empire, assailed on every side by the barbarians, required on every side the presence of a great army and of an emperor. With this view, he resolved once more to divide his unwieldy power, and, with the inferior title of *Cæsars*, to confer on two generals of approved merit an equal share of the sovereign authority. Galerius, surnamed Armentarius, from his original profession of a herdsman, and Constantius, who from his pale complexion had acquired the denomination of Chlorus, were the two persons invested with the second honours of the Imperial purple. In describing the country, extraction, and manners of Herculius, we have already delineated those of Galerius, who was often, and not improperly, styled the younger Maximian, though, in many instances both of virtue and ability, he appears to have possessed a manifest superiority over the elder. The birth of Constantius was less obscure than that of his colleagues. Eutropius, his father, was one of the most considerable nobles of Dardania, and his mother was the niece of the emperor Claudius. Although the youth of Constantius had been spent in arms, he was endowed with a mild and amiable disposition, and the popular voice had long since acknowledged him worthy of the rank which he at last attained. To strengthen the bonds of political, by those of domestic, union, each of the emperors assumed the character of a father to one of the Cæsars, Diocletian to Galerius, and Maximian to Constantius; and each, obliging them to repudiate their former wives, bestowed his daughter in marriage on his adopted son. These four princes distributed among themselves the wide extent of the Roman empire. The defence of Gaul, Spain, and Britain was intrusted to Constantius: Galerius was stationed on the banks of the Danube, as the safeguard of the Illyrian provinces. Italy and Africa were considered as the department of Maximian; and for his peculiar portion Diocletian reserved Thrace, Egypt, and the rich countries of Asia. Every one was sovereign within his own jurisdiction; but their united authority extended over the whole monarchy, and each of them was prepared to assist his colleagues with his counsels or presence. The Cæsars, in their exalted rank, revered the majesty of the emperors, and the three younger princes invariably acknowledged, by their gratitude and obedience, the common parent of their fortunes. The suspicious jealousy of power found not any place among them; and the singular happiness of their union has been compared to a chorus of music, whose harmony was regulated and maintained by the skilful hand of the first artist.

This important measure was not carried into execution till about six years after the association of Maximian, and that interval of time had not been destitute of memorable incidents. But we have preferred, for the sake of perspicuity, first to describe the more perfect form of Diocletian's government, and afterwards to relate the actions of his reign, following rather the natural order of the events than the dates of a very doubtful chronology.

Maximian subdued a peasant revolt in Gaul. Carausius, gaining control of the channel fleet, assumed the Imperial purple in Britain, but his assassination led to the recovery of Britain by Constantius. The two Cæsars defended the Rhine and Danube frontiers. Diocletian, after suppressing a rebellion in Egypt, turned his attention to the East. He established a friendly prince, Tiridates, in Armenia, ceded the provinces beyond the Tigris to Persia and concluded a peace which lasted forty years.

TRIUMPH AND NEW ORDER OF DIOCLETIAN

As soon as Diocletian entered into the twentieth year of his reign, he celebrated that memorable era, as well as the success of his arms, by the pomp of a Roman triumph. Maximian, the equal partner of his power, was his only companion in the glory of that day. The two Cæsars had fought and conquered, but the merit of their exploits was ascribed, according to the rigour of ancient maxims, to the auspicious influence of their fathers and emperors. The triumph of Diocletian and Maximian was less magnificent, perhaps, than those of Aurelian and Probus, but it was dignified by several circumstances of superior fame and good fortune. Africa and Britain, the Rhine, the Danube, and the Nile, furnished their respective trophies; but the most distinguished ornament was of a more singular nature, a Persian victory followed by an important conquest. The representations of rivers, mountains, and provinces were carried before the Imperial car. The images of the captive wives, the sisters, and the children of the Great King afforded a new and grateful spectacle to the vanity of the people. In the eyes of posterity this triumph is remarkable by a distinction of a less honourable kind. It was the last that Rome ever beheld. Soon after this period the emperors ceased to vanquish, and Rome ceased to be the capital of the empire.

The spot on which Rome was founded had been consecrated by ancient ceremonies and imaginary miracles. The presence of some god, or the memory of some hero, seemed to animate every part of the city, and the empire of the world had been promised to the Capitol. The native Romans felt and confessed the power of this agreeable illusion. It was derived from their ancestors, had grown up with their earliest habits of life, and was protected, in some measure, by the opinion of political utility. The form and the seat of government were intimately blended together, nor was it esteemed possible to transport the one without destroying the other. But the sovereignty of the capital was gradually annihilated in the extent of conquest; the provinces rose to the same level, and the vanquished nations acquired the name and privileges, without imbibing the partial affections, of Romans. During a long period, however, the remains of the ancient constitution and the influence of custom preserved the dignity of Rome. The emperors, though perhaps of African or Illyrian extraction, respected their adopted country, as the seat of their power and the centre of their extensive dominions. The emergencies of war very frequently required their presence on the frontiers; but Diocletian and Maximian were the first Roman princes who fixed, in time of peace, their ordinary residence in the provinces; and their conduct, however it might be suggested by private motives, was justified by very specious considerations of policy. The court of the emperor of the West was, for the most part, established at Milan, whose situation, at the foot of the Alps, appeared far more convenient than that of Rome, for the important purpose of watching the motions of the barbarians of Germany. Milan soon assumed the splendour of an Imperial city. The houses are described as numerous and well built; the manners of the people as polished and liberal. A circus, a theatre, a mint, a palace, baths, which bore the name of their founder Maximian; porticoes adorned with statues, and a double circumference of walls, contributed to the beauty of the new capital; nor did it seem oppressed even by the proximity of Rome. To rival the majesty of Rome was the ambition likewise of Diocletian, who employed his leisure, and the wealth of the East, in the embellishment of Nicomedia, a city placed on the verge of Europe and Asia, almost at an equal distance between the Danube and the Euphrates. By the taste of the monarch, and at the expense of the people, Nicomedia acquired, in the space of a few years, a degree of magnificence which might appear to have required the labour of ages, and became inferior only to Rome, Alexandria, and Antioch, in extent of populousness. The life of Diocletian and Maximian was a life of action, and a considerable portion of it was spent in camps, or in their long and frequent marches; but whenever the public business allowed them any relaxation, they seem to have retired with pleasure to their favourite residences of Nicomedia and Milan. Till Diocletian, in the twentieth year of his reign, celebrated his Roman triumph, it is extremely doubtful whether he ever visited the ancient capital of the empire. Even on that memorable occasion his stay did not exceed two months. Disgusted with the licentious familiarity of the people, he quitted Rome with precipitation thirteen days before it was expected that he should have appeared in the senate, invested with the ensigns of the consular dignity.

The dislike expressed by Diocletian towards Rome and Roman freedom was not the effect of momentary caprice, but the result of the most artful policy. That crafty prince had framed a new system of Imperial government, which was afterwards completed by the family of Constantine; and as the image of the old constitution was religiously preserved in the senate, he resolved to deprive that order of its small remains of power and consideration. We may recollect, about eight years before the elevation of Diocletian, the transient greatness and the ambitious hopes of the Roman senate. As long as that enthusiasm prevailed, many of the nobles imprudently displayed their zeal in the cause of freedom; and after the successors of Probus had withdrawn their countenance from the republican party, the senators were unable to disguise their impotent resentment. As the sovereign of Italy, Maximian was intrusted with the care of extinguishing this troublesome, rather than dangerous spirit, and the task was perfectly suited to his cruel temper. The most illustrious members of the senate, whom Diocletian always affected to esteem, were involved, by his colleague, in the accusation of imaginary plots; and the possession of an elegant villa, or a well-cultivated estate, was interpreted as a convincing evidence of guilt. The camp of the Prætorians, which had so long oppressed, began to protect, the majesty of Rome; and as those haughty troops were conscious of the decline of their power, they were naturally disposed to unite their strength with the authority of the senate. By the prudent measures of Diocletian, the numbers of the Prætorians were insensibly reduced, their privileges abolished, and their place supplied by two faithful legions of Illyricum, who, under the new titles of Jovians and Herculians, were appointed to perform the service of the Imperial guards. But the most fatal though secret wound which the senate received from the hands of Diocletian and Maximian was inflicted by the inevitable operation of their absence. As long as the emperors resided at Rome, that assembly might be oppressed, but it could scarcely be neglected. The successors of Augustus exercised the power of dictating whatever laws their wisdom or caprice might suggest; but those laws were ratified by the sanction of the senate. The model of ancient freedom was preserved in its deliberations and decrees; and wise princes, who respected the prejudices of the Roman people, were in some measure obliged to assume the language and behaviour suitable to the general and first magistrate of the republic. In the armies and in the provinces they displayed the dignity of monarchs; and when they fixed their residence at a distance from the capital, they for ever laid aside the dissimulation which Augustus had recommended to his successors. In the exercise of the legislative as well as the executive power, the sovereign advised with his ministers, instead of consulting the great council of the nation. The name of the senate was mentioned with honour till the last period of the empire; the vanity of its members was still flattered with honorary distinctions; but the assembly which had so long been the source, and so long the instrument of power, was respectfully suffered to sink into oblivion. The senate of Rome, losing all connexion with the Imperial court and the actual constitution, was left a venerable but useless monument of antiquity on the Capitoline hill.

When the Roman princes had lost sight of the senate and of their ancient capital, they easily forgot the origin and nature of their legal power. The civil offices of consul, of proconsul, of censor, and of tribune, by the union of which it had been formed, betrayed to the people its republican extraction. Those modest titles were laid aside; and if they still distinguished their high station by the appellation of Emperor, or IMPERATOR, that word was understood in a new and more dignified sense, and no longer denoted the general of the Roman armies, but the sovereign of the Roman world. The name of Emperor, which was at first of a military nature, was associated with another of a more servile kind. The epithet of DOMINUS, or Lord, in its primitive signification, was expressive not of the authority of a prince over his subjects, or of a commander over his soldiers, but of the despotic power of a master over his domestic slaves. Viewing it in that odious light, it had been rejected with abhorrence by the first Cæsars. Their resistance insensibly became more feeble, and the name less odious; till at length the style of *our Lord and Emperor* was not only bestowed by flattery, but was regularly admitted into the laws and public monuments. Such lofty epithets were sufficient to elate and satisfy the most excessive vanity; and if the successors of Diocletian still declined the title of King, it seems to have been the effect not so much of their moderation as of their delicacy.

Wherever the Latin tongue was in use (and it was the language of government throughout the empire), the Imperial title, as it was peculiar to themselves, conveyed a more respectable idea than the name of king, which they must have shared with an hundred barbarian chieftains; or which, at the best, they could derive only from Romulus, or from Tarquin. But the sentiments of the East were very different from those of the West. From the earliest period of history, the sovereigns of Asia had been celebrated in the Greek language by the title of BASILEUS, or King; and since it was considered as the first distinction among men, it was soon employed by the servile provincials of the East in their humble addresses to the Roman throne. Even the attributes, or at least the titles, of the DIVINITY, were usurped by Diocletian and Maximian, who transmitted them to a succession of Christian emperors. Such extravagant compliments, however, soon lose their impiety by losing their meaning; and when the ear is once accustomed to the sound, they are heard with indifference as vague though excessive professions of respect.

GROWTH OF COURT CEREMONIAL

From the time of Augustus to that of Diocletian, the Roman princes, conversing in a familiar manner among their fellow-citizens, were saluted only with the same respect that was usually paid to senators and magistrates. Their principal distinction was the Imperial or military robe of purple; whilst the senatorial garment was marked by a broad, and the equestrian by a narrow, band or stripe of the same honourable colour. The pride, or rather the policy, of Diocletian, engaged that artful prince to introduce the stately magnificence of the court of Persia. He ventured to assume the diadem, an ornament detested by the Romans as the odious ensign of royalty, and the use of which had been considered as the most desperate act of the madness of Caligula. It was no more than a broad white fillet set with pearls, which encircled the emperor's head. The sumptuous robes of Diocletian and his successors were of silk and gold; and it is remarked with indignation that even their shoes were studded with the most precious gems. The access to their sacred person was every day rendered more difficult by the institution of new forms and ceremonies. The avenues of the palace were strictly guarded by the various *schools*, as they began to be called, of domestic officers. The interior apartments were intrusted to the jealous vigilance of the eunuchs; the increase of whose numbers and influence was the most infallible symptom of the progress of despotism. When a subject was at length admitted to the Imperial presence, he was obliged, whatever might be his rank, to fall prostrate on the ground, and to adore, according to the eastern fashion, the divinity of his lord and master. Diocletian was a man of sense, who, in the course of private as well as public life, had formed a just estimate both of himself and of mankind: nor is it easy to conceive that in substituting the manners of

Persia to those of Rome he was seriously actuated by so mean a principle as that of vanity. He flattered himself that an ostentation of splendour and luxury would subdue the imagination of the multitude; that the monarch would be less exposed to the rude licence of the people and the soldiers, as his person was secluded from the public view; and that habits of submission would insensibly be productive of sentiments of veneration. Like the modesty affected by Augustus, the state maintained by Diocletian was a theatrical representation; but it must be confessed that, of the two comedies, the former was of a much more liberal and manly character than the latter. It was the aim of the one to disguise, and the object of the other to display, the unbounded power which the emperors possessed over the Roman world.

Ostentation was the first principle of the new system instituted by Diocletian. The second was division. He divided the empire, the provinces, and every branch of the civil as well as military administration. He multiplied the wheels of the machine of government, and rendered its operations less rapid but more secure. Whatever advantages and whatever defects might attend these innovations, they must be ascribed in a very great degree to the first inventor; but as the new frame of policy was gradually improved and completed by succeeding princes, it will be more satisfactory to delay the consideration of it till the season of its full maturity and perfection. Reserving, therefore, for the reign of Constantine a more exact picture of the new empire, we shall content ourselves with describing the principal and decisive outline, as it was traced by the hand of Diocletian. He had associated three colleagues in the exercise of the supreme power; and as he was convinced that the abilities of a single man were inadequate to the public defence, he considered the joint administration of four princes not as a temporary expedient, but as a fundamental law of the constitution. It was his intention that the two elder princes should be distinguished by the use of the diadem, and the title of *Augusti*; that, as affection or esteem might direct their choice, they should regularly call to their assistance two subordinate colleagues; and that the *Cæsars*, rising in their turn to the first rank, should supply an uninterrupted succession of emperors. The empire was divided into four parts. The East and Italy were the most honourable, the Danube and the Rhine the most laborious stations. The former claimed the presence of the *Augusti*, the latter were intrusted to the administration of the *Cæsars*. The strength of the legions was in the hands of the four partners of sovereignty, and the despair of successively vanquishing four formidable rivals might intimidate the ambition of an aspiring general. In their civil government the emperors were supposed to exercise the undivided power of the monarch, and their edicts, inscribed with their joint names, were received in all the provinces, as promulgated by their mutual councils and authority. Notwithstanding these precautions, the political union of the Roman world was gradually dissolved, and a principle of division was introduced, which, in the course of a few years, occasioned the perpetual separation of the eastern and western empires.

The system of Diocletian was accompanied with another very material disadvantage, which cannot even at present be totally overlooked; a more expensive establishment, and consequently an increase of taxes, and the oppression of the people. Instead of a modest family of slaves and freedmen, such as had contented the simple greatness of Augustus and Trajan, three or four magnificent courts were established in the various parts of the empire, and as many Roman *kings* contended with each other and with the Persian monarch for the vain superiority of pomp and luxury. The number of ministers, of magistrates, of officers, and of servants, who filled the different departments of the state, was multiplied beyond the example of former times; and (if we may borrow the warm expression of a contemporary) "when the proportion of those who received exceeded the proportion of those who contributed, the provinces were oppressed by the weight of tributes." From this period to the extinction of the empire, it would be easy to deduce an uninterrupted series of clamours and complaints. According to his religion and situation, each writer chooses either Diocletian, or Constantine, or Valens, or Theodosius, for the object of his invectives; but they unanimously agree in representing the burden of the public impositions, and particularly the land-tax and capitation, as the intolerable and increasing grievance of their own times. From such a concurrence, an impartial historian, who is obliged to extract truth from satire, as well as from panegyric, will be inclined to divide the blame among the princes whom they accuse, and to ascribe their exactions much less to their personal vices than to the uniform system of their administration. The emperor Diocletian was indeed the author of that system; but during his reign the growing evil was confined within the bounds of modesty and discretion, and he deserves the reproach of establishing pernicious precedents, rather than of exercising actual oppression. It may be added, that his revenues were managed with prudent economy; and that, after all the current expenses were discharged, there still remained in the Imperial treasury an ample provision either for judicious liberality or for any emergency of the state.

ABDICATION AND DEATH OF DIOCLETIAN

It was in the twenty-first year of his reign that Diocletian executed his memorable resolution of abdicating the empire; an action more naturally to have been expected from the elder or the younger Antoninus than from a prince who had never practised the lessons of philosophy either in the attainment or in the use of supreme power. Diocletian acquired the glory of giving to the world the first example of a resignation which has not been very frequently imitated by succeeding monarchs. The parallel of Charles the Fifth, however, will naturally offer itself to our mind, not only since the eloquence of a modern historian has rendered that name so familiar to an English reader, but from the very striking resemblance between the characters of the two emperors, whose political abilities were superior to their military genius, and whose specious virtues were much less the effect of nature than of art. The abdication of Charles appears to have been hastened by the vicissitude of fortune; and the disappointment of his favourite schemes urged him to relinquish a power which he found inadequate to his ambition. But the reign of Diocletian had flowed with a tide of uninterrupted success; nor was it till after he had vanquished all his enemies, and accomplished all his designs, that he seems to have entertained any serious thoughts of resigning the empire. Neither Charles nor Diocletian were arrived at a very advanced period of life; since the one was only fifty-five, and the other was no more than fifty-nine years of age; but the active life of those princes, their wars and journeys, the cares of royalty, and their application to business, had already impaired their constitution, and brought on the infirmities of a premature old age.

Notwithstanding the severity of a very cold and rainy winter, Diocletian left Italy soon after the ceremony of his triumph, and began his progress towards the East round the circuit of the Illyrian provinces. From the inclemency of the weather and the fatigue of the journey, he soon contracted a slow illness; and though he made easy marches, and was generally carried in a close litter, his disorder, before he arrived at Nicomedia, about the end of the summer, was become very serious and alarming. During the whole winter he was confined to his palace; his danger inspired a general and unaffected concern; but the people could only judge of the various alterations of his health from the joy or consternation which they discovered in the countenances and behaviour of his attendants. The rumour of his death was for some time universally believed, and it was supposed to be concealed with a view to prevent the troubles that might have happened during the absence of the Cæsar Galerius. At length, however, on the first of March, Diocletian once more appeared in public, but so pale and emaciated, that he could scarcely have been recognised by those to whom his person was the most familiar. It was time to put an end to the painful struggle, which he had sustained during more than a year, between the care of his health and that of his dignity. The former required indulgence and relaxation, the latter compelled him to direct, from the bed of sickness, the administration of a great empire. He resolved to pass the remainder of his days in honourable repose, to place his glory beyond the reach of fortune, and to relinquish the theatre of the world to his younger and more active associates.

The ceremony of his abdication was performed in a spacious plain, about three miles from Nicomedia. The emperor ascended a lofty throne, and, in a speech full of reason and dignity, declared his intention, both to the people and to the soldiers who were assembled on this extraordinary occasion. As soon as he had divested himself of the purple, he withdrew from the gazing multitude, and, traversing the city in a covered chariot, proceeded without delay to the favourite retirement which he had chosen in his native country of Dalmatia. On the same day, which was the first of May, Maximian, as it had been previously concerted, made his resignation of the Imperial dignity at Milan. Even in the splendour of the Roman triumph, Diocletian had meditated his design of abdicating the government. As he wished to secure the obedience of Maximian, he exacted from him either a general assurance that he would submit his actions to the authority of his benefactor, or a particular promise that he would descend from the throne whenever he should receive the advice and the example. This engagement, though it was confirmed by the solemnity of an oath before the altar of the Capitoline Jupiter, would have proved a feeble restraint on the fierce temper of Maximian, whose passion was the love of power, and who neither desired present tranquillity nor future reputation. But he yielded, however reluctantly, to the ascendant which his wiser colleague had acquired over him, and retired immediately after his abdication to a villa in Lucania, where it was almost impossible that such an impatient spirit could find any lasting tranquillity.

Diocletian, who, from a servile origin, had raised himself to the throne, passed the nine last years of his life in a private condition. Reason had dictated, and content seems to have accompanied, his retreat, in which he enjoyed for a long time the respect of those princes to whom he had resigned the possession of the world. It is seldom that minds long exercised in business have formed any habits of conversing with themselves, and in the loss of power they principally regret the want of occupation. The amusements of letters and of devotion, which afford so many resources in solitude, were incapable of fixing the attention of Diocletian; but he had preserved, or at least he soon recovered, a taste for the most innocent as well as natural pleasures, and his leisure hours were sufficiently employed in building, planting, and gardening. His answer to Maximian is deservedly celebrated. He was solicited by that restless old man to reassume the reins of government and the Imperial purple. He rejected the temptation with a smile of pity, calmly observing that, if he could show Maximian the cabbages which he had planted with his own hands at Salona, he should no longer be urged to relinquish the enjoyment of happiness for the pursuit of power. In his conversations with his friends, he frequently acknowledged, that of all arts the most difficult was the art of reigning; and he expressed himself on that favourite topic with a degree of warmth which could be the result only of experience. "How often," was he accustomed to say, "is it the interest of four or five ministers to combine together to deceive their sovereign! Secluded from mankind by his exalted dignity, the truth is concealed from his knowledge; he can see only with their eyes, he hears nothing but their misrepresentations. He confers the most important offices upon vice and weakness, and disgraces the most virtuous and deserving among his subjects. By such infamous arts," added Diocletian, "the best and wisest princes are sold to the venal corruption of their courtiers." A just estimate of greatness, and the assurance of immortal fame, improve our relish for the pleasures of retirement; but the Roman emperor had filled too important a character in the world to enjoy without alloy the comforts and security of a private condition. It was impossible that he could remain ignorant of the troubles which afflicted the empire after his abdication. It was impossible that he could be indifferent to their consequences. Fear, sorrow, and discontent sometimes pursued him into the solitude of Salona. His tenderness, or at least his pride, was deeply wounded by the misfortunes of his wife and daughter; and the last moments of Diocletian were embittered by some affronts, which Licinius and Constantine might have spared the father of so many emperors, and the first author of their own fortune. A report, though of a very doubtful nature, has reached our times, that he prudently withdrew himself from their power by a voluntary death.

Before we dismiss the consideration of the life and character of Diocletian, we may for a moment direct our view to the place of his retirement. Salona, a principal city of his native province of Dalmatia, was near two hundred Roman miles (according to the measurement of the public highways) from Aquileia and the confines of Italy, and about two hundred and seventy from Sirmium, the usual residence of the emperors whenever they visited the Illyrian frontier. A miserable village still preserves the name of Salona; but so late as the sixteenth century the remains of a theatre, and a confused prospect of broken arches and marble columns, continued to attest its ancient splendour. About six or seven miles from the city Diocletian constructed a magnificent palace, and we may infer, from the greatness of the work, how long he had meditated his design of abdicating the empire. The choice of a spot which united all that could contribute either to health or to luxury did not require the partiality of a native. "The soil was dry and fertile, the air is pure and wholesome, and, though extremely hot during the summer months, this country seldom feels those sultry and noxious winds to which the coasts of Istria and some parts of Italy are exposed. The views from the palace are no less beautiful than the soil and climate were inviting. Towards the west lies the fertile shore that stretches along the Adriatic, in which a number of small islands are scattered in such a manner as to give this part of the sea the appearance of a great lake. On the north side lies the bay, which led to the ancient city of Salona; and the country beyond it, appearing in sight, forms a proper contrast to that more extensive prospect of water which the Adriatic presents both to the south and to the east. Towards the north the view is terminated by high and irregular mountains, situated at a proper distance, and in many places covered with villages, woods, and vineyards." [1]

Though Constantine, from a very obvious prejudice, affects to mention the palace of Diocletian with contempt, yet one of their successors, who could only see it in a neglected and mutilated state, celebrates its magnificence in terms of the highest admiration. It covered an extent of ground consisting of between nine and ten English acres. The form was quadrangular, flanked with sixteen towers. Two of the sides were near six hundred, and the other two near seven hundred, feet in length. The whole was constructed of a beautiful free-stone, extracted from the neighbouring quarries of Trau, or Tragutium, and very little inferior to marble itself. Four streets, intersecting each other at right angles, divided the several parts of this great edifice, and the approach to the principal apartment was from a very stately entrance, which is still denominated the Golden Gate. The approach was terminated by a *peristylium* of granite columns, on one side of which we discover the square temple of Æsculapius, on the other the octagon temple of Jupiter. The latter of those deities Diocletian revered as the patron of his fortunes, the former as the protector of his health. By comparing the present remains with the precepts of Vitruvius, the several parts of the building, the baths, bedchamber, the *atrium*, the *basilica*, and the Cyzicene, Corinthian, and Egyptian halls have been described with some degree of precision, or at least of probability. Their forms were various, their proportions just, but they were all attended with two imperfections, very repugnant to our modern notions of taste and conveniency. These stately rooms had neither windows nor chimneys. They were lighted from the top (for the building seems to have consisted of no more than one story), and they received their heat by the help of pipes that were conveyed along the walls. The range of principal apartments was protected towards the south-west by a portico five hundred and seventeen feet long, which must have formed a very noble and delightful walk, when the beauties of painting and sculpture were added to those of the prospect.

DECLINE OF THE ARTS

Had this magnificent edifice remained in a solitary country, it would have been exposed to the ravages of time; but it might, perhaps, have escaped the rapacious industry of man. The village of Aspalathus, and,

---

[1] Adam's Antiquities of Diocletian's Palace at Spalatro, p. 6. We may add a circumstance or two from the Abate Fortis: the little stream of the Hyader, mentioned by Lucan, produces most exquisite trout, which a sagacious writer, perhaps a monk, supposes to have been one of the principal reasons that determined Diocletian in the choice of his retirement. The same author observes that a taste for agriculture is reviving at Spalatro; and that an experimental farm has lately been established near the city by a society of gentlemen.

long afterwards, the provincial town of Spalatro, have grown out of its ruins. The Golden Gate now opens into the market-place. St. John the Baptist has usurped the honours of Æsculapius; and the temple of Jupiter, under the protection of the Virgin, is converted into the cathedral church. For this account of Diocletian's palace we are principally indebted to an ingenious artist of our own time and country, whom a very liberal curiosity carried into the heart of Dalmatia. But there is room to suspect that the elegance of his designs and engraving has somewhat flattered the objects which it was their purpose to represent. We are informed by a more recent and very judicious traveller that the awful ruins of Spalatro are not less expressive of the decline of the arts than of the greatness of the Roman empire in the time of Diocletian. If such was indeed the state of architecture, we must naturally believe that painting and sculpture had experienced a still more sensible decay. The practice of architecture is directed by a few general and even mechanical rules. But sculpture, and, above all, painting, propose to themselves the imitation not only of the forms of nature, but of the characters and passions of the human soul. In those sublime arts the dexterity of the hand is of little avail, unless it is animated by fancy and guided by the most correct taste and observation.

It is almost unnecessary to remark that the civil distractions of the empire, the licence of the soldiers, the inroads of the barbarians, and the progress of despotism, had proved very unfavourable to genius, and even to learning. The succession of Illyrian princes restored the empire without restoring the sciences. Their military education was not calculated to inspire them with the love of letters; and even the mind of Diocletian, however active and capacious in business, was totally uninformed by study or speculation. The professions of law and physic are of such common use and certain profit that they will always secure a sufficient number of practitioners endowed with a reasonable degree of abilities and knowledge; but it does not appear that the students in those two faculties appeal to any celebrated masters who have flourished within that period. The voice of poetry was silent. History was reduced to dry and confused abridgments, alike destitute of amusement and instruction. A languid and affected eloquence was still retained in the pay and service of the emperors, who encouraged not any arts except those which contributed to the gratification of their pride or the defence of their power.

The declining age of learning and of mankind is marked, however, by the rise and rapid progress of the new Platonists. The school of Alexandria silenced those of Athens; and the ancient sects enrolled themselves under the banners of the more fashionable teachers, who recommended their system by the novelty of their method and the austerity of their manners. Several of these masters—Ammonius, Plotinus, Amelius, and Porphyry—were men of profound thought and intense application; but, by mistaking the true object of philosophy, their labours contributed much less to improve than to corrupt the human understanding. The knowledge that is suited to our situation and powers, the whole compass of moral, natural, and mathematical science, was neglected by the new Platonists; whilst they exhausted their strength in the verbal disputes of metaphysics, attempted to explore the secrets of the invisible world, and studied to reconcile Aristotle with Plato, on subjects of which both these philosophers were as ignorant as the rest of mankind. Consuming their reason in these deep but unsubstantial meditations, their minds were exposed to illusions of fancy. They flattered themselves that they possessed the secret of disengaging the soul from its corporeal prison; claimed a familiar intercourse with dæmons and spirits; and, by a very singular revolution, converted the study of philosophy into that of magic. The ancient sages had derided the popular superstition; after disguising its extravagance by the thin pretence of allegory, the disciples of Plotinus and Porphyry became its most zealous defenders. As they agreed with the Christians in a few mysterious points of faith, they attacked the remainder of their theological system with all the fury of civil war. The new Platonists would scarcely deserve a place in the history of science, but in that of the church the mention of them will very frequently occur.

Chapter 14

CONSTANTINE IN ROME. HIS LEGAL REFORMS

The initial and fatal flaw in Diocletian's organisation lay in the fact that Maximian and Constantius both had sons, Maxentius and Constantine, respectively. Paternal favour overruled the electoral system. Galerius tried to separate Constantine from his father. Nevertheless the young man joined his father in Britain and on his death at York was proclaimed Augustus. In the same year Maxentius broke his pact and emerged from retirement.

The main thread in the tangle of wars and political manœuvres lies in Constantine's masterly strategy. Constantine administered Gaul while Maxentius exercised a tyrannical rule over Italy and Africa. He then invaded Italy. Maxentius was defeated and killed at the Milvian bridge outside Rome. It was before this battle that Constantine was alleged to have seen the vision which decided his conversion to Christianity.

CONSTANTINE IN ROME

IN the use of victory Constantine neither deserved the praise of clemency nor incurred the censure of immoderate rigor. He inflicted the same treatment to which a defeat would have exposed his own person and family, put to death the two sons of the tyrant, and carefully extirpated his whole race. The most distinguished adherents of Maxentius must have expected to share his fate, as they had shared his prosperity and his crimes; but when the Roman people loudly demanded a greater number of victims, the conqueror resisted, with firmness and humanity, those servile clamours, which were dictated by flattery as well as by resentment. Informers were punished and discouraged; the innocent who had suffered under the late tyranny were recalled from exile, and restored to their estates. A general act of oblivion quieted the minds and settled the property of the people both in Italy and in Africa. The first time that Constantine honoured the senate with his presence he recapitulated his own services and exploits in a modest oration, assured that illustrious order of his sincere regard, and promised to re-establish its ancient dignity and privileges. The grateful senate repaid these unmeaning professions by the empty titles of honour which it was yet in their power to bestow; and, without presuming to ratify the authority of Constantine, they passed a decree to assign him the first rank among the three *Augusti* who governed the Roman world. Games and festivals were instituted to preserve the fame of his victory, and several edifices, raised at the expense of Maxentius, were dedicated to the honour of his successful rival. The triumphal arch of Constantine still remains a melancholy proof of the decline of the arts, and a singular testimony of the meanest vanity. As it was not possible to find in the capital of the empire a sculptor who was capable of adorning that public monument, the arch of Trajan, without any respect either for his memory or for the rules of propriety, was stripped of its most elegant figures. The difference of times and persons, of actions and characters, was totally disregarded. The Parthian captives appear prostrate at the feet of a prince who never carried his arms beyond the Euphrates; and curious antiquarians can still discover the head of Trajan on the trophies of Constantine. The new ornaments which it was necessary to introduce between the vacancies of ancient sculpture are executed in the rudest and most unskilful manner.

The final abolition of the Prætorian guards was a measure of prudence as well as of revenge. Those haughty troops, whose numbers and privileges had been restored, and even augmented, by Maxentius, were for ever suppressed by Constantine. Their fortified camp was destroyed, and the few Prætorians who had escaped the fury of the sword were dispersed among the legions and banished to the frontiers of the empire, where they might be serviceable without again becoming dangerous. By suppressing the troops which were usually stationed in Rome, Constantine gave the fatal blow to the dignity of the senate and people, and the disarmed capital was exposed, without protection, to the insults or neglect of its distant master. We may observe that, in this last effort to preserve their expiring freedom, the Romans, from the apprehension of a tribute, had raised Maxentius to the throne. He exacted that tribute from the senate under the name of a free gift. They implored the assistance of Constantine. He vanquished the tyrant, and converted the free gift into a perpetual tax. The senators, according to the declaration which was required of their property, were divided into several classes. The most opulent paid annually eight pounds of gold, the next class paid four, the last two, and those whose poverty might have claimed an exemption were assessed however at seven pieces of gold. Besides the regular members of the senate, their sons, their descendants, and even their relations, enjoyed the vain privileges and supported the heavy burdens of the senatorial order; nor will it any longer excite our surprise that Constantine should be attentive to increase the number of persons who were included under so useful a description. After the defeat of Maxentius the victorious emperor passed no more than two or three months in Rome, which he visited twice during the remainder of his life to celebrate the solemn festivals of the tenth and of the twentieth years of his reign. Constantine was almost perpetually in motion, to exercise the legions or to inspect the state of the provinces. Treves, Milan,

Aquileia, Sirmium, Naissus, and Thessalonica were the occasional places of his residence till he founded a NEW ROME on the confines of Europe and Asia.

Constantine first formed an alliance with Licinius and was then at war with him. After the battles of Cibalis and Mardia they were reconciled.

CONSTANTINE'S LEGAL REFORMS

The reconciliation of Constantine and Licinius, though it was embittered by resentment and jealousy, by the remembrance of recent injuries, and by the apprehension of future dangers, maintained, however, above eight years, the tranquillity of the Roman world. As a very regular series of the Imperial laws commences about this period, it would not be difficult to transcribe the civil regulations which employed the leisure of Constantine. But the most important of his institutions are intimately connected with the new system of policy and religion, which was not perfectly established till the last and peaceful years of his reign. There are many of his laws which, as far as they concern the rights and property of individuals, and the practice of the bar, are more properly referred to the private than to the public jurisprudence of the empire; and he published many edicts of so local and temporary a nature, that they would ill deserve the notice of a general history. Two laws, however, may be selected from the crowd; the one for its importance, the other for its singularity; the former for its remarkable benevolence, the latter for its excessive severity. 1. The horrid practice, so familiar to the ancients, of exposing or murdering their new-born infants, was become every day more frequent in the provinces, and especially in Italy. It was the effect of distress; and the distress was principally occasioned by the intolerable burden of taxes, and by the vexations as well as cruel prosecutions of the officers of the revenue against their insolvent debtors. The less opulent or less industrious part of mankind, instead of rejoicing in an increase of family, deemed it an act of paternal tenderness to release their children from the impending miseries of a life which they themselves were unable to support. The humanity of Constantine, moved, perhaps, by some recent and extraordinary instances of despair, engaged him to address an edict to all the cities of Italy, and afterwards of Africa, directing immediate and sufficient relief to be given to those parents who should produce before the magistrates the children whom their own poverty would not allow them to educate. But the promise was too liberal, and the provision too vague, to effect any general or permanent benefit. The law, though it may merit some praise, served rather to display than to alleviate the public distress. It still remains an authentic monument to contradict and confound those venal orators who were too well satisfied with their own situation to discover either vice or misery under the government of a generous sovereign. 2. The laws of Constantine against rapes were dictated with very little indulgence for the most amiable weaknesses of human nature; since the description of that crime was applied not only to the brutal violence which compelled, but even to the gentle seduction which might persuade, an unmarried woman, under the age of twenty-five, to leave the house of her parents. "The successful ravisher was punished with death; and as if simple death was inadequate to the enormity of his guilt, he was either burnt alive, or torn in pieces by wild beasts in the amphitheatre. The virgin's declaration that she had been carried away with her own consent, instead of saving her lover, exposed her to share his fate. The duty of a public prosecution was intrusted to the parents of the guilty or unfortunate maid; and if the sentiments of nature prevailed on them to dissemble the injury, and to repair by a subsequent marriage the honour of their family, they were themselves punished by exile and confiscation. The slaves, whether male or female, who were convicted of having been accessary to the rape or seduction, were burnt alive, or put to death by the ingenious torture of pouring down their throats a quantity of melted lead. As the crime was of a public kind, the accusation was permitted even to strangers. The commencement of the action was not limited to any term of years, and the consequences of the sentence were extended to the innocent offspring of such an irregular union." But whenever the offence inspires less horror than the punishment, the rigour of penal law is obliged to give way to the common feelings of mankind. The most odious parts of this edict were softened or repealed in the subsequent reigns; and even Constantine himself very frequently alleviated, by partial acts of mercy, the stern temper of his general institutions. Such, indeed, was the singular humour of that emperor, who showed himself as indulgent, and even remiss, in the execution of his laws, as he was severe, and even cruel, in the enacting of them. It is scarcely possible to observe a more decisive symptom of weakness, either in the character of the prince, or in the constitution of the government.

Civil war broke out again between Constantine and Licinius in 323. After the battles of Adrianople and Chrysopolis and the death of Licinius, Constantine attained the sole mastery of the empire.

THE RISE OF CHRISTIANITY

Chapter 15

FIVE CAUSES OF THE GROWTH OF CHRISTIANITY. CON-
DITIONS FAVOURABLE TO ITS PROGRESS. THE NUMBERS AND
CONDITION OF THE PRIMITIVE CHRISTIANS

A CANDID but rational inquiry into the progress and establishment of Christianity may be considered as a very essential part of
the history of the Roman empire. While that great body was
invaded by open violence, or undermined by slow decay, a pure and
humble religion gently insinuated itself into the minds of men, grew up
in silence and obscurity, derived new vigour from opposition, and finally
erected the triumphant banner of the Cross on the ruins of the Capitol.
Nor was the influence of Christianity confined to the period or to the
limits of the Roman empire. After a revolution of thirteen or fourteen
centuries, that religion is still professed by the nations of Europe, the
most distinguished portion of human kind in arts and learning as well
as in arms. By the industry and zeal of the Europeans it has been widely
diffused to the most distant shores of Asia and Africa; and by the means
of their colonies has been firmly established from Canada to Chile, in
a world unknown to the ancients.

But this inquiry, however useful or entertaining, is attended with
two peculiar difficulties. The scanty and suspicious materials of ecclesiastical history seldom enable us to dispel the dark cloud that hangs
over the first age of the church. The great law of impartiality too often
obliges us to reveal the imperfections of the uninspired teachers and
believers of the Gospel; and, to a careless observer, *their* faults may
seem to cast a shade on the faith which they professed. But the scandal
of the pious Christian, and the fallacious triumph of the Infidel, should
cease as soon as they recollect not only *by whom*, but likewise *to whom*,
the Divine Revelation was given. The theologian may indulge the
pleasing task of describing Religion as she descended from Heaven,
arrayed in her native purity. A more melancholy duty is imposed on
the historian. He must discover the inevitable mixture of error and
corruption which she contracted in a long residence upon earth, among
a weak and degenerate race of beings.

Our curiosity is naturally prompted to inquire by what means the
Christian faith obtained so remarkable a victory over the established
religions of the earth. To this inquiry an obvious but satisfactory
answer may be returned; that it was owing to the convincing evidence
of the doctrine itself, and to the ruling providence of its great Author.

But as truth and reason seldom find so favourable a reception in the world, and as the wisdom of Providence frequently condescends to use the passions of the human heart, and the general circumstances of mankind, as instruments to execute its purpose, we may still be permitted, though with becoming submission, to ask, not indeed what were the first, but what were the secondary causes of the rapid growth of the Christian church? It will, perhaps, appear that it was most effectually favoured and assisted by the five following causes:—I. The inflexible, and, if we may use the expression, the intolerant zeal of the Christians, derived, it is true, from the Jewish religion, but purified from the narrow and unsocial spirit which, instead of inviting, had deterred the Gentiles from embracing the law of Moses. II. The doctrine of a future life, improved by every additional circumstance which could give weight and efficacy to that important truth. III. The miraculous powers ascribed to the primitive church. IV. The pure and austere morals of the Christians. V. The union and discipline of the Christian republic, which gradually formed an independent and increasing state in the heart of the Roman empire.

THE INFLEXIBLE ZEAL OF THE CHRISTIANS INHERITED FROM THE JEWS

I. We have already described the religious harmony of the ancient world, and the facility with which the most different and even hostile nations embraced, or at least respected, each other's superstitions. A single people refused to join in the common intercourse of mankind. The Jews, who, under the Assyrian and Persian monarchies, had languished for many ages the most despised portion of their slaves, emerged from obscurity under the successors of Alexander; and as they multiplied to a surprising degree in the East, and afterwards in the West, they soon excited the curiosity and wonder of other nations. The sullen obstinacy with which they maintained their peculiar rites and unsocial manners seemed to mark them out a distinct species of men, who boldly professed, or who faintly disguised, their implacable hatred to the rest of human-kind. Neither the violence of Antiochus, nor the arts of Herod, nor the example of the circumjacent nations, could ever persuade the Jews to associate with the institutions of Moses the elegant mythology of the Greeks. According to the maxims of universal toleration, the Romans protected a superstition which they despised. The polite Augustus condescended to give orders that sacrifices should be offered for his prosperity in the temple of Jerusalem; while the meanest of the posterity of Abraham, who should have paid the same homage to the Jupiter of the Capitol, would have been an object of abhorrence to himself and to his brethren. But the moderation of the conquerors was insufficient to appease the jealous prejudices of their subjects, who were alarmed and scandalised at the ensigns of paganism, which necessarily introduced themselves into a Roman province. The mad attempt of Caligula to place his own statue in the temple of Jerusalem was defeated by the unanimous resolution of a people who dreaded death much less than such an idolatrous profanation. Their attachment to the law of Moses was equal to their detestation of foreign religions. The current of zeal and devotion, as it was contracted into a narrow channel, ran with the strength, and sometimes with the fury, of a torrent.

This inflexible perseverance, which appeared so odious or so ridiculous to the ancient world, assumes a more awful character, since Providence has designed to reveal to us the mysterious history of the chosen people. But the devout and even scrupulous attachment to the Mosaic religion, so conspicuous among the Jews who lived under the second temple, becomes still more surprising, if it is compared with the stubborn incredulity of their forefathers. When the law was given in thunder from Mount Sinai; when the tides of the ocean and the course of the planets were suspended for the convenience of the Israelites; and when temporal rewards and punishments were the immediate consequences of their piety or disobedience, they perpetually relapsed into rebellion against the visible majesty of their Divine King, placed the idols of the nations in the sanctuary of Jehovah, and imitated every fantastic ceremony that was practised in the tents of the Arabs, or in the cities of Phœnicia. As the protection of Heaven was deservedly withdrawn from the ungrateful race, their faith acquired a proportionable degree of vigour and purity. The contemporaries of Moses and Joshua had beheld with careless indifference the most amazing miracles. Under the pressure of every calamity, the belief of those miracles has preserved the Jews of a later period from the universal contagion of idolatry; and in contradiction to every known principle of the human mind, that singular people seems to have yielded a stronger and more ready assent to the traditions of their remote ancestors than to the evidence of their own senses.[1]

The Jewish religion was admirably fitted for defence, but it was never designed for conquest; and it seems probable that the number of proselytes was never much superior to that of apostates. The divine promises were originally made, and the distinguishing rite of circumcision was enjoined, to a single family. When the posterity of Abraham had multiplied like the sands of the sea, the Deity, from whose mouth they received a system of laws and ceremonies, declared himself the proper and as it were the national God of Israel; and with the most jealous care separated his favourite people from the rest of mankind. The conquest of the land of Canaan was accompanied with so many wonderful

---

[1] "How long will this people provoke me? and how long will it be ere they *believe* me, for all the *signs* which I have shewn among them?" (Numbers xiv. 11.) It would be easy, but it would be unbecoming, to justify the complaint of the Deity from the whole tenor of the Mosaic history.

and with so many bloody circumstances, that the victorious Jews were left in a state of irreconcileable hostility with all their neighbours. They had been commanded to extirpate some of the most idolatrous tribes, and the execution of the Divine will had seldom been retarded by the weakness of humanity. With the other nations they were forbidden to contract any marriages or alliances; and the prohibition of receiving them into the congregation, which in some cases was perpetual, almost always extended to the third, to the seventh, or even to the tenth generation. The obligation of preaching to the Gentiles the faith of Moses had never been inculcated as a precept of the law, nor were the Jews inclined to impose it on themselves as a voluntary duty.

In the admission of new citizens that unsocial people was actuated by the selfish vanity of the Greeks, rather than by the generous policy of Rome. The descendants of Abraham were flattered by the opinion that they alone were the heirs of the covenant, and they were apprehensive of diminishing the value of their inheritance by sharing it too easily with the strangers of the earth. A larger acquaintance with mankind extended their knowledge without correcting their prejudices; and whenever the God of Israel acquired any new votaries, he was much more indebted to the inconstant humour of polytheism than to the active zeal of his own missionaries. The religion of Moses seems to be instituted for a particular country as well as for a single nation; and if a strict obedience had been paid to the order that every male, three times in the year, should present himself before the Lord Jehovah, it would have been impossible that the Jews could ever have spread themselves beyond the narrow limits of the promised land. That obstacle was indeed removed by the destruction of the temple of Jerusalem; but the most considerable part of the Jewish religion was involved in its destruction; and the Pagans, who had long wondered at the strange report of an empty sanctuary, were at a loss to discover what could be the object, or what could be the instruments, of a worship which was destitute of temples and of altars, of priests and of sacrifices. Yet even in their fallen state, the Jews, still asserting their lofty and exclusive privileges, shunned, instead of courting, the society of strangers. They still insisted with inflexible rigour on those parts of the law which it was in their power to practise. Their peculiar distinctions of days, of meats, and a variety of trivial though burdensome observances, were so many objects of disgust and aversion for the other nations, to whose habits and prejudices they were diametrically opposite. The painful and even dangerous rite of circumcision was alone capable of repelling a willing proselyte from the door of the synagogue.

Under these circumstances, Christianity offered itself to the world, armed with the strength of the Mosaic law, and delivered from the weight of its fetters. An exclusive zeal for the truth of religion and the unity of God was as carefully inculcated in the new as in the ancient system: and whatever was now revealed to mankind concerning the nature and designs of the Supreme Being was fitted to increase their reverence for that mysterious doctrine. The divine authority of Moses and the prophets was admitted, and even established, as the firmest basis of Christianity. From the beginning of the world an uninterrupted series of predictions had announced and prepared the long-expected coming of the Messiah, who, in compliance with the gross apprehensions of the Jews, had been more frequently represented under the character of a King and Conqueror, than under that of a Prophet, a Martyr, and the Son of God. By his expiatory sacrifice the imperfect sacrifices of the temple were at once consummated and abolished. The ceremonial law, which consisted only of types and figures, was succeeded by a pure and spiritual worship, equally adapted to all climates, as well as to every condition of mankind; and to the initiation of blood, was substituted a more harmless initiation of water. The promise of divine favour, instead of being partially confined to the posterity of Abraham, was universally proposed to the freeman and the slave, to the Greek and to the barbarian, to the Jew and to the Gentile. Every privilege that could raise the proselyte from earth to heaven, that could exalt his devotion, secure his happiness, or even gratify that secret pride which, under the semblance of devotion, insinuates itself into the human heart, was still reserved for the members of the Christian church; but at the same time all mankind was permitted, and even solicited, to accept the glorious distinction, which was not only proffered as a favour, but imposed as an obligation. It became the most sacred duty of a new convert to diffuse amongst his friends and relations the inestimable blessing which he had received, and to warn them against a refusal that would be severely punished as a criminal disobedience to the will of a benevolent but all-powerful Deity.

The enfranchisement of the church from the bonds of the synagogue was a work, however, of some time and of some difficulty. The Jewish converts, who acknowledged Jesus in the character of the Messiah foretold by their ancient oracles, respected him as a prophetic teacher of virtue and religion; but they obstinately adhered to the ceremonies of their ancestors, and were desirous of imposing them on the Gentiles, who continually augmented the number of believers. These Judaising Christians seem to have argued with some degree of plausibility from the Divine origin of the Mosaic law, and from the immutable perfections of its great Author. They affirmed, *that*, if the Being who is the same through all eternity had designed to abolish those sacred rites which had served to distinguish his chosen people, the repeal of them would have been no less clear and solemn than their first promulgation: *that*, instead of those frequent declarations which either suppose or assert the perpetuity of the Mosaic religion, it would have been represented as a provisionary scheme intended to last only till the coming of the

Messiah, who should instruct mankind in a more perfect mode of faith and of worship: *that* the Messiah himself, and his disciples who conversed with him on earth, instead of authorising by their example the most minute observances of the Mosaic law, would have published to the world the abolition of those useless and obsolete ceremonies, without suffering Christianity to remain during so many years obscurely confounded among the sects of the Jewish church. Arguments like these appear to have been used in the defence of the expiring cause of the Mosaic law; but the industry of our learned divines has abundantly explained the ambiguous language of the Old Testament, and the ambiguous conduct of the apostolic teachers. It was proper gradually to unfold the system of the Gospel, and to pronounce with the utmost caution and tenderness a sentence of condemnation so repugnant to the inclination and prejudices of the believing Jews.

The history of the church of Jerusalem affords a lively proof of the necessity of those precautions, and of the deep impression which the Jewish religion had made on the minds of its sectaries. The first fifteen bishops of Jerusalem were all circumcised Jews; and the congregation over which they presided united the law of Moses with the doctrine of Christ. It was natural that the primitive tradition of a church which was founded only forty days after the death of Christ, and was governed almost as many years under the immediate inspection of his apostle, should be received as the standard of orthodoxy. The distant churches very frequently appealed to the authority of their venerable Parent, and relieved her distresses by a liberal contribution of alms. But when numerous and opulent societies were established in the great cities of the empire, in Antioch, Alexandria, Ephesus, Corinth, and Rome, the reverence which Jerusalem had inspired to all the Christian colonies insensibly diminished. The Jewish converts, or, as they were afterwards called, the Nazarenes, who had laid the foundations of the church, soon found themselves overwhelmed by the increasing multitudes that from all the various religions of polytheism enlisted under the banner of Christ: and the Gentiles, who, with the approbation of their peculiar apostle, had rejected the intolerable weight of Mosaic ceremonies, at length refused to their more scrupulous brethren the same toleration which at first they had humbly solicited for their own practice. The ruin of the temple, of the city, and of the public religion of the Jews, was severely felt by the Nazarenes; as in their manners, though not in their faith, they maintained so intimate a connexion with their impious countrymen, whose misfortunes were attributed by the Pagans to the contempt, and more justly ascribed by the Christians to the wrath, of the Supreme Deity. The Nazarenes retired from the ruins of Jerusalem to the little town of Pella beyond the Jordan, where that ancient church languished above sixty years in solitude and obscurity. They still enjoyed the comfort of making frequent and devout visits to the *Holy*

City, and the hope of being one day restored to those seats which both nature and religion taught them to love as well as to revere. But at length, under the reign of Hadrian, the desperate fanaticism of the Jews filled up the measure of their calamities; and the Romans, exasperated by their repeated rebellions, exercised the rights of victory with unusual rigour. The emperor founded, under the name of Ælia Capitolina, a new city on Mount Sion, to which he gave the privileges of a colony; and denouncing the severest penalties against any of the Jewish people who should dare to approach its precincts, he fixed a vigilant garrison of a Roman cohort to enforce the execution of his orders. The Nazarenes had only one way left to escape the common proscription, and the force of truth was on this occasion assisted by the influence of temporal advantages. They elected Marcus for their bishop, a prelate of the race of the Gentiles, and most probably a native either of Italy or of some of the Latin provinces. At his persuasion the most considerable part of the congregation renounced the Mosaic law, in the practice of which they had persevered above a century. By this sacrifice of their habits and prejudices they purchased a free admission into the colony of Hadrian, and more firmly cemented their union with the Catholic church.

When the name and honours of the church of Jerusalem had been restored to Mount Sion, the crimes of heresy and schism were imputed to the obscure remnant of the Nazarenes which refused to accompany their Latin bishop. They still preserved their former habitation of Pella, spread themselves into the villages adjacent to Damascus, and formed an inconsiderable church in the city of Berœa, or, as it is now called, of Aleppo, in Syria. The name of Nazarenes was deemed too honourable for those Christian Jews, and they soon received, from the supposed poverty of their understanding, as well as of their condition, the contemptuous epithet of Ebionites. In a few years after the return of the church of Jerusalem, it became a matter of doubt and controversy whether a man who sincerely acknowledged Jesus as the Messiah, but who still continued to observe the law of Moses, could possibly hope for salvation. The humane temper of Justin Martyr inclined him to answer this question in the affirmative; and though he expressed himself with the most guarded diffidence, he ventured to determine in favour of such an imperfect Christian, if he were content to practise the Mosaic ceremonies without pretending to assert their general use or necessity. But when Justin was pressed to declare the sentiment of the church, he confessed that there were very many among the orthodox Christians who not only excluded their Judaising brethren from the hope of salvation, but who declined any intercourse with them in the common offices of friendship, hospitality, and social life. The more rigorous opinion prevailed, as it was natural to expect, over the milder; and an eternal bar of separation was fixed between the disciples of Moses and those of Christ. The unfortunate Ebionites, rejected from one religion as apostates, and from the other as heretics, found themselves compelled to assume a more decided character; and although some traces of that obsolete sect may be discovered as late as the fourth century, they insensibly melted away either into the church or the synagogue.

While the orthodox church preserved a just medium between excessive veneration and improper contempt for the law of Moses, the various heretics deviated into equal but opposite extremes of error and extravagance. From the acknowledged truth of the Jewish religion, the Ebionites had concluded that it could never be abolished. From its supposed imperfections, the Gnostics as hastily inferred that it never was instituted by the wisdom of the Deity. There are some objections against the authority of Moses and the prophets which too readily present themselves to the sceptical mind; though they can only be derived from our ignorance of remote antiquity, and from our incapacity to form an adequate judgment of the Divine economy. These objections were eagerly embraced and as petulantly urged by the vain science of the Gnostics. As those heretics were, for the most part, averse to the pleasures of sense, they morosely arraigned the polygamy of the patriarchs, the gallantries of David, and the seraglio of Solomon. The conquest of the land of Canaan, and the extirpation of the unsuspecting natives, they were at a loss how to reconcile with the common notions of humanity and justice. But when they recollected the sanguinary list of murders, of executions, and of massacres, which stain almost every page of the Jewish annals, they acknowledged that the barbarians of Palestine had exercised as much compassion towards their idolatrous enemies as they had ever shown to their friends or countrymen. Passing from the sectaries of the law to the law itself, they asserted that it was impossible that a religion which consisted only of bloody sacrifices and trifling ceremonies, and whose rewards as well as punishments were all of a carnal and temporal nature, could inspire the love of virtue, or restrain the impetuosity of passion. The Mosaic account of the creation and fall of man was treated with profane derision by the Gnostics, who would not listen with patience to the repose of the Deity after six days' labour, to the rib of Adam, the garden of Eden, the trees of life and of knowledge, the speaking serpent, the forbidden fruit, and the condemnation pronounced against human kind for the venial offence of their first progenitors. The God of Israel was impiously represented by the Gnostics as a being liable to passion and to error, capricious in his favour, implacable in his resentment, meanly jealous of his superstitious worship, and confining his partial providence to a single people, and to this transitory life. In such a character they could discover none of the features of the wise and omnipotent Father of the universe. They allowed that the religion of the Jews was somewhat less criminal than the idolatry of the Gentiles: but it was their fundamental doctrine that the Christ whom they adored as the first and brightest emanation of the Deity appeared upon earth to rescue mankind from their various errors, and to reveal a *new* system of truth and perfection. The most learned of the fathers, by a very singular condescension, have imprudently admitted the sophistry of the Gnostics. Acknowledging that the literal sense is repugnant to every principle of faith as well as reason, they deem themselves secure and invulnerable behind the ample veil of allegory, which they carefully spread over every tender part of the Mosaic dispensation.

It has been remarked with more ingenuity than truth that the virgin purity of the church was never violated by schism or heresy before the reign of Trajan or Hadrian, about one hundred years after the death of Christ. We may observe with much more propriety, that, during that period, the disciples of the Messiah were indulged in a freer latitude both of faith and practice than has ever been allowed in succeeding ages. As the terms of communion were insensibly narrowed, and the spiritual authority of the prevailing party was exercised with increasing severity, many of its most respectable adherents, who were called upon to renounce, were provoked to assert their private opinions, to pursue the consequences of their mistaken principles, and openly to erect the standard of rebellion against the unity of the church. The Gnostics were distinguished as the most polite, the most learned, and the most wealthy of the Christian name; and that general appellation, which expressed a superiority of knowledge, was either assumed by their own pride, or ironically bestowed by the envy of their adversaries. They were almost without exception of the race of the Gentiles, and their principal founders seem to have been natives of Syria or Egypt, where the warmth of the climate disposes both the mind and the body to indolent and contemplative devotion. The Gnostics blended with the faith of Christ many sublime but obscure tenets, which they derived from oriental philosophy, and even from the religion of Zoroaster, concerning the eternity of matter, the existence of two principles, and the mysterious hierarchy of the invisible world. As soon as they launched out into that vast abyss, they delivered themselves to the guidance of a disordered imagination; and as the paths of error are various and infinite, the Gnostics were imperceptibly divided into more than fifty particular sects, of whom the most celebrated appear to have been the Basilidians, the Valentinians, the Marcionites, and, in a still later period, the Manichæans. Each of these sects could boast of its bishops and congregations, of its doctors and martyrs; and, instead of the Four Gospels adopted by the church, the heretics produced a multitude of histories, in which the actions and discourses of Christ and of his apostles were adapted to their respective tenets. The success of the Gnostics was rapid and extensive. They covered Asia and Egypt, established themselves in Rome, and sometimes penetrated into the provinces of the West. For the most part they arose in the second century, flourished during the third, and were suppressed in the fourth or fifth, by the prevalence of more fashionable controversies, and by the superior ascendant of the reigning power. Though they constantly disturbed the peace, and frequently disgraced the name, of religion, they contributed to assist rather than to retard the progress of Christianity. The Gentile converts, whose strongest objections and prejudices were directed against the law of Moses, could find admission into many Christian societies, which required not from their untutored mind any belief of an antecedent revelation. Their faith was insensibly fortified and enlarged, and the church was ultimately benefited by the conquests of its most inveterate enemies.

But whatever difference of opinion might subsist between the Orthodox, the Ebionites, and the Gnostics, concerning the divinity or the obligation of the Mosaic law, they were all equally animated by the same exclusive zeal, and by the same abhorrence for idolatry, which had distinguished the Jews from the other nations of the ancient world. The philosopher, who considered the system of polytheism as a composition of human fraud and error, could disguise a smile of contempt under the mask of devotion, without apprehending that either the mockery or the compliance would expose him to the resentment of any invisible, or, as he conceived them, imaginary powers. But the established religions of Paganism were seen by the primitive Christians in a much more odious and formidable light. It was the universal sentiment both of the church and of heretics, that the dæmons were the authors, the patrons, and the objects of idolatry. Those rebellious spirits who had been degraded from the rank of angels, and cast down into the infernal pit, were still permitted to roam upon earth, to torment the bodies and to seduce the minds of sinful men. The dæmons soon discovered and abused the natural propensity of the human heart towards devotion, and, artfully withdrawing the adoration of mankind from their Creator, they usurped the place and honours of the Supreme Deity. By the success of their malicious contrivances, they at once gratified their own vanity and revenge, and obtained the only comfort of which they were yet susceptible, the hope of involving the human species in the participation of their guilt and misery. It was confessed, or at least it was imagined, that they had distributed among themselves the most important characters of polytheism, one dæmon assuming the name and attributes of Jupiter, another of Æsculapius, a third of Venus, and a fourth perhaps of Apollo; and that, by the advantage of their long experience and aërial nature, they were enabled to execute, with sufficient skill and dignity, the parts which they had undertaken. They lurked in the temples, instituted festivals and sacrifices, invented fables, pronounced oracles, and were frequently allowed to perform miracles. The Christians, who, by the interposition of evil spirits, could so readily explain every præternatural appearance, were disposed and even desirous to admit the most extravagant fictions of the Pagan mythology. But the belief of the Christian was accompanied with horror. The most trifling mark of respect to the national worship he considered as a direct homage yielded to the dæmon, and as an act of rebellion against the majesty of God.

In consequence of this opinion, it was the first but arduous duty of a Christian to preserve himself pure and undefiled by the practice of idolatry. The religion of the nations was not merely a speculative doctrine professed in the schools or preached in the temples. The innumerable deities and rites of polytheism were closely interwoven with every circumstance of business or pleasure, of public or of private life; and it seemed impossible to escape the observance of them, without, at the same time, renouncing the commerce of mankind, and all the offices and amusements of society. The important transactions of peace and war were prepared or concluded by solemn sacrifices, in which the magistrate, the senator, and the soldier, were obliged to preside or to participate.[1] The public spectacles were an essential part of the cheerful devotion of the Pagans, and the gods were supposed to accept, as the most grateful offering, the games that the prince and people celebrated in honour of their peculiar festivals.[2] The Christian, who with pious horror avoided the abomination of the circus or the theatre, found himself encompassed with infernal snares in every convivial entertainment, as often as his friends, invoking the hospitable deities, poured out libations to each other's happiness. When the bride, struggling with well-affected reluctance, was forced in hymenæal pomp over the threshold of her new habitation, or when the sad procession of the dead slowly moved towards the funeral pile,[3] the Christian, on these interesting occasions, was compelled to desert the persons who were the dearest to him, rather than contract the guilt inherent to those impious ceremonies. Every art and every trade that was in the least concerned in the framing or adorning of idols was polluted by the stain of idolatry; a severe sentence, since it devoted to eternal misery the far greater part of the community which is employed in the exercise of liberal or mechanic professions. If we cast our eyes over the numerous remains of antiquity, we shall perceive that, besides the immediate representations

---

[1] The Roman senate was always held in a temple or consecrated place. Before they entered on business, every senator dropped some wine and frankincense on the altar.

[2] See Tertullian, De Spectaculis. This severe reformer shows no more indulgence to a tragedy of Euripides than to a combat of gladiators. The dress of the actors particularly offends him. By the use of the lofty buskin they impiously strive to add a cubit to their stature.

[3] The ancient funerals (in those of Misenus and Pallas) are no less accurately described by Virgil than they are illustrated by his commentator Servius. The pile itself was an altar, the flames were fed with the blood of victims, and all the assistants were sprinkled with lustral water.

of the gods and the holy instruments of their worship, the elegant forms
and agreeable fictions consecrated by the imagination of the Greeks
were introduced as the richest ornaments of the houses, the dress, and
the furniture of the Pagans. Even the arts of music and painting, of
eloquence and poetry, flowed from the same impure origin. In the style
of the fathers, Apollo and the Muses were the organs of the infernal
spirit; Homer and Virgil were the most eminent of his servants; and
the beautiful mythology which pervades and animates the compositions
of their genius is destined to celebrate the glory of the dæmons. Even
the common language of Greece and Rome abounded with familiar
but impious expressions, which the imprudent Christian might too
carelessly utter, or too patiently hear.[1]

The dangerous temptations which on every side lurked in ambush
to surprise the unguarded believer assailed him with redoubled violence
on the days of solemn festivals. So artfully were they framed and
disposed throughout the year, that superstition always wore the appearance of pleasure, and often of virtue. Some of the most sacred festivals
in the Roman ritual were destined to salute the new calends of January
with vows of public and private felicity; to indulge the pious remembrance of the dead and living; to ascertain the inviolable bounds of
property; to hail, on the return of spring, the genial powers of fecundity; to perpetuate the two memorable eras of Rome, the foundation
of the city, and that of the republic; and to restore, during the humane
licence of the Saturnalia, the primitive equality of mankind. Some idea
may be conceived of the abhorrence of the Christians for such impious
ceremonies, by the scrupulous delicacy which they displayed on a much
less alarming occasion. On days of general festivity it was the custom
of the ancients to adorn their doors with lamps and with branches of
laurel, and to crown their heads with a garland of flowers. This innocent and elegant practice might perhaps have been tolerated as a mere
civil institution. But it most unluckily happened that the doors were
under the protection of the household gods, that the laurel was sacred
to the lover of Daphne, and that garlands of flowers, though frequently
worn as a symbol either of joy or mourning, had been dedicated in their
first origin to the service of superstition. The trembling Christians, who
were persuaded in this instance to comply with the fashion of their
country and the commands of the magistrate, laboured under the most
gloomy apprehensions, from the reproaches of their own conscience,
the censures of the church, and the denunciations of divine vengeance.

Such was the anxious diligence which was required to guard the
chastity of the Gospel from the infectious breath of idolatry. The
superstitious observances of public or private rites were carelessly

---

[1] Tertullian de Idololatria. If a Pagan friend (on the occasion perhaps of sneezing)
used the familiar expression of "Jupiter bless you," the Christian was obliged to
protest against the divinity of Jupiter.

practised, from education and habit, by the followers of the established religion. But as often as they occurred, they afforded the Christians an opportunity of declaring and confirming their zealous opposition. By these frequent protestations their attachment to the faith was continually fortified; and in proportion to the increase of zeal, they combated with the more ardour and success in the holy war which they had undertaken against the empire of the dæmons.

THE DOCTRINE OF A FUTURE LIFE

II. The writings of Cicero represent in the most lively colours the ignorance, the errors, and the uncertainty of the ancient philosophers with regard to the immortality of the soul. When they are desirous of arming their disciples against the fear of death, they inculcate, as an obvious, though melancholy position, that the fatal stroke of our dissolution releases us from the calamities of life; and that those can no longer suffer who no longer exist. Yet there were a few sages of Greece and Rome who had conceived a more exalted, and, in some respects, a juster idea of human nature, though it must be confessed that, in the sublime inquiry, their reason had been often guided by their imagination, and that their imagination had been prompted by their vanity. When they viewed with complacency the extent of their own mental powers, when they exercised the various faculties of memory, of fancy, and of judgment, in the most profound speculations or the most important labours, and when they reflected on the desire of fame, which transported them into future ages, far beyond the bounds of death and of the grave, they were unwilling to confound themselves with the beasts of the field, or to suppose that a being, for whose dignity they entertained the most sincere admiration, could be limited to a spot of earth, and to a few years of duration. With this favourable prepossession they summoned to their aid the science, or rather the language of Metaphysics. They soon discovered that, as none of the properties of matter will apply to the operations of the mind, the human soul must consequently be a substance distinct from the body, pure, simple, and spiritual, incapable of dissolution, and susceptible of a much higher degree of virtue and happiness after the release from its corporeal prison. From these specious and noble principles the philosophers who trod in the footsteps of Plato deduced a very unjustifiable conclusion, since they asserted, not only the future immortality, but the past eternity of the human soul, which they were too apt to consider as a portion of the infinite and self-existing spirit which pervades and sustains the universe. A doctrine thus removed beyond the senses and the experience of mankind might serve to amuse the leisure of a philosophic mind; or, in the silence of solitude, it might sometimes impart a ray of comfort to desponding virtue; but the faint impression which had been received in the schools was soon obliterated by the commerce and business of active life. We are sufficiently acquainted with the eminent persons who flourished in the age of Cicero and of the first Cæsars, with their actions, their characters, and their motives, to be assured that their conduct in this life was never regulated by any serious conviction of the rewards or punishments of a future state. At the bar and in the senate of Rome the ablest orators were not apprehensive of giving offence to their hearers by exposing that doctrine as an idle and extravagant opinion, which was rejected with contempt by every man of a liberal education and understanding.

Since therefore the most sublime efforts of philosophy can extend no farther than feebly to point out the desire, the hope, or, at most, the probability, of a future state, there is nothing, except a divine revelation, that can ascertain the existence, and describe the condition, of the invisible country which is destined to receive the souls of men after their separation from the body. But we may perceive several defects inherent to the popular religions of Greece and Rome, which rendered them very unequal to so arduous a task. 1. The general system of their mythology was unsupported by any solid proofs; and the wisest among the Pagans had already disclaimed its usurped authority. 2. The description of the infernal regions had been abandoned to the fancy of painters and of poets, who peopled them with so many phantoms and monsters, who dispensed their rewards and punishments with so little equity, that a solemn truth, the most congenial to the human heart, was oppressed and disgraced by the absurd mixture of the wildest fictions. 3. The doctrine of a future state was scarcely considered among the devout polytheists of Greece and Rome as a fundamental article of faith. The providence of the gods, as it related to public communities rather than to private individuals, was principally displayed on the visible theatre of the present world. The petitions which were offered on the altars of Jupiter or Apollo expressed the anxiety of their worshippers for temporal happiness, and their ignorance or indifference concerning a future life. The important truth of the immortality of the soul was inculcated with more diligence as well as success in India, in Assyria, in Egypt, and in Gaul; and since we cannot attribute such a difference to the superior knowledge of the barbarians, we must ascribe it to the influence of an established priesthood, which employed the motives of virtue as the instrument of ambition.

We might naturally expect that a principle so essential to religion would have been revealed in the clearest terms to the chosen people of Palestine, and that it might safely have been intrusted to the hereditary priesthood of Aaron. It is incumbent on us to adore the mysterious dispensations of Providence, when we discover that the doctrine of the immortality of the soul is omitted in the law of Moses; it is darkly insinuated by the prophets; and during the long period which elapsed between the Egyptian and the Babylonian servitudes, the hopes as well as fears of the Jews appear to have been confined within the narrow compass of the present life. After Cyrus had permitted the exiled nation to return into the promised land, and after Ezra had restored the ancient records of their religion, two celebrated sects, the Sadducees and the Pharisees, insensibly arose at Jerusalem. The former, selected from the more opulent and distinguished ranks of society, were strictly attached to the literal sense of the Mosaic law, and they piously rejected the immortality of the soul, as an opinion that received no countenance from the divine book, which they revered as the only rule of their faith. To the authority of Scripture the Pharisees added that of tradition, and they accepted, under the name of traditions, several speculative tenets from the philosophy or religion of the eastern nations. The doctrines of fate or predestination, of angels and spirits, and of a future state of rewards and punishments, were in the number of these new articles of belief; and as the Pharisees, by the austerity of their manners, had drawn into their party the body of the Jewish people, the immortality of the soul became the prevailing sentiment of the synagogue under the reign of the Asmonæan princes and pontiffs. The temper of the Jews was incapable of contenting itself with such a cold and languid assent as might satisfy the mind of a Polytheist; and as soon as they admitted the idea of a future state, they embraced it with the zeal which has always formed the characteristic of the nation. Their zeal, however, added nothing to its evidence, or even probability: and it was still necessary that the doctrine of life and immortality, which had been dictated by nature, approved by reason, and received by superstition, should obtain the sanction of divine truth from the authority and example of Christ.

When the promise of eternal happiness was proposed to mankind on condition of adopting the faith, and of observing the precepts, of the Gospel, it is no wonder that so advantageous an offer should have been accepted by great numbers of every religion, of every rank, and of every province in the Roman empire. The ancient Christians were animated by a contempt for their present existence, and by a just confidence of immortality, of which the doubtful and imperfect faith of modern ages cannot give us any adequate notion. In the primitive church the influence of truth was very powerfully strengthened by an opinion which, however it may deserve respect for its usefulness and antiquity, has not been found agreeable to experience. It was universally believed that the end of the world, and the kingdom of heaven, were at hand. The near approach of this wonderful event had been predicted by the apostles; the tradition of it was preserved by their earliest disciples, and those who understood in their literal sense the discourses of Christ himself were obliged to expect the second and glorious coming of the Son of Man in the clouds, before that generation was totally extinguished which had beheld his humble condition upon earth, and which might still be witness of the calamities of the Jews under Vespasian or Hadrian. The revolution of seventeen centuries has instructed us not to press too closely to the mysterious language of prophecy and revelation; but as long as, for wise purposes, this error was permitted to subsist in the church, it was productive of the most salutary effects on the faith and practice of Christians, who lived in the awful expectation of that moment when the globe itself, and all the various race of mankind, should tremble at the appearance of their divine Judge.

The ancient and popular doctrine of the Millennium was intimately connected with the second coming of Christ. As the works of the creation had been finished in six days, their duration in their present state, according to a tradition which was attributed to the prophet Elijah, was fixed to six thousand years. By the same analogy it was inferred that this long period of labour and contention, which was now almost elapsed, would be succeeded by a joyful Sabbath of a thousand years; and that Christ, with the triumphant band of the saints and the elect who had escaped death, or who had been miraculously revived, would reign upon earth till the time appointed for the last and general resurrection. So pleasing was this hope to the mind of believers, that the *New Jerusalem*, the seat of this blissful kingdom, was quickly adorned with all the gayest colours of the imagination. A felicity consisting only of pure and spiritual pleasure would have appeared too refined for its inhabitants, who were still supposed to possess their human nature and senses. A garden of Eden, with the amusements of the pastoral life, was no longer suited to the advanced state of society which prevailed under the Roman empire. A city was therefore erected of gold and precious stones, and a supernatural plenty of corn and wine was bestowed on the adjacent territory; in the free enjoyment of whose spontaneous productions the happy and benevolent people was never to be restrained by any jealous laws of exclusive property. The assurance of such a Millennium was carefully inculcated by a succession of fathers from Justin Martyr and Irenæus, who conversed with the immediate disciples of the apostles, down to Lactantius, who was preceptor to the son of Constantine. Though it might not be universally received, it appears to have been the reigning sentiment of the orthodox believers; and it seems so well adapted to the desires and apprehensions of mankind, that it must have contributed in a very considerable degree to the progress of the Christian faith. But when the edifice of the church was almost completed, the temporary support was laid aside. The doctrine of Christ's reign upon earth was at first treated as a profound allegory, was considered by degrees as a doubtful and useless opinion, and was at length rejected as the absurd invention of heresy and fanaticism. A mysterious prophecy, which still forms a part of the sacred canon, but which was thought to favour the exploded sentiment, has very narrowly escaped the proscription of the church.

Whilst the happiness and glory of a temporal reign were promised to the disciples of Christ, the most dreadful calamities were denounced against an unbelieving world. The edification of the new Jerusalem was to advance by equal steps with the destruction of the mystic Babylon; and as long as the emperors who reigned before Constantine persisted in the profession of idolatry, the epithet of Babylon was applied to the city and to the empire of Rome. A regular series was prepared of all the moral and physical evils which can afflict a flourishing nation; intestine discord, and the invasion of the fiercest barbarians from the unknown regions of the North; pestilence and famine, comets and eclipses, earthquakes and inundations. All these were only so many preparatory and alarming signs of the great catastrophe of Rome, when the country of the Scipios and Cæsars should be consumed by a flame from Heaven, and the city of the seven hills, with her palaces, her temples, and her triumphal arches, should be buried in a vast lake of fire and brimstone. It might, however, afford some consolation to Roman vanity, that the period of their empire would be that of the world itself; which, as it had once perished by the element of water, was destined to experience a second and a speedy destruction from the element of fire. In the opinion of a general conflagration the faith of the Christian very happily coincided with the tradition of the East, the philosophy of the Stoics, and the analogy of Nature; and even the country which, from religious motives, had been chosen for the origin and principal scene of the conflagration, was the best adapted for that purpose by natural and physical causes—by its deep caverns, beds of sulphur, and numerous volcanoes, of which those of Ætna, of Vesuvius, and of Lipari, exhibit a very imperfect representation. The calmest and most intrepid sceptic could not refuse to acknowledge that the destruction of the present system of the world by fire was in itself extremely probable. The Christian, who founded his belief much less on the fallacious arguments of reason than on the authority of tradition and the interpretation of Scripture, expected it with terror and confidence as a certain and approaching event; and as his mind was perpetually filled with the solemn idea, he considered every disaster that happened to the empire as an infallible symptom of an expiring world.

The condemnation of the wisest and most virtuous of the Pagans, on account of their ignorance or disbelief of the divine truth, seems to offend the reason and the humanity of the present age. But the primitive church, whose faith was of a much firmer consistence, delivered over, without hesitation, to eternal torture, the far greater part of the human species. A charitable hope might perhaps be indulged in favour of Socrates, or some other sages of antiquity, who had consulted the light of reason before that of the Gospel had arisen. But it was unanimously affirmed that those who, since the birth or the death of Christ, had obstinately persisted in the worship of the dæmons, neither deserved nor

could expect a pardon from the irritated justice of the Deity. These
rigid sentiments, which had been unknown to the ancient world, appear
to have infused a spirit of bitterness into a system of love and harmony.
The ties of blood and friendship were frequently torn asunder by the
difference of religious faith; and the Christians, who, in this world,
found themselves oppressed by the power of the Pagans, were sometimes
seduced by resentment and spiritual pride to delight in the prospect of
their future triumph. "You are fond of spectacles," exclaims the stern
Tertullian, "expect the greatest of all spectacles, the last and eternal
judgment of the universe. How shall I admire, how laugh, how rejoice,
how exult, when I behold so many proud monarchs, and fancied gods,
groaning in the lowest abyss of darkness; so many magistrates, who
persecuted the name of the Lord, liquefying in fiercer fires than they
ever kindled against the Christians; so many sage philosophers blushing
in red-hot flames with their deluded scholars; so many celebrated poets
trembling before the tribunal, not of Minos, but of Christ; so many
tragedians, more tuneful in the expression of their own sufferings; so
many dancers——" But the humanity of the reader will permit me to
draw a veil over the rest of this infernal description, which the zealous
African pursues in a long variety of affected and unfeeling witticisms.

Doubtless there were many among the primitive Christians of a
temper more suitable to the meekness and charity of their profession.
There were many who felt a sincere compassion for the danger of their
friends and countrymen, and who exerted the most benevolent zeal to
save them from the impending destruction. The careless Polytheist,
assailed by new and unexpected terrors, against which neither his priests
nor his philosophers could afford him any certain protection, was very
frequently terrified and subdued by the menace of eternal tortures. His
fears might assist the progress of his faith and reason; and if he could
once persuade himself to suspect that the Christian religion might
possibly be true, it became an easy task to convince him that it was the
safest and most prudent party that he could possibly embrace.

MIRACULOUS POWERS OF THE PRIMITIVE CHURCH

III. The supernatural gifts, which even in this life were ascribed to
the Christians above the rest of mankind, must have conduced to their
own comfort, and very frequently to the conviction of infidels. Besides
the occasional prodigies, which might sometimes be effected by the immediate interposition of the Deity when he suspended the laws of
Nature for the service of religion, the Christian church, from the time
of the apostles and their first disciples, has claimed an uninterrupted
succession of miraculous powers, the gift of tongues, of vision, and of
prophecy, the power of expelling dæmons, of healing the sick, and of
raising the dead. The knowledge of foreign languages was frequently
communicated to the contemporaries of Irenæus, though Irenæus him-

self was left to struggle with the difficulties of a barbarous dialect whilst he preached the Gospel to the natives of Gaul. The divine inspiration, whether it was conveyed in the form of a waking or of a sleeping vision, is described as a favour very liberally bestowed on all ranks of the faithful, on women as on elders, on boys as well as upon bishops. When their devout minds were sufficiently prepared by a course of prayer, of fasting, and of vigils, to receive the extraordinary impulse, they were transported out of their senses, and delivered in extasy what was inspired, being mere organs of the Holy Spirit, just as a pipe or flute is of him who blows into it. We may add that the design of these visions was, for the most part, either to disclose the future history, or to guide the present administration, of the church. The expulsion of the dæmons from the bodies of those unhappy persons whom they had been permitted to torment was considered as a signal though ordinary triumph of religion, and is repeatedly alleged by the ancient apologists as the most convincing evidence of the truth of Christianity. The awful ceremony was usually performed in a public manner, and in the presence of a great number of spectators; the patient was relieved by the power or skill of the exorcist, and the vanquished dæmon was heard to confess that he was one of the fabled gods of antiquity, who had impiously usurped the adoration of mankind. But the miraculous cure of diseases of the most inveterate or even preternatural kind can no longer occasion any surprise, when we recollect that in the days of Irenæus, about the end of the second century, the resurrection of the dead was very far from being esteemed an uncommon event; that the miracle was frequently performed on necessary occasions, by great fasting and the joint supplication of the church of the place, and that the persons thus restored to their prayers had lived afterwards amongst them many years. At such a period, when faith could boast of so many wonderful victories over death, it seems difficult to account for the scepticism of those philosophers who still rejected and derided the doctrine of the resurrection. A noble Grecian had rested on this important ground the whole controversy, and promised Theophilus, bishop of Antioch, that, if he could be gratified with the sight of a single person who had been actually raised from the dead, he would immediately embrace the Christian religion. It is somewhat remarkable that the prelate of the first eastern church, however anxious for the conversion of his friend, thought proper to decline this fair and reasonable challenge.

The miracles of the primitive church, after obtaining the sanction of ages, have been lately attacked in a very free and ingenious inquiry; which, though it has met with the most favourable reception from the public, appears to have excited a general scandal among the divines of our own as well as of the other Protestant churches of Europe. Our different sentiments on this subject will be much less influenced by any particular arguments than by our habits of study and reflection, and,

above all, by the degree of the evidence which we have accustomed ourselves to require for the proof of a miraculous event. The duty of an
historian does not call upon him to interpose his private judgment in
this nice and important controversy; but he ought not to dissemble the
difficulty of adopting such a theory as may reconcile the interest of
religion with that of reason, of making a proper application of that
theory, and of defining with precision the limits of that happy period,
exempt from error and from deceit, to which we might be disposed to
extend the gift of supernatural powers. From the first of the fathers to
the last of the popes, a succession of bishops, of saints, of martyrs, and
of miracles, is continued without interruption; and the progress of
superstition was so gradual and almost imperceptible, that we know
not in what particular link we should break the chain of tradition.
Every age bears testimony to the wonderful events by which it was
distinguished, and its testimony appears no less weighty and respectable
than that of the preceding generation, till we are insensibly led on to
accuse our own inconsistency if, in the eighth or in the twelfth century,
we deny to the venerable Bede, or to the holy Bernard, the same degree
of confidence which, in the second century, we had so liberally granted
to Justin or to Irenæus.[1] If the truth of any of those miracles is appre-
ciated by their apparent use and propriety, every age had unbelievers to
convince, heretics to confute, and idolatrous nations to convert; and
sufficient motives might always be produced to justify the interposition
of Heaven. And yet, since every friend to revelation is persuaded of the
reality, and every reasonable man is convinced of the cessation, of
miraculous powers, it is evident that there must have been *some period*
in which they were either suddenly or gradually withdrawn from the
Christian church. Whatever era is chosen for that purpose, the death
of the apostles, the conversion of the Roman empire, or the extinction
of the Arian heresy,[2] the insensibility of the Christians who lived at that
time will equally afford a just matter of surprise. They still supported
their pretensions after they had lost their power. Credulity performed
the office of faith; fanaticism was permitted to assume the language of
inspiration, and the effects of accident or contrivance were ascribed to
supernatural causes. The recent experience of genuine miracles should
have instructed the Christian world in the ways of Providence, and
habituated their eye (if we may use a very inadequate expression) to the
style of the Divine artist. Should the most skilful painter of modern

---

[1] It may seem somewhat remarkable that Bernard of Clairvaux, who records so
many miracles of his friend St. Malachi, never takes any notice of his own, which, in
their turn, however, are carefully related by his companions and disciples. In the
long series of ecclesiastical history, does there exist a single instance of a saint asserting that he himself possessed the gift of miracles?

[2] The conversion of Constantine is the era which is most usually fixed by Protestants. The more rational divines are unwilling to admit the miracles of the ivth, whilst
the more credulous are unwilling to reject those of the vth century.

Italy presume to decorate his feeble imitations with the name of Raphael
or of Correggio, the insolent fraud would be soon discovered and indignantly rejected.

Whatever opinion may be entertained of the miracles of the primitive
church since the time of the apostles, this unresisting softness of temper,
so conspicuous among the believers of the second and third centuries,
proved of some accidental benefit to the cause of truth and religion.
In modern times, a latent and even involuntary scepticism adheres to
the most pious dispositions. Their admission of supernatural truths is
much less an active consent than a cold and passive acquiescence.
Accustomed long since to observe and to respect the invariable order of
Nature, our reason, or at least our imagination, is not sufficiently prepared to sustain the visible action of the Deity. But in the first ages of
Christianity the situation of mankind was extremely different. The most
curious, or the most credulous, among the Pagans, were often persuaded
to enter into a society which asserted an actual claim of miraculous
powers. The primitive Christians perpetually trod on mystic ground,
and their minds were exercised by the habits of believing the most
extraordinary events. They felt, or they fancied, that on every side they
were incessantly assaulted by dæmons, comforted by visions, instructed
by prophecy, and surprisingly delivered from danger, sickness, and from
death itself, by the supplications of the church. The real or imaginary
prodigies, of which they so frequently conceived themselves to be the
objects, the instruments, or the spectators, very happily disposed them
to adopt with the same ease, but with far greater justice, the authentic
wonders of the evangelic history; and thus miracles that exceeded not
the measure of their own experience inspired them with the most lively
assurance of mysteries which were acknowledged to surpass the limits
of their understanding. It is this deep impression of supernatural truths
which has been so much celebrated under the name of faith; a state of
mind described as the surest pledge of the Divine favour and of future
felicity, and recommended as the first or perhaps the only merit of a
Christian. According to the more rigid doctors, the moral virtues,
which may be equally practised by infidels, are destitute of any value or
efficacy in the work of our justification.

AUSTERE MORALS OF THE FIRST CHRISTIANS

IV. But the primitive Christian demonstrated his faith by his virtues;
and it was very justly supposed that the Divine persuasion, which enlightened or subdued the understanding, must at the same time purify
the heart and direct the actions of the believer. The first apologists of
Christianity who justify the innocence of their brethren, and the writers
of a later period who celebrate the sanctity of their ancestors, display,
in the most lively colours, the reformation of manners which was
introduced into the world by the preaching of the Gospel. As it is my

intention to remark only such human causes as were permitted to second the influence of revelation, I shall slightly mention two motives which might naturally render the lives of the primitive Christians much purer and more austere than those of their Pagan contemporaries or their degenerate successors—repentance for their past sins, and the laudable desire of supporting the reputation of the society in which they were engaged.

It is a very ancient reproach, suggested by the ignorance or the malice of infidelity, that the Christians allured into their party the most atrocious criminals, who, as soon as they were touched by a sense of remorse, were easily persuaded to wash away, in the water of baptism, the guilt of their past conduct, for which the temples of the gods refused to grant them any expiation. But this reproach, when it is cleared from misrepresentation, contributes as much to the honour as it did to the increase of the church. The friends of Christianity may acknowledge without a blush that many of the most eminent saints had been before their baptism the most abandoned sinners. Those persons who in the world had followed, though in an imperfect manner, the dictates of benevolence and propriety, derived such a calm satisfaction from the opinion of their own rectitude as rendered them much less susceptible of the sudden emotions of shame, of grief, and of terror, which have given birth to so many wonderful conversions. After the example of their Divine Master, the missionaries of the Gospel disdained not the society of men, and especially of women, oppressed by the consciousness, and very often by the effects, of their vices. As they emerged from sin and superstition to the glorious hope of immortality, they resolved to devote themselves to a life, not only of virtue, but of penitence. The desire of perfection became the ruling passion of their soul; and it is well known that, while reason embraces a cold mediocrity, our passions hurry us with rapid violence over the space which lies between the most opposite extremes.

When the new converts had been enrolled in the number of the faithful, and were admitted to the sacraments of the church, they found themselves restrained from relapsing into their past disorders by another consideration of a less spiritual but of a very innocent and respectable nature. Any particular society that has departed from the great body of the nation, or the religion to which it belonged, immediately becomes the object of universal as well as invidious observation. In proportion to the smallness of its numbers, the character of the society may be affected by the virtue and vices of the persons who compose it; and every member is engaged to watch with the most vigilant attention over his own behaviour, and over that of his brethren, since, as he must expect to incur a part of the common disgrace, he may hope to enjoy a share of the common reputation. When the Christians of Bithynia were brought before the tribunal of the younger Pliny, they assured the proconsul that, far from being engaged in any unlawful conspiracy, they were bound by a solemn obligation to abstain from the commission of those crimes which disturb the private or public peace of society, from theft, robbery, adultery, perjury, and fraud. Near a century afterwards, Tertullian with an honest pride could boast that very few Christians had suffered by the hand of the executioner, except on account of their religion. Their serious and sequestered life, averse to the gay luxury of the age, inured them to chastity, temperance, economy, and all the sober and domestic virtues. As the greater number were of some trade or profession, it was incumbent on them, by the strictest integrity and the fairest dealing, to remove the suspicions which the profane are too apt to conceive against the appearances of sanctity. The contempt of the world exercised them in the habits of humility, meekness, and patience. The more they were persecuted, the more closely they adhered to each other. Their mutual charity and unsuspecting confidence has been remarked by infidels, and was too often abused by perfidious friends.

It is a very honourable circumstance for the morals of the primitive Christians, that even their faults, or rather errors, were derived from an excess of virtue. The bishops and doctors of the church, whose evidence attests, and whose authority might influence, the professions, the principles, and even the practice of their contemporaries, had studied the Scriptures with less skill than devotion; and they often received in the most literal sense those rigid precepts of Christ and the apostles to which the prudence of succeeding commentators has applied a looser and more figurative mode of interpretation. Ambitious to exalt the perfection of the Gospel above the wisdom of philosophy, the zealous fathers have carried the duties of self-mortification, of purity, and of patience, to a height which it is scarcely possible to attain, and much less to preserve, in our present state of weakness and corruption. A doctrine so extraordinary and so sublime must inevitably command the veneration of the people; but it was ill calculated to obtain the suffrage of those worldly philosophers who, in the conduct of this transitory life, consult only the feelings of nature and the interests of society.

There are two very natural propensities which we may distinguish in the most virtuous and liberal dispositions, the love of pleasure and the love of action. If the former is refined by art and learning, improved by the charms of social intercourse, and corrected by a just regard to economy, to health, and to reputation, it is productive of the greatest part of the happiness of private life. The love of action is a principle of a much stronger and more doubtful nature. It often leads to anger, to ambition, and to revenge; but when it is guided by the sense of propriety and benevolence, it becomes the parent of every virtue, and, if those virtues are accompanied with equal abilities, a family, a state, or an empire, may be indebted for their safety and prosperity to the undaunted courage of a single man. To the love of pleasure we may therefore ascribe most of the agreeable, to the love of action we may attribute most of the useful and respectable, qualifications. The character in which both the one and the other should be united and harmonised would seem to constitute the most perfect idea of human nature. The insensible and inactive disposition, which should be supposed alike destitute of both, would be rejected, by the common consent of mankind, as utterly incapable of procuring any happiness to the individual, or any public benefit to the world. But it was not in *this* world that the primitive Christians were desirous of making themselves either agreeable or useful.

The acquisition of knowledge, the exercise of our reason or fancy, and the cheerful flow of unguarded conversation, may employ the leisure of a liberal mind. Such amusements, however, were rejected with abhorrence, or admitted with the utmost caution, by the severity of the fathers, who despised all knowledge that was not useful to salvation, and who considered all levity of discourse as a criminal abuse of the gift of speech. In our present state of existence the body is so inseparably connected with the soul, that it seems to be our interest to taste, with innocence and moderation, the enjoyments of which that faithful companion is susceptible. Very different was the reasoning of our devout predecessors; vainly aspiring to imitate the perfection of angels, they disdained, or they affected to disdain, every earthly and corporeal delight. Some of our senses indeed are necessary for our preservation, others for our subsistence, and others again for our information; and thus far it was impossible to reject the use of them. The first sensation of pleasure was marked as the first moment of their abuse. The unfeeling candidate for heaven was instructed, not only to resist the grosser allurements of the taste or smell, but even to shut his ears against the profane harmony of sounds, and to view with indifference the most finished productions of human art. Gay apparel, magnificent houses, and elegant furniture, were supposed to unite the double guilt of pride and of sensuality: a simple and mortified appearance was more suitable to the Christian who was certain of his sins and doubtful of his salvation. In their censures of luxury the fathers are extremely minute and circumstantial; and among the various articles which excite their pious indignation we may enumerate false hair, garments of any colour except white, instruments of music, vases of gold or silver, downy pillows (as Jacob reposed his head on a stone), white bread, foreign wines, public salutations, the use of warm baths, and the practice of shaving the beard, which, according to the expression of Tertullian, is a lie against our own faces, and an impious attempt to improve the works of the Creator. When Christianity was introduced among the rich and the polite, the observation of these singular laws was left, as it would be at present, to the few who were ambitious of superior sanctity. But it is always easy, as well as agreeable, for the inferior ranks of mankind to claim a merit from the contempt of that pomp and pleasure which fortune has placed beyond their reach. The virtue of the primitive Christians, like that of the first Romans, was very frequently guarded by poverty and ignorance.

The chaste severity of the fathers in whatever related to the commerce of the two sexes flowed from the same principle—their abhorrence of every enjoyment which might gratify the sensual, and degrade the spiritual nature of man. It was their favourite opinion, that if Adam had preserved his obedience to the Creator, he would have lived for ever in a state of virgin purity, and that some harmless mode of vegetation might have peopled paradise with a race of innocent and immortal beings. The use of marriage was permitted only to his fallen posterity, as a necessary expedient to continue the human species, and as a restraint, however imperfect, on the natural licentiousness of desire. The hesitation of the orthodox casuists on this interesting subject betrays the perplexity of men unwilling to approve an institution which they were compelled to tolerate. The enumeration of the very whimsical laws which they most circumstantially imposed on the marriage-bed would force a smile from the young and a blush from the fair. It was their unanimous sentiment that a first marriage was adequate to all the purposes of nature and of society. The sensual connection was refined into a resemblance of the mystic union of Christ with his church, and was pronounced to be indissoluble either by divorce or by death. The practice of second nuptials was branded with the name of a legal adultery; and the persons who were guilty of so scandalous an offence against Christian purity were soon excluded from the honours, and even from the arms, of the church. Since desire was imputed as a crime, and marriage was tolerated as a defect, it was consistent with the same principles to consider a state of celibacy as the nearest approach to the Divine perfection. It was with the utmost difficulty that ancient Rome could support the institution of six vestals; [1] but the primitive church was filled with a great number of persons of either sex who had devoted themselves to the profession of perpetual chastity. A few of these, among whom we may reckon the learned Origen, judged it the most prudent to disarm the tempter. [2] Some were insensible and some were invincible against the assaults of the flesh. Disdaining an ignominious flight, the virgins of the warm climate of Africa encountered the enemy in the closest engagement; they permitted priests and deacons to share their bed, and gloried amidst the flames in their unsullied purity. But

---

[1] Notwithstanding the honours and rewards which were bestowed on those virgins, it was difficult to procure a sufficient number; nor could the dread of the most horrible death always restrain their incontinence.

[2] Before the fame of Origen had excited envy and persecution, this extraordinary action was rather admired than censured. As it was his general practice to allegorize Scripture, it seems unfortunate that, in this instance only, he should have adopted the literal sense.

insulted Nature sometimes vindicated her rights, and this new species of martyrdom served only to introduce a new scandal into the church.[1] Among the Christian ascetics, however (a name which they soon acquired from their painful exercise), many, as they were less presumptuous, were probably more successful. The loss of sensual pleasure was supplied and compensated by spiritual pride. Even the multitude of Pagans were inclined to estimate the merit of the sacrifice by its apparent difficulty; and it was in the praise of these chaste spouses of Christ that the fathers have poured forth the troubled stream of their eloquence. Such are the early traces of monastic principles and institutions, which, in a subsequent age, have counterbalanced all the temporal advantages of Christianity.

The Christians were not less averse to the business than to the pleasures of this world. The defence of our persons and property they knew not how to reconcile with the patient doctrine which enjoined an unlimited forgiveness of past injuries, and commanded them to invite the repetition of fresh insults. Their simplicity was offended by the use of oaths, by the pomp of magistracy, and by the active contention of public life; nor could their humane ignorance be convinced that it was lawful on any occasion to shed the blood of our fellow-creatures, either by the sword of justice or by that of war, even though their criminal or hostile attempts should threaten the peace and safety of the whole community. It was acknowledged that, under a less perfect law, the powers of the Jewish constitution had been exercised, with the approbation of Heaven, by inspired prophets and by anointed kings. The Christians felt and confessed that such institutions might be necessary for the present system of the world, and they cheerfully submitted to the authority of their Pagan governors. But while they inculcated the maxims of passive obedience, they refused to take any active part in the civil administration or the military defence of the empire. Some indulgence might perhaps be allowed to those persons who, before their conversion, were already engaged in such violent and sanguinary occupations; but it was impossible that the Christians, without renouncing a more sacred duty, could assume the character of soldiers, of magistrates, or of princes.[2] This indolent, or even criminal disregard to the public welfare, exposed them to the contempt and reproaches of the Pagans, who very frequently asked, what must be the fate of the empire, attacked on every side by the barbarians, if all mankind should adopt the pusillanimous sentiments of the new sect? To this insulting question the Christian apologists returned obscure and ambiguous answers, as

[1] Something like this rash attempt was long afterwards imputed to the founder of the order of Fontevrault. Bayle has amused himself and his readers on that very delicate subject.

[2] Tertullian suggested to them the expedient of deserting; a counsel which, if it had been generally known, was not very proper to conciliate the favour of the emperors towards the Christian sect. .

they were unwilling to reveal the secret cause of their security; the expectation that, before the conversion of mankind was accomplished, war, government, the Roman empire, and the world itself, would be no more. It may be observed that, in this instance likewise, the situation of the first Christians coincided very happily with their religious scruples, and that their aversion to an active life contributed rather to excuse them from the service than to exclude them from the honours of the state and army.

THE DEVELOPMENT OF CHURCH GOVERNMENT

V. But the human character, however it may be exalted or depressed by a temporary enthusiasm, will return by degrees to its proper and natural level, and will resume those passions that seem the most adapted to its present condition. The primitive Christians were dead to the business and pleasures of the world; but their love of action, which could never be entirely extinguished, soon revived, and found a new occupation in the government of the church. A separate society, which attacked the established religion of the empire, was obliged to adopt some form of internal policy, and to appoint a sufficient number of ministers, intrusted not only with the spiritual functions, but even with the temporal direction of the Christian commonwealth. The safety of that society, its honour, its aggrandisement, were productive, even in the most pious minds, of a spirit of patriotism, such as the first of the Romans had felt for the republic, and sometimes of a similar indifference in the use of whatever means might probably conduce to so desirable an end. The ambition of raising themselves or their friends to the honours and offices of the church was disguised by the laudable intention of devoting to the public benefit the power and consideration which, for that purpose only, it became their duty to solicit. In the exercise of their functions they were frequently called upon to detect the errors of heresy or the arts of faction, to oppose the designs of perfidious brethren, to stigmatise their characters with deserved infamy, and to expel them from the bosom of a society whose peace and happiness they had attempted to disturb. The ecclesiastical governors of the Christians were taught to unite the wisdom of the serpent with the innocence of the dove; but as the former was refined, so the latter was insensibly corrupted, by the habits of government. In the church as well as in the world, the persons who were placed in any public station rendered themselves considerable by their eloquence and firmness, by their knowledge of mankind, and by their dexterity in business; and while they concealed from others, and perhaps from themselves, the secret motives of their conduct, they too frequently relapsed into all the turbulent passions of active life, which were tinctured with an additional degree of bitterness and obstinacy from the infusion of spiritual zeal.

The government of the church has often been the subject, as well as the prize, of religious contention. The hostile disputants of Rome, of Paris, of Oxford, and of Geneva, have alike struggled to reduce the primitive and apostolic model [1] to the respective standards of their own policy. The few who have pursued this inquiry with more candour and impartiality are of opinion that the apostles declined the office of legislation, and rather chose to endure some partial scandals and divisions, than to exclude the Christians of a future age from the liberty of varying their forms of ecclesiastical government according to the changes of times and circumstances. The scheme of policy which, under their approbation, was adopted for the use of the first century, may be discovered from the practice of Jerusalem, of Ephesus, or of Corinth. The societies which were instituted in the cities of the Roman empire were united only by the ties of faith and charity. Independence and equality formed the basis of their internal constitution. The want of discipline and human learning was supplied by the occasional assistance of the *prophets*, who were called to that function without distinction of age, of sex, or of natural abilities, and who, as often as they felt the divine impulse, poured forth the effusions of the Spirit in the assembly of the faithful. But these extraordinary gifts were frequently abused or misapplied by the prophetic teachers. They displayed them at an improper season, presumptuously disturbed the service of the assembly, and by their pride or mistaken zeal they introduced, particularly into the apostolic church of Corinth, a long and melancholy train of disorders. As the institution of prophets became useless, and even pernicious, their powers were withdrawn, and their office abolished. The public functions of religion were solely intrusted to the established ministers of the church, the *bishops* and the *presbyters*; two appellations which, in their first origin, appear to have distinguished the same office and the same order of persons. The name of Presbyter was expressive of their age, or rather of their gravity and wisdom. The title of Bishop denoted their inspection over the faith and manners of the Christians who were committed to their pastoral care. In proportion to the respective numbers of the faithful, a larger or smaller number of these *episcopal presbyters* guided each infant congregation with equal authority and with united counsels.

But the most perfect equality of freedom requires the directing hand of a superior magistrate: and the order of public deliberations soon introduces the office of a president, invested at least with the authority of collecting the sentiments, and of executing the resolutions, of the assembly. A regard for the public tranquillity, which would so frequently have been interrupted by annual or by occasional elections, induced the primitive Christians to constitute an honourable and perpe-

---

[1] The aristocratical party in France, as well as in England, has strenuously maintained the divine origin of bishops. But the Calvinistical presbyters were impatient of a superior; and the Roman Pontiff refused to acknowledge an equal.

tual magistracy, and to choose one of the wisest and most holy amongst their presbyters to execute, during his life, the duties of their ecclesiastical governor. It was under these circumstances that the lofty title of Bishop began to raise itself above the humble appellation of Presbyter; and while the latter remained the most natural distinction for the members of every Christian senate, the former was appropriated to the dignity of its new president. The advantages of this episcopal form of government, which appears to have been introduced before the end of the first century,[1] were so obvious, and so important for the future greatness, as well as the present peace, of Christianity, that it was adopted without delay by all the societies which were already scattered over the empire, had acquired in a very early period the sanction of antiquity,[2] and is still revered by the most powerful churches, both of the East and of the West, as a primitive and even as a divine establishment.[3] It is needless to observe that the pious and humble presbyters who were first dignified with the episcopal title could not possess, and would probably have rejected, the power and pomp which now encircles the tiara of the Roman pontiff, or the mitre of a German prelate. But we may define in a few words the narrow limits of their original jurisdiction, which was chiefly of a spiritual, though in some instances of a temporal nature. It consisted in the administration of the sacraments and discipline of the church, the superintendency of religious ceremonies, which imperceptibly increased in number and variety, the consecration of ecclesiastical ministers, to whom the bishop assigned their respective functions, the management of the public fund, and the determination of all such differences as the faithful were unwilling to expose before the tribunal of an idolatrous judge. These powers, during a short period, were exercised according to the advice of the presbyteral college, and with the consent and approbation of the assembly of Christians. The primitive bishops were considered only as the first of their equals, and the honourable servants of a free people. Whenever the episcopal chair became vacant by death, a new president was chosen among the presbyters by the suffrage of the whole congregation, every member of which supposed himself invested with a sacred and sacerdotal character.

Such was the mild and equal constitution by which the Christians were governed more than an hundred years after the death of the

---

[1] See the introduction to the Apocalypse. Bishops, under the name of angels, were already instituted in the seven cities of Asia. And yet the epistle of Clemens (which is probably of as ancient a date) does not lead us to discover any traces of episcopacy either at Corinth or Rome.

[2] Nulla Ecclesia sine Episcopo, has been a fact as well as a maximum since the time of Tertullian and Irenæus.

[3] After we have passed the difficulties of the first century, we find the episcopal government universally established, till it was interrupted by the republican genius of the Swiss and German reformers.

apostles. Every society formed within itself a separate and independent republic; and although the most distant of these little states maintained a mutual as well as friendly intercourse of letters and deputations, the Christian world was not yet connected by any supreme authority or legislative assembly. As the numbers of the faithful were gradually multiplied, they discovered the advantages that might result from a closer union of their interest and designs. Towards the end of the second century, the churches of Greece and Asia adopted the useful institutions of provincial synods, and they may justly be supposed to have borrowed the model of a representative council from the celebrated examples of their own country, the Amphictyons, the Achæan league, or the assemblies of the Ionian cities. It was soon established as a custom and as a law, that the bishops of the independent churches should meet in the capital of the province at the stated periods of spring and autumn. Their deliberations were assisted by the advice of a few distinguished presbyters, and moderated by the presence of a listening multitude. Their decrees, which were styled Canons, regulated every important controversy of faith and discipline; and it was natural to believe that a liberal effusion of the Holy Spirit would be poured on the united assembly of the delegates of the Christian people. The institution of synods was so well suited to private ambition and to public interest, that in the space of a few years it was received throughout the whole empire. A regular correspondence was established between the provincial councils, which mutually communicated and approved their respective proceedings; and the catholic church soon assumed the form, and acquired the strength, of a great fœderative republic.

As the legislative authority of the particular churches was insensibly superseded by the use of councils, the bishops obtained by their alliance a much larger share of executive and arbitrary power; and as soon as they were connected by a sense of their common interest, they were enabled to attack, with united vigour, the original rights of their clergy and people. The prelates of the third century imperceptibly changed the language of exhortation into that of command, scattered the seeds of future usurpations, and supplied, by Scripture allegories and declamatory rhetoric, their deficiency of force and of reason. They exalted the unity and power of the church, as it was represented in the EPISCOPAL OFFICE, of which every bishop enjoyed an equal and undivided portion. Princes and magistrates, it was often repeated, might boast an earthly claim to a transitory dominion: it was the episcopal authority alone which was derived from the Deity, and extended itself over this and over another world. The bishops were the vicegerents of Christ, the successors of the apostles, and the mystic substitutes of the high priest of the Mosaic law. Their exclusive privilege of conferring the sacerdotal character invaded the freedom both of clerical and of popular elections: and if, in the administration of the church, they still consulted the judgment of the presbyters or the inclination of the people, they most carefully inculcated the merit of such a voluntary condescension. The bishops acknowledged the supreme authority which resided in the assembly of their brethren; but in the government of his peculiar diocese each of them exacted from his *flock* the same implicit obedience as if that favourite metaphor had been literally just, and as if the shepherd had been of a more exalted nature than that of his sheep. This obedience, however, was not imposed without some efforts on one side, and some resistance on the other. The democratical part of the constitution was, in many places, very warmly supported by the zealous or interested opposition of the inferior clergy. But their patriotism received the ignominious epithets of faction and schism, and the episcopal cause was indebted for its rapid progress to the labours of many active prelates, who, like Cyprian of Carthage, could reconcile the arts of the most ambitious statesman with the Christian virtues which seem adapted to the character of a saint and martyr.[1]

The same causes which at first had destroyed the equality of the presbyters introduced among the bishops a pre-eminence of rank, and from thence a superiority of jurisdiction. As often as in the spring and autumn they met in provincial synod, the difference of personal merit and reputation was very sensibly felt among the members of the assembly, and the multitude was governed by the wisdom and eloquence of the few. But the order of public proceedings required a more regular and less invidious distinction; the office of perpetual presidents in the councils of each province was conferred on the bishops of the principal city; and these aspiring prelates, who soon acquired the lofty titles of Metropolitans and Primates, secretly prepared themselves to usurp over their episcopal brethren the same authority which the bishops had so lately assumed above the college of presbyters. Nor was it long before an emulation of pre-eminence and power prevailed among the Metropolitans themselves, each of them affecting to display, in the most pompous terms, the temporal honours and advantages of the city over which he presided; the numbers and opulence of the Christians who were subject to their pastoral care; the saints and martyrs who had arisen among them; and the purity with which they preserved the tradition of the faith as it had been transmitted through a series of orthodox bishops from the apostle or the apostolic disciple to whom the foundation of their church was ascribed. From every cause, either of a civil or of an ecclesiastical nature, it was easy to foresee that Rome must enjoy the respect, and would soon claim the obedience, of the provinces. The society of the faithful bore a just proportion to the capital of the empire; and the Roman church was the greatest, the most numerous,

---

[1] If Novatus, Felicissimus, &c., whom the bishop of Carthage expelled from his church, and from Africa, were not the most detestable monsters of wickedness, the zeal of Cyprian must occasionally have prevailed over his veracity.

and, in regard to the West, the most ancient of all the Christian establishments, many of which had received their religion from the pious labours of her missionaries. Instead of *one* apostolic founder, the utmost boast of Antioch, of Ephesus, or of Corinth, the banks of the Tiber were supposed to have been honoured with the preaching and martyrdom of the *two* most eminent among the apostles; and the bishops of Rome very prudently claimed the inheritance of whatsoever prerogatives were attributed either to the person or to the office of St. Peter.[1] The bishops of Italy and of the provinces were disposed to allow them a primacy of order and association (such was their very accurate expression) in the Christian aristocracy. But the power of a monarch was rejected with abhorrence, and the aspiring genius of Rome experienced from the nations of Asia and Africa a more vigorous resistance to her spiritual than she had formerly done to her temporal dominion. The patriotic Cyprian, who ruled with the most absolute sway the church of Carthage and the provincial synods, opposed with resolution and success the ambition of the Roman pontiff, artfully connected his own cause with that of the eastern bishops, and, like Hannibal, sought out new allies in the heart of Asia. If this Punic war was carried on without any effusion of blood, it was owing much less to the moderation than to the weakness of the contending prelates. Invectives and excommunications were *their* only weapons; and these, during the progress of the whole controversy, they hurled against each other with equal fury and devotion. The hard necessity of censuring either a pope or a saint and martyr distresses the modern Catholics whenever they are obliged to relate the particulars of a dispute in which the champions of religion indulged such passions as seem much more adapted to the senate or to the camp.

The progress of the ecclesiastical authority gave birth to the memorable distinction of the laity and of the clergy, which had been unknown to the Greeks and Romans.[2] The former of these appellations comprehended the body of the Christian people; the latter, according to the signification of the word, was appropriated to the chosen portion that had been set apart for the service of religion; a celebrated order of men which has furnished the most important, though not always the most edifying, subjects for modern history. Their mutual hostilities sometimes disturbed the peace of the infant church, but their zeal and activity were united in the common cause, and the love of power, which (under the most artful disguises) could insinuate itself into the breasts of bishops and martyrs, animated them to increase the number of their subjects, and to enlarge the limits of the Christian empire. They were destitute of any temporal force, and they were for a long time discouraged and

---

[1] It is in French only that the famous allusion to St. Peter's name is exact. Tu es *Pierre*, et sur cette *pierre*.—The same is imperfect in Greek, Latin, Italian, &c., and totally unintelligible in our Teutonic languages.

[2] The distinction of *Clerus* and *Laicus* was established before the time of Tertullian.

oppressed, rather than assisted, by the civil magistrate; but they had acquired, and they employed within their own society, the two most efficacious instruments of government, rewards and punishments; the former derived from the pious liberality, the latter from the devout apprehensions, of the faithful.

I. The community of goods, which had so agreeably amused the imagination of Plato, and which subsisted in some degree among the austere sect of the Essenians, was adopted for a short time in the primitive church. The fervour of the first proselytes prompted them to sell those worldly possessions which they despised, to lay the price of them at the feet of the apostles, and to content themselves with receiving an equal share out of the general distribution. The progress of the Christian religion relaxed, and gradually abolished, this generous institution, which, in hands less pure than those of the apostles, would too soon have been corrupted and abused by the returning selfishness of human nature; and the converts who embraced the new religion were permitted to retain the possession of their patrimony, to receive legacies and inheritances, and to increase their separate property by all the lawful means of trade and industry. Instead of an absolute sacrifice, a moderate proportion was accepted by the ministers of the Gospel; and in their weekly or monthly assemblies every believer, according to the exigency of the occasion, and the measure of his wealth and piety, presented his voluntary offering for the use of the common fund. Nothing, however inconsiderable, was refused; but it was diligently inculcated that, in the article of tithes, the Mosaic law was still of divine obligation; and that, since the Jews, under a less perfect discipline, had been commanded to pay a tenth part of all that they possessed, it would become the disciples of Christ to distinguish themselves by a superior degree of liberality, and to acquire some merit by resigning a superfluous treasure, which must so soon be annihilated with the world itself.[1] It is almost unnecessary to observe that the revenue of each particular church, which was of so uncertain and fluctuating a nature, must have varied with the poverty or the opulence of the faithful, as they were dispersed in obscure villages, or collected in the great cities of the empire. In the time of the emperor Decius it was the opinion of the magistrates that the Christians of Rome were possessed of very considerable wealth, that vessels of gold and silver were used in their religious worship, and that many among their proselytes had sold their lands and houses to increase the public riches of the sect, at the expense, indeed, of their unfortunate children, who found themselves beggars because their parents had been saints. We should listen with distrust to the suspicions of strangers and enemies; on this occasion, however, they receive a very specious and probable

---

[1] The same opinion, which prevailed about the year one thousand, was productive of the same effects. Most of the donations express their motive, "appropinquante mundi fine."

colour from the two following circumstances, the only ones that have reached our knowledge which define any precise sums or convey any distinct idea. Almost at the same period the bishop of Carthage, from a society less opulent than that of Rome, collected an hundred thousand sesterces (above eight hundred and fifty pounds sterling), on a sudden call of charity to redeem the brethren of Numidia, who had been carried away captives by the barbarians of the desert. About an hundred years before the reign of Decius the Roman church had received, in a single donation, the sum of two hundred thousand sesterces from a stranger of Pontus, who proposed to fix his residence in the capital. These oblations, for the most part, were made in money; nor was the society of Christians either desirous or capable of acquiring, to any considerable degree, the incumbrance of landed property. It had been provided by several laws, which were enacted with the same design as our statutes of mortmain, that no real estates should be given or bequeathed to any corporate body without either a special privilege or a particular dispensation from the emperor or from the senate; who were seldom disposed to grant them in favour of a sect, at first the object of their contempt, and at last of their fears and jealousy. A transaction, however, is related under the reign of Alexander Severus, which discovers that the restraint was sometimes eluded or suspended, and that the Christians were permitted to claim and to possess lands within the limits of Rome itself. The progress of Christianity, and the civil confusion of the empire, contributed to relax the severity of the laws; and, before the close of the third century, many considerable estates were bestowed on the opulent churches of Rome, Milan, Carthage, Antioch, Alexandria, and the other great cities of Italy and the provinces.

The bishop was the natural steward of the church; the public stock was intrusted to his care without account or control; the presbyters were confined to their spiritual functions, and the more dependent order of deacons was solely employed in the management and distribution of the ecclesiastical revenue. If we may give credit to the vehement declamations of Cyprian, there were too many among his African brethren who, in the execution of their charge, violated every precept, not only of evangelic perfection, but even of moral virtue. By some of these unfaithful stewards the riches of the church were lavished in sensual pleasures; by others they were perverted to the purposes of private gain, of fraudulent purchases, and of rapacious usury. But as long as the contributions of the Christian people were free and unconstrained, the abuse of their confidence could not be very frequent, and the general uses to which their liberality was applied reflected honour on the religious society. A decent portion was reserved for the maintenance of the bishop and his clergy; a sufficient sum was allotted for the expenses of the public worship, of which the feasts of love, the *agapæ*, as they were called, constituted a very pleasing part. The whole remainder

was the sacred patrimony of the poor. According to the discretion of
the bishop, it was distributed to support widows and orphans, the lame,
the sick, and the aged of the community; to comfort strangers and
pilgrims, and to alleviate the misfortunes of prisoners and captives,
more especially when their sufferings had been occasioned by their firm
attachment to the cause of religion. A generous intercourse of charity
united the most distant provinces, and the smaller congregations were
cheerfully assisted by the alms of their more opulent brethren. Such an
institution, which paid less regard to the merit than to the distress of
the object, very materially conduced to the progress of Christianity.
The pagans, who were actuated by a sense of humanity, while they
derided the doctrines, acknowledged the benevolence, of the new sect.[1]
The prospect of immediate relief and of future protection allured into its
hospitable bosom many of those unhappy persons whom the neglect of
the world would have abandoned to the miseries of want, of sickness,
and of old age. There is some reason likewise to believe that great
numbers of infants who, according to the inhuman practice of the times,
had been exposed by their parents, were frequently rescued from death,
baptised, educated, and maintained by the piety of the Christians, and
at the expense of the public treasure.[2]

II. It is the undoubted right of every society to exclude from its communion and benefits such among its members as reject or violate those
regulations which have been established by general consent. In the
exercise of this power the censures of the Christian church were chiefly
directed against scandalous sinners, and particularly those who were
guilty of murder, of fraud, or of incontinence; against the authors, or the
followers, of any heretical opinions which had been condemned by the
judgment of the episcopal order; and against those unhappy persons
who, whether from choice or from compulsion, had polluted themselves
after their baptism by any act of idolatrous worship. The consequences
of excommunication were of a temporal as well as a spiritual nature.
The Christian against whom it was pronounced was deprived of any
part in the oblations of the faithful. The ties both of religious and of
private friendship were dissolved: he found himself a profane object of
abhorrence to the persons whom he the most esteemed, or by whom he
had been the most tenderly beloved; and as far as an expulsion from a
respectable society could imprint on his character a mark of disgrace, he
was shunned or suspected by the generality of mankind. The situation
of these unfortunate exiles was in itself very painful and melancholy;
but, as it usually happens, their apprehensions far exceeded their

[1] Julian seems mortified that the Christian charity maintains not only their
own, but likewise the heathen poor.

[2] Such, at least, has been the laudable conduct of more modern missionaries, under
the same circumstances. Above three thousand new-born infants are annually exposed in the streets of Pekin.

sufferings. The benefits of the Christian communion were those of eternal life; nor could they erase from their minds the awful opinion that to those ecclesiastical governors by whom they were condemned the Deity had committed the keys of Hell and of Paradise. The heretics, indeed, who might be supported by the consciousness of their intentions, and by the flattering hope that they alone had discovered the true path of salvation, endeavoured to regain, in their separate assemblies, those comforts, temporal as well as spiritual, which they no longer derived from the great society of Christians. But almost all those who had reluctantly yielded to the power of vice or idolatry were sensible of their fallen condition, and anxiously desirous of being restored to the benefits of the Christian communion.

With regard to the treatment of these penitents, two opposite opinions, the one of justice, the other of mercy, divided the primitive church. The more rigid and inflexible casuists refused them for ever, and without exception, the meanest place in the holy community which they had disgraced or deserted; and leaving them to the remorse of a guilty conscience, indulged them only with a faint ray of hope that the contrition of their life and death might possibly be accepted by the Supreme Being.[1] A milder sentiment was embraced, in practice as well as in theory, by the purest and most respectable of the Christian churches. The gates of reconciliation and of heaven were seldom shut against the returning penitent; but a severe and solemn form of discipline was instituted, which, while it served to expiate his crime, might powerfully deter the spectators from the imitation of his example. Humbled by a public confession, emaciated by fasting, and clothed in sackcloth, the penitent lay prostrate at the door of the assembly, imploring with tears the pardon of his offences, and soliciting the prayers of the faithful.[2] If the fault was of a very heinous nature, whole years of penance were esteemed an inadequate satisfaction to the Divine justice; and it was always by slow and painful gradations that the sinner, the heretic, or the apostate was readmitted into the bosom of the church. A sentence of perpetual excommunication was, however, reserved for some crimes of an extraordinary magnitude, and particularly for the inexcusable relapses of those penitents who had already experienced and abused the clemency of their ecclesiastical superiors. According to the circumstances or the number of the guilty, the exercise of the Christian discipline was varied by the discretion of the bishops. The councils of Ancyra and Illiberis were held about the same time, the one in Galatia, the other in Spain; but their respective canons, which are still extant, seem to breathe a very different spirit. The Galatian, who

---

[1] The Montanists and the Novatians, who adhered to this opinion with the greatest rigour and obstinacy, found *themselves* at last in the number of excommunicated heretics.

[2] The admirers of antiquity regret the loss of this public penance.

after his baptism had repeatedly sacrificed to idols, might obtain his pardon by a penance of seven years; and if he had seduced others to imitate his example, only three years more were added to the term of his exile. But the unhappy Spaniard who had committed the same offence was deprived of the hope of reconciliation even in the article of death; and his idolatry was placed at the head of a list of seventeen other crimes, against which a sentence no less terrible was pronounced. Among these we may distinguish the inexpiable guilt of calumniating a bishop, a presbyter, or even a deacon.

The well-tempered mixture of liberality and rigour, the judicious dispensation of rewards and punishments, according to the maxims of policy as well as justice, constituted the *human* strength of the church. The bishops, whose paternal care extended itself to the government of both worlds, were sensible of the importance of these prerogatives; and, covering their ambition with the fair pretence of the love of order, they were jealous of any rival in the exercise of a discipline so necessary to prevent the desertion of those troops which had enlisted themselves under the banner of the Cross, and whose numbers every day became more considerable. From the imperious declamations of Cyprian we should naturally conclude that the doctrines of excommunication and penance formed the most essential part of religion; and that it was much less dangerous for the disciples of Christ to neglect the observance of the moral duties than to despise the censures and authority of their bishops. Sometimes we might imagine that we were listening to the voice of Moses, when he commanded the earth to open, and to swallow up, in consuming flames, the rebellious race which refused obedience to the priesthood of Aaron; and we should sometimes suppose that we heard a Roman consul asserting the majesty of the republic, and declaring his inflexible resolution to enforce the rigour of the laws. "If such irregularities are suffered with impunity" (it is thus that the bishop of Carthage chides the lenity of his colleague), "if such irregularities are suffered, there is an end of EPISCOPAL VIGOUR; an end of the sublime and divine power of governing the Church; and end of Christianity itself." Cyprian had renounced those temporal honours which it is probable he would never have obtained; but the acquisition of such absolute command over the consciences and understanding of a congregation, however obscure or despised by the world, is more truly grateful to the pride of the human heart than the possession of the most despotic power imposed by arms and conquest on a reluctant people.

In the course of this important, though perhaps tedious, inquiry, I have attempted to display the secondary causes which so efficaciously assisted the truth of the Christian religion. If among these causes we have discovered any artificial ornaments, any accidental circumstances, or any mixture of error and passion, it cannot appear surprising that mankind should be the most sensibly affected by such motives as were suited to their imperfect nature. It was by the aid of these causes—exclusive zeal, the immediate expectation of another world, the claim of miracles, the practice of rigid virtue, and the constitution of the primitive church—that Christianity spread itself with so much success in the Roman empire. To the first of these the Christians were indebted for their invincible valour, which disdained to capitulate with the enemy whom they were resolved to vanquish. The three succeeding causes supplied their valour with the most formidable arms. The last of these causes united their courage, directed their arms, and gave their efforts that irresistible weight which even a small band of well-trained and intrepid volunteers has so often possessed over an undisciplined multitude, ignorant of the subject and careless of the event of the war. In the various religions of Polytheism, some wandering fanatics of Egypt and Syria, who addressed themselves to the credulous superstition of the populace, were perhaps the only order of priests that derived their whole support and credit from their sacerdotal profession, and were very deeply affected by a personal concern for the safety or prosperity of their tutelar deities. The ministers of Polytheism, both in Rome and in the provinces, were, for the most part, men of a noble birth and of an affluent fortune, who received, as an honourable distinction, the care of a celebrated temple or of a public sacrifice, exhibited, very frequently at their own expense, the sacred games, and with cold indifference performed the ancient rites, according to the laws and fashion of their country. As they were engaged in the ordinary occupations of life, their zeal and devotion were seldom animated by a sense of interest, or by the habits of an ecclesiastical character. Confined to their respective temples and cities, they remained without any connection of discipline or government; and whilst they acknowledged the supreme jurisdiction of the senate, of the college of pontiffs, and of the emperor, those civil magistrates contented themselves with the easy task of maintaining in peace and dignity the general worship of mankind. We have already seen how various, how loose, and how uncertain were the religious sentiments of Polytheists. They were abandoned, almost without control, to the natural workings of a superstitious fancy. The accidental circumstances of their life and situation determined the object as well as the degree of their devotion; and as long as their adoration was successively prostituted to a thousand deities, it was scarcely possible that their hearts could be susceptible of a very sincere or lively passion for any of them.

CONDITIONS FAVOURABLE TO THE PROGRESS OF CHRISTIANITY

When Christianity appeared in the world, even these faint and imperfect impressions had lost much of their original power. Human reason, which by its unassisted strength is incapable of perceiving the mysteries of faith, had already obtained an easy triumph over the folly of Paganism; and when Tertullian or Lactantius employ their labours in exposing its falsehood and extravagance, they are obliged to transcribe the eloquence of Cicero or the wit of Lucian. The contagion of these sceptical writings had been diffused far beyond the number of their readers. The fashion of incredulity was communicated from the philosopher to the man of pleasure or business, from the noble to the plebeian, and from the master to the menial slave who waited at his table, and who eagerly listened to the freedom of his conversation. On public occasions the philosophic part of mankind affected to treat with respect and decency the religious institutions of their country, but their secret contempt penetrated through the thin and awkward disguise; and even the people, when they discovered that their deities were rejected and derided by those whose rank or understanding they were accustomed to reverence, were filled with doubts and apprehensions concerning the truth of those doctrines to which they had yielded the most implicit belief. The decline of ancient prejudice exposed a very numerous portion of human kind to the danger of a painful and comfortless situation. A state of scepticism and suspense may amuse a few inquisitive minds. But the practice of superstition is so congenial to the multitude that, if they are forcibly awakened, they still regret the loss of their pleasing vision. Their love of the marvellous and supernatural, their curiosity with regard to future events, and their strong propensity to extend their hopes and fears beyond the limits of the visible world, were the principal causes which favoured the establishment of Polytheism. So urgent on the vulgar is the necessity of believing, that the fall of any system of mythology will most probably be succeeded by the introduction of some other mode of superstition. Some deities of a more recent and fashionable cast might soon have occupied the deserted temples of Jupiter and Apollo, if, in the decisive moment, the wisdom of Providence had not interposed a genuine revelation fitted to inspire the most rational esteem and conviction, whilst, at the same time, it was adorned with all that could attract the curiosity, the wonder, and the veneration of the people. In their actual disposition, as many were almost disengaged from their artificial prejudices, but equally susceptible and desirous of a devout attachment, an object much less deserving would have been sufficient to fill the vacant place in their hearts, and to gratify the uncertain eagerness of their passions. Those who are inclined to pursue this reflection, instead of viewing with astonishment the rapid progress of Christianity, will perhaps be surprised that its success was not still more rapid and still more universal.

It has been observed, with truth as well as propriety, that the conquests of Rome prepared and facilitated those of Christianity. In the second chapter of this work we have attempted to explain in what manner the most civilized provinces of Europe, Asia, and Africa were united under the dominion of one sovereign, and gradually connected by the most intimate ties of laws, of manners, and of language. The Jews of Palestine, who had fondly expected a temporal deliverer, gave so cold a reception to the miracles of the divine prophet, that it was found unnecessary to publish, or at least to preserve, any Hebrew gospel. The authentic histories of the actions of Christ were composed in the Greek language, at a considerable distance from Jerusalem, and after the Gentile converts were grown extremely numerous. As soon as those histories were translated into the Latin tongue they were perfectly intelligible to all the subjects of Rome, excepting only to the peasants of Syria and Egypt, for whose benefit particular versions were afterwards made. The public highways, which had been constructed for the use of the legions, opened an easy passage for the Christian missionaries from Damascus to Corinth, and from Italy to the extremity of Spain or Britain; nor did those spiritual conquerors encounter any of the obstacles which usually retard or prevent the introduction of a foreign religion into a distant country. There is the strongest reason to believe that before the reigns of Diocletian and Constantine the faith of Christ had been preached in every province, and in all the great cities of the empire; but the foundation of the several congregations, the numbers of the faithful who composed them, and their proportion to the unbelieving multitude, are now buried in obscurity or disguised by fiction and declamation. Such imperfect circumstances, however, as have reached our knowledge concerning the increase of the Christian name in Asia and Greece, in Egypt, in Italy, and in the West, we shall now proceed to relate, without neglecting the real or imaginary acquisitions which lay beyond the frontiers of the Roman empire.

The rich provinces that extend from the Euphrates to the Ionian sea were the principal theatre on which the apostle of the Gentiles displayed his zeal and piety. The seeds of the Gospel, which he had scattered in a fertile soil, were diligently cultivated by his disciples; and it should seem that, during the two first centuries, the most considerable body of Christians was contained within those limits. Among the societies which were instituted in Syria, none were more ancient or more illustious than those of Damascus, of Berœa or Aleppo, and of Antioch. The prophetic introduction of the Apocalypse has described and immortalised the seven churches of Asia—Ephesus, Smyrna, Pergamus, Thyatira, Sardes, Laodicea, and Philadelphia; and their colonies were soon diffused over that populous country. In a very early period, the islands of Cyprus and Crete, the provinces of Thrace and Macedonia, gave a favourable reception to the new religion; and Christian republics were soon founded in the cities of Corinth, of Sparta, and of Athens. The antiquity of the Greek and Asiatic churches allowed a sufficient space of time for their increase and multiplication; and even the swarms of Gnostics and other heretics serve to display the flourishing condition of the orthodox church, since the appellation of heretics has always been applied to the less numerous party. To these domestic testimonies we may add the confession, the complaints, and the apprehensions of the Gentiles themselves. From the writings of Lucian, a philosopher who had studied mankind, and who describes their manners in the most lively colours, we may learn that, under the reign of Commodus, his native country of Pontus was filled with Epicureans and *Christians*. Within fourscore years after the death of Christ, the humane Pliny laments the magnitude of the evil which he vainly attempted to eradicate. In his very curious epistle to the emperor Trajan he affirms that the temples were almost deserted, that the sacred victims scarcely found any purchasers, and that the superstition had not only infected the cities, but had even spread itself into the villages and the open country of Pontus and Bithynia.

Without descending into a minute scrutiny of the expressions or of the motives of those writers who either celebrate or lament the progress of Christianity in the East, it may in general be observed that none of them have left us any grounds from whence a just estimate might be formed of the real numbers of the faithful in those provinces. One circumstance, however, has been fortunately preserved, which seems to cast a more distinct light on this obscure but interesting subject. Under the reign of Theodosius, after Christianity had enjoyed, during more than sixty years, the sunshine of Imperial favour, the ancient and illustrious church of Antioch consisted of one hundred thousand persons, three thousand of whom were supported out of the public oblations. The splendour and dignity of the queen of the East, the acknowledged populousness of Cæsarea, Seleucia, and Alexandria, and the destruction of two hundred and fifty thousand souls in the earthquake which afflicted Antioch under the elder Justin, are so many convincing proofs that the whole number of its inhabitants was not less than half a million, and that the Christians, however multiplied by zeal and power, did not exceed a fifth part of that great city. How different a proportion must we adopt when we compare the persecuted with the triumphant church, the West with the East, remote villages with populous towns, and countries recently converted to the faith with the place where the believers first received the appellation of Christians! It must not, however, be dissembled that, in another passage, Chrysostom, to whom we are indebted for this useful information, computes the multitude of the faithful as even superior to that of the Jews and Pagans. But the solution of this apparent difficulty is easy and obvious. The eloquent preacher draws a parallel between the civil and the ecclesiastical constitution of Antioch; between the list of Christians who had acquired heaven by baptism, and the list of citizens who had a right to share the public liberality. Slaves, strangers, and infants were comprised in the former; they were excluded from the latter.

The extensive commerce of Alexandria, and its proximity to Palestine, gave an easy entrance to the new religion. It was at first embraced by great numbers of the Therapeutæ, or Essenians, of the lake Mareotis, a Jewish sect which had abated much of its reverence for the Mosaic ceremonies. The austere life of the Essenians, their fasts and excommunications, the community of goods, the love of celibacy, their zeal for martyrdom, and the warmth though not the purity of their faith, already offered a very lively image of the primitive discipline. It was in the school of Alexandria that the Christian theology appears to have assumed a regular and scientifical form; and when Hadrian visited Egypt, he found a church composed of Jews and of Greeks, sufficiently important to attract the notice of that inquisitive prince. But the progress of Christianity was for a long time confined within the limits of a single city, which was itself a foreign colony, and till the close of the second century the predecessors of Demetrius were the only prelates of the Egyptian church. Three bishops were consecrated by the hands of Demetrius, and the number was increased to twenty by his successor Heraclas. The body of the natives, a people distinguished by a sullen inflexibility of temper, entertained the new doctrine with coldness and reluctance; and even in the time of Origen it was rare to meet with an Egyptian who had surmounted his early prejudices in favour of the sacred animals of his country. As soon, indeed, as Christianity ascended the throne, the zeal of those barbarians obeyed the prevailing impulsion; the cities of Egypt were filled with bishops, and the deserts of Thebais swarmed with hermits.

A perpetual stream of strangers and provincials flowed into the capacious bosom of Rome. Whatever was strange or odious, whoever was guilty or suspected, might hope, in the obscurity of that immense capital, to elude the vigilance of the law. In such a various conflux of nations, every teacher, either of truth or of falsehood, every founder, whether of a virtuous or a criminal association, might easily multiply his disciples or accomplices. The Christians of Rome, at the time of the accidental persecution of Nero, are represented by Tacitus as already amounting to a very great multitude, and the language of that great historian is almost similar to the style employed by Livy, when he relates the introduction and the suppression of the rites of Bacchus. After the Bacchanals had awakened the severity of the senate, it was likewise apprehended that a very great multitude, as it were *another people*, had been initiated into those abhorred mysteries. A more careful inquiry soon demonstrated that the offenders did not exceed seven thousand; a number indeed sufficiently alarming when considered as the object of public justice. It is with the same candid allowance that we should interpret the vague expressions of Tacitus, and in a former instance of Pliny, when they exaggerate the crowds of deluded fanatics who had forsaken the established worship of the gods. The church of Rome was undoubtedly the first and most populous of the empire; and we are possessed of an authentic record which attests the state of religion in that city about the middle of the third century, and after a peace of thirty-eight years. The clergy, at that time, consisted of a bishop, forty-six presbyters, seven deacons, as many sub-deacons, forty-two acolythes, and fifty readers, exorcists, and porters. The number of widows, of the infirm, and of the poor, who were maintained by the oblations of the faithful, amounted to fifteen hundred. From reason, as well as from the analogy of Antioch, we may venture to estimate the Christians of Rome at about fifty thousand. The populousness of that great capital cannot perhaps be exactly ascertained; but the most modest calculation will not surely reduce it lower than a million of inhabitants, of whom the Christians might constitute at the most a twentieth part.

The western provincials appeared to have derived the knowledge of Christianity from the same source which had diffused among them the language, the sentiments, and the manners of Rome. In this more important circumstance, Africa, as well as Gaul, was gradually fashioned to the imitation of the capital. Yet notwithstanding the many favourable occasions which might invite the Roman missionaries to visit their Latin provinces, it was late before they passed either the sea or the Alps; nor can we discover in those great countries any assured traces either of faith or of persecution that ascend higher than the reign of the Antonines. The slow progress of the Gospel in the cold climate of Gaul was extremely different from the eagerness with which it seems to have been received on the burning sands of Africa. The African Christians soon formed one of the principal members of the primitive church. The practice introduced into that province of appointing bishops to the most inconsiderable towns, and very frequently to the most obscure villages, contributed to multiply the splendour and importance of their religious societies, which during the course of the third century were animated by the zeal of Tertullian, directed by the abilities of Cyprian, and adorned by the eloquence of Lactantius. But if, on the contrary, we turn our eyes towards Gaul, we must content ourselves with discovering, in the time of Marcus Antoninus, the feeble and united congregations of Lyons and Vienne; and even as late as the reign of Decius we are assured that in a few cities only—Arles, Narbonne, Toulouse, Limoges, Clermont, Tours, and Paris—some scattered churches were supported by the devotion of a small number of Christians. Silence is indeed very consistent with devotion; but as it is seldom compatible with zeal, we may perceive and lament the languid state of Christianity in those provinces which had exchanged the Celtic for the Latin tongue, since they did not, during the three first centuries, give birth to a single ecclesiastical writer. From Gaul, which claimed a just pre-eminence of learning and authority over all the countries on this side of the Alps, the light of the Gospel was more faintly reflected on the remote provinces of Spain and Britain; and if we may credit the vehement assertions of Tertullian, they had already received the first rays of the faith when he addressed his Apology to the magistrates of the emperor Severus. But the obscure and imperfect origin of the western churches of Europe has been so negligently recorded, that, if we would relate the time and manner of their foundation, we must supply the silence of antiquity by those legends which avarice or superstition long afterwards dictated to the monks in the lazy gloom of their convents. Of these holy romances, that of the apostle St. James can alone, by its singular extravagance, deserve to be mentioned. From a peaceful fisherman of the lake of Gennesareth, he was transformed into a valorous knight, who charged at the head of the Spanish chivalry in their battles against the Moors. The gravest historians have celebrated his exploits; the miraculous shrine of Compostella displayed his power; and the sword of a military order, assisted by the terrors of the Inquisition, was sufficient to remove every objection of profane criticism.

The progress of Christianity was not confined to the Roman empire; and, according to the primitive fathers, who interpret facts by prophecy, the new religion, within a century after the death of its Divine Author, had already visited every part of the globe. "There exists not," says Justin Martyr, "a people, whether Greek or barbarian, or any other race of men, by whatsoever appellation or manners they may be distinguished, however ignorant of arts or agriculture, whether they dwell under tents, or wander about in covered waggons, among whom prayers are not offered up in the name of a crucified Jesus to the Father and Creator of all things." But this splendid exaggeration, which even at present it would be extremely difficult to reconcile with the real state of mankind, can be considered only as the rash sally of a devout but careless writer, the measure of whose belief was regulated by that of his wishes. But neither the belief nor the wishes of the fathers can alter the truth of history. It will still remain an undoubted fact that the barbarians of Scythia and Germany, who afterwards subverted the Roman monarchy, were involved in the darkness of paganism; and that even the conversion of Iberia, of Armenia, or of Ethiopia, was not attempted with any degree of success till the sceptre was in the hands of an orthodox emperor. Before that time the various accidents of war and commerce might indeed diffuse an imperfect knowledge of the Gospel among the tribes of Caledonia, and among the borderers of the Rhine, the Danube, and the Euphrates. Beyond the last-mentioned river, Edessa was distinguished by a firm and early adherence to the faith. From Edessa the principles of Christianity were easily introduced into the Greek and Syrian cities which obeyed the successors of Artaxerxes; but they do not appear to have made any deep impression on the minds of the Persians, whose religious system, by the labours of a well disciplined order of priests, had been constructed with much more art and solidity than the uncertain mythology of Greece and Rome.

THE NUMBERS AND CONDITION OF THE PRIMITIVE CHRISTIANS

From this impartial though imperfect survey of the progress of Christianity, it may perhaps seem probable that the number of its proselytes has been excessively magnified by fear on the one side, and by devotion on the other. According to the irreproachable testimony of Origen, the proportion of the faithful was very inconsiderable, when compared with the multitude of an unbelieving world; but, as we are left without any distinct information, it is impossible to determine, and it is difficult even to conjecture, the real numbers of the primitive Christians. The most favourable calculation, however, that can be deduced from the examples of Antioch and of Rome will not permit us to imagine that more than a twentieth part of the subjects of the empire had enlisted themselves under the banner of the Cross before the important conversion of Constantine. But their habits of faith, of zeal, and of union, seemed to multiply their numbers; and the same causes which contributed to their future increase served to render their actual strength more apparent and more formidable.

Such is the constitution of civil society, that, whilst a few persons are distinguished by riches, by honours, and by knowledge, the body of the people is condemned to obscurity, ignorance, and poverty. The Christian religion, which addressed itself to the whole human race, must consequently collect a far greater number of proselytes from the lower than from the superior ranks of life. This innocent and natural circumstance has been improved into a very odious imputation, which seems to be less strenuously denied by the apologists than it is urged by the adversaries of the faith; that the new sect of Christians was almost entirely composed of the dregs of the populace, of peasants and mechanics, of boys and women, of beggars and slaves, the last of whom might sometimes introduce the missionaries into the rich and noble families to which they belonged. These obscure teachers (such was the charge of malice and infidelity) are as mute in public as they are loquacious and dogmatical in private. Whilst they cautiously avoid the dangerous encounter of philosophers, they mingle with the rude and illiterate crowd, and insinuate themselves into those minds whom their age, their sex, or their education has the best disposed to receive the impression of superstitious terrors.

This unfavourable picture, though not devoid of a faint resemblance, betrays, by its dark colouring the distorted features, the pencil of an enemy. As the humble faith of Christ diffused itself through the world, it was embraced by several persons who derived some consequence from the advantages of nature or fortune. Aristides, who presented an eloquent apology to the emperor Hadrian, was an Athenian philosopher. Justin Martyr had sought divine knowledge in the schools of Zeno, of Aristotle, of Pythagoras, and of Plato, before he fortunately was accosted by the old man, or rather the angel, who turned his attention to the study of the Jewish prophets. Clemens of Alexandria had acquired much various reading in the Greek, and Tertullian in the Latin, language. Julius Africanus and Origen possessed a very considerable share of the learning of their times; and although the style of Cyprian is very different from that of Lactantius, we might almost discover that both those writers had been public teachers of rhetoric. Even the study of philosophy was at length introduced among the Christians, but it was not always productive of the most salutary effects; knowledge was as often the parent of heresy as of devotion, and the description which was designed for the followers of Artemon may, with equal propriety, be applied to the various sects that resisted the successors of the apostles. "They presume to alter the holy Scriptures, to abandon the ancient rule of faith, and to form their opinions according to the subtile precepts of logic. The science of the church is neglected for the study of geometry, and they lose sight of heaven while they are employed in measuring the earth. Euclid is perpetually in their hands. Aristotle and Theophrastus are the objects of their admiration; and they express an uncommon reverence for the works of Galen. Their errors are derived from the abuse of the arts and sciences of the infidels, and they corrupt the simplicity of the Gospel by the refinements of human reason."

Nor can it be affirmed with truth that the advantages of birth and fortune were always separated from the profession of Christianity. Several Roman citizens were brought before the tribunal of Pliny, and he soon discovered that a great number of persons of *every order* of men in Bithynia had deserted the religion of their ancestors. His unsuspected testimony may, in this instance, obtain more credit than the bold challenge of Tertullian, when he addresses himself to the fears as well as to the humanity of the proconsul of Africa, by assuring him that if he persists in his cruel intentions he must decimate Carthage, and that he will find among the guilty many persons of his own rank, senators and matrons of noblest extraction, and the friends or relations of his most intimate friends. It appears, however, that about forty years afterwards the emperor Valerian was persuaded of the truth of this assertion, since in one of his rescripts he evidently supposes that senators, Roman knights, and ladies of quality, were engaged in the Christian sect. The church still continued to increase its outward splendour as it lost its internal purity; and, in the reign of Diocletian, the palace, the courts of justice, and even the army, concealed a multitude of

Christians, who endeavoured to reconcile the interests of the present with those of a future life.

And yet these exceptions are either too few in number, or too recent in time, entirely to remove the imputation of ignorance and obscurity which has been so arrogantly cast on the first proselytes of Christianity. Instead of employing in our defence the fictions of later ages, it will be more prudent to convert the occasion of scandal into a subject of edification. Our serious thoughts will suggest to us that the apostles themselves were chosen by Providence among the fishermen of Galilee, and that, the lower we depress the temporal condition of the first Christians, the more reason we shall find to admire their merit and success. It is incumbent on us diligently to remember that the kingdom of heaven was promised to the poor in spirit, and that minds afflicted by calamity and the contempt of mankind cheerfully listen to the divine promise of future happiness; while, on the contrary, the fortunate are satisfied with the possession of this world; and the wise abuse in doubt and dispute their vain superiority of reason and knowledge.

We stand in need of such reflections to comfort us for the loss of some illustrious characters, which in our eyes might have seemed the most worthy of the heavenly present. The names of Seneca, of the elder and the younger Pliny, of Tacitus, of Plutarch, of Galen, of the slave Epictetus, and of the emperor Marcus Antoninus, adorn the age in which they flourished, and exalt the dignity of human nature. They filled with glory their respective stations, either in active or contemplative life; their excellent understandings were improved by study; philosophy had purified their minds from the prejudices of the popular superstition; and their days were spent in the pursuit of truth and the practice of virtue. Yet all these sages (it is no less an object of surprise than of concern) overlooked or rejected the perfection of the Christian system. Their language or their silence equally discover their contempt for the growing sect which in their time had diffused itself over the Roman empire. Those among them who condescend to mention the Christians consider them only as obstinate and perverse enthusiasts, who exacted an implicit submission to their mysterious doctrines, without being able to produce a single argument that could engage the attention of men of sense and learning.

It is at least doubtful whether any of these philosophers perused the apologies which the primitive Christians repeatedly published in behalf of themselves and of their religion; but it is much to be lamented that such a cause was not defended by abler advocates, They expose with superfluous wit and eloquence the extravagance of Polytheism. They interest our compassion by displaying the innocence and sufferings of their injured brethren. But when they would demonstrate the divine origin of Christianity, they insist much more strongly on the predictions which announced, than on the miracles which accompanied, the appearance of the Messiah. Their favourite argument might serve to edify a Christian or to convert a Jew, since both the one and the other acknowledge the authority of those prophecies, and both are obliged, with devout reverence, to search for their sense and their accomplishment. But this mode of persuasion loses much of its weight and influence when it is addressed to those who neither understand nor respect the Mosaic dispensation and the prophetic style. In the unskilful hands of Justin and of the succeeding apologists, the sublime meaning of the Hebrew oracles evaporates in distant types, affected conceits, and cold allegories; and even their authenticity was rendered suspicious to an unenlightened Gentile, by the mixture of pious forgeries which, under the names of Orpheus, Hermes, and the Sibyls,[1] were obtruded on him as of equal value with the genuine inspirations of Heaven. The adoption of fraud and sophistry in the defence of revelation too often reminds us of the injudicious conduct of those poets who load their *invulnerable* heroes with a useless weight of cumbersome and brittle armour.

But how shall we excuse the supine inattention of the Pagan and philosophic world to those evidences which were presented by the hand of Omnipotence, not to their reason, but to their senses? During the age of Christ, of his apostles, and of their first disciples, the doctrine which they preached was confirmed by innumerable prodigies. The lame walked, the blind saw, the sick were healed, the dead were raised, dæmons were expelled, and the laws of Nature were frequently suspended for the benefit of the church. But the sages of Greece and Rome turned aside from the awful spectacle, and, pursuing the ordinary occupations of life and study, appeared unconscious of any alterations in the moral or physical government of the world. Under the reign of Tiberius, the whole earth, or at least a celebrated province of the Roman empire, was involved in a preternatural darkness of three hours. Even this miraculous event, which ought to have excited the wonder, the curiosity, and the devotion of mankind, passed without notice in an age of science and history. It happened during the lifetime of Seneca and the elder Pliny, who must have experienced the immediate effects, or received the earliest intelligence, of the prodigy. Each of these philosophers, in a laborious work, has recorded all the great phenomena of Nature, earthquakes, meteors, comets, and eclipses, which his indefatigable curiosity could collect. Both the one and the other had omitted to mention the greatest phenomenon to which the mortal eye has been witness since the

---

[1] The philosophers, who derided the more ancient predictions of the Sibyls, would easily have detected the Jewish and Christian forgeries, which have been so triumphantly quoted by the fathers, from Justin Martyr to Lactantius. When the Sib. 'line verses had performed their appointed task, they, like the system of the millennium, were quietly laid aside. The Christian Sibyl had unluckily fixed the ruin of Rome for the year 195, A. U. C. 948.

creation of the globe. A distinct chapter of Pliny is designed for eclipses of an extraordinary nature and unusual duration; but he contents himself with describing the singular defect of light which followed the murder of Cæsar, when, during the greatest part of a year, the orb of the sun appeared pale and without splendour. This season of obscurity, which cannot surely be compared with the preternatural darkness of the Passion, had been already celebrated by most of the poets and historians of that memorable age.

Chapter 16

THE CONDUCT OF THE ROMAN GOVERNMENT TOWARDS
THE CHRISTIANS. THE ATTITUDE OF THE EMPERORS. THE
MARTYRDOM OF CYPRIAN. VARYING POLICIES OF PERSE-
CUTION. THE CHURCH UNDER DIOCLETIAN AND HIS
SUCCESSORS. GALERIUS'S EDICT OF TOLERATION

IF we seriously consider the purity of the Christian religion, the
sanctity of its moral precepts, and the innocent as well as austere
lives of the greater number of those who during the first ages embraced the faith of the Gospel, we should naturally suppose that so
benevolent a doctrine would have been received with due reverence
even by the unbelieving world; that the learned and the polite, however
they might deride the miracles, would have esteemed the virtues of the
new sect; and that the magistrates, instead of persecuting, would have
protected an order of men who yielded the most passive obedience to
the laws, though they declined the active cares of war and government.
If, on the other hand, we recollect the universal toleration of Polytheism,
as it was invariably maintained by the faith of the people, the incredulity
of philosophers, and the policy of the Roman senate and emperors, we
are at a loss to discover what new offence the Christians had committed, what new provocation could exasperate the mild indifference
of antiquity, and what new motives could urge the Roman princes, who
beheld without concern a thousand forms of religion subsisting in
peace under their gentle sway, to inflict a severe punishment on any part
of their subjects who had chosen for themselves a singular but an
inoffensive mode of faith and worship.

The religious policy of the ancient world seems to have assumed a
more stern and intolerant character to oppose the progress of Christianity. About fourscore years after the death of Christ, his innocent disciples were punished with death by the sentence of a proconsul of the
most amiable and philosophic character, and according to the laws of
an emperor distinguished by the wisdom and justice of his general
administration. The apologies which were repeatedly addressed to the
successors of Trajan are filled with the most pathetic complaints that the
Christians, who obeyed the dictates and solicited the liberty of conscience, were alone, among all the subjects of the Roman empire, excluded from the common benefits of their auspicious government. The
deaths of a few eminent martyrs have been recorded with care; and
from the time that Christianity was invested with the supreme power,

the governors of the church have been no less diligently employed in displaying the cruelty, than in imitating the conduct, of their Pagan adversaries. To separate (if it be possible) a few authentic as well as interesting facts from an undigested mass of fiction and error, and to relate, in a clear and rational manner, the causes, the extent, the duration, and the most important circumstances of the persecutions to which the first Christians were exposed, is the design of the present chapter.

The sectaries of a persecuted religion, depressed by fear, animated with resentment, and perhaps heated by enthusiasm, are seldom in a proper temper of mind calmly to investigate, or candidly to appreciate, the motives of their enemies, which often escape the impartial and discerning view even of those who are placed at a secure distance from the flames of persecution. A reason has been assigned for the conduct of the emperors towards the primitive Christians, which may appear the more specious and probable as it is drawn from the acknowledged genius of Polytheism. It has already been observed that the religious concord of the world was principally supported by the implicit assent and reverence which the nations of antiquity expressed for their respective traditions and ceremonies. It might therefore be expected that they would unite with indignation against any sect or people which should separate itself from the communion of mankind, and, claiming the exclusive possession of divine knowledge, should disdain every form of worship except its own as impious and idolatrous. The rights of toleration were held by mutual indulgence: they were justly forfeited by a refusal of the accustomed tribute. As the payment of this tribute was inflexibly refused by the Jews, and by them alone, the consideration of the treatment which they experienced from the Roman magistrates will serve to explain how far these speculations are justified by facts, and will lead us to discover the true causes of the persecution of Christianity.

Without repeating what has been already mentioned of the reverence of the Roman princes and governors for the temple of Jerusalem, we shall only observe that the destruction of the temple and city was accompanied and followed by every circumstance that could exasperate the minds of the conquerors, and authorise religious persecution by the most specious arguments of political justice and the public safety. From the reign of Nero to that of Antoninus Pius, the Jews discovered a fierce impatience of the dominion of Rome, which repeatedly broke out in the most furious massacres and insurrections. Humanity is shocked at the recital of the horrid cruelties which they committed in the cities of Egypt, of Cyprus, and of Cyrene, where they dwelt in treacherous friendship with the unsuspecting natives; and we are tempted to applaud the severe retaliation which was exercised by the arms of the legions against a race of fanatics whose dire and credulous superstition seemed to render them the implacable enemies not only of the Roman government, but of human kind. The enthusiasm of the Jews was supported by the opinion that it was unlawful for them to pay taxes to an idolatrous master, and by the flattering promise which they derived from their ancient oracles, that a conquering Messiah would soon arise, destined to break their fetters, and to invest the favourites of heaven with the empire of the earth. It was by announcing himself as their long-expected deliverer, and by calling on all the descendants of Abraham to assert the hope of Israel, that the famous Barchochebas collected a formidable army, with which he resisted during two years the power of the emperor Hadrian.

Notwithstanding these repeated provocations, the resentment of the Roman princes expired after the victory, nor were their apprehensions continued beyond the period of war and danger. By the general indulgence of Polytheism, and by the mild temper of Antoninus Pius, the Jews were restored to their ancient privileges, and once more obtained the permission of circumcising their children, with the easy restraint that they should never confer on any foreign proselyte that distinguishing mark of the Hebrew race. The numerous remains of that people, though they were still excluded from the precincts of Jerusalem, were permitted to form and to maintain considerable establishments both in Italy and in the provinces, to acquire the freedom of Rome, to enjoy municipal honours, and to obtain at the same time an exemption from the burdensome and expensive offices of society. The moderation or the contempt of the Romans gave a legal sanction to the form of ecclesiastical police which was instituted by the vanquished sect. The patriarch, who had fixed his residence at Tiberias, was empowered to appoint his subordinate ministers and apostles, to exercise a domestic jurisdiction, and to receive from his dispersed brethren an annual contribution. New synagogues were frequently erected in the principal cities of the empire; and the sabbaths, the fasts, and the festivals, which were either commanded by the Mosaic law or enjoined by the traditions of the Rabbis, were celebrated in the most solemn and public manner. Such gentle treatment insensibly assuaged the stern temper of the Jews. Awakened from their dream of prophecy and conquest, they assumed the behaviour of peaceable and industrious subjects. Their irreconcilable hatred of mankind, instead of flaming out in acts of blood and violence, evaporated in less dangerous gratifications. They embraced every opportunity of overreaching the idolaters in trade, and they pronounced secret and ambiguous imprecations against the haughty kingdom of Edom.

Since the Jews, who rejected with abhorrence the deities adored by their sovereign and by their fellow-subjects, enjoyed, however, the free exercise of their unsocial religion, there must have existed some other cause which exposed the disciples of Christ to those severities from which the posterity of Abraham was exempt. The difference between them is simple and obvious, but, according to the sentiments of antiquity, it was of the highest importance. The Jews were a *nation*, the Christians were a *sect*: and if it was natural for every community to respect the sacred institutions of their neighbours, it was incumbent on them to persevere in those of their ancestors. The voice of oracles, the precepts of philosophers, and the authority of the laws, unanimously enforced this national obligation. By their lofty claim of superior sanctity the Jews might provoke the Polytheists to consider them as an odious and impure race. By disdaining the intercourse of other nations they might deserve their contempt. The laws of Moses might be for the most part frivolous or absurd; yet, since they had been received during many ages by a large society, his followers were justified by the example of mankind, and it was universally acknowledged that they had a right to practise what it would have been criminal in them to neglect. But this principle, which protected the Jewish synagogue, afforded not any favour or security to the primitive church. By embracing the faith of the Gospel the Christians incurred the supposed guilt of an unnatural and unpardonable offence. They dissolved the sacred ties of custom and education, violated the religious institutions of their country, and presumptuously despised whatever their fathers had believed as true or had reverenced as sacred. Nor was this apostacy (if we may use the expression) merely of a partial or local kind; since the pious deserter who withdrew himself from the temples of Egypt or Syria would equally disdain to seek an asylum in those of Athens or Carthage. Every Christian rejected with contempt the superstitions of his family, his city, and his province. The whole body of Christians unanimously refused to hold any communion with the gods of Rome, of the empire, and of mankind. It was in vain that the oppressed believer asserted the inalienable rights of conscience and private judgment. Though his situation might excite the pity, his arguments could never reach the understanding, either of the philosophic or of the believing part of the Pagan world. To their apprehensions it was no less a matter of surprise that any individuals should entertain scruples against complying with the established mode of worship than if they had conceived a sudden abhorrence to the manners, the dress, or the language of their native country.

The surprise of the Pagans was soon succeeded by resentment, and the most pious of men were exposed to the unjust but dangerous imputation of impiety. Malice and prejudice concurred in representing the Christians as a society of atheists, who, by the most daring attack on the religious constitution of the empire, had merited the severest animadversion of the civil magistrate. They had separated themselves (they gloried in the confession) from every mode of superstition which was received in any part of the globe by the various temper of Polytheism: but it was not altogether so evident what deity, or what form of worship, they had substituted to the gods and temples of antiquity.

The pure and sublime idea which they entertained of the Supreme Being escaped the gross conception of the Pagan multitude, who were at a loss to discover a spiritual and solitary God, that was neither represented under any corporeal figure or visible symbol, nor was adored with the accustomed pomp of libations and festivals, of altars and sacrifices. The sages of Greece and Rome, who had elevated their minds to the contemplation of the existence and attributes of the First Cause, were induced by reason or by vanity to reserve for themselves and their chosen disciples the privilege of this philosophical devotion. They were far from admitting the prejudices of mankind as the standard of truth, but they considered them as flowing from the original disposition of human nature; and they supposed that any popular mode of faith and worship which presumed to disclaim the assistance of the senses would, in proportion as it receded from superstition, find itself incapable of restraining the wanderings of the fancy and the visions of fanaticism. The careless glance which men of wit and learning condescended to cast on the Christian revelation served only to confirm their hasty opinion, and to persuade them that the principle, which they might have revered, of the Divine Unity, was defaced by the wild enthusiasm, and annihilated by the airy speculations, of the new sectaries. The author of a celebrated dialogue, which has been attributed to Lucian, whilst he affects to treat the mysterious subject of the Trinity in a style of ridicule and contempt, betrays his own ignorance of the weakness of human reason, and of the inscrutable nature of the Divine perfections.

It might appear less surprising that the founder of Christianity should not only be revered by his disciples as a sage and a prophet, but that he should be adored as a God. The Polytheists were disposed to adopt every article of faith which seemed to offer any resemblance, however distant or imperfect, with the popular mythology; and the legends of Bacchus, of Hercules, and of Æsculapius, had, in some measure, prepared their imagination for the appearance of the Son of God under a human form. But they were astonished that the Christians should abandon the temples of those ancient heroes who, in the infancy of the world, had invented arts, instituted laws, and vanquished the tyrants or monsters who infested the earth; in order to choose for the exclusive object of their religious worship an obscure teacher, who, in a recent age, and among a barbarous people, had fallen a sacrifice either to the malice of his own countrymen, or to the jealousy of the Roman government. The Pagan multitude, reserving their gratitude for temporal benefits alone, rejected the inestimable present of life and immortality which was offered to mankind by Jesus of Nazareth. His mild constancy in the midst of cruel and voluntary sufferings, his universal benevolence, and the sublime simplicity of his actions and character, were insufficient, in the opinion of those carnal men, to compensate for the want of fame, of empire, and of success; and whilst they refused to acknowledge his stupendous triumph over the powers of darkness and of the grave, they misrepresented, or they insulted, the equivocal birth, wandering life, and ignominious death, of the divine Author of Christianity.

The personal guilt which every Christian had contracted, in thus preferring his private sentiment to the national religion, was aggravated in a very high degree by the number and union of the criminals. It is well known, and has been already observed, that Roman policy viewed with the utmost jealousy and distrust any association among its subjects; and that the privileges of private corporations, though formed for the most harmless or beneficial purposes, were bestowed with a very sparing hand. The religious assemblies of the Christians, who had separated themselves from the public worship, appeared of a much less innocent nature: they were illegal in their principle, and in their consequences might become dangerous; nor were the emperors conscious that they violated the laws of justice, when, for the peace of society, they prohibited those secret and sometimes nocturnal meetings. The pious disobedience of the Christians made their conduct, or perhaps their designs, appear in a much more serious and criminal light; and the Roman princes, who might perhaps have suffered themselves to be disarmed by a ready submission, deeming their honour concerned in the execution of their commands, sometimes attempted, by rigorous punishments, to subdue this independent spirit, which boldly acknowledged an authority superior to that of the magistrate. The extent and duration of this spiritual conspiracy seemed to render it every day more deserving of his animadversion. We have already seen that the active and successful zeal of the Christians had insensibly diffused them through every province and almost every city of the empire. The new converts seemed to renounce their family and country, that they might connect themselves in an indissoluble band of union with a peculiar society, which everywhere assumed a different character from the rest of mankind. Their gloomy and austere aspect, their abhorrence of the common business and pleasures of life, and their frequent predictions of impending calamities, inspired the Pagans with the apprehension of some danger which would arise from the new sect, the more alarming as it was the more obscure. "Whatever," says Pliny, "may be the principle of their conduct, their inflexible obstinacy appeared deserving of punishment."

The precautions with which the disciples of Christ performed the offices of religion were at first dictated by fear and necessity; but they were continued from choice. By imitating the awful secrecy which reigned in the Eleusinian mysteries, the Christians had flattered themselves that they should render their sacred institutions more respectable in the eyes of the Pagan world. But the event, as it often happens to the operations of subtile policy, deceived their wishes and their expectations. It was concluded that they only concealed what they would have blushed to disclose. Their mistaken prudence afforded an opportunity for malice to invent, and for suspicious credulity to believe, the horrid tales which described the Christians as the most wicked of human kind, who practised in their dark recesses every abomination that a depraved fancy could suggest, and who solicited the favour of their unknown God by the sacrifice of every moral virtue. There were many who pretended to confess or to relate the ceremonies of this abhorred society. It was asserted, "that a new-born infant, entirely covered over with flour, was presented, like some mystic symbol of initiation, to the knife of the proselyte, who unknowingly inflicted many a secret and mortal wound on the innocent victim of his error; that as soon as the cruel deed was perpetrated, the sectaries drank up the blood, greedily tore asunder the quivering members, and pledged themselves to eternal secrecy, by a mutual consciousness of guilt. It was as confidently affirmed that this inhuman sacrifice was succeeded by a suitable entertainment, in which intemperance served as a provocative to brutal lust; till, at the appointed moment, the lights were suddenly extinguished, shame was banished, nature was forgotten; and, as accident might direct, the darkness of the night was polluted by the incestuous commerce of sisters and brothers, of sons and of mothers."

But the perusal of the ancient apologies was sufficient to remove even the slightest suspicion from the mind of a candid adversary. The Christians, with the intrepid security of innocence, appeal from the voice of rumour to the equity of the magistrates. They acknowledge that, if any proof can be produced of the crimes which calumny has imputed to them, they are worthy of the most severe punishment. They provoke the punishment, and they challenge the proof. At the same time they urge, with equal truth and propriety, that the charge is not less devoid of probability than it is destitute of evidence; they ask whether any one can seriously believe that the pure and holy precepts of the Gospel, which so frequently restrain the use of the most lawful enjoyments, should inculcate the practice of the most abominable crimes; that a large society should resolve to dishonour itself in the eyes of its own members; and that a great number of persons, of either sex, and every age and character, insensible to the fear of death or infamy, should consent to violate those principles which nature and education had imprinted most deeply in their minds. Nothing, it should seem, could weaken the force or destroy the effect of so unanswerable a justification, unless it were the injudicious conduct of the apologists themselves, who betrayed the common cause of religion, to gratify their devout hatred to the domestic enemies of the church. It was sometimes faintly insinuated, and sometimes boldly asserted, that the same bloody sacrifices, and the same incestuous festivals, which were so falsely ascribed to the orthodox believers, were in reality celebrated by the Marcionites, by the Carpocratians, and by several other sects of the Gnostics, who, notwithstanding they might deviate into the paths of heresy, were still actuated by the sentiments of men, and still governed by the precepts of Christianity. Accusations of a similar kind were retorted upon the church by the schismatics who had departed from its communion, and it was confessed on all sides that the most scandalous licentiousness of manners prevailed among great numbers of those who affected the name of Christians. A Pagan magistrate, who possessed neither leisure nor abilities to discern the almost imperceptible line which divides the orthodox faith from heretical pravity, might easily have imagined that their mutual animosity had extorted the discovery of their common guilt. It was fortunate for the repose, or at least for the reputation, of the first Christians, that the magistrates sometimes proceeded with more temper and moderation than is usually consistent with religious zeal, and that they reported, as the impartial result of their judicial inquiry, that the sectaries who had deserted the established worship appeared to them sincere in their professions and blameless in their manners, however they might incur, by their absurd and excessive superstition, the censure of the laws.

THE ATTITUDE OF THE EMPERORS TOWARDS CHRISTIANS

History, which undertakes to record the transactions of the past, for the instruction of future ages, would ill deserve that honourable office, if she condescended to plead the cause of tyrants, or to justify the maxims of persecution. It must, however, be acknowledged that the conduct of the emperors who appeared the least favourable to the primitive church is by no means so criminal as that of modern sovereigns who have employed the arm of violence and terror against the religious opinions of any part of their subjects. From their reflections, or even from their own feelings, a Charles V. or a Louis XIV. might have acquired a just knowledge of the rights of conscience, of the obligation of faith, and of the innocence of error. But the princes and magistrates of ancient Rome were strangers to those principles which inspired and authorised the inflexible obstinacy of the Christians in the cause of truth, nor could they themselves discover in their own breasts any motive which would have prompted them to refuse a legal, and as it were a natural, submission to the sacred institutions of their country. The same reason which contributes to alleviate the guilt, must have tended to abate the rigour, of their persecutions. As they were actuated, not by the furious zeal of bigots, but by the temperate policy of legislators, contempt must often have relaxed, and humanity must frequently have suspended, the execution of those laws which they enacted against the humble and obscure followers of Christ. From the general view of their character and motives we might naturally conclude: I. That a considerable time elapsed before they considered the new sectaries as an object deserving of the attention of government. II. That in the conviction of any of their subjects who were accused of so very singular a crime, they proceeded with caution and reluctance. III. That they were moderate in the use of punishments; and IV. That the afflicted church enjoyed many intervals of peace and tranquillity. Notwithstanding the careless indifference which the most copious and the most minute of the Pagan writers have shown to the affairs of the Christians, it may still be in our power to confirm each of these probable suppositions by the evidence of authentic facts.

I. By the wise dispensation of Providence a mysterious veil was cast over the infancy of the church, which, till the faith of the Christians was matured, and their numbers were multiplied, served to protect them not only from the malice but even from the knowledge of the Pagan world. The slow and gradual abolition of the Mosaic ceremonies afforded a safe and innocent disguise to the more early proselytes of the Gospel. As they were for the greater part of the race of Abraham, they were distinguished by the peculiar mark of circumcision, offered up their devotions in the Temple of Jerusalem till its final destruction, and received both the Law and the Prophets as the genuine inspirations of the Deity. The Gentile converts who by a spiritual adoption had been associated to the hope of Israel, were likewise confounded under the garb and appearance of Jews; and as the Polytheists paid less regard to articles of faith than to the external worship, the new sect, which carefully concealed, or faintly announced, its future greatness and ambition, was permitted to shelter itself under the general toleration which was granted to an ancient and celebrated people in the Roman empire. It was not long, perhaps, before the Jews themselves, animated with a fiercer zeal and a more jealous faith, perceived the gradual separation of their Nazarene brethren from the doctrine of the synagogue: and they would gladly have extinguished the dangerous heresy in the blood of its adherents. But the decrees of Heaven had already disarmed their malice; and though they might sometimes exert the licentious privilege of sedition, they no longer possessed the administration of criminal justice; nor did they find it easy to infuse into the calm breast of a Roman magistrate the rancour of their own zeal and prejudice. The provincial governors declared themselves ready to listen to any accusation that might affect the public safety; but as soon as they were informed that it was a question not of facts but of words, a dispute relating only to the interpretation of the Jewish laws and prophecies, they deemed it unworthy of the majesty of Rome seriously to discuss the obscure differences which might arise among a barbarous and superstitious people. The innocence of the first Christians was protected by ignorance and contempt; and the tribunal of the Pagan magistrate often proved their most assured refuge against the fury of the synagogue. If, indeed, we were disposed to adopt the traditions of a too credulous antiquity, we might relate the distant peregrinations, the wonderful achievements, and the various deaths of the twelve apostles: but a more accurate inquiry will induce us to doubt whether any of those persons who had been witnesses to the miracles of Christ were permitted, beyond the limits of Palestine, to seal with their blood the truth of their testimony.[1] From the ordinary term of human life, it may very naturally be presumed that most of them were deceased before the discontent of the Jews broke out into that furious war which was terminated only by the ruin of Jerusalem. During a long period, from the death of Christ to that memorable rebellion, we cannot discover any traces of Roman intolerance, unless they are to be found in the sudden, the transient, but the cruel persecution, which was exercised by Nero against the Christians of the capital, thirty-five years after the former, and only two years before the latter, of those great events. The character of the philosophic historian, to whom we are principally indebted for the knowledge of this singular transaction, would alone be sufficient to recommend it to our most attentive consideration.

In the tenth year of the reign of Nero the capital of the empire was afflicted by a fire which raged beyond the memory or example of former ages. The monuments of Grecian art and of Roman virtue, the trophies of the Punic and Gallic wars, the most holy temples, and the most splendid palaces were involved in one common destruction. Of the fourteen regions or quarters into which Rome was divided, four only subsisted entire, three were levelled with the ground, and the remaining seven, which had experienced the fury of the flames, displayed a melancholy prospect of ruin and desolation. The vigilance of government appears not to have neglected any of the precautions which might alleviate the sense of so dreadful a calamity. The Imperial gardens were thrown open to the distressed multitude, temporary buildings were erected for their accommodation, and a plentiful supply of corn and provisions was distributed at a very moderate price. The most generous policy seemed to have dictated the edicts which regulated the disposition of the streets and the construction of private houses; and, as it usually happens in an age of prosperity, the conflagration of Rome, in the course of a few years, produced a new city, more regular and more beautiful than the former. But all the prudence and humanity affected by Nero on this occasion were insufficient to preserve him from the popular suspicion. Every crime might be imputed to the assassin of his

---

[1] In the time of Tertullian and Clemens of Alexandria the glory of martyrdom was confined to St. Peter, St. Paul, and St. James. It was gradually bestowed on the rest of the apostles by the more recent Greeks, who prudently selected for the theatre of their preaching and sufferings some remote country beyond the limits of the Roman empire.

wife and mother; nor could the prince who prostituted his person and dignity on the theatre be deemed incapable of the most extravagant folly. The voice of rumour accused the emperor as the incendiary of his own capital; and, as the most incredible stories are the best adapted to the genius of an enraged people, it was gravely reported, and firmly believed, that Nero, enjoying the calamity which he had occasioned, amused himself with singing to his lyre the destruction of ancient Troy. To divert a suspicion which the power of despotism was unable to suppress, the emperor resolved to substitute in his own place some fictitious criminals. "With this view (continues Tacitus) he inflicted the most exquisite tortures on those men who, under the vulgar appellation of Christians, were already branded with deserved infamy. They derived their name and origin from Christ, who, in the reign of Tiberius, had suffered death by the sentence of the procurator Pontius Pilate. For a while this dire superstition was checked, but it again burst forth; and not only spread itself over Judæa, the first seat of this mischievous sect, but was even introduced into Rome, the common asylum which receives and protects whatever is impure, whatever is atrocious. The confessions of those who were seized discovered a great multitude of their accomplices, and they were all convicted, not so much for the crime of setting fire to the city as for their hatred of human kind. They died in torments, and their torments were embittered by insult and derision. Some were nailed on crosses; others sewn up in the skins of wild beasts, and exposed to the fury of dogs; others again, smeared over with combustible materials, were used as torches to illuminate the darkness of the night. The gardens of Nero were destined for the melancholy spectacle, which was accompanied with a horse-race, and honoured with the presence of the emperor, who mingled with the populace in the dress and attitude of a charioteer. The guilt of the Christians deserved indeed the most exemplary punishment, but the public abhorrence was changed into commiseration, from the opinion that those unhappy wretches were sacrificed, not so much to the public welfare as to the cruelty of a jealous tyrant." Those who survey with a curious eye the revolutions of mankind may observe that the gardens and circus of Nero on the Vatican, which were polluted with the blood of the first Christians, have been rendered still more famous by the triumph and by the abuse of the persecuted religion. On the same spot a temple, which far surpasses the ancient glories of the Capitol, has been since erected by the Christian Pontiffs, who, deriving their claim of universal dominion from an humble fisherman of Galilee, have succeeded to the throne of the Cæsars, given laws to the barbarian conquerors of Rome, and extended their spiritual jurisdiction from the coast of the Baltic to the shores of the Pacific Ocean.

But it would be improper to dismiss this account of Nero's persecution till we have made some observations that may serve to remove the difficulties with which it is perplexed, and to throw some light on the subsequent history of the church.

1. The most sceptical criticism is obliged to respect the truth of this extraordinary fact, and the integrity of this celebrated passage of Tacitus. The former is confirmed by the diligent and accurate Suetonius, who mentions the punishment which Nero inflicted on the Christians, a sect of men who had embraced a new and criminal superstition. The latter may be proved by the consent of the most ancient manuscripts; by the inimitable character of the style of Tacitus; by his reputation, which guarded his text from the interpolations of pious fraud; and by the purport of his narration, which accused the first Christians of the most atrocious crimes, without insinuating that they possessed any miraculous or even magical powers above the rest of mankind. 2. Notwithstanding it is probable that Tacitus was born some years before the fire of Rome, he could derive only from reading and conversation the knowledge of an event which happened during his infancy. Before he gave himself to the public he calmly waited till his genius had attained its full maturity, and he was more than forty years of age when a grateful regard for the memory of the virtuous Agricola extorted from him the most early of those historical compositions which will delight and instruct the most distant posterity. After making a trial of his strength in the life of Agricola, and the description of Germany, he conceived, and at length executed, a more arduous work—the history of Rome, in thirty books, from the fall of Nero to the accession of Nerva. The administration of Nerva introduced an age of justice and prosperity, which Tacitus had destined for the occupation of his old age; but when he took a nearer view of his subject, judging, perhaps, that it was a more honourable or a less invidious office to record the vices of past tyrants than to celebrate the virtues of a reigning monarch, he chose rather to relate, under the form of annals, the actions of the four immediate successors of Augustus. To collect, to dispose, and to adorn a series of fourscore years in an immortal work, every sentence of which is pregnant with the deepest observations and the most lively images, was an undertaking sufficient to exercise the genius of Tacitus himself during the greatest part of his life. In the last years of the reign of Trajan, whilst the victorious monarch extended the power of Rome beyond its ancient limits, the historian was describing, in the second and fourth books of his Annals, the tyranny of Tiberius; and the emperor Hadrian must have succeeded to the throne before Tacitus, in the regular prosecution of his work, could relate the fire of the capital and the cruelty of Nero towards the unfortunate Christians. At the distance of sixty years it was the duty of the annalist to adopt the narratives of contemporaries; but it was natural for the philosopher to indulge himself in the description of the origin, the progress, and the character of the new sect, not so much according to the knowledge or prejudices of the age of

Nero, as according to those of the time of Hadrian. 3. Tacitus very frequently trusts to the curiosity or reflection of his readers to supply those intermediate circumstances and ideas which, in his extreme conciseness, he has thought proper to suppress. We may therefore presume to imagine some probable cause which could direct the cruelty of Nero against the Christians of Rome, whose obscurity, as well as innocence, should have shielded them from his indignation, and even from his notice. The Jews, who were numerous in the capital and oppressed in their own country, were a much fitter object for the suspicions of the emperor and of the people: nor did it seem unlikely that a vanquished nation, who already discovered their abhorrence of the Roman yoke, might have recourse to the most atrocious means of gratifying their implacable revenge. But the Jews possessed very powerful advocates in the palace, and even in the heart of the tyrant; his wife and mistress, the beautiful Poppæa, and a favourite player of the race of Abraham, who had already employed their intercession on behalf of the obnoxious people. In their room it was necessary to offer some other victims, and it might easily be suggested that, although the genuine followers of Moses were innocent of the fire of Rome, there had arisen among them a new and pernicious sect of GALILÆANS, which was capable of the most horrid crimes. Under the appellation of GALILÆANS two distinctions of men were confounded, the most opposite to each other in their manners and principles; the disciples who had embraced the faith of Jesus of Nazareth, and the zealots who had followed the standard of Judas the Gaulonite. The former were the friends, the latter were the enemies, of human kind; and the only resemblance between them consisted in the same inflexible constancy which, in the defence of their cause, rendered them insensible of death and tortures. The followers of Judas, who impelled their countrymen into rebellion, were soon buried under the ruins of Jerusalem; whilst those of Jesus, known by the more celebrated name of Christians, diffused themselves over the Roman empire. How natural was it for Tacitus, in the time of Hadrian, to appropriate to the Christians the guilt and the sufferings which he might, with far greater truth and justice, have attributed to a sect whose odious memory was almost extinguished! 4. Whatever opinion may be entertained of this conjecture (for it is no more than a conjecture), it is evident that the effect, as well as the cause, of Nero's persecution, were confined to the walls of Rome; that the religious tenets of the Galilæans, or Christians, were never made a subject of punishment, or even of inquiry; and that, as the idea of their sufferings was, for a long time, connected with the idea of cruelty and injustice, the moderation of succeeding princes inclined them to spare a sect oppressed by a tyrant whose rage had been usually directed against virtue and innocence.

It is somewhat remarkable that the flames of war consumed almost at the same time the Temple of Jerusalem and the Capitol of Rome;

and it appears no less singular that the tribute which devotion had destined to the former should have been converted by the power of an assaulting victor to restore and adorn the splendour of the latter. The emperors levied a general capitation tax on the Jewish people; and although the sum assessed on the head of each individual was inconsiderable, the use for which it was designed, and the severity with which it was exacted, were considered as an intolerable grievance. Since the officers of the revenue extended their unjust claim to many persons who were strangers to the blood or religion of the Jews, it was impossible that the Christians, who had so often sheltered themselves under the shade of the synagogue, should now escape this rapacious persecution. Anxious as they were to avoid the slightest infection of idolatry, their conscience forbade them to contribute to the honour of that dæmon who had assumed the character of the Capitoline Jupiter. As a very numerous though declining party among the Christians still adhered to the law of Moses, their efforts to dissemble their Jewish origin were detected by the decisive test of circumcision; nor were the Roman magistrates at leisure to inquire into the difference of their religious tenets. Among the Christians who were brought before the tribunal of the emperor, or, as it seems more probable, before that of the procurator of Judæa, two persons are said to have appeared, distinguished by their extraction, which was more truly noble than that of the greatest monarchs. These were the grandsons of St. Jude the apostle, who himself was the brother of Jesus Christ. Their natural pretensions to the throne of David might perhaps attract the respect of the people, and excite the jealousy of the governor; but the meanness of their garb and the simplicity of their answers soon convinced him that they were neither desirous nor capable of disturbing the peace of the Roman empire. They frankly confessed their royal origin, and their near relation to the Messiah; but they disclaimed any temporal views, and professed that his kingdom, which they devoutly expected, was purely of a spiritual and angelic nature. When they were examined concerning their fortune and occupation, they showed their hands hardened with daily labour, and declared that they derived their whole subsistence from the cultivation of a farm near the village of Cocaba, of the extent of about twenty-four English acres, and of the value of nine thousand drachms, or three hundred pounds sterling. The grandsons of St. Jude were dismissed with compassion and contempt.

But although the obscurity of the house of David might protect them from the suspicions of a tyrant, the present greatness of his own family alarmed the pusillanimous temper of Domitian, which could only be appeased by the blood of those Romans whom he either feared, or hated, or esteemed. Of the two sons of his uncle Flavius Sabinus, the elder was soon convicted of treasonable intentions, and the younger, who bore the name of Flavius Clemens, was indebted for his safety to his want of courage and ability. The emperor for a long time distinguished so harmless a kinsman by his favour and protection, bestowed on him his own niece Domitilla, adopted the children of that marriage to the hope of the succession, and invested their father with the honours of the consulship. But he had scarcely finished the term of his annual magistracy, when on a slight pretence he was condemned and executed; Domitilla was banished to a desolate island on the coast of Campania; and sentences either of death or of confiscation were pronounced against a great number of persons who were involved in the same accusation. The guilt imputed to their charge was that of *Atheism* and *Jewish manners*; a singular association of ideas, which cannot with any propriety be applied except to the Christians, as they were obscurely and imperfectly viewed by the magistrates and by the writers of that period. On the strength of so probable an interpretation, and too eagerly admitting the suspicions of a tyrant as an evidence of their honourable crime, the church has placed both Clemens and Domitilla among its first martyrs, and has branded the cruelty of Domitian with the name of the second persecution. But this persecution (if it deserves that epithet) was of no long duration. A few months after the death of Clemens and the banishment of Domitilla, Stephen, a freedman belonging to the latter, who had enjoyed the favour, but who had not surely embraced the faith, of his mistress, assassinated the emperor in his palace. The memory of Domitian was condemned by the senate; his acts were rescinded; his exiles recalled; and under the gentle administration of Nerva, while the innocent were restored to their rank and fortunes, even the most guilty either obtained pardon or escaped punishment.

II. About ten years afterwards, under the reign of Trajan, the younger Pliny was intrusted by his friend and master with the government of Bithynia and Pontus. He soon found himself at a loss to determine by what rule of justice or of law he should direct his conduct in the execution of an office the most repugnant to his humanity. Pliny had never assisted at any judicial proceedings against the Christians, with whose name alone he seems to be acquainted; and he was totally uninformed with regard to the nature of their guilt, the method of their conviction, and the degree of their punishment. In this perplexity he had recourse to his usual expedient, of submitting to the wisdom of Trajan an impartial, and, in some respects, a favourable account of the new superstition, requesting the emperor that he would condescend to resolve his doubts and to instruct his ignorance. The life of Pliny had been employed in the acquisition of learning, and in the business of the world. Since the age of nineteen he had pleaded with distinction in the tribunals of Rome, filled a place in the senate, had been invested with the honours of the consulship, and had formed very numerous connections with every order of men, both in Italy and in the provinces. From *his* ignorance therefore we may derive some useful information. We may assure ourselves that when he accepted the government of Bithynia there were no general laws or decrees of the senate in force against the Christians; that neither Trajan nor any of his virtuous predecessors, whose edicts were received into the civil and criminal jurisprudence, had publicly declared their intentions concerning the new sect; and that, whatever proceedings had been carried on against the Christians, there were none of sufficient weight and authority to establish a precedent for the conduct of a Roman magistrate.

The answer of Trajan, to which the Christians of the succeeding age have frequently appealed, discovers as much regard for justice and humanity as could be reconciled with his mistaken notions of religious policy. Instead of displaying the implacable zeal of an Inquisitor, anxious to discover the most minute particles of heresy, and exulting in the number of his victims, the emperor expresses much more solicitude to protect the security of the innocent than to prevent the escape of the guilty. He acknowledges the difficulty of fixing any general plan; but he lays down two salutary rules, which often afforded relief and support to the distressed Christians. Though he directs the magistrates to punish such persons as are legally convicted, he prohibits them, with a very humane inconsistency, from making any inquiries concerning the supposed criminals. Nor was the magistrate allowed to proceed on every kind of information. Anonymous charges the emperor rejects, as too repugnant to the equity of his government; and he strictly requires, for the conviction of those to whom the guilt of Christianity is imputed, the positive evidence of a fair and open accuser. It is likewise probable that the persons who assumed so invidious an office were obliged to declare the grounds of their suspicions, to specify (both in respect to time and place) the secret assemblies which their Christian adversary had frequented, and to disclose a great number of circumstances which were concealed with the most vigilant jealousy from the eye of the profane. If they succeeded in their prosecution, they were exposed to the resentment of a considerable and active party, to the censure of the more liberal portion of mankind, and to the ignominy which, in every age and country, has attended the character of an informer. If, on the contrary, they failed in their proofs, they incurred the severe and perhaps capital penalty, which, according to a law published by the emperor Hadrian, was inflicted on those who falsely attributed to their fellow-citizens the crime of Christianity. The violence of personal or superstitious animosity might sometimes prevail over the most natural apprehensions of disgrace and danger; but it cannot surely be imagined that accusations of so unpromising an appearance were either lightly or frequently undertaken by the Pagan subjects of the Roman empire.

The expedient which was employed to elude the prudence of the laws affords a sufficient proof how effectually they disappointed the mischievous designs of private malice or superstitious zeal. In a large and tumultuous assembly the restraints of fear and shame, so forcibly on the minds of individuals, are deprived of the greatest part of their influence. The pious Christian, as he was desirous to obtain, or to escape, the glory of martyrdom, expected, either with impatience or with terror, the stated returns of the public games and festivals. On those occasions the inhabitants of the great cities of the empire were collected in the circus or the theatre, where every circumstance of the place, as well as of the ceremony, contributed to kindle their devotion and to extinguish their humanity. Whilst the numerous spectators, crowned with garlands, perfumed with incense, purified with the blood of victims, and surrounded with the altars and statues of their tutelar deities, resigned themselves to the enjoyment of pleasures which they considered as an essential part of their religious worship, they recollected that the Christians alone abhorred the gods of mankind, and, by their absence and melancholy on these solemn festivals, seemed to insult or to lament the public felicity. If the empire had been afflicted by any recent calamity, by a plague, a famine, or an unsuccessful war; if the Tiber had, or if the Nile had not, risen beyond its banks; if the earth had shaken, or if the temperate order of the seasons had been interrupted, the superstitious Pagans were convinced that the crimes and the impiety of the Christians, who were spared by the excessive lenity of the government, had at length provoked the Divine justice. It was not among a licentious and exasperated populace that the forms of legal proceedings could be observed; it was not in an amphitheatre, stained with the blood of wild beasts and gladiators, that the voice of compassion could be heard. The impatient clamours of the multitude denounced the Christians as the enemies of gods and men, doomed them to the severest tortures, and, venturing to accuse by name some of the most distinguished of the new sectaries, required with irresistible vehemence that they should be instantly apprehended and cast to the lions. The provincial governors and magistrates who presided in the public spectacles were usually inclined to gratify the inclinations, and to appease the rage of the people, by the sacrifice of a few obnoxious victims. But the wisdom of the emperors protected the church from the danger of these tumultuous clamours and irregular accusations, which they justly censured as repugnant both to the firmness and to the equity of their administration. The edicts of Hadrian and of Antoninus Pius expressly declared that the voice of the multitude should never be admitted as legal evidence to convict or to punish those unfortunate persons who had embraced the enthusiasm of the Christians.

III. Punishment was not the inevitable consequence of conviction, and the Christians whose guilt was the most clearly proved by the testimony of witnesses, or even by their voluntary confession, still retained in their own power the alternative of life or death. It was not so much the past offence, as the actual resistance, which excited the indignation of the magistrate. He was persuaded that he offered them an easy pardon, since, if they consented to cast a few grains of incense upon the altar, they were dismissed from the tribunal in safety and with applause. It was esteemed the duty of a humane judge to endeavour to reclaim, rather than to punish, those deluded enthusiasts. Varying his tone according to the age, the sex, or the situation of the prisoners, he frequently condescended to set before their eyes every circumstance which could render life more pleasing, or death more terrible; and to solicit, nay to intreat them, that they would show some compassion to themselves, to their families, and to their friends. If threats and persuasions proved ineffectual, he had often recourse to violence; the scourge and the rack were called in to supply the deficiency of argument, and every art of cruelty was employed to subdue such inflexible, and, as it appeared to the Pagans, such criminal obstinacy. The ancient apologists of Christianity have censured, with equal truth and severity, the irregular conduct of their persecutors, who, contrary to every principle of judicial proceeding, admitted the use of torture, in order to obtain, not a confession, but a denial, of the crime which was the object of their inquiry. The monks of succeeding ages, who, in their peaceful solitudes, entertained themselves with diversifying the deaths and sufferings of the primitive martyrs, have frequently invented torments of a much more refined and ingenious nature. In particular, it has pleased them to suppose that the zeal of the Roman magistrates, disdaining every consideration of moral virtue or public decency, endeavoured to seduce those whom they were unable to vanquish, and that by their orders the most brutal violence was offered to those whom they found it impossible to seduce. It is related that pious females, who were prepared to despise death, were sometimes condemned to a more severe trial, and called upon to determine whether they set a higher value on their religion or on their chastity. The youths to whose licentious embraces they were abandoned received a solemn exhortation from the judge to exert their most strenuous efforts to maintain the honour of Venus against the impious virgin who refused to burn incense on her altars. Their violence, however, was commonly disappointed, and the seasonable interposition of some miraculous power preserved the chaste spouses of Christ from the dishonour even of an involuntary defeat. We should not indeed neglect to remark that the more ancient as well as authentic memorials of the church are seldom polluted with these extravagant and indecent fictions.[1]

The total disregard of truth and probability in the representation of these primitive martyrdoms was occasioned by a very natural mistake.

---

[1] Jerome, in his Legend of Paul the Hermit, tells a strange story of a young man who was chained naked on a bed of flowers, and assaulted by a beautiful and wanton courtezan. He quelled the rising temptation by biting off his tongue.

The ecclesiastical writers of the fourth or fifth centuries ascribed to the magistrates of Rome the same degree of implacable and unrelenting zeal which filled their own breasts against the heretics or the idolaters of their own times. It is not improbable that some of those persons who were raised to the dignities of the empire might have imbibed the prejudices of the populace, and that the cruel disposition of others might occasionally be stimulated by motives of avarice or of personal resentment.[1] But it is certain, and we may appeal to the grateful confessions of the first Christians, that the greatest part of those magistrates who exercised in the provinces the authority of the emperor or of the senate, and to whose hands alone the jurisdiction of life and death was intrusted, behaved like men of polished manners and liberal educations, who respected the rules of justice, and who were conversant with the precepts of philosophy. They frequently declined the odious task of persecution, dismissed the charge with contempt, or suggested to the accused Christian some legal evasion by which he might elude the severity of the laws. Whenever they were invested with a discretionary power, they used it much less for the oppression than for the relief and benefit of the afflicted church. They were far from condemning all the Christians who were accused before their tribunal, and very far from punishing with death all those who were convicted of an obstinate adherence to the new superstition. Contenting themselves, for the most part, with the milder chastisements of imprisonment, exile, or slavery in the mines, they left the unhappy victims of their justice some reason to hope that a prosperous event, the accession, the marriage, or the triumph of an emperor, might speedily restore them by a general pardon to their former state. The martyrs, devoted to immediate execution by the Roman magistrates, appear to have been selected from the most opposite extremes. They were either bishops and presbyters, the persons the most distinguished among the Christians by their rank and influence, and whose example might strike terror into the whole sect; or else they were the meanest and most abject among them, particularly those of the servile condition, whose lives were esteemed of little value, and whose sufferings were viewed by the ancients with too careless an indifference. The learned Origen, who, from his experience as well as reading, was intimately acquainted with the history of the Christians, declares, in the most express terms, that the number of martyrs was very inconsiderable. His authority would alone be sufficient to annihilate that formidable army of martyrs, whose relics, drawn for the most part from the catacombs of Rome, have replenished so many churches,[2]

---

[1] The conversion of his wife provoked Claudius Herminianus, governor of Cappadocia, to treat the Christians with uncommon severity.

[2] If we recollect that all the Plebeians of Rome were not Christians, and that all the Christians were not saints and martyrs, we may judge with how much safety religious honours can be ascribed to bones or urns indiscriminately taken from the

and whose marvellous achievements have been the subject of so many volumes of holy romance.[1] But the general assertion of Origen may be explained and confirmed by the particular testimony of his friend Dionysius, who, in the immense city of Alexandria, and under the rigorous persecution of Decius, reckons only ten men and seven women who suffered for the profession of the Christian name.

THE MARTYRDOM OF CYPRIAN

During the same period of persecution, the zealous, the eloquent, the ambitious Cyprian governed the church, not only of Carthage, but even of Africa. He possessed every quality which could engage the reverence of the faithful, or provoke the suspicions and resentment of the Pagan magistrates. His character as well as his station seemed to mark out that holy prelate as the most distinguished object of envy and of danger. The experience, however, of the life of Cyprian is sufficient to prove that our fancy has exaggerated the perilous situation of a Christian bishop; and that the dangers to which he was exposed were less imminent than those which temporal ambition is always prepared to encounter in the pursuit of honours. Four Roman emperors, with their families, their favourites, and their adherents, perished by the sword in the space of ten years, during which the bishop of Carthage guided by his authority and eloquence the councils of the African church. It was only in the third year of his administration that he had reason, during a few months, to apprehend the severe edicts of Decius, the vigilance of the magistrate, and the clamours of the multitude, who loudly demanded that Cyprian, the leader of the Christians, should be thrown to the lions. Prudence suggested the necessity of a temporary retreat, and the voice of prudence was obeyed. He withdrew himself into an obscure solitude, from whence he could maintain a constant correspondence with the clergy and people of Carthage; and, concealing himself till the tempest was past, he preserved his life, without relinquishing either his power or his reputation. His extreme caution did not however escape the censure of the more rigid Christians, who lamented, or the reproaches of his personal enemies, who insulted, a conduct which they

---

public burial-place. After ten centuries of a very free and open trade some suspicions have arisen among the more learned Catholics. They now require, as a proof of sanctity and martyrdom, the letters B. M., a vial full of red liquor supposed to be blood, or the figure of a palm-tree. But the two former signs are of little weight, and with regard to the last, it is observed by the critics—1. That the figure, as it is called, of a palm, is perhaps a cypress, and perhaps only a stop, the flourish of a comma used in the monumental inscriptions. 2. That the palm was the symbol of victory among the Pagans. 3. That among the Christians it served as the emblem, not only of martyrdom, but in general of a joyful resurrection.

[1] As a specimen of these legends, we may be satisfied with 10,000 Christian soldiers crucified in one day, either by Trajan or Hadrian, on Mount Ararat. The abbreviation of Mil., which may signify either *soldiers* or *thousands*, is said to have occasioned some extraordinary mistakes.

considered as a pusillanimous and criminal desertion of the most sacred duty. The propriety of reserving himself for the future exigencies of the church, the example of several holy bishops, and the divine admonitions which, as he declares himself, he frequently received in visions and ecstasies, were the reasons alleged in his justification. But his best apology may be found in the cheerful resolution with which, about eight years afterwards, he suffered death in the cause of religion. The authentic history of his martyrdom has been recorded with unusual candour and impartiality. A short abstract therefore of its most important circumstances will convey the clearest information of the spirit and of the forms of the Roman persecutions.

When Valerian was consul for the third, and Gallienus for the fourth time, Paternus, proconsul of Africa, summoned Cyprian to appear in his private council-chamber. He there acquainted him with the imperial mandate which he had just received, that those who had abandoned the Roman religion should immediately return to the practice of the ceremonies of their ancestors. Cyprian replied without hesitation that he was a Christian and a bishop, devoted to the worship of the true and only Deity, to whom he offered up his daily supplications for the safety and prosperity of the two emperors, his lawful sovereigns. With modest confidence he pleaded the privilege of a citizen in refusing to give any answer to some invidious and indeed illegal questions which the proconsul had proposed. A sentence of banishment was pronounced as the penalty of Cyprian's disobedience; and he was conducted without delay to Curubis, a free and maritime city of Zeugitana, in a pleasant situation, a fertile territory, and at the distance of about forty miles from Carthage. The exiled bishop enjoyed the conveniences of life and the consciousness of virtue. His reputation was diffused over Africa and Italy; an account of his behaviour was published for the edification of the Christian world; and his solitude was frequently interrupted by the letters, the visits, and the congratulations of the faithful. On the arrival of a new proconsul in the province the fortune of Cyprian appeared for some time to wear a still more favourable aspect. He was recalled from banishment, and, though not yet permitted to return to Carthage, his own gardens in the neighbourhood of the capital were assigned for the place of his residence.

At length, exactly one year after Cyprian was first apprehended, Galerius Maximus, proconsul of Africa, received the imperial warrant for the execution of the Christian teachers. The bishop of Carthage was sensible that he should be singled out for one of the first victims, and the frailty of nature tempted him to withdraw himself, by a secret flight, from the danger and the honour of martyrdom; but, soon recovering that fortitude which his character required, he returned to his gardens, and patiently expected the ministers of death. Two officers of rank, who were intrusted with that commission, placed Cyprian between them in a chariot, and, as the proconsul was not then at leisure, they conducted him, not to a prison, but to a private house in Carthage, which belonged to one of them. An elegant supper was provided for the entertainment of the bishop, and his Christian friends were permitted for the last time to enjoy his society, whilst the streets were filled with a multitude of the faithful, anxious and alarmed at the approaching fate of their spiritual father. In the morning he appeared before the tribunal of the proconsul, who, after informing himself of the name and situation of Cyprian, commanded him to offer sacrifice, and pressed him to reflect on the consequences of his disobedience. The refusal of Cyprian was firm and decisive, and the magistrate, when he had taken the opinion of his council, pronounced, with some reluctance, the sentence of death. It was conceived in the following terms: "That Thascius Cyprianus should be immediately beheaded, as the enemy of the gods of Rome, and as the chief and ringleader of a criminal association, which he had seduced into an impious resistance against the laws of the most holy emperors Valerian and Gallienus." The manner of his execution was the mildest and least painful that could be inflicted on a person convicted of any capital offence: nor was the use of torture admitted to obtain from the bishop of Carthage either the recantation of his principles or the discovery of his accomplices.

As soon as the sentence was proclaimed, a general cry of "We will die with him" arose at once among the listening multitude of Christians who waited before the palace gates. The generous effusions of their zeal and affection were neither serviceable to Cyprian nor dangerous to themselves. He was led away under a guard of tribunes and centurions, without resistance and without insult, to the place of his execution, a spacious and level plain near the city, which was already filled with great numbers of spectators. His faithful presbyters and deacons were permitted to accompany their holy bishop. They assisted him in laying aside his upper garment, spread linen on the ground to catch the precious relics of his blood, and received his orders to bestow five-and-twenty pieces of gold on the executioner. The martyr then covered his face with his hands, and at one blow his head was separated from his body. His corpse remained during some hours exposed to the curiosity of the Gentiles, but in the night it was removed, and transported, in a triumphal procession and with a splendid illumination, to the burial-place of the Christians. The funeral of Cyprian was publicly celebrated without receiving any interruption from the Roman magistrates; and those among the faithful who had performed the last offices to his person and his memory were secure from the danger of inquiry or of punishment. It is remarkable that, of so great a multitude of bishops in the province of Africa, Cyprian was the first who was esteemed worthy to obtain the crown of martyrdom.

It was in the choice of Cyprian either to die a martyr or to live an apostate, but on that choice depended the alternative of honour or infamy. Could we suppose that the bishop of Carthage had employed the profession of the Christian faith only as the instrument of his avarice or ambition, it was still incumbent on him to support the character which he had assumed, and, if he possessed the smallest degree of manly fortitude, rather to expose himself to the most cruel tortures than by a single act to exchange the reputation of a whole life for the abhorrence of his Christian brethren and the contempt of the Gentile world. But if the zeal of Cyprian was supported by the sincere conviction of the truth of those doctrines which he preached, the crown of martyrdom must have appeared to him as an object of desire rather than of terror. It is not easy to extract any distinct ideas from the vague though eloquent declamations of the Fathers, or to ascertain the degree of immortal glory and happiness which they confidently promised to those who were so fortunate as to shed their blood in the cause of religion. They inculcated with becoming diligence that the fire of martyrdom supplied every defect and expiated every sin; that, while the souls of ordinary Christians were obliged to pass through a slow and painful purification, the triumphant sufferers entered into the immediate fruition of eternal bliss, where, in the society of the patriarchs, the apostles, and the prophets, they reigned with Christ, and acted as his assessors in the universal judgment of mankind. The assurance of a lasting reputation upon earth, a motive so congenial to the vanity of human nature, often served to animate the courage of the martyrs. The honours which Rome or Athens bestowed on those citizens who had fallen in the cause of their country were cold and unmeaning demonstrations of respect, when compared with the ardent gratitude and devotion which the primitive church expressed towards the victorious champions of the faith. The annual commemoration of their virtues and sufferings was observed as a sacred ceremony, and at length terminated in religious worship. Among the Christians who had publicly confessed their religious principles, those who (as it very frequently happened) had been dismissed from the tribunal or the prisons of the Pagan magistrates obtained such honours as were justly due to their imperfect martyrdom and their generous resolution. The most pious females courted the permission of imprinting kisses on the fetters which they had worn, and on the wounds which they had received. Their persons were esteemed holy, their decisions were admitted with deference, and they too often abused, by their spiritual pride and licentious manners, the pre-eminence which their zeal and intrepidity had acquired.[1] Distinctions like these, whilst they display the exalted merit, betray the inconsiderable number, of those who suffered and of those who died for the profession of Christianity.

[1] The number of pretended martyrs has been very much multiplied by the custom which was introduced of bestowing that honourable name on confessors.

The sober discretion of the present age will more readily censure than admire, but can more easily admire than imitate, the fervour of the first Christians, who, according to the lively expression of Sulpicius Severus, desired martyrdom with more eagerness than his own contemporaries solicited a bishopric. The epistles which Ignatius composed as he was carried in chains through the cities of Asia breathe sentiments the most repugnant to the ordinary feelings of human nature. He earnestly beseeches the Romans that, when he should be exposed in the amphitheatre, they would not, by their kind but unseasonable intercession, deprive him of the crown of glory; and he declares his resolution to provoke and irritate the wild beasts which might be employed as the instruments of his death. Some stories are related of the courage of martyrs who actually performed what Ignatius had intended, who exasperated the fury of the lions, pressed the executioner to hasten his office, cheerfully leaped into the fires which were kindled to consume them, and discovered a sensation of joy and pleasure in the midst of the most exquisite tortures. Several examples have been preserved of a zeal impatient of those restraints which the emperors had provided for the security of the church. The Christians sometimes supplied by their voluntary declaration the want of an accuser, rudely disturbed the public service of paganism, and, rushing in crowds round the tribunal of the magistrates, called upon them to pronounce and to inflict the sentence of the law. The behaviour of the Christians was too remarkable to escape the notice of the ancient philosophers, but they seem to have considered it with much less admiration than astonishment. Incapable of conceiving the motives which sometimes transported the fortitude of believers beyond the bounds of prudence or reason, they treated such an eagerness to die as the strange result of obstinate despair, of stupid insensibility, or of superstitious frenzy. "Unhappy men!" exclaimed the proconsul Antoninus to the Christians of Asia, "unhappy men! if you are thus weary of your lives, is it so difficult for you to find ropes and precipices?" He was extremely cautious (as it is observed by a learned and pious historian) of punishing men who had found no accusers but themselves, the imperial laws not having made any provision for so unexpected a case; condemning therefore a few as a warning to their brethren, he dismissed the multitude with indignation and contempt. Notwithstanding this real or affected disdain, the intrepid constancy of the faithful was productive of more salutary effects on those minds which nature or grace had disposed for the easy reception of religious truth. On these melancholy occasions there were many among the Gentiles who pitied, who admired, and who were converted. The generous enthusiasm was communicated from the sufferer to the spectators, and the blood of martyrs, according to a well-known observation, became the seed of the church.

VARYING POLICIES OF PERSECUTION

But although devotion had raised, and eloquence continued to inflame, this fever of the mind, it insensibly gave way to the more natural hopes and fears of the human heart, to the love of life, the apprehension of pain, and the horror of dissolution. The more prudent rulers of the church found themselves obliged to restrain the indiscreet ardour of their followers, and to distrust a constancy which too often abandoned them in the hour of trial. As the lives of the faithful became less mortified and austere, they were every day less ambitious of the honours of martyrdom; and the soldiers of Christ, instead of distinguishing themselves by voluntary deeds of heroism, frequently deserted their post, and fled in confusion before the enemy whom it was their duty to resist. There were three methods, however, of escaping the flames of persecution, which were not attended with an equal degree of guilt: the first indeed was generally allowed to be innocent; the second was of a doubtful, or at least of a venial, nature; but the third implied a direct and criminal apostacy from the Christian faith.

I. A modern Inquisitor would hear with surprise, that, whenever an information was given to a Roman magistrate of any person within his jurisdiction who had embraced the sect of the Christians, the charge was communicated to the party accused, and that a convenient time was allowed him to settle his domestic concerns, and to prepare an answer to the crime which was imputed to him. If he entertained any doubt of his own constancy, such a delay afforded him the opportunity of preserving his life and honour by flight, of withdrawing himself into some obscure retirement or some distant province, and of patiently expecting the return of peace and security. A measure so consonant to reason was soon authorised by the advice and example of the most holy prelates; and seems to have been censured by few, except by the Montanists, who deviated into heresy by their strict and obstinate adherence to the rigour of ancient discipline.[1] II. The provincial governors, whose zeal was less prevalent than their avarice, had countenanced the practice of selling certificates (or libels as they were called), which attested that the persons therein mentioned had complied with the laws, and sacrificed to the Roman deities. By producing these false declarations, the opulent and timid Christians were enabled to silence the malice of an informer, and to reconcile in some measure their safety with their religion. A slight penance atoned for this profane dissimulation. III. In every persecution there were great numbers of unworthy Christians who publicly disowned or renounced the faith which they

---

[1] Tertullian considers flight from persecution as an imperfect, but very criminal, apostasy, as an impious attempt to elude the will of God, &c. &c. He has written a treatise on this subject, which is filled with the wildest fanaticism and the most incoherent declamation. It is, however, somewhat remarkable that Tertullian did not suffer martyrdom himself.

had professed; and who confirmed the sincerity of their abjuration by the legal acts of burning incense or of offering sacrifices. Some of these apostates had yielded on the first menace of exhortation of the magistrate; whilst the patience of others had been subdued by the length and repetition of tortures. The affrighted countenances of some betrayed their inward remorse, while others advanced with confidence and alacrity to the altars of the gods. But the disguise which fear had imposed subsisted no longer than the present danger. As soon as the severity of the persecution was abated, the doors of the churches were assailed by the returning multitude of penitents, who detested their idolatrous submission, and who solicited with equal ardour, but with various success, their readmission into the society of Christians.

IV. Notwithstanding the general rules established for the conviction and punishment of the Christians, the fate of those sectaries, in an extensive and arbitrary government, must still, in a great measure, have depended on their own behaviour, the circumstances of the times, and the temper of their supreme as well as subordinate rulers. Zeal might sometimes provoke, and prudence might sometimes avert or assuage, the superstitious fury of the Pagans. A variety of motives might dispose the provincial governors either to enforce or to relax the execution of the laws; and of these motives the most forcible was their regard not only for the public edicts, but for the secret intentions of the emperor, a glance from whose eye was sufficient to kindle or to extinguish the flames of persecution. As often as any occasional severities were exercised in the different parts of the empire, the primitive Christians lamented and perhaps magnified their own sufferings; but the celebrated number of *ten* persecutions has been determined by the ecclesiastical writers of the fifth century, who possessed a more distinct view of the prosperous or adverse fortunes of the church from the age of Nero to that of Diocletian. The ingenious parallels of the *ten* plagues of Egypt, and of the *ten* horns of the Apocalypse, first suggested this calculation to their minds; and in their application of the faith of prophecy to the truth of history they were careful to select those reigns which were indeed the most hostile to the Christian cause. But these transient persecutions served only to revive the zeal and to restore the discipline of the faithful; and the moments of extraordinary rigour were compensated by much longer intervals of peace and security. The indifference of some princes and the indulgence of others permitted the Christians to enjoy, though not perhaps a legal, yet an actual and public toleration of their religion.

The Apology of Tertullian contains two very ancient, very singular, but at the same time very suspicious instances of Imperial clemency; the edicts published by Tiberius and by Marcus Antoninus, and designed not only to protect the innocence of the Christians, but even to proclaim those stupendous miracles which had attested the truth of their doctrine. The first of these examples is attended with some difficulties which might perplex a sceptical mind. We are required to believe *that* Pontius Pilate informed the emperor of the unjust sentence of death which he had pronounced against an innocent, and, as it appeared, a divine person; and that, without acquiring the merit, he exposed himself to the danger, of martyrdom; *that* Tiberius, who avowed his contempt for all religion, immediately conceived the design of placing the Jewish Messiah among the gods of Rome; *that* his servile senate ventured to disobey the commands of their master; *that* Tiberius, instead of resenting their refusal, contented himself with protecting the Christians from the severity of the laws, many years before such laws were enacted or before the church had assumed any distinct name or existence; and lastly, *that* the memory of this extraordinary transaction was preserved in the most public and authentic records, which escaped the knowledge of the historians of Greece and Rome, and were only visible to the eyes of an African Christian, who composed his Apology one hundred and sixty years after the death of Tiberius. The edict of Marcus Antoninus is supposed to have been the effect of his devotion and gratitude for the miraculous deliverance which he had obtained in the Marcomannic war. The distress of the legions, the seasonable tempest of rain and hail, of thunder and of lightning, and the dismay and defeat of the barbarians, have been celebrated by the eloquence of several Pagan writers. If there were any Christians in that army, it was natural that they should ascribe some merit to the fervent prayers which, in the moment of danger, they had offered up for their own and the public safety. But we are still assured by monuments of brass and marble, by the Imperial medals, and by the Antonine column, that neither the prince nor the people entertained any sense of this signal obligation, since they unanimously attribute their deliverance to the providence of Jupiter, and to the interposition of Mercury. During the whole course of his reign Marcus despised the Christians as a philosopher, and punished them as a sovereign.

By a singular fatality, the hardships which they had endured under the government of a virtuous prince immediately ceased on the accession of a tyrant; and as none except themselves had experienced the injustice of Marcus, so they alone were protected by the lenity of Commodus. The celebrated Marcia, the most favoured of his concubines, and who at length contrived the murder of her Imperial lover, entertained a singular affection for the oppressed church; and though it was impossible that she could reconcile the practice of vice with the precepts of the Gospel, she might hope to atone for the frailties of her sex and profession by declaring herself the patroness of the Christians. Under the gracious protection of Marcia they passed in safety the thirteen years of a cruel tyranny; and when the empire was established in the house of Severus, they formed a domestic but more honourable connection with the new court. The emperor was persuaded that, in a dangerous sickness, he had derived some benefit, either spiritual or physical, from the holy oil with which one of his slaves had anointed him. He always treated with peculiar distinction several persons of both sexes who had embraced the new religion. The nurse as well as the preceptor of Caracalla were Christians; and if that young prince ever betrayed a sentiment of humanity, it was occasioned by an incident which, however trifling, bore some relation to the cause of Christianity. Under the reign of Severus the fury of the populace was checked; the rigour of ancient laws was for some time suspended; and the provincial governors were satisfied with receiving an annual present from the churches within their jurisdiction, as the price, or as the reward, of their moderation. The controversy concerning the precise time of the celebration of Easter armed the bishops of Asia and Italy against each other, and was considered as the most important business of this period of leisure and tranquillity. Nor was the peace of the church interrupted till the increasing numbers of proselytes seem at length to have attracted the attention, and to have alienated the mind, of Severus. With the design of restraining the progress of Christianity, he published an edict, which, though it was designed to affect only the new converts, could not be carried into strict execution without exposing to danger and punishment the most zealous of their teachers and missionaries. In this mitigated persecution we may still discover the indulgent spirit of Rome and of Polytheism, which so readily admitted every excuse in favour of those who practised the religious ceremonies of their fathers.

But the laws which Severus had enacted soon expired with the authority of that emperor; and the Christians, after this accidental tempest, enjoyed a calm of thirty-eight years. Till this period they had usually held their assemblies in private houses and sequestered places. They were now permitted to erect and consecrate convenient edifices for the purpose of religious worship; to purchase lands, even at Rome itself, for the use of the community; and to conduct the elections of their ecclesiastical ministers in so public, but at the same time in so exemplary a manner, as to deserve the respectful attention of the Gentiles. This long repose of the church was accompanied with dignity. The reigns of those princes who derived their extraction from the Asiatic provinces proved the most favourable to the Christians; the eminent persons of the sect, instead of being reduced to implore the protection of a slave or concubine, were admitted into the palace in the honourable characters of priests and philosophers; and their mysterious doctrines, which were already diffused among the people, insensibly attracted the curiosity of their sovereign. When the empress Mamæa passed through Antioch, she expressed a desire of conversing with the celebrated Origen, the fame of whose piety and learning was spread over the East. Origen obeyed so flattering an invitation, and, though he could not expect to succeed in the conversion of an artful and ambitious woman, she listened with pleasure to his eloquent exhortations, and honourably dismissed him to his retirement in Palestine. The sentiments of Mamæa were adopted by her son Alexander, and the philosophic devotion of that emperor was marked by a singular but injudicious regard for the Christian religion. In his domestic chapel he placed the statues of Abraham, of Orpheus, of Apollonius, and of Christ, as an honour justly due to those respectable sages who had instructed mankind in the various modes of addressing their homage to the supreme and universal Deity. A purer faith, as well as worship, was openly professed and practised among his household. Bishops, perhaps for the first time, were seen at court; and, after the death of Alexander, when the inhuman Maximin discharged his fury on the favourites and servants of his unfortunate benefactor, a great number of Christians, of every rank, and of both sexes, were involved in the promiscuous massacre, which, on their account, has improperly received the name of Persecution.

Notwithstanding the cruel disposition of Maximin, the effects of his resentment against the Christians were of a very local and temporary nature, and the pious Origen, who had been proscribed as a devoted victim, was still reserved to convey the truths of the Gospel to the ear of monarchs. He addressed several edifying letters to the emperor Philip, to his wife, and to his mother; and as soon as that prince, who was born in the neighbourhood of Palestine, had usurped the Imperial sceptre, the Christians acquired a friend and a protector. The public and even partial favour of Philip towards the sectaries of the new religion, and his constant reverence for the ministers of the church, gave some colour to the suspicion, which prevailed in his own times, that the emperor himself was become a convert to the faith; and afforded some grounds for a fable which was afterwards invented, that he had been purified by confession and penance from the guilt contracted by the murder of his innocent predecessor. The fall of Philip introduced, with the change of masters, a new system of government, so oppressive to the Christians, that their former condition, ever since the time of Domitian, was represented as a state of perfect freedom and security, if compared with the rigorous treatment which they experienced under the short reign of Decius. The virtues of that prince will scarcely allow us to suspect that he was actuated by a mean resentment against the favourites of his predecessor; and it is more reasonable to believe that, in the prosecution of his general design to restore the purity of Roman manners, he was desirous of delivering the empire from what he condemned as a recent and criminal superstition. The bishops of the most considerable cities were removed by exile or death: the vigilance of the magistrates prevented the clergy of Rome during sixteen months from proceeding to a new election; and it was the opinion of the Christians that the emperor would more patiently endure a competitor for the purple than a bishop in the capital. Were it possible to suppose that the penetration of Decius had discovered pride under the disguise of humility, or that he could foresee the temporal dominion which might insensibly arise from the claims of spiritual authority, we might be less suprised that he should consider the successors of St. Peter as the most formidable rivals to those of Augustus.

The administration of Valerian was distinguished by a levity and inconstancy ill suited to the gravity of the *Roman Censor*. In the first part of his reign he surpassed in clemency those princes who had been suspected of an attachment to the Christian faith. In the last three years and a half, listening to the insinuations of a minister addicted to the susperstitions of Egypt, he adopted the maxims, and imitated the severity, of his predecessor Decius. The accession of Gallienus, which increased the calamities of the empire, restored peace to the church; and the Christians obtained the free exercise of their religion by an edict addressed to the bishops, and conceived in such terms as seemed to acknowledge their office and public character. The ancient laws, without being formally repealed, were suffered to sink into oblivion; and (excepting only some hostile intentions which are attributed to the emperor Aurelian) the disciples of Christ passed above forty years in a state of prosperity, far more dangerous to their virtue than the severest trials of persecution.

The story of Paul of Samosata, who filled the metropolitan see of Antioch whilst the East was in the hands of Odenathus and Zenobia, may serve to illustrate the condition and character of the times. The wealth of that prelate was a sufficient evidence of his guilt, since it was neither derived from the inheritance of his fathers, nor acquired by the arts of honest industry. But Paul considered the service of the church as a very lucrative profession. His ecclesiastical jurisdiction was venal and rapacious; he extorted frequent contributions from the most opulent of the faithful, and converted to his own use a considerable part of the public revenue. By his pride and luxury the Christian religion was rendered odious in the eyes of the Gentiles. His council chamber and his throne, the splendour with which he appeared in public, the suppliant crowd who solicited his attention, the multitude of letters and petitions to which he dictated his answers, and the perpetual hurry of business in which he was involved, were circumstances much better suited to the state of a civil magistrate [1] than to the humility of a primitive bishop. When he harangued his people from the pulpit, Paul affected the figurative style and the theatrical gestures of an Asiatic sophist, while the

---

[1] Simony was not unknown in those times; and the clergy sometimes bought what they intended to sell. It appears that the bishopric of Carthage was purchased by a wealthy matron, named Lucilla, for her servant Majorinus. The price was 400 *Folles*. Every *Follis* contained 125 pieces of silver, and the whole sum may be computed at about 2400*l*.

cathedral resounded with the loudest and most extravagant acclamations in the praise of his divine eloquence. Against those who resisted his power, or refused to flatter his vanity, the prelate of Antioch was arrogant, rigid, and inexorable; but he relaxed the discipline, and lavished the treasures of the church on his dependent clergy, who were permitted to imitate their master in the gratification of every sensual appetite. For Paul indulged himself very freely in the pleasures of the table, and he had received into the episcopal palace two young and beautiful women, as the constant companions of his leisure moments.[1]

Notwithstanding these scandalous vices, if Paul of Samosata had preserved the purity of the orthodox faith, his reign over the capital of Syria would have ended only with his life; and had a seasonable persecution intervened, an effort of courage might perhaps have placed him in the rank of saints and martyrs. Some nice and subtle errors, which he imprudently adopted and obstinately maintained, concerning the doctrine of the Trinity, excited the zeal and indignation of the Eastern churches. From Egypt to the Euxine Sea, the bishops were in arms and in motion. Several councils were held, confutations were published, excommunications were pronounced, ambiguous explanations were by turns accepted and refused, treaties were concluded and violated, and at length Paul of Samosata was degraded from his episcopal character by the sentence of seventy or eighty bishops who assembled for that purpose at Antioch, and who, without consulting the rights of the clergy or people, appointed a successor by their own authority. The manifest irregularity of this proceeding increased the numbers of the discontented faction; and as Paul, who was no stranger to the arts of courts, had insinuated himself into the favour of Zenobia, he maintained above four years the possession of the episcopal house and office. The victory of Aurelian changed the face of the East, and the two contending parties, who applied to each other the epithets of schism and heresy, were either commanded or permitted to plead their cause before the tribunal of the conqueror. This public and very singular trial affords a convincing proof that the existence, the property, the privileges, and the internal policy of the Christians, were acknowledged, if not by the laws, at least by the magistrates of the empire. As a Pagan and as a soldier, it could scarcely be expected that Aurelian should enter into the discussion, whether the sentiments of Paul or those of his adversaries were most agreeable to the true standard of the orthodox faith. His determination, however, was founded on the general principles of equity and reason. He considered the bishops of Italy as the most impartial and respectable judges among the Christians, and, as soon as he was informed that they had unanimously approved the sentence of the council, he acquiesced in ʰheir

---

[1] If we are desirous of extenuating the vices of Paul, we must suspect the assembled bishops of the East of publishing the most malicious calumnies in circular epistles addressed to all the churches of the empire.

opinion, and immediately gave orders that Paul should be compelled to relinquish the temporal possessions belonging to an office, of which, in the judgment of his brethren, he had been regularly deprived. But whilst we applaud the justice, we should not overlook the policy of Aurelian, who was desirous of restoring and cementing the dependence of the provinces on the capital, by every means which could bind the interest or prejudices of any part of his subjects.

THE CHURCH UNDER DIOCLETIAN AND HIS SUCCESSORS

Amidst the frequent revolutions of the empire the Christians still flourished in peace and prosperity; and notwithstanding a celebrated era of martyrs has been deduced from the accession of Diocletian, the new system of policy, introduced and maintained by the wisdom of that prince, continued, during more than eighteen years, to breathe the mildest and most liberal spirit of religious toleration. The mind of Diocletian himself was less adapted indeed to speculative inquiries than to the active labours of war and government. His prudence rendered him averse to any great innovation, and, though his temper was not very susceptible of zeal or enthusiasm, he always maintained an habitual regard for the ancient deities of the empire. But the leisure of the two empresses, of his wife Prisca, and of Valeria his daughter, permitted them to listen with more attention and respect to the truths of Christianity, which in every age has acknowledged its important obligations to female devotion. The principal eunuchs, Lucian and Dorotheus, Gorgonius and Andrew, who attended the person, possessed the favour, and governed the household of Diocletian, protected by their powerful influence the faith which they had embraced. Their example was imitated by many of the most considerable officers of the palace, who, in their respective stations, had the care of the Imperial ornaments, of the robes, of the furniture, of the jewels, and even of the private treasury; and, though it might sometimes be incumbent on them to accompany the emperor when he sacrificed in the temple, they enjoyed, with their wives, their children, and their slaves, the free exercise of the Christian religion. Diocletian and his colleagues frequently conferred the most important offices on those persons who avowed their abhorrence for the worship of the gods, but who had displayed abilities proper for the service of the state. The bishops held an honourable rank in their respective provinces and were treated with distinction and respect, not only by the people, but by the magistrates themselves. Almost in every city the ancient churches were found insufficient to contain the increasing multitude of proselytes; and in their place more stately and capacious edifices were erected for the public worship of the faithful. The corruption of manners and principles, so forcibly lamented by Eusebius, may be considered, not only as a consequence, but as a proof, of the liberty which the Christians enjoyed and abused under the reign of Diocletian. Prosperity had relaxed the nerves of discipline. Fraud, envy, and malice prevailed in every congregation. The presbyters aspired to the episcopal office, which every day became an object more worthy of their ambition. The bishops, who contended with each other for ecclesiastical pre-eminence, appeared by their conduct to claim a secular and tyrannical power in the church; and the lively faith which still distinguished the Christians from the Gentiles was shown much less in their lives than in their controversial writings.

Notwithstanding this seeming security, an attentive observer might discern some symptoms that threatened the church with a more violent persecution than any which she had yet endured. The zeal and rapid progress of the Christians awakened the Polytheists from their supine indifference in the cause of those deities whom custom and education had taught them to revere. The mutual provocations of a religious war, which had already continued above two hundred years, exasperated the animosity of the contending parties. The Pagans were incensed at the rashness of a recent and obscure sect, which presumed to accuse their countrymen of error, and to devote their ancestors to eternal misery. The habits of justifying the popular mythology against the invectives of an implacable enemy, produced in their minds some sentiments of faith and reverence for a system which they had been accustomed to consider with the most careless levity. The supernatural powers assumed by the church inspired at the same time terror and emulation. The followers of the established religion intrenched themselves behind a similar fortification of prodigies; invented new modes of sacrifice, of expiation, and of initiation;[1] attempted to revive the credit of their expiring oracles; and listened with eager credulity to every impostor who flattered their prejudices by a tale of wonders. Both parties seemed to acknowledge the truth of those miracles which were claimed by their adversaries; and while they were contented with ascribing them to the arts of magic, and to the power of dæmons, they mutually concurred in restoring and establishing the reign of superstition.[2] Philosophy, her most dangerous enemy, was now converted into her most useful ally. The groves of the Academy, the gardens of Epicurus, and even the portico of the Stoics, were almost deserted, as so many different schools of scepticism or impiety; and many among the Romans were desirous that the writings of Cicero should be condemned and suppressed by the authority of the senate. The prevailing sect of the new Platonicians judged it prudent to

[1] We might quote, among a great number of instances, the mysterious worship of Mithras and the Taurobolia; the latter of which became fashionable in the time of the Antonines. The romance of Apuleius is as full of devotion as of satire.

[2] It is seriously to be lamented that the Christian fathers, by acknowledging the supernatural, or, as they deem it, the infernal part of Paganism, destroy with their own hands the great advantage which we might otherwise derive from the liberal concessions of our adversaries.

connect themselves with the priests, whom perhaps they despised, against the Christians, whom they had reason to fear. These fashionable philosophers prosecuted the design of extracting allegorical wisdom from the fictions of the Greek poets; instituted mysterious rites of devotion for the use of their chosen disciples; recommended the worship of the ancient gods as the emblems or ministers of the Supreme Deity, and composed against the faith of the Gospel many elaborate treatises, which have since been committed to the flames by the prudence of orthodox emperors.

Although the policy of Diocletian and the humanity of Constantius inclined them to preserve inviolate the maxims of toleration, it was soon discovered that their two associates, Maximian and Galerius, entertained the most implacable aversion for the name and religion of the Christians. The minds of those princes had never been enlightened by science; education had never softened their temper. They owed their greatness to their swords, and in their most elevated fortune they still retained their superstitious prejudices of soldiers and peasants. In the general administration of the provinces they obeyed the laws which their benefactor had established; but they frequently found occasions of exercising within their camp and palaces a secret persecution, for which the imprudent zeal of the Christians sometimes offered the most specious pretences. A sentence of death was executed upon Maximilianus, an African youth, who had been produced by his own father before the magistrate as a sufficient and legal recruit, but who obstinately persisted in declaring that his conscience would not permit him to embrace the profession of a soldier. It could scarcely be expected that any government should suffer the action of Marcellus the centurion to pass with impunity. On the day of a public festival, that officer threw away his belt, his arms, and the ensigns of his office, and exclaimed with a loud voice that he would obey none but Jesus Christ the eternal King, and that he renounced for ever the use of carnal weapons, and the service of an idolatrous master. The soldiers, as soon as they recovered from their astonishment, secured the person of Marcellus. He was examined in the city of Tingi by the president of that part of Mauritania; and as he was convicted by his own confession, he was condemned and beheaded for the crime of desertion. Examples of such a nature savour much less of religious persecution than of martial or even civil law: but they served to alienate the mind of the emperors, to justify the severity of Galerius, who dismissed a great number of Christian officers from their employments; and to authorise the opinion that a sect of enthusiasts, which avowed principles so repugnant to the public safety, must either remain useless, or would soon become dangerous subjects of the empire.

After the success of the Persian war had raised the hopes and the reputation of Galerius, he passed a winter with Diocletian in the palace of Nicomedia; and the fate of Christianity became the object of their secret consultations. The experienced emperor was still inclined to pursue measures of lenity; and though he readily consented to exclude the Christians from holding any employments in the household or the army, he urged in the strongest terms the danger as well as cruelty of shedding the blood of those deluded fanatics. Galerius at length extorted from him the permission of summoning a council, composed of a few persons the most distinguished in the civil and military departments of the state. The important question was agitated in their presence, and those ambitious courtiers easily discerned that it was incumbent on them to second, by their eloquence, the importunate violence of the Cæsar. It may be presumed that they insisted on every topic which might interest the pride, the piety, or the fears, of their sovereign in the destruction of Christianity. Perhaps they represented that the glorious work of the deliverance of the empire was left imperfect, as long as an independent people was permitted to subsist and multiply in the heart of the provinces. The Christians (it might speciously be alleged), renouncing the gods and the institutions of Rome, had constituted a distinct republic, which might yet be suppressed before it had acquired any military force; but which was already governed by its own laws and magistrates, was possessed of a public treasure, and was intimately connected in all its parts by the frequent assemblies of the bishops, to whose decrees their numerous and opulent congregations yielded an implicit obedience. Arguments like these may seem to have determined the reluctant mind of Diocletian to embrace a new system of persecution: but though we may suspect, it is not in our power to relate, the secret intrigues of the palace, the private views and resentments, the jealousy of women or eunuchs, and all those trifling but decisive causes which so often influence the fate of empires and the councils of the wisest monarchs.

The pleasure of the emperors was at length signified to the Christians, who, during the course of this melancholy winter, had expected, with anxiety, the result of so many secret consultations. The twenty-third of February, which coincided with the Roman festival of the Terminalia, was appointed (whether from accident or design) to set bounds to the progress of Christianity. At the earliest dawn of day the Prætorian prefect, accompanied by several generals, tribunes, and officers of the revenue, repaired to the principal church of Nicomedia, which was situated on an eminence in the most populous and beautiful part of the city. The doors were instantly broke open; they rushed into the sanctuary; and as they searched in vain for some visible object of worship, they were obliged to content themselves with committing to the flames the volumes of Holy Scripture. The ministers of Diocletian were followed by a numerous body of guards and pioneers, who marched in order of battle, and were provided with all the instruments used in the destruction of fortified cities. By their incessant labour, a sacred edifice, which towered above the Imperial palace, and had long excited the indignation and envy of the Gentiles, was in a few hours levelled with the ground.

The next day the general edict of persecution was published; and though Diocletian, still averse to the effusion of blood, had moderated the fury of Galerius, who proposed that every one refusing to offer sacrifice should immediately be burnt alive, the penalties inflicted on the obstinacy of the Christians might be deemed sufficiently rigorous and effectual. It was enacted that their churches, in all the provinces of the empire, should be demolished to their foundations; and the punishment of death was denounced against all who should presume to hold any secret assemblies for the purpose of religious worship. The philosophers, who now assumed the unworthy office of directing the blind zeal of persecution, had diligently studied the nature and genius of the Christian religion; and as they were not ignorant that the speculative doctrines of the faith were supposed to be contained in the writings of the prophets, of the evangelists, and of the apostles, they most probably suggested the order that the bishops and presbyters should deliver all their sacred books into the hands of the magistrates; who were commanded, under the severest penalties, to burn them in a public and solemn manner. By the same edict, the property of the church was at once confiscated; and the several parts of which it might consist were either sold to the highest bidder, united to the Imperial domain, bestowed on the cities and corporations, or granted to the solicitations of rapacious courtiers. After taking such effectual measures to abolish the worship and to dissolve the government of the Christians, it was thought necessary to subject to the most intolerable hardships the condition of those perverse individuals who should still reject the religion of nature, of Rome, and of their ancestors. Persons of a liberal birth were declared incapable of holding any honours or employments; slaves were for ever deprived of the hopes of freedom; and the whole body of the people were put out of the protection of the law. The judges were authorised to hear and to determine every action that was brought against a Christian. But the Christians were not permitted to complain of any injury which they themselves had suffered; and thus those unfortunate sectaries were exposed to the severity, while they were excluded from the benefits, of public justice. This new species of martyrdom, so painful and lingering, so obscure and ignominious, was, perhaps, the most proper to weary the constancy of the faithful: nor can it be doubted that the passions and interest of mankind were disposed on this occasion to second the designs of the emperors. But the policy of a well-ordered government must sometimes have interposed in behalf of the oppressed Christians; nor was it possible for the Roman princes entirely to remove the apprehension of punishment, or to connive at every act of fraud and violence, without exposing their own authority and the rest of their subjects to the most alarming dangers.

This edict was scarcely exhibited to the public view, in the most conspicuous place of Nicomedia, before it was torn down by the hands of a Christian, who expressed at the same time, by the bitterest invectives, his contempt as well as abhorrence for such impious and tyrannical governors. His offence, according to the mildest laws, amounted to treason, and deserved death. And if it be true that he was a person of rank and education, those circumstances could serve only to aggravate his guilt. He was burnt, or rather roasted, by a slow fire; and his executioners, zealous to revenge the personal insult which had been offered to the emperors, exhausted every refinement of cruelty, without being able to subdue his patience, or to alter the steady and insulting smile which, in his dying agonies, he still preserved in his countenance. The Christians, though they confessed that his conduct had not been strictly conformable to the laws of prudence, admired the divine fervour of his zeal; and the excessive commendations which they lavished on the memory of their hero and martyr contributed to fix a deep impression of terror and hatred in the mind of Diocletian.

His fears were soon alarmed by the view of a danger from which he very narrowly escaped. Within fifteen days the palace of Nicomedia, and even the bedchamber of Diocletian, were twice in flames; and though both times they were extinguished without any material damage, the singular repetition of the fire was justly considered as an evident proof that it had not been the effect of chance or negligence. The suspicion naturally fell on the Christians; and it was suggested, with some degree of probability, that those desperate fanatics, provoked by their present sufferings, and apprehensive of impending calamities, had entered into a conspiracy with their faithful brethren, the eunuchs of the palace, against the lives of two emperors whom they detested as the irreconcilable enemies of the church of God. Jealousy and resentment prevailed in every breast, but especially in that of Diocletian. A great number of persons, distinguished either by the offices which they had filled, or by the favour which they had enjoyed, were thrown into prison. Every mode of torture was put in practice, and the court, as well as city, was polluted with many bloody executions. But as it was found impossible to extort any discovery of this mysterious transaction, it seems incumbent on us either to presume the innocence, or to admire the resolution, of the sufferers. A few days afterwards Galerius hastily withdrew himself from Nicomedia, declaring that, if he delayed his departure from that devoted palace, he should fall a sacrifice to the rage of the Christians. The ecclesiastical historians, from whom alone we derive a partial and imperfect knowledge of this persecution, are at a loss how to account for the fears and danger of the emperors. Two of these writers, a prince and a rhetorician, were eye-witnesses of the fire of Nicomedia. The one ascribes it to lightning and the divine wrath, the other affirms that it was kindled by the malice of Galerius himself.

As the edict against the Christians was designed for a general law of the whole empire, and as Diocletian and Galerius, though they might not wait for the consent, were assured of the concurrence, of the Western princes, it would appear more consonant to our ideas of policy that the governors of all the provinces should have received secret instructions to publish, on one and the same day, this declaration of war within their respective departments. It was at least to be expected that the convenience of the public highways and established posts would have enabled the emperors to transmit their orders with the utmost despatch from the palace of Nicomedia to the extremities of the Roman world; and that they would not have suffered fifty days to elapse before the edict was published in Syria, and near four months before it was signified to the cities of Africa. This delay may perhaps be imputed to the cautious temper of Diocletian, who had yielded a reluctant consent to the measures of persecution, and who was desirous of trying the experiment under his more immediate eye before he gave way to the disorders and discontent which it must inevitably occasion in the distant provinces. At first, indeed, the magistrates were restrained from the effusion of blood; but the use of every other severity was permitted, and even recommended to their zeal; nor could the Christians, though they cheerfully resigned the ornaments of their churches, resolve to interrupt their religious assemblies, or to deliver their sacred books to the flames. The pious obstinacy of Felix, an African bishop, appears to have embarrassed the subordinate ministers of the government. The curator of his city sent him in chains to the proconsul. The proconsul transmitted him to the Prætorian prefect of Italy; and Felix, who disdained even to give an evasive answer, was at length beheaded at Venusia, in Lucania, a place on which the birth of Horace has conferred fame. This precedent, and perhaps some Imperial rescript, which was issued in consequence of it, appeared to authorise the governors of provinces in punishing with death the refusal of the Christians to deliver up their sacred books. There were undoubtedly many persons who embraced this opportunity of obtaining the crown of martyrdom; but there were likewise too many who purchased an ignominious life by discovering and betraying the Holy Scripture into the hands of infidels. A great number even of bishops and presbyters acquired, by this criminal compliance, the opprobrious epithet of *Traditors*; and their offence was productive of much present scandal and of much future discord in the African church.

The copies as well as the versions of Scripture were already so multiplied in the empire, that the most severe inquisition could no longer be attended with any fatal consequences; and even the sacrifice of those volumes which, in every congregation, were preserved for public use, required the consent of some treacherous and unworthy Christians. But the ruin of the churches was easily effected by the authority of the government and by the labour of the Pagans. In some provinces, however, the magistrates contented themselves with shutting up the places of religious worship. In others they more literally complied with the terms of the edict; and, after taking away the doors, the benches, and the pulpit, which they burnt as it were in a funeral pile, they completely demolished the remainder of the edifice. It is perhaps to this melancholy occasion that we should apply a very remarkable story, which is related with so many circumstances of variety and improbability that it serves rather to excite than to satisfy our curiosity. In a small town in Phrygia, of whose name as well as situation we are left ignorant, it should seem that the magistrates and the body of the people had embraced the Christian faith; and as some resistance might be apprehended to the execution of the edict, the governor of the province was supported by a numerous detachment of legionaries. On their approach the citizens threw themselves into the church, with the resolution either of defending by arms that sacred edifice or of perishing in its ruins. They indignantly rejected the notice and permission which was given them to retire, till the soldiers, provoked by their obstinate refusal, set fire to the building on all sides, and consumed, by this extraordinary kind of martyrdom, a great number of Phrygians, with their wives and children.

Some slight disturbances, though they were suppressed almost as soon as excited, in Syria and the frontiers of Armenia, afforded the enemies of the church a very plausible occasion to insinuate that those troubles had been secretly fomented by the intrigues of the bishops, who had already forgotten their ostentatious professions of passive and unlimited obedience. The resentment, or the fears, of Diocletian at length transported him beyond the bounds of moderation which he had hitherto preserved, and he declared, in a series of cruel edicts, his intention of abolishing the Christian name. By the first of these edicts the governors of the provinces were directed to apprehend all persons of the ecclesiastical order; and the prisons destined for the vilest criminals were soon filled with a multitude of bishops, presbyters, deacons, readers, and exorcists. By a second edict the magistrates were commanded to employ every method of severity which might reclaim them from their odious superstition, and oblige them to return to the established worship of the gods. This rigorous order was extended, by a subsequent edict, to the whole body of Christians, who were exposed to a violent and general persecution. Instead of those salutary restraints which had required the direct and solemn testimony of an accuser, it became the duty as well as the interest of the Imperial officers to discover, to pursue, and to torment the most obnoxious among the faithful. Heavy penalties were denounced against all who should presume to save a proscribed sectary from the just indignation of the gods and of the emperors. Yet, notwithstanding the severity of this law, the virtuous courage of many of the Pagans, in concealing their friends or relations, affords an honourable proof that the rage of superstition had not extinguished in their minds the sentiments of nature and humanity.

Diocletian had no sooner published his edicts against the Christians, than, as if he had been desirous of committing to other hands the work of persecution, he divested himself of the Imperial purple. The character and situation of his colleagues and successors sometimes urged them to enforce, and sometimes inclined them to suspend, the execution of these rigorous laws; nor can we acquire a just and distinct idea of this important period of ecclesiastical history unless we separately consider the state of Christianity, in the different parts of the empire, during the space of ten years which elapsed between the first edicts of Diocletian and the final peace of the church.

The mild and humane temper of Constantius was averse to the oppression of any part of his subjects. The principal offices of his palace were exercised by Christians. He loved their persons, esteemed their fidelity, and entertained not any dislike to their religious principles. But as long as Constantius remained in the subordinate station of Cæsar, it was not in his power openly to reject the edicts of Diocletian, or to disobey the commands of Maximian. His authority contributed, however, to alleviate the sufferings which he pitied and abhorred. He consented with reluctance to the ruin of the churches, but he ventured to protect the Christians themselves from the fury of the populace and from the rigour of the laws. The provinces of Gaul (under which we may probably include those of Britain) were indebted for the singular tranquillity which they enjoyed to the gentle interposition of their sovereign. But Datianus, the president or governor of Spain, actuated either by zeal or policy, chose rather to execute the public edicts of the emperors than to understand the secret intentions of Constantius; and it can scarcely be doubted that his provincial administration was stained with the blood of a few martyrs. The elevation of Constantius to the supreme and independent dignity of Augustus gave a free scope to the exercise of his virtues, and the shortness of his reign did not prevent him from establishing a system of toleration of which he left the precept and the example to his son Constantine. His fortunate son, from the first moment of his accession declaring himself the protector of the church, at length deserved the appellation of the first emperor who publicly professed and established the Christian religion. The motives of his conversion, as they may variously be deduced from benevolence, from policy, from conviction, or from remorse, and the progress of the revolution, which, under his powerful influence and that of his sons, rendered Christianity the reigning religion of the Roman empire, will form a very interesting and important chapter in the third volume of this history. At present it may be sufficient to observe that every victory of Constantine was productive of some relief or benefit to the church.

The provinces of Italy and Africa experienced a short but violent persecution. The rigorous edicts of Diocletian were strictly and cheerfully executed by his associate Maximian, who had long hated the Christians, and who delighted in acts of blood and violence. In the autumn of the first year of the persecution the two emperors met at Rome to celebrate their triumph; several oppressive laws appear to have issued from their secret consultations, and the diligence of the magistrates was animated by the presence of their sovereigns. After Diocletian had divested himself of the purple, Italy and Africa were administered under the name of Severus, and were exposed, without defence, to the implacable resentment of his master Galerius. Among the martyrs of Rome, Adauctus deserves the notice of posterity. He was of a noble family in Italy, and had raised himself, through the successive honours of the palace, to the important office of treasurer of the private demesnes. Adauctus is the more remarkable for being the only person of rank and distinction who appears to have suffered death during the whole course of this general persecution.

The revolt of Maxentius immediately restored peace to the churches of Italy and Africa, and the same tyrant who oppressed every other class of his subjects showed himself just, humane, and even partial, towards the afflicted Christians. He depended on their gratitude and affection, and very naturally presumed that the injuries which they had suffered, and the dangers which they still apprehended, from his most inveterate enemy, would secure the fidelity of a party already considerable by their numbers and opulence. Even the conduct of Maxentius towards the bishops of Rome and Carthage may be considered as the proof of his toleration, since it is probable that the most orthodox princes would adopt the same measures with regard to their established clergy. Marcellus, the former of those prelates, had thrown the capital into confusion by the severe penance which he imposed on a great number of Christians who, during the late persecution, had renounced or dissembled their religion. The rage of faction broke out in frequent and violent seditions; the blood of the faithful was shed by each other's hands; and the exile of Marcellus, whose prudence seems to have been less eminent than his zeal, was found to be the only measure capable of restoring peace to the distracted church of Rome. The behaviour of Mensurius, bishop of Carthage, appears to have been still more reprehensible. A deacon of that city had published a libel against the emperor. The offender took refuge in the episcopal palace, and, though it was somewhat early to advance any claims of ecclesiastical immunities, the bishop refused to deliver him up to the officers of justice. For this treasonable resistance Mensurius was summoned to court, and, instead of receiving a legal sentence of death or banishment, he was permitted, after a short examination, to return to his diocese. Such was the happy condition of the Christian subjects of Maxentius, that, whenever they were desirous of procuring for their own use any bodies of martyrs, they were obliged to purchase them from the most distant provinces of the East. A story is related of Aglae, a Roman lady, descended from a consular family, and possessed of so ample an estate that it required the management of seventy-three stewards. Among these Boniface was the favourite of his mistress, and, as Aglae mixed love with devotion, it is reported that he was admitted to share her bed. Her fortune enabled her to gratify the pious desire of obtaining some sacred relics from the East. She intrusted Boniface with a considerable sum of gold and a large quantity of aromatics, and her lover, attended by twelve horsemen and three covered chariots, undertook a remote pilgrimage as far as Tarsus in Cilicia.

GALERIUS'S EDICT OF TOLERATION

The sanguinary temper of Galerius, the first and principal author of the persecution, was formidable to those Christians whom their misfortunes had placed within the limits of his dominions; and it may fairly be presumed that many persons of a middle rank, who were not confined by the chains either of wealth or of poverty, very frequently deserted their native country, and sought a refuge in the milder climate of the West. As long as he commanded only the armies and provinces of Illyricum, he could with difficulty either find or make a considerable number of martyrs in a warlike country which had entertained the missionaries of the Gospel with more coldness and reluctance than any other part of the empire. But when Galerius had obtained the supreme power and the government of the East, he indulged in their fullest extent his zeal and cruelty, not only in the provinces of Thrace and Asia, which acknowledged his immediate jurisdiction, but in those of Syria, Palestine, and Egypt, where Maximin gratified his own inclination by yielding a rigorous obedience to the stern commands of his benefactor. The frequent disappointments of his ambitious views, the experience of six years of persecution, and the salutary reflections which a lingering and painful distemper suggested to the mind of Galerius, at length convinced him that the most violent efforts of despotism are insufficient to extirpate a whole people, or to subdue their religious prejudices. Desirous of repairing the mischief that he had occasioned, he published in his own name, and in those of Licinius and Constantine, a general edict, which, after a pompous recital of the Imperial titles, proceeded in the following manner:

"Among the important cares which have occupied our mind for the utility and preservation of the empire, it was our intention to correct and re-establish all things according to the ancient laws and public discipline of the Romans. We were particularly desirous of reclaiming into the way of reason and nature the deluded Christians who had renounced the religion and ceremonies instituted by their fathers, and,

presumptuously despising the practice of antiquity, had invented extravagant laws and opinions according to the dictates of their fancy, and
had collected a various society from the different provinces of our
empire. The edicts which we have published to enforce the worship of
the gods having exposed many of the Christians to danger and distress,
many having suffered death, and many more, who still persist in their
impious folly, being left destitute of *any* public exercise of religion, we
are disposed to extend to those unhappy men the effects of our wonted
clemency. We permit them, therefore, freely to profess their private
opinions, and to assemble in their conventicles without fear or molestation, provided always that they preserve a due respect to the established
laws and government. By another rescript we shall signify our intentions
to the judges and magistrates, and we hope that our indulgence will
engage the Christians to offer up their prayers to the Deity whom they
adore for our safety and prosperity, for their own, and for that of the
republic." It is not usually in the language of edicts and manifestos that
we should search for the real character or the secret motives of princes;
but as these were the words of a dying emperor, his situation, perhaps,
may be admitted as a pledge of his sincerity.

When Galerius subscribed this edict of toleration, he was well assured
that Licinius would readily comply with the inclinations of his friend
and benefactor, and that any measures in favour of the Christians would
obtain the approbation of Constantine. But the emperor would not venture to insert in the preamble the name of Maximin, whose consent was
of the greatest importance, and who succeeded a few days afterwards to
the provinces of Asia. In the first six months, however, of his new reign,
Maximin affected to adopt the prudent counsels of his predecessor; and
though he never condescended to secure the tranquillity of the church
by a public edict, Sabinus, his Prætorian prefect, addressed a circular
letter to all the governors and magistrates of the provinces, expatiating
on the Imperial clemency, acknowledging the invincible obstinacy of the
Christians, and directing the officers of justice to cease their ineffectual
prosecutions, and to connive at the secret assemblies of those enthusiasts. In consequence of these orders, great numbers of Christians were
released from prison, or delivered from the mines. The confessors, singing hymns of triumph, returned into their own countries; and those who
had yielded to the violence of the tempest, solicited with tears of repentance their re-admission into the bosom of the church.

But this treacherous calm was of short duration; nor could the
Christians of the East place any confidence in the character of their
sovereign. Cruelty and superstition were the ruling passions of the soul
of Maximin. The former suggested the means, the latter pointed out the
objects, of persecution. The emperor was devoted to the worship of the
gods, to the study of magic, and to the belief of oracles. The prophets or
philosophers, whom he revered as the favourites of Heaven, were fre-

quently raised to the government of provinces, and admitted into his most secret councils. They easily convinced him that the Christians had been indebted for their victories to their regular discipline, and that the weakness of polytheism had principally flowed from a want of union and subordination among the ministers of religion. A system of government was therefore instituted, which was evidently copied from the policy of the church. In all the great cities of the empire, the temples were repaired and beautified by the order of Maximin, and the officiating priests of the various deities were subjected to the authority of a superior pontiff destined to oppose the bishop, and to promote the cause of paganism. These pontiffs acknowledged, in their turn, the supreme jurisdiction of the metropolitans or high priests of the province, who acted as the immediate vicegerents of the emperor himself. A white robe was the ensign of their dignity; and these new prelates were carefully selected from the most noble and opulent families. By the influence of the magistrates, and of the sacerdotal order, a great number of dutiful addresses were obtained, particularly from the cities of Nicomedia, Antioch, and Tyre, which artfully represented the well-known intentions of the court as the general sense of the people; solicited the emperor to consult the laws of justice rather than the dictates of his clemency; expressed their abhorrence of the Christians, and humbly prayed that those impious sectaries might at least be excluded from the limits of their respective territories. The answer of Maximin to the address which he obtained from the citizens of Tyre is still extant. He praises their zeal and devotion in terms of the highest satisfaction, descants on the obstinate impiety of the Christians, and betrays, by the readiness with which he consents to their banishment, that he considered himself as receiving, rather than as conferring, an obligation. The priests as well as the magistrates were empowered to enforce the execution of his edicts, which were engraved on tables of brass; and though it was recommended to them to avoid the effusion of blood, the most cruel and ignominious punishments were inflicted on the refractory Christians.

The Asiatic Christians had everything to dread from the severity of a bigoted monarch who prepared his measures of violence with such deliberate policy. But a few months had scarcely elapsed before the edicts published by the two Western emperors obliged Maximin to suspend the prosecution of his designs; the civil war which he so rashly undertook against Licinius employed all his attention; and the defeat and death of Maximin soon delivered the church from the last and most implacable of her enemies.

In this general view of the persecution which was first authorised by the edicts of Diocletian, I have purposely refrained from describing the particular sufferings and deaths of the Christian martyrs. It would have been an easy task, from the history of Eusebius, from the declamations of Lactantius, and from the most ancient acts, to collect a long series of

horrid and disgustful pictures, and to fill many pages with racks and
scourges, with iron hooks and red-hot beds, and with all the variety of
tortures which fire and steel, savage beasts, and more savage executioners,
could inflict on the human body. These melancholy scenes might be
enlivened by a crowd of visions and miracles destined either to delay the
death, to celebrate the triumph, or to discover the relics of those canonised saints who suffered for the name of Christ. But I cannot determine
what I ought to transcribe, till I am satisfied how much I ought to
believe. The gravest of the ecclesiastical historians, Eusebius himself,
indirectly confesses that he has related whatever might redound to the
glory, and that he has suppressed all that could tend to the disgrace, of
religion. Such an acknowledgment will naturally excite a suspicion that
a writer who has so openly violated one of the fundamental laws of
history has not paid a very strict regard to the observance of the other;
and the suspicion will derive additional credit from the character of
Eusebius, which was less tinctured with credulity, and more practised in
the arts of courts, than that of almost any of his contemporaries. On
some particular occasions, when the magistrates were exasperated by
some personal motives of interest or resentment, when the zeal of the
martyrs urged them to forget the rules of prudence, and perhaps of
decency, to overturn the altars, to pour out imprecations against the
emperors, or to strike the judge as he sat on his tribunal, it may be presumed that every mode of torture which cruelty could invent, or constancy could endure, was exhausted on those devoted victims. Two
circumstances, however, have been unwarily mentioned, which insinuate
that the general treatment of the Christians who had been apprehended
by the officers of justice was less intolerable than it is usually imagined
to have been. 1. The confessors who were condemned to work in the
mines were permitted by the humanity or the negligence of their keepers
to build chapels, and freely to profess their religion in the midst of those
dreary habitations. 2. The bishops were obliged to check and to censure
the forward zeal of the Christians, who voluntarily threw themselves
into the hands of the magistrates. Some of these were persons oppressed
by poverty and debts, who blindly sought to terminate a miserable
existence by a glorious death. Others were allured by the hope that a
short confinement would expiate the sins of a whole life; and others
again were actuated by the less honourable motive of deriving a plentiful
subsistence, and perhaps a considerable profit, from the alms which the
charity of the faithful bestowed on the prisoners. After the church had
triumphed over all her enemies, the interest as well as vanity of the
captives prompted them to magnify the merit of their respective suffering. A convenient distance of time or place gave an ample scope to the
progress of fiction; and the frequent instances which might be alleged
of holy martyrs whose wounds had been instantly healed, whose strength
had been renewed, and whose lost members had miraculously been

restored, were extremely convenient for the purpose of removing every difficulty, and of silencing every objection. The most extravagant legends, as they conduced to the honour of the church, were applauded by the credulous multitude, countenanced by the power of the clergy, and attested by the suspicious evidence of ecclesiastical history.

The vague descriptions of exile and imprisonment, of pain and torture, are so easily exaggerated or softened by the pencil of an artful orator, that we are naturally induced to inquire into a fact of a more distinct and stubborn kind; the number of persons who suffered death in consequence of the edicts published by Diocletian, his associates, and his successors. The recent legendaries record whole armies and cities which were at once swept away by the undistinguishing rage of persecution. The more ancient writers content themselves with pouring out a liberal effusion of loose and tragical invectives, without condescending to ascertain the precise number of those persons who were permitted to seal with their blood their belief of the Gospel. From the history of Eusebius it may however be collected that only nine bishops were punished with death; and we are assured, by his particular enumeration of the martyrs of Palestine, that no more than ninety-two Christians were entitled to that honourable appellation.[1] As we are unacquainted with the degree of episcopal zeal and courage which prevailed at that time, it is not in our power to draw any useful inferences from the former of these facts: but the latter may serve to justify a very important and probable conclusion. According to the distribution of Roman provinces, Palestine may be considered as the sixteenth part of the Eastern empire: and since there were some governors who, from a real or affected clemency, had preserved their hands unstained with the blood of the faithful, it is reasonable to believe that the country which had given birth to Christianity produced at least the sixteenth part of the martyrs who suffered death within the dominions of Galerius and Maximin; the whole might consequently amount to about fifteen hundred, a number which, if it is

---

[1] He closes his narration by assuring us that these were the martyrdoms inflicted in Palestine during the *whole* course of the persecution. The 9th chapter of his viiith book, which relates to the province of Thebais in Egypt, may seem to contradict our moderate computation; but it will only lead us to admire the artful management of the historian. Choosing for the scene of the most exquisite cruelty the most remote and sequestered country of the Roman empire, he relates that in Thebais from ten to one hundred persons had frequently suffered martyrdom in the same day. But when he proceeds to mention his own journey into Egypt, his language insensibly becomes more cautious and moderate. Instead of a large but definite number, he speaks of many Christians, and most artfully selects two ambiguous words which may signify either what he had seen or what he had heard; either the expectation or the execution of the punishment. Having thus provided a secure evasion, he commits the equivocal passage to his readers and translators; justly conceiving that their piety would induce them to prefer the most favourable sense. There was perhaps some malice in the remark of Theodorus Metochita, that all who, like Eusebius, had been conversant with the Egyptians, delighted in an obscure and intricate style.

equally divided between the ten years of the persecution, will allow an annual consumption of one hundred and fifty martyrs. Allotting the same proportion to the provinces of Italy, Africa, and perhaps Spain, where, at the end of two or three years, the rigour of the penal laws was either suspended or abolished, the multitude of Christians in the Roman empire, on whom a capital punishment was inflicted by a judicial sentence, will be reduced to somewhat less than two thousand persons. Since it cannot be doubted that the Christians were more numerous, and their enemies more exasperated, in the time of Diocletian than they had ever been in any former persecution, this probable and moderate computation may teach us to estimate the number of primitive saints and martyrs who sacrificed their lives for the important purpose of introducing Christianity into the world.

We shall conclude this chapter by a melancholy truth which obtrudes itself on the reluctant mind; that, even admitting, without hesitation or inquiry, all that history has recorded, or devotion has feigned, on the subject of martyrdoms, it must still be acknowledged that the Christians, in the course of their intestine dissensions, have inflicted far greater severities on each other than they had experienced from the zeal of infidels. During the ages of ignorance which followed the subversion of the Roman empire in the West, the bishops of the Imperial city extended their dominion over the laity as well as clergy of the Latin church. The fabric of superstition which they had erected, and which might long have defied the feeble efforts of reason, was at length assaulted by a crowd of daring fanatics, who, from the twelfth to the sixteenth century, assumed the popular character of reformers. The church of Rome defended by violence the empire which she had acquired by fraud; a system of peace and benevolence was soon disgraced by proscriptions, wars, massacres, and the institution of the holy office. And as the reformers were animated by the love of civil as well as of religious freedom, the Catholic princes connected their own interest with that of the clergy, and enforced by fire and the sword the terrors of spiritual censures. In the Netherlands alone more than one hundred thousand of the subjects of Charles V. are said to have suffered by the hand of the executioner; and this extraordinary number is attested by Grotius, a man of genius and learning, who preserved his moderation amidst the fury of contending sects, and who composed the annals of his own age and country at a time when the invention of printing had facilitated the means of intelligence and increased the danger of detection. If we are obliged to submit our belief to the authority of Grotius, it must be allowed that the number of Protestants who were executed in a single province and a single reign far exceeded that of the primitive martyrs in the space of three centuries and of the Roman empire. But if the improbability of the fact itself should prevail over the weight of evidence; if Grotius should be convicted of exaggerating the merit and sufferings of the reformers; we shall be naturally led to inquire what confidence can be placed in the doubtful and imperfect monuments of ancient credulity; what degree of credit can be assigned to a courtly bishop and a passionate declaimer, who, under the protection of Constantine, enjoyed the exclusive privilege of recording the persecutions inflicted on the Christians by the vanquished rivals or disregarded predecessors of their gracious sovereign.

THE MOVEMENT TOWARDS
THE EAST

Chapter 17

THE NEW ROME. THE FOUNDATION AND DEDICATION OF CONSTANTINOPLE. DIVISIONS OF OFFICE IN THE NEW ORDER OF GOVERNMENT. BEGINNINGS OF THE POLICE STATE

THE unfortunate Licinius was the last rival who opposed the greatness, and the last captive who adorned the triumph of Constantine. After a tranquil and prosperous reign the conqueror bequeathed to his family the inheritance of the Roman empire; a new capital, a new policy, and a new religion; and the innovations which he established have been embraced and consecrated by succeeding generations. The age of the great Constantine and his sons is filled with important events; but the historian must be oppressed by their number and variety, unless he diligently separates from each other the scenes which are connected only by the order of time. He will describe the political institutions that gave strength and stability to the empire before he proceeds to relate the wars and revolutions which hastened its decline. He will adopt the division unknown to the ancients of civil and ecclesiastical affairs: the victory of the Christians, and their intestine discord, will supply copious and distinct materials both for edification and for scandal.

After the defeat and abdication of Licinius his victorious rival proceeded to lay the foundations of a city destined to reign in future times the mistress of the East, and to survive the empire and religion of Constantine. The motives, whether of pride or of policy, which first induced Diocletian to withdraw himself from the ancient seat of government, had acquired additional weight by the example of his successors and the habits of forty years. Rome was insensibly confounded with the dependent kingdoms which had once acknowledged her supremacy; and the country of the Cæsars was viewed with cold indifference by a martial prince, born in the neighbourhood of the Danube, educated in the courts and armies of Asia, and invested with the purple by the legions of Britain. The Italians, who had received Constantine as their deliverer, submissively obeyed the edicts which he sometimes condescended to address to the senate and people of Rome; but they were seldom honoured with the presence of their new sovereign. During the vigour of his age Constantine, according to the various exigencies of peace and

240

war, moved with slow dignity or with active diligence along the frontiers of his extensive dominions; and was always prepared to take the field either against a foreign or a domestic enemy. But as he gradually reached the summit of prosperity and the decline of life, he began to meditate the design of fixing in a more permanent station the strength as well as majesty of the throne. In the choice of an advantageous situation he preferred the confines of Europe and Asia; to curb with a powerful arm the barbarians who dwelt between the Danube and the Tanais; to watch with an eye of jealousy the conduct of the Persian monarch, who indignantly supported the yoke of an ignominious treaty. With these views Diocletian had selected and embellished the residence of Nicomedia: but the memory of Diocletian was justly abhorred by the protector of the church; and Constantine was not insensible to the ambition of founding a city which might perpetuate the glory of his own name. During the late operations of the war against Licinius he had sufficient opportunity to contemplate, both as a soldier and as a statesman, the incomparable position of Byzantium; and to observe how strongly it was guarded by nature against an hostile attack, whilst it was accessible on every side to the benefits of commercial intercourse. Many ages before Constantine, one of the most judicious historians of antiquity had described the advantages of a situation from whence a feeble colony of Greeks derived the command of the sea, and the honours of a flourishing and independent republic.

If we survey Byzantium in the extent which it acquired with the august name of Constantinople, the figure of the Imperial city may be represented under that of an unequal triangle. The obtuse point, which advances towards the east and the shores of Asia, meets and repels the waves of the Thracian Bosphorus. The northern side of the city is bounded by the harbour, and the southern is washed by the Propontis or Sea of Marmara. The basis of the triangle is opposed to the west, and terminates the continent of Europe. But the admirable form and division of the circumjacent land and water cannot, without a more ample explanation, be clearly or sufficiently understood.

The winding channel through which the waters of the Euxine flow with a rapid and incessant course towards the Mediterranean received the appellation of Bosphorus, a name not less celebrated in the history than in the fables of antiquity. A crowd of temples and of votive altars, profusely scattered along its steep and woody banks, attested the unskilfulness, the terrors, and the devotion of the Grecian navigators who, after the example of the Argonauts, explored the dangers of the inhospitable Euxine. On these banks tradition long preserved the memory of the palace of Phineus, infested by the obscene harpies; and of the sylvan reign of Amycus, who defied the son of Leda to the combat of the Cestus. The straits of the Bosphorus are terminated by the Cyanean rocks, which, according to the description of the poets, had once floated on the face of the waters, and were destined by the gods to protect the entrance of the Euxine against the eye of profane curiosity. From the Cyanean rocks to the point and harbour of Byzantium the winding length of the Bosphorus extends about sixteen miles, and its most ordinary breadth may be computed at about one mile and a half. The *new* castles of Europe and Asia are constructed, on either continent, upon the foundations of two celebrated temples, of Serapis and of Jupiter Urius. The *old* castles, a work of the Greek emperors, command the narrowest part of the channel, in a place where the opposite banks advance within five hundred paces of each other. These fortresses were restored and strengthened by Mahomet the Second when he meditated the siege of Constantinople: but the Turkish conqueror was most probably ignorant that, near two thousand years before his reign, Darius had chosen the same situation to connect the two continents by a bridge of boats. At a small distance from the old castles we discover the little town of Chrysopolis, or Scutari, which may almost be considered as the Asiatic suburb of Constantinople. The Bosphorus, as it begins to open into the Propontis, passes between Byzantium and Chalcedon. The latter of those cities was built by the Greeks a few years before the former; and the blindness of its founders, who overlooked the superior advantages of the opposite coast, has been stigmatised by a proverbial expression of contempt.

The harbour of Constantinople, which may be considered as an arm of the Bosphorus, obtained, in a very remote period, the denomination of the *Golden Horn*. The curve which it describes might be compared to the horn of a stag, or as it should seem, with more propriety, to that of an ox. The epithet of *golden* was expressive of the riches which every wind wafted from the most distant countries into the secure and capacious port of Constantinople. The river Lycus, formed by the conflux of two little streams, pours into the harbour a perpetual supply of fresh water, which serves to cleanse the bottom and to invite the periodical shoals of fish to seek their retreat in that convenient recess. As the vicissitudes of tides are scarcely felt in those seas, the constant depth of the harbour allows goods to be landed on the quays without the assistance of boats; and it has been observed that, in many places, the largest vessels may rest their prows against the houses while their sterns are floating in the water. From the mouth of the Lycus to that of the harbour this arm of the Bosphorus is more than seven miles in length. The entrance is about five hundred yards broad, and a strong chain could be occasionally drawn across it to guard the port and city from the attack of an hostile navy.

Between the Bosphorus and the Hellespont, the shores of Europe and Asia receding on either side enclose the Sea of Marmara, which was known to the ancients by the denomination of Propontis. The navigation from the issue of the Bosphorus to the entrance of the Hellespont is about one hundred and twenty miles. Those who steer their westward course through the middle of the Propontis may at once descry the high lands of Thrace and Bithynia, and never lose sight of the lofty summit of Mount Olympus, covered with eternal snows. They leave on the left a deep gulf, at the bottom of which Nicomedia was seated, the imperial residence of Diocletian; and they pass the small islands of Cyzicus and Proconnesus before they cast anchor at Gallipoli, where the sea, which separates Asia from Europe, is again contracted into a narrow channel.

The geographers who, with the most skilful accuracy, have surveyed the form and extent of the Hellespont, assign about sixty miles for the winding course, and about three miles for the ordinary breadth, of those celebrated straits. But the narrowest part of the channel is found to the northward of the old Turkish castles, between the cities of Sestus and Abydus. It was here that the adventurous Leander braved the passage of the flood for the possession of his mistress. It was here likewise, in a place where the distance between the opposite banks cannot exceed five hundred paces, that Xerxes imposed a stupendous bridge of boats, for the purpose of transporting into Europe a hundred and seventy myriads of barbarians. A sea contracted within such narrow limits may seem but ill to deserve the singular epithet of *broad*, which Homer, as well as Orpheus, has frequently bestowed on the Hellespont. But our ideas of greatness are of a relative nature: the traveller, and especially the poet, who sailed along the Hellespont, who pursued the windings of the stream, and contemplated the rural scenery, which appeared on every side to terminate the prospect, insensibly lost the remembrance of the sea; and his fancy painted those celebrated straits with all the attributes of a mighty river, flowing with a swift current, in the midst of a woody and inland country, and at length, through a wide mouth, discharging itself into the Ægean or Archipelago. Ancient Troy, seated on an eminence at the foot of Mount Ida, overlooked the mouth of the Hellespont, which scarcely received an accession of waters from the tribute of those immortal rivulets the Simois and Scamander. The Grecian camp had stretched twelve miles along the shore, from the Sigean to the Rhœtean promontory; and the flanks of the army were guarded by the bravest chiefs who fought under the banners of Agamemnon. The first of those promontories was occupied by Achilles with his invincible myrmidons, and the dauntless Ajax pitched his tents on the other. After Ajax had fallen a sacrifice to his disappointed pride and to the ingratitude of the Greeks, his sepulchre was erected on the ground where he had defended the navy against the rage of Jove and of Hector; and the citizens of the rising town of Rhœteum celebrated his memory with divine honours. Before Constantine gave a just preference to the situation of Byzantium, he had conceived the design of erecting the seat of empire on this celebrated spot, from whence the Romans derived their fabulous origin. The extensive plain which lies below ancient Troy, towards the Rhœtean promontory and the tomb of Ajax, was first chosen for his new capital; and, though the undertaking was soon relinquished, the stately remains of unfinished walls and towers attracted the notice of all who sailed through the straits of the Hellespont.

We are at present qualified to view the advantageous position of Constantinople, which appears to have been formed by nature for the centre and capital of a great monarchy. Situated in the forty-first degree of latitude, the Imperial city commanded, from her seven hills, the opposite shores of Europe and Asia; the climate was healthy and temperate, the soil fertile, the harbour secure and capacious, and the approach on the side of the continent was of small extent and easy defence. The Bosphorus and the Hellespont may be considered as the two gates of Constantinople, and the prince who possessed those important passages could always shut them against a naval enemy and open them to the fleets of commerce. The preservation of the eastern provinces may, in some degree, be ascribed to the policy of Constantine, as the barbarians of the Euxine, who in the preceding age had poured their armaments into the heart of the Mediterranean, soon desisted from the exercise of piracy, and despaired of forcing this insurmountable barrier. When the gates of the Hellespont and Bosphorus were shut, the capital still enjoyed within their spacious enclosure every production which could supply the wants or gratify the luxury of its numerous inhabitants. The sea-coasts of Thrace and Bithynia, which languish under the weight of Turkish oppression, still exhibit a rich prospect of vineyards, of gardens, and of plentiful harvests; and the Propontis has ever been renowned for an inexhaustible store of the most exquisite fish, that are taken in their stated seasons, without skill, and almost without labour. But when the passages of the straits were thrown open for trade, they alternately admitted the natural and artificial riches of the north and south, of the Euxine, and of the Mediterranean. Whatever rude commodities were collected in the forests of Germany and Scythia, as far as the sources of the Tanais and the Borysthenes; whatsoever was manufactured by the skill of Europe or Asia; the corn of Egypt, and the gems and spices of the farthest India, were brought by the varying winds into the port of Constantinople, which, for many ages, attracted the commerce of the ancient world.

THE FOUNDATION OF THE CITY

The prospect of beauty, of safety, and of wealth, united in a single spot, was sufficient to justify the choice of Constantine. But as some decent mixture of prodigy and fable has, in every age, been supposed to reflect a becoming majesty on the origin of great cities, the emperor was desirous of ascribing his resolution not so much to the uncertain counsels of human policy as to the infallible and eternal decrees of divine wisdom. In one of his laws he has been careful to instruct posterity that, in obedience to the commands of God, he laid the everlasting foundations of Constantinople; and though he has not condescended to relate in what manner the celestial inspiration was communicated to his mind, the defect of his modest silence has been liberally supplied by the ingenuity of succeeding writers, who describe the nocturnal vision which appeared to the fancy of Constantine as he slept within the walls of Byzantium. The tutelar genius of the city, a venerable matron sinking under the weight of years and infirmities, was suddenly transformed into a blooming maid, whom his own hands adorned with all the symbols of Imperial greatness. The monarch awoke, interpreted the auspicious omen, and obeyed, without hesitation, the will of Heaven. The day which gave birth to a city or colony was celebrated by the Romans with such ceremonies as had been ordained by a generous superstition; and though Constantine might omit some rites which savoured too strongly of their Pagan origin, yet he was anxious to leave a deep impression of hope and respect on the minds of the spectators. On foot, with a lance in his hand, the emperor himself led the solemn procession, and directed the line which was traced as the boundary of the destined capital, till the growing circumference was observed with astonishment by the assistants, who, at length, ventured to observe that he had already exceeded the most ample measure of a great city. "I shall still advance," replied Constantine, "till HE, the invisible guide who marches before me, thinks proper to stop." Without presuming to investigate the nature or motives of this extraordinary conductor, we shall content ourselves with the more humble task of describing the extent and limits of Constantinople.

In the actual state of the city, the palace and gardens of the Seraglio occupy the eastern promontory, the first of the seven hills, and cover about one hundred and fifty acres of our own measure. The seat of Turkish jealousy and despotism is erected on the foundations of a Grecian republic; but it may be supposed that the Byzantines were tempted by the conveniency of the harbour to extend their habitations on that side beyond the modern limits of the Seraglio. The new walls of Constantine stretched from the port to the Propontis across the enlarged breadth of the triangle, at the distance of fifteen stadia from the ancient fortification, and with the city of Byzantium they enclosed five of the seven hills which, to the eyes of those who approach Constantinople, appear to rise above each other in beautiful order. About a century after the death of the founder, the new buildings, extending on one side up the harbour, and on the other along the Propontis, already covered the narrow ridge of the sixth and the broad summit of the seventh hill. The necessity of protecting those suburbs from the incessant inroads of the barbarians engaged the younger Theodosius to surround his capital with an adequate and permanent enclosure of walls. From the eastern promontory to the golden gate, the extreme length of Constantinople was about three Roman miles, the circumference measured between ten and eleven, and the surface might be computed as equal to about two thousand English acres. It is impossible to justify the vain and credulous exaggerations of modern travellers, who have sometimes stretched the limits of Constantinople over the adjacent villages of the European and even of the Asiatic coast. But the suburbs of Pera and Galata, though situate beyond the harbour, may deserve to be considered as a part of the city; and this addition may perhaps authorise the measure of a Byzantine historian, who assigns sixteen Greek (about fourteen Roman) miles for the circumference of his native city. Such an extent may seem not unworthy of an Imperial residence. Yet Constantinople must yield to Babylon and Thebes, to ancient Rome, to London, and even to Paris.

The master of the Roman world, who aspired to erect an eternal monument of the glories of his reign, could employ in the prosecution of that great work the wealth, the labour, and all that yet remained of the genius, of obedient millions. Some estimate may be formed of the expense bestowed with Imperial liberality on the foundation of Constantinople by the allowance of about two millions five hundred thousand pounds for the construction of the walls, the porticoes, and the aqueducts. The forests that overshadowed the shores of the Euxine, and the celebrated quarries of white marble in the little island of Proconnesus, supplied an inexhaustible stock of materials, ready to be conveyed, by the convenience of a short water-carriage, to the harbour of Byzantium. A multitude of labourers and artificers urged the conclusion of the work with incessant toil; but the impatience of Constantine soon discovered that, in the decline of the arts, the skill as well as numbers of his architects bore a very unequal proportion to the greatness of his designs. The magistrates of the most distant provinces were therefore directed to institute schools, to appoint professors, and, by the hopes of rewards and privileges, to engage in the study and practice of architecture a sufficient number of ingenious youths who had received a liberal education. The buildings of the new city were executed by such artificers as the reign of Constantine could afford; but they were decorated by the hands of the most celebrated masters of the age of Pericles and Alexander. To revive the genius of Phidias and Lysippus surpassed indeed the power of a Roman emperor; but the immortal productions which they had bequeathed to posterity were exposed without defence to the rapacious vanity of a despot. By his commands the cities of Greece and Asia were despoiled of their most valuable ornaments. The trophies of memorable wars, the objects of religious veneration, the most finished statues of the gods and heroes, of the sages and poets of ancient times, contributed to the splendid triumph of Constantinople; and gave occasion to the remark of the historian Cedrenus, who observes, with some enthusiasm, that nothing seemed wanting except the souls of the illustrious men whom those admirable monuments were intended to represent. But it is not in the city of Constantine, nor in the declining period of an empire, when the human mind was depressed by civil and religious slavery, that we should seek for the souls of Homer and of Demosthenes.

During the siege of Byzantium the conqueror had pitched his tent on the commanding eminence of the second hill. To perpetuate the memory of his success, he chose the same advantageous position for the principal Forum, which appears to have been of a circular, or rather elliptical form. The two opposite entrances formed triumphal arches; the porticoes, which enclosed it on every side, were filled with statues, and the centre of the Forum was occupied by a lofty column, of which a mutilated fragment is now degraded by the appellation of the *burnt pillar*. This column was erected on a pedestal of white marble twenty feet high, and was composed of ten pieces of porphyry, each of which measured about ten feet in height, and about thirty-three in circumference. On the summit of the pillar, above one hundred and twenty feet from the ground, stood the colossal statue of Apollo. It was of bronze, had been transported either from Athens or from a town of Phrygia, and was supposed to be the work of Phidias. The artist had represented the god of day, or, as it was afterwards interpreted, the emperor Constantine himself, with a sceptre in his right hand, the globe of the world in his left, and a crown of rays glittering on his head. The Circus, or Hippodrome, was a stately building about four hundred paces in length, and one hundred in breadth. The space between the two *metæ* or goals was filled with statues and obelisks; and we may still remark a very singular fragment of antiquity, the bodies of three serpents twisted into one pillar of brass. Their triple heads had once supported the golden tripod which, after the defeat of Xerxes, was consecrated in the temple of Delphi by the victorious Greeks. The beauty of the Hippodrome has been long since defaced by the rude hands of the Turkish conquerors, but, under the similar appellation of Atmeidan, it still serves as a place of exercise for their horses. From the throne, whence the emperor viewed the Circensian games, a winding staircase descended to the palace; a magnificent edifice, which scarcely yielded to the residence of Rome itself, and which, together with the dependent courts, gardens, and porticoes, covered a considerable extent of ground upon the banks of the Propontis, between the Hippodrome and the church of St. Sophia. We might likewise celebrate the baths, which still retained the name of Zeuxippus, after they had been enriched, by the munificence of Constantine, with lofty columns, various marbles, and above threescore statues of bronze. But we should deviate from the design of this history if we attempted minutely to describe the different buildings or quarters of the city. It may be sufficient to observe that whatever could adorn the dignity of a great capital, or contribute to the benefit or pleasure of its numerous inhabitants, was contained within the walls of Constantinople. A particular description, composed about a century after its foundation, enumerates a capitol or school of learning, a circus, two theatres, eight public and one hundred and fifty-three private baths, fifty-two porticoes, five granaries, eight aqueducts or reservoirs of water, four spacious halls for the meetings of the senate or courts of justice, fourteen churches, fourteen palaces, and four thousand three hundred and eighty-eight houses which, for their size or beauty, deserved to be distinguished from the multitude of plebeian habitations.

The populousness of his favoured city was the next and most serious object of the attention of its founder. In the dark ages which succeeded the translation of the empire, the remote and the immediate consequences of that memorable event were strangely confounded by the vanity of the Greeks and the credulity of the Latins. It was asserted and believed that all the noble families of Rome, the senate, and the equestrian order, with their innumerable attendants, had followed their emperor to the banks of the Propontis; that a spurious race of strangers and plebeians was left to possess the solitude of the ancient capital; and that the lands of Italy, long since converted into gardens, were at once deprived of cultivation and inhabitants. In the course of this history such exaggerations will be reduced to their just value; yet, since the growth of Constantinople cannot be ascribed to the general increase of mankind and of industry, it must be admitted that this artificial colony was raised at the expense of the ancient cities of the empire. Many opulent senators of Rome and of the eastern provinces were probably invited by Constantine to adopt for their country the fortunate spot which he had chosen for his own residence. The invitations of a master are scarcely to be distinguished from commands, and the liberality of the emperor obtained a ready and cheerful obedience. He bestowed on his favourites the palaces which he had built in the several quarters of the city, assigned them lands and pensions for the support of their dignity, and alienated the demesnes of Pontus and Asia to grant hereditary estates by the easy tenure of maintaining a house in the capital. But these encouragements and obligations can become superfluous, and were gradually abolished. Wherever the seat of government is fixed, a considerable part of the public revenue will be expended by the prince himself, by his ministers, by the officers of justice, and by the domestics of the palace. The most wealthy of the provincials will be attracted by the powerful motives of interest and duty, of amusement and curiosity. A third and more numerous class of inhabitants will insensibly be formed, of servants, of artificers, and of merchants, who derive their subsistence from their own labour, and from the wants or luxury of the superior ranks. In less than a century Constantinople disputed with Rome itself the pre-eminence of riches and numbers. New piles of buildings, crowded together with too little regard to health or convenience, scarcely allowed the intervals of narrow streets for the perpetual throng of men, of horses, and of carriages. The allotted space of ground was insufficient to contain the increasing people, and the additional foundations, which on either side were advanced into the sea, might alone have composed a very considerable city.

The frequent and regular distributions of wine and oil, of corn or bread, of money or provisions, had almost exempted the poorer citizens of Rome from the necessity of labour. The magnificence of the first Cæsars was in some measure imitated by the founder of Constantinople: but his liberality, however it might excite the applause of the people, has incurred the censure of posterity. A nation of legislators and conquerors might assert their claim to the harvests of Africa, which had been purchased with their blood; and it was artfully contrived by Augustus, that, in the enjoyment of plenty, the Romans should lose the memory of freedom. But the prodigality of Constantine could not be excused by any consideration either of public or private interest; and the annual tribute of corn imposed upon Egypt for the benefit of his new capital was applied to feed a lazy and insolent populace, at the expense of the husbandmen of an industrious province. Some other regulations of this emperor are less liable to blame, but they are less deserving of notice. He divided Constantinople into fourteen regions or quarters, dignified the public council with the appellation of senate, communicated to the citizens the privileges of Italy, and bestowed on the rising city the title of Colony, the first and most favoured daughter of ancient Rome. The venerable parent still maintained the legal and acknowledged supremacy, which was due to her age, to her dignity, and to the remembrance of her former greatness.

THE DEDICATION OF THE CITY

As Constantine urged the progress of the work with the impatience of a lover, the walls, the porticoes, and the principal edifices were completed in a few years, or, according to another account, in a few months: but this extraordinary diligence should excite the less admiration, since many of the buildings were finished in so hasty and imperfect a manner, that, under the succeeding reign, they were preserved with difficulty from impending ruin. But while they displayed the vigour and freshness of youth, the founder prepared to celebrate the dedication of his city. The games and largesses which crowned the pomp of this memorable festival may easily be supposed; but there is one circumstance of a more singular and permanent nature, which ought not entirely to be overlooked. As often as the birthday of the city returned, the statue of Constantine, framed by his order, of gilt wood, and bearing in its right hand a small image of the genius of the place, was erected on a triumphal car. The guards, carrying white tapers, and clothed in their richest apparel, accompanied the solemn procession as it moved through the Hippodrome. When it was opposite to the throne of the reigning emperor, he rose from his seat, and with grateful reverence adored the memory of his predecessor. At the festival of the dedication, an edict, engraved on a column of marble, bestowed the title of SECOND or NEW ROME on the city of Constantine. But the name of Constantinople has prevailed over that honourable epithet, and after the revolution of fourteen centuries still perpetuates the fame of its author.

THE NEW ORDER OF GOVERNMENT

The foundation of a new capital is naturally connected with the establishment of a new form of civil and military administration. The distinct view of the complicated system of policy introduced by Diocletian, improved by Constantine, and completed by his immediate successors, may not only amuse the fancy by the singular picture of a great empire, but will tend to illustrate the secret and internal causes of its rapid decay. In the pursuit of any remarkable institution, we may be frequently led into the more early or the more recent times of the Roman history; but the proper limits of this inquiry will be included within a period of about one hundred and thirty years, from the accession of Constantine to the publication of the Theodosian code; from which, as well as from the *Notitia* of the East and West, we derive the most copious and authentic information of the state of the empire. This variety of objects will suspend, for some time, the course of the narrative; but the interruption will be censured only by those readers who are insensible to the importance of laws and manners, while they peruse, with eager curiosity, the transient intrigues of a court, or the accidental event of a battle.

The manly pride of the Romans, content with substantial power, had left to the vanity of the East the forms and ceremonies of ostentatious greatness. But when they lost even the semblance of those virtues which were derived from their ancient freedom, the simplicity of Roman manners was insensibly corrupted by the stately affectation of the courts of Asia. The distinctions of personal merit and influence, so conspicuous in a republic, so feeble and obscure under a monarchy, were abolished by the despotism of the emperors; who substituted in their room a severe subordination of rank and office, from the titled slaves who were seated on the steps of the throne, to the meanest instruments of arbitrary power. This multitude of abject dependents was interested in the support of the actual government, from the dread of a revolution which might at once confound their hopes and intercept the reward of their services. In this divine hierarchy (for such it is frequently styled) every rank was marked with the most scrupulous exactness, and its dignity was displayed in a variety of trifling and solemn ceremonies, which it was a study to learn, and a sacrilege to neglect. The purity of the Latin language was debased, by adopting, in the intercourse of pride and flattery, a profusion of epithets which Tully would scarcely have understood, and which Augustus would have rejected with indignation. The principal officers of the empire were saluted, even by the sovereign himself, with the deceitful titles of your *Sincerity*, your *Gravity*, your *Excellency*, your *Eminence*, your *sublime and wonderful Magnitude*, your *illustrious and magnificent Highness*. The codicils or patents of their office were curiously emblazoned with such emblems as were best adapted to explain its nature and high dignity—the image or portrait of the reigning emperors; a triumphal car; the book of mandates placed on a table, covered with a rich carpet, and illuminated by four tapers; the allegorical figures of the provinces which they governed; or the appellations and standards of the troops whom they commanded. Some of these official ensigns were really exhibited in their hall of audience; others preceded their pompous march whenever they appeared in public; and every circumstance of their demeanour, their dress, their ornaments, and their train, was calculated to inspire a deep reverence for the representatives of supreme majesty. By a philosophic observer the system of the Roman government might have been mistaken for a splendid theatre, filled with players of every character and degree, who repeated the language, and imitated the passions, of their original model.

All the magistrates of sufficient importance to find a place in the general state of the empire were accurately divided into three classes—1. The *Illustrious*; 2. The *Spectabiles*, or *Respectable*; and, 3. The *Clarissimi*, whom we may translate by the word *Honourable*. In the times of Roman simplicity, the last-mentioned epithet was used only as a vague expression of deference, till it became at length the peculiar and appropriated title of all who were members of the senate, and consequently of all who, from that venerable body, were selected to govern the provinces. The vanity of those who, from their rank and office, might claim a superior distinction above the rest of the senatorial order, was long afterwards indulged with the new appellation of *Respectable*: but the title of *Illustrious* was always reserved to some eminent personages who were obeyed or reverenced by the two subordinate classes. It was communicated only, I. To the consuls and patricians; II. To the Prætorian prefects, with the prefects of Rome and Constantinople; III. To the masters general of the cavalry and the infantry; and, IV. To the seven ministers of the palace, who exercised their *sacred* functions about the person of the emperor. Among those illustrious magistrates who were esteemed co-ordinate with each other, the seniority of appointment gave place to the union of dignities. By the expedient of honorary codicils, the emperors, who were fond of multiplying their favours, might sometimes gratify the vanity, though not the ambition, of impatient courtiers.

THE CONSULS AND PATRICIANS

I. As long as the Roman consuls were the first magistrates of a free state, they derived their right to power from the choice of the people.

As long as the emperors condescended to disguise the servitude which they imposed, the consuls were still elected by the real or apparent suffrage of the senate. From the reign of Diocletian even these vestiges of liberty were abolished, and the successful candidates, who were invested with the annual honours of the consulship, affected to deplore the humiliating condition of their predecessors. The Scipios and the Catos had been reduced to solicit the votes of plebeians, to pass through the tedious and expensive forms of a popular election, and to expose their dignity to the shame of a public refusal; while their own happier fate had reserved them for an age and government in which the rewards of virtue were assigned by the unerring wisdom of a gracious sovereign. In the epistles which the emperor addressed to the two consuls elect, it was declared that they were created by his sole authority. Their names and portraits, engraved on gilt tablets of ivory, were dispersed over the empire as presents to the provinces, the cities, the magistrates, the senate, and the people. Their solemn inauguration was performed at the place of the Imperial residence; and during a period of one hundred and twenty years Rome was constantly deprived of the presence of her ancient magistrates. On the morning of the first of January the consuls assumed the ensigns of their dignity. Their dress was a robe of purple, embroidered in silk and gold, and sometimes ornamented with costly gems. On this solemn occasion they were attended by the most eminent officers of the state and army in the habit of senators; and the useless fasces, armed with the once formidable axes, were borne before them by the lictors. The procession moved from the palace to the Forum or principal square of the city; where the consuls ascended their tribunal, and seated themselves in the curule chairs, which were framed after the fashion of ancient times. They immediately exercised an act of jurisdiction, by the manumission of a slave who was brought before them for that purpose; and the ceremony was intended to represent the celebrated action of the elder Brutus, the author of liberty and of the consulship, when he admitted among his fellow-citizens the faithful Vindex, who had revealed the conspiracy of the Tarquins. The public festival was continued during several days in all the principal cities; in Rome, from custom; in Constantinople, from imitation; in Carthage, Antioch, and Alexandria, from the love of pleasure and the superfluity of wealth. In the two capitals of the empire the annual games of the theatre, the circus, and the amphitheatre cost four thousand pounds of gold, (about) one hundred and sixty thousand pounds sterling; and if so heavy an expense surpassed the faculties or the inclination of the magistrates themselves, the sum was supplied from the Imperial treasury. As soon as the consuls had discharged these customary duties, they were at liberty to retire into the shade of private life, and to enjoy during the remainder of the year the undisturbed contemplation of their own greatness. They no longer presided in the national councils;

they no longer executed the resolutions of peace or war. Their abilities (unless they were employed in more effective offices) were of little moment; and their names served only as the legal date of the year in which they had filled the chair of Marius and of Cicero. Yet it was still felt and acknowledged, in the last period of Roman servitude, that this empty name might be compared, and even preferred, to the possession of substantial power. The title of consul was still the most splendid object of ambition, the noblest reward of virtue and loyalty. The emperors themselves, who disdained the faint shadow of the republic, were conscious that they acquired an additional splendour and majesty as often as they assumed the annual honours of the consular dignity.

The proudest and most perfect separation which can be found in any age or country between the nobles and the people is perhaps that of the Patricians and the Plebeians, as it was established in the first age of the Roman republic. Wealth and honours, the offices of the state, and the ceremonies of religion, were almost exclusively possessed by the former; who, preserving the purity of their blood with the most insulting jealousy, held their clients in a condition of specious vassalage. But these distinctions, so incompatible with the spirit of a free people, were removed, after a long struggle, by the persevering efforts of the Tribunes. The most active and successful of the Plebeians accumulated wealth, aspired to honours, deserved triumphs, contracted alliances, and, after some generations, assumed the pride of ancient nobility. The Patrician families, on the other hand, whose original number was never recruited till the end of the commonwealth, either failed in the ordinary course of nature, or were extinguished in so many foreign and domestic wars, or, through a want of merit or fortune, insensibly mingled with the mass of the people. Very few remained who could derive their pure and genuine origin from the infancy of the city, or even from that of the republic, when Cæsar and Augustus, Claudius and Vespasian, created from the body of the senate a competent number of new Patrician families, in the hope of perpetuating an order which was still considered as honourable and sacred. But these artificial supplies (in which the reigning house was always included) were rapidly swept away by the rage of tyrants, by frequent revolutions, by the change of manners, and by the intermixture of nations. Little more was left when Constantine ascended the throne than a vague and imperfect tradition that the Patricians had once been the first of the Romans. To form a body of nobles, whose influence may restrain while it secures the authority of the monarch, would have been very inconsistent with the character and policy of Constantine; but, had he seriously entertained such a design, it might have exceeded the measure of his power to ratify by an arbitrary edict an institution which must expect the sanction of time and of opinion. He revived, indeed, the title of PATRICIANS, but he revived it as a personal, not as an hereditary distinction. They yielded only to the transient superiority of the annual consuls; but they enjoyed the pre-eminence over all the great officers of state, with the most familiar access to the person of the prince. This honourable rank was bestowed on them for life; and, as they were usually favourites and ministers who had grown old in the Imperial court, the true etymology of the word was perverted by ignorance and flattery; and the Patricians of Constantine were reverenced as the adopted *Fathers* of the emperor and the republic.

THE PREFECTS, PROCONSULS, AND GOVERNORS

II. The fortunes of the Prætorian prefects were essentially different from those of the consuls and Patricians. The latter saw their ancient greatness evaporate in a vain title. The former, rising by degrees from the most humble condition, were invested with the civil and military administration of the Roman world. From the reign of Severus to that of Diocletian, the guards and the palace, the laws and the finances, the armies and the provinces, were intrusted to their superintending care; and, like the viziers of the East, they held with one hand the seal, and with the other the standard, of the empire. The ambition of the prefects, always formidable, and sometimes fatal to the masters whom they served, was supported by the strength of the Prætorian bands; but, after those haughty troops had been weakened by Diocletian and finally suppressed by Constantine, the prefects, who survived their fall, were reduced without difficulty to the station of useful and obedient ministers. When they were no longer responsible for the safety of the emperor's person, they resigned the jurisdiction which they had hitherto claimed and exercised over all the departments of the palace. They were deprived by Constantine of all military command as soon as they had ceased to lead into the field, under their immediate orders, the flower of the Roman troops; and, at length, by a singular revolution, the captains of the guards were transformed into the civil magistrates of the provinces. According to the plan of government instituted by Diocletian, the four princes had each their Prætorian prefect; and after the monarchy was once more united in the person of Constantine, he still continued to create the same number of FOUR PREFECTS, and intrusted to their care the same provinces which they already administered. 1. The prefect of the East stretched his ample jurisdiction into the three parts of the globe which were subject to the Romans, from the cataracts of the Nile to the banks of the Phasis, and from the mountains of Thrace to the frontiers of Persia. 2. The important provinces of Pannonia, Dacia, Macedonia, and Greece once acknowledged the authority of the prefect of Illyricum. 3. The power of the prefect of Italy was not confined to the country from whence he derived his title; it extended over the additional territory of Rhætia as far as the banks of the Danube, over the dependent islands of the Mediterranean, and over that part of the continent of Africa which lies between the confines of Cyrene and those of Tingitania. 4. The prefect of the Gauls comprehended under that plural denomination the kindred provinces of Britain and Spain, and his authority was obeyed from the wall of Antoninus to the foot of Mount Atlas.

After the Prætorian prefects had been dismissed from all military command, the civil functions which they were ordained to exercise over so many subject nations were adequate to the ambition and abilities of the most consummate ministers. To their wisdom was committed the supreme administration of justice and of the finances, the two objects which, in a state of peace, comprehend almost all the respective duties of the sovereign and of the people; of the former, to protect the citizens who are obedient to the laws; of the latter, to contribute the share of their property which is required for the expenses of the state. The coin, the highways, the posts, the granaries, the manufactures, whatever could interest the public prosperity, was moderated by the authority of the Prætorian prefects. As the immediate representatives of the Imperial majesty, they were empowered to explain, to enforce, and on some occasions to modify, the general edicts by their discretionary proclamations. They watched over the conduct of the provincial governors, removed the negligent, and inflicted punishments on the guilty. From all the inferior jurisdictions an appeal in every matter of importance, either civil or criminal, might be brought before the tribunal of the prefect: but *his* sentence was final and absolute; and the emperors themselves refused to admit any complaints against the judgment or the integrity of a magistrate whom they honoured with such unbounded confidence. His appointments were suitable to his dignity; and, if avarice was his ruling passion, he enjoyed frequent opportunities of collecting a rich harvest of fees, of presents, and of perquisites. Though the emperors no longer dreaded the ambition of their prefects, they were attentive to counterbalance the power of this great office by the uncertainty and shortness of its duration.

From their superior importance and dignity, Rome and Constantinople were alone excepted from the jurisdiction of the Prætorian prefects. The immense size of the city, and the experience of the tardy, ineffectual operation of the laws, had furnished the policy of Augustus with a specious pretence for introducing a new magistrate, who alone could restrain a servile and turbulent populace by the strong arm of arbitrary power. Valerius Messalla was appointed the first prefect of Rome, that his reputation might countenance so invidious a measure; but at the end of a few days that accomplished citizen resigned his office, declaring, with a spirit worthy of the friend of Brutus, that he found himself incapable of exercising a power incompatible with public freedom. As the sense of liberty became less exquisite, the advantages of order were more clearly understood; and the prefect, who seemed to have been designed as a terror only to slaves and vagrants, was permitted to extend his civil and criminal jurisdiction over the equestrian and noble families of Rome. The prætors, annually created as the judges of law and equity, could not long dispute the possession of the Forum with a vigorous and permanent magistrate who was usually admitted into the confidence of the prince. Their courts were deserted; their number, which had once fluctuated between twelve and eighteen, was gradually reduced to two or three; and their important functions were confined to the expensive obligation of exhibiting games for the amusement of the people. After the office of Roman consuls had been changed into a vain pageant, which was rarely displayed in the capital, the prefects assumed their vacant place in the senate, and were soon acknowledged as the ordinary presidents of that venerable assembly. They received appeals from the distance of one hundred miles; and it was allowed as a principle of jurisprudence that all municipal authority was derived from them alone. In the discharge of his laborious employment the governor of Rome was assisted by fifteen officers, some of whom had been originally his equals, or even his superiors. The principal departments were relative to the command of a numerous watch, established as a safeguard against fires, robberies, and nocturnal disorders; the custody and distribution of the public allowance of corn and provisions; the care of the port, of the aqueducts, of the common sewers, and of the navigation and bed of the Tiber; the inspection of the markets, the theatres, and of the private as well as public works. Their vigilance ensured the three principal objects of a regular police—safety, plenty, and cleanliness; and, as a proof of the attention of government to preserve the splendour and ornaments of the capital, a particular inspector was appointed for the statues; the guardian, as it were, of that inanimate people, which, according to the extravagant computation of an old writer, was scarcely inferior in number to the living inhabitants of Rome. About thirty years after the foundation of Constantinople a similar magistrate was created in that rising metropolis, for the same uses and with the same powers. A perfect equality was established between the dignity of the *two* municipal and that of the *four* Prætorian prefects.

Those who in the Imperial hierarchy were distinguished by the title of *Respectable* formed an intermediate class between the *illustrious* prefects and the *honourable* magistrates of the provinces. In this class the proconsuls of Asia, Achaia, and Africa claimed a pre-eminence, which was yielded to the remembrance of their ancient dignity; and the appeal from their tribunal to that of the prefects was almost the only mark of their dependence. But the civil government of the empire was distributed into thirteen great DIOCESES, each of which equalled the just measure of a powerful kingdom. The first of these dioceses was subject to the jurisdiction of the *count* of the East; and we may convey some idea of the importance and variety of his functions by observing that six hundred apparitors, who would be styled at present either secretaries, or clerks, or ushers, or messengers, were employed in his immediate office. The place of *Augustal prefect* of Egypt was no longer filled by a Roman knight; but the name was retained; and the extraordinary powers which the situation of the country and the temper of the inhabitants had once made indispensable were still continued to the governor. The eleven remaining dioceses—of Asiana, Pontica, and Thrace; of Macedonia, Dacia, and Pannonia, or Western Illyricum; of Italy and Africa; of Gaul, Spain, and Britain—were governed by twelve *vicars* or *vice-prefects*, whose name sufficiently explains the nature and dependence of their office. It may be added that the lieutenant-generals of the Roman armies, the military counts and dukes, who will be hereafter mentioned, were allowed the rank and title of *Respectable*.

As the spirit of jealousy and ostentation prevailed in the councils of the emperors, they proceeded with anxious diligence to divide the substance and to multiply the titles of power. The vast countries which the Roman conquerors had united under the same simple form of administration were imperceptibly crumbled into minute fragments, till at length the whole empire was distributed into one hundred and sixteen provinces, each of which supported an expensive and splendid establishment. Of these, three were governed by *proconsuls*, thirty-seven by *consulars*, five by *correctors*, and seventy-one by *presidents*. The appellations of these magistrates were different; they ranked in successive order, the ensigns of their dignity were curiously varied, and their situation, from accidental circumstances, might be more or less agreeable or advantageous. But they were all (excepting only the proconsuls) alike included in the class of *honourable* persons; and they were alike intrusted, during the pleasure of the prince, and under the authority of the prefects or their deputies, with the administration of justice and the finances in their respective districts. The ponderous volumes of the Codes and Pandects would furnish ample materials for a minute inquiry into the system of provincial government, as in the space of six centuries it was improved by the wisdom of the Roman statesmen and lawyers. It may be sufficient for the historian to select two singular and salutary provisions, intended to restrain the abuse of authority. 1. For the preservation of peace and order, the governors of the provinces were armed with the sword of justice. They inflicted corporal punishments, and they exercised, in capital offences, the power of life and death. But they were not authorised to indulge the condemned criminal with the choice of his own execution, or to pronounce a sentence of the mildest and most honourable kind of exile. These prerogatives were reserved to the prefects, who alone could impose the heavy fine of fifty pounds of gold: their vicegerents were confined to the trifling weight of a few ounces. This distinction, which seems to grant the larger while it denies the smaller degree of authority, was founded on a very rational motive. The smaller degree was infinitely more liable to abuse. The passions of a provincial magistrate might frequently provoke him into acts of oppression, which affected only the freedom or the fortunes of the subject; though, from a principle of prudence, perhaps of humanity, he might still be terrified by the guilt of innocent blood. It may likewise be considered that exile, considerable fines, or the choice of an easy death, relate more particularly to the rich and the noble; and the persons the most exposed to the avarice or resentment of a provincial magistrate were thus removed from his obscure persecution to the more august and impartial tribunal of the Prætorian prefect. 2. As it was reasonably apprehended that the integrity of the judge might be biassed, if his interest was concerned or his affections were engaged, the strictest regulations were established to exclude any person, without the special dispensation of the emperor, from the government of the province where he was born; and to prohibit the governor or his son from contracting marriage with a native or an inhabitant; or from purchasing slaves, lands, or houses within the extent of his jurisdiction. Notwithstanding these rigorous precautions, the emperor Constantine, after a reign of twenty-five years, still deplores the venal and oppressive administration of justice, and expresses the warmest indignation that the audience of the judge, his despatch of business, his seasonable delays, and his final sentence, were publicly sold, either by himself or by the officers of his court. The continuance, and perhaps the impunity, of these crimes is attested by the repetition of impotent laws and ineffectual menaces.

All the civil magistrates were drawn from the profession of the law. The celebrated Institutes of Justinian are addressed to the youth of his dominions who had devoted themselves to the study of Roman jurisprudence; and the sovereign condescends to animate their diligence by the assurance that their skill and ability would in time be rewarded by an adequate share in the government of the republic. The rudiments of this lucrative science were taught in all the considerable cities of the East and West; but the most famous school was that of Berytus, on the coast of Phœnicia, which flourished above three centuries from the time of Alexander Severus, the author perhaps of an institution so advantageous to his native country. After a regular course of education, which lasted five years, the students dispersed themselves through the provinces in search of fortune and honours; nor could they want an inexhaustible supply of business in a great empire already corrupted by the multiplicity of laws, of arts, and of vices. The court of the Prætorian prefect of the East could alone furnish employment for one hundred and fifty advocates, sixty-four of whom were distinguished by peculiar privileges, and two were annually chosen with a salary of sixty pounds of gold to defend the causes of the treasury. The first experiment was made of their judicial talents by appointing them to act occasionally as assessors to the magistrates; from thence they were often raised to preside in the tribunals before which they had pleaded. They obtained the government of a province; and, by the aid of merit, of reputation, or of favour, they ascended, by successive steps, to the *illustrious* dignities of the state. In the practice of the bar these men had considered reason as the instrument of dispute; they interpreted the laws according to the dictates of private interest; and the same pernicious habits might still adhere to their characters in the public administration of the state. The honour of a liberal profession has indeed been vindicated by ancient and modern advocates, who have filled the most important stations with pure integrity and consummate wisdom; but in the decline of Roman jurisprudence the ordinary promotion of lawyers was pregnant with mischief and disgrace. The noble art, which had once been preserved as the sacred inheritance of the patricians, was fallen into the hands of freedmen and plebeians, who, with cunning rather than with skill, exercised a sordid and pernicious trade. Some of them procured admittance into families for the purpose of fomenting differences, of encouraging suits, and of preparing a harvest of gain for themselves or their brethren. Others, recluse in their chambers, maintained the gravity of legal professors, by furnishing a rich client with subtleties to confound the plainest truth, and with arguments to colour the most unjustifiable pretensions. The splendid and popular class was composed of the advocates, who filled the Forum with the sound of their turgid and loquacious rhetoric. Careless of fame and of justice, they are described for the most part as ignorant and rapacious guides, who conducted their clients through a maze of expense, of delay, and of disappointment; from whence, after a tedious series of years, they were at length dismissed, when their patience and fortune were almost exhausted.

*   *   *   *   *

THE SEVEN MINISTERS OF THE PALACE

Besides the magistrates and generals, who at a distance from the court diffused their delegated authority over the provinces and armies, the emperor conferred the rank of *Illustrious* on seven of his more immediate servants, to whose fidelity he intrusted his safety, or his counsels, or his treasures. 1. The private apartments of the palace were governed by a favourite eunuch, who, in the language of that age, was styled the *præpositus*, or prefect of the sacred bedchamber. His duty was to attend the emperor in his hours of state or in those of amusement, and to perform about his person all those menial services which can only derive their splendour from the influence of royalty. Under a prince who deserved to reign, the great chamberlain (for such we may call him) was an useful and humble domestic; but an artful domestic,

who improves every occasion of unguarded confidence, will insensibly
acquire over a feeble mind that ascendant which harsh wisdom and
uncomplying virtue can seldom obtain. The degenerate grandsons of
Theodosius, who were invisible to their subjects, and contemptible to
their enemies, exalted the prefects of their bedchamber above the heads
of all the ministers of the palace; and even his deputy, the first of the
splendid train of slaves who waited in the presence, was thought worthy
to rank before the *respectable* proconsuls of Greece or Asia. The jurisdiction of the chamberlain was acknowledged by the *counts*, or super-
intendents, who regulated the two important provinces of the magnificence of the wardrobe, and of the luxury of the Imperial table. 2. The
principal administration of public affairs was committed to the diligence
and abilities of the *master of the offices*. He was the supreme magistrate
of the palace, inspected the discipline of the civil and military *schools*,
and received appeals from all parts of the empire, in the causes which
related to that numerous army of privileged persons who, as the servants of the court, had obtained for themselves and families a right to
decline the authority of the ordinary judges. The correspondence between the prince and his subjects was managed by the four *scrinia*, or
offices of this minister of state. The first was appropriated to memorials,
the second to epistles, the third to petitions, and the fourth to papers and
orders of a miscellaneous kind. Each of these was directed by an inferior *master* of *respectable* dignity, and the whole business was despatched by a hundred and forty-eight secretaries, chosen for the most
part from the profession of the law, on account of the variety of
abstracts of reports and references which frequently occurred in the
exercise of their several functions. From a condescension which in
former ages would have been esteemed unworthy of the Roman
majesty, a particular secretary was allowed for the Greek language; and
interpreters were appointed to receive the ambassadors of the barbarians; but the department of foreign affairs, which constitutes so
essential a part of modern policy, seldom diverted the attention of the
master of the offices. His mind was more seriously engaged by the
general direction of the posts and arsenals of the empire. There were
thirty-four cities, fifteen in the East and nineteen in the West, in which
regular companies of workmen were perpetually employed in fabricat-
ing defensive armour, offensive weapons of all sorts, and military
engines, which were deposited in the arsenals, and occasionally delivered for the service of the troops. 3. In the course of nine centuries
the office of *quæstor* had experienced a very singular revolution. In the
infancy of Rome, two inferior magistrates were annually elected by
the people, to relieve the consuls from the invidious management of the
public treasure; a similar assistant was granted to every proconsul and
to every prætor who exercised a military or provincial command; with
the extent of conquest, the two quæstors were gradually multiplied to

the number of four, of eight, of twenty, and for a short time, perhaps, of forty; and the noblest citizens ambitiously solicited an office which gave them a seat in the senate, and a just hope of obtaining the honours of the republic. Whilst Augustus affected to maintain the freedom of election, he consented to accept the annual privilege of recommending, or rather indeed of nominating, a certain proportion of candidates; and it was his custom to select one of these distinguished youths to read his orations or epistles in the assemblies of the senate. The practice of Augustus was imitated by succeeding princes; the occasional commission was established as a permanent office; and the favoured quæstor, assuming a new and more illustrious character, alone survived the suppression of his ancient and useless colleagues. As the orations which he composed in the name of the emperor acquired the force, and at length the form, of absolute edicts, he was considered as the representative of the legislative power, the oracle of the council, and the original source of the civil jurisprudence. He was sometimes invited to take his seat in the supreme judicature of the Imperial consistory, with the Prætorian prefects and the master of the offices; and he was frequently requested to resolve the doubts of inferior judges: but as he was not oppressed with a variety of subordinate business, his leisure and talents were employed to cultivate that dignified style of eloquence which, in the corruption of taste and language, still preserves the majesty of the Roman laws. In some respects the office of the Imperial quæstor may be compared with that of a modern chancellor; but the use of a great seal, which seems to have been adopted by the illiterate barbarians, was never introduced to attest the public acts of the emperors. 4. The extraordinary title of *count of the sacred largesses* was bestowed on the treasurer-general of the revenue, with the intention perhaps of inculcating that every payment flowed from the voluntary bounty of the monarch. To conceive the almost infinite detail of the annual and daily expense of the civil and military administration in every part of a great empire would exceed the powers of the most vigorous imagination. The actual account employed several hundred persons, distributed into eleven different offices, which were artfully contrived to examine and control their respective operations. The multitude of these agents had a natural tendency to increase; and it was more than once thought expedient to dismiss to their native homes the useless supernumeraries, who, deserting their honest labours, had pressed with too much eagerness into the lucrative profession of the finances. Twenty-nine provincial receivers, of whom eighteen were honoured with the title of count, corresponded with the treasurer; and he extended his jurisdiction over the mines from whence the precious metals were extracted, over the mints, in which they were converted into the current coin, and over the public treasuries of the most important cities, where they were deposited for the service of the state. The foreign trade of the empire was regulated by this minister, who directed likewise all the linen and woollen manufactures, in which the successive operations of spinning, weaving, and dyeing were executed, chiefly by women of a servile condition, for the use of the palace and army. Twenty-six of these institutions are enumerated in the West, where the arts had been more recently introduced, and a still larger proportion may be allowed for the industrious provinces of the East. 5. Besides the public revenue, which an absolute monarch might levy and expend according to his pleasure, the emperors, in the capacity of opulent citizens, possessed a very extensive property, which was administered by the *count* or treasurer of *the private estate*. Some part had perhaps been the ancient demesnes of kings and republics; some accessions might be derived from the families which were successively invested with the purple; but the most considerable portion flowed from the impure source of confiscations and forfeitures. The Imperial estates were scattered through the provinces from Mauritania to Britain; but the rich and fertile soil of Cappadocia tempted the monarch to acquire in that country his fairest possessions, and either Constantine or his successors embraced the occasion of justifying avarice by religious zeal. They suppressed the rich temple of Comana, where the high-priest of the goddess of war supported the dignity of a sovereign prince; and they applied to their private use the consecrated lands, which were inhabited by six thousand subjects or slaves of the deity and her ministers. But these were not the valuable inhabitants: the plains that stretch from the foot of Mount Argæus to the banks of the Sarus bred a generous race of horses, renowned above all other in the ancient world for their majestic shape and incomparable swiftness. These *sacred* animals, destined for the service of the palace and the Imperial games, were protected by the laws from the profanation of a vulgar master. The demesnes of Cappadocia were important enough to require the inspection of a *count*; officers of an inferior rank were stationed in the other parts of the empire and the deputies of the private, as well as those of the public treasurer, were maintained in the exercise of their independent functions, and encouraged to control the authority of the provincial magistrates. 6, 7. The chosen bands of cavalry and infantry, which guarded the person of the emperor, were under the immediate command of the *two counts of the domestics*. The whole number consisted of three thousand five hundred men, divided into seven *schools*, or troops, of five hundred each; and in the East this honourable service was almost entirely appropriated to the Armenians. Whenever, on public ceremonies, they were drawn up in the courts and porticos of the palace, their lofty stature, silent order, and splendid arms of silver and gold, displayed a martial pomp not unworthy of the Roman majesty. From the seven schools two companies of horse and foot were selected, of the *protectors*, whose advantageous station was the hope and reward of the most deserving soldiers. They mounted guard in the interior apartments, and were occasionally despatched into the provinces, to execute with celerity and vigour the orders of their master. The counts of the domestics had succeeded to the office of the Prætorian prefects; like the prefects, they aspired from the service of the palace to the command of armies.

THE BEGINNINGS OF THE POLICE STATE

The perpetual intercourse between the court and the provinces was facilitated by the construction of roads and the institution of posts. But these beneficial establishments were accidentally connected with a pernicious and intolerable abuse. Two or three hundred *agents* or messengers were employed, under the jurisdiction of the master of the offices, to announce the names of the annual consuls, and the edicts or victories of the emperors. They insensibly assumed the licence of reporting whatever they could observe of the conduct either of magistrates or of private citizens; and were soon considered as the eyes of the monarch and the scourge of the people. Under the warm influence of a feeble reign they multiplied to the incredible number of ten thousand, disdained the mild though frequent admonitions of the laws, and exercised in the profitable management of the posts a rapacious and insolent oppression. These official spies, who regularly corresponded with the palace, were encouraged, by favour and reward, anxiously to watch the progress of every treasonable design, from the faint and latent symptoms of disaffection, to the actual preparation of an open revolt. Their careless or criminal violation of truth and justice was covered by the consecrated mask of zeal; and they might securely aim their poisoned arrows at the breast either of the guilty or the innocent, who had provoked their resentment, or refused to purchase their silence. A faithful subject, of Syria perhaps, or of Britain, was exposed to the danger, or at least to the dread, of being dragged in chains to the court of Milan or Constantinople, to defend his life and fortune against the malicious charge of these privileged informers. The ordinary administration was conducted by those methods which extreme necessity can alone palliate; and the defects of evidence were diligently supplied by the use of torture.

The deceitful and dangerous experiment of the criminal *quæstion*, as it is emphatically styled, was admitted, rather than approved, in the jurisprudence of the Romans. They applied this sanguinary mode of examination only to servile bodies, whose sufferings were seldom weighed by those haughty republicans in the scale of justice or humanity; but they would never consent to violate the sacred person of a citizen till they possessed the clearest evidence of his guilt. The annals of tyranny, from the reign of Tiberius to that of Domitian, circumstantially relate the executions of many innocent victims; but, as long as the faintest remembrance was kept alive of the national freedom and honour, the last hours of a Roman were secure from the danger of ignominious torture.[1] The conduct of the provincial magistrates was not, however, regulated by the practice of the city, or the strict maxims of the civilians. They found the use of torture established not only among the slaves of oriental despotism, but among the Macedonians, who obeyed a limited monarch; among the Rhodians, who flourished by the liberty of commerce; and even among the sage Athenians, who had asserted and adorned the dignity of human kind. The acquiescence of the provincials encouraged their governors to acquire, or perhaps to usurp, a discretionary power of employing the rack, to extort from vagrants or plebeian criminals the confession of their guilt, till they insensibly proceeded to confound the distinctions of rank, and to disregard the privileges of Roman citizens. The apprehensions of the subjects urged them to solicit, and the interest of the sovereign engaged him to grant, a variety of special exemptions, which tacitly allowed, and even authorised, the general use of torture. They protected all persons of illustrious or honourable rank, bishops and their presbyters, professors of the liberal arts, soldiers and their families, municipal officers, and their posterity to the third generation, and all children under the age of puberty. But a fatal maxim was introduced into the new jurisprudence of the empire, that in the case of treason, which included every offence that the subtlety of lawyers could derive from an *hostile intention* towards the prince or republic, all privileges were suspended, and all conditions were reduced to the same ignominious level. As the safety of the emperor was avowedly preferred to every consideration of justice or humanity, the dignity of age and the tenderness of youth were alike exposed to the most cruel tortures; and the terrors of a malicious information, which might select them as the accomplices, or even as the witnesses, perhaps, of an imaginary crime, perpetually hung over the heads of the principal citizens of the Roman world.

*   *   *   *   *

A people elated by pride, or soured by discontent, is seldom qualified to form a just estimate of their actual situation. The subjects of Constantine were incapable of discerning the decline of genius and manly virtue, which so far degraded them below the dignity of their ancestors; but they could feel and lament the rage of tyranny, the relaxation of discipline, and the increase of taxes. The impartial historian, who acknowledges the justice of their complaints, will observe some favourable circumstances which tended to alleviate the misery of their condition. The threatening tempest of barbarians, which so soon subverted the foundations of Roman greatness, was still repelled, or suspended, on

---

[1] In the conspiracy of Piso against Nero, Epicharis (libertina mulier) was the only person tortured; the rest were *intacti tormentis.* It would be superfluous to add a weaker, and it would be difficult to find a stronger, example. Tacit. Annal. xv. 57.

the frontiers. The arts of luxury and literature were cultivated, and the elegant pleasures of society were enjoyed, by the inhabitants of a considerable portion of the globe. The forms, the pomp, and the expense of the civil administration contributed to restrain the irregular licence of the soldiers; and although the laws were violated by power, or perverted by subtlety, the sage principles of the Roman jurisprudence preserved a sense of order and equity unknown to the despotic governments of the East. The rights of mankind might derive some protection from religion and philosophy; and the name of freedom, which could no longer alarm, might sometimes admonish, the successors of Augustus, that they did not reign over a nation of Slaves or Barbarians.

Chapter 18

THE CHARACTER OF CONSTANTINE. HIS
FAMILY. HIS DEATH. THE RISE OF PERSIA UNDER SAPOR II

THE character of the prince who removed the seat of empire, and introduced such important changes into the civil and religious constitution of his country, has fixed the attention, and divided the opinions, of mankind. By the grateful zeal of the Christians the deliverer of the church has been decorated with every attribute of a hero, and even of a saint; while the discontent of the vanquished party has compared Constantine to the most abhorred of those tyrants who, by their vice and weakness, dishonoured the Imperial purple. The same passions have, in some degree, been perpetuated to succeeding generations, and the character of Constantine is considered, even in the present age, as an object either of satire or of panegyric. By the impartial union of those defects which are confessed by his warmest admirers, and of those virtues which are acknowledged by his most implacable enemies, we might hope to delineate a just portrait of that extraordinary man, which the truth and candour of history should adopt without a blush. But it would soon appear that the vain attempt to blend such discordant colours, and to reconcile such inconsistent qualities, must produce a figure monstrous rather than human, unless it is viewed in its proper and distinct lights by a careful separation of the different periods of the reign of Constantine.

The person, as well as the mind, of Constantine had been enriched by nature with her choicest endowments. His stature was lofty, his countenance majestic, his deportment graceful; his strength and activity were displayed in every manly exercise, and, from his earliest youth to a very advanced season of life, he preserved the vigour of his constitution by a strict adherence to the domestic virtues of chastity and temperance. He delighted in the social intercourse of familiar conversation; and though he might sometimes indulge his disposition to raillery with less reserve than was required by the severe dignity of his station, the courtesy and liberality of his manners gained the hearts of all who approached him. The sincerity of his friendship has been suspected; yet he showed, on some occasions, that he was not incapable of a warm and lasting attachment. The disadvantage of an illiterate education had not prevented him from forming a just estimate of the value of learning; and the arts and sciences derived some encouragement from the munificent protection of Constantine. In the despatch of business his diligence was

266

indefatigable; and the active powers of his mind were almost continually exercised in reading, writing, or meditating, in giving audience to ambassadors, and in examining the complaints of his subjects. Even those who censured the propriety of his measures were compelled to acknowledge that he possessed magnanimity to conceive, and patience to execute, the most arduous designs, without being checked either by the prejudices of education or by the clamours of the multitude. In the field he infused his own intrepid spirit into the troops, whom he conducted with the talents of a consummate general; and to his abilities, rather than to his fortune, we may ascribe the signal victories which he obtained over the foreign and domestic foes of the republic. He loved glory as the reward, perhaps as the motive, of his labours. The boundless ambition which, from the moment of his accepting the purple at York, appears as the ruling passion of his soul, may be justified by the dangers of his own situation, by the character of his rivals, by the consciousness of superior merit, and by the prospect that his success would enable him to restore peace and order to the distracted empire. In his civil wars against Maxentius and Licinius he had engaged on his side the inclinations of the people, who compared the undissembled vices of those tyrants with the spirit of wisdom and justice which seemed to direct the general tenor of the administration of Constantine.

Had Constantine fallen on the banks of the Tiber, or even in the plains of Hadrianople, such is the character which, with a few exceptions, he might have transmitted to posterity. But the conclusion of his reign (according to the moderate and indeed tender sentence of a writer of the same age) degraded him from the rank which he had acquired among the most deserving of the Roman princes. In the life of Augustus we behold the tyrant of the republic converted almost by imperceptible degrees into the father of his country and of human kind. In that of Constantine we may contemplate a hero, who had so long inspired his subjects with love and his enemies with terror, degenerating into a cruel and dissolute monarch, corrupted by his fortune, or raised by conquest above the necessity of dissimulation. The general peace which he maintained during the last fourteen years of his reign was a period of apparent splendour rather than of real prosperity; and the old age of Constantine was disgraced by the opposite yet reconcileable vices of rapaciousness and prodigality. The accumulated treasures found in the palaces of Maxentius and Licinius were lavishly consumed; the various innovations introduced by the conqueror were attended with an increasing expense; the cost of his buildings, his court, and his festivals required an immediate and plentiful supply; and the oppression of the people was the only fund which could support the magnificence of the sovereign. His unworthy favourites, enriched by the boundless liberality of their master, usurped with impunity the privilege of rapine and corruption. A secret but universal decay was felt in every part of the public administration, and the emperor himself, though he still retained the obedience, gradually lost the esteem, of his subjects. The dress and manners which, towards the decline of life, he chose to affect, served only to degrade him in the eyes of mankind. The Asiatic pomp which had been adopted by the pride of Diocletian assumed an air of softness and effeminacy in the person of Constantine. He is represented with false hair of various colours, laboriously arranged by the skilful artists of the times; a diadem of a new and more expensive fashion; a profusion of gems and pearls, of collars and bracelets; and a variegated flowing robe of silk, most curiously embroidered with flowers of gold. In such apparel, scarcely to be excused by the youth and folly of Elagabalus, we are at a loss to discover the wisdom of an aged monarch and the simplicity of a Roman veteran. A mind thus relaxed by prosperity and indulgence was incapable of rising to that magnanimity which disdains suspicion and dares to forgive. The deaths of Maximian and Licinius may perhaps be justified by the maxims of policy as they are taught in the schools of tyrants; but an impartial narrative of the executions, or rather murders, which sullied the declining age of Constantine, will suggest to our most candid thoughts the idea of a prince who could sacrifice, without reluctance, the laws of justice and the feelings of nature to the dictates either of his passions or of his interest.

THE FAMILY OF CONSTANTINE

The same fortune which so invariably followed the standard of Constantine seemed to secure the hopes and comforts of his domestic life. Those among his predecessors who had enjoyed the longest and most prosperous reigns, Augustus, Trajan, and Diocletian, had been disappointed of posterity; and the frequent revolutions had never allowed sufficient time for any Imperial family to grow up and multiply under the shade of the purple. But the royalty of the Flavian line, which had been first ennobled by the Gothic Claudius, descended through several generations; and Constantine himself derived from his royal father the hereditary honours which he transmitted to his children. The emperor had been twice married. Minervina, the obscure but lawful object of his youthful attachment, had left him only one son, who was called Crispus. By Fausta, the daughter of Maximian, he had three daughters, and three sons known by the kindred names of Constantine, Constantius, and Constans. The unambitious brothers of the great Constantine, Julius Constantius, Dalmatius, and Hannibalianus, were permitted to enjoy the most honourable rank and the most affluent fortune that could be consistent with a private station. The youngest of the three lived without a name and died without posterity. His two elder brothers obtained in marriage the daughters of wealthy senators, and propagated new branches of the Imperial race. Gallus and Julian afterwards became the most illustrious of the children of Julius Constantius, the *Patrician*. The two sons of Dalmatius, who had been decorated with the vain title of *Censor*, were named Dalmatius and Hannibalianus. The two sisters of the great Constantine, Anastasia and Eutropia, were bestowed on Optatus and Nepotianus, two senators of noble birth and of consular dignity. His third sister, Constantia, was distinguished by her pre-eminence of greatness and of misery. She remained the widow of the vanquished Licinius; and it was by her entreaties that an innocent boy, the offspring of their marriage, preserved, for some time, his life, the title of Cæsar, and a precarious hope of the succession. Besides the females and the allies of the Flavian house, ten or twelve males, to whom the language of modern courts would apply the title of prince of the blood, seemed, according to the order of their birth, to be destined either to inherit or to support the throne of Constantine. But in less than thirty years this numerous and increasing family was reduced to the persons of Constantius and Julian, who alone had survived a series of crimes and calamities such as the tragic poets have deplored in the devoted lines of Pelops and of Cadmus.

Crispus, the eldest son of Constantine, and the presumptive heir of the empire, is represented by impartial historians as an amiable and accomplished youth. The care of his education, or at least of his studies, was intrusted to Lactantius, the most eloquent of the Christians; a preceptor admirably qualified to form the taste and to excite the virtues of his illustrious disciple. At the age of seventeen Crispus was invested with the title of Cæsar, and the administration of the Gallic provinces, where the inroads of the Germans gave him an early occasion of signalising his military prowess. In the civil war which broke out soon afterwards, the father and son divided their powers; and this history has already celebrated the valour as well as conduct displayed by the latter in forcing the straits of the Hellespont, so obstinately defended by the superior fleet of Licinius. This naval victory contributed to determine the event of the war, and the names of Constantine and of Crispus were united in the joyful acclamations of their eastern subjects, who loudly proclaimed that the world had been subdued, and was now governed, by an emperor endowed with every virtue, and by his illustrious son, a prince beloved of Heaven, and the lively image of his father's perfections. The public favour, which seldom accompanies old age, diffused its lustre over the youth of Crispus. He deserved the esteem and he engaged the affections of the court, the army, and the people. The experienced merit of a reigning monarch is acknowledged by his subjects with reluctance, and frequently denied with partial and discontented murmurs; while, from the opening virtues of his successor, they fondly conceive the most unbounded hopes of private as well as public felicity.

This dangerous popularity soon excited the attention of Constantine, who, both as a father and as a king, was impatient of an equal. Instead of attempting to secure the allegiance of his son by the generous ties of confidence and gratitude, he resolved to prevent the mischiefs which might be apprehended from dissatisfied ambition. Crispus soon had reason to complain that, while his infant brother Constantius was sent with the title of Cæsar to reign over his peculiar department of the Gallic provinces, *he*, a prince of mature years, who had performed such recent and signal services, instead of being raised to the superior rank of Augustus, was confined almost a prisoner to his father's court, and exposed, without power or defence, to every calumny which the malice of his enemies could suggest. Under such painful circumstances the royal youth might not always be able to compose his behaviour or suppress his discontent; and we may be assured that he was encompassed by a train of indiscreet or perfidious followers, who assiduously studied to inflame, and who were perhaps instructed to betray, the unguarded warmth of his resentment. An edict of Constantine, published about this time, manifestly indicates his real or affected suspicions that a secret conspiracy had been formed against his person and government. By all the allurements of honours and rewards he invites informers of every degree to accuse, without exception, his magistrates or ministers, his friends or his most intimate favourites, protesting, with a solemn asseveration, that he himself will listen to the charge, that he himself will revenge his injuries; and concluding with a prayer, which discovers some apprehension of danger, that the providence of the Supreme Being may still continue to protect the safety of the emperor and of the empire.

The informers who complied with so liberal an invitation were sufficiently versed in the arts of courts to select the friends and adherents of Crispus as the guilty persons; nor is there any reason to distrust the veracity of the emperor, who had promised an ample measure of revenge and punishment. The policy of Constantine maintained, however, the same appearances of regard and confidence towards a son whom he began to consider as his most irreconcileable enemy. Medals were struck with the customary vows for the long and auspicious reign of the young Cæsar; and as the people, who was not admitted into the secrets of the palace, still loved his virtues and respected his dignity, a poet, who solicits his recall from exile, adores with equal devotion the majesty of the father and that of the son. The time was now arrived for celebrating the august ceremony of the twentieth year of the reign of Constantine, and the emperor, for that purpose, removed his court from Nicomedia to Rome, where the most splendid preparations had been made for his reception. Every eye and every tongue affected to express their sense of the general happiness, and the veil of ceremony and dissimulation was drawn for a while over the darkest designs of revenge and murder. In the midst of the festival the unfortunate Crispus was apprehended by order of the emperor, who laid aside the tenderness of a father without assuming the equity of a judge. The examination was short and private; and as it was thought decent to conceal the fate of the young prince from the eyes of the Roman people, he was sent under a strong guard to Pola, in Istria, where, soon afterwards, he was put to death, either by the hand of the executioner or by the more gentle operation of poison. The Cæsar Licinius, a youth of amiable manners, was involved in the ruin of Crispus, and the stern jealousy of Constantine was unmoved by the prayers and tears of his favourite sister, pleading for the life of a son whose rank was his only crime, and whose loss she did not long survive. The story of these unhappy princes, the nature and evidence of their guilt, the forms of their trial, and the circumstances of their death, were buried in mysterious obscurity, and the courtly bishop, who has celebrated in an elaborate work the virtues and piety of his hero, observes a prudent silence on the subject of these tragic events. Such haughty contempt for the opinion of mankind, whilst it imprints an indelible stain on the memory of Constantine, must remind us of the very different behaviour of one of the greatest monarchs of the present age. The Czar Peter, in the full possession of despotic power, submitted to the judgment of Russia, of Europe, and of posterity, the reasons which had compelled him to subscribe the condemnation of a criminal, or at least of a degenerate, son.

The innocence of Crispus was so universally acknowledged that the modern Greeks, who adore the memory of their founder, are reduced to palliate the guilt of a parricide which the common feelings of human nature forbade them to justify. They pretend that, as soon as the afflicted father discovered the falsehood of the accusation by which his credulity had been so fatally misled, he published to the world his repentance and remorse; that he mourned forty days, during which he abstained from the use of the bath and all the ordinary comforts of life; and that, for the lasting instruction of posterity, he erected a golden statue of Crispus, with this memorable inscription,—To MY SON, WHOM I UNJUSTLY CONDEMNED. A tale so moral and so interesting would deserve to be supported by less exceptionable authority; but if we consult the more ancient and authentic writers, they will inform us that the repentance of Constantine was manifested only in acts of blood and revenge, and that he atoned for the murder of an innocent son by the execution, perhaps, of a guilty wife. They ascribe the misfortunes of Crispus to the arts of his stepmother Fausta, whose implacable hatred or whose disappointed love renewed in the palace of Constantine the ancient tragedy of Hippolytus and of Phædra. Like the daughter of Minos, the daughter of Maximian accused her son-in-law of an incestuous attempt on the chastity of his father's wife, and easily obtained, from the jealousy of the emperor, a sentence of death against a young prince whom she considered with reason as the most formidable rival of her own children. But Helena, the aged mother of Constantine, lamented and revenged the untimely fate of her grandson Crispus; nor was it long before a real or pretended discovery was made that Fausta herself entertained a criminal connection with a slave belonging to the Imperial stables. Her condemnation and punishment were the instant consequences of the charge, and the adulteress was suffocated by the steam of a bath, which, for that purpose, had been heated to an extraordinary degree. By some it will perhaps be thought that the remembrance of a conjugal union of twenty years, and the honour of their common offspring, the destined heirs of the throne, might have softened the obdurate heart of Constantine, and persuaded him to suffer his wife, however guilty she might appear, to expiate her offences in a solitary prison. But it seems a superfluous labour to weigh the propriety, unless we could ascertain the truth, of this singular event, which is attended with some circumstances of doubt and perplexity. Those who have attacked, and those who have defended, the character of Constantine, have alike disregarded two very remarkable passages of two orations pronounced under the succeeding reign. The former celebrates the virtues, the beauty, and the fortune of the empress Fausta, the daughter, wife, sister, and mother of so many princes. The latter asserts, in explicit terms, that the mother of the younger Constantine, who was slain three years after his father's death, survived to weep over the fate of her son. Notwithstanding the positive testimony of several writers of the Pagan as well as of the Christian religion, there may still remain some reason to believe, or at least to suspect, that Fausta escaped the blind and suspicious cruelty of her husband. The deaths of a son and of a nephew, with the execution of a great number of respectable and perhaps innocent friends, who were involved in their fall, may be sufficient, however, to justify the discontent of the Roman people, and to explain the satirical verses affixed to the palace-gate, comparing the splendid and bloody reigns of Constantine and Nero.

By the death of Crispus the inheritance of the empire seemed to devolve on the three sons of Fausta, who have been already mentioned under the names of Constantine, of Constantius, and of Constans. These young princes were successively invested with the title of Cæsar, and the dates of their promotion may be referred to the tenth, the twentieth, and the thirtieth years of the reign of their father. This conduct, though it tended to multiply the future masters of the Roman world, might be excused by the partiality of paternal affection; but it is not so easy to understand the motives of the emperor, when he endangered the safety both of his family and of his people by the unnecessary elevation of his two nephews, Dalmatius and Hannibalianus. The former was raised, by the title of Cæsar, to an equality with his cousins. In favour of the latter, Constantine invented the new and singular appellation of *Nobilissimus*, to which he annexed the flattering distinction of a robe of purple and gold. But of the whole series of

Roman princes in any age of the empire Hannibalianus alone was distinguished by the title of KING, a name which the subjects of Tiberius would have detested as the profane and cruel insult of capricious tyranny. The use of such a title, even as it appears under the reign of Constantine, is a strange and unconnected fact, which can scarcely be admitted on the joint authority of Imperial medals and contemporary writers.

The whole empire was deeply interested in the education of these five youths, the acknowledged successors of Constantine. The exercises of the body prepared them for the fatigues of war and the duties of active life. Those who occasionally mention the education or talents of Constantius allow that he excelled in the gymnastic arts of leaping and running; that he was a dexterous archer, a skilful horseman, and a master of all the different weapons used in the service either of the cavalry or of the infantry. The same assiduous cultivation was bestowed, though not perhaps with equal success, to improve the minds of the sons and nephews of Constantine. The most celebrated professors of the Christian faith, of the Grecian philosophy, and of the Roman jurisprudence, were invited by the liberality of the emperor, who reserved for himself the important task of instructing the royal youths in the science of government and the knowledge of mankind. But the genius of Constantine himself had been formed by adversity and experience. In the free intercourse of private life, and amidst the dangers of the court of Galerius, he had learned to command his own passions, to encounter those of his equals, and to depend for his present safety and future greatness on the prudence and firmness of his personal conduct. His destined successors had the misfortune of being born and educated in the Imperial purple. Incessantly surrounded with a train of flatterers, they passed their youth in the enjoyment of luxury and the expectation of a throne; nor would the dignity of their rank permit them to descend from that elevated station from whence the various characters of human nature appear to wear a smooth and uniform aspect. The indulgence of Constantine admitted them, at a very tender age, to share the administration of the empire; and they studied the art of reigning, at the expense of the people intrusted to their care. The younger Constantine was appointed to hold his court in Gaul; and his brother Constantius exchanged that department, the ancient patrimony of their father, for the more opulent, but less martial, countries of the East. Italy, the Western Illyricum, and Africa, were accustomed to revere Constans, the third of his sons, as the representative of the great Constantine. He fixed Dalmatius on the Gothic frontier, to which he annexed the government of Thrace, Macedonia, and Greece. The city of Cæsarea was chosen for the residence of Hannibalianus; and the provinces of Pontus, Cappadocia, and the Lesser Armenia, were designed to form the extent of his new kingdom. For each of these princes a suitable establishment was provided. A just proportion of guards, of legions, and of auxiliaries, was allotted for their respective dignity and defence. The ministers and generals who were placed about their persons were such as Constantine could trust to assist, and even to control, these youthful sovereigns in the exercise of their delegated power. As they advanced in years and experience, the limits of their authority were insensibly enlarged: but the emperor always reserved for himself the title of Augustus; and while he showed the *Cæsars* to the armies and provinces, he maintained every part of the empire in equal obedience to its supreme head. The tranquillity of the last fourteen years of his reign was scarcely interrupted by the contemptible insurrection of a cameldriver in the island of Cyprus, or by the active part which the policy of Constantine engaged him to assume in the wars of the Goths and Sarmatians.

Inconclusive wars with Sarmatians and Goths occupied Constantine's last years.

THE DEATH OF CONSTANTINE

By chastising the pride of the Goths, and by accepting the homage of a suppliant nation, Constantine asserted the majesty of the Roman empire; and the ambassadors of Ethiopia, Persia, and the most remote countries of India, congratulated the peace and prosperity of his government. If he reckoned among the favours of fortune the death of his eldest son, of his nephew, and perhaps of his wife, he enjoyed an uninterrupted flow of private as well as public felicity till the thirtieth year of his reign; a period which none of his predecessors, since Augustus, had been permitted to celebrate. Constantine survived that solemn festival about ten months; and, at the mature age of sixty-four, after a short illness, he ended his memorable life at the palace of Achyrion, in the suburbs of Nicomedia, whither he had retired for the benefit of the air, and with the hope of recruiting his exhausted strength by the use of the warm baths. The excessive demonstrations of grief, or at least of mourning, surpassed whatever had been practised on any former occasion. Notwithstanding the claims of the senate and people of ancient Rome, the corpse of the deceased emperor, according to his last request, was transported to the city which was destined to preserve the name and memory of its founder. The body of Constantine, adorned with the vain symbols of greatness, the purple and diadem, was deposited on a golden bed in one of the apartments of the palace, which for that purpose had been splendidly furnished and illuminated. The forms of the court were strictly maintained. Every day, at the appointed hours, the principal officers of the state, the army, and the household, approaching the person of their sovereign with bended knees and a composed countenance, offered their respectful homage as seriously as if he had been still alive. From motives of policy, this theatrical representation was for some time continued; nor could flattery neglect the opportunity of remarking that Constantine alone, by the peculiar indulgence of Heaven, had reigned after his death.

But this reign could subsist only in empty pageantry; and it was soon discovered that the will of the most absolute monarch is seldom obeyed when his subjects have no longer anything to hope from his favour, or to dread from his resentment. The same ministers and generals who bowed with such reverential awe before the inanimate corpse of their deceased sovereign were engaged in secret consultations to exclude his two nephews, Dalmatius and Hannibalianus, from the share which he had assigned them in the succession of the empire. We are too imperfectly acquainted with the court of Constantine to form any judgment of the real motives which influenced the leaders of the conspiracy; unless we should suppose that they were actuated by a spirit of jealousy and revenge against the prefect Ablavius, a proud favourite, who had long directed the counsels and abused the confidence of the late emperor. The arguments by which they solicited the concurrence of the soldiers and people are of a more obvious nature: and they might with decency, as well as truth, insist on the superior rank of the children of Constantine, the danger of multiplying the number of sovereigns, and the impending mischiefs which threatened the republic, from the discord of so many rival princes who were not connected by the tender sympathy of fraternal affection. The intrigue was conducted with zeal and secrecy, till a loud and unanimous declaration was procured from the troops that they would suffer none except the sons of their lamented monarch to reign over the Roman empire. The younger Dalmatius, who was united with his collateral relations by the ties of friendship and interest, is allowed to have inherited a considerable share of the abilities of the great Constantine; but, on this occasion, he does not appear to have concerted any measures for supporting by arms the just claims which himself and his royal brother derived from the liberality of their uncle. Astonished and overwhelmed by the tide of popular fury, they seem to have remained, without the power of flight or of resistance, in the hands of their implacable enemies. Their fate was suspended till the arrival of Constantius, the second, and perhaps the most favoured, of the sons of Constantine.

The voice of the dying emperor had recommended the care of his funeral to the piety of Constantius; and that prince, by the vicinity of his eastern station, could easily prevent the diligence of his brothers, who resided in their distant government of Italy and Gaul. As soon as he had taken possession of the palace of Constantinople, his first care was to remove the apprehensions of his kinsmen, by a solemn oath which he pledged for their security. His next employment was to find some specious pretence which might release his conscience from the obligation of an imprudent promise. The arts of fraud were made subservient to the designs of cruelty; and a manifest forgery was attested by a person of the most sacred character. From the hands of the bishop of Nicomedia, Constantius received a fatal scroll, affirmed to be the genuine testament of his father; in which the emperor expressed his suspicions that he had been poisoned by his brothers; and conjured his sons to revenge his death, and to consult their own safety, by the punishment of the guilty. Whatever reasons might have been alleged by these unfortunate princes to defend their life and honour against so incredible an accusation, they were silenced by the furious clamours of the soldiers, who declared themselves, at once, their enemies, their judges, and their executioners. The spirit, and even the forms, of legal proceedings were repeatedly violated in a promiscuous massacre; which involved the two uncles of Constantius, seven of his cousins, of whom Dalmatius and Hannibalianus were the most illustrious, the Patrician Optatus, who had married a sister of the late emperor, and the prefect Ablavius, whose power and riches had inspired him with some hopes of obtaining the purple. If it were necessary to aggravate the horrors of this bloody scene, we might add that Constantius himself had espoused the daughter of his uncle Julius, and that he had bestowed his sister in marriage on his cousin Hannibalianus. These alliances, which the policy of Constantine, regardless of the public prejudice, had formed between the several branches of the Imperial house, served only to convince mankind that these princes were as cold to the endearments of conjugal affection, as they were insensible to the ties of consanguinity and the moving entreaties of youth and innocence. Of so numerous a family, Gallus and Julian alone, the two youngest children of Julius Constantius, were saved from the hands of the assassins, till their rage, satiated with slaughter, had in some measure subsided. The emperor Constantius, who, in the absence of his brothers, was the most obnoxious to guilt and reproach, discovered, on some future occasions, a faint and transient remorse for those cruelties which the perfidious counsels of his ministers, and the irresistible violence of the troops, had extorted from his unexperienced youth.

The massacre of the Flavian race was succeeded by a new division of the provinces, which was ratified in a personal interview of the three brothers. Constantine, the eldest of the Cæsars, obtained, with a certain pre-eminence of rank, the possession of the new capital, which bore his own name and that of his father. Thrace and the countries of the East were allotted for the patrimony of Constantius; and Constans was acknowledged as the lawful sovereign of Italy, Africa, and the western Illyricum. The armies submitted to their hereditary right, and they condescended, after some delay, to accept from the Roman senate the title of *Augustus*. When they first assumed the reins of government, the eldest of these princes was twenty-one, the second twenty, and the third only seventeen, years of age.

THE RISE OF PERSIA UNDER SAPOR II

While the martial nations of Europe followed the standards of his brothers, Constantius, as the head of the effeminate troops of Asia, was left to sustain the weight of the Persian war. At the decease of Constantine, the throne of the East was filled by Sapor, son of Hormouz, or Hormisdas, and grandson of Narses, who, after the victory of Galerius, had humbly confessed the superiority of the Roman power. Although Sapor was in the thirtieth year of his long reign, he was still in the vigour of youth, as the date of his accession, by a very strange fatality, had preceded that of his birth. The wife of Hormouz remained pregnant at the time of her husband's death, and the uncertainty of the sex, as well as of the event, excited the ambitious hopes of the princes of the house of Sassan. The apprehensions of civil war were at length removed by the positive assurance of the Magi that the widow of Hormouz had conceived, and would safely produce a son. Obedient to the voice of superstition, the Persians prepared, without delay, the ceremony of his coronation. A royal bed, on which the queen lay in state, was exhibited in the midst of the palace; the diadem was placed on the spot which might be supposed to conceal the future heir of Artaxerxes, and the prostrate satraps adored the majesty of their invisible and insensible sovereign. If any credit can be given to this marvellous tale, which seems, however, to be countenanced by the manners of the people and by the extraordinary duration of his reign, we must admire not only the fortune but the genius of Sapor. In the soft sequestered education of a Persian harem the royal youth could discover the importance of exercising the vigour of his mind and body, and by his personal merit deserved a throne on which he had been seated while he was yet unconscious of the duties and temptations of absolute power. His minority was exposed to the almost inevitable calamities of domestic discord; his capital was surprised and plundered by Thair, a powerful king of Yemen or Arabia, and the majesty of the royal family was degraded by the captivity of a princess, the sister of the deceased king. But as soon as Sapor attained the age of manhood the presumptuous Thair, his nation, and his country, fell beneath the first effort of the young warrior, who used his victory with so judicious a mixture of rigour and clemency that he obtained from the fears and gratitude of the Arabs the title of *Dhoulacnaf*, or protector of the nation.

Constantine II was defeated at Aquileia by Constans in 340 who became the ruler of the West. Constantius ruling the East had to face the attacks of the Persians under Sapor II. The Persian invasion of Armenia was a threat to the growth of Christianity in the

East. A victory at Singara in 348 was turned by carelessness into a crushing defeat. The fortress of Nisibis sustained three sieges and peace was made in 350. In the same year Constans was removed by Magnetius while Vetranio assumed the purple on Constantius's behalf. Eventually Constantius overcame Magnentius at Mursa in 351 in the valley of the Save and finally in 353 Constantius ruled over an undivided empire.

Chapter 19

THE RISE OF JULIAN. HIS CIVIL ADMINIS-
TRATION IN GAUL. HIS LOVE FOR THE CITY OF PARIS

THE divided provinces of the empire were again united by the victory of Constantius; but as that feeble prince was destitute of personal merit either in peace or war; as he feared his generals, and distrusted his ministers; the triumph of his arms served only to establish the reign of the *eunuchs* over the Roman world. Those unhappy beings, the ancient production of Oriental jealousy and despotism, were introduced into Greece and Rome by the contagion of Asiatic luxury. Their progress was rapid; and the eunuchs, who, in the time of Augustus, had been abhorred, as the monstrous retinue of an Egyptian queen, were gradually admitted into the families of matrons, of senators, and of the emperors themselves. Restrained by the severe edicts of Domitian and Nerva, cherished by the pride of Diocletian, reduced to an humble station by the prudence of Constantine, they multiplied in the palaces of his degenerate sons, and insensibly acquired the knowledge, and at length the direction, of the secret councils of Constantius. The aversion and contempt which mankind has so uniformly entertained for that imperfect species appears to have degraded their character, and to have rendered them almost as incapable as they were supposed to be of conceiving any generous sentiment, or of performing any worthy action. But the eunuchs were skilled in the arts of flattery and intrigue; and they alternately governed the mind of Constantius by his fears, his indolence, and his vanity. Whilst he viewed in a deceitful mirror the fair appearance of public prosperity, he supinely permitted them to intercept the complaints of the injured provinces; to accumulate immense treasures by the sale of justice and of honours; to disgrace the most important dignities by the promotion of those who had purchased at their hands the powers of oppression; and to gratify their resentment against the few independent spirits who arrogantly refused to solicit the protection of slaves. Of these slaves the most distinguished was the chamberlain Eusebius, who ruled the monarch and the palace with such absolute sway, that Constantius, according to the sarcasm of an impartial historian, possessed some credit with his haughty favourite. By his artful suggestions, the emperor was persuaded to subscribe the condemnation of the unfortunate Gallus, and to add a new crime to the long list of unnatural murders which pollute the honour of the house of Constantine.

When the two nephews of Constantine, Gallus and Julian, were saved from the fury of the soldiers, the former was about twelve, and the latter about six, years of age; and, as the eldest was thought to be of a sickly constitution, they obtained with the less difficulty a precarious and dependent life from the affected pity of Constantius, who was sensible that the execution of these helpless orphans would have been esteemed, by all mankind, an act of the most deliberate cruelty. Different cities of Ionia and Bithynia were assigned for the places of their exile and education; but as soon as their growing years excited the jealousy of the emperor, he judged it more prudent to secure those unhappy youths in the strong castle of Macellum, near Cæsarea. The treatment which they experienced during a six years' confinement was partly such as they could hope from a careful guardian, and partly such as they might dread from a suspicious tyrant. Their prison was an ancient palace, the residence of the kings of Cappadocia; the situation was pleasant, the building stately, the enclosure spacious. They pursued their studies, and practised their exercises, under the tuition of the most skilful masters; and the numerous household appointed to attend, or rather to guard, the nephews of Constantine, was not unworthy of the dignity of their birth. But they could not disguise to themselves that they were deprived of fortune, of freedom, and of safety; secluded from the society of all whom they could trust or esteem, and condemned to pass their melancholy hours in the company of slaves devoted to the commands of a tyrant who had already injured them beyond the hope of reconciliation. At length, however, the emergencies of the state compelled the emperor, or rather his eunuchs, to invest Gallus, in the twenty-fifth year of his age, with the title of Cæsar, and to cement this political connection by his marriage with the princess Constantina. After a formal interview, in which the two princes mutually engaged their faith never to undertake anything to the prejudice of each other, they repaired without delay to their respective stations. Constantius continued his march towards the West, and Gallus fixed his residence at Antioch; from whence, with a delegated authority, he administered the five great dioceses of the eastern prefecture. In this fortunate change, the new Cæsar was not unmindful of his brother Julian, who obtained the honours of his rank, the appearances of liberty, and the restitution of an ample patrimony.

Gallus proved unfit to rule and was removed by murder. Julian, although not originally thought of as a possible emperor, gradually advanced in experience and power and in 355 was declared Cæsar. While Constantius was engaged on the Danube frontier he defended Gaul against invasions by the Alemanni and Franks. He immediately set himself to rebuild and restore the cities of Gaul, "a work more congenial to his humane and philosophic temper."

CIVIL ADMINISTRATION OF JULIAN IN GAUL

A tender regard for the peace and happiness of his subjects was the ruling principle which directed, or seemed to direct, the administration of Julian. He devoted the leisure of his winter-quarters to the offices of civil government; and affected to assume with more pleasure the character of a magistrate than that of a general. Before he took the field he devolved on the provincial governors most of the public and private causes which had been referred to his tribunal; but, on his return, he carefully revised their proceedings, mitigated the rigour of the law, and pronounced a second judgment on the judges themselves. Superior to the last temptation of virtuous minds, an indiscreet and intemperate zeal for justice, he restrained, with calmness and dignity, the warmth of an advocate who prosecuted, for extortion, the president of the Narbonnese province. "Who will ever be found guilty," exclaimed the vehement Delphidius, "if it be enough to deny?" "And who," replied Julian, "will ever be innocent, if it is sufficient to affirm?" In the general administration of peace and war, the interest of the sovereign is commonly the same as that of his people; but Constantius would have thought himself deeply injured, if the virtues of Julian had defrauded him of any part of the tribute which he extorted from an oppressed and exhausted country. The prince who was invested with the ensigns of royalty might sometimes presume to correct the rapacious insolence of the inferior agents, to expose their corrupt arts, and to introduce an equal and easier mode of collection. But the management of the finances was more safely intrusted to Florentius, Prætorian prefect of Gaul, an effeminate tyrant, incapable of pity or remorse: and the haughty minister complained of the most decent and gentle opposition, while Julian himself was rather inclined to censure the weakness of his own behaviour. The Cæsar had rejected with abhorrence a mandate for the levy of an extraordinary tax; a new superindiction, which the prefect had offered for his signature; and the faithful picture of the public misery, by which he had been obliged to justify his refusal, offended the court of Constantius. We may enjoy the pleasure of reading the sentiments of Julian, as he expresses them with warmth and freedom in a letter to one of his most intimate friends. After stating his own conduct, he proceeds in the following terms:—"Was it possible for the disciple of Plato and Aristotle to act otherwise than I have done? Could I abandon the unhappy subjects intrusted to my care? Was I not called upon to defend them from the repeated injuries of these unfeeling robbers? A tribune who deserts his post is punished with death, and deprived of the honours of burial. With what justice could I pronounce *his* sentence, if, in the hour of danger, I myself neglected a duty far more sacred and far more important? God has placed me in this elevated post; his providence will guard and support me. Should I be condemned to suffer, I

shall derive comfort from the testimony of a pure and upright conscience. Would to Heaven that I still possessed a counsellor like Sallust!
If they think proper to send me a successor, I shall submit without reluctance; and had much rather improve the short opportunity of doing
good, than enjoy a long and lasting impunity of evil." The precarious
and dependent situation of Julian displayed his virtues and concealed
his defects. The young hero who supported, in Gaul, the throne of
Constantius, was not permitted to reform the vices of the government;
but he had courage to alleviate or to pity the distress of the people.
Unless he had been able to revive the martial spirit of the Romans, or
to introduce the arts of industry and refinement among their savage
enemies, he could not entertain any rational hopes of securing the public
tranquillity, either by the peace or conquest of Germany. Yet the
victories of Julian suspended for a short time the inroads of the barbarians, and delayed the ruin of the Western Empire.

JULIAN AND THE CITY OF PARIS

His salutary influence restored the cities of Gaul, which had been so
long exposed to the evils of civil discord, barbarian war, and domestic
tyranny; and the spirit of industry was revived with the hopes of enjoyment. Agriculture, manufactures, and commerce, again flourished
under the protection of the laws; and the *curiæ*, or civil corporations,
were again filled with useful and respectable members: the youth were
no longer apprehensive of marriage; and married persons were no
longer apprehensive of posterity: the public and private festivals were
celebrated with customary pomp; and the frequent and secure intercourse of the provinces displayed the image of national prosperity. A
mind like that of Julian must have felt the general happiness of which
he was the author; but he viewed with peculiar satisfaction and complacency the city of Paris, the seat of his winter residence, and the object
of his partial affection. That splendid capital, which now embraces an
ample territory on either side of the Seine, was originally confined to the
small island in the midst of the river, from whence the inhabitants derived a supply of pure and salubrious water. The river bathed the foot
of the walls; and the town was accessible only by two wooden bridges.
A forest overspread the northern side of the Seine, but on the south, the
ground which now bears the name of the University was insensibly
covered with houses, and adorned with a palace and amphitheatre,
baths, an aqueduct, and a field of Mars for the exercise of the Roman
troops. The severity of the climate was tempered by the neighbourhood
of the ocean; and with some precautions, which experience had taught,
the vine and fig-tree were successfully cultivated. But in remarkable
winters the Seine was deeply frozen; and the huge pieces of ice that
floated down the stream might be compared, by an Asiatic, to the blocks
of white marble which were extracted from the quarries of Phrygia.

The licentiousness and corruption of Antioch recalled to the memory of Julian the severe and simple manners of his beloved Lutetia, where the amusements of the theatre were unknown or despised. He indignantly contrasted the effeminate Syrians with the brave and honest simplicity of the Gauls, and almost forgave the intemperance which was the only stain of the Celtic character. If Julian could now revisit the capital of France, he might converse with men of science and genius, capable of understanding and of instructing a disciple of the Greeks; he might excuse the lively and graceful follies of a nation whose martial spirit has never been enervated by the indulgence of luxury; and he must applaud the perfection of that inestimable art which softens and refines and embellishes the intercourse of social life.

THE RECOGNITION OF CHRISTIANITY
THE BEGINNINGS OF HERESY

Chapter 20

THE CONVERSION OF CONSTANTINE. HIS EDICT OF TOLERA-
TION. HIS VISION AND HIS BAPTISM. THE LEGAL ESTAB-
LISHMENT OF CHRISTIANITY. DISTINCTION OF SPIRITUAL
AND TEMPORAL POWERS

THE public establishment of Christianity may be considered as one of those important and domestic revolutions which excite the most lively curiosity, and afford the most valuable instruction. The victories and the civil policy of Constantine no longer influence the state of Europe; but a considerable portion of the globe still retains the impression which it received from the conversion of that monarch; and the ecclesiastical institutions of his reign are still connected, by an indissoluble chain, with the opinions, the passions, and the interests of the present generation.

In the consideration of a subject which may be examined with impartiality, but cannot be viewed with indifference, a difficulty immediately arises of a very unexpected nature—that of ascertaining the real and precise date of the conversion of Constantine. The eloquent Lactantius, in the midst of his court, seems impatient to proclaim to the world the glorious example of the sovereign of Gaul; who, in the first moments of his reign, acknowledged and adored the majesty of the true and only God. The learned Eusebius has ascribed the faith of Constantine to the miraculous sign which was displayed in the heavens whilst he meditated and prepared the Italian expedition. The historian Zosimus maliciously asserts that the emperor had imbrued his hands in the blood of his eldest son before he publicly renounced the gods of Rome and of his ancestors. The perplexity produced by these discordant authorities is derived from the behaviour of Constantine himself. According to the strictness of ecclesiastical language, the first of the *Christian* emperors was unworthy of that name till the moment of his death; since it was only during his last illness that he received, as a catechumen, the imposition of hands, and was afterwards admitted, by the initiatory rites of baptism, into the number of the faithful. The Christianity of Constantine must be allowed in a much more vague and qualified sense; and the nicest accuracy is required in tracing the slow and almost imperceptible gradations by which the monarch declared himself the protector, and at length the proselyte, of the church. It was an arduous task to eradicate the habits and prejudices of his education, to acknowledge the divine power of Christ, and to understand that the truth of *his* revelation was incompatible with the worship of the gods. The obstacles which he had probably experienced in his own mind instructed him to proceed with caution in the momentous change of a national religion; and he insensibly discovered his new opinions, as far as he could enforce them with safety and with effect. During the whole course of his reign, the stream of Christianity flowed with a gentle, though accelerated, motion: but its general direction was sometimes checked, and sometimes diverted, by the accidental circumstances of the times, and by the prudence, or possibly by the caprice, of the monarch. His ministers were permitted to signify the intentions of the master in the various languages which was best adapted to their respective principles; and he artfully balanced the hopes and fears of his subjects, by publishing in the same year two edicts; the first of which enjoined the solemn observance of Sunday, and the second directed the regular consultation of the Aruspices. While this important revolution yet remained in suspense, the Christians and the Pagans watched the conduct of their sovereign with the same anxiety, but with very opposite sentiments. The former were prompted by every motive of zeal, as well as vanity, to exaggerate the marks of his favour and the evidences of his faith. The latter, till their just apprehensions were changed into despair and resentment, attempted to conceal from the world, and from themselves, that the gods of Rome could no longer reckon the emperor in the number of their votaries. The same passions and prejudices have engaged the partial writers of the times to connect the public profession of Christianity with the most glorious or the most ignominious era of the reign of Constantine.

Whatever symptoms of Christian piety might transpire in the discourses or actions of Constantine, he persevered till he was near forty years of age in the practice of the established religion; and the same conduct which in the court of Nicomedia might be imputed to his fear, could be ascribed only to the inclination or policy of the sovereign of Gaul. His liberality restored and enriched the temples of the gods; the medals which issued from his Imperial mint are impressed with the figures and attributes of Jupiter and Apollo, of Mars and Hercules; and his filial piety increased the council of Olympus by the solemn apotheosis of his father Constantius. But the devotion of Constantine was more peculiarly directed to the genius of the Sun, the Apollo of Greek and Roman mythology; and he was pleased to be represented with the symbols of the God of Light and Poetry. The unerring shafts of that deity, the brightness of his eyes, his laurel wreath, immortal beauty, and elegant accomplishments, seem to point him out as the patron of a young hero. The altars of Apollo were crowned with the votive offerings of Constantine; and the credulous multitude were taught to believe that the emperor was permitted to behold with mortal eyes the visible majesty of their tutelar deity; and that, either waking or in a vision, he was blessed with the auspicious omens of a long and victorious reign. The Sun was universally celebrated as the invincible guide and protector of Constantine; and the Pagans might reasonably expect that the insulted god would pursue with unrelenting vengeance the impiety of his ungrateful favourite.

As long as Constantine exercised a limited sovereignty over the provinces of Gaul, his Christian subjects were protected by the authority, and perhaps by the laws, of a prince who wisely left to the gods the care of vindicating their own honour. If we may credit the assertion of Constantine himself, he had been an indignant spectator of the savage cruelties which were inflicted, by the hands of Roman soldiers, on those citizens whose religion was their only crime.[1] In the East and in the West he had seen the different effects of severity and indulgence; and as the former was rendered still more odious by the example of Galerius, his implacable enemy, the latter was recommended to his imitation by the authority and advice of a dying father. The son of Constantius immediately suspended or repealed the edicts of persecution, and granted the free exercise of their religious ceremonies to all those who had already professed themselves members of the church. They were soon encouraged to depend on the favour as well as on the justice of their sovereign, who had imbibed a secret and sincere reverence for the name of Christ, and for the God of the Christians.

THE EDICT OF TOLERATION

About five months after the conquest of Italy, the emperor made a solemn and authentic declaration of his sentiments by the celebrated edict of Milan, which restored peace to the catholic church. In the personal interview of the two western princes, Constantine, by the ascendant of genius and power, obtained the ready concurrence of his colleague, Licinius; the union of their names and authority disarmed the fury of Maximin; and, after the death of the tyrant of the East, the edict of Milan was received as a general and fundamental law of the Roman world.

The wisdom of the emperors provided for the restitution of all the civil and religious rights of which the Christians had been so unjustly deprived. It was enacted that the places of worship, and public lands, which had been confiscated, should be restored to the church, without dispute, without delay, and without expense: and this severe injunction was accompanied with a gracious promise, that, if any of the purchasers

---

[1] But it might easily be shown that the Greek translator has improved the sei.‿e of the Latin original; and the aged emperor might recollect the persecution of Diocletian with a more lively abhorrence than he had actually felt in the days of his youth and Paganism.

had paid a fair and adequate price, they should be indemnified from the Imperial treasury. The salutary regulations which guard the future tranquillity of the faithful are framed on the principles of enlarged and equal toleration; and such an equality must have been interpreted by a recent sect as an advantageous and honourable distinction. The two emperors proclaim to the world that they have granted a free and absolute power to the Christians, and to all others, of following the religion which each individual thinks proper to prefer, to which he has addicted his mind, and which he may deem the best adapted to his own use. They carefully explain every ambiguous word, remove every exception, and exact from the governors of the provinces a strict obedience to the true and simple meaning of an edict which was designed to establish and secure, without any limitation, the claims of religious liberty. They condescend to assign two weighty reasons which have induced them to allow this universal toleration: the humane intention of consulting the peace and happiness of their people; and the pious hope that by such a conduct they shall appease and propitiate *the Deity*, whose seat is in Heaven. They gratefully acknowledge the many signal proofs which they have received of the divine favour; and they trust that the same Providence will for ever continue to protect the prosperity of the prince and people. From these vague and indefinite expressions of piety three suppositions may be deduced, of a different, but not of an incompatible nature. The mind of Constantine might fluctuate between the Pagan and the Christian religions. According to the loose and complying notions of Polytheism, he might acknowledge the God of the Christians as *one* of the *many* deities who compose the hierarchy of Heaven. Or perhaps he might embrace the philosophic and pleasing idea that, notwithstanding the variety of names, of rites, and of opinions, all the sects and all the nations of mankind are united in the worship of the common Father and Creator of the universe.

But the counsels of princes are more frequently influenced by views of temporal advantage than by considerations of abstract and speculative truth. The partial and increasing favour of Constantine may naturally be referred to the esteem which he entertained for the moral character of the Christians, and to a persuasion that the propagation of the Gospel would inculcate the practice of private and public virtue. Whatever latitude an absolute monarch may assume in his own conduct, whatever indulgence he may claim for his own passions, it is undoubtedly his interest that all his subjects should respect the natural and civil obligations of society. But the operation of the wisest laws is imperfect and precarious. They seldom inspire virtue, they cannot always restrain vice. Their power is insufficient to prohibit all that they condemn, nor can they always punish the actions which they prohibit. The legislators of antiquity had summoned to their aid the powers of education and of opinion. But every principle which had once maintained the vigour and purity of Rome and Sparta was long since extinguished in a declining and despotic empire. Philosophy still exercised her temperate sway over the human mind, but the cause of virtue derived very feeble support from the influence of the Pagan superstition. Under these discouraging circumstances a prudent magistrate might observe with pleasure the progress of a religion which diffused among the people a pure, benevolent, and universal system of ethics, adapted to every duty and every condition of life, recommended as the will and reason of the supreme Deity, and enforced by the sanction of eternal rewards or punishments. The experience of Greek and Roman history could not inform the world how far the system of national manners might be reformed and improved by the precepts of a divine revelation; and Constantine might listen with some confidence to the flattering, and indeed reasonable, assurances of Lactantius. The eloquent apologist seemed firmly to expect, and almost ventured to promise, *that* the establishment of Christianity would restore the innocence and felicity of the primitive age; *that* the worship of the true God would extinguish war and dissension among those who mutually considered themselves as the children of a common parent; *that* every impure desire, every angry or selfish passion, would be restrained by the knowledge of the Gospel; and *that* the magistrates might sheath the sword of justice among a people who would be universally actuated by the sentiments of truth and piety, of equity and moderation, of harmony and universal love.

The passive and unresisting obedience which bows under the yoke of authority, or even of oppression, must have appeared in the eyes of an absolute monarch the most conspicuous and useful of the evangelic virtues. The primitive Christians derived the institution of civil government, not from the consent of the people, but from the decrees of Heaven. The reigning emperor, though he had usurped the sceptre by treason and murder, immediately assumed the sacred character of vicegerent of the Deity. To the Deity alone he was accountable for the abuse of his power; and his subjects were indissolubly bound by their oath of fidelity to a tyrant who had violated every law of nature and society. The humble Christians were sent into the world as sheep among wolves; and since they were not permitted to employ force even in the defence of their religion, they should be still more criminal if they were tempted to shed the blood of their fellow-creatures in disputing the vain privileges or the sordid possessions of this transitory life. Faithful to the doctrine of the apostle, who in the reign of Nero had preached the duty of unconditional submission, the Christians of the three first centuries preserved their conscience pure and innocent of the guilt of secret conspiracy or open rebellion. While they experienced the rigour of persecution, they were never provoked either to meet their tyrants in the field, or indignantly to withdraw themselves into some remote and sequestered corner of the globe. The protestants of France,

of Germany, and of Britain, who asserted with such intrepid courage
their civil and religious freedom, have been insulted by the invidious
comparison between the conduct of the primitive and of the reformed
Christians. Perhaps, instead of censure, some applause may be due to
the superior sense and spirit of our ancestors, who had convinced themselves that religion cannot abolish the unalienable rights of human
nature. Perhaps the patience of the primitive church may be ascribed
to its weakness as well as to its virtue. A sect of unwarlike plebeians,
without leaders, without arms, without fortifications, must have encountered inevitable destruction in a rash and fruitless resistance to the
master of the Roman legions. But the Christians, when they deprecated
the wrath of Diocletian, or solicited the favour of Constantine, could
allege, with truth and confidence, that they held the principle of passive
obedience, and that, in the space of three centuries, their conduct had
always been conformable to their principles. They might add that the
throne of the emperors would be established on a fixed and permanent
basis if all their subjects, embracing the Christian doctrine, should learn
to suffer and to obey.

In the general order of Providence princes and tyrants are considered
as the ministers of Heaven, appointed to rule or to chastise the nations
of the earth. But sacred history affords many illustrious examples of
the more immediate interposition of the Deity in the government of his
chosen people. The sceptre and the sword were committed to the hands
of Moses, of Joshua, of Gideon, of David, of the Maccabees; the virtues
of those heroes were the motive or the effect of the divine favour, the
success of their arms was destined to achieve the deliverance or the
triumph of the church. If the judges of Israel were occasional and
temporary magistrates, the kings of Judah derived from the royal
unction of their great ancestor an hereditary and indefeasible right,
which could not be forfeited by their own vices, nor recalled by the
caprice of their subjects. The same extraordinary providence, which
was no longer confined to the Jewish people, might elect Constantine
and his family as the protectors of the Christian world; and the devout
Lactantius announces, in a prophetic tone, the future glories of his long
and universal reign. Galerius and Maximin, Maxentius and Licinius,
were the rivals who shared with the favourite of Heaven the provinces
of the empire. The tragic deaths of Galerius and Maximin soon gratified
the resentment, and fulfilled the sanguine expectations, of the Christians.
The success of Constantine against Maxentius and Licinius removed the
two formidable competitors who still opposed the triumph of the second
David, and his cause might seem to claim the peculiar interposition of
Providence. The character of the Roman tyrant disgraced the purple
and human nature; and though the Christians might enjoy his precarious favour, they were exposed, with the rest of his subjects, to the
effects of his wanton and capricious cruelty. The conduct of Licinius

soon betrayed the reluctance with which he had consented to the wise and humane regulations of the edict of Milan. The convocation of provincial synods was prohibited in his dominions; his Christian officers were ignominiously dismissed; and if he avoided the guilt, or rather danger, of a general persecution, his partial oppressions were rendered still more odious by the violation of a solemn and voluntary engagement. While the East, according to the lively expression of Eusebius, was involved in the shades of infernal darkness, the auspicious rays of celestial light warmed and illuminated the provinces of the West. The piety of Constantine was admitted as an unexceptionable proof of the justice of his arms; and his use of victory confirmed the opinion of the Christians, that their hero was inspired and conducted by the Lord of Hosts. The conquest of Italy produced a general edict of toleration; and as soon as the defeat of Licinius had invested Constantine with the sole dominion of the Roman world, he immediately, by circular letters, exhorted all his subjects to imitate, without delay, the example of their sovereign, and to embrace the divine truth of Christianity.

The assurance that the elevation of Constantine was intimately connected with the designs of Providence instilled into the minds of the Christians two opinions, which, by very different means, assisted the accomplishment of the prophecy. Their warm and active loyalty exhausted in his favour every resource of human industry; and they confidently expected that their strenuous efforts would be seconded by some divine and miraculous aid. The enemies of Constantine have imputed to interested motives the alliance which he insensibly contracted with the catholic church, and which apparently contributed to the success of his ambition. In the beginning of the fourth century the Christians still bore a very inadequate proportion to the inhabitants of the empire; but among a degenerate people, who viewed the change of masters with the indifference of slaves, the spirit and union of a religious party might assist the popular leader, to whose service, from a principle of conscience, they had devoted their lives and fortunes. The example of his father had instructed Constantine to esteem and to reward the merit of the Christians; and in the distribution of public offices he had the advantage of strengthening his government by the choice of ministers or generals in whose fidelity he could repose a just and unreserved confidence. By the influence of these dignified missionaries the proselytes of the new faith must have multiplied in the court and army; the barbarians of Germany, who filled the ranks of the legions, were of a careless temper, which acquiesced without resistance in the religion of their commander; and when they passed the Alps it may fairly be presumed that a great number of the soldiers had already consecrated their swords to the service of Christ and of Constantine. The habits of mankind and the interest of religion gradually abated the horror of war and bloodshed which had so long prevailed among the Christians; and in the councils which were assembled under the gracious protection of Constantine the authority of the bishops was seasonably employed to ratify the obligation of the military oath, and to inflict the penalty of excommunication on those soldiers who threw away their arms during the peace of the church. While Constantine in his own dominions increased the number and zeal of his faithful adherents, he could depend on the support of a powerful faction in those provinces which were still possessed or usurped by his rivals. A secret disaffection was diffused among the Christian subjects of Maxentius and Licinius; and the resentment which the latter did not attempt to conceal served only to engage them still more deeply in the interest of his competitor. The regular correspondence which connected the bishops of the most distant provinces enabled them freely to communicate their wishes and their designs, and to transmit without danger any useful intelligence, or any pious contributions, which might promote the service of Constantine, who publicly declared that he had taken up arms for the deliverance of the church.

THE VISION OF CONSTANTINE

The enthusiasm which inspired the troops, and perhaps the emperor himself, had sharpened their swords while it satisfied their conscience. They marched to battle with the full assurance that the same God who had formerly opened a passage to the Israelites through the waters of Jordan, and had thrown down the walls of Jericho at the sound of the trumpets of Joshua, would display his visible majesty and power in the victory of Constantine. The evidence of ecclesiastical history is prepared to affirm that their expectations were justified by the conspicuous miracle to which the conversion of the first Christian emperor had been almost unanimously ascribed. The real or imaginery cause of so important an event deserves and demands the attention of posterity; and I shall endeavour to form a just estimate of the famous vision of Constantine, by a distinct consideration of the *standard*, the *dream*, and the *celestial sign*; by separating the historical, the natural, and the marvellous parts of this extraordinary story, which, in the composition of a specious argument, have been artfully confounded in one splendid and brittle mass.

1. An instrument of the tortures which were inflicted only on slaves and strangers became an object of horror in the eyes of a Roman citizen; and the ideas of guilt, of pain, and of ignominy, were closely united with the idea of the cross.[1] The piety, rather than the humanity,

---

[1] The Christian writers, Justin, Minucius Felix, Tertullian, Jerom, and Maximus of Turin, have investigated with tolerable success the figure or likeness of a cross in almost every object of nature or art; in the intersection of the meridian and equator, the human face, a bird flying, a man swimming, a mast and yard, a plough, a *standard*, &c. &c. &c.

of Constantine soon abolished in his dominions the punishment which
the Saviour of mankind had condescended to suffer; but the emperor
had already learned to despise the prejudices of his education and of
his people, before he could erect in the midst of Rome his own statue,
bearing a cross in its right hand, with an inscription which referred the
victory of his arms, and the deliverance of Rome, to the virtue of that
salutary sign, the true symbol of force and courage. The same symbol
sanctified the arms of the soldiers of Constantine; the cross glittered on
their helmet, was engraved on their shields, was interwoven into their
banners; and the consecrated emblems which adorned the person of the
emperor himself were distinguished only by richer materials and more
exquisite workmanship. But the principal standard which displayed the
triumph of the cross was styled the *Labarum*, an obscure, though celebrated, name, which has been vainly derived from almost all the languages of the world. It is described as a long pike intersected by a
transversal beam. The silken veil which hung down from the beam was
curiously inwrought with the images of the reigning monarch and his
children. The summit of the pike supported a crown of gold, which
enclosed the mysterious monogram, at once expressive of the figure of
the cross and the initial letters of the name of Christ. The safety of the
labarum was intrusted to fifty guards of approved valour and fidelity;
their station was marked by honours and emoluments; and some for-
tinate accidents soon introduced an opinion that as long as the guards
of the labarum were engaged in the execution of their office they were
secure and invulnerable amidst the darts of the enemy. In the second
civil war Licinus felt and dreaded the power of this consecrated banner,
the sight of which in the distress of battle animated the soldiers of
Constantine with an invincible enthusiasm, and scattered terror and
dismay through the ranks of the adverse legions. The Christian emperors, who respected the example of Constantine, displayed in all their
military expeditions the standard of the cross; but when the degenerate
successors of Theodosius had ceased to appear in person at the head of
their armies, the labarum was deposited as a venerable but useless relic
in the palace of Constantinople. Its honours are still preserved on the
medals of the Flavian family. Their grateful devotion has placed the
monogram of Christ in the midst of the ensigns of Rome. The solemn
epithets of safety of the republic, glory of the army, restoration of
public happiness, are equally applied to the religious and military
trophies; and there is still extant a medal of the emperor Constantius,
where the standard of the labarum is accompanied with these memorable words, BY THIS SIGN THOU SHALT CONQUER.

II. In all occasions of danger or distress it was the practice of the
primitive Christians to fortify their minds and bodies by the sign of the
cross, which they used in all their ecclesiastical rites, in all the daily
occurrences of life, as an infallible preservative against every species of

spiritual or temporal evil. The authority of the church might alone have had sufficient weight to justify the devotion of Constantine, who, in the same prudent and gradual progress, acknowledged the truth and assumed the symbol of Christianity. But the testimony of a contemporary writer, who in a formal treatise has avenged the cause of religion, bestows on the piety of the emperor a more awful and sublime character. He affirms, with the most perfect confidence, that, in the night which preceded the last battle against Maxentius, Constantine was admonished in a dream to inscribe the shields of his soldiers with the *celestial sign of God*, the sacred monogram of the name of Christ; that he executed the commands of Heaven, and that his valour and obedience were rewarded by the decisive victory of the Milvian Bridge. Some considerations might perhaps incline a sceptical mind to suspect the judgment or the veracity of the rhetorician, whose pen, either from zeal or interest, was devoted to the cause of the prevailing faction. He appears to have published his Deaths of the Persecutors at Nicomedia about three years after the Roman victory; but the interval of a thousand miles, and a thousand days, will allow an ample latitude for the invention of declaimers, the credulity of party, and the tacit approbation of the emperor himself; who might listen without indignation to a marvellous tale which exalted his fame and promoted his designs. In favour of Licinius, who still dissembled his animosity to the Christians, the same author has provided a similar vision, of a form of prayer, which was communicated by an angel, and repeated by the whole army before they engaged the legions of the tyrant Maximin. The frequent repetition of miracles serves to provoke, where it does not subdue, the reason of mankind; but if the dream of Constantine is separately considered, it may be naturally explained either by the policy or the enthusiasm of the emperor. Whilst his anxiety for the approaching day, which must decide the fate of the empire, was suspended by a short and interrupted slumber, the venerable form of Christ, and the well-known symbol of his religion, might forcibly offer themselves to the active fancy of a prince who reverenced the name, and had perhaps secretly implored the power, of the God of the Christians. As readily might a consummate statesman indulge himself in the use of one of those military stratagems, one of those pious frauds, which Philip and Sertorius had employed with such art and effect. The preternatural origin of dreams was universally admitted by the nations of antiquity, and a considerable part of the Gallic army was already prepared to place their confidence in the salutary sign of the Christian religion. The secret vision of Constantine could be disproved only by the event; and the intrepid hero who had passed the Alps and the Apennine might view with careless despair the consequences of a defeat under the walls of Rome. The senate and people, exulting in their own deliverance from an odious tyrant, acknowledged that the victory of Constantine surpassed the powers of man, without daring to insinuate that it had been obtained by the protection of the *gods*. The triumphal arch, which was erected about three years after the event, proclaims, in ambiguous language, that, by the greatness of his own mind, and by an *instinct* or impulse of the Divinity, he had saved and avenged the Roman republic. The Pagan orator, who had seized an earlier opportunity of celebrating the virtues of the conqueror, supposes that he alone enjoyed a secret and intimate commerce with the Supreme Being, who delegated the care of mortals to his subordinate deities; and thus assigns a very plausible reason why the subjects of Constantine should not presume to embrace the new religion of their sovereign.

III. The philosopher, who with calm suspicion examines the dreams and omens, the miracles and prodigies, of profane or even of ecclesiastical history, will probably conclude that, if the eyes of the spectators have sometimes been deceived by fraud, the understanding of the readers has much more frequently been insulted by fiction. Every event, or appearance, or accident, which seems to deviate from the ordinary course of nature, has been rashly ascribed to the immediate action of the Deity; and the astonished fancy of the multitude has sometimes given shape and colour, language and motion, to the fleeting but uncommon meteors of the air. Nazarius and Eusebius are the two most celebrated orators who, in studied panegyrics, have laboured to exalt the glory of Constantine. Nine years after the Roman victory Nazarius describes an army of divine warriors, who seemed to fall from the sky; he marks their beauty, their spirit, their gigantic forms, the stream of light which beamed from their celestial armour, their patience in suffering themselves to be heard, as well as seen, by mortals; and their declaration that they were sent, that they flew, to the assistance of the great Constantine. For the truth of this prodigy the Pagan orator appeals to the whole Gallic nation, in whose presence he was then speaking; and seems to hope that the ancient apparitions would now obtain credit from this recent and public event. The Christian fable of Eusebius, which, in the space of twenty-six years, might arise from the original dream, is cast in a much more correct and elegant mould. In one of the marches of Constantine he is reported to have seen with his own eyes the luminous trophy of the cross, placed above the meridian sun, and inscribed with the following words: BY THIS CONQUER. This amazing object in the sky astonished the whole army, as well as the emperor himself, who was yet undetermined in the choice of a religion: but his astonishment was converted into faith by the vision of the ensuing night. Christ appeared before his eyes; and displaying the same celestial sign of the cross, he directed Constantine to frame a similar standard, and to march, with an assurance of victory, against Maxentius and all his enemies. The learned bishop of Cæsarea appears to be sensible that the recent discovery of this marvellous anecdote would excite some surprise and distrust among the most pious of his readers. Yet, instead of ascertaining the precise circumstances of time and place, which always serve to detect falsehood or establish truth; instead of collecting and recording the evidence of so many living witnesses, who must have been spectators of this stupendous miracle, Eusebius contents himself with alleging a very singular testimony, that of the deceased Constantine, who, many years after the event, in the freedom of conversation, had related to him this extraordinary incident of his own life, and had attested the truth of it by a solemn oath. The prudence and gratitude of the learned prelate forbade him to suspect the veracity of his victorious master; but he plainly intimates that, in a fact of such a nature, he should have refused his assent to any meaner authority. This motive of credibility could not survive the power of the Flavian family; and the celestial sign, which the Infidels might afterwards deride, was disregarded by the Christians of the age which immediately followed the conversion of Constantine. But the catholic church, both of the East and of the West, has adopted a prodigy which favours, or seems to favour, the popular worship of the cross. The vision of Constantine maintained an honourable place in the legend of superstition till the bold and sagacious spirit of criticism presumed to depreciate the triumph, and to arraign the truth, of the first Christian emperor.

THE BAPTISM OF CONSTANTINE

The protestant and philosophic readers of the present age will incline to believe that, in the account of his own conversion Constantine attested a wilful falsehood by a solemn and deliberate perjury. They may not hesitate to pronounce that, in the choice of a religion, his mind was determined only by a sense of interest; and that (according to the expression of a profane poet) he used the altars of the church as a convenient footstool to the throne of the empire. A conclusion so harsh and so absolute is not, however, warranted by our knowledge of human nature, of Constantine, or of Christianity. In an age of religious fervour the most artful statesmen are observed to feel some part of the enthusiasm which they inspire; and the most orthodox saints assume the dangerous privilege of defending the cause of truth by the arms of deceit and falsehood. Personal interest is often the standard of our belief, as well as of our practice; and the same motives of temporal advantage which might influence the public conduct and professions of Constantine would insensibly dispose his mind to embrace a religion so propitious to his fame and fortunes. His vanity was gratified by the flattering assurance that *he* had been chosen by Heaven to reign over the earth: success had justified his divine title to the throne, and that title was founded on the truth of the Christian revelation. As real virtue is sometimes excited by undeserved applause, the specious piety of Constantine, if at first it was only specious, might gradually, by the influence of praise, of habit, and of example, be matured into serious faith and fervent devotion. The bishops and teachers of the new sect, whose dress and manners had not qualified them for the residence of a court, were admitted to the Imperial table; they accompanied the monarch in his expeditions; and the ascendant which one of them, an Egyptian or a Spaniard, acquired over his mind was imputed by the Pagans to the effect of magic. Lactantius, who has adorned the precepts of the Gospel with the eloquence of Cicero, and Eusebius, who has consecrated the learning and philosophy of the Greeks to the service of religion, were both received into the friendship and familiarity of their sovereign; and those able masters of controversy could patiently watch the soft and yielding moments of persuasion, and dexterously apply the arguments which were the best adapted to his character and understanding. Whatever advantages might be derived from the acquisition of an Imperial proselyte, he was distinguished by the splendour of his purple, rather than by the superiority of wisdom or virtue, from the many thousands of his subjects who had embraced the doctrines of Christianity. Nor can it be deemed incredible that the mind of an unlettered soldier should have yielded to the weight of evidence which, in a more enlightened age, has satisfied or subdued the reason of a Grotius, a Pascal, or a Locke. In the midst of the incessant labours of his great office this soldier employed, or affected to employ, the hours of the night in the diligent study of the Scriptures, and the composition of theological discourses, which he afterwards pronounced in the presence of a numerous and applauding audience. In a very long discourse, which is still extant, the royal preacher expatiates on the various proofs of religion; but he dwells with peculiar complacency on the Sibylline verses, and the fourth eclogue of Virgil. Forty years before the birth of Christ, the Mantuan bard, as if inspired by the celestial muse of Isaiah, had celebrated, with all the pomp of oriental metaphor, the return of the Virgin, the fall of the serpent, the approaching birth of a godlike child, the offspring of the great Jupiter, who should expiate the guilt of human kind and govern the peaceful universe with the virtues of his father; the rise and appearance of an heavenly race, a primitive nation throughout the world; and the gradual restoration of the innocence and felicity of the golden age. The poet was perhaps unconscious of the secret sense and object of these sublime predictions, which have been so unworthily applied to the infant son of a consul, or a triumvir: but if a more splendid, and indeed specious, interpretation of the fourth eclogue contributed to the conversion of the first Christian emperor, Virgil may deserve to be ranked among the most successful missionaries of the Gospel.

The awful mysteries of the Christian faith and worship were concealed from the eyes of strangers, and even of catechumens, with an affected secrecy, which served to excite their wonder and curiosity. But the severe rules of discipline which the prudence of the bishops had instituted were relaxed by the same prudence in favour of an Imperial proselyte, whom it was so important to allure, by every gentle condescension, into the pale of the church; and Constantine was permitted, at least by a tacit dispensation, to enjoy *most* of the privileges, before he had contracted *any* of the obligations, of a Christian. Instead of retiring from the congregation when the voice of the deacon dismissed the profane multitude, he prayed with the faithful, disputed with the bishops, preached on the most sublime and intricate subjects of theology, celebrated with sacred rites the vigil of Easter, and publicly declared himself, not only a partaker, but, in some measure, a priest and hierophant of the Christian mysteries. The pride of Constantine might assume, and his services had deserved, some extraordinary distinction; an ill-timed rigour might have blasted the unripened fruits of his conversion; and if the doors of the church had been strictly closed against a prince who had deserted the altars of the gods, the master of the empire would have been left destitute of any form of religious worship. In his last visit to Rome he piously disclaimed and insulted the superstition of his ancestors, by refusing to lead the military procession of the equestrian order, and to offer the public vows to the Jupiter of the Capitoline Hill. Many years before his baptism and death Constantine had proclaimed to the world that neither his person nor his image should ever more be seen within the walls of an idolatrous temple; while he distributed through the provinces a variety of medals and pictures which represented the emperor in an humble and suppliant posture of Christian devotion.

The pride of Constantine, who refused the privileges of a catechumen, cannot easily be explained or excused; but the delay of his baptism may be justified by the maxims and the practice of ecclesiastical antiquity. The sacrament of baptism was regularly administered by the bishop himself, with his assistant clergy, in the cathedral church of the diocese, during the fifty days between the solemn festivals of Easter and Pentecost; and this holy term admitted a numerous band of infants and adult persons into the bosom of the church. The discretion of parents often suspended the baptism of their children till they could understand their obligations which they contracted: the severity of ancient bishops exacted from the new converts a noviciate of two or three years; and the catechumens themselves, from different motives of a temporal or a spiritual nature, were seldom impatient to assume the character of perfect and initiated Christians. The sacrament of baptism was supposed to contain a full and absolute expiation of sin; and the soul was instantly restored to its original purity, and entitled to the promise of eternal salvation. Amongst the proselytes of Christianity there were many who judged it imprudent to precipitate a salutary rite which could not be repeated; to throw away an inestimable privilege which could never be recovered. By the delay of their baptism they could venture freely to indulge their passions in the enjoyment of this world, while they still retained in their own hands the means of a sure and easy absolution.[1] The sublime theory of the Gospel had made a much fainter impression on the heart than on the understanding of Constantine himself. He pursued the great object of his ambition through the dark and bloody paths of war and policy; and, after the victory, he abandoned himself, without moderation, to the abuse of his fortune. Instead of asserting his just superiority above the imperfect heroism and profane philosophy of Trajan and the Antonines, the mature age of Constantine forfeited the reputation which he had acquired in his youth. As he gradually advanced in the knowledge of truth, he proportionably declined in the practice of virtue; and the same year of his reign in which he convened the council of Nice was polluted by the execution, or rather murder, of his eldest son. This date is alone sufficient to refute the ignorant and malicious suggestions of Zosimus, who affirms that, after the death of Crispus, the remorse of his father accepted from the ministers of Christianity the expiation which he had vainly solicited from the Pagan pontiffs. At the time of the death of Crispus the emperor could no longer hesitate in the choice of a religion; he could no longer be ignorant that the church was possessed of an infallible remedy, though he chose to defer the application of it till the approach of death had removed the temptation and danger of a relapse. The bishops whom he summoned in his last illness to the palace of Nicomedia were edified by the fervour with which he requested and received the sacrament of baptism, by the solemn protestation that the remainder of his life should be worthy of a disciple of Christ, and by his humble refusal to wear the Imperial purple after he had been clothed in the white garment of a Neophyte. The example and reputation of Constantine seemed to countenance the delay of baptism. Future tyrants were encouraged to believe that the innocent blood which they might shed in a long reign would instantly be washed away in the waters of regeneration; and the abuse of religion dangerously undermined the foundations of moral virtue.

THE LEGAL ESTABLISHMENT OF CHRISTIANITY

The gratitude of the church has exalted the virtues and excused the failings of a generous patron, who seated Christianity on the throne of

---

[1] The Fathers, who censured this criminal delay, could not deny the certain and victorious efficacy even of a death-bed baptism. The ingenious rhetoric of Chrysostom could find only three arguments against these prudent Christians. 1. That we should love and pursue virtue for her own sake, and not merely for the reward. 2. That we may be surprised by death without an opportunity of baptism. 3. That, although we shall be placed in heaven, we shall only twinkle like little stars, when compared to the suns of righteousness who have run their appointed course with labour, with success, and with glory. I believe that this delay of baptism, though attended with the most pernicious consequences, was never condemned by any general or provincial council, or by any public act or declaration of the church. The zeal of the bishops was easily kindled on much slighter occasions.

the Roman world; and the Greeks, who celebrate the festival of the Imperial saint, seldom mention the name of Constantine without adding the title of *equal to the Apostles*. Such a comparison, if it alludes to the character of those divine missionaries, must be imputed to the extravagance of impious flattery. But if the parallel is confined to the extent and number of their evangelic victories, the success of Constantine might perhaps equal that of the Apostles themselves. By the edicts of toleration he removed the temporal disadvantages which had hitherto retarded the progress of Christianity; and its active and numerous ministers received a free permission, a liberal encouragement, to recommend the salutary truths of revelation by every argument which could affect the reason or piety of mankind. The exact balance of the two religions continued but a moment; and the piercing eye of ambition and avarice soon discovered that the profession of Christianity might contribute to the interest of the present, as well as of a future life. The hopes of wealth and honours, the example of an emperor, his exhortations, his irresistible smiles, diffused conviction among the venal and obsequious crowds which usually fill the apartments of a palace. The cities which signalised a forward zeal by the voluntary destruction of their temples were distinguished by municipal privileges and rewarded with popular donatives; and the new capital of the East gloried in the singular advantage that Constantinople was never profaned by the worship of idols. As the lower ranks of society are governed by imitation, the conversion of those who possessed any eminence of birth, of power, or of riches, was soon followed by dependent multitudes. The salvation of the common people was purchased at an easy rate, if it be true that, in one year, twelve thousand men were baptised at Rome, besides a proportionable number of women and children, and that a white garment, with twenty pieces of gold had been promised by the emperor to every convert. The powerful influence of Constantine was not circumscribed by the narrow limits of his life or of his dominions. The education which he bestowed on his sons and nephews secured to the empire a race of princes whose faith was still more lively and sincere, as they imbibed, in their earliest infancy, the spirit, or at least the doctrine, of Christianity. War and commerce had spread the knowledge of the Gospel beyond the confines of the Roman provinces; and the barbarians, who had disdained an humble and proscribed sect, soon learned to esteem a religion which had been so lately embraced by the greatest monarch and the most civilised nation of the globe. The Goths and Germans, who enlisted under the standard of Rome, revered the cross which glittered at the head of the legions, and their fierce countrymen received at the same time the lessons of faith and of humanity. The kings of Iberia and Armenia worshipped the God of their protector; and their subjects, who have invariably preserved the name of Christians, soon formed a sacred and perpetual connexion within their Roman brethren. The Christians of Persia were suspected, in time of war, of preferring their religion to their country; but as long as peace subsisted between the two empires, the persecuting spirit of the Magi was effectually restrained by the interposition of Constantine. The rays of the Gospel Illuminated the coast of India. The colonies of Jews who had penetrated into Arabia and Ethiopia opposed the progress of Christianity; but the labour of the missionaries was in some measure facilitated by a previous knowledge of the Mosaic revelation; and Abyssinia still reveres the memory of Frumentius, who, in the time of Constantine, devoted his life to the conversion of those sequested regions. Under the reign of his son Constantius, Theophilus, who was himself of Indian extraction, was invested with the double character of ambassador and bishop. He embarked on the Red Sea with two hundred horses of the purest breed of Cappadocia, which were sent by the emperor to the prince of the Sabæans, or Homerites. Theophilus was intrusted with many other useful or curious presents, which might raise the admiration and conciliate the friendship of the barbarians; and he successfully employed several years in a pastoral visit to the churches of the torrid zone.

The irresistible power of the Roman emperors was displayed in the important and dangerous change of the national religion. The terrors of a military force silenced the faint and unsupported murmurs of the Pagans, and there was reason to expect that the cheerful submission of the Christian clergy, as well as people, would be the result of conscience and gratitude. It was long since established as a fundamental maxim of the Roman constitution, that every rank of citizens was alike subject to the laws, and that the care of religion was the right as well as duty of the civil magistrate. Constantine and his successors could not easily persuade themselves that they had forfeited, by their conversion, any branch of the Imperial prerogatives, or that they were incapable of giving laws to a religion which they had protected and embraced. The emperors still continued to exercise a supreme jurisdiction over the ecclesiastical order; and the sixteenth book of the Theodosian code represents, under a variety of titles, the authority which they assumed in the government of the catholic church.

DISTINCTION OF SPIRITUAL AND TEMPORAL POWERS

But the distinction of the spiritual and temporal powers, which had never been imposed on the free spirit of Greece and Rome, was introduced and confirmed by the legal establishment of Christianity. The office of supreme pontiff, which, from the time of Numa to that of Augustus, had always been exercised by one of the most eminent of the senators, was at length united to the Imperial dignity. The first magistrate of the state, as often as he was prompted by superstition or policy, performed with his own hands the sacerdotal functions; nor was there any order of priests, either at Rome or in the provinces, who claimed a more sacred character amongst men, or a more intimate communication with the gods. But in the Christian church, which intrusts the service of the altar to a perpetual succession of consecrated ministers, the monarch, whose spiritual rank is less honourable than that of the meanest deacon, was seated below the rails of the sanctuary, and confounded with the rest of the faithful multitude. The emperor might be saluted as the father of his people, but he owed a filial duty and reverence to the fathers of the church; and the same marks of respect which Constantine had paid to the persons of saints and confessors were soon exacted by the pride of the episcopal order. A secret conflict between the civil and ecclesiastical jurisdictions embarrassed the operations of the Roman government; and a pious emperor was alarmed by the guilt and danger of touching with a profane hand the ark of the covenant. The separation of men into the two orders of the clergy and of the laity was, indeed, familiar to many nations of antiquity; and the priests of India, of Persia, of Assyria, of Judea, of Ethiopia, of Egypt, and of Gaul, derived from a celestial origin the temporal power and possessions which they had acquired. These venerable institutions had gradually assimilated themselves to the manners and government of their respective countries, but the opposition or contempt of the civil power served to cement the discipline of the primitive church. The Christians had been obliged to elect their own magistrates, to raise and distribute a peculiar revenue, and to regulate the internal policy of their republic by a code of laws, which were ratified by the consent of the people and the practice of three hundred years. When Constantine embraced the faith of the Christians, he seemed to contract a perpetual alliance with a distinct and independent society; and the privileges granted or confirmed by that emperor, or by his successors, were accepted, not as the precarious favours of the court, but as the just and inalienable rights of the ecclesiastical order.

The catholic church was administered by the spiritual and legal jurisdiction of eighteen hundred bishops; of whom one thousand were seated in the Greek, and eight hundred in the Latin, provinces of the empire. The extent and boundaries of their respective dioceses had been variously and accidently decided by the zeal and success of the first missionaries, by the wishes of the people, and by the propagation of the Gospel. Episcopal churches were closely planted along the banks of the Nile, on the sea-coast of Africa, in the proconsular Asia, and through the southern provinces of Italy. The bishops of Gaul and Spain, of Thrace and Pontus, reigned over an ample territory, and delegated their rural suffragans to execute the subordinate duties of the pastoral office. A Christian diocese might be spread over a province, or reduced to a village; but all the bishops possessed an equal and indelible character; they all derived the same powers and privileges from the apostles, from the people, and from the laws. While the *civil* and *military* professions were separated by the policy of Constantine, a new and perpetual order of *ecclesiastical* ministers, always respectable, sometimes dangerous, was established in the church and state. The important review of their station and attributes may be distributed under the following heads: I. Popular election. II. Ordination of the clergy. III. Property. IV. Civil jurisdiction. V. Spiritual censures. VI. Exercise of public oratory. VII. Privilege of legislative assemblies.

I. The freedom of elections subsisted long after the legal establishment of Christianity, and the subjects of Rome enjoyed in the church the privilege which they had lost in the republic, of choosing the magistrates whom they were bound to obey. As soon as a bishop had closed his eyes, the metropolitan issued a commission to one of his suffragans to administer the vacant see, and prepare, within a limited time, the future election. The right of voting was vested in the inferior clergy, who were best qualified to judge of the merit of the candidates; in the senators or nobles of the city, all those who were distinguished by their rank or property; and finally in the whole body of the people, who on the appointed day flocked in multitudes from the most remote parts of the diocese, and sometimes silenced, by their tumultuous acclamations, the voice of reason and the laws of discipline. These acclamations might accidentally fix on the head of the most deserving competitor, of some ancient presbyter, some holy monk, or some layman conspicuous for his zeal and piety. But the episcopal chair was solicited, especially in the great and opulent cities of the empire, as a temporal rather than as a spiritual dignity. The interested views, the selfish and angry passions, the arts of perfidy and dissimulation, the secret corruption, the open and even bloody violence which had formerly disgraced the freedom of election in the commonwealths of Greece and Rome, too often influenced the choice of the successors of the apostles. While one of the candidates boasted the honours of his family, a second allured his judges by the delicacies of a plentiful table, and a third, more guilty than his rivals, offered to share the plunder of the church among the accomplices of his sacrilegious hopes. The civil as well as ecclesiastical laws attempted to exclude the populace from this solemn and important transaction. The canons of ancient discipline, by requiring several episcopal qualifications of age, station, &c., restrained in some measure the indiscriminate caprice of the electors. The authority of the provincial bishops, who were assembled in the vacant church to consecrate the choice of the people, was interposed to moderate their passions and to correct their mistakes. The bishops could refuse to ordain an unworthy candidate, and the rage of contending factions sometimes accepted their impartial mediation. The submission or the resistance of the clergy and people, on various occasions, afforded different precedents, which were insensibly converted into positive laws and provincial customs: but it was everywhere admitted, as a fundamental maxim of religious policy, that no bishop could be imposed on an orthodox church without the consent of its members. The emperors, as the guardians of the public peace, and as the first citizens of Rome and Constantinople, might effectually declare their wishes in the choice of a primate; but those absolute monarchs respected the freedom of ecclesiastical elections, and, while they distributed and resumed the honours of the state and army, they allowed eighteen hundred perpetual magistrates to receive their important offices from the free suffrages of the people. It was agreeable to the dictates of justice that these magistrates should not desert an honourable station from which they could not be removed; but the wisdom of councils endeavoured, without much success, to enforce the residence, and to prevent the translation, of bishops. The discipline of the West was indeed less relaxed than that of the East; but the same passions which made those regulations necessary rendered them ineffectual. The reproaches which angry prelates have so vehemently urged against each other serve only to expose their common guilt and their mutual indiscretion.

II. The bishops alone possessed the faculty of *spiritual* generation, and this extraordinary privilege might compensate, in some degree, for the painful celibacy which was imposed as a virtue, as a duty, and at length as a positive obligation. The religions of antiquity, which established a separate order of priests, dedicated a holy race, a tribe or family, to the perpetual service of the gods. Such institutions were founded for possession rather than conquest. The children of the priests enjoyed, with proud and indolent security, their sacred inheritance; and the fiery spirit of enthusiam was abated by the cares, the pleasures, and the endearments of domestic life. But the Christian sanctuary was open to every ambitious candidate who aspired to its heavenly promises or temporal possessions. The office of priests, like that of soldiers or magistrates, was strenuously exercised by those men whose temper and abilities had prompted them to embrace the ecclesiastical profession, or who had been selected by a discerning bishop as the best qualified to promote the glory and interest of the church. The bishops (till the abuse was restrained by the prudence of the laws) might constrain the reluctant and protect the distressed, and the imposition of hands for ever bestowed some of the most valuable privileges of civil society. The whole body of the catholic clergy, more numerous, perhaps, than the legions, was exempted by the emperors from all service, private or public, all municipal offices, and all personal taxes and contributions, which pressed on their fellow-citizens with intolerable weight; and the duties of their holy profession were accepted as a full discharge of their obligations to the republic. Each bishop acquired an absolute and indefeasible right to the perpetual obedience of the clerk whom he ordained; the clergy of each episcopal church, with its dependent parishes, formed a regular and permanent society; and the cathedrals of Constantinople [1] and Carthage maintained their peculiar establishment of five hundred ecclesiastical ministers. Their ranks and numbers were insensibly multiplied by the superstition of the times, which introduced into the church the splendid ceremonies of a Jewish or Pagan temple; and a long train of priests, deacons, sub-deacons, acolythes, exorcists, readers, singers, and doorkeepers contributed, in their respective stations, to swell the pomp and harmony of religious worship. The clerical name and privilege were extended to many pious fraternities, who devoutly supported the ecclesiastical throne. Six hundred *parabolani*, or adventurers, visited the sick at Alexandria; eleven hundred *copiatæ*, or gravediggers, buried the dead at Constantinople; and the swarms of monks, who arose from the Nile, overspread and darkened the face of the Christian world.

III. The edict of Milan secured the revenue as well as the peace of the church. The Christians not only recovered the lands and houses of which they had been stripped by the persecuting laws of Diocletian, but they acquired a perfect title to all the possessions which they had hitherto enjoyed by the connivance of the magistrate. As soon as Christianity became the religion of the emperor and the empire, the national clergy might claim a decent and honourable maintenance: and the payment of an annual tax might have delivered the people from the more oppressive tribute which superstition imposes on her votaries. But as the wants and expenses of the church increased with her prosperity, the ecclesiastical order was still supported and enriched by the voluntary oblations of the faithful. Eight years after the edict of Milan, Constantine granted to all his subjects the free and universal permission of bequeathing their fortunes to the holy catholic church; and their devout liberality, which during their lives was checked by luxury or avarice, flowed with a profuse stream at the hour of their death. The wealthy Christians were encouraged by the example of their sovereign. An absolute monarch, who is rich without patrimony, may be charitable without merit; and Constantine too easily believed that he should purchase the favour of Heaven if he maintained the idle at the expense of the industrious, and distributed amongst the saints the wealth of the republic. The same messenger who carried over to Africa the head of Maxentius might be intrusted with an epistle to Cæcilian, bishop of Carthage. The emperor acquaints him that the treasures of the province are directed to pay into his hands the sum of three thousand *folles*, or eighteen thousand pounds sterling, and to obey his

---

[1] Sixty presbyters or priests, one hundred deacons, forty deaconesses, ninety sub-deacons, one hundred and ten readers, twenty-five chanters, and one hundred doorkeepers; in all, five hundred and twenty-five. This moderate number was fixed by the emperor to relieve the distress of the church, which had been involved in debt and usury by the expense of a much higher establishment.

farther requisitions for the relief of the churches of Africa, Numidia, and Mauritania. The liberality of Constantine increased in a just proportion to his faith and to his vices. He assigned in each city a regular allowance of corn to supply the fund of ecclesiastical charity, and the persons of both sexes who embraced the monastic life became the peculiar favourites of their sovereign. The Christian temples of Antioch, Alexandria, Jerusalem, Constantinople, &c., displayed the ostentatious piety of a prince ambitious in a declining age to equal the perfect labours of antiquity. The form of these religious edifices was simple and oblong, though they might sometimes swell into the shape of a dome, and sometimes branch into the figure of a cross. The timbers were framed for the most part of cedars of Libanus; the roof was covered with tiles, perhaps of gilt brass; and the walls, the columns, the pavement, were incrusted with variegated marbles. The most precious ornaments of gold and silver, of silk and gems, were profusely dedicated to the service of the altar, and this specious magnificence was supported on the solid and perpetual basis of landed property. In the space of two centuries, from the reign of Constantine to that of Justinian, the eighteen hundred churches of the empire were enriched by the frequent and unalienable gifts of the prince and people. An annual income of six hundred pounds sterling may be reasonably assigned to the bishops, who were placed at an equal distance between riches and poverty, but the standard of their wealth insensibly rose with the dignity and opulence of the cities which they governed. An authentic but imperfect [1] rent-roll specifies some houses, shops, gardens, and farms, which belonged to the three *Basilicæ* of Rome—St. Peter, St. Paul, and St. John Lateran—in the provinces of Italy, Africa, and the East. They produce, besides a reserved rent of oil, linen, paper, aromatics, &c., a clear annual revenue of twenty-two thousand pieces of gold, or twelve thousand pounds sterling. In the age of Constantine and Justinian the bishops no longer possessed, perhaps they no longer deserved, the unsuspecting confidence of their clergy and people. The ecclesiastical revenues of each diocese were divided into four parts, for the respective uses of the bishop himself, of his inferior clergy, of the poor, and of the public worship; and the abuse of this sacred trust was strictly and repeatedly checked. The patrimony of the church was still subject to all the public impositions of the state. The clergy of Rome, Alexandria, Thessalonica, &c., might solicit and obtain some partial exemptions; but the premature attempt of the great council of Rimini, which aspired to universal freedom, was successfully resisted by the son of Constantine.

IV. The Latin clergy, who erected their tribunal on the ruins of the

---

[1] Every record which comes from the Vatican is justly suspected; yet these rent-rolls have an ancient and authentic colour; and it is at least evident that, if forged, they were forged in a period when *farms*, not *kingdoms*, were the objects of papal avarice.

civil and common law, have modestly accepted, as the gift of Constantine,[1] the independent jurisdiction which was the fruit of time, of accident, and of their own industry. But the liberality of the Christian emperors had actually endowed them with some legal prerogatives which secured and dignified the sacerdotal character.[2] 1. Under a despotic government, the bishops alone enjoyed and asserted the inestimable privilege of being tried only by their *peers*; and even in a capital accusation, a synod of their brethren were the sole judges of their guilt or innocence. Such a tribunal, unless it was inflamed by personal resentment or religious discord, might be favourable, or even partial, to the sacerdotal order: but Constantine was satisfied that secret impunity would be less pernicious than public scandal, and the Nicene council was edified by his public declaration, that, if he surprised a bishop in the act of adultery, he should cast his Imperial mantle over the episcopal sinner. 2. The domestic jurisdiction of the bishops was at once a privilege and a restraint of the ecclesiastical order, whose civil causes were decently withdrawn from the cognizance of a secular judge. Their venial offences were not exposed to the shame of a public trial or punishment; and the gentle correction which the tenderness of youth may endure from its parents or instructors was inflicted by the temperate severity of the bishops. But if the clergy were guilty of any crime which could not be sufficiently expiated by their degradation from an honourable and beneficial profession, the Roman magistrate drew the sword of justice, without any regard to ecclesiastical immunities. 3. The arbitration of the bishops was ratified by a positive law; and the judges were instructed to execute, without appeal or delay, the episcopal decrees, whose validity had hitherto depended on the consent of the parties. The conversion of the magistrates themselves, and of the whole empire, might gradually remove the fears and scruples of the Christians. But they still resorted to the tribunal of the bishops, whose abilities and integrity they esteemed; and the venerable Austin enjoyed the satisfac-

---

[1] From Eusebius and Sozomen we are assured that the episcopal jurisdiction was extended and confirmed by Constantine; but the forgery of a famous edict, which was never fairly inserted in the Theodosian Code is demonstrated by Godefroy in the most satisfactory manner. It is strange that M. de Montesquieu, who was a lawyer as well as a philosopher, should allege this edict of Constantine without intimating any suspicion.

[2] The subject of ecclesiastical jurisdiction has been involved in a mist of passion, of prejudice, and of interest. Two of the fairest books which have fallen into my hands are the Institutes of Canon Law, by the Abbé de Fleury, and the Civil History of Naples, by Giannone. Their moderation was the effect of situation as well as of temper. Fleury was a French ecclesiastic, who respected the authority of the parliaments; Giannone was an Italian lawyer, who dreaded the power of the church. And here let me observe that, as the general propositions which I advance are the result of *many* particular and imperfect facts, I must either refer the reader to those modern authors who have expressly treated the subject, or swell these notes to a disagreeable and disproportioned size.

tion of complaining that his spiritual functions were perpetually interrupted by the invidious labour of deciding the claim or the possession of silver and gold, of lands and cattle. 4. The ancient privilege of sanctuary was transferred to the Christian temples, and extended, by the liberal piety of the younger Theodosius, to the precincts of consecrated ground. The fugitive, and even guilty, suppliants were permitted to implore either the justice or the mercy of the Deity and his ministers. The rash violence of despotism was suspended by the mild interposition of the church, and the lives or fortunes of the most eminent subjects might be protected by the mediation of the bishop.

V. The bishop was the perpetual censor of the morals of his people. The discipline of penance was digested into a system of canonical jurisprudence, which accurately defined the duty of private or public confession, the rules of evidence, the degrees of guilt, and the measure of punishment. It was impossible to execute this spiritual censure, if the Christian pontiff, who punished the obscure sins of the multitude, respected the conspicuous vices and destructive crimes of the magistrate: but it was impossible to arraign the conduct of the magistrate without controlling the administration of civil government. Some considerations of religion, or loyalty, or fear, protected the sacred persons of the emperors from the zeal or resentment of the bishops; but they boldly censured and excommunicated the subordinate tyrants who were not invested with the majesty of the purple. St. Athanasius excommunicated one of the ministers of Egypt, and the interdict which he pronounced of fire and water was solemnly transmitted to the churches of Cappadocia. Under the reign of the younger Theodosius, the polite and eloquent Synesius, one of the descendants of Hercules, filled the episcopal seat of Ptolemais, near the ruins of ancient Cyrene, and the philosophic bishop supported with dignity the character which he had assumed with reluctance.[1] He vanquished the monster of Libya, the president Andronicus, who abused the authority of a venal office, invented new modes of rapine and torture, and aggravated the guilt of oppression by that of sacrilege. After a fruitless attempt to reclaim the haughty magistrate by mild and religious admonition, Synesius proceeds to inflict the last sentence of ecclesiastical justice, which devotes Andronicus, with his associates and their *families*, to the abhorrence of earth and heaven. The impenitent sinners, more cruel than Phalaris or Sennacherib, more destructive than war, pestilence, or a cloud of locusts, are deprived of the name and privileges of Christians, of the participation of the sacraments, and of the hope of Paradise. The bishop exhorts the clergy,

---

[1] Synesius had previously represented his own disqualifications. He loved profane studies and profane sports; he was incapable of supporting a life of celibacy; he disbelieved the resurrection; and he refused to preach *fables* to the people, unless he might be permitted to *philosophise* at home. Theophilus, primate of Egypt, who knew his merit, accepted this extraordinary compromise.

the magistrates, and the people to renounce all society with the enemies of Christ, to exclude them from their houses and tables, and to refuse them the common offices of life, and the decent rites of burial. The church of Ptolemais, obscure and contemptible as she may appear, addresses this declaration to all her sister churches of the world; and the profane who reject her decrees will be involved in the guilt and punishment of Andronicus and his impious followers. These spiritual terrors were enforced by a dexterous application to the Byzantine court; the trembling president implored the mercy of the church, and the descendent of Hercules enjoyed the satisfaction of raising a prostrate tyrant from the ground. Such principles and such examples insensibly prepared the triumph of the Roman pontiffs, who have trampled on the necks of kings.

VI. Every popular government has experienced the effects of rude or artificial eloquence. The coldest nature is animated, the firmest reason is moved, by the rapid communication of the prevailing impulse; and each hearer is affected by his own passions and by those of the surrounding multitude. The ruin of civil liberty had silenced the demagogues of Athens and the tribunes of Rome; the custom of preaching, which seems to constitute a considerable part of Christian devotion, had not been introduced into the temples of antiquity; and the ears of monarchs were never invaded by the harsh sound of popular eloquence till the pulpits of the empire were filled with sacred orators, who possessed some advantages unknown to their profane predecessors. The arguments and rhetoric of the tribune were instantly opposed, with equal arms, by skilful and resolute antagonists; and the cause of truth and reason might derive an accidental support from the conflict of hostile passions. The bishop, or some distinguished presbyter to whom he cautiously delegated the powers of preaching, harangued, without the danger of interruption or reply, a submissive multitude, whose minds had been prepared and subdued by the awful ceremonies of religion. Such was the strict subordination of the catholic church, that the same concerted sounds might issue at once from an hundred pulpits of Italy or Egypt, if they were *tuned* [1] by the master-hand of the Roman or Alexandrian primate. The design of this institution was laudable, but the fruits were not always salutary. The preachers recommended the practice of the social duties; but they exalted the perfection of monastic virtue, which is painful to the individual, and useless to mankind. Their charitable exhortations betrayed a secret wish that the clergy might be permitted to manage the wealth of the faithful for the benefit of the poor. The most sublime representations of the attributes

---

[1] Queen Elizabeth used this expression and practised this art whenever she wished to prepossess the minds of her people in favour of any extraordinary measure of government. The hostile effects of this *music* were apprehended by her successor, and severely felt by his son. "When pulpit, drum ecclesiastic," &c.

and laws of the Deity were sullied by an idle mixture of metaphysical subtleties, puerile rites, and fictitious miracles: and the expatiated, with the most fervent zeal, on the religious merit of hating the adversaries and obeying the ministers of the church. When the public peace was distracted by heresy and schism, the sacred orators sounded the trumpet of discord, and perhaps of sedition. The understandings of their congregations were perplexed by mystery, their passions were inflamed by invectives; and they rushed from the Christian temples of Antioch or Alexandria, prepared either to suffer or to inflict martyrdom. The corruption of taste and language is strongly marked in the vehement declamations of the Latin bishops; but the compositions of Gregory and Chrysostom have been compared with the most splendid models of Attic, or at least of Asiatic, eloquence.[1]

VII. The representatives of the Christian republic were regularly assembled in the spring and autumn of each year; and these synods diffused the spirit of ecclesiastical discipline and legislation through the hundred and twenty provinces of the Roman world. The archbishop or metropolitan was empowered by the laws to summon the suffragan bishops of his province; to revise their conduct, to vindicate their rights, to declare their faith, and to examine the merit of the candidates who were elected by the clergy and people to supply the vacancies of the episcopal college. The primates of Rome, Alexandria, Antioch, Carthage, and afterwards Constantinople, who exercised a more ample jurisdiction, convened the numerous assembly of their dependent bishops. But the convocation of great and extraordinary synods was the prerogative of the emperor alone. Whenever the emergencies of the church required this decisive measure, he despatched a peremptory summons to the bishops or the deputies of each province, with an order for the use of post-horses and a competent allowance for the expenses of their journey. At an early period, when Constantine was the protector rather than the proselyte of Christianity, he referred the African controversy to the council of Arles; in which the bishops of York, of Trèves, of Milan, and of Carthage, met as friends and brethren, to debate in their native tongue on the common interest of the Latin or Western church. Eleven years afterwards, a more numerous and celebrated assembly was convened at Nice in Bithynia, to extinguish, by their final sentence, the subtle disputes which had arisen in Egypt on the subject of the Trinity. Three hundred and eighteen bishops obeyed the summons of their indulgent master; the ecclesiastics of every rank, and sect, and denomination have been computed at two thousand and forty-eight persons; the Greeks appeared in person; and the consent of the Latins was expressed by the legates of the Roman pontiff. The session, which lasted about two months, was frequently honoured by

---

[1] Those modest orators acknowledge that, as they were destitute of the gift of miracles, they endeavoured to acquire the arts of eloquence.

the presence of the emperor. Leaving his guards at the door, he seated himself (with the permission of the council) on a low stool in the midst of the hall. Constantine listened with patience and spoke with modesty; and while he influenced the debates, he humbly professed that he was the minister, not the judge, of the successors of the apostles, who had been established as priests and as gods upon earth. Such profound reverence of an absolute monarch towards a feeble and unarmed assembly of his own subjects can only be compared to the respect with which the senate had been treated by the Roman princes who adopted the policy of Augustus. Within the space of fifty years, a philosophic spectator of the vicissitudes of human affairs might have contemplated Tacitus in the senate of Rome, and Constantine in the council of Nice. The fathers of the Capitol and those of the church had alike degenerated from the virtues of their founders; but as the bishops were more deeply rooted in the public opinion, they sustained their dignity with more decent pride, and sometimes opposed with a manly spirit the wishes of their sovereign. The progress of time and superstition erased the memory of the weakness, the passion, the ignorance, which disgraced these ecclesiastical synods; and the catholic world has unanimously submitted to the *infallible* decrees of the general councils.

Chapter 21

ARIANISM. COUNCIL OF NICÆA AND THE *HOMOOUSION*.
THE EMPERORS AND THE ARIAN CONTROVERSY. CHARACTER
AND ADVENTURES OF ATHANASIUS. COUNCILS OF ARLES
AND MILAN. GENERAL CHARACTER OF THE CHRISTIAN
SECTS

*Early in his reign Constantine was faced with the problem of
Christian heresy. In Africa the followers of Donatus, a rival bishop
of Carthage, began a schism which was to last in that province for
three hundred years—for as long as Christianity itself in Africa.
But the most widespread and fundamental dispute of the age concerned the Trinity, a doctrine which could be traced at least as far
back as the cosmology of Plato. In the first century A.D. the
question of the nature of the Son of God gave rise to the opposite
heresies of the Ebionites and the Gnostics. At the end of the century
these two heresies were confuted by the fourth evangelist, St. John,
who gave a Christian interpretation to the Platonic cosmology: he
revealed that Jesus Christ was the incarnation of Plato's Logos, or
Reason, which had been with God from the beginning. This eternal
relationship between the Logos and the Father was now disputed by
Arius. Arianism, which was to last until the times of Theodoric and
Clovis, became a major faction in the Christian world.*

AFTER the edict of toleration had restored peace and leisure to
the Christians, the Trinitarian controversy was revived in the
ancient seat of Platonism, the learned, the opulent, the tumultuous city of Alexandria; and the flame of religious discord was rapidly
communicated from the schools to the clergy, the people, the province,
and the East. The abstruse question of the eternity of the *Logos* was
agitated in ecclesiastic conferences and popular sermons; and the hetero-
dox opinions of Arius were soon made public by his own zeal and by
that of his adversaries. His most implacable adversaries have acknowledged the learning and blameless life of that eminent presbyter, who, in
a former election, had declined, and perhaps generously declined, his
pretensions to the episcopal throne. His competitor Alexander assumed
the office of his judge. The important cause was argued before him; and
if at first he seemed to hesitate, he at length pronounced his final sentence
as an absolute rule of faith. The undaunted presbyter, who presumed
to resist the authority of his angry bishop, was separated from the

communion of the church. But the pride of Arius was supported by the applause of a numerous party. He reckoned among his immediate followers two bishops of Egypt, seven presbyters, twelve deacons, and (what may appear almost incredible) seven hundred virgins. A large majority of the bishops of Asia appeared to support or favour his cause; and their measures were conducted by Eusebius of Cæsarea, the most learned of the Christian prelates; and by Eusebius of Nicomedia, who had acquired the reputation of a statesman without forfeiting that of a saint. Synods in Palestine and Bithynia were opposed to the synods of Egypt. The attention of the prince and people was attracted by this theological dispute; and the decision, at the end of six years, was referred to the supreme authority of the general council of Nice.

When the mysteries of the Christian faith were dangerously exposed to public debate, it might be observed that the human understanding was capable of forming three distinct, though imperfect, systems concerning the nature of the Divine Trinity, and it was pronounced that none of these systems, in a pure and absolute sense, were exempt from heresy and error. I. According to the first hypothesis, which was maintained by Arius and his disciples, the *Logos* was a dependent and spontaneous production, created from nothing by the will of the Father. The Son, by whom all things were made,[1] had been begotten before all worlds, and the longest of the astronomical periods could be compared only as a fleeting moment to the extent of his duration; yet this duration was not infinite, and there *had* been a time which preceded the ineffable generation of the *Logos*. On this only-begotten Son the Almighty Father had transfused his ample spirit, and impressed the effulgence of his glory. Visible image of invisible perfection, he saw, at an immeasurable distance beneath his feet, the thrones of the brightest archangels; yet he shone only with a reflected light, and, like the sons of the Roman emperors, who were invested with the titles of Cæsar or Augustus, he governed the universe in obedience to the will of his Father and Monarch. II. In the second hypothesis, the *Logos* possessed all the inherent, incommunicable perfections which religion and philosophy appropriate to the Supreme God. Three distinct and infinite minds or substances, three co-equal and co-eternal beings, composed the Divine Essence; and it would have implied contradiction that any of them should not have existed, or that they should ever cease to exist. The advocates of a system which seemed to establish three independent Deities attempted to preserve the unity of the First Cause, so conspicuous in the design and order of the world, by the perpetual concord of their administration and the essential agreement of their will. A faint resemblance of this unity of action may be discovered in the societies of men, and even of animals.

[1] As the doctrine of absolute creation from nothing was gradually introduced among the Christians, the dignity of the *workman* very naturally rose with that of the *work*.

The causes which disturb their harmony proceed only from the imperfection and inequality of their faculties; but the omnipotence which is guided by infinite wisdom and goodness cannot fail of choosing the same means for the accomplishment of the same ends. III. Three beings, who, by the self-derived necessity of their existence, possess all the divine attributes in the most perfect degree, who are eternal in duration, infinite in space, and intimately present to each other and to the whole universe, irresistibly force themselves on the astonished mind as one and the same Being, who, in the economy of grace, as well as in that of nature, may manifest himself under different forms, and be considered under different aspects. By this hypothesis a real substantial trinity is refined into a trinity of names and abstract modifications that subsist only in the mind which conceives them. The *Logos* is no longer a person, but an attribute; and it is only in a figurative sense that the epithet of Son can be applied to the eternal reason which was with God from the beginning, and by *which*, not by *whom*, all things were made. The incarnation of the *Logos* is reduced to a mere inspiration of the Divine Wisdom, which filled the soul and directed all the actions of the man Jesus. Thus, after revolving round the theological circle, we are surprised to find that the Sabellian ends where the Ebionite had begun, and that the incomprehensible mystery which excites our adoration eludes our inquiry.

COUNCIL OF NICE AND THE *HOMOOUSION*

If the bishops of the council of Nice had been permitted to follow the unbiassed dictates of their conscience, Arius and his associates could scarcely have flattered themselves with the hopes of obtaining a majority of votes in favour of an hypothesis so directly adverse to the two most popular opinions of the catholic world. The Arians soon perceived the danger of their situation, and prudently assumed those modest virtues which, in the fury of civil and religious dissensions, are seldom practised, or even praised, except by the weaker party. They recommended the exercise of Christian charity and moderation, urged the incomprehensible nature of the controversy, disclaimed the use of any terms or definitions which could not be found in the Scriptures, and offered, by very liberal concessions, to satisfy their adversaries without renouncing the integrity of their own principles. The victorious faction received all their proposals with haughty suspicion, and anxiously sought for some irreconcileable mark of distinction, the rejection of which might involve the Arians in the guilt and consequences of heresy. A letter was publicly read and ignominiously torn, in which their patron, Eusebius of Nicomedia, ingenuously confessed that the admission of the HOMOOUSION, or Consubstantial, a word already familiar to the Platonists, was incompatible with the principles of their theological system.

The fortunate opportunity was eagerly embraced by the bishops, who governed the resolutions of the synod, and, accordingly to the lively expression of Ambrose, they used the sword, which heresy itself had drawn from the scabbard, to cut off the head of the hated monster. The consubstantiality of the Father and the Son was established by the council of Nice, and has been unanimously received as a fundamental article of the Christian faith by the consent of the Greek, the Latin, the Oriental, and the Protestant churches. But if the same word had not served to stigmatise the heretics and to unite the catholics, it would have been inadequate to the purpose of the majority by whom it was introduced into the orthodox creed. This majority was divided into two parties, distinguished by a contrary tendency to the sentiments of the Tritheists and of the Sabellians. But as those opposite extremes seemed to overthrow the foundations either of natural or revealed religion, they mutually agreed to qualify the rigour of their principles, and to disavow the just, but invidious, consequences which might be urged by their antagonists. The interest of the common cause inclined them to join their numbers and to conceal their differences; their animosity was softened by the healing counsels of toleration, and their disputes were suspended by the use of the mysterious *Homoousion*, which either party was free to interpret according to their peculiar tenets. The Sabellian sense, which, about fifty years before, had obliged the council of Antioch to prohibit this celebrated term, had endeared it to those theologians who entertained a secret but partial affection for a nominal Trinity. But the more fashionable saints of the Arian times, the intrepid Athanasius, the learned Gregory Nazianzen, and the other pillars of the church, who supported with ability and success the Nicene doctrine, appeared to consider the expression of *substance* as if it had been synonymous with that of *nature*; and they ventured to illustrate their meaning by affirming that three men, as they belong to the same common species, are consubstantial or homoousian to each other. This pure and distinct equality was tempered, on the one hand, by the internal connexion and spiritual penetration which indissolubly unites the divine persons; and, on the other, by the pre-eminence of the Father, which was acknowledged as far as it is compatible with the independence of the Son. Within these limits the almost invisible and tremulous ball of orthodoxy was allowed securely to vibrate. On either side, beyond this consecrated ground, the heretics and the dæmons lurked in ambush to surprise and devour the unhappy wanderer. But as the degrees of theological hatred depend on the spirit of the war rather than on the importance of the controversy, the heretics who degraded were treated with more severity than those who annihilated the person of the Son. The life of Athanasius was consumed in irreconcileable opposition to the impious *madness* of the Arians, but he defended above twenty years the Sabellianism of Marcellus of Ancyra; and when at last he was compelled to withdraw himself from his communion, he continued to mention with an ambiguous smile the venial errors of his respectable friend.

The authority of a general council, to which the Arians themselves had been compelled to submit, inscribed on the banners of the orthodox party the mysterious characters of the word *Homoousion*, which essentially contributed, notwithstanding some obscure disputes, some nocturnal combats, to maintain and perpetuate the uniformity of faith, or at least of language. The Consubstantialists, who by their success have deserved and obtained the title of Catholics, gloried in the simplicity and steadiness of their own creed, and insulted the repeated variations of their adversaries, who were destitute of any certain rule of faith. The sincerity or the cunning of the Arian chiefs, the fear of the laws or of the people, their reverence for Christ, their hatred of Athanasius, all the causes, human and divine, that influence and disturb the counsels of a theological faction, introduced among the sectaries a spirit of discord and inconstancy, which in the course of a few years erected eighteen different models of religion, and avenged the violated dignity of the church. The zealous Hilary, who, from the peculiar hardships of his situation, was inclined to extenuate rather than to aggravate the errors of the Oriental clergy, declares that, in the wide extent of the ten provinces of Asia to which he had been banished, there could be found very few prelates who had preserved the knowledge of the true God. The oppression which he had felt, the disorders of which he was the spectator and the victim, appeased, during a short interval, the angry passions of his soul; and in the following passage, of which I shall transcribe a few lines, the bishop of Poitiers unwarily deviates into the style of a Christian philosopher. "It is a thing," says Hilary, "equally deplorable and dangerous, that there are as many creeds as opinions among men, as many doctrines as inclinations, and as many sources of blasphemy as there are faults among us; because we make creeds arbitrarily, and explain them as arbitrarily. The Homoousion is rejected, and received, and explained away by successive synods. The partial or total resemblance of the Father and of the Son is a subject of dispute for these unhappy times. Every year, nay, every moon, we make new creeds to describe invisible mysteries. We repent of what we have done, we defend those who repent, we anathematise those whom we defended. We condemn either the doctrine of others in ourselves, or our own in that of others; and, reciprocally tearing one another to pieces, we have been the cause of each other's ruin."

It will not be expected, it would not perhaps be endured, that I should swell this theological digression by a minute examination of the eighteen creeds, the authors of which, for the most part, disclaimed the odious name of their parent Arius. It is amusing enough to delineate the form, and to trace the vegetation, of a singular plant; but the tedious detail of leaves without flowers, and of branches without fruit, would soon exhaust the patience and disappoint the curiosity of the laborious student. One question, which gradually arose from the Arian controversy, may, however, be noticed, as it served to produce and discriminate the three sects who were united only by their common aversion to the Homoousion of the Nicene synod. 1. If they were asked whether the Son was *like* unto the Father, the question was resolutely answered in the negative by the heretics who adhered to the principles of Arius, or indeed to those of philosophy, which seem to establish an infinite difference between the Creator and the most excellent of his creatures. This obvious consequence was maintained by Aëtius, on whom the zeal of his adversaries bestowed the surname of the Atheist. His restless and aspiring spirit urged him to try almost every profession of human life. He was successively a slave, or at least a husbandman, a travelling tinker, a goldsmith, a physician, a schoolmaster, a theologian, and at last the apostle of a new church, which was propagated by the abilities of his disciple Eunomius. Armed with texts of Scripture, and with captious syllogisms from the logic of Aristotle, the subtle Aëtius had acquired the fame of an invincible disputant, whom it was impossible either to silence or to convince. Such talents engaged the friendship of the Arian bishops, till they were forced to renounce and even to persecute a dangerous ally, who, by the accuracy of his reasoning, had prejudiced their cause in the popular opinion, and offended the piety of their most devoted followers. 2. The omnipotence of the Creator suggested a specious and respectful solution of the *likeness* of the Father and the Son; and faith might humbly receive what reason could not presume to deny, that the Supreme God might communicate his infinite perfections, and create a being similar only to himself. These Arians were powerfully supported by the weight and abilities of their leaders, who had succeeded to the management of the Eusebian interest, and who occupied the principal throne of the East. They detested, perhaps with some affection, the impiety of Aëtius; they professed to believe, either without reserve or according to the Scriptures, that the Son was different from all *other* creatures, and similar only to the Father. But they denied that he was either of the same or of a similar substance; sometimes boldly justifying their dissent, and sometimes objecting to the use of the word substance, which seems to imply an adequate, or at least a distinct, notion of the nature of the Deity. 3. The sect which asserted the doctrine of a similar substance was the most numerous, at least in the provinces of Asia; and when the leaders of both parties were assembled in the council of Seleucia, *their* opinion would have prevailed by a majority of one hundred and five to forty-three bishops. The Greek word which was chosen to express this mysterious resemblance bears so close an affinity to the orthodox symbol, that the profane of every age have derided the furious contests which the difference of a single diphthong excited between the Homoousians and the Homoiousians. As it frequently happens that the sounds and characters which approach the nearest to each other accidentally represent the most opposite ideas, the observation would be itself ridiculous, if it were possible to mark any real and sensible distinction between the doctrine of the Semi-Arians, as they were improperly styled, and that of the Catholics themselves. The bishop of Poitiers, who in his Phrygian exile very wisely aimed at a coalition of parties, endeavours to prove that, by a pious and faithful interpretation, the *Homoiousion* may be reduced to a consubstantial sense. Yet he confesses that the word has a dark and suspicious aspect; and, as if darkness were congenial to theological disputes, the Semi-Arians, who advanced to the doors of the church, assailed them with the most unrelenting fury.

THE EMPERORS AND THE ARIAN CONTROVERSY

The provinces of Egypt and Asia, which cultivated the language and manners of the Greeks, had deeply imbibed the venom of the Arian controversy. The unfamiliar study of the Platonic system, a vain and argumentative disposition, a copious and flexible idiom, supplied the clergy and people of the East with an inexhaustible flow of words and distinctions; and, in the midst of their fierce contentions, they easily forgot the doubt which is recommended by philosophy, and the submission which is enjoined by religion. The inhabitants of the West were of a less inquisitive spirit; their passions were not so forcibly moved by invisible objects, their minds were less frequently exercised by the habits of dispute; and such was the happy ignorance of the Gallican church, that Hilary himself, above thirty years after the first general council, was still a stranger to the Nicene creed. The Latins had received the rays of divine knowledge through the dark and doubtful medium of a translation. The poverty and stubbornness of their native tongue was not always capable of affording just equivalents for the Greek terms, for the technical words of the Platonic philosophy, which had been consecrated, by the Gospel or by the church, to express the mysteries of the Christian faith, and a verbal defect might introduce into the Latin theology a long train of error or perplexity. But as the western provincials had the good fortune of deriving their religion from an orthodox source, they preserved with steadiness the doctrine which they had accepted with docility; and when the Arian pestilence approached their frontiers, they were supplied with the seasonable preservative of the Homoousion by the paternal care of the Roman pontiff. Their sentiments and their temper were displayed in the memorable synod of Rimini, which surpassed in numbers the council of Nice, since it was composed of above four hundred bishops of Italy, Africa, Spain, Gaul, Britain, and Illyricum. From the first debates it appeared that only fourscore prelates adhered to the party, though *they* affected to anathematise the name and memory of Arius. But this inferiority was compensated by the advantages of skill, of experience, and of discipline; and the minority was conducted by Valens and Ursacius, two bishops of Illyricum, who had spent their lives in the intrigues of courts and councils, and who had been trained under the Eusebian banner in the religious wars of the East. By their arguments and negotiations they embarrassed, they confounded, they at last deceived the honest simplicity of the Latin bishops, who suffered the palladium of the faith to be extorted from their hands by fraud and importunity, rather than by open violence. The council of Rimini was not allowed to separate till the members had imprudently subscribed a captious creed, in which some expressions, susceptible of an heretical sense, were inserted in the room of the Homoousion. It was on this occasion that, according to Jerom, the world was surprised to find itself Arian. But the bishops of the Latin provinces had no sooner reached their respective dioceses than they discovered their mistake, and repented of their weakness. The ignominious capitulation was rejected with disdain and abhorrence, and the Homoousian standard, which had been shaken but not overthrown, was more firmly replanted in all the churches of the West.

Such was the rise and progress, and such were the natural revolutions, of those theological disputes which disturbed the peace of Christianity under the reigns of Constantine and of his sons. But as those princes presumed to extend their despotism over the faith, as well as over the lives and fortunes, of their subjects, the weight of their suffrage sometimes inclined the ecclesiastical balance: and the prerogatives of the King of Heaven were settled, or changed, or modified, in the cabinet of an earthly monarch.

The unhappy spirit of discord which pervaded the provinces of the East interrupted the triumph of Constantine; but the emperor continued for some time to view with cool and careless indifference the object of the dispute. As he was yet ignorant of the difficulty of appeasing the quarrels of theologians, he addressed to the contending parties, to Alexander and to Arius, a moderating epistle; [1] which may be ascribed with far greater reason to the untutored sense of a soldier and statesman than to the dictates of any of his episcopal counsellors. He attributes the origin of the whole controversy to a trifling and subtle question concerning an incomprehensible point of the law, which was foolishly asked by the bishop, and imprudently resolved by the presbyter. He laments that the Christian people, who had the same God, the same religion, and the same worship, should be divided by such inconsiderable distinctions; and he seriously recommends to the clergy of Alexandria the example of the Greek philosophers, who could maintain their argu-

---

[1] The principles of toleration and religious indifference contained in this epistle have given great offence to Baronius, Tillemont, &c., who suppose that the emperor had some evil counsellor, either Satan or Eusebius, at his elbow.

ments without losing their temper, and assert their freedom without violating their friendship. The indifference and contempt of the sovereign would have been, perhaps, the most effectual method of silencing the dispute, if the popular current had been less rapid and impetuous, and if Constantine himself, in the midst of faction and fanaticism, could have preserved the calm possession of his own mind. But his ecclesiastical ministers soon contrived to seduce the impartiality of the magistrate, and to awaken the zeal of the proselyte. He was provoked by the insults which had been offered to his statues; he was alarmed by the real as well as the imaginary magnitude of the spreading mischief; and he extinguished the hope of peace and toleration, from the moment that he assembled three hundred bishops within the walls of the same palace. The presence of the monarch swelled the importance of the debate; his attention multiplied the arguments; and he exposed his person with a patient intrepidity which animated the valour of the combatants. Notwithstanding the applause which has been bestowed on the eloquence and sagacity of Constantine, a Roman general, whose religion might be still a subject of doubt, and whose mind had not been enlightened either by study or by inspiration, was indifferently qualified to discuss, in the Greek language, a metaphysical question, or an article of faith. But the credit of his favourite Osius, who appears to have presided in the council of Nice, might dispose the emperor in favour of the orthodox party; and a well-timed insinuation, that the same Eusebius of Nicomedia, who now protected the heretic, had lately assisted the tyrant, might exasperate him against their adversaries. The Nicene creed was ratified by Constantine; and his firm declaration, that those who resisted the divine judgment of the synod must prepare themselves for an immediate exile, annihilated the murmurs of a feeble opposition; which, from seventeen, was almost instantly reduced to two, protesting bishops. Eusebius of Cæsarea yielded a reluctant and ambiguous consent to the Homoousion; and the wavering conduct of the Nicomedian Eusebius served only to delay about three months his disgrace and exile. The impious Arius was banished into one of the remote provinces of Illyricum; his person and disciples were branded, by law, with the odious name of Porphyrians; his writings were condemned to the flames, and a capital punishment was denounced against those in whose possession they should be found. The emperor had now imbibed the spirit of controversy, and the angry sarcastic style of his edicts was designed to inspire his subjects with the hatred which he had conceived against the enemies of Christ.

But, as if the conduct of the emperor had been guided by passion instead of principle, three years from the council of Nice were scarcely elapsed before he discovered some symptoms of mercy, and even of indulgence, towards the proscribed sect, which was secretly protected by his favourite sister. The exiles were recalled; and Eusebius, who gradually resumed his influence over the mind of Constantine, was restored to the episcopal throne, from which he had been ignominiously degraded. Arius himself was treated by the whole court with the respect which would have been due to an innocent and oppressed man. His faith was approved by the synod of Jerusalem; and the emperor seemed impatient to repair his injustice, by issuing an absolute command that he should be solemnly admitted to the communion in the cathedral of Constantinople. On the same day which had been fixed for the triumph of Arius, he expired; and the strange and horrid circumstances of his death might excite a suspicion that the orthodox saints had contributed more efficaciously than by their prayers to deliver the church from the most formidable of her enemies.[1] The three principal leaders of the catholics, Athanasius of Alexandria, Eustathius of Antioch, and Paul of Constantinople, were deposed on various accusations, by the sentence of numerous councils; and were afterwards banished into distant provinces by the first of the Christian emperors, who, in the last moments of his life, received the rites of baptism from the Arian bishop of Nicomedia. The ecclesiastical government of Constantine cannot be justified from the reproach of levity and weakness. But the credulous monarch, unskilled in the stratagems of theological warfare, might be deceived by the modest and specious professions of the heretics, whose sentiments he never perfectly understood; and while he protected Arius, and persecuted Athanasius, he still considered the council of Nice as the bulwark of the Christian faith, and the peculiar glory of his own reign.

The sons of Constantine must have been admitted from their childhood into the rank of catechumens, but they imitated, in the delay of their baptism, the example of their father. Like him they presumed to pronounce their judgment on mysteries into which they had never been regularly initiated: and the fate of the Trinitarian controversy depended, in a great measure, on the sentiments of Constantius, who inherited the provinces of the East, and acquired the possession of the whole empire. The Arian presbyter or bishop, who had secreted for his use the testament of the deceased emperor, improved the fortunate occasion which had introduced him to the familiarity of a prince whose public counsels were always swayed by his domestic favourites. The eunuchs and slaves diffused the spiritual poison through the palace, and the dangerous infection was communicated by the female attendants to the guards, and by the empress to her unsuspicious husband.[2] The partiality which

---

[1] We derive the original story from Athanasius, who expresses some reluctance to stigmatise the memory of the dead. He might exaggerate; but the perpetual commerce of Alexandria and Constantinople would have rendered it dangerous to invent. Those who press the literal narrative of the death of Arius (his bowels suddenly burst out in a privy) must make their option between *poison* and *miracle*.

[2] He observes that the eunuchs are the natural enemies of the *Son*. Compare Dr. Jortin's Remarks on Ecclesiastical History, vol. iv. p. 3, with a certain genealogy in *Candide* (ch. iv.), which ends with one of the first companions of Christopher Columbus.

Constantius always expressed towards the Eusebian faction was insensibly fortified by the dexterous management of their leaders; and his victory over the tyrant Magnentius increased his inclination, as well as ability, to employ the arms of power in the cause of Arianism. While the two armies were engaged in the plains of Mursa, and the fate of the two rivals depended on the chance of war, the son of Constantine passed the anxious moments in a church of the martyrs, under the walls of the city. His spiritual comforter, Valens, the Arian bishop of the diocese, employed the most artful precautions to obtain such early intelligence as might secure either his favour or his escape. A secret chain of swift and trusty messengers informed him of the vicissitudes of the battle; and while the courtiers stood trembling round their affrighted master, Valens assured him that the Gallic legions gave way; and insinuated, with some presence of mind, that the glorious event had been revealed to him by an angel. The grateful emperor ascribed his success to the merits and intercession of the bishop of Mursa, whose faith had deserved the public and miraculous approbation of Heaven. The Arians, who considered as their own the victory of Constantius, preferred his glory to that of his father.[1] Cyril, bishop of Jerusalem, immediately composed the description of a celestial cross, encircled with a splendid rainbow, which, during the festival of Pentecost, about the third hour of the day, had appeared over the Mount of Olives, to the edification of the devout pilgrims and the people of the holy city. The size of the meteor was gradually magnified; and the Arian historian has ventured to affirm that it was conspicuous to the two armies in the plains of Pannonia; and that the tyrant, who is purposely represented as an idolater, fled before the auspicious sign of orthodox Christianity.

The sentiments of a judicious stranger, who has impartially considered the progress of civil or ecclesiastical discord, are always entitled to our notice: and a short passage of Ammianus, who served in the armies, and studied the character, of Constantius, is perhaps of more value than many pages of theological invectives. "The Christian religion, which, in itself," says that moderate historian, "is plain and simple, *he* confounded by the dotage of superstition. Instead of reconciling the parties by the weight of his authority, he cherished and propagated, by verbal disputes, the differences which his vain curiosity had excited. The highways were covered with troops of bishops galloping from every side to the assemblies, which they call synods; and while they laboured to reduce the whole sect to their own particular opinions, the public

---

[1] Cyril expressly observes that in the reign of Constantine the cross had been found in the bowels of the earth; but that it had appeared, in the reign of Constantius, in the midst of the heavens. This opposition evidently proves that Cyril was ignorant of the stupendous miracle to which the conversion of Constantine is attributed; and this ignorance is the more surprising, since it was no more than twelve years after his death that Cyril was consecrated bishop of Jerusalem by the immediate successor of Eusebius of Cæsarea.

establishment of the posts was almost ruined by their hasty and repeated journeys." Our more intimate knowledge of the ecclesiastical transactions of the reign of Constantius would furnish an ample commentary on this remarkable passage; which justifies the rational apprehensions of Athanasius, that the restless activity of the clergy, who wandered round the empire in search of the true faith, would excite the contempt and laughter of the unbelieving world. As soon as the emperor was relieved from the terrors of the civil war, he devoted the leisure of his winter-quarters at Arles, Milan, Sirmium, and Constantinople, to the amusement or toils of controversy: the sword of the magistrate, and even of the tyrant, was unsheathed, to enforce the reasons of the theologian; and as he opposed the orthodox faith of Nice, it is readily confessed that his incapacity and ignorance were equal to his presumption. The eunuchs, the women, and the bishops, who governed the vain and feeble mind of the emperor, had inspired him with an insuperable dislike to the Homoousion; but his timid conscience was alarmed by the impiety of Aëtius. The guilt of that atheist was aggravated by the suspicious favour of the unfortunate Gallus; and even the deaths of the Imperial ministers who had been massacred at Antioch were imputed to the suggestions of that dangerous sophist. The mind of Constantius, which could neither be moderated by reason nor fixed by faith, was blindly impelled to either side of the dark and empty abyss, by his horror of the opposite extreme; he alternately embraced and condemned the sentiments, he successively banished and recalled the leaders, of the Arian and Semi-Arian factions. During the season of public business or festivity, he employed whole days, and even nights, in selecting the words, and weighing the syllables, which composed his fluctuating creeds. The subject of his meditations still pursued and occupied his slumbers: the incoherent dreams of the emperor were received as celestial visions, and he accepted with complacency the lofty title of bishop of bishops, from those ecclesiastics who forgot the interest of their order for the gratification of their passions. The design of establishing an uniformity of doctrine, which had engaged him to convene so many synods in Gaul, Italy, Illyricum, and Asia, was repeatedly baffled by his own levity, by the divisions of the Arians, and by the resistance of the catholics; and he resolved, as the last and decisive effort, imperiously to dictate the decrees of a general council. The destructive earthquake of Nicomedia, the difficulty of finding a convenient place, and perhaps some secret motives of policy, produced an alteration in the summons. The bishops of the East were directed to meet at Seleucia, in Isauria; while those of the West held their deliberations at Rimini, on the coast of the Hadriatic; and instead of two or three deputies from each province, the whole episcopal body was ordered to march. The Eastern council, after consuming four days in fierce and unavailing debate, separated without any definitive conclusion. The council of the West was protracted till the seventh month. Taurus, the

Prætorian prefect, was instructed not to dismiss the prelates till they should all be united in the same opinion; and his efforts were supported by a power of banishing fifteen of the most refractory, and a promise of the consulship if he achieved so difficult an adventure. His prayers and threats, the authority of the sovereign, the sophistry of Valens and Ursacius, the distress of cold and hunger, and the tedious melancholy of a hopeless exile, at length extorted the reluctant consent of the bishops of Rimini. The deputies of the East and of the West attended the emperor in the palace of Constantinople, and he enjoyed the satisfaction of imposing on the world a profession of faith which established the *likeness*, without expressing the *consubstantiality*, of the Son of God. But the triumph of Arianism had been preceded by the removal of the orthodox clergy, whom it was impossible either to intimidate or to corrupt; and the reign of Constantius was disgraced by the unjust and ineffectual persecution of the great Athanasius.

THE CHARACTER AND ADVENTURES OF ATHANASIUS

We have seldom an opportunity of observing, either in active or speculative life, what effect may be produced, or what obstacles may be surmounted, by the force of a single mind, when it is inflexibly applied to the pursuit of a single object. The immortal name of Athanasius will never be separated from the catholic doctrine of the Trinity, to whose defence he consecrated every moment and every faculty of his being. Educated in the family of Alexander, he had vigorously opposed the early progress of the Arian heresy: he exercised the important functions of secretary under the aged prelate; and the fathers of the Nicene council beheld with surprise and respect the rising virtues of the young deacon. In a time of public danger the dull claims of age and of rank are sometimes superseded; and within five months after his return from Nice the deacon Athanasius was seated on the archiepiscopal throne of Egypt. He filled that eminent station above forty-six years, and his long administration was spent in a perpetual combat against the powers of Arianism. Five times was Athanasius expelled from his throne; twenty years he passed as an exile or a fugitive; and almost every province of the Roman empire was successively witness to his merit, and his sufferings in the cause of the Homoousion, which he considered as the sole pleasure and business, as the duty, and as the glory of his life. Amidst the storms of persecution, the archbishop of Alexandria was patient of labour, jealous of fame, careless of safety; and although his mind was tainted by the contagion of fanaticism, Athanasius displayed a superiority of character and abilities which would have qualified him, far better than the degenerate sons of Constantine, for the government of a great monarchy. His learning was much less profound and extensive than that of Eusebius of Cæsarea, and his rude eloquence could not be compared with the polished oratory of Gregory of Basil; but whenever the primate of Egypt was called upon to justify his sentiments or his conduct, his unpremeditated style, either of speaking or writing, was clear, forcible, and persuasive. He has always been revered in the orthodox school as one of the most accurate masters of the Christian theology; and he was supposed to possess two profane sciences, less adapted to the episcopal character— the knowledge of jurisprudence, and that of divination. Some fortunate conjectures of future events, which impartial reasoners might ascribe to the experience and judgment of Athanasius, were attributed by his friends to heavenly inspiration, and imputed by his enemies to infernal magic.

But as Athanasius was continually engaged with the prejudices and passions of every order of men, from the monk to the emperor, the knowledge of human nature was his first and most important science. He preserved a distinct and unbroken view of a scene which was incessantly shifting; and never failed to improve those decisive moments which are irrevocably past before they are perceived by a common eye. The archbishop of Alexandria was capable of distinguishing how far he might boldly command, and where he must dexterously insinuate; how long he might contend with power, and when he must withdraw from persecution; and while he directed the thunders of the church against heresy and rebellion, he could assume, in the bosom of his own party, the flexible and indulgent temper of a prudent leader. The election of Athanasius has not escaped the reproach of irregularity and precipitation; but the propriety of his behaviour conciliated the affections both of the clergy and of the people. The Alexandrians were impatient to rise in arms for the defence of an eloquent and liberal pastor. In his distress he always derived support, or at least consolation, from the faithful attachment of his parochial clergy; and the hundred bishops of Egypt adhered, with unshaken zeal, to the cause of Athanasius. In the modest equipage which pride and policy would affect, he frequently performed the episcopal visitation of his provinces, from the mouth of the Nile to the confines of Ethiopia; familiarly conversing with the meanest of the populace, and humbly saluting the saints and hermits of the desert. Nor was it only in ecclesiastical assemblies, among men whose education and manners were similar to his own, that Athanasius displayed the ascendancy of his genius. He appeared with easy and respectful firmness in the courts of princes; and in the various turns of his prosperous and adverse fortune he never lost the confidence of his friends, or the esteem of his enemies.

In his youth the primate of Egypt resisted the great Constantine, who had repeatedly signified his will that Arius should be restored to the catholic communion. The emperor respected, and might forgive, this inflexible resolution; and the faction who considered Athanasius as their most formidable enemy were constrained to dissemble their hatred, and silently to prepare an indirect and distant assault. They scattered rumours and suspicions, represented the archbishop as a proud and oppressive tyrant, and boldly accused him of violating the treaty which had been ratified in the Nicene council with the schismatic followers of Meletius. Athanasius had openly disapproved that ignominious peace, and the emperor was disposed to believe that he had abused his ecclesiastical and civil power to persecute those odious sectaries; that he had sacrilegiously broken a chalice in one of their churches of Mareotis; that he had whipped or imprisoned six of their bishops; and that Arsenius, a seventh bishop of the same party, had been murdered, or at least mutilated, by the cruel hand of the primate. These charges, which affected his honour and his life, were referred by Constantine to his brother Dalmatius, the censor, who resided at Antioch; the synods of Cæsarea and Tyre were successively convened; and the bishops of the East were instructed to judge the cause of Athanasius before they proceeded to consecrate the new church of the Resurrection at Jerusalem. The primate might be conscious of his innocence; but he was sensible that the same implacable spirit which had dictated the accusation would direct the proceeding and pronounce the sentence. He prudently declined the tribunal of his enemies, despised the summons of the synod of Cæsarea; and, after a long and artful delay, submitted to the peremptory commands of the emperor, who threatened to punish his criminal disobedience if he refused to appear in the council of Tyre. Before Athanasius, at the head of fifty Egyptian prelates, sailed from Alexandria, he had wisely secured the alliance of the Meletians; and Arsenius himself, his imaginary victim, and his secret friend, was privately concealed in his train. The synod of Tyre was conducted by Eusebius of Cæsarea, with more passion, and with less art, than his learning and experience might promise; his numerous faction repeated the names of homicide and tyrant; and their clamours were encouraged by the seeming patience of Athanasius, who expected the decisive moment to produce Arsenius alive and unhurt in the midst of the assembly. The nature of the other charges did not admit of such clear and satisfactory replies; yet the archbishop was able to prove that, in the village where he was accused of breaking a consecrated chalice, neither church nor altar nor chalice could really exist. The Arians, who had secretly determined the guilt and condemnation of their enemy, attempted, however, to disguise their injustice by the imitation of judicial forms: the synod appointed an episcopal commission of six delegates to collect evidence on the spot; and this measure, which was vigorously opposed by the Egyptian bishops, opened new scenes of violence and perjury. After the return of the deputies from Alexandria, the majority of the council pronounced the final sentence of degradation and exile against the primate of Egypt. The decree, expressed in the fiercest language of malice and revenge, was communicated to the emperor and the catholic church; and the bishops immediately resumed a mild and devout aspect, such as became their holy pilgrimage to the Sepulchre of Christ.

But the injustice of these ecclesiastical judges had not been countenanced by the submission, or even by the presence, of Athanasius. He resolved to make a bold and dangerous experiment, whether the throne was inaccessible to the voice of truth; and before the final sentence could be pronounced at Tyre, the intrepid primate threw himself into a bark which was ready to hoist sail for the Imperial city. The request of a formal audience might have been opposed or eluded; but Athanasius concealed his arrival, watched the moment of Constantine's return from an adjacent villa, and boldly encountered his angry sovereign as he passed on horseback through the principal street of Constantinople. So strange an apparition excited his surprise and indignation; and the guards were ordered to remove the importunate suitor; but his resentment was subdued by involuntary respect; and the haughty spirit of the emperor was awed by the courage and eloquence of a bishop who implored his justice and awakened his conscience. Constantine listened to the complaints of Athanasius with impartial and even gracious attention; the members of the synod of Tyre were summoned to justify their proceedings; and the arts of the Eusebian faction would have been confounded if they had not aggravated the guilt of the primate by the dexterous supposition of an unpardonable offence—a criminal design to intercept and detain the corn-fleet of Alexandria, which supplied the subsistence of the new capital.[1] The emperor was satisfied that the peace of Egypt would be secured by the absence of a popular leader; but he refused to fill the vacancy of the archiepiscopal throne; and the sentence which, after long hesitation, he pronounced, was that of a jealous ostracism rather than of an ignominious exile. In the remote province of Gaul, but in the hospitable court of Treves, Athanasius passed about twenty-eight months. The death of the emperor changed the face of public affairs; and, amidst the general indulgence of a young reign, the primate was restored to his country by an honourable edict of the younger Constantine, who expressed a deep sense of the innocence and merit of his venerable guest.

The death of that prince exposed Athanasius to a second persecution; and the feeble Constantius, the sovereign of the East, soon became the secret accomplice of the Eusebians. Ninety bishops of that sect or faction assembled at Antioch, under the specious pretence of dedicating

---

[1] Eunapius has related a strange example of the cruelty and credulity of Constantine on a similar occasion. The eloquent Sopater, a Syrian philosopher, enjoyed his friendship, and provoked the resentment of Ablavius, his Prætorian prefect. The corn-fleet was detained for want of a south wind; the people of Constantinople were discontented; and Sopater was beheaded, on a charge that he had *bound* the winds by the power of magic. Suidas adds, that Constantine wished to prove, by this execution, that he had absolutely renounced the superstition of the Gentiles.

the cathedral. They composed an ambiguous creed, which is faintly tinged with the colours of Semi-Arianism, and twenty-five canons, which still regulate the discipline of the orthodox Greeks. It was decided, with some appearance of equity, that a bishop, deprived by a synod, should not resume his episcopal functions till he had been absolved by the judgment of an equal synod; the law was immediately applied to the case of Athanasius; the council of Antioch pronounced, or rather confirmed, his degradation: a stranger, named Gregory, was seated on his throne; and Philagrius, the prefect of Egypt, was instructed to support the new primate with the civil and military powers of the province. Oppressed by the conspiracy of the Asiatic prelates, Athanasius withdrew from Alexandria and passed three years as an exile and a suppliant on the holy threshold of the Vatican. By the assiduous study of the Latin language he soon qualified himself to negotiate with the western clergy; his decent flattery swayed and directed the haughty Julius: the Roman pontiff was persuaded to consider his appeal as the peculiar interest of the Apostolic see; and his innocence was unanimously declared in a council of fifty bishops of Italy. At the end of three years the primate was summoned to the court of Milan by the emperor Constans, who, in the indulgence of unlawful pleasures, still professed a lively regard for the orthodox faith. The cause of truth and justice was promoted by the influence of gold, and the ministers of Constans advised their sovereign to require the convocation of an ecclesiastical assembly, which might act as the representatives of the catholic church. Ninety-four bishops of the West, seventy-six bishops of the East, encountered each other at Sardica, on the verge of the two empires, but in the dominions of the protector of Athanasius. Their debates soon degenerated into hostile altercations; the Asiatics, apprehensive for their personal safety, retired to Philippopolis in Thrace; and the rival synods reciprocally hurled their spiritual thunders against their enemies, whom they piously condemned as the enemies of the true God. Their decrees were published and ratified in the respective provinces: and Athanasius, who in the West was revered as a saint, was exposed as a criminal to the abhorrence of the East. The council of Sardica reveals the first symptoms of discord and schism between the Greek and Latin churches, which were separated by the accidental difference of faith and the permanent distinction of language.

During his second exile in the West, Athanasius was frequently admitted to the Imperial presence—at Capua, Lodi, Milan, Verona, Padua, Aquileia, and Treves. The bishop of the diocese usually assisted at these interviews; the master of the offices stood before the veil or curtain of the sacred apartment; and the uniform moderation of the primate might be attested by these respectable witnesses, to whose evidence he solemnly appeals. Prudence would undoubtedly suggest the mild and respectful tone that became a subject and a bishop. In these familiar conferences with the sovereign of the West, Athanasius might lament the error of Constantius, but he boldly arraigned the guilt of his eunuchs and his Arian prelates; deplored the distress and danger of the catholic church; and excited Constans to emulate the zeal and glory of his father. The emperor declared his resolution of employing the troops and treasures of Europe in the orthodox cause; and signified, by a concise and peremptory epistle to his brother Constantius, that, unless he consented to the immediate restoration of Athanasius, he himself, with a fleet and army, would seat the archbishop on the throne of Alexandria. But this religious war, so horrible to nature, was prevented by the timely compliance of Constantius; and the emperor of the East condescended to solicit a reconciliation with a subject whom he had injured. Athanasius waited with decent pride till he had received three successive epistles full of the strongest assurances of the protection, the favour, and the esteem of his sovereign; who invited him to resume his episcopal seat, and who added the humiliating precaution of engaging his principal ministers to attest the sincerity of his intentions. They were manifested in a still more public manner by the strict orders which were despatched into Egypt to recall the adherents of Athanasius, to restore their privileges, to proclaim their innocence, and to erase from the public registers the illegal proceedings which had been obtained during the prevalence of the Eusebian faction. After every satisfaction and security had been given which justice or even delicacy could require, the primate proceeded, by slow journeys, through the provinces of Thrace, Asia, and Syria; and his progress was marked by the abject homage of the Oriental bishops, who excited his contempt without deceiving his penetration. At Antioch he saw the emperor Constantius; sustained, with modest firmness, the embraces and protestations of his master; and eluded the proposal of allowing the Arians a single church at Alexandria by claiming, in the other cities of the empire, a similar toleration for his own party; a reply which might have appeared just and moderate in the mouth of an independent prince. The entrance of the archbishop into his capital was a triumphal procession; absence and persecution had endeared him to the Alexandrians; his authority, which he exercised with rigour, was more firmly established; and his fame was diffused from Ethiopia to Britain, over the whole extent of the Christian world.

But the subject who has reduced his prince to the necessity of dissembling can never expect a sincere and lasting forgiveness; and the tragic fate of Constans soon deprived Athanasius of a powerful and generous protector. The civil war between the assassin and the only surviving brother of Constans, which afflicted the empire above three years, secured an interval of repose to the catholic church; and the two contending parties were desirous to conciliate the friendship of a bishop who, by the weight of his personal authority, might determine the fluctuating resolutions of an important province. He gave audience to the ambassadors of the tyrant, with whom he was afterwards accused of holding a secret correspondence; and the emperor Constantius repeatedly assured his dearest father, the most reverend Athanasius, that, notwithstanding the malicious rumours which were circulated by their common enemies, he had inherited the sentiments, as well as the throne, of his deceased brother. Gratitude and humanity would have disposed the primate of Egypt to deplore the untimely fate of Constans, and to abhor the guilt of Magnentius; but as he clearly understood that the apprehensions of Constantius were his only safeguard, the fervour of his prayers for the success of the righteous cause might perhaps be somewhat abated. The ruin of Athanasius was no longer contrived by the obscure malice of a few bigoted or angry bishops, who abused the authority of a credulous monarch. The monarch himself avowed the resolution, which he had so long suppressed, of avenging his private injuries; and the first winter after his victory, which he passed at Arles, was employed against an enemy more odious to him than the vanquished tyrant of Gaul.

THE COUNCILS OF ARLES AND MILAN

If the emperor had capriciously decreed the death of the most eminent and virtuous citizen of the republic, the cruel order would have been executed without hesitation by the ministers of open violence or of specious injustice. The caution, the delay, the difficulty with which he proceeded in the condemnation and punishment of a popular bishop, discovered to the world that the privileges of the church had already revived a sense of order and freedom in the Roman government. The sentence which was pronounced in the synod of Tyre, and subscribed by a large majority of the Eastern bishops, had never been expressly repealed; and as Athanasius had been once degraded from his episcopal dignity by the judgment of his brethren, every subsequent act might be considered as irregular, and even criminal. But the memory of the firm and effectual support which the primate of Egypt had derived from the attachment of the Western church engaged Constantius to suspend the execution of the sentence till he had obtained the concurrence of the Latin bishops. Two years were consumed in ecclesiastical negotiations; and the important cause between the emperor and one of his subjects was solemnly debated, first in the synod of Arles, and afterwards in the great council of Milan, which consisted of above three hundred bishops. Their integrity was gradually undermined by the arguments of the Arians, the dexterity of the eunuchs, and the pressing solicitations of a prince who gratified his revenge at the expense of his dignity, and exposed his own passions whilst he influenced those of the clergy. Corruption, the most infallible symptom of constitutional liberty, was successfully practised; honours, gifts, and immunities were offered and accepted as the price of an episcopal vote;[1] and the condemnation of the Alexandrian primate was artfully represented as the only measure which could restore the peace and union of the catholic church. The friends of Athanasius were not, however, wanting to their leader, or to their cause. With a manly spirit, which the sanctity of their character rendered less dangerous, they maintained, in public debate, and in private conference with the emperor, the eternal obligation of religion and justice. They declared that neither the hope of his favour, nor the fear of his displeasure, should prevail on them to join in the condemnation of an absent, an innocent, a respectable brother. They affirmed, with apparent reason, that the illegal and obsolete decrees of the council of Tyre had long since been tacitly abolished by the Imperial edicts, the honourable re-establishment of the archbishop of Alexandria, and the silence or recantation of his most clamorous adversaries. They alleged that his innocence had been attested by the unanimous bishops of Egypt, and had been acknowledged in the councils of Rome and Sardica by the impartial judgment of the Latin church. They deplored the hard condition of Athanasius, who, after enjoying so many years his seat, his reputation, and the seeming confidence of his sovereign, was again called upon to confute the most groundless and extravagant accusations. Their language was specious; their conduct was honourable: but in this long and obstinate contest, which fixed the eyes of the whole empire on a single bishop, the ecclesiastical factions were prepared to sacrifice truth and justice to the more interesting object of defending or removing the intrepid champion of the Nicene faith. The Arians still thought it prudent to disguise, in ambiguous language, their real sentiments and designs; but the orthodox bishops, armed with the favour of the people and the decrees of a general council, insisted on every occasion, and particularly at Milan, that their adversaries should purge themselves from the suspicion of heresy, before they presumed to arraign the conduct of the great Athanasius.

But the voice of reason (if reason was indeed on the side of Athanasius) was silenced by the clamours of a factious or venal majority; and the councils of Arles and Milan were not dissolved till the archbishop of Alexandria had been solemnly condemned and deposed by the judgment of the Western, as well as of the Eastern, church. The bishops who had opposed were required to subscribe the sentence; and to unite in religious communion with the suspected leaders of the adverse party. A formulary of consent was transmitted by the messengers of state to the absent bishops: and all those who refused to submit their private opinion to the public and inspired wisdom of the councils of Arles and Milan were

---

[1] The honours, presents, feasts, which seduced so many bishops, are mentioned with indignation by those who were too pure or too proud to accept them. "We combat (says Hilary of Poitiers) against Constantius the Antichrist, who strokes the belly instead of scourging the back;" qui non dorsa cædit, sed ventrem palpat.

immediately banished by the emperor, who affected to execute the decrees of the catholic church. Among those prelates who led the honourable band of confessors and exiles, Liberius of Rome, Osius of Cordova, Paulinus of Treves, Dionysius of Milan, Eusebius of Vercellæ, Lucifer of Cagliari, and Hilary of Poitiers, may deserve to be particularly distinguished. The eminent station of Liberius, who governed the capital of the empire; the personal merit and long experience of the venerable Osius, who was revered as the favourite of the great Constantine, and the father of the Nicene faith; place those prelates at the head of the Latin church: and their example, either of submission or resistance, would probably be imitated by the episcopal crowd. But the repeated attempts of the emperor to seduce or to intimidate the bishops of Rome and Cordova were for some time ineffectual. The Spaniard declared himself ready to suffer under Constantius, as he had suffered threescore years before under his grandfather Maximian. The Roman, in the presence of his sovereign, asserted the innocence of Athanasius, and his own freedom. When he was banished to Beræa in Thrace, he sent back a large sum which had been offered for the accommodation of his journey; and insulted the court of Milan by the haughty remark, that the emperor and his eunuchs might want that gold to pay their soldiers and their bishops. The resolution of Liberius and Osius was at length subdued by the hardships of exile and confinement. The Roman pontiff purchased his return by some criminal compliances; and afterwards expiated his guilt by a seasonable repentance. Persuasion and violence were employed to extort the reluctant signature of the decrepit bishop of Cordova, whose strength was broken, and whose faculties were perhaps impaired, by the weight of a hundred years; and the insolent triumph of the Arians provoked some of the orthodox party to treat with inhuman severity the character, or rather the memory, of an unfortunate old man, to whose former services Christianity itself was so deeply indebted.

The fall of Liberius and Osius reflected a brighter lustre on the firmness of those bishops who still adhered, with unshaken fidelity, to the cause of Athanasius and religious truth. The ingenious malice of their enemies had deprived them of the benefit of mutual comfort and advice, separated those illustrious exiles into distant provinces, and carefully selected the most inhospitable spots of a great empire.[1] Yet they soon experienced that the deserts of Libya, and the most barbarous tracts of Cappadocia, were less inhospitable than the residence of those cities in

---

[1] The confessors of the West were successively banished to the deserts of Arabia or Thebaïs, the lonely places of Mount Taurus, the wildest parts of Phrygia, which were in the possession of the impious Montanists, &c. When the heretic Aëtius was too favourably entertained at Mopsuestia in Cilicia, the place of his exile was changed, by the advice of Acacius, to Amblada, a district inhabited by savages, and infested by war and pestilence.

which an Arian bishop could satiate, without restraint, the exquisite rancour of theological hatred. Their consolation was derived from the consciousness of rectitude and independence, from the applause, the visits, the letters, and the liberal alms of their adherents; and from the satisfaction which they soon enjoyed of observing the intestine divisions of the adversaries of the Nicene faith. Such was the nice and capricious taste of the emperor Constantius, and so easily was he offended by the slightest deviation from his imaginary standard of Christian truth, that he persecuted, with equal zeal, those who defended the *consubstantiality*, those who asserted the *similar substance*, and those who denied the *likeness*, of the Son of God. Three bishops, degraded and banished for those adverse opinions, might possibly meet in the same place of exile; and, according to the difference of their temper, might either pity or insult the blind enthusiasm of their antagonists, whose present sufferings would never be compensated by future happiness.

The disgrace and exile of the orthodox bishops of the West were designed as so many preparatory steps to the ruin of Athanasius himself. Six-and-twenty months had elapsed, during which the Imperial court secretly laboured, by the most insidious arts, to remove him from Alexandria, and to withdraw the allowance which supplied his popular liberality. But when the primate of Egypt, deserted and proscribed by the Latin church, was left destitute of any foreign support, Constantius despatched two of his secretaries with a verbal commission to announce and execute the order of his banishment. As the justice of the sentence was publicly avowed by the whole party, the only motive which could restrain Constantius from giving his messengers the sanction of a written mandate must be imputed to his doubt of the event; and to a sense of the danger to which he might expose the second city and the most fertile province of the empire, if the people should persist in the resolution of defending, by force of arms, the innocence of their spiritual father. Such extreme caution afforded Athanasius a specious pretence respectfully to dispute the truth of an order which he could not reconcile either with the equity or with the former declarations of his gracious master. The civil powers of Egypt found themselves inadequate to the task of persuading or compelling the primate to abdicate his episcopal throne; and they were obliged to conclude a treaty with the popular leaders of Alexandria, by which it was stipulated that all proceedings and all hostilities should be suspended till the emperor's pleasure had been more distinctly ascertained. By this seeming moderation the catholics were deceived into a false and fatal security; while the legions of the Upper Egypt, and of Libya, advanced, by secret orders and hasty marches, to besiege, or rather to surprise, a capital habituated to sedition, and inflamed by religious zeal. The position of Alexandria, between the sea and the lake Mareotis, facilitated the approach and landing of the troops, who were introduced into the heart of the city before any effectual measures could be taken, either to shut the gates, or to occupy the important posts of defence. At the hour of midnight, twenty-three days after the signature of the treaty, Syrianus, duke of Egypt, at the head of five thousand soldiers, armed and prepared for an assault, unexpectedly invested the church of St. Theonas, where the archbishop, with a part of his clergy and people, performed their nocturnal devotions. The doors of the sacred edifice yielded to the impetuosity of the attack, which was accompanied with every horrid circumstance of tumult and bloodshed; but, as the bodies of the slain, and the fragments of military weapons, remained the next day an unexceptionable evidence in the possession of the catholics, the enterprise of Syrianus may be considered as a successful irruption rather than as an absolute conquest. The other churches of the city were profaned by similar outrages; and, during at least four months, Alexandria was exposed to the insults of a licentious army, stimulated by the ecclesiastics of an hostile faction. Many of the faithful were killed, who may deserve the name of martyrs if their deaths were neither provoked nor revenged; bishops and presbyters were treated with cruel ignominy; consecrated virgins were stripped naked, scourged, and violated; the houses of wealthy citizens were plundered; and, under the mask of religious zeal, lust, avarice, and private resentment were gratified with impunity, and even with applause. The Pagans of Alexandria, who still formed a numerous and discontented party, were easily persuaded to desert a bishop whom they feared and esteemed. The hopes of some peculiar favours, and the apprehension of being involved in the general penalties of rebellion, engaged them to promise their support to the destined successor of Athanasius, the famous George of Cappadocia. The usurper, after receiving the consecration of an Arian synod, was placed on the episcopal throne by the arms of Sebastian, who had been appointed count of Egypt for the execution of that important design. In the use, as well as in the acquisition, of power, the tyrant George disregarded the laws of religion, of justice, and of humanity; and the same scenes of violence and scandal which had been exhibited in the capital were repeated in more than ninety episcopal cities of Egypt. Encouraged by success, Constantius ventured to approve the conduct of his ministers. By a public and passionate epistle, the emperor congratulates the deliverance of Alexandria from a popular tyrant, who deluded his blind votaries by the magic of his eloquence; expatiates on the virtues and piety of the most reverend George, the elected bishop; and aspires, as the patron and benefactor of the city, to surpass the fame of Alexander himself. But he solemnly declares his unalterable resolution to pursue with fire and sword the seditious adherents of the wicked Athanasius, who, by flying from justice, has confessed his guilt, and escaped the ignominious death which he had so often deserved.

Athanasius had indeed escaped from the most imminent dangers;

and the adventures of that extraordinary man deserve and fix our attention. On the memorable night when the church of St. Theonas was invested by the troops of Syrianus, the archbishop, seated on his throne, expected, with calm and intrepid dignity, the approach of death. While the public devotion was interrupted by shouts of rage and cries of terror, he animated his trembling congregation to express their religious confidence by chanting one of the psalms of David which celebrates the triumph of the God of Israel over the haughty and impious tyrant of Egypt. The doors were at length burst open: a cloud of arrows was discharged among the people; the soldiers, with drawn swords, rushed forwards into the sanctuary; and the dreadful gleam of their armour was reflected by the holy luminaries which burnt round the altar. Athanasius still rejected the pious importunity of the monks and presbyters who were attached to his person; and nobly refused to desert his episcopal station till he had dismissed in safety the last of the congregation. The darkness and tumult of the night favoured the retreat of the archbishop; and though he was oppressed by the waves of an agitated multitude, though he was thrown to the ground, and left without sense or motion, he still recovered his undaunted courage, and eluded the eager search of the soldiers, who were instructed by their Arian guides that the head of Athanasius would be the most acceptable present to the emperor. From that moment the primate of Egypt disappeared from the eyes of his enemies, and remained above six years concealed in impenetrable obscurity.

The despotic power of his implacable enemy filled the whole extent of the Roman world; and the exasperated monarch had endeavoured, by a very pressing epistle to the Christian princes of Ethiopia, to exclude Athanasius from the most remote and sequestered regions of the earth. Counts, prefects, tribunes, whole armies, were successively employed to pursue a bishop and a fugitive; the vigilance of the civil and military powers was excited by the Imperial edicts; liberal rewards were promised to the man who should produce Athanasius, either alive or dead; and the most severe penalties were denounced against those who should dare to protect the public enemy. But the deserts of Thebaïs were now peopled by a race of wild, yet submissive fanatics, who preferred the commands of their abbot to the laws of their sovereign. The numerous disciples of Antony and Pachomius received the fugitive primate as their father, admired the patience and humility with which he conformed to their strictest institutions, collected every word which dropped from his lips as the genuine effusions of inspired wisdom; and persuaded themselves that their prayers, their fasts, and their vigils, were less meritorious than the zeal which they expressed, and the dangers which they braved, in the defence of truth and innocence. The monasteries of Egypt were seated in lonely and desolate places, on the summit of mountains, or in the islands of the Nile; and the sacred horn or trumpet of Tabenne was the well-known signal which assembled several thousand robust and determined monks, who, for the most part, had been the peasants of the adjacent country. When their dark retreats were invaded by a military force which it was impossible to resist, they silently stretched out their necks to the executioner; and supported their national character, that tortures could never wrest from an Egyptian the confession of a secret which he was resolved not to disclose. The archbishop of Alexandria, for whose safety they eagerly devoted their lives, was lost among a uniform and well-disciplined multitude; and on the nearer approach of danger, he was swiftly removed, by their officious hands from one place of concealment to another, till he reached the formidable deserts, which the gloomy and credulous temper of superstition had peopled with dæmons and savage monsters. The retirement of Athanasius, which ended only with the life of Constantius, was spent, for the most part, in the society of the monks, who faithfully served him as guards, as secretaries, and as messengers; but the importance of maintaining a more intimate connection with the catholic party tempted him, whenever the diligence of the pursuit was abated, to emerge from the desert, to introduce himself into Alexandria, and to trust his person to the discretion of his friends and adherents. His various adventures might have furnished the subject of a very entertaining romance. He was once secreted in a dry cistern, which he had scarcely left before he was betrayed by the treachery of a female slave; and he was once concealed in a still more extraordinary asylum, the house of a virgin, only twenty years of age, and who was celebrated in the whole city for her exquisite beauty. At the hour of midnight, as she related the story many years afterwards, she was surprised by the appearance of the archbishop in a loose undress, who, advancing with hasty steps, conjured her to afford him the protection which he had been directed by a celestial vision to seek under her hospitable roof. The pious maid accepted and preserved the sacred pledge which was intrusted to her prudence and courage. Without imparting the secret to any one, she instantly conducted Athanasius into her most secret chamber, and watched over his safety with the tenderness of a friend and the assiduity of a servant. As long as the danger continued, she regularly supplied him with books and provisions, washed his feet, managed his correspondence, and dexterously concealed from the eye of suspicion this familiar and solitary intercourse between a saint whose character required the most unblemished chastity, and a female whose charms might excite the most dangerous emotions.[1] During the six years of persecution and exile,

[1] Palladius the original author of this anecdote, had conversed with the damsel, who in her old age still remembered with pleasure so pious and honourable a connexion. I cannot indulge the delicacy of Baronius, Valesius, Tillemont, &c., who almost reject a story so unworthy, as they deem it, of the gravity of ecclesiastical history.

Athanasius repeated his visits to his fair and faithful companion; and the formal declaration that he *saw* the councils of Rimini and Seleucia, forces us to believe that he was secretly present at the time and place of their convocation. The advantage of personally negotiating with his friends, and of observing and improving the divisions of his enemies, might justify, in a prudent statesman, so bold and dangerous an enterprise: and Alexandria was connected by trade and navigation with every seaport of the Mediterranean. From the depth of his inaccessible retreat the intrepid primate waged an incessant and offensive war against the protector of the Arians; and his seasonable writings, which were diligently circulated and eagerly perused, contributed to unite and animate the orthodox party. In his public apologies, which he addressed to the emperor himself, he sometimes affected the praise of moderation; whilst at the same time, in secret and vehement invectives, he exposed Constantius as a weak and wicked prince, the executioner of his family, the tyrant of the republic, and the Antichrist of the church. In the height of his prosperity, the victorious monarch, who had chastised the rashness of Gallus, and suppressed the revolt of Sylvanus, who had taken the diadem from the head of Vetranio, and vanquished in the field the legions of Magnentius, received from an invisible hand a wound which he could neither heal nor revenge; and the son of Constantine was the first of the Christian princes who experienced the strength of those principles which, in the cause of religion, could resist the most violent exertions of the civil power.

*   *   *   *   *

THE GENERAL CHARACTER OF THE CHRISTIAN SECTS

The simple narrative of the intestine divisions which distracted the peace, and dishonoured the triumph, of the church, will confirm the remark of a Pagan historian, and justify the complaint of a venerable bishop. The experience of Ammianus had convinced him that the enmity of the Christians towards each other surpassed the fury of savage beasts against man; and Gregory Nazianzen most pathetically laments that the kingdom of heaven was converted by discord into the image of chaos, of a nocturnal tempest, and of hell itself. The fierce and partial writers of the times, ascribing *all* virtue to themselves, and imputing *all* guilt to their adversaries, have painted the battle of the angels and dæmons. Our calmer reason will reject such pure and perfect monsters of vice or sanctity, and will impute an equal, or at least an indiscriminate, measure of good and evil to the hostile sectaries, who assumed and bestowed the appellations of orthodox and heretics. They had been educated in the same religion and the same civil society. Their hopes and fears in the present, or in a future life, were balanced in the same proportion. On either side the error might be innocent, the faith sincere, the practice meritorious or corrupt. Their passions were excited by similar objects; and they might alternately abuse the favour of the court, or of the people. The metaphysical opinions of the Athanasians and the Arians could not influence their moral character; and they were alike actuated by the intolerant spirit which has been extracted from the pure and simple maxims of the Gospel.

A modern writer, who, with a just confidence, has prefixed to his own history the honourable epithets of political and philosophical, accuses the timid prudence of Montesquieu, for neglecting to enumerate, among the causes of the decline of the empire, a law of Constantine, by which the exercise of the Pagan worship was absolutely suppressed, and a considerable part of his subjects was left destitute of priests, of temples, and of any public religion. The zeal of the philosophic historian for the rights of mankind has induced him to acquiesce in the ambiguous testimony of those ecclesiastics who have too lightly ascribed to their favourite hero the *merit* of a general persecution. Instead of alleging this imaginary law, which would have blazed in the front of the Imperial codes, we may safely appeal to the original epistle which Constantine addressed to the followers of the ancient religion, at a time when he no longer disguised his conversion, nor dreaded the rivals of his throne. He invites and exhorts, in the most pressing terms, the subjects of the Roman empire to imitate the example of their master; but he declares that those who still refuse to open their eyes to the celestial light may freely enjoy their temples and their fancied gods. A report that the ceremonies of Paganism were suppressed is formally contradicted by the emperor himself, who wisely assigns, as the principle of his moderation, the invincible force of habit, of prejudice, and of superstition. Without violating the sanctity of his promise, without alarming the fears of the Pagans, the artful monarch advanced, by slow and cautious steps, to undermine the irregular and decayed fabric of polytheism. The partial acts of severity which he occasionally exercised, though they were secretly prompted by a Christian zeal, were coloured by the fairest pretences of justice and the public good; and while Constantine designed to ruin the foundations, he seemed to reform the abuses, of the ancient religion. After the example of the wisest of his predecessors, he condemned, under the most rigorous penalties, the occult and impious arts of divination, which excited the vain hopes, and sometimes the criminal attempts, of those who were discontented with their present condition. An ignominious silence was imposed on the oracles, which had been publicly convicted of fraud and falsehood; the effeminate priests of the Nile were abolished; and Constantine discharged the duties of a Roman censor, when he gave orders for the demolition of several temples of Phœnicia, in which every mode of prostitution was devoutly practised in the face of day, and to the honour of Venus. The Imperial city of Constantinople was, in some measure, raised at the expense, and was adorned with the spoils, of the opulent temples of Greece and Asia; the sacred property was confiscated; the statues of gods and heroes were transported, with rude familiarity, among a people who considered them as objects, not of adoration, but of curiosity; the gold and silver were restored to circulation; and the magistrates, the bishops, and the eunuchs, improved the fortunate occasion of gratifying, at once, their zeal, their avarice, and their resentment. But these depredations were confined to a small part of the Roman world; and the provinces had been long since accustomed to endure the same sacrilegious rapine, from the tyranny of princes and proconsuls who could not be suspected of any design to subvert the established religion.

The sons of Constantine trod in the footsteps of their father, with more zeal, and with less discretion. The pretences of rapine and oppression were insensibly multiplied; [1] every indulgence was shown to the illegal behaviour of the Christians; every doubt was explained to the disadvantage of Paganism; and the demolition of the temples was celebrated as one of the auspicious events of the reign of Constans and Constantius. The name of Constantius is prefixed to a concise law, which might have superseded the necessity of any future prohibitions. "It is our pleasure that in all places, and in all cities, the temples be immediately shut and carefully guarded, that none may have the power of offending. It is likewise our pleasure that all our subjects should abstain from sacrifices. If any one should be guilty of such an act, let him feel the sword of vengeance, and, after his execution, let his property be confiscated to the public use. We denounce the same penalties against the governors of the provinces, if they neglect to punish the criminals." But there is the strongest reason to believe that this formidable edict was either composed without being published, or was published without being executed. The evidence of facts, and the monuments which are still extant of brass and marble, continue to prove the public exercise of the Pagan worship during the whole reign of the sons of Constantine. In the East as well as in the West, in cities as well as in the country, a great number of temples were respected, or at least were spared; and the devout multitude still enjoyed the luxury of sacrifices, of festivals, and of processions, by the permission, or by the connivance, of the civil government. About four years after the supposed date of his bloody edict, Constantius visited the temples of Rome; and the decency of his behaviour is recommended by a Pagan orator as an example worthy of the imitation of succeeding princes. "That emperor," says Symmachus, "suffered the privileges of the vestal virgins to remain

---

[1] Ammianus speaks of some court eunuchs who were spoliis templorum pasti. Libanius says that the emperor often gave away a temple, like a dog, or a horse, or a slave, or a gold cup: but the devout philosopher takes care to observe that these sacrilegious favourites very seldom prospered.

inviolate; he bestowed the sacerdotal dignities on the nobles of Rome, granted the customary allowance to defray the expenses of the public rites and sacrifices; and, though he had embraced a different religion, he never attempted to deprive the empire of the sacred worship of antiquity." The senate still presumed to consecrate, by solemn decrees, the *divine* memory of their sovereigns; and Constantine himself was associated, after his death, to those gods whom he had renounced and insulted during his life. The title, the ensigns, the prerogatives, of SOVEREIGN PONTIFF, which had been instituted by Numa, and assumed by Augustus, were accepted, without hesitation, by seven Christian emperors; who were invested with a more absolute authority over the religion which they had deserted than over that which they professed.

The divisions of Christianity suspended the ruin of *Paganism*;[1] and the holy war against the infidels was less vigorously prosecuted by princes and bishops who were more immediately alarmed by the guilt and danger of domestic rebellion. The extirpation of *idolatry* might have been justified by the established principles of intolerance: but the hostile sects, which alternately reigned in the Imperial court, were mutually apprehensive of alienating, and perhaps exasperating, the minds of a powerful, though declining faction. Every motive of authority and fashion, of interest and reason, now militated on the side of Christianity; but two or three generations elapsed before their victorious influence was universally felt. The religion which had so long and so lately been established in the Roman empire was still revered by a numerous people, less attached indeed to speculative opinion than to ancient custom. The honours of the state and army were indifferently

---

[1] As I have freely anticipated the use of *pagans* and paganism, I shall now trace the singular revolutions of those celebrated words. 1. Παγη, in the Doric dialect, so familiar to the Italians, signifies a fountain; and the rural neighbourhood which frequented the same fountain derived the common appellation of *pagus* and *pagans*. 2. By an easy extension of the word, *pagan* and rural became almost synonymous; and the meaner rustics acquired that name, which has been corrupted into *peasants* in the modern languages of Europe. 3. The amazing increase of the military order introduced the necessity of a correlative term; and all the *people* who were not enlisted in the service of the prince were branded with the contemptuous epithet of pagans. 4. The Christians were the soldiers of Christ; their adversaries who refused his *sacrament*, or military oath of baptism, might deserve the metaphorical name of pagans; and this popular reproach was introduced as early as the reign of Valentinian (A.D. 365) into Imperial laws and theological writings. 5. Christianity gradually filled the cities of the empire: the old religion, in the time of Prudentius, retired and languished in obscure villages; and the word *pagans*, with its new signification, reverted to its primitive origin. 6. Since the worship of Jupiter and his family has expired, the vacant title of Pagans has been successively applied to all the idolaters and polytheists of the old and new world. 7. The Latin Christians bestowed it, without scruple, on their mortal enemies the Mahometans; and the purest *Unitarians* were branded with the unjust reproach of idolatry and paganism. [Gibbon was mistaken in supposing that the Latin pagus was connected with the Greek word πηγή or παγή (Doric) although this was a very ancient belief.—D.M.L.]

bestowed on all the subjects of Constantine and Constantius; and a considerable portion of knowledge and wealth and valour was still engaged in the service of polytheism. The superstition of the senator and of the peasant, of the poet and the philosopher, was derived from very different causes, but they met with equal devotion in the temples of the gods. Their zeal was insensibly provoked by the insulting triumph of a proscribed sect; and their hopes were revived by the well-grounded confidence that the presumptive heir of the empire, a young and valiant hero, who had delivered Gaul from the arms of the barbarians, had secretly embraced the religion of his ancestors.

THE PAGAN
COUNTER-REFORMATION

Chapter 22

THE SUCCESSION OF JULIAN. HIS CHARACTER

Constantius after a tyrannical reign died in 361 on the eve of a civil war with Julian, who thus became sole emperor. Julian's brief reign was guided by two motives derived from his early studies. One was to realise the ideal of the philosopher-king. This he blended with practical reforms and economies and an attempt to exchange the orientalism of his predecessors' court for the simplicity of ancient manners. Secondly he had an ambition to emulate Alexander the Great in eastern conquests. Julian's special significance for posterity has been his rejection of Christianity and his attempt to reform as well as re-establish the pagan cults.

THE SUCCESSION OF JULIAN

IMPATIENT to visit the place of his birth and the new capital of the empire, he advanced from Naissus through the mountains of Hæmus and the cities of Thrace. When he reached Heraclea, at the distance of sixty miles, all Constantinople was poured forth to receive him; and he made his triumphal entry amidst the dutiful acclamations of the soldiers, the people, and the senate. An innumerable multitude pressed around him with eager respect, and were perhaps disappointed when they beheld the small stature and simple garb of a hero, whose unexperienced youth had vanquished the barbarians of Germany, and who had now traversed, in a successful career, the whole continent of Europe from the shores of the Atlantic to those of the Bosphorus. A few days afterwards, when the remains of the deceased emperor were landed in the harbour, the subjects of Julian applauded the real or affected humanity of their sovereign. On foot, without his diadem, and clothed in a mourning habit, he accompanied the funeral as far as the church of the Holy Apostles, where the body was deposited: and if these marks of respect may be interpreted as a selfish tribute to the birth and dignity of his Imperial kinsman, the tears of Julian professed to the world that he had forgot the injuries, and remembered only the obligations, which he had received from Constantius. As soon as the legions of Aquileia were assured of the death of the emperor, they opened the gates of the city, and, by the sacrifice of their guilty leaders, obtained an easy pardon from the prudence or lenity of Julian; who, in the thirty-second year of his age, acquired the undisputed possession of the Roman empire.

Philosophy had instructed Julian to compare the advantages of action and retirement; but the elevation of his birth and the accidents of his life never allowed him the freedom of choice. He might perhaps sincerely have preferred the groves of the Academy and the society of Athens; but he was constrained, at first by the will, and afterwards by the injustice of Constantius, to expose his person and fame to the dangers of Imperial greatness; and to make himself accountable to the world and to posterity for the happiness of millions. Julian recollected with terror the observation of his master Plato, that the government of our flocks and herds is always committed to beings of a superior species; and that the conduct of nations requires and deserves the celestial powers of the Gods or of the Genii. From this principle he justly concluded that the man who presumes to reign should aspire to the perfection of the divine nature; that he should purify his soul from her mortal and terrestrial part; that he should extinguish his appetites, enlighten his understanding, regulate his passions, and subdue the wild beast which, according to the lively metaphor of Aristotle, seldom fails to ascend the throne of a despot. The throne of Julian, which the death of Constantius fixed on an independent basis, was the seat of reason, of virtue, and perhaps of vanity. He despised the honours, renounced the pleasures, and discharged with incessant diligence the duties of his exalted station: and there were few among his subjects who would have consented to relieve him from the weight of the diadem, had they been obliged to submit their time and their actions to the rigorous laws which their philosophic emperor imposed on himself. One of his most intimate friends, who had often shared the frugal simplicity of his table, has remarked that his light and sparing diet (which was usually of the vegetable kind) left his mind and body always free and active for the various and important business of an author, a pontiff, a magistrate, a general, and a prince. In one and the same day he gave audience to several ambassadors, and wrote or dictated a great number of letters to his generals, his civil magistrates, his private friends, and the different cities of his dominions. He listened to the memorials which had been received, considered the subject of the petitions, and signified his intentions more rapidly than they could be taken in short-hand by the diligence of his secretaries. He possessed such flexibility of thought, and such firmness of attention, that he could employ his hand to write, his ear to listen, and his voice to dictate; and pursue at once three several trains of ideas without hesitation, and without error. While his ministers reposed, the prince flew with agility from one labour to another; and, after a hasty dinner, retired into his library till the public business which he had appointed for the evening summoned him to interrupt the prosecution of his studies. The supper of the emperor was still less substantial than the former meal; his sleep was never clouded by the fumes of indigestion; and, except in the short interval of a marriage which was the effect of policy rather than love, the chaste Julian never shared his bed with a female companion. He was soon awakened by the entrance of fresh secretaries, who had slept the preceding day; and his servants were obliged to wait alternately, while their indefatigable master allowed himself scarcely any other refreshment than the change of occupations. The predecessors of Julian, his uncle, his brother, and his cousin, indulged their puerile taste for the games of the Circus, under the specious pretence of complying with the inclinations of the people; and they frequently remained the greatest part of the day as idle spectators, and as a part of the splendid spectacle, till the ordinary round of twenty-four races was completely finished. On solemn festivals, Julian, who felt and professed an unfashionable dislike to these frivolous amusements, condescended to appear in the Circus; and, after bestowing a careless glance on five or six of the races, he hastily withdrew with the impatience of a philosopher, who considered every moment as lost that was not devoted to the advantage of the public or the improvement of his own mind. By this avarice of time he seemed to protract the short duration of his reign; and, if the dates were less securely ascertained, we should refuse to believe that only sixteen months elapsed between the death of Constantius and the departure of his successor for the Persian war. The actions of Julian can only be preserved by the care of the historian; but the portion of his voluminous writings which is still extant remains as a monument of the application, as well as of the genius, of the emperor. The Misopogon, the Cæsars, several of his orations, and his elaborate work against the Christian religion, were composed in the long nights of the two winters, the former of which he passed at Constantinople, and the latter at Antioch.

*   *   *   *   *

THE CHARACTER OF JULIAN

The laborious administration of military and civil affairs, which were multiplied in proportion to the extent of the empire, exercised the abilities of Julian; but he frequently assumed the two characters of Orator and of Judge, which are almost unknown to the modern sovereigns of Europe. The arts of persuasion, so diligently cultivated by the first Cæsars, were neglected by the military ignorance and Asiatic pride of their successors, and, if they condescended to harangue the soldiers, whom they feared, they treated with silent disdain the senators, whom they despised. The assemblies of the senate, which Constantius had avoided, were considered by Julian as the place where he could exhibit with the most propriety the maxims of a republican and the talents of a rhetorician. He alternately practised, as in a school of declamation, the several modes of praise, of censure, of exhortation; and his friend Libanius has remarked that the study of Homer taught him to imitate the simple, concise style of Menelaus, the copiousness of Nestor, whose words descended like the flakes of a winter's snow, or the pathetic and forcible eloquence of Ulysses. The functions of a judge, which are sometimes incompatible with those of a prince, were exercised by Julian not only as a duty, but as an amusement; and although he might have trusted the integrity and discernment of his Prætorian prefects, he often placed himself by their side on the seat of judgment. The acute penetration of his mind was agreeably occupied in detecting and defeating the chicanery of the advocates, who laboured to disguise the truth of facts and to pervert the sense of the laws. He sometimes forgot the gravity of his station, asked indiscreet or unseasonable questions, and betrayed, by the loudness of his voice and the agitation of his body, the earnest vehemence with which he maintained his opinion against the judges, the advocates, and their clients. But his knowledge of his own temper prompted him to encourage, and even to solicit, the reproof of his friends and ministers: and whenever they ventured to oppose the irregular sallies of his passions, the spectators could observe the shame as well as the gratitude of their monarch. The decrees of Julian were almost always founded on the principles of justice, and he had the firmness to resist the two most dangerous temptations which assault the tribunal of a sovereign under the specious forms of compassion and equity. He decided the merits of the cause without weighing the circumstances of the parties; and the poor, whom he wished to relieve, were condemned to satisfy the just demands of a noble and wealthy adversary. He carefully distinguished the judge from the legislator; and though he meditated a necessary reformation of the Roman jurisprudence, he pronounced sentence according to the strict and literal interpretation of those laws which the magistrates were bound to execute and the subjects to obey.

The generality of princes, if they were stripped of their purple and cast naked into the world, would immediately sink to the lowest rank of society, without a hope of emerging from their obscurity. But the personal merit of Julian was, in some measure, independent of his fortune. Whatever had been his choice of life, by the force of intrepid courage, lively wit, and intense application, he would have obtained, or at least he would have deserved, the highest honours of his profession, and Julian might have raised himself to the rank of minister or general of the state in which he was born a private citizen. If the jealous caprice of power had disappointed his expectations; if he had prudently declined the paths of greatness, the employment of the same talents in studious solitude would have placed beyond the reach of kings his present happiness and his immortal fame. When we inspect with minute, or perhaps malevolent, attention the portrait of Julian, something seems wanting to the grace and perfection of the whole figure. His genius was less power-ful and sublime than that of Cæsar, nor did he possess the consummate prudence of Augustus. The virtues of Trajan appear more steady and natural, and the philosophy of Marcus is more simple and consistent. Yet Julian sustained adversity with firmness, and prosperity with moderation. After an interval of one hundred and twenty years from the death of Alexander Severus, the Romans beheld an emperor who made no distinction between his duties and his pleasures, who laboured to relieve the distress and to revive the spirit of his subjects, and who endeavoured always to connect authority with merit, and happiness with virtue. Even faction, and religious faction, was constrained to acknowledge the superiority of his genius in peace as well as in war, and to confess, with a sigh, that the apostate Julian was a lover of his country, and that he deserved the empire of the world.

Chapter 23

THE RELIGION OF JULIAN. HIS FANATICISM. HIS RESTORA-
TION AND REFORM OF PAGANISM. HIS CONDUCT TOWARDS
THE JEWS. HIS OPPRESSION OF THE CHRISTIANS. THE
TEMPLE AND SACRED GROVE OF DAPHNE. ST. GEORGE.
JULIAN AND ATHANASIUS

THE character of Apostate has injured the reputation of Julian;
and the enthusiasm which clouded his virtues has exaggerated
the real and apparent magnitude of his faults. Our partial ignorance may represent him as a philosophic monarch, who studied to protect, with an equal hand, the religious factions of the empire, and to
allay the theological fever which had inflamed the minds of the people
from the edicts of Diocletian to the exile of Athanasius. A more
accurate view of the character and conduct of Julian will remove this
favourable prepossession for a prince who did not escape the general
contagion of the times. We enjoy the singular advantage of comparing
the pictures which have been delineated by his fondest admirers and his
implacable enemies. The actions of Julian are faithfully related by a
judicious and candid historian, the impartial spectator of his life and
death. The unanimous evidence of his contemporaries is confirmed by
the public and private declarations of the emperor himself; and his
various writings express the uniform tenor of his religious sentiments,
which policy would have prompted him to dissemble rather than to
affect. A devout and sincere attachment for the gods of Athens and
Rome constituted the ruling passion of Julian; the powers of an enlightened understanding were betrayed and corrupted by the influence
of superstitious prejudice; and the phantoms which existed only in the
mind of the emperor had a real and pernicious effect on the government
of the empire. The vehement zeal of the Christians, who despised the
worship, and overturned the altars, of those fabulous deities, engaged
their votary in a state of irreconcilable hostility with a very numerous
party of his subjects; and he was sometimes tempted, by the desire of
victory or the shame of a repulse, to violate the laws of prudence, and
even of justice. The triumph of the party which he deserted and opposed
has fixed a stain of infamy on the name of Julian; and the unsuccessful
apostate has been overwhelmed with a torrent of pious invectives, of
which the signal was given by the sonorous trumpet of Gregory Nazianzen. The interesting nature of the events which were crowded into
the short reign of this active emperor deserves a just and circumstantial

narrative. His motives, his counsels, and his actions, as far as they are connected with the history of religion, will be the subject of the present chapter.

The cause of his strange and fatal apostasy may be derived from the early period of his life when he was left an orphan in the hands of the murderers of his family. The names of Christ and of Constantius, the ideas of slavery and of religion, were soon associated in a youthful imagination, which was susceptible of the most lively impressions. The care of his infancy was intrusted to Eusebius, bishop of Nicomedia, who was related to him on the side of his mother; and till Julian reached the twentieth year of his age, he received from his Christian preceptors the education not of a hero but of a saint. The emperor, less jealous of a heavenly than of an earthly crown, contented himself with the imperfect character of a catechumen, while he bestowed the advantages of baptism on the nephews of Constantine. They were even admitted to the inferior offices of the ecclesiastical order; and Julian publicly read the Holy Scriptures in the church of Nicomedia. The study of religion, which they assiduously cultivated, appeared to produce the fairest fruits of faith and devotion. They prayed, they fasted, they distributed alms to the poor, gifts to the clergy, and oblations to the tombs of the martyrs; and the splendid monument of St. Mamas, at Cæsarea, was erected, or at least was undertaken, by the joint labour of Gallus and Julian. They respectfully conversed with the bishops who were eminent for superior sanctity, and solicited the benediction of the monks and hermits who had introduced into Cappadocia the voluntary hardships of the ascetic life. As the two princes advanced towards the years of manhood, they discovered, in their religious sentiments, the difference of their characters. The dull and obstinate understanding of Gallus embraced, with implicit zeal, the doctrines of Christianity, which never influenced his conduct, or moderated his passions. The mild disposition of the younger brother was less repugnant to the precepts of the Gospel; and his active curiosity might have been gratified by a theological system which explains the mysterious essence of the Deity, and opens the boundless prospect of invisible and future worlds. But the independent spirit of Julian refused to yield the passive and unresisting obedience which was required, in the name of religion, by the haughty ministers of the church. Their speculative opinions were imposed as positive laws, and guarded by the terrors of eternal punishments; but while they prescribed the rigid formulary of the thoughts, the words, and the actions of the young prince; whilst they silenced his objections, and severely checked the freedom of his inquiries, they secretly provoked his impatient genius to disclaim the authority of his ecclesiastical guides. He was educated in the Lesser Asia, amidst the scandals of the Arian controversy. The fierce contests of the Eastern bishops, the incessant alterations of their creeds, and the profane motives which appeared to actuate their conduct, insensibly strengthened the prejudice of Julian that they neither understood nor believed the religion for which they so fiercely contended. Instead of listening to the proofs of Christianity with that favourable attention which adds weight to the most respectable evidence, he heard with suspicion, and disputed with obstinacy and acuteness, the doctrines for which he already entertained an invincible aversion. Whenever the young princes were directed to compose declamations on the subject of the prevailing controversies, Julian always declared himself the advocate of Paganism, under the specious excuse that, in the defence of the weaker cause, his learning and in-genuity might be more advantageously exercised and displayed.

As soon as Gallus was invested with the honours of the purple, Julian was permitted to breathe the air of freedom, of literature, and of Paganism. The crowd of sophists, who were attracted by the taste and liberality of their royal pupil, had formed a strict alliance between the learning and the religion of Greece; and the poems of Homer, instead of being admired as the original productions of human genius, were seri-ously ascribed to the heavenly inspiration of Apollo and the Muses. The deities of Olympus, as they are painted by the immortal bard, im-print themselves on the minds which are the least addicted to super-stitious credulity. Our familiar knowledge of their names and characters, their forms and attributes, *seems* to bestow on those airy beings a real and substantial existence; and the pleasing enchantment produces an imperfect and momentary assent of the imagination to those fables which are the most repugnant to our reason and experience. In the age of Julian every circumstance contributed to prolong and fortify the illusion—the magnificent temples of Greece and Asia; the works of those artists who had expressed, in painting or in sculpture, the divine conceptions of the poet; the pomp of festivals and sacrifices; the success-ful arts of divination; the popular traditions of oracles and prodigies; and the ancient practice of two thousand years. The weakness of poly-theism was, in some measure, excused by the moderation of its claims; and the devotion of the Pagans was not incompatible with the most licentious scepticism. Instead of an indivisible and regular system, which occupies the whole extent of the believing mind, the mythology of the Greeks was composed of a thousand loose and flexible parts, and the servant of the gods was at liberty to define the degree and measure of his religious faith. The creed which Julian adopted for his own use was of the largest dimensions; and, by a strange contradiction, he dis-dained the salutary yoke of the Gospel, whilst he made a voluntary offering of his reason on the altars of Jupiter and Apollo. One of the orations of Julian is consecrated to the honour of Cybele, the mother of the gods, who required from her effeminate priests the bloody sacri-fice so rashly performed by the madness of the Phrygian boy. The pious emperor condescends to relate, without a blush and without a smile, the voyage of the goddess from the shores of Pergamus to the mouth of the Tiber; and the stupendous miracle which convinced the senate and people of Rome that the lump of clay which their ambassadors had transported over the seas was endowed with life, and sentiment, and divine power. For the truth of this prodigy he appeals to the public monuments of the city; and censures, with some acrimony, the sickly and affected taste of those men who impertinently derided the sacred traditions of their ancestors.

But the devout philosopher, who sincerely embraced, and warmly encouraged, the superstition of the people, reserved for himself the privilege of a liberal interpretation, and silently withdrew from the foot of the altars into the sanctuary of the temple. The extravagance of the Grecian mythology proclaimed, with a clear and audible voice, that the pious inquirer, instead of being scandalised or satisfied with the literal sense, should diligently explore the occult wisdom, which had been disguised, by the prudence of antiquity, under the mask of folly and of fable.[1] The philosophers of the Platonic school, Plotinus, Porphyry, and the divine Iamblichus, were admired as the most skilful masters of this allegorical science, which laboured to soften and harmonise the deformed features of Paganism. Julian himself, who was directed in the mysterious pursuit by Ædesius, the venerable successor of Iamblichus, aspired to the possession of a treasure which he esteemed, if we may credit his solemn asseverations, far above the empire of the world. It was indeed a treasure which derived its value only from opinion; and every artist who flattered himself that he had extracted the precious ore from the surrounding dross claimed an equal right of stamping the name and figure the most agreeable to his peculiar fancy. The fable of Atys and Cybele had been already explained by Porphyry; but his labours served only to animate the pious industry of Julian, who invented and published his own allegory of that ancient and mystic tale. This freedom of interpretation, which might gratify the pride of the Platonists, exposed the vanity of their art. Without a tedious detail the modern reader could not form a just idea of the strange allusions, the forced etymologies, the solemn trifling, and the impenetrable obscurity of these sages, who professed to reveal the system of the universe. As the traditions of Pagan mythology were variously related, the sacred interpreters were at liberty to select the most convenient circumstances; and as they translated an arbitrary cipher, they could extract from any fable any sense which was adapted to their favourite system of religion and philosophy. The lascivious form of a naked Venus was tortured into the discovery of some moral precept, or some physical truth; and the

---

[1] See the principles of allegory in Julian. His reasoning is less absurd than that of some modern theologians, who assert that an extravagant or contradictory doctrine must be divine, since no man alive could have thought of inventing it.

castration of Atys explained the revolution of the sun between the tropics, or the separation of the human soul from vice and error.[1]

The theological system of Julian appears to have contained the sublime and important principles of natural religion. But as the faith which is not founded on revelation must remain destitute of any firm assurance, the disciple of Plato imprudently relapsed into the habits of vulgar superstition; and the popular and philosophic notion of the Deity seems to have been confounded in the practice, the writings, and even in the mind of Julian. The pious emperor acknowledged and adored the Eternal Cause of the universe, to whom he ascribed all the perfections of an infinite nature, invisible to the eyes and inaccessible to the understanding of feeble mortals. The Supreme God had created, or rather, in the Platonic language, had generated, the gradual succession of dependent spirits, of gods, of dæmons, of heroes, and of men; and every being which derived its existence immediately from the First Cause received the inherent gift of immortality. That so precious an advantage might not be lavished upon unworthy objects, the Creator had intrusted to the skill and power of the inferior gods the office of forming the human body, and of arranging the beautiful harmony of the animal, the vegetable, and the mineral kingdoms. To the conduct of these divine ministers he delegated the temporal government of this lower world; but their imperfect administration is not exempt from discord or error. The earth and its inhabitants are divided among them, and the characters of Mars or Minerva, of Mercury or Venus, may be distinctly traced in the laws and manners of their peculiar votaries. As long as our immortal souls are confined in a mortal prison, it is our interest, as well as our duty, to solicit the favour, and to deprecate the wrath, of the powers of heaven; whose pride is gratified by the devotion of mankind, and whose grosser parts may be supposed to derive some nourishment from the fumes of sacrifice. The inferior gods might sometimes condescend to animate the statues, and to inhabit the temples, which were dedicated to their honour. They might occasionally visit the earth, but the heavens were the proper throne and symbol of their glory. The invariable order of the sun, moon, and stars was hastily admitted by Julian as a proof of their *eternal* duration; and their eternity was a sufficient evidence that they were the workmanship, not of an inferior deity, but of the Omnipotent King. In the system of the Platonists the visible was a type of the invisible world. The celestial bodies, as they were informed by a divine spirit, might be considered as the objects the most worthy of religious worship. The Sun, whose genial influence pervades and sustains the universe, justly claimed the adora-

---

[1] See the fifth oration of Julian. But all the allegories which ever issued fro... the Platonic school are not worth the short poem of Catullus on the same extraordinary subject. The transition of Atys from the wildest enthusiasm to sober pathetic complaint for his irretrievable loss, must inspire a man with pity, a eunuch with despair.

tion of mankind, as the bright representative of the Logos, the lively, the rational, the beneficent image of the intellectual Father.

THE FANATICISM OF JULIAN

In every age the absence of genuine inspiration is supplied by the strong illusions of enthusiasm and the mimic arts of imposture. If, in the time of Julian, these arts had been practised only by the Pagan priests, for the support of an expiring cause, some indulgence might perhaps be allowed to the interest and habits of the sacerdotal character. But it may appear a subject of surprise and scandal that the philosophers themselves should have contributed to abuse the superstitious credulity of mankind,[1] and that the Grecian mysteries should have been supported by the magic or theurgy of the modern Platonists. They arrogantly pretended to control the order of nature, to explore the secrets of futurity, to command the service of the inferior dæmons, to enjoy the view and conversation of the superior gods, and, by disengaging the soul from her material bands, to re-unite that immortal particle with the Infinite and Divine Spirit.

The devout and fearless curiosity of Julian tempted the philosophers with the hopes of an easy conquest, which, from the situation of their young proselyte, might be productive of the most important consequences. Julian imbibed the first rudiments of the Platonic doctrines from the mouth of Ædesius, who had fixed at Pergamus his wandering and persecuted school. But as the declining strength of that venerable sage was unequal to the ardour, the diligence, the rapid conception of his pupil, two of his most learned disciples, Chrysanthes and Eusebius, supplied, at his own desire, the place of their aged master. These philosophers seem to have prepared and distributed their respective parts; and they artfully contrived, by dark hints and affected disputes, to excite the impatient hopes of the *aspirant* till they delivered him into the hands of their associate, Maximus, the boldest and most skilful master of the Theurgic science. By his hands Julian was secretly initiated at Ephesus, in the twentieth year of his age. His residence at Athens confirmed this unnatural alliance of philosophy and superstition. He obtained the privilege of a solemn initiation into the mysteries of Eleusis, which, amidst the general decay of the Grecian worship, still retained some vestiges of their primæval sanctity; and such was the zeal of Julian that he afterwards invited the Eleusinian pontiff to the court of Gaul, for the sole purpose of consummating, by mystic rites and sacrifices, the great work of his sanctification. As these ceremonies

---

[1] The sophists of Eunapius perform as many miracles as the saints of the desert; and the only circumstance in their favour is, that they are of a less gloomy complexion. Instead of devils with horns and tails, Iamblichus evoked the genii of love, Eros and Anteros, from two adjacent fountains. Two beautiful boys issued from the water, fondly embraced him as their father, and retired at his command.

were performed in the depth of caverns and in the silence of the night, and as the inviolable secret of the mysteries was preserved by the discretion of the initiated, I shall not presume to describe the horrid sounds and fiery apparitions which were presented to the senses or the imagination of the credulous aspirant,[1] till the visions of comfort and knowledge broke upon him in a blaze of celestial light. In the caverns of Ephesus and Eleusis the mind of Julian was penetrated with sincere, deep, and unalterable enthusiasm; though he might sometimes exhibit the vicissitudes of pious fraud and hypocrisy which may be observed, or at least suspected, in the characters of the most conscientious fanatics. From that moment he consecrated his life to the service of the gods; and while the occupations of war, of government, and of study seemed to claim the whole measure of his time, a stated portion of the hours of the night was invariably reserved for the exercise of private devotion. The temperance which adorned the severe manners of the soldier and the philosopher was connected with some strict and frivolous rules of religious abstinence; and it was in honour of Pan or Mercury, of Hecate or Isis, that Julian, on particular days, denied himself the use of some particular food, which might have been offensive to his tutelar deities. By these voluntary fasts he prepared his senses and his understanding for the frequent and familiar visits with which he was honoured by the celestial powers. Notwithstanding the modest silence of Julian himself, we may learn from his faithful friend, the orator Libanius, that he lived in a perpetual intercourse with the gods and goddesses; that they descended upon earth to enjoy the conversation of their favourite hero; that they gently interrupted his slumbers by touching his hand or his hair; that they warned him of every impending danger, and conducted him, by their infallible wisdom, in every action of his life; and that he had acquired such an intimate knowledge of his heavenly guests, as readily to distinguish the voice of Jupiter from that of Minerva, and the form of Apollo from the figure of Hercules. These sleeping or waking visions, the ordinary effects of abstinence and fanaticism, would almost degrade the emperor to the level of an Egyptian monk. But the useless lives of Antony or Pachomius were consumed in these vain occupations. Julian could break from the dream of superstition to arm himself for battle; and after vanquishing in the field the enemies of Rome, he calmly retired into his tent, to dictate the wise and salutary laws of an empire, or to indulge his genius in the elegant pursuits of literature and philosophy.

The important secret of the apostasy of Julian was intrusted to the fidelity of the *initiated*, with whom he was united by the sacred ties of

---

[1] When Julian, in a momentary panic, made the sign of the cross, the dæmons instantly disappeared. Gregory supposes that they were frightened, but the priests declared that they were indignant. The reader, according to the measure of his faith, will determine this profound question.

friendship and religion. The pleasing rumour was cautiously circulated among the adherents of the ancient worship; and his future greatness became the object of the hopes, the prayers, and the predictions of the Pagans in every province of the empire. From the zeal and virtues of their royal proselyte they fondly expected the cure of every evil and the restoration of every blessing; and instead of disapproving of the ardour of their pious wishes, Julian ingenuously confessed that he was ambitious to attain a situation in which he might be useful to his country and to his religion. But this religion was viewed with an hostile eye by the successor of Constantine, whose capricious passions alternately saved and threatened the life of Julian. The arts of magic and divination were strictly prohibited under a despotic government which condescended to fear them; and if the Pagans were reluctantly indulged in the exercise of their superstition, the rank of Julian would have excepted him from the general toleration. The apostate soon became the presumptive heir of the monarchy, and his death could alone have appeased the just apprehensions of the Christians. But the young prince, who aspired to the glory of a hero rather than of a martyr, consulted his safety by dissembling his religion; and the easy temper of polytheism permitted him to join in the public worship of a sect which he inwardly despised. Libanius has considered the hypocrisy of his friend as a subject, not of censure, but of praise. "As the statues of the gods," says that orator, "which have been defiled with filth are again placed in a magnificent temple, so the beauty of truth was seated in the mind of Julian after it had been purified from the errors and follies of his education. His sentiments were changed; but as it would have been dangerous to have avowed his sentiments, his conduct still continued the same. Very different from the ass in Æsop, who disguised himself with a lion's hide, our lion was obliged to conceal himself under the skin of an ass; and, while he embraced the dictates of reason, to obey the laws of prudence and necessity." The dissimulation of Julian lasted above ten years, from his secret initiation at Ephesus to the beginning of the civil war; when he declared himself at once the implacable enemy of Christ and of Constantius. This state of constraint might contribute to strengthen his devotion; and as soon as he had satisfied the obligation of assisting, on solemn festivals, at the assemblies of the Christians, Julian returned, with the impatience of a lover, to burn his free and voluntary incense on the domestic chapels of Jupiter and Mercury. But as every act of dissimulation must be painful to an ingenuous spirit, the profession of Christianity increased the aversion of Julian for a religion which oppressed the freedom of his mind, and compelled him to hold a conduct repugnant to the noblest attributes of human nature—sincerity and courage.

The inclination of Julian might prefer the gods of Homer and of the Scipios to the new faith which his uncle had established in the Roman empire, and in which he himself had been sanctified by the sacrament of baptism. But, as a philosopher, it was incumbent on him to justify his dissent from Christianity, which was supported by the number of its converts, by the chain of prophecy, the splendour of miracles, and the weight of evidence. The elaborate work which he composed amidst the preparations of the Persian war contained the substance of those arguments which he had long revolved in his mind. Some fragments have been transcribed and preserved by his adversary, the vehement Cyril of Alexandria; and they exhibit a very singular mixture of wit and learning, of sophistry and fanaticism. The elegance of the style and the rank of the author recommended his writings to the public attention; and in the impious list of the enemies of Christianity the celebrated name of Porphyry was effaced by the superior merit or reputation of Julian. The minds of the faithful were either seduced, or scandalised, or alarmed; and the Pagans, who sometimes presumed to engage in the unequal dispute, derived, from the popular work of their Imperial missionary, an inexhaustible supply of fallacious objections. But in the assiduous prosecution of these theological studies the emperor of the Romans imbibed the illiberal prejudices and passions of a polemic divine. He contracted an irrevocable obligation to maintain and propagate his religious opinions; and whilst he secretly applauded the strength and dexterity with which he wielded the weapons of controversy, he was tempted to distrust the sincerity, or to despise the understandings, of his antagonists, who could obstinately resist the force of reason and eloquence.

The Christians, who beheld with horror and indignation the apostasy of Julian, had much more to fear from his power than from his arguments. The Pagans, who were conscious of his fervent zeal, expected, perhaps with impatience, that the flames of persecution should be immediately kindled against the enemies of the gods; and that the ingenious malice of Julian would invent some cruel refinements of death and torture which had been unknown to the rude and inexperienced fury of his predecessors. But the hopes, as well as the fears, of the religious factions were apparently disappointed by the prudent humanity of a prince who was careful of his own fame, of the public peace, and of the rights of mankind. Instructed by history and reflection, Julian was persuaded that, if the diseases of the body may sometimes be cured by salutary violence, neither steel nor fire can eradicate the erroneous opinions of the mind. The reluctant victim may be dragged to the foot of the altar; but the heart still abhors and disclaims the sacrilegious act of the hand. Religious obstinacy is hardened and exasperated by oppression; and, as soon as the persecution subsides, those who have yielded are restored as penitents, and those who have resisted are honoured as saints and martyrs. If Julian adopted the unsuccessful cruelty of Diocletian and his colleagues, he was sensible that he should stain his memory with the name of tyrant, and add new glories to the catholic church, which had derived strength and increase from the severity of the Pagan magistrates. Actuated by these motives, and apprehensive of disturbing the repose of an unsettled reign, Julian surprised the world by an edict which was not unworthy of a statesman or a philosopher. He extended to all the inhabitants of the Roman world the benefits of a free and equal toleration; and the only hardship which he inflicted on the Christians was to deprive them of the power of tormenting their fellow-subjects, whom they stigmatised with the odious titles of idolaters and heretics. The Pagans received a gracious permission, or rather an express order, to open ALL their temples; and they were at once delivered from the oppressive laws and arbitrary vexations which they had sustained under the reign of Constantine and of his sons. At the same time, the bishops and clergy who had been banished by the Arian monarch were recalled from exile, and restored to their respective churches; the Donatists, the Novatians, the Macedonians, the Eunomians, and those who, with a more prosperous fortune, adhered to the doctrine of the council of Nice. Julian, who understood and derided their theological disputes, invited to the palace the leaders of the hostile sects, that he might enjoy the agreeable spectacle of their furious encounters. The clamour of controversy sometimes provoked the emperor to exclaim, "Hear me! the Franks have heard me, and the Alemanni "; but he soon discovered that he was now engaged with more obstinate and implacable enemies; and though he exerted the powers of oratory to persuade them to live in concord, or at least in peace, he was perfectly satisfied, before he dismissed them from his presence, that he had nothing to dread from the union of the Christians. The impartial Ammianus has ascribed this affected clemency to the desire of fomenting the intestine divisions of the church; and the insidious design of undermining the foundations of Christianity was inseparably connected with the zeal which Julian professed to restore the ancient religion of the empire.

JULIAN'S RESTORATION AND REFORM OF PAGANISM

As soon as he ascended the throne, he assumed, according to the custom of his predecessors, the character of supreme pontiff; not only as the most honourable title of Imperial greatness, but as a sacred and important office, the duties of which he was resolved to execute with pious diligence. As the business of the state prevented the emperor from joining every day in the public devotion of his subjects, he dedicated a domestic chapel to his tutelar deity the Sun; his gardens were filled with statues and altars of the gods; and each apartment of the palace displayed the appearance of a magnificent temple. Every morning he saluted the parent of light with a sacrifice; the blood of another victim was shed at the moment when the Sun sunk below the horizon; and the

Moon, the Stars, and the Genii of the night received their respective and seasonable honours from the indefatigable devotion of Julian. On solemn festivals he regularly visited the temple of the god or goddess to whom the day was peculiarly consecrated, and endeavoured to excite the religion of the magistrates and people by the example of his own zeal. Instead of maintaining the lofty state of a monarch, distinguished by the splendour of his purple, and encompassed by the golden shields of his guards, Julian solicited, with respectful eagerness, the meanest offices which contributed to the worship of the gods. Amidst the sacred but licentious crowd of priests, of inferior ministers, and of female dancers, who were dedicated to the service of the temple, it was the business of the emperor to bring the wood, to blow the fire, to handle the knife, to slaughter the victim, and, thrusting his bloody hands into the bowels of the expiring animal, to draw forth the heart or liver, and to read, with the consummate skill of an haruspex, the imaginary signs of future events. The wisest of the Pagans censured this extravagant superstition, which affected to despise the restraints of prudence and decency. Under the reign of a prince who practised the rigid maxims of economy, the expense of religious worship consumed a very large portion of the revenue; a constant supply of the scarcest and most beautiful birds was transported from distant climates, to bleed on the altars of the gods; an hundred oxen were frequently sacrificed by Julian on one and the same day; and it soon became a popular jest, that, if he should return with conquest from the Persian war, the breed of horned cattle must infallibly be extinguished. Yet this expense may appear inconsiderable, when it is compared with the splendid presents which were offered, either by the hand or by order of the emperor, to all the celebrated places of devotion in the Roman world; and with the sums allotted to repair and decorate the ancient temples, which had suffered the silent decay of time, or the recent injuries of Christian rapine. Encouraged by the example, the exhortations, the liberality of their pious sovereign, the cities and families resumed the practice of their neglected ceremonies. "Every part of the world," exclaims Libanius, with devout transport, "displayed the triumph of religion, and the grateful prospect of flaming altars, bleeding victims, the smoke of incense, and a solemn train of priests and prophets, without fear and without danger. The sound of prayer and of music was heard on the tops of the highest mountains; and the same ox afforded a sacrifice for the gods, and a supper for their joyous votaries."

But the genius and power of Julian were unequal to the enterprise of restoring a religion which was destitute of theological principles, of moral precepts, and of ecclesiastical discipline; which rapidly hastened to decay and dissolution, and was not susceptible of any solid or consistent reformation. The jurisdiction of the supreme pontiff, more especially after that office had been united with the Imperial dignity, comprehended the whole extent of the Roman empire. Julian named for his vicars, in the several provinces, the priests and philosophers, whom he esteemed the best qualified to co-operate in the execution of his great design; and his pastoral letters, if we may use that name, still represent a very curious sketch of his wishes and intentions. He directs that in every city the sacerdotal order should be composed, without any distinction of birth or fortune, of those persons who were the most conspicuous for their love of the gods and of men. "If they are guilty," continues he, "of any scandalous offence, they should be censured or degraded by the superior pontiff; but as long as they retain their rank, they are entitled to the respect of the magistrates and people. Their humility may be shown in the plainness of their domestic garb; their dignity, in the pomp of holy vestments. When they are summoned in their turn to officiate before the altar, they ought not, during the appointed number of days, to depart from the precincts of the temple; nor should a single day be suffered to elapse without the prayers and the sacrifice which they are obliged to offer for the prosperity of the state and of individuals. The exercise of their sacred functions requires an immaculate purity both of mind and body; and even when they are dismissed from the temple to the occupations of common life, it is incumbent on them to excel in decency and virtue the rest of their fellow-citizens. The priest of the gods should never be seen in theatres or taverns. His conversation should be chaste, his diet temperate, his friends of honourable reputation; and if he sometimes visits the Forum or the Palace, he should appear only as the advocate of those who have vainly solicited either justice or mercy. His studies should be suited to the sanctity of his profession. Licentious tales, or comedies, or satires, must be banished from his library, which ought solely to consist of historical and philosophical writings; of history, which is founded in truth, and of philosophy, which is connected with religion. The impious opinions of the Epicureans and sceptics deserve his abhorrence and contempt;[1] but he should diligently study the systems of Pythagoras, of Plato, and of the Stoics, which unanimously teach that there *are* gods; that the world is governed by their providence; that their goodness is the source of every temporal blessing; and that they have prepared for the human soul a future state of reward or punishment." The Imperial pontiff inculcates, in the most persuasive language, the duties of benevolence and hospitality; exhorts his inferior clergy to recommend the universal practice of those virtues; promises to assist their indigence from the public treasury; and declares his resolution of establishing hospitals in every city, where the poor should be received without any invidious distinction of country or of religion. Julian beheld with envy

---

[1] The exultation of Julian that these impious sects, and even their writings, are extinguished, may be consistent enough with the sacerdotal character; but it is unworthy of a philosopher to wish that any opinions and arguments the most repugnant to his own should be concealed from the knowledge of mankind.

the wise and humane regulations of the church; and he very frankly confesses his intention to deprive the Christians of the applause, as well as advantage, which they had acquired by the exclusive practice of charity and beneficence.[1] The same spirit of imitation might dispose the emperor to adopt several ecclesiastical institutions, the use and importance of which were approved by the success of his enemies. But if these imaginary plans of reformation had been realised, the forced and imperfect copy would have been less beneficial to Paganism than honourable to Christianity. The Gentiles, who peaceably followed the customs of their ancestors, were rather surprised than pleased with the introduction of foreign manners; and, in the short period of his reign, Julian had frequent occasions to complain of the want of fervour of his own party.

The enthusiasm of Julian prompted him to embrace the friends of Jupiter as his personal friends and brethren; and though he partially overlooked the merit of Christian constancy, he admired and rewarded the noble perseverance of those Gentiles who had preferred the favour of the gods to that of the emperor. If they cultivated the literature as well as the religion of the Greeks, they acquired an additional claim to the friendship of Julian, who ranked the Muses in the number of his tutelar deities. In the religion which he had adopted, piety and learning were almost synonymous; and a crowd of poets, of rhetoricians, and of philosophers, hastened to the Imperial court to occupy the vacant places of the bishops who had seduced the credulity of Constantius. His successor esteemed the ties of common initiation as far more sacred than those of consanguinity; he chose his favourites among the sages who were deeply skilled in the occult sciences of magic and divination, and every impostor who pretended to reveal the secrets of futurity was assured of enjoying the present hour in honour and affluence. Among the philosophers, Maximus obtained the most eminent rank in the friendship of his royal disciple, who communicated, with unreserved confidence, his actions, his sentiments, and his religious designs, during the anxious suspense of the civil war. As soon as Julian had taken possession of the palace of Constantinople, he despatched an honourable and pressing invitation to Maximus, who then resided at Sardes in Lydia, with Chrysanthius, the associate of his art and studies. The prudent and superstitious Chrysanthius refused to undertake a journey which showed itself, according to the rules of divination, with the most threatening and malignant aspect; but his companion, whose fanaticism was of a bolder cast, persisted in his interrogations till he had extorted from the gods a seeming consent to his own wishes and those of the emperor. The journey of Maximus through the cities of Asia displayed

---

[1] Yet he insinuates that the Christians, under the pretence of charity, inveigled children from their religion and parents, conveyed them on shipboard, and devoted those victims to a life of poverty or servitude in a remote country. Had the charge been proved, it was his duty not to complain but to punish.

the triumph of philosophic vanity, and the magistrates vied with each other in the honourable reception which they prepared for the friend of their sovereign. Julian was pronouncing an oration before the senate, when he was informed of the arrival of Maximus. The emperor immediately interrupted his discourse, advanced to meet him, and, after a tender embrace, conducted him by the hand into the midst of the assembly, where he publicly acknowledged the benefits which he had derived from the instructions of the philosopher. Maximus, who soon acquired the confidence, and influenced the councils, of Julian, was insensibly corrupted by the temptations of a court. His dress became more splendid, his demeanour more lofty, and he was exposed, under a succeeding reign, to a disgraceful inquiry into the means by which the disciple of Plato had accumulated, in the short duration of his favour, a very scandalous proportion of wealth. Of the other philosophers and sophists who were invited to the Imperial residence by the choice of Julian, or by the success of Maximus, few were able to preserve their innocence or their reputation. The liberal gifts of money, lands, and houses were insufficient to satiate their rapacious avarice, and the indignation of the people was justly excited by the remembrance of their abject poverty and disinterested professions. The penetration of Julian could not always be deceived, but he was unwilling to despise the characters of those men whose talents deserved his esteem; he desired to escape the double reproach of imprudence and inconstancy, and he was apprehensive of degrading, in the eyes of the profane, the honour of letters and of religion.

The favour of Julian was almost equally divided between the Pagans who had firmly adhered to the worship of their ancestors, and the Christians who prudently embraced the religion of their sovereign. The acquisition of new proselytes [1] gratified the ruling passions of his soul, superstition and vanity; and he was heard to declare, with the enthusiasm of a missionary, that if he could render each individual richer than Midas, and every city greater than Babylon, he should not esteem himself the benefactor of mankind unless, at the same time, he could reclaim his subjects from their impious revolt against the immortal gods. A prince, who had studied human nature, and who possessed the treasures of the Roman empire, could adapt his arguments, his promises, and his rewards to every order of Christians; and the merit of a seasonable conversion was allowed to supply the defects of a candidate, or even to expiate the guilt of a criminal. As the army is the most forcible engine of absolute power, Julian applied himself, with peculiar diligence, to corrupt the religion of his troops, without whose hearty concurrence

---

[1] Under the reign of Louis XIV. his subjects of every rank aspired to the glorious title of *Convertisseur*, expressive of their zeal and success in making proselytes. The word and the idea are growing obsolete in France; may they never be introduced into England!

every measure must be dangerous and unsuccessful, and the natural temper of soldiers made this conquest as easy as it was important. The legions of Gaul devoted themselves to the faith, as well as to the fortunes, of their victorious leader; and even before the death of Constantius, he had the satisfaction of announcing to his friends that they assisted, with fervent devotion and voracious appetite, at the sacrifices, which were repeatedly offered in his camp, of whole hecatombs of fat oxen. The armies of the East, which had been trained under the standard of the cross and of Constantius, required a more artful and expensive mode of persuasion. On the days of solemn and public festivals the emperor received the homage, and rewarded the merit, of the troops. His throne of state was encircled with the military ensigns of Rome and the republic; the holy name of Christ was erased from the *Labarum*; and the symbols of war, of majesty, and of Pagan superstition were so dexterously blended that the faithful subject incurred the guilt of idolatry when he respectfully saluted the person or image of his sovereign. The soldiers passed successively in review, and each of them, before he received from the hand of Julian a liberal donative, proportioned to his rank and services, was required to cast a few grains of incense into the flame which burnt upon the altar. Some Christian confessors might resist, and others might repent; but the far greater number, allured by the prospect of gold and awed by the presence of the emperor, contracted the criminal engagement, and their future perseverance in the worship of the gods was enforced by every consideration of duty and of interest. By the frequent repetition of these arts, and at the expense of sums which would have purchased the service of half the nations of Scythia, Julian gradually acquired for his troops the imaginary protection of the gods, and for himself the firm and effectual support of the Roman legions. It is indeed more than probable that the restoration and encouragement of Paganism revealed a multitude of pretended Christians, who, from motives of temporal advantage, had acquiesced in the religion of the former reign, and who afterwards returned, with the same flexibility of conscience, to the faith which was professed by the successors of Julian.

JULIAN AND THE JEWS

While the devout monarch incessantly laboured to restore and propagate the religion of his ancestors, he embraced the extraordinary design of rebuilding the temple of Jerusalem. In a public epistle to the nation of community of the Jews dispersed through the provinces, he pities their misfortunes, condemns their oppressors, praises their constancy, declares himself their gracious protector, and expresses a pious hope that, after his return from the Persian war, he may be permitted to pay his grateful vows to the Almighty in his holy city of Jerusalem. The blind superstition and abject slavery of those unfortunate exiles must excite the contempt of a philosophic emperor, but they deserved the friendship of Julian by their implacable hatred of the Christian name. The barren synagogue abhorred and envied the fecundity of the rebellious church; the power of the Jews was not equal to their malice, but their gravest rabbis approved the private murder of an apostate, and their seditious clamours had often awakened the indolence of the Pagan magistrates. Under the reign of Constantine, the Jews became the subjects of their revolted children, nor was it long before they experienced the bitterness of domestic tyranny. The civil immunities which had been granted or confirmed by Severus were gradually repealed by the Christian princes; and a rash tumult, excited by the Jews of Palestine, seemed to justify the lucrative modes of oppression which were invented by the bishops and eunuchs of the court of Constantius. The Jewish patriarch, who was still permitted to exercise a precarious jurisdiction, held his residence at Tiberias, and the neighbouring cities of Palestine were filled with the remains of a people who fondly adhered to the promised land. But the edict of Hadrian was renewed and enforced, and they viewed from afar the walls of the holy city, which were profaned in their eyes by the triumph of the cross and the devotion of the Christians.

In the midst of a rocky and barren country the walls of Jerusalem enclosed the two mountains of Sion and Acra within an oval figure of about three English miles. Towards the south, the upper town and the fortress of David were erected on the lofty ascent of Mount Sion; on the north side, the buildings of the lower town covered the spacious summit of Mount Acra; and a part of the hill, distinguished by the name of Moriah, and levelled by human industry, was crowned with the stately temple of the Jewish nation. After the final destruction of the temple by the arms of Titus and Hadrian a ploughshare was drawn over the consecrated ground, as a sign of perpetual interdiction. Sion was deserted, and the vacant space of the lower city was filled with the public and private edifices of the Ælian colony, which spread themselves over the adjacent hill of Calvary. The holy places were polluted with monuments of idolatry, and, either from design or accident, a chapel was dedicated to Venus on the spot which had been sanctified by the death and resurrection of Christ. Almost three hundred years after those stupendous events, the profane chapel of Venus was demolished by the order of Constantine, and the removal of the earth and stones revealed the holy sepulchre to the eyes of mankind. A magnificent church was erected on that mystic ground by the first Christian emperor, and the effects of his pious munificence were extended to every spot which had been consecrated by the footsteps of patriarchs, of prophets, and of the Son of God.

The passionate desire of contemplating the original monuments of their redemption attracted to Jerusalem a successive crowd of pilgrims from the shores of the Atlantic ocean and the most distant countries of the East: and their piety was authorised by the example of the empress Helena, who appears to have united the credulity of age with the warm feelings of a recent conversion. Sages and heroes, who have visited the memorable scenes of ancient wisdom or glory, have confessed the inspiration of the genius of the place; and the Christian who knelt before the holy sepulchre ascribed his lively faith and his fervent devotion to the more immediate influence of the Divine Spirit. The zeal, perhaps the avarice, of the clergy of Jerusalem cherished and multiplied these beneficial visits. They fixed, by unquestionable tradition, the scene of each memorable event. They exhibited the instruments which had been used in the passion of Christ; the nails and the lance that had pierced his hands, his feet, and his side; the crown of thorns that was planted on his head; the pillar at which he was scourged; and, above all, they showed the cross on which he suffered, and which was dug out of the earth in the reign of those princes who inserted the symbol of Christianity in the banners of the Roman legions. Such miracles as seemed necessary to account for its extraordinary preservation and seasonable discovery were gradually propagated without opposition. The custody of the *true cross*, which on Easter Sunday was solemnly exposed to the people, was intrusted to the bishop of Jerusalem; and he alone might gratify the curious devotion of the pilgrims by the gift of small pieces, which they enchased in gold or gems, and carried away in triumph to their respective countries. But as this gainful branch of commerce must soon have been annihilated, it was found convenient to suppose that the marvellous wood possessed a secret power of vegetation, and that its substance, though continually diminished, still remained entire and unimpaired. It might perhaps have been expected that the influence of the place and the belief of a perpetual miracle should have produced some salutary effects on the morals, as well as on the faith, of the people. Yet the most respectable of the ecclesiastical writers have been obliged to confess, not only that the streets of Jerusalem were filled with the incessant tumult of business and pleasure, but that every species of vice—adultery, theft, idolatry, poisoning, murder—was familiar to the inhabitants of the holy city. The wealth and pre-eminence of the church of Jerusalem excited the ambition of Arian as well as orthodox candidates; and the virtues of Cyril, who since his death has been honoured with the title of Saint, were displayed in the exercise, rather than in the acquisition, of his episcopal dignity.[1]

The vain and ambitious mind of Julian might aspire to restore the ancient glory of the temple of Jerusalem. As the Christians were firmly

---

[1] He renounced his orthodox ordination, officiated as a deacon, and was re-ordained by the hands of the Arians. But Cyril afterwards changed with the times, and prudently conformed to the Nicene faith. Tillemont, who treats his memory with tenderness and respect, has thrown his virtues into the text, and his faults into the notes, in decent obscurity, at the end of the volume.

persuaded that a sentence of everlasting destruction had been pronounced against the whole fabric of the Mosaic law, the Imperial
sophist would have converted the success of his undertaking into a
specious argument against the faith of prophecy and the truth of revelation.[1] He was displeased with the spiritual worship of the synagogue;
but he approved the institutions of Moses, who had not disdained to
adopt many of the rites and ceremonies of Egypt. The local and
national deity of the Jews was sincerely adored by a polytheist who
desired only to multiply the number of the gods; and such was the
appetite of Julian for bloody sacrifice, that his emulation might be
excited by the piety of Solomon, who had offered at the feast of the
dedication twenty-two thousand oxen and one hundred and twenty
thousand sheep. These considerations might influence his designs; but
the prospect of an immediate and important advantage would not suffer
the impatient monarch to expect the remote and uncertain event of the
Persian war. He resolved to erect, without delay, on the commanding
eminence of Moriah, a stately temple, which might eclipse the splendour
of the church of the Resurrection on the adjacent hill of Calvary; to
establish an order of priests, whose interested zeal would detect the arts
and resist the ambition of their Christian rivals; and to invite a numerous
colony of Jews, whose stern fanaticism would be always prepared to
second, and even to anticipate, the hostile measures of the Pagan
government. Among the friends of the emperor (if the names of
emperor and of friend are not incompatible) the first place was assigned,
by Julian himself, to the virtuous and learned Alypius. The humanity
of Alypius was tempered by severe justice and manly fortitude; and
while he exercised his abilities in the civil administration of Britain, he
imitated, in his poetical compositions, the harmony and softness of the
odes of Sappho. This minister, to whom Julian communicated, without reserve, his most careless levities and his most serious counsels, received an extraordinary commission to restore, in its pristine beauty, the
temple of Jerusalem; and the diligence of Alypius required and obtained
the strenuous support of the governor of Palestine. At the call of their
great deliverer, the Jews from all the provinces of the empire assembled
on the holy mountain of their fathers; and their insolent triumph
alarmed and exasperated the Christian inhabitants of Jerusalem. The
desire of rebuilding the temple has in every age been the ruling passion
of the children of Israel. In this propitious moment the men forgot their
avarice, and the women their delicacy; spades and pickaxes of silver
were provided by the vanity of the rich, and the rubbish was transported

---

[1] The secret intentions of Julian are revealed by the late bishop of Gloucester, the
learned and dogmatic Warburton; who, with the authority of a theologian, prescribes
the motives and conduct of the Supreme Being. The discourse entitled *Julian* is
strongly marked with all the peculiarities which are imputed to the Warburtonian
school.

in mantles of silk and purple. Every purse was opened in liberal contributions, every hand claimed a share in the pious labour; and the commands of a great monarch was executed by the enthusiasm of a whole people.

Yet, on this occasion, the joint efforts of power and enthusiasm were unsuccessful; and the ground of the Jewish temple, which is now covered by a Mahometan mosque, still continued to exhibit the same edifying spectacle of ruin and desolation. Perhaps the absence and death of the emperor, and the new maxims of a Christian reign, might explain the interruption of an arduous work, which was attempted only in the last six months of the life of Julian. But the Christians entertained a natural and pious expectation that in this memorable contest the honour of religion would be vindicated by some signal miracle. An earthquake, a whirlwind, and a fiery eruption, which overturned and scattered the new foundations of the temple, are attested, with some variations, by contemporary and respectable evidence. This public event is described by Ambrose, bishop of Milan, in an epistle to the emperor Theodosius, which must provoke the severe animadversion of the Jews; by the eloquent Chrysostom, who might appeal to the memory of the elder part of his congregation at Antioch; and by Gregory Nazianzen, who published his account of the miracle before the expiration of the same year. The last of these writers has boldly declared that this preternatural event was not disputed by the infidels; and his assertion, strange as it may seem, is confirmed by the unexceptionable testimony of Ammianus Marcellinus. The philosophic soldier, who loved the virtues without adopting the prejudices of his master, has recorded, in his judicious and candid history of his own times, the extraordinary obstacles which interrupted the restoration of the temple of Jerusalem. "Whilst Alypius, assisted by the governor of the province, urged with vigour and diligence the execution of the work, horrible balls of fire, breaking out near the foundations, with frequent and reiterated attacks, rendered the place, from time to time, inaccessible to the scorched and blasted workmen; and, the victorious element continuing in this manner obstinately and resolutely bent, as it were, to drive them to a distance, the undertaking was abandoned." Such authority should satisfy a believing, and must astonish an incredulous, mind. Yet a philosopher may still require the original evidence of impartial and intelligent spectators. At this important crisis any singular accident of nature would assume the appearance, and produce the effects, of a real prodigy. This glorious deliverance would be speedily improved and magnified by the pious art of the clergy of Jerusalem, and the active credulity of the Christian world; and, at the distance of twenty years, a Roman historian, careless of theological disputes, might adorn his work with the specious and splendid miracle.

JULIAN'S OPPRESSION OF THE CHRISTIANS

The restoration of the Jewish temple was secretly connected with the ruin of the Christian church. Julian still continued to maintain the freedom of religious worship, without distinguishing whether this universal toleration proceeded from his justice or his clemency. He affected to pity the unhappy Christians, who were mistaken in the most important object of their lives; but his pity was degraded by contempt, his contempt was embittered by hatred; and the sentiments of Julian were expressed in a style of sarcastic wit, which inflicts a deep and deadly wound whenever it issues from the mouth of a sovereign. As he was sensible that the Christians gloried in the name of their Redeemer, he countenanced, and perhaps enjoined, the use of the less honourable appellation of GALILÆANS. He declared that, by the folly of the Galilæans, whom he describes as a sect of fanatics, contemptible to men and odious to the gods, the empire had been reduced to the brink of destruction; and he insinuates in a public edict that a frantic patient might sometimes be cured by salutary violence. An ungenerous distinction was admitted into the mind and counsels of Julian, that, according to the difference of their religious sentiments, one part of his subjects deserved his favour and friendship, while the other was entitled only to the common benefits that his justice could not refuse to an obedient people. According to a principle pregnant with mischief and oppression, the emperor transferred to the pontiffs of his own religion the management of the liberal allowances from the public revenue which had been granted to the church by the piety of Constantine and his sons. The proud system of clerical honours and immunities, which had been constructed with so much art and labour, was levelled to the ground; the hopes of testamentary donations were intercepted by the rigour of the laws; and the priests of the Christian sect were confounded with the last and most ignominious class of the people. Such of these regulations as appeared necessary to check the ambition and avarice of the ecclesiastics were soon afterwards imitated by the wisdom of an orthodox prince. The peculiar distinctions which policy has bestowed, or superstition has lavished, on the sacerdotal order, *must* be confined to those priests who profess the religion of the state. But the will of the legislator was not excempt from prejudice and passion; and it was the object of the insidious policy of Julian to deprive the Christians of all the temporal honours and advantages which rendered them respectable in the eyes of the world.

A just and severe censure has been inflicted on the law which prohibited the Christians from teaching the arts of grammar and rhetoric. The motives alleged by the emperor to justify this partial and oppressive measure might command, during his lifetime, the silence of slaves and the applause of flatterers. Julian abuses the ambiguous meaning of a word which might be indifferently applied to the language and the religion of the GREEKS: he contemptuously observes that the men who exalt the merit of implicit faith are unfit to claim or to enjoy the advantages of science; and he vainly contends that, if they refuse to adore the gods of Homer and Demosthenes, they ought to content themselves with expounding Luke and Matthew in the churches of the Galilæans. In all the cities of the Roman world the education of the youth was intrusted to masters of grammar and rhetoric, who were elected by the magistrates, maintained at the public expense, and distinguished by many lucrative and honourable privileges. The edict of Julian appears to have included the physicians, and professors of all the liberal arts; and the emperor, who reserved to himself the approbation of the candidates, was authorised by the laws to corrupt, or to punish, the religious constancy of the most learned of the Christians. As soon as the resignation of the more obstinate teachers had established the unrivalled dominion of the Pagan sophists, Julian invited the rising generation to resort with freedom to the public schools, in a just confidence that their tender minds would receive the impressions of literature and idolatry. If the greatest part of the Christian youth should be deterred by their own scruples, or by those of their parents, from accepting this dangerous mode of instruction, they must, at the same time, relinquish the benefits of a liberal education. Julian had reason to expect that, in the space of a few years, the church would relapse into its primæval simplicity, and that the theologians, who possessed an adequate share of the learning and eloquence of the age, would be succeeded by a generation of blind and ignorant fanatics, incapable of defending the truth of their own principles, or of exposing the various follies of Polytheism.

It was undoubtedly the wish and the design of Julian to deprive the Christians of the advantages of wealth, of knowledge, and of power; but the injustice of excluding them from all offices of trust and profit seems to have been the result of his general policy, rather than the immediate consequence of any positive law. Superior merit might deserve and obtain some extraordinary exceptions; but the greater part of the Christian officers were gradually removed from their employments in the state, the army, and the provinces. The hopes of future candidates were extinguished by the declared partiality of a prince who maliciously reminded them that it was unlawful for a Christian to use the sword, either of justice or of war, and who studiously guarded the camp and the tribunals with the ensigns of idolatry. The powers of government were intrusted to the Pagans, who professed an ardent zeal for the religion of their ancestors; and as the choice of the emperor was often directed by the rules of divination, the favourites whom he preferred as the most agreeable to the gods did not always obtain the approbation of mankind. Under the administration of their enemies, the Christians had much to suffer, and more to apprehend. The temper of Julian was averse to cruelty; and the care of his reputation, which was exposed to the eyes of the universe, restrained the philosophic monarch from violating the laws of justice and toleration which he himself had so recently established. But the provincial ministers of his authority were placed in a less conspicuous station. In the exercise of arbitrary power, they consulted the wishes, rather than the commands, of their sovereign; and ventured to exercise a secret and vexatious tyranny against the sectaries on whom they were not permitted to confer the honours of martyrdom. The emperor, who dissembled as long as possible his knowledge of the injustice that was exercised in his name, expressed his real sense of the conduct of his officers by gentle reproofs and substantial rewards.

The most effectual instrument of oppression with which they were armed was the law that obliged the Christians to make full and ample satisfaction for the temples which they had destroyed under the preceding reign. The zeal of the triumphant church had not always expected the sanction of the public authority; and the bishops, who were secure of impunity, had often marched at the head of their congregations to attack and demolish the fortresses of the prince of darkness. The consecrated lands, which had increased the patrimony of the sovereign or of the clergy, were clearly defined, and easily restored. But on these lands, and on the ruins of Pagan superstition, the Christians had frequently erected their own religious edifices: and as it was necessary to remove the church before the temple could be rebuilt, the justice and piety of the emperor were applauded by one party, while the other deplored and execrated his sacrilegious violence. After the ground was cleared, the restitution of those stately structures which had been levelled with the dust, and of the precious ornaments which had been converted to Christian uses, swelled into a very large account of damages and debt. The authors of the injury had neither the ability nor the inclination to discharge this accumulated demand: and the impartial wisdom of a legislator would have been displayed in balancing the adverse claims and complaints by an equitable and temperate arbitration. But the whole empire, and particularly the East, was thrown into confusion by the rash edicts of Julian; and the Pagan magistrates, inflamed by zeal and revenge, abused the rigorous privilege of the Roman law, which substitutes, in the place of his inadequate property, the person of the insolvent debtor. Under the preceding reign, Mark, bishop of Arethusa, had laboured in the conversion of his people with arms more effectual than those of persuasion. The magistrates required the full value of a temple which had been destroyed by his intolerant zeal; but as they were satisfied of his poverty, they desired only to bend his inflexible spirit to the promise of the slightest compensation. They apprehended the aged prelate, they inhumanly scourged him, they tore his beard; and his naked body, anointed with honey, was suspended, in a net, between heaven and earth, and exposed to the stings of insects and the rays of a Syrian sun. From this lofty station, Mark still persisted to glory in his crime, and to insult the impotent rage of his persecutors. He was at length rescued from their hands, and dismissed to enjoy the honour of his divine triumph. The Arians celebrated the virtue of their pious confessor; the catholics ambitiously claimed his alliance, and the Pagans, who might be susceptible of shame or remorse, were deterred from the repetition of such unavailing cruelty. Julian spared his life: but if the bishop of Arethusa had saved the infancy of Julian, posterity will condemn the ingratitude, instead of praising the clemency, of the emperor.

THE TEMPLE AND SACRED GROVE OF DAPHNE

At the distance of five miles from Antioch, the Macedonian kings of Syria had consecrated to Apollo one of the most elegant places of devotion in the Pagan world. A magnificent temple rose in honour of the god of light; and his colossal figure almost filled the capacious sanctuary, which was enriched with gold and gems, and adorned by the skill of the Grecian artists. The deity was represented in a bending attitude, with a golden cup in his hand, pouring out a libation on the earth; as if he supplicated the venerable mother to give to his arms the cold and beauteous DAPHNE: for the spot was ennobled by fiction; and the fancy of the Syrian poets had transported the amorous tale from the banks of the Peneus to those of the Orontes. The ancient rites of Greece were imitated by the royal colony of Antioch. A stream of prophecy, which rivalled the truth and reputation of the Delphic oracle, flowed from the *Castalian* fountain of Daphne. In the adjacent fields a stadium was built by a special privilege, which had been purchased from Elis; the Olympic games were celebrated at the expense of the city; and a revenue of thirty thousand pounds sterling was annually applied to the public pleasures. The perpetual resort of pilgrims and spectators insensibly formed, in the neighbourhood of the temple, the stately and populous village of Daphne, which emulated the splendour, without acquiring the title, of a provincial city. The temple and the village were deeply bosomed in a thick grove of laurels and cypresses, which reached as far as a circumference of ten miles, and formed in the most sultry summers a cool and impenetrable shade. A thousand streams of the purest water, issuing from every hill, preserved the verdure of the earth and the temperature of the air; the senses were gratified with harmonious sounds and aromatic odours; and the peaceful grove was consecrated to health and joy, to luxury and love. The vigorous youth pursued, like Apollo, the object of his desires; and the blushing maid was warned, by the fate of Daphne, to shun the folly of unseasonable coyness. The soldier and the philosopher wisely avoided the temptation of this sensual paradise; where pleasure, assuming the character of religion, imperceptibly dissolved the firmness of manly virtue. But the groves of Daphne continued for many ages to enjoy the veneration of natives and strangers; the privileges of the holy ground were enlarged by the munificence of succeeding emperors; and every generation added new ornaments to the splendour of the temple.

When Julian, on the day of the annual festival, hastened to adore the Apollo of Daphne, his devotion was raised to the highest pitch of eagerness and impatience. His lively imagination anticipated the grateful pomp of victims, of libations, and of incense; a long procession of youths and virgins, clothed in white robes, the symbol of their innocence; and the tumultuous concourse of an innumerable people. But the zeal of Antioch was diverted, since the reign of Christianity, into a different channel. Instead of hecatombs of fat oxen sacrificed by the tribes of a wealthy city to their tutelar deity, the emperor complains that he found only a single goose, provided at the expense of a priest, the pale and solitary inhabitant of this decayed temple.[1] The altar was deserted, the oracle had been reduced to silence, and the holy ground was profaned by the introduction of Christian and funereal rites. After Babylas (a bishop of Antioch, who died in prison in the persecution of Decius) had rested near a century in his grave, his body, by the order of the Cæsar Gallus, was transported into the midst of the grove of Daphne. A magnificent church was erected over his remains; a portion of the sacred lands was usurped for the maintenance of the clergy, and for the burial of the Christians of Antioch, who were ambitious of lying at the feet of their bishop; and the priests of Apollo retired, with their affrighted and indignant votaries. As soon as another revolution seemed to restore the fortune of Paganism, the church of St. Babylas was demolished, and new buildings were added to the mouldering edifice which had been raised by the piety of Syrian kings. But the first and most serious care of Julian was to deliver his oppressed deity from the odious presence of the dead and living Christians, who had so effectually suppressed the voice of fraud or enthusiasm. The scene of infection was purified, according to the forms of ancient rituals; the bodies were decently removed; and the ministers of the church were permitted to convey the remains of St. Babylas to their former habitation within the walls of Antioch. The modest behaviour which might have assuaged the jealousy of an hostile government, was neglected on this occasion by the zeal of the Christians. The lofty car that transported the relics of Babylas was followed, and accompanied, and received, by an innumerable multitude, who chanted, with thundering acclamations, the Psalms of David the most expressive of their contempt for idols and idolaters. The return of the saint was a triumph; and the triumph was an insult on the religion of the emperor, who exerted his pride to dissemble his resentment. During the night which terminated this indiscreet procession the temple of Daphne was in

---

[1] Julian (*Misopogon*) discovers his own character with that *naïveté*, that unconscious simplicity, which always constitutes genuine humour.

flames; the statue of Apollo was consumed; and the walls of the edifice were left a naked and awful monument of ruin. The Christians of Antioch asserted, with religious confidence, that the powerful intercession of St. Babylas had pointed the lightnings of heaven against the devoted roof: but as Julian was reduced to the alternative of believing either a crime or a miracle, he chose, without hesitation, without evidence, but with some colour of probability, to impute the fire of Daphne to the revenge of the Galilæans. Their offence, had it been sufficiently proved, might have justified the retaliation, which was immediately executed by the order of Julian, of shutting the doors, and confiscating the wealth, of the cathedral of Antioch. To discover the criminals who were guilty of the tumult, of the fire, or of secreting the riches of the church, several ecclesiastics were tortured; and a presbyter, of the name of Theodoret, was beheaded by the sentence of the count of the East. But this hasty act was blamed by the emperor, who lamented, with real or affected concern, that the imprudent zeal of his ministers would tarnish his reign with the disgrace of persecution.

The zeal of the ministers of Julian was instantly checked by the frown of their sovereign; but when the father of his country declares himself the leader of a faction, the licence of popular fury cannot easily be restrained, nor consistently punished. Julian, in a public composition, applauds the devotion and loyalty of the holy cities of Syria, whose pious inhabitants had destroyed, at the first signal, the sepulchres of the Galilæans; and faintly complains that they had revenged the injuries of the gods with less moderation than he should have recommended. This imperfect and reluctant confession may appear to confirm the ecclesiastical narratives—that in the cities of Gaza, Ascalon, Cæsarea, Heliopolis, &c., the Pagans abused, without prudence or remorse, the moment of their prosperity; that the unhappy objects of their cruelty were released from torture only by death; that, as their mangled bodies were dragged through the streets, they were pierced (such was the universal rage) by the spits of cooks, and the distaffs of enraged women; and that the entrails of Christian priests and virgins, after they had been tasted by those bloody fanatics, were mixed with barley, and contemptuously thrown to the unclean animals of the city. Such scenes of religious madness exhibit the most contemptible and odious picture of human nature; but the massacre of Alexandria attracts still more attention, from the certainty of the fact, the rank of the victims, and the splendour of the capital of Egypt.

ST. GEORGE

George, from his parents or his education, surnamed the Cappadocian, was born at Epiphania in Cilicia, in a fuller's shop. From this obscure and servile origin he raised himself by the talents of a parasite; and the patrons whom he assiduously flattered procured for their worthless dependent a lucrative commission, or contract, to supply the army with bacon. His employment was mean; he rendered it infamous. He accumulated wealth by the basest arts of fraud and corruption; but his malversations were so notorious, that George was compelled to escape from the pursuits of justice. After this disgrace, in which he appears to have saved his fortune at the expense of his honour, he embraced, with real or affected zeal, the profession of Arianism. From the love, cr the ostentation, of learning, he collected a valuable library of history, rhetoric, philosophy, and theology;[1] and the choice of the prevailing faction promoted George of Cappadocia to the throne of Athanasius. The entrance of the new archbishop was that of a barbarian conqueror; and each moment of his reign was polluted by cruelty and avarice. The catholics of Alexandria and Egypt were abandoned to a tyrant, qualified, by nature and education, to exercise the office of persecution; but he oppressed with an impartial hand the various inhabitants of his extensive diocese. The primate of Egypt assumed the pomp and insolence of his lofty station; but he still betrayed the vices of his base and servile extraction. The merchants of Alexandria were impoverished by the unjust and almost universal monopoly, which he acquired, of nitre, salt, paper, funerals, &c.: and the spiritual father of a great people condescended to practise the vile and pernicious arts of an informer. The Alexandrians could never forget, nor forgive, the tax which he suggested on all the houses of the city, under an obsolete claim that the royal founder had conveyed to his successors, the Ptolemies and the Cæsars, the perpetual property of the soil. The Pagans, who had been flattered with the hopes of freedom and toleration, excited his devout avarice; and the rich temples of Alexandria were either pillaged or insulted by the haughty prelate, who exclaimed in a loud and threatening tone, "How long will these sepulchres be permitted to stand?" Under the reign of Constantius he was expelled by the fury, or rather by the justice, of the people; and it was not without a violent struggle that the civil and military powers of the state could restore his authority, and gratify his revenge. The messenger who proclaimed at Alexandria the accession of Julian announced the downfall of the archbishop. George, with two of his obsequious ministers, count Diodorus, and Dracontius, master of the mint, were ignominiously dragged in chains to the public prison. At the end of twenty-four days the prison was forced open by the rage of a superstitious multitude, impatient of the tedious forms of judicial proceedings. The enemies of gods and men expired under their cruel

---

[1] After the massacre of George, the emperor Julian repeatedly sent orders to preserve the library for his own use, and to torture the slaves who might be suspected of secreting any books. He praises the merit of the collection, from whence he had borrowed and transcribed several manuscripts while he pursued his studies in Cappadocia. He could wish indeed that the works of the Galilæans might perish; but he requires an exact account even of those theological volumes, lest other treatises more valuable should be confounded in their loss.

insults; the lifeless bodies of the archbishop and his associates were carried in triumph through the streets on the back of a camel; and the inactivity of the Athanasian party was esteemed a shining example of evangelical patience. The remains of these guilty wretches were thrown into the sea; and the popular leaders of the tumult declared their resolution to disappoint the devotion of the Christians, and to intercept the future honours of these *martyrs*, who had been punished, like their predecessors, by the enemies of their religion. The fears of the Pagans were just, and their precautions ineffectual. The meritorious death of the archbishop obliterated the memory of his life. The rival of Athanasius was dear and sacred to the Arians, and the seeming conversion of those sectaries introduced his worship into the bosom of the catholic church. The odious stranger, disguising every circumstance of time and place, assumed the mask of a martyr, a saint, and a Christian hero;[1] and the infamous George of Cappadocia has been transformed [2] into the renowned St. George of England, the patron of arms, of chivalry, and of the garter.[3]

About the same time that Julian was informed of the tumult of Alexandria he received intelligence from Edessa that the proud and wealthy faction of the Arians had insulted the weakness of the Valentinians, and committed such disorders as ought not to be suffered with impunity in a well-regulated state. Without expecting the slow forms of justice, the exasperated prince directed his mandate to the magistrates of Edessa, by which he confiscated the whole property of the church: the money was distributed among the soldiers; the lands were added to the domain; and this act of oppression was aggravated by the most ungenerous irony. "I show myself," says Julian, "the true friend of the Galilæans. Their *admirable* law has promised the kingdom of heaven to the poor; and they will advance with more diligence in the paths of virtue and salvation when they are relieved by my assistance from the load of temporal possessions. Take care," pursued the monarch, in a more serious tone, "take care how you provoke my patience and humanity. If these disorders continue, I will revenge on the magistrates the crimes of the people; and you will have reason to dread, not only

---

[1] The saints of Cappadocia, Basil and the Gregories, were ignorant of their holy companion. Pope Gelasius (A.D. 494), the first catholic who acknowledges St. George, places him among the martyrs "qui Deo magis quam hominibus noti sunt." He rejects his Acts as the composition of heretics. Some, perhaps not the oldest, of the spurious Acts, are still extant; and, through a cloud of fiction, we may yet distinguish the combat which St. George of Cappadocia sustained, in the presence of Queen *Alexandra*, against the *magician Athanasius*.

[2] This transformation is not given as absolutely certain, but as *extremely* probable.

[3] A curious history of the worship of St. George, from the sixth century (when he was already revered in Palestine, in Armenia, at Rome, and at Treves in Gaul), might be extracted from Dr. Heylin (History of St. George), and the Bollandists. His fame and popularity in Europe, and especially in England, proceeded from the Crusades.

confiscation and exile, but fire and the sword." The tumults of Alexandria were doubtless of a more bloody and dangerous nature: but a Christian bishop had fallen by the hands of the Pagans; and the public epistle of Julian affords a very lively proof of the partial spirit of his administration. His reproaches to the citizens of Alexandria are mingled with expressions of esteem and tenderness; and he laments that, on this occasion, they should have departed from the gentle and generous manners which attested their Grecian extraction. He gravely censures the offence which they had committed against the laws of justice and humanity; but he recapitulates, with visible complacency, the intolerable provocations which they had so long endured from the impious tyranny of George of Cappadocia. Julian admits the principle that a wise and vigorous government should chastise the insolence of the people; yet, in consideration of their founder Alexander, and of Serapis their tutelar deity, he grants a free and gracious pardon to the guilty city, for which he again feels the affection of a brother.

JULIAN AND ATHANASIUS

After the tumult of Alexandria had subsided, Athanasius, amidst the public acclamations, seated himself on the throne from whence his unworthy competitor had been precipitated: and as the zeal of the archbishop was tempered with discretion, the exercise of his authority tended not to inflame, but to reconcile, the minds of the people. His pastoral labours were not confined to the narrow limits of Egypt. The state of the Christian world was present to his active and capacious mind; and the age, the merit, the reputation of Athanasius, enabled him to assume, in a moment of danger, the office of Ecclesiastical Dictator. Three years were not yet elapsed since the majority of the bishops of the West had, ignorantly or reluctantly, subscribed the Confession of Rimini. They repented, they believed, but they dreaded the unseasonable rigour of their orthodox brethren; and if their pride was stronger than their faith, they might throw themselves into the arms of the Arians, to escape the indignity of a public penance, which must degrade them to the condition of obscure laymen. At the same time the domestic differences concerning the union and distinction of the divine persons were agitated with some heat among the catholic doctors; and the progress of this metaphysical controversy seemed to threaten a public and lasting division of the Greek and Latin churches. By the wisdom of a select synod, to which the name and presence of Athanasius gave the authority of a general council, the bishops who had unwarily deviated into error were admitted to the communion of the church, on the easy condition of subscribing the Nicene Creed, without any formal acknowledgment of their past fault, or any minute definition of their scholastic opinions. The advice of the primate of Egypt had already prepared the clergy of Gaul and Spain, of Italy and Greece, for the reception of this salutary measure; and, notwithstanding the opposition of some ardent spirits, the fear of the common enemy promoted the peace and harmony of the Christians.

The skill and diligence of the primate of Egypt had improved the season of tranquillity before it was interrupted by the hostile edicts of the emperor. Julian, who despised the Christians, honoured Athanasius with his sincere and peculiar hatred. For his sake alone he introduced an arbitrary distinction, repugnant at least to the spirit of his former declarations. He maintained that the Galilæans whom he had recalled from exile were not restored, by that general indulgence, to the possession of their respective churches; and he expressed his astonishment that a criminal, who had been repeatedly condemned by the judgment of the emperors, should dare to insult the majesty of the laws, and insolently usurp the archiepiscopal throne of Alexandria, without expecting the orders of his sovereign. As a punishment for the imaginary offence, he again banished Athanasius from the city; and he was pleased to suppose that this act of justice would be highly agreeable to his pious subjects. The pressing solicitations of the people soon convinced him that the majority of the Alexandrians were Christians; and that the greatest part of the Christians were firmly attached to the cause of their oppressed primate. But the knowledge of their sentiments, instead of persuading him to recall his decree, provoked him to extend to all Egypt the term of the exile of Athanasius. The zeal of the multitude rendered Julian still more inexorable: he was alarmed by the danger of leaving at the head of a tumultuous city a daring and popular leader; and the language of his resentment discovers the opinion which he entertained of the courage and abilities of Athanasius. The execution of the sentence was still delayed, by the caution or negligence of Ecdicius, prefect of Egypt, who was at length awakened from his lethargy by a severe reprimand. "Though you neglect," says Julian, "to write to me on any other subject, at least it is your duty to inform me of your conduct towards Athanasius, the enemy of the gods. My intentions have been long since communicated to you. I swear by the great Serapis, that unless, on the calends of December, Athanasius has departed from Alexandria, nay from Egypt, the officers of your government shall pay a fine of one hundred pounds of gold. You know my temper: I am slow to condemn, but I am still slower to forgive." This epistle was enforced by a short postscript written with the emperor's own hand. "The contempt that is shown for all the gods fills me with grief and indignation. There is nothing that I shall see, nothing that I should hear, with more pleasure, than the expulsion of Athanasius from all Egypt. The abominable wretch! Under my reign, the baptism of several Grecian ladies of the highest rank has been the effect of his persecutions." The death of Athanasius was not *expressly* commanded; but the prefect of Egypt understood that it was safer for him to exceed than to neglect the orders of an irritated master. The archbishop prudently retired to the monasteries of the Desert; eluded, with his usual dexterity, the snares of the enemy; and lived to triumph over the ashes of a prince who, in words of formidable import, had declared his wish that the whole venom of the Galilæan school were contained in the single person of Athanasius.

I have endeavoured faithfully to represent the artful system by which Julian proposed to obtain the effects, without incurring the guilt or reproach, of persecution. But if the deadly spirit of fanaticism perverted the heart and understanding of a virtuous prince, it must, at the same time, be confessed, that the *real* sufferings of the Christians were inflamed and magnified by human passions and religious enthusiasm. The meekness and resignation which had distinguished the primitive disciples of the Gospel was the object of the applause, rather than of the imitation, of their successors. The Christians, who had now possessed above forty years the civil and ecclesiastical government of the empire, had contracted the insolent vices of prosperity, and the habit of believing that the saints alone were entitled to reign over the earth. As soon as the enmity of Julian deprived the clergy of the privileges which had been conferred by the favour of Constantine, they complained of the most cruel oppression; and the free toleration of idolaters and heretics was a subject of grief and scandal to the orthodox party. The acts of violence, which were no longer countenanced by the magistrates, were still committed by the zeal of the people. At Pessinus the altar of Cybele was overturned almost in the presence of the emperor; and in the city of Cæsarea, in Cappadocia, the temple of Fortune, the sole place of worship which had been left to the Pagans, was destroyed by the rage of a popular tumult. On these occasions, a prince who felt for the honour of the gods was not disposed to interrupt the course of justice; and his mind was still more deeply exasperated when he found that the fanatics, who had deserved and suffered the punishment of incendiaries, were rewarded with the honours of martyrdom. The Christian subjects of Julian were assured of the hostile designs of their sovereign; and, to their jealous apprehension, every circumstance of his government might afford some grounds of discontent and suspicion. In the ordinary administration of the laws, the Christians, who formed so large a part of the people, must frequently be condemned; but their indulgent brethren, without examining the merits of the cause, presumed their innocence, allowed their claims, and imputed the severity of their judge to the partial malice of religious persecution. These present hardships, intolerable as they might appear, were represented as a slight prelude of the impending calamities. The Christians considered Julian as a cruel and crafty tyrant, who suspended the execution of his revenge till he should return victorious from the Persian war. They expected that, as soon as he had triumphed over the foreign enemies of Rome, he would lay aside the irksome mask of dissimulation; that the amphitheatres would stream with the blood of hermits and bishops; and that the Christians who still persevered in the profession of the faith would be deprived of the common benefits of nature and society. Every calumny that could wound the reputation of the Apostate was credulously embraced by the fears and hatred of his adversaries; and their indiscreet clamours provoked the temper of a sovereign whom it was their duty to respect, and their interest to flatter. They still protested that prayers and tears were their only weapons against the impious tyrant, whose head they devoted to the justice of offended Heaven. But they insinuated, with sullen resolution, that their submission was no longer the effect of weakness; and that, in the imperfect state of human virtue, the patience which is founded on principle may be exhausted by persecution. It is impossible to determine how far the zeal of Julian would have prevailed over his good sense and humanity; but, if we seriously reflect on the strength and spirit of the church, we shall be convinced that, before the emperor could have extinguished the religion of Christ, he must have involved his country in the horrors of a civil war.

Chapter 24

ELECTION OF JOVIAN.
REFLECTIONS ON THE DEATH OF JULIAN

Julian took the field with some success against the Persians. He was compelled however to withdraw and during a critical battle beyond the river Tigris he was mortally wounded. He died on June 26th, 363.

THE ELECTION OF JOVIAN

THE triumph of Christianity, and the calamities of the empire, may, in some measure, be ascribed to Julian himself, who had neglected to secure the future execution of his designs by the timely and judicious nomination of an associate and successor. But the royal race of Constantius Chlorus was reduced to his own person; and if he entertained any serious thoughts of investing with the purple the most worthy among the Romans, he was diverted from his resolution by the difficulty of the choice, the jealousy of power, the fear of ingratitude, and the natural presumption of health, of youth, and of prosperity. His unexpected death left the empire without a master, and without an heir, in a state of perplexity and danger which, in the space of fourscore years, had never been experienced, since the election of Diocletian. In a government which had almost forgotten the distinction of pure and noble blood, the superiority of birth was of little moment; the claims of official rank were accidental and precarious; and the candidates who might aspire to ascend the vacant throne could be supported only by the consciousness of personal merit, or by the hopes of popular favour. But the situation of a famished army, encompassed on all sides by an host of barbarians, shortened the moments of grief and deliberation. In these scenes of terror and distress, the body of the deceased prince, according to his own directions, was decently embalmed; and, at the dawn of day, the generals convened a military senate, at which the commanders of the legions, and the officers both of cavalry and infantry, were invited to assist. Three or four hours of the night had not passed away without some secret cabals; and when the election of an emperor was proposed, the spirit of faction began to agitate the assembly. Victor and Arinthæus collected the remains of the court of Constantius; the friends of Julian attached themselves to the Gallic chiefs Dagalaiphus and Nevitta; and the most fatal consequences might be apprehended from the discord of two factions, so opposite in their character and interest, in their maxims of government, and perhaps in their religious principles. The superior virtues of Sallust could alone reconcile their divisions and unite their suffrages; and the venerable prefect would immediately have been declared the successor of Julian, if he himself, with sincere and modest firmness, had not alleged his age and infirmities, so unequal to the weight of the diadem. The generals, who were surprised and perplexed by his refusal, showed some disposition to adopt the salutary advice of an inferior officer, that they should act as they would have acted in the absence of the emperor; that they should exert their abilities to extricate the army from the present distress; and, if they were fortunate enough to reach the confines of Mesopotamia, they should proceed with united and deliberate counsels in the election of a lawful sovereign. While they debated, a few voices saluted Jovian, who was no more than *first* of the domestics, with the names of Emperor and Augustus. The tumultuary acclamation was instantly repeated by the guards who surrounded the tent, and passed, in a few minutes, to the extremities of the line. The new prince, astonished with his own fortune, was hastily invested with the Imperial ornaments, and received an oath of fidelity from the generals, whose favour and protection he so lately solicited. The strongest recommendation of Jovian was the merit of his father, Count Varronian, who enjoyed, in honourable retirement, the fruit of his long services. In the obscure freedom of a private station, the son indulged his taste for wine and women; yet he supported, with credit, the character of a Christian and a soldier. Without being conspicuous for any of the ambitious qualifications which excite the admiration and envy of mankind, the comely person of Jovian, his cheerful temper, and familiar wit, had gained the affection of his fellow-soldiers; and the generals of both parties acquiesced in a popular election which had not been conducted by the arts of their enemies. The pride of this unexpected elevation was moderated by the just apprehension that the same day might terminate the life and reign of the new emperor. The pressing voice of necessity was obeyed without delay; and the first orders issued by Jovian, a few hours after his predecessor had expired, were to prosecute a march which could alone extricate the Romans from their actual distress.

The esteem of an enemy is most sincerely expressed by his fears; and the degree of fear may be accurately measured by the joy with which he celebrates his deliverance. The welcome news of the death of Julian, which a deserter revealed to the camp of Sapor, inspired the desponding monarch with a sudden confidence of victory. He immediately detached the royal cavalry, perhaps the ten thousand *Immortals*, to second and support the pursuit; and discharged the whole weight of his united forces on the rear-guard of the Romans. The rear-guard was thrown into disorder; the renowned legions, which derived their titles from Diocletian and his warlike colleague, were broke and trampled down by the elephants; and three tribunes lost their lives in attempting to stop the flight of their soldiers. The battle was at length restored by the persevering valour of the Romans; the Persians were repulsed with a great slaughter of men and elephants; and the army, after marching and fighting a long summer's day, arrived, in the evening, at Samara, on the banks of the Tigris, about one hundred miles above Ctesiphon. On the ensuing day the barbarians, instead of harassing the march, attacked the camp, of Jovian, which had been seated in a deep and sequestered valley. From the hills, the archers of Persia insulted and annoyed the wearied legionaries; and a body of cavalry, which had penetrated with desperate courage through the Prætorian gate, was cut in pieces, after a doubtful conflict, near the Imperial tent. In the succeeding night the camp of Carche was protected by the lofty dykes of the river; and the Roman army, though incessantly exposed to the vexatious pursuit of the Saracens, pitched their tents near the city of Dura four days after the death of Julian. The Tigris was still on their left; their hopes and provisions were almost consumed; and the impatient soldiers, who had fondly persuaded themselves that the frontiers of the empire were not far distant, requested their new sovereign that they might be permitted to hazard the passage of the river. With the assistance of his wisest officers, Jovian endeavoured to check their rashness, by representing that, if they possessed sufficient skill and vigour to stem the torrent of a deep and rapid stream, they would only deliver themselves naked and defenceless to the barbarians, who had occupied the opposite banks. Yielding at length to their clamorous importunities, he consented, with reluctance, that five hundred Gauls and Germans, accustomed from their infancy to the waters of the Rhine and Danube, should attempt the bold adventure, which might serve either as an encouragement or as a warning for the rest of the army. In the silence of the night they swam the Tigris, surprised an unguarded post of the enemy, and displayed at the dawn of day the signal of their resolution and fortune. The success of this trial disposed the emperor to listen to the promises of his architects, who proposed to construct a floating bridge of the inflated skins of sheep, oxen, and goats, covered with a floor of earth and fascines. Two important days were spent in the ineffectual labour; and the Romans, who already endured the miseries of famine, cast a look of despair on the Tigris, and upon the barbarians, whose numbers and obstinacy increased with the distress of the Imperial army.

In this hopeless situation, the fainting spirits of the Romans were revived by the sound of peace. The transient presumption of Sapor had vanished: he observed, with serious concern, that, in the repetition of doubtful combats, he had lost his most faithful and intrepid nobles, his bravest troops, and the greatest part of his train of elephants: and the experienced monarch feared to provoke the resistance of despair, the vicissitudes of fortune, and the exhausted powers of the Roman empire, which might soon advance to relieve, or to revenge, the successor of Julian. The Surenas himself, accompanied by another satrap, appeared in the camp of Jovian, and declared that the clemency of his sovereign was not averse to signify the conditions on which he would consent to . spare and to dismiss the Cæsar with the relics of his captive army. The hopes of safety subdued the firmness of the Romans; the emperor was compelled, by the advice of his council and the cries of the soldiers, to embrace the offer of peace; and the prefect Sallust was immediately sent, with the general Arinthæus, to understand the pleasure of the Great King. The crafty Persian delayed, under various pretences, the conclusion of the agreement; started difficulties, required explanations, suggested expedients, receded from his concessions, increased his demands, and wasted four days in the arts of negociation, till he had consumed the stock of provisions which yet remained in the camp of the Romans. Had Jovian been capable of executing a bold and prudent measure, he would have continued his march with unremitting diligence; the progress of the treaty would have suspended the attacks of the barbarians; and, before the expiration of the fourth day, he might have safely reached the fruitful province of Corduene, at the distance only of one hundred miles. The irresolute emperor, instead of breaking through the toils of the enemy, expected his fate with patient resignation; and accepted the humiliating conditions of peace which it was no longer in his power to refuse. The five provinces beyond the Tigris, which had been ceded by the grandfather of Sapor, were restored to the Persian monarchy. He acquired, by a single article, the impregnable city of Nisibis, which had sustained, in three successive sieges, the effort of his arms. Singara, and the castle of the Moors, one of the strongest places of Mesopotamia, were likewise dismembered from the empire. It was considered as an indulgence that the inhabitants of those fortresses were permitted to retire with their effects; but the conqueror rigorously insisted that the Romans should for ever abandon the king and kingdom of Armenia. A peace, or rather a long truce, of thirty years, was stipulated between the hostile nations; the faith of the treaty was ratified by solemn oaths and religious ceremonies; and hostages of distinguished rank were reciprocally delivered to secure the performance of the conditions.

The sophist of Antioch, who saw with indignation the sceptre of his hero in the feeble hand of a Christian successor, professes to admire the moderation of Sapor in contenting himself with so small a portion of the Roman empire. If he had stretched as far as the Euphrates the claims of his ambition, he might have been secure, says Libanius, of not meeting with a refusal. If he had fixed, as the boundary of Persia, the Orontes, the Cydnus, the Sangarius, or even the Thracian Bosphorus, flatterers would not have been wanting in the court of Jovian to convince the timid monarch that his remaining provinces would still afford the most ample gratifications of power and luxury. Without adopting in its full force this malicious insinuation, we must acknowledge that the conclusion of so ignominious a treaty was facilitated by the private ambition of Jovian. The obscure domestic, exalted to the throne by fortune, rather than by merit, was impatient to escape from the hands of the Persians, that he might prevent the designs of Procopius, who commanded the army of Mesopotamia, and establish his doubtful reign over the legions and provinces which were still ignorant of the hasty and tumultuous choice of the camp beyond the Tigris. In the neighbourhood of the same river, at no very considerable distance from the fatal station of Dura, the ten thousand Greeks, without general, or guides, or provisions, were abandoned, above twelve hundred miles from their native country, to the resentment of a victorious monarch. The difference of *their* conduct and success depended much more on their character than on their situation. Instead of tamely resigning themselves to the secret deliberations and private views of a single person, the united councils of the Greeks were inspired by the generous enthusiasm of a popular assembly, where in the mind of each citizen is filled with the love of glory, the pride of freedom, and the contempt of death. Conscious of their superiority over the barbarians in arms and discipline, they disdained to yield, they refused to capitulate: every obstacle was surmounted by the patience, courage, and military skill; and the memorable retreat of the ten thousand exposed and insulted the weakness of the Persian monarchy.

As the price of his disgraceful concessions, the emperor might perhaps have stipulated that the camp of the hungry Romans should be plentifully supplied, and that they should be permitted to pass the Tigris on the bridge which was constructed by the hands of the Persians. But if Jovian presumed to solicit those equitable terms, they were sternly refused by the haughty tyrant of the East, whose clemency had pardoned the invaders of his country. The Saracens sometimes intercepted the stragglers of the march; but the generals and troops of Sapor respected the cessation of arms, and Jovian was suffered to explore the most convenient place for the passage of the river. The small vessels which had been saved from the conflagration of the fleet performed the most essential service. They first conveyed the emperor and his favourites, and afterwards transported, in many successive voyages, a great part of the army. But, as every man was anxious for his personal safety and apprehensive of being left on the hostile shore, the soldiers, who were too impatient to wait the slow returns of the boats, boldly ventured themselves on light hurdles or inflated skins, and drawing after them their horses, attempted, with various success, to swim across the river. Many of these daring adventurers were swallowed by the waves; many others, who were carried along by the violence of the stream, fell an easy prey to the avarice or cruelty of the wild Arabs; and the loss which the army sustained in the passage of the Tigris was not inferior to the carnage of a day of battle. As soon as the Romans had landed on the western bank, they were delivered from the hostile pursuit of the barbarians; but in a laborious march of two hundred miles over the plains of Mesopotamia they endured the last extremities of thirst and hunger. They were obliged to traverse a sandy desert, which, in the extent of seventy miles, did not afford a single blade of sweet grass nor a single spring of fresh water, and the rest of the inhospitable waste was untrod by the footsteps either of friends or enemies. Whenever a small measure of flour could be discovered in the camp, twenty pounds weight were greedily purchased with ten pieces of gold, the beasts of burden were slaughtered and devoured, and the desert was strewed with the arms and baggage of the Roman soldiers, whose tattered garments and meagre countenances displayed their past sufferings and actual misery. A small convoy of provisions advanced to meet the army as far as the castle of Ur; and the supply was the more grateful, since it declared the fidelity of Sebastian and Procopius. At Thilsaphata the emperor most graciously received the generals of Mesopotamia, and the remains of a once flourishing army at length reposed themselves under the walls of Nisibis. The messengers of Jovian had already proclaimed, in the language of flattery, his election, his treaty, and his return, and the new prince had taken the most effectual measure to secure the allegiance of the armies and provinces of Europe by placing the military command in the hands of those officers who, from motives of interest or inclination, would firmly support the cause of their benefactor.

The friends of Julian had confidently announced the success of his expedition. They entertained a fond persuasion that the temples of the gods would be enriched with the spoils of the East; that Persia would be reduced to the humble state of a tributary province, governed by the laws and magistrates of Rome; that the barbarians would adopt the dress, and manners, and language of their conquerors; and that the youth of Ecbatana and Susa would study the art of rhetoric under Grecian masters. The progress of the arms of Julian interrupted his communication with the empire, and, from the moment that he passed the Tigris, his affectionate subjects were ignorant of the fate and fortunes of their prince. Their contemplation of fancied triumphs was disturbed by the melancholy rumour of his death, and they persisted to doubt, after they could no longer deny, the truth of that fatal event. The messengers of Jovian promulgated the specious tale of a prudent and necessary peace; the voice of fame, louder and more sincere, revealed the disgrace of the emperor and the conditions of the ignominious treaty. The minds of the people were filled with astonishment and grief, with indignation and terror, when they were informed that the unworthy successor of Julian relinquished the five provinces which had been acquired by the victory of Galerius, and that he shamefully surrendered to the barbarians the important city of Nisibis, the firmest bulwark of the provinces of the East. The deep and dangerous question, how far the public faith should be observed when it becomes incompatible with the public safety, was freely agitated in popular conversation, and some hopes were entertained that the emperor would redeem his pusillanimous behaviour by a splendid act of patriotic perfidy. The inflexible spirit of the Roman senate had always disclaimed the unequal conditions which were extorted from the distress of her captive armies; and, if it were necessary to satisfy the national honour by delivering the guilty general into the hands of the barbarians, the greatest part of the subjects of Jovian would have cheerfully acquiesced in the precedent of ancient times.

But the emperor, whatever might be the limits of his constitutional authority, was the absolute master of the laws and arms of the state; and the same motives which had forced him to subscribe, now pressed him to execute the treaty of peace. He was impatient to secure an empire at the expense of a few provinces, and the respectable names of religion and honour concealed the personal fears and the ambition of Jovian. Notwithstanding the dutiful solicitations of the inhabitants, decency, as well as prudence, forbade the emperor to lodge in the palace of Nisibis; but the next morning after his arrival, Bineses, the ambassador of Persia, entered the place, displayed from the citadel the standard of the Great King, and proclaimed, in his name, the cruel alternative of exile or servitude. The principal citizens of Nisibis, who, till that fatal moment, had confided in the protection of their sovereign, threw themselves at his feet. They conjured him not to abandon, or, at least, not to deliver, a faithful colony to the rage of a barbarian tyrant, exasperated by the three successive defeats which he had experienced under the walls of Nisibis. They still possessed arms and courage to repel the invaders of their country; they requested only the permission of using them in their own defence, and, as soon as they had asserted their independence, they should implore the favour of being again admitted into the rank of his subjects. Their arguments, their eloquence, their tears, were ineffectual. Jovian alleged, with some confusion, the sanctity of oaths; and as the reluctance with which he accepted the present of a crown of gold convinced the citizens of their hopeless condition, the advocate Sylvanus was provoked to exclaim, "O emperor! may you thus be crowned by all the cities of your dominions!" Jovian, who in a few weeks had assumed the habits of a prince,[1] was displeased with freedom, and offended with truth; and as he reasonably supposed that the discontent of the people might incline them to submit to the Persian government, he published an edict, under pain of death, that they should leave the city within the

---

[1] At Nisibis he performed a *royal* act. A brave officer, his namesake, who had been thought worthy of the purple, was dragged from supper, thrown into a well, and stoned to death without any form of trial or evidence of guilt.

term of three days. Ammianus has delineated in lively colours the
scene of universal despair, which he seems to have viewed with an eye of
compassion. The martial youth deserted, with indignant grief, the walls
which they had so gloriously defended; the disconsolate mourner
dropped a last tear over the tomb of a son or husband, which must soon
be profaned by the rude hand of a barbarian master; and the aged
citizen kissed the threshold and clung to the doors of the house where he
had passed the cheerful and careless hours of infancy. The highways were
crowded with a trembling multitude; the distinctions of rank, and sex,
and age, were lost in the general calamity. Every one strove to bear
away some fragment from the wreck of his fortunes; and as they could
not command the immediate service of an adequate number of horses or
waggons, they were obliged to leave behind them the greatest part of
their valuable effects. The savage insensibility of Jovian appears to have
aggravated the hardships of these unhappy fugitives. They were seated,
however, in a new-built quarter of Amida; and that rising city, with the
reinforcement of a very considerable colony, soon recovered its former
splendour and became the capital of Mesopotamia. Similar orders were
despatched by the emperor for the evacuation of Singara and the castle
of the Moors, and for the restitution of the five provinces beyond the
Tigris. Sapor enjoyed the glory and the fruits of his victory; and this
ignominious peace has justly been considered as a memorable era in the
decline and fall of the Roman empire. The predecessors of Jovian had
sometimes reliquished the dominion of distant and unprofitable provinces; but, since the foundation of the city, the genius of Rome, the god
Terminus, who guarded the boundaries of the republic, had never
retired before the sword of a victorious enemy.

REFLECTIONS ON THE DEATH OF JULIAN

After Jovian had performed those engagements which the voice of
his people might have tempted him to violate, he hastened away from
the scene of his disgrace, and proceeded with his whole court to enjoy
the luxury of Antioch. Without consulting the dictates of religious zeal,
he was prompted, by humanity and gratitude, to bestow the last honours
on the remains of his deceased sovereign; and Procopius, who sincerely
bewailed the loss of his kinsman, was removed from the command of the
army, under the decent pretence of conducting the funeral. The corpse
of Julian was transported from Nisibis to Tarsus, in a slow march of
fifteen days, and, as it passed through the cities of the East, was saluted
by the hostile factions with mournful lamentations and clamorous
insults. The Pagans already placed their beloved hero in the rank of
those gods whose worship he had restored, while the invectives of the
Christians pursued the soul of the apostate to hell, and his body to the
grave. One party lamented the approaching ruin of their altars, the
other celebrated the marvellous deliverance of the church. The Chris-

tians applauded, in lofty ambiguous strains, the stroke of divine vengeance which had been so long suspended over the guilty head of Julian. They acknowledged that the death of the tyrant, at the instant he expired beyond the Tigris, was *revealed* to the saints of Egypt, Syria, and Cappadocia; and instead of suffering him to fall by the Persian darts, their indiscretion ascribed the heroic deed to the obscure hand of some mortal or immortal champion of the faith. Such imprudent declarations were eagerly adopted by the malice or credulity of their adversaries, who darkly insinuated or confidently asserted that the governors of the church had instigated and directed the fanaticism of a domestic assassin. Above sixteen years after the death of Julian, the charge was solemnly and vehemently urged in a public oration addressed by Libanius to the emperor Theodosius. His suspicions are unsupported by fact or argument, and we can only esteem the generous zeal of the sophist of Antioch for the cold and neglected ashes of his friend.

It was an ancient custom in the funerals, as well as in the triumphs of the Romans, that the voice of praise should be corrected by that of satire and ridicule, and that, in the midst of the splendid pageants which displayed the glory of the living or of the dead, their imperfections should not be concealed from the eyes of the world. This custom was practised in the funeral of Julian. The comedians, who resented his contempt and aversion for the theatre, exhibited, with the applause of a Christian audience, the lively and exaggerated representation of the faults and follies of the deceased emperor. His various character and singular manners afforded an ample scope for pleasantry and ridicule. In the exercise of his uncommon talents he often descended below the majesty of his rank. Alexander was transformed into Diogenes,—the philosopher was degraded into a priest. The purity of his virtue was sullied by excessive vanity; his superstition disturbed the peace and endangered the safety of a mighty empire; and his irregular sallies were the less entitled to indulgence, as they appeared to be the laborious efforts of art, or even of affection. The remains of Julian were interred at Tarsus in Cilicia; but his stately tomb, which arose in that city on the banks of the cold and limpid Cydnus, was displeasing to the faithful friends who loved and revered the memory of that extraordinary man. The philosopher expressed a very reasonable wish that the disciple of Plato might have reposed amidst the groves of the Academy, while the soldier exclaimed, in bolder accents, that the ashes of Julian should have been mingled with those of Cæsar, in the field of Mars, and among the ancient monuments of Roman virtue. The history of princes does not very frequently renew the example of a similar competition.

THE RETURN OF CHRISTIANITY
TO FAVOR

Chapter 25

THE CHRISTIANS UNDER JOVIAN

THE death of Julian had left the public affairs of the empire in a very doubtful and dangerous situation. The Roman army was saved by an inglorious, perhaps a necessary, treaty; [1] and the first moments of peace were consecrated by the pious Jovian to restore the domestic tranquillity of the church and state. The indiscretion of his predecessor, instead of reconciling, had artfully fomented the religious war; and the balance which he affected to preserve between the hostile factions served only to perpetuate the contest by the vicissitudes of hope and fear, by the rival claims of ancient possession and actual favour. The Christians had forgotten the spirit of the Gospel, and the Pagans had imbibed the spirit of the church. In private families the sentiments of nature were extinguished by the blind fury of zeal and revenge; the majesty of the laws was violated or abused; the cities of the East were stained with blood; and the most implacable enemies of the Romans were in the bosom of their country. Jovian was educated in the profession of Christianity; and as he marched from Nisibis to Antioch, the banner of the Cross, the LABARUM of Constantine, which was again displayed at the head of the legions, announced to the people the faith of their new emperor. As soon as he ascended the throne he transmitted a circular epistle to all the governors of provinces, in which he confessed the divine truth and secured the legal establishment of the Christian religion. The insidious edicts of Julian were abolished, the ecclesiastical immunities were restored and enlarged, and Jovian condescended to lament that the distress of the times obliged him to diminish the measure of charitable distributions. The Christians were unanimous in the loud and sincere applause which they bestowed on the pious successor of Julian; but they were still ignorant what creed or what synod he would choose for the standard of orthodoxy, and the peace of the church immediately revived those eager disputes which had been suspended during the season of persecution. The episcopal leaders of the contending sects, convinced from experience how much their fate would depend on the earliest impressions that were made on the mind of an untutored soldier, hastened to the court of Edessa, or Antioch. The highways of

---

[1] The medals of Jovian adorn him with victories, laurel crowns, and prostrate captives. Flattery is a foolish suicide; she destroys herself with her own hands.

386

the East were crowded with Homoousian, and Arian, and Semi-Arian, and Eunomian bishops, who struggled to outstrip each other in the holy race; the apartments of the palace resounded with their clamours, and the ears of the prince were assaulted, and perhaps astonished, by the singular mixture of metaphysical argument and passionate invective. The moderation of Jovian, who recommended concord and charity, and referred the disputants to the sentence of a future council, was interpreted as a symptom of indifference; but his attachment to the Nicene Creed was at length discovered and declared by the reverence which he expressed for the *celestial* virtues of the great Athanasius. The intrepid veteran of the faith, at the age of seventy, had issued from his retreat on the first intelligence of the tyrant's death. The acclamations of the people seated him once more on the archiepiscopal throne, and he wisely accepted or anticipated the invitation of Jovian. The venerable figure of Athanasius, his calm courage and insinuating eloquence, sustained the reputation which he had already acquired in the courts of four successive princes. As soon as he had gained the confidence and secured the faith of the Christian emperor, he returned in triumph to his diocese, and continued, with mature counsels and undiminished vigour, to direct, ten years longer, the ecclesiastical government of Alexandria, Egypt, and the catholic church. Before his departure from Antioch, he assured Jovian that his orthodox devotion would be rewarded with a long and peaceful reign. Athanasius had reason to hope that he should be allowed either the merit of a successful prediction, or the excuse of a grateful though ineffectual prayer.

Jovian died after a reign of only eight months. After Jovian Valentinian became emperor and associated his brother Valens. The western and eastern provinces were now formally divided. Valentinian maintained religious toleration in the West. Valens professed Arianism in the East.

Barbarian pressure was increasing on different frontiers, in Gaul from the Alemanni and Burgundians, in Britain from the Picts and Scots, on the Danube from the Goths and Sarmatians. These peoples were now being pushed forward by the Huns. As a result of this pressure the Visigoths were allowed to settle within the Danube. Here however they revolted and threatened Constantinople. Valens met them at Adrianople and was defeated and killed in a decisive battle which in tactics asserted the supremacy of cavalry over infantry which was to endure until the battle of Crecy and which inflicted losses in men and damage to the prestige of the Roman army from which it never recovered.

In the general calamities which followed, the investiture of Theodosius as emperor in the East marks a turning point in secular and ecclesiastical government. He defeated the Goths and made treaties with them which none the less involved further settlements within the empire. He earned the title of the Great by his enforcement of Catholic orthodoxy. After the deaths of Gratian, Valentinian II and a usurper, Eugenius, Theodosius was the last sole ruler of the empire in the West and the East. These events are narrated in the remainder of this chapter and in Chapter 26.[1]

[1] The origin of the Huns discussed by Gibbon in Chapter 26 remains somewhat obscure. The best modern account is E. A. Thompson's *Attila and the Huns* 1948.

Chapter 27

AMBROSE, ARCHBISHOP OF MILAN. VIRTUES AND FAULTS
OF THEODOSIUS. SEDITION OF ANTIOCH AND MASSACRE OF
THESSALONICA. PENANCE OF THEODOSIUS. CHARACTER
AND DEATH OF VALENTINIAN. DEATH OF THEODOSIUS.

*Constantinople had been a stronghold of Arianism for forty years.
Theodosius was the first emperor to be baptised in the orthodox faith
of the Trinity. In 380 an orthodox bishop, Gregory Nazianzen, was
established in Constantinople and Arianism was driven from the
East. At the Council of Constantinople in 381 the theological system
of the Trinity, which had been established by the Council of Nicœa,
was completed. Between 380 and 394 Theodosius promulgated a
number of severe edicts against the heretics.*

*Meanwhile the lazy disposition of Gratian, emperor of the West,
had aroused discontent among the Roman troops. Maximus, leading
a revolt from Britain, defeated him near Lyons before Theodosius
could march to his relief. Gratian was assassinated and Theodosius
formed an alliance with Maximus, by which Maximus reigned
beyond the Alps and Gratian's brother Valentinian was confirmed in
the sovereignty of Italy.*

AMBROSE, ARCHBISHOP OF MILAN

AMONG the ecclesiastics who illustrated the reign of Theodosius, Gregory Nazianzen was distinguished by the talents of
an eloquent preacher; the reputation of miraculous gifts added
weight and dignity to the monastic virtues of Martin of Tours; but the
palm of episcopal vigour and ability was justly claimed by the intrepid
Ambrose. He was descended from a noble family of Romans; his
father had exercised the important office of Prætorian prefect of Gaul;
and the son, after passing through the studies of a liberal education,
attained, in the regular gradation of civil honours, the station of consular of Liguria, a province which included the Imperial residence of
Milan. At the age of thirty-four, and before he had received the sacrament of baptism, Ambrose, to his own surprise and to that of the world,
was suddenly transformed from a governor to an archbishop. Without
the least mixture, as it is said, of art or intrigue, the whole body of the
people unanimously saluted him with the episcopal title; the concord and
perseverance of their acclamations were ascribed to a præternatural
impulse; and the reluctant magistrate was compelled to undertake a

spiritual office for which he was not prepared by the habits and occupations of his former life. But the active force of his genius soon qualified him to exercise, with zeal and prudence, the duties of his ecclesiastical jurisdiction; and while he cheerfully renounced the vain and splendid trappings of temporal greatness, he condescended, for the good of the church, to direct the conscience of the emperors, and to control the administration of the empire. Gratian loved and revered him as a father; and the elaborate treatise on the faith of the Trinity was designed for the instruction of the young prince. After his tragic death, at a time when the empress Justina trembled for her own safety, and for that of her son Valentinian, the archbishop of Milan was despatched on two different embassies to the court of Trèves. He exercised, with equal firmness and dexterity, the powers of his spiritual and political characters; and perhaps contributed, by his authority and eloquence, to check the ambition of Maximus, and to protect the peace of Italy. Ambrose had devoted his life and his abilities to the service of the church. Wealth was the object of his contempt; he had renounced his private patrimony; and he sold, without hesitation, the consecrated plate for the redemption of captives. The clergy and people of Milan were attached to their archbishop; and he deserved the esteem, without soliciting the favour, or apprehending the displeasure, of his feeble sovereigns.

The government of Italy, and of the young emperor, naturally devolved to his mother Justina, a woman of beauty and spirit, but who, in the midst of an orthodox people, had the misfortune of professing the Arian heresy, which she endeavoured to instil into the mind of her son. Justina was persuaded that a Roman emperor might claim, in his own dominions, the public exercise of his religion; and she proposed to the archbishop, as a moderate and reasonable concession, that he should resign the use of a single church, either in the city or suburbs of Milan. But the conduct of Ambrose was governed by very different principles. The palaces of the earth might indeed belong to Cæsar, but the churches were the houses of God; and, within the limits of his diocese, he himself, as the lawful successor of the apostles, was the only minister of God. The privileges of Christianity, temporal as well as spiritual, were confined to the true believers; and the mind of Ambrose was satisfied that his own theological opinions were the standard of truth and orthodoxy. The archbishop, who refused to hold any conference or negociation with the instruments of Satan, declared, with modest firmness, his resolution to die a martyr, rather than to yield to the impious sacrilege; and Justina, who resented the refusal as an act of insolence and rebellion, hastily determined to exert the Imperial prerogative of her son. As she desired to perform her public devotions on the approaching festival of Easter, Ambrose was ordered to appear before the council. He obeyed the summons with the respect of a faithful subject, but he was followed, without his consent, by an innumerable people: they pressed, with impetuous zeal, against the gates of the palace; and the affrighted ministers of Valentinian, instead of pronouncing a sentence of exile on the archbishop of Milan, humbly requested that he would interpose his authority to protect the person of the emperor, and to restore the tranquillity of the capital. But the promises which Ambrose received and communicated were soon violated by a perfidious court; and, during six of the most solemn days which Christian piety has set apart for the exercise of religion, the city was agitated by the irregular convulsions of tumult and fanaticism. The officers of the household were directed to prepare, first the Portian, and afterwards the new, *Basilica*, for the immediate reception of the emperor and his mother. The splendid canopy and hangings of the royal seat were arranged in the customary manner; but it was found necessary to defend them, by a strong guard, from the insults of the populace. The Arian ecclesiastics who ventured to show themselves in the streets were exposed to the most imminent danger of their lives; and Ambrose enjoyed the merit and reputation of rescuing his personal enemies from the hands of the enraged multitude.

But while he laboured to restrain the effects of their zeal, the pathetic vehemence of his sermons continually inflamed the angry and seditious temper of the people of Milan. The characters of Eve, of the wife of Job, of Jezebel, of Herodias, were indecently applied to the mother of the emperor; and her desire to obtain a church for the Arians was compared to the most cruel persecutions which Christianity had endured under the reign of Paganism. The measures of the court served only to expose the magnitude of the evil. A fine of two hundred pounds of gold was imposed on the corporate body of merchants and manufacturers: an order was signified, in the name of the emperor, to all the officers and inferior servants of the courts of justice, that, during the continuance of the public disorders, they should strictly confine themselves to their houses: and the ministers of Valentinian imprudently confessed that the most respectable part of the citizens of Milan was attached to the cause of their archbishop. He was again solicited to restore peace to his country, by a timely compliance with the will of his sovereign. The reply of Ambrose was couched in the most humble and respectful terms, which might, however, be interpreted as a serious declaration of civil war. "His life and fortune were in the hands of the emperor; but he would never betray the church of Christ, or degrade the dignity of the episcopal character. In such a cause he was prepared to suffer whatever the malice of the dæmon could inflict; and he only wished to die in the presence of his faithful flock, and at the foot of the altar; *he* had not contributed to excite, but it was in the power of God alone to appease, the rage of the people: he deprecated the scenes of blood and confusion which were likely to ensue; and it was his fervent prayer that he might not survive to behold the ruin of a flourishing city, and perhaps the desolation of all Italy." The obstinate bigotry of Justina would have endangered the empire of her son, if, in this contest with the church and people of Milan, she could have depended on the active obedience of the troops of the palace. A large body of Goths had marched to occupy the *Basilica*, which was the object of the dispute: and it might be expected from the Arian principles and barbarous manners of these foreign mercenaries, that they would not entertain any scruples in the execution of the most sanguinary orders. They were encountered on the sacred threshold by the archbishop, who, thundering against them a sentence of excommunication, asked them, in the tone of a father and a master, Whether it was to invade the house of God that they had implored the hospitable protection of the republic? The suspense of the barbarians allowed some hours for a more effectual negociation; and the empress was persuaded by the advice of her wisest counsellors to leave the catholics in possession of all the churches of Milan; and to dissemble, till a more convenient season, her intentions of revenge. The mother of Valentinian could never forgive the triumph of Ambrose: and the royal youth uttered a passionate exclamation, that his own servants were ready to betray him into the hands of an insolent priest.

The laws of the empire, some of which were inscribed with the name of Valentinian, still condemned the Arian heresy, and seemed to excuse the resistance of the catholics. By the influence of Justina, an edict of toleration was promulgated in all the provinces which were subject to the court of Milan; the free exercise of their religion was granted to those who professed the faith of Rimini; and the emperor declared that all persons who should infringe this sacred and salutary constitution should be capitally punished, as the enemies of the public peace. The character and language of the archbishop of Milan may justify the suspicion that his conduct soon afforded a reasonable ground, or at least a specious pretence, to the Arian ministers, who watched the opportunity of surprising him in some act of disobedience to a law which he strangely represents as a law of blood and tyranny. A sentence of easy and honourable banishment was pronounced, which enjoined Ambrose to depart from Milan without delay, whilst it permitted him to choose the place of his exile and the number of his companions. But the authority of the saints, who have preached and practised the maxims of passive loyalty, appeared to Ambrose of less moment than the extreme and pressing danger of the church. He boldly refused to obey; and his refusal was supported by the unanimous consent of his faithful people. They guarded by turns the person of their archbishop; the gates of the cathedral and the episcopal palace were strongly secured; and the Imperial troops, who had formed the blockade, were unwilling to risk the attack of that impregnable fortress. The numerous poor, who had been relieved by the liberality of Ambrose, embraced the fair occasion of signalising their zeal and gratitude; and as the patience of the multitude might have been exhausted by the length and uniformity of nocturnal vigils, he prudently introduced into the church of Milan the useful institution of a loud and regular psalmody. While he maintained this arduous contest, he was instructed, by a dream, to open the earth in a place where the remains of two martyrs, Gervasius and Protasius, had been deposited above three hundred years. Immediately under the pavement of the church two perfect skeletons were found, with the heads separated from their bodies, and a plentiful effusion of blood. The holy relics were presented, in solemn pomp, to the veneration of the people; and every circumstance of this fortunate discovery was admirably adapted to promote the designs of Ambrose. The bones of the martyrs, their blood, their garments, were supposed to contain a healing power; and the preternatural influence was communicated to the most distant objects, without losing any part of its original virtue. The extraordinary cure of a blind man, and the reluctant confessions of several dæmoniacs, appeared to justify the faith and sanctity of Ambrose; and the truth of those miracles is attested by Ambrose himself, by his secretary Paulinus, and by his proselyte, the celebrated Augustin, who, at that time, professed the art of rhetoric in Milan. The reason of the present age may possibly approve the incredulity of Justina and her Arian court, who derided the theatrical representations which were exhibited by the contrivance, and at the expense, of the archbishop. Their effect, however, on the minds of the people, was rapid and irresistible; and the feeble sovereign of Italy found himself unable to contend with the favourite of Heaven. The powers likewise of the earth interposed in the defence of Ambrose: the disinterested advice of Theodosius was the genuine result of piety and friendship; and the mask of religious zeal concealed the hostile and ambitious designs of the tyrant of Gaul.

Maximus invaded Italy in 387. Valentinian and his mother fled to Theodosius in Thessalonica. Theodosius married Valentinian's sister and ended the civil war by defeating and beheading Maximus.

THE VIRTUES AND FAULTS OF THEODOSIUS

The orator, who may be silent without danger, may praise without difficulty and without reluctance; and posterity will confess that the character of Theodosius might furnish the subject of a sincere and ample panegyric. The wisdom of his laws and the success of his arms rendered his administration respectable in the eyes both of his subjects and of his enemies. He loved and practised the virtues of domestic life, which seldom hold their residence in the palaces of kings. Theodosius was chaste and temperate; he enjoyed, without excess, the sensual and social

pleasures of the table, and the warmth of his amorous passions was
never diverted from their lawful objects. The proud titles of Imperial
greatness were adorned by the tender names of a faithful husband, an
indulgent father; his uncle was raised, by his affectionate esteem, to the
rank of a second parent; Theodosius embraced, as his own, the children
of his brother and sister, and the expressions of his regard were extended
to the most distant and obscure branches of his numerous kindred.
His familiar friends were judiciously selected from amongst those persons who, in the equal intercourse of private life, had appeared before
his eyes without a mask; the consciousness of personal and superior
merit enabled him to despise the accidental distinction of the purple,
and he proved by his conduct that he had forgotten all the injuries,
while he most gratefully remembered all the favours and services, which
he had received before he ascended the throne of the Roman empire.
The serious or lively tone of his conversation was adapted to the age,
the rank, or the character of his subjects whom he admitted into his
society; and the affability of his manners displayed the image of his
mind. Theodosius respected the simplicity of the good and virtuous:
every art, every talent, of an useful or even of an innocent nature, was
rewarded by his judicious liberality; and, except the heretics, whom he
persecuted with implacable hatred, the diffusive circle of his benevolence
was circumscribed only by the limits of the human race. The government of a mighty empire may assuredly suffice to occupy the time and
the abilities of a mortal; yet the diligent prince, without aspiring to the
unsuitable reputation of profound learning, always reserved some
moments of his leisure for the instructive amusement of reading.
History, which enlarged his experience, was his favourite study. The
annals of Rome, in the long period of eleven hundred years, presented
him with a various and splendid picture of human life; and it has been
particularly observed that, whenever he perused the cruel acts of Cinna,
of Marius, or of Sylla, he warmly expressed his generous detestation of
those enemies of humanity and freedom. His disinterested opinion of
past events was usefully applied as the rule of his own actions, and
Theodosius has deserved the singular commendation that his virtues
always seemed to expand with his fortune; the season of his prosperity
was that of his moderation, and his clemency appeared the most conspicuous after the danger and success of the civil war. The Moorish
guards of the tyrant had been massacred in the first heat of the victory,
and a small number of the most obnoxious criminals suffered the
punishment of the law. But the emperor showed himself much more
attentive to relieve the innocent than to chastise the guilty. The oppressed subjects of the West, who would have deemed themselves happy
in the restoration of their lands, were astonished to receive a sum of
money equivalent to their losses; and the liberality of the conqueror
supported the aged mother and educated the orphan daughters of

Maximus. A character thus accomplished might almost excuse the extravagant supposition of the orator Pacatus that, if the elder Brutus could be permitted to revisit the earth, the stern republican would abjure, at the feet of Theodosius, his hatred of kings; and ingenuously confess that such a monarch was the most faithful guardian of the happiness and dignity of the Roman people.

Yet the piercing eye of the founder of the republic must have discerned two essential imperfections, which might, perhaps, have abated his recent love of despotism. The virtuous mind of Theodosius was often relaxed by indolence, and it was sometimes inflamed by passion. In the pursuit of an important object his active courage was capable of the most vigorous exertions; but as soon as the design was accomplished, or the danger was surmounted, the hero sunk into inglorious repose, and, forgetful that the time of a prince is the property of his people, resigned himself to the enjoyment of the innocent but trifling pleasures of a luxurious court. The natural disposition of Theodosius was hasty and choleric; and, in a station where none could resist and few would dissuade the fatal consequence of his resentment, the humane monarch was justly alarmed by the consciousness of his infirmity and of his power. It was the constant study of his life to suppress or regulate the intemperate sallies of passion; and the success of his efforts enhanced the merit of his clemency. But the painful virtue which claims the merit of victory is exposed to the danger of defeat; and the reign of a wise and merciful prince was polluted by an act of cruelty which would stain the annals of Nero or Domitian. Within the space of three years the inconsistent historian of Theodosius must relate the generous pardon of the citizens of Antioch, and the inhuman massacre of the people of Thessalonica.

THE SEDITION OF ANTIOCH

The lively impatience of the inhabitants of Antioch was never satisfied with their own situation, or with the character and conduct of their successive sovereigns. The Arian subjects of Theodosius deplored the loss of their churches; and, as three rival bishops disputed the throne of Antioch, the sentence which decided their pretensions excited the murmurs of the two unsuccessful congregations. The exigencies of the Gothic war, and the inevitable expense that accompanied the conclusion of the peace, had constrained the emperor to aggravate the weight of the public impositions; and the provinces of Asia, as they had not been involved in the distress, were the less inclined to contribute to the relief of Europe. The auspicious period now approached of the tenth year of his reign; a festival more grateful to the soldiers, who received a liberal donative, than to the subjects, whose voluntary offerings had been long since converted into an extraordinary and oppressive burden. The edicts of taxation interrupted the repose and pleasures of Antioch;

and the tribunal of the magistrate was besieged by a suppliant crowd, who, in pathetic, but at first in respectful language, solicited the redress of their grievances. They were gradually incensed by the pride of their haughty rulers, who treated their complaints as a criminal resistance; their satirical wit degenerated into sharp and angry invectives; and, from the subordinate powers of government, the invectives of the people insensibly rose to attack the sacred character of the emperor himself. Their fury, provoked by a feeble opposition, discharged itself on the images of the Imperial family which were erected, as objects of public veneration, in the most conspicuous places of the city. The statues of Theodosius, of his father, of his wife Flaccilla, of his two sons Arcadius and Honorius, were insolently thrown down from their pedestals, broken in pieces, or dragged with contempt through the streets; and the indignities which were offered to the representations of Imperial majesty sufficiently declared the impious and treasonable wishes of the populace. The tumult was almost immediately suppressed by the arrival of a body of archers; and Antioch had leisure to reflect on the nature and consequences of her crime. According to the duty of his office, the governor of the province despatched a faithful narrative of the whole transaction, while the trembling citizens intrusted the confession of their crime and the assurances of their repentance to the zeal of Flavian their bishop, and to the eloquence of the senator Hilarius, the friend, and most probably the disciple, of Libanius, whose genius on the melancholy occasion was not useless to his country. But the two capitals, Antioch and Constantinople, were separated by the distance of eight hundred miles; and, notwithstanding the diligence of the Imperial posts, the guilty city was severely punished by a long and dreadful interval of suspense. Every rumour agitated the hopes and fears of the Antiochans, and they heard with terror that their sovereign, exasperated by the insult which had been offered to his own statues, and more especially to those of his beloved wife, had resolved to level with the ground the offending city, and to massacre, without distinction of age or sex, the criminal inhabitants, many of whom were actually driven, by their apprehensions, to seek a refuge in the mountains of Syria and the adjacent desert. At length, twenty-four days after the sedition, the general Hellebicus, and Cæsarius, master of the offices, declared the will of the emperor and the sentence of Antioch. That proud capital was degraded from the rank of a city; and the metropolis of the East, stripped of its lands, its privileges, and its revenues, was subjected, under the humiliating denomination of a village, to the jurisdiction of Laodicea. The baths, the circus, and the theatres were shut; and, that every source of plenty and pleasure might at the same time be intercepted, the distribution of corn was abolished by the severe instructions of Theodosius. His commissioners then proceeded to inquire into the guilt of individuals—of those who had perpetrated, and of those who had not prevented, the destruction of the sacred statues. The tribunal of Hellebicus and Cæsarius, encompassed with armed soldiers, was erected in the midst of the Forum. The noblest and most wealthy of the citizens of Antioch appeared before them in chains; the examination was assisted by the use of torture, and their sentence was pronounced or suspended, according to the judgment of these extraordinary magistrates. The houses of the criminals were exposed to sale, their wives and children were suddenly reduced from affluence and luxury to the most abject distress, and a bloody execution was expected to conclude the horrors of a day which the preacher of Antioch, the eloquent Chrysostom, has represented as a lively image of the last and universal judgment of the world. But the ministers of Theodosius performed with reluctance the cruel task which had been assigned them; they dropped a gentle tear over the calamities of the people, and they listened with reverence to the pressing solicitations of the monks and hermits, who descended in swarms from the mountains. Hellebicus and Cæsarius were persuaded to suspend the execution of their sentence; and it was agreed that the former should remain at Antioch, while the latter returned, with all possible speed, to Constantinople, and presumed once more to consult the will of his sovereign. The resentment of Theodosius had already subsided; the deputies of the people, both the bishop and the orator, had obtained a favourable audience; and the reproaches of the emperor were the complaints of injured friendship rather than the stern menaces of pride and power. A free and general pardon was granted to the city and citizens of Antioch; the prison-doors were thrown open; the senators, who despaired of their lives, recovered the possession of their houses and estates; and the capital of the East was restored to the enjoyment of her ancient dignity and splendour. Theodosius condescended to praise the senate of Constantinople, who had generously interceded for their distressed brethren; he rewarded the eloquence of Hilarius with the government of Palestine, and dismissed the bishop of Antioch with the warmest expressions of his respect and gratitude. A thousand new statues arose to the clemency of Theodosius; the applause of his subjects was ratified by the approbation of his own heart; and the emperor confessed that, if the exercise of justice is the most important duty, the indulgence of mercy is the most exquisite pleasure of a sovereign.

THE MASSACRE OF THESSALONICA

The sedition of Thessalonica is ascribed to a more shameful cause, and was productive of much more dreadful consequences. That great city, the metropolis of all the Illyrian provinces, had been protected from the dangers of the Gothic war by strong fortifications and a numerous garrison. Botheric, the general of those troops, and, as it should seem from his name, a barbarian, had amongst his slaves a beautiful boy, who excited the impure desires of one of the charioteers of the circus. The insolent and brutal lover was thrown into prison by the order of Botheric; and he sternly rejected the importunate clamours of the multitude, who, on the day of the public games, lamented the absence of their favourite, and considered the skill of a charioteer as an object of more importance than his virtue. The resentment of the people was embittered by some previous disputes; and, as the strength of the garrison had been drawn away for the service of the Italian war, the feeble remnant, whose numbers were reduced by desertion, could not save the unhappy general from their licentious fury. Botheric and several of his principal officers were inhumanly murdered; their mangled bodies were dragged about the streets; and the emperor, who then resided at Milan, was surprised by the intelligence of the audacious and wanton cruelty of the people of Thessalonica. The sentence of a dispassionate judge would have inflicted a severe punishment on the authors of the crime; and the merit of Botheric might contribute to exasperate the grief and indignation of his master. The fiery and choleric temper of Theodosius was impatient of the dilatory forms of a judicial inquiry; and he hastily resolved that the blood of his lieutenant should be expiated by the blood of the guilty people. Yet his mind still fluctuated between the counsels of clemency and of revenge; the zeal of the bishops had almost extorted from the reluctant emperor the promise of a general pardon; his passion was again inflamed by the flattering suggestions of his minister Rufinus; and, after Theodosius had despatched the messengers of death, he attempted, when it was too late, to prevent the execution of his orders. The punishment of a Roman city was blindly committed to the undistinguishing sword of the barbarians; and the hostile preparations were concerted with the dark and perfidious artifice of an illegal conspiracy. The people of Thessalonica were treacherously invited, in the name of their sovereign, to the games of the circus; and such was their insatiate avidity for those amusements that every consideration of fear or suspicion was disregarded by the numerous spectators. As soon as the assembly was complete, the soldiers, who had secretly been posted round the circus, received the signal, not of the races, but of a general massacre. The promiscuous carnage continued three hours, without discrimination of strangers or natives, of age or sex, of innocence or guilt; the most moderate accounts state the number of the slain at seven thousand; and it is affirmed by some writers that more than fifteen thousand victims were sacrificed to the manes of Botheric. A foreign merchant, who had probably no concern in his murder, offered his own life and all his wealth to supply the place of *one* of his two sons; but, while the father hesitated with equal tenderness, while he was doubtful to choose, and unwilling to condemn, the soldiers determined his suspense by plunging their daggers at the same moment into the breasts of the defenceless youths. The apology of the assassins, that they were obliged to produce the prescribed number of heads, serves only to increase, by an appearance of order and design, the horrors of the massacre, which was executed by the commands of Theodosius. The guilt of the emperor is aggravated by his long and frequent residence at Thessalonica. The situation of the unfortunate city, the aspect of the streets and buildings, the dress and faces of the inhabitants, were familiar, and even present, to his imagination; and Theodosius possessed a quick and lively sense of the existence of the people whom he destroyed.

The respectful attachment of the emperor for the orthodox clergy had disposed him to love and admire the character of Ambrose, who united all the episcopal virtues in the most eminent degree. The friends and ministers of Theodosius imitated the example of their sovereign; and he observed, with more surprise than displeasure, that all his secret counsels were immediately communicated to the archbishop, who acted from the laudable persuasion that every measure of civil government may have some connexion with the glory of God and the interest of the true religion. The monks and populace of Callinicum, an obscure town on the frontier of Persia, excited by their own fanaticism, and by that of their bishop, had tumultuously burnt a conventicle of the Valentinians and a synagogue of the Jews. The seditious prelate was condemned by the magistrate of the province either to rebuild the synagogue or to repay the damage; and this moderate sentence was confirmed by the emperor. But it was not confirmed by the archbishop of Milan. He dictated an epistle of censure and reproach, more suitable, perhaps, if the emperor had received the mark of circumcision and renounced the faith of his baptism. Ambrose considers the toleration of the Jewish as the persecution of the Christian religion; boldly declares that he himself and every true believer would eagerly dispute with the bishop of Callinicum the merit of the deed and the crown of martyrdom; and laments, in the most pathetic terms, that the execution of the sentence would be fatal to the fame and salvation of Theodosius. As this private admonition did not produce an immediate effect, the archbishop from his pulpit publicly addressed the emperor on his throne; nor would he consent to offer the oblation of the altar till he had obtained from Theodosius a solemn and positive declaration which secured the impunity of the bishop and monks of Callinicum. The recantation of Theodosius was sincere; and, during the term of his residence at Milan, his affection for Ambrose was continually increased by the habits of pious and familiar conversation.

THE PENANCE OF THEODOSIUS

When Ambrose was informed of the massacre of Thessalonica, his mind was filled with horror and anguish. He retired into the country to indulge his grief and to avoid the presence of Theodosius. But as the archbishop was satisfied that a timid silence would render him the accomplice of his guilt, he represented in a private letter the enormity of the crime, which could only be effaced by the tears of penitence. The episcopal vigour of Ambrose was tempered by prudence; and he contented himself with signifying an indirect sort of excommunication, by the assurance that he had been warned in a vision not to offer the oblation in the name or in the presence of Theodosius, and by the advice that he would confine himself to the use of prayer, without presuming to approach the altar of Christ, or to receive the holy eucharist with those hands that were still polluted with the blood of an innocent people. The emperor was deeply affected by his own reproaches and by those of his spiritual father; and after he had bewailed the mischievous and irreparable consequences of his rash fury, he proceeded in the accustomed manner to perform his devotions in the great church of Milan. He was stopped in the porch by the archbishop, who, in the tone and language of an ambassador of Heaven, declared to his sovereign that private contrition was not sufficient to atone for a public fault or to appease the justice of the offended Deity. Theodosius humbly represented that, if he had contracted the guilt of homicide, David, the man after God's own heart, had been guilty not only of murder but of adultery. "You have imitated David in his crime, imitate then his repentance," was the reply of the undaunted Ambrose. The rigorous conditions of peace and pardon were accepted; and the public penance of the emperor Theodosius has been recorded as one of the most honourable events in the annals of the church. According to the mildest rules of ecclesiastical discipline which were established in the fourth century, the crime of homicide was expiated by the penitence of twenty years: and as it was impossible in the period of human life to purge the accumulated guilt of the massacre of Thessalonica, the murderer should have been excluded from the holy communion till the hour of his death. But the archbishop, consulting the maxims of religious policy, granted some indulgence to the rank of his illustrious penitent, who humbled in the dust the pride of the diadem; and the public edification might be admitted as a weighty reason to abridge the duration of his punishment. It was sufficient that the emperor of the Romans, stripped of the ensigns of royalty, should appear in a mournful and suppliant posture; and that, in the midst of the church of Milan, he should humbly solicit, with sighs and tears, the pardon of his sins. In this spiritual cure Ambrose employed the various methods of mildness and severity. After a delay of about eight months Theodosius was restored to the communion of the faithful; and the edict, which interposes a salutary interval of thirty days between the sentence and the execution, may be accepted as the worthy fruits of his repentance. Posterity has applauded the virtuous firmness of the archbishop: and the example of Theodosius may prove the beneficial influence of those principles which could force a monarch, exalted above the apprehension of human punishment, to respect the laws and ministers of an invisible Judge. "The prince," says Montesquieu, "who is actuated by the hopes and fears of religion, may be compared to a lion, docile only to the voice, and tractable to the hand, of his keeper." The motions of the royal animal will therefore depend on the inclination and interest of the man who has acquired such dangerous authority over him; and the priest who holds in his hand the conscience of a king may inflame or moderate his sanguinary passions. The cause of humanity and that of persecution have been asserted by the same Ambrose with equal energy and with equal success.

After the defeat and death of the tyrant of Gaul, the Roman world was in the possession of Theodosius. He derived from the choice of Gratian his honourable title to the provinces of the East; he had acquired the West by the right of conquest; and the three years which he spent in Italy were usefully employed to restore the authority of the laws and to correct the abuses which had prevailed with impunity under the usurpation of Maximus and the minority of Valentinian. The name of Valentinian was regularly inserted in the public acts, but the tender age and doubtful faith of the son of Justina appeared to require the prudent care of an orthodox guardian, and his specious ambition might have excluded the unfortunate youth, without a struggle and almost without a murmur, from the administration and even from the inheritance of the empire. If Theodosius had consulted the rigid maxims of interest and policy, his conduct would have been justified by his friends, but the generosity of his behaviour on this memorable occasion has extorted the applause of his most inveterate enemies. He seated Valentinian on the throne of Milan, and without stipulating any present or future advantages, restored him to the absolute dominion of all the provinces from which he had been driven by the arms of Maximus. To the restitution of his ample patrimony Theodosius added the free and generous gift of the countries beyond the Alps which his successful valour had recovered from the assassin of Gratian. Satisfied with the glory which he had acquired by revenging the death of his benefactor and delivering the West from the yoke of tyranny, the emperor returned from Milan to Constantinople, and, in the peaceful possession of the East, insensibly relapsed into his former habits of luxury and indolence. Theodosius discharged his obligation to the brother, he indulged his conjugal tenderness to the sister, of Valentinian; and posterity, which admires the pure and singular glory of his elevation, must applaud his unrivalled generosity in the use of victory.

THE CHARACTER AND DEATH OF VALENTINIAN

The empress Justina did not long survive her return to Italy, and, though she beheld the triumph of Theodosius, she was not allowed to influence the government of her son. The pernicious attachment to the Arian sect which Valentinian had imbibed from her example and instructions was soon erased by the lessons of a more orthodox education.

His growing zeal for the faith of Nice, and his filial reverence for the character and authority of Ambrose, disposed the catholics to entertain the most favourable opinion of the virtues of the young emperor of the West.[1] They applauded his chastity and temperance, his contempt of pleasure, his application to business, and his tender affection for his two sisters, which could not, however, seduce his impartial equity to pronounce an unjust sentence against the meanest of his subjects. But this amiable youth, before he had accomplished the twentieth year of his age, was oppressed by domestic treason, and the empire was again involved in the horrors of a civil war. Arbogastes, a gallant soldier of the nation of the Franks, held the second rank in the service of Gratian. On the death of his master he joined the standard of Theodosius, contributed, by his valour and military conduct, to the destruction of the tyrant, and was appointed, after the victory, master-general of the armies of Gaul. His real merit and apparent fidelity had gained the confidence both of the prince and people; his boundless liberality corrupted the allegiance of the troops; and, whilst he was universally esteemed as the pillar of the state, the bold and crafty barbarian was secretly determined either to rule or to ruin the empire of the West. The important commands of the army were distributed among the Franks; the creatures of Arbogastes were promoted to all the honours and offices of the civil government; the progress of the conspiracy removed every faithful servant from the presence of Valentinian; and the emperor, without power and without intelligence, insensibly sunk into the precarious and dependent condition of a captive. The indignation which he expressed, though it might arise only from the rash and impatient temper of youth, may be candidly ascribed to the generous spirit of a prince who felt that he was not unworthy to reign. He secretly invited the archbishop of Milan to undertake the office of a mediator, as the pledge of his sincerity and the guardian of his safety. He contrived to apprise the emperor of the East of his helpless situation, and he declared that, unless Theodosius could speedily march to his assistance, he must attempt to escape from the palace, or rather prison, of Vienne, in Gaul, where he had imprudently fixed his residence in the midst of the hostile faction. But the hopes of relief were distant and doubtful; and, as every day furnished some new provocation, the emperor, without strength or counsel, too hastily resolved to risk an immediate contest with his powerful general. He received Arbogastes on the throne, and, as the count approached with some appearance of respect, delivered to him a paper which dismissed him from all his employments. "My authority," replied Arbogastes, with insulting coolness, "does not depend on the smile or the frown of a monarch;" and he

---

[1] When the young emperor gave an entertainment, he fasted himself; he refused to see an handsome actress, &c. Since he ordered his wild beasts to be killed, it is ungenerous in Philostorgius to reproach him with the love of that amusement.

contemptuously threw the paper on the ground. The indignant monarch snatched at the sword of one of the guards, which he struggled to draw from its scabbard, and it was not without some degree of violence that he was prevented from using the deadly weapon against his enemy or against himself. A few days after this extraordinary quarrel, in which he had exposed his resentment and his weakness, the unfortunate Valentinian was found strangled in his apartment, and some pains were employed to disguise the manifest guilt of Arbogastes, and to persuade the world that the death of the young emperor had been the voluntary effect of his own despair. His body was conducted with decent pomp to the sepulchre of Milan, and the archbishop pronounced a funeral oration to commemorate his virtue and his misfortunes. On this occasion the humanity of Ambrose tempted him to make a singular breach in his theological system, and to comfort the weeping sisters of Valentinian by the firm assurance that their pious brother, though he had not received the sacrament of baptism, was introduced, without difficulty, into the mansions of eternal bliss.

The prudence of Arbogastes had prepared the success of his ambitious designs, and the provincials, in whose breasts every sentiment of patriotism or loyalty was extinguished, expected, with tame resignation, the unknown master whom the choice of a Frank might place on the Imperial throne. But some remains of pride and prejudice still opposed the elevation of Arbogastes himself, and the judicious barbarian thought it more advisable to reign under the name of some dependent Roman. He bestowed the purple on the rhetorician Eugenius, whom he had already raised from the place of his domestic secretary to the rank of master of the offices. In the course both of his private and public service the count had always approved the attachment and abilities of Eugenius; his learning and eloquence, supported by the gravity of his manners, recommended him to the esteem of the people, and the reluctance with which he seemed to ascend the throne may inspire a favourable prejudice of his virtue and moderation. The ambassadors of the new emperor were immediately despatched to the court of Theodosius, to communicate with affected grief, the unfortunate accident of the death of Valentinian, and, without mentioning the name of Arbogastes, to request that the monarch of the East would embrace as his lawful colleague the respectable citizen who had obtained the unanimous suffrage of the armies and provinces of the West. Theodosius was justly provoked that the perfidy of a barbarian should have destroyed in a moment the labours and the fruit of his former victory; and he was excited by the tears of his beloved wife to revenge the fate of her unhappy brother, and once more to assert by arms the violated majesty of the throne. But as the second conquest of the West was a task of difficulty and danger, he dismissed, with splendid presents and an ambiguous answer, the ambassadors of Eugenius, and almost two years were consumed in the preparations of the civil war. Before he formed any decisive resolution, the pious emperor was anxious to discover the will of Heaven; and as the progress of Christianity had silenced the oracles of Delphi and Dodona, he consulted an Egyptian monk, who possessed, in the opinion of the age, the gift of miracles and the knowledge of futurity. Eutropius, one of the favourite eunuchs of the palace of Constantinople, embarked for Alexandria, from whence he sailed up the Nile as far as the city of Lycopolis, or of Wolves, in the remote province of Thebais. In the neighbourhood of that city, and on the summit of a lofty mountain, the holy John had constructed with his own hands an humble cell, in which he had dwelt above fifty years, without opening his door, without seeing the face of a woman, and without tasting any food that had been prepared by fire or any human art. Five days of the week he spent in prayer and meditation, but on Saturdays and Sundays he regularly opened a small window, and gave audience to the crowd of suppliants who successively flowed from every part of the Christian world. The eunuch of Theodosius approached the window with respectful steps, proposed his questions concerning the event of the civil war, and soon returned with a favourable oracle, which animated the courage of the emperor by the assurance of a bloody but infallible victory. The accomplishment of the prediction was forwarded by all the means that human prudence could supply. The industry of the two master-generals, Stilicho and Timasius, was directed to recruit the numbers and to revive the discipline of the Roman legions. The formidable troops of barbarians marched under the ensigns of their national chieftains. The Iberian, the Arab, and the Goth, who gazed on each other with mutual astonishment, were enlisted in the service of the same prince; and the renowned Alaric acquired, in the school of Theodosius, the knowledge of the art of war which he afterwards so fatally exerted for the destruction of Rome.

The emperor of the West, or, to speak more properly, his general Arbogastes, was instructed by the misconduct and misfortune of Maximus how dangerous it might prove to extend the line of defence against a skilful antagonist, who was free to press or to suspend, to contract or to multiply, his various methods of attack. Arbogastes fixed his station on the confines of Italy; the troops of Theodosius were permitted to occupy, without resistance, the provinces of Pannonia, as far as the foot of the Julian Alps; and even the passes of the mountains were negligently, or perhaps artfully, abandoned to the bold invader. He descended from the hills, and beheld, with some astonishment, the formidable camp of the Gauls and Germans that covered with arms and tents the open country which extends to the walls of Aquileia and the banks of the Frigidus, or Cold River. This narrow theatre of the war, circumscribed by the Alps and the Adriatic, did not allow much room for the operations of military skill; the spirit of Arbogastes would have disdained a pardon; his guilt extinguished the hope of a negociation; and Theodosius was impatient to satisfy his glory and revenge by the chastisement of the assassins of Valentinian. Without weighing the natural and artificial obstacles that opposed his efforts, the emperor of the East immediately attacked the fortifications of his rivals, assigned the post of honourable danger to the Goths, and cherished a secret wish that the bloody conflict might diminish the pride and numbers of the conquerors. Ten thousand of those auxiliaries, and Bacurius, general of the Iberians, died bravely on the field of battle. But the victory was not purchased by their blood; the Gauls maintained their advantage, and the approach of night protected the disorderly flight, or retreat, of the troops of Theodosius. The emperor retired to the adjacent hills, where he passed a disconsolate night, without sleep, without provisions, and without hopes,[1] except that strong assurance which, under the most desperate circumstances, the independent mind may derive from the contempt of fortune and of life. The triumph of Eugenius was celebrated by the insolent and dissolute joy of his camp, whilst the active and vigilant Arbogastes secretly detached a considerable body of troops to occupy the passes of the mountains and to encompass the rear of the Eastern army. The dawn of day discovered to the eyes of Theodosius the extent and the extremity of his danger, but his apprehensions were soon dispelled by a friendly message from the leaders of those troops, who expressed their inclination to desert the standard of the tyrant. The honourable and lucrative rewards which they stipulated as the price of their perfidy were granted without hesitation, and, as ink and paper could not easily be procured, the emperor subscribed on his own tablets the ratification of the treaty. The spirit of his soldiers was revived by this seasonable reinforcement, and they again marched with confidence to surprise the camp of a tyrant whose principal officers appeared to distrust either the justice or the success of his arms. In the heat of the battle a violent tempest, such as is often felt among the Alps, suddenly arose from the East. The army of Theodosius was sheltered by their position from the impetuosity of the wind, which blew a cloud of dust in the faces of the enemy, disordered their ranks, wrested their weapons from their hands, and diverted or repelled their ineffectual javelins. This accidental advantage was skilfully improved: the violence of the storm was magnified by the superstitious terrors of the Gauls, and they yielded without shame to the invisible powers of heaven, who seemed to militate on the side of the pious emperor. His victory was decisive, and the deaths of his two rivals were distinguished only by the difference of their characters. The rhetorician Eugenius, who had almost acquired the dominion of the world, was reduced to implore the mercy of the conqueror, and the unrelenting soldiers separated his head from his body as he lay prostrate at the feet

[1] Theodoret affirms that St. John and St. Philip appeared to the waking or sleeping emperor, on horseback, &c. This is the first instance of apostolic chivalry, which afterwards became so popular in Spain and in the Crusades.

of Theodosius. Arbogastes, after the loss of a battle in which he had discharged the duties of a soldier and a general, wandered several days among the mountains. But when he was convinced that his cause was desperate, and his escape impracticable, the intrepid barbarian imitated the example of the ancient Romans, and turned his sword against his own breast. The fate of the empire was determined in a narrow corner of Italy; and the legitimate successor of the house of Valentinian embraced the archbishop of Milan, and graciously received the submission of the provinces of the West. Those provinces were involved in the guilt of rebellion; while the inflexible courage of Ambrose alone had resisted the claims of successful usurpation. With a manly freedom, which might have been fatal to any other subject, the archbishop rejected the gifts of Eugenius, declined his correspondence, and withdrew himself from Milan to avoid the odious presence of a tyrant whose downfall he predicted in discreet and ambiguous language. The merit of Ambrose was applauded by the conqueror, who secured the attachment of the people by his alliance with the church: and the clemency of Theodosius is ascribed to the humane intercession of the archbishop of Milan.

THE DEATH OF THEODOSIUS

After the defeat of Eugenius, the merit, as well as the authority, of Theodosius was cheerfully acknowledged by all the inhabitants of the Roman world. The experience of his past conduct encouraged the most pleasing expectations of his future reign; and the age of the emperor, which did not exceed fifty years, seemed to extend the prospect of the public felicity. His death, only four months after his victory, was considered by the people as an unforeseen and fatal event, which destroyed in a moment the hopes of the rising generation. But the indulgence of ease and luxury had secretly nourished the principles of disease. The strength of Theodosius was unable to support the sudden and violent transition from the palace to the camp; and the increasing symptoms of a dropsy announced the speedy dissolution of the emperor. The opinion, and perhaps the interest, of the public had confirmed the division of the Eastern and Western empires; and the two royal youths, Arcadius and Honorius, who had already obtained, from the tenderness of their father, the title of Augustus, were destined to fill the thrones of Constantinople and of Rome. Those princes were not permitted to share the danger and glory of the civil war; but as soon as Theodosius had triumphed over his unworthy rivals, he called his younger son, Honorius, to enjoy the fruits of the victory, and to receive the sceptre of the West from the hands of his dying father. The arrival of Honorius at Milan was welcomed by a splendid exhibition of the games of the circus; and the emperor, though he was oppressed by the weight of his disorder, contributed by his presence to the public joy. But the remains of his strength were exhausted by the painful effort which he made to assist at the spectacles of the morning. Honorius supplied, during the rest of the day, the place of his father; and the great Theodosius expired in the ensuing night. Notwithstanding the recent animosities of a civil war, his death was universally lamented. The barbarians, whom he had vanquished, and the churchmen, by whom he had been subdued, celebrated with loud and sincere applause the qualities of the deceased emperor which appeared the most valuable in their eyes. The Romans were terrified by the impending dangers of a feeble and divided administration; and every disgraceful moment of the unfortunate reigns of Arcadius and Honorius revived the memory of their irreparable loss.

In the faithful picture of the virtues of Theodosius, his imperfections have not been dissembled; the act of cruelty, and the habits of indolence, which tarnished the glory of one of the greatest of the Roman princes. An historian perpetually adverse to the fame of Theodosius has exaggerated his vices and their pernicious effects; he boldly asserts that every rank of subjects imitated the effeminate manners of their sovereign; that every species of corruption polluted the course of public and private life; and that the feeble restraints of order and decency were insufficient to resist the progress of that degenerate spirit which sacrifices, without a blush, the consideration of duty and interest to the base indulgence of sloth and appetite. The complaints of contemporary writers, who deplore the increase of luxury and depravation of manners, are commonly expressive of their peculiar temper and situation. There are few observers who possess a clear and comprehensive view of the revolutions of society, and who are capable of discovering the nice and secret springs of action which impel, in the same uniform direction, the blind and capricious passions of a multitude of individuals. If it can be affirmed, with any degree of truth, that the luxury of the Romans was more shameless and dissolute in the reign of Theodosius than in the age of Constantine, perhaps, or of Augustus, the alteration cannot be ascribed to any beneficial improvements which had gradually increased the stock of national riches. A long period of calamity or decay must have checked the industry and diminished the wealth of the people; and their profuse luxury must have been the result of that indolent despair which enjoys the present hour and declines the thoughts of futurity. The uncertain condition of their property discouraged the subjects of Theodosius from engaging in those useful and laborious undertakings which require an immediate expense, and promise a slow and distant advantage. The frequent examples of ruin and desolation tempted them not to spare the remains of a patrimony which might, every hour, become the prey of the rapacious Goth. And the mad prodigality which prevails in the confusion of a shipwreck or a siege may serve to explain the progress of luxury amidst the misfortunes and terrors of a sinking nation.

The effeminate luxury, which infected the manners of courts and cities, had instilled a secret and destructive poison into the camps of the legions;

and their degeneracy has been marked by the pen of a military writer, who had accurately studied the genuine and ancient principles of Roman discipline. It is the just and important observation of Vegetius, that the infantry was invariably covered with defensive armour from the foundation of the city to the reign of the emperor Gratian. The relaxation of discipline and the disuse of exercise rendered the soldiers less able and less willing to support the fatigues of the service; they complained of the weight of the armour, which they seldom wore; and they successively obtained the permission of laying aside both their cuirasses and their helmets. The heavy weapons of their ancestors, the short sword and the formidable *pilum*, which had subdued the world, insensibly dropped from their feeble hands. As the use of the shield is incompatible with that of the bow, they reluctantly marched into the field, condemned to suffer either the pain of wounds or the ignominy of flight, and always disposed to prefer the more shameful alternative. The cavalry of the Goths, the Huns, and the Alani, had felt the benefits and adopted the use of defensive armour; and, as they excelled in the management of missile weapons, they easily overwhelmed the naked and trembling legions, whose heads and breasts were exposed, without defence, to the arrows of the barbarians. The loss of armies, the destruction of cities, and the dishonour of the Roman name, ineffectually solicited the successors of Gratian to restore the helmets and cuirasses of the infantry. The enervated soldiers abandoned their own and the public defence; and their pusillanimous indolence may be considered as the immediate cause of the downfall of the empire.

Chapter 28

THE END OF PAGANISM. DESTRUCTION OF THE TEMPLE OF
SERAPIS. PROHIBITION OF PAGAN RITES. WORSHIP OF
THE CHRISTIAN MARTYRS AND REVIVAL OF POLYTHEISTIC
PRACTICES

THE ruin of Paganism, in the age of Theodosius, is perhaps the only example of the total extirpation of any ancient and popular superstition, and may therefore deserve to be considered as a singular event in the history of the human mind. The Christians, more especially the clergy, had impatiently supported the prudent delays of Constantine and the equal toleration of the elder Valentinian; nor could they deem their conquest perfect or secure as long as their adversaries were permitted to exist. The influence which Ambrose and his brethren had acquired over the youth of Gratian and the piety of Theodosius was employed to infuse the maxims of persecution into the breasts of their Imperial proselytes. Two specious principles of religious jurisprudence were established, from whence they deduced a direct and rigorous conclusion against the subjects of the empire who still adhered to the ceremonies of their ancestors: *that* the magistrate is, in some measure, guilty of the crimes which he neglects to prohibit or to punish; and *that* the idolatrous worship of fabulous deities and real dæmons is the most abominable crime against the supreme majesty of the Creator. The laws of Moses and the examples of Jewish history were hastily, perhaps erroneously, applied by the clergy to the mild and universal reign of Christianity. The zeal of the emperors was excited to vindicate their own honour and that of the Deity; and the temples of the Roman world were subverted about sixty years after the conversion of Constantine.

From the age of Numa to the reign of Gratian, the Romans preserved succession of the several colleges of the sacerdotal order. Fifteen PONTIFFS exercised their supreme jurisdiction over all things and persons that were consecrated to the service of the gods; and the various questions which perpetually arose in a loose and traditionary system were submitted to the judgment of their holy tribunal. Fifteen grave and learned AUGURS observed the face of the heavens, and prescribed the actions of heroes according to the flight of birds. Fifteen keepers of the Sibylline books (their name of QUINDECEMVIRS was derived from their number) occasionally consulted the history of future, and, as it should seem, of contingent events. Six VESTALS devoted their virginity to the guard of the sacred fire and of the unknown pledges of the duration of

Rome, which no mortal had been suffered to behold with impunity. Seven EPULOS prepared the table of the gods, conducted the solemn procession, and regulated the ceremonies of the annual festival. The three FLAMENS of Jupiter, of Mars, and of Quirinus, were considered as the peculiar ministers of the three most powerful deities, who watched over the fate of Rome and of the universe. The KING of the SACRIFICES represented the person of Numa and of his successors in the religious functions, which could be performed only by royal hands. The confraternities of the SALIANS, the LUPERCALS, &c., practised such rites as might extort a smile of contempt from every reasonable man, with a lively confidence of recommending themselves to the favour of the immortal gods. The authority which the Roman priests had formerly obtained in the counsels of the republic was gradually abolished by the establishment of monarchy and the removal of the seat of empire. But the dignity of their sacred character was still protected by the laws and manners of their country; and they still continued, more especially the college of pontiffs, to exercise in the capital, and sometimes in the provinces, the rights of their ecclesiastical and civil jurisdiction. Their robes of purple, chariots of state, and sumptuous entertainments, attracted the admiration of the people; and they received, from the consecrated lands and the public revenue, an ample stipend, which liberally supported the splendour of the priesthood and all the expenses of the religious worship of the state. As the service of the altar was not incompatible with the command of armies, the Romans, after their consulships and triumphs, aspired to the place of pontiff or of augur; the seats of Cicero and Pompey were filled, in the fourth century, by the most illustrious members of the senate; and the dignity of their birth reflected additional splendour on their sacerdotal character. The fifteen priests who composed the college of pontiffs enjoyed a more distinguished rank as the companions of their sovereign; and the Christian emperors condescended to accept the robe and ensigns which were appropriated to the office of supreme pontiff. But when Gratian ascended the throne, more scrupulous or more enlightened, he sternly rejected those profane symbols; applied to the service of the state or of the church the revenues of the priests and vestals; abolished their honours and immunities; and dissolved the ancient fabric of Roman superstition, which was supported by the opinions and habits of eleven hundred years. Paganism was still the constitutional religion of the senate. The hall or temple in which they assembled was adorned by the statue and altar of Victory; a majestic female standing on a globe, with flowing garments, expanded wings, and a crown of laurel in her outstretched hand. The senators were sworn on the altar of the goddess to observe the laws of the emperor and of the empire; and a solemn offering of wine and incense was the ordinary prelude of their public deliberations. The removal of this ancient monument was the only injury which Constantius had offered to the superstition of the Romans. The altar of Victory was again restored by Julian, tolerated by Valentinian, and once more banished from the senate by the zeal of Gratian. But the emperor yet spared the statues of the gods which were exposed to the public veneration: four hundred and twenty-four temples, or chapels, still remained to satisfy the devotion of the people, and in every quarter of Rome the delicacy of the Christians was offended by the fumes of idolatrous sacrifice.

But the Christians formed the least numerous party in the senate of Rome; and it was only by their absence that they could express their dissent from the legal, though profane, acts of a Pagan majority. In that assembly the dying embers of freedom were, for a moment, revived and inflamed by the breath of fanaticism. Four respectable deputations were successively voted to the Imperial court, to represent the grievances of the priesthood and the senate, and to solicit the restoration of the altar of Victory. The conduct of this important business was intrusted to the eloquent Symmachus, a wealthy and noble senator, who united the sacred characters of pontiff and augur with the civil dignities of pro-consul of Africa and prefect of the city. The breast of Symmachus was animated by the warmest zeal for the cause of expiring Paganism; and his religious antagonists lamented the abuse of his genius and the in-efficacy of his moral virtues. The orator, whose petition is extant to the emperor Valentinian, was conscious of the difficulty and danger of the office which he had assumed. He cautiously avoids every topic which might appear to reflect on the religion of his sovereign; humbly declares that prayers and entreaties are his only arms; and artfully draws his arguments from the schools of rhetoric rather than from those of philosophy. Symmachus endeavours to seduce the imagination of a young prince, by displaying the attributes of the goddess of Victory; he insinuates that the confiscation of the revenues which were consecrated to the service of the gods was a measure unworthy of his liberal and dis-interested character; and he maintains that the Roman sacrifices would be deprived of their force and energy, if they were no longer celebrated at the expense as well as in the name of the republic. Even scepticism is made to supply an apology for superstition. The great and incompre-hensible *secret* of the universe eludes the inquiry of man. Where reason cannot instruct, custom may be permitted to guide; and every nation seems to consult the dictates of prudence, by a faithful attachment to those rites and opinions which have received the sanction of ages. If those ages have been crowned with glory and prosperity; if the devout people has frequently obtained the blessings which they have solicited at the altars of the gods,—it must appear still more advisable to persist in the same salutary practice, and not to risk the unknown perils that may attend any rash innovations. The test of antiquity and success was applied with singular advantage to the religion of Numa; and ROME her-self, the celestial genius that presided over the fates of the city, is introduced by the orator to plead her own cause before the tribunal of the emperors. "Most excellent princes," says the venerable matron, "fathers of your country! pity and respect my age, which has hitherto flowed in an uninterrupted course of piety. Since I do not repent, permit me to continue in the practice of my ancient rites. Since I am born free, allow me to enjoy my domestic institutions. This religion has reduced the world under my laws. These rites have repelled Hannibal from the city, and the Gauls from the Capitol. Were my grey hairs reserved for such intolerable disgrace? I am ignorant of the new system that I am required to adopt; but I am well assured that the correction of old age is always an ungrateful and ignominious office." The fears of the people supplied what the discretion of the orator had suppressed; and the calamities which afflicted or threatened the declining empire were unanimously imputed by the Pagans to the new religion of Christ and of Constantine.

But the hopes of Symmachus were repeatedly baffled by the firm and dexterous opposition of the archbishop of Milan, who fortified the emperors against the fallacious eloquence of the advocate of Rome. In this controversy Ambrose condescends to speak the language of a philosopher, and to ask, with some contempt, why it should be thought necessary to introduce an imaginary and invisible power as the cause of those victories, which were sufficiently explained by the valour and discipline of the legions. He justly derides the absurd reverence for antiquity, which could only tend to discourage the improvements of art and to replunge the human race into their original barbarism. From thence gradually rising to a more lofty and theological tone, he pronounces that Christianity alone is the doctrine of truth and salvation, and that every mode of Polytheism conducts its deluded votaries through the paths of error to the abyss of eternal perdition. Arguments like these, when they were suggested by a favourite bishop, had power to prevent the restoration of the altar of Victory; but the same arguments fell with much more energy and effect from the mouth of a conqueror, and the gods of antiquity were dragged in triumph at the chariot-wheels of Theodosius. In a full meeting of the senate the emperor proposed, according to the forms of the republic, the important question, whether the worship of Jupiter or that of Christ should be the religion of the Romans? The liberty of suffrages, which he affected to allow, was destroyed by the hopes and fears that his presence inspired; and the arbitrary exile of Symmachus was a recent admonition that it might be dangerous to oppose the wishes of the monarch. On a regular division of the senate, Jupiter was condemned and degraded by the sense of a very large majority; and it is rather surprising that any members should be found bold enough to declare, by their speeches and votes, that they were still attached to the interest of an abdicated deity. The hasty conversion of the senate must be attributed either to supernatural or to sordid motives; and many of these reluctant proselytes betrayed, on every favourable occasion, their secret disposition to throw aside the mask of odious dissimulation. But they were gradually fixed in the new religion, as the cause of the ancient became more hopeless; they yielded to the authority of the emperor, to the fashion of the times, and to the entreaties of their wives and children, who were instigated and governed by the clergy of Rome and the monks of the East. The edifying example of the Anician family was soon imitated by the rest of the nobility: the Bassi, the Paullini, the Gracchi, embraced the Christian religion; and "the luminaries of the world, the venerable assembly of Catos (such are the high-flown expressions of Prudentius), were impatient to strip themselves of their pontifical garment; to cast the skin of the old serpent; to assume the snowy robes of baptismal innocence; and to humble the pride of the consular fasces before the tombs of the martyrs." The citizens, who subsisted by their own industry, and the populace, who were supported by the public liberality, filled the churches of the Lateran and Vatican with an incessant throng of devout proselytes. The decrees of the senate, which proscribed the worship of idols, were ratified by the general consent of the Romans; the splendour of the Capitol was defaced, and the solitary temples were abandoned to ruin and contempt. Rome submitted to the yoke of the Gospel; and the vanquished provinces had not yet lost their reverence for the name and authority of Rome.

The filial piety of the emperors themselves engaged them to proceed with some caution and tenderness in the reformation of the eternal city. Those absolute monarchs acted with less regard to the prejudices of the provincials. The pious labour, which had been suspended near twenty years since the death of Constantius, was vigorously resumed, and finally accomplished, by the zeal of Theodosius. Whilst that warlike prince yet struggled with the Goths, not for the glory, but for the safety of the republic, he ventured to offend a considerable party of his subjects, by some acts which might perhaps secure the protection of Heaven, but which must seem rash and unseasonable in the eye of human prudence. The success of his first experiments against the Pagans encouraged the pious emperor to reiterate and enforce his edicts of proscription: the same laws which had been originally published in the provinces of the East, were applied, after the defeat of Maximus, to the whole extent of the Western empire; and every victory of the orthodox Theodosius contributed to the triumph of the Christian and catholic faith. He attacked superstition in her most vital part, by prohibiting the use of sacrifices, which he declared to be criminal as well as infamous; and if the terms of his edicts more strictly condemned the impious curiosity which examined the entrails of the victims, every subsequent explanation tended to involve in the same guilt the general practice of *immolation*, which essentially constituted the religion of the Pagans. As the temples had been erected for the purpose of sacrifice, it was the duty of a benevolent prince to remove from his subjects the dangerous temptation of offending against the laws which he had enacted. A special commission was granted to Cynegius, the Prætorian prefect of the East, and afterwards to the counts Jovius and Gaudentius, two officers of distinguished rank in the West, by which they were directed to shut the temples, to seize or destroy the instruments of idolatry, to abolish the privileges of the priests, and to confiscate the consecrated property for the benefit of the emperor, of the church, or of the army. Here the desolation might have stopped: and the naked edifices, which were no longer employed in the service of idolatry, might have been protected from the destructive rage of fanaticism. Many of those temples were the most splendid and beautiful monuments of Grecian architecture: and the emperor himself was interested not to deface the splendour of his own cities, or to diminish the value of his own possessions. Those stately edifices might be suffered to remain, as so many lasting trophies of the victory of Christ. In the decline of the arts, they might be usefully converted into magazines, manufactures, or places of public assembly: and perhaps, when the walls of the temple had been sufficiently purified by holy rites, the worship of the true Deity might be allowed to expiate the ancient guilt of idolatry. But as long as they subsisted, the Pagans fondly cherished the secret hope that an auspicious revolution, a second Julian, might again restore the altars of the gods: and the earnestness with which they addressed their unavailing prayers to the throne increased the zeal of the Christian reformers to extirpate, without mercy, the root of superstition. The laws of the emperors exhibit some symptoms of a milder disposition: but their cold and languid efforts were insufficient to stem the torrent of enthusiasm and rapine, which was conducted, or rather impelled, by the spiritual rulers of the church. In Gaul, the holy Martin, bishop of Tours,[1] marched at the head of his faithful monks to destroy the idols, the temples, and the consecrated trees of his extensive diocese; and, in the execution of this arduous task, the prudent reader will judge whether Martin was supported by the aid of miraculous powers or of carnal weapons. In Syria, the divine and excellent Marcellus, as he is styled by Theodoret, a bishop animated with apostolic fervour, resolved to level with the ground the stately temples within the diocese of Apamea. His attack was resisted by the skill and solidity with which the temple of Jupiter had been constructed. The building was seated on an eminence: on each of the four sides the lofty roof was supported by fifteen massy columns, sixteen feet in circumference; and the large stones of which they were composed were firmly cemented with lead and iron. The force of the strongest and sharpest tools had been tried without effect. It was found necessary to undermine the foundations of the columns, which fell down as soon as the temporary wooden props had

---

[1] See the Life of Martin by Sulpicius Severus. The saint once mistook (as Don Quixote might have done) an harmless funeral for an idolatrous procession, and imprudently committed a miracle.

been consumed with fire; and the difficulties of the enterprise are
described under the allegory of a black dæmon, who retarded, though he
could not defeat, the operations of the Christian engineers. Elated with
victory, Marcellus took the field in person against the powers of darkness; a numerous troop of soldiers and gladiators marched under the
episcopal banner, and he successively attacked the villages and country
temples of the diocese of Apamea. Whenever any resistance or danger
was apprehended, the champion of the faith, whose lameness would not
allow him either to fight or fly, placed himself at a convenient distance,
beyond the reach of darts. But this prudence was the occasion of his
death; he was surprised and slain by a body of exasperated rustics; and
the synod of the province pronounced, without hesitation, that the holy
Marcellus had sacrificed his life in the cause of God. In the support of
this cause, the monks, who rushed with tumultuous fury from the
desert, distinguished themselves by their zeal and diligence. They deserved the enmity of the Pagans; and some of them might deserve the
reproaches of avarice and intemperance—of avarice, which they gratified
with holy plunder; and of intemperance, which they indulged at the expense of the people, who foolishly admired their tattered garments, loud
psalmody, and artificial paleness.[1] A small number of temples was
protected by the fears, the venality, the taste, or the prudence of the civil
and ecclesiastical governors. The temple of the Celestial Venus at
Carthage, whose sacred precincts formed a circumference of two miles,
was judiciously converted into a Christian church; and a similar consecration has preserved inviolate the majestic dome of the Pantheon at
Rome. But in almost every province of the Roman world, an army of
fanatics, without authority and without discipline, invaded the peaceful
inhabitants; and the ruin of the fairest structures of antiquity still displays the ravages of *those* barbarians who alone had time and inclination
to execute such laborious destruction.

THE DESTRUCTION OF THE TEMPLE OF SERAPIS

In this wide and various prospect of devastation, the spectator may
distinguish the ruins of the temple of Serapis, at Alexandria. Serapis
does not appear to have been one of the native gods, or monsters, who
sprung from the fruitful soil of superstitious Egypt. The first of the
Ptolemies had been commanded, by a dream, to import the mysterious
stranger from the coast of Pontus, where he had been long adored by
the inhabitants of Sinope; but his attributes and his reign were so imperfectly understood, that it became a subject of dispute whether he
represented the bright orb of day, or the gloomy monarch of the subterraneous regions. The Egyptians, who were obstinately devoted to the
religion of their fathers, refused to admit this foreign deity within the

[1] Libanius. He rails at these black-garbed men, the Christian monks, who eat
more than elephants. Poor elephants! *they* are temperate animals.

walls of their cities. But the obsequious priests, who were seduced by the liberality of the Ptolemies, submitted, without resistance, to the power of the god of Pontus: an honourable and domestic genealogy was provided; and this fortunate usurper was introduced into the throne and bed of Osiris, the husband of Isis, and the celestial monarch of Egypt. Alexandria, which claimed his peculiar protection, gloried in the name of the city of Serapis. His temple, which rivalled the pride and magnificence of the Capitol, was erected on the spacious summit of an artificial mount, raised one hundred steps above the level of the adjacent parts of the city; and the interior cavity was strongly supported by arches, and distributed into vaults and subterraneous apartments. The consecrated buildings were surrounded by a quadrangular portico; the stately halls and exquisite statues displayed the triumph of the arts; and the treasures of ancient learning were preserved in the famous Alexandrian library, which had arisen with new splendour from its ashes. After the edicts of Theodosius had severely prohibited the sacrifices of the Pagans, they were still tolerated in the city and temple of Serapis; and this singular indulgence was imprudently ascribed to the superstitious terrors of the Christians themselves: as if they had feared to abolish those ancient rites which could alone secure the inundations of the Nile, the harvests of Egypt, and the subsistence of Constantinople.

At that time the archiepiscopal throne of Alexandria was filled by Theophilus, the perpetual enemy of peace and virtue; a bold, bad man, whose hands were alternately polluted with gold and with blood. His pious indignation was excited by the honours of Serapis; and the insults which he offered to an ancient chapel of Bacchus convinced the Pagans that he meditated a more important and dangerous enterprise. In the tumultuous capital of Egypt, the slightest provocation was sufficient to inflame a civil war. The votaries of Serapis, whose strength and numbers were much inferior to those of their antagonists, rose in arms at the instigation of the philosopher Olympius, who exhorted them to die in the defence of the altars of the gods. These Pagan fanatics fortified themselves in the temple, or rather fortress, of Serapis; repelled the besiegers by daring sallies and resolute defence; and, by the inhuman cruelties which they exercised on their Christian prisoners, obtained the last consolation of despair. The efforts of the prudent magistrate were usefully exerted for the establishment of a truce till the answer of Theodosius should determine the fate of Serapis. The two parties assembled, without arms, in the principal square; and the Imperial rescript was publicly read. But when a sentence of destruction against the idols of Alexandria was pronounced, the Christians sent up a shout of joy and exultation, whilst the unfortunate Pagans, whose fury had given way to consternation, retired with hasty and silent steps, and eluded, by their flight or obscurity, the resentment of their enemies. Theophilus proceeded to demolish the temple of Serapis, without any other difficulties

than those which he found in the weight and solidity of the materials;
but these obstacles proved so insuperable, that he was obliged to leave
the foundations, and to content himself with reducing the edifice itself
to a heap of rubbish, a part of which was soon afterwards cleared away,
to make room for a church erected in honour of the Christian martyrs.
The valuable library of Alexandria was pillaged or destroyed; and near
twenty years afterwards, the appearance of the empty shelves excited
the regret and indignation of every spectator whose mind was not totally
darkened by religious prejudice. The compositions of ancient genius,
so many of which have irretrievably perished, might surely have been
excepted from the wreck of idolatry, for the amusement and instruction
of succeeding ages; and either the zeal or the avarice of the archbishop
might have been satiated with the rich spoils which were the reward of
his victory. While the images and vases of gold and silver were carefully
melted, and those of a less valuable metal were contemptuously broken
and cast into the streets, Theophilus laboured to expose the frauds and
vices of the ministers of the idols: their dexterity in the management of
the loadstone; their secret methods of introducing an human actor into
a hollow statue; and their scandalous abuse of the confidence of devout
husbands and unsuspecting females.[1] Charges like these may seem to
deserve some degree of credit, as they are not repugnant to the crafty
and interested spirit of superstition. But the same spirit is equally prone
to the base practice of insulting and calumniating a fallen enemy; and
our belief is naturally checked by the reflection that it is much less
difficult to invent a fictitious story than to support a practical fraud.
The colossal statue of Serapis was involved in the ruin of his temple and
religion. A great number of plates of different metals, artificially joined
together, composed the majestic figure of the deity, who touched on
either side the walls of the sanctuary. The aspect of Serapis, his sitting
posture, and the sceptre which he bore in his left hand, were extremely
similar to the ordinary representations of Jupiter. He was distinguished
from Jupiter by the basket, or bushel, which was placed on his head;
and by the emblematic monster which he held in his right hand; the
head and body of a serpent branching into three tails, which were again
terminated by the triple heads of a dog, a lion, and a wolf. It was confidently affirmed, that, if any impious hand should dare to violate the
majesty of the god, the heavens and the earth would instantly return to
their original chaos. An intrepid soldier, animated by zeal, and armed
with a weighty battle-axe, ascended the ladder; and even the Christian
multitude expected with some anxiety the event of the combat. He

---

[1] Rufinus names the priest of Saturn who, in the character of the god, familiarly
conversed with many pious ladies of quality; till he betrayed himself, in a moment of
transport, when he could not disguise the tone of his voice. The authentic and impartial narrative of Æschines, and the adventure of Mundus, may prove that such
amorous frauds have been practised with success.

aimed a vigorous stroke against the cheek of Serapis; the cheek fell to the ground; the thunder was still silent, and both the heavens and the earth continued to preserve their accustomed order and tranquillity. The victorious soldier repeated his blows: the huge idol was overthrown and broken in pieces; and the limbs of Serapis were ignominiously dragged through the streets of Alexandria. His mangled carcase was burnt in the amphitheatre, amidst the shouts of the populace; and many persons attributed their conversion to this discovery of the impotence of their tutelar deity. The popular modes of religion, that propose any visible and material objects of worship, have the advantage of adapting and familiarising themselves to the senses of mankind; but this advantage is counterbalanced by the various and inevitable accidents to which the faith of the idolater is exposed. It is scarcely possible that, in every disposition of mind, he should preserve his implicit reverence for the idols, or the relics, which the naked eye and the profane hand are unable to distinguish from the most common productions of art or nature; and if, in the hour of danger, their secret and miraculous virtue does not operate for their own preservation, he scorns the vain apologies of his priests, and justly derides the object and the folly of his superstitious attachment. After the fall of Serapis, some hopes were still entertained by the Pagans that the Nile would refuse his annual supply to the impious masters of Egypt; and the extraordinary delay of the inundation seemed to announce the displeasure of the river-god. But this delay was soon compensated by the rapid swell of the waters. They suddenly rose to such an unusual height as to comfort the discontented party with the pleasing expectation of a deluge; till the peaceful river again subsided to the well-known and fertilising level of sixteen cubits, or about thirty English feet.

THE PROHIBITION OF PAGAN RITES

The temples of the Roman empire were deserted or destroyed; but the ingenious superstition of the Pagans still attempted to elude the laws of Theodosius, by which all sacrifices had been severely prohibited. The inhabitants of the country, whose conduct was less exposed to the eye of malicious curiosity, disguised their *religious* under the appearance of *convivial* meetings. On the days of solemn festivals they assembled in great numbers under the spreading shade of some consecrated trees; sheep and oxen were slaughtered and roasted; and this rural entertainment was sanctified by the use of incense and by the hymns which were sung in honour of the gods. But it was alleged that, as no part of the animal was made a burnt-offering, as no altar was provided to receive the blood, and as the previous oblation of salt-cakes and the concluding ceremony of libations were carefully omitted, these festal meetings did not involve the guests in the guilt or penalty of an illegal sacrifice.

Whatever might be the truth of the facts or the merit of the distinction, these vain pretences were swept away by the last edict of Theodosius, which inflicted a deadly wound on the superstition of the Pagans. This prohibitory law is expressed in the most absolute and comprehensive terms. "It is our will and pleasure," says the emperor, "that none of our subjects, whether magistrates or private citizens, however exalted or however humble may be their rank and condition, shall presume in any city or in any place to worship an inanimate idol by the sacrifice of a guiltless victim." The act of sacrificing and the practice of divination by the entrails of the victim are declared (without any regard to the object of the inquiry) a crime of high-treason against the state, which can be expiated only by the death of the guilty. The rites of Pagan superstition which might seem less bloody and atrocious are abolished as highly injurious to the truth and honour of religion; luminaries, garlands, frankincense, and libations of wine are specially enumerated and condemned; and the harmless claims of the domestic genius, of the household gods are included in this rigorous proscription. The use of any of these profane and illegal ceremonies subjects the offender to the forfeiture of the house or estate where they have been performed; and if he has artfully chosen the property of another for the scene of his impiety, he is compelled to discharge, without delay, a heavy fine of twenty-five pounds of gold, or more than one thousand pounds sterling. A fine not less considerable is imposed on the connivance of the secret enemies of religion who shall neglect the duty of their respective stations, either to reveal or to punish the guilt of idolatry. Such was the persecuting spirit of the laws of Theodosius, which were repeatedly enforced by his sons and grandsons, with the loud and unanimous applause of the Christian world.

In the cruel reigns of Decius and Diocletian Christianity had been proscribed, as a revolt from the ancient and hereditary religion of the empire; and the unjust suspicions which were entertained of a dark and dangerous faction were in some measure countenanced by the inseparable union and rapid conquests of the catholic church. But the same excuses of fear and ignorance cannot be applied to the Christian emperors, who violated the precepts of humanity and of the Gospel. The experience of ages had betrayed the weakness as well as folly of Paganism; the light of reason and of faith had already exposed to the greatest part of mankind the vanity of idols; and the declining sect, which still adhered to their worship, might have been permitted to enjoy in peace and obscurity the religious customs of their ancestors. Had the Pagans been animated by the undaunted zeal which possessed the minds of the primitive believers, the triumph of the church must have been stained with blood; and the martyrs of Jupiter and Apollo might have embraced the glorious opportunity of devoting their lives and fortunes at the foot of their altars. But such obstinate zeal was not congenial to the loose and careless temper of Polytheism. The violent and repeated strokes of the orthodox princes were broken by the soft and yielding substance against which they were directed; and the ready obedience of the Pagans protected them from the pains and penalties of the Theodosian Code. Instead of asserting that the authority of the gods was superior to that of the emperor, they desisted, with a plaintive murmur, from the use of those sacred rites which their sovereign had condemned. If they were sometimes tempted by a sally of passion, or by the hopes of concealment, to indulge their favourite superstition, their humble repentance disarmed the severity of the Christian magistrate, and they seldom refused to atone for their rashness by submitting, with some secret reluctance, to the yoke of the Gospel. The churches were filled with the increasing multitude of these unworthy proselytes, who had conformed, from temporal motives, to the reigning religion; and whilst they devoutly imitated the postures and recited the prayers of the faithful, they satisfied their conscience by the silent and sincere invocation of the gods of antiquity. If the Pagans wanted patience to suffer, they wanted spirit to resist; and the scattered myriads, who deplored the ruin of the temples, yielded, without a contest, to the fortune of their adversaries. The disorderly opposition of the peasants of Syria and the populace of Alexandria to the rage of private fanaticism was silenced by the name and authority of the emperor. The Pagans of the West, without contributing to the elevation of Eugenius, disgraced by their partial attachment the cause and character of the usurper. The clergy vehemently exclaimed that he aggravated the crime of rebellion by the guilt of apostacy; that, by his permission, the altar of Victory was again restored; and that the idolatrous symbols of Jupiter and Hercules were displayed in the field against the invincible standard of the cross. But the vain hopes of the Pagans were soon annihilated by the defeat of Eugenius; and they were left exposed to the resentment of the conqueror, who laboured to deserve the favour of Heaven by the extirpation of idolatry.

A nation of slaves is always prepared to applaud the clemency of their master who, in the abuse of absolute power, does not proceed to the last extremes of injustice and oppression. Theodosius might undoubtedly have proposed to his Pagan subjects the alternative of baptism or of death; and the eloquent Libanius has praised the moderation of a prince who never enacted, by any positive law, that all his subjects should immediately embrace and practise the religion of their sovereign. The profession of Christianity was not made an essential qualification for the enjoyment of the civil rights of society, nor were any peculiar hardships imposed on the sectaries who credulously received the fables of Ovid and obstinately rejected the miracles of the Gospel. The palace, the schools, the army, and the senate were filled with declared and devout Pagans; they obtained, without distinction, the civil and military honours of the empire. Theodosius distinguished his liberal regard for virtue and genius by the consular dignity which he bestowed on Symmachus, and by the personal friendship which he expressed to Libanius; and the two eloquent apologists of Paganism were never required either to change or to dissemble their religious opinions. The Pagans were indulged in the most licentious freedom of speech and writing; the historical and philosophic remains of Eunapius, Zosimus, and the fanatic teachers of the school of Plato, betray the most furious animosity, and contain the sharpest invectives, against the sentiments and conduct of their victorious adversaries. If these audacious libels were publicly known, we must applaud the good sense of the Christian princes, who viewed with a smile of contempt the last struggles of superstition and despair. But the Imperial laws which prohibited the sacrifices and ceremonies of Paganism were rigidly executed; and every hour contributed to destroy the influence of a religion which was supported by custom rather than by argument. The devotion of the poet or the philosopher may be secretly nourished by prayer, meditation, and study; but the exercise of public worship appears to be the only solid foundation of the religious sentiments of the people, which derive their force from imitation and habit. The interruption of that public exercise may consummate, in the period of a few years, the important work of a national revolution. The memory of theological opinions cannot long be preserved without the artificial helps of priests, of temples, and of books. The ignorant vulgar, whose minds are still agitated by the blind hopes and terrors of superstition, will be soon persuaded by their superiors to direct their vows to the reigning deities of the age; and will insensibly imbibe an ardent zeal for the support and propagation of the new doctrine, which spiritual hunger at first compelled them to accept. The generation that arose in the world after the promulgation of the Imperial laws was attracted within the pale of the catholic church: and so rapid, yet so gentle, was the fall of Paganism, that only twenty-eight years after the death of Theodosius the faint and minute vestiges were no longer visible to the eye of the legislator.

WORSHIP OF THE CHRISTIAN MARTYRS AND REVIVAL OF POLYTHEISTIC PRACTICES

The ruin of the Pagan religion is described by the sophists as a dreadful and amazing prodigy, which covered the earth with darkness and restored the ancient dominion of chaos and of night. They relate in solemn and pathetic strains that the temples were converted into sepulchres, and that the holy places, which had been adorned by the statues of the gods, were basely polluted by the relics of Christian martyrs. "The monks" (a race of filthy animals, to whom Eunapius is tempted to refuse the name of men) "are the authors of the new worship, which, in the place of those deities who are conceived by the understanding, has substituted the meanest and most contemptible slaves. The heads, salted and pickled, of those infamous malefactors, who for the multitude of their crimes have suffered a just and ignominious death; their bodies, still marked by the impression of the lash and the scars of those tortures which were inflicted by the sentence of the magistrate; such" (continues Eunapius) "are the gods which the earth produces in our days; such are the martyrs, the supreme arbitrators of our prayers and petitions to the Deity, whose tombs are now consecrated as the objects of the veneration of the people." Without approving the malice, it is natural enough to share the surprise of the sophist, the spectator of a revolution which raised those obscure victims of the laws of Rome to the rank of celestial and invisible protectors of the Roman empire. The grateful respect of the Christians for the martyrs of the faith was exalted, by time and victory, into religious adoration; and the most illustrious of the saints and prophets were deservedly associated to the honours of the martyrs. One hundred and fifty years after the glorious deaths of St. Peter and St. Paul, the Vatican and the Ostian road were distinguished by the tombs, or rather by the trophies, of those spiritual heroes. In the age which followed the conversion of Constantine, the emperors, the consuls, and the generals of armies devoutly visited the sepulchres of a tentmaker and a fisherman; and their venerable bones were deposited under the altars of Christ, on which the bishops of the royal city continually offered the unbloody sacrifice. The new capital of the Eastern world, unable to produce any ancient and domestic trophies, was enriched by the spoils of dependent provinces. The bodies of St. Andrew, St. Luke, and St. Timothy had reposed near three hundred years in the obscure graves from whence they were transported, in solemn pomp, to the church of the apostles, which the magnificence of Constantine had founded on the banks of the Thracian Bosphorus. About fifty years afterwards the same banks were honoured by the presence of Samuel, the judge and prophet of the people of Israel. His ashes, deposited in a golden vase, and covered with a silken veil, were delivered by the bishops into each other's hands. The relics of Samuel were received by the people with the same joy and reverence which they would have shown to the living prophet; the highways, from Palestine to the gates of Constantinople, were filled with an uninterrupted procession; and the emperor Arcadius himself, at the head of the most illustrious members of the clergy and senate, advanced to meet his extraordinary guest, who had always deserved and claimed the homage of kings. The example of Rome and Constantinople confirmed the faith and discipline of the catholic world. The honours of the saints and martyrs, after a feeble and ineffectual murmur of profane reason, were universally established; and in the age of Ambrose and Jerom something was still deemed wanting to the sanctity of a Christian church, till it had been consecrated by some portion of holy relics, which fixed and inflamed the devotion of the faithful. In the long period of twelve hundred years, which elapsed between the reign of Constantine and the reformation of Luther, the worship of saints and relics corrupted the pure and perfect simplicity of the Christian model: and some symptoms of degeneracy may be observed even in the first generations which adopted and cherished this pernicious innovation.

I. The satisfactory experience that the relics of saints were more valuable than gold or precious stones stimulated the clergy to multiply the treasures of the church. Without much regard for truth or probability, they invented names for skeletons, and actions for names. The fame of the apostles, and of the holy men who had imitated their virtues, was darkened by religious fiction. To the invincible band of genuine and primitive martyrs they added myriads of imaginary heroes, who had never existed, except in the fancy of crafty or credulous legendaries; and there is reason to suspect that Tours might not be the only diocese in which the bones of a malefactor were adored instead of those of a saint.[1] A superstitious practice, which tended to increase the temptations of fraud and credulity, insensibly extinguished the light of history and of reason in the Christian world.

II. But the progress of superstition would have been much less rapid and victorious if the faith of the people had not been assisted by the seasonable aid of visions and miracles to ascertain the authenticity and virtue of the most suspicious relics. In the reign of the younger Theodosius, Lucian, a presbyter of Jerusalem, and the ecclesiastical minister of the village of Caphargamala, about twenty miles from the city, related a very singular dream, which, to remove his doubts, had been repeated on three successive Saturdays. A venerable figure stood before him, in the silence of the night, with a long beard, a white robe, and a gold rod; announced himself by the name of Gamaliel; and revealed to the astonished presbyter, that his own corpse, with the bodies of his son Abibas, his friend Nicodemus, and the illustrious Stephen, the first martyr of the Christian faith, were secretly buried in the adjacent field. He added, with some impatience, that it was time to release himself and his companions from their obscure prison; that their appearance would be salutary to a distressed world; and that they had made choice of Lucian to inform the bishop of Jerusalem of their situation and their wishes. The doubts and difficulties which still retarded this important discovery were successively removed by new visions; and the ground was opened by the bishop, in the presence of an innumerable multitude. The coffins of Gamaliel, of his son, and of his friend, were found in regular order; but when the fourth coffin, which contained the remains of

---

[1] Martin of Tours extorted this confession from the mouth of the dead man. The error is allowed to be natural; the discovery is supposed to be miraculous. Which of the two was likely to happen most frequently?

Stephen, was shown to the light, the earth trembled, and an odour such as that of Paradise was smelt, which instantly cured the various diseases of seventy-three of the assistants. The companions of Stephen were left in their peaceful residence of Caphargamala; but the relics of the first martyr were transported, in solemn procession, to a church constructed in their honour on Mount Sion; and the minute particles of those relics, a drop of blood,[1] or the scrapings of a bone, were acknowledged, in almost every province of the Roman world, to possess a divine and miraculous virtue. The grave and learned Augustin,[2] whose understanding scarcely admits the excuse of credulity, has attested the innumerable prodigies which were performed in Africa by the relics of St. Stephen; and this marvellous narrative is inserted in the elaborate work of the City of God, which the bishop of Hippo designed as a solid and immortal proof of the truth of Christianity. Augustin solemnly declares that he has selected those miracles only which were publicly certified by the persons who were either the objects, or the spectators, of the power of the martyr. Many prodigies were omitted or forgotten; and Hippo had been less favourably treated than the other cities of the province. And yet the bishop enumerates above seventy miracles, of which three were resurrections from the dead, in the space of two years, and within the limits of his own diocese.[3] If we enlarge our view to all the dioceses, and all the saints, of the Christian world, it will not be easy to calculate the fables, and the errors, which issued from this inexhaustible source. But we may surely be allowed to observe that a miracle, in that age of superstition and credulity, lost its name and its merit, since it could scarcely be considered as a deviation from the ordinary and established laws of nature.

III. The innumerable miracles, of which the tombs of the martyrs were the perpetual theatre, revealed to the pious believer the actual state and constitution of the invisible world; and his religious speculations appeared to be founded on the firm basis of fact and experience. Whatever might be the condition of vulgar souls in the long interval between the dissolution and the resurrection of their bodies, it was evident that the superior spirits of the saints and martyrs did not consume that portion of their existence in silent and inglorious sleep. It was evident (without presuming to determine the place of their habitation, or the

[1] A phial of St. Stephen's blood was annually liquefied at Naples till he was superseded by St. Januarius.

[2] Augustin composed the two-and-twenty books de Civitate Dei in the space of thirteen years, A.D. 413–426. His learning is too often borrowed, and his arguments are too often his own; but the whole work claims the merit of a magnificent design, vigorously, and not unskilfully, executed.

[3] See Augustin de Civitate Dei, l. xxii. c. 22, and the Appendix, which contains two books of St. Stephen's miracles, by Evodius, bishop of Uzalis. Freculphus has preserved a Gallic or Spanish proverb, "Whoever pretends to have read all the miracles of St. Stephen, he lies."

nature of their felicity) that they enjoyed the lively and active consciousness of their happiness, their virtue, and their powers; and that they had
already secured the possession of their eternal reward. The enlargement
of their intellectual faculties surpassed the measure of the human imagination; since it was proved by *experience* that they were capable of
hearing and understanding the various petitions of their numerous
votaries, who, in the same moment of time, but in the most distant parts
of the world, invoked the name and assistance of Stephen or of Martin.
The confidence of their petitioners was founded on the persuasion that
the saints, who reigned with Christ, cast an eye of pity upon earth; that
they were warmly interested in the prosperity of the catholic church; and
that the individuals who imitated the example of their faith and piety
were the peculiar and favourite objects of their most tender regard.
Sometimes, indeed, their friendship might be influenced by considerations of a less exalted kind: they viewed with partial affection the places
which had been consecrated by their birth, their residence, their death,
their burial, or the possession of their relics. The meaner passions of
pride, avarice, and revenge, may be deemed unworthy of a celestial
breast; yet the saints themselves condescended to testify their grateful
approbation of the liberality of their votaries; and the sharpest bolts of
punishment were hurled against those impious wretches who violated
their magnificent shrines, or disbelieved their supernatural power.
Atrocious, indeed, must have been the guilt, and strange would have
been the scepticism, of those men, if they had obstinately resisted the
proofs of a divine agency, which the elements, the whole range of
the animal creation, and even the subtle and invisible operations of the
human mind, were compelled to obey. The immediate, and almost in-
stantaneous, effects, that were supposed to follow the prayer, or the
offence, satisfied the Christians of the ample measure of favour and
authority which the saints enjoyed in the presence of the Supreme God;
and it seemed almost superfluous to inquire whether they were continually obliged to intercede before the throne of grace, or whether they
might not be permitted to exercise, according to the dictates of their
benevolence and justice, the delegated powers of their subordinate
ministry. The imagination, which had been raised by a painful effort to
the contemplation and worship of the Universal Cause, eagerly embraced such inferior objects of adoration as were more proportioned to
its gross conceptions and imperfect faculties. The sublime and simple
theology of the primitive Christians was gradually corrupted: and the
MONARCHY of heaven, already clouded by metaphysical subtleties, was
degraded by the introduction of a popular mythology, which tended to
restore the reign of polytheism.

IV. As the objects of religion were gradually reduced to the standard
of the imagination, the rites and ceremonies were introduced that seemed
most powerfully to affect the senses of the vulgar. If, in the beginning of

the fifth century, Tertullian, or Lactantius, had been suddenly raised from the dead, to assist at the festival of some popular saint or martyr, they would have gazed with astonishment and indignation on the profane spectacle which had succeeded to the pure and spiritual worship of a Christian congregation. As soon as the doors of the church were thrown open, they must have been offended by the smoke of incense, the perfume of flowers, and the glare of lamps and tapers, which diffused, at noon-day, a gaudy, superfluous, and, in their opinion, a sacrilegious light. If they approached the balustrade of the altar, they made their way through the prostrate crowd, consisting, for the most part, of strangers and pilgrims, who resorted to the city on the vigil of the feast; and who already felt the strong intoxication of fanaticism, and, perhaps, of wine. Their devout kisses were imprinted on the walls and pavement of the sacred edifice; and their fervent prayers were directed, whatever might be the language of their church, to the bones, the blood, or the ashes of the saint, which were usually concealed, by a linen or silken veil, from the eyes of the vulgar. The Christians frequented the tombs of the martyrs, in the hope of obtaining, from their powerful intercession, every sort of spiritual, but more especially of temporal, blessings. They implored the preservation of their health, or the cure of their infirmities; the fruitfulness of their barren wives, or the safety and happiness of their children. Whenever they undertook any distant or dangerous journey, they requested that the holy martyrs would be their guides and protectors on the road; and if they returned without having experienced any misfortune, they again hastened to the tombs of the martyrs, to celebrate, with grateful thanksgivings, their obligations to the memory and relics of those heavenly patrons. The walls were hung round with symbols of the favours which they had received; eyes, and hands, and feet, of gold and silver: and edifying pictures, which could not long escape the abuse of indiscreet or idolatrous devotion, represented the image, the attributes, and the miracles of the tutelar saint. The same uniform original spirit of superstition might suggest, in the most distant ages and countries, the same methods of deceiving the credulity, and of affecting the senses of mankind: but it must ingenuously be confessed that the ministers of the catholic church imitated the profane model which they were impatient to destroy. The most respectable bishops had persuaded themselves that the ignorant rustics would more cheerfully renounce the superstitions of Paganism, if they found some resemblance, some compensation, in the bosom of Christianity. The religion of Constantine achieved, in less than a century, the final conquest of the Roman empire: but the victors themselves were insensibly subdued by the arts of their vanquished rivals.

After Theodosius the western and eastern halves of the empire were finally separated. His sons Arcadius and Honorius ruled respectively in the East and the West. Honorius was a feeble character and the dominant figures in the West were his administrator Rufinus and Stilicho, a Vandal, able both as a general and a negotiator. His part in the latter role is obscure, and in his campaigns he was thwarted by the growing antipathy between the East and West.

In the years from 395 to 398 the Goths under Alaric invaded Greece and were almost cut off in the Peloponnese. Alaric extricated himself with Stilicho's connivance, made a secret agreement with the eastern government, was made master general of the forces in eastern Illyria and was proclaimed King of the Visigoths. Alaric made a first incursion into Italy but was repulsed. Honorius celebrated a triumph in Rome and then fixed his residence at Ravenna. In 406 Radagaisus invaded Italy. His army was destroyed by Stilicho, who opened negotiations with Alaric but was overthrown by a palace intrigue and put to death.

These events are described by Gibbon in Chapters 29 and 30.

THE GREAT INVASIONS

Chapter 31

INVASION OF ITALY BY ALARIC. CHARACTER OF THE
NOBLES AND PEOPLE OF ROME. THREE SIEGES AND SACK
OF ROME. RETREAT OF THE GOTHS AND DEATH OF ALARIC

THE incapacity of weak and distracted government may often assume the appearance and produce the effects of a treasonable correspondence with the public enemy. If Alaric himself had been introduced into the council of Ravenna, he would probably have advised the same measures which were actually pursued by the ministers of Honorius. The king of the Goths would have conspired, perhaps with some reluctance, to destroy the formidable adversary by whose arms, in Italy as well as in Greece, he had been twice overthrown. *Their* active and interested hatred laboriously accomplished the disgrace and ruin of the great Stilicho. The valour of Sarus, his fame in arms, and his personal or hereditary influence over the confederate barbarians, could recommend him only to the friends of their country who despised or detested the worthless characters of Turpilio, Varanes, and Vigilantius. By the pressing instances of the new favourites, these generals, unworthy as they had shown themselves of the name of soldiers, were promoted to the command of the cavalry, of the infantry, and of the domestic troops. The Gothic prince would have subscribed with pleasure the edict which the fanaticism of Olympius dictated to the simple and devout emperor. Honorius excluded all persons who were adverse to the catholic church from holding any office in the state; obstinately rejected the service of all those who dissented from his religion; and rashly disqualified many of his bravest and most skilful officers who adhered to the Pagan worship or who had imbibed the opinions of Arianism. These measures, so advantageous to an enemy, Alaric would have approved, and might perhaps have suggested; but it may seem doubtful whether the barbarian would have promoted his interest at the expense of the inhuman and absurd cruelty which was perpetrated by the direction, or at least with the connivance, of the Imperial ministers. The foreign auxiliaries who had been attached to the person of Stilicho lamented his death; but the desire of revenge was checked by a natural apprehension for the safety of their wives and children, who were detained as hostages in the strong cities of Italy, where they had likewise deposited their most valuable effects. At the same hour, and as if by a common signal, the cities of Italy were polluted by the same horrid scenes of universal massacre and pillage, which involved in promiscuous destruction the families and fortunes of the barbarians. Exasperated by such an injury, which might have awakened the tamest and most servile spirit, they cast a look of indignation and hope towards the camp of Alaric, and unanimously swore to pursue with just and implacable war the perfidious nation that had so basely violated the laws of hospitality. By the imprudent conduct of the ministers of Honorius the republic lost the assistance, and deserved the enmity, of thirty thousand of her bravest soldiers; and the weight of that formidable army, which alone might have determined the event of the war, was transferred from the scale of the Romans into that of the Goths.

In the arts of negociation, as well as in those of war, the Gothic king maintained his superior ascendant over an enemy whose seeming changes proceeded from the total want of counsel and design. From his camp, on the confines of Italy, Alaric attentively observed the revolutions of the palace, watched the progress of faction and discontent, disguised the hostile aspect of a barbarian invader, and assumed the more popular appearance of the friend and ally of the great Stilicho; to whose virtues, when they were no longer formidable, he could pay a just tribute of sincere praise and regret. The pressing invitation of the malcontents, who urged the king of the Goths to invade Italy, was enforced by a lively sense of his personal injuries; and he might speciously complain that the Imperial ministers still delayed and eluded the payment of the four thousand pounds of gold which had been granted by the Roman senate either to reward his services or to appease his fury. His decent firmness was supported by an artful moderation, which contributed to the success of his designs. He required a fair and reasonable satisfaction; but he gave the strongest assurances that, as soon as he had obtained it, he would immediately retire. He refused to trust the faith of the Romans, unless Aëtius and Jason, the sons of two great officers of state, were sent as hostages to his camp: but he offered to deliver in exchange several of the noblest youths of the Gothic nation. The modesty of Alaric was interpreted by the ministers of Ravenna as a sure evidence of his weakness and fear. They disdained either to negociate a treaty or to assemble an army; and with a rash confidence, derived only from their ignorance of the extreme danger, irretrievably wasted the decisive moments of peace and war. While they expected, in sullen silence, that the barbarians should evacuate the confines of Italy, Alaric, with bold and rapid marches, passed the Alps and the Po; hastily pillaged the cities of Aquileia, Altinum, Concordia, and Cremona, which yielded to his arms; increased his forces by the accession of thirty thousand auxiliaries; and, without meeting a single enemy in the field, advanced as far as the edge of the morass which protected the impregnable residence of the emperor of the West. Instead of attempting the hopeless siege of Ravenna, the prudent leader of the Goths proceeded to Rimini, stretched his ravages along the sea-coast of the Adriatic, and meditated the conquest of the ancient mistress of the world. An Italian hermit, whose zeal and sanctity were respected by the barbarians themselves, encountered the victorious monarch, and boldly denounced the indignation of Heaven against the oppressors of the earth: but the saint himself was confounded by the solemn asseveration of Alaric that he felt a secret and preternatural impulse, which directed, and even compelled, his march to the gates of Rome. He felt that his genius and his fortune were equal to the most arduous enterprises; and the enthusiasm which he communicated to the Goths insensibly removed the popular and almost superstitious reverence of the nations for the majesty of the Roman name. His troops, animated by the hopes of spoil, followed the course of the Flaminian way, occupied the unguarded passes of the Apennine,[1] descended into the rich plains of Umbria; and, as they lay encamped on the banks of the Clitumnus, might wantonly slaughter and devour the milk-white oxen which had been so long reserved for the use of Roman triumphs. A lofty situation and a seasonable tempest of thunder and lightning preserved the little city of Narni: but the king of the Goths, despising the ignoble prey, still advanced with unabated vigour; and after he had passed through the stately arches, adorned with the spoils of barbaric victories, he pitched his camp under the walls of Rome.

During a period of six hundred and nineteen years the seat of empire had never been violated by the presence of a foreign enemy. The unsuccessful expedition of Hannibal served only to display the character of the senate and people; of a senate degraded, rather than ennobled, by the comparison of an assembly of kings; and of a people to whom the ambassador of Pyrrhus ascribed the inexhaustible resources of the Hydra. Each of the senators in the time of the Punic war had accomplished his term of military service, either in a subordinate or a superior station; and the decree which invested with temporary command all those who had been consuls, or censors, or dictators, gave the republic the immediate assistance of many brave and experienced generals. In the beginning of the war the Roman people consisted of two hundred and fifty thousand citizens of an age to bear arms. Fifty thousand had already died in the defence of their country; and the twenty-three legions which were employed in the different camps of Italy, Greece, Sardinia, Sicily, and Spain, required about one hundred thousand men. But there still remained an equal number in Rome and the adjacent territory who were animated by the same intrepid courage; and every citizen was trained from his earliest youth in the discipline and exercises of a soldier. Hannibal was astonished by the constancy of the senate, who, without

---

[1] Addison has given a very picturesque description of the road through the Apennine. The Goths were not at leisure to observe the beauties of the prospect; but they were pleased to find that the Saxa Intercisa, a narrow passage which Vespasian had cut through the rock, was totally neglected.

raising the siege of Capua or recalling their scattered forces, expected his approach. He encamped on the banks of the Anio, at the distance of three miles from the city: and he was soon informed that the ground on which he had pitched his tent was sold for an adequate price at a public auction; and that a body of troops was dismissed by an opposite road to reinforce the legions of Spain. He led his Africans to the gates of Rome, where he found three armies in order of battle prepared to receive him; but Hannibal dreaded the event of a combat from which he could not hope to escape unless he destroyed the last of his enemies; and his speedy retreat confessed the invincible courage of the Romans.

THE CHARACTER OF THE ROMAN NOBLES

From the time of the Punic war the uninterrupted succession of senators had preserved the name and image of the republic; and the degenerate subjects of Honorius ambitiously derived their descent from the heroes who had repulsed the arms of Hannibal and subdued the nations of the earth. The temporal honours which the devout Paula inherited and despised are carefully recapitulated by Jerom, the guide of her conscience and the historian of her life. The genealogy of her father, Rogatus, which ascended as high as Agamemnon, might seem to betray a Grecian origin; but her mother, Blæsilla, numbered the Scipios, Æmilius Paulus, and the Gracchi in the list of her ancestors; and Toxotius, the husband of Paula, deduced his royal lineage from Æneas, the father of the Julian line. The vanity of the rich, who desired to be noble, was gratified by these lofty pretensions. Encouraged by the applause of their parasites, they easily imposed on the credulity of the vulgar; and were countenanced in some measure by the custom of adopting the name of their patron, which had always prevailed among the freedmen and clients of illustrious families. Most of those families, however, attacked by so many causes of external violence or internal decay, were gradually extirpated: and it would be more reasonable to seek for a lineal descent of twenty generations among the mountains of the Alps or in the peaceful solitude of Apulia, than on the theatre of Rome, the seat of fortune, of danger, and of perpetual revolutions. Under each successive reign and from every province of the empire a crowd of hardy adventurers, rising to eminence by their talents or their vices, usurped the wealth, the honours, and the palaces of Rome; and oppressed or protected the poor and humble remains of consular families, who were ignorant, perhaps, of the glory of their ancestors.

In the time of Jerom and Claudian the senators unanimously yielded the pre-eminence to the Anician line; and a slight view of *their* history will serve to appreciate the rank and antiquity of the noble families which contended only for the second place. During the five first ages of the city the name of the Anicians was unknown; they appear to have derived their origin from Præneste; and the ambition of those new citizens was long satisfied with the plebeian honours of tribunes of the people. One hundred and sixty-eight years before the Christian era the family was ennobled by the prætorship of Anicius, who gloriously terminated the Illyrian war by the conquest of the nation and the captivity of their king. From the triumph of that general three consulships in distant periods mark the succession of the Anician name. From the reign of Diocletian to the final extinction of the Western empire that name shone with a lustre which was not eclipsed in the public estimation by the majesty of the Imperial purple. The several branches to whom it was communicated united, by marriage or inheritance, the wealth and titles of the Annian, the Petronian, and the Olybrian houses; and in each generation the number of consulships was multiplied by an hereditary claim. The Anician family excelled in faith and in riches: they were the first of the Roman senate who embraced Christianity; and it is probable that Anicius Julian, who was afterwards consul and prefect of the city, atoned for his attachment to the party of Maxentius by the readiness with which he accepted the religion of Constantine. Their ample patrimony was increased by the industry of Probus, the chief of the Anician family, who shared with Gratian the honours of the consulship, and exercised four times the high office of Prætorian prefect. His immense estates were scattered over the wide extent of the Roman world; and though the public might suspect or disapprove the methods by which they had been acquired, the generosity and magnificence of that fortunate statesman deserved the gratitude of his clients and the admiration of strangers. Such was the respect entertained for his memory, that the two sons of Probus, in their earliest youth and at the request of the senate, were associated in the consular dignity: a memorable distinction, without example in the annals of Rome.

"The marbles of the Anician palace" were used as a proverbial expression of opulence and splendour; but the nobles and senators of Rome aspired in due gradation to imitate that illustrious family. The accurate description of the city, which was composed in the Theodosian age, enumerates one thousand seven hundred and eighty *houses*, the residence of wealthy and honourable citizens. Many of these stately mansions might almost excuse the exaggeration of the poet—that Rome contained a multitude of palaces, and that each palace was equal to a city: since it included within its own precincts everything which could be subservient either to use or luxury; markets, hippodromes, temples, fountains, baths, porticos, shady groves, and artificial aviaries. The historian Olympiodorus, who represents the state of Rome when it was besieged by the Goths, continues to observe that several of the richest senators received from their estates an annual income of four thousand pounds of gold, above one hundred and sixty thousand pounds sterling; without computing the stated provision of corn and wine, which, had they been sold, might have equalled in value one-third of the money.

Compared to this immoderate wealth, an ordinary revenue of a thousand or fifteen hundred pounds of gold might be considered as no more than adequate to the dignity of the senatorian rank, which required many expenses of a public and ostentatious kind. Several examples are recorded in the age of Honorius of vain and popular nobles who celebrated the year of their prætorship by a festival which lasted seven days and cost above one hundred thousand pounds sterling. The estates of the Roman senators, which so far exceed the proportion of modern wealth, were not confined to the limits of Italy. Their possessions extended far beyond the Ionian and Ægean seas to the most distant provinces: the city of Nicopolis, which Augustus had founded as an eternal monument of the Actian victory, was the property of the devout Paula; and it is observed by Seneca, that the rivers which had divided hostile nations now flowed through the lands of private citizens. According to their temper and circumstances, the estates of the Romans were either cultivated by the labour of their slaves, or granted, for a certain and stipulated rent, to the industrious farmer. The economical writers of antiquity strenuously recommend the former method wherever it may be practicable; but if the object should be removed by its distance or magnitude from the immediate eye of the master, they prefer the active care of an old hereditary tenant, attached to the soil and interested in the produce, to the mercenary administration of a negligent, perhaps an unfaithful, steward.

The opulent nobles of an immense capital, who were never excited by the pursuit of military glory, and seldom engaged in the occupations of civil government, naturally resigned their leisure to the business and amusements of private life. At Rome commerce was always held in contempt; but the senators, from the first age of the republic, increased their patrimony and multiplied their clients by the lucrative practice of usury, and the obsolete laws were eluded or violated by the mutual inclinations and interest of both parties. A considerable mass of treasure must always have existed at Rome, either in the current coin of the empire, or in the form of gold and silver plate; and there were many sideboards in the time of Pliny which contained more solid silver than had been transported by Scipio from vanquished Carthage. The greater part of the nobles, who dissipated their fortunes in profuse luxury, found themselves poor in the midst of wealth, and idle in a constant round of dissipation. Their desires were continually gratified by the labour of a thousand hands; of the numerous train of their domestic slaves, who were actuated by the fear of punishment; and of the various professions of artificers and merchants, who were more powerfully impelled by the hopes of gain. The ancients were destitute of many of the conveniences of life which have been invented or improved by the progress of industry; and the plenty of glass and linen has diffused more real comforts among the modern nations of Europe than the senators of Rome could derive from all the refinements of pompous or sensual luxury.[1] Their luxury and their manners have been the subject of minute and laborious disquisition; but as such inquiries would divert me too long from the design of the present work, I shall produce an authentic state of Rome and its inhabitants which is more peculiarly applicable to the period of the Gothic invasion. Ammianus Marcellinus who prudently chose the capital of the empire as the residence the best adapted to the historian of his own times, has mixed with the narrative of public events a lively representation of the scenes with which he was familiarly conversant. The judicious reader will not always approve the asperity of censure, the choice of circumstances, or the style of expression; he will perhaps detect the latent prejudices and personal resentments which soured the temper of Ammianus himself; but he will surely observe, with philosophic curiosity, the interesting and original picture of the manners of Rome.[2]

"The greatness of Rome (such is the language of the historian) was founded on the rare and almost incredible alliance of virtue and of fortune. The long period of her infancy was employed in a laborious struggle against the tribes of Italy, the neighbours and enemies of the rising city. In the strength and ardour of youth she sustained the storms of war, carried her victorious arms beyond the seas and the mountains, and brought home triumphal laurels from every country of the globe. At length, verging towards old age, and sometimes conquering by the terror only of her name, she sought the blessings of ease and tranquillity. The VENERABLE CITY, which had trampled on the necks of the fiercest nations, and established a system of laws, the perpetual guardians of justice and freedom, was content, like a wise and wealthy parent, to devolve on the Cæsars, her favourite sons, the care of governing her ample patrimony. A secure and profound peace, such as had been once enjoyed in the reign of Numa, succeeded to the tumults of a republic; while Rome was still adored as the queen of the earth, and the subject nations still reverenced the name of her people and the majesty of the senate. But this native splendour (continues Ammianus) is degraded and sullied by the conduct of some nobles, who, unmindful of their own dignity and of that of their country, assume an unbounded licence of vice and folly. They contend with each other in the empty vanity of titles and surnames,

---

[1] The learned Arbuthnot has observed with humour, and I believe with truth, that Augustus had neither glass to his windows nor a shirt to his back. Under the lower-empire the use of linen and glass became somewhat more common.

[2] It is incumbent on me to explain the liberties which I have taken with the text of Ammianus. 1. I have melted down into one piece the sixth chapter of the fourteenth and the fourth of the twenty-eighth book. 2. I have given order and connexion to the confused mass of materials. 3. I have softened some extravagant hyperboles and pared away some superfluities of the original. 4. I have developed some observations which were insinuated rather than expressed. With these allowances my version will be found, not literal indeed, but faithful and exact.

and curiously select or invent the most lofty and sonorous appellations —Reburrus or Fabunius, Pagonius or Tarrasius—which may impress the ears of the vulgar with astonishment and respect. From a vain ambition of perpetuating their memory, they affect to multiply their likeness in statues of bronze and marble; nor are they satisfied unless those statues are covered with plates of gold; an honourable distinction, first granted to Acilius the consul, after he had subdued by his arms and counsels the power of king Antiochus. The ostentation of displaying, of magnifying perhaps, the rent-roll of the estates which they possess in all the provinces, from the rising to the setting sun, provokes the just resentment of every man who recollects that their poor and invincible ancestors were not distinguished from the meanest of the soldiers by the delicacy of their food or the splendour of their apparel. But the modern nobles measure their rank and consequence according to the loftiness of their chariots,[1] and the weighty magnificence of their dress. Their long robes of silk and purple float in the wind; and as they are agitated, by art or accident, they occasionally discover the under garments, the rich tunics, embroidered with the figures of various animals.[2] Followed by a train of fifty servants, and tearing up the pavement, they move along the streets with the same impetuous speed as if they travelled with post-horses; and the example of the senators is boldly imitated by the matrons and ladies, whose covered carriages are continually driving round the immense space of the city and suburbs. Whenever these persons of high distinction condescend to visit the public baths, they assume, on their entrance, a tone of loud and insolent command, and appropriate to their own use the conveniences which were designed for the Roman people. If, in these places of mixed and general resort, they meet any of the infamous ministers of their pleasures, they express their affection by a tender embrace, while they proudly decline the salutations of their fellow-citizens, who are not permitted to aspire above the honour of kissing their hands or their knees. As soon as they have indulged themselves in the refreshment of the bath, they resume their rings and the other ensigns of their dignity, select from their private

---

[1] The *carrucæ*, or coaches of the Romans, were often of solid silver curiously carved and engraved; and the trappings of the mules or horses were embossed with gold. This magnificence continued from the reign of Nero to that of Honorius; and the Appian way was covered with the splendid equipages of the nobles, who came out to meet St. Melania when she returned to Rome six years before the Gothic siege. Yet pomp is well exchanged for convenience; and a plain modern coach that is hung upon springs is much preferable to the silver or gold *carts* of antiquity, which rolled on the axletree, and were exposed, for the most part, to the inclemency of the weather.

[2] In a homily of Asterius, bishop of Amasia, M. de Valois has discovered that this was a new fashion; that bears, wolves, lions, and tigers, woods, hunting-matches, &c., were represented in embroidery; and that the more pious coxcombs substituted the figure or legend of some favourite saint.

wardrobe of the finest linen, such as might suffice for a dozen persons, the garments the most agreeable to their fancy, and maintain till their departure the same haughty demeanour, which perhaps might have been excused in the great Marcellus after the conquest of Syracuse. Sometimes indeed these heroes undertake more arduous achievements: they visit their estates in Italy, and procure themselves, by the toil of servile hands, the amusements of the chase. If at any time, but more especially on a hot day, they have courage to sail in their painted galleys from the Lucrine lake to their elegant villas on the sea-coast of Puteoli and Caieta, they compare their own expeditions to the marches of Cæsar and Alexander. Yet should a fly presume to settle on the silken folds of their gilded umbrellas, should a sunbeam penetrate through some unguarded and imperceptible chink, they deplore their intolerable hardships, and lament in affected language that they were not born in the land of the Cimmerians, the regions of eternal darkness. In these journeys into the country the whole body of the household marches with their master. In the same manner as the cavalry and infantry, the heavy and the light armed troops, the advanced guard and the rear, are marshalled by the skill of their military leaders, so the domestic officers, who bear a rod as an ensign of authority, distribute and arrange the numerous train of slaves and attendants. The baggage and wardrobe move in the front, and are immediately followed by a multitude of cooks and inferior ministers employed in the service of the kitchens and of the table. The main body is composed of a promiscuous crowd of slaves, increased by the accidental concourse of idle or dependent plebeians. The rear is closed by the favourite band of eunuchs, distributed from age to youth, according to the order of seniority. Their numbers and their deformity excite the horror of the indignant spectators, who are ready to execrate the memory of Semiramis for the cruel art which she invented of frustrating the purposes of nature, and of blasting in the bud the hopes of future generations. In the exercise of domestic jurisdiction the nobles of Rome express an exquisite sensibility for any personal injury, and a contemptuous indifference for the rest of the human species. When they have called for warm water, if a slave has been tardy in his obedience, he is instantly chastised with three hundred lashes; but should the same slave commit a wilful murder, the master will mildly observe that he is a worthless fellow, but that if he repeats the offence he shall not escape punishment. Hospitality was formerly the virtue of the Romans; and every stranger who could plead either merit or misfortune was relieved or rewarded by their generosity. At present, if a foreigner, perhaps of no contemptible rank, is introduced to one of the proud and wealthy senators, he is welcomed indeed in the first audience with such warm professions and such kind inquiries, that he retires enchanted with the affability of his illustrious friend, and full of regret that he had so long delayed his journey to Rome, the native seat of manners as well as of empire. Secure of a favourable reception, he repeats his visit the ensuing day, and is mortified by the discovery that his person, his name, and his country are already forgotten. If he still has resolution to persevere, he is gradually numbered in the train of dependents, and obtains the permission to pay his assiduous and unprofitable court to a haughty patron, incapable of gratitude or friendship, who scarcely deigns to remark his presence, his departure, or his return. Whenever the rich prepare a solemn and popular entertainment, whenever they celebrate with profuse and pernicious luxury their private banquets, the choice of the guests is the subject of anxious deliberation. The modest, the sober, and the learned are seldom preferred; and the nomenclators, who are commonly swayed by interested motives, have the address to insert in the list of invitations the obscure names of the most worthless of mankind. But the frequent and familiar companions of the great are those parasites who practise the most useful of all arts, the art of flattery; who eagerly applaud each word and every action of their immortal patron; gaze with rapture on his marble columns and variegated pavements, and strenuously praise the pomp and elegance which he is taught to consider as a part of his personal merit. At the Roman tables the birds, the *squirrels*,[1] or the fish, which appear of an uncommon size, are contemplated with curious attention; a pair of scales is accurately applied to ascertain their real weight; and, while the more rational guests are disgusted by the vain and tedious repetition, notaries are summoned to attest by an authentic record the truth of such a marvellous event. Another method of introduction into the houses and society of the great is derived from the profession of gaming, or, as it is more politely styled, of play. The confederates are united by a strict and indissoluble bond of friendship, or rather of conspiracy; a superior degree of skill in the *Tesserarian* art (which may be interpreted the game of dice and tables [2]) is a sure road to wealth and reputation.

[1] The want of an English name obliges me to refer to the common genus of squirrels, the Latin *glis*, the French *loir*; a little animal who inhabits the woods and remains torpid in cold weather. The art of rearing and fattening great numbers of *glires* was practised in Roman villas as a profitable article of rural economy. The excessive demand of them for luxurious tables was increased by the foolish prohibitions of the censors; and it is reported that they are still esteemed in modern Rome, and are frequently sent as presents by the Colonna princes.

[2] This game, which might be translated by the more familiar names of *trictrac*, or *backgammon*, was a favourite amusement of the gravest Romans; and old Mucius Scævola, the lawyer, had the reputation of a very skilful player. It was called *ludus duodecim scriptorum*, from the twelve *scripta* or lines which equally divided the *alveolus* or table. On these the two armies, the white and the black, each consisting of fifteen men, or *calculi*, were regularly placed and alternately moved according to the laws of the game and the chances of the *tesseræ* or dice. Dr. Hyde, who diligently traces the history and varieties of the *nerdiludium* (a name of Persic etymology) from Ireland to Japan, pours forth on this trifling subject a copious torrent of classic and Oriental learning.

A master of that sublime science, who in a supper or assembly is placed below a magistrate, displays in his countenance the surprise and indignation which Cato might be supposed to feel when he was refused the prætorship by the votes of a capricious people. The acquisition of knowledge seldom engages the curiosity of the nobles, who abhor the fatigue and disdain the advantages of study; and the only books which they peruse are the Satires of Juvenal, and the verbose and fabulous histories of Marius Maximus. The libraries which they have inherited from their fathers are secluded, like dreary sepulchres, from the light of day. But the costly instruments of the theatre, flutes, and enormous lyres, and hydraulic organs, are constructed for their use; and the harmony of vocal and instrumental music is incessantly repeated in the palaces of Rome. In those palaces sound is preferred to sense, and the care of the body to that of the mind. It is allowed as a salutary maxim, that the light and frivolous suspicion of a contagious malady is of sufficient weight to excuse the visits of the most intimate friends; and even the servants who are despatched to make the decent inquiries are not suffered to return home till they have undergone the ceremony of a previous ablution. Yet this selfish and unmanly delicacy occasionally yields to the more imperious passion of avarice. The prospect of gain will urge a rich and gouty senator as far as Spoleto; every sentiment of arrogance and dignity is subdued by the hopes of an inheritance, or even of a legacy; and a wealthy childless citizen is the most powerful of the Romans. The art of obtaining the signature of a favourable testament, and sometimes of hastening the moment of its execution, is perfectly understood; and it has happened that in the same house, though in different apartments, a husband and a wife, with the laudable design of overreaching each other, have summoned their respective lawyers, to declare at the same time their mutual but contradictory intentions. The distress which follows and chastises extravagant luxury often reduces the great to the use of the most humiliating expedients. When they desire to borrow, they employ the base and supplicating style of the slave in the comedy; but when they are called upon to pay, they assume the royal and tragic declamation of the grandsons of Hercules. If the demand is repeated, they readily procure some trusty sycophant, instructed to maintain a charge of poison, or magic, against the insolent creditor, who is seldom released from prison till he has signed a discharge of the whole debt. These vices, which degrade the moral character of the Romans, are mixed with a puerile superstition that disgraces their understanding. They listen with confidence to the predictions of haruspices, who pretend to read in the entrails of victims the signs of future greatness and prosperity; and there are many who do not presume either to bathe or to dine, or to appear in public, till they have diligently consulted, according to the rules of astrology, the situation of Mercury and the aspect of the moon. It is singular enough that this vain credulity may often be discovered among the profane sceptics who impiously doubt or deny the existence of a celestial power."

THE PEOPLE OF ROME

In populous cities, which are the seat of commerce and manufactures, the middle ranks of inhabitants, who derive their subsistence from the dexterity or labour of their hands, are commonly the most prolific, the most useful, and, in that sense, the most respectable part of the community. But the plebeians of Rome, who disdained such sedentary and servile arts, had been oppressed from the earliest times by the weight of debt and usury, and the husbandman, during the term of his military service, was obliged to abandon the cultivation of his farm. The lands of Italy, which had been originally divided among the families of free and indigent proprietors, were insensibly purchased or usurped by the avarice of the nobles; and in the age which preceded the fall of the republic, it was computed that only two thousand citizens were possessed of any independent substance. Yet as long as the people bestowed by their suffrages the honours of the state, the command of the legions, and the administration of wealthy provinces, their conscious pride alleviated in some measure the hardships of poverty; and their wants were seasonably supplied by the ambitious liberality of the candidates, who aspired to secure a venal majority in the thirty-five tribes, or the hundred and ninety-three centuries, of Rome. But when the prodigal commons had imprudently alienated not only the *use*, but the *inheritance*, of power, they sunk, under the reign of the Cæsars, into a vile and wretched populace, which must, in a few generations, have been totally extinguished, if it had not been continually recruited by the manumission of slaves and the influx of strangers. As early as the time of Hadrian it was the just complaint of the ingenuous natives that the capital had attracted the vices of the universe and the manners of the most opposite nations. The intemperance of the Gauls, the cunning and levity of the Greeks, the savage obstinacy of the Egyptians and Jews, the servile temper of the Asiatics, and the dissolute, effeminate prostitution of the Syrians, were mingled in the various multitude, which, under the proud and false denomination of Romans, presumed to despise their fellow-subjects, and even their sovereigns, who dwelt beyond the precincts of the ETERNAL CITY.

Yet the name of that city was still pronounced with respect: the frequent and capricious tumults of its inhabitants were indulged with impunity; and the successors of Constantine, instead of crushing the last remains of the democracy by the strong arm of military power, embraced the mild policy of Augustus, and studied to relieve the poverty and to amuse the idleness of an innumerable people. I. For the convenience of the lazy plebeians, the monthly distributions of corn were converted into a daily allowance of bread; a great number of ovens were constructed and maintained at the public expense; and at the appointed hour, each citizen, who was furnished with a ticket, ascended the flight of steps which had been assigned to his peculiar quarter or division, and received, either as a gift or at a very low price, a loaf of bread of the weight of three pounds for the use of his family. II. The forests of Lucania, whose acorns fattened large droves of wild hogs, afforded, as a species of tribute, a plentiful supply of cheap and wholesome meat. During five months of the year a regular allowance of bacon was distributed to the poorer citizens; and the annual consumption of the capital, at a time when it was much declined from its former lustre, was ascertained, by an edict of Valentinian the Third, at three millions six hundred and twenty-eight thousand pounds. III. In the manners of antiquity the use of oil was indispensable for the lamp as well as for the bath, and the annual tax which was imposed on Africa for the benefit of Rome amounted to the weight of three millions of pounds, to the measure, perhaps, of three hundred thousand English gallons. IV. The anxiety of Augustus to provide the metropolis with sufficient plenty of corn was not extended beyond that necessary article of human subsistence; and when the popular clamour accused the dearness and scarcity of wine, a proclamation was issued by the grave reformer to remind his subjects that no man could reasonably complain of thirst, since the aqueducts of Agrippa had introduced into the city so many copious streams of pure and salubrious water. This rigid sobriety was insensibly relaxed; and, although the generous design of Aurelian does not appear to have been executed in its full extent, the use of wine was allowed on very easy and liberal terms. The administration of the public cellars was delegated to a magistrate of honourable rank; and a considerable part of the vintage of Campania was reserved for the fortunate inhabitants of Rome.

The stupendous aqueducts, so justly celebrated by the praises of Augustus himself, replenished the *Thermæ*, or baths, which had been constructed in every part of the city, with Imperial magnificence. The baths of Antoninus Caracalla, which were open, at stated hours, for the indiscriminate service of the senators and the people, contained above sixteen hundred seats of marble; and more than three thousand were reckoned in the baths of Diocletian. The walls of the lofty apartments were covered with curious mosaics, that imitated the art of the pencil in the elegance of design and the variety of colours. The Egyptian granite was beautifully encrusted with the precious green marble of Numidia; the perpetual stream of hot water was poured into the capacious basons through so many wide mouths of bright and massy silver; and the meanest Roman could purchase, with a small copper coin, the daily enjoyment of a scene of pomp and luxury which might excite the envy of the kings of Asia. From these stately palaces issued a swarm of dirty and ragged plebeians, without shoes and without a mantle; who loitered away whole days in the street or Forum to hear news and to hold disputes; who dissipated in extravagant gaming the miserable pittance of their wives and children; and spent the hours of the night in obscure taverns and brothels in the indulgence of gross and vulgar sensuality.

But the most lively and splendid amusement of the idle multitude depended on the frequent exhibition of public games and spectacles. The piety of Christian princes had suppressed the inhuman combats of gladiators; but the Roman people still considered the Circus as their home, their temple, and the seat of the republic. The impatient crowd rushed at the dawn of day to secure their places, and there were many who passed a sleepless and anxious night in the adjacent porticos. From the morning to the evening, careless of the sun or of the rain, the spectators, who sometimes amounted to the number of four hundred thousand, remained in eager attention; their eyes fixed on the horses and charioteers, their minds agitated with hope and fear for the success of the *colours* which they espoused; and the happiness of Rome appeared to hang on the event of a race. The same immoderate ardour inspired their clamours and their applause as often as they were entertained with the hunting of wild beasts and the various modes of theatrical representation. These representations in modern capitals may deserve to be considered as a pure and elegant school of taste, and perhaps of virtue. But the Tragic and Comic Muse of the Romans, who seldom aspired beyond the imitation of Attic genius, had been almost totally silent since the fall of the republic; and their place was unworthily occupied by licentious farce, effeminate music, and splendid pageantry. The pantomimes, who maintained their reputation from the age of Augustus to the sixth century, expressed, without the use of words, the various fables of the gods and heroes of antiquity; and the perfection of their art, which sometimes disarmed the gravity of the philosopher, always excited the applause and wonder of the people. The vast and magnificent theatres of Rome were filled by three thousand female dancers, and by three thousand singers, with the masters of the respective choruses. Such was the popular favour which they enjoyed, that, in a time of scarcity, when all strangers were banished from the city, the merit of contributing to the public pleasures exempted *them* from a law which was strictly executed against the professors of the liberal arts.

It is said that the foolish curiosity of Elagabalus attempted to discover, from the quantity of spiders' webs, the number of the inhabitants of Rome. A more rational method of inquiry might not have been undeserving of the attention of the wisest princes, who could easily have resolved a question so important for the Roman government and so interesting to succeeding ages. The births and deaths of the citizens were duly registered; and if any writer of antiquity had condescended to mention the annual amount, or the common average, we might now produce some satisfactory calculation which would destroy the extravagant assertions of critics, and perhaps confirm the modest and probable conjectures of philosophers. The most diligent researches have collected only the following circumstances, which, slight and imperfect as they are, may tend in some degree to illustrate the question of the populousness of ancient Rome. I. When the capital of the empire was besieged by the Goths, the circuit of the walls was accurately measured by Ammonius, the mathematician, who found it equal to twenty-one miles. It should not be forgotten that the form of the city was almost that of a circle; the geometrical figure which is known to contain the largest space within any given circumference. II. The architect Vitruvius, who flourished in the Augustan age, and whose evidence, on this occasion, has peculiar weight and authority, observes that the innumerable habitations of the Roman people would have spread themselves far beyond the narrow limits of the city; and that the want of ground, which was probably contracted on every side by gardens and villas, suggested the common, though inconvenient practice of raising the houses to a considerable height in the air. But the loftiness of these buildings, which often consisted of hasty work and insufficient materials, was the cause of frequent and fatal accidents; and it was repeatedly enacted by Augustus, as well as by Nero, that the height of private edifices within the walls of Rome should not exceed the measure of seventy feet from the ground. III. Juvenal laments, as it should seem from his own experience, the hardships of the poorer citizens, to whom he addresses the salutary advice of emigrating, without delay, from the smoke of Rome, since they might purchase in the little towns of Italy a cheerful, commodious dwelling at the same price which they annually paid for a dark and miserable lodging. House-rent was therefore immoderately dear: the rich acquired, at an enormous expense, the ground, which they covered with palaces and gardens; but the body of the Roman people was crowded into a narrow space; and the different floors and apartments of the same house were divided, as it is still the custom of Paris and other cities, among several families of plebeians. IV. The total number of houses in the fourteen regions of the city is accurately stated in the description of Rome composed under the reign of Theodosius, and they amount to forty-eight thousand three hundred and eighty-two. The two classes of *domus* and of *insulæ*, into which they are divided, include all the habitations of the capital, of every rank and condition, from the marble palace of the Anicii, with a numerous establishment of freedmen and slaves, to the lofty and narrow lodging-house where the poet Codrus and his wife were permitted to hire a wretched garret immediately under the tiles. If we adopt the same average which, under similar circumstances, has been found applicable to Paris, and indifferently allow about twenty-five persons for each house, of every degree, we may fairly estimate the inhabitants of Rome at twelve hundred thousand: a number which cannot be thought excessive for the capital of a mighty empire, though it exceeds the populousness of the greatest cities of modern Europe.

THE FIRST SIEGE OF ROME

Such was the state of Rome under the reign of Honorius, at the time when the Gothic army formed the siege, or rather the blockade, of the city. By a skilful disposition of his numerous forces, who impatiently watched the moment of an assault, Alaric encompassed the walls, commanded the twelve principal gates, intercepted all communication with the adjacent country, and vigilantly guarded the navigation of the Tiber, from which the Romans derived the surest and most plentiful supply of provisions. The first emotions of the nobles and of the people were those of surprise and indignation, that a vile barbarian should dare to insult the capital of the world; but their arrogance was soon humbled by misfortune; and their unmanly rage, instead of being directed against an enemy in arms, was meanly exercised on a defenceless and innocent victim. Perhaps in the person of Serena the Romans might have respected the niece of Theodosius, the aunt, nay even the adoptive mother, of the reigning emperor; but they abhorred the widow of Stilicho; and they listened with credulous passion to the tale of calumny which accused her of maintaining a secret and criminal correspondence with the Gothic invader. Actuated, or overawed, by the same popular frenzy, the senate, without requiring any evidence of her guilt, pronounced the sentence of her death. Serena was ignominiously strangled; and the infatuated multitude were astonished to find that this cruel act of injustice did not immediately produce the retreat of the barbarians and the deliverance of the city. That unfortunate city gradually experienced the distress of scarcity, and at length the horrid calamities of famine. The daily allowance of three pounds of bread was reduced to one-half, to one-third, to nothing; and the price of corn still continued to rise in a rapid and extravagant proportion. The poorer citizens, who were unable to purchase the necessaries of life, solicited the precarious charity of the rich; and for a while the public misery was alleviated by the humanity of Læta, the widow of the emperor Gratian, who had fixed her residence at Rome, and consecrated, to the use of the indigent, the princely revenue which she annually received from the grateful successors of her husband. But these private and temporary donatives were insufficient to appease the hunger of a numerous people; and the progress of famine invaded the marble palaces of the senators themselves. The persons of both sexes, who had been educated in the enjoyment of ease and luxury, discovered how little is requisite to supply the demands of nature; and lavished their unavailing treasures of gold and silver to obtain the coarse and scanty sustenance which they would formerly have rejected with disdain. The food the most repugnant to sense or imagination, the aliments the most unwholesome and pernicious to the constitution, were eagerly devoured, and fiercely disputed, by the rage of hunger. A dark suspicion was entertained that some desperate wretches fed on the bodies of their fellow-creatures whom they had secretly murdered; and even mothers (such was the horrid conflict of the two most powerful instincts implanted by nature in the human breast), even mothers are said to have tasted the flesh of their slaughtered infants! Many thousands of the inhabitants of Rome expired in their houses, or in the streets, for want of sustenance; and as the public sepulchres without the walls were in the power of the enemy, the stench which arose from so many putrid and unburied carcasses infected the air; and the miseries of famine were succeeded and aggravated by the contagion of a pestilential disease. The assurances of speedy and effectual relief, which were repeatedly transmitted from the court of Ravenna, supported, for some time, the fainting resolution of the Romans, till at length the despair of any human aid tempted them to accept the offers of a preternatural deliverance. Pompeianus, prefect of the city, had been persuaded, by the art or fanaticism of some Tuscan diviners, that, by the mysterious force of spells and sacrifices, they could extract the lightning from the clouds, and point those celestial fires against the camp of the barbarians. The important secret was communicated to Innocent, the bishop of Rome; and the successor of St. Peter is accused, perhaps without foundation, of preferring the safety of the republic to the rigid severity of the Christian worship. But when the question was agitated in the senate; when it was proposed, as an essential condition, that those sacrifices should be performed in the Capitol, by the authority, and in the presence, of the magistrates; the majority of that respectable assembly, apprehensive either of the Divine or of the Imperial displeasure, refused to join in an act which appeared almost equivalent to the public restoration of Paganism.

The last resource of the Romans was in the clemency, or at least in the moderation, of the king of the Goths. The senate, who in an emergency assumed the supreme powers of government, appointed two ambassadors to negociate with the enemy. This important trust was delegated to Basilius, a senator of Spanish extraction, and already conspicuous in the administration of provinces; and to John, the first tribune of the notaries, who was peculiarly qualified, by his dexterity in business, as well as by his former intimacy with the Gothic prince. When they were introduced into his presence, they declared, perhaps in a more lofty style than became their abject condition, that the Romans were resolved to maintain their dignity, either in peace or war; and that, if Alaric refused them a fair and honourable capitulation, he might sound his trumpets, and prepare to give battle to an innumerable people, exercised in arms and animated by despair. "The thicker the hay, the easier it is mowed," was the concise reply of the barbarian; and this rustic metaphor was accompanied by a loud and insulting laugh, expressive of his contempt for the menaces of an unwarlike populace, enervated by luxury before they were emaciated by famine. He then condescended to fix the ransom which he would accept as the price of his retreat from the walls of Rome: *all* the gold and silver in the city, whether it were the property of the state, or of individuals; *all* the rich and precious moveables; and *all* the slaves who could prove their title to the name of *barbarians*. The ministers of the senate presumed to ask, in a modest and suppliant tone, "If such, O king! are your demands, what do you intend to leave us?" "YOUR LIVES," replied the haughty conqueror: they trembled and retired. Yet before they retired, a short suspension of arms was granted, which allowed some time for a more temperate negociation. The stern features of Alaric were insensibly relaxed; he abated much of the rigour of his terms; and at length consented to raise the siege, on the immediate payment of five thousand pounds of gold, of thirty thousand pounds of silver, of four thousand robes of silk, of three thousand pieces of fine scarlet cloth, and of three thousand pounds weight of pepper.[1] But the public treasury was exhausted; the annual rents of the great estates in Italy and the provinces were intercepted by the calamities of war; the gold and gems had been exchanged, during the famine, for the vilest sustenance; the hoards of secret wealth were still concealed by the obstinacy of avarice; and some remains of consecrated spoils afforded the only resource that could avert the impending ruin of the city. As soon as the Romans had satisfied the rapacious demands of Alaric, they were restored, in some measure, to the enjoyment of peace and plenty. Several of the gates were cautiously opened; the importation of provisions from the river and the adjacent country was no longer obstructed by the Goths; the citizens resorted in crowds to the free market which was held during three days in the suburbs; and while the merchants who undertook this gainful trade made a considerable profit, the future subsistence of the city was secured by the ample magazines which were deposited in the public and private granaries. A more regular discipline than could have been expected was maintained in the camp of Alaric; and the wise barbarian justified his regard for the faith of treaties, by the just severity with which he chastised a party of licentious Goths who had insulted some Roman citizens on the road to Ostia. His army, enriched by the contributions of the capital, slowly advanced into the fair and fruitful province of Tuscany, where he proposed to establish his winter-quarters;

---

[1] Pepper was a favourite ingredient of the most expensive Roman cookery, and the best sort commonly sold for fifteen denarii, or ten shillings, the pound. It was brought from India; and the same country, the coast of Malabar, still affords the greatest plenty; but the improvement of trade and navigation has multiplied the quantity and reduced the price.

and the Gothic standard became the refuge of forty thousand barbarian slaves, who had broke their chains, and aspired, under the command of their great deliverer, to revenge the injuries and the disgrace of their cruel servitude. About the same time he received a more honourable reinforcement of Goths and Huns, whom Adolphus,[1] the brother of his wife, had conducted, at his pressing invitation, from the banks of the Danube to those of the Tiber, and who had cut their way, with some difficulty and loss, through the superior numbers of the Imperial troops. A victorious leader, who united the daring spirit of a barbarian with the art and discipline of a Roman general, was at the head of an hundred thousand fighting men; and Italy pronounced with terror and respect the formidable name of Alaric.

At the distance of fourteen centuries we may be satisfied with relating the military exploits of the conquerors of Rome, without presuming to investigate the motives of their political conduct. In the midst of his apparent prosperity, Alaric was conscious, perhaps, of some secret weakness, some internal defect; or perhaps the moderation which he displayed was intended only to deceive and disarm the easy credulity of the ministers of Honorius. The king of the Goths repeatedly declared that it was his desire to be considered as the friend of peace and of the Romans. Three senators, at his earnest request, were sent ambassadors to the court of Ravenna, to solicit the exchange of hostages and the conclusion of the treaty; and the proposals which he more clearly expressed during the course of the negociations could only inspire a doubt of his sincerity, as they might seem inadequate to the state of his fortune. The barbarian still aspired to the rank of master-general of the armies of the West; he stipulated an annual subsidy of corn and money; and he chose the provinces of Dalmatia, Noricum, and Venetia for the seat of his new kingdom, which would have commanded the important communication between Italy and the Danube. If these modest terms should be rejected, Alaric showed a disposition to relinquish his pecuniary demands, and even to content himself with the possession of Noricum; an exhausted and impoverished country, perpetually exposed to the inroads of the barbarians of Germany. But the hopes of peace were disappointed by the weak obstinacy, or interested views, of the minister Olympius. Without listening to the salutary remonstrances of the senate, he dismissed their ambassadors under the conduct of a military escort, too numerous for a retinue of honour, and too feeble for an army of defence. Six thousand Dalmatians, the flower of the Imperial legions, were ordered to march from Ravenna to Rome, through an open country which was occupied by the formidable myriads of the barbarians.

[1] This Gothic chieftain is called, by Jornandes and Isidore, *Athaulphus*; by Zosimus and Orosius, *Ataulphus*; and by Olympiodorus, *Adaoulphus*. I have used the celebrated name of *Adolphus*, which seems to be authorised by the practice of the Swedes, the sons or brothers of the ancient Goths.

These brave legionaries, encompassed and betrayed, fell a sacrifice to ministerial folly; their general, Valens, with an hundred soldiers, escaped from the field of battle; and one of the ambassadors, who could no longer claim the protection of the law of nations, was obliged to purchase his freedom with a ransom of thirty thousand pieces of gold. Yet Alaric, instead of resenting this act of impotent hostility, immediately renewed his proposals of peace; and the second embassy of the Roman senate, which derived weight and dignity from the presence of Innocent, bishop of the city, was guarded from the dangers of the road by a detachment of Gothic soldiers.

Olympius might have continued to insult the just resentment of a people who loudly accused him as the author of the public calamities, but his power was undermined by the secret intrigues of the palace. The favourite eunuchs transferred the government of Honorius and the empire to Jovius, the Prætorian prefect—an unworthy servant, who did not atone by the merit of personal attachment for the errors and misfortunes of his administration. The exile, or escape, of the guilty Olympius reserved him for more vicissitudes of fortune: he experienced the adventures of an obscure and wandering life; he again rose to power; he fell a second time into disgrace; his ears were cut off—he expired under the lash—and his ignominious death afforded a grateful spectacle to the friends of Stilicho. After the removal of Olympius, whose character was deeply tainted with religious fanaticism, the Pagans and heretics were delivered from the impolitic proscription which excluded them from the dignities of the state. The brave Gennerid, a soldier of barbarian origin, who still adhered to the worship of his ancestors, had been obliged to lay aside the military belt; and though he was repeatedly assured by the emperor himself that laws were not made for persons of his rank or merit, he refused to accept any partial dispensation, and persevered in honourable disgrace till he had extorted a general act of justice from the distress of the Roman government. The conduct of Gennerid in the important station to which he was promoted or restored, of master-general of Dalmatia, Pannonia, Noricum, and Rhætia, seemed to revive the discipline and spirit of the republic. From a life of idleness and want his troops were soon habituated to severe exercise and plentiful subsistence, and his private generosity often supplied the rewards which were denied by the avarice or poverty of the court of Ravenna. The valour of Gennerid, formidable to the adjacent barbarians, was the firmest bulwark of the Illyrian frontier; and his vigilant care assisted the empire with a reinforcement of ten thousand Huns, who arrived on the confines of Italy, attended by such a convoy of provisions, and such a numerous train of sheep and oxen, as might have been sufficient not only for the march of an army but for the settlement of a colony. But the court and councils of Honorius still remained a scene of weakness and distraction, of corruption and anarchy. Instigated by the prefect

Jovius, the guards rose in furious mutiny and demanded the heads of two generals and of the two principal eunuchs. The generals, under a perfidious promise of safety, were sent on ship-board and privately executed; while the favour of the eunuchs procured them a mild and secure exile at Milan and Constantinople. Eusebius the eunuch and the barbarian Allobich succeeded to the command of the bed-chamber and of the guards; and the mutual jealousy of the subordinate ministers was the cause of their mutual destruction. By the insolent order of the count of the domestics, the great chamberlain was shamefully beaten to death with sticks before the eyes of the astonished emperor; and the subsequent assassination of Allobich, in the midst of a public procession, is the only circumstance of his life in which Honorius discovered the faintest symptom of courage or resentment. Yet before they fell, Eusebius and Allobich had contributed their part to the ruin of the empire by opposing the conclusion of a treaty which Jovius, from a selfish, and perhaps a criminal motive, had negociated with Alaric, in a personal interview under the walls of Rimini. During the absence of Jovius the emperor was persuaded to assume a lofty tone of inflexible dignity, such as neither his situation nor his character could enable him to support; and a letter, signed with the name of Honorius, was immediately despatched to the Prætorian prefect, granting him a free permission to dispose of the public money, but sternly refusing to prostitute the military honours of Rome to the proud demands of a barbarian. This letter was imprudently communicated to Alaric himself; and the Goth, who in the whole transaction had behaved with temper and decency, expressed in the most outrageous language his lively sense of the insult so wantonly offered to his person and to his nation. The conference of Rimini was hastily interrupted; and the prefect Jovius, on his return to Ravenna, was compelled to adopt, and even to encourage, the fashionable opinions of the court. By his advice and example the principal officers of the state and army were obliged to swear, that, without listening in *any* circumstances to *any* conditions of peace, they would still persevere in perpetual and implacable war against the enemy of the republic. This rash engagement opposed an insuperable bar to all future negociation. The ministers of Honorius were heard to declare, that, if they had only invoked the name of the Deity, they would consult the public safety, and trust their souls to the mercy of Heaven: but they had sworn by the sacred head of the emperor himself; they had touched in solemn ceremony that august seat of majesty and wisdom; and the violation of their oath would expose them to the temporal penalties of sacrilege and rebellion.

THE SECOND SIEGE OF ROME

While the emperor and his court enjoyed with sullen pride the security of the marshes and fortifications of Ravenna, they abandoned Rome, almost without defence, to the resentment of Alaric. Yet such was the moderation which he still preserved, or affected, that as he moved with his army along the Flaminian way he successively despatched the bishops of the towns of Italy to reiterate his offers of peace, and to conjure the emperor that he would save the city and its inhabitants from hostile fire and the sword of the barbarians. These impending calamities were however averted, not indeed by the wisdom of Honorius, but by the prudence or humanity of the Gothic king, who employed a milder though not less effectual, method of conquest. Instead of assaulting the capital he successfully directed his efforts against the *Port* of Ostia, one of the boldest and most stupendous works of Roman magnificence. The accidents to which the precarious subsistence of the city was continually exposed in a winter navigation and an open road had suggested to the genius of the first Cæsar the useful design which was executed under the reign of Claudius. The artificial moles which formed the narrow entrance advanced far into the sea, and firmly repelled the fury of the waves, while the largest vessels securely rode at anchor within three deep and capacious basons which received the northern branch of the Tiber about two miles from the ancient colony of Ostia.[1] The Roman *Port* insensibly swelled to the size of an episcopal city, where the corn of Africa was deposited in spacious granaries for the use of the capital. As soon as Alaric was in possession of that important place he summoned the city to surrender at discretion; and his demands were enforced by the positive declaration that a refusal, or even a delay, should be instantly followed by the destruction of the magazines on which the life of the Roman people depended. The clamours of that people and the terror of famine subdued the pride of the senate; they listened without reluctance to the proposal of placing a new emperor on the throne of the unworthy Honorius; and the suffrage of the Gothic conqueror bestowed the purple on Attalus, prefect of the city. The grateful monarch immediately acknowledged his protector as master-general of the armies of the West; Adolphus, with the rank of count of the domestics, obtained the custody of the person of Attalus; and the two hostile nations seemed to be united in the closest bands of friendship and alliance.

[1] The *Ostia Tiberina*, in the plural number, the two mouths of the Tiber, were separated by the Holy Island, an equilateral triangle, whose sides were each of them computed at about two miles. The colony of Ostia was founded immediately beyond the left, or southern, and the *Port* immediately beyond the right, or northern, branch of the river; and the distance between their remains measures something more than two miles on Cingolani's map. In the time of Strabo the sand and mud deposited by the Tiber had choked the harbour of Ostia; the progress of the same cause has added much to the size of the Holy Island, and gradually left both Ostia and the Port at a considerable distance from the shore. The dry channels and the large estuaries mark the changes of the river and the efforts of the sea. Consult, for the present state of this dreary and desolate tract, the excellent map of the ecclesiastical state by the mathematicians of Benedict XIV; an actual survey of the *Agro Romano*, in six sheets, by Cingolani, which contains 113,819 *rubbia* (about 570,000 acres); and the large topographical map of Ameti, in eight sheets.

The gates of the city were thrown open, and the new emperor of the Romans, encompassed on every side by the Gothic arms, was conducted in tumultuous procession to the palace of Augustus and Trajan. After he had distributed the civil and military dignities among his favourites and followers, Attalus convened an assembly of the senate, before whom, in a formal and florid speech, he asserted his resolution of restoring the majesty of the republic, and of uniting to the empire the provinces of Egypt and the East which had once acknowledged the sovereignty of Rome. Such extravagant promises inspired every reasonable citizen with a just contempt for the character of an unwarlike usurper, whose elevation was the deepest and most ignominious wound which the republic had yet sustained from the insolence of the barbarians. But the populace, with their usual levity, applauded the change of masters. The public discontent was favourable to the rival of Honorius; and the sectaries, oppressed by his persecuting edicts, expected some degree of countenance, or at least of toleration, from a prince who, in his native country of Ionia, had been educated in the Pagan superstition, and who had since received the sacrament of baptism from the hands of an Arian bishop. The first days of the reign of Attalus were fair and prosperous. An officer of confidence was sent with an inconsiderable body of troops to secure the obedience of Africa; the greatest part of Italy submitted to the terror of the Gothic powers; and though the city of Bologna made a vigorous and effectual resistance, the people of Milan, dissatisfied perhaps with the absence of Honorius, accepted with loud acclamations the choice of the Roman senate. At the head of a formidable army, Alaric conducted his royal captive almost to the gates of Ravenna; and a solemn embassy of the principal ministers—of Jovius the Prætorian prefect, of Valens, master of the cavalry and infantry, of the quæstor Potamius, and of Julian, the first of the notaries—was introduced with martial pomp into the Gothic camp. In the name of their sovereign they consented to acknowledge the lawful election of his competitor, and to divide the provinces of Italy and the West between the two emperors. Their proposals were rejected with disdain; and the refusal was aggravated by the insulting clemency of Attalus, who condescended to promise that if Honorius would instantly resign the purple he should be permitted to pass the remainder of his life in the peaceful exile of some remote island. So desperate indeed did the situation of the son of Theodosius appear to those who were the best acquainted with his strength and resources, that Jovius and Valens, his minister and his general, betrayed their trust, infamously deserted the sinking cause of their benefactor, and devoted their treacherous allegiance to the service of his more fortunate rival. Astonished by such examples of domestic treason, Honorius trembled at the approach of every servant, at the arrival of every messenger. He dreaded the secret enemies who might lurk in his capital, his palace, his bed-chamber; and some ships lay ready in the harbour of Ravenna to transport the abdicated monarch to the dominions of his infant nephew, the emperor of the East.

But there *is* a Providence (such at least was the opinion of the historian Procopius) that watches over innocence and folly, and the pretensions of Honorius to its peculiar care cannot reasonably be disputed. At the moment when his despair, incapable of any wise or manly resolution, meditated a shameful flight, a seasonable reinforcement of four thousand veterans unexpectedly landed in the port of Ravenna. To these valiant strangers, whose fidelity had not been corrupted by the factions of the court, he committed the walls and gates of the city, and the slumbers of the emperor were no longer disturbed by the apprehension of imminent and internal danger. The favourable intelligence which was received from Africa suddenly changed the opinions of men and the state of public affairs. The troops and officers whom Attalus had sent into that province were defeated and slain, and the active zeal of Heraclian maintained his own allegiance and that of his people. The faithful count of Africa transmitted a large sum of money, which fixed the attachment of the Imperial guards; and his vigilance in preventing the exportation of corn and oil introduced famine, tumult, and discontent into the walls of Rome. The failure of the African expedition was the source of mutual complaint and recrimination in the party of Attalus, and the mind of his protector was insensibly alienated from the interest of a prince who wanted spirit to command or docility to obey. The most imprudent measures were adopted, without the knowledge or against the advice of Alaric, and the obstinate refusal of the senate to allow in the embarkation the mixture even of five hundred Goths, betrayed a suspicious and distrustful temper which in their situation was neither generous nor prudent. The resentment of the Gothic king was exasperated by the malicious arts of Jovius, who had been raised to the rank of patrician, and who afterwards excused his double perfidy by declaring without a blush that he had only *seemed* to abandon the service of Honorius more effectually to ruin the cause of the usurper. In a large plain near Rimini, and in the presence of an innumerable multitude of Romans and barbarians, the wretched Attalus was publicly despoiled of the diadem and purple; and those ensigns of royalty were sent by Alaric as the pledge of peace and friendship to the son of Theodosius. The officers who returned to their duty were reinstated in their employments, and even the merit of a tardy repentance was graciously allowed; but the degraded emperor of the Romans, desirous of life and insensible of disgrace, implored the permission of following the Gothic camp in the train of a haughty and capricious barbarian.

THE THIRD SIEGE AND SACK OF ROME

The degradation of Attalus removed the only real obstacle to the conclusion of the peace, and Alaric advanced within three miles of

Ravenna to press the irresolution of the Imperial ministers, whose insolence soon returned with the return of fortune. His indignation was kindled by the report that a rival chieftain, that Sarus, the personal enemy of Adolphus, and the hereditary foe of the house of Balti, had been received into the palace. At the head of three hundred followers that fearless barbarian immediately sallied from the gates of Ravenna, surprised and cut in pieces a considerable body of Goths, re-entered the city in triumph, and was permitted to insult his adversary by the voice of a herald, who publicly declared that the guilt of Alaric had for ever excluded him from the friendship and alliance of the emperor. The crime and folly of the court of Ravenna was expiated a third time by the calamities of Rome. The king of the Goths, who no longer dissembled his appetite for plunder and revenge, appeared in arms under the walls of the capital; and the trembling senate, without any hopes of relief, prepared by a desperate resistance to delay the ruin of their country. But they were unable to guard against the secret conspiracy of their slaves and domestics, who either from birth or interest were attached to the cause of the enemy. At the hour of midnight the Salarian gate was silently opened, and the inhabitants were awakened by the tremendous sound of the Gothic trumpet. Eleven hundred and sixty-three years after the foundation of Rome, the Imperial city, which had subdued and civilised so considerable a part of mankind, was delivered to the licentious fury of the tribes of Germany and Scythia.

The proclamation of Alaric, when he forced his entrance into a vanquished city, discovered, however, some regard for the laws of humanity and religion. He encouraged his troops boldly to seize the rewards of valour, and to enrich themselves with the spoils of a wealthy and effeminate people; but he exhorted them at the same time to spare the lives of the unresisting citizens, and to respect the churches of the apostles St. Peter and St. Paul as holy and inviolable sanctuaries. Amidst the horrors of a nocturnal tumult several of the Christian Goths displayed the fervour of a recent conversion; and some instances of their uncommon piety and moderation are related, and perhaps adorned, by the zeal of ecclesiastical writers.[1] While the barbarians roamed through the city in quest of prey, the humble dwelling of an aged virgin, who had devoted her life to the service of the altar, was forced open by one of the powerful Goths. He immediately demanded, though in civil language, all the gold and silver in her possession, and was astonished at the readiness with which she conducted him to a splendid hoard of

---

[1] Orosius applauds the piety of the Christian Goths without seeming to perceive that the greatest part of them were Arian heretics. Jornandes and Isidore of Seville, who were both attached to the Gothic cause, have repeated and embellished these edifying tales. According to Isidore, Alaric himself was heard to say that he waged war with the Romans, and not with the Apostles. Such was the style of the seventh century: two hundred years before, the fame and merit had been ascribed, not to the Apostles, but to Christ.

massy plate of the richest materials and the most curious workmanship. The barbarian viewed with wonder and delight this valuable acquisition, till he was interrupted by a serious admonition, addressed to him in the following words: "These," said she, "are the consecrated vessels belonging to St. Peter: if you presume to touch them, the sacrilegious deed will remain on your conscience. For my part, I dare not keep what I am unable to defend." The Gothic captain, struck with reverential awe, despatched a messenger to inform the king of the treasure which he had discovered, and received a peremptory order from Alaric, that all the consecrated plate and ornaments should be transported, without damage or delay, to the church of the apostle. From the extremity, perhaps, of the Quirinal hill to the distant quarter of the Vatican, a numerous detachment of Goths, marching in order of battle through the principal streets, protected with glittering arms the long train of their devout companions who bore aloft on their heads the sacred vessels of gold and silver, and the martial shouts of the barbarians were mingled with the sound of religious psalmody. From all the adjacent houses a crowd of Christians hastened to join this edifying procession, and a multitude of fugitives, without distinction of age or rank, or even of sect, had the good fortune to escape to the secure and hospitable sanctuary of the Vatican. The learned work concerning the *City of God* was professedly composed by St. Augustin, to justify the ways of Providence in the destruction of the Roman greatness. He celebrates with peculiar satisfaction this memorable triumph of Christ, and insults his adversaries by challenging them to produce some similar example of a town taken by storm, in which the fabulous gods of antiquity had been able to protect either themselves or their deluded votaries.

In the sack of Rome some rare and extraordinary examples of barbarian virtue have been deservedly applauded. But the holy precincts of the Vatican and the apostolic churches could receive a very small proportion of the Roman people: many thousand warriors, more especially of the Huns who served under the standard of Alaric, were strangers to the name, or at least to the faith of Christ, and we may suspect, without any breach of charity or candour, that in the hour of savage licence, when every passion was inflamed and every restraint was removed, the precepts of the Gospel seldom influenced the behaviour of the Gothic Christians. The writers tho boot disposed to exaggerate their clemency have freely confessed that a cruel slaughter was made of the Romans, and that the streets of the city were filled with dead bodies, which remained without burial during the general consternation. The despair of the citizens was sometimes converted into fury; and whenever the barbarians were provoked by opposition, they extended the promiscuous massacre to the feeble, the innocent, and the helpless. The private revenge of forty thousand slaves was exercised without pity or remorse; and the ignominious lashes which they had formerly received were washed away in the blood of the guilty or obnoxious families. The matrons and virgins of Rome were exposed to injuries more dreadful, in the apprehension of chastity, than death itself; and the ecclesiastical historian has selected an example of female virtue for the admiration of future ages.[1] A Roman lady, of singular beauty and orthodox faith, had excited the impatient desires of a young Goth, who, according to the sagacious remark of Sozomen, was attached to the Arian heresy. Exasperated by her obstinate resistance, he drew his sword, and, with the anger of a lover, slightly wounded her neck. The bleeding heroine still continued to brave his resentment and to repel his love, till the ravisher desisted from his unavailing efforts, respectfully conducted her to the sanctuary of the Vatican, and gave six pieces of gold to the guards of the church on condition that they should restore her inviolate to the arms of her husband. Such instances of courage and generosity were not extremely common. The brutal soldiers satisfied their sensual appetites without consulting either the inclination or the duties of their female captives; and a nice question of casuistry was seriously agitated, Whether those tender victims, who had inflexibly refused their consent to the violation which they sustained, had lost, by their misfortune, the glorious crown of virginity. There were other losses indeed of a more substantial kind and more general concern. It cannot be presumed that all the barbarians were at all times capable of perpetrating such amorous outrages; and the want of youth, or beauty, or chastity, protected the greatest part of the Roman women from the danger of a rape. But avarice is an insatiate and universal passion; since the enjoyment of almost every object that can afford pleasure to the different tastes and tempers of mankind may be procured by the possession of wealth. In the pillage of Rome a just preference was given to gold and jewels, which contain the greatest value in the smallest compass and weight; but, after these portable riches had been removed by the more diligent robbers, the palaces of Rome were rudely stripped of their splendid and costly furniture. The sideboards of massy plate, and the variegated wardrobes of silk and purple, were irregularly piled in the waggons that always followed the march of a Gothic army. The most exquisite works of art were roughly handled or wantonly destroyed: many a statue was melted for the sake of the precious materials; and many a vase, in the division of the spoil, was shivered into fragments by the stroke of a battle-axe. The acquisition of riches served only to stimulate the avarice of the rapacious barbarians, who proceeded by threats, by blows, and

---

[1] Augustin intimates that some virgins or matrons actually killed themselves to escape violation; and though he admires their spirit, he is obliged, by his theology, to condemn their rash presumption. Perhaps the good bishop of Hippo was too easy in the belief, as well as too rigid in the censure, of this act of female heroism. The twenty maidens (if they ever existed) who threw themselves into the Elbe when Magdeburg was taken by storm, have been multiplied to the number of twelve hundred.

by tortures, to force from their prisoners the confession of hidden treasure. Visible splendour and expense were alleged as the proof of a plentiful fortune; the appearance of poverty was imputed to a parsimonious disposition; and the obstinacy of some misers, who endured the most cruel torments before they would discover the secret object of their affection, was fatal to many unhappy wretches, who expired under the lash for refusing to reveal their imaginary treasures. The edifices of Rome, though the damage has been much exaggerated, received some injury from the violence of the Goths. At their entrance through the Salarian gate they fired the adjacent houses to guide their march and to distract the attention of the citizens; the flames, which encountered no obstacle in the disorder of the night, consumed many private and public buildings, and the ruins of the palace of Sallust remained in the age of Justinian a stately monument of the Gothic conflagration. Yet a contemporary historian has observed that fire could scarcely consume the enormous beams of solid brass, and that the strength of man was insufficient to subvert the foundations of ancient structures. Some truth may possibly be concealed in his devout assertion, that the wrath of Heaven supplied the imperfections of hostile rage, and that the proud Forum of Rome, decorated with the statues of so many gods and heroes, was levelled in the dust by the stroke of lightning.

Whatever might be the numbers, of equestrian or plebeian rank, who perished in the massacre of Rome, it is confidently affirmed that only one senator lost his life by the sword of the enemy. But it was not easy to compute the multitudes who, from an honourable station and a prosperous fortune, were suddenly reduced to the miserable condition of captives and exiles. As the barbarians had more occasion for money than for slaves, they fixed at a moderate price the redemption of their indigent prisoners; and the ransom was often paid by the benevolence of their friends, or the charity of strangers. The captives, who were regularly sold, either in open market, or by private contract, would have legally regained their native freedom, which it was impossible for a citizen to lose or to alienate. But as it was soon discovered that the vindication of their liberty would endanger their lives, and that the Goths, unless they were tempted to sell, might be provoked to murder their useless prisoners, the civil jurisprudence had been already qualified by a wise regulation, that they should be obliged to serve the moderate term of five years, till they had discharged by their labour the price of their redemption. The nations who invaded the Roman empire had driven before them, into Italy, whole troops of hungry and affrighted provincials, less apprehensive of servitude than of famine. The calamities of Rome and Italy dispersed the inhabitants to the most lonely, the most secure, the most distant places of refuge. While the Gothic cavalry spread terror and desolation along the seacoast of Campania and Tuscany, the little island of Igilium, separated by a narrow channel from the Argentarian promontory, repulsed, or eluded, their hostile attempts; and at so small a distance from Rome, great numbers of citizens were securely concealed in the thick woods of the sequestered spot. The ample patrimonies which many senatorian families possessed in Africa invited them, if they had time and prudence to escape from the ruin of their country, to embrace the shelter of that hospitable province. The most illustrious of these fugitives was the noble and pious Proba,[1] the widow of the prefect Petronius. After the death of her husband, the most powerful subject of Rome, she had remained at the head of the Anician family, and successively supplied, from her private fortune, the expense of the consulships of her three sons. When the city was besieged and taken by the Goths, Proba supported with Christian resignation the loss of immense riches; embarked in a small vessel, from whence she beheld, at sea, the flames of her burning palace; and fled with her daughter Læta, and her grand-daughter, the celebrated virgin Demetrias, to the coast of Africa. The benevolent profusion with which the matron distributed the fruits or the price of her estates contributed to alleviate the misfortunes of exile and captivity. But even the family of Proba herself was not exempt from the rapacious oppression of Count Heraclian, who basely sold, in matrimonial prostitution, the noblest maidens of Rome to the lust or avarice of the Syrian merchants. The Italian fugitives were dispersed through the provinces, along the coast of Egypt and Asia, as far as Constantinople and Jerusalem; and the village of Bethlem, the solitary residence of St. Jerom and his female converts, was crowded with illustrious beggars, of either sex and every age, who excited the public compassion by the remembrance of their past fortune. This awful catastrophe of Rome filled the astonished empire with grief and terror. So interesting a contrast of greatness and ruin disposed the fond credulity of the people to deplore, and even to exaggerate, the afflictions of the queen of cities. The clergy, who applied to recent events the lofty metaphors of Oriental prophecy, were sometimes tempted to confound the destruction of the capital and the dissolution of the globe.

There exists in human nature a strong propensity to depreciate the advantages, and to magnify the evils, of the present times. Yet, when the first emotions had subsided, and a fair estimate was made of the real damage, the more learned and judicious contemporaries were forced to confess that infant Rome had formerly received more essential injury from the Gauls than she had now sustained from the Goths in her de-

_____
[1] As the adventures of Proba and her family are connected with the life of St. Augustin, they are diligently illustrated by Tillemont. Some time after their arrival in Africa, Demetrias took the veil and made a vow of virginity; an event which was considered as of the highest importance to Rome and to the world. All the *Saints* wrote congratulatory letters to her; that of Jerome is still extant, and contains a mixture of absurd reasoning, spirited declamation, and curious facts, some of which relate to the siege and sack of Rome.

clining age. The experience of eleven centuries has enabled posterity to produce a much more singular parallel; and to affirm with confidence, that the ravages of the barbarians whom Alaric had led from the banks of the Danube were less destructive than the hostilities exercised by the troops of Charles the Fifth, a catholic prince, who styled himself Emperor of the Romans. The Goths evacuated the city at the end of six days, but Rome remained above nine months in the possession of the Imperialists; and every hour was stained by some atrocious act of cruelty, lust, and rapine. The authority of Alaric preserved some order and moderation among the ferocious multitude which acknowledged him for their leader and king; but the constable of Bourbon had gloriously fallen in the attack of the walls; and the death of the general removed every restraint of discipline from an army which consisted of three independent nations, the Italians, the Spaniards, and the Germans. In the beginning of the sixteenth century the manners of Italy exhibited a remarkable scene of the depravity of mankind. They united the sanguinary crimes that prevail in an unsettled state of society, with the polished vices which spring from the abuse of art and luxury; and the loose adventurers, who had violated every prejudice of patriotism and superstition to assault the palace of the Roman pontiff, must deserve to be considered as the most profligate of the *Italians*. At the same era the *Spaniards* were the terror both of the Old and New World; but their high-spirited valour was disgraced by gloomy pride, rapacious avarice, and unrelenting cruelty. Indefatigable in the pursuit of fame and riches, they had improved, by repeated practice, the most exquisite and effectual methods of torturing their prisoners: many of the Castilians who pillaged Rome were familiars of the holy inquisition; and some volunteers, perhaps, were lately returned from the conquest of Mexico. The *Germans* were less corrupt than the Italians, less cruel than the Spaniards; and the rustic, or even savage, aspect of those *Tramontane* warriors, often disguised a simple and merciful disposition. But they had imbibed, in the first fervour of the Reformation, the spirit, as well as the principles, of Luther. It was their favourite amusement to insult, or destroy, the consecrated objects of catholic superstition; they indulged, without pity or remorse, a devout hatred against the clergy of every denomination and degree who form so considerable a part of the inhabitants of modern Rome; and their fanatic zeal might aspire to subvert the throne of Antichrist, to purify, with blood and fire, the abominations of the spiritual Babylon.

THE RETREAT OF THE GOTHS AND THE DEATH OF ALARIC

The retreat of the victorious Goths, who evacuated Rome on the sixth day, might be the result of prudence, but it was not surely the effect of fear.[1] At the head of an army encumbered with rich and weighty spoils,

---

[1] Socrates pretends, without any colour of truth or reason, that Alaric fled on the report that the armies of the Eastern empire were in full march to attack him.

their intrepid leader advanced along the Appian Way into the southern provinces of Italy, destroying whatever dared to oppose his passage, and contenting himself with the plunder of the unresisting country. The fate of Capua, the proud and luxurious metropolis of Campania, and which was respected, even in its decay, as the eighth city of the empire, is buried in oblivion; whilst the adjacent town of Nola has been illustrated, on this occasion, by the sanctity of Paulinus, who was successively a consul, a monk, and a bishop. At the age of forty he renounced the enjoyment of wealth and honour, of society and literature, to embrace a life of solitude and penance; and the loud applause of the clergy encouraged him to despise the reproaches of his worldly friends, who ascribed this desperate act to some disorder of the mind or body. An early and passionate attachment determined him to fix his humble dwelling in one of the suburbs of Nola, near the miraculous tomb of St. Felix, which the public devotion had already surrounded with five large and populous churches. The remains of his fortune, and of his understanding, were dedicated to the service of the glorious martyr; whose praise, on the day of his festival, Paulinus never failed to celebrate by a solemn hymn; and in whose name he erected a sixth church, of superior elegance and beauty, which was decorated with many curious pictures from the history of the Old and New Testament. Such assiduous zeal secured the favour of the saint,[1] or at least of the people; and, after fifteen years' retirement, the Roman consul was compelled to accept the bishopric of Nola, a few months before the city was invested by the Goths. During the siege, some religious persons were satisfied that they had seen, either in dreams or visions, the divine form of their tutelar patron; yet it soon appeared by the event, that Felix wanted power, or inclination, to preserve the flock of which he had formerly been the shepherd. Nola was not saved from the general devastation; and the captive bishop was protected only by the general opinion of his innocence and poverty. Above four years elapsed from the successful invasion of Italy by the arms of Alaric, to the voluntary retreat of the Goths under the conduct of his successor Adolphus; and, during the whole time, they reigned without control over a country which, in the opinion of the ancients, had united all the various excellences of nature and art. The prosperity, indeed, which Italy had attained in the auspicious age of the Antonines, had gradually declined with the decline of the empire. The fruits of a long peace perished under the rude grasp of the barbarians; and they themselves were incapable of tasting the more elegant refinements of luxury which had been prepared for the use of the soft and polished Italians. Each soldier, however, claimed an ample portion of the substantial plenty, the corn and cattle, oil and wine, that was daily collected and consumed in the Gothic camp; and the principal

[1] The humble Paulinus once presumed to say that he believed St. Felix *did* love him; at least, as a master loves his little dog.

warriors insulted the villas and gardens, once inhabited by Lucullus and Cicero, along the beauteous coast of Campania. Their trembling captives, the sons and daughters of Roman senators, presented, in goblets of gold and gems, large draughts of Falernian wine to the haughty victors, who stretched their huge limbs under the shade of plane-trees, artificially disposed to exclude the scorching rays, and to admit the genial warmth, of the sun. These delights were enhanced by the memory of past hardships: the comparison of their native soil, the bleak and barren hills of Scythia, and the frozen banks of the Elbe and Danube, added new charms to the felicity of the Italian climate.

Whether fame, or conquest, or riches were the object of Alaric, he pursued that object with an indefatigable ardour which could neither be quelled by adversity nor satiated by success. No sooner had he reached the extreme land of Italy then he was attracted by the neighbouring prospect of a fertile and peaceful island. Yet even the possession of Sicily he considered only as an intermediate step to the important expedition which he already meditated against the continent of Africa. The straits of Rhegium and Messina are twelve miles in length, and in the narrowest passage about one mile and a half broad; and the fabulous monsters of the deep, the rocks of Scylla and the whirlpool of Charybdis, could terrify none but the most timid and unskilful mariners. Yet as soon as the first division of the Goths had embarked, a sudden tempest arose, which sunk or scattered many of the transports; their courage was daunted by the terrors of a new element; and the whole design was defeated by the premature death of Alaric, which fixed, after a short illness, the fatal term of his conquests. The ferocious character of the barbarians was displayed in the funeral of a hero whose valour and fortune they celebrated with mournful applause. By the labour of a captive multitude they forcibly diverted the course of the Busentinus, a small river that washes the walls of Consentia. The royal sepulchre, adorned with the splendid spoils and trophies of Rome, was constructed in the vacant bed; the waters were then restored to their natural channel; and the secret spot where the remains of Alaric had been deposited was for ever concealed by the inhuman massacre of the prisoners who had been employed to execute the work.

Adolphus, who now became King of the Goths, concluded a peace with the Romans and married Placidia, the half-sister of Honorius. He marched into Spain to expel an invasion of the Suevi, Vandals, and Alani but was treacherously murdered. His successor, Wallia, recovered Spain for Honorius, confining the Vandals in the northwestern part of the peninsula, and then established the Goths in Aquitaine.

Chapter 32

THE REIGN OF ARCADIUS. ST. JOHN CHRYSOSTOM. DEATH
OF ARCADIUS AND SUCCESSION OF THEODOSIUS THE
YOUNGER. ADMINISTRATION OF PULCHERIA. ADVEN-
TURES OF EUDOCIA

THE division of the Roman world between the sons of Theodosius
marks the final establishment of the empire of the East, which
from the reign of Arcadius to the taking of Constantinople by the
Turks, subsisted one thousand and fifty-eight years in a state of premature and perpetual decay. The sovereign of that empire assumed and
obstinately retained the vain, and at length fictitious, title of Emperor of
the ROMANS; and the hereditary appellations of CÆSAR and AUGUSTUS
continued to declare that he was the legitimate successor of the first of
men, who had reigned over the first of nations. The palace of Constantinople rivalled, and perhaps excelled, the magnificence of Persia; and
the eloquent sermons of St. Chrysostom celebrate, while they condemn,
the pompous luxury of the reign of Arcadius. "The emperor," says he,
"wears on his head either a diadem or a crown of gold, decorated with
precious stones of inestimable value. These ornaments and his purple
garments are reserved for his sacred person alone; and his robes of silk
are embroidered with the figures of golden dragons. His throne is of
massy gold. Whenever he appears in public he is surrounded by his
courtiers, his guards, and his attendants. Their spears, their shields,
their cuirasses, the bridles and trappings of their horses, have either the
substance, or the appearance of gold; and the large splendid boss in the
midst of their shield is encircled with smaller bosses, which represent
the shape of the human eye. The two mules that draw the chariot of
the monarch are perfectly white, and shining all over with gold. The
chariot itself, of pure and solid gold, attracts the admiration of the
spectators, who contemplate the purple curtains, the snowy carpet,
the size of the precious stones, and the resplendent plates of gold, that
glitter as they are agitated by the motion of the carriage. The Imperial
pictures are white, on a blue ground; the emperor appears seated on his
throne, with his arms, his horses, and his guards beside him; and his
vanquished enemies in chains at his feet." The successors of Constantine established their perpetual residence in the royal city which he had
erected on the verge of Europe and Asia. Inaccessible to the menaces
of their enemies, and perhaps to the complaints of their people, they
received with each wind the tributary productions of every climate;

while the impregnable strength of their capital continued for ages to defy the hostile attempts of the barbarians. Their dominions were bounded by the Adriatic and the Tigris; and the whole interval of twenty-five days' navigation, which separated the extreme cold of Scythia from the torrid zone of Ethiopia, was comprehended within the limits of the empire of the East. The populous countries of that empire were the seat of art and learning, of luxury and wealth; and the inhabitants, who had assumed the language and manners of Greeks, styled themselves, with some appearance of truth, the most enlightened and civilised portion of the human species. The form of government was a pure and simple monarchy; the name of the ROMAN REPUBLIC, which so long preserved a faint tradition of freedom, was confined to the Latin provinces; and the princes of Constantinople measured their greatness by the servile obedience of their people. They were ignorant how much this passive disposition enervates and degrades every faculty of the mind. The subjects who had resigned their will to the absolute commands of a master were equally incapable of guarding their lives and fortunes against the assaults of the barbarians, or of defending their reason from the terrors of superstition.

During the first five years of the reign of Arcadius the administration was controlled by his chamberlain, the cruel and avaricious eunuch Eutropius. Eutropius was brought down by a rebellion of the Ostrogoths under Tribigild and Gainas and at the instigation of the Empress Eudoxia. The rebellion was subsequently defeated.

ST. JOHN CHRYSOSTOM

After the death of the indolent Nectarius, the successor of Gregory Nazianzen, the church of Constantinople was distracted by the ambition of rival candidates, who were not ashamed to solicit, with gold or flattery, the suffrage of the people or of the favourite. On this occasion Eutropius seems to have deviated from his ordinary maxims; and his uncorrupted judgment was determined only by the superior merit of a stranger. In a late journey into the East he had admired the sermons of John, a native and presbyter of Antioch, whose name has been distinguished by the epithet of Chrysostom, or the Golden Mouth. A private order was despatched to the governor of Syria, and as the people might be unwilling to resign their favourite preacher, he was transported, with speed and secrecy, in a post-chariot, from Antioch to Constantinople. The unanimous and unsolicited consent of the court, the clergy, and the people ratified the choice of the minister; and, both as a saint and as an orator, the new archbishop surpassed the sanguine expectations of the public. Born of a noble and opulent family in the capital of Syria, Chrysostom had been educated, by the care of a tender mother, under the tuition of the most skilful masters. He studied the art of rhetoric in the school of Libanius; and that celebrated sophist, who soon discovered the talents of his disciple, ingenuously confessed that John would have deserved to succeed him had he not been stolen away by the Christians. His piety soon disposed him to receive the sacrament of baptism; to renounce the lucrative and honourable profession of the law; and to bury himself in the adjacent desert, where he subdued the lusts of the flesh by an austere penance of six years. His infirmities compelled him to return to the society of mankind; and the authority of Meletius devoted his talents to the service of the church: but in the midst of his family, and afterwards on the archiepiscopal throne, Chrysostom still persevered in the practice of the monastic virtues. The ample revenues, which his predecessors had consumed in pomp and luxury, he diligently applied to the establishment of hospitals; and the multitudes who were supported by his charity preferred the eloquent and edifying discourses of their archbishop to the amusements of the theatre or the circus. The monuments of that eloquence, which was admired near twenty years at Antioch and Constantinople, have been carefully preserved; and the possession of near one thousand sermons or homilies has authorised the critics [1] of succeeding times to appreciate the genuine merit of Chrysostom. They unanimously attribute to the Christian orator the free command of an elegant and copious language; the judgment to conceal the advantages which he derived from the knowledge of rhetoric and philosophy; an inexhaustible fund of metaphors and similitudes, of ideas and images, to vary and illustrate the most familiar topics; the happy art of engaging the passions in the service of virtue, and of exposing the folly as well as the turpitude of vice almost with the truth and spirit of a dramatic representation.

The pastoral labours of the archbishop of Constantinople provoked and gradually united against him two sorts of enemies; the aspiring clergy, who envied his success, and the obstinate sinners, who were offended by his reproofs. When Chrysostom thundered from the pulpit of St. Sophia against the degeneracy of the Christians, his shafts were spent among the crowd, without wounding or even marking the character of any individual. When he declaimed against the peculiar vices of the rich, poverty might obtain a transient consolation from his invectives: but the guilty were still sheltered by their numbers; and the reproach itself was dignified by some ideas of superiority and enjoyment. But as the pyramid rose towards the summit, it insensibly diminished to a point; and the magistrates, the ministers, the favourite eunuchs, the

---

[1] As I am *almost* a stranger to the voluminous sermons of Chrysostom, I have given my confidence to the two most judicious and moderate of the ecclesiastical critics, Erasmus and Dupin; yet the good taste of the former is sometimes vitiated by an excessive love of antiquity, and the good sense of the latter is always restrained by prudential considerations.

ladies of the court,[1] the empress Eudoxia herself, had a much larger share of guilt to divide among a smaller proportion of criminals. The personal applications of the audience were anticipated or confirmed by the testimony of their own conscience; and the intrepid preacher assumed the dangerous right of exposing both the offence and the offender to the public abhorrence. The secret resentment of the court encouraged the discontent of the clergy and monks of Constantinople, who were too hastily reformed by the fervent zeal of their archbishop. He had condemned from the pulpit the domestic females of the clergy of Constantinople, who, under the name of servants or sisters, afforded a perpetual occasion either of sin or of scandal. The silent and solitary ascetics, who had secluded themselves from the world, were entitled to the warmest approbation of Chrysostom; but he despised and stigmatised, as the disgrace of their holy profession, the crowd of degenerate monks, who, from some unworthy motives of pleasure or profit, so frequently infested the streets of the capital. To the voice of persuasion the archbishop was obliged to add the terrors of authority; and his ardour in the exercise of ecclesiastical jurisdiction was not always exempt from passion; nor was it always guided by prudence. Chrysostom was naturally of a choleric disposition.[2] Although he struggled, according to the precepts of the Gospel, to love his private enemies, he indulged himself in the privilege of hating the enemies of God and of the church; and his sentiments were sometimes delivered with too much energy of countenance and expression. He still maintained, from some considerations of health or abstinence, his former habits of taking his repasts alone; and this inhospitable custom,[3] which his enemies imputed to pride, contributed at least to nourish the infirmity of a morose and unsocial humour. Separated from that familiar intercourse which facilitates the knowledge and the despatch of business, he reposed an unsuspecting confidence in his deacon Serapion; and seldom applied his speculative knowledge of human nature to the particular characters either of his dependents or

[1] The females of Constantinople distinguished themselves by their enmity or their attachment to Chrysostom. Three noble and opulent widows—Marsa, Castricia, and Eugraphia—were the leaders of the persecution. It was impossible that they should forgive a preacher who reproached their affectation to conceal, by the ornaments of dress, their age and ugliness. Olympias, by equal zeal, displayed in a more pious cause, has obtained the title of saint.

[2] Sozomen, and more especially Socrates, have defined the real character of Chrysostom with a temperate and impartial freedom very offensive to his blind admirers. Those historians lived in the next generation, when party violence was abated, and had conversed with many persons intimately acquainted with the virtues and imperfections of the saint.

[3] Palladius very seriously defends the archbishop. 1. He never tasted wine. 2. The weakness of his stomach required a peculiar diet. 3. Business, or study, or devotion, often kept him fasting till sunset. 4. He detested the noise and levity of great dinners. 5. He saved the expense for the use of the poor. 6. He was apprehensive, in a capital like Constantinople, of the envy and reproach of partial invitations.

of his equals. Conscious of the purity of his intentions, and perhaps of the superiority of his genius, the archbishop of Constantinople extended the jurisdiction of the Imperial city, that he might enlarge the sphere of his pastoral labours; and the conduct which the profane imputed to an ambitious motive, appeared to Chrysostom himself in the light of a sacred and indispensable duty. In his visitation through the Asiatic provinces he deposed thirteen bishops of Lydia and Phrygia; and indiscreetly declared that a deep corruption of simony and licentiousness had infected the whole episcopal order.[1] If those bishops were innocent, such a rash and unjust condemnation must excite a well-grounded discontent. If they were guilty, the numerous associates of their guilt would soon discover that their own safety depended on the ruin of the archbishop, whom they studied to represent as the tyrant of the Eastern church.

This ecclesiastical conspiracy was managed by Theophilus, archbishop of Alexandria, an active and ambitious prelate, who displayed the fruits of rapine in monuments of ostentation. His national dislike to the rising greatness of a city which degraded him from the second to the third rank in the Christian world was exasperated by some personal disputes with Chrysostom himself. By the private invitation of the empress, Theophilus landed at Constantinople, with a stout body of Egyptian mariners, to encounter the populace; and a train of dependent bishops, to secure by their voices the majority of a synod. The synod was convened in the suburb of Chalcedon, surnamed the *Oak*, where Rufinus had erected a stately church and monastery; and their proceedings were continued during fourteen days or sessions. A bishop and a deacon accused the archbishop of Constantinople; but the frivolous or improbable nature of the forty-seven articles which they presented against him may justly be considered as a fair and unexceptionable panegyric. Four successive summons were signified to Chrysostom; but he still refused to trust either his person or his reputation in the hands of his implacable enemies, who, prudently declining the examination of any particular charges, condemned his contumacious disobedience, and hastily pronounced a sentence of deposition. The synod of the *Oak* immediately addressed the emperor to ratify and execute their judgment, and charitably insinuated that the penalties of treason might be inflicted on the audacious preacher, who had reviled, under the name of Jezebel, the empress Eudoxia herself. The archbishop was rudely arrested, and conducted through the city, by one of the Imperial messengers, who landed him, after a short navigation, near the entrance of the Euxine; from whence, before the expiration of two days, he was gloriously recalled.

The first astonishment of his faithful people had been mute and passive: they suddenly rose with unanimous and irresistible fury.

----

[1] Chrysostom declares his free opinion that the number of bishops who might be saved bore a very small proportion to those who would be damned.

Theophilus escaped, but the promiscuous crowd of monks and Egyptian mariners was slaughtered without pity in the streets of Constantinople. A seasonable earthquake justified the interposition of Heaven; the torrent of sedition rolled forwards to the gates of the palace; and the empress, agitated by fear or remorse, threw herself at the feet of Arcadius, and confessed that the public safety could be purchased only by the restoration of Chrysostom. The Bosphorus was covered with innumerable vessels; the shores of Europe and Asia were profusely illuminated; and the acclamations of a victorious people accompanied, from the port to the cathedral, the triumph of the archbishop, who too easily consented to resume the exercise of his functions, before his sentence had been legally reversed by the authority of an ecclesiastical synod. Ignorant, or careless, of the impending danger, Chrysostom indulged his zeal, or perhaps his resentment; declaimed with peculiar asperity against *female* vices; and condemned the profane honours which were addressed, almost in the precincts of St. Sophia, to the statue of the empress. His imprudence tempted his enemies to inflame the haughty spirit of Eudoxia, by reporting, or perhaps inventing, the famous exordium of a sermon, "Herodias is again furious; Herodias again dances; she once more requires the head of John:" an insolent allusion, which, as a woman and a sovereign, it was impossible for her to forgive. The short interval of a perfidious truce was employed to concert more effectual measures for the disgrace and ruin of the archbishop. A numerous council of the Eastern prelates, who were guided from a distance by the advice of Theophilus, confirmed the validity, without examining the justice, of the former sentence; and a detachment of barbarian troops was introduced into the city, to suppress the emotions of the people. On the vigil of Easter the solemn administration of baptism was rudely interrupted by the soldiers, who alarmed the modesty of the naked catechumens, and violated, by their presence, the awful mysteries of the Christian worship. Arsacius occupied the church of St. Sophia and the archiepiscopal throne. The catholics retreated to the baths of Constantine, and afterwards to the fields, where they were still pursued and insulted by the guards, the bishops, and the magistrates. The fatal day of the second and final exile of Chrysostom was marked by the conflagration of the cathedral, of the senate-house, and of the adjacent buildings; and this calamity was imputed, without proof, but not without probability, to the despair of a persecuted faction.

Cicero might claim some merit if his voluntary banishment preserved the peace of the republic; but the submission of Chrysostom was the indispensable duty of a Christian and a subject. Instead of listening to his humble prayer that he might be permitted to reside at Cyzicus or Nicomedia, the inflexible empress assigned for his exile the remote and desolate town of Cucusus, among the ridges of Mount Taurus, in the Lesser Armenia. A secret hope was entertained that the archbishop might perish in a difficult and dangerous march of seventy days in the heat of summer, through the provinces of Asia Minor, where he was continually threatened by the hostile attacks of the Isaurians, and the more implacable fury of the monks. Yet Chrysostom arrived in safety at the place of his confinement; and the three years which he spent at Cucusus, and the neighbouring town of Arabissus, were the last and most glorious of his life. His character was consecrated by absence and persecution; the faults of his administration were no longer remembered; but every tongue repeated the praises of his genius and virtue: and the respectful attention of the Christian world was fixed on a desert spot among the mountains of Taurus. From that solitude the archbishop, whose active mind was invigorated by misfortunes, maintained a strict and frequent correspondence with the most distant provinces; exhorted the separate congregation of his faithful adherents to persevere in their allegiance; urged the destruction of the temples of Phœnicia, and the extirpation of heresy in the isle of Cyprus; extended his pastoral care to the missions of Persia and Scythia; negociated, by his ambassadors, with the Roman pontiff and the emperor Honorius; and boldly appealed, from a partial synod, to the supreme tribunal of a free and general council. The mind of the illustrious exile was still independent; but his captive body was exposed to the revenge of the oppressors, who continued to abuse the name and authority of Arcadius. An order was despatched for the instant removal of Chrysostom to the extreme desert of Pityus: and his guards so faithfully obeyed their cruel instructions, that, before he reached the sea-coast of the Euxine, he expired at Comana, in Pontus, in the sixtieth year of his age. The succeeding generation acknowledged his innocence and merit. The archbishops of the East, who might blush that their predecessors had been the enemies of Chrysostom, were gradually disposed, by the firmness of the Roman pontiff, to restore the honours of that venerable name. At the pious solicitation of the clergy and people of Constantinople, his relics, thirty years after his death, were transported from their obscure sepulchre to the royal city. The emperor Theodosius advanced to receive them as far as Chalcedon; and, falling prostrate on the coffin, implored, in the name of his guilty parents, Arcadius and Eudoxia, the forgiveness of the injured saint.

THE DEATH OF ARCADIUS AND SUCCESSION OF THEODOSIUS THE YOUNGER

Yet a reasonable doubt may be entertained whether any stain of hereditary guilt could be derived from Arcadius to his successor. Eudoxia was a young and beautiful woman, who indulged her passions and despised her husband: Count John enjoyed, at least, the familiar confidence of the empress; and the public named him as the real father of Theodosius the younger. The birth of a son was accepted, however, by the pious husband, as an event the most fortunate and honourable to himself, to his family, and to the Eastern world: and the royal infant, by an unprecedented favour, was invested with the titles of Cæsar and Augustus. In less than four years afterwards, Eudoxia, in the bloom of youth, was destroyed by the consequences of a miscarriage; and this untimely death confounded the prophecy of a holy bishop, who, amidst the universal joy, had ventured to foretell that she should behold the long and auspicious reign of her glorious son. The catholics applauded the justice of Heaven, which avenged the persecution of St. Chrysostom; and perhaps the emperor was the only person who sincerely bewailed the loss of the haughty and rapacious Eudoxia. Such a domestic misfortune afflicted *him* more deeply than the public calamities of the East —the licentious excursions, from Pontus to Palestine, of the Isaurian robbers, whose impunity accused the weakness of the government; and the earthquakes, the conflagrations, the famine, and the flights of locusts, which the popular discontent was equally disposed to attribute to the incapacity of the monarch. At length, in the thirty-first year of his age, after a reign (if we may abuse that word) of thirteen years, three months, and fifteen days, Arcadius expired in the palace of Constantinople. It is impossible to delineate his character; since, in a period very copiously furnished with historical materials, it has not been possible to remark one action that properly belongs to the son of the great Theodosius.

The historian Procopius has indeed illuminated the mind of the dying emperor with a ray of human prudence, or celestial wisdom. Arcadius considered, with anxious foresight, the helpless condition of his son Theodosius, who was no more than seven years of age, the dangerous factions of a minority, and the aspiring spirit of Jezdegerd, the Persian monarch. Instead of tempting the allegiance of an ambitious subject by the participation of supreme power, he boldly appealed to the magnanimity of a king, and placed, by a solemn testament, the sceptre of the East in the hands of Jezdegerd himself. The royal guardian accepted and discharged this honourable trust with unexampled fidelity; and the infancy of Theodosius was protected by the arms and councils of Persia. Such is the singular narrative of Procopius; and his veracity is not disputed by Agathias, while he presumes to dissent from his judgment, and to arraign the wisdom of a Christian emperor, who, so rashly, though so fortunately, committed his son and his dominions to the unknown faith of a stranger, a rival, and a heathen. At the distance of one hundred and fifty years, this political question might be debated in the court of Justinian; but a prudent historian will refuse to examine the *propriety*, till he has ascertained the *truth*, of the testament of Arcadius. As it stands without a parallel in the history of the world, we may justly require that it should be attested by the positive and unanimous evidence of contemporaries. The strange novelty of the event, which excites our distrust, must have attracted their notice; and their universal silence annihilates the vain tradition of the succeeding age.

The maxims of Roman jurisprudence, if they could fairly be transferred from private property to public dominion, would have adjudged to the emperor Honorius the guardianship of his nephew, till he had attained, at least, the fourteenth year of his age. But the weakness of Honorius, and the calamities of his reign, disqualified him from prosecuting this natural claim; and such was the absolute separation of the two monarchies, both in interest and affection, that Constantinople would have obeyed with less reluctance the orders of the Persian, than those of the Italian court. Under a prince whose weakness is disguised by the external signs of manhood and discretion, the most worthless favourites may secretly dispute the empire of the palace, and dictate to submissive provinces the commands of a master whom they direct and despise. But the ministers of a child, who is incapable of arming them with the sanction of the royal name, must acquire and exercise an independent authority. The great officers of the state and army, who had been appointed before the death of Arcadius, formed an aristocracy, which might have inspired them with the idea of a free republic; and the government of the Eastern empire was fortunately assumed by the prefect Anthemius, who obtained, by his superior abilities, a lasting ascendant over the minds of his equals. The safety of the young emperor proved the merit and integrity of Anthemius; and his prudent firmness sustained the force and reputation of an infant reign. Uldin, with a formidable host of barbarians, was encamped in the heart of Thrace; he proudly rejected all terms of accommodation; and, pointing to the rising sun, declared to the Roman ambassadors that the course of that planet should alone terminate the conquests of the Huns. But the desertion of his confederates, who were privately convinced of the justice and liberality of the Imperial ministers, obliged Uldin to repass the Danube: the tribe of the Scyrri, which composed his rear-guard, was almost extirpated; and many thousand captives were dispersed, to cultivate, with servile labour, the fields of Asia. In the midst of the public triumph, Constantinople was protected by a strong enclosure of new and more extensive walls; the same vigilant care was applied to restore the fortifications of the Illyrian cities; and a plan was judiciously conceived, which, in the space of seven years, would have secured the command of the Danube, by establishing on that river a perpetual fleet of two hundred and fifty armed vessels.

THE ADMINISTRATION OF PULCHERIA

But the Romans had so long been accustomed to the authority of a monarch, that the first, even among the females of the Imperial family, who displayed any courage or capacity, was permitted to ascend the vacant throne of Theodosius. His sister Pulcheria, who was only two years older than himself, received at the age of sixteen the title of *Augusta*; and though her favour might be sometimes clouded by caprice or intrigue, she continued to govern the Eastern empire near forty years; during the long minority of her brother, and after his death in her own name, and in the name of Marcian, her nominal husband. From a motive either of prudence or religion, she embraced a life of celibacy; and notwithstanding some aspersions on the chastity of Pulcheria, this resolution, which she communicated to her sisters Arcadia and Marina, was celebrated by the Christian world as the sublime effort of heroic piety. In the presence of the clergy and people the three daughters of Arcadius dedicated their virginity to God; and the obligation of their solemn vow was inscribed on a tablet of gold and gems, which they publicly offered in the great church of Constantinople. Their palace was converted into a monastery, and all males—except the guides of their conscience, the saints who had forgotten the distinction of sexes—were scrupulously excluded from the holy threshold. Pulcheria, her two sisters, and a chosen train of favourite damsels, formed a religious community: they renounced the vanity of dress, interrupted by frequent fasts their simple and frugal diet, allotted a portion of their time to works of embroidery, and devoted several hours of the day and night to the exercises of prayer and psalmody. The piety of a Christian virgin was adorned by the zeal and liberality of an empress. Ecclesiastical history describes the splendid churches which were built at the expense of Pulcheria in all the provinces of the East, her charitable foundations for the benefit of strangers and the poor, the ample donations which she assigned for the perpetual maintenance of monastic societies, and the active severity with which she laboured to suppress the opposite heresies of Nestorius and Eutyches. Such virtues were supposed to deserve the peculiar favour of the Deity: and the relics of martyrs, as well as the knowledge of future events, were communicated in visions and revelations to the Imperial saint.[1] Yet the devotion of Pulcheria never diverted her indefatigable attention from temporal affairs; and she alone, among all the descendants of the great Theodosius, appears to have inherited any share of his manly spirit and abilities. The elegant and familiar use which she had acquired both of the Greek and Latin languages was readily applied to the various occasions of speaking or writing on public business: her deliberations were maturely weighed; her actions were prompt and decisive; and while she moved without noise or ostentation the wheel of government, she discreetly attributed to

[1] She was admonished, by repeated dreams, of the place where the relics of the forty martyrs had been buried. The ground had successively belonged to the house and garden of a woman of Constantinople, to a monastery of Macedonian monks, and to a church of St. Thyrsus, erected by Cæsarius, who was consul A.D. 397; and the memory of the relics was almost obliterated. Notwithstanding the charitable wishes of Dr. Jortin, it is not easy to acquit Pulcheria of some share in the pious fraud, which must have been transacted when she was more than five-and-thirty years of age.

the genius of the emperor the long tranquillity of his reign. In the last years of his peaceful life Europe was indeed afflicted by the arms of Attila; but the more extensive provinces of Asia still continued to enjoy a profound and permanent repose. Theodosius the younger was never reduced to the disgraceful necessity of encountering and punishing a rebellious subject: and since we cannot applaud the vigour, some praise may be due to the mildness and prosperity, of the administration of Pulcheria.

The Roman world was deeply interested in the education of its master. A regular course of study and exercise was judiciously instituted; of the military exercises of riding, and shooting with the bow; of the liberal studies of grammar, rhetoric, and philosophy: the most skilful masters of the East ambitiously solicited the attention of their royal pupil, and several noble youths were introduced into the palace to animate his diligence by the emulation of friendship. Pulcheria alone discharged the important task of instructing her brother in the arts of government; but her precepts may countenance some suspicion of the extent of her capacity or of the purity of her intentions She taught him to maintain a grave and majestic deportment; to walk, to hold his robes, to seat himself on his throne in a manner worthy of a great prince; to abstain from laughter, to listen with condescension, to return suitable answers; to assume by turns a serious or a placid countenance; in a word, to re-present with grace and dignity the external figure of a Roman emperor. But Theodosius was never excited to support the weight and glory of an illustrious name; and, instead of aspiring to imitate his ancestors, he degenerated (if we may presume to measure the degrees of incapacity) be-low the weakness of his father and his uncle. Arcadius and Honorius had been assisted by the guardian care of a parent, whose lessons were en-forced by his authority and example. But the unfortunate prince who is born in the purple must remain a stranger to the voice of truth; and the son of Arcadius was condemned to pass his perpetual infancy encom-passed only by a servile train of women and eunuchs. The ample leisure which he acquired by neglecting the essential duties of his high office was filled by idle amusements and unprofitable studies. Hunting was the only active pursuit that could tempt him beyond the limits of the palace; but he most assiduously laboured, sometimes by the light of a midnight lamp, in the mechanic occupations of painting and carving; and the elegance with which he transcribed religious books entitled the Roman emperor to the singular epithet of *Calligraphes*, or a fair writer. Separated from the world by an impenetrable veil, Theodosius trusted the persons he loved; he loved those who were accustomed to amuse and flatter his indolence; and as he never perused the papers that were pre-sented for the royal signature, the acts of injustice the most repugnant to his character were frequently perpetrated in his name. The emperor himself was chaste, temperate, liberal, and merciful; but these qualities

—which can only deserve the name of virtues when they are supported by courage and regulated by discretion—were seldom beneficial, and they sometimes proved mischievous, to mankind. His mind, enervated by a royal education, was oppressed and degraded by abject superstition: he fasted, he sung psalms, he blindly accepted the miracles and doctrines with which his faith was continually nourished. Theodosius devoutly worshipped the dead and living saints of the catholic church; and he once refused to eat till an insolent monk, who had cast an excommunication on his sovereign, condescended to heal the spiritual wound which he had inflicted.

THE ADVENTURES OF EUDOCIA

The story of a fair and virtuous maiden, exalted from a private condition to the Imperial throne, might be deemed an incredible romance, if such a romance had not been verified in the marriage of Theodosius. The celebrated Athenais was educated by her father Leontius in the religion and sciences of the Greeks; and so advantageous was the opinion which the Athenian philosopher entertained of his contemporaries, that he divided his patrimony between his two sons, bequeathing to his daughter a small legacy of one hundred pieces of gold, in the lively confidence that her beauty and merit would be a sufficient portion. The jealousy and avarice of her brothers soon compelled Athenais to seek a refuge at Constantinople, and with some hopes, either of justice or favour, to throw herself at the feet of Pulcheria. That sagacious princess listened to her eloquent complaint, and secretly destined the daughter of the philosopher Leontius for the future wife of the emperor of the East, who had now attained the twentieth year of his age. She easily excited the curiosity of her brother by an interesting picture of the charms of Athenais: large eyes, a well-proportioned nose, a fair complexion, golden locks, a slender person, a graceful demeanour, an understanding improved by study, and a virtue tried by distress. Theodosius, concealed behind a curtain in the apartment of his sister, was permitted to behold the Athenian virgin: the modest youth immediately declared his pure and honourable love, and the royal nuptials were celebrated amidst the acclamations of the capital and the provinces. Athenais, who was easily persuaded to renounce the errors of Paganism, received at her baptism the Christian name of Eudocia: but the cautious Pulcheria withheld the title of Augusta till the wife of Theodosius had approved her fruitfulness by the birth of a daughter, who espoused fifteen years afterwards the emperor of the West. The brothers of Eudocia obeyed, with some anxiety, her Imperial summons; but as she could easily forgive their fortunate unkindness, she indulged the tenderness, or perhaps the vanity, of a sister, by promoting them to the rank of consuls and prefects. In the luxury of the palace she still cultivated those ingenuous arts which had contributed to her greatness, and wisely dedicated her talents to the honour of religion and of her husband. Eudocia composed a poetical paraphrase of the first eight books of the Old Testament and of the prophecies of Daniel and Zachariah; a cento of the verses of Homer, applied to the life and miracles of Christ, the legend of St. Cyprian, and a panegyric on the Persian victories of Theodosius: and her writings, which were applauded by a servile and superstitious age, have not been disdained by the candour of impartial criticism. The fondness of the emperor was not abated by time and possession; and Eudocia, after the marriage of her daughter, was permitted to discharge her grateful vows by a solemn pilgrimage to Jerusalem. Her ostentatious progress through the East may seem inconsistent with the spirit of Christian humility: she pronounced from a throne of gold and gems an eloquent oration to the senate of Antioch, declared her royal intention of enlarging the walls of the city, bestowed a donative of two hundred pounds of gold to restore the public baths, and accepted the statues which were decreed by the gratitude of Antioch. In the Holy Land her alms and pious foundations exceeded the munificence of the great Helena; and though the public treasure might be impoverished by this excessive liberality, she enjoyed the conscious satisfaction of returning to Constantinople with the chains of St. Peter, the right arm of St. Stephen, and an undoubted picture of the Virgin, painted by St. Luke. But this pilgrimage was the fatal term of the glories of Eudocia. Satiated with empty pomp, and unmindful perhaps of her obligations to Pulcheria, she ambitiously aspired to the government of the Eastern empire: the palace was distracted by female discord; but the victory was at last decided by the superior ascendant of the sister of Theodosius. The execution of Paulinus, master of the offices, and the disgrace of Cyrus, Prætorian prefect of the East, convinced the public that the favour of Eudocia was insufficient to protect her most faithful friends, and the uncommon beauty of Paulinus encouraged the secret rumour that his guilt was that of a successful lover. As soon as the empress perceived that the affection of Theodosius was irretrievably lost, she requested the permission of retiring to the distant solitude of Jerusalem. She obtained her request, but the jealousy of Theodosius, or the vindictive spirit of Pulcheria, pursued her in her last retreat; and Saturninus, count of the domestics, was directed to punish with death two ecclesiastics, her most favoured servants. Eudocia instantly revenged them by the assassination of the count: the furious passions which she indulged on this suspicious occasion seemed to justify the severity of Theodosius; and the empress, ignominiously stripped of the honours of her rank, was disgraced, perhaps unjustly, in the eyes of the world. The remainder of the life of Eudocia, about sixteen years, was spent in exile and devotion; and the approach of age, the death of Theodosius, the misfortunes of her only daughter, who was led a captive from Rome to Carthage, and the society of the Holy Monks of Palestine, insensibly confirmed the religious temper of her mind. After a full experience of the vicissitudes of human life, the daughter of the philosopher Leontius expired at Jerusalem, in the sixty-seventh year of her age; protesting with her dying breath that she had never transgressed the bounds of innocence and friendship.

An inconclusive war with Persia led to a peace of eighty years. Armenia was divided between the Persians and the Romans.

Chapter 33

THE INVASION OF AFRICA BY THE VANDALS. ST. AUGUSTIN
AND THE SIEGE OF HIPPO. SACK OF CARTHAGE. FABLE
OF THE SEVEN SLEEPERS

*Honorius died of dropsy in 423. He was eventually succeeded by
Valentinian III, the six-year-old son of Galla Placidia and the
general Constantius (whom she had married after the death of
Adolphus) and the cousin of Theodosius the Younger. Placidia
reigned for twenty-five years in her son's name. Her armies were
commanded by Aëtius and Boniface, whom Gibbon describes as "the
last of the Romans". After Aëtius had conspired to discredit him in
the eyes of Placidia, Boniface rashly proposed an alliance with the
Vandals in Spain and invited them to settle in Africa. This invitation,
which Boniface regretted too late, was accepted by the savage Vandal
king, Genseric.*

INVASION OF AFRICA BY THE VANDALS

THE long and narrow tract of the African coast was filled with
frequent monuments of Roman art and magnificence; and the
respective degrees of improvement might be accurately measured
by the distance from Carthage and the Mediterranean. A simple reflection will impress every thinking mind with the clearest idea of fertility
and cultivation: the country was extremely populous; the inhabitants
reserved a liberal subsistence for their own use; and the annual exportation, particularly of wheat, was so regular and plentiful, that Africa
deserved the name of the common granary of Rome and of mankind.
On a sudden the seven fruitful provinces, from Tangier to Tripoli, were
overwhelmed by the invasion of the Vandals, whose destructive rage has
perhaps been exaggerated by popular animosity, religious zeal, and
extravagant declamation. War in its fairest form implies a perpetual
violation of humanity and justice; and the hostilities of barbarians are
inflamed by the fierce and lawless spirit which incessantly disturbs their
peaceful and domestic society. The Vandals, where they found resistance, seldom gave quarter; and the deaths of their valient countrymen
were expiated by the ruin of the cities under whose walls they had fallen.
Careless of the distinctions of age, or sex, or rank, they employed every
species of indignity and torture to force from the captives a discovery of
their hidden wealth. The stern policy of Genseric justified his frequent
examples of military execution: he was not always the master of his own

passions or of those of his followers; and the calamities of war were aggravated by the licentiousness of the Moors and the fanaticism of the Donatists. Yet I shall not easily be persuaded that it was the common practice of the Vandals to extirpate the olives and other fruit-trees of a country where they intended to settle: nor can I believe that it was a usual stratagem to slaughter great numbers of their prisoners before the walls of a besieged city, for the sole purpose of infecting the air and producing a pestilence, of which they themselves must have been the first victims.[1]

ST. AUGUSTIN AND THE SIEGE OF HIPPO

The generous mind of Count Boniface was tortured by the exquisite distress of beholding the ruin which he had occasioned, and whose rapid progress he was unable to check. After the loss of a battle he retired into Hippo Regius, where he was immediately besieged by an enemy who considered him as the real bulwark of Africa. The maritime colony of *Hippo*, about two hundred miles westward of Carthage, had formerly acquired the distinguishing epithet of *Regius*, from the residence of Numidian kings; and some remains of trade and populousness still adhere to the modern city, which is known in Europe by the corrupted name of Bona. The military labours and anxious reflections of Count Boniface were alleviated by the edifying conversation of his friend St. Augustin; till that bishop, the light and pillar of the catholic church, was gently released, in the third month of the siege and in the seventy-sixth year of his age, from the actual and the impending calamities of his country. The youth of Augustin had been stained by the vices and errors which he so ingenuously confesses; but from the moment of his conversion to that of his death the manners of the bishop of Hippo were pure and austere, and the most conspicuous of his virtues was an ardent zeal against heretics of every denomination—the Manichæans, the Donatists, and the Pelagians, against whom he waged a perpetual controversy. When the city, some months after his death, was burnt by the Vandals, the library was fortunately saved which contained his voluminous writings—two hundred and thirty-two separate books or treatises on theological subjects, besides a complete exposition of the psalter and the gospel, and a copious magazine of epistles and homilies. According to the judgment of the most impartial critics, the superficial learning of

---

[1] The original complaints of the desolation of Africa are contained—1. In a letter from Capreolus, bishop of Carthage, to excuse his absence from the council of Ephesus. 2. In the Life of St. Augustin by his friend and colleague Possidius. 3. In the History of the Vandalic Persecution, by Victor Vitensis. The last picture, which was drawn sixty years after the event, is more expressive of the author's passions than of the truth of facts.

Augustin was confined to the Latin language;[1] and his style, though sometimes animated by the eloquence of passion, is usually clouded by false and affected rhetoric. But he possessed a strong, capacious, argumentative mind; he boldly sounded the dark abyss of grace, predestination, free-will, and original sin; and the rigid system of Christianity which he framed or restored has been entertained with public applause and secret reluctance by the Latin church.[2]

By the skill of Boniface, and perhaps by the ignorance of the Vandals, the siege of Hippo was protracted above fourteen months: the sea was continually open; and when the adjacent country had been exhausted by irregular rapine, the besiegers themselves were compelled by famine to relinquish their enterprise. The importance and danger of Africa were deeply felt by the regent of the West. Placidia implored the assistance of her Eastern ally; and the Italian fleet and army were reinforced by Aspar, who sailed from Constantinople with a powerful armament. As soon as the force of the two empires was united under the command of Boniface, he boldly marched against the Vandals; and the loss of a second battle irretrievably decided the fate of Africa. He embarked with the precipitation of despair; and the people of Hippo were permitted, with their families and effects, to occupy the vacant place of the soldiers, the greatest part of whom were either slain or made prisoners by the Vandals. The count, whose fatal credulity had wounded the vitals of the republic, might enter the palace of Ravenna with some anxiety, which was soon removed by the smiles of Placidia. Boniface accepted with gratitude the rank of patrician and the dignity of master-general of the Roman armies; but he must have blushed at the sight of those medals in which he was represented with the name and attributes of victory. The discovery of his fraud, the displeasure of the empress, and the distinguished favour of his rival, exasperated the haughty and perfidious soul of Aëtius. He hastily returned from Gaul to Italy, with a retinue, or rather with an army, of barbarian followers; and such was the weakness of the government, that the two generals decided their private quarrel in a bloody battle. Boniface was successful; but he received in the conflict a mortal wound from the spear of his adversary,

---

[1] In his early youth, St. Augustin disliked and neglected the study of Greek; and he frankly owns that he read the Platonists in a Latin version. Some modern critics have thought that his ignorance of Greek disqualified him from expounding the Scriptures; and Cicero or Quintilian would have required the knowledge of that language in a professor of rhetoric.

[2] The church of Rome has canonised Augustin and reprobated Calvin. Yet, as the *real* difference between them is invisible even to a theological microscope, the Molinists are oppressed by the authority of the saint, and the Jansenists are disgraced by their resemblance to the heretic. In the mean while the Protestant Arminians stand aloof and deride the mutual perplexity of the disputants. Perhaps a reasoner still more independent may smile in *his* turn when he peruses an Arminian Commentary on the Epistle to the Romans.

of which he expired within a few days, in such Christian and charitable sentiments that he exhorted his wife, a rich heiress of Spain, to accept Aëtius for her second husband. But Aëtius could not derive any immediate advantage from the generosity of his dying enemy: he was proclaimed a rebel by the justice of Placidia; and though he attempted to defend some strong fortresses, erected on his patrimonial estate, the Imperial power soon compelled him to retire into Pannonia, to the tents of his faithful Huns. The republic was deprived by their mutual discord of the service of her two most illustrious champions.

THE SACK OF CARTHAGE

It might naturally be expected, after the retreat of Boniface, that the Vandals would achieve without resistance or delay the conquest of Africa. Eight years however elapsed from the evacuation of Hippo to the reduction of Carthage. In the midst of that interval the ambitious Genseric, in the full tide of apparent prosperity, negociated a treaty of peace, by which he gave his son Hunneric for an hostage, and consented to leave the Western emperor in the undisturbed possession of the three Mauritanias. This moderation, which cannot be imputed to the justice, must be ascribed to the policy, of the conqueror. His throne was encompassed with domestic enemies, who accused the baseness of his birth, and asserted the legitimate claims of his nephews, the sons of Gonderic. Those nephews, indeed, he sacrificed to his safety; and their mother, the widow of the deceased king, was precipitated by his order into the river Ampsaga. But the public discontent burst forth in dangerous and frequent conspiracies; and the warlike tyrant is supposed to have shed more Vandal blood by the hand of the executioner than in the field of battle. The convulsions of Africa, which had favoured his attack, opposed the firm establishment of his power; and the various seditions of the Moors and Germans, the Donatists and catholics, continually disturbed or threatened the unsettled reign of the conqueror. As he advanced towards Carthage he was forced to withdraw his troops from the Western provinces; the sea-coast was exposed to the naval enterprises of the Romans of Spain and Italy; and, in the heart of Numidia, the strong inland city of Cirta still persisted in obstinate independence. These difficulties were gradually subdued by the spirit, the perseverance, and the cruelty of Genseric; who alternately applied the arts of peace and war to the establishment of his African kingdom. He subscribed a solemn treaty, with the hope of deriving some advantage from the term of its continuance and the moment of its violation. The vigilance of his enemies was relaxed by the protestations of friendship which concealed his hostile approach; and Carthage was at length surprised by the Vandals, five hundred and eighty-five years after the destruction of the city and republic by the younger Scipio.

A new city had arisen from its ruins, with the title of a colony; and though Carthage might yield to the royal prerogatives of Constantinople, and perhaps to the trade of Alexandria, or the splendour of Antioch, she still maintained the second rank in the West; as the *Rome* (if we may use the style of contemporaries) of the African world. That wealthy and opulent metropolis displayed, in a dependent condition, the image of a flourishing republic. Carthage contained the manufactures, the arms, and the treasures of the six provinces. A regular subordination of civil honours gradually ascended from the procurators of the streets and quarters of the city to the tribunal of the supreme magistrate, who, with the title of proconsul, represented the state and dignity of a consul of ancient Rome. Schools and *gymnasia* were instituted for the education of the African youth; and the liberal arts and manners, grammar, rhetoric, and philosophy, were publicly taught in the Greek and Latin languages. The buildings of Carthage were uniform and magnificent: a shady grove was planted in the midst of the capital; the *new* port, a secure and capacious harbour, was subservient to the commercial industry of citizens and strangers; and the splendid games of the circus and theatre were exhibited almost in the presence of the barbarians. The reputation of the Carthaginians was not equal to that of their country, and the reproach of Punic faith still adhered to their subtle and faithless character. The habits of trade and the abuse of luxury had corrupted their manners; but their impious contempt of monks and the shameless practice of unnatural lusts are the two abominations which excite the pious vehemence of Salvian, the preacher of the age.[1] The king of the Vandals severely reformed the vices of a voluptuous people; and the ancient, noble, ingenuous freedom of Carthage (these expressions of Victor are not without energy) was reduced by Genseric into a state of ignominious servitude. After he had permitted his licentious troops to satiate their rage and avarice, he instituted a more regular system of rapine and oppression. An edict was promulgated, which enjoined all persons, without fraud or delay, to deliver their gold, silver, jewels, and valuable furniture or apparel to the royal officers; and the attempt to secrete any part of their patrimony was inexorably punished with death and torture as an act of treason against the state. The lands of the proconsular province, which formed the immediate district of Carthage, were accurately measured and divided among the barbarians; and the conqueror reserved for his peculiar domain the fertile territory of Byzacium and the adjacent parts of Numidia and Gætulia.

It was natural enough that Genseric should hate those whom he had

[1] He declares that the peculiar vices of each country were collected in the sink of Carthage. In the indulgence of vice the Africans applauded their manly virtue. Et illi se magis virilis fortitudinis esse crederent, qui maxime viros fæminei usus probrositate fregissent. The streets of Carthage were polluted by effeminate wretches, who publicly assumed the countenance, the dress, and the character, of women. If a monk appeared in the city, the holy man was pursued with impious scorn and ridicule; detestantibus ridentium cachinnis.

injured: the nobility and senators of Carthage were exposed to his jealousy and resentment; and all those who refused the ignominious terms which their honour and religion forbade them to accept were compelled by the Arian tyrant to embrace the condition of perpetual banishment. Rome, Italy, and the provinces of the East, were filled with a crowd of exiles, of fugitives, and of ingenuous captives, who solicited the public compassion: and the benevolent epistles of Theodoret still preserve the names and misfortunes of Cælestian and Maria. The Syrian bishop deplores the misfortunes of Cælestian, who, from the state of a noble and opulent senator of Carthage, was reduced, with his wife and family, and servants, to beg his bread in a foreign country; but he applauds the resignation of the Christian exile, and the philosophic temper which, under the pressure of such calamities, could enjoy more real happiness than was the ordinary lot of wealth and prosperity. The story of Maria, the daughter of the magnificent Eudæmon, is singular and interesting. In the sack of Carthage she was purchased from the Vandals by some merchants of Syria, who afterwards sold her as a slave in their native country. A female attendant, transported in the same ship, and sold in the same family, still continued to respect a mistress whom fortune had reduced to the common level of servitude; and the daughter of Eudæmon received from her grateful affection the domestic services which she had once required from her obedience. This remarkable behaviour divulged the real condition of Maria, who, in the absence of the bishop of Cyrrhus, was redeemed from slavery by the generosity of some soldiers of the garrison. The liberality of Theodoret provided for her decent maintenance; and she passed ten months among the deaconesses of the church, till she was unexpectedly informed that her father, who had escaped from the ruin of Carthage, exercised an honourable office in one of the Western provinces. Her filial impatience was seconded by the pious bishop: Theodoret, in a letter still extant, recommends Maria to the bishop of Ægæ, a maritime city of Cilicia, which was frequented, during the annual fair, by the vessels of the West; most earnestly requesting that his colleague would use the maiden with a tenderness suitable to her birth; and that he would intrust her to the care of such faithful merchants as would esteem it a sufficient gain if they restored a daughter, lost beyond all human hope, to the arms of her afflicted parent.

THE FABLE OF THE SEVEN SLEEPERS

Among the insipid legends of ecclesiastical history, I am tempted to distinguish the memorable fable of the SEVEN SLEEPERS; whose imaginary date corresponds with the reign of the younger Theodosius, and the conquest of Africa by the Vandals. When the emperor Decius persecuted the Christians, seven noble youths of Ephesus concealed themselves in a spacious cavern in the side of an adjacent mountain; where they were doomed to perish by the tyrant, who gave orders that the entrance should be firmly secured with a pile of huge stones. They immediately fell into a deep slumber, which was miraculously prolonged, without injuring the powers of life, during a period of one hundred and eighty-seven years. At the end of that time, the slaves of Adolius, to whom the inheritance of the mountain had descended, removed the stones, to supply materials for some rustic edifice: the light of the sun darted into the cavern, and the Seven Sleepers were permitted to awake. After a slumber, as they thought of a few hours, they were pressed by the calls of hunger; and resolved that Jamblichus, one of their number, should secretly return to the city to purchase bread for the use of his companions. The youth (if we may still employ that appellation) could no longer recognise the once familiar aspect of his native country; and his surprise was increased by the appearance of a large cross, triumphantly erected over the principal gate of Ephesus. His singular dress and obsolete language confounded the baker, to whom he offered an ancient medal of Decius as the current coin of the empire; and Jamblichus, on the suspicion of a secret treasure, was dragged before the judge. Their mutual inquiries produced the amazing discovery that two centuries were almost elapsed since Jamblichus and his friends had escaped from the rage of a Pagan tyrant. The bishop of Ephesus, the clergy, the magistrates, the people, and, as it is said, the emperor Theodosius himself, hastened to visit the cavern of the Seven Sleepers; who bestowed their benediction, related their story, and at the same instant peaceably expired. The origin of this marvellous fable cannot be ascribed to the pious fraud and credulity of the *modern* Greeks, since the authentic tradition may be traced within half a century of the supposed miracle. James of Sarug, a Syrian bishop, who was born only two years after the death of the younger Theodosius, has devoted one of his two hundred and thirty homilies to the praise of the young men of Ephesus. Their legend, before the end of the sixth century, was translated from the Syriac into the Latin language, by the care of Gregory of Tours. The hostile communions of the East preserve their memory with equal reverence; and their names are honourably inscribed in the Roman, the Abyssinian, and the Russian calendar. Nor has their reputation been confined to the Christian world. This popular tale, which Mahomet might learn when he drove his camels to the fairs of Syria, is introduced, as a divine revelation, into the Koran.[1] The story of the Seven Sleepers has been adopted and adorned by the nations, from Bengal to Africa, who profess the Mahometan religion; and some vestiges of a similar

---

[1] With such an ample privilege Mahomet has not shown much taste or ingenuity. He has invented the dog (Al Rakim) of the Seven Sleepers; the respect of the sun, who altered his course twice a day that he might not shine into the cavern; and the care of God himself, who preserved their bodies from putrefaction by turning them to the right and left.

tradition have been discovered in the remote extremities of Scandinavia.[1] This easy and universal belief, so expressive of the sense of mankind, may be ascribed to the genuine merit of the fable itself. We imperceptibly advance from youth to age without observing the gradual, but incessant, change of human affairs; and even in our larger experience of history, the imagination is accustomed, by a perpetual series of causes and effects, to unite the most distant revolutions. But if the interval between two memorable eras could be instantly annihilated; if it were possible, after a momentary slumber of two hundred years, to display the *new* world to the eyes of a spectator who still retained a lively and recent impression of the *old*, his surprise and his reflections would furnish the pleasing subject of a philosophical romance. The scene could not be more advantageously placed than in the two centuries which elapsed between the reigns of Decius and of Theodosius the Younger. During this period the seat of government had been transported from Rome to a new city on the banks of the Thracian Bosphorus; and the abuse of military spirit had been suppressed by an artificial system of tame and ceremonious servitude. The throne of the persecuting Decius was filled by a succession of Christian and orthodox princes, who had extirpated the fabulous gods of antiquity: and the public devotion of the age was impatient to exalt the saints and martyrs of the catholic church on the altars of Diana and Hercules. The union of the Roman empire was dissolved; its genius was humbled in the dust; and armies of unknown barbarians, issuing from the frozen regions of the North, had established their victorious reign over the fairest provinces of Europe and Africa.

[1] Paul, the deacon of Aquileia, who lived towards the end of the eighth century, has placed in a cavern under a rock on the shore of the ocean the Seven Sleepers of the North, whose long repose was respected by the barbarians. Their dress declared them to be Romans; and the deacon conjectures that they were reserved by Providence as the future apostles of those unbelieving countries.

THE END OF THE
EMPIRE IN THE WEST

Chapter 35

INVASION OF GAUL AND ITALY BY ATTILA. FOUNDATION
OF VENICE. DEATH OF ATTILA AND DESTRUCTION OF HIS
EMPIRE. MURDER OF AËTIUS AND DEATH OF VALENTINIAN
III. SYMPTOMS OF DECAY IN THE ROMAN EMPIRE OF THE
WEST

*The progress of invasions by the Goths and kindred peoples had
been accelerated by the pressure in their rear by the Huns. In
Chapter 34 Gibbon describes the first appearance of Attila and
the establishment of the Huns in modern Hungary. Between 430–
440 Persia had been invaded and in 466 Attila, after ravaging
Europe as far as Constantinople, signed a treaty with the Eastern
empire. Theodosius the Younger died in 450 and was succeeded in
the empire of the East by his sister Pulcheria, who thus became
the first woman to rule the Romans. She soon however married
a senator, Marcian, who was himself invested with the Imperial
purple.*

*Meanwhile Attila, the king of the Huns, prepared to invade Gaul.
Here Theodoric, the son of Alaric, had become king of the Visigoths
on the death of Wallia. Aëtius, who had previously cultivated an
alliance with the Huns, now allied the Romans with the Goths. In
451 Attila invaded Gaul and besieged Orleans. Aëtius and Theodoric
marched to its relief.*

THE INVASION OF GAUL BY ATTILA

THE facility with which Attila had penetrated into the heart of
Gaul may be ascribed to his insidious policy as well as to the
terror of his arms. His public declarations were skilfully mitigated
by his private assurances; he alternately soothed and threatened the
Romans and the Goths; and the courts of Ravenna and Toulouse,
mutually suspicious of each other's intentions, beheld with supine indifference the approach of their common enemy. Aëtius was the sole
guardian of the public safety; but his wisest measures were embarrassed
by a faction which, since the death of Placidia, infested the Imperial
palace: the youth of Italy trembled at the sound of the trumpet; and the
barbarians, who from fear or affection were inclined to the cause of

Attila, awaited with doubtful and venal faith the event of the war. The patrician passed the Alps at the head of some troops whose strength and numbers scarcely deserved the name of an army. But on his arrival at Arles or Lyons he was confounded by the intelligence that the Visigoths, refusing to embrace the defence of Gaul, had determined to expect within their own territories the formidable invader whom they professed to despise. The senator Avitus, who after the honourable exercise of the Prætorian prefecture had retired to his estate in Auvergne, was persuaded to accept the important embassy, which he executed with ability and success. He represented to Theodoric that an ambitious conqueror who aspired to the dominion of the earth could be resisted only by the firm and unanimous alliance of the powers whom he laboured to oppress. The lively eloquence of Avitus inflamed the Gothic warriors by the description of the injuries which their ancestors had suffered from the Huns, whose implacable fury still pursued them from the Danube to the foot of the Pyrenees. He strenuously urged that it was the duty of every Christian to save from sacrilegious violation the churches of God and the relics of the saints; that it was the interest of every barbarian who had acquired a settlement in Gaul to defend the fields and vineyards, which were cultivated for his use, against the desolation of the Scythian shepherds. Theodoric yielded to the evidence of truth, adopted the measure at once the most prudent and the most honourable, and declared that as the faithful ally of Aëtius and the Romans he was ready to expose his life and kingdom for the common safety of Gaul. The Visigoths, who at that time were in the mature vigour of their fame and power, obeyed with alacrity the signal of war, prepared their arms and horses, and assembled under the standard of their aged king, who was resolved, with his two eldest sons, Torismond and Theodoric, to command in person his numerous and valiant people. The example of the Goths determined several tribes or nations that seemed to fluctuate between the Huns and the Romans. The indefatigable diligence of the patrician gradually collected the troops of Gaul and Germany, who had formerly acknowledged themselves the subjects or soldiers of the republic, but who now claimed the rewards of voluntary service and the rank of independent allies; the Læti, the Armoricans, the Breones, the Saxons, the Burgundians, the Sarmatians or Alani, the Ripuarians, and the Franks who followed Meroveus as their lawful prince. Such was the various army which, under the conduct of Aëtius and Theodoric, advanced by rapid marches to relieve Orleans, and to give battle to the innumerable host of Attila.

On their approach the king of the Huns immediately raised the siege, and sounded a retreat to recall the foremost of his troops from the pillage of a city which they had already entered. The valour of Attila was always guided by his prudence; and as he foresaw the fatal consequences of a defeat in the heart of Gaul, he repassed the Seine, and expected the enemy in the plains of Châlons, whose smooth and level surface was adapted to the operations of his Scythian cavalry. But in this tumultuary retreat the vanguard of the Romans and their allies continually pressed, and sometimes engaged, the troops whom Attila had posted in the rear; the hostile columns, in the darkness of the night and the perplexity of the roads, might encounter each other without design; and the bloody conflict of the Franks and Gepidæ, in which fifteen thousand barbarians were slain, was a prelude to a more general and decisive action. The Catalaunian fields spread themselves round Châlons, and extend, according to the vague measurement of Jornandes, to the length of one hundred and fifty, and the breadth of one hundred miles, over the whole province, which is entitled to the appellation of a *champaign* country. This spacious plain was distinguished, however, by some inequalities of ground; and the importance of an height which commanded the camp of Attila was understood and disputed by the two generals. The young and valiant Torismond first occupied the summit; the Goths rushed with irresistible weight on the Huns, who laboured to ascend from the opposite side: and the possession of this advantageous post inspired both the troops and their leaders with a fair assurance of victory. The anxiety of Attila prompted him to consult his priests and haruspices. It was reported that, after scrutinising the entrails of victims and scraping their bones, they revealed, in mysterious language, his own defeat, with the death of his principal adversary; and that the barbarian, by accepting the equivalent, expressed his involuntary esteem for the superior merit of Aëtius. But the unusual despondency which seemed to prevail among the Huns engaged Attila to use the expedient, so familiar to the generals of antiquity, of animating his troops by a military oration; and his language was that of a king who had often fought and conquered at their head. He pressed them to consider their past glory, their actual danger, and their future hopes. The same fortune which opened the deserts and morasses of Scythia to their unarmed valour, which had laid so many warlike nations prostrate at their feet, had reserved the *joys* of this memorable field for the consummation of their victories. The cautious steps of their enemies, their strict alliance, and their advantageous posts, he artfully represented as the effects, not of prudence, but of fear. The Visigoths alone were the strength and nerves of the opposite army; and the Huns might securely trample on the degenerate Romans, whose close and compact order betrayed their apprehensions, and who were equally incapable of supporting the dangers or the fatigues of a day of battle. The doctrine of predestination, so favourable to martial virtue, was carefully inculcated by the king of the Huns; who assured his subjects that the warriors, protected by Heaven, were safe and invulnerable amidst the darts of the enemy; but that the unerring Fates would strike their victims in the bosom of inglorious peace. "I myself," continued Attila, "will throw the first javelin, and the wretch who refuses to imitate the example of his sovereign is devoted to inevitable death." The spirit of the barbarians was rekindled by the presence, the voice, and the example of their intrepid leader; and Attila, yielding to their impatience, immediately formed his order of battle. At the head of his brave and faithful Huns, he occupied in person the centre of the line. The nations subject to his empire, the Rugians, the Heruli, the Thuringians, the Franks, the Burgundians, were extended, on either hand, over the ample space of the Catalaunian fields; the right wing was commanded by Ardaric, king of the Gepidæ; and the three valiant brothers who reigned over the Ostrogoths were posted on the left to oppose the kindred tribes of the Visigoths. The disposition of the allies was regulated by a different principle. Sangiban, the faithless king of the Alani, was placed in the centre: where his motions might be strictly watched, and his treachery might be instantly punished. Aëtius assumed the command of the left, and Theodoric of the right wing; while Torismond still continued to occupy the heights which appear to have stretched on the flank, and perhaps the rear, of the Scythian army. The nations from the Volga to the Atlantic were assembled on the plain of Châlons; but many of these nations had been divided by faction, or conquest, or emigration; and the appearance of similar arms and ensigns, which threatened each other, presented the image of a civil war.

The discipline and tactics of the Greeks and Romans form an interesting part of their national manners. The attentive study of the military operations of Xenophon, or Cæsar, or Frederic, when they are described by the same genius which conceived and executed them, may tend to improve (if such improvement can be wished) the art of destroying the human species. But the battle of Châlons [1] can only excite our curiosity by the magnitude of the object; since it was decided by the blind impetuosity of barbarians, and has been related by partial writers, whose civil or ecclesiastical profession secluded them from the knowledge of military affairs. Cassiodorus, however, had familiarly conversed with many Gothic warriors who served in that memorable engagement; "a conflict," as they informed him, "fierce, various, obstinate, and bloody; such as could not be paralleled either in the present or in past ages." The number of the slain amounted to one hundred and sixty-two thousand, or, according to another account, three hundred thousand persons; and these incredible exaggerations suppose a real and effective loss, sufficient to justify the historian's remark that whole generations may be swept away by the madness of kings in the space of a single hour. After the mutual and repeated discharge of missile weapons, in which the archers of Scythia might signalise their superior dexterity, the

[1] Gibbon and others after him were mistaken in giving the name of Châlons to the scene of Attila's defeat. It is now accepted that the action occurred in the plain of Maurica.—D.M.L.

cavalry and infantry of the two armies were furiously mingled in closer combat. The Huns, who fought under the eyes of their king, pierced through the feeble and doubtful centre of the allies, separated their wings from each other, and wheeling, with a rapid effort, to the left, directed their whole force against the Visigoths. As Theodoric rode along the ranks to animate his troops, he received a mortal stroke from the javelin of Andages, a noble Ostrogoth, and immediately fell from his horse. The wounded king was oppressed in the general disorder and trampled under the feet of his own cavalry; and this important death served to explain the ambiguous prophecy of the haruspices. Attila already exulted in the confidence of victory, when the valiant Torismond descended from the hills, and verified the remainder of the prediction. The Visigoths, who had been thrown into confusion by the flight, or defection, of the Alani, gradually restored their order of battle; and the Huns were undoubtedly vanquished, since Attila was compelled to retreat. He had exposed his person with the rashness of a private soldier; but the intrepid troops of the centre had pushed forwards beyond the rest of the line; their attack was faintly supported; their flanks were unguarded; and the conquerors of Scythia and Germany were saved by the approach of the night from a total defeat. They retired within the circle of waggons that fortified their camp; and the dismounted squadrons prepared themselves for a defence to which neither their arms nor their temper were adapted. The event was doubtful: but Attila had secured a last and honourable resource. The saddles and rich furniture of the cavalry were collected by his order into a funeral pile; and the magnanimous barbarian had resolved, if his entrenchments should be forced, to rush headlong into the flames, and to deprive his enemies of the glory which they might have acquired by the death or captivity of Attila.

But his enemies had passed the night in equal disorder and anxiety. The inconsiderate courage of Torismond was tempted to urge the pursuit, till be unexpectedly found himself, with a few followers, in the midst of the Scythian waggons. In the confusion of a nocturnal combat he was thrown from his horse; and the Gothic prince must have perished like his father, if his youthful strength and the intrepid zeal of his companions had not rescued him from this dangerous situation. In the same manner, but on the left of the line, Aëtius himself, separated from his allies, ignorant of their victory, and anxious for their fate, encountered and escaped the hostile troops that were scattered over the plains of Châlons; and at length reached the camp of the Goths, which he could only fortify with a slight rampart of shields till the dawn of day. The Imperial general was soon satisfied of the defeat of Attila, who still remained inactive within his entrenchments; and when he contemplated the bloody scene, he observed, with secret satisfaction, that the loss had principally fallen on the barbarians. The body of Theodoric, pierced with honourable wounds, was discovered under a heap of the slain: his subjects bewailed the death of their king and father; but their tears were mingled with songs and acclamations, and his funeral rites were performed in the face of a vanquished enemy. The Goths, clashing their arms, elevated on a buckler his eldest son Torismond, to whom they justly ascribed the glory of their success; and the new king accepted the obligation of revenge as a sacred portion of his paternal inheritance. Yet the Goths themselves were astonished by the fierce and undaunted aspect of their formidable antagonist; and their historian has compared Attila to a lion encompassed in his den and threatening his hunters with redoubled fury. The kings and nations who might have deserted his standard in the hour of distress were made sensible that the displeasure of their monarch was the most imminent and inevitable danger. All his instruments of martial music incessantly sounded a loud and animating strain of defiance; and the foremost troops, who advanced to the assault, were checked or destroyed by showers of arrows from every side of the entrenchments. It was determined in a general council of war to besiege the king of the Huns in his camp, to intercept his provisions, and to reduce him to the alternative of a disgraceful treaty or an unequal combat. But the impatience of the barbarians soon disdained these cautious and dilatory measures: and the mature policy of Aëtius was apprehensive that, after the extirpation of the Huns, the republic would be oppressed by the pride and power of the Gothic nation. The patrician exerted the superior ascendant of authority and reason to calm the passions which the son of Theodoric considered as a duty; represented, with seeming affection and real truth, the dangers of absence and delay; and persuaded Torismond to disappoint, by his speedy return, the ambitious designs of his brothers, who might occupy the throne and treasures of Toulouse. After the departure of the Goths, and the separation of the allied army, Attila was surprised at the vast silence that reigned over the plains of Châlons: the suspicion of some hostile stratagem detained him several days within the circle of his waggons, and his retreat beyond the Rhine confessed the last victory which was achieved in the name of the Western empire. Meroveus and his Franks, observing a prudent distance, and magnifying the opinion of their strength by the numerous fires which they kindled every night, continued to follow the rear of the Huns till they reached the confines of Thuringia. The Thuringians served in the army of Attila: they traversed, both in their march and in their return, the territories of the Franks; and it was perhaps in this war that they exercised the cruelties which, about fourscore years afterwards, were revenged by the son of Clovis. They massacred their hostages, as well as their captives: two hundred young maidens were tortured with exquisite and unrelenting rage; their bodies were torn asunder by wild horses, or their bones were crushed under the weight of rolling waggons; and their unburied limbs were abandoned on the public roads as a prey to dogs and vultures. Such were those savage ancestors whose imaginary virtues have sometimes excited the praise and envy of civilised ages!

THE INVASION OF ITALY

Neither the spirit, nor the forces, nor the reputation of Attila were impaired by the failure of the Gallic expedition. In the ensuing spring he repeated his demand of the princess Honoria and her patrimonial treasures. The demand was again rejected or eluded; and the indignant lover immediately took the field, passed the Alps, invaded Italy, and besieged Aquileia with an innumerable host of barbarians. Those barbarians were unskilled in the methods of conducting a regular siege, which, even among the ancients, required some knowledge, or at least some practice, of the mechanic arts. But the labour of many thousand provincials and captives, whose lives were sacrificed without pity, might execute the most painful and dangerous work. The skill of the Roman artists might be corrupted to the destruction of their country. The walls of Aquileia were assaulted by a formidable train of battering rams, moveable turrets, and engines that threw stones, darts, and fire;[1] and the monarch of the Huns employed the forcible impulse of hope, fear, emulation, and interest, to subvert the only barrier which delayed the conquest of Italy. Aquileia was at that period one of the richest, the most populous, and the strongest of the maritime cities of the Adriatic coast. The Gothic auxiliaries, who appear to have served under their native princes, Alaric and Antala, communicated their intrepid spirit and the citizens still remembered the glorious and successful resistance which their ancestors had opposed to a fierce, inexorable barbarian, who disgraced the majesty of the Roman purple. Three months were consumed without effect in the siege of Aquileia; till the want of provisions and the clamours of his army compelled Attila to relinquish the enterprise, and reluctantly to issue his orders that the troops should strike their tents the next morning, and begin their retreat. But as he rode round the walls, pensive, angry, and disappointed, he observed a stork preparing to leave her nest in one of the towers, and to fly with her infant family towards the country. He seized, with the ready penetration of a statesman, this trifling incident which chance had offered to superstition; and exclaimed, in a loud and cheerful tone, that such a domestic bird, so constantly attached to human society, would never have abandoned her ancient seats unless those towers had been devoted

---

[1] In the thirteenth century the Moguls battered the cities of China with large engines constructed by the Mahometans or Christians in their service, which threw stones from 150 to 300 pounds weight. In the defence of their country the Chinese used gunpowder, and even bombs, above an hundred years before they were known in Europe; yet even those celestial, or infernal, arms were insufficient to protect a pusillanimous nation.

to impending ruin and solitude. The favourable omen inspired an assurance of victory; the siege was renewed, and prosecuted with fresh vigour; a large breach was made in the part of the wall from whence the stork had taken her flight; the Huns mounted to the assault with irresistible fury; and the succeeding generation could scarcely discover the ruins of Aquileia. After this dreadful chastisement, Attila pursued his march; and as he passed, the cities of Altinum, Concordia, and Padua were reduced into heaps of stones and ashes. The inland towns, Vicenza, Verona, and Bergamo, were exposed to the rapacious cruelty of the Huns. Milan and Pavia submitted, without resistance, to the loss of their wealth; and applauded the unusual clemency which preserved from the flames the public as well as private buildings, and spared the lives of the captive multitude. The popular traditions of Comum, Turin, or Modena may justly be suspected; yet they concur with more authentic evidence to prove that Attila spread his ravages over the rich plains of modern Lombardy, which are divided by the Po, and bounded by the Alps and Apennine. When he took possession of the royal palace of Milan, he was surprised and offended at the sight of a picture which represented the Cæsars seated on their throne, and the princes of Scythia prostrate at their feet. The revenge which Attila inflicted on this monument of Roman vanity was harmless and ingenious. He commanded a painter to reverse the figures and the attitudes; and the emperors were delineated on the same canvas approaching in a suppliant posture to empty their bags of tributary gold before the throne of the Scythian monarch. The spectators must have confessed the truth and propriety of the alteration; and were perhaps tempted to apply, on this singular occasion, the well-known fable of the dispute between the lion and the man.

THE FOUNDATION OF VENICE

It is a saying worthy of the ferocious pride of Attila, that the grass never grew on the spot where his horse had trod. Yet the savage destroyer undesignedly laid the foundations of a republic which revived, in the feudal state of Europe, the art and spirit of commercial industry. The celebrated name of Venice, or Venetia, was formerly diffused over a large and fertile province of Italy, from the confines of Pannonia to the river Addua, and from the Po to the Rhætian and Julian Alps. Before the irruption of the barbarians, fifty Venetian cities flourished in peace and prosperity: Aquileia was placed in the most conspicuous station: but the ancient dignity of Padua was supported by agriculture and manufactures; and the property of five hundred citizens, who were entitled to the equestrian rank, must have amounted, at the strictest computation, to one million seven hundred thousand pounds. Many families of Aquileia, Padua, and the adjacent towns, who fled from the sword of the Huns, found a safe, though obscure, refuge in the neigh-bouring islands.[1] At the extremity of the Gulf, where the Adriatic feebly imitates the tides of the ocean, near an hundred small islands are separated by shallow water from the continent, and protected from the waves by several long slips of land, which admit the entrance of vessels through some secret and narrow channels. Till the middle of the fifth century these remote and sequestered spots remained without cultiva-tion, with few inhabitants, and almost without a name. But the manners of the Venetian fugitives, their arts and their government, were gradually formed by their new situation; and one of the epistles of Cassiodorus, which describes their condition about seventy years afterwards, may be considered as the primitive monument of the republic. The minister of Theodoric compares them, in his quaint declamatory style, to water-fowl, who had fixed their nests on the bosom of the waves; and though he allows that the Venetian provinces had formerly contained many noble families, he insinuates that they were now reduced by misfortune to the same level of humble poverty. Fish was the common, and almost the universal, food of every rank: their only treasure consisted in the plenty of salt which they extracted from the sea: and the exchange of that commodity, so essential to human life, was substituted in the neighbouring markets to the currency of gold and silver. A people whose habitations might be doubtfully assigned to the earth or water soon became alike familiar with the two elements; and the demands of avarice succeeded to those of necessity. The islanders, who, from Grado to Chiozza, were intimately connected with each other, penetrated into the heart of Italy, by the secure, though laborious, navigation of the rivers and inland canals. Their vessels, which were continually in-creasing in size and number, visited all the harbours of the Gulf; and the marriage which Venice annually celebrates with the Adriatic was contracted in her early infancy. The epistle of Cassiodorus, the Prætorian prefect, is addressed to the maritime tribunes; and he exhorts them, in a mild tone of authority, to animate the zeal of their country-men for the public service, which required their assistance to transport the magazines of wine and oil from the province of Istria to the royal city of Ravenna. The ambiguous office of these magistrates is explained by the tradition, that, in the twelve principal islands, twelve tribunes, or judges, were created by an annual and popular election. The existence of the Venetian republic under the Gothic kingdom of Italy is attested by the same authentic record which annihilates their lofty claim of origi-nal and perpetual independence.

The Italians, who had long since renounced the exercise of arms, were

[1] Venice is now held to have had its beginnings during the later invasions of the Lombards. There need be no doubt, however, that some people fleeing from Attila took refuge in the Lagoon. Gibbon's description therefore may be accepted with this *caveat*.—D.M.L.

surprised, after forty years' peace, by the approach of a formidable barbarian, whom they abhorred as the enemy of their religion as well as of their republic. Amidst the general consternation, Aëtius alone was incapable of fear; but it was impossible that he should achieve alone and unassisted any military exploits worthy of his former renown. The barbarians who had defended Gaul refused to march to the relief of Italy; and the succours promised by the Eastern emperor were distant and doubtful. Since Aëtius, at the head of his domestic troops, still maintained the field, and harassed or retarded the march of Attila, he never showed himself more truly great than at the time when his conduct was blamed by an ignorant and ungrateful people. If the mind of Valentinian had been susceptible of any generous sentiments, he would have chosen such a general for his example and his guide. But the timid grandson of Theodosius, instead of sharing the dangers, escaped from the sound, of war; and his hasty retreat from Ravenna to Rome, from an impregnable fortress to an open capital, betrayed his secret intention of abandoning Italy as soon as the danger should approach his Imperial person. This shameful abdication was suspended, however, by the spirit of doubt and delay which commonly adheres to pusillanimous counsels, and sometimes corrects their pernicious tendency. The Western emperor, with the senate and people of Rome, embraced the more salutary resolution of deprecating, by a solemn and suppliant embassy, the wrath of Attila. This important commission was accepted by Avienus, who, from his birth and riches, his consular dignity, the numerous train of his clients, and his personal abilities, held the first rank in the Roman senate. The specious and artful character of Avienus was admirably qualified to conduct a negociation either of public or private interest: his colleague Trigetius had exercised the Prætorian prefecture of Italy; and Leo, bishop of Rome, consented to expose his life for the safety of his flock. The genius of Leo was exercised and displayed in the public misfortunes; and he has deserved the appellation of *Great* by the successful zeal with which he laboured to establish his opinions and his authority, under the venerable names of orthodox faith and ecclesiastical discipline. The Roman ambassadors were introduced to the tent of Attila, as he lay encamped at the place where the slow-winding Mincius is lost in the foaming waves of the lake Benacus, and trampled, with his Scythian cavalry, the farms of Catullus and Virgil. The barbarian monarch listened with favourable, and even respectful, attention; and the deliverance of Italy was purchased by the immense ransom or dowry of the princess Honoria. The state of his army might facilitate the treaty and hasten his retreat. Their martial spirit was relaxed by the wealth and indolence of a warm climate. The shepherds of the North, whose ordinary food consisted of milk and raw flesh, indulged themselves too freely in the use of bread, of wine, and of meat prepared and seasoned by the arts of cookery; and the progress of disease revenged in some measure the injuries of the Italians. When Attila declared his resolution of carrying his victorious arms to the gates of Rome, he was admonished by his friends, as well as by his enemies, that Alaric had not long survived the conquest of the eternal city. His mind, superior to real danger, was assaulted by imaginary terrors; nor could he escape the influence of superstition, which had so often been subservient to his designs. The pressing eloquence of Leo, his majestic aspect and sacerdotal robes, excited the veneration of Attila for the spiritual father of the Christians. The apparition of the two apostles St. Peter and St. Paul, who menaced the barbarian with instant death if he rejected the prayer of their successor, is one of the noblest legends of ecclesiastical tradition. The safety of Rome might deserve the interposition of celestial beings; and some indulgence is due to a fable which has been represented by the pencil of Raphael and the chisel of Algardi.

THE DEATH OF ATTILA AND DESTRUCTION OF HIS EMPIRE

Before the king of the Huns evacuated Italy, he threatened to return more dreadful, and more implacable, if his bride, the princess Honoria, were not delivered to his ambassadors within the term stipulated by the treaty. Yet, in the mean while, Attila relieved his tender anxiety by adding a beautiful maid, whose name was Ildico, to the list of his innumerable wives. Their marriage was celebrated with barbaric pomp and festivity, at his wooden palace beyond the Danube; and the monarch, oppressed with wine and sleep, retired at a late hour from the banquet to the nuptial bed. His attendants continued to respect his pleasures or his repose the greatest part of the ensuing day, till the unusual silence alarmed their fears and suspicions; and, after attempting to awaken Attila by loud and repeated cries, they at length broke into the royal apartment. They found the trembling bride sitting by the bedside, hiding her face with her veil, and lamenting her own danger, as well as the death of the king, who had expired during the night. An artery had suddenly burst: and as Attila lay in a supine posture, he was suffocated by a torrent of blood, which, instead of finding a passage through the nostrils, regurgitated into the lungs and stomach. His body was solemnly exposed in the midst of the plain, under a silken pavilion; and the chosen squadrons of the Huns, wheeling round in measured evolutions, chanted a funeral song to the memory of a hero, glorious in his life, invincible in his death, the father of his people, the scourge of his enemies, and the terror of the world. According to their national custom, the barbarians cut off a part of their hair, gashed their faces with unseemly wounds, and bewailed their valiant leader as he deserved, not with the tears of women, but with the blood of warriors. The remains of Attila were enclosed within three coffins, of gold, of silver, and of iron, and privately buried in the night: the spoils of nations were thrown into his grave; the captives who had opened the ground were inhumanly massacred; and the same Huns, who had indulged such excessive grief, feasted, with dissolute and intemperate mirth, about the recent sepulchre of their king. It was reported at Constantinople that, on the fortunate night in which he expired, Marcian beheld in a dream the bow of Attila broken asunder: and the report may be allowed to prove how seldom the image of that formidable barbarian was absent from the mind of a Roman emperor.

The revolution which subverted the empire of the Huns established the fame of Attila, whose genius alone had sustained the huge and disjointed fabric. After his death the boldest chieftains aspired to the rank of kings; the most powerful kings refused to acknowledge a superior; and the numerous sons whom so many various mothers bore to the deceased monarch divided and disputed like a private inheritance the sovereign command of the nations of Germany and Scythia. The bold Ardaric felt and represented the disgrace of this servile partition; and his subjects, the warlike Gepidæ, with the Ostrogoths, under the conduct of three valiant brothers, encouraged their allies to vindicate the rights of freedom and royalty. In a bloody and decisive conflict on the banks of the river Netad in Pannonia, the lance of the Gepidæ, the sword of the Goths, the arrows of the Huns, the Suevic infantry, the light arms of the Heruli, and the heavy weapons of the Alani, encountered or supported each other; and the victory of Ardaric was accompanied with the slaughter of thirty thousand of his enemies. Ellac, the eldest son of Attila, lost his life and crown in the memorable battle of Netad: his early valour had raised him to the throne of the Acatzires, a Scythian people, whom he subdued; and his father, who loved the superior merit, would have envied the death, of Ellac. His brother Dengisich, with an army of Huns still formidable in their flight and ruin, maintained his ground above fifteen years on the banks of the Danube. The palace of Attila, with the old country of Dacia, from the Carpathian hills to the Euxine, became the seat of a new power which was erected by Ardaric, king of the Gepidæ. The Pannonian conquests, from Vienna to Sirmium, were occupied by the Ostrogoths; and the settlements of the tribes who had so bravely asserted their native freedom were irregularly distributed according to the measure of their respective strength. Surrounded and oppressed by the multitude of his father's slaves, the kingdom of Dengisich was confined to the circle of his waggons; his desperate courage urged him to invade the Eastern empire: he fell in battle, and his head, ignominiously exposed in the Hippodrome, exhibited a grateful spectacle to the people of Constantinople. Attila had fondly or superstitiously believed that Irnac, the youngest of his sons, was destined to perpetuate the glories of his race. The character of that prince, who attempted to moderate the rashness of his brother Dengisich, was more suitable to the declining condition of the Huns; and Irnac, with his subject hordes, retired into the heart of the Lesser Scythia. They were soon overwhelmed by a torrent of new barbarians, who followed the same road which their own ancestors had formerly discovered. The *Geougen*, or Avares, whose residence is assigned by the Greek writers to the shores of the ocean, impelled the adjacent tribes; till at length the Igours of the North, issuing from the cold Siberian regions which produce the most valuable furs, spread themselves over the desert as far as the Borysthenes and the Caspian gates, and finally extinguished the empire of the Huns.

THE MURDER OF AËTIUS AND DEATH OF VALENTINIAN III

Such an event might contribute to the safety of the Eastern empire under the reign of a prince who conciliated the friendship, without forfeiting the esteem, of the barbarians. But the emperor of the West, the feeble and dissolute Valentinian, who had reached his thirty-fifth year without attaining the age of reason or courage, abused this apparent security to undermine the foundations of his own throne by the murder of the patrician Aëtius. From the instinct of a base and jealous mind, he hated the man who was universally celebrated as the terror of the barbarians and the support of the republic; and his new favourite, the eunuch Heraclius, awakened the emperor from the supine lethargy which might be disguised during the life of Placidia [1] by the excuse of filial piety. The fame of Aëtius, his wealth and dignity, the numerous and martial train of barbarian followers, his powerful dependents who filled the civil offices of the state, and the hopes of his son Gaudentius, who was already contracted to Eudoxia, the emperor's daughter, had raised him above the rank of a subject. The ambitious designs, of which he was secretly accused, excited the fears as well as the resentment of Valentinian. Aëtius himself, supported by the consciousness of his merit, his services, and perhaps his innocence, seems to have maintained a haughty and indiscreet behaviour. The patrician offended his sovereign by an hostile declaration; he aggravated the offence by compelling him to ratify with a solemn oath a treaty of reconciliation and alliance; he proclaimed his suspicions, he neglected his safety; and from a vain confidence that the enemy whom he despised was incapable even of a manly crime, he rashly ventured his person in the palace of Rome. Whilst he urged, perhaps with intemperate vehemence, the marriage of

---

[1] Placidia died at Rome, November 27, A.D. 450. She was buried at Ravenna, where her sepulchre, and even her corpse, seated in a chair of cypress-wood, were preserved for ages. The empress received many compliments from the orthodox clergy; and St. Peter Chrysologus assured her that her zeal for the Trinity had been recompensed by an august trinity of children.

his son, Valentinian, drawing his sword—the first sword he had ever drawn—plunged it in the breast of a general who had saved his empire: his courtiers and eunuchs ambitiously struggled to imitate their master; and Aëtius, pierced with an hundred wounds, fell dead in the royal presence. Boethius, the Prætorian prefect, was killed at the same moment; and before the event could be divulged, the principal friends of the patrician were summoned to the palace and separately murdered. The horrid deed, palliated by the specious names of justice and necessity, was immediately communicated by the emperor to his soldiers, his subjects, and his allies. The nations who were strangers or enemies to Aëtius generously deplored the unworthy fate of a hero; the barbarians who had been attached to his service dissembled their grief and resentment; and the public contempt which had been so long entertained for Valentinian was at once converted into deep and universal abhorrence. Such sentiments seldom pervade the walls of a palace; yet the emperor was confounded by the honest reply of a Roman whose approbation he had not disdained to solicit. "I am ignorant, sir, of your motives or provocations; I only know that you have acted like a man who cuts off his right hand with his left."

The luxury of Rome seems to have attracted the long and frequent visits of Valentinian, who was consequently more despised at Rome than in any other part of his dominions. A republican spirit was insensibly revived in the senate, as their authority, and even their supplies, became necessary for the support of his feeble government. The stately demeanour of an hereditary monarch offended their pride, and the pleasures of Valentinian were injurious to the peace and honour of noble families. The birth of the empress Eudoxia was equal to his own, and her charms and tender affection deserved those testimonies of love which her inconstant husband dissipated in vague and unlawful amours. Petronius Maximus, a wealthy senator of the Anician family, who had been twice consul, was possessed of a chaste and beautiful wife: her obstinate resistance served only to irritate the desires of Valentinian, and he resolved to accomplish them either by stratagem or force. Deep gaming was one of the vices of the court; the emperor, who, by chance or contrivance, had gained from Maximus a considerable sum, uncourteously exacted his ring as a security for the debt, and sent it by a trusty messenger to his wife, with an order in her husband's name that she should immediately attend the empress Eudoxia. The unsuspecting wife of Maximus was conveyed in her litter to the Imperial palace; the emissaries of her impatient lover conducted her to a remote and silent bed-chamber; and Valentinian violated, without remorse, the laws of hospitality. Her tears when she returned home, her deep affliction, and her bitter reproaches against a husband whom she considered as the accomplice of his own shame, excited Maximus to a just revenge; the desire of revenge was stimulated by ambition; and he might reasonably aspire, by the free suffrage of the Roman senate, to the throne of a detested and despicable rival. Valentinian, who supposed that every human breast was devoid like his own of friendship and gratitude, had imprudently admitted among his guards several domestics and followers of Aëtius. Two of these, of barbarian race, were persuaded to execute a sacred and honourable duty by punishing with death the assassin of their patron; and their intrepid courage did not long expect a favourable moment. Whilst Valentinian amused himself in the field of Mars with the spectacle of some military sports, they suddenly rushed upon him with drawn weapons, despatched the guilty Heraclius, and stabbed the emperor to the heart, without the least opposition from his numerous train, who seemed to rejoice in the tyrant's death. Such was the fate of Valentinian the Third, the last Roman emperor of the family of Theodosius. He faithfully imitated the hereditary weakness of his cousin and his two uncles, without inheriting the gentleness, the purity, the innocence, which alleviate in their characters the want of spirit and ability. Valentinian was less excusable, since he had passions without virtues: even his religion was questionable; and though he never deviated into the paths of heresy, he scandalised the pious Christians by his attachment to the profane arts of magic and divination.

SYMPTOMS OF DECAY IN THE ROMAN EMPIRE
OF THE WEST

As early as the time of Cicero and Varro it was the opinion of the Roman augurs that the *twelve vultures* which Romulus had seen represented the *twelve centuries* assigned for the fatal period of his city. This prophecy, disregarded perhaps in the season of health and prosperity, inspired the people with gloomy apprehensions when the twelfth century, clouded with disgrace and misfortune, was almost elapsed; and even posterity must acknowledge with some surprise that the arbitrary interpretation of an accidental or fabulous circumstance has been seriously verified in the downfall of the Western empire. But its fall was announced by a clearer omen than the flight of vultures: the Roman government appeared every day less formidable to its enemies, more odious and oppressive to its subjects. The taxes were multiplied with the public distress; economy was neglected in proportion as it became necessary; and the injustice of the rich shifted the unequal burden from themselves to the people, whom they defrauded of the *indulgences* that might sometimes have alleviated their misery. The severe inquisition, which confiscated their goods and tortured their persons, compelled the subjects of Valentinian to prefer the more simple tyranny of the barbarians, to fly to the woods and mountains, or to embrace the vile and abject condition of mercenary servants. They abjured and abhorred the name of Roman citizens, which had formerly excited the ambition of mankind. The Armorican provinces of Gaul and the greatest part of Spain were thrown into a state of disorderly independence by the confederations of the Bagaudæ, and the Imperial ministers pursued with proscriptive laws and ineffectual arms the rebels whom they had made. If all the barbarian conquerors had been annihilated in the same hour, their total destruction would not have restored the empire of the West: and if Rome still survived, she survived the loss of freedom, of virtue, and of honour.

Chapter 36

THE EMPEROR MAJORIAN. ODOACER, KING OF ITALY

Although the Huns had made but a transitory sojourn in Italy, the organisation of the West was now shaken beyond repair. Within three months of Valentinian's death (455) Genseric (Gaiseric) had brought his fleet to the mouth of the Tiber and sacked Rome.

The next twenty years witnessed the final collapse of the West under a series of emperors who are but names. Some respite was obtained in the short reign (457–461) of Majorian.

THE EMPEROR MAJORIAN

THE successor of Avitus presents the welcome discovery of a great and heroic character, such as sometimes arise, in a degenerate age, to vindicate the honour of the human species. The emperor Majorian has deserved the praises of his contemporaries and of posterity; and these praises may be strongly expressed in the words of a judicious and disinterested historian: "That he was gentle to his subjects; that he was terrible to his enemies; and that he excelled in *every* virtue *all* his predecessors who had reigned over the Romans." Such a testimony may justify at least the panegyric of Sidonius; and we may acquiesce in the assurance that, although the obsequious orator would have flattered with equal zeal the most worthless of princes, the extraordinary merit of his object confined him, on this occasion, within the bounds of truth. Majorian derived his name from his maternal grandfather, who, in the reign of the great Theodosius, had commanded the troops of the Illyrian frontier. He gave his daughter in marriage to the father of Majorian, a respectable officer, who administered the revenues of Gaul with skill and integrity; and generously preferred the friendship of Aëtius to the tempting offers of an insidious court. His son, the future emperor, who was educated in the profession of arms, displayed, from his early youth, intrepid courage, premature wisdom, and unbounded liberality in a scanty fortune. He followed the standard of Aëtius, contributed to his success, shared, and sometimes eclipsed, his glory, and at last excited the jealousy of the patrician, or rather of his wife, who forced him to retire from the service. Majorian, after the death of Aëtius, was recalled and promoted: and his intimate connection with Count Ricimer was the immediate step by which he ascended the throne of the Western empire. During the vacancy that succeeded the abdication of Avitus,

498

the ambitious barbarian, whose birth excluded him from the Imperial
dignity, governed Italy, with the title of Patrician; resigned to his friend
the conspicuous station of master-general of the cavalry and infantry;
and, after an interval of some months, consented to the unanimous wish
of the Romans, whose favour Majorian had solicited by a recent victory
over the Alemanni. He was invested with the purple at Ravenna: and
the epistle which he addressed to the senate will best describe his situation and his sentiments. "Your election, Conscript Fathers! and the
ordinance of the most valiant army, have made me your emperor. May
the propitious Deity direct and prosper the counsels and events of my
administration to your advantage and to the public welfare! For my
own part, I did not aspire, I have submitted, to reign; nor should I have
discharged the obligations of a citizen if I had refused, with base and
selfish ingratitude, to support the weight of those labours which were
imposed by the republic. Assist, therefore, the prince whom you have
made; partake the duties which you have enjoined; and may our common endeavours promote the happiness of an empire which I have
accepted from your hands. Be assured that, in our times, justice shall
resume her ancient vigour, and that virtue shall become not only innocent but meritorious. Let none, except the authors themselves, be
apprehensive of *delations*, which, as a subject, I have always condemned,
and, as a prince, will severely punish. Our own vigilance, and that of
our father, the patrician Ricimer, shall regulate all military affairs and
provide for the safety of the Roman world, which we have saved from
foreign and domestic enemies. You now understand the maxims of my
government: you may confide in the faithful love and sincere assurances
of a prince who has formerly been the companion of your life and
dangers, who still glories in the name of senator, and who is anxious that
you should never repent of the judgment which you have pronounced in
his favour." The emperor, who, amidst the ruins of the Roman world,
revived the ancient language of law and liberty, which Trajan would not
have disclaimed, must have derived those generous sentiments from his
own heart, since they were not suggested to his imitation by the customs
of his age or the example of his predecessors.

The private and public actions of Majorian are very imperfectly
known: but his laws, remarkable for an original cast of thought and
expression, faithfully represent the character of a sovereign who loved
his people, who sympathised in their distress, who had studied the
causes of the decline of the empire, and who was capable of applying (as
far as such reformation was practicable) judicious and effectual remedies
to the public disorders. His regulations concerning the finances manifestly tended to remove, or at least to mitigate, the most intolerable
grievances. I. From the first hour of his reign, he was solicitous (I
translate his own words) to relieve the *weary* fortunes of the provincials,
oppressed by the accumulated weight of indictions and superindictions.

With this view, he granted an universal amnesty, a final and absolute discharge of all arrears of tribute, of all debts which, under any pretence, the fiscal officers might demand from the people. This wise dereliction of obsolete, vexatious, and unprofitable claims, improved and purified the sources of the public revenue; and the subject, who could now look back without despair, might labour with hope and gratitude for himself and for his country. II. In the assessment and collection of taxes Majorian restored the ordinary jurisdiction of the provincial magistrates, and suppressed the extraordinary commissions which had been introduced in the name of the emperor himself or of the Prætorian prefects. The favourite servants who obtained such irregular powers were insolent in their behaviour and arbitrary in their demands: they affected to despise the subordinate tribunals, and they were discontented if their fees and profits did not twice exceed the sum which they condescended to pay into the treasury. One instance of their extortion would appear incredible were it not authenticated by the legislator himself. They exacted the whole payment in gold: but they refused the current coin of the empire, and would accept only such ancient pieces as were stamped with the names of Faustina or the Antonines. The subject who was unprovided with these curious medals had recourse to the expedient of compounding with their rapacious demands; or, if he succeeded in the research, his imposition was doubled according to the weight and value of the money of former times. III. "The municipal corporations (says the emperor), the lesser senates (so antiquity has justly styled them), deserve to be considered as the heart of the cities and the sinews of the republic. And yet so low are they now reduced, by the injustice of magistrates and the venality of collectors, that many of their members, renouncing their dignity and their country, have taken refuge in distant and obscure exile." He urges, and even compels, their return to their respective cities; but he removes the grievance which had forced them to desert the exercise of their municipal functions. They are directed, under the authority of the provincial magistrates, to resume their office of levying the tribute; but, instead of being made responsible for the whole sum assessed on their district, they are only required to produce a regular account of the payments which they have actually received, and of the defaulters who are still indebted to the public. IV. But Majorian was not ignorant that these corporate bodies were too much inclined to retaliate the injustice and oppression which they had suffered, and he therefore revives the useful office of the *defenders of cities*. He exhorts the people to elect, in a full and free assembly, some man of discretion and integrity who would dare to assert their privileges, to represent their grievances, to protect the poor from the tyranny of the rich, and to inform the emperor of the abuses that were committed under the sanction of his name and authority.

The spectator who casts a mournful view over the ruins of ancient

Rome is tempted to accuse the memory of the Goths and Vandals for the mischief which they had neither leisure, nor power, nor perhaps inclination, to perpetrate. The tempest of war might strike some lofty turrets to the ground; but the destruction which undermined the foundations of those massy fabrics was prosecuted, slowly and silently, during a period of ten centuries; and the motives of interest, that afterwards operated without shame or control, were severely checked by the taste and spirit of the emperor Majorian. The decay of the city had gradually impaired the value of the public works. The circus and theatres might still excite, but they seldom gratified, the desires of the people: the temples which had escaped the zeal of the Christians were no longer inhabited either by gods or men; the diminished crowds of the Romans were lost in the immense space of their baths and porticoes; and the stately libraries and halls of justice became useless to an indolent generation whose repose was seldom disturbed either by study or business. The monuments of consular or Imperial greatness were no longer revered as the immortal glory of the capital: they were only esteemed as an inexhaustible mine of materials, cheaper, and more convenient, than the distant quarry. Specious petitions were continually addressed to the easy magistrates of Rome which stated the want of stones or bricks for some necessary service: the fairest forms of architecture were rudely defaced for the sake of some paltry or pretended repairs; and the degenerate Romans, who converted the spoil to their own emolument, demolished, with sacrilegious hands, the labours of their ancestors. Majorian, who had often sighed over the desolation of the city, applied a severe remedy to the growing evil. He reserved to the prince and senate the sole cognizance of the extreme cases which might justify the destruction of an ancient edifice; imposed a fine of fifty pounds of gold (two thousand pounds sterling) on every magistrate who should presume to grant such illegal and scandalous licence; and threatened to chastise the criminal obedience of their subordinate officers by a severe whipping and the amputation of both their hands. In the last instance the legislator might seem to forget the proportion of guilt and punishment; but his zeal arose from a generous principle, and Majorian was anxious to protect the monuments of those ages in which he would have desired and deserved to live. The emperor conceived that it was his interest to increase the number of his subjects; that it was his duty to guard the purity of the marriage-bed: but the means which he employed to accomplish these salutary purposes are of an ambiguous, and perhaps exceptionable, kind. The pious maids who consecrated their virginity to Christ were restrained from taking the veil till they had reached their fortieth year. Widows under that age were compelled to form a second alliance within the term of five years, by the forfeiture of half their wealth to their nearest relations or to the state. Unequal marriages were condemned or annulled. The punishment of confiscation and exile was deemed so inadequate to the guilt of adultery, that, if the criminal returned to Italy, he might, by the express declaration of Majorian, be slain with impunity.

While the emperor Majorian assiduously laboured to restore the happiness and virtue of the Romans, he encountered the arms of Genseric, from his character and situation their most formidable enemy. A fleet of Vandals and Moors landed at the mouth of the Liris or Garigliano; but the Imperial troops surprised and attacked the disorderly barbarians, who were encumbered with the spoils of Campania; they were chased with slaughter to their ships, and their leader, the king's brother-in-law, was found in the number of the slain. Such vigilance might announce the character of the new reign, but the strictest vigilance and the most numerous forces were insufficient to protect the long-extended coast of Italy from the depredations of a naval war. The public opinion had imposed a nobler and more arduous task on the genius of Majorian. Rome expected from him alone the restitution of Africa, and the design which he formed of attacking the Vandals in their new settlements was the result of bold and judicious policy. If the intrepid emperor could have infused his own spirit into the youth of Italy; if he could have revived in the field of Mars the manly exercises in which he had always surpassed his equals; he might have marched against Genseric at the head of a *Roman* army. Such a reformation of national manners might be embraced by the rising generation; but it is the misfortune of those princes who laboriously sustain a declining monarchy, that, to obtain some immediate advantage, or to avert some impending danger, they are forced to countenance, and even to multiply, the most pernicious abuses. Majorian, like the weakest of his predecessors, was reduced to the disgraceful expedient of substituting barbarian auxiliaries in the place of his unwarlike subjects: and his superior abilities could only be displayed in the vigour and dexterity with which he wielded a dangerous instrument, so apt to recoil on the hand that used it. Besides the confederates who were already engaged in the service of the empire, the fame of his liberality and valour attracted the nations of the Danube, the Borysthenes, and perhaps of the Tanais. Many thousands of the bravest subjects of Attila, the Gepidæ, the Ostrogoths, the Rugians, the Burgundians, the Suevi, the Alani, assembled in the plains of Liguria, and their formidable strength was balanced by their mutual animosities. They passed the Alps in a severe winter. The emperor led the way on foot and in complete armour, sounding with his long staff the depth of the ice or snow, and encouraging the Scythians, who complained of the extreme cold, by the cheerful assurance that they should be satisfied with the heat of Africa. The citizens of Lyons had presumed to shut their gates: they soon implored, and experienced, the clemency of Majorian. He vanquished Theodoric in the field, and admitted to his friendship and alliance a king whom he had found not unworthy of his arms. The beneficial though precarious reunion of the greatest part of Gaul and Spain was the effect of persuasion as well as of force; and the independent Bagaudæ, who had escaped or resisted the oppression of former reigns, were disposed to confide in the virtues of Majorian. His camp was filled with barbarian allies; his throne was supported by the zeal of an affectionate people; but the emperor had foreseen that it was impossible without a maritime power to achieve the conquest of Africa. In the first Punic war the republic had exerted such incredible diligence, that, within sixty days after the first stroke of the axe had been given in the forest, a fleet of one hundred and sixty galleys proudly rode at anchor in the sea. Under circumstances much less favourable, Majorian equalled the spirit and perseverance of the ancient Romans. The woods of the Apennine were felled; the arsenals and manufactures of Ravenna and Misenum were restored; Italy and Gaul vied with each other in liberal contributions to the public service; and the Imperial navy of three hundred large galleys, with an adequate proportion of transports and smaller vessels, was collected in the secure and capacious harbour of Carthagena in Spain. The intrepid countenance of Majorian animated his troops with a confidence of victory; and if we might credit the historian Procopius, his courage sometimes hurried him beyond the bounds of prudence. Anxious to explore with his own eyes the state of the Vandals, he ventured, after disguising the colour of his hair, to visit Carthage in the character of his own ambassador: and Genseric was afterwards mortified by the discovery that he had entertained and dismissed the emperor of the Romans. Such an anecdote may be rejected as an improbable fiction, but it is a fiction which would not have been imagined unless in the life of a hero.

Without the help of a personal interview, Genseric was sufficiently acquainted with the genius and designs of his adversary. He practised his customary arts of fraud and delay, but he practised them without success. His applications for peace became each hour more submissive, and perhaps more sincere; but the inflexible Majorian had adopted the ancient maxim that Rome could not be safe as long as Carthage existed in a hostile state. The king of the Vandals distrusted the valour of his native subjects, who were enervated by the luxury of the South; he suspected the fidelity of the vanquished people, who abhorred him as an Arian tyrant; and the desperate measure which he executed of reducing Mauritania into a desert could not defeat the operations of the Roman emperor, who was at liberty to land his troops on any part of the African coast. But Genseric was saved from impending and inevitable ruin by the treachery of some powerful subjects, envious or apprehensive of their master's success. Guided by their secret intelligence, he surprised the unguarded fleet in the bay of Carthagena: many of the ships were sunk, or taken, or burnt; and the preparations of three years were destroyed in a single day. After this event the behaviour of the two antagonists showed them superior to their fortune. The Vandal, instead of being elated by this accidental victory, immediately renewed his solicitations for peace. The emperor of the West, who was capable of forming great designs and of supporting heavy disappointments, consented to a treaty, or rather to a suspension of arms, in the full assurance that before he could restore his navy he should be supplied with provocations to justify a second war. Majorian returned to Italy to prosecute his labours for the public happiness; and as he was conscious of his own integrity, he might long remain ignorant of the dark conspiracy which threatened his throne and his life. The recent misfortune of Carthagena sullied the glory which had dazzled the eyes of the multitude: almost every description of civil and military officers were exasperated against the Reformer, since they all derived some advantage from the abuses which he endeavoured to suppress; and the patrician Ricimer impelled the inconstant passions of the barbarians against a prince whom he esteemed and hated. The virtues of Majorian could not protect him from the impetuous sedition which broke out in the camp near Tortona at the foot of the Alps. He was compelled to abdicate the Imperial purple; five days after his abdication it was reported that he died of a dysentery; and the humble tomb which covered his remains was consecrated by the respect and gratitude of succeeding generations. The private character of Majorian inspired love and respect. Malicious calumny and satire excited his indignation, or, if he himself were the object, his contempt; but he protected the freedom of wit, and in the hours which the emperor gave to the familiar society of his friends he could indulge his taste for pleasantry without degrading the majesty of his rank.

Between 461 and 471 Ricimer ruled Italy in fact if not in name. In 471, after disagreement with the Emperor Anthemius, he sacked Rome but died soon after. In 476 Romulus Augustulus became the last emperor. The traditional date of the extinction of the Western Empire is linked with his accidentally significant name. Between 476 and 490 Odoacer established a Gothic kingdom in Italy while nominally acting as vice-gerent for the Emperor in Constantinople.

ODOACER, KING OF ITALY

Odoacer was the first barbarian who reigned in Italy, over a people who had once asserted their just superiority above the rest of mankind. The disgrace of the Romans still excites our respectful compassion, and we fondly sympathise with the imaginary grief and indignation of their degenerate posterity. But the calamities of Italy had gradually subdued the proud consciousness of freedom and glory. In the age of Roman virtue the provinces were subject to the arms, and the citizens to the laws, of the republic, till those laws were subverted by civil discord, and both the city and the provinces became the servile property of a tyrant. The forms of the constitution, which alleviated or disguised their abject slavery, were abolished by time and violence; the Italians alternately lamented the presence or the absence of the sovereigns whom they detested or despised; and the succession of five centuries inflicted the various evils of military licence, capricious despotism, and elaborate oppression. During the same period, the barbarians had emerged from obscurity and contempt, and the warriors of Germany and Scythia were introduced into the provinces, as the servants, the allies, and at length the masters, of the Romans, whom they insulted or protected. The hatred of the people was suppressed by fear; they respected the spirit and splendour of the martial chiefs who were invested with the honours of the empire; and the fate of Rome had long depended on the sword of those formidable strangers. The stern Ricimer, who trampled on the ruins of Italy, had exercised the power, without assuming the title, of a king; and the patient Romans were insensibly prepared to acknowledge the royalty of Odoacer and his barbaric successors.

The king of Italy was not unworthy of the high station to which his valour and fortune had exalted him: his savage manners were polished by the habits of conversation; and he respected, though a conqueror and a barbarian, the institutions, and even the prejudices, of his subjects. After an interval of seven years, Odoacer restored the consulship of the West. For himself, he modestly, or proudly, declined an honour which was still accepted by the emperors of the East; but the curule chair was successively filled by eleven of the most illustrious senators; and the list is adorned by the respectable name of Basilius, whose virtues claimed the friendship and grateful applause of Sidonius, his client. The laws of the emperors were strictly enforced, and the civil administration of Italy was still exercised by the Prætorian prefect and his subordinate officers. Odoacer devolved on the Roman magistrates the odious and oppressive task of collecting the public revenue; but he reserved for himself the merit of seasonable and popular indulgence. Like the rest of the barbarians, he had been instructed in the Arian heresy; but he revered the monastic and episcopal characters; and the silence of the catholics attests the toleration which they enjoyed. The peace of the city required the interposition of his prefect Basilius in the choice of a Roman pontiff: the decree which restrained the clergy from alienating their lands was ultimately designed for the benefit of the people, whose devotion would have been taxed to repair the dilapidations of the church. Italy was protected by the arms of its conqueror; and its frontiers were respected by the barbarians of Gaul and Germany, who had so long insulted the feeble race of Theodosius. Odoacer passed the Adriatic, to chastise the assassins of the emperor Nepos, and to acquire the maritime province of Dalmatia. He passed the Alps, to rescue the remains of Noricum from Fava, or Feletheus, king of the Rugians, who held his residence beyond the Danube. The king was vanquished in battle, and led away prisoner; a numerous colony of captives and subjects was transplanted into Italy; and Rome, after a long period of defeat and disgrace, might claim the triumph of her barbarian master.

Notwithstanding the prudence and success of Odoacer, his kingdom exhibited the sad prospect of misery and desolation. Since the age of Tiberius, the decay of agriculture had been felt in Italy; and it was a just subject of complaint that the life of the Roman people depended on the accidents of the winds and waves. In the division and the decline of the empire, the tributary harvests of Egypt and Africa were withdrawn; the numbers of the inhabitants continually diminished with the means of subsistence; and the country was exhausted by the irretrievable losses of war, famine, and pestilence. St. Ambrose has deplored the ruin of a populous district, which had been once adorned with the flourishing cities of Bologna, Modena, Rhegium, and Placentia. Pope Gelasius was a subject of Odoacer; and he affirms, with strong exaggeration, that in Æmilia, Tuscany, and the adjacent provinces, the human species was almost extirpated. The plebeians of Rome, who were fed by the hand of their master, perished or disappeared as soon as his liberality was suppressed; the decline of the arts reduced the industrious mechanic to idleness and want; and the senators, who might support with patience the ruin of their country, bewailed their private loss of wealth and luxury. One third of those ample estates, to which the ruin of Italy is originally imputed, was extorted for the use of the conquerors. Injuries were aggravated by insults; the sense of actual sufferings was embittered by the fear of more dreadful evils; and as new lands were allotted to new swarms of barbarians, each senator was apprehensive lest the arbitrary surveyors should approach his favourite villa, or his most profitable farm. The least unfortunate were those who submitted without a murmur to the power which it was impossible to resist. Since they desired to live, they owed some gratitude to the tyrant who had spared their lives; and since he was the absolute master of their fortunes, the portion which he left must be accepted as his pure and voluntary gift. The distress of Italy was mitigated by the prudence and humanity of Odoacer, who had bound himself, as the price of his elevation, to satisfy the demands of a licentious and turbulent multitude. The kings of the barbarians were frequently resisted, deposed, or murdered, by their *native* subjects; and the various bands of Italian mercenaries, who associated under the standard of an elective general, claimed a larger privilege of freedom and rapine. A monarchy destitute of national union and hereditary right hastened to its dissolution. After a reign of fourteen years Odoacer was oppressed by the superior genius of Theodoric, king of the Ostrogoths; a hero alike excellent in the arts of war and of government, who restored an age of peace and prosperity, and whose name still excites and deserves the attention of mankind.

Chapter 37

ORIGIN OF THE MONKS. CAUSES OF THE RAPID PROGRESS
OF MONASTICISM. ST. SIMEON STYLITES. CONVERSION OF
THE BARBARIANS TO CHRISTIANITY

THE indissoluble connexion of civil and ecclesiastical affairs had compelled and encouraged me to relate the progress, the persecutions, the establishment, the divisions, the final triumph, and the gradual corruption of Christianity. I have purposely delayed the consideration of two religious events interesting in the study of human nature, and important in the decline and fall of the Roman empire. I. The institution of the monastic life; and, II. The conversion of the northern barbarians.

I. Prosperity and peace introduced the distinction of the *vulgar* and the *Ascetic Christians*. The loose and imperfect practice of religion satisfied the conscience of the multitude. The prince or magistrate, the soldier or merchant, reconciled their fervent zeal and implicit faith with the exercise of their profession, the pursuit of their interest, and the indulgence of their passions: but the Ascetics, who obeyed and abused the rigid precepts of the Gospel, were inspired by the savage enthusiasm which represents man as a criminal, and God as a tyrant. They seriously renounced the business and the pleasures of the age; abjured the use of wine, of flesh, and of marriage; chastised their body, mortified their affections, and embraced a life of misery, as the price of eternal happiness. In the reign of Constantine the Ascetics fled from a profane and degenerate world to perpetual solitude or religious society. Like the first Christians of Jerusalem, they resigned the use or the property of their temporal possessions; established regular communities of the same sex and a similar disposition; and assumed the names of *Hermits*, *Monks*, and *Anachorets*, expressive of their lonely retreat in a natural or artificial desert. They soon acquired the respect of the world, which they despised; and the loudest applause was bestowed on this DIVINE PHILOSOPHY, which surpassed, without the aid of science or reason, the laborious virtues of the Grecian schools. The monks might indeed contend with the Stoics in the contempt of fortune, of pain, and of death: the Pythagorean silence and submission were revived in their servile discipline; and they disdained as firmly as the Cynics themselves all the forms and decencies of civil society. But the votaries of this Divine Philosophy aspired to imitate a purer and more perfect model. They trod in the footsteps of the prophets, who had retired to the desert; and

507

they restored the devout and contemplative life, which had been instituted by the Essenians in Palestine and Egypt. The philosophic eye of Pliny had surveyed with astonishment a solitary people, who dwelt among the palm-trees near the Dead Sea; who subsisted without money; who were propagated without women; and who derived from the disgust and repentance of mankind a perpetual supply of voluntary associates.

Egypt, the fruitful parent of superstition, afforded the first example of the monastic life. Antony, an illiterate youth of the lower parts of Thebais, distributed his patrimony, deserted his family and native home, and executed his *monastic* penance with original and intrepid fanaticism. After a long and painful noviciate, among the tombs, and in a ruined tower, he boldly advanced into the desert three days' journey to the eastward of the Nile; discovered a lonely spot, which possessed the advantages of shade and water; and fixed his last residence on Mount Colzim, near the Red Sea, where an ancient monastery still preserves the name and memory of the saint. The curious devotion of the Christians pursued him to the desert; and when he was obliged to appear at Alexandria, in the face of mankind, he supported his fame with discretion and dignity. He enjoyed the friendship of Athanasius, whose doctrine he approved; and the Egyptian peasant respectfully declined a respectful invitation from the emperor Constantine. The venerable patriarch (for Antony attained the age of one hundred and five years) beheld the numerous progeny which had been formed by his example and his lessons. The prolific colonies of monks multiplied with rapid increase on the sands of Libya, upon the rocks of Thebais, and in the cities of the Nile. To the south of Alexandria, the mountain, and adjacent desert, of Nitria, was peopled by five thousand anachorets; and the traveller may still investigate the ruins of fifty monasteries, which were planted in that barren soil by the disciples of Antony. In the Upper Thebais, the vacant island of Tabenne was occupied by Pachomius and fourteen hundred of his brethren. That holy abbot successively founded nine monasteries of men, and one of women; and the festival of Easter sometimes collected fifty thousand religious persons, who followed his *angelic* rule of discipline. The stately and populous city of Oxyrhyuchus, the seat of Christian orthodoxy, had devoted the temples, the public edifices, and even the ramparts, to pious and charitable uses; and the bishop, who might preach in twelve churches, computed ten thousand females, and twenty thousand males, of the monastic profession. The Egyptians, who gloried in this marvellous revolution, were disposed to hope, and to believe, that the number of the monks was equal to the remainder of the people; and posterity might repeat the saying which had formerly been applied to the sacred animals of the same country, that in Egypt it was less difficult to find a god than a man.

Athanasius introduced into Rome the knowledge and practice of the monastic life; and a school of this new philosophy was opened by the disciples of Antony, who accompanied their primate to the holy threshold of the Vatican. The strange and savage appearance of these Egyptians excited, at first, horror and contempt, and, at length, applause and zealous imitation. The senators, and more especially the matrons, transformed their palaces and villas into religious houses; and the narrow institution of *six* Vestals was eclipsed by the frequent monasteries, which were seated on the ruins of ancient temples, and in the midst of the Roman forum. Inflamed by the example of Antony, a Syrian youth, whose name was Hilarion,[1] fixed his dreary abode on a sandy beach between the sea and a morass, about seven miles from Gaza. The austere penance, in which he persisted forty-eight years, diffused a similar enthusiasm; and the holy man was followed by a train of two or three thousand anachorets, whenever he visited the innumerable monasteries of Palestine. The fame of Basil is immortal in the monastic history of the East. With a mind that had tasted the learning and eloquence of Athens; with an ambition scarcely to be satisfied by the archbishopric of Cæsarea, Basil retired to a savage solitude in Pontus; and deigned, for a while, to give laws to the spiritual colonies which he profusely scattered along the coast of the Black Sea. In the West, Martin of Tours,[2] a soldier, an hermit, a bishop, and a saint, established the monasteries of Gaul; two thousand of his disciples followed him to the grave; and his eloquent historian challenges the deserts of Thebais to produce, in a more favourable climate, a champion of equal virtue. The progress of the monks was not less rapid or universal than that of Christianity itself. Every province, and, at last, every city, of the empire, was filled with their increasing multitudes; and the bleak and barren isles, from Lerins to Lipari, that arise out of the Tuscan sea, were chosen by the anachorets for the place of their voluntary exile. An easy and perpetual intercourse by sea and land connected the provinces of the Roman world; and the life of Hilarion displays the facility with which an indigent hermit of Palestine might traverse Egypt, embark for Sicily, escape to Epirus, and finally settle in the island of Cyprus.[3] The Latin Christians embraced the religious institutions of Rome. The pilgrims who visited Jerusalem eagerly copied, in the most distant climates of the earth, the faithful model of the monastic life. The disciples of Antony spread themselves beyond the

---

[1] See the Life of Hilarion, by St. Jerom. The stories of Paul, Hilarion, and Malchus, by the same author, are admirably told; and the only defect of these pleasing compositions is the want of truth and common sense.

[2] See his Life, and the three Dialogues by Sulpicius Severus, who asserts that the booksellers of Rome were delighted with the quick and ready sale of his popular work.

[3] When Hilarion sailed from Parætonium to Cape Pachynus, he offered to pay his passage with a book of the Gospels. Posthumian, a Gallic monk, who had visited Egypt, found a merchant-ship bound from Alexandria to Marseilles, and performed the voyage in thirty days. Athanasius, who addressed his Life of St. Antony to the foreign monks, was obliged to hasten the composition, that it might be ready for the sailing of the fleets.

tropic, over the Christian empire of Ethiopia. The monastery of Banchor, in Flintshire, which contained above two thousand brethren, dispersed a numerous colony among the barbarians of Ireland; and Iona, one of the Hebrides, which was planted by the Irish monks, diffused over the northern regions a doubtful ray of science and superstition.

CAUSES OF THE RAPID PROGRESS OF MONASTICISM

These unhappy exiles from social life were impelled by the dark and implacable genius of superstition. Their mutual resolution was supported by the example of millions, of either sex, of every age, and of every rank; and each proselyte who entered the gates of a monastery was persuaded that he trod the steep and thorny path of eternal happiness.[1] But the operation of these religious motives was variously determined by the temper and situation of mankind. Reason might subdue, or passion might suspend, their influence; but they acted most forcibly on the infirm minds of children and females; they were strengthened by secret remorse, or accidental misfortune; and they might derive some aid from the temporal considerations of vanity or interest. It was naturally supposed that the pious and humble monks, who had renounced the world to accomplish the work of their salvation, were the best qualified for the spiritual government of the Christians. The reluctant hermit was torn from his cell, and seated, amidst the acclamations of the people, on the episcopal throne: the monasteries of Egypt, of Gaul, and of the East, supplied a regular succession of saints and bishops; and ambition soon discovered the secret road which led to the possession of wealth and honours. The popular monks, whose reputation was connected with the fame and success of the order, assiduously laboured to multiply the number of their fellow-captives. They insinuated themselves into noble and opulent families; and the specious arts of flattery and seduction were employed to secure those proselytes who might bestow wealth or dignity on the monastic profession. The indignant father bewailed the loss, perhaps, of an only son; the credulous maid was betrayed by vanity to violate the laws of nature; and the matron aspired to imaginary perfection by renouncing the virtues of domestic life. Paula yielded to the persuasive eloquence of Jerom;[2] and the profane title of mother-in-law

---

[1] Chrysostom has consecrated three books to the praise and defence of the monastic life. He is encouraged, by the example of the ark, to presume that none but the elect (the monks) can possibly be saved. Elsewhere, indeed, he becomes more merciful, and allows different degrees of glory, like the sun, moon, and stars. In his lively comparison of a king and a monk, he supposes (what is hardly fair) that the king will be more sparingly rewarded, and more rigorously punished.

[2] Jerom's devout ladies form a very considerable portion of his works: the particular treatise, which he styles the Epitaph of Paula, is an elaborate and extravagant panegyric. The exordium is ridiculously turgid:—"If all the members of my body were changed into tongues, and if all my limbs resounded with a human voice, yet should I be incapable," &c.

of God tempted that illustrious widow to consecrate the virginity of her daughter Eustochium. By the advice, and in the company, of her spiritual guide, Paula abandoned Rome and her infant son; retired to the holy village of Bethlem; founded an hospital and four monasteries; and acquired, by her alms and penance, an eminent and conspicuous station in the catholic church. Such rare and illustrious penitents were celebrated as the glory and example of their age; but the monasteries were filled by a crowd of obscure and abject plebeians, who gained in the cloister much more than they had sacrificed in the world. Peasants, slaves, and mechanics, might escape from poverty and contempt to a safe and honourable profession, whose apparent hardships were mitigated by custom, by popular applause, and by the secret relaxation of discipline.[1] The subjects of Rome, whose persons and fortunes were made responsible for unequal and exorbitant tributes, retired from the oppression of the Imperial government; and the pusillanimous youth preferred the penance of a monastic, to the dangers of a military life. The affrighted provincials of every rank, who fled before the barbarians, found shelter and subsistence; whole legions were buried in these religious sanctuaries; and the same cause which relieved the distress of individuals impaired the strength and fortitude of the empire.

The monastic profession of the ancients was an act of voluntary devotion. The inconstant fanatic was threatened with the eternal vengeance of the God whom he deserted; but the doors of the monastery were still open for repentance. Those monks whose conscience was fortified by reason or passion were at liberty to resume the character of men and citizens; and even the spouses of Christ might accept the legal embraces of an earthly lover. The examples of scandal, and the progress of superstition, suggested the propriety of more forcible restraints. After a sufficient trial, the fidelity of the novice was secured by a solemn and perpetual vow; and his irrevocable engagement was ratified by the laws of the church and state. A guilty fugitive was pursued, arrested, and restored to his perpetual prison; and the interposition of the magistrate oppressed the freedom and merit which had alleviated, in some degree, the abject slavery of the monastic discipline. The actions of a monk, his words, and even his thoughts, were determined by an inflexible rule, or a capricious superior: the slightest offences were corrected by disgrace or confinement, extraordinary fasts, or bloody flagellation; and disobedience, murmur, or delay, were ranked in the catalogue of the most heinous sins.[2] A blind submission to the commands of the abbot,

---

[1] A Dominican friar, who lodged at Cadiz in a convent of his brethren, soon understood that their repose was never interrupted by nocturnal devotion; "quoiqu'on ne laisse pas de sonner pour l'édification du peuple".

[2] The rule of Columbanus, so prevalent in the West, inflicts one hundred lashes for very slight offences. Before the time of Charlemagne the abbots indulged themselves in mutilating their monks, or putting out their eyes—a punishment much less

however absurd, or even criminal, they might seem, was the ruling principle, the first virtue of the Egyptian monks; and their patience was frequently exercised by the most extravagant trials. They were directed to remove an enormous rock; assiduously to water a barren staff that was planted in the ground, till, at the end of three years, it should vegetate and blossom like a tree; to walk into a fiery furnace; or to cast their infant into a deep pond; and several saints, or madmen, have been immortalised in monastic story, by their thoughtless and fearless obedience. The freedom of the mind, the source of every generous and rational sentiment, was destroyed by the habits of credulity and submission; and the monk, contracting the vices of a slave, devoutly followed the faith and passions of his ecclesiastical tyrant. The peace of the Eastern church was invaded by a swarm of fanatics, incapable of fear, or reason, or humanity; and the Imperial troops acknowledged, without shame, that they were much less apprehensive of an encounter with the fiercest barbarians.

Superstition has often framed and consecrated the fantastic garments of the monks: but their apparent singularity sometimes proceeds from their uniform attachment to a simple and primitive model, which the revolutions of fashion have made ridiculous in the eyes of mankind. The father of the Benedictines expressly disclaims all idea of choice or merit; and soberly exhorts his disciples to adopt the coarse and convenient dress of the countries which they may inhabit. The monastic habits of the ancients varied with the climate and the mode of life; and they assumed, with the same indifference, the sheepskin of the Egyptian peasants, or the cloak of the Grecian philosophers. They allowed themselves the use of linen in Egypt, where it was a cheap and domestic manufacture; but in the West they rejected such an expensive article of foreign luxury. It was the practice of the monks either to cut or shave their hair; they wrapped their heads in a cowl, to escape the sight of profane objects; their legs and feet were naked, except in the extreme cold of winter; and their slow and feeble steps were supported by a long staff. The aspect of a genuine anachoret was horrid and disgusting: every sensation that is offensive to man was thought acceptable to God; and the angelic rule of Tabenne condemned the salutary custom of bathing the limbs in water, and of anointing them with oil. The austere monks slept on the ground, on a hard mat, or a rough blanket; and the same bundle of palm-leaves served them as a seat in the day, and a pillow in the night. Their original cells were low narrow huts, built of the slightest materials; which formed, by the regular distribution of the streets, a large and populous village, enclosing, within the common wall,

---

cruel than the tremendous *vade in pace* (the subterraneous dungeon, or sepulchre), which was afterwards invented. See an admirable discourse of the learned Mabillon, who, on this occasion, seems to be inspired by the genius of humanity. For such an effort, I can forgive his defence of the holy tear of Vendôme.

a church, an hospital, perhaps a library, some necessary offices, a garden, and a fountain or reservoir of fresh water. Thirty or forty brethren composed a family of separate discipline and diet; and the great monasteries of Egypt consisted of thirty or forty families.

Pleasure and guilt are synonymous terms in the language of the monks, and they had discovered, by experience, that rigid fasts and abstemious diet are the most effectual preservatives against the impure desires of the flesh. The rules of abstinence which they imposed, or practised, were not uniform or perpetual: the cheerful festival of the Pentecost was balanced by the extraordinary mortification of Lent: the fervour of new monasteries was insensibly relaxed; and the voracious appetite of the Gauls could not imitate the patient and temperate virtue of the Egyptians. The disciples of Antony and Pachomius were satisfied with the daily pittance [1] of twelve ounces of bread, or rather biscuit, which they divided into two frugal repasts, of the afternoon and of the evening. It was esteemed a merit, and almost a duty, to abstain from the boiled vegetables which were provided for the refectory; but the extraordinary bounty of the abbot sometimes indulged them with the luxury of cheese, fruit, salad, and the small dried fish of the Nile. A more ample latitude of sea and river fish was gradually allowed or assumed; but the use of flesh was long confined to the sick or travellers: and when it gradually prevailed in the less rigid monasteries of Europe, a singular distinction was introduced; as if birds, whether wild or domestic, had been less profane than the grosser animals of the field. Water was the pure and innocent beverage of the primitive monks; and the founder of the Benedictines regrets the daily portion of half a pint of wine, which had been extorted from him by the intemperance of the age. Such an allowance might be easily supplied by the vineyards of Italy; and his victorious disciples, who passed the Alps, the Rhine, and the Baltic, required, in the place of wine, an adequate compensation of strong beer or cider.

The candidate who aspired to the virtue of evangelical poverty, abjured, at his first entrance into a regular community, the idea, and even the name, of all separate or exclusive possession. [2] The brethren were supported by their manual labour; and the duty of labour was strenuously recommended as a penance, as an exercise, and as the most laudable means of securing their daily subsistence. The garden and fields, which the industry of the monks had often rescued from the forest or the morass, were diligently cultivated by their hands. They performed,

---

[1] "Those who drink only water, and have no nutritious liquor, ought at least to have a pound and a half (*twenty-four ounces*) of bread every day." State of Prisons, p. 40, by Mr. Howard. [*The State of the Prisons in England and Wales* 1784.]

[2] Such expressions as *my* book, *my* cloak, *my* shoes, were not less severely prohibited among the Western monks, and the Rule of Columbanus punished them with six lashes. The ironical author of the *Ordres Monastiques*, who laughs at the foolish nicety of modern convents, seems ignorant that the ancients were equally absurd.

without reluctance, the menial offices of slaves and domestics; and the several trades that were necessary to provide their habits, their utensils, and their lodging, were exercised within the precincts of the great monasteries. The monastic studies have tended, for the most part, to darken, rather than to dispel, the cloud of superstition. Yet the curiosity or zeal of some learned solitaries has cultivated the ecclesiastical, and even the profane sciences: and posterity must gratefully acknowledge that the monuments of Greek and Roman literature have been preserved and multiplied by their indefatigable pens. But the more humble industry of the monks, especially in Egypt, was contented with the silent, sedentary occupation of making wooden sandals, or of twisting the leaves of the palm-tree into mats and baskets. The superfluous stock, which was not consumed in domestic use, supplied, by trade, the wants of the community: the boats of Tabenne, and the other monasteries of Thebais, descended the Nile as far as Alexandria; and, in a Christian market, the sanctity of the workmen might enhance the intrinsic value of the work.

But the necessity of manual labour was insensibly superseded. The novice was tempted to bestow his fortune on the saints in whose society he was resolved to spend the remainder of his life; and the pernicious indulgence of the laws permitted him to receive, for their use, any future accessions of legacy or inheritance. Melania contributed her plate, three hundred pounds' weight of silver, and Paula contracted an immense debt, for the relief of their favourite monks, who kindly imparted the merits of their prayers and penance to a rich and liberal sinner.[1] Time continually increased, and accidents could seldom diminish, the estates of the popular monasteries, which spread over the adjacent country and cities: and, in the first century of the institution, the infidel Zosimus has maliciously observed, that, for the benefit of the poor, the Christian monks had reduced a great part of mankind to a state of beggary. As long as they maintained their original fervour, they approved themselves, however, the faithful and benevolent stewards of the charity which was intrusted to their care. But their discipline was corrupted by prosperity: they gradually assumed the pride of wealth, and at last indulged the luxury of expense. Their public luxury might be excused by the magnificence of religious worship, and the decent motive of erecting durable habitations for an immortal society. But every age of the church has accused the licentiousness of the degenerate monks; who no longer remembered the object of their institution, embraced the vain and sensual pleasures of the world which they had renounced, and scandalously abused the riches which had been acquired

---

[1] The monk Pambo made a sublime answer to Melania, who wished to specify the value of her gift:—"Do you offer it to me, or to God? If to God, HE who suspends the mountains in a balance need not be informed of the weight of your plate."

by the austere virtues of their founders.[1] Their natural descent, from such painful and dangerous virtue, to the common vices of humanity, will not, perhaps, excite much grief or indignation in the mind of a philosopher.

The lives of the primitive monks were consumed in penance and solitude, undisturbed by the various occupations which fill the time, and exercise the faculties, of reasonable, active, and social beings. Whenever they were permitted to step beyond the precincts of the monastery, two jealous companions were the mutual guards and spies of each other's actions; and, after their return, they were condemned to forget, or, at least, to suppress, whatever they had seen or heard in the world. Strangers, who professed the orthodox faith, were hospitably entertained in a separate apartment; but their dangerous conversation was restricted to some chosen elders of approved discretion and fidelity. Except in their presence, the monastic slave might not receive the visits of his friends or kindred; and it was deemed highly meritorious, if he afflicted a tender sister, or an aged parent, by the obstinate refusal of a word or look. The monks themselves passed their lives, without personal attachments, among a crowd which had been formed by accident, and was detained, in the same prison, by force or prejudice. Recluse fanatics have few ideas or sentiments to communicate: a special licence of the abbot regulated the time and duration of their familiar visits; and, at their silent meals, they were enveloped in their cowls, inaccessible, and almost invisible, to each other. Study is the resource of solitude; but education had not prepared and qualified for any liberal studies the mechanics and peasants who filled the monastic communities. They might work; but the vanity of spiritual perfection was tempted to disdain the exercise of manual labour; and the industry must be faint and languid which is not excited by the sense of personal interest.

According to their faith and zeal, they might employ the day, which they passed in their cells, either in vocal or mental prayer: they assembled in the evening, and they were awakened in the night, for the public worship of the monastery. The precise moment was determined by the stars, which are seldom clouded in the serene sky of Egypt; and a rustic horn, or trumpet, the signal of devotion, twice interrupted the vast silence of the desert. Even sleep, the last refuge of the unhappy, was rigorously measured: the vacant hours of the monk heavily rolled along, without business or pleasure; and, before the close of each day, he had repeatedly accused the tedious progress of the sun. In this comfortless state, superstition still pursued and tormented her wretched votaries. The repose which they had sought in the cloister was disturbed by tardy

[1] I have somewhere heard or read the frank confession of a Benedictine abbot: "My vow of poverty has given me an hundred thousand crowns a year; my vow of obedience has raised me to the rank of a sovereign prince." I forget the consequences of his vow of chastity.

repentance, profane doubts, and guilty desires; and, while they considered each natural impulse as an unpardonable sin, they perpetually trembled on the edge of a flaming and bottomless abyss. From the painful struggles of disease and despair, these unhappy victims were sometimes relieved by madness or death; and, in the sixth century, an hospital was founded at Jerusalem for a small portion of the austere penitents who were deprived of their senses. Their visions, before they attained this extreme and acknowledged term of frenzy, have afforded ample materials of supernatural history. It was their firm persuasion that the air which they breathed was peopled with invisible enemies; with innumerable dæmons, who watched every occasion, and assumed every form, to terrify, and above all to tempt, their unguarded virtue. The imagination, and even the senses, were deceived by the illusions of distempered fanaticism; and the hermit, whose midnight prayer was oppressed by involuntary slumber, might easily confound the phantoms of horror or delight which had occupied his sleeping and his waking dreams.

ST. SIMEON STYLITES

The monks were divided into two classes: the *Cœnobites*, who lived under a common and regular discipline; and the *Anachorets*, who indulged their unsocial, independent fanaticism. The most devout, or the most ambitious, of the spiritual brethren, renounced the convent, as they had renounced the world. The fervent monasteries of Egypt, Palestine, and Syria, were surrounded by a *Laura*, a distant circle of solitary cells; and the extravagant penance of the Hermits was stimulated by applause and emulation. They sunk under the painful weight of crosses and chains; and their emaciated limbs were confined by collars, bracelets, gauntlets, and greaves of massy and rigid iron. All superfluous incumbrance of dress they contemptuously cast away; and some savage saints of both sexes have been admired, whose naked bodies were only covered by their long hair. They aspired to reduce themselves to the rude and miserable state in which the human brute is scarcely distinguished above his kindred animals; and the numerous sect of Anachorets derived their name from their humble practice of grazing in the fields of Mesopotamia with the common herd. They often usurped the den of some wild beast whom they affected to resemble; they buried themselves in some gloomy cavern, which art or nature had scooped out of the rock; and the marble quarries of Thebais are still inscribed with the monuments of their penance. The most perfect Hermits are supposed to have passed many days without food, many nights without sleep, and many years without speaking; and glorious was the *man* (I abuse that name) who contrived any cell, or seat, of a peculiar construction, which might expose him, in the most inconvenient posture, to the inclemency of the seasons.

Among these heroes of the monastic life, the name and genius of Simeon Stylites have been immortalised by the singular invention of an aërial penance. At the age of thirteen the young Syrian deserted the profession of a shepherd, and threw himself into an austere monastery. After a long and painful noviciate, in which Simeon was repeatedly saved from pious suicide, he established his residence on a mountain, about thirty or forty miles to the east of Antioch. Within the space of a *mandra*, or circle of stones, to which he had attached himself by a ponderous chain, he ascended a column, which was successively raised from the height of nine, to that of sixty, feet from the ground. In this last and lofty station, the Syrian Anachoret resisted the heat of thirty summers, and the cold of as many winters. Habit and exercise instructed him to maintain his dangerous situation without fear or giddiness, and successively to assume the different postures of devotion. He sometimes prayed in an erect attitude, with his outstretched arms in the figure of a cross; but his most familiar practice was that of bending his meagre skeleton from the forehead to the feet; and a curious spectator, after numbering twelve hundred and forty-four repetitions, at length desisted from the endless account. The progress of an ulcer in his thigh [1] might shorten, but it could not disturb, this *celestial* life; and the patient Hermit expired without descending from his column. A prince, who should capriciously inflict such tortures, would be deemed a tyrant; but it would surpass the power of a tyrant to impose a long and miserable existence on the reluctant victims of his cruelty. This voluntary martyrdom must have gradually destroyed the sensibility both of the mind and body; nor can it be presumed that the fanatics who torment themselves are susceptible of any lively affection for the rest of mankind. A cruel unfeeling temper has distinguished the monks of every age and country: their stern indifference, which is seldom mollified by personal friendship, is inflamed by religious hatred; and their merciless zeal has strenuously administered the holy office of the Inquisition.

The monastic saints, who excite only the contempt and pity of a philosopher, were respected and almost adored by the prince and people. Successive crowds of pilgrims from Gaul and India saluted the divine pillar of Simeon; the tribes of Saracens disputed in arms the honour of his benediction; the queens of Arabia and Persia gratefully confessed his supernatural virtue; and the angelic Hermit was consulted by the younger Theodosius in the most important concerns of the church and state. His remains were transported from the mountain of Telenissa, by a solemn procession of the patriarch, the master-general of the East, six bishops, twenty-one counts or tribunes, and six thousand soldiers; and

---

[1] I must not conceal a piece of ancient scandal concerning the origin of this ulcer. It has been reported that the Devil, assuming an angelic form, invited him to ascend, like Elijah, into a fiery chariot. The saint too hastily raised his foot, and Satan seized the moment of inflicting this chastisement on his vanity.

Antioch revered his bones as her glorious ornament and impregnable defence. The fame of the apostles and martyrs was gradually eclipsed by these recent and popular Anachorets; the Christian world fell prostrate before their shrines; and the miracles ascribed to their relics exceeded, at least in number and duration, the spiritual exploits of their lives. But the golden legend of their lives was embellished by the artful credulity of their interested brethren; and a believing age was easily persuaded that the slightest caprice of an Egyptian or a Syrian monk had been sufficient to interrupt the eternal laws of the universe. The favourites of Heaven were accustomed to cure inveterate diseases with a touch, a word, or a distant message; and to expel the most obstinate dæmons from the souls or bodies which they possessed. They familiarly accosted, or imperiously commanded, the lions and serpents of the desert; infused vegetation into a sapless trunk; suspended iron on the surface of the water; passed the Nile on the back of a crocodile; and refreshed themselves in a fiery furnace. These extravagant tales, which display the fiction, without the genius, of poetry, have seriously affected the reason, the faith, and the morals of the Christians. Their credulity debased and vitiated the faculties of the mind: they corrupted the evidence of history; and superstition gradually extinguished the hostile light of philosophy and science. Every mode of religious worship which had been practised by the saints, every mysterious doctrine which they believed, was fortified by the sanction of divine revelation, and all the manly virtues were oppressed by the servile and pusillanimous reign of the monks. If it be possible to measure the interval between the philosophic writings of Cicero and the sacred legend of Theodoret, between the character of Cato and that of Simeon, we may appreciate the memorable revolution which was accomplished in the Roman empire within a period of five hundred years.

II. The progress of Christianity has been marked by two glorious and decisive victories: over the learned and luxurious citizens of the Roman empire; and over the warlike barbarians of Scythia and Germany, who subverted the empire and embraced the religion of the Romans. The Goths were the foremost of these savage proselytes; and the nation was indebted for its conversion to a countryman, or at least to a subject, worthy to be ranked among the inventors of useful arts who have deserved the remembrance and gratitude of posterity. A great number of Roman provincials had been led away into captivity by the Gothic bands who ravaged Asia in the time of Gallienus; and of these captives many were Christians, and several belonged to the ecclesiastical order. Those involuntary missionaries, dispersed as slaves in the villages of Dacia, successively laboured for the salvation of their masters. The seeds which they planted of the evangelic doctrine were gradually propagated; and before the end of a century the pious work was achieved by the labours of Ulphilas, whose ancestors had been transported beyond the Danube from a small town of Cappadocia.

Ulphilas, the bishop and apostle of the Goths, acquired their love and reverence by his blameless life and indefatigable zeal, and they received with implicit confidence the doctrines of truth and virtue which he preached and practised. He executed the arduous task of translating the Scriptures into their native tongue, a dialect of the German or Teutonic language; but he prudently suppressed the four books of Kings, as they might tend to irritate the fierce and sanguinary spirit of the barbarians. The rude, imperfect idiom of soldiers and shepherds, so ill qualified to communicate any spiritual ideas, was improved and modulated by his genius; and Ulphilas, before he could frame his version, was obliged to compose a new alphabet of twenty-four letters; four of which he invented to express the peculiar sounds that were unknown to the Greek and Latin pronunciation. But the prosperous state of the Gothic church was soon afflicted by war and intestine discord, and the chieftains were divided by religion as well as by interest. Fritigern, the friend of the Romans, became the proselyte of Ulphilas; while the haughty soul of Athanaric disdained the yoke of the empire and of the Gospel. The faith of the new converts was tried by the persecution which he excited. A waggon, bearing aloft the shapeless image of Thor, perhaps, or of Woden, was conducted in solemn procession through the streets of the camp, and the rebels who refused to worship the god of their fathers were immediately burnt with their tents and families. The character of Ulphilas recommended him to the esteem of the Eastern court, where he twice appeared as the minister of peace; he pleaded the cause of the distressed Goths, who implored the protection of Valens; and the name of *Moses* was applied to this spiritual guide, who conducted his people through the deep waters of the Danube to the Land of Promise. The devout shepherds, who were attached to his person and tractable to his voice, acquiesced in their settlement at the foot of the Mæsian mountains, in a country of woodlands and pastures, which supported their flocks and herds, and enabled them to purchase the corn and wine of the more plentiful provinces. These harmless barbarians multiplied in obscure peace and the profession of Christianity.

Their fiercer brethren, the formidable Visigoths, universally adopted the religion of the Romans, with whom they maintained a perpetual intercourse of war, of friendship, or of conquest. In their long and victorious march from the Danube to the Atlantic ocean they converted their allies; they educated the rising generation; and the devotion which reigned in the camp of Alaric, or the court of Toulouse, might edify or disgrace the palaces of Rome and Constantinople. During the same period Christianity was embraced by almost all the barbarians who established their kingdoms on the ruins of the Western empire; the Burgundians in Gaul, the Suevi in Spain, the Vandals in Africa, the

Ostrogoths in Pannonia, and the various bands of mercenaries that raised Odoacer to the throne of Italy. The Franks and the Saxons still persevered in the errors of Paganism; but the Franks obtained the monarchy of Gaul by their submission to the example of Clovis; and the Saxon conquerors of Britain were reclaimed from their savage superstitions by the missionaries of Rome. These barbarian proselytes displayed an ardent and successful zeal in the propagation of the faith. The Merovingian kings and their successors, Charlemagne and the Othos, extended by their laws and victories the dominion of the cross. England produced the apostle of Germany; and the evangelic light was gradually diffused from the neighbourhood of the Rhine to the nations of the Elbe, the Vistula, and the Baltic.

The different motives which influenced the reason of the passions of the barbarian converts cannot easily be ascertained. They were often capricious and accidental; a dream, an omen, the report of a miracle, the example of some priest or hero, the charms of a believing wife, and, above all, the fortunate event of a prayer or vow which, in a moment of danger, they had addressed to the God of the Christians. The early prejudices of education were insensibly erased by the habits of frequent and familiar society; the moral precepts of the Gospel were protected by the extravagant virtues of the monks; and a spiritual theology was supported by the visible power of relics, and the pomp of religious worship. But the rational and ingenious mode of persuasion which a Saxon bishop suggested to a popular saint might sometimes be employed by the missionaries who laboured for the conversion of infidels. "Admit," says the sagacious disputant, "whatever they are pleased to assert of the fabulous and carnal genealogy of their gods and goddesses, who are propagated from each other. From this principle deduce their imperfect nature and human infirmities, the assurance they were *born*, and the probability that they will *die*. At what time, by what means, from what cause, were the eldest of the gods or goddesses produced? Do they still continue, or have they ceased, to propagate? If they have ceased, summon your antagonists to declare the reason of this strange alteration. If they still continue, the number of the gods must become infinite; and shall we not risk, by the indiscreet worship of some impotent deity, to excite the resentment of his jealous superior? The visible heavens and earth, the whole system of the universe, which may be conceived by the mind, is it created or eternal? If created, how or where could the gods themselves exist before the creation? If eternal, how could they assume the empire of an independent and pre-existing world? Urge these arguments with temper and moderation; insinuate, at seasonable intervals, the truth and beauty of the Christian revelation; and endeavour to make the unbelievers ashamed without making them angry." This metaphysical reasoning, too refined perhaps for the barbarians of Germany, was fortified by the grosser weight of authority and

popular consent. The advantage of temporal prosperity had deserted the
Pagan cause and passed over to the service of Christianity. The Romans
themselves, the most powerful and enlightened nation of the globe, had
renounced their ancient superstition; and if the ruin of their empire
seemed to accuse the efficacy of the new faith, the disgrace was already
retrieved by the conversion of the victorious Goths. The valiant and
fortunate barbarians who subdued the provinces of the West successively
received and reflected the same edifying example. Before the age of
Charlemagne, the Christian nations of Europe might exult in the exclusive possession of the temperate climates, of the fertile lands which
produced corn, wine, and oil; while the savage idolaters and their helpless idols were confined to the extremities of the earth, the dark and
frozen regions of the North.

Christianity, which opened the gates of Heaven to the barbarians,
introduced an important change in their moral and political condition.
They received, at the same time, the use of letters, so essential to a
religion whose doctrines are contained in a sacred book; and while they
studied the divine truth, their minds were insensibly enlarged by the
distant view of history, of nature, of the arts, and of society. The
version of the Scriptures into their native tongue, which had facilitated
their conversion, must excite, among their clergy, some curiosity to read
the original text, to understand the sacred liturgy of the church, and to
examine, in the writings of the fathers, the chain of ecclesiastical tradition. These spiritual gifts were preserved in the Greek and Latin languages, which concealed the inestimable monuments of ancient learning.
The immortal productions of Virgil, Cicero, and Livy, which were accessible to the Christian barbarians, maintained a silent intercourse between
the reign of Augustus and the times of Clovis and Charlemagne. The
emulation of mankind was encouraged by the remembrance of a more
perfect state; and the flame of science was secretly kept alive, to warm
and enlighten the mature age of the Western world. In the most corrupt
state of Christianity the barbarians might learn justice from the *law*, and
mercy from the *gospel*; and if the knowledge of their duty was insufficient
to guide their actions or to regulate their passions, they were sometimes
restrained by conscience, and frequently punished by remorse. But the
direct authority of religion was less effectual than the holy communion,
which united them with their Christian brethren in spiritual friendship.
The influence of these sentiments contributed to secure their fidelity in
the service or the alliance of the Romans, to alleviate the horrors of war,
to moderate the insolence of conquest, and to preserve, in the downfall
of the empire, a permanent respect for the name and institutions of
Rome. In the days of Paganism the priests of Gaul and Germany
reigned over the people, and controlled the jurisdiction of the magistrates; and the zealous proselytes transferred an equal, or more ample,
measure of devout obedience to the pontiffs of the Christian faith. The

sacred character of the bishops was supported by their temporal possessions; they obtained an honourable seat in the legislative assemblies of
soldiers and freemen; and it was their interest, as well as their duty, to
mollify by peaceful counsels the fierce spirit of the barbarians. The
perpetual correspondence of the Latin clergy, the frequent pilgrimages
to Rome and Jerusalem, and the growing authority of the popes, cemented the union of the Christian republic, and gradually produced the
similar manners and common jurisprudence which have distinguished
from the rest of mankind the independent, and even hostile, nations of
modern Europe.

*   *   *   *   *

Chapter 38

THE FALL OF
THE ROMAN EMPIRE IN THE WEST. GENERAL OBSERVATIONS

Between 476 and 496 Clovis, king of the Franks, established his power in Gaul and was converted to Christianity. After the conquests of Aquitaine and Burgundy a French monarchy was founded in Gaul in 536. The Visigoths, expelled from Gaul, achieved the conquest of Spain. The Saxons established themselves in Britain in 455–582.

FALL OF THE ROMAN EMPIRE IN THE WEST

I HAVE now accomplished the laborious narrative of the decline and fall of the Roman empire, from the fortunate age of Trajan and the Antonines to its total extinction in the West, about five centuries after the Christian era. At that unhappy period the Saxons fiercely struggled with the natives for the possession of Britain: Gaul and Spain were divided between the powerful monarchies of the Franks and Visigoths and the dependent kingdoms of the Suevi and Burgundians: Africa was exposed to the cruel persecution of the Vandals and the savage insults of the Moors: Rome and Italy, as far as the banks of the Danube, were afflicted by an army of barbarian mercenaries, whose lawless tyranny was succeeded by the reign of Theodoric the Ostrogoth. All the subjects of the empire, who, by the use of the Latin language, more particularly deserved the name and privileges of Romans, were oppressed by the disgrace and calamities of foreign conquest; and the victorious nations of Germany established a new system of manners and government in the western countries of Europe. The majesty of Rome was faintly represented by the princes of Constantinople, the feeble and imaginary successors of Augustus. Yet they continued to reign over the East, from the Danube to the Nile and Tigris; the Gothic and Vandal kingdoms of Italy and Africa were subverted by the arms of Justinian; and the history of the Greek emperors may still afford a long series of instructive lessons and interesting revolutions.

GENERAL OBSERVATIONS ON THE FALL OF THE ROMAN EMPIRE IN THE WEST

The Greeks, after their country had been reduced into a province, imputed the triumphs of Rome, not to the merit, but to the FORTUNE, of the republic. The inconstant goddess, who so blindly distributes and resumes her favours, had *now* consented (such was the language of envious flattery) to resign her wings, to descend from her globe, and to fix her firm and immutable throne on the banks of the Tiber. A wiser Greek, who has composed, with a philosophic spirit, the memorable history of his own times, deprived his countrymen of this vain and delusive comfort, by opening to their view the deep foundations of the greatness of Rome. The fidelity of the citizens to each other and to the state was confirmed by the habits of education and the prejudices of religion. Honour, as well as virtue, was the principle of the republic; the ambitious citizens laboured to deserve the solemn glories of a triumph; and the ardour of the Roman youth was kindled into active emulation as often as they beheld the domestic images of their ancestors. The temperate struggles of the patricians and plebeians had finally established the firm and equal balance of the constitution, which united the freedom of popular assemblies with the authority and wisdom of a senate and the executive powers of a regal magistrate. When the consul displayed the standard of the republic, each citizen bound himself, by the obligation of an oath, to draw his sword in the cause of his country till he had discharged the sacred duty by a military service of ten years. This wise institution continually poured into the field the rising generations of freemen and soldiers; and their numbers were reinforced by the warlike and populous states of Italy, who, after a brave resistance, had yielded to the valour and embraced the alliance of the Romans. The sage historian, who excited the virtue of the younger Scipio and beheld the ruin of Carthage, has accurately described their military system; their levies, arms, exercises, subordination, marches, encampments; and the invincible legion, superior in active strength to the Macedonian phalanx of Philip and Alexander. From these institutions of peace and war Polybius has deduced the spirit and success of a people incapable of fear and impatient of repose. The ambitious design of conquest, which might have been defeated by the seasonable conspiracy of mankind, was attempted and achieved; and the perpetual violation of justice was maintained by the political virtues of prudence and courage. The arms of the republic, sometimes vanquished in battle, always victorious in war, advanced with rapid steps to the Euphrates, the Danube, the Rhine, and the Ocean; and the images of gold, or silver, or brass, that might serve to represent the nations and their kings, were successively broken by the *iron* monarchy of Rome.

The rise of a city, which swelled into an empire, may deserve, as a singular prodigy, the reflection of a philosophic mind. But the decline of Rome was the natural and inevitable effect of immoderate greatness. Prosperity ripened the principle of decay; the causes of destruction multiplied with the extent of conquest; and as soon as time or accident had removed the artificial supports, the stupendous fabric yielded to the pressure of its own weight. The story of its ruin is simple and obvious;

and instead of inquiring *why* the Roman empire was destroyed, we should rather be surprised that it had subsisted so long. The victorious legions, who, in distant wars, acquired the vices of strangers and mercenaries, first oppressed the freedom of the republic, and afterwards violated the majesty of the purple. The emperors, anxious for their personal safety and the public peace, were reduced to the base expedient of corrupting the discipline which rendered them alike formidable to their sovereign and to the enemy; the vigour of the military government was relaxed and finally dissolved by the partial institutions of Constantine; and the Roman world was overwhelmed by a deluge of barbarians.

The decay of Rome has been frequently ascribed to the translation of the seat of empire; but this history has already shown that the powers of government were *divided*, rather than *removed*. The throne of Constantinople was erected in the East; while the West was still possessed by a series of emperors who held their residence in Italy, and claimed their equal inheritance of the legions and provinces. This dangerous novelty impaired the strength and fomented the vices of a double reign: the instruments of an oppressive and arbitrary system were multiplied; and a vain emulation of luxury, not of merit, was introduced and supported between the degenerate successors of Theodosius. Extreme distress, which unites the virtue of a free people, embitters the factions of a declining monarchy. The hostile favourites of Arcadius and Honorius betrayed the republic to its common enemies; and the Byzantine court beheld with indifference, perhaps with pleasure, the disgrace of Rome, the misfortunes of Italy, and the loss of the West. Under the succeeding reigns the alliance of the two empires was restored; but the aid of the Oriental Romans was tardy, doubtful, and ineffectual; and the national schism of the Greeks and Latins was enlarged by the perpetual difference of language and manners, of interests, and even of religion. Yet the salutary event approved in some measure the judgment of Constantine. During a long period of decay his impregnable city repelled the victorious armies of barbarism, protected the wealth of Asia, and commanded, both in peace and war, the important straits which connect the Euxine and Mediterranean seas. The foundation of Constantinople more essentially contributed to the preservation of the East than to the ruin of the West.

As the happiness of a *future* life is the great object of religion, we may hear without surprise or scandal that the introduction, or at least the abuse of Christianity, had some influence on the decline and fall of the Roman empire. The clergy successfully preached the doctrines of patience and pusillanimity; the active virtues of society were discouraged; and the last remains of military spirit were buried in the cloister: a large portion of public and private wealth was consecrated to the specious demands of charity and devotion; and the soldiers' pay was lavished on the useless multitudes of both sexes who could only plead the merits of abstinence and chastity. Faith, zeal, curiosity, and the more earthly passions of malice and ambition, kindled the flame of theological discord; the church, and even the state, were distracted by religious factions, whose conflicts were sometimes bloody and always implacable; the attention of the emperors was diverted from camps to synods; the Roman world was oppressed by a new species of tyranny; and the persecuted sects became the secret enemies of their country. Yet party-spirit, however pernicious or absurd, is a principle of union as well as of dissension. The bishops, from eighteen hundred pulpits, inculcated the duty of passive obedience to a lawful and orthodox sovereign; their frequent assemblies and perpetual correspondence maintained the communion of distant churches; and the benevolent temper of the Gospel was strengthened, though confined, by the spiritual alliance of the catholics. The sacred indolence of the monks was devoutly embraced by a servile and effeminate age; but if superstition had not afforded a decent retreat, the same vices would have tempted the unworthy Romans to desert, from baser motives, the standard of the republic. Religious precepts are easily obeyed which indulge and sanctify the natural inclinations of their votaries; but the pure and genuine influence of Christianity may be traced in its beneficial, though imperfect, effects on the barbarian proselytes of the North. If the decline of the Roman empire was hastened by the conversion of Constantine, his victorious religion broke the violence of the fall, and mollified the ferocious temper of the conquerors.

This awful revolution may be usefully applied to the instruction of the present age. It is the duty of a patriot to prefer and promote the exclusive interest and glory of his native country: but a philosopher may be permitted to enlarge his views, and to consider Europe as one great republic, whose various inhabitants have attained almost the same level of politeness and cultivation. The balance of power will continue to fluctuate, and the prosperity of our own or the neighbouring kingdoms may be alternately exalted or depressed; but these partial events cannot essentially injure our general state of happiness, the system of arts, and laws, and manners, which so advantageously distinguish, above the rest of mankind, the Europeans and their colonies. The savage nations of the globe are the common enemies of civilised society; and we may inquire, with anxious curiosity, whether Europe is still threatened with a repetition of those calamities which formerly oppressed the arms and institutions of Rome. Perhaps the same reflections will illustrate the fall of that mighty empire, and explain the probable causes of our actual security.

I. The Romans were ignorant of the extent of their danger and the number of their enemies. Beyond the Rhine and Danube the northern countries of Europe and Asia were filled with innumerable tribes of hunters and shepherds, poor, voracious, and turbulent; bold in arms, and impatient to ravish the fruits of industry. The barbarian world was agitated by the rapid impulse of war; and the peace of Gaul or Italy was shaken by the distant revolutions of China. The Huns, who fled before a victorious enemy, directed their march towards the West; and the torrent was swelled by the gradual accession of captives and allies. The flying tribes who yielded to the Huns assumed in *their* turn the spirit of conquest; the endless column of barbarians pressed on the Roman empire with accumulated weight; and, if the foremost were destroyed, the vacant space was instantly replenished by new assailants. Such formidable emigrations no longer issue from the North; and the long repose, which has been imputed to the decrease of population, is the happy consequence of the progress of arts and agriculture. Instead of some rude villages thinly scattered among its woods and morasses, Germany now produces a list of two thousand three hundred walled towns: the Christian kingdoms of Denmark, Sweden, and Poland have been successively established; and the Hanse merchants, with the Teutonic knights, have extended their colonies along the coast of the Baltic as far as the Gulf of Finland. From the Gulf of Finland to the Eastern Ocean, Russia now assumes the form of a powerful and civilised empire. The plough, the loom, and the forge are introduced on the banks of the Volga, the Oby, and the Lena; and the fiercest of the Tartar hordes have been taught to tremble and obey. The reign of independent barbarism is now contracted to a narrow span; and the remnant of Calmucks or Uzbecks, whose forces may be almost numbered, cannot seriously excite the apprehensions of the great republic of Europe. Yet this apparent security should not tempt us to forget that new enemies and unknown dangers may *possibly* arise from some obscure people, scarcely visible in the map of the world. The Arabs or Saracens, who spread their conquests from India to Spain, had languished in poverty and contempt till Mahomet breathed into those savage bodies the soul of enthusiasm.

II. The empire of Rome was firmly established by the singular and perfect coalition of its members. The subject nations, resigning the hope and even the wish of independence, embraced the character of Roman citizens; and the provinces of the West were reluctantly torn by the barbarians from the bosom of their mother country. But this union was purchased by the loss of national freedom and military spirit; and the servile provinces, destitute of life and motion, expected their safety from the mercenary troops and governors who were directed by the orders of a distant court. The happiness of an hundred millions depended on the personal merit of one or two men, perhaps children, whose minds were corrupted by education, luxury, and despotic power. The deepest wounds were inflicted on the empire during the minorities of the sons and grandsons of Theodosius; and, after those incapable princes seemed to attain the age of manhood, they abandoned the church to the bishops, the state to the eunuchs, and the provinces to the barbarians. Europe is now divided into twelve powerful, though unequal kingdoms, three respectable commonwealths, and a variety of smaller, though independent states: the chances of royal and ministerial talents are multiplied, at least, with the number of its rulers; and a Julian, or Semiramis, may reign in the North, while Arcadius and Honorius again slumber on the thrones of the South. The abuses of tyranny are restrained by the mutual influence of fear and shame; republics have acquired order and stability; monarchies have imbibed the principles of freedom, or, at least, of moderation; and some sense of honour and justice is introduced into the most defective constitutions by the general manners of the times. In peace, the progress of knowledge and industry is accelerated by the emulation of so many active rivals: in war, the European forces are exercised by temperate and undecisive contests. If a savage conqueror should issue from the deserts of Tartary, he must repeatedly vanquish the robust peasants of Russia, the numerous armies of Germany, the gallant nobles of France, and the intrepid freemen of Britain; who, perhaps, might confederate for their common defence. Should the victorious barbarians carry slavery and desolation as far as the Atlantic Ocean, ten thousand vessels would transport beyond their pursuit the remains of civilised society; and Europe would revive and flourish in the American world, which is already filled with her colonies and institutions.[1]

III. Cold, poverty, and a life of danger and fatigue fortify the strength and courage of barbarians. In every age they have oppressed the polite and peaceful nations of China, India, and Persia, who neglected, and still neglect, to counterbalance these natural powers by the resources of military art. The warlike states of antiquity, Greece, Macedonia, and Rome, educated a race of soldiers; exercised their bodies, disciplined their courage, multiplied their forces by regular evolutions, and converted the iron which they possessed into strong and serviceable weapons. But this superiority insensibly declined with their laws and manners: and the feeble policy of Constantine and his successors armed and instructed, for the ruin of the empire, the rude valour of the barbarian mercenaries. The military art has been changed by the invention of gunpowder; which enables man to command the two most powerful agents of nature, air and fire. Mathematics, chemistry, mechanics, architecture, have been applied to the service of war; and the adverse parties oppose to each other the most elaborate modes of attack and of defence. Historians may indignantly observe that the preparations of a siege

[1] America now contains about six millions of European blood and descent; and their numbers, at least in the North, are continually increasing. Whatever may be the changes of their political situation, they must preserve the manners of Europe; and we may reflect with some pleasure that the English language will probably be diffused over an immense and populous continent.

would found and maintain a flourishing colony; yet we cannot be displeased that the subversion of a city should be a work of cost and difficulty; or that an industrious people should be protected by those arts which survive and supply the decay of military virtue. Cannon and fortifications now form an impregnable barrier against the Tartar horse; and Europe is secure from any future irruption of barbarians; since, before they can conquer, they must cease to be barbarous. Their gradual advances in the science of war would always be accompanied, as we may learn from the example of Russia, with a proportionable improvement in the arts of peace and civil policy; and they themselves must deserve a place among the polished nations whom they subdue.

Should these speculations be found doubtful or fallacious, there still remains a more humble source of comfort and hope. The discoveries of ancient and modern navigators, and the domestic history or tradition of the most enlightened nations, represent the *human savage* naked both in mind and body, and destitute of laws, of arts, of ideas, and almost of language.[1] From this abject condition, perhaps the primitive and universal state of man, he has gradually arisen to command the animals, to fertilise the earth, to traverse the ocean, and to measure the heavens. His progress in the improvement and exercise of his mental and corporeal faculties has been irregular and various; infinitely slow in the beginning, and increasing by degrees with redoubled velocity: ages of laborious ascent have been followed by a moment of rapid downfall; and the several climates of the globe have felt the vicissitudes of light and darkness. Yet the experience of four thousand years should enlarge our hopes and diminish our apprehensions: we cannot determine to what height the human species may aspire in their advances towards perfection; but it may safely be presumed that no people, unless the face of nature is changed, will relapse into their original barbarism. The improvements of society may be viewed under a threefold aspect. 1. The poet or philosopher illustrates his age and country by the efforts of a *single* mind; but these superior powers of reason or fancy are rare and spontaneous productions; and the genius of Homer, or Cicero, or Newton, would excite less admiration if they could be created by the will of a prince or the lessons of a preceptor. 2. The benefits of law and policy, of trade and manufactures, of arts and sciences, are more solid and permanent; and *many* individuals may be qualified, by education and discipline, to promote, in their respective stations, the interest of

---

[1] It would be an easy, though tedious, task to produce the authorities of poets, philosophers, and historians. I shall therefore content myself with appealing to the decisive and authentic testimony of Diodorus Siculus. The Ichthyophagi, who in his time wandered along the shores of the Red Sea, can only be compared to the natives of New Holland. Fancy, or perhaps reason, may still suppose an extreme and absolute state of nature far below the level of these savages, who had acquired some arts and instruments.

the community. But this general order is the effect of skill and labour; and the complex machinery may be decayed by time, or injured by violence. 3. Fortunately for mankind, the more useful, or, at least, more necessary arts, can be performed without superior talents or national subordination; without the powers of *one*, or the union of *many*. Each village, each family, each individual, must always possess both ability and inclination to perpetuate the use of fire and of metals; the propagation and service of domestic animals; the methods of hunting and fishing; the rudiments of navigation; the imperfect cultivation of corn or other nutritive grain; and the simple practice of the mechanic trades. Private genius and public industry may be extirpated; but these hardy plants survive the tempest, and strike an everlasting root into the most unfavourable soil. The splendid days of Augustus and Trajan were eclipsed by a cloud of ignorance; and the barbarians subverted the laws and palaces of Rome. But the scythe, the invention or emblem of Saturn, still continued annually to mow the harvests of Italy; and the human feasts of the Læstrigons have never been renewed on the coast of Campania.

Since the first discovery of the arts, war, commerce, and religious zeal have diffused among the savages of the Old and New World these inestimable gifts: they have been successively propagated; they can never be lost. We may therefore acquiesce in the pleasing conclusion that every age of the world has increased and still increases the real wealth, the happiness, the knowledge, and perhaps the virtue, of the human race.[1]

[1] The merit of discovery has too often been stained with avarice, cruelty, and fanaticism; and the intercourse of nations has produced the communication of disease and prejudice. A singular exception is due to the virtue of our own times and country. The five great voyages, successively undertaken by the command of his present Majesty, were inspired by the pure and generous love of science and of mankind. The same prince, adapting his benefactions to the different stages of society, has founded a school of painting in his capital, and has introduced into the islands of the South Sea the vegetables and animals most useful to human life.

THE STATE OF ITALY

Chapter 39

THE REIGN OF THEODORIC THE OSTROGOTH. PROSPERITY OF ROME AND ITALY. ARIANISM OF THEODORIC. EXECUTION OF BOETHIUS. DEATH OF THEODORIC

With the approval of Zeno, the emperor of the East, Theodoric invaded Italy and defeated Odoacer. Odoacer was murdered in 493. In the same year Zeno was succeeded in Constantinople by Anastasius. Theodoric reigned over a Gothic kingdom in Italy, 494–526.

THE REIGN OF THEODORIC

AMONG the barbarians of the West the victory of Theodoric had spread a general alarm. But as soon as it appeared that he was satisfied with conquest and desirous of peace, terror was changed into respect, and they submitted to a powerful mediation, which was uniformly employed for the best purposes of reconciling their quarrels and civilising their manners. The ambassadors who resorted to Ravenna from the most distant countries of Europe admired his wisdom, magnificence, and courtesy; and if he sometimes accepted either slaves or arms, white horses or strange animals, the gift of a sun-dial, a water-clock, or a musician, admonished even the princes of Gaul of the superior art and industry of his Italian subjects. His domestic alliances, a wife, two daughters, a sister, and a niece, united the family of Theodoric with the kings of the Franks, the Burgundians, the Visigoths, the Vandals, and the Thuringians, and contributed to maintain the harmony, or at least the balance, of the great republic of the West. It is difficult in the dark forests of Germany and Poland to pursue the emigrations of the Heruli, a fierce people who disdained the use of armour, and who condemned their widows and aged parents not to survive the loss of their husbands or the decay of their strength. The king of these savage warriors solicited the friendship of Theodoric, and was elevated to the rank of his son, according to the barbaric rites of a military adoption. From the shores of the Baltic the Æstians or Livonians laid their offerings of native amber at the feet of a prince whose fame had excited them to undertake an unknown and dangerous journey of fifteen hundred miles. With the country from whence the Gothic nation derived their origin he maintained a frequent and friendly correspondence: the Italians were clothed in the rich sables of Sweden; and one of its sovereigns, after a voluntary or reluctant abdication, found an hospitable retreat in the palace of Ravenna. He had reigned over one of the thirteen populous tribes who cultivated a small portion of the great island or peninsula of Scandinavia, to which the vague appellation of Thule has been sometimes applied. That northern region was peopled, or had been explored, as high as the sixty-eighth degree of latitude, where the natives of the polar circle enjoy and lose the presence of the sun at each summer and winter solstice during an equal period of forty days. The long night of his absence or death was the mournful season of distress and anxiety, till the messengers, who had been sent to the mountain tops, descried the first rays of returning light, and proclaimed to the plain below the festival of his resurrection.

The life of Theodoric represents the rare and meritorious example of a barbarian who sheathed his sword in the pride of victory and the vigour of his age. A reign of three and thirty years was consecrated to the duties of civil government, and the hostilities, in which he was sometimes involved, were speedily terminated by the conduct of his lieutenants, the discipline of his troops, the arms of his allies, and even by the terror of his name. He reduced, under a strong and regular government, the unprofitable countries of Rhætia, Noricum, Dalmatia, and Pannonia, from the source of the Danube and the territory of the Bavarians to the petty kingdom erected by the Gepidæ on the ruins of Sirmium. His prudence could not safely intrust the bulwark of Italy to such feeble and turbulent neighbours; and his justice might claim the lands which they oppressed, either as a part of his kingdom, or as the inheritance of his father. The greatness of a servant, who was named perfidious because he was successful, awakened the jealousy of the emperor Anastasius; and a war was kindled on the Dacian frontier, by the protection which the Gothic king, in the vicissitude of human affairs, had granted to one of the descendants of Attila. Sabinian, a general illustrious by his own and father's merit, advanced at the head of ten thousand Romans; and the provisions and arms, which filled a long train of waggons, were distributed to the fiercest of the Bulgarian tribes. But in the fields of Margus the Eastern powers were defeated by the inferior forces of the Goths and Huns; the flower and even the hope of the Roman armies was irretrievably destroyed; and such was the temperance with which Theodoric had inspired his victorious troops, that, as their leader had not given the signal of pillage, the rich spoils of the enemy lay untouched at their feet. Exasperated by this disgrace, the Byzantine court despatched two hundred ships and eight thousand men to plunder the sea-coast of Calabria and Apulia: they assaulted the ancient city of Tarentum, interrupted the trade and agriculture of an happy country, and sailed back to the Hellespont, proud of their piratical victory over a people whom they still presumed to consider as their *Roman* brethren. Their retreat was possibly hastened by the activity of Theodoric; Italy was covered by a fleet of a thousand light vessels, which he constructed with incredible despatch; and his firm moderation was soon rewarded by a solid and honourable peace. He maintained with a powerful hand the balance of the West, till it was at length overthrown by the ambition of Clovis; and although unable to assist his rash and unfortunate kinsman the king of the Visigoths, he saved the remains of his family and people, and checked the Franks in the midst of their victorious career. I am not desirous to prolong or repeat this narrative of military events, the least interesting of the reign of Theodoric; and shall be content to add that the Alemanni were protected, that an inroad of the Burgundians was severely chastised, and that the conquest of Arles and Marseilles opened a free communication with the Visigoths, who revered him both as their national protector, and as the guardian of his grandchild, the infant son of Alaric. Under this respectable character, the king of Italy restored the Prætorian prefecture of the Gauls, reformed some abuses in the civil government of Spain, and accepted the annual tribute and apparent submission of its military governor, who wisely refused to trust his person in the palace of Ravenna. The Gothic sovereignty was established from Sicily to the Danube, from Sirmium or Belgrade to the Atlantic Ocean; and the Greeks themselves have acknowledged that Theodoric reigned over the fairest portion of the Western empire.

The union of the Goths and Romans might have fixed for ages the transient happiness of Italy; and the first of nations, a new people of free subjects and enlightened soldiers, might have gradually arisen from the mutual emulation of their respective virtues. But the sublime merit of guiding or seconding such a revolution was not reserved for the reign of Theodoric: he wanted either the genius or the opportunities of a legislator; and while he indulged the Goths in the enjoyment of rude liberty, he servilely copied the institutions, and even the abuses, of the political system which had been framed by Constantine and his successors. From a tender regard to the expiring prejudices of Rome, the barbarian declined the name, the purple, and the diadem of the emperors; but he assumed, under the hereditary title of king, the whole substance and plenitude of Imperial prerogative. His addresses to the Eastern throne were respectful and ambiguous: he celebrated in pompous style the harmony of the two republics, applauded his own government as the perfect similitude of a sole and undivided empire, and claimed above the kings of the earth the same pre-eminence which he modestly allowed to the person or rank of Anastasius. The alliance of the East and West was annually declared by the unanimous choice of two consuls; but it should seem that the Italian candidate, who was named by Theodoric, accepted a formal confirmation from the sovereign of Constantinople. The Gothic palace of Ravenna reflected the image of the court of Theodosius or Valentinian. The Prætorian prefect, the prefect of Rome, the quæstor, the master of the offices, with the public and patrimonial treasurers, whose functions are painted in gaudy colours by the rhetoric of Cassiodorus, still continued to act as the ministers of state. And the subordinate care of justice and the revenue was delegated to seven consulars, three correctors, and five presidents, who governed the fifteen *regions* of Italy according to the principles, and even the forms, of Roman jurisprudence. The violence of the conquerors was abated or eluded by the slow artifice of judicial proceedings; the civil administration, with its honours and emoluments, was confined to the Italians; and the people still preserved their dress and language, their laws and customs, their personal freedom, and two-thirds of their landed property. It had been the object of Augustus to conceal the introduction of monarchy; it was the policy of Theodoric to disguise the reign of a barbarian. If his subjects were sometimes awakened from this pleasing vision of a Roman government, they derived more substantial comfort from the character of a Gothic prince who had penetration to discern, and firmness to pursue, his own and the public interest. Theodoric loved the virtues which he possessed, and the talents of which he was destitute. Liberius was promoted to the office of Prætorian prefect for his unshaken fidelity to the unfortunate cause of Odoacer. The ministers of Theodoric, Cassiodorus and Boethius, have reflected on his reign the lustre of their genius and learning. More prudent or more fortunate than his collegue, Cassiodorus preserved his own esteem without forfeiting the royal favour; and after passing thirty years in the honours of the world, he was blessed with an equal term of repose in the devout and studious solitude of Squillace.

PROSPERITY OF ROME AND ITALY

As the patron of the republic, it was the interest and duty of the Gothic king to cultivate the affections of the senate and people. The nobles of Rome were flattered by sonorous epithets and formal professions of respect, which had been more justly applied to the merit and authority of their ancestors. The people enjoyed, without fear or danger, the three blessings of a capital, order, plenty, and public amusements. A visible diminution of their numbers may be found even in the measure of liberality; yet Apulia, Calabria, and Sicily poured their tribute of corn into the granaries of Rome; an allowance of bread and meat was distributed to the indigent citizens; and every office was deemed honourable which was consecrated to the care of their health and happiness. The public games, such as a Greek ambassador might politely applaud, exhibited a faint and feeble copy of the magnificence of the Cæsars: yet the musical, the gymnastic, and the pantomime arts, had not totally sunk in oblivion; the wild beasts of Africa still exercised in the amphitheatre the courage and dexterity of the hunters; and the indulgent Goth either patiently tolerated or gently restrained the blue and green factions, whose contests so often filled the circus with clamour, and even with blood. In the seventh year of his peaceful reign, Theodoric visited the old capital of the world; the senate and people advanced in solemn procession to salute a second Trajan, a new Valentinian; and he nobly supported that character, by the assurance of a just and legal government, in a discourse which he was not afraid to pronounce in public, and to inscribe on a tablet of brass. Rome, in this august ceremony, shot a last ray of declining glory; and a saint, the spectator of this pompous scene, could only hope, in his pious fancy, that it was excelled by the celestial splendour of the New Jerusalem. During a residence of six months, the fame, the person, and the courteous demeanour of the Gothic king, excited the admiration of the Romans, and he contemplated, with equal curiosity and surprise, the monuments that remained of their ancient greatness. He imprinted the footsteps of a conqueror on the Capitoline hill, and frankly confessed that each day he viewed with fresh wonder the forum of Trajan and his lofty column. The theatre of Pompey appeared, even in its decay, as a huge mountain artificially hollowed and polished, and adorned by human industry; and he vaguely computed that a river of gold must have been drained to erect the colossal amphitheatre of Titus. From the mouths of fourteen aqueducts a pure and copious stream was diffused into every part of the city; among these the Claudian water, which arose at the distance of thirty-eight miles in the Sabine mountains, was conveyed along a gentle though constant declivity of solid arches, till it descended on the summit of the Aventine hill. The long and spacious vaults which had been constructed for the purpose of common sewers subsisted after twelve centuries in their pristine strength; and these subterraneous channels have been preferred to all the visible wonders of Rome. The Gothic kings, so injuriously accused of the ruin of antiquity, were anxious to preserve the monuments of the nation whom they had subdued. The royal edicts were framed to prevent the abuses, the neglect, or the depredations of the citizens themselves; and a professed architect, the annual sum of two hundred pounds of gold, twenty-five thousand tiles, and the receipt of customs from the Lucrine port, were assigned for the ordinary repairs of the walls and public edifices. A similar care was extended to the statues of metal or marble of men or animals. The spirit of the horses which have given a modern name to the Quirinal was applauded by the barbarians; the brazen elephants of the *Via sacra* were diligently restored; the famous heifer of Myron deceived the cattle, as they were driven through the forum of peace; and an officer was created to protect those works of art, which Theodoric considered as the noblest ornament of his kingdom.

After the example of the last emperors, Theodoric preferred the residence of Ravenna, where he cultivated an orchard with his own hands. As often as the peace of his kingdom was threatened (for it was never invaded) by the barbarians, he removed his court to Verona on the northern frontier, and the image of his palace, still extant on a coin, represents the oldest and most authentic model of Gothic architecture. These two capitals, as well as Pavia, Spoleto, Naples, and the rest of the Italian cities, acquired under his reign the useful or splendid decorations of churches, aqueducts, baths, porticoes, and palaces. But the happiness of the subject was more truly conspicuous in the busy scene of labour and luxury, in the rapid increase and bold enjoyment of national wealth. From the shades of Tibur and Præneste, the Roman senators still retired in the winter season to the warm sun and salubrious springs of Baiæ; and their villas, which advanced on solid moles into the bay of Naples, commanded the various prospect of the sky, the earth, and the water. On the eastern side of the Adriatic a new Campania was formed in the fair and fruitful province of Istria, which communicated with the palace of Ravenna by an easy navigation of one hundred miles. The rich productions of Lucania and the adjacent provinces were exchanged at the Marcilian fountain, in a populous fair annually dedicated to trade, intemperance, and superstition. In the solitude of Comum, which had once been animated by the mild genius of Pliny, a transparent basin above sixty miles in length still reflected the rural seats which encompassed the margin of the Larian lake; and the gradual ascent of the hills was covered by a triple plantation of olives, of vines, and of chestnut-trees. Agriculture revived under the shadow of peace, and the number of husbandmen was multiplied by the redemption of captives.[1] The iron-mines of Dalmatia, a gold-mine in Bruttium, were carefully explored, and the Pomptine marshes, as well as those of Spoleto, were drained and cultivated by private undertakers, whose distant reward must depend on the continuance of the public prosperity. Whenever the seasons were less propitious, the doubtful precautions of forming magazines of corn, fixing the price, and prohibiting the exportation, attested at least the benevolence of the state; but such was the extraordinary plenty which an industrious people produced from a grateful soil, that a gallon of wine was sometimes sold in Italy for less than three farthings, and a quarter of wheat at about five shillings and sixpence. A country possessed of so many valuable objects of exchange soon attracted the merchants of the world, whose beneficial traffic was encouraged and protected by the liberal spirit of Theodoric. The free intercourse of the provinces by land and water was restored and extended; the city gates were never shut either by day or by night; and the

---

[1] St. Epiphanius of Pavia redeemed by prayer or ransom 600 captives from the Burgundians of Lyons and Savoy. Such deeds are the best of miracles.

common saying, that a purse of gold might be safely left in the fields, was expressive of the conscious security of the inhabitants.

ARIANISM OF THEODORIC

A difference of religion is always pernicious and often fatal to the harmony of the prince and people: the Gothic conqueror had been educated in the profession of Arianism, and Italy was devoutly attached to the Nicene faith. But the persuasion of Theodoric was not infected by zeal: and he piously adhered to the heresy of his fathers, without condescending to balance the subtle arguments of theological metaphysics. Satisfied with the private toleration of his Arian sectaries, he justly conceived himself to be the guardian of the public worship, and his external reverence for a superstition which he despised may have nourished in his mind the salutary indifference of a statesman or philosopher. The catholics of his dominions acknowledged, perhaps with reluctance, the peace of the church; their clergy, according to the degrees of rank or merit, were honourably entertained in the palace of Theodoric; he esteemed the living sanctity of Cæsarius and Epiphanius, the orthodox bishops of Arles and Pavia; and presented a decent offering on the tomb of St. Peter, without any scrupulous inquiry into the creed of the apostle. His favourite Goths, and even his mother, were permitted to retain or embrace the Athanasian faith, and his long reign could not afford the example of an Italian catholic who, either from choice or compulsion, had deviated into the religion of the conqueror. The people, and the barbarians themselves, were edified by the pomp and order of religious worship; the magistrates were instructed to defend the just immunities of ecclesiastical persons and possessions; the bishops held their synods, the metropolitans exercised their jurisdiction, and the privileges of sanctuary were maintained or moderated according to the spirit of the Roman jurisprudence. With the protection, Theodoric assumed the legal supremacy, of the church; and his firm administration restored or extended some useful prerogatives which had been neglected by the feeble emperors of the West. He was not ignorant of the dignity and importance of the Roman pontiff, to whom the venerable name of POPE was now appropriated. The peace or the revolt of Italy might depend on the character of a wealthy and popular bishop, who claimed such ample dominion both in heaven and earth; who had been declared in a numerous synod to be pure from all sin, and exempt trom all judgment. When the chair of St. Peter was disputed by Symmachus and Laurence, they appeared at his summons before the tribunal of an Arian monarch, and he confirmed the election of the most worthy or the most obsequious candidate. At the end of his life, in a moment of jealousy and resentment, he prevented the choice of the Romans, by nominating a pope in the palace of Ravenna. The danger and furious contests of a schism were mildly restrained, and the last decree of the senate was enacted to extinguish, if it were possible, the scandalous venality of the papal elections.

I have descanted with pleasure on the fortunate condition of Italy, but our fancy must not hastily conceive that the golden age of the poets, a race of men without vice or misery, was realised under the Gothic conquest. The fair prospect was sometimes overcast with clouds; the wisdom of Theodoric might be deceived, his power might be resisted, and the declining age of the monarch was sullied with popular hatred and patrician blood. In the first insolence of victory he had been tempted to deprive the whole party of Odoacer of the civil and even the natural rights of society; a tax, unseasonably imposed after the calamities of war, would have crushed the rising agriculture of Liguria; a rigid pre-emption of corn, which was intended for the public relief, must have aggravated the distress of Campania. These dangerous projects were defeated by the virtue and eloquence of Epiphanius and Boethius, who, in the presence of Theodoric himself, successfully pleaded the cause of the people: but, if the royal ear was open to the voice of truth, a saint and a philosopher are not always to be found at the ear of kings. The privileges of rank, or office, or favour were too frequently abused by Italian fraud and Gothic violence, and the avarice of the king's nephew was publicly exposed, at first by the usurpation, and afterwards by the restitution, of the estates which he had unjustly extorted from his Tuscan neighbours. Two hundred thousand barbarians, formidable even to their master, were seated in the heart of Italy; they indignantly supported the restraints of peace and discipline; the disorders of their march were always felt and sometimes compensated; and where it was dangerous to punish, it might be prudent to dissemble, the sallies of their native fierceness. When the indulgence of Theodoric had remitted two-thirds of the Ligurian tribute, he condescended to explain the difficulties of his situation, and to lament the heavy though inevitable burdens which he imposed on his subjects for their own defence. These ungrateful subjects could never be cordially reconciled to the origin, the religion, or even the virtues, of the Gothic conqueror; past calamities were forgotten, and the sense or suspicion of injuries was rendered still more exquisite by the present felicity of the times.

Even the religious toleration which Theodoric had the glory of introducing into the Christian world was painful and offensive to the orthodox zeal of the Italians. They respected the armed heresy of the Goths; but their pious rage was safely pointed against the rich and defenceless Jews, who had formed their establishments at Naples, Rome, Ravenna, Milan, and Genoa, for the benefit of trade, and under the sanction of the laws. Their persons were insulted, their effects were pillaged, and their synagogues were burnt by the mad populace of Ravenna and Rome, inflamed, as it should seem, by the most frivolous or extravagant pretences. The government which could neglect, would have deserved such an outrage. A legal inquiry was instantly directed; and, as the authors of the tumult had escaped in the crowd, the whole community was condemned to repair the damage, and the obstinate bigots, who refused their contributions, were whipped through the streets by the hand of the executioner. This simple act of justice exasperated the discontent of the catholics, who applauded the merit and patience of these holy confessors. Three hundred pulpits deplored the persecution of the church; and if the chapel of St. Stephen at Verona was demolished by the command of Theodoric, it is probable that some miracle hostile to his name and dignity had been performed on that sacred theatre. At the close of a glorious life, the king of Italy discovered that he had excited the hatred of a people whose happiness he had so assiduously laboured to promote; and his mind was soured by indignation, jealousy, and the bitterness of unrequited love. The Gothic conqueror condescended to disarm the unwarlike natives of Italy, interdicting all weapons of offence, and excepting only a small knife for domestic use. The deliverer of Rome was accused of conspiring with the vilest informers against the lives of senators whom he suspected of a secret and treasonable correspondence with the Byzantine court. After the death of Anastasius, the diadem had been placed on the head of a feeble old man, but the powers of government were assumed by his nephew Justinian, who already meditated the extirpation of heresy and the conquest of Italy and Africa. A rigorous law, which was published at Constantinople, to reduce the Arians, by the dread of punishment, within the pale of the church, awakened the just resentment of Theodoric, who claimed for his distressed brethren of the East the same indulgence which he had so long granted to the catholics of his dominions. At his stern command the Roman pontiff, with four *illustrious* senators, embarked on an embassy of which he must have alike dreaded the failure or the success. The singular veneration shown to the first pope who had visited Constantinople was punished as a crime by his jealous monarch; the artful or peremptory refusal of the Byzantine court might excuse an equal, and would provoke a larger, measure of retaliation; and a mandate was prepared in Italy to prohibit, after a stated day, the exercise of the catholic worship. By the bigotry of his subjects and enemies the most tolerant of princes was driven to the brink of persecution, and the life of Theodoric was too long, since he lived to condemn the virtue of Boethius and Symmachus.

THE EXECUTION OF BOETHIUS

The senator Boethius is the last of the Romans whom Cato or Tully could have acknowledged for their countryman. As a wealthy orphan, he inherited the patrimony and honours of the Anician family, a name ambitiously assumed by the kings and emperors of the age, and the appellation of Manlius asserted his genuine or fabulous descent from a race of consuls and dictators who had repulsed the Gauls from the Capitol, and sacrificed their sons to the discipline of the republic. In the youth of Boethius the studies of Rome were not totally abandoned; a Virgil is now extant corrected by the hand of a consul; and the professors of grammar, rhetoric, and jurisprudence were maintained in their privileges and pensions by the liberality of the Goths. But the erudition of the Latin language was insufficient to satiate his ardent curiosity; and Boethius is said to have employed eighteen laborious years in the schools of Athens, which were supported by the zeal, the learning, and the diligence of Proclus and his disciples. The reason and piety of their Roman pupil were fortunately saved from the contagion of mystery and magic which polluted the groves of the Academy; but he imbibed the spirit, and imitated the method, of his dead and living masters, who attempted to reconcile the strong and subtle sense of Aristotle with the devout contemplation and sublime fancy of Plato. After his return to Rome, and his marriage with the daughter of his friend the patrician Symmachus, Boethius still continued, in a palace of ivory and marble, to prosecute the same studies. The church was edified by his profound defence of the orthodox creed against the Arian, the Eutychian, and the Nestorian heresies; and the catholic unity was explained or exposed in a formal treatise by the *indifference* of three distinct though consubstantial persons. For the benefit of his Latin readers, his genius submitted to teach the first elements of the arts and sciences of Greece. The geometry of Euclid, the music of Pythagoras, the arithmetic of Nicomachus, the mechanics of Archimedes, the astronomy of Ptolemy, the theology of Plato, and the logic of Aristotle, with the commentary of Porphyry, were translated and illustrated by the indefatigable pen of the Roman senator. And he alone was esteemed capable of describing the wonders of art, a sun-dial, a water-clock, or a sphere which represented the motions of the planets. From these abstruse speculations Boethius stooped—or, to speak more truly, he rose—to the social duties of public and private life; the indigent were relieved by his liberality, and his eloquence, which flattery might compare to the voice of Demosthenes or Cicero, was uniformly exerted in the cause of innocence and humanity. Such conspicuous merit was felt and rewarded by a discerning prince: the dignity of Boethius was adorned with the titles of consul and patrician, and his talents were usefully employed in the important station of master of the offices. Notwithstanding the equal claims of the East and West, his two sons were created, in their tender youth, the consuls of the same year. On the memorable day of their inauguration they proceeded in solemn pomp from their palace to the forum amidst the applause of the senate and people; and their joyful father, the true consul of Rome, after pronouncing an oration in the praise of his royal benefactor, distributed a triumphal largess in the games of the circus. Prosperous in his fame and fortunes, in his public honours and private alliances, in the cultivation of science and the consciousness of virtue, Boethius might have been styled happy, if that precarious epithet could be safely applied before the last term of the life of man.

A philosopher, liberal of his wealth and parsimonious of his time, might be insensible to the common allurements of ambition, the thirst of gold and employment. And some credit may be due to the asseveration of Boethius, that he had reluctantly obeyed the divine Plato, who enjoins every virtuous citizen to rescue the state from the usurpation of vice and ignorance. For the integrity of his public conduct he appeals to the memory of his country. His authority had restrained the pride and oppression of the royal officers, and his eloquence had delivered Paulianus from the dogs of the palace. He had always pitied, and often relieved, the distress of the provincials, whose fortunes were exhausted by public and private rapine; and Boethius alone had courage to oppose the tyranny of the barbarians, elated by conquest, excited by avarice, and, as he complains, encouraged by impunity. In these honourable contests his spirit soared above the consideration of danger, and perhaps of prudence; and we may learn from the example of Cato that a character of pure and inflexible virtue is the most apt to be misled by prejudice, to be heated by enthusiasm, and to confound private enmities with public justice. The disciple of Plato might exaggerate the infirmities of nature and the imperfections of society; and the mildest form of a Gothic kingdom, even the weight of allegiance and gratitude, must be insupportable to the free spirit of a Roman patriot. But the favour and fidelity of Boethius declined in just proportion with the public happiness, and an unworthy colleague was imposed to divide and control the power of the master of the offices. In the last gloomy season of Theodoric he indignantly felt that he was a slave; but as his master had only power over his life, he stood, without arms and without fear, against the face of an angry barbarian, who had been provoked to believe that the safety of the senate was incompatible with his own. The senator Albinus was accused and already convicted on the presumption of *hoping*, as it was said, the liberty of Rome. "If Albinus be criminal," exclaimed the orator, "the senate and myself are all guilty of the same crime. If we are innocent, Albinus is equally entitled to the protection of the laws." These laws might not have punished the simple and barren wish of an unattainable blessing; but they would have shown less indulgence to the rash confession of Boethius, that, had he known of a conspiracy, the tyrant never should. The advocate of Albinus was soon involved in the danger and perhaps the guilt of his client; their signature (which they denied as a forgery) was affixed to the original address inviting the emperor to deliver Italy from the Goths; and three witnesses of honourable rank, perhaps of infamous reputation, attested the treasonable designs of the Roman patrician. Yet his innocence must be

presumed, since he was deprived by Theodoric of the means of justification, and rigorously confined in the tower of Pavia, while the senate, at
the distance of five hundred miles, pronounced a sentence of confiscation and death against the most illustrious of its members. At the command of the barbarians, the occult science of a philosopher was stigmatised with the names of sacrilege and magic.[1] A devout and dutiful
attachment to the senate was condemned as criminal by the trembling
voices of the senators themselves; and their ingratitude deserved the
wish or prediction of Boethius, that, after him, none should be found
guilty of the same offence.

While Boethius, oppressed with fetters, expected each moment the
sentence or the stroke of death, he composed in the tower of Pavia the
Consolation of Philosophy; a golden volume not unworthy of the leisure
of Plato or Tully, but which claims incomparable merit from the barbarism of the times and the situation of the author. The celestial guide
whom he had so long invoked at Rome and Athens now condescended
to illumine his dungeon, to revive his courage, and to pour into his
wounds her salutary balm. She taught him to compare his long prosperity and his recent distress, and to conceive new hopes from the inconstancy of fortune. Reason had informed him of the precarious
condition of her gifts; experience had satisfied him of their real value;
he had enjoyed them without guilt, he might resign them without a sigh,
and calmly disdain the impotent malice of his enemies, who had left him
happiness, since they had left him virtue. From the earth Boethius
ascended to heaven in search of the SUPREME GOOD; explored the metaphysical labyrinth of chance and destiny, of prescience and free-will, of
time and eternity; and generously attempted to reconcile the perfect
attributes of the Deity with the apparent disorders of his moral and
physical government. Such topics of consolation, so obvious, so vague,
or so abstruse, are ineffectual to subdue the feelings of human nature.
Yet the sense of misfortune may be diverted by the labour of thought;
and the sage who could artfully combine in the same work the various
riches of philosophy, poetry, and eloquence, must already have possessed the intrepid calmness which he affected to seek. Suspense, the
worst of evils, was at length determined by the ministers of death, who
executed, and perhaps exceeded, the inhuman mandate of Theodoric.
A strong cord was fastened round the head of Boethius, and forcibly
tightened till his eyes almost started from their sockets; and some mercy
may be discovered in the milder torture of beating him with clubs till he
expired. But his genius survived to diffuse a ray of knowledge over the
darkest ages of the Latin world; the writings of the philosopher were
translated by the most glorious of the English kings, and the third

[1] A severe inquiry was instituted into the crime of magic; and it was believed that
many necromancers had escaped by making their gaolers mad: for *mad*, I should
read *drunk*.

emperor of the name of Otho removed to a more honourable tomb the bones of a catholic saint who, from his Arian persecutors, had acquired the honours of martyrdom and the fame of miracles.[1] In the last hours of Boethius he derived some comfort from the safety of his two sons, of his wife, and of his father-in-law, the venerable Symmachus. But the grief of Symmachus was indiscreet, and perhaps disrespectful: he had presumed to lament, he might dare to revenge, the death of an injured friend. He was dragged in chains from Rome to the palace of Ravenna, and the suspicions of Theodoric could only be appeased by the blood of an innocent and aged senator.

THE DEATH OF THEODORIC

Humanity will be disposed to encourage any report which testifies the jurisdiction of conscience and the remorse of kings; and philosophy is not ignorant that the most horrid spectres are sometimes created by the powers of a disordered fancy, and the weakness of a distempered body. After a life of virtue and glory, Theodoric was now descending with shame and guilt into the grave: his mind was humbled by the contrast of the past, and justly alarmed by the invisible terrors of futurity. One evening, as it is related, when the head of a large fish was served on the royal table, he suddenly exclaimed that he beheld the angry countenance of Symmachus, his eyes glaring fury and revenge, and his mouth armed with long sharp teeth, which threatened to devour him. The monarch instantly retired to his chamber, and, as he lay trembling with aguish cold under a weight of bed-clothes, he expressed in broken murmurs to his physician Elpidius his deep repentance for the murders of Boethius and Symmachus. His malady increased, and, after a dysentery which continued three days, he expired in the palace of Ravenna, in the thirty-third, or, if we compute from the invasion of Italy, in the thirty-seventh year of his reign. Conscious of his approaching end, he divided his treasures and provinces between his two grandsons, and fixed the Rhône as their common boundary. Amalaric was restored to the throne of Spain. Italy, with all the conquests of the Ostrogoths, was bequeathed to Athalaric, whose age did not exceed ten years, but who was cherished as the last male offspring of the line of Amali, by the short-lived marriage of his mother Amalasuntha with a royal fugitive of the same blood. In the presence of the dying monarch the Gothic chiefs and Italian magistrates mutually engaged their faith and loyalty to the young prince and to his guardian mother; and received, in the same awful moment, his

---

[1] The inscription on his new tomb was composed by the preceptor of Otho the Third, the learned pope Silvester II, who, like Boethius himself, was styled a magician by the ignorance of the times. The catholic martyr had carried his head in his hands a considerable way; yet on a similar tale, a lady of my acquaintance once observed, "La distance n'y fait rien; il n'y a que le premier pas qui coûte." [Madame du Deffand. She was speaking of the similar miracle of St. Denis.—D.M.L.]

last salutary advice to maintain the laws, to love the senate and people of Rome, and to cultivate with decent reverence the friendship of the emperor. The monument of Theodoric was erected by his daughter Amalasuntha in a conspicuous situation, which commanded the city of Ravenna, the harbour, and the adjacent coast. A chapel of a circular form, thirty feet in diameter, is crowned by a dome of one entire piece of granite: from the centre of the dome four columns arose, which supported in a vase of porphyry the remains of the Gothic king, surrounded by the brazen statues of the twelve apostles. His spirit, after some previous expiation, might have been permitted to mingle with the benefactors of mankind, if an Italian hermit had not been witness in a vision to the damnation of Theodoric, whose soul was plunged by the ministers of divine vengeance into the volcano of Lipari, one of the flaming mouths of the infernal world.

THE AGE OF JUSTINIAN

Chapter 40

THE REIGN OF JUSTINIAN. THE EMPRESS THEODORA. THE
NIKA RIOTS. IMPORTATION OF SILK FROM CHINA. THE
CHURCH OF ST. SOPHIA. SUPPRESSION OF THE SCHOOLS
OF ATHENS AND OF THE ROMAN CONSULSHIP

THE emperor Justinian was born near the ruins of Sardica (the
modern Sophia), of an obscure race of barbarians, the inhabitants
of a wild and desolate country, to which the names of Dardania,
of Dacia, and of Bulgaria, have been successively applied. His elevation
was prepared by the adventurous spirit of his uncle Justin, who, with
two other peasants of the same village, deserted for the profession of
arms the more useful employment of husbandmen or shepherds. On
foot, with a scanty provision of biscuit in their knapsacks, the three
youths followed the high road of Constantinople, and were soon enrolled, for their strength and stature, among the guards of the emperor
Leo. Under the two succeeding reigns, the fortunate peasant emerged
to wealth and honours; and his escape from some dangers which
threatened his life was afterwards ascribed to the guardian angel who
watches over the fate of kings. His long and laudable service in the
Isaurian and Persian wars would not have preserved from oblivion the
name of Justin; yet they might warrant the military promotion which,
in the course of fifty years, he gradually obtained—the rank of tribune,
of count, and of general, the dignity of senator, and the command of the
guards, who obeyed him as their chief at the important crisis when the
emperor Anastasius was removed from the world. The powerful kinsmen whom he had raised and enriched were excluded from the throne;
and the eunuch Amantius, who reigned in the palace, had secretly resolved to fix the diadem on the head of the most obsequious of his
creatures. A liberal donative, to conciliate the suffrage of the guards,
was entrusted for that purpose in the hands of their commander. But
these weighty arguments were treacherously employed by Justin in his
own favour; and as no competitor presumed to appear, the Dacian
peasant was invested with the purple by the unanimous consent of the
soldiers, who knew him to be brave and gentle; of the clergy and people,
who believed him to be orthodox; and of the provincials, who yielded a
blind and implicit submission to the will of the capital. The elder Justin,
as he is distinguished from another emperor of the same family and
name, ascended the Byzantine throne at the age of sixty-eight years; and,
had he been left to his own guidance, every moment of a nine-years'

reign must have exposed to his subjects the impropriety of their choice. His ignorance was similar to that of Theodoric; and it is remarkable that, in an age not destitute of learning, two contemporary monarchs had never been instructed in the knowledge of the alphabet. But the genius of Justin was far inferior to that of the Gothic king: the experience of a soldier had not qualified him for the government of an empire; and though personally brave, the consciousness of his own weakness was naturally attended with doubt, distrust, and political apprehension. But the official business of the state was diligently and faithfully transacted by the quæstor Proclus; and the aged emperor adopted the talents and ambition of his nephew Justinian, an aspiring youth, whom his uncle had drawn from the rustic solitude of Dacia, and educated at Constantinople as the heir of his private fortune, and at length of the Eastern empire.

Since the eunuch Amantius had been defrauded of his money, it became necessary to deprive him of his life. The task was easily accomplished by the charge of a real or fictitious conspiracy; and the judges were informed, as an accumulation of guilt, that he was secretly addicted to the Manichæan heresy. Amantius lost his head; three of his companions, the first domestics of the palace, were punished either with death or exile; and their unfortunate candidate for the purple was cast into a deep dungeon, overwhelmed with stones, and ignominiously thrown without burial into the sea. The ruin of Vitalian was a work of more difficulty and danger. That Gothic chief had rendered himself popular by the civil war which he boldly waged against Anastasius for the defence of the orthodox faith; and after the conclusion of an advantageous treaty, he still remained in the neighbourhood of Constantinople at the head of a formidable and victorious army of barbarians. By the frail security of oaths he was tempted to relinquish this advantageous situation, and to trust his person within the walls of a city whose inhabitants, particularly the *blue* faction, were artfully incensed against him by the remembrance even of his pious hostilities. The emperor and his nephew embraced him as the faithful and worthy champion of the church and state, and gratefully adorned their favourite with the titles of consul and general; but in the seventh month of his consulship Vitalian was stabbed with seventeen wounds at the royal banquet, and Justinian, who inherited the spoil, was accused as the assassin of a spiritual brother, to whom he had recently pledged his faith in the participation of the Christian mysteries. After the fall of his rival, he was promoted, without any claim of military service, to the office of master-general of the Eastern armies, whom it was his duty to lead into the field against the public enemy. But, in the pursuit of fame, Justinian might have lost his present dominion over the age and weakness of his uncle; and instead of acquiring by Scythian or Persian trophies the applause of his countrymen, the prudent warrior solicited their favour in the churches, the circus, and the senate of Constantinople. The catholics were attached to the nephew of Justin, who between the Nestorian and Eutychian heresies, trod the narrow path of inflexible and intolerant orthodoxy. In the first days of the new reign he prompted and gratified the popular enthusiasm against the memory of the deceased emperor. After a schism of thirty-four years, he reconciled the proud and angry spirit of the Roman pontiff, and spread among the Latins a favourable report of his pious respect for the apostolic see. The thrones of the East were filled with catholic bishops devoted to his interest, the clergy and the monks were gained by his liberality, and the people were taught to pray for their future sovereign, the hope and pillar of the true religion. The magnificence of Justinian was displayed in the superior pomp of his public spectacles, an object not less sacred and important in the eyes of the multitude than the creed of Nice or Chalcedon: the expense of his consulship was esteemed at two hundred and eighty-eight thousand pieces of gold; twenty lions and thirty leopards were produced at the same time in the amphitheatre; and a numerous train of horses, with their rich trappings, was bestowed as an extraordinary gift on the victorious charioteers of the circus. While he indulged the people of Constantinople, and received the addresses of foreign kings, the nephew of Justin assiduously cultivated the friendship of the senate. That venerable name seemed to qualify its members to declare the sense of the nation, and to regulate the succession of the Imperial throne. The feeble Anastasius had permitted the vigour of government to degenerate into the form or substance of an aristocracy, and the military officers who had obtained the senatorial rank were followed by their domestic guards, a band of veterans whose arms or acclamations might fix in a tumultuous moment the diadem of the East. The treasures of the state were lavished to procure the voices of the senators, and their unanimous wish that he would be pleased to adopt Justinian for his colleague was communicated to the emperor. But this request, which too clearly admonished him of his approaching end, was unwelcome to the jealous temper of an aged monarch desirous to retain the power which he was incapable of exercising; and Justin, holding his purple with both his hands, advised them to prefer, since an election was so profitable, some older candidate. Notwithstanding this reproach, the senate proceeded to decorate Justinian with the royal epithet of *nobilissimus*; and their decree was ratified by the affection or the fears of his uncle. After some time the languour of mind and body to which he was reduced by an incurable wound in his thigh indispensably required the aid of a guardian. He summoned the patriarch and senators, and in their presence solemnly placed the diadem on the head of his nephew, who was conducted from the palace to the circus, and saluted by the loud and joyful applause of the people. The life of Justin was prolonged about four months; but from the instant of this ceremony he was considered as dead to the empire, which acknowledged Justinian, in the forty-ninth year of his age, for the lawful sovereign of the East.

From his elevation to his death, Justinian governed the Roman empire thirty-eight years, seven months, and thirteen days. The events of his reign, which excite our curious attention by their number, variety, and importance, are diligently related by the secretary of Belisarius, a rhetorician, whom eloquence had promoted to the rank of senator and prefect of Constantinople. According to the vicissitudes of courage or servitude, of favour or disgrace, Procopius successively composed the *history*, the *panegyric*, and the *satire* of his own times. The eight books of the Persian, Vandalic, and Gothic wars, which are continued in the five books of Agathias, deserve our esteem as a laborious and successful imitation of the Attic, or at least of the Asiatic, writers of ancient Greece. His facts are collected from the personal experience and free conversation of a soldier, a statesman, and a traveller; his style continually aspires, and often attains to the merit of strength and elegance; his reflections, more especially in the speeches, which he too frequently inserts, contain a rich fund of political knowledge; and the historian, excited by the generous ambition of pleasing and instructing posterity, appears to disdain the prejudices of the people and the flattery of courts. The writings of Procopius were read and applauded by his contemporaries: but, although he respectfully laid them at the foot of the throne, the pride of Justinian must have been wounded by the praise of an hero who perpetually eclipses the glory of his inactive sovereign. The conscious dignity of independence was subdued by the hopes and fears of a slave; and the secretary of Belisarius laboured for pardon and reward in the six books of the Imperial *edifices*. He had dexterously chosen a subject of apparent splendour, in which he could loudly celebrate the genius, the magnificence, and the piety of a prince who, both as a conqueror and legislator, has surpassed the puerile virtues of Themistocles and Cyrus. Disappointment might urge the flatterer to secret revenge; and the first glance of favour might again tempt him to suspend and suppress a libel in which the Roman Cyrus is degraded into an odious and contemptible tyrant, in which both the emperor and his consort Theodora are seriously represented as two dæmons who had assumed an human form for the destruction of mankind.[1] Such base inconsistency must doubtless sully the reputation, and detract from the credit, of Procopius: yet after the venom of his malignity has been suffered to exhale, the residue of the *anecdotes*, even the most disgraceful facts, some of which had been tenderly hinted in his public history, are established by their internal

[1] Justinian an ass—the perfect likeness of Domitian—Theodora's lovers driven from her bed by rival dæmons—her marriage foretold with a great dæmon—a monk saw the prince of the dæmons, instead of Justinian, on the throne—the servants who watched beheld a face without features, a body walking without an head, &c. &c. Procopius declares his own and his friends' belief in these diabolical stories.

evidence, or the authentic monuments of the times. From these various materials I shall now proceed to describe the reign of Justinian, which will deserve and occupy an ample space. The present chapter will explain the elevation and character of Theodora, the factions of the circus, and the peaceful administration of the sovereign of the East. In the three succeeding chapters I shall relate the wars of Justinian, which achieved the conquest of Africa and Italy; and I shall follow the victories of Belisarius and Narses, without disguising the vanity of their triumphs, or the hostile virtue of the Persian and Gothic heroes. The series of this volume will embrace the jurisprudence and theology of the emperor; the controversies and sects which still divide the Oriental church; the reformation of the Roman law which is obeyed or respected by the nations of modern Europe.

THE EMPRESS THEODORA

In the exercise of supreme power, the first act of Justinian was to divide it with the woman whom he loved, the famous Theodora, whose strange elevation cannot be applauded as the triumph of female virtue. Under the reign of Anastasius, the care of the wild beasts maintained by the green faction at Constantinople was intrusted to Acacius, a native of the isle of Cyprus, who, from his employment, was surnamed the master of the bears. This honourable office was given after his death to another candidate, notwithstanding the diligence of his widow, who had already provided a husband and a successor. Acacius had left three daughters, Comito, THEODORA, and Anastasia, the eldest of whom did not then exceed the age of seven years. On a solemn festival, these helpless orphans were sent by their distressed and indignant mother, in the garb of suppliants, into the midst of the theatre: the green faction received them with contempt, the blues with compassion; and this difference, which sunk deep into the mind of Theodora, was felt long afterwards in the administration of the empire. As they improved in age and beauty, the three sisters were successively devoted to the public and private pleasures of the Byzantine people; and Theodora, after following Comito on the stage, in the dress of a slave, with a stool on her head, was at length permitted to exercise her independent talents. She neither danced, nor sung, nor played on the flute; her skill was confined to the pantomime arts; she excelled in buffoon characters; and as often as the comedian swelled her cheeks, and complained with a ridiculous tone and gesture of the blows that were inflicted, the whole theatre of Constantinople resounded with laughter and applause. The beauty of Theodora was the subject of more flattering praise, and the source of more exquisite delight. Her features were delicate and regular; her complexion, though somewhat pale, was tinged with a natural colour; every sensation was instantly expressed by the vivacity of her eyes; her easy motions displayed the graces of a small but elegant figure; and either love or adulation might proclaim that painting and poetry were incapable of delineating the matchless excellence of her form. But this form was degraded by the facility with which it was exposed to the public eye, and prostituted to licentious desire. Her venal charms were abandoned to a promiscuous crowd of citizens and strangers, of every rank and of every profession: the fortunate lover who had been promised a night of enjoyment was often driven from her bed by a stronger or more wealthy favourite; and when she passed through the streets, her presence was avoided by all who wished to escape either the scandal or the temptation. The satirical historian has not blushed to describe the naked scenes which Theodora was not ashamed to exhibit in the theatre. After exhausting the arts of sensual pleasure, she most ungratefully murmured against the parsimony of Nature; but her murmurs, her pleasures, and her arts, must be veiled in the obscurity of a learned language. After reigning for some time the delight and contempt of the capital, she condescended to accompany Ecebolus, a native of Tyre, who had obtained the government of the African Pentapolis. But this union was frail and transient: Ecebolus soon rejected an expensive or faithless concubine; she was reduced at Alexandria to extreme distress; and in her laborious return to Constantinople, every city of the East admired and enjoyed the fair Cyprian, whose merit appeared to justify her descent from the peculiar island of Venus. The vague commerce of Theodora, and the most detestable precautions, preserved her from the danger which she feared; yet once, and once only, she became a mother. The infant was saved and educated in Arabia by his father, who imparted to him on his death-bed that he was the son of an empress. Filled with ambitious hopes, the unsuspecting youth immediately hastened to the palace of Constantinople, and was admitted to the presence of his mother. As he was never more seen, even after the decease of Theodora, she deserved the foul imputation of extinguishing with his life a secret so offensive to her imperial virtue.

In the most abject state of her fortune and reputation, some vision, either of sleep or of fancy, had whispered to Theodora the pleasing assurance that she was destined to become the spouse of a potent monarch. Conscious of her approaching greatness, she returned from Paphlagonia to Constantinople; assumed, like a skilful actress, a more decent character; relieved her poverty by the laudable industry of spinning wool; and affected a life of chastity and solitude in a small house, which she afterwards changed into a magnificent temple. Her beauty, assisted by art or accident, soon attracted, captivated, and fixed, the patrician Justinian, who already reigned with absolute sway under the name of his uncle. Perhaps she contrived to enhance the value of a gift which she had so often lavished on the meanest of mankind; perhaps she inflamed, at first by modest delays, and at last by sensual allurements, the desires of a lover who, from nature or devotion, was addicted to long vigils and abstemious diet. When his first transports had subsided, she still maintained the same ascendant over his mind by the more solid merit of temper and understanding. Justinian delighted to ennoble and enrich the object of his affection: the treasures of the East were poured at her feet, and the nephew of Justin was determined, perhaps by religious scruples, to bestow on his concubine the sacred and legal character of a wife. But the laws of Rome expressly prohibited the marriage of a senator with any female who had been dishonoured by a servile origin or theatrical profession: the empress Lupicina or Euphemia, a barbarian of rustic manners, but of irreproachable virtue, refused to accept a prostitute for her niece; and even Vigilantia, the superstitious mother of Justinian, though she acknowledged the wit and beauty of Theodora, was seriously apprehensive lest the levity and arrogance of that artful paramour might corrupt the piety and happiness of her son. These obstacles were removed by the inflexible constancy of Justinian. He patiently expected the death of the empress; he despised the tears of his mother, who soon sunk under the weight of her affliction; and a law was promulgated, in the name of the emperor Justin, which abolished the rigid jurisprudence of antiquity. A glorious repentance (the words of the edict) was left open for the unhappy females who had prostituted their persons on the theatre, and they were permitted to contract a legal union with the most illustrious of the Romans. This indulgence was speedily followed by the solemn nuptials of Justinian and Theodora; her dignity was gradually exalted with that of her lover; and, as soon as Justin had invested his nephew with the purple, the patriarch of Constantinople placed the diadem on the heads of the emperor and empress of the East. But the usual honours which the severity of Roman manners had allowed to the wives of princes could not satisfy either the ambition of Theodora or the fondness of Justinian. He seated her on the throne as an equal and independent colleague in the sovereignty of the empire, and an oath of allegiance was imposed on the governors of the provinces in the joint names of Justinian and Theodora. The Eastern world fell prostrate before the genius and fortune of the daughter of Acacius. The prostitute who, in the presence of innumerable spectators, had polluted the theatre of Constantinople, was adorned as a queen in the same city, by grave magistrates, orthodox bishops, victorious generals, and captive monarchs.[1]

Those who believe that the female mind is totally depraved by the loss of chastity will eagerly listen to all the invectives of private envy or popular resentment, which have dissembled the virtues of Theodora, exaggerated her vices, and condemned with rigour the venal or voluntary sins of the youthful harlot. From a motive of shame or contempt,

---

[1] "Let greatness own her, and she's mean no more," &c.

Without Warburton's critical telescope I should never have seen, in this general picture of triumphant vice, any personal allusion to Theodora.

she often declined the servile homage of the multitude, escaped from the odious light of the capital, and passed the greatest part of the year in the palaces and gardens which were pleasantly seated on the sea-coast of the Propontis and the Bosphorus. Her private hours were devoted to the prudent as well as grateful care of her beauty, the luxury of the bath and table, and the long slumber of the evening and the morning. Her secret apartments were occupied by the favourite women and eunuchs, whose interests and passions she indulged at the expense of justice: the most illustrious personages of the state were crowded into a dark and sultry antechamber; and when at last, after tedious attendance, they were admitted to kiss the feet of Theodora, they experienced, as her humour might suggest, the silent arrogance of an empress or the capricious levity of a comedian. Her rapacious avarice to accumulate an immense treasure may be excused by the apprehension of her husband's death, which could leave no alternative between ruin and the throne; and fear as well as ambition might exasperate Theodora against two generals who, during a malady of the emperor, had rashly declared that they were not disposed to acquiesce in the choice of the capital. But the reproach of cruelty, so repugnant even to her softer vices, has left an indelible stain on the memory of Theodora. Her numerous spies observed and zealously reported every action, or word, or look, injurious to their royal mistress. Whomsoever they accused were cast into her peculiar prisons, inaccessible to the inquirers of justice; and it was rumoured that the torture of the rack or scourge had been inflicted in the presence of a female tyrant, insensible to the voice of prayer or of pity. Some of these unhappy victims perished in deep unwholesome dungeons, while others were permitted, after the loss of their limbs, their reason, or their fortune, to appear in the world, the living monuments of her vengeance, which was commonly extended to the children of those whom she had suspected or injured. The senator or bishop whose death or exile Theodora had pronounced, was delivered to a trusty messenger, and his diligence was quickened by a menace from her own mouth. "If you fail in the execution of my commands, I swear by him who liveth for ever that your skin shall be flayed from your body."

If the creed of Theodora had not been tainted with heresy, her exemplary devotion might have atoned, in the opinion of her contemporaries, for pride, avarice, and cruelty; but if she employed her influence to assuage the intolerant fury of the emperor, the present age will allow some merit to her religion, and much indulgence to her speculative errors. The name of Theodora was introduced, with equal honour, in all the pious and charitable foundations of Justinian; and the most benevolent institution of his reign may be ascribed to the sympathy of the empress for her less fortunate sisters, who had been seduced or compelled to embrace the trade of prostitution. A palace, on the Asiatic side of the Bosphorus, was converted into a stately and spacious monastery, and a liberal maintenance was assigned to five hundred women who had been collected from the streets and brothels of Constantinople. In this safe and holy retreat they were devoted to perpetual confinement; and the despair of some, who threw themselves headlong into the sea, was lost in the gratitude of the penitents who had been delivered from sin and misery by the generous benefactress. The prudence of Theodora is celebrated by Justinian himself; and his laws are attributed to the sage counsels of his most reverend wife, whom he had received as the gift of the Deity. Her courage was displayed amidst the tumult of the people and the terrors of the court. Her chastity, from the moment of her union with Justinian, is founded on the silence of her implacable enemies; and although the daughter of Acacius might be satiated with love, yet some applause is due to the firmness of a mind which could sacrifice pleasure and habit to the stronger sense either of duty or interest. The wishes and prayers of Theodora could never obtain the blessing of a lawful son, and she buried an infant daughter, the sole offspring of her marriage. Notwithstanding this disappointment, her dominion was permanent and absolute; she preserved, by art or merit, the affections of Justinian; and their seeming dissensions were always fatal to the courtiers who believed them to be sincere. Perhaps her health had been impaired by the licentiousness of her youth; but it was always delicate, and she was directed by her physicians to use the Pythian warm-baths. In this journey the empress was followed by the Prætorian prefect, the great treasurer, several counts and patricians, and a splendid train of four thousand attendants: the highways were repaired at her approach; a palace was erected for her reception; and as she passed through Bithynia she distributed liberal alms to the churches, the monasteries, and the hospitals, that they might implore Heaven for the restoration of her health. At length, in the twenty-fourth year of her marriage, and the twenty-second of her reign, she was consumed by a cancer; and the irreparable loss was deplored by her husband, who, in the room of a theatrical prostitute, might have selected the purest and most noble virgin of the East.

THE *NIKA* RIOTS

A material difference may be observed in the games of antiquity: the most eminent of the Greeks were actors, the Romans were merely spectators. The Olympic stadium was open to wealth, merit, and ambition; and if the candidates could depend on their personal skill and activity, they might pursue the footsteps of Diomede and Menelaus, and conduct their own horses in the rapid career. Ten, twenty, forty chariots, were allowed to start at the same instant; a crown of leaves was the reward of the victor, and his fame, with that of his family and country, was chanted in lyric strains more durable than monuments of brass and marble. But a senator, or even a citizen, conscious of his dignity, would have blushed to expose his person or his horses in the circus of Rome. The games were exhibited at the expense of the republic, the magistrates, or the emperors; but the reins were abandoned to servile hands; and if the profits of a favourite charioteer sometimes exceeded those of an advocate, they must be considered as the effects of popular extravagance, and the high wages of a disgraceful profession. The race, in its first institution, was a simple contest of two chariots, whose drivers were distinguished by *white* and *red* liveries: two additional colours, a light *green* and a cærulean *blue*, were afterwards introduced; and, as the races were repeated twenty-five times, one hundred chariots contributed in the same day to the pomp of the circus. The four *factions* soon acquired a legal establishment and a mysterious origin, and their fanciful colours were derived from the various appearances of nature in the four seasons of the year; the red dog-star of summer, the snows of winter, the deep shades of autumn, and the cheerful verdure of the spring. Another interpretation preferred the elements to the seasons, and the struggle of the green and blue was supposed to represent the conflict of the earth and sea. Their respective victories announced either a plentiful harvest or a prosperous navigation, and the hostility of the husbandmen and mariners was somewhat less absurd than the blind ardour of the Roman people, who devoted their lives and fortunes to the colour which they had espoused. Such folly was disdained and indulged by the wisest princes; but the names of Caligula, Nero, Vitellius, Verus, Commodus, Caracalla, and Elagabalus, were enrolled in the blue or green factions of the circus: they frequented their stables, applauded their favourites, chastised their antagonists, and deserved the esteem of the populace by the natural or affected imitation of their manners. The bloody and tumultuous contest continued to disturb the public festivity till the last age of the spectacles of Rome; and Theodoric, from a motive of justice or affection, interposed his authority to protect the greens against the violence of a consul and a patrician who were passionately addicted to the blue faction of the circus.

Constantinople adopted the follies, though not the virtues, of ancient Rome; and the same factions which had agitated the circus raged with redoubled fury in the hippodrome. Under the reign of Anastasius, this popular frenzy was inflamed by religious zeal; and the greens, who had treacherously concealed stones and daggers under baskets of fruit, massacred at a solemn festival three thousand of their blue adversaries. From the capital this pestilence was diffused into the provinces and cities of the East, and the sportive distinction of two colours produced two strong and irreconcileable factions, which shook the foundations of a feeble government. The popular dissensions, founded on the most serious interest or holy pretence, have scarcely equalled the obstinacy of this wanton discord, which invaded the peace of families, divided friends and brothers, and tempted the female sex, though seldom seen in the circus, to espouse the inclinations of their lovers, or to contradict the wishes of their husbands. Every law, either human or divine, was trampled under foot; and as long as the party was successful, its deluded followers appeared careless of private distress or public calamity. The licence, without the freedom, of democracy, was revived at Antioch and Constantinople, and the support of a faction became necessary to every candidate for civil or ecclesiastical honours. A secret attachment to the family or sect of Anastasius was imputed to the greens; the blues were zealously devoted to the cause of orthodoxy and Justinian, and their grateful patron protected, above five years, the disorders of a faction whose seasonable tumults overawed the palace, the senate, and the capitals of the East. Insolent with royal favour, the blues affected to strike terror by a peculiar and barbaric dress—the long hair of the Huns, their close sleeves and ample garments, a lofty step, and a sonorous voice. In the day they concealed the two-edged poniards, but in the night they boldly assembled in arms and in numerous bands, prepared for every act of violence and rapine. Their adversaries of the green faction, or even inoffensive citizens, were stripped and often murdered by these nocturnal robbers, and it became dangerous to wear any gold buttons or girdles, or to appear at a late hour in the streets of a peaceful capital. A daring spirit, rising with impunity, proceeded to violate the safeguard of private houses; and fire was employed to facilitate the attack, or to conceal the crimes, of these factious rioters. No place was safe or sacred from their depredations; to gratify either avarice or revenge they profusely spilt the blood of the innocent; churches and altars were polluted by atrocious murders, and it was the boast of the assassins that their dexterity could always inflict a mortal wound with a single stroke of their dagger. The dissolute youth of Constantinople adopted the blue livery of disorder; the laws were silent, and the bonds of society were relaxed; creditors were compelled to resign their obligations; judges to reverse their sentence; masters to enfranchise their slaves; fathers to supply the extravagance of their children; noble matrons were prostituted to the lust of their servants; beautiful boys were torn from the arms of their parents; and wives, unless they preferred a voluntary death, were ravished in the presence of their husbands. The despair of the greens, who were persecuted by their enemies and deserted by the magistrate, assumed the privilege of defence, perhaps of retaliation; but those who survived the combat were dragged to execution, and the unhappy fugitives, escaping to woods and caverns, preyed without mercy on the society from whence they were expelled. Those ministers of justice who had courage to punish the crimes and to brave the resentment of the blues became the victims of their indiscreet zeal: a prefect of Constantinople fled for refuge to the holy sepulchre, a count of the East was ignominiously whipped, and a governor of Cilicia was hanged, by the order of Theodora, on the tomb of two assassins whom he had condemned for the murder of his groom, and a daring attack upon his own life. An aspiring candidate may be tempted to build his greatness on the public confusion, but it is the interest as well as duty of a sovereign to maintain the authority of the laws. The first edict of Justinian, which was often repeated and some-times executed, announced his firm resolution to support the innocent, and to chastise the guilty, of every denomination and *colour*. Yet the balance of justice was still inclined in favour of the blue faction, by the secret affection, the habits, and the fears of the emperor; his equity, after an apparent struggle, submitted without reluctance to the implacable passions of Theodora, and the empress never forgot or forgave the injuries of the comedian. At the accession of the younger Justin, the proclamation of equal and rigorous justice indirectly condemned the partiality of the former reign. "Ye blues, Justinian is no more! ye greens, he is still alive!"

A sedition, which almost laid Constantinople in ashes, was excited by the mutual hatred and momentary reconciliation of the two factions.[1] In the fifth year of his reign Justinian celebrated the festival of the ides of January: the games were incessantly disturbed by the clamorous dis-content of the greens; till the twenty-second race the emperor maintained his silent gravity; at length, yielding to his impatience, he condescended to hold, in abrupt sentences, and by the voice of a crier, the most singular dialogue that ever passed between a prince and his subjects. Their first complaints were respectful and modest; they accused the subordinate ministers of oppression, and proclaimed their wishes for the long life and victory of the emperor. "Be patient and attentive ye insolent railers!" exclaimed Justinian; "be mute, ye Jews, Samaritans, and Manichæans!" The greens still attempted to awaken his com-passion. "We are poor, we are innocent, we are injured, we dare not pass through the streets: a general persecution is exercised against our name and colour. Let us die, O emperor! but let us die by your com-mand, and for your service!" But the repetition of partial and passionate invectives degraded, in their eyes, the majesty of the purple; they re-nounced allegiance to the prince who refused justice to his people, lamented that the father of Justinian had been born, and branded his son with the opprobrious names of an homicide, an ass, and a perjured tyrant. "Do you despise your lives?" cried the indignant monarch. The blues rose with fury from their seats, their hostile clamours thun-dered in the hippodrome, and their adversaries, deserting the unequal contest, spread terror and despair through the streets of Constantinople.

---

[1] The real cause of the *Nika* riots was resentment at the extortions of Justinian's reckless administration. Gibbon does not bring this out nor was he aware that the factions of the Circus were in fact the atrophied demes or parishes of the city. They were therefore to some extent still the constitutional means of communication be-tween the people and the emperor.—D.M.L.

At this dangerous moment, seven notorious assassins of both factions, who had been condemned by the prefect, were carried round the city, and afterwards transported to the place of execution in the suburb of Pera. Four were immediately beheaded; a fifth was hanged; but, when the same punishment was inflicted on the remaining two, the rope broke, they fell alive to the ground, the populace applauded their escape, and the monks of St. Conon, issuing from the neighbouring convent, conveyed them in a boat to the sanctuary of the church. As one of these criminals was of the blue, and the other of the green, livery, the two factions were equally provoked by the cruelty of their oppressor or the ingratitude of their patron, and a short truce was concluded till they had delivered their prisoners and satisfied their revenge. The palace of the prefect, who withstood the seditious torrent, was instantly burnt, his officers and guards were massacred, the prisons were forced open, and freedom was restored to those who could use it for the public destruction. A military force which had been despatched to the aid of the civil magistrate was fiercely encountered by an armed multitude, whose numbers and boldness continually increased: and the Heruli, the wildest barbarians in the service of the empire, overturned the priests and their relics, which, from a pious motive, had been rashly interposed to separate the bloody conflict. The tumult was exasperated by this sacrilege; the people fought with enthusiasm in the cause of God; the women, from the roofs and windows, showered stones on the heads of the soldiers, who darted firebrands against the houses; and the various flames, which had been kindled by the hands of citizens and strangers, spread without control over the face of the city. The conflagration involved the cathedral of St. Sophia, the baths of Zeuxippus, a part of the palace from the first entrance to the altar of Mars, and the long portico from the palace to the forum of Constantine: a large hospital, with the sick patients, was consumed; many churches and stately edifices were destroyed; and an immense treasure of gold and silver was either melted or lost. From such scenes of horror and distress the wise and wealthy citizens escaped over the Bosphorus to the Asiatic side, and during five days Constantinople was abandoned to the factions, whose watchword, Nika, *vanquish*! has given a name to this memorable sedition.

As long as the factions were divided, the triumphant blues and desponding greens appeared to behold with the same indifference the disorders of the state. They agreed to censure the corrupt management of justice and the finance; and the two responsible ministers, the artful Tribonian and the rapacious John of Cappadocia, were loudly arraigned as the authors of the public misery. The peaceful murmurs of the people would have been disregarded: they were heard with respect when the city was in flames; the quæstor and the prefect were instantly removed, and their offices were filled by two senators of blameless integrity. After this popular concession Justinian proceeded to the hippodrome to confess his own errors, and to accept the repentance of his grateful subjects; but they distrusted his assurances, though solemnly pronounced in the presence of the holy gospels; and the emperor, alarmed by their distrust, retreated with precipitation to the strong fortress of the palace. The obstinacy of the tumult was now imputed to a secret and ambitious conspiracy, and a suspicion was entertained that the insurgents, more especially the green faction, had been supplied with arms and money by Hypatius and Pompey, two patricians who could neither forget with honour, nor remember with safety, that they were the nephews of the emperor Anastasius. Capriciously trusted, disgraced, and pardoned by the jealous levity of the monarch, they had appeared as loyal servants before the throne, and, during five days of the tumult, they were detained as important hostages; till at length, the fears of Justinian prevailing over his prudence, he viewed the two brothers in the light of spies, perhaps of assassins, and sternly commanded them to depart from the palace. After a fruitless representation that obedience might lead to involuntary treason, they retired to their houses, and in the morning of the sixth day Hypatius was surrounded and seized by the people, who, regardless of his virtuous resistance and the tears of his wife, transported their favourite to the forum of Constantine, and, instead of a diadem, placed a rich collar on his head. If the usurper, who afterwards pleaded the merit of his delay, had complied with the advice of his senate, and urged the fury of the multitude, their first irresistible effort might have oppressed or expelled his trembling competitor. The Byzantine palace enjoyed a free communication with the sea, vessels lay ready at the garden-stairs, and a secret resolution was already formed to convey the emperor with his family and treasures to a safe retreat at some distance from the capital.

Justinian was lost, if the prostitute whom he raised from the theatre had not renounced the timidity as well as the virtues of her sex. In the midst of a council where Belisarius was present, Theodora alone displayed the spirit of an hero, and she alone, without apprehending his future hatred, could save the emperor from the imminent danger and his unworthy fears. "If flight," said the consort of Justinian, "were the only means of safety, yet I should disdain to fly. Death is the condition of our birth, but they who have reigned should never survive the loss of dignity and dominion. I implore Heaven that I may never be seen, not a day, without my diadem and purple; that I may no longer behold the light when I cease to be saluted with the name of queen. If you resolve, O Cæsar! to fly, you have treasures; behold the sea, you have ships; but tremble lest the desire of life should expose you to wretched exile and ignominious death. For my own part, I adhere to the maxim of antiquity, that the throne is a glorious sepulchre." The firmness of a woman restored the courage to deliberate and act, and courage soon discovers the resources of the most desperate situation. It was an easy and a decisive measure to revive the animosity of the factions; the blues were astonished at their own guilt and folly, that a trifling injury should provoke them to conspire with their implacable enemies against a gracious and liberal benefactor; they again proclaimed the majesty of Justinian; and the greens, with their upstart emperor, were left alone in the hippodrome. The fidelity of the guards was doubtful; but the military force of Justinian consisted in three thousand veterans, who had been trained to valour and discipline in the Persian and Illyrian wars. Under the command of Belisarius and Mundus, they silently marched in two divisions from the palace, forced their obscure way through narrow passages, expiring flames, and falling edifices, and burst open at the same moment the two opposite gates of the hippodrome. In this narrow space the disorderly and affrighted crowd was incapable of resisting on either side a firm and regular attack; the blues signalised the fury of their repentance, and it is computed that above thirty thousand persons were slain in the merciless and promiscuous carnage of the day. Hypatius was dragged from his throne, and conducted with his brother Pompey to the feet of the emperor; they implored his clemency, but their crime was manifest, their innocence uncertain, and Justinian had been too much terrified to forgive. The next morning the two nephews of Anastasius, with eighteen *illustrious* accomplices, of patrician or consular rank, were privately executed by the soldiers, their bodies were thrown into the sea, their palaces razed, and their fortunes confiscated. The hippodrome itself was condemned, during several years, to a mournful silence; with the restoration of the games the same disorders revived, and the blue and green factions continued to afflict the reign of Justinian, and to disturb the tranquillity of the Eastern empire.

IMPORTATION OF SILK FROM CHINA

That empire, after Rome was barbarous, still embraced the nations whom she had conquered beyond the Adriatic, and as far as the frontiers of Ethiopia and Persia. Justinian reigned over sixty-four provinces and nine hundred and thirty-five cities; his dominions were blessed by nature with the advantages of soil, situation, and climate, and the improvements of human art had been perpetually diffused along the coast of the Mediterranean and the banks of the Nile from ancient Troy to the Egyptian Thebes. Abraham had been relieved by the well-known plenty of Egypt; the same country, a small and populous tract, was still capable of exporting each year two hundred and sixty thousand quarters of wheat for the use of Constantinople; and the capital of Justinian was supplied with the manufactures of Sidon fifteen centuries after they had been celebrated in the poems of Homer. The annual powers of vegetation, instead of being exhausted by two thousand harvests, were renewed and invigorated by skilful husbandry, rich manure, and seasonable repose. The breed of domestic animals was infinitely multiplied.

Plantations, buildings, and the instruments of labour and luxury, which are more durable than the term of human life, were accumulated by the care of successive generations. Tradition preserved, and experience simplified, the humble practice of the arts; society was enriched by the division of labour and the facility of exchange; and every Roman was lodged, clothed, and subsisted by the industry of a thousand hands. The invention of the loom and distaff has been piously ascribed to the gods. In every age a variety of animal and vegetable productions, hair, skins, wool, flax, cotton, and at length *silk*, have been skilfully manufactured to hide or adorn the human body; they were stained with an infusion of permanent colours, and the pencil was successfully employed to improve the labours of the loom. In the choice of those colours which imitate the beauties of nature, the freedom of taste and fashion was indulged; but the deep purple which the Phœnicians extracted from a shell-fish was restrained to the sacred person and palace of the emperor, and the penalties of treason were denounced against the ambitious subjects who dared to usurp the prerogative of the throne.

I need not explain that *silk* [1] is originally spun from the bowels of a caterpillar, and that it composes the golden tomb from whence a worm emerges in the form of a butterfly. Till the reign of Justinian, the silkworms who feed on the leaves of the white mulberry-tree were confined to China; those of the pine, the oak, and the ash were common in the forests both of Asia and Europe; but as their education is more difficult, and their produce more uncertain, they were generally neglected, except in the little island of Ceos, near the coast of Attica. A thin gauze was procured from their webs, and this Cean manufacture, the invention of a woman, for female use, was long admired both in the East and at Rome. Whatever suspicions may be raised by the garments of the Medes and Assyrians, Virgil is the most ancient writer who expressly mentions the soft wool which was combed from the trees of the Seres or Chinese; and this natural error, less marvellous than the truth, was slowly corrected by the knowledge of a valuable insect, the first artificer of the luxury of nations. That rare and elegant luxury was censured, in the reign of Tiberius, by the gravest of the Romans; and Pliny, in affected though forcible language, has condemned the thirst of gain, which explored the last confines of the earth for the pernicious purpose of exposing to the public eye naked draperies and transparent matrons. A dress which showed the turn of the limbs and colour of the skin might gratify vanity or provoke desire; the silks which had been closely woven

[1] In the history of insects (far more wonderful than Ovid's Metamorphoses) the silkworm holds a conspicuous place. The bombyx of the isle of Ceos, as described by Pliny, may be illustrated by a similar species in China; but our silkworm, as well as the white mulberry-tree, were unknown to Theophrastus and Pliny. [Gibbon has confused Cos with Ceos. Aristotle was the first Greek writer to mention silk. It is probable that raw silk was brought from Asia to Cos and there manufactured.—D.M.L.]

in China were sometimes unravelled by the Phœnician women, and the precious materials were multiplied by a looser texture, and the intermixture of linen threads. Two hundred years after the age of Pliny the use of pure or even of mixed silks was confined to the female sex, till the opulent citizens of Rome and the provinces were insensibly familiarised with the example of Elagabalus, the first who, by this effeminate habit, had sullied the dignity of an emperor and a man. Aurelian complained that a pound of silk was sold at Rome for twelve ounces of gold; but the supply increased with the demand, and the price diminished with the supply. If accident or monopoly sometimes raised the value even above the standard of Aurelian, the manufacturers of Tyre and Berytus were sometimes compelled, by the operation of the same causes, to content themselves with a ninth part of that extravagant rate. A law was thought necessary to discriminate the dress of comedians from that of senators, and of the silk exported from its native country the far greater part was consumed by the subjects of Justinian. They were still more intimately acquainted with a shell-fish of the Mediterranean, surnamed the silkworm of the sea: the fine wool or hair by which the mother-of-pearl affixes itself to the rock is now manufactured for curiosity rather than use; and a robe obtained from the same singular materials was the gift of the Roman emperor to the satraps of Armenia.

A valuable merchandise of small bulk is capable of defraying the expense of land-carriage, and the caravans traversed the whole latitude of Asia in two hundred and forty-three days from the Chinese ocean to the sea-coast of Syria. Silk was immediately delivered to the Romans by the Persian merchants, who frequented the fairs of Armenia and Nisibis; but this trade, which in the intervals of truce was oppressed by avarice and jealousy, was totally interrupted by the long wars of the rival monarchies. The Great King might proudly number Sogdiana, and even *Serica*, among the provinces of his empire, but his real dominion was bounded by the Oxus, and his useful intercourse with the Sogdoites, beyond the river, depended on the pleasure of their conquerors, the white Huns and the Turks, who successively reigned over that industrious people. Yet the most savage dominion has not extirpated the seeds of agriculture and commerce in a region which is celebrated as one of the four gardens of Asia; the cities of Samarcand and Bochara are advantageously seated for the exchange of its various productions, and their merchants purchased from the Chinese [1] the raw

---

[1] The blind admiration of the Jesuits confounds the different periods of the Chinese history. They are more critically distinguished by M. de Guignes, who discovers the gradual progress of the truth of the annals and the extent of the monarchy, till the Christian era. He has searched with a curious eye the connexions of the Chinese with the nations of the West; but these connexions are slight, casual, and obscure; nor did the Romans entertain a suspicion that the Seres or Sinæ possessed an empire not inferior to their own.

or manufactured silk which they transported into Persia for the use of the Roman empire. In the vain capital of China the Sogdian caravans were entertained as the suppliant embassies of tributary kingdoms, and, if they returned in safety, the bold adventure was rewarded with exorbitant gain. But the difficult and perilous march from Samarcand to the first town of Shensi could not be performed in less than sixty, eighty, or one hundred days; as soon as they had passed the Jaxartes they entered the desert, and the wandering hordes, unless they are restrained by armies and garrisons, have always considered the citizen and the traveller as the objects of lawful rapine. To escape the Tartar robbers and the tyrants of Persia, the silk-caravans explored a more southern road: they traversed the mountains of Thibet, descended the streams of the Ganges or the Indus, and patiently expected, in the ports of Guzerat and Malabar, the annual fleets of the West.[1] But the dangers of the desert were found less intolerable than toil, hunger, and the loss of time; the attempt was seldom renewed, and the only European who has passed that unfrequented way applauds his own diligence that, in nine months after his departure from Pekin, he reached the mouth of the Indus. The ocean, however, was open to the free communication of mankind. From the great river to the tropic of Cancer the provinces of China were subdued and civilised by the emperors of the North; they were filled about the time of the Christian era with cities and men, mulberry-trees and their precious inhabitants; and if the Chinese, with the knowledge of the compass, had possessed the genius of the Greeks or Phœnicians, they might have spread their discoveries over the southern hemisphere. I am not qualified to examine, and I am not disposed to believe, their distant voyages to the Persian Gulf or the Cape of Good Hope; but their ancestors might equal the labours and success of the present race, and the sphere of their navigation might extend from the isles of Japan to the straits of Malacca, the Pillars, if we may apply that name, of an Oriental Hercules. Without losing sight of land, they might sail along the coast to the extreme promontory of Achin, which is annually visited by ten or twelve ships laden with the productions, the manufactures, and even the artificers of China; the island of Sumatra and the opposite peninsula are faintly delineated as the regions of gold and silver, and the trading cities named in the geography of Ptolemy may indicate that this wealth was not solely derived from the mines. The direct interval between Sumatra and Ceylon is about three hundred leagues; the Chinese and Indian navigators were conducted by the flight of birds and periodical winds, and the ocean might be securely traversed in square-built ships, which instead of iron, were sewed together with the strong thread of the cocoa-nut. Ceylon,

[1] The roads from China to Persia and Hindostan may be investigated in the relations of Hackluyt and Thevenot. A communication through Thibet has been lately explored by the English sovereigns of Bengal.

Serendib, or Taprobana was divided between two hostile princes, one of whom possessed the mountains, the elephants, and the luminous carbuncle, and the other enjoyed the more solid riches of domestic industry, foreign trade, and the capacious harbour of Trinquemale, which received and dismissed the fleets of the East and West. In this hospitable isle, at an equal distance (as it was computed) from their respective countries, the silk-merchants of China, who had collected in their voyages aloes, cloves, nutmeg, and sandal-wood, maintained a free and beneficial commerce with the inhabitants of the Persian Gulf. The subjects of the Great King exalted, without a rival, his power and magnificence; and the Roman, who confounded their vanity by comparing his paltry coin with a gold medal of the emperor Anastasius, had sailed to Ceylon, in an Ethiopian ship, as a simple passenger.

As silk became of indispensable use, the emperor Justinian saw with concern that the Persians had occupied by land and sea the monopoly of this important supply, and that the wealth of his subjects was continually drained by a nation of enemies and idolators. An active government would have restored the trade of Egypt and the navigation of the Red Sea, which had decayed with the prosperity of the empire; and the Roman vessels might have sailed for the purchase of silk to the ports of Ceylon, of Malacca, or even of China. Justinian embraced a more humble expedient, and solicited the aid of his Christian allies, the Ethiopians of Abyssinia, who had recently acquired the arts of navigation, the spirit of trade, and the seaport of Adulis, still decorated with the trophies of a Grecian conqueror. Along the African coast they penetrated to the equator in search of gold, emeralds, and aromatics; but they wisely declined an unequal competition, in which they must be always prevented by the vicinity of the Persians to the markets of India: and the emperor submitted to the disappointment till his wishes were gratified by an unexpected event. The Gospel had been preached to the Indians: a bishop already governed the Christians of St. Thomas on the pepper-coast of Malabar; a church was planted in Ceylon, and the missionaries pursued the footsteps of commerce to the extremities of Asia. Two Persian monks had long resided in China, perhaps in the royal city of Nankin, the seat of a monarch addicted to foreign superstitions, and who actually received an embassy from the isle of Ceylon. Amidst their pious occupations they viewed with a curious eye the common dress of the Chinese, the manufactures of silk, and the myriads of silkworms, whose education (either on trees or in houses) had once been considered as the labour of queens. They soon discovered that it was impracticable to transport the short-lived insect, but that in the eggs a numerous progeny might be preserved and multiplied in a distant climate. Religion or interest had more power over the Persian monks than the love of their country: after a long journey they arrived at Constantinople, imparted their project to the emperor, and were liberally encouraged by the gifts and promises of Justinian. To the historians of that prince a campaign at the foot of Mount Caucasus has seemed more deserving of a minute relation than the labours of these missionaries of commerce, who again entered China, deceived a jealous people by concealing the eggs of the silkworm in a hollow cane, and returned in triumph with the spoils of the East. Under their direction the eggs were hatched at the proper season by the artificial heat of dung; the worms were fed with mulberry-leaves; they lived and laboured in a foreign climate; a sufficient number of butterflies was saved to propagate the race, and trees were planted to supply the nourishment of the rising generations. Experience and reflection corrected the errors of a new attempt, and the Sogdoite ambassadors acknowledged in the succeeding reign that the Romans were not inferior to the natives of China in the education of the insects and the manufactures of silk, in which both China and Constantinople have been surpassed by the industry of modern Europe. I am not insensible of the benefits of elegant luxury; yet I reflect with some pain that if the importers of silk had introduced the art of printing, already practised by the Chinese, the comedies of Menander and the entire decads of Livy would have been perpetuated in the editions of the sixth century. A larger view of the globe might at least have promoted the improvement of speculative science; but the Christian geography was forcibly extracted from texts of Scripture, and the study of nature was the surest symptom of an unbelieving mind. The orthodox faith confined the habitable world to *one* temperate zone, and represented the earth as an oblong surface, four hundred days' journey in length, two hundred in breadth, encompassed by the ocean and covered by the solid crystal of the firmament.

*   *   *   *   *

THE CHURCH OF ST. SOPHIA

The *edifices* of Justinian were cemented with the blood and treasure of his people; but those stately structures appeared to announce the prosperity of the empire, and actually displayed the skill of their architects. Both the theory and practice of the arts which depend on mathematical science and mechanical power were cultivated under the patronage of the emperors; the fame of Archimedes was rivalled by Proclus and Anthemius; and if their *miracles* had been related by intelligent spectators, they might now enlarge the speculations, instead of exciting the distrust, of philosophers. A tradition has prevailed that the Roman fleet was reduced to ashes in the port of Syracuse by the burning-glasses of Archimedes; and it is asserted that a similar expedient was employed by Proclus to destroy the Gothic vessels in the harbour of Constantinople, and to protect his benefactor Anastasius against the bold enterprise of Vitalian. A machine was fixed on the walls of the city, consisting of an hexagon mirror of polished brass, with many smaller and moveable polygons to receive and reflect the rays of the meridian sun; and a consuming flame was darted, to the distance, perhaps, of two hundred feet. The truth of these two extraordinary facts is invalidated by the silence of the most authentic historians; and the use of burning-glasses was never adopted in the attack or defence of places. Yet the admirable experiments of a French philosopher have demonstrated the possibility of such a mirror; and, since it is possible, I am more disposed to attribute the art to the greatest mathematicians of antiquity, than to give the merit of the fiction to the idle fancy of a monk or a sophist. According to another story, Proclus applied sulphur to the destruction of the Gothic fleet; in a modern imagination, the name of sulphur is instantly connected with the suspicion of gunpowder, and that suspicion is propagated by the secret arts of his disciple Anthemius. A citizen of Tralles in Asia had five sons, who were all distinguished in their respective professions by merit and success. Olympius excelled in the knowledge and practice of the Roman jurisprudence. Dioscorus and Alexander became learned physicians; but the skill of the former was exercised for the benefit of his fellow-citizens, while his more ambitious brother acquired wealth and reputation at Rome. The fame of Metrodorus the grammarian, and of Anthemius the mathematician and architect, reached the ears of the emperor Justinian, who invited them to Constantinople; and while the one instructed the rising generation in the schools of eloquence, the other filled the capital and provinces with more lasting monuments of his art. In a trifling dispute relative to the walls or windows of their contiguous houses, he had been vanquished by the eloquence of his neighbour Zeno; but the orator was defeated in his turn by the master of mechanics, whose malicious, though harmless, stratagems are darkly represented by the ignorance of Agathias. In a lower room, Anthemius arranged several vessels or caldrons of water, each of them covered by the wide bottom of a leathern tube, which rose to a narrow top, and was artificially conveyed among the joists and rafters of the adjacent building. A fire was kindled beneath the caldron; the steam of the boiling water ascended through the tubes; the house was shaken by the efforts of imprisoned air, and its trembling inhabitants might wonder that the city was unconscious of the earthquake which they had felt. At another time, the friends of Zeno, as they sat at table, were dazzled by the intolerable light which flashed in their eyes from the reflecting mirrors of Anthemius; they were astonished by the noise which he produced from the collision of certain minute and sonorous particles; and the orator declared in tragic style to the senate, that a mere mortal must yield to the power of an antagonist who shook the earth with the trident of Neptune, and imitated the thunder and lightning of Jove himself. The genius of Anthemius, and his colleague Isidore the Milesian, was excited and employed by a prince whose taste for architecture had

degenerated into a mischievous and costly passion. His favourite architects submitted their designs and difficulties to Justinian, and discreetly
confessed how much their laborious meditations were surpassed by the
intuitive knowledge or celestial inspiration of an emperor whose views
were always directed to the benefit of his people, the glory of his reign,
and the salvation of his soul.

The principal church, which was dedicated by the founder of Constantinople to Saint Sophia, or the eternal wisdom, had been twice destroyed
by fire; after the exile of John Chrysostom, and during the *Nika* of the
blue and green factions. No sooner did the tumult subside than the
Christian populace deplored their sacrilegious rashness; but they might
have rejoiced in the calamity, had they foreseen the glory of the new
temple, which at the end of forty days was strenuously undertaken by
the piety of Justinian. The ruins were cleared away, a more spacious
plan was described, and, as it required the consent of some proprietors
of ground, they obtained the most exorbitant terms from the eager
desires and timorous conscience of the monarch. Anthemius formed
the design, and his genius directed the hands of ten thousand workmen,
whose payment in pieces of fine silver was never delayed beyond the
evening. The emperor himself, clad in a linen tunic, surveyed each day
their rapid progress, and encouraged their diligence by his familiarity,
his zeal, and his rewards. The new cathedral of St. Sophia was consecrated by the patriarch, five years, eleven months, and ten days from
the first foundation; and in the midst of the solemn festival Justinian
exclaimed with devout vanity, "Glory be to God, who hath thought me
worthy to accomplish so great a work; I have vanquished thee, O
Solomon!" But the pride of the Roman Solomon, before twenty years
had elapsed, was humbled by an earthquake, which overthrew the
eastern part of the dome. Its splendour was again restored by the perseverance of the same prince; and in the thirty-sixth year of his reign
Justinian celebrated the second dedication of a temple which remains,
after twelve centuries, a stately monument of his fame. The architecture
of St. Sophia, which is now converted into the principal mosque, has
been imitated by the Turkish sultans, and that venerable pile continues
to excite the fond admiration of the Greeks, and the more rational
curiosity of European travellers. The eye of the spectator is disappointed
by an irregular prospect of half-domes and shelving roofs: the western
front, the principal approach, is destitute of simplicity and magnificence;
and the scale of dimensions has been much surpassed by several of the
Latin cathedrals. But the architect who first erected an *aërial* cupola is
entitled to the praise of bold design and skilful execution. The dome of
St. Sophia, illuminated by four-and-twenty windows, is formed with so
small a curve, that the depth is equal only to one-sixth of its diameter;
the measure of that diameter is one hundred and fifteen feet, and the
lofty centre, where a crescent has supplanted the cross, rises to the per-

pendicular height of one hundred and eighty feet above the pavement. The circle which encompasses the dome lightly reposes on four strong arches, and their weight is firmly supported by four massy piles, whose strength is assisted on the northern and southern sides by four columns of Egyptian granite. A Greek cross, inscribed in a quadrangle, represents the form of the edifice; the exact breadth is two hundred and forty-three feet, and two hundred and sixty-nine may be assigned for the extreme length, from the sanctuary in the east to the nine western doors which open into the vestibule, and from thence into the *narthex* or exterior portico. That portico was the humble station of the penitents. The nave or body of the church was filled by the congregation of the faithful; but the two sexes were prudently distinguished, and the upper and lower galleries were allotted for the more private devotion of the women. Beyond the northern and southern piles, a balustrade, terminated on either side by the thrones of the emperor and the patriarch, divided the nave from the choir; and the space, as far as the steps of the altar, was occupied by the clergy and singers. The altar itself, a name which insensibly became familiar to Christian ears, was placed in the eastern recess, artificially built in the form of a demicylinder; and this sanctuary communicated by several doors with the sacristy, the vestry, the baptistery, and the contiguous buildings, subservient either to the pomp of worship, or the private use of the ecclesiastical ministers. The memory of past calamities inspired Justinian with a wise resolution, that no wood, except for the doors, should be admitted into the new edifice; and the choice of the materials was applied to the strength, the lightness, or the splendour of the respective parts. The solid piles which sustained the cupola were composed of huge blocks of freestone, hewn into squares and triangles, fortified by circles of iron, and firmly cemented by the infusion of lead and quicklime; but the weight of the cupola was diminished by the levity of its substance, which consists either of pumice-stone that floats in the water, or of bricks, from the isle of Rhodes, five times less ponderous than the ordinary sort. The whole frame of the edifice was constructed of brick; but those base materials were concealed by a crust of marble; and the inside of St. Sophia, the cupola, the two larger and the six smaller semidomes, the walls, the hundred columns, and the pavement, delight even the eyes of barbarians with a rich and variegated picture.

A poet, who beheld the primitive lustre of St. Sophia, enumerates the colours, the shades, and the spots of ten or twelve marbles, jaspers, and porphyries, which nature had profusely diversified, and which were blended and contrasted as it were by a skilful painter. The triumph of Christ was adorned with the last spoils of Paganism, but the greater part of these costly stones was extracted from the quarries of Asia Minor, the isles and continent of Greece, Egypt, Africa, and Gaul. Eight columns of porphyry, which Aurelian had placed in the Temple of the

Sun, were offered by the piety of a Roman matron; eight others of green marble were presented by the ambitious zeal of the magistrates of Ephesus: both are admirable by their size and beauty, but every order of architecture disclaims their fantastic capitals. A variety of ornaments and figures was curiously expressed in mosaic; and the images of Christ, of the Virgin, of saints, and of angels, which have been defaced by Turkish fanaticism, were dangerously exposed to the superstition of the Greeks. According to the sanctity of each object, the precious metals were distributed in thin leaves or in solid masses. The balustrade of the choir, the capitals of the pillars, the ornaments of the doors and galleries, were of gilt bronze. The spectator was dazzled by the glittering aspect of the cupola. The sanctuary contained forty thousand pound weight of silver, and the holy vases and vestments of the altar were of the purest gold, enriched with inestimable gems. Before the structure of the church had arisen two cubits above the ground, forty-five thousand two hundred pounds were already consumed, and the whole expense amounted to three hundred and twenty thousand. Each reader, according to the measure of his belief, may estimate their value either in gold or silver; but the sum of one million sterling is the result of the lowest computation. A magnificent temple is a laudable monument of national taste and religion, and the enthusiast who entered the dome of St. Sophia might be tempted to suppose that it was the residence, or even the workmanship, of the Deity. Yet how dull is the artifice, how insignificant is the labour, if it be compared with the formation of the vilest insect that crawls upon the surface of the temple!

So minute a description of an edifice which time has respected may attest the truth and excuse the relation of the innumerable works, both in the capital and provinces, which Justinian constructed on a smaller scale and less durable foundations. In Constantinople alone, and the adjacent suburbs, he dedicated twenty-five churches to the honour of Christ, the Virgin, and the saints. Most of these churches were decorated with marble and gold; and their various situation was skilfully chosen in a populous square or a pleasant grove, on the margin of the sea-shore, or on some lofty eminence which overlooked the continents of Europe and Asia. The church of the Holy Apostles at Constantinople, and that of St. John at Ephesus, appear to have been framed on the same model: their domes aspired to imitate the cupolas of St. Sophia, but the altar was more judiciously placed under the centre of the dome, at the junction of four stately porticoes, which more accurately expressed the figure of the Greek cross. The Virgin of Jerusalem might exult in the temple erected by her imperial votary on a most ungrateful spot, which afforded neither ground nor materials to the architect. A level was formed by raising part of a deep valley to the height of the mountain. The stones of a neighbouring quarry were hewn into regular forms; each block was fixed on a peculiar carriage drawn by forty of the strongest oxen, and the roads were widened for the passage of such enormous weights. Lebanon furnished her loftiest cedars for the timbers of the church; and the seasonable discovery of a vein of red marble supplied its beautiful columns, two of which, the supporters of the exterior portico, were esteemed the largest in the world. The pious munificence of the emperor was diffused over the Holy Land; and if reason should condemn the monasteries of both sexes which were built or restored by Justinian, yet charity must applaud the wells which he sunk, and the hospitals which he founded, for the relief of the weary pilgrims. The schismatical temper of Egypt was ill entitled to the royal bounty; but in Syria and Africa some remedies were applied to the disasters of wars and earthquakes, and both Carthage and Antioch, emerging from their ruins, might revere the name of their gracious benefactor. Almost every saint in the calendar acquired the honours of a temple—almost every city of the empire obtained the solid advantages of bridges, hospitals, and aqueducts; but the severe liberality of the monarch disdained to indulge his subjects in the popular luxury of baths and theatres. While Justinian laboured for the public service, he was not unmindful of his own dignity and ease. The Byzantine palace, which had been damaged by the conflagration, was restored with new magnificence; and some notion may be conceived of the whole edifice by the vestibule or hall, which, from the doors perhaps, or the roof, was surnamed *chalce*, or the brazen. The dome of a spacious quadrangle was supported by massy pillars; the pavement and walls were incrusted with many-coloured marbles—the emerald green of Laconia, the fiery red, and the white Phrygian stone, intersected with veins of a sea-green hue. The mosaic paintings of the dome and sides represented the glories of the African and Italian triumphs. On the Asiatic shore of the Propontis, at a small distance to the east of Chalcedon, the costly palace and gardens of Heræum were prepared for the summer residence of Justinian, and more especially of Theodora. The poets of the age have celebrated the rare alliance of nature and art, the harmony of the nymphs of the groves, the fountains and the waves; yet the crowd of attendants who followed the court complained of their inconvenient lodgings, and the nymphs were too often alarmed by the famous Porphyrio, a whale of ten cubits in breadth and thirty in length, who was stranded at the mouth of the river Sangaris after he had infested more than half a century the seas of Constantinople.

*　　*　　*　　*　　*

SUPPRESSION OF THE SCHOOLS OF ATHENS

Justinian suppressed the schools of Athens and the consulship of Rome, which had given so many sages and heroes to mankind. Both these institutions had long since degenerated from their primitive glory, yet some reproach may be justly inflicted on the avarice and jealousy of a prince by whose hand such venerable ruins were destroyed.

Athens, after her Persian triumphs, adopted the philosophy of Ionia and the rhetoric of Sicily; and these studies became the patrimony of a city whose inhabitants, about thirty thousand males, condensed, within the period of a single life, the genius of ages and millions. Our sense of the dignity of human nature is exalted by the simple recollection that Isocrates was the companion of Plato and Xenophon; that he assisted, perhaps with the historian Thucydides, at the first representations of the Œdipus of Sophocles and the Iphigenia of Euripides; and that his pupils Æschines and Demosthenes contended for the crown of patriotism in the presence of Aristotle, the master of Theophrastus, who taught at Athens with the founders of the Stoic and Epicurean sects. The ingenuous youth of Attica enjoyed the benefits of their domestic education, which was communicated without envy to the rival cities. Two thousand disciples heard the lessons of Theophrastus; the schools of rhetoric must have been still more populous than those of philosophy; and a rapid succession of students diffused the fame of their teachers as far as the utmost limits of the Grecian language and name. Those limits were enlarged by the victories of Alexander; the arts of Athens survived her freedom and dominion; and the Greek colonies which the Macedonians planted in Egypt, and scattered over Asia, undertook long and frequent pilgrimages to worship the Muses in their favourite temple on the banks of the Ilissus. The Latin conquerors respectfully listened to the instructions of their subjects and captives; the names of Cicero and Horace were enrolled in the schools of Athens; and after the perfect settlement of the Roman empire, the natives of Italy, of Africa, and of Britain, conversed in the groves of the Academy with their fellow-students of the East. The studies of philosophy and eloquence are congenial to a popular state, which encourages the freedom of inquiry, and submits only to the force of persuasion. In the republics of Greece and Rome the art of speaking was the powerful engine of patriotism or ambition; and the schools of rhetoric poured forth a colony of statesmen and legislators. When the liberty of public debate was suppressed, the orator, in the honourable profession of an advocate, might plead the cause of innocence and justice; he might abuse his talents in the more profitable trade of panegyric; and the same precepts continued to dictate the fanciful declamations of the sophist, and the chaster beauties of historical composition. The systems which professed to unfold the nature of God, of man, and of the universe, entertained the curiosity of the philosophic student; and according to the temper of his mind, he might doubt with the Sceptics, or decide with the Stoics, sublimely speculate with Plato, or severely argue with Aristotle. The pride of the adverse sects had fixed an unattainable term of moral happiness and perfection: but the race was glorious and salutary; the disciples of Zeno, and even those of

Epicurus, were taught both to act and to suffer; and the death of
Petronius was not less effectual than that of Seneca to humble a tyrant
by the discovery of his impotence. The light of science could not indeed
be confined within the walls of Athens. Her incomparable writers
address themselves to the human race; the living masters emigrated to
Italy and Asia; Berytus, in later times, was devoted to the study of the
law; astronomy and physic were cultivated in the musæum of Alexandria; but the Attic schools of rhetoric and philosophy maintained their
superior reputation from the Peloponnesian war to the reign of Justinian. Athens, though situate in a barren soil, possessed a pure air, a free
navigation, and the monuments of ancient art. That sacred retirement
was seldom disturbed by the business of trade or government; and the
last of the Athenians were distinguished by their lively wit, the purity
of their taste and language, their social manners, and some traces, at
least in discourse, of the magnanimity of their fathers. In the suburbs
of the city, the *Academy* of the Platonists, the *Lycæum* of the Peripatetics,
the *Portico* of the Stoics, and the *Garden* of the Epicureans, were planted
with trees and decorated with statues; and the philosophers, instead of
being immured in a cloister, delivered their instructions in spacious and
pleasant walks, which, at different hours, were consecrated to the exercises of the mind and body. The genius of the founders still lived in
those venerable seats; the ambition of succeeding to the masters of
human reason excited a generous emulation; and the merit of the candidates was determined, on each vacancy, by the free voices of an enlightened people. The Athenian professors were paid by their disciples:
according to their mutual wants and abilities, the price appears to have
varied from a mina to a talent; and Isocrates himself, who derides the
avarice of the sophists, required, in his school of rhetoric, about thirty
pounds from each of his hundred pupils. The wages of industry are just
and honourable, yet the same Isocrates shed tears at the first receipt of a
stipend: the Stoic might blush when he was hired to preach the contempt of money; and I should be sorry to discover that Aristotle or Plato
so far degenerated from the example of Socrates as to exchange knowledge for gold. But some property of lands and houses was settled, by
the permission of the laws, and the legacies of deceased friends, on the
philosophic chairs of Athens. Epicurus bequeathed to his disciples the
gardens which he had purchased for eighty minæ or two hundred and
fifty pounds, with a fund sufficient for their frugal subsistence and
monthly festivals; and the patrimony of Plato afforded an annual rent,
which, in eight centuries, was gradually increased from three to one
thousand pieces of gold. The schools of Athens were protected by the
wisest and most virtuous of the Roman princes. The library, which
Hadrian founded, was placed in a portico adorned with pictures, statues,
and a roof of alabaster, and supported by one hundred columns of
Phrygian marble. The public salaries were assigned by the generous

spirit of the Antonines; and each professor, of politics, of rhetoric, of the Platonic, the Peripatetic, the Stoic, and the Epicurean philosophy, received an annual stipend of ten thousand drachmæ, or more than three hundred pounds sterling. After the death of Marcus, these liberal donations, and the privileges attached to the *thrones* of science, were abolished and revived, diminished and enlarged; but some vestige of royal bounty may be found under the successors of Constantine; and their arbitrary choice of an unworthy candidate might tempt the philosophers of Athens to regret the days of independence and poverty. It is remarkable that the impartial favour of the Antonines was bestowed on the four adverse sects of philosophy, which they considered as equally useful, or at least as equally innocent. Socrates had formerly been the glory and the reproach of his country; and the first lessons of Epicurus so strangely scandalised the pious ears of the Athenians, that by his exile, and that of his antagonists, they silenced all vain disputes concerning the nature of the gods. But in the ensuing year they recalled the hasty decree, restored the liberty of the schools, and were convinced by the experience of ages that the moral character of philosophers is not affected by the diversity of their theological speculations.

The Gothic arms were less fatal to the schools of Athens than the establishment of a new religion, whose ministers superseded the exercise of reason, resolved every question by an article of faith, and condemned the infidel or sceptic to eternal flames. In many a volume of laborious controversy they exposed the weakness of the understanding and the corruption of the heart, insulted human nature in the sages of antiquity, and proscribed the spirit of philosophical inquiry, so repugnant to the doctrine, or at least to the temper, of an humble believer. The surviving sect of the Platonists, whom Plato would have blushed to acknowledge, extravagantly mingled a sublime theory with the practice of superstition and magic; and as they remained alone in the midst of a Christian world, they indulged a secret rancour against the government of the church and state, whose severity was still suspended over their heads. About a century after the reign of Julian, Proclus was permitted to teach in the philosophic chair of the Academy; and such was his industry, that he frequently, in the same day, pronounced five lessons, and composed seven hundred lines. His sagacious mind explored the deepest questions of morals and metaphysics, and he ventured to urge eighteen arguments against the Christian doctrine of the creation of the world. But in the intervals of study he *personally* conversed with Pan, Æsculapius, and Minerva, in whose mysteries he was secretly initiated, and whose prostrate statues he adored; in the devout persuasion that the philosopher, who is a citizen of the universe, should be the priest of its various deities. An eclipse of the sun announced his approaching end; and his Life, with that of his scholar Isidore, compiled by two of their most learned disciples, exhibits a deplorable picture of the second childhood of human reason. Yet the golden chain, as it was fondly styled, of the Platonic succession, continued forty-four years from the death of Proclus to the edict of Justinian, which imposed a perpetual silence on the schools of Athens, and excited the grief and indignation of the few remaining votaries of Grecian science and superstition. Seven friends and philosophers, Diogenes and Hermias, Eulalius and Priscian, Damascius, Isidore, and Simplicius, who dissented from the religion of their sovereign, embraced the resolution of seeking in a foreign land the freedom which was denied in their native country. They had heard, and they credulously believed, that the republic of Plato was realised in the despotic government of Persia, and that a patriot king reigned over the happiest and most virtuous of nations. They were soon astonished by the natural discovery that Persia resembled the other countries of the globe; that Chosroes, who affected the name of a philosopher, was vain, cruel, and ambitious; that bigotry, and a spirit of intolerance, prevailed among the Magi; that the nobles were haughty, the courtiers servile, and the magistrates unjust; that the guilty sometimes escaped, and that the innocent were often oppressed. The disappointment of the philosophers provoked them to overlook the real virtues of the Persians; and they were scandalised, more deeply perhaps than became their profession, with the plurality of wives and concubines, the incestuous marriages, and the custom of exposing dead bodies to the dogs and vultures, instead of hiding them in the earth, or consuming them with fire. Their repentance was expressed by a precipitate return, and they loudly declared that they had rather die on the borders of the empire than enjoy the wealth and favour of the barbarian. From this journey, however, they derived a benefit which reflects the purest lustre on the character of Chosroes. He required that the seven sages who had visited the court of Persia should be exempted from the penal laws which Justinian enacted against his Pagan subjects; and this privilege, expressly stipulated in a treaty of peace, was guarded by the vigilance of a powerful mediator. Simplicius and his companions ended their lives in peace and obscurity; and as they left no disciples, they terminate the long list of Grecian philosophers, who may be justly praised, notwithstanding their defects, as the wisest and most virtuous of their contemporaries. The writings of Simplicius are now extant. His physical and metaphysical commentaries on Aristotle have passed away with the fashion of the times; but his moral interpretation of Epictetus is preserved in the library of nations, as a classic book, most excellently adapted to direct the will, to purify the heart, and to confirm the understanding, by a just confidence in the nature both of God and man.

EXTINCTION OF THE ROMAN CONSULSHIP

About the same time that Pythagoras first invented the appellation of philosopher, liberty and the consulship were founded at Rome by the elder Brutus. The revolutions of the consular office, which may be viewed in the successive lights of a substance, a shadow, and a name, have been occasionally mentioned in the present history. The first magistrates of the republic had been chosen by the people, to exercise, in the senate and in the camp, the powers of peace and war, which were afterwards translated to the emperors. But the tradition of ancient dignity was long revered by the Romans and barbarians. A Gothic historian applauds the consulship of Theodoric as the height of all temporal glory and greatness; the king of Italy himself congratulates those annual favourites of fortune who, without the cares, enjoyed the splendour of the throne; and at the end of a thousand years, two consuls were created by the sovereigns of Rome and Constantinople for the sole purpose of giving a date to the year and a festival to the people. But the expenses of this festival, in which the wealthy and the vain aspired to surpass their predecessors, insensibly arose to the enormous sum of fourscore thousand pounds; the wisest senators declined an useless honour which involved the certain ruin of their families, and to this reluctance I should impute the frequent chasms in the last age of the consular *Fasti*. The predecessors of Justinian had assisted from the public treasures the dignity of the less opulent candidates; the avarice of that prince preferred the cheaper and more convenient method of advice and regulation. Seven *processions* or spectacles were the number to which his edict confined the horse and chariot races, the athletic sports, the music and pantomimes of the theatre, and the hunting of wild beasts; and small pieces of silver were discreetly substituted to the gold medals, which had always excited tumult and drunkenness when they were scattered with a profuse hand among the populace. Notwithstanding these precautions and his own example, the succession of consuls finally ceased in the thirteenth year of Justinian, whose despotic temper might be gratified by the silent extinction of a title which admonished the Romans of their ancient freedom. Yet the annual consulship still lived in the minds of the people; they fondly expected its speedy restoration; they applauded the gracious condescension of successive princes, by whom it was assumed in the first year of their reign; and three centuries elapsed, after the death of Justinian, before that obsolete dignity, which had been suppressed by custom, could be abolished by law. The imperfect mode of distinguishing each year by the name of a magistrate was usefully supplied by the date of a permanent era: the creation of the world, according to the Septuagint version, was adopted by the Greeks; and the Latins, since the age of Charlemagne, have computed their time from the birth of Christ.

Under the glories of Justinian's reign lay two fatally unsound conditions. One was his economic extravagance. The other was that theologically and politically he failed to reconcile the eastern and western provinces. His very able wife Theodora had been a Monophysite. After her death in 548 Justinian tried to conciliate the Monophysite elements. Had he been successful he might have retained the allegiance of the eastern provinces. But in fact Monophysite doctrines were so much akin to those of Islam that when that power arose the eastern provinces easily and inevitably fell away.

In Chapter 41 Gibbon describes Justinian's Conquests (533–540). Through his generals Belisarius and Narses Justinian held the eastern frontier, recovered Africa and part of Spain from the Vandals and made the Mediterranean a Roman sea once more. Belisarius overthrew the Ostrogothic power in Italy, recovering Rome and successfully resisting a siege of Rome by the Goths, and subsequently besieging and taking Ravenna.

In Chapter 42 Gibbon relates the rise of the Lombards and the appearance of Slav and Turkish peoples.

Chapter 43

LAST VICTORY AND DEATH OF BELISARIUS. CHARACTER
AND DEATH OF JUSTINIAN. COMETS, EARTHQUAKES, AND
PLAGUE DURING THE REIGN OF JUSTINIAN

*The Goths revolted under Totila and took Rome in 546. It was
recovered by Belisarius but taken again after his recall. In 552
the eunuch Narses defeated Totila and liberated Rome. He
subsequently defeated Totila's successor, Teias, the last king of the
Goths, and crushed an invasion of the Franks and Alemanni. The
throne of the Gothic kings was now filled by the exarchs of Ravenna,
the representatives of the emperor in Constantinople. Narses himself
became the first exarch and administered the entire kingdom of Italy
for over fifteen years.*

THE LAST VICTORY AND DEATH OF BELISARIUS

I DESIRE to believe, but I dare not affirm, that Belisarius sincerely
rejoiced in the triumph of Narses. Yet the consciousness of his own
exploits might teach him to esteem, without jealousy, the merit of a
rival; and the repose of the aged warrior was crowned by a last victory,
which saved the emperor and the capital. The barbarians, who annually
visited the provinces of Europe, were less discouraged by some accidental defeats than they were excited by the double hope of spoil and
of subsidy. In the thirty-second winter of Justinian's reign the Danube
was deeply frozen; Zabergan led the cavalry of the Bulgarians, and his
standard was followed by a promiscuous multitude of Sclavonians. The
savage chief passed, without opposition, the river and the mountains,
spread his troops over Macedonia and Thrace, and advanced with no
more than seven thousand horse to the long walls which should have
defended the territory of Constantinople. But the works of man are
impotent against the assaults of nature: a recent earthquake had shaken
the foundations of the walls; and the forces of the empire were employed
on the distant frontiers of Italy, Africa, and Persia. The seven *schools*,
or companies, of the guards or domestic troops, had been augmented
to the number of five thousand five hundred men, whose ordinary
station was in the peaceful cities of Asia. But the places of the brave
Armenians were insensibly supplied by lazy citizens, who purchased an
exemption from the duties of civil life without being exposed to the

576

dangers of military service. Of such soldiers few could be tempted to sally from the gates; and none could be persuaded to remain in the field, unless they wanted strength and speed to escape from the Bulgarians. The report of the fugitives exaggerated the numbers and fierceness of an enemy who had polluted holy virgins and abandoned new-born infants to the dogs and vultures; a crowd of rustics, imploring food and protection, increased the consternation of the city; and the tents of Zabergan were pitched at the distance of twenty miles, on the banks of a small river which encircles Melanthias and afterwards falls into the Propontis. Justinian trembled: and those who had only seen the emperor in his old age were pleased to suppose that he had *lost* the alacrity and vigour of his youth. By his command the vessels of gold and silver were removed from the churches in the neighbourhood, and even the suburbs, of Constantinople: the ramparts were lined with trembling spectators; the golden gate was crowded with useless generals and tribunes; and the senate shared the fatigues and the apprehensions of the populace.

But the eyes of the prince and people were directed to a feeble veteran, who was compelled by the public danger to resume the armour in which he had entered Carthage and defended Rome. The horses of the royal stables, of private citizens, and even of the circus, were hastily collected; the emulation of the old and young was roused by the name of Belisarius, and his first encampment was in the presence of a victorious enemy. His prudence, and the labour of the friendly peasants, secured, with a ditch and rampart, the repose of the night; innumerable fires and clouds of dust were artfully contrived to magnify the opinion of his strength; his soldiers suddenly passed from despondency to presumption; and, while ten thousand voices demanded the battle, Belisarius dissembled his knowledge that in the hour of trial he must depend on the firmness of three hundred veterans. The next morning the Bulgarian cavalry advanced to the charge. But they heard the shouts of multitudes, they beheld the arms and discipline of the front; they were assaulted on the flanks by two ambuscades which rose from the woods; their foremost warriors fell by the hand of the aged hero and his guards; and the swiftness of their evolutions was rendered useless by the close attack and rapid pursuit of the Romans. In this action (so speedy was their flight) the Bulgarians lost only four hundred horse: but Constantinople was saved; and Zabergan, who felt the hand of a master, withdrew to a respectful distance. But his friends were numerous in the councils of the emperor, and Belisarius obeyed with reluctance the commands of envy and Justinian, which forbade him to achieve the deliverance of his country. On his return to the city, the people, still conscious of their danger, accompanied his triumph with acclamations of joy and gratitude, which were imputed as a crime to the victorious general. But when he entered the palace the courtiers were silent, and the emperor, after a cold and thankless embrace, dismissed him to mingle with the train of slaves. Yet

so deep was the impression of his glory on the minds of men, that
Justinian, in the seventy-seventh year of his age, was encouraged to
advance near forty miles from the capital, and to inspect in person the
restoration of the long wall. The Bulgarians wasted the summer in the
plains of Thrace; but they were inclined to peace by the failure of their
rash attempts on Greece and the Chersonesus. A menace of killing their
prisoners quickened the payment of heavy ransoms; and the departure
of Zabergan was hastened by the report that double-prowed vessels were
built on the Danube to intercept his passage. The danger was soon
forgotten; and a vain question, whether their sovereign had shown
more wisdom or weakness, amused the idleness of the city.

About two years after the last victory of Belisarius, the emperor returned from a Thracian journey of health, or business, or devotion.
Justinian was afflicted by a pain in his head; and his private entry
countenanced the rumour of his death. Before the third hour of the day,
the bakers' shops were plundered of their bread, the houses were shut,
and every citizen, with hope or terror, prepared for the impending
tumult. The senators themselves, fearful and suspicious, were convened
at the ninth hour; and the prefect received their commands to visit every
quarter of the city and proclaim a general illumination for the recovery
of the emperor's health. The ferment subsided; but every accident betrayed the impotence of the government and the factious temper of the
people: the guards were disposed to mutiny as often as their quarters
were changed, or their pay was withheld: the frequent calamities of
fires and earthquakes afforded the opportunities of disorder; the disputes of the blues and greens, of the orthodox and heretics, degenerated
into bloody battles; and, in the presence of the Persian ambassador,
Justinian blushed for himself and for his subjects. Capricious pardon
and arbitrary punishment embittered the irksomeness and discontent of
a long reign: a conspiracy was formed in the palace; and, unless we are
deceived by the names of Marcellus and Sergius, the most virtuous and
the most profligate of the courtiers were associated in the same designs.
They had fixed the time of the execution; their rank gave them access
to the royal banquet; and their black slaves were stationed in the vestibule and porticoes to announce the death of the tyrant, and to excite
a sedition in the capital. But the indiscretion of an accomplice saved
the poor remnant of the days of Justinian. The conspirators were detected and seized with daggers hidden under their garments; Marcellus
died by his own hand, and Sergius was dragged from the sanctuary.
Pressed by remorse, or tempted by the hopes of safety, he accused two
officers of the household of Belisarius, and torture forced them to
declare that they had acted according to the secret instructions of their
patron. Posterity will not hastily believe that an hero who in the vigour
of life had disdained the fairest offers of ambition and revenge should
stoop to the murder of his prince, whom he could not long expect to

survive. His followers were impatient to fly; but flight must have been supported by rebellion, and he had lived enough for nature and for glory. Belisarius appeared before the council with less fear than indignation: after forty years' service the emperor had prejudged his guilt; and injustice was sanctified by the presence and authority of the patriarch. The life of Belisarius was graciously spared, but his fortunes were sequestered; and, from December to July, he was guarded as a prisoner in his own palace. At length his innocence was acknowledged; his freedom and honours were restored; and death, which might be hastened by resentment and grief, removed him from the world about eight months after his deliverance. The name of Belisarius can never die: but, instead of the funeral, the monuments, the statues, so justly due to his memory, I only read that his treasures, the spoils of the Goths and Vandals, were immediately confiscated by the emperor. Some decent portion was reserved, however, for the use of his widow: and as Antonina had much to repent, she devoted the last remains of her life and fortune to the foundation of a convent. Such is the simple and genuine narrative of the fall of Belisarius, and the ingratitude of Justinian. That he was deprived of his eyes, and reduced by envy to beg his bread, "Give a penny to Belisarius the general!" is a fiction of later times, which has obtained credit, or rather favour, as a strange example of the vicissitudes of fortune.

THE CHARACTER AND DEATH OF JUSTINIAN

If the emperor could rejoice in the death of Belisarius, he enjoyed the base satisfaction only eight months, the last period of a reign of thirty-eight and a life of eighty-three years. It would be difficult to trace the character of a prince who is not the most conspicuous object of his own times: but the confessions of an enemy may be received as the safest evidence of his virtues. The resemblance of Justinian to the bust of Domitian is maliciously urged, with the acknowledgement, however, of a well-proportioned figure, a ruddy complexion, and a pleasing countenance. The emperor was easy of access, patient of hearing, courteous and affable in discourse, and a master of the angry passions which rage with such destructive violence in the breast of a despot. Procopius praises his temper, to reproach him with calm and deliberate cruelty: but in the conspiracies which attacked his authority and person, a more candid judge will approve the justice, or admire the clemency, of Justinian. He excelled in the private virtues of chastity and temperance; but the impartial love of beauty would have been less mischievous than his conjugal tenderness for Theodora; and his abstemious diet was regulated, not by the prudence of a philosopher, but the superstition of a monk. His repasts were short and frugal: on solemn fasts he contented himself with water and vegetables; and such was his strength as well as fervour, that he frequently passed two days, and as many nights, without tasting any food. The measure of his sleep was not less rigorous: after the repose of a single hour, the body was awakened by the soul, and, to the astonishment of his chamberlains, Justinian walked or studied till the morning light. Such restless application prolonged his time for the acquisition of knowledge and the despatch of business; and he might seriously deserve the reproach of confounding, by minute and preposterous diligence, the general order of his administration. The emperor professed himself a musician and architect, a poet and philosopher, a lawyer and theologian; and if he failed in the enterprise of reconciling the Christian sects, the review of the Roman jurisprudence is a noble monument of his spirit and industry. In the government of the empire he was less wise, or less successful: the age was unfortunate; the people was oppressed and discontented; Theodora abused her power; a succession of bad ministers disgraced his judgment; and Justinian was neither beloved in his life nor regretted at his death. The love of fame was deeply implanted in his breast, but he condescended to the poor ambition of titles, honours, and contemporary praise; and while he laboured to fix the admiration, he forfeited the esteem and affection, of the Romans. The design of the African and Italian wars was boldly conceived and executed; and his penetration discovered the talents of Belisarius in the camp, of Narses in the palace. But the name of the emperor is eclipsed by the names of his victorious generals; and Belisarius still lives, to upbraid the envy and ingratitude of his sovereign. The partial favour of mankind applauds the genius of a conqueror who leads and directs his subjects in the exercise of arms. The characters of Philip the Second and of Justinian are distinguished by the cold ambition which delights in war, and declines the dangers of the field. Yet a colossal statue of bronze represented the emperor on horseback, preparing to march against the Persians in the habit and armour of Achilles. In the great square before the church of St. Sophia, this monument was raised on a brass column and a stone pedestal of seven steps; and the pillar of Theodosius, which weighed seven thousand four hundred pounds of silver, was removed from the same place by the avarice and vanity of Justinian. Future princes were more just or indulgent to *his* memory; the elder Andronicus, in the beginning of the fourteenth century, repaired and beautified his equestrian statue: since the fall of the empire it has been melted into cannon by the victorious Turks.

COMETS

I shall conclude this chapter with the comets, the earthquakes, and the plague, which astonished or afflicted the age of Justinian.

In the fifth year of his reign, and in the month of September, a comet was seen during twenty days in the western quarter of the heavens, and which shot its rays into the north. Eight years afterwards, while the sun was in Capricorn, another comet appeared to follow in the Sagittary: the size was gradually increasing; the head was in the east, the tail in the west, and it remained visible above forty days. The nations, who gazed with astonishment, expected wars and calamities from their baleful influence; and these expectations were abundantly fulfilled. The astronomers dissembled their ignorance of the nature of these blazing stars, which they affected to represent as the floating meteors of the air; and few among them embraced the simple notion of Seneca and the Chaldæans, that they are only planets of a longer period and more eccentric motion. Time and science have justified the conjectures and predictions of the Roman sage: the telescope has opened new worlds to the eyes of astronomers; and, in the narrow space of history and fable, one and the same comet is already found to have revisited the earth in *seven* equal revolutions of five hundred and seventy-five years. The *first*, which ascends beyond the Christian era one thousand seven hundred and sixty-seven years, is coëval with Ogyges, the father of Grecian antiquity. And this appearance explains the tradition which Varro has preserved, that under his reign the planet Venus changed her colour, size, figure, and course; a prodigy without example either in past or succeeding ages. The *second* visit, in the year eleven hundred and ninety-three, is darkly implied in the fable of Electra, the seventh of the Pleiads, who have been reduced to six since the time of the Trojan war. That nymph, the wife of Dardanus, was unable to support the ruin of her country: she abandoned the dances of her sister orbs, fled from the zodiac to the north pole, and obtained, from her dishevelled locks, the name of the *comet*. The *third* period expires in the year six hundred and eighteen, a date that exactly agrees with the tremendous comet of the Sibyl, and perhaps of Pliny, which arose in the West two generations before the reign of Cyrus. The *fourth* apparition, forty-four years before the birth of Christ, is of all others the most splendid and important. After the death of Cæsar, a long-haired star was conspicuous to Rome and to the nations during the games which were exhibited by young Octavian in honour of Venus and his uncle. The vulgar opinion, that it conveyed to heaven the divine soul of the dictator, was cherished and consecrated by the piety of a statesman; while his secret superstition referred the comet to the glory of his own times. The *fifth* visit has been already ascribed to the fifth year of Justinian, which coincides with the five hundred and thirty-first of the Christian era. And it may deserve notice, that in this, as in the preceding instance, the comet was followed, though at a longer interval, by a remarkable paleness of the sun. The *sixth* return, in the year eleven hundred and six, is recorded by the chronicles of Europe and China: and in the first fervour of the Crusades, the Christians and the Mahometans might surmise, with equal reason, that it portended the destruction of the Infidels. The *seventh* phenomenon, of one thousand six hundred and eighty, was presented to the eyes of an enlightened age. The philosophy of Bayle dispelled a prejudice which Milton's muse had so recently adorned, that the comet, "from its horrid hair shakes pestilence and war." Its road in the heavens was observed with exquisite skill by Flamsteed and Cassini: and the mathematical science of Bernoulli, Newton, and Halley investigated the laws of its revolutions. At the *eighth* period, in the year two thousand three hundred and fifty-five, their calculations may perhaps be verified by the astronomers of some future capital in the Siberian or American wilderness.

EARTHQUAKES

The near approach of a comet may injure or destroy the globe which we inhabit; but the changes on its surface have been hitherto produced by the action of volcanoes and earthquakes. The nature of the soil may indicate the countries most exposed to these formidable concussions, since they are caused by subterraneous fires, and such fires are kindled by the union and fermentation of iron and sulphur. But their times and effects appear to lie beyond the reach of human curiosity; and the philosopher will discreetly abstain from the prediction of earthquakes, till he has counted the drops of water that silently filtrate on the inflammable mineral, and measured the caverns which increase by resistance the explosion of the imprisoned air. Without assigning the cause, history will distinguish the periods in which these calamitous events have been rare or frequent, and will observe that this fever of the earth raged with uncommon violence during the reign of Justinian. Each year is marked by the repetition of earthquakes, of such duration that Constantinople has been shaken above forty days; of such extent that the shock has been communicated to the whole surface of the globe, or at least of the Roman empire. An impulsive or vibratory motion was felt, enormous chasms were opened, huge and heavy bodies were discharged into the air, the sea alternately advanced and retreated beyond its ordinary bounds, and a mountain was torn from Libanus and cast into the waves where it protected, as a mole, the new harbour of Botrys in Phœnicia. The stroke that agitates an ant-hill may crush the insect-myriads in the dust; yet truth must extort a confession that man has industriously laboured for his own destruction. The institution of great cities, which include a nation within the limits of a wall, almost realises the wish of Caligula that the Roman people had but one neck. Two hundred and fifty thousand persons are said to have perished in the earthquake of Antioch, whose domestic multitudes were swelled by the conflux of strangers to the festival of the Ascension. The loss of Berytus was of smaller account, but of much greater value. That city, on the coast of Phœnicia, was illustrated by the study of the civil law, which opened the surest road to wealth and dignity: the schools of Berytus were filled with the rising spirits of the age, and many a youth was lost in the earthquake who might have lived to be the scourge or

the guardian of his country. In these disasters the architect becomes
the enemy of mankind. The hut of a savage, or the tent of an Arab,
may be thrown down without injury to the inhabitant; and the Peruvians
had reason to deride the folly of their Spanish conquerors, who with
so much cost and labour erected their own sepulchres. The rich marbles
of a patrician are dashed on his own head; a whole people is buried
under the ruins of public and private edifices; and the conflagration is
kindled and propagated by the innumerable fires which are necessary
for the subsistence and manufactures of a great city. Instead of the
mutual sympathy which might comfort and assist the distressed, they
dreadfully experience the vices and passions which are released from
the fear of punishment: the tottering houses are pillaged by intrepid
avarice; revenge embraces the moment and selects the victim; and the
earth often swallows the assassin, or the ravisher, in the consummation
of their crimes. Superstition involves the present danger with invisible
terrors; and if the image of death may sometimes be subservient to the
virtue or repentance of individuals, an affrighted people is more forcibly
moved to expect the end of the world, or to deprecate with servile
homage the wrath of an avenging Deity.

THE PLAGUE

Ethiopia and Egypt have been stigmatised in every age as the original
source and seminary of the plague. In a damp, hot, stagnating air, this
African fever is generated from the putrefaction of animal substances,
and especially from the swarms of locusts, not less destructive to mankind in their death than in their lives. The fatal disease which depopulated the earth in the time of Justinian and his successors first appeared
in the neighbourhood of Pelusium, between the Serbonian bog and the
eastern channel of the Nile. From thence, tracing as it were a double
path, it spread to the East, over Syria, Persia, and the Indies, and penetrated to the West, along the coast of Africa and over the continent of
Europe. In the spring of the second year Constantinople, during three or
four months, was visited by the pestilence; and Procopius, who observed
its progress and symptoms with the eyes of a physician, has emulated the
skill and diligence of Thucydides in the description of the plague of
Athens. The infection was sometimes announced by the visions of a distempered fancy, and the victim despaired as soon as he had heard the
menace and felt the stroke of an invisible spectre. But the greater number, in their beds, in the streets, in their usual occupation, were surprised
by a slight fever; so slight, indeed, that neither the pulse nor the colour
of the patient gave any signs of the approaching danger. The same,
the next, or the succeeding day, it was declared by the swelling of the
glands, particularly those of the groin, of the armpits, and under the
ear; and when these buboes or tumours were opened, they were found
to contain a *coal*, or black substance, of the size of a lentil. If they

came to a just swelling and suppuration, the patient was saved by this kind of natural discharge of the morbid humour; but if they continued hard and dry, a mortification quickly ensued, and the fifth day was commonly the term of his life. The fever was often accompanied with lethargy or delirium; the bodies of the sick were covered with black pustules or carbuncles, the symptoms of immediate death; and in the constitutions too feeble to produce an eruption, the vomiting of blood was followed by a mortification of the bowels. To pregnant women the plague was generally mortal; yet one infant was drawn alive from his dead mother, and three mothers survived the loss of their infected fœtus. Youth was the most perilous season, and the female sex was less susceptible than the male; but every rank and profession was attacked with indiscriminate rage, and many of those who escaped were deprived of the use of their speech, without being secure from a return of the disorder. The physicians of Constantinople were zealous and skilful; but their art was baffled by the various symptoms and pertinacious vehemence of the disease: the same remedies were productive of contrary effects, and the event capriciously disappointed their prognostics of death or recovery. The order of funerals and the right of sepulchres were confounded; those who were left without friends or servants lay unburied in the streets, or in their desolate houses; and a magistrate was authorised to collect the promiscuous heaps of dead bodies, to transport them by land or water, and to inter them in deep pits beyond the precincts of the city. Their own danger and the prospect of public distress awakened some remorse in the minds of the most vicious of mankind: the confidence of health again revived their passions and habits; but philosophy must disdain the observation of Procopius, that the lives of such men were guarded by the peculiar favour of fortune or Providence. He forgot, or perhaps he secretly recollected, that the plague had touched the person of Justinian himself; but the abstemious diet of the emperor may suggest, as in the case of Socrates, a more rational and honourable cause for his recovery.[1] During his sickness the public consternation was expressed in the habits of the citizens; and their idleness and despondence occasioned a general scarcity in the capital of the East.

Contagion is the inseparable symptom of the plague; which, by mutual respiration, is transfused from the infected persons to the lungs and stomach of those who approach them. While philosophers believe and tremble, it is singular that the existence of a real danger should have been denied by a people most prone to vain and imaginary terrors.[2]

[1] It was thus that Socrates had been saved by his temperance, in the plague of Athens. Dr. Mead accounts for the peculiar salubrity of religious houses by the two advantages of seclusion and abstinence.

[2] Mead proves that the plague is contagious, from Thucydides, Lucretius, Aristotle, Galen, and common experience; and he refutes the contrary opinion of the French

Yet the fellow-citizens of Procopius were satisfied, by some short and partial experience, that the infection could not be gained by the closest conversation; and this persuasion might support the assiduity of friends or physicians in the care of the sick, whom inhuman prudence would have condemned to solitude and despair. But the fatal security, like the predestination of the Turks, must have aided the progress of the contagion; and those salutary precautions to which Europe is indebted for her safety were unknown to the government of Justinian. No restraints were imposed on the free and frequent intercourse of the Roman provinces: from Persia to France the nations were mingled and infected by wars and emigrations; and the pestilential odour which lurks for years in a bale of cotton was imported, by the abuse of trade, into the most distant regions. The mode of its propagation is explained by the remark of Procopius himself, that it always spread from the sea-coast to the inland country: the most sequestered islands and mountains were successively visited; the places which had escaped the fury of its first passage were alone exposed to the contagion of the ensuing year. The winds might diffuse that subtle venom; but unless the atmosphere be previously disposed for its reception, the plague would soon expire in the cold or temperate climates of the earth. Such was the universal corruption of the air, that the pestilence which burst forth in the fifteenth year of Justinian was not checked or alleviated by any difference of the seasons. In time its first malignity was abated and dispersed; the disease alternately languished and revived; but it was not till the end of a calamitous period of fifty-two years that mankind recovered their health, or the air resumed its pure and salubrious quality. No facts have been preserved to sustain an account, or even a conjecture, of the numbers that perished in this extraordinary mortality. I only find that, during three months, five and at length ten thousand persons died each day at Constantinople; that many cities of the East were left vacant; and that in several districts of Italy the harvest and the vintage withered on the ground. The triple scourge of war, pestilence, and famine, afflicted the subjects of Justinian; and his reign is disgraced by a visible decrease of the human species, which has never been repaired in some of the fairest countries of the globe.

The supreme achievement of Justinian's reign was the codification of the Roman law. This is described by Gibbon in Chapter 44, omitted here.

---

physicians who visited Marseilles in the year 1720. Yet these were the recent and enlightened spectators of a plague which, in a few months, swept away 50,000 inhabitants of a city that, in the present hour of prosperity and trade, contains no more than 90,000 souls.

Chapter 45

MISERY OF ROME AT THE CLOSE OF THE SIXTH
CENTURY. THE PONTIFICATE OF GREGORY THE GREAT

*Between 568 and 570, after the death of Narses, the Lombards
under Alboin conquered the greater part of Italy. For two hundred
years Italy was divided between the Lombard kingdom and the
exarchate of Ravenna.*

MISERY OF ROME AT THE CLOSE OF THE SIXTH CENTURY

AMIDST the arms of the Lombards, and under the despotism of
the Greeks, we again inquire into the fate of Rome, which had
reached, about the close of the sixth century, the lowest period
of her depression. By the removal of the seat of empire and the successive loss of the provinces, the sources of public and private opulence
were exhausted: the lofty tree, under whose shade the nations of the
earth had reposed, was deprived of its leaves and branches, and the
sapless trunk was left to wither on the ground. The ministers of command and the messengers of victory no longer met on the Appian or
Flaminian way, and the hostile approach of the Lombards was often
felt and continually feared. The inhabitants of a potent and peaceful
capital, who visit without an anxious thought the garden of the adjacent
country, will faintly picture in their fancy the distress of the Romans:
they shut or opened their gates with a trembling hand, beheld from the
walls the flames of their houses, and heard the lamentations of their
brethren, who were coupled together like dogs, and dragged away into
distant slavery beyond the sea and the mountains. Such incessant alarms
must annihilate the pleasures and interrupt the labours of a rural life;
and the Campagna of Rome was speedily reduced to the state of a
dreary wilderness, in which the land is barren, the waters are impure, and
the air is infectious. Curiosity and ambition no longer attracted the
nations to the capital of the world; but, if chance or necessity directed
the steps of a wandering stranger, he contemplated with horror the
vacancy and solitude of the city, and might be tempted to ask, where is
the senate, and where are the people? In a season of excessive rains the
Tiber swelled above its banks, and rushed with irresistible violence into
the valleys of the seven hills. A pestilential disease arose from the stag-
nation of the deluge, and so rapid was the contagion that fourscore
persons expired in an hour in the midst of a solemn procession which
implored the mercy of Heaven. A society in which marriage is en-

586

couraged and industry prevails soon repairs the accidental losses of pestilence and war; but, as the far greater part of the Romans was condemned to hopeless indigence and celibacy, the depopulation was constant and visible, and the gloomy enthusiasts might expect the approaching failure of the human race. Yet the number of citizens still exceeded the measure of subsistence: their precarious food was supplied from the harvests of Sicily or Egypt, and the frequent repetition of famine betrays the inattention of the emperor to a distant province. The edifices of Rome were exposed to the same ruin and decay; the mouldering fabrics were easily overthrown by inundations, tempests, and earthquakes; and the monks, who had occupied the most advantageous stations, exulted in their base triumph over the ruins of antiquity. It is commonly believed that pope Gregory the First attacked the temples and mutilated the statues of the city; that, by the command of the barbarian, the Palatine library was reduced to ashes, and that the history of Livy was the peculiar mark of his absurd and mischievous fanaticism. The writings of Gregory himself reveal his implacable aversion to the monuments of classic genius, and he points his severest censure against the profane learning of a bishop who taught the art of grammar, studied the Latin poets, and pronounced with the same voice the praises of Jupiter and those of Christ. But the evidence of his destructive rage is doubtful and recent: the Temple of Peace or the Theatre of Marcellus have been demolished by the slow operation of ages, and a formal proscription would have multiplied the copies of Virgil and Livy in the countries which were subject to the ecclesiastical dictator.

THE PONTIFICATE OF GREGORY THE GREAT

Like Thebes, or Babylon, or Carthage, the name of Rome might have been erased from the earth, if the city had not been animated by a vital principle, which again restored her to honour and dominion. A vague tradition was embraced, that two Jewish teachers, a tent-maker and a fisherman, had formerly been executed in the circus of Nero, and at the end of five hundred years their genuine or fictitious relics were adored as the Palladium of Christian Rome. The pilgrims of the East and West resorted to the holy threshold; but the shrines of the apostles were guarded by miracles and invisible terrors, and it was not without fear that the pious catholic approached the object of his worship. It was fatal to touch, it was dangerous to behold, the bodies of the saints; and those who, from the purest motives, presumed to disturb the repose of the sanctuary were affrighted by visions or punished with sudden death. The unreasonable request of an empress, who wished to deprive the Romans of their sacred treasure, the head of St. Paul, was rejected with the deepest abhorrence; and the pope asserted, most probably with truth, that a linen which had been sanctified in the neighbourhood of his body, or the filings of his chain, which it was sometimes easy and sometimes impossible to obtain, possessed an equal degree of miraculous virtue. But the power as well as virtue of the apostles resided with living energy in the breast of their successors: and the chair of St. Peter was filled under the reign of Maurice by the first and greatest of the name of Gregory. His grandfather Felix had himself been pope, and, as the bishops were already bound by the law of celibacy, his consecration must have been preceded by the death of his wife. The parents of Gregory, Sylvia and Gordian, were the noblest of the senate, and the most pious of the church of Rome; his female relations were numbered among the saints and virgins, and his own figure, with those of his father and mother, were represented near three hundred years in a family portrait which he offered to the monastery of St. Andrew. The design and colouring of this picture afford an honourable testimony that the art of painting was cultivated by the Italians of the sixth century; but the most abject ideas must be entertained of their taste and learning, since the epistles of Gregory, his sermons, and his dialogues, are the work of a man who was second in erudition to none of his contemporaries: his birth and abilities had raised him to the office of prefect of the city, and he enjoyed the merit of renouncing the pomp and vanities of this world. His ample patrimony was dedicated to the foundation of seven monasteries, one in Rome and six in Sicily; and it was the wish of Gregory that he might be unknown in this life, and glorious only in the next. Yet his devotion, and it might be sincere, pursued the path which would have been chosen by a crafty and ambitious statesman. The talents of Gregory, and the splendour which accompanied his retreat, rendered him dear and useful to the church, and implicit obedience has been always inculcated as the first duty of a monk. As soon as he had received the character of deacon, Gregory was sent to reside at the Byzantine court, the nuncio or minister of the apostolic see; and he boldly assumed, in the name of St. Peter, a tone of independent dignity which would have been criminal and dangerous in the most illustrious layman of the empire. He returned to Rome with a just increase of reputation, and, after a short exercise of the monastic virtues, he was dragged from the cloister to the papal throne by the unanimous voice of the clergy, the senate, and the people. He alone resisted, or seemed to resist, his own elevation; and his humble petition that Maurice would be pleased to reject the choice of the Romans could only serve to exalt his character in the eyes of the emperor and the public. When the fatal mandate was proclaimed, Gregory solicited the aid of some friendly merchants to convey him in a basket beyond the gates of Rome, and modestly conceal himself some days among the woods and mountains, till his retreat was discovered, as it is said, by a celestial light.

The pontificate of Gregory the *Great*, which lasted thirteen years, six months, and ten days, is one of the most edifying periods of the history of the church. His virtues, and even his faults, a singular mixture of simplicity and cunning, of pride and humility, of sense and superstition, were happily suited to his station and to the temper of the times. In his rival, the patriarch of Constantinople, he condemned the antichristian title of universal bishop, which the successor of St. Peter was too haughty to concede and too feeble to assume; and the ecclesiastical jurisdiction of Gregory was confined to the triple character of Bishop of Rome, Primate of Italy, and Apostle of the West. He frequently ascended the pulpit, and kindled, by his rude though pathetic eloquence, the congenial passions of his audience: the language of the Jewish prophets was interpreted and applied; and the minds of a people depressed by their present calamities were directed to the hopes and fears of the invisible world. His precepts and example defined the model of the Roman liturgy; the distribution of the parishes, the calendar of festivals, the order of processions, the service of the priests and deacons, the variety and change of sacerdotal garments. Till the last days of his life he officiated in the canon of the mass, which continued above three hours: the Gregorian chant has preserved the vocal and instrumental music of the theatre, and the rough voices of the barbarians attempted to imitate the melody of the Roman school. Experience had shown him the efficacy of these solemn and pompous rites to soothe the distress, to confirm the faith, to mitigate the fierceness, and to dispel the dark enthusiasm of the vulgar, and he readily forgave their tendency to promote the reign of priesthood and superstition. The bishops of Italy and the adjacent islands acknowledged the Roman pontiff as their special metropolitan. Even the existence, the union, or the translation of episcopal seats was decided by his absolute discretion: and his successful inroads into the provinces of Greece, of Spain, and of Gaul, might countenance the more lofty pretensions of succeeding popes. He interposed to prevent the abuses of popular elections; his jealous care maintained the purity of faith and discipline; and the apostolic shepherd assiduously watched over the faith and discipline of the subordinate pastors. Under his reign the Arians of Italy and Spain were reconciled to the catholic church, and the conquest of Britain reflects less glory on the name of Cæsar than on that of Gregory the First. Instead of six legions, forty monks were embarked for that distant island, and the pontiff lamented the austere duties which forbade him to partake the perils of their spiritual warfare. In less than two years he could announce to the archbishop of Alexandria that they had baptised the king of Kent with ten thousand of his Anglo-Saxons; and that the Roman missionaries, like those of the primitive church, were armed only with spiritual and supernatural powers. The credulity or the prudence of Gregory was always disposed to confirm the truths of religion by the evidence of ghosts, miracles, and resurrections; and posterity has paid to *his* memory the same tribute which he freely granted to the virtue of his own or the preceding generation. The celestial honours have been liberally bestowed by the authority of the popes, but Gregory is the last of their own order whom they have presumed to inscribe in the calendar of saints.

Their temporal power insensibly arose from the calamities of the times; and the Roman bishops, who have deluged Europe and Asia with blood, were compelled to reign as the ministers of charity and peace. I. The church of Rome, as it has been formerly observed, was endowed with ample possessions in Italy, Sicily, and the more distant provinces; and her agents, who were commonly subdeacons, had acquired a civil and even criminal jurisdiction over their tenants and husbandmen. The successor of St. Peter administered his patrimony with the temper of a vigilant and moderate landlord; and the epistles of Gregory are filled with salutary instructions to abstain from doubtful or vexatious law-suits, to preserve the integrity of weights and measures, to grant every reasonable delay, and to reduce the capitation of the slaves of the glebe, who purchased the right of marriage by the payment of an arbitrary fine. The rent or the produce of these estates was transported to the mouth of the Tiber, at the risk and expense of the pope: in the use of wealth he acted like a faithful steward of the church and the poor, and liberally applied to their wants the inexhaustible resources of abstinence and order. The voluminous account of his receipts and disbursements was kept above three hundred years in the Lateran, as the model of Christian economy. On the four great festivals he divided their quarterly allowance to the clergy, to his domestics, to the monasteries, the churches, the places of burial, the almshouses, and the hospitals of Rome, and the rest of the diocese. On the first day of every month he distributed to the poor, according to the season, their stated portion of corn, wine, cheese, vegetables, oil, fish, fresh provisions, clothes, and money; and his treasurers were continually summoned to satisfy, in his name, the extraordinary demands of indigence and merit. The instant distress of the sick and helpless, of strangers and pilgrims, was relieved by the bounty of each day and of every hour; nor would the pontiff indulge himself in a frugal repast till he had sent the dishes from his own table to some objects deserving of his compassion. The misery of the times had reduced the nobles and matrons of Rome to accept, without a blush, the benevolence of the church: three thousand virgins received their food and raiment from the hand of their benefactor; and many bishops of Italy escaped from the barbarians to the hospitable threshold of the Vatican. Gregory might justly be styled the Father of his country; and such was the extreme sensibility of his conscience, that, for the death of a beggar who had perished in the streets, he interdicted himself during several days from the exercise of sacerdotal functions. II. The misfortunes of Rome involved the apostolical pastor in the business of peace and war; and it might be doubtful to himself whether piety or ambition prompted him to supply the place of his absent sovereign.

Gregory awakened the emperor from a long slumber; exposed the guilt or incapacity of the exarch and his inferior ministers; complained that the veterans were withdrawn from Rome for the defence of Spoleto; encouraged the Italians to guard their cities and altars; and condescended, in the crisis of danger, to name the tribunes and to direct the operations of the provincial troops. But the martial spirit of the pope was checked by the scruples of humanity and religion: the imposition of tribute, though it was employed in the Italian war, he freely condemned as odious and oppressive; whilst he protected, against the Imperial edicts, the pious cowardice of the soldiers who deserted a military for a monastic life. If we may credit his own declarations, it would have been easy for Gregory to exterminate the Lombards by their domestic factions, without leaving a king, a duke, or a count, to save that unfortunate nation from the vengeance of their foes. As a Christian bishop, he preferred the salutary offices of peace; his mediation appeased the tumult of arms; but he was too conscious of the arts of the Greeks and the passions of the Lombards to engage his sacred promise for the observance of the truce. Disappointed in the hope of a general and lasting treaty, he presumed to save his country without the consent of the emperor or the exarch. The sword of the enemy was suspended over Rome; it was averted by the mild eloquence and seasonable gifts of the pontiff, who commanded the respect of heretics and barbarians. The merits of Gregory were treated by the Byzantine court with reproach and insult; but in the attachment of a grateful people he found the purest reward of a citizen, and the best right of a sovereign.

In the following chapter, 46, Gibbon describes the end of the dynasty of Justinian and the beginning of the new dynasty of Heraclius.

The end of the dynasty of Justinian first under Maurice (582–602) and then Phocas (602–610) witnessed a progress from extreme weakness almost to sheer anarchy with foreign invasions and internal disruption.

During the reign of Heraclius (610–642) the Persians in a long war sacked Jerusalem, invaded Egypt and with the Avars nearly took Constantinople. The Persian power, however, was crushed forever in 628 by Heraclius, who also held the Slavs in the Balkans in check.

The key to the endless theories of the Incarnation which Gibbon discusses in Chapter 47 is the difference between the Nicaean Doctrine and that of the Monophysites. The latter appealed widely to the peoples of the eastern provinces, who recognised in Jesus simply a god incarnate. The body was of human form but the nature was single and divine.

THEOLOGICAL INFLUENCES

Chapter 47

HISTORY OF THE DOCTRINE OF THE INCARNATION. THE EBIONITES AND GNOSTICS. OPPOSITE THEORIES OF CERINTHUS AND APOLLINARIS, CYRIL, NESTORIUS AND THE FIRST COUNCIL OF EPHESUS. HERESY OF EUTYCHES AND THE SECOND COUNCIL OF EPHESUS. THE COUNCIL OF CHALCEDON. THE *HENOTICON* OF ZENO. THEOLOGY OF JUSTINIAN

AFTER the extinction of paganism, the Christians in peace and piety might have enjoyed their solitary triumph. But the principle of discord was alive in their bosom, and they were more solicitous to explore the nature, than to practise the laws, of their founder. I have already observed that the disputes of the TRINITY were succeeded by those of the INCARNATION; alike scandalous to the church, alike pernicious to the state, still more minute in their origin, still more durable in their effects. It is my design to comprise in the present chapter a religious war of two hundred and fifty years, to represent the ecclesiastical and political schism of the Oriental sects, and to introduce their clamorous or sanguinary contests, by a modest inquiry into the doctrines of the primitive church.

THE EBIONITES

I. A laudable regard for the honour of the first proselytes has countenanced the belief, the hope, the wish, that the Ebionites, or at least the Nazarenes, were distinguished only by their obstinate perseverance in the practice of the Mosaic rites. Their churches have disappeared, their books are obliterated: their obscure freedom might allow a latitude of faith, and the softness of their infant creed would be variously moulded by the zeal or prudence of three hundred years. Yet the most charitable criticism must refuse these sectaries any knowledge of the pure and proper divinity of Christ. Educated in the school of Jewish prophecy and prejudice, they had never been taught to elevate their hopes above an human and temporal Messiah. If they had courage to hail their king when he appeared in a plebeian garb, their grosser apprehensions were incapable of discerning their God, who had studiously disguised his celestial character under the name and person of a mortal.[1] The familiar companions of Jesus of Nazareth conversed with their

---

[1] Chrysostom and Athanasius are obliged to confess that the divinity of Christ is rarely mentioned by himself or his apostles.

friend and countryman, who, in all the actions of rational and animal life, appeared of the same species with themselves. His progress from infancy to youth and manhood was marked by a regular increase in stature and wisdom; and after a painful agony of mind and body, he expired on the cross. He lived and died for the service of mankind: but the life and death of Socrates had likewise been devoted to the cause of religion and justice; and although the stoic or the hero may disdain the humble virtues of Jesus, the tears which he shed over his friend and country may be esteemed the purest evidence of his humanity. The miracles of the gospel could not astonish a people who held with intrepid faith the more splendid prodigies of the Mosaic law. The prophets of ancient days had cured diseases, raised the dead, divided the sea, stopped the sun, and ascended to heaven in a fiery chariot. And the metaphorical style of the Hebrews might ascribe to a saint and martyr the adoptive title of SON OF GOD.

Yet in the insufficient creed of the Nazarenes and the Ebionites a distinction is faintly noticed between the heretics, who confounded the generation of Christ in the common order of nature, and the less guilty schismatics, who revered the virginity of his mother, and excluded the aid of an earthly father. The incredulity of the former was countenanced by the visible circumstances of his birth, the legal marriage of his reputed parents, Joseph and Mary, and his lineal claim to the kingdom of David and the inheritance of Judah. But the secret and authentic history has been recorded in several copies of the Gospel according to St. Matthew, which these sectaries long preserved in the original Hebrew, as the sole evidence of their faith. The natural suspicions of the husband, conscious of his own chastity, were dispelled by the assurance (in a dream) that his wife was pregnant of the Holy Ghost: and as this distant and domestic prodigy could not fall under the personal observation of the historian, he must have listened to the same voice which dictated to Isaiah the future conception of a virgin. The son of a virgin, generated by the ineffable operation of the Holy Spirit, was a creature without example or resemblance, superior in every attribute of mind and body to the children of Adam. Since the introduction of the Greek or Chaldean philosophy, the Jews were persuaded of the pre-existence, transmigration, and immortality of souls; and Providence was justified by a supposition that they were confined in their earthly prisons to expiate the stains which they had contracted in a former state. But the degrees of purity and corruption are almost immeasurable. It might be fairly presumed that the most sublime and virtuous of human spirits was infused into the offspring of Mary and the Holy Ghost; that his abasement was the result of his voluntary choice; and that the object of his mission was to purify, not his own, but the sins of the world. On his return to his native skies he received the immense reward of his obedience: the everlasting kingdom of the Messiah, which had been darkly foretold by the prophets, under the carnal images of peace, of conquest, and of dominion. Omnipotence could enlarge the human faculties of Christ to the extent of his celestial office. In the language of antiquity, the title of God has not been severely confined to the first parent; and his incomparable minister, his only begotten Son, might claim, without presumption, the religious, though secondary, worship of a subject world.

THE GNOSTICS

II. The seeds of the faith, which had slowly arisen in the rocky and ungrateful soil of Judea, were transplanted, in full maturity, to the happier climes of the Gentiles; and the strangers of Rome or Asia, who never beheld the manhood, were the more readily disposed to embrace the divinity, of Christ. The polytheist and the philosopher, the Greek and the barbarian, were alike accustomed to conceive a long succession, an infinite chain of angels, or dæmons, or deities, or æons, or emanations, issuing from the throne of light. Nor could it seem strange or incredible that the first of these æons, the *Logos*, or Word of God, of the same substance with the Father, should descend upon earth, to deliver the human race from vice and error, and to conduct them in the paths of life and immortality. But the prevailing doctrine of the eternity and inherent pravity of matter infected the primitive churches of the East. Many among the Gentile proselytes refused to believe that a celestial spirit, an undivided portion of the first essence, had been personally united with a mass of impure and contaminated flesh: and, in their zeal for the divinity, they piously abjured the humanity, of Christ. While his blood was still recent on Mount Calvary, the *Docetes*, a numerous and learned sect of Asiatics, invented the *phantastic* system, which was afterwards propagated by the Marcionites, the Manichæans, and the various names of the Gnostic heresy. They denied the truth and authenticity of the gospels, as far as they relate the conception of Mary, the birth of Christ, and the thirty years that preceded the exercise of his ministry. He first appeared on the banks of the Jordan in the form of perfect manhood; but it was a form only, and not a substance; an human figure created by the hand of Omnipotence to imitate the faculties and actions of a man, and to impose a perpetual illusion on the senses of his friends and enemies. Articulate sounds vibrated on the ears of the disciples; but the image which was impressed on their optic nerve eluded the more stubborn evidence of the touch; and they enjoyed the spiritual, not the corporeal, presence of the Son of God. The rage of the Jews was idly wasted against an impassive phantom; and the mystic scenes of the passion and death, the resurrection and ascension of Christ, were represented on the theatre of Jerusalem for the benefit of mankind. If it were urged that such ideal mimicry, such incessant deception, was unworthy of the God of truth, the Docetes agreed with too many of their orthodox brethren in the justification of pious falsehood. In the system of the Gnostics the Jehovah of Israel, the Creator of this lower world, was a rebellious, or at least an ignorant, spirit. The Son of God descended upon earth to abolish his temple and his law; and, for the accomplishment of this salutary end, he dexterously transferred to his own person the hope and prediction of a temporal Messiah.

One of the most subtle disputants of the Manichæan school has pressed the danger and indecency of supposing that the God of the Christians, in the state of an human fœtus, emerged at the end of nine months from a female womb. The pious horror of his antagonists provoked them to disclaim all sensual circumstances of conception and delivery; to maintain that the divinity passed through Mary like a sunbeam through a plate of glass; and to assert that the seal of her virginity remained unbroken even at the moment when she became the mother of Christ. But the rashness of these concessions has encouraged a milder sentiment of those Docetes who taught, not that Christ was a phantom, but that he was clothed with an impassible and incorruptible body. Such, indeed, in the more orthodox system, he has acquired since his resurrection, and such he must have always possessed, if it were capable of pervading, without resistance or injury, the density of intermediate matter. Devoid of its most essential properties, it might be exempt from the attributes and infirmities of the flesh. A fœtus that could increase from an invisible point to its full maturity; a child that could attain the stature of perfect manhood, without deriving any nourishment from the ordinary sources, might continue to exist without repairing a daily waste by a daily supply of external matter. Jesus might share the repasts of his disciples without being subject to the calls of thirst or hunger; and his virgin purity was never sullied by the involuntary stains of sensual concupiscence. Of a body thus singularly constituted, a question would arise, by what means and of what materials it was originally framed; and our sounder theology is startled by an answer which was not peculiar to the Gnostics, that both the form and the substance proceeded from the divine essence. The idea of pure and absolute spirit is a refinement of modern philosophy: the incorporeal essence, ascribed by the ancients to human souls, celestial beings, and even the Deity himself, does not exclude the notion of extended space; and their imagination was satisfied with a subtle nature of air, or fire, or æther, incomparably more perfect than the grossness of the material world. If we define the place, we must describe the figure, of the Deity. Our experience, perhaps our vanity, represents the powers of reason and virtue under an human form. The Anthropomorphites, who swarmed among the monks of Egypt and the Catholics of Africa, could produce the express declaration of Scripture, that man was made after the image of his Creator. The venerable Serapion, one of the saints of the Nitrian desert, relinquished, with many a tear, his darling prejudice; and bewailed, like an infant, his unlucky conversion, which had stolen away his God, and left his mind without any visible object of faith or devotion.

OPPOSITE THEORIES OF CERINTHUS AND APOLLINARIS

III. Such were the fleeting shadows of the Docetes. A more substantial, though less simple hypothesis, was contrived by Cerinthus of Asia,[1] who dared to oppose the last of the apostles. Placed on the confines of the Jewish and Gentile world, he laboured to reconcile the Gnostic with the Ebionite, by confessing in the same Messiah the supernatural union of a man and a God; and this mystic doctrine was adopted with many fanciful improvements by Carpocrates, Basilides, and Valentine, the heretics of the Egyptian school. In their eyes Jesus of Nazareth was a mere mortal, the legitimate son of Joseph and Mary: but he was the best and wisest of the human race, selected as the worthy instrument to restore upon earth the worship of the true and supreme Deity. When he was baptized in the Jordan, the Christ, the first of the æons, the Son of God himself, descended on Jesus in the form of a dove, to inhabit his mind and direct his actions during the allotted period of his ministry. When the Messiah was delivered into the hands of the Jews, the Christ, an immortal and impassible being, forsook his earthly tabernacle, flew back to the *pleroma* or world of spirits, and left the solitary Jesus to suffer, to complain, and to expire. But the justice and generosity of such a desertion are strongly questionable; and the fate of an innocent martyr, at first impelled, and at length abandoned, by his divine companion, might provoke the pity and indignation of the profane. Their murmurs were variously silenced by the sectaries who espoused and modified the double system of Cerinthus. It was alleged that, when Jesus was nailed to the cross, he was endowed with a miraculous apathy of mind and body, which rendered him insensible of his apparent sufferings. It was affirmed that these momentary, though real pangs, would be abundantly repaid by the temporal reign of a thousand years reserved for the Messiah in his kingdom of the new Jerusalem. It was insinuated that if he suffered, he deserved to suffer; that human nature is never absolutely perfect; and that the cross and passion might serve to expiate the venial transgressions of the son of Joseph, before his mysterious union with the Son of God.

IV. All those who believe the immateriality of the soul, a specious and noble tenet, must confess, from their present experience, the incompre-

---

[1] St. John and Cerinthus accidentally met in the public bath of Ephesus; but the apostle fled from the heretic lest the building should tumble on their heads. This foolish story, reprobated by Dr. Middleton is related however by Irenæus, on the evidence of Polycarp, and was probably suited to the time and residence of Cerinthus. The obsolete, yet probably the true, reading of 1 John iv. 3—ὁ λύει τὸν Ἰησοῦν—alludes to the double nature of that primitive heretic.

hensible union of mind and matter. A similar union is not inconsistent with a much higher, or even with the highest, degree of mental faculties; and the incarnation of an æon or archangel, the most perfect of created spirits, does not involve any positive contradiction or absurdity. In the age of religious freedom, which was determined by the council of Nice, the dignity of Christ was measured by private judgment according to the indefinite rule of Scripture, or reason, or tradition. But when his pure and proper divinity had been established on the ruins of Arianism, the faith of the Catholics trembled on the edge of a precipice where it was impossible to recede, dangerous to stand, dreadful to fall; and the manifold inconveniences of their creed were aggravated by the sublime character of their theology. They hesitated to pronounce—*that* God himself, the second person of an equal and consubstantial trinity, was manifested in the flesh;[1] *that* a being who pervades the universe had been confined in the womb of Mary; *that* his eternal duration had been marked by the days, and months, and years of human existence; *that* the Almighty had been scourged and crucified; *that* his impassible essence had felt pain and anguish; *that* his omniscience was not exempt from ignorance; and *that* the source of life and immortality expired on Mount Calvary. These alarming consequences were affirmed with unblushing simplicity by Apollinaris, bishop of Laodicea, and one of the luminaries of the church. The son of a learned grammarian, he was skilled in all the sciences of Greece; eloquence, erudition, and philosophy, conspicuous in the volumes of Apollinaris, were humbly devoted to the service of religion. The worthy friend of Athanasius, the worthy antagonist of Julian, he bravely wrestled with the Arians and Polytheists, and, though he affected the rigour of geometrical demonstration, his commentaries revealed the literal and allegorical sense of the Scriptures. A mystery which had long floated in the looseness of popular belief was defined by his perverse diligence in a technical form; and he first proclaimed the memorable words, "One incarnate nature of Christ," which are still re-echoed with hostile clamours in the churches of Asia, Egypt, and Ethiopia. He taught that the Godhead was united or mingled with the body of a man; and that the *Logos*, the eternal wisdom, supplied in the flesh the place and office of an human soul. Yet, as the profound doctor

---

[1] This strong expression might be justified by the language of St. Paul (1 Tim. iii. 16); but we are deceived by our modern Bibles. The word ὅ (*which*) was altered to θεός (*God*) at Constantinople in the beginning of the vith century: the true reading, which is visible in the Latin and Syriac versions, still exists in the reasoning of the Greek as well as of the Latin fathers; and this fraud, with that of the *three witnesses of St. John*, is admirably detected by Sir Isaac Newton. I have weighed the arguments, and may yield to the authority of the first of philosophers, who was deeply skilled in critical and theological studies. [It should be ὅς. The weight of authority is so much against the common reading on both these points, that they are no longer urged by prudent controversialists. Would Gibbon's deference for the *first of philosophers* have extended to *all* his theological conclusions?—Milman.]

had been terrified at his own rashness, Apollinaris was heard to mutter some faint accents of excuse and explanation. He acquiesced in the old distinction of the Greek philosophers between the rational and sensitive soul of man; that he might reserve the *Logos* for intellectual functions, and employ the subordinate human principle in the meaner actions of animal life. With the moderate Docetes he revered Mary as the spiritual, rather than as the carnal, mother of Christ, whose body either came from heaven, impassible and incorruptible, or was absorbed, and as it were transformed, into the essence of the Deity. The system of Apollinaris was strenuously encountered by the Asiatic and Syrian divines, whose schools are honoured by the names of Basil, Gregory, and Chrysostom, and tainted by those of Diodorus, Theodore, and Nestorius. But the person of the aged bishop of Laodicea, his character and dignity, remained inviolate; and his rivals, since we may not suspect them of the weakness of toleration, were astonished, perhaps, by the novelty of the argument, and diffident of the final sentence of the Catholic church. Her judgment at length inclined in their favour; the heresy of Apollinaris was condemned, and the separate congregations of his disciples were proscribed by the Imperial laws. But his principles were secretly entertained in the monasteries of Egypt, and his enemies felt the hatred of Theophilus and Cyril, the successive patriarchs of Alexandria.

V. The grovelling Ebionite and the fantastic Docetes were rejected and forgotten: the recent zeal against the errors of Apollinaris reduced the Catholics to a seeming agreement with the double nature of Cerinthus. But instead of a temporary and occasional alliance, *they* established, and *we* still embrace, the substantial, indissoluble, and everlasting union of a perfect God with a perfect man, of the second person of the trinity with a reasonable soul and human flesh. In the beginning of the fifth century the *unity* of the *two natures* was the prevailing doctrine of the church. On all sides it was confessed that the mode of their co-existence could neither be represented by our ideas nor expressed by our language. Yet a secret and incurable discord was cherished between those who were most apprehensive of confounding, and those who were most fearful of separating, the divinity and the humanity of Christ. Impelled by religious frenzy, they fled with adverse haste from the error which they mutually deemed most destructive of truth and salvation. On either hand they were anxious to guard, they were jealous to defend, the union and the distinction of the two natures, and to invent such forms of speech, such symbols of doctrine, as were least susceptible of doubt or ambiguity. The poverty of ideas and language tempted them to ransack art and nature for every possible comparison, and each comparison misled their fancy in the explanation of an incomparable mystery. In the polemic microscope an atom is enlarged to a monster, and each party was skilful to exaggerate the absurd or impious conclusions that might be extorted from the principles of their adversaries.

To escape from each other they wandered through many a dark and devious thicket, till they were astonished by the horrid phantoms of Cerinthus and Apollinaris, who guarded the opposite issues of the theological labyrinth. As soon as they beheld the twilight of sense and heresy, they started, measured back their steps, and were again involved in the gloom of impenetrable orthodoxy. To purge themselves from the guilt or reproach of damnable error, they disavowed their consequences, explained their principles, excused their indiscretions, and unanimously pronounced the sounds of concord and faith. Yet a latent and almost invisible spark still lurked among the embers of controversy: by the breath of prejudice and passion it was quickly kindled to a mighty flame, and the verbal disputes of the Oriental sects have shaken the pillars of the church and state.

CYRIL, NESTORIUS AND THE FIRST
COUNCILS OF EPHESUS

The name of CYRIL of Alexandria is famous in controversial story, and the title of *saint* is a mark that his opinions and his party have finally prevailed. In the house of his uncle, the archbishop Theophilus, he imbibed the orthodox lessons of zeal and dominion, and five years of his youth were profitably spent in the adjacent monasteries of Nitria. Under the tuition of the abbot Serapion, he applied himself to ecclesiastical studies with such indefatigable ardour, that in the course of *one* sleepless night he had perused the four gospels, the catholic epistles, and the epistle to the Romans. Origen he detested; but the writings of Clemens and Dionysius, of Athanasius and Basil, were continually in his hands: by the theory and practice of dispute, his faith was confirmed and his wit was sharpened; he extended round his cell the cobwebs of scholastic theology, and meditated the works of allegory and metaphysics, whose remains, in seven verbose folios, now peaceably slumber by the side of their rivals. Cyril prayed and fasted in the desert, but his thoughts (it is the reproach of a friend) were still fixed on the world; and the call of Theophilus, who summoned him to the tumult of cities and synods, was too readily obeyed by the aspiring hermit. With the approbation of his uncle he assumed the office and acquired the fame of a popular preacher. His comely person adorned the pulpit; the harmony of his voice resounded in the cathedral; his friends were stationed to lead or second the applause of the congregation; and the hasty notes of the scribes preserved his discourses, which, in their effect, though not in their composition, might be compared with those of the Athenian orators. The death of Theophilus expanded and realised the hopes of his nephew. The clergy of Alexandria was divided; the soldiers and their general supported the claims of the archdeacon; but a resistless multitude, with voices and with hands, asserted the cause of their favourite;

and after a period of thirty-nine years Cyril was seated on the throne of Athanasius.

The prize was not unworthy of his ambition. At a distance from the court, and at the head of an immense capital, the patriarch, as he was now styled, of Alexandria had gradually usurped the state and authority of a civil magistrate. The public and private charities of the city were managed by his discretion; his voice inflamed or appeased the passions of the multitude; his commands were blindly obeyed by his numerous and fanatic *parabolani*, familiarised in their daily office with scenes of death; and the prefects of Egypt were awed or provoked by the temporal power of these Christian pontiffs. Ardent in the prosecution of heresy, Cyril auspiciously opened his reign by oppressing the Novatians, the most innocent and harmless of the sectaries. The interdiction of their religious worship appeared in his eyes a just and meritorious act; and he confiscated their holy vessels, without apprehending the guilt of sacrilege. The toleration, and even the privileges of the Jews, who had multiplied to the number of forty thousand, were secured by the laws of the Cæsars and Ptolemies, and a long prescription of seven hundred years since the foundation of Alexandria. Without any legal sentence, without any royal mandate, the patriarch, at the dawn of day, led a seditious multitude to the attack of the synagogues. Unarmed and unprepared, the Jews were incapable of resistance; their houses of prayer were levelled with the ground, and the episcopal warrior, after rewarding his troops with the plunder of their goods, expelled from the city the remnant of the unbelieving nation. Perhaps he might plead the insolence of their prosperity, and their deadly hatred of the Christians, whose blood they had recently shed in a malicious or accidental tumult. Such crimes would have deserved the animadversion of the magistrate; but in this promiscuous outrage the innocent were confounded with the guilty, and Alexandria was impoverished by the loss of a wealthy and industrious colony. The zeal of Cyril exposed him to the penalties of the Julian law; but in a feeble government and a superstitious age he was secure of impunity, and even of praise. Orestes complained; but his just complaints were too quickly forgotten by the ministers of Theodosius, and too deeply remembered by a priest who affected to pardon, and continued to hate, the prefect of Egypt. As he passed through the streets his chariot was assaulted by a band of five hundred of the Nitrian monks; his guards fled from the wild beasts of the desert; his protestations that he was a Christian and a Catholic were answered by a volley of stones, and the face of Orestes was covered with blood. The loyal citizens of Alexandria hastened to his rescue; he instantly satisfied his justice and revenge against the monk by whose hand he had been wounded, and Ammonius expired under the rod of the lictor. At the command of Cyril his body was raised from the ground, and transported in solemn procession to the cathedral; the name of Ammonius was changed to that of Thaumasius, the *wonderful*; his tomb was decorated with the trophies of martyrdom; and the patriarch ascended the pulpit to celebrate the magnanimity of an assassin and a rebel. Such honours might incite the faithful to combat and die under the banners of the saint; and he soon prompted, or accepted, the sacrifice of a virgin, who professed the religion of the Greeks, and cultivated the friendship of Orestes. Hypatia, the daughter of Theon the mathematician, was initiated in her father's studies; her learned comments have elucidated the geometry of Apollonius and Diophantus; and she publicly taught, both at Athens and Alexandria, the philosophy of Plato and Aristotle. In the bloom of beauty, and in the maturity of wisdom, the modest maid refused her lovers and instructed her disciples; the persons most illustrious for their rank or merit were impatient to visit the female philosopher; and Cyril beheld with a jealous eye the gorgeous train of horses and slaves who crowded the door of her academy. A rumour was spread among the Christians that the daughter of Theon was the only obstacle to the reconciliation of the prefect and the archbishop; and that obstacle was speedily removed. On a fatal day, in the holy season of Lent, Hypatia was torn from her chariot, stripped naked, dragged to the church, and inhumanly butchered by the hands of Peter the reader and a troop of savage and merciless fanatics: her flesh was scraped from her bones with sharp oyster-shells, and her quivering limbs were delivered to the flames. The just progress of inquiry and punishment was stopped by seasonable gifts; but the murder of Hypatia has imprinted an indelible stain on the character and religion of Cyril of Alexandria.

Superstition, perhaps, would more gently expiate the blood of a virgin than the banishment of a saint; and Cyril had accompanied his uncle to the iniquitous synod of the Oak. When the memory of Chrysostom was restored and consecrated, the nephew of Theophilus, at the head of a dying faction, still maintained the justice of his sentence; nor was it till after a tedious delay and an obstinate resistance that he yielded to the consent of the Catholic world. His enmity to the Byzantine pontiffs was a sense of interest, not a sally of passion: he envied their fortunate station in the sunshine of the Imperial court; and he dreaded their upstart ambition, which oppressed the metropolitans of Europe and Asia, invaded the provinces of Antioch and Alexandria, and measured their diocese by the limits of the empire. The long moderation of Atticus, the mild usurper of the throne of Chrysostom, suspended the animosities of the Eastern patriarchs; but Cyril was at length awakened by the exaltation of a rival more worthy of his esteem and hatred. After the short and troubled reign of Sisinnius, bishop of Constantinople, the factions of the clergy and people were appeased by the choice of the emperor, who, on this occasion, consulted the voice of fame, and invited the merit of a stranger. Nestorius, a native of Germanicia, and a monk of Antioch, was recommended by the austerity of his life and the eloquence

of his sermons; but the first homily which he preached before the devout
Theodosius betrayed the acrimony and impatience of his zeal. "Give me
O Cæsar!" he exclaimed, "give me the earth purged of heretics, and I
will give you in exchange the kingdom of heaven. Exterminate with me
the heretics, and with you I will exterminate the Persians." On the fifth
day, as if the treaty had been already signed, the patriarch of Constantinople discovered, surprised, and attacked a secret conventicle of the
Arians; they preferred death to submission; the flames that were kindled
by their despair soon spread to the neighbouring houses, and the
triumph of Nestorius was clouded by the name of *incendiary*. On either
side of the Hellespont his episcopal vigour imposed a rigid formulary of
faith and discipline—a chronological error concerning the festival of
Easter was punished as an offence against the church and state. Lydia
and Caria, Sardes and Miletus, were purified with the blood of the
obstinate Quartodecimans; and the edict of the emperor, or rather of
the patriarch, enumerates three-and-twenty degrees and denominations
in the guilt and punishment of heresy. But the sword of persecution
which Nestorius so furiously wielded was soon turned against his own
breast. Religion was the pretence; but, in the judgment of a contemporary saint, ambition was the genuine motive of episcopal warfare.

In the Syrian school Nestorius had been taught to abhor the confusion of the two natures, and nicely to discriminate the humanity of his
master Christ from the divinity of the *Lord* Jesus. The Blessed Virgin
he revered as the mother of Christ, but his ears were offended with the
rash and recent title of mother of God, which had been insensibly
adopted since the origin of the Arian controversy. From the pulpit of
Constantinople, a friend of the patriarch, and afterwards the patriarch
himself, repeatedly preached against the use, or the abuse, of a word
unknown to the apostles, unauthorised by the church, and which could
only tend to alarm the timorous, to mislead the simple, to amuse the
profane, and to justify, by a seeming resemblance, the old genealogy of
Olympus. In his calmer moments Nestorius confessed that it might be
tolerated or excused by the union of the two natures, and the communication of their *idioms*: but he was exasperated by contradiction to disclaim the worship of a new-born, an infant Deity, to draw his inadequate
similes from the conjugal or civil partnerships of life, and to describe
the manhood of Christ as the robe, the instrument, the tabernacle of his
Godhead. At these blasphemous sounds the pillars of the sanctuary were
shaken. The unsuccessful competitors of Nestorius indulged their pious
or personal resentment, the Byzantine clergy was secretly displeased
with the intrusion of a stranger: whatever is superstitious or absurd
might claim the protection of the monks; and the people was interested
in the glory of their virgin patroness. The sermons of the archbishop,
and the service of the altar, were disturbed by seditious clamour; his
authority and doctrine were renounced by separate congregations; every

wind scattered round the empire the leaves of controversy; and the voice of the combatants on a sonorous theatre re-echoed in the cells of Palestine and Egypt. It was the duty of Cyril to enlighten the zeal and ignorance of his innumerable monks: in the school of Alexandria he had imbibed and professed the incarnation of one nature; and the successor of Athanasius consulted his pride and ambition when he rose in arms against another Arius, more formidable and more guilty, on the second throne of the hierarchy. After a short correspondence, in which the rival prelates disguised their hatred in the hollow language of respect and charity, the patriarch of Alexandria denounced to the prince and people, to the East and to the West, the damnable errors of the Byzantine pontiff. From the East, more especially from Antioch, he obtained the ambiguous counsels of toleration and silence, which were addressed to both parties while they favoured the cause of Nestorius. But the Vatican received with open arms the messengers of Egypt. The vanity of Celestine was flattered by the appeal; and the partial version of a monk decided the faith of the pope, who, with his Latin clergy, was ignorant of the language, the arts, and the theology of the Greeks. At the head of an Italian synod, Celestine weighed the merits of the cause, approved the creed of Cyril, condemned the sentiments and person of Nestorius, degraded the heretic from his episcopal dignity, allowed a respite of ten days for recantation and penance, and delegated to his enemy the execution of this rash and illegal sentence. But the patriarch of Alexandria, whilst he darted the thunders of a god, exposed the errors and passions of a mortal; and his twelve anathemas still torture the orthodox slaves who adore the memory of a saint without forfeiting their allegiance to the synod of Chalcedon. These bold assertions are indelibly tinged with the colours of the Apollinarian heresy; but the serious, and perhaps the sincere, professions of Nestorius have satisfied the wiser and less partial theologians of the present times.

Yet neither the emperor nor the primate of the East were disposed to obey the mandate of an Italian priest; and a synod of the Catholic, or rather of the Greek, church was unanimously demanded as the sole remedy that could appease or decide this ecclesiastical quarrel. Ephesus, on all sides accessible by sea and land, was chosen for the place, the festival of Pentecost for the day, of the meeting; a writ of summons was despatched to each metropolitan, and a guard was stationed to protect and confine the fathers till they should settle the mysteries of heaven and the faith of the earth. Nestorius appeared not as a criminal, but as a judge; he depended on the weight rather than the number of his prelates, and his sturdy slaves from the baths of Zeuxippus were armed for every service of injury or defence. But his adversary Cyril was more powerful in the weapons both of the flesh and of the spirit. Disobedient to the letter, or at least to the meaning, of the royal summons, he was attended by fifty Egyptian bishops, who expected from their patriarch's nod the inspiration of the Holy Ghost. He had contracted an intimate alliance with Memnon bishop of Ephesus. The despotic primate of Asia disposed of the ready succours of thirty or forty episcopal votes: a crowd of peasants, the slaves of the church, was poured into the city to support with blows and clamours a metaphysical argument; and the people zealously asserted the honour of the Virgin, whose body reposed within the walls of Ephesus.[1] The fleet which had transported Cyril from Alexandria was laden with the riches of Egypt; and he disembarked a numerous body of mariners, slaves, and fanatics, enlisted with blind obedience under the banner of St. Mark and the mother of God. The fathers, and even the guards, of the church were awed by this martial array; the adversaries of Cyril and Mary were insulted in the streets, or threatened in their houses; his eloquence and liberality made a daily increase in the number of his adherents; and the Egyptian soon computed that he might command the attendance and the voices of two hundred bishops. But the author of the twelve anathemas foresaw and dreaded the opposition of John of Antioch, who, with a small though respectable train of metropolitans and divines, was advancing by slow journeys from the distant capital of the East. Impatient of a delay which he stigmatised as voluntary and culpable, Cyril announced the opening of the synod sixteen days after the festival of Pentecost. Nestorius, who depended on the near approach of his Eastern friends, persisted, like his predecessor Chrysostom, to disclaim the jurisdiction, and to disobey the summons, of his enemies: they hastened his trial, and his accuser presided in the seat of judgment. Sixty-eight bishops, twenty-two of metropolitan rank, defended his cause by a modest and temperate protest: they were excluded from the councils of their brethren. Candidian, in the emperor's name, requested a delay of four days; the profane magistrate was driven with outrage and insult from the assembly of the saints. The whole of this momentous transaction was crowded into the compass of a summer's day: the bishops delivered their separate opinions; but the uniformity of style reveals the influence or the hand of a master, who has been accused of corrupting the public evidence of their acts and subscriptions. Without a dissenting voice they recognised in the epistles of Cyril the Nicene creed and the doctrine of the fathers: but the partial extracts from the letters and homilies of Nestorius were interrupted by curses and anathemas; and the heretic was degraded from his episcopal and ecclesiastical dignity. The sentence, maliciously inscribed to the new Judas, was affixed and proclaimed in the streets of Ephesus: the weary prelates, as they issued from the church of the

---

[1] The Christians of the four first centuries were ignorant of the death and burial of Mary. The tradition of Ephesus is affirmed by the synod; yet it has been superseded by the claim of Jerusalem; and her *empty* sepulchre, as it was shown to the pilgrims, produced the fable of her resurrection and assumption, in which the Greek and Latin churches have piously acquiesced.

mother of God, were saluted as her champions; and her victory was celebrated by the illuminations, the songs, and the tumult of the night.

On the fifth day the triumph was clouded by the arrival and indignation of the Eastern bishops. In a chamber of the inn, before he had wiped the dust from his shoes, John of Antioch gave audience to Candidian the Imperial minister, who related his ineffectual efforts to prevent or to annul the hasty violence of the Egyptian. With equal haste and violence the Oriental synod of fifty bishops degraded Cyril and Memnon from their episcopal honours; condemned, in the twelve anathemas, the purest venom of the Apollinarian heresy; and described the Alexandrian primate as a monster, born and educated for the destruction of the church. *His* throne was distant and inaccessible; but they instantly resolved to bestow on the flock of Ephesus the blessing of a faithful shepherd. By the vigilance of Memnon the churches were shut against them, and a strong garrison was thrown into the cathedral. The troops, under the command of Candidian, advanced to the assault; the outguards were routed and put to the sword, but the place was impregnable: the besiegers retired; their retreat was pursued by a vigorous sally; they lost their horses, and many of the soldiers were dangerously wounded with clubs and stones. Ephesus, the city of the Virgin, was defiled with rage and clamour, with sedition and blood; the rival synods darted anathemas and excommunications from their spiritual engines; and the court of Theodosius was perplexed by the adverse and contradictory narratives of the Syrian and Egyptian factions. During a busy period of three months the emperor tried every method, except the most effectual means of indifference and contempt, to reconcile this theological quarrel. He attempted to remove or intimidate the leaders by a common sentence of acquittal or condemnation; he invested his representatives at Ephesus with ample power and military force; he summoned from either party eight chosen deputies to a free and candid conference in the neighbourhood of the capital, far from the contagion of popular frenzy. But the Orientals refused to yield, and the Catholics, proud of their numbers and of their Latin allies, rejected all terms of union or toleration. The patience of the meek Theodosius was provoked, and he dissolved in anger this episcopal tumult, which at the distance of thirteen centuries assumes the venerable aspect of the third oecumenical council. "God is my witness," said the pious prince, "that I am not the author of this confusion. His providence will discern and punish the guilty. Return to your provinces, and may your private virtues repair the mischief and scandal of your meeting." They returned to their provinces; but the same passions which had distracted the synod of Ephesus were diffused over the Eastern world. After three obstinate and equal campaigns, John of Antioch and Cyril of Alexandria condescended to explain and embrace: but their seeming re-union must be imputed rather to prudence than to reason, to the mutual lassitude rather than to the Christian charity of the patriarchs.

The Byzantine pontiff had instilled into the royal ear a baleful prejudice against the character and conduct of his Egyptian rival. An epistle of menace and invective, which accompanied the summons, accused him as a busy, insolent, and envious priest, who perplexed the simplicity of the faith, violated the peace of the church and state, and, by his artful and separate addresses to the wife and sister of Theodosius, presumed to suppose, or to scatter, the seeds of discord in the Imperial family. At the stern command of his sovereign, Cyril had repaired to Ephesus, where he was resisted, threatened, and confined, by the magistrates in the interest of Nestorius and the Orientals, who assembled the troops of Lydia and Ionia to suppress the fanatic and disorderly train of the patriarch. Without expecting the royal licence, he escaped from his guards, precipitately embarked, deserted the imperfect synod, and retired to his episcopal fortress of safety and independence. But his artful emissaries, both in the court and city, successfully laboured to appease the resentment, and to conciliate the favour, of the emperor. The feeble son of Arcadius was alternately swayed by his wife and sister, by the eunuchs and women of the palace: superstition and avarice were their ruling passions; and the orthodox chiefs were assiduous in their endeavours to alarm the former and to gratify the latter. Constantinople and the suburbs were sanctified with frequent monasteries, and the holy abbots, Dalmatius and Eutyches, had devoted their zeal and fidelity to the cause of Cyril, the worship of Mary, and the unity of Christ. From the first moment of their monastic life they had never mingled with the world, or trod the profane ground of the city. But in this awful moment of the danger of the church, their vow was superseded by a more sublime and indispensable duty. At the head of a long order of monks and hermits, who carried burning tapers in their hands, and chanted litanies to the mother of God, they proceeded from their monasteries to the palace. The people was edified and inflamed by this extraordinary spectacle, and the trembling monarch listened to the prayers and adjurations of the saints, who boldly pronounced that none could hope for salvation unless they embraced the person and the creed of the orthodox successor of Athanasius. At the same time every avenue of the throne was assaulted with gold. Under the decent names of *eulogies* and *benedictions*, the courtiers of both sexes were bribed according to the measure of their power and rapaciousness. But their incessant demands despoiled the sanctuaries of Constantinople and Alexandria; and the authority of the patriarch was unable to silence the just murmur of his clergy, that a debt of sixty thousand pounds had already been contracted to support the expense of this scandalous corruption. Pulcheria, who relieved her brother from the weight of an empire, was the firmest pillar of orthodoxy; and so intimate was the alliance between the thunders of the synod and the whispers of the court, that Cyril was assured of success if he could displace one eunuch, and substitute another in the favour of Theodosius. Yet the Egyptian could not boast of a glorious or decisive victory. The emperor, with unaccustomed firmness, adhered to his promise of protecting the innocence of the Oriental bishops; and Cyril softened his anathemas, and confessed, with ambiguity and reluctance, a twofold nature of Christ, before he was permitted to satiate his revenge against the unfortunate Nestorius.

The rash and obstinate Nestorius, before the end of the synod, was oppressed by Cyril, betrayed by the court, and faintly supported by his Eastern friends. A sentiment of fear or indignation prompted him, while it was yet time, to affect the glory of a voluntary abdication: his wish, or at least his request, was readily granted; he was conducted with honour from Ephesus to his old monastery of Antioch; and, after a short pause, his successors, Maximian and Proclus, were acknowledged as the lawful bishops of Constantinople. But in the silence of his cell the degraded patriarch could no longer resume the innocence and security of a private monk. The past he regretted, he was discontented with the present, and the future he had reason to dread: the Oriental bishops successively disengaged their cause from his unpopular name, and each day decreased the number of the schismatics who revered Nestorius as the confessor of the faith. After a residence at Antioch of four years, the hand of Theodosius subscribed an edict which ranked him with Simon the magician, proscribed his opinions and followers, condemned his writings to the flames, and banished his person first to Petra in Arabia, and at length to Oasis, one of the *islands* of the Libyan desert. Secluded from the church and from the world, the exile was still pursued by the rage of bigotry and war. A wandering tribe of the Blemmyes or Nubians invaded his solitary prison: in their retreat they dismissed a crowd of useless captives; but no sooner had Nestorius reached the banks of the Nile, than he would gladly have escaped from a Roman and orthodox city to the milder servitude of the savages. His flight was punished as a new crime: the soul of the patriarch inspired the civil and ecclesiastical powers of Egypt; the magistrates, the soldiers, the monks, devoutly tortured the enemy of Christ and St. Cyril; and, as far as the confines of Ethiopia, the heretic was alternately dragged and recalled, till his aged body was broken by the hardships and accidents of these reiterated journeys. Yet his mind was still independent and erect; the president of Thebais was awed by his pastoral letters; he survived the Catholic tyrant of Alexandria, and, after sixteen years' banishment, the synod of Chalcedon would perhaps have restored him to the honours, or at least to the communion, of the church. The death of Nestorius prevented his obedience to their welcome summons; and his disease might afford some colour to the scandalous report, that his tongue, the organ of blasphemy, had been eaten by the worms. He was buried in a city of Upper Egypt, known by the names of Chemnis, or Panopolis, or Akmim; but the immortal malice of the Jacobites has persevered for ages to cast stones against his sepulchre, and to propagate the foolish tradition that it was never watered by the rain of heaven, which equally descends on the righteous and the ungodly. Humanity may drop a tear on the fate of Nestorius; yet justice must observe that he suffered the persecution which he had approved and inflicted.

HERESY OF EUTYCHES AND SECOND COUNCIL OF EPHESUS

The death of the Alexandrian primate, after a reign of thirty-two years, abandoned the Catholics to the intemperance of zeal and the abuse of victory. The *monophysite* doctrine (one incarnate nature) was rigorously preached in the churches of Egypt and the monasteries of the East; the primitive creed of Apollinaris was protected by the sanctity of Cyril; and the name of EUTYCHES, his venerable friend, has been applied to the sect most adverse to the Syrian heresy of Nestorius. His rival Eutyches was the abbot, or archimandrite, or superior of three hundred monks; but the opinions of a simple and illiterate recluse might have expired in the cell where he had slept above seventy years, if the resentment or indiscretion of Flavian, the Byzantine pontiff, had not exposed the scandal to the eyes of the Christian world. His domestic synod was instantly convened, their proceedings were sullied with clamour and artifice, and the aged heretic was surprised into a seeming confession that Christ had not derived his body from the substance of the Virgin Mary. From their partial decree Eutyches appealed to a general council; and his cause was vigorously asserted by his godson Chrysaphius, the reigning eunuch of the palace, and his accomplice Dioscorus, who had succeeded to the throne, the creed, the talents, and the vices of the nephew of Theophilus. By the special summons of Theodosius, the second synod of Ephesus was judiciously composed of ten metropolitans and ten bishops from each of the six dioceses of the Eastern empire: some exceptions of favour or merit enlarged the number to one hundred and thirty-five; and the Syrian Barsumas, as the chief and representative of the monks, was invited to sit and vote with the successors of the apostles. But the despotism of the Alexandrian patriarch again oppressed the freedom of debate: the same spiritual and carnal weapons were again drawn from the arsenals of Egypt; the Asiatic veterans, a band of archers, served under the orders of Dioscorus; and the more formidable monks, whose minds were inaccessible to reason or mercy, besieged the doors of the cathedral. The general, and, as it should seem, the unconstrained voice of the fathers accepted the faith and even the anathemas of Cyril; and the heresy of the two natures was formally condemned in the persons and writings of the most learned Orientals. "May those who divide Christ be divided with the sword, may they be hewn in pieces, may they be burned alive!" were the charitable wishes of a Christian synod. The innocence and sanctity of Eutyches were acknowledged without hestitation; but the prelates, more especially those of Thrace and Asia, were unwilling to depose their patriarch for the use or even the abuse of his lawful jurisdiction. They embraced the knees of Dioscorus, as he stood with a threatening aspect on the footstool of his throne, and conjured him to forgive the offences and to respect the dignity of his brother. "Do you mean to raise a sedition?" exclaimed the relentless tyrant. "Where are the officers?" At these words a furious multitude of monks and soldiers, with staves, and swords, and chains, burst into the church: the trembling bishops hid themselves behind the altar, or under the benches; and as they were not inspired with the zeal of martyrdom, they successively subscribed a blank paper, which was afterwards filled with the condemnation of the Byzantine pontiff. Flavian was instantly delivered to the wild beasts of this spiritual amphitheatre: the monks were stimulated by the voice and example of Barsumas to avenge the injuries of Christ: it is said that the patriarch of Alexandria reviled, and buffeted, and kicked, and trampled his brother of Constantinople: it is certain that the victim, before he could reach the place of his exile, expired on the third day of the wounds and bruises which he had received at Ephesus. The second synod has been justly branded as a gang of robbers and assassins; yet the accusers of Dioscorus would magnify his violence, to alleviate the cowardice and inconstancy of their own behaviour.

THE COUNCIL OF CHALCEDON

The faith of Egypt had prevailed: but the vanquished party was supported by the same pope who encountered without fear the hostile rage of Attila and Genseric. The theology of Leo, his famous *tome* or epistle on the mystery of the incarnation, had been disregarded by the synod of Ephesus: his authority, and that of the Latin church, was insulted in his legates, who escaped from slavery and death to relate the melancholy tale of the tyranny of Dioscorus and the martyrdom of Flavian. His provincial synod annulled the irregular proceedings of Ephesus; but as this step was itself irregular, he solicited the convocation of a general council in the free and orthodox provinces of Italy. From his independent throne the Roman bishop spoke and acted without danger as the head of the Christians, and his dictates were obsequiously transcribed by Placidia and her son Valentinian, who addressed their Eastern colleague to restore the peace and unity of the church. But the pageant of Oriental royalty was moved with equal dexterity by the hand of the eunuch; and Theodosius could pronounce, without hesitation, that the church was already peaceful and triumphant, and that the recent flame had been extinguished by the just punishment of the Nestorians. Perhaps the Greeks would be still involved in the heresy of the Monophysites, if the emperor's horse had not fortunately stumbled; Theodosius

expired; his orthodox sister, Pulcheria, with a nominal husband, succeeded to the throne; Chrysaphius was burnt, Dioscorus was disgraced,
the exiles were recalled, and the *tome* of Leo was subscribed by the
Oriental bishops. Yet the pope was disappointed in his favourite project
of a Latin council: he disdained to preside in the Greek synod which
was speedily assembled at Nice in Bithynia; his legates required in a
peremptory tone the presence of the emperor; and the weary fathers
were transported to Chalcedon under the immediate eye of Marcian and
the senate of Constantinople. A quarter of a mile from the Thracian
Bosphorus the church of St. Euphemia was built on the summit of a
gentle though lofty ascent: the triple structure was celebrated as a
prodigy of art, and the boundless prospect of the land and sea might
have raised the mind of a sectary to the contemplation of the God of
the universe. Six hundred and thirty bishops were ranged in order in the
nave of the church; but the patriarchs of the East were preceded by the
legates, of whom the third was a simple priest; and the place of honour
was reserved for twenty laymen of consular or senatorian rank. The
gospel was ostentatiously displayed in the centre, but the rule of faith
was defined by the papal and imperial ministers, who moderated the
thirteen sessions of the council of Chalcedon. Their partial interposition
silenced the intemperate shouts and execrations which degraded the
episcopal gravity; but, on the formal accusation of the legates, Dioscorus
was compelled to descend from his throne to the rank of a criminal,
already condemned in the opinion of his judges. The Orientals, less
adverse to Nestorius than to Cyril, accepted the Romans as their
deliverers: Thrace, and Pontus, and Asia, were exasperated against the
murderer of Flavian, and the new patriarchs of Constantinople and
Antioch secured their places by the sacrifice of their benefactor. The
bishops of Palestine, Macedonia, and Greece were attached to the faith
of Cyril; but in the face of the synod, in the heat of the battle, the
leaders, with their obsequious train, passed from the right to the left
wing, and decided the victory by this seasonable desertion. Of the
seventeen suffragans who sailed from Alexandria, four were tempted
from their allegiance, and the thirteen, falling prostrate on the ground,
implored the mercy of the council, with sighs and tears, and a pathetic
declaration, that, if they yielded, they should be massacred, on their
return to Egypt, by the indignant people. A tardy repentance was
allowed to expiate the guilt or error of the accomplices of Dioscorus:
but their sins were accumulated on his head; he neither asked nor hoped
for pardon, and the moderation of those who pleaded for a general
amnesty was drowned in the prevailing cry of victory and revenge. To
save the reputation of his late adherents, some *personal* offences were
skilfully detected; his rash and illegal excommunication of the pope, and
his contumacious refusal (while he was detained a prisoner) to attend
the summons of the synod. Witnesses were introduced to prove the

special facts of his pride, avarice, and cruelty; and the fathers heard with abhorrence that the alms of the church were lavished on the female dancers, that his palace, and even his bath, was open to the prostitutes of Alexandria, and that the infamous Pansophia, or Irene, was publicly entertained as the concubine of the patriarch.

For these scandalous offences Dioscorus was deposed by the synod, and banished by the emperor; but the purity of his faith was declared in the presence, and with the tacit approbation, of the fathers. Their prudence supposed rather than pronounced the heresy of Eutyches, who was never summoned before their tribunal; and they sat silent and abashed, when a bold Monophysite, casting at their feet a volume of Cyril, challenged them to anathematise in his person the doctrine of the saint. If we fairly peruse the acts of Chalcedon as they are recorded by the orthodox party, we shall find that a great majority of the bishops embraced the simple unity of Christ; and the ambiguous concession that he was formed OF or FROM two natures might imply either their previous existence, or their subsequent confusion, or some dangerous interval between the conception of the man and the assumption of the God. The Roman theology, more positive and precise, adopted the term most offensive to the ears of the Egyptians, that Christ existed IN two natures; and this momentous particle (which the memory, rather than the understanding, must retain) had almost produced a schism among the Catholic bishops. The *tome* of Leo had been respectfully, perhaps sincerely, subscribed; but they protested, in two successive debates, that it was neither expedient nor lawful to transgress the sacred landmarks which had been fixed at Nice, Constantinople, and Ephesus, according to the rule of Scripture and tradition. At length they yielded to the importunities of their masters, but their infallible decree, after it had been ratified with deliberate votes and vehement acclamations, was overturned in the next session by the opposition of the legates and their Oriental friends. It was in vain that a multitude of episcopal voices repeated in chorus, "The definition of the fathers is orthodox and immutable! The heretics are now discovered! Anathema to the Nestorians! Let them depart from the synod! Let them repair to Rome." The legates threatened, the emperor was absolute, and a committee of eighteen bishops prepared a new decree, which was imposed on the reluctant assembly. In the name of the fourth general council, the Christ in one person, but *in* two natures, was announced to the Catholic world: an invisible line was drawn between the heresy of Apollinaris and the faith of St. Cyril; and the road to paradise, a bridge as sharp as a razor, was suspended over the abyss by the master-hand of the theological artist. During ten centuries of blindness and servitude Europe received her religious opinions from the oracle of the Vatican; and the same doctrine, already varnished with the rust of antiquity, was admitted without dispute into the creed of the reformers, who disclaimed the supremacy of the Roman pontiff. The synod of Chalcedon still triumphs in the Protestant churches; but the ferment of controversy has subsided, and the most pious Christians of the present day are ignorant, or careless, of their own belief concerning the mystery of the incarnation.

Far different was the temper of the Greeks and Egyptians under the orthodox reigns of Leo and Marcian. Those pious emperors enforced with arms and edicts the symbol of their faith; and it was declared by the conscience or honour of five hundred bishops, that the decrees of the synod of Chalcedon might be lawfully supported, even with blood. The Catholics observed with satisfaction that the same synod was odious both to the Nestorians and the Monophysites; but the Nestorians were less angry, or less powerful, and the East was distracted by the obstinate and sanguinary zeal of the Monophysites. Jerusalem was occupied by an army of monks; in the name of the one incarnate nature, they pillaged, they burnt, they murdered; the sepulchre of Christ was defiled with blood; and the gates of the city were guarded in tumultuous rebellion against the troops of the emperor. After the disgrace and exile of Dioscorus, the Egyptians still regretted their spiritual father, and detested the usurpation of his successor, who was introduced by the fathers of Chalcedon. The throne of Proterius was supported by a guard of two thousand soldiers; he waged a five years' war against the people of Alexandria; and on the first intelligence of the death of Marcian, he became the victim of their zeal. On the third day before the festival of Easter the patriarch was besieged in the cathedral, and murdered in the baptistery. The remains of his mangled corpse were delivered to the flames, and his ashes to the wind: and the deed was inspired by the vision of a pretended angel; an ambitious monk who, under the name of Timothy the Cat, succeeded to the place and opinions of Dioscorus. This deadly superstition was inflamed on either side by the principle and the practice of retaliation: in the pursuit of a metaphysical quarrel many thousands were slain, and the Christians of every degree were deprived of the substantial enjoyments of social life, and of the invisible gifts of baptism and the holy communion. Perhaps an extravagant fable of the times may conceal an allegorical picture of these fanatics, who tortured each other and themselves. "Under the consulship of Venantius and Celer," says a grave bishop, "the people of Alexandria, and all Egypt, were seized with a strange and diabolical frenzy: great and small, slaves and freedmen, monks and clergy, the natives of the land, who opposed the synod of Chalcedon, lost their speech and reason, barked like dogs, and tore, with their own teeth, the flesh from their hands and arms."

THE *HENOTICON* OF ZENO

The disorders of thirty years at length produced the famous HENO-TICON of the emperor Zeno, which in his reign, and in that of Anastasius, was signed by all the bishops of the East, under the penalty of degradation and exile if they rejected or infringed this salutary and fundamental law. The clergy may smile or groan at the presumption of a layman who defines the articles of faith; yet, if he stoops to the humiliating task, his mind is less infected by prejudice or interest, and the authority of the magistrate can only be maintained by the concord of the people. It is in ecclesiastical story that Zeno appears least contemptible; and I am not able to discern any Manichæan or Eutychian guilt in the generous saying of Anastasius, That it was unworthy of an emperor to persecute the worshippers of Christ and the citizens of Rome. The Henoticon was most pleasing to the Egyptians; yet the smallest blemish has not been descried by the jealous and even jaundiced eyes of our orthodox schoolmen, and it accurately represents the Catholic faith of the incarnation, without adopting or disclaiming the peculiar terms or tenets of the hostile sects. A solemn anathema is pronounced against Nestorius and Eutyches; against all heretics by whom Christ is divided, or confounded, or reduced to a phantom. Without defining the number or the article of the word *nature*, the pure system of St. Cyril, the faith of Nice, Constantinople, and Ephesus, is respectfully confirmed; but, instead of bowing at the name of the fourth council, the subject is dismissed by the censure of all contrary doctrines, *if* any such have been taught either elsewhere or at Chalcedon. Under this ambiguous expression the friends and the enemies of the last synod might unite in a silent embrace. The most reasonable Christians acquiesced in this mode of toleration; but their reason was feeble and inconstant, and their obedience was despised as timid and servile by the vehement spirit of their brethren. On a subject which engrossed the thoughts and discourses of men, it was difficult to preserve an exact neutrality; a book, a sermon, a prayer, rekindled the flame of controversy; and the bonds of communion were alternately broken and renewed by the private animosity of the bishops. The space between Nestorius and Eutyches was filled by a thousand shades of language and opinion; the *acephali* of Egypt, and the Roman pontiffs, of equal valour, though of unequal strength, may be found at the two extremities of the theological scale. The acephali, without a king or a bishop, were separated above three hundred years from the patriarchs of Alexandria, who had accepted the communion of Constantinople, without exacting a formal condemnation of the synod of Chalcedon. For accepting the communion of Alexandria, without a formal approbation of the same synod, the patriarchs of Constantinople were anathematised by the popes. Their inflexible despotism involved the most orthodox of the Greek churches in this spiritual contagion, denied or doubted the validity of their sacraments, and fomented, thirty-five years, the schism of the East and West, till they finally abolished the memory of four Byzantine pontiffs who had dared to oppose the supremacy of St. Peter. Before that period the precarious truce of Constantinople and Egypt had been violated by the zeal of the rival prelates. Macedonius, who was suspected of the Nestorian heresy, asserted, in disgrace and exile, the synod of Chalcedon, while the successor of Cyril would have purchased its overthrow with a bribe of two thousand pounds of gold.

In the fever of the times the sense, or rather the sound of a syllable, was sufficient to disturb the peace of an empire. The TRISAGION (thrice holy), "Holy, holy, holy, Lord God of Hosts!" is supposed by the Greeks to be the identical hymn which the angels and cherubim eternally repeat before the throne of God, and which, about the middle of the fifth century, was miraculously revealed to the church of Constantinople. The devotion of Antioch soon added, "who was crucified for us!" and this grateful address, either to Christ alone, or to the whole Trinity, may be justified by the rules of theology, and has been gradually adopted by the Catholics of the East and West. But it had been imagined by a Monophysite bishop; the gift of an enemy was at first rejected as a dire and dangerous blasphemy, and the rash innovation had nearly cost the emperor Anastasius his throne and his life. The people of Constantinople was devoid of any rational principles of freedom; but they held, as a lawful cause of rebellion, the colour of a livery in the races, or the colour of a mystery in the schools. The Trisagion, with and without this obnoxious addition, was chanted in the cathedral by two adverse choirs, and, when their lungs were exhausted, they had recourse to the more solid arguments of sticks and stones; the aggressors were punished by the emperor, and defended by the patriarch; and the crown and mitre were staked on the event of this momentous quarrel. The streets were instantly crowded with innumerable swarms of men, women, and children; the legions of monks, in regular array, marched, and shouted, and fought at their head. "Christians! this is the day of martyrdom: let us not desert our spiritual father; anathema to the Manichæan tyrant! he is unworthy to reign." Such was the Catholic cry; and the galleys of Anastasius lay upon their oars before the palace, till the patriarch had pardoned his penitent, and hushed the waves of the troubled multitude. The triumph of Macedonius was checked by a speedy exile; but the zeal of his flock was again exasperated by the same question, "Whether one of the Trinity had been crucified?" On this momentous occasion the blue and green factions of Constantinople suspended their discord, and the civil and military powers were annihilated in their presence. The keys of the city, and the standards of the guards, were deposited in the forum of Constantine, the principal station and camp of the faithful. Day and night they were incessantly busied either in singing hymns to the honour of their God, or in pillaging and murdering the servants of their prince. The head of his favourite monk, the friend, as they styled him, of the enemy of the Holy Trinity, was borne aloft on a spear; and the fire-brands, which had been darted against heretical structures, diffused the undistinguishing flames over the most orthodox buildings.

The statues of the emperor were broken, and his person was concealed in a suburb, till, at the end of three days, he dared to implore the mercy of his subjects. Without his diadem, and in the posture of a suppliant, Anastasius appeared on the throne of the circus. The Catholics, before his face, rehearsed their genuine Trisagion; they exulted in the offer which he proclaimed by the voice of a herald of abdicating the purple; they listened to the admonition, that, since *all* could not reign, they should previously agree in the choice of a sovereign: and they accepted the blood of two unpopular ministers, whom their master without hesitation condemned to the lions. These furious but transient seditions were encouraged by the success of Vitalian, who, with an army of Huns and Bulgarians, for the most part idolaters, declared himself the champion of the Catholic faith. In this pious rebellion he depopulated Thrace, besieged Constantinople, exterminated sixty-five thousand of his fellow-Christians, till he obtained the recall of the bishops, the satisfaction of the pope, and the establishment of the council of Chalcedon, an orthodox treaty, reluctantly signed by the dying Anastasius, and more faithfully performed by the uncle of Justinian. And such was the event of the *first* of the religious wars which have been waged in the name and by the disciples of the God of Peace.

THEOLOGY OF JUSTINIAN

Justinian has been already seen in the various lights of a prince, a conqueror, and a lawgiver: the theologian still remains, and it affords an unfavourable prejudice that his theology should form a very prominent feature of his portrait. The sovereign sympathised with his subjects in their superstitious reverence for living and departed saints: his Code, and more especially his Novels, confirm and enlarge the privileges of the clergy; and in every dispute between a monk and a layman, the partial judge was inclined to pronounce that truth and innocence and justice were always on the side of the church. In his public and private devotions the emperor was assiduous and exemplary; his prayers, vigils, and fasts displayed the austere penance of a monk; his fancy was amused by the hope or belief of personal inspiration; he had secured the patronage of the Virgin and St. Michael the archangel; and his recovery from a dangerous disease was ascribed to the miraculous succour of the holy martyrs Cosmas and Damian. The capital and the provinces of the East were decorated with the monuments of his religion; and though the far greater part of these costly structures may be attributed to his taste or ostentation, the zeal of the royal architect was probably quickened by a genuine sense of love and gratitude towards his invisible benefactors. Among the titles of Imperial greatness the name of *Pious* was most pleasing to his ear; to promote the temporal and spiritual interest of the church was the serious business of his life; and the duty of father of his country was often sacrificed to that of defender of the faith. The controversies of the times were congenial to his temper and understanding; and the theological professors must inwardly deride the diligence of a stranger who cultivated their art and neglected his own. "What can ye fear," said a bold conspirator to his associates, "from your bigoted tyrant? Sleepless and unarmed he sits whole nights in his closet debating with reverend greybeards, and turning over the pages of ecclesiastical volumes." The fruits of these lucubrations were displayed in many a conference, where Justinian might shine as the loudest and most subtle of the disputants; in many a sermon, which, under the name of edicts and epistles, proclaimed to the empire the theology of their master. While the barbarians invaded the provinces, while the victorious legions marched under the banners of Belisarius and Narses, the successor of Trajan, unknown to the camp, was content to vanquish at the head of a synod. Had he invited to these synods a disinterested and rational spectator, Justinian might have learned "*that* religious controversy is the offspring of arrogance and folly; *that* true piety is most laudably expressed by silence and submission; *that* man, ignorant of his own nature, should not presume to scrutinise the nature of his God; and *that* it is sufficient for us to know that power and benevolence are the perfect attributes of the Deity."

Toleration was not the virtue of the times, and indulgence to rebels has seldom been the virtue of princes. But when the prince descends to the narrow and peevish character of a disputant, he is easily provoked to supply the defect of argument by the plenitude of power, and to chastise without mercy the perverse blindness of those who wilfully shut their eyes against the light of demonstration. The reign of Justinian was an uniform yet various scene of persecution; and he appears to have surpassed his indolent predecessors, both in the contrivance of his laws and the rigour of their execution. The insufficient term of three months was assigned for the conversion or exile of all heretics; and if he still connived at their precarious stay, they were deprived, under his iron yoke, not only of the benefits of society, but of the common birthright of men and Christians. At the end of four hundred years the Montanists of Phrygia still breathed the wild enthusiasm of perfection and prophecy which they had imbibed from their male and female apostles, the special organs of the Paraclete. On the approach of the Catholic priests and soldiers, they grasped with alacrity the crown of martyrdom; the conventicle and the congregation perished in the flames, but these primitive fanatics were not extinguished three hundred years after the death of their tyrant. Under the protection of the Gothic confederates, the church of the Arians at Constantinople had braved the severity of the laws: their clergy equalled the wealth and magnificence of the senate; and the gold and silver which were seized by the rapacious hand of Justinian might perhaps be claimed as the spoils of the provinces and the trophies of the barbarians. A secret remnant of pagans, who still lurked in the most refined and most rustic conditions of mankind, excited the indignation of the Christians, who were perhaps unwilling that any strangers should be the witnesses of their intestine quarrels. A bishop was named as the inquisitor of the faith, and his diligence soon discovered, in the court and city, the magistrates, lawyers, physicians, and sophists, who still cherished the superstition of the Greeks. They were sternly informed that they must choose without delay between the displeasure of Jupiter or Justinian, and that their aversion to the gospel could no longer be disguised under the scandalous mask of indifference or impiety. The patrician Photius perhaps alone was resolved to live and to die like his ancestors: he enfranchised himself with the stroke of a dagger, and left his tyrant the poor consolation of exposing with ignominy the lifeless corpse of the fugitive. His weaker brethren submitted to their earthly monarch, underwent the ceremony of baptism, and laboured, by their extraordinary zeal, to erase the suspicion, or to expiate the guilt, of idolatry. The native country of Homer, and the theatre of the Trojan war, still retained the last sparks of his mythology: by the care of the same bishop, seventy thousand pagans were detected and converted in Asia, Phrygia, Lydia, and Caria; ninety-six churches were built for the new proselytes; and linen vestments, bibles and liturgies, and vases of gold and silver, were supplied by the pious munificence of Justinian. The Jews, who had been gradually stripped of their immunities, were oppressed by a vexatious law, which compelled them to observe the festival of Easter the same day on which it was celebrated by the Christians. And they might complain with the more reason, since the Catholics themselves did not agree with the astronomical calculations of their sovereign: the people of Constantinople delayed the beginning of their Lent a whole week after it had been ordained by authority; and they had the pleasure of fasting seven days, while meat was exposed for sale by the command of the emperor. The Samaritans of Palestine were a motley race, an ambiguous sect, rejected as Jews by the pagans, by the Jews as schismatics, and by the Christians as idolaters. The abomination of the cross had already been planted on their holy mount of Garizim, but the persecution of Justinian offered only the alternative of baptism or rebellion. They chose the latter: under the standard of a desperate leader they rose in arms, and retaliated their wrongs on the lives, the property, and the temples of a defenceless people. The Samaritans were finally subdued by the regular forces of the East: twenty thousand were slain, twenty thousand were sold by the Arabs to the infidels of Persia and India, and the remains of that unhappy nation atoned for the crime of treason by the sin of hypocrisy. It has been computed that one hundred thousand Roman subjects were extirpated in the Samaritan war, which converted the once fruitful province into a desolate and smoking wilderness. But in the creed of Justinian the guilt of murder could not be applied to the slaughter of unbelievers; and he piously laboured to establish with fire and sword the unity of the Christian faith.

With these sentiments, it was incumbent on him, at least, to be always in the right. In the first years of his administration he signalised his zeal as the disciple and patron of orthodoxy: the reconciliation of the Greeks and Latins established the *tome* of St. Leo as the creed of the emperor and the empire; the Nestorians and Eutychians were exposed, on either side, to the double edge of persecution; and the four synods, of Nice, Constantinople, Ephesus, and *Chalcedon*, were ratified by the code of a Catholic lawgiver. But while Justinian strove to maintain the uniformity of faith and worship, his wife Theodora, whose vices were not incompatible with devotion, had listened to the Monophysite teachers; and the open or clandestine enemies of the church revived and multiplied at the smile of their gracious patroness. The capital, the palace, the nuptial bed, were torn by spiritual discord; yet so doubtful was the sincerity of the royal consorts, that their seeming disagreement was imputed by many to a secret and mischievous confederacy against the religion and happiness of their people. The famous dispute of the THREE CHAPTERS, which has filled more volumes than it deserves lines, is deeply marked with this subtle and disingenuous spirit. It was now three hundred years since the body of Origen had been eaten by the worms: his soul, of which he held the pre-existence, was in the hands of its Creator; but his writings were eagerly perused by the monks of Palestine. In these writings the piercing eye of Justinian descried more than ten metaphysical errors; and the primitive doctor, in the company of Pythagoras and Plato, was devoted by the clergy to the *eternity* of hell-fire, which he had presumed to deny. Under the cover of this precedent a treacherous blow was aimed at the council of Chalcedon. The fathers had listened without impatience to the praise of Theodore of Mopsuestia; and their justice or indulgence had restored both Theodoret of Cyrrhus and Ibas of Edessa to the communion of the church. But the characters of these Oriental bishops were tainted with the reproach of heresy; the first had been the master, the two others were the friends, of Nestorius: their most suspicious passages were accused under the title of the *three chapters*; and the condemnation of their memory must involve the honour of a synod whose name was pronounced with sincere or affected reverence by the Catholic world. If these bishops, whether innocent or guilty, were annihilated in the sleep of death, they would not probably be awakened by the clamour which, after an hundred years, was raised over their grave. If they were already in the fangs of the dæmon, their torments could neither be aggravated nor assuaged by human industry. If in the company of saints and angels they enjoyed the rewards of piety, they must have smiled at the idle fury of the theological insects who still crawled on the surface of the earth. The foremost of these insects, the emperor of the Romans, darted his sting, and distilled his venom, per-

haps without discerning the true motives of Theodora and her ecclesiastical faction. The victims were no longer subject to his power, and the
vehement style of his edicts could only proclaim their damnation, and
invite the clergy of the East to join in a full chorus of curses and
anathemas. The East, with some hesitation, consented to the voice of
her sovereign: the fifth general council, of three patriarchs and one
hundred and sixty-five bishops, was held at Constantinople; and the
authors, as well as the defenders of the three chapters, were separated
from the communion of the saints, and solemnly delivered to the prince
of darkness. But the Latin churches were more jealous of the honour of
Leo and the synod of Chalcedon; and if they had fought as they usually
did under the standard of Rome, they might have prevailed in the cause
of reason and humanity. But their chief was a prisoner in the hands of
the enemy; the throne of St. Peter, which had been disgraced by the
simony, was betrayed by the cowardice, of Vigilius, who yielded, after a
long and inconsistent struggle, to the despotism of Justinian and the
sophistry of the Greeks. His apostasy provoked the indignation of the
Latins, and no more than two bishops could be found who would
impose their hands on his deacon and successor Pelagius. Yet the
perseverance of the popes insensibly transferred to their adversaries the
appellation of schismatics; the Illyrian, African, and Italian churches
were oppressed by the civil and ecclesiastical powers, not without some
effort of military force; the distant barbarians transcribed the creed of
the Vatican, and, in the period of a century, the schism of the three
chapters expired in an obscure angle of the Venetian province. But the
religious discontent of the Italians had already promoted the conquests
of the Lombards, and the Romans themselves were accustomed to
suspect the faith, and to detest the government, of their Byzantine
tyrant.

Justinian was neither steady nor consistent in the nice process of
fixing his volatile opinions and those of his subjects. In his youth he was
offended by the slightest deviation from the orthodox line; in his old age
he transgressed the measure of temperate heresy, and the Jacobites, not
less than the Catholics, were scandalised by his declaration that the body
of Christ was incorruptible, and that his manhood was never subject to
any wants and infirmities, the inheritance of our mortal flesh. This
fantastic opinion was announced in the last edicts of Justinian; and at
the moment of his seasonable departure, the clergy had refused to subscribe, the prince was prepared to persecute, and the people were resolved to suffer or resist. A bishop of Treves, secure beyond the limits
of his power, addressed the monarch of the East in the language of
authority and affection. "Most gracious Justinian, remember your
baptism and your creed. Let not your grey hairs be defiled with heresy.
Recall your fathers from exile, and your followers from perdition. You
cannot be ignorant that Italy and Gaul, Spain and Africa, already

deplore your fall, and anathematise your name. Unless, without delay, you destroy what you have taught; unless you exclaim with a loud voice, I have erred, I have sinned, anathema to Nestorius, anathema to Eutyches, you deliver your soul to the same flames in which *they* will eternally burn." He died and made no sign. His death restored in some degree the peace of the church, and the reigns of his four successors, Justin, Tiberius, Maurice, and Phocas, are distinguished by a rare, though fortunate, vacancy in the ecclesiastical history of the East.

Heraclius tried to conciliate the Monophysites by the monothelite doctrine, the proposition that Christ had only one will. His victory and diplomatic theology came too late. The Arabian invasions were imminent.

In Chapter 48, which is omitted here, Gibbon outlined the plan of his last two quarto volumes and gave a conspectus of the imperial succession in four main dynasties from Heraclius (610–641) to the Latin conquest of Constantinople in 1204.

The following table is offered in its place.

HERACLIAN DYNASTY A.D. 610–717

Heraclius defeated the Persians and made a first stand against Islam. His defeat in 636 on the banks of the Yarmak resulted in the loss of Syria to the Empire. Jerusalem was captured in 638 and Alexandria in 647 (see below, Chapter 51).

In 679 the Bulgars crossed the Danube, and the latter end of the Heraclian dynasty was a period of decline.

ISAURIAN DYNASTY A.D. 717–867, THE ICONOCLASTS

Leo III the Isaurian, 717–740, foiled a large-scale attack by the Arabs on Constantinople.

In 754 the Seventh Ecumenical Council held at Constantinople condemned the worship of images.

The Empress Irene (797–802) temporarily restored the use of images which was finally re-established by Theodora in 843 (see below, Chapter 49).

The disputes about images tend to obscure the fact that the Iconoclasts gave the empire a new civil and military organisation, and tried to adapt Roman law to current needs and to free the civil power from the influence of the monks.

The Isaurian dynasty ended with the murder of Leo V (813–820) and was followed by the short Phrygian dynasty (820–867).

THE MACEDONIAN DYNASTY A.D. 867–1057

Basil I, 867–886, established this dynasty. Among his successors may be noted Constantine VII Porphyrogenitus, 912–959, and his stepfather Romanus I Lecapenus (919–944), and John I Zimisces (969–970), who left three daughters Eudoxia a nun, Theodora, and Zoe. The personal and political complications of the last two ladies dominated the imperial scene until Theodora's death in 1056. The dynasty survived for one more year with Michael Stratioticus her nominee.

During this period a new political antithesis arose in Europe between the Emperor and the Patriarch in the East and the Emperor and the Pope in the West. Schism was created between the churches and became final in 1054. Politically the Slav nations became more important to the Roman Empire than the nations of the West.

The ninth and tenth centuries brought about some recovery of power and territory. Constantine VII initiated reforms of law and an intellectual revival (see below, Chapter 53). Nicephorus Phocas in 963–969 and John Zimisces (969–976) recovered Syria and Mesopotamia from Islam. Basil II Bulgaroctonus i.e. the slayer of the Bulgars (963–1025) broke the power of the Slavs. After his death the power and prosperity of the Empire declined once more.

THE COMNENIAN DYNASTY A.D. 1057–1204

Isaac I Comnenus, 1057–1059, abdicated and was followed by a disastrous period marked by the victory of the Seljuk Turks at Manzikert in 1071, the prelude to the total loss of Asia minor (see below, Chapter 57). Isaac's nephew founded a dynasty in 1081 and inaugurated a period of reform. Appeals were now made to the West, and the West in various ways recognised advantages to be got from the East. In 1095 the First Crusade began. A mortal blow to the Empire was dealt in 1204 when the Fourth Crusade captured and sacked Constantinople and ended the Comnenian dynasty. (See below, Chapter 60.)

Chapter 49

THE WORSHIP OF IMAGES. LEO THE ICONOCLAST. REVOLT OF ITALY. RELATIONS OF PEPIN AND CHARLEMAGNE WITH THE POPES. RESTORATION OF IMAGES IN THE EAST. FINAL SEPARATION OF THE POPES FROM THE EASTERN EMPIRE. REIGN AND CHARACTER OF CHARLEMAGNE. REIGN OF CHARLES IV AND COMPARISON WITH AUGUSTUS

IN the connection of the church and state I have considered the former as subservient only, and relative, to the latter; a salutary maxim, if in fact as well as in narrative it had ever been held sacred. The oriental philosophy of the Gnostics, the dark abyss of predestination and grace, and the strange transformation of the Eucharist from the sign to the substance of Christ's body, I have purposely abandoned to the curiosity of speculative divines. But I have reviewed with diligence and pleasure the objects of ecclesiastical history by which the decline and fall of the Roman empire were materially affected, the propagation of Christianity, the constitution of the Catholic church, the ruin of Paganism, and the sects that arose from the mysterious controversies concerning the Trinity and incarnation. At the head of this class we may justly rank the worship of images, so fiercely disputed in the eighth and ninth centuries; since a question of popular superstition produced the revolt of Italy, the temporal power of the popes, and the restoration of the Roman empire in the West.

The primitive Christians were possessed with an unconquerable repugnance to the use and abuse of images; and this aversion may be ascribed to their descent from the Jews, and their enmity to the Greeks. The Mosaic law had severely proscribed all representations of the Deity; and that precept was firmly established in the principles and practice of the chosen people. The wit of the Christian apologists was pointed against the foolish idolaters who bowed before the workmanship of their own hands; the images of brass and marble, which, had *they* been endowed with sense and motion, should have started rather from the pedestal to adore the creative powers of the artist. Perhaps some recent and imperfect converts of the Gnostic tribe might crown the statues of Christ and St. Paul with the profane honours which they paid to those of Aristotle and Pythagoras; but the public religion of the Catholics was uniformly simple and spiritual; and the first notice of the use of pictures is in the censure of the council of Illiberis, three hundred years after the Christian era. Under the successors of Constantine, in the peace and luxury of the triumphant church, the more prudent bishops condescended to indulge a visible superstition for the benefit of the multitude; and after the ruin of Paganism they were no longer restrained by the apprehension of an odious parallel. The first introduction of a symbolic worship was in the veneration of the cross and of relics. The saints and martyrs, whose intercession was implored, were seated on the right hand of God; but the gracious and often supernatural favours which, in the popular belief, were showered round their tomb, conveyed an unquestionable sanction of the devout pilgrims who visited, and touched, and kissed these lifeless remains, the memorials of their merits and sufferings. But a memorial more interesting than the skull or the sandals of a departed worthy is the faithful copy of his person and features, delineated by the arts of painting or sculpture. In every age such copies, so congenial to human feelings, have been cherished by the zeal of private friendship or public esteem: the images of the Roman emperors were adored with civil and almost religious honours; a reverence less ostentatious, but more sincere, was applied to the statues of sages and patriots; and these profane virtues, these splendid sins, disappeared in the presence of the holy men who had died for their celestial and everlasting country. At first the experiment was made with caution and scruple; and the venerable pictures were discreetly allowed to instruct the ignorant, to awaken the cold, and to gratify the prejudices of the heathen proselytes. By a slow though inevitable progression the honours of the original were transferred to the copy: the devout Christian prayed before the image of a saint; and the Pagan rites of genuflexion, luminaries, and incense again stole into the Catholic church. The scruples of reason or piety were silenced by the strong evidence of visions and miracles; and the pictures which speak, and move, and bleed, must be endowed with a divine energy, and may be considered as the proper objects of religious adoration. The most audacious pencil might tremble in the rash attempt of defining by forms and colours the infinite Spirit, the eternal Father, who pervades and sustains the universe. But the superstitious mind was more easily reconciled to paint and to worship the angels, and, above all, the Son of God, under the human shape which on earth they have condescended to assume. The second person of the Trinity had been clothed with a real and mortal body; but that body had ascended into heaven: and had not some similitude been presented to the eyes of his disciples, the spiritual worship of Christ might have been obliterated by the visible relics and representations of the saints. A similar indulgence was requisite and propitious for the Virgin Mary: the place of her burial was unknown; and the assumption of her soul and body into heaven was adopted by the credulity of the Greeks and Latins. The use, and even the worship, of images was firmly established before the end of the sixth century: they were fondly cherished by the warm imagination of the Greeks and Asiatics: the Pantheon and Vatican were adorned with the emblems of a new superstition; but this semblance of idolatry was more coldly entertained by the rude barbarians and the Arian clergy of the West. The bolder forms of sculpture, in brass or marble, which peopled the temples of antiquity, were offensive to the fancy or conscience of the Christian Greeks; and a smooth surface of colours has ever been esteemed a more decent and harmless mode of imitation.

The merit and effect of a copy depends on its resemblance with the original; but the primitive Christians were ignorant of the genuine features of the Son of God, his mother, and his apostles: the statue of Christ at Paneas, in Palestine, was more probably that of some temporal saviour; the Gnostics and their profane monuments were reprobated, and the fancy of the Christian artists could only be guided by the clandestine imitation of some heathen model. In this distress a bold and dexterous invention assured at once the likeness of the image and the innocence of the worship. A new superstructure of fable was raised on the popular basis of a Syrian legend on the correspondence of Christ and Abgarus, so famous in the days of Eusebius, so reluctantly deserted by our modern advocates. The bishop of Cæsarea records the epistle, but he most strangely forgets the picture of Christ—the perfect impression of his face on a linen, with which he gratified the faith of the royal stranger who had invoked his healing power, and offered the strong city of Edessa to protect him against the malice of the Jews. The ignorance of the primitive church is explained by the long imprisonment of the image in a niche of the wall, from whence, after an oblivion of five hundred years, it was released by some prudent bishop, and seasonably presented to the devotion of the times. Its first and most glorious exploit was the deliverance of the city from the arms of Chosroes Nushirvan; and it was soon revered as a pledge of the divine promise that Edessa should never be taken by a foreign enemy. It is true, indeed, that the text of Procopius ascribes the double deliverance of Edessa to the wealth and valour of her citizens, who purchased the absence and repelled the assaults of the Persian monarch. He was ignorant, the profane historian, of the testimony which he is compelled to deliver in the ecclesiastical page of Evagrius, that the Palladium was exposed on the rampart, and that the water which had been sprinkled on the holy face, instead of quenching, added new fuel to the flames of the besieged. After this important service the image of Edessa was preserved with respect and gratitude; and if the Armenians rejected the legend, the more credulous Greeks adored the similitude, which was not the work of any mortal pencil, but the immediate creation of the divine original. The style and sentiments of a Byzantine hymn will declare how far their worship was removed from the grossest idolatry. "How can we with mortal eyes contemplate this image, whose celestial splendour the host of heaven presumes not to behold? HE who dwells in heaven condescends this day to visit us by his venerable image; HE who is seated on the cherubim visits us this day by a picture, which the Father has delineated with his immaculate hand, which he has formed in an ineffable manner, and which we sanctify by adoring it with fear and love." Before the end of the sixth century these images, *made without hands* (in Greek it is a single word), were propagated in the camps and cities of the Eastern empire; they were the objects of worship, and the instruments of miracles; and in the hour of danger or tumult their venerable presence could revive the hope, rekindle the courage, or repress the fury of the Roman legions. Of these pictures the far greater part, the transcripts of a human pencil, could only pretend to a secondary likeness and improper title; but there were some of higher descent, who derived their resemblance from an immediate contact with the original, endowed for that purpose with a miraculous and prolific virtue. The most ambitious aspired from a filial to a fraternal relation with the image of Edessa; and such is the *veronica* of Rome, or Spain, or Jerusalem, which Christ in his agony and bloody sweat applied to his face, and delivered to a holy matron. The fruitful precedent was speedily transferred to the Virgin Mary, and the saints and martyrs. In the church of Diospolis, in Palestine, the features of the Mother of God were deeply inscribed in a marble column: the East and West have been decorated by the pencil of St. Luke; and the Evangelist, who was perhaps a physician, has been forced to exercise the occupation of a painter, so profane and odious in the eyes of the primitive Christians. The Olympian Jove, created by the muse of Homer and the chisel of Phidias, might inspire a philosophic mind with momentary devotion; but these Catholic images were faintly and flatly delineated by monkish artists in the last degeneracy of taste and genius.[1]

LEO THE ICONOCLAST

The worship of images had stolen into the church by insensible degrees, and each petty step was pleasing to the superstitious mind, as productive of comfort and innocent of sin. But in the beginning of the eighth century, in the full magnitude of the abuse, the more timorous Greeks were awakened by an apprehension that, under the mask of Christianity, they had restored the religion of their fathers: they heard, with grief and impatience, the name of idolaters—the incessant charge of the Jews and Mahometans, who derived from the Law and the Koran an immortal hatred to graven images and all relative worship. The servitude of the Jews might curb their zeal and depreciate their authority, but the triumphant Musulmans, who reigned at Damascus, and threatened Constantinople, cast into the scale of reproach the accumulated weight of truth and victory. The cities of Syria, Palestine, and Egypt had been fortified with the images of Christ, his mother, and his saints;

[1] "Your scandalous figures stand quite out from the canvas: they are as bad as a group of statues!" It was thus that the ignorance and bigotry of a Greek priest applauded the pictures of Titian, which he had ordered, and refused to accept.

and each city presumed on the hope or promise of miraculous defence. In a rapid conquest of ten years the Arabs subdued those cities and these images; and, in their opinion, the Lord of Hosts pronounced a decisive judgment between the adoration and contempt of these mute and inanimate idols. For a while Edessa had braved the Persian assaults; but the chosen city, the spouse of Christ, was involved in the common ruin; and his divine resemblance became the slave and trophy of the infidels. After a servitude of three hundred years, the Palladium was yielded to the devotion of Constantinople, for a ransom of twelve thousand pounds of silver, the redemption of two hundred Musulmans, and a perpetual truce for the territory of Edessa. In this season of distress and dismay the eloquence of the monks was exercised in the defence of images; and they attempted to prove that the sin and schism of the greatest part of the Orientals had forfeited the favour and annihilated the virtue of these precious symbols. But they were now opposed by the murmurs of many simple or rational Christians, who appealed to the evidence of texts, of facts, and of the primitive times, and secretly desired the reformation of the church. As the worship of images had never been established by any general or positive law, its progress in the Eastern empire had been retarded, or accelerated, by the differences of men and manners, the local degrees of refinement, and the personal characters of the bishops. The splendid devotion was fondly cherished by the levity of the capital and the inventive genius of the Byzantine clergy; while the rude and remote districts of Asia were strangers to this innovation of sacred luxury. Many large congregations of Gnostics and Arians maintained, after their conversion, the simple worship which had preceded their separation; and the Armenians, the most warlike subjects of Rome, were not reconciled, in the twelfth century, to the sight of images. These various denominations of men afforded a fund of prejudice and aversion, of small account in the villages of Anatolia or Thrace, but which, in the fortune of a soldier, a prelate, or an eunuch, might be often connected with the powers of the church and state.

Of such adventurers the most fortunate was the emperor Leo the Third, who, from the mountains of Isauria, ascended the throne of the East. He was ignorant of sacred and profane letters; but his education, his reason, perhaps his intercourse with the Jews and Arabs, had inspired the martial peasant with an hatred of images; and it was held to be the duty of a prince to impose on his subjects the dictates of his own conscience. But in the outset of an unsettled reign, during ten years of toil and danger, Leo submitted to the meanness of hypocrisy, bowed before the idols which he despised, and satisfied the Roman pontiff with the annual professions of his orthodoxy and zeal. In the reformation of religion his first steps were moderate and cautious: he assembled a great council of senators and bishops, and enacted, with their consent, that all the images should be removed from the sanctuary and altar to a proper height in the churches, where they might be visible to the eyes, and inaccessible to the superstition, of the people. But it was impossible on either side to check the rapid though adverse impulse of veneration and abhorrence: in their lofty position the sacred images still edified their votaries and reproached the tyrant. He was himself provoked by resistance and invective; and his own party accused him of an imperfect discharge of his duty, and urged for his imitation the example of the Jewish king, who had broken without scruple the brazen serpent of the temple. By a second edict he proscribed the existence as well as the use of religious pictures; the churches of Constantinople and the provinces were cleansed from idolatry; the images of Christ, the Virgin, and the saints were demolished, or a smooth surface of plaster was spread over the walls of the edifice. The sect of the Iconoclasts was supported by the zeal and despotism of six emperors, and the East and West were involved in a noisy conflict of one hundred and twenty years. It was the design of Leo the Isaurian to pronounce the condemnation of images as an article of faith, and by the authority of a general council: but the convocation of such an assembly was reserved for his son Constantine; and though it is stigmatised by triumphant bigotry as a meeting of fools and atheists, their own partial and mutilated acts betray many symptoms of reason and piety. The debates and decrees of many provincial synods introduced the summons of the general council which met in the suburbs of Constantinople, and was composed of the respectable number of three hundred and thirty-eight bishops of Europe and Anatolia; for the patriarchs of Antioch and Alexandria were the slaves of the caliph, and the Roman pontiff had withdrawn the churches of Italy and the West from the communion of the Greeks. This Byzantine synod assumed the rank and powers of the seventh general council; yet even this title was a recognition of the six preceding assemblies, which had laboriously built the structure of the Catholic faith. After a serious deliberation of six months, the three hundred and thirty-eight bishops pronounced and subscribed an unanimous decree, that all visible symbols of Christ, except in the Eucharist, were either blasphemous or heretical; that image-worship was a corruption of Christianity and a renewal of Paganism; that all such monuments of idolatry should be broken or erased; and that those who should refuse to deliver the objects of their private superstition were guilty of disobedience to the authority of the church and of the emperor. In their loud and loyal acclamations they celebrated the merits of their temporal redeemer; and to his zeal and justice they intrusted the execution of their spiritual censures. At Constantinople, as in the former councils, the will of the prince was the rule of episcopal faith; but on this occasion I am inclined to suspect that a large majority of the prelates sacrificed their secret conscience to the temptations of hope and fear. In the long night of superstition the Christians had wandered far away from the simplicity of the Gospel:

nor was it easy for them to discern the clue, and tread back the mazes of the labyrinth. The worship of images was inseparably blended, at least to a pious fancy, with the Cross, the Virgin, the saints and their relics; the holy ground was involved in a cloud of miracles and visions; and the nerves of the mind, curiosity and scepticism, were benumbed by the habits of obedience and belief. Constantine himself is accused of indulging a royal licence to doubt, or deny, or deride the mysteries of the Catholics, but they were deeply inscribed in the public creed of his bishops; and the boldest Iconoclast might assault with a secret horror the monuments of popular devotion, which were consecrated to the honour of his celestial patrons. In the reformation of the sixteenth century freedom and knowledge had expanded all the faculties of man: the thirst of innovation superseded the reverence of antiquity; and the vigour of Europe could disdain those phantoms which terrified the sickly and servile weakness of the Greeks.

The scandal of an abstract heresy can be only proclaimed to the people by the blast of the ecclesiastical trumpet; but the most ignorant can perceive, the most torpid must feel, the profanation and downfall of their visible deities. The first hostilities of Leo were directed against a lofty Christ on the vestibule, and above the gate, of the palace. A ladder had been planted for the assault, but it was furiously shaken by a crowd of zealots and women: they beheld, with pious transports, the ministers of sacrilege tumbling from on high and dashed against the pavement; and the honours of the ancient martyrs were prostituted to these criminals, who justly suffered for murder and rebellion. The execution of the Imperial edicts was resisted by frequent tumults in Constantinople and the provinces: the person of Leo was endangered, his officers were massacred, and the popular enthusiasm was quelled by the strongest efforts of the civil and military power. Of the Archipelago, or Holy Sea, the numerous islands were filled with images and monks: their votaries abjured, without scruple, the enemy of Christ, his mother, and the saints; they armed a fleet of boats and galleys, displayed their consecrated banners, and boldly steered for the harbour of Constantinople, to place on the throne a new favourite of God and the people. They depended on the succour of a miracle: but their miracles were inefficient against the *Greek fire*; and, after the defeat and conflagration of their fleet, the naked islands were abandoned to the clemency or justice of the conqueror. The son of Leo, in the first year of his reign, had undertaken an expedition against the Saracens: during his absence the capital, the palace, and the purple were occupied by his kinsman Artavasdes, the ambitious champion of the orthodox faith. The worship of images was triumphantly restored: the patriarch renounced his dissimulation, or dissembled his sentiments; and the righteous claim of the usurper was acknowledged, both in the new and in ancient Rome. Constantine flew for refuge to his paternal mountains; but he descended at the head of the bold and affectionate Isaurians; and his final victory confounded the arms and predictions of the fanatics. His long reign was distracted with clamour, sedition, conspiracy, and mutual hatred and sanguinary revenge: the persecution of images was the motive or pretence of his adversaries; and, if they missed a temporal diadem, they were rewarded by the Greeks with the crown of martyrdom. In every act of open and clandestine treason the emperor felt the unforgiving enmity of the monks, the faithful slaves of the superstition to which they owed their riches and influence. They prayed, they preached, they absolved, they inflamed, they conspired; the solitude of Palestine poured forth a torrent of invective; and the pen of St. John Damascenus,[1] the last of the Greek fathers, devoted the tyrant's head, both in this world and the next. I am not at leisure to examine how far the monks provoked, nor how much they have exaggerated, their real and pretended sufferings, nor how many lost their lives or limbs, their eyes or their beards, by the cruelty of the emperor. From the chastisement of individuals he proceeded to the abolition of the order; and, as it was wealthy and useless, his resentment might be stimulated by avarice, and justified by patriotism. The formidable name and mission of the *Dragon*, his visitor-general, excited the terror and abhorrence of the *black* nation: the religious communities were dissolved, the buildings were converted into magazines or barracks; the lands, moveables, and cattle were confiscated; and our modern precedents will support the charge, that much wanton or malicious havoc was exercised against the relics, and even the books, of the monasteries. With the habit and profession of monks, the public and private worship of images was rigorously proscribed; and it should seem that a solemn abjuration of idolatry was exacted from the subjects, or at least from the clergy, of the Eastern empire.

REVOLT OF ITALY

The patient East abjured with reluctance her sacred images; they were fondly cherished, and vigorously defended, by the independent zeal of the Italians. In ecclesiastical rank and jurisdiction the patriarch of Constantinople and the pope of Rome were nearly equal. But the Greek prelate was a domestic slave under the eye of his master, at whose nod he alternately passed from the convent to the throne, and from the throne to the convent. A distant and dangerous station, amidst the

---

[1] John, or Mansur, was a noble Christian of Damascus, who held a considerable office in the service of the caliph. His zeal in the cause of images exposed him to the resentment and treachery of the Greek emperor; and, on the suspicion of a treasonable correspondence, he was deprived of his right hand, which was miraculously restored by the Virgin. After this deliverance he resigned his office, distributed his wealth, and buried himself in the monastery of St. Sabas, between Jerusalem and the Dead Sea. The legend is famous; but his learned editor, Father Lequien, has unluckily proved that St. John Damascenus was already a monk before the Iconoclast dispute.

barbarians of the West, excited the spirit and freedom of the Latin bishops. Their popular election endeared them to the Romans: the public and private indigence was relieved by their ample revenue; and the weakness of neglect of the emperors compelled them to consult, both in peace and war, the temporal safety of the city. In the school of adversity the priest insensibly imbibed the virtues and the ambition of a prince; the same character was assumed, the same policy was adopted, by the Italian, the Greek, or the Syrian, who ascended the chair of St. Peter; and, after the loss of her legions and provinces, the genius and fortune of the popes again restored the supremacy of Rome. It is agreed that in the eighth century their dominion was founded on rebellion, and that the rebellion was produced, and justified, by the heresy of the Iconoclasts; but the conduct of the second and third Gregory, in this memorable contest, is variously interpreted by the wishes of their friends and enemies. The Byzantine writers unanimously declare that, after a fruitless admonition, they pronounced the separation of the East and West, and deprived the sacrilegious tyrant of the revenue and sovereignty of Italy. Their excommunication is still more clearly expressed by the Greeks, who beheld the accomplishment of the papal triumphs; and as they are more strongly attached to their religion than to their country, they praise, instead of blaming, the zeal and orthodoxy of these apostolic men. The modern champions of Rome are eager to accept the praise and the precedent: this great and glorious example of the deposition of royal heretics is celebrated by the cardinals Baronius and Bellarmine; and if they are asked why the same thunders were not hurled against the Neros and Julians of antiquity? they reply, that the weakness of the primitive church was the sole cause of her patient loyalty. On this occasion the effects of love and hatred are the same; and the zealous Protestants, who seek to kindle the indignation and to alarm the fears of princes and magistrates, expatiate on the insolence and treason of the two Gregories against their lawful sovereign. They are defended only by the moderate Catholics, for the most part of the Gallican church, who respect the saint without approving the sin. These common advocates of the crown and the mitre circumscribe the truth of facts by the rule of equity, Scripture, and tradition, and appeal to the evidence of the Latins, and the lives and epistles of the popes themselves.

Two original epistles, from Gregory the Second to the emperor Leo, are still extant; and if they cannot be praised as the most perfect models of eloquence and logic, they exhibit the portrait, or at least the mask, of the founder of the papal monarchy. "During ten pure and fortunate years," says Gregory to the emperor, "we have tasted the annual comfort of your royal letters, subscribed in purple ink with your own hand, the sacred pledges of your attachment to the orthodox creed of our fathers. How deplorable is the change! how tremendous the scandal! You now accuse the Catholics of idolatry; and, by the accusation, you betray your own impiety and ignorance. To this ignorance we are compelled to adapt the grossness of our style and arguments: the first elements of holy letters are sufficient for your confusion; and were you to enter a grammar-school, and avow yourself the enemy of our worship, the simple and pious children would be provoked to cast their horn-books at your head." After this decent salutation the pope attempts the usual distinction between the idols of antiquity and the Christian images. The former were the fanciful representations of phantoms or dæmons, at a time when the true God had not manifested his person in any visible likeness. The latter are the geniune forms of Christ, his mother, and his saints, who had approved, by a crowd of miracles, the innocence and merit of this relative worship. He must indeed have trusted to the ignorance of Leo, since he could assert the perpetual use of images from the apostolic age, and their venerable presence in the six synods of the Catholic church. A more specious argument is drawn from the present possession and recent practice: the harmony of the Christian world supersedes the demand of a general council; and Gregory confesses that such assemblies can only be useful under the reign of an orthodox prince. To the impudent and inhuman Leo, more guilty than a heretic, he recommends peace, silence, and implicit obedience to his spiritual guides of Constantinople and Rome. The limits of civil and ecclesiastical powers are defined by the pontiff. To the former he appropriates the body; to the latter the soul: the sword of justice is in the hands of the magistrate: the more formidable weapon of excommunication is intrusted to the clergy; and in the exercise of their divine commission a zealous son will not spare his offending father: the successor of St. Peter may lawfully chastise the kings of the earth. "You assault us, O tyrant! with a carnal and military hand: unarmed and naked we can only implore the Christ, the prince of the heavenly host, that he will send unto you a devil for the destruction of your body and the salvation of your soul. You declare, with foolish arrogance, I will despatch my orders to Rome: I will break in pieces the image of St. Peter; and Gregory, like his predecessor Martin, shall be transported in chains and in exile to the foot of the imperial throne. Would to God that I might be permitted to tread in the footsteps of the holy Martin! but may the fate of Constans serve as a warning to the persecutors of the church! After his just condemnation by the bishops of Sicily, the tyrant was cut off in the fulness of his sins, by a domestic servant: the saint is still adored by the nations of Scythia, among whom he ended his banishment and his life. But it is our duty to live for the edification and support of the faithful people; nor are we reduced to risk our safety on the event of a combat. Incapable as you are of defending Roman subjects, the maritime situation of the city may perhaps expose it to your depredation; but we can remove to the distance of four-and-twenty *stadia*, to the first fortress of the Lombards, and then——you may pursue the winds. Are you ignorant that the popes are the bond of union, the mediators of peace between the East and West? The eyes of the nations are fixed on our humility; and they revere, as a God upon earth, the apostle St. Peter, whose image you threaten to destroy. The remote and interior kingdoms of the West present their homage to Christ and his vicegerent; and we now prepare to visit one of their most powerful monarchs who desires to receive from our hands the sacrament of baptism. The barbarians have submitted to the yoke of the Gospel, while you alone are deaf to the voice of the shepherd. These pious barbarians are kindled into rage: they thirst to avenge the persecution of the East. Abandon your rash and fatal enterprise; reflect, tremble, and repent. If you persist, we are innocent of the blood that will be spilt in the contest; may it fall on your own head!"

The first assault of Leo against the images of Constantinople had been witnessed by a crowd of strangers from Italy and the West, who related with grief and indignation the sacrilege of the emperor. But on the reception of his proscriptive edict they trembled for their domestic deities; the images of Christ and the Virgin, of the angels, martyrs, and saints, were abolished in all the churches of Italy; and a strong alternative was proposed to the Roman pontiff, the royal favour as the price of his compliance, degradation and exile as the penalty of his disobedience. Neither zeal nor policy allowed him to hesitate; and the haughty strain in which Gregory addressed the emperor displays his confidence in the truth of his doctrine or the powers of resistance. Without depending on prayers or miracles, he boldly armed against the public enemy, and his pastoral letters admonished the Italians of their danger and their duty. At this signal, Ravenna, Venice, and the cities of the Exarchate and Pentapolis adhered to the cause of religion; their military force by sea and land consisted, for the most part, of the natives; and the spirit of patriotism and zeal was transfused into the mercenary strangers. The Italians swore to live and die in the defence of the pope and the holy images; the Roman people was devoted to their father, and even the Lombards were ambitious to share the merit and advantage of his holy war. The most treasonable act, but the most obvious revenge, was the destruction of the statues of Leo himself: the most effectual and pleasing measure of rebellion was the withholding the tribute of Italy, and depriving him of a power which he had recently abused by the imposition of a new capitation. A form of administration was preserved by the election of magistrates and governors; and so high was the public indignation, that the Italians were prepared to create an orthodox emperor, and to conduct him with a fleet and army to the palace of Constantinople. In that palace the Roman bishops, the second and third Gregory, were condemned as the authors of the revolt, and every attempt was made, either by fraud or force, to seize their persons and to strike at their lives. The city was repeatedly visited or assaulted by captains of the guards, and dukes and exarchs of high dignity or secret trust; they landed with foreign troops, they obtained some domestic aid, and the superstition of Naples may blush that her fathers were attached to the cause of heresy. But these clandestine or open attacks were repelled by the courage and vigilance of the Romans; the Greeks were overthrown and massacred, their leaders suffered an ignominious death, and the popes, however inclined to mercy, refused to intercede for these guilty victims. At Ravenna, the several quarters of the city had long exercised a bloody and hereditary feud; in religious controversy they found a new aliment of faction: but the votaries of images were superior in numbers or spirit, and the exarch, who attempted to stem the torrent, lost his life in a popular sedition. To punish this flagitious deed, and restore his dominion in Italy, the emperor sent a fleet and army into the Adriatic gulf. After suffering from the winds and waves much loss and delay, the Greeks made their descent in the neighbourhood of Ravenna: they threatened to depopulate the guilty capital, and to imitate, perhaps to surpass, the example of Justinian the Second, who had chastised a former rebellion by the choice and execution of fifty of the principal inhabitants. The women and clergy, in sackcloth and ashes, lay prostrate in prayer; the men were in arms for the defence of their country; the common danger had united the factions, and the event of a battle was preferred to the slow miseries of a siege. In a hard-fought day, as the two armies alternately yielded and advanced, a phantom was seen, a voice was heard, and Ravenna was victorious by the assurance of victory. The strangers retreated to their ships, but the populous seacoast poured forth a multitude of boats; the waters of the Po were so deeply infected with blood, that during six years the public prejudice abstained from the fish of the river; and the institution of an annual feast perpetuated the worship of images and the abhorrence of the Greek tyrant. Amidst the triumph of the Catholic arms, the Roman pontiff convened a synod of ninety-three bishops against the heresy of the Iconoclasts. With their consent, he pronounced a general excommunication against all who by word or deed should attack the tradition of the fathers and the images of the saints: in this sentence the emperor was tacitly involved, but the vote of a last and hopeless remonstrance may seem to imply that the anathema was yet suspended over his guilty head. No sooner had they confirmed their own safety, the worship of images, and the freedom of Rome and Italy, than the popes appear to have relaxed of their severity, and to have spared the relics of the Byzantine dominion. Their moderate counsels delayed and prevented the election of a new emperor, and they exhorted the Italians not to separate from the body of the Roman monarchy. The exarch was permitted to reside within the walls of Ravenna, a captive rather than a master; and till the Imperial coronation of Charlemagne, the government of Rome and Italy was exercised in the name of the successors of Constantine.

The liberty of Rome, which had been oppressed by the arms and arts of Augustus, was rescued, after seven hundred and fifty years of servitude, from the persecution of Leo the Isaurian. By the Cæsars the triumphs of the consuls had been annihilated: in the decline and fall of the empire, the god Terminus, the sacred boundary, had insensibly receded from the ocean, the Rhine, the Danube, and the Euphrates; and Rome was reduced to her ancient territory from Viterbo to Terracina, and from Narni to the mouth of the Tiber. When the kings were banished, the republic reposed on the firm basis which had been founded by their wisdom and virtue. Their perpetual jurisdiction was divided between two annual magistrates: the senate continued to exercise the powers of administration and counsel; and the legislative authority was distributed in the assemblies of the people by a well-proportioned scale of property and service. Ignorant of the arts of luxury, the primitive Romans had improved the science of government and war: the will of the community was absolute: the rights of individuals were sacred: one hundred and thirty thousand citizens were armed for defence of conquest; and a band of robbers and outlaws was moulded into a nation, deserving of freedom and ambitious of glory. When the sovereignty of the Greek emperors was extinguished, the ruins of Rome presented the sad image of depopulation and decay: her slavery was a habit, her liberty an accident; the effect of superstition, and the object of her own amazement and terror. The last vestige of the substance, or even the forms, of the constitution, was obliterated from the practice and memory of the Romans; and they were devoid of knowledge, or virtue, again to build the fabric of a commonwealth. Their scanty remnant, the offspring of slaves and strangers, was despicable in the eyes of the victorious barbarians. As often as the Franks or Lombards expressed their most bitter contempt of a foe, they called him a Roman; "and in this name," says the bishop Liutprand, "we include whatever is base, whatever is cowardly, whatever is perfidious, the extremes of avarice and luxury, and every vice that can prostitute the dignity of human nature." By the necessity of their situation, the inhabitants of Rome were cast into the rough model of a republican government: they were compelled to elect some judges in peace and some leaders in war: the nobles assembled to deliberate, and their resolves could not be executed without the union and consent of the multitude. The style of the Roman senate and people was revived, but the spirit was fled; and their new independence was disgraced by the tumultuous conflict of licentiousness and oppression. The want of laws could only be supplied by the influence of religion, and their foreign and domestic counsels were moderated by the authority of the bishop. His alms, his sermons, his correspondence with the kings and prelates of the West, his recent services, their gratitude and oath, accustomed the Romans to consider him as the first magistrate or prince of the city. The Christian humility

of the popes was not offended by the name of *Dominus*, or Lord; and
their face and inscription are still apparent on the most ancient coins.
Their temporal dominion is now confirmed by the reverence of a
thousand years; and their noblest title is the free choice of a people
whom they had redeemed from slavery.

*The Lombards subdued Ravenna, putting an end to the exarchate,
and attacked Rome. Rome was delivered by Pepin, king of the
Franks, and the Lombards finally surrendered to his son, Charlemagne, in 774.*

RELATIONS OF PEPIN AND CHARLEMAGNE WITH THE POPES

The mutual obligations of the popes and the Carlovingian family
form the important link of ancient and modern, of civil and ecclesiastical,
history. In the conquest of Italy, the champions of the Roman church
obtained a favourable occasion, a specious title, the wishes of the people,
the prayers and intrigues of the clergy. But the most essential gifts of
the popes to the Carlovingian race were the dignities of king of France
and of patrician of Rome. I. Under the sacerdotal monarchy of St.
Peter the nations began to resume the practice of seeking, on the banks
of the Tiber, their kings, their laws, and the oracles of their fate. The
Franks were perplexed between the name and substance of their government. All the powers of royalty were exercised by Pepin, mayor of the
palace; and nothing, except the regal title, was wanting to his ambition.
His enemies were crushed by his valour; his friends were multiplied by
his liberality; his father had been the saviour of Christendom; and the
claims of personal merit were repeated and ennobled in a descent of
four generations. The name and image of royalty was still preserved in
the last descendant of Clovis, the feeble Childeric; but his obsolete right
could only be used as an instrument of sedition: the nation was desirous
of restoring the simplicity of the constitution; and Pepin, a subject and
a prince, was ambitious to ascertain his own rank and the fortune of
his family. The mayor and the nobles were bound, by an oath of fidelity,
to the royal phantom: the blood of Clovis was pure and sacred in their
eyes; and their common ambassadors addressed the Roman pontiff to
dispel their scruples or to absolve their promise. The interest of Pope
Zachary, the successor of the two Gregories, prompted him to decide
in their favour: he pronounced that the nation might lawfully unite, in
the same person, the title and authority of king; and that the unfortunate
Childeric, a victim of the public safety, should be degraded, shaved, and
confined in a monastery for the remainder of his days. An answer so
agreeable to their wishes was accepted by the Franks, as the opinion of
a casuist, the sentence of a judge, or the oracle of a prophet: the Merovingian race disappeared from the earth; and Pepin was exalted on a
buckler by the suffrage of a free people, accustomed to obey his laws

and to march under his standard. His coronation was twice performed, with the sanction of the popes, by their most faithful servant St. Boniface, the apostle of Germany, and by the grateful hands of Stephen the Third, who, in the monastery of St. Denys, placed the diadem on the head of his benefactor. The royal unction of the kings of Israel was dexterously applied: the successor of St. Peter assumed the character of a divine ambassador: a German chieftain was transformed into the Lord's anointed; and this Jewish rite has been diffused and maintained by the superstition and vanity of modern Europe. The Franks were absolved from their ancient oath; but a dire anathema was thundered against them and their posterity, if they should dare to renew the same freedom of choice, or to elect a king, except in the holy and meritorious race of the Carlovingian princes. Without apprehending the future danger, these princes gloried in their present security: the secretary of Charlemagne affirms that the French sceptre was transferred by the authority of the popes; and, in their boldest enterprises, they insist, with confidence, on this signal and successful act of temporal jurisdiction.

II. In the change of manners and language the patricians of Rome were far removed from the senate of Romulus, or the palace of Constantine—from the free nobles of the republic, or the fictitious parents of the emperor. After the recovery of Italy and Africa by the arms of Justinian, the importance and danger of those remote provinces required the presence of a supreme magistrate; he was indifferently styled the exarch or the patrician; and these governors of Ravenna, who fill their place in the chronology of princes, extended their jurisdiction over the Roman city. Since the revolt of Italy and the loss of the Exarchate, the distress of the Romans had exacted some sacrifice of their independence. Yet, even in this act, they exercised the right of disposing of themselves; and the decrees of the senate and people successively invested Charles Martel and his posterity with the honours of patrician of Rome. The leaders of a powerful nation would have disdained a servile title and subordinate office; but the reign of the Greek emperors was suspended; and, in the vacancy of the empire, they derived a more glorious commission from the pope and the republic. The Roman ambassadors presented these patricians with the keys of the shrine of St. Peter, as a pledge and symbol of sovereignty; with a holy banner which it was their right and duty to unfurl in the defence of the church and city. In the time of Charles Martel and of Pepin, the interposition of the Lombard kingdom covered the freedom, while it threatened the safety, of Rome; and the *patriciate* represented only the title, the service, the alliance, of these distant protectors. The power and policy of Charlemagne annihilated an enemy and imposed a master. In his first visit to the capital he was received with all the honours which had formerly been paid to the exarch, the representative of the emperor; and these honours obtained some new decorations from the joy and gratitude of Pope Adrian the

First. No sooner was he informed of the sudden approach of the monarch, than he despatched the magistrates and nobles of Rome to meet him, with the banner, about thirty miles from the city. At the distance of one mile the Flaminian Way was lined with the *schools*, or national communities, of Greeks, Lombards, Saxons, &c.: the Roman youth was under arms; and the children of a more tender age, with palms and olive-branches in their hands, chanted the praises of their great deliverer. At the aspect of the holy crosses, and ensigns of the saints, he dismounted from his horse, led the procession of his nobles to the Vatican, and, as he ascended the stairs, devoutly kissed each step of the threshold of the apostles. In the portico, Adrian expected him at the head of his clergy: they embraced, as friends and equals; but in their march to the altar, the king or patrician assumed the right hand of the pope. Nor was the Frank content with these vain and empty demonstrations of respect. In the twenty-six years that elapsed between the conquest of Lombardy and his Imperial coronation, Rome, which had been delivered by the sword, was subject, as his own, to the sceptre of Charlemagne. The people swore allegiance to his person and family: in his name money was coined and justice was administered; and the election of the popes was examined and confirmed by his authority. Except an original and self-inherent claim of sovereignty, there was not any prerogative remaining which the title of emperor could add to the patrician of Rome.

The gratitude of the Carlovingians was adequate to these obligations, and their names are consecrated as the saviours and benefactors of the Roman church. Her ancient patrimony of farms and houses was transformed by their bounty into the temporal dominion of cities and provinces; and the donation of the Exarchate was the first-fruits of the conquests of Pepin. Astolphus with a sigh relinquished his prey; the keys and the hostages of the principal cities were delivered to the French ambassador; and, in his master's name, he presented them before the tomb of St. Peter. The ample measure of the Exarchate might comprise all the provinces of Italy which had obeyed the emperor and his vicegerent; but its strict and proper limits were included in the territories of Ravenna, Bologna, and Ferrara: its inseparable dependency was the Pentapolis, which stretched along the Adriatic from Rimini to Ancona, and advanced into the midland country as far as the ridges of the Apennine. In this transaction the ambition and avarice of the popes had been severely condemned. Perhaps the humility of a Christian priest should have rejected an earthly kingdom, which it was not easy for him to govern without renouncing the virtues of his profession. Perhaps a faithful subject, or even a generous enemy, would have been less impatient to divide the spoils of the barbarian; and if the emperor had intrusted Stephen to solicit in his name the restitution of the Exarchate, I will not absolve the pope from the reproach of treachery and falsehood.

But in the rigid interpretation of the laws, every one may accept, without injury, whatever his benefactor can bestow without injustice. The Greek emperor had abdicated or forfeited his right to the Exarchate; and the sword of Astolphus was broken by the stronger sword of the Carlovingian. It was not in the cause of the Iconoclast that Pepin had exposed his person and army in a double expedition beyond the Alps: he possessed, and might lawfully alienate, his conquests: and to the importunities of the Greeks he piously replied that no human consideration should tempt him to resume the gift which he had conferred on the Roman pontiff for the remission of his sins and the salvation of his soul. The splendid donation was granted in supreme and absolute dominion, and the world beheld for the first time a Christian bishop invested with the prerogatives of a temporal prince—the choice of magistrates, the exercise of justice, the imposition of taxes, and the wealth of the palace of Ravenna. In the dissolution of the Lombard kingdom the inhabitants of the duchy of Spoleto sought a refuge from the storm, shaved their heads after the Roman fashion, declared themselves the servants and subjects of St. Peter, and completed, by this voluntary surrender, the present circle of the ecclesiastical state. That mysterious circle was enlarged to an indefinite extent by the verbal or written donation of Charlemagne, who, in the first transports of his victory, despoiled himself and the Greek emperor of the cities and islands which had formerly been annexed to the Exarchate. But in the cooler moments of absence and reflection he viewed with an eye of jealousy and envy the recent greatness of his ecclesiastical ally. The execution of his own and his father's promises was respectfully eluded: the king of the Franks and Lombards asserted the inalienable rights of the empire; and, in his life and death, Ravenna, as well as Rome, was numbered in the list of his metropolitan cities. The sovereignty of the Exarchate melted away in the hands of the popes; they found in the archbishops of Ravenna a dangerous and domestic rival: the nobles and people disdained the yoke of a priest; and in the disorders of the time they could only retain the memory of an ancient claim, which, in a more prosperous age, they have revived and realised.

Fraud is the resource of weakness and cunning; and the strong, though ignorant, barbarian was often entangled in the net of sacerdotal policy. The Vatican and Lateran were an arsenal and manufacture which, according to the occasion, have produced or concealed a various collection of false or genuine, of corrupt or suspicious acts, as they tended to promote the interest of the Roman church. Before the end of the eighth century some apostolical scribe, perhaps the notorious Isidore, composed the decretals and the donation of Constantine, the two magic pillars of the spiritual and temporal monarchy of the popes. This memorable donation was introduced to the world by an epistle of Adrian the First, who exhorts Charlemagne to imitate the liberality and revive the name of the great Constantine. According to the legend, the first of the Christian emperors was healed of the leprosy, and purified in the waters of baptism, by St. Silvester, the Roman bishop; and never was physician more gloriously recompensed. His royal proselyte withdrew from the seat and patrimony of St. Peter; declared his resolution of founding a new capital in the East; and resigned to the popes the free and perpetual sovereignty of Rome, Italy, and the provinces of the West. This fiction was productive of the most beneficial effects. The Greek princes were convicted of the guilt of usurpation; and the revolt of Gregory was the claim of his lawful inheritance. The popes were delivered from their debt of gratitude; and the nominal gifts of the Carlovingians were no more than the just and irrevocable restitution of a scanty portion of the ecclesiastical state. The sovereignty of Rome no longer depended on the choice of a fickle people; and the successors of St. Peter and Constantine were invested with the purple and prerogatives of the Cæsars. So deep was the ignorance and credulity of the times that the most absurd of fables was received with equal reverence in Greece and in France, and is still enrolled among the decrees of the canon law. The emperors and the Romans were incapable of discerning a forgery that subverted their rights and freedom; and the only opposition proceeded from a Sabine monastery, which in the beginning of the twelfth century disputed the truth and validity of the donation of Constantine. In the revival of letters and liberty this fictitious deed was transpierced by the pen of Laurentius Valla, the pen of an eloquent critic and a Roman patriot. His contemporaries of the fifteenth century were astonished at his sacrilegious boldness; yet such is the silent and irresistible progress of reason, that before the end of the next age the fable was rejected by the contempt of historians and poets, and the tacit or modest censure of the advocates of the Roman church. The popes themselves have indulged a smile at the credulity of the vulgar; but a false and obsolete title still sanctifies their reign; and by the same fortune which has attended the decretals and the Sibylline oracles, the edifice has subsisted after the foundations have been undermined.

RESTORATION OF IMAGES IN THE EAST

While the popes established in Italy their freedom and dominion, the images, the first cause of their revolt, were restored in the Eastern empire. Under the reign of Constantine the Fifth, the union of civil and ecclesiastical power had overthrown the tree, without extirpating the root, of superstition. The idols, for such they were now held, were secretly cherished by the order and the sex most prone to devotion; and the fond alliance of the monks and females obtained a final victory over the reason and authority of man. Leo the Fourth maintained with less rigour the religion of his father and grandfather; but his wife, the fair and ambitious Irene, had imbibed the zeal of the Athenians, the heirs of the idolatry, rather than the philosophy, of their ancestors. During the life of her husband these sentiments were inflamed by danger and dissimulation, and she could only labour to protect and promote some favourite monks whom she drew from their caverns and seated on the metropolitan thrones of the East. But as soon as she reigned in her own name and that of her son, Irene more seriously undertook the ruin of the Iconoclasts; and the first step of her future persecution was a general edict for liberty of conscience. In the restoration of the monks a thousand images were exposed to the public veneration; a thousand legends were invented of their sufferings and miracles. By the opportunities of death or removal the episcopal seats were judiciously filled; the most eager competitors for earthly or celestial favour anticipated and flattered the judgment of their sovereign; and the promotion of her secretary Tarasius gave Irene the patriarch of Constantinople, and the command of the Oriental church. But the decrees of a general council could only be repealed by a similar assembly: the Iconoclasts whom she convened were bold in possession, and averse to debate; and the feeble voice of the bishops was re-echoed by the more formidable clamour of the soldiers and people of Constantinople. The delay and intrigues of a year, the separation of the disaffected troops, and the choice of Nice for a second orthodox synod, removed these obstacles; and the episcopal conscience was again, after the Greek fashion, in the hands of the prince. No more than eighteen days were allowed for the consummation of this important work: the Iconoclasts appeared, not as judges, but as criminals or penitents: the scene was decorated by the legates of Pope Adrian and the Eastern patriarchs; the decrees were framed by the president Tarasius, and ratified by the acclamations and subscriptions of three hundred and fifty bishops. They unanimously pronounced that the worship of images is agreeable to Scripture and reason, to the fathers and councils of the church: but they hesitate whether that worship be relative or direct; whether the Godhead and the figure of Christ be entitled to the same mode of adoration. Of this second Nicene council the acts are still extant; a curious monument of superstition and ignorance, of falsehood and folly. I shall only notice the judgment of the bishops, on the comparative merit of image-worship and morality. A monk had concluded a truce with the dæmon of fornication, on condition of interrupting his daily prayers to a picture that hung in his cell. His scruples prompted him to consult the abbot. "Rather than abstain from adoring Christ and his Mother in their holy images, it would be better for you," replied the casuist, "to enter every brothel, and visit every prostitute, in the city." For the honour of orthodoxy, at least the orthodoxy of the Roman church, it is somewhat unfortunate that the two princes who convened the two councils of Nice are both stained with the blood of their sons. The second of these assemblies was approved and rigorously executed by the despotism of Irene, and she refused her adversaries the toleration which at first she had granted to her friends. During the five succeeding reigns, a period of thirty-eight years, the contest was maintained with unabated rage and various success between the worshippers and the breakers of the images; but I am not inclined to pursue with minute diligence the repetition of the same events. Nicephorus allowed a general liberty of speech and practice; and the only virtue of his reign is accused by the monks as the cause of his temporal and eternal perdition. Superstition and weakness formed the character of Michael the First, but the saints and images were incapable of supporting their votary on the throne. In the purple, Leo the Fifth asserted the name and religion of an Armenian; and the idols, with their seditious adherents, were condemned to a second exile. Their applause would have sanctified the murder of an impious tyrant, but his assassin and successor, the second Michael, was tainted from his birth with the Phrygian heresies: he attempted to mediate between the contending parties; and the intractable spirit of the Catholics insensibly cast him into the opposite scale. His moderation was guarded by timidity; but his son Theophilus, alike ignorant of fear and pity, was the last and most cruel of the Iconoclasts. The enthusiasm of the times ran strongly against them; and the emperors, who stemmed the torrent, were exasperated and punished by the public hatred. After the death of Theophilus the final victory of the images was achieved by a second female, his widow Theodora, whom he left the guardian of the empire. Her measures were bold and decisive. The fiction of a tardy repentance absolved the fame and the soul of her deceased husband; the sentence of the Iconoclast patriarch was commuted from the loss of his eyes to a whipping of two hundred lashes: the bishops trembled, the monks shouted, and the festival of orthodoxy preserves the annual memory of the triumph of the images. A single question yet remained, whether they are endowed with any proper and inherent sanctity; it was agitated by the Greeks of the eleventh century; and as this opinion has the strongest recommendation of absurdity, I am surprised that it was not more explicitly decided in the affirmative. In the West, Pope Adrian the First accepted and announced the decrees of the Nicene assembly, which is now revered by the Catholics as the seventh in rank of the general councils. Rome and Italy were docile to the voice of their father; but the greatest part of the Latin Christians were far behind in the race of superstition. The churches of France, Germany, England, and Spain steered a middle course between the adoration and the destruction of images, which they admitted into their temples, not as objects of worship, but as lively and useful memorials of faith and history. An angry book of controversy was composed and published in the name of Charlemagne: under his authority a synod of three hundred bishops was assembled at Frankfort: they blamed the fury of the Iconoclasts, but they pronounced a more severe censure against the superstition of the Greeks, and the decrees of their pretended council, which was long despised by the barbarians of the West. Among them the worship of images advanced with a silent and insensible progress; but a large atonement is made for their hesitation and delay by the gross idolatry of the ages which precede the reformation, and of the countries, both in Europe and America, which are still immersed in the gloom of superstition.

THE FINAL SEPARATION OF THE POPES FROM THE EASTERN EMPIRE

It was after the Nicene synod, and under the reign of the pious Irene, that the popes consummated the separation of Rome and Italy, by the translation of the empire to the less orthodox Charlemagne. They were compelled to choose between the rival nations: religion was not the sole motive of their choice; and while they dissembled the failings of their friends, they beheld, with reluctance and suspicion, the Catholic virtues of their foes. The difference of language and manners had perpetuated the enmity of the two capitals; and they were alienated from each other by the hostile opposition of seventy years. In that schism the Romans had tasted of freedom, and the popes of sovereignty: their submission would have exposed them to the revenge of a jealous tyrant; and the revolution of Italy had betrayed the impotence, as well as the tyranny of the Byzantine court. The Greek emperors had restored the images, but they had not restored the Calabrian estates and the Illyrian diocese, which the Iconoclasts had torn away from the successors of St. Peter; and Pope Adrian threatens them with a sentence of excommunication unless they speedily abjure this practical heresy. The Greeks were now orthodox; but their religion might be tainted by the breath of the reigning monarch: the Franks were now contumacious; but a discerning eye might discern their approaching conversion, from the use, to the adoration, of images. The name of Charlemagne was stained by the polemic acrimony of his scribes; but the conqueror himself conformed, with the temper of a statesman, to the various practice of France and Italy. In his four pilgrimages or visits to the Vatican he embraced the popes in the communion of friendship and piety; knelt before the tomb, and consequently before the image, of the apostle; and joined, without scruple, in all the prayers and processions of the Roman liturgy. Would prudence or gratitude allow the pontiffs to renounce their benefactor? Had they a right to alienate his gift of the Exarchate? Had they power to abolish his government of Rome? The title of patrician was below the merit and greatness of Charlemagne; and it was only by reviving the Western empire that they could pay their obligations or secure their establishment. By this decisive measure they would finally eradicate the claims of the Greeks: from the debasement of a provincial town, the majesty of Rome would be restored; the Latin Christians would be united, under a supreme head, in their ancient metropolis; and the conquerors of the West would receive their crown from the successors of St. Peter. The Roman church would acquire a zealous and respectable advocate; and, under the shadow of the Carlovingian power, the bishop might exercise, with honour and safety, the government of the city.

Before the ruin of Paganism in Rome the competition for a wealthy bishopric had often been productive of tumult and bloodshed. The people was less numerous, but the times were more savage, the prize more important, and the chair of St. Peter was fiercely disputed by the leading ecclesiastics who aspired to the rank of sovereign. The reign of Adrian the First surpasses the measure of past or succeeding ages; the walls of Rome, the sacred patrimony, the ruin of the Lombards, and the friendship of Charlemagne, were the trophies of his fame: he secretly edified the throne of his successors, and displayed in a narrow space the virtues of a great prince. His memory was revered; but in the next election, a priest of the Lateran, Leo the Third, was preferred to the nephew and the favourite of Adrian, whom he had promoted to the first dignities of the church. Their acquiescence or repentance disguised, above four years, the blackest intention of revenge, till the day of a procession, when a furious band of conspirators dispersed the unarmed multitude, and assaulted with blows and wounds the sacred person of the pope. But their enterprise on his life or liberty was disappointed, perhaps by their own confusion and remorse. Leo was left for dead on the ground: on his revival from the swoon, the effect of his loss of blood, he recovered his speech and sight; and this natural event was improved to the miraculous restoration of his eyes and tongue, of which he had been deprived, twice deprived, by the knife of the assassins. From his prison he escaped to the Vatican: the duke of Spoleto hastened to his rescue, Charlemagne sympathised in his injury, and in his camp of Paderborn in Westphalia accepted, or solicited, a visit from the Roman pontiff. Leo repassed the Alps with a commission of counts and bishops, the guards of his safety and the judges of his innocence; and it was not without reluctance that the conqueror of the Saxons delayed till the ensuing year the personal discharge of this pious office. In his fourth and last pilgrimage he was received at Rome with the due honours of king and patrician: Leo was permitted to purge himself by oath of the crimes imputed to his charge: his enemies were silenced, and the sacrilegious attempt against his life was punished by the mild and insufficient penalty of exile. On the festival of Christmas, the last year of the eighth century, Charlemagne appeared in the church of St. Peter; and to gratify the vanity of Rome, he had exchanged the simple dress of his country for the habit of a patrician. After the celebration of the holy mysteries, Leo suddenly placed a precious crown on his head, and the dome resounded with the acclamations of the people, "Long life and victory to Charles, the most pious Augustus, crowned by God the great and pacific emperor of the Romans!" The head and body of Charlemagne were consecrated by the royal unction: after the example of the Cæsars, he was saluted or adored by the pontiff: his coronation oath represents a promise to maintain the faith and privileges of the church; and the first-fruits were paid in his rich offerings to the shrine of the apostle. In his familiar conversation the emperor protested his ignorance of the intentions of Leo, which he would have disappointed by his absence on that memorable day. But the preparations of the ceremony must have disclosed the secret; and the journey of Charlemagne reveals his knowledge and expectation: he had acknowledged that the Imperial title was the object of his ambition, and a Roman synod had pronounced that it was the only adequate reward of his merit and services.

THE REIGN AND CHARACTER OF CHARLEMAGNE

The appellation of *great* has been often bestowed, and sometimes deserved, but Charlemagne is the only prince in whose favour the title has been indissolubly blended with the name. That name, with the addition of *saint*, is inserted in the Roman calendar; and the saint, by a rare felicity, is crowned with the praises of the historians and philosophers of an enlightened age. His *real* merit is doubtless enhanced by the barbarism of the nation and the times from which he emerged: but the *apparent* magnitude of an object is likewise enlarged by an unequal comparison; and the ruins of Palmyra derive a casual splendour from the nakedness of the surrounding desert. Without injustice to his fame, I may discern some blemishes in the sanctity and greatness of the restorer of the Western empire. Of his moral virtues, chastity is not the most conspicuous:[1] but the public happiness could not be materially injured by his nine wives or concubines, the various indulgence of meaner or more transient amours, the multitude of his bastards whom he bestowed on the church, and the long celibacy and licentious manners of his daughters,[2] whom the father was suspected of loving with too fond a passion. I shall be scarcely permitted to accuse the ambition of a conqueror; but in a day of equal retribution, the sons of his brother Carloman, the Merovingian princes of Aquitain, and the four thousand five hundred Saxons who were beheaded on the same spot, would have something to allege against the justice and humanity of Charlemagne. His treatment of the vanquished Saxons was an abuse of the right of

[1] The vision of Weltin, composed by a monk eleven years after the death of Charlemagne, shows him in purgatory, with a vulture, who is perpetually gnawing the guilty member, while the rest of his body, the emblem of his virtues, is sound and perfect.

[2] The marriage of Eginhard with Imma, daughter of Charlemagne, is, in my opinion, sufficiently refuted by the *probrum* and *suspicio* that sullied these fair damsels, without excepting his own wife. The husband must have been too strong for the historian.

conquest; his laws were not less sanguinary than his arms, and, in the discussion of his motives, whatever is subtracted from bigotry must be imputed to temper. The sedentary reader is amazed by his incessant activity of mind and body; and his subjects and enemies were not less astonished at his sudden presence at the moment when they believed him at the most distant extremity of the empire; neither peace nor war, nor summer nor winter, were a season of repose; and our fancy cannot easily reconcile the annals of his reign with the geography of his expeditions. But this activity was a national, rather than a personal virtue: the vagrant life of a Frank was spent in the chase, in pilgrimage, in military adventures; and the journeys of Charlemagne were distinguished only by a more numerous train and a more important purpose. His military renown must be tried by the scrutiny of his troops, his enemies, and his actions. Alexander conquered with the arms of Philip, but the *two* heroes who preceded Charlemagne bequeathed him their name, their examples, and the companions of their victories. At the head of his veteran and superior armies he oppressed the savage or degenerate nations, who were incapable of confederating for their common safety; nor did he ever encounter an equal antagonist in numbers, in discipline, or in arms. The science of war has been lost and revived with the arts of peace; but his campaigns are not illustrated by any siege or battle of singular difficulty and success; and he might behold with envy the Saracen trophies of his grandfather. After his Spanish expedition his rear-guard was defeated in the Pyrenæan mountains; and the soldiers, whose situation was irretrievable, and whose valour was useless, might accuse, with their last breath, the want of skill or caution of their general. I touch with reverence the laws of Charlemagne, so highly applauded by a respectable judge. They compose not a system, but a series, of occasional and minute edicts, for the correction of abuses, the reformation of manners, the economy of his farms, the care of his poultry, and even the sale of his eggs. He wished to improve the laws and the character of the Franks; and his attempts, however feeble and imperfect, are deserving of praise: the inveterate evils of the times were suspended or mollified by his government; but in his institutions I can seldom discover the general views and the immortal spirit of a legislator, who survives himself for the benefit of posterity. The union and stability of his empire depended on the life of a single man; he imitated the dangerous practice of dividing his kingdoms among his sons; and, after his numerous diets, the whole constitution was left to fluctuate between the disorders of anarchy and despotism. His esteem for the piety and knowledge of the clergy tempted him to intrust that aspiring order with temporal dominion and civil jurisdiction; and his son Lewis, when he was stripped and degraded by the bishops, might accuse, in some measure, the imprudence of his father. His laws enforced the imposition of tithes, because the dæmons had proclaimed in the air that the default of payment had been the cause of the last scarcity. The literary merits of Charlemagne are attested by the foundation of schools, the introduction of arts, the works which were published in his name, and his familiar connection with the subjects and strangers whom he invited to his court to educate both the prince and people. His own studies were tardy, laborious, and imperfect; if he spoke Latin, and understood Greek, he derived the rudiments of knowledge from conversation, rather than from books; and, in his mature age, the emperor strove to acquire the practice of writing, which every peasant now learns in his infancy. The grammar and logic, the music and astronomy, of the times were only cultivated as the handmaids of superstition; but the curiosity of the human mind must ultimately tend to its improvement, and the encouragement of learning reflects the purest and most pleasing lustre on the character of Charlemagne. The dignity of his person, the length of his reign, the prosperity of his arms, the vigour of his government, and the reverence of distant nations, distinguish from the royal crowd: and Europe dates a new era from his restoration of the Western empire.

In 962 Otho, king of Germany, subdued Italy and appropriated the Western empire. The Imperial Crown was now vested in the name and nation of Germany.

THE EMPEROR CHARLES IV

It is in the fourteenth century that we may view in the strongest light the state and contrast of the Roman empire of Germany, which no longer held, except on the borders of the Rhine and Danube, a single province of Trajan or Constantine. Their unworthy successors were the counts of Hapsburg, of Nassau, of Luxemburg, and of Schwartzenburg: the emperor Henry the Seventh procured for his son the crown of Bohemia, and his grandson Charles the Fourth was born among a people strange and barbarous in the estimation of the Germans themselves. After the excommunication of Lewis of Bavaria, he received the gift or promise of the vacant empire from the Roman pontiffs, who, in the exile and captivity of Avignon, affected the dominion of the earth. The death of his competitors united the electoral college, and Charles was unanimously saluted king of the Romans, and future emperor; a title which in the same age was prostituted to the Cæsars of Germany and Greece. The German emperor was no more than the elective and impotent magistrate of an aristocracy of princes, who had not left him a village that he might call his own. His best prerogative was the right of presiding and proposing in the national senate, which was convened at his summons; and his native kingdom of Bohemia, less opulent than the adjacent city of Nuremberg, was the firmest seat of his power and the richest source of his revenue. The army with which he passed the Alps consisted of three hundred horse. In the cathedral of St. Ambrose,

Charles was crowned with the *iron* crown, which tradition ascribed to the Lombard monarchy; but he was admitted only with a peaceful train; the gates of the city were shut upon him; and the king of Italy was held a captive by the arms of the Visconti, whom he confirmed in the sovereignty of Milan. In the Vatican he was again crowned with the *golden* crown of the empire; but, in obedience to a secret treaty, the Roman emperor immediately withdrew, without reposing a single night within the walls of Rome. The eloquent Petrarch, whose fancy revived the visionary glories of the Capitol, deplores and upbraids the ignominious flight of the Bohemian; and even his contemporaries could observe that the sole exercise of his authority was in the lucrative sale of privileges and titles. The gold of Italy secured the election of his son; but such was the shameful poverty of the Roman emperor, that his person was arrested by a butcher in the streets of Worms, and was detained in the public inn as a pledge or hostage for the payment of his expenses.

From this humiliating scene let us turn to the apparent majesty of the same Charles in the diets of the empire. The golden bull, which fixes the Germanic constitution, is promulgated in the style of a sovereign and legislator. An hundred princes bowed before his throne, and exalted their own dignity by the voluntary honours which they yielded to their chief or minister. At the royal banquet the hereditary great officers, the seven electors, who in rank and title were equal to kings, performed their solemn and domestic service of the palace. The seals of the triple kingdom were borne in state by the archbishops of Maintz, Cologne, and Treves, the perpetual arch-chancellors of Germany, Italy, and Arles. The great marshal, on horseback, exercised his function with a silver measure of oats, which he emptied on the ground, and immediately dismounted to regulate the order of the guests. The great steward, the count palatine of the Rhine, placed the dishes on the table. The great chamberlain, the margrave of Brandenburg, presented, after the repast, the golden ewer and basin, to wash. The king of Bohemia, as great cupbearer, was represented by the emperor's brother, the duke of Luxembourg and Brabant; and the procession was closed by the great huntsmen, who introduced a boar and a stag, with a loud chorus of horns and hounds. Nor was the supremacy of the emperor confined to Germany alone: the hereditary monarchs of Europe confessed the preeminence of his rank and dignity: he was the first of the Christian princes, the temporal head of the great republic of the West: to his person the title of majesty was long appropriated; and he disputed with the pope the sublime prerogative of creating kings and assembling councils. The oracle of the civil law, the learned Bartolus, was a pensioner of Charles the Fourth; and his school resounded with the doctrine that the Roman emperor was the rightful sovereign of the earth, from the rising to the setting sun. The contrary opinion was condemned, not as an error, but as an heresy, since even the Gospel had pronounced, "And there went forth a decree from Cæsar Augustus, that *all the world* should be taxed."

COMPARISON OF CHARLES IV AND AUGUSTUS

If we annihilate the interval of time and space between Augustus and Charles, strong and striking will be the contrast between the two Cæsars: the Bohemian, who concealed his weakness under the mask of ostentation, and the Roman, who disguised his strength under the semblance of modesty. At the head of his victorious legions, in his reign over the sea and land, from the Nile and Euphrates to the Atlantic Ocean, Augustus professed himself the servant of the state and the equal of his fellow-citizens. The conqueror of Rome and her provinces assumed the popular and legal form of a censor, a consul, and a tribune. His will was the law of mankind, but in the declaration of his laws he borrowed the voice of the senate and people; and, from their decrees, their master accepted and renewed his temporary commission to administer the republic. In his dress, his domestics, his titles, in all the offices of social life, Augustus maintained the character of a private Roman; and his most artful flatterers respected the secret of his absolute and perpetual monarchy.

THE COMING OF ISLAM

Chapter 50

DESCRIPTION OF ARABIA. CHARACTER AND RELIGION OF
THE ARABS. THE RISE OF MAHOMET. HIS PRECEPTS. HIS
FLIGHT FROM MECCA TO MEDINA. HIS DECLARATION OF
WAR AGAINST THE INFIDELS. DEATH OF MAHOMET. HIS
CHARACTER AND PRIVATE LIFE. ASSESSMENT OF HIS
INFLUENCE

AFTER pursuing above six hundred years the fleeting Cæsars of
Constantinople and Germany, I now descend, in the reign of
Heraclius, on the eastern borders of the Greek monarchy. While
the state was exhausted by the Persian war, and the church was distracted by the Nestorian and Monophysite sects, Mahomet, with the
sword in one hand and the Koran in the other, erected his throne on the
ruins of Christianity and of Rome. The genius of the Arabian prophet,
the manners of his nation, and the spirit of his religion, involve the
causes of the decline and fall of the Eastern empire; and our eyes are
curiously intent on one of the most memorable revolutions which have
impressed a new and lasting character on the nations of the globe.[1]

In the vacant space between Persia, Syria, Egypt, and Ethiopia, the
Arabian peninsula may be conceived as a triangle of spacious but irregular dimensions. From the northern point of Beles, on the Euphrates,
a line of fifteen hundred miles is terminated by the Straits of Babel-
mandeb and the land of frankincense. About half this length may be
allowed for the middle breadth, from east to west, from Bassora to Suez,
from the Persian Gulf to the Red Sea. The sides of the triangle are
gradually enlarged, and the southern basis presents a front of a thousand
miles to the Indian Ocean. The entire surface of the peninsula exceeds
in a fourfold proportion that of Germany or France; but the far greater
part has been justly stigmatised with the epithets of the *stony* and the
sandy. Even the wilds of Tartary are decked, by the hand of nature, with
lofty trees and luxuriant herbage; and the lonesome traveller derives a
sort of comfort and society from the presence of vegetable life. But in
the dreary waste of Arabia a boundless level of sand is intersected by
sharp and naked mountains; and the face of the desert, without shade
or shelter, is scorched by the direct and intense rays of a tropical sun.

[1] As in this and the following chapter I shall display much Arabic learning, I must
profess my total ignorance of the Oriental tongues, and my gratitude to the learned
interpreters, who have transfused their science into the Latin, French, and English
languages. Their collections, versions, and histories, I shall occasionally notice.

Instead of refreshing breezes, the winds, particularly from the south-west, diffuse a noxious and even deadly vapour; the hillocks of sand which they alternately raise and scatter are compared to the billows of the ocean, and whole caravans, whole armies, have been lost and buried in the whirlwind. The common benefits of water are an object of desire and contest; and such is the scarcity of wood, that some art is requisite to preserve and propagate the element of fire. Arabia is destitute of navigable rivers, which fertilise the soil, and convey its produce to the adjacent regions: the torrents that fall from the hills are imbibed by the thirsty earth: the rare and hardy plants, the tamarind or the acacia that strike their roots into the clefts of the rocks, are nourished by the dews of the night: a scanty supply of rain is collected in cisterns and aqueducts: the wells and springs are the secret treasure of the desert; and the pilgrim of Mecca, after many a dry and sultry march, is disgusted by the taste of the waters which have rolled over a bed of sulphur or salt. Such is the general and genuine picture of the climate of Arabia. The experience of evil enhances the value of any local or partial enjoyments. A shady grove, a green pasture, a stream of fresh water, are sufficient to attract a colony of sedentary Arabs to the fortunate spots which can afford food and refreshment to themselves and their cattle, and which encourage their industry in the cultivation of the palm-tree and the vine. The high lands that border on the Indian Ocean are distinguished by their superior plenty of wood and water: the air is more temperate, the fruits are more delicious, the animals and the human race more numerous: the fertility of the soil invites and rewards the toil of the husbandman; and the peculiar gifts of frankincense and coffee have attracted in different ages the merchants of the world. If it be compared with the rest of the peninsula, this sequestered region may truly deserve the appellation of the *happy*; and the splendid colouring of fancy and fiction has been suggested by contrast and countenanced by distance. It was for this earthly paradise that nature had reserved her choicest favours and her most curious workmanship: the incompatible blessings of luxury and innocence were ascribed to the natives: the soil was impregnated with gold and gems, and both the land and sea were taught to exhale the odours of aromatic sweets. This division of the *sandy*, the *stony*, and the *happy*, so familiar to the Greeks and Latins, is unknown to the Arabians themselves; and it is singular enough, that a country whose language and inhabitants have ever been the same should scarcely retain a vestige of its ancient geography. The maritime districts of *Bahrein* and *Oman* are opposite to the realms of Persia. The kingdom of *Yemen* displays the limits, or at least the situation, of Arabia Felix: the name of *Neged* is extended over the inland space; and the birth of Mahomet has illustrated the province of *Hejaz* along the coast of the Red Sea.

The measure of population is regulated by the means of subsistence; and the inhabitants of this vast peninsula might be out-numbered by the subjects of a fertile and industrious province. Along the shores of the Persian Gulf, of the ocean, and even of the Red Sea, the *Ichthyophagi*, or fish-eaters, continued to wander in quest of their precarious food. In this primitive and abject state, which ill deserves the name of society, the human brute, without arts or laws, almost without sense or language, is poorly distinguished from the rest of the animal creation. Generations and ages might roll away in silent oblivion, and the helpless savage was restrained from multiplying his race by the wants and pursuits which confined his existence to the narrow margin of the sea-coast. But in an early period of antiquity the great body of the Arabs had emerged from this scene of misery; and as the naked wilderness could not maintain a people of hunters, they rose at once to the more secure and plentiful condition of the pastoral life. The same life is uniformly pursued by the roving tribes of the desert; and in the portrait of the modern *Bedoweens* we may trace the features of their ancestors, who, in the age of Moses or Mahomet, dwelt under similar tents, and conducted their horses, and camels, and sheep to the same springs and the same pastures. Our toil is lessened, and our wealth is increased, by our dominion over the useful animals; and the Arabian shepherd had acquired the absolute possession of a faithful friend and a laborious slave. Arabia in the opinion of the naturalist, is the genuine and original country of the *horse*; the climate most propitious, not indeed to the size, but to the spirit and swiftness, of that generous animal. The merit of the Barb, the Spanish, and the English breed is derived from a mixture of Arabian blood: the Bedoweens preserve, with superstitious care, the honours and the memory of the purest race: the males are sold at a high price, but the females are seldom alienated; and the birth of a noble foal was esteemed among the tribes as a subject of joy and mutual congratulation. These horses are educated in the tents, among the children of the Arabs, with a tender familiarity, which trains them in the habits of gentleness and attachment. They are accustomed only to walk and to gallop: their sensations are not blunted by the incessant abuse of the spur and the whip: their powers are reserved for the moments of flight and pursuit: but no sooner do they feel the touch of the hand or the stirrup, than they dart away with the swiftness of the wind; and if their friend be dismounted in the rapid career, they instantly stop till he has recovered his seat. In the sands of Africa and Arabia the *camel* is a sacred and precious gift. That strong and patient beast of burden can perform, without eating or drinking, a journey of several days; and a reservoir of fresh water is preserved in a large bag, a fifth stomach of the animal, whose body is imprinted with the marks of servitude: the larger breed is capable of transporting a weight of a thousand pounds; and the dromedary, of a lighter and more active frame, outstrips the fleetest courser in the race. Alive or dead, almost every part of the camel is serviceable to man: her milk is plentiful and nutritious: the young and tender flesh has the taste of veal: a valuable salt is extracted from the urine: the dung supplies the deficiency of fuel: and the long hair, which falls each year and is renewed, is coarsely manufactured into the garments, the furniture, and the tents of the Bedoweens. In the rainy seasons they consume the rare and insufficient herbage of the desert: during the heats of summer and the scarcity of winter they remove their encampments to the sea-coast, the hills of Yemen, or the neighbourhood of the Euphrates, and have often extorted the dangerous licence of visiting the banks of the Nile and the villages of Syria and Palestine. The life of a wandering Arab is a life of danger and distress; and though sometimes, by rapine or exchange, he may appropriate the fruits of industry, a private citizen in Europe is in the possession of more solid and pleasing luxury than the proudest emir who marches in the field at the head of ten thousand horse.

Yet an essential difference may be found between the hordes of Scythia and the Arabian tribes; since many of the latter were collected into towns, and employed in the labours of trade and agriculture. A part of their time and industry was still devoted to the management of their cattle: they mingled, in peace and war, with their brethren of the desert; and the Bedoweens derived from their useful intercourse some supply of their wants, and some rudiments of art and knowledge. Among the forty-two cities of Arabia, enumerated by Abulfeda, the most ancient and populous were situate in the *happy* Yemen: the towers of Saana, and the marvellous reservoir of Merab, were constructed by the kings of the Homerites; but their profane lustre was eclipsed by the prophetic glories of MEDINA and MECCA, near the Red Sea, and at the distance from each other of two hundred and seventy miles. The last of these holy places was known to the Greeks under the name of Macoraba; and the termination of the word is expressive of its greatness, which has not indeed, in the most flourishing period, exceeded the size and populousness of Marseilles. Some latent motive, perhaps of superstition, must have impelled the founders in the choice of a most unpromising situation. They erected their habitations of mud or stone in a plain about two miles long and one mile broad, at the foot of three barren mountains: the soil is a rock; the water even of the holy well of Zemzem is bitter or brackish; the pastures are remote from the city; and grapes are transported above seventy miles from the gardens of Tayef. The fame and spirit of the Koreishites, who reigned in Mecca, were conspicuous among the Arabian tribes; but their ungrateful soil refused the labours of agriculture, and their position was favourable to the enterprises of trade. By the seaport of Gedda, at the distance only of forty miles, they maintained an easy correspondence with Abyssinia; and that Christian kingdom afforded the first refuge to the disciples of Mahomet. The treasures of Africa were conveyed over the peninsula to Gerrha or Katif, in the province of Bahrein, a city built, as it is said, of rock-salt, by the Chaldæan exiles; and from thence, with the native pearls of the Persian Gulf, they were floated on rafts to the

mouth of the Euphrates. Mecca is placed almost at an equal distance, a
month's journey, between Yemen on the right and Syria on the left hand.
The former was the winter, the latter the summer, station of her caravans; and their seasonable arrival relieved the ships of India from the
tedious and troublesome navigation of the Red Sea. In the markets of
Saana and Merab, in the harbours of Oman and Aden, the camels of the
Koreishites were laden with a precious cargo of aromatics; a supply of
corn and manufactures was purchased in the fairs of Bostra and Damascus; the lucrative exchange diffused plenty and riches in the streets
of Mecca; and the noblest of her sons united the love of arms with the
profession of merchandise.

CHARACTER OF THE ARABS

The perpetual independence of the Arabs has been the theme of praise
among strangers and natives; and the arts of controversy transform this
singular event into a prophecy and a miracle in favour of the posterity of
Ismael. Some exceptions, that can neither be dissembled nor eluded,
render this mode of reasoning as indiscreet as it is superfluous; the kingdom of Yemen has been successively subdued by the Abyssinians, the
Persians, the sultans of Egypt, and the Turks: the holy cities of Mecca
and Medina have repeatedly bowed under a Scythian tyrant; and the
Roman province of Arabia embraced the peculiar wilderness in which
Ismael and his sons must have pitched their tents in the face of their
brethren. Yet these exceptions are temporary or local; the body of the
nation has escaped the yoke of the most powerful monarchies: the arms
of Sesostris and Cyrus, of Pompey and Trajan, could never achieve the
conquest of Arabia; the present sovereign of the Turks may exercise a
shadow of jurisdiction, but his pride is reduced to solicit the friendship of
a people whom it is dangerous to provoke and fruitless to attack. The
obvious causes of their freedom are inscribed on the character and country of the Arabs. Many ages before Mahomet, their intrepid valour had
been severely felt by their neighbours in offensive and defensive war. The
patient and active virtues of a soldier are insensibly nursed in the habits
and discipline of a pastoral life. The care of the sheep and camels is
abandoned to the women of the tribe; but the martial youth, under the
banner of the emir, is ever on horseback, and in the field, to practise the
exercise of the bow, the javelin, and the scymetar. The long memory of
their independence is the firmest pledge of its perpetuity, and succeeding
generations are animated to prove their descent and to maintain their
inheritance. Their domestic feuds are suspended on the approach of a
common enemy; and in their last hostilities against the Turks, the caravan of Mecca was attacked and pillaged by fourscore thousand of the
confederates. When they advance to battle, the hope of victory is in the
front; in the rear, the assurance of a retreat. Their horses and camels,

who in eight or ten days can perform a march of four or five hundred miles, disappear before the conqueror; the secret waters of the desert elude his search; and his victorious troops are consumed with thirst, hunger, and fatigue in the pursuit of an invisible foe, who scorns his efforts, and safely reposes in the heart of the burning solitude. The arms and deserts of the Bedoweens are not only the safeguards of their own freedom, but the barriers also of the happy Arabia, whose inhabitants, remote from war, are enervated by the luxury of the soil and climate. The legions of Augustus melted away in disease and lassitude; and it is only by a naval power that the reduction of Yemen has been successfully attempted. When Mahomet erected his holy standard, that kingdom was a province of the Persian empire; yet seven princes of the Homerites still reigned in the mountains; and the vicegerent of Chosroes was tempted to forget his distant country and his unfortunate master. The historians of the age of Justinian represent the state of the independent Arabs, who were divided by interest or affection in the long quarrel of the East: the tribe of *Gassan* was allowed to encamp on the Syrian territory: the princes of *Hira* were permitted to form a city about forty miles to the southward of the ruins of Babylon. Their service in the field was speedy and vigorous; but their friendship was venal, their faith inconstant, their enmity capricious: it was an easier task to excite than to disarm these roving barbarians; and, in the familiar intercourse of war, they learned to see and to despise the splendid weakness both of Rome and of Persia. From Mecca to the Euphrates, the Arabian tribes were confounded by the Greeks and Latins under the general appellation of SARACENS, a name which every Christian mouth has been taught to pronounce with terror and abhorrence.

The slaves of domestic tyranny may vainly exult in their national independence: but the Arab is personally free; and he enjoys, in some degree, the benefits of society, without forfeiting the prerogatives of nature. In every tribe, superstition, or gratitude, or fortune has exalted a particular family above the heads of their equals. The dignities of sheickh and emir invariably descend in this chosen race; but the order of succession is loose and precarious; and the most worthy or aged of the noble kinsmen are preferred to the simple though important office of composing disputes by their advice, and guiding valour by their example. Even a female of sense and spirit has been permitted to command the countrymen of Zenobia. The momentary junction of several tribes produces an army: their more lasting union constitutes a nation: and the supreme chief, the emir of emirs, whose banner is displayed at their head, may deserve, in the eyes of strangers, the honours of the kingly name. If the Arabian princes abuse their power, they are quickly punished by the desertion of their subjects, who had been accustomed to a mild and parental jurisdiction. Their spirit is free, their steps are unconfined, the desert is open, and the tribes and families are held together by a mutual and voluntary compact. The softer natives of Yemen supported the pomp and majesty of a monarch; but if he could not leave his palace without endangering his life, the active powers of government must have been devolved on his nobles and magistrates. The cities of Mecca and Medina present, in the heart of Asia, the form, or rather the substance, of a commonwealth. The grandfather of Mahomet, and his lineal ancestors, appear in foreign and domestic transactions as the princes of their country; but they reigned, like Pericles at Athens, or the Medici at Florence, by the opinion of their wisdom and integrity; their influence was divided with their patrimony; and the sceptre was transferred from the uncles of the prophet to a younger branch of the tribe of Koreish. On solemn occasions they convened the assembly of the people; and, since mankind must be either compelled or persuaded to obey, the use and reputation of oratory among the ancient Arabs is the clearest evidence of public freedom. But their simple freedom was of a very different cast from the nice and artificial machinery of the Greek and Roman republics, in which each member possessed an undivided share of the civil and political rights of the community. In the more simple state of the Arabs, the nation is free, because each of her sons disdains a base submission to the will of a master. His breast is fortified with the austere virtues of courage, patience, and sobriety; the love of independence prompts him to exercise the habits of self-command; and the fear of dishonour guards him from the meaner apprehension of pain, of danger, and of death. The gravity and firmness of the mind is conspicuous in his outward demeanour: his speech is slow, weighty, and concise; he is seldom provoked to laughter; his only gesture is that of stroking his beard, the venerable symbol of manhood; and the sense of his own importance teaches him to accost his equals without levity, and his superiors without awe. The liberty of the Saracens survived their conquests: the first caliphs indulged the bold and familiar language of their subjects: they ascended the pulpit to persuade and edify the congregation; nor was it before the seat of empire was removed to the Tigris that the Abbassides adopted the proud and pompous ceremonial of the Persian and Byzantine courts.

In the study of nations and men we may observe the causes that render them hostile or friendly to each other, that tend to narrow or enlarge, to mollify or exasperate, the social character. The separation of the Arabs from the rest of mankind has accustomed them to confound the ideas of stranger and enemy; and the poverty of the land has introduced a maxim of jurisprudence which they believe and practise to the present hour. They pretend that, in the division of the earth, the rich and fertile climates were assigned to the other branches of the human family; and that the posterity of the outlaw Ismael might recover, by fraud or force, the portion of inheritance of which he had been unjustly deprived. According to the remark of Pliny, the Arabian tribes are equally addicted to theft and merchandise: the caravans that traverse the desert are ransomed or pillaged; and their neighbours, since the remote times of Job and Sesostris, have been the victims of their rapacious spirit. If a Bedoween discovers from afar a solitary traveller, he rides furiously against him, crying, with a loud voice, "Undress thyself, thy aunt (*my wife*) is without a garment." A ready submission entitles him to mercy; resistance will provoke the aggressor, and his own blood must expiate the blood which he presumes to shed in legitimate defence. A single robber, or a few associates, are branded with their genuine name; but the exploits of a numerous band assume the character of lawful and honourable war. The temper of a people thus armed against mankind was doubly inflamed by the domestic licence of rapine, murder, and revenge. In the constitution of Europe, the right of peace and war is now confined to a small, and the actual exercise to a much smaller, list of respectable potentates; but each Arab, with impunity and renown, might point his javelin against the life of his countryman. The union of the nation consisted only in a vague resemblance of language and manners; and in each community the jurisdiction of the magistrate was mute and impotent. Of the time of ignorance which preceded Mahomet, seventeen hundred battles are recorded by tradition: hostility was embittered with rancour of civil faction: and the recital, in prose or verse, of an obsolete feud, was sufficient to rekindle the same passions among the descendants of the hostile tribes. In private life every man, at least every family, was the judge and avenger of its own cause. The nice sensibility of honour, which weighs the insult rather than the injury, sheds its deadly venom on the quarrels of the Arabs: the honour of their women, and of their *beards*, is most easily wounded; an indecent action, a contemptuous word, can be expiated only by the blood of the offender; and such is their patient inveteracy, that they expect whole months and years the opportunity of revenge. A fine or compensation for murder is familiar to the barbarians of every age: but in Arabia the kinsmen of the dead are at liberty to accept the atonement, or to exercise with their own hands the law of retaliation. The refined malice of the Arabs refuses even the head of the murderer, substitutes an innocent to the guilty person, and transfers the penalty to the best and most considerable of the race by whom they have been injured. If he falls by their hands, they are exposed in their turn to the danger of reprisals; the interest and principal of the bloody debt are accumulated: the individuals of either family lead a life of malice and suspicion, and fifty years may sometimes elapse before the account or vengeance be finally settled. This sanguinary spirit, ignorant of pity of forgiveness, had been moderated, however, by the maxims of honour, which require in every private encounter some decent equality of age and strength, of numbers and weapons. An annual festival of two, perhaps of four, months, was observed by the Arabs before the time of Mahomet, during which their swords were religiously sheathed both in foreign and domestic hostility; and this partial truce is more strongly expressive of the habits of anarchy and warfare.

But the spirit of rapine and revenge was attempered by the milder influence of trade and literature. The solitary peninsula is encompassed by the most civilised nations of the ancient world; the merchant is the friend of mankind; and the annual caravans imported the first seeds of knowledge and politeness into the cities and even the camps of the desert. Whatever may be the pedigree of the Arabs, their language is derived from the same original stock with the Hebrew, the Syriac, and the Chaldæan tongues; the independence of the tribes was marked by their peculiar dialects; but each, after their own, allowed a just preference to the pure and perspicuous idiom of Mecca. In Arabia, as well as in Greece, the perfection of language outstripped the refinement of manners; and her speech could diversify the fourscore names of honey, the two hundred of a serpent, the five hundred of a lion, the thousand of a sword, at a time when this copious dictionary was intrusted to the memory of an illiterate people. The monuments of the Homerites were inscribed with an obsolete and mysterious character; but the Cufic letters, the groundwork of the present alphabet, were invented on the banks of the Euphrates; and the recent invention was taught at Mecca by a stranger who settled in that city after the birth of Mahomet. The arts of grammar, of metre, and of rhetoric were unknown to the freeborn eloquence of the Arabians; but their penetration was sharp, their fancy luxuriant, their wit strong and sententious, and their more elaborate compositions were addressed with energy and effect to the minds of their hearers. The genius and merit of a rising poet was celebrated by the applause of his own and the kindred tribes. A solemn banquet was prepared, and a chorus of women, striking their tymbals, and displaying the pomp of their nuptials, sung in the presence of their sons and husbands the felicity of their native tribe—that a champion had now appeared to vindicate their rights—that a herald had raised his voice to immortalise their renown. The distant or hostile tribes resorted to an annual fair, which was abolished by the fanaticism of the first Moslems—a national assembly that must have contributed to refine and harmonise the barbarians. Thirty days were employed in the exchange, not only of the corn and wine, but of eloquence and poetry. The prize was disputed by the generous emulation of the bards; the victorious performance was deposited in the archives of princes and emirs; and we may read in our own language the seven original poems which were inscribed in letters of gold, and suspended in the temple of Mecca. The Arabian poets were the historians and moralists of the age; and if they sympathised with the prejudices, they inspired and crowned the virtues, of their countrymen. The indissoluble union of generosity and valour was the darling theme of their song; and when they pointed their keenest satire against a despicable race, they affirmed, in the bitterness of reproach, that the men knew not how to give, nor the women to deny. The same hospitality which was practised by Abraham, and celebrated by Homer, is still renewed in the camps of the Arabs. The ferocious Bedoweens, the terror of the desert, embrace, without inquiry or hesitation, the stranger who dares to confide in their honour and to enter their tent. His treatment is kind and respectful: he shares the wealth or the poverty of his host; and, after a needful repose, he is dismissed on his way with thanks, with blessings, and perhaps with gifts. The heart and hand are more largely expanded by the wants of a brother or a friend; but the heroic acts that could deserve the public applause must have surpassed the narrow measure of discretion and experience. A dispute had arisen, who among the citizens of Mecca was entitled to the prize of generosity; and a successive application was made to the three who were deemed most worthy of the trial. Abdallah, the son of Abbas, had undertaken a distant journey, and his foot was in the stirrup, when he heard the voice of a suppliant, "O son of the uncle of the apostle of God, I am a traveller, and in distress!" He instantly dismounted to present the pilgrim with his camel, her rich caparison, and a purse of four thousand pieces of gold, excepting only the sword, either for its intrinsic value, or as the gift of an honoured kinsman. The servant of Kais informed the second suppliant that his master was asleep: but he immediately added, "Here is a purse of seven thousand pieces of gold (it is all we have in the house), and here is an order that will entitle you to a camel and a slave;" the master, as soon as he awoke, praised and enfranchised his faithful steward, with a gentle reproof, that by respecting his slumbers he had stinted his bounty. The third of the heroes, the blind Arabah, at the hour of prayer, was supporting his steps on the shoulders of two slaves. "Alas!" he replied, "my coffers are empty! but these you may sell; if you refuse, I renounce them." At these words, pushing away the youths, he groped along the wall with his staff. The character of Hatem is the perfect model of Arabian virtue: he was brave and liberal, an eloquent poet, and a successful robber: forty camels were roasted at his hospitable feasts; and at the prayer of a suppliant enemy he restored both the captives and the spoil. The freedom of his countrymen disdained the laws of justice; they proudly indulged the spontaneous impulse of pity and benevolence.

THE RELIGION OF THE ARABS

The religion of the Arabs, as well as of the Indians, consisted in the worship of the sun, the moon, and the fixed stars; a primitive and specious mode of superstition. The bright luminaries of the sky display the visible image of a Deity: their number and distance convey to a philosophic, or even a vulgar, eye the idea of boundless space: the character of eternity is marked on these solid globes, that seem incapable of corruption or decay: the regularity of their motions may be ascribed to a principle of reason or instinct; and their real or imaginary influence encourages the vain belief that the earth and its inhabitants are the object of their peculiar care. The science of astronomy was cultivated at Babylon; but the school of the Arabs was a clear firmament and a naked plain. In their nocturnal marches they steered by the guidance of the stars; their names, and order, and daily station were familiar to the curiosity and devotion of the Bedoween; and he was taught by experience to divide in twenty-eight parts the zodiac of the moon, and to bless the constellations who refreshed with salutary rains the thirst of the desert. The reign of the heavenly orbs could not be extended beyond the visible sphere; and some metaphysical powers were necessary to sustain the transmigration of souls and the resurrection of bodies: a camel was left to perish on the grave, that he might serve his master in another life; and the invocation of departed spirits implies that they were still endowed with consciousness and power. I am ignorant, and I am careless, of the blind mythology of the barbarians—of the local deities, of the stars, the air, and the earth, of their sex or titles, their attributes of subordination. Each tribe, each family, each independent warrior, created and changed the rites and the object of his fantastic worship; but the nation, in every age, has bowed to the religion as well as to the language of Mecca. The genuine antiquity of the CAABA ascends beyond the Christian era: in describing the coast of the Red Sea the Greek historian Diodorus has remarked, between the Thamudites and the Sabæans, a famous temple, whose superior sanctity was revered by *all* the Arabians; the linen or silken veil, which is annually renewed by the Turkish emperor, was first offered by a pious king of the Homerites, who reigned seven hundred years before the time of Mahomet. A tent or a cavern might suffice for the worship of the savages, but an edifice of stone and clay has been erected in its place; and the art and power of the monarchs of the East have been confined to the simplicity of the original model. A spacious portico encloses the quadrangle of the Caaba—a square chapel twenty-four cubits long, twenty-three broad, and twenty-seven high: a door and a window admit the light; the double roof is supported by three pillars of wood; a spout (now of gold) discharges the rain-water, and the well Zemzem is protected by a dome from accidental pollution. The tribe of Koreish, by fraud or force, had acquired the custody of the Caaba: the sacerdotal office devolved through four lineal descents to the grandfather of Mahomet; and the family of the Hashemites, from whence he sprung, was the most respectable and sacred in the eyes of their country. The precincts of Mecca enjoyed the rights of sanctuary; and in the last month of each year the city and the temple were crowded with a long train of pilgrims, who presented their vows and offerings in the house of God. The same rites which are now accomplished by the faithful Musulman were invented and practised by the superstition of the idolaters. At an awful distance they cast away their garments: seven times with hasty steps they encircled the Caaba, and kissed the black stone: seven times they visited and adored the adjacent mountains: seven times they threw stones into the valley of Mina: and the pilgrimage was achieved, as at the present hour, by a sacrifice of sheep and camels, and the burial of their hair and nails in the consecrated ground. Each tribe either found or introduced in the Caaba their domestic worship: the temple was adorned, or defiled, with three hundred and sixty idols of men, eagles, lions, and antelopes; and most conspicuous was the statue of Hebal, of red agate, holding in his hand seven arrows without heads or feathers, the instruments and symbols of profane divination. But this statue was a monument of Syrian arts: the devotion of the ruder ages was content with a pillar or a tablet; and the rocks of the desert were hewn into gods or altars in imitation of the black stone of Mecca, which is deeply tainted with the reproach of an idolatrous origin. From Japan to Peru the use of sacrifice has universally prevailed; and the votary has expressed his gratitude or fear by destroying or consuming, in honour of the gods, the dearest and most precious of their gifts. The life of a man is the most precious oblation to deprecate a public calamity: the altars of Phœnicia and Egypt, of Rome and Carthage, have been polluted with human gore: the cruel practice was long preserved among the Arabs; in the third century a boy was annually sacrificed by the tribe of the Dumatians; and a royal captive was piously slaughtered by the prince of the Saracens, the ally and soldier of the emperor Justinian. A parent who drags his son to the altar exhibits the most painful and sublime effort of fanaticism: the deed or the intention was sanctified by the example of saints and heroes; and the father of Mahomet himself was devoted by a rash vow, and hardly ransomed for the equivalent of an hundred camels. In the time of ignorance the Arabs, like the Jews and Egyptians, abstained from the taste of swine's flesh; they circumcised [1] their children at the age of puberty: the same customs, without the censure or the precept of the Koran, have been silently transmitted to their posterity and proselytes. It has been sagaciously conjectured that the artful legislator indulged the stubborn prejudices of his countrymen. It is more simple to believe that he adhered to the habits and opinions of his youth, without foreseeing that a practice congenial to the climate of Mecca might become useless or inconvenient on the banks of the Danube or the Volga.

Arabia was free: the adjacent kingdoms were shaken by the storms of conquest and tyranny, and the persecuted sects fled to the happy land where they might profess what they thought, and practise what they professed. The religions of the Sabians and Magians, of the Jews and Christians, were disseminated from the Persian Gulf to the Red Sea.

---

[1] The Mahometan doctors are not fond of the subject; yet they hold circumcision necessary to salvation, and even pretend that Mahomet was miraculously born without a foreskin.

In a remote period of antiquity Sabianism was diffused over Asia by the science of the Chaldæans and the arms of the Assyrians. From the observations of two thousand years the priests and astronomers of Babylon deduced the eternal laws of nature and providence. They adored the seven gods, or angels, who directed the course of the seven planets, and shed their irresistible influence on the earth. The attributes of the seven planets, with the twelve signs of the zodiac, and the twenty-four constellations of the northern and southern hemisphere, were represented by images and talismans; the seven days of the week were dedicated to their respective deities; the Sabians prayed thrice each day; and the temple of the moon at Haran was the term of their pilgrimage. But the flexible genius of their faith was always ready either to teach or to learn: in the tradition of the creation, the deluge, and the patriarchs, they held a singular agreement with their Jewish captives; they appealed to the secret books of Adam, Seth, and Enoch; and a slight infusion of the Gospel has transformed the last remnant of the Polytheists into the Christians of St. John, in the territory of Bassora. The altars of Babylon were overturned by the Magians; but the injuries of the Sabians were revenged by the sword of Alexander; Persia groaned above five hundred years under a foreign yoke; and the purest disciples of Zoroaster escaped from the contagion of idolatry, and breathed with their adversaries the freedom of the desert. Seven hundred years before the death of Mahomet the Jews were settled in Arabia; and a far greater multitude was expelled from the Holy Land in the wars of Titus and Hadrian. The industrious exiles aspired to liberty and power: they erected synagogues in the cities, and castles in the wilderness; and their Gentile converts were confounded with the children of Israel, whom they resembled in the outward mark of circumcision. The Christian missionaries were still more active and successful: the Catholics asserted their universal reign; the sects whom they oppressed successively retired beyond the limits of the Roman empire; the Marcionites and Manichæans dispersed their *fantastic* opinions and apocryphal gospels; the churches of Yemen, and the princes of Hira and Gassan, were instructed in a purer creed by the Jacobite and Nestorian bishops. The liberty of choice was presented to the tribes: each Arab was free to elect or to compose his private religion; and the rude superstition of his house was mingled with the sublime theology of saints and philosophers. A fundamental article of faith was inculcated by the consent of the learned strangers; the existence of one supreme God, who is exalted above the powers of heaven and earth, but who has often revealed himself to mankind by the ministry of his angels and prophets, and whose grace or justice has interrupted, by seasonable miracles, the order of nature. The most rational of the Arabs acknowledged his power, though they neglected his worship; and it was habit rather than conviction that still attached them to the relics of idolatry. The Jews and Christians were the people of the *Book*; the Bible was already translated into the Arabic language, and the volume of the Old Testament was accepted by the concord of these implacable enemies. In the story of the Hebrew patriarchs the Arabs were pleased to discover the fathers of their nation. They applauded the birth and promises of Ismael; revered the faith and virtue of Abraham; traced his pedigree and their own to the creation of the first man, and imbibed with equal credulity the prodigies of the holy text, and the dreams and traditions of the Jewish rabbis.

THE RISE OF MAHOMET

The base and plebeian origin of Mahomet is an unskilful calumny of the Christians, who exalt instead of degrading the merit of their adversary. His descent from Ismael was a national privilege or fable; but if the first steps of the pedigree are dark and doubtful, he could produce many generations of pure and genuine nobility: he sprung from the tribe of Koreish and the family of Hashem, the most illustrious of the Arabs, the princes of Mecca, and the hereditary guardians of the Caaba. The grandfather of Mahomet was Abdol Motalleb, the son of Hashem, a wealthy and generous citizen, who relieved the distress of famine with the supplies of commerce. Mecca, which had been fed by the liberality of the father, was saved by the courage of the son. The kingdom of Yemen was subject to the Christian princes of Abyssinia: their vassal Abrahah was provoked by an insult to avenge the honour of the cross; and the holy city was invested by a train of elephants and an army of Africans. A treaty was proposed; and, in the first audience, the grandfather of Mahomet demanded the restitution of his cattle. "And why," said Abrahah, "do you not rather implore my clemency in favour of your temple, which I have threatened to destroy?" "Because," replied the intrepid chief, "the cattle is my own; the Caaba belongs to the gods, and *they* will defend their house from injury and sacrilege." The want of provisions, or the valour of the Koreish, compelled the Abyssinians to a disgraceful retreat: their discomfiture has been adorned with a miraculous flight of birds, who showered down stones on the heads of the infidels; and the deliverance was long commemorated by the era of the elephant. The glory of Abdol Motalleb was crowned with domestic happiness; his life was prolonged to the age of one hundred and ten years; and he became the father of six daughters and thirteen sons. His best beloved Abdallah was the most beautiful and modest of the Arabian youth; and in the first night, when he consummated his marriage with Amina, of the noble race of the Zahrites, two hundred virgins are said to have expired of jealousy and despair. Mahomet, or more properly Mohammed, the only son of Abdallah and Amina, was born at Mecca, four years after the death of Justinian, and two months after the defeat of the Abyssinians, whose victory would have introduced into the Caaba the religion of the Christians. In his early infancy he was deprived of his father, his mother, and his grandfather; his uncles were strong and numerous; and, in the division of the inheritance, the orphan's share was reduced to five camels and an Ethiopian maid-servant. At home and abroad, in peace and war, Abu Taleb, the most respectable of his uncles, was the guide and guardian of his youth; in his twenty-fifth year he entered into the service of Cadijah, a rich and noble widow of Mecca, who soon rewarded his fidelity with the gift of her hand and fortune. The marriage contract, in the simple style of antiquity, recites the mutual love of Mahomet and Cadijah; describes him as the most accomplished of the tribe of Koreish; and stipulates a dowry of twelve ounces of gold and twenty camels, which was supplied by the liberality of his uncle. By this alliance the son of Abdallah was restored to the station of his ancestors; and the judicious matron was content with his domestic virtues, till, in the fortieth year of his age, he assumed the title of a prophet, and proclaimed the religion of the Koran.

According to the tradition of his companions, Mahomet was distinguished by the beauty of his person, an outward gift which is seldom despised, except by those to whom it has been refused. Before he spoke, the orator engaged on his side the affections of a public or private audience. They applauded his commanding presence, his majestic aspect, his piercing eye, his gracious smile, his flowing beard, his countenance that painted every sensation of the soul, and his gestures that enforced each expression of the tongue. In the familiar offices of life he scrupulously adhered to the grave and ceremonious politeness of his country: his respectful attention to the rich and powerful was dignified by his condescension and affability to the poorest citizens of Mecca: the frankness of his manner concealed the artifice of his views; and the habits of courtesy were imputed to personal friendship or universal benevolence. His memory was capacious and retentive; his wit easy and social; his imagination sublime; his judgment clear, rapid, and decisive. He possessed the courage both of thought and action; and, although his designs might gradually expand with his success, the first idea which he entertained of his divine mission bears the stamp of an original and superior genius. The son of Abdallah was educated in the bosom of the noblest race, in the use of the purest dialect of Arabia; and the fluency of his speech was corrected and enhanced by the practice of discreet and seasonable silence. With these powers of eloquence, Mahomet was an illiterate barbarian: his youth had never been instructed in the arts of reading and writing; the common ignorance exempted him from shame or reproach, but he was reduced to a narrow circle of existence, and deprived of those faithful mirrors which reflect to our mind the minds of sages and heroes. Yet the book of nature and of man was open to his view; and some fancy has been indulged in the political and philosophical observations which are ascribed to the Arabian *traveller*. He compares the nations and the religions of the earth; discovers the weakness of the

Persian and Roman monarchies; beholds with pity and indignation the degeneracy of the times; and resolves to unite under one God and one king the invincible spirit and primitive virtues of the Arabs. Our more accurate inquiry will suggest, that, instead of visiting the courts, the camps, the temples of the East, the two journeys of Mahomet into Syria were confined to the fairs of Bostra and Damascus; that he was only thirteen years of age when he accompanied the caravan of his uncle; and that his duty compelled him to return as soon as he had disposed of the merchandise of Cadijah. In these hasty and superficial excursions the eye of genius might discern some objects invisible to his grosser companions; some seeds of knowledge might be cast upon a fruitful soil; but his ignorance of the Syriac language must have checked his curiosity; and I cannot perceive in the life or writings of Mahomet that his prospect was far extended beyond the limits of the Arabian world. From every region of that solitary world the pilgrims of Mecca were annually assembled by the calls of devotion and commerce: in the free concourse of multitudes, a simple citizen, in his native tongue, might study the political state and character of the tribes, the theory and practice of the Jews and Christians. Some useful strangers might be tempted, or forced, to implore the rights of hospitality; and the enemies of Mahomet have named the Jew, the Persian, and the Syrian monk, whom they accuse of lending their secret aid to the composition of the Koran. Conversation enriches the understanding, but solitude is the school of genius; and the uniformity of a work denotes the hand of a single artist. From his earliest youth Mahomet was addicted to religious contemplation; each year, during the month of Ramadan, he withdrew from the world and from the arms of Cadijah: in the cave of Hera, three miles from Mecca, he consulted the spirit of fraud or enthusiasm, whose abode is not in the heavens, but in the mind of the prophet. The faith which, under the name of *Islam*, he preached to his family and nation, is compounded of an eternal truth and a necessary fiction, THAT THERE IS ONLY ONE GOD, AND THAT MAHOMET IS THE APOSTLE OF GOD.

It is the boast of the Jewish apologists, that, while the learned nations of antiquity were deluded by the fables of polytheism, their simple ancestors of Palestine preserved the knowledge and worship of the true God. The moral attributes of Jehovah may not easily be reconciled with the standard of *human* virtue: his metaphysical qualities are darkly expressed; but each page of the Pentateuch and the Prophets is an evidence of his power: the unity of his name is inscribed in the first table of the law; and his sanctuary was never defiled by any visible image of the invisible essence. After the ruin of the temple, the faith of the Hebrew exiles was purified, fixed, and enlightened by the spiritual devotion of the synagogue; and the authority of Mahomet will not justify his perpetual reproach that the Jews of Mecca or Medina adored Ezra as the son of God. But the children of Israel had ceased to be a people;

and the religions of the world were guilty, at least in the eyes of the prophet, of giving sons, or daughters, or companions to the supreme God. In the rude idolatry of the Arabs the crime is manifest and audacious: the Sabians are poorly excused by the pre-eminence of the first planet, or intelligence, in their celestial hierarchy; and in the Magian system the conflict of the two principles betrays the imperfection of the conqueror. The Christians of the seventh century had insensibly relapsed into a semblance of paganism; their public and private vows were addressed to the relics and images that disgraced the temples of the East: the throne of the Almighty was darkened by a cloud of martyrs, and saints, and angels, the objects of popular veneration; and the Collyridian heretics, who flourished in the fruitful soil of Arabia, invested the Virgin Mary with the name and honours of a goddess. The mysteries of the Trinity and Incarnation *appear* to contradict the principle of the divine unity. In their obvious sense, they introduce three equal deities, and transform the man Jesus into the substance of the Son of God: an orthodox commentary will satisfy only a believing mind: intemperate curiosity and zeal had torn the veil of the sanctuary: and each of the Oriental sects was eager to confess that all, except themselves, deserved the reproach of idolatry and polytheism. The creed of Mahomet is free from suspicion or ambiguity; and the Koran is a glorious testimony to the unity of God. The prophet of Mecca rejected the worship of idols and men, of stars and planets, on the rational principle that whatever rises must set, that whatever is born must die, that whatever is corruptible must decay and perish. In the Author of the universe his rational enthusiasm confessed and adored an infinite and eternal being, without form or place, without issue or similitude, present to our most secret thoughts, existing by the necessity of his own nature, and deriving from himself all moral and intellectual perfection. These sublime truths, thus announced in the language of the prophet, are firmly held by his disciples, and defined with metaphysical precision by the interpreters of the Koran. A philosophic theist might subscribe the popular creed of the Mahometans: a creed too sublime perhaps for our present faculties. What object remains for the fancy, or even the understanding, when we have abstracted from the unknown substance all ideas of time and space, of motion and matter, of sensation and reflection? The first principle of reason and revelation was confirmed by the voice of Mahomet: his proselytes, from India to Morocco, are distinguished by the name of *Unitarians*; and the danger of idolatry has been prevented by the interdiction of images. The doctrine of eternal decrees and absolute predestination is strictly embraced by the Mahometans; and they struggle with the common difficulties, *how* to reconcile the prescience of God with the freedom and responsibility of man; *how* to explain the permission of evil under the reign of infinite power and infinite goodness.

The God of nature has written his existence on all his works, and his law in the heart of man. To restore the knowledge of the one, and the practice of the other, has been the real or pretended aim of the prophets of every age: the liberality of Mahomet allowed to his predecessors the same credit which he claimed for himself; and the chain of inspiration was prolonged from the fall of Adam to the promulgation of the Koran. During that period some rays of prophetic light had been imparted to one hundred and twenty-four thousand of the elect, discriminated by their respective measure of virtue and grace; three hundred and thirteen apostles were sent with a special commission to recall their country from idolatry and vice; one hundred and four volumes have been dictated by the Holy Spirit; and six legislators of transcendent brightness have announced to mankind the six successive revelations of various rites, but of one immutable religion. The authority and station of Adam, Noah, Abraham, Moses, Christ, and Mahomet, rise in just gradation above each other; but whosoever hates or rejects any one of the prophets is numbered with the infidels. The writings of the patriarchs were extant only in the apocryphal copies of the Greeks and Syrians: the conduct of Adam had not entitled him to the gratitude of his children; the seven precepts of Noah were observed by an inferior and imperfect class of the proselytes of the synagogue; and the memory of Abraham was obscurely revered by the Sabians in his native land of Chaldæa: of the myriads of prophets, Moses and Christ alone lived and reigned; and the remnant of the inspired writings was comprised in the books of the Old and the New Testament. The miraculous story of Moses is consecrated and embellished in the Koran; and the captive Jews enjoy the secret revenge of imposing their own belief on the nations whose recent creeds they deride. For the author of Christianity, the Mahometans are taught by the prophet to entertain a high and mysterious reverence. "Verily, Christ Jesus, the son of Mary, is the apostle of God, and his word, which he conveyed unto Mary, and a Spirit proceeding from him: honourable in this world, and in the world to come; and one of those who approach near to the presence of God." The wonders of the genuine and apocryphal gospels are profusely heaped on his head; and the Latin church has not disdained to borrow from the Koran the immaculate conception [1] of his virgin mother. Yet Jesus was a mere mortal; and, at the day of judgment, his testimony will serve to condemn both the Jews, who reject him as a prophet, and the Christians, who adore him as the Son of God. The malice of his enemies aspersed his reputation, and conspired against his life; but their intention only was guilty; a phantom or a criminal was substituted on the cross; and the innocent saint was translated to the seventh heaven. During six hundred years the Gospel was the way of truth and salvation; but the

---

[1] It is darkly hinted in the Koran, and more clearly explained by the tradition of the Sonnites. In the xiith century, the immaculate conception was condemned by St. Bernard as a presumptuous novelty.

Christians insensibly forgot both the laws and the example of their
founder; and Mahomet was instructed by the Gnostics to accuse the
church, as well as the synagogue, of corrupting the integrity of the
sacred text. The piety of Moses and of Christ rejoiced in the assurance
of a future Prophet, more illustrious than themselves: the evangelic
promise of the *Paraclete*, or Holy Ghost, was prefigured in the name,
and accomplished in the person, of Mahomet, the greatest and the last
of the apostles of God.

The communication of ideas requires a similitude of thought and
language: the discourse of a philosopher would vibrate without effect
on the ear of a peasant; yet how minute is the distance of *their* understandings, if it be compared with the contact of an infinite and a finite
mind, with the word of God expressed by the tongue or the pen of a
mortal? The inspiration of the Hebrew prophets, of the apostles and
evangelists of Christ, might not be incompatible with the exercise of
their reason and memory; and the diversity of their genius is strongly
marked in the style and composition of the books of the Old and New
Testament. But Mahomet was content with a character more humble,
yet more sublime, of a simple editor; the substance of the Koran,
according to himself or his disciples, is uncreated and eternal; subsisting
in the essence of the Deity, and inscribed with a pen of light on the table
of his everlasting decrees. A paper copy, in a volume of silk and gems,
was brought down to the lowest heaven by the angel Gabriel, who, under
the Jewish economy, had indeed been despatched on the most important
errands; and this trusty messenger successively revealed the chapters and
verses to the Arabian prophet. Instead of a perpetual and perfect
measure of the divine will, the fragments of the Koran were produced at
the discretion of Mahomet; each revelation is suited to the emergencies
of his policy or passion; and all contradiction is removed by the saving
maxim that any text of Scripture is abrogated or modified by any
subsequent passage. The word of God and of the apostle was diligently
recorded by his disciples on palm-leaves and the shoulder-bones of
mutton; and the pages, without order or connection, were cast into a
domestic chest in the custody of one of his wives. Two years after the
death of Mahomet, the sacred volume was collected and published by
his friend and successor Abubeker: the work was revised by the caliph
Othman, in the thirtieth year of the Hegira; and the various editions of
the Koran assert the same miraculous privilege of an uniform and in
corruptible text. In the spirit of enthusiasm or vanity, the prophet rests
the truth of his mission on the merit of his book; audaciously challenges
both men and angels to imitate the beauties of a single page; and presumes to assert that God alone could dictate this incomparable performance. This argument is most powerfully addressed to a devout
Arabian, whose mind is attuned to faith and rapture; whose ear is delighted by the music of sounds; and whose ignorance is incapable of

comparing the productions of human genius. The harmony and copiousness of style will not reach, in a version, the European infidel: he will
peruse with impatience the endless incoherent rhapsody of fable, and
precept, and declamation, which seldom excites a sentiment or an idea,
which sometimes crawls in the dust, and is sometimes lost in the clouds.
The divine attributes exalt the fancy of the Arabian missionary; but his
loftiest strains must yield to the sublime simplicity of the book of Job,
composed in a remote age, in the same country, and in the same
language. If the composition of the Koran exceed the faculties of a man,
to what superior intelligence should we ascribe the Iliad of Homer, or the
Philippics of Demosthenes? In all religions the life of the founder
supplies the silence of his written revelation: the sayings of Mahomet
were so many lessons of truth; his actions so many examples of virtue;
and the public and private memorials were preserved by his wives and
companions. At the end of two hundred years the *Sonna*, or oral law,
was fixed and consecrated by the labours of Al Bochari, who discriminated seven thousand two hundred and seventy-five genuine traditions, from a mass of three hundred thousand reports of a more doubtful
or spurious character. Each day the pious author prayed in the temple
of Mecca, and performed his ablutions with the water of Zemzem: the
pages were successively deposited on the pulpit and the sepulchre of the
apostle; and the work has been approved by the four orthodox sects of
the Sonnites.

The mission of the ancient prophets, of Moses and of Jesus, had been
confirmed by many splendid prodigies; and Mahomet was repeatedly
urged, by the inhabitants of Mecca and Medina, to produce a similar
evidence of his divine legation; to call down from heaven the angel or the
volume of his revelation, to create a garden in the desert, or to kindle a
conflagration in the unbelieving city. As often as he is pressed by the
demands of the Koreish, he involves himself in the obscure boast of
vision and prophecy, appeals to the internal proofs of his doctrine, and
shields himself behind the providence of God, who refuses those signs and
wonders that would depreciate the merit of faith and aggravate the guilt
of infidelity. But the modest or angry tone of his apologies betrays his
weakness and vexation; and these passages of scandal established beyond
suspicion the integrity of the Koran. The votaries of Mahomet are more
assured than himself of his miraculous gifts; and their confidence and
credulity increase as they are farther removed from the time and place of
his spiritual exploits. They believe or affirm that trees went forth to meet
him; that he was saluted by stones; that water gushed from his fingers;
that he fed the hungry, cured the sick, and raised the dead; that a beam
groaned to him; that a camel complained to him; that a shoulder of
mutton informed him of its being poisoned; and that both animate and
inanimate nature were equally subject to the apostle of God. His dream
of a nocturnal journey is seriously described as a real and corporeal

transaction. A mysterious animal, the Borak, conveyed him from the temple of Mecca to that of Jerusalem: with his companion Gabriel he successively ascended the seven heavens, and received and repaid the salutations of the patriarchs, the prophets, and the angels, in their respective mansions. Beyond the seventh heaven Mahomet alone was permitted to proceed; he passed the veil of unity within two bow-shots of the throne, and felt a cold that pierced him to the heart, when his shoulder was touched by the hand of God. After this familiar though important conversation, he again descended to Jerusalem, remounted the Borak, returned to Mecca, and performed in the tenth part of a night the journey of many thousand years. According to another legend, the apostle confounded in a national assembly the malicious challenge of the Koreish. His resistless word split asunder the orb of the moon: the obedient planet stooped from her station in the sky, accomplished the seven revolutions round the Caaba, saluted Mahomet in the Arabian tongue, and, suddenly contracting her dimensions, entered at the collar, and issued forth through the sleeve, of his shirt. The vulgar are amused with these marvellous tales; but the gravest of the Musulman doctors imitate the modesty of their master, and indulge a latitude of faith or interpretation. They might speciously allege, that in preaching the religion it was needless to violate the harmony of nature; that a creed unclouded with mystery may be excused from miracles; and that the sword of Mahomet was not less potent than the rod of Moses.

PRECEPTS OF MAHOMET

The polytheist is oppressed and distracted by the variety of superstition: a thousand rites of Egyptian origin were interwoven with the essence of the Mosaic law; and the spirit of the Gospel had evaporated in the pageantry of the church. The prophet of Mecca was tempted by prejudice, or policy, or patriotism, to sanctify the rites of the Arabians, and the custom of visiting the holy stone of the Caaba. But the precepts of Mahomet himself inculcate a more simple and rational piety: prayer, fasting, and alms are the religious duties of a Musulman; and he is encouraged to hope that prayer will carry him half way to God, fasting will bring him to the door of his palace, and alms will gain him admittance. I. According to the tradition of the nocturnal journey, the apostle, in his personal conference with the Deity, was commanded to impose on his disciples the daily obligation of fifty prayers. By the advice of Moses, he applied for an alleviation of this intolerable burden; the number was gradually reduced to five; without any dispensation of business or pleasure, or time or place: the devotion of the faithful is repeated at daybreak, at noon, in the afternoon, in the evening, and at the first watch of the night; and in the present decay of religious fervour, our travellers are edified by the profound humility and attention of the Turks and Persians. Cleanliness is the key of prayer: the frequent lustration of the hands, the face, and the body, which was practised of old by the Arabs, is solemnly enjoined by the Koran; and a permission is formally granted to supply with sand the scarcity of water. The words and attitudes of supplication, as it is performed either sitting, or standing, or prostrate on the ground, are prescribed by custom or authority; but the prayer is poured forth in short and fervent ejaculations; the measure of zeal is not exhausted by a tedious liturgy; and each Musulman for his own person is invested with the character of a priest. Among the theists, who reject the use of images, it has been found necessary to restrain the wanderings of the fancy, by directing the eye and the thought towards a *kebla* or visible point of the horizon. The prophet was at first inclined to gratify the Jews by the choice of Jerusalem; but he soon returned to a more natural partiality; and five times every day the eyes of the nations at Astracan, at Fez, at Delhi, are devoutly turned to the holy temple of Mecca. Yet every spot for the service of God is equally pure: the Mahometans indifferently pray in their chamber or in the street. As a distinction from the Jews and Christians, the Friday in each week is set apart for the useful institution of public worship: the people is assembled in the mosch; and the imam, some respectable elder, ascends the pulpit, to begin the prayer and pronounce the sermon. But the Mahometan religion is destitute of priesthood or sacrifice; and the independent spirit of fanaticism looks down with contempt on the ministers and the slaves of superstition. II. The voluntary penance of the ascetics, the torment and glory of their lives, was odious to a prophet who censured in his companions a rash vow of abstaining from flesh, and women, and sleep; and firmly declared that he would suffer no monks in his religion. Yet he instituted, in each year, a fast of thirty days; and strenuously recommended the observance as a discipline which purifies the soul and subdues the body, as a salutary exercise of obedience to the will of God and his apostle. During the month of Ramadan, from the rising to the setting of the sun, the Musulman abstains from eating, and drinking, and women, and baths, and perfumes; from all nourishment that can restore his strength, from all pleasure that can gratify his senses. In the revolution of the lunar year, the Ramadan coincides, by turns, with the winter cold and the summer heat; and the patient martyr, without assuaging his thirst with a drop of water, must expect the close of a tedious and sultry day. The interdiction of wine, peculiar to some orders of priests or hermits, is converted by Mahomet alone into a positive and general law; and a considerable portion of the globe has abjured, at his command, the use of that salutary, though dangerous liquor. These painful restraints are, doubtless, infringed by the libertine, and eluded by the hypocrite; but the legislator, by whom they are enacted, cannot surely be accused of alluring his proselytes by the indulgence of their sensual appetites. III. The charity of the Mahometans descends to the animal creation; and the Koran repeatedly inculcates, not as a merit,

but as a strict and indispensable duty, the relief of the indigent and unfortunate. Mahomet, perhaps, is the only lawgiver who has defined the
precise measure of charity: the standard may vary with the degree and
nature of property, as it consists either in money, in corn or cattle, in
fruits or merchandise: but the Musulman does not accomplish the law,
unless he bestows a *tenth* of his revenue; and if his conscience accuses
him of fraud or extortion, the tenth, under the idea of restitution, is
enlarged to a *fifth*.[1] Benevolence is the foundation of justice, since we
are forbid to injure those whom we are bound to assist. A prophet may
reveal the secrets of heaven and of futurity: but in his moral precepts
he can only repeat the lessons of our own hearts.

The two articles of belief, and the four practical duties, of Islam, are
guarded by rewards and punishments; and the faith of the Musulman is
devoutly fixed on the event of the judgment and the last day. The prophet has not presumed to determine the moment of that awful catastrophe, though he darkly announces the signs, both in heaven and earth,
which will precede the universal dissolution, when life shall be destroyed,
and the order of creation shall be confounded in the primitive chaos. At
the blast of the trumpet new worlds will start into being; angels, genii,
and men will arise from the dead, and the human soul will again be
united to the body. The doctrine of the resurrection was first entertained
by the Egyptians; and their mummies were embalmed, their pyramids
were constructed, to preserve the ancient mansion of the soul during a
period of three thousand years. But the attempt is partial and unavailing;
and it is with a more philosophic spirit that Mahomet relies on the
omnipotence of the Creator, whose word can re-animate the breathless
clay, and collect the innumerable atoms that no longer retain their form
or substance. The intermediate state of the soul it is hard to decide; and
those who most firmly believe her immaterial nature, are at a loss to
understand how she can think or act without the agency of the organs
of sense.

The re-union of the soul and body will be followed by the final judgment of mankind; and in his copy of the Magian picture, the prophet
has too faithfully represented the forms of proceeding, and even the
slow and successive operations, of an earthly tribunal. By his intolerant
adversaries he is upbraided for extending, even to themselves, the hope
of salvation; for asserting the blackest heresy, that every man who be-
lieves in God, and accomplishes good works, may expect in the last day
a favourable sentence. Such rational indifference is ill adapted to the

---

[1] The jealousy of Maracci prompts him to enumerate the more liberal alms of the
Catholics of Rome. Fifteen great hospitals are open to many thousand patients and
pilgrims; fifteen hundred maidens are annually portioned; fifty-six charity-schools are
founded for both sexes; one hundred and twenty confraternities relieve the wants
of their brethren, &c. The benevolence of London is still more extensive; but I am
afraid that much more is to be ascribed to the humanity than to the religion of the
people.

character of a fanatic; nor is it probable that a messenger from heaven should depreciate the value and necessity of his own revelation. In the idiom of the Koran, the belief of God is inseparable from that of Mahomet: the good works are those which he has enjoined; and the two qualifications imply the profession of Islam, to which all nations and all sects are equally invited. Their spiritual blindness, though excused by ignorance and crowned with virtue, will be scourged with everlasting torments; and the tears which Mahomet shed over the tomb of his mother, for whom he was forbidden to pray, display a striking contrast of humanity and enthusiasm. The doom of the infidels is common: the measure of their guilt and punishment is determined by the degree of evidence which they have rejected, by the magnitude of the errors which they have entertained: the eternal mansions of the Christians, the Jews, the Sabians, the Magians, and the idolators are sunk below each other in the abyss: and the lowest hell is reserved for the faithless hypocrites who have assumed the mask of religion. After the greater part of mankind has been condemned for their opinions, the true believers only will be judged by their actions. The good and evil of each Musulman will be accurately weighed in a real or allegorical balance; and a singular mode of compensation will be allowed for the payment of injuries: the aggressor will refund an equivalent of his own good actions, for the benefit of the person whom he has wronged; and if he should be destitute of any moral property, the weight of his sins will be loaded with an adequate share of the demerits of the sufferer. According as the shares of guilt or virtue shall preponderate, the sentence will be pronounced, and all, without distinction, will pass over the sharp and perilous bridge of the abyss; but the innocent, treading in the footsteps of Mahomet, will gloriously enter the gates of paradise, while the guilty will fall into the first and mildest of the seven hells. The term of expiation will vary from nine hundred to seven thousand years; but the prophet has judiciously promised that *all* his disciples, whatever may be their sins, shall be saved, by their own faith and his intercession, from eternal damnation. It is not surprising that superstition should act most powerfully on the fears of her votaries, since the human fancy can paint with more energy the misery than the bliss of a future life. With the two simple elements of darkness and fire we create a sensation of pain, which may be aggravated to an infinite degree by the idea of endless duration. But the same idea operates with an opposite effect on the continuity of pleasure; and too much of our present enjoyments is obtained from the relief, or the comparison, of evil. It is natural enough that an Arabian prophet should dwell with rapture on the groves, the fountains, and the rivers of paradise; but instead of inspiring the blessed inhabitants with a liberal taste for harmony and science, conversation and friendship, he idly celebrates the pearls and diamonds, the robes of silk, palaces of marble, dishes of gold, rich wines, artificial dainties, numerous attendants, and the whole train of sensual and costly luxury, which becomes insipid to the owner, even in the short period of this mortal life. Seventy-two *Houris*, or black-eyed girls, of resplendent beauty, blooming youth, virgin purity, and exquisite sensibility, will be created for the use of the meanest believer; a moment of pleasure will be prolonged to a thousand years, and his faculties will be increased an hundred fold, to render him worthy of his felicity. Notwithstanding a vulgar prejudice, the gates of heaven will be open to both sexes; but Mahomet has not specified the male companions of the female elect, lest he should either alarm the jealousy of their former husbands, or disturb their felicity by the suspicion of an everlasting marriage. This image of a carnal paradise has provoked the indignation, perhaps the envy, of the monks: they declaim against the impure religion of Mahomet; and his modest apologists are driven to the poor excuse of figures and allegories. But the sounder and more consistent party adhere, without shame, to the literal interpretation of the Koran: useless would be the resurrection of the body, unless it were restored to the possession and exercise of its worthiest faculties; and the union of sensual and intellectual enjoyment is requisite to complete the happiness of the double animal, the perfect man. Yet the joys of the Mahometan paradise will not be confined to the indulgence of luxury and appetite; and the prophet has expressly declared that all meaner happiness will be forgotten and despised by the saints and martyrs, who shall be admitted to the beatitude of the divine vision.

MAHOMET'S FLIGHT FROM MECCA TO MEDINA

The first and most arduous conquests of Mahomet were those of his wife, his servant, his pupil, and his friend; since he presented himself as a prophet to those who were most conversant with his infirmities as a man. Yet Cadijah believed the words, and cherished the glory, of her husband; the obsequious and affectionate Zeid was tempted by the prospect of freedom; the illustrious Ali, the son of Abu Taleb, embraced the sentiments of his cousin with the spirit of a youthful hero; and the wealth, the moderation, the veracity of Abubeker, confirmed the religion of the prophet whom he was destined to succeed. By his persuasion ten of the most respectable citizens of Mecca were introduced to the private lessons of Islam; they yielded to the voice of reason and enthusiasm; they repeated the fundamental creed, "There is but one God, and Mahomet is the apostle of God;" and their faith, even in this life, was rewarded with riches and honours, with the command of armies and the government of kingdoms. Three years were silently employed in the conversion of fourteen proselytes, the first-fruits of his mission; but in the fourth year he assumed the prophetic office, and, resolving to impart to his family the light of divine truth, he prepared a banquet, a lamb, as it is said, and a bowl of milk, for the entertainment of forty guests of the race of Hashem. "Friends and kinsmen," said Mahomet to the assembly, "I offer you, and I alone can offer, the most precious of gifts, the treasures of this world and of the world to come. God has commanded me to call you to his service. Whom among you will support my burden? Who among you will be my companion and my vizir?" No answer was returned, till the silence of astonishment, and doubt, and contempt was at length broken by the impatient courage of Ali, a youth in the fourteenth year of his age. "O prophet, I am the man: whosoever rises against thee, I will dash out his teeth, tear out his eyes, break his legs, rip up his belly. O prophet, I will be thy vizir over them." Mahomet accepted his offer with transport, and Abu Taleb was ironically exhorted to respect the superior dignity of his son. In a more serious tone, the father of Ali advised his nephew to relinquish his impracticable design. "Spare your remonstrances," replied the intrepid fanatic to his uncle and benefactor; "if they should place the sun on my right hand, and the moon on my left, they should not divert me from my course." He persevered ten years in the exercise of his mission; and the religion which has overspread the East and the West advanced with a slow and painful progress within the walls of Mecca. Yet Mahomet enjoyed the satisfaction of beholding the increase of his infant congregation of Unitarians, who revered him as a prophet, and to whom he seasonably dispensed the spiritual nourishment of the Koran. The number of proselytes may be esteemed by the absence of eighty-three men and eighteen women, who retired to Ethiopia in the seventh year of his mission; and his party was fortified by the timely conversion of his uncle Hamza, and of the fierce and inflexible Omar, who signalised in the cause of Islam the same zeal which he had exerted for its destruction. Nor was the charity of Mahomet confined to the tribe of Koreish, or the precincts of Mecca: on solemn festivals, in the days of pilgrimage, he frequented the Caaba, accosted the strangers of every tribe, and urged, both in private converse and public discourse, the belief and worship of a sole Deity. Conscious of his reason and of his weakness, he asserted the liberty of conscience, and disclaimed the use of religious violence: but he called the Arabs to repentance, and conjured them to remember the ancient idolaters of Ad and Thamud, whom the divine justice had swept away from the face of the earth.

The people of Mecca were hardened in their unbelief by superstition and envy. The elders of the city, the uncles of the prophet, affected to despise the presumption of an orphan, the reformer of his country: the pious orations of Mahomet in the Caaba were answered by the clamours of Abu Taleb. "Citizens and pilgrims, listen not to the tempter, hearken not to his impious novelties. Stand fast in the worship of Al Lâta and Al Uzzah." Yet the son of Abdallah was ever dear to the aged chief: and he protected the fame and person of his nephew against the assaults of the Koreishites, who had long been jealous of the pre-eminence of the family of Hashem. Their malice was coloured with the pretence of religion: in the age of Job the crime of impiety was punished by the Arabian magistrate; and Mahomet was guilty of deserting and denying the national deities. But so loose was the policy of Mecca, that the leaders of the Koreish, instead of accusing a criminal, were compelled to employ the measures of persuasion or violence. They repeatedly addressed Abu Taleb in the style of reproach and menace. "Thy nephew reviles our religion; he accuses our wise forefathers of ignorance and folly; silence him quickly, lest he kindle tumult and discord in the city. If he persevere, we shall draw our swords against him and his adherents, and thou wilt be responsible for the blood of thy fellow-citizens." The weight and moderation of Abu Taleb eluded the violence of religious faction; the most helpless or timid of the disciples retired to Ethiopia, and the prophet withdrew himself to various places of strength in the town and country. As he was still supported by his family, the rest of the tribe of Koreish engaged themselves to renounce all intercourse with the children of Hashem—neither to buy nor sell, neither to marry nor to give in marriage, but to pursue them with implacable enmity, till they should deliver the person of Mahomet to the justice of the gods. The decree was suspended in the Caaba before the eyes of the nation: the messengers of the Koreish pursued the Musulman exiles in the heart of Africa; they besieged the prophet and his most faithful followers, intercepted their water, and inflamed their mutual animosity by the retaliation of injuries and insults. A doubtful truce restored the appearances of concord, till the death of Abu Taleb abandoned Mahomet to the power of his enemies, at the moment when he was deprived of his domestic comforts by the loss of his faithful and generous Cadijah. Abu Sophian, the chief of the branch of Ommiyah, succeeded to the principality of the republic of Mecca. A zealous votary of the idols, a mortal foe of the line of Hashem, he convened an assembly of the Koreishites and their allies to decide the fate of the apostle. His imprisonment might provoke the despair of his enthusiasm; and the exile of an eloquent and popular fanatic would diffuse the mischief through the provinces of Arabia. His death was resolved; and they agreed that a sword from each tribe should be buried in his heart, to divide the guilt of his blood, and baffle the vengeance of the Hashemites. An angel or a spy revealed their conspiracy, and flight was the only resource of Mahomet. At the dead of night, accompanied by his friend Abubeker, he silently escaped from his house: the assassins watched at the door; but they were deceived by the figure of Ali, who reposed on the bed, and was covered with the green vestment, of the apostle. The Koreish respected the piety of the heroic youth; but some verses of Ali, which are still extant, exhibit an interesting picture of his anxiety, his tenderness, and his religious confidence. Three days Mahomet and his companion were concealed in the cave of Thor, at the distance of a league from Mecca; and in the close of each evening they received from the son and daughter of Abubeker a secret supply of intelligence and food. The diligence of the Koreish explored every haunt in the neighbourhood of the city: they arrived at the entrance of the cavern; but the providential deceit of a spider's web and a pigeon's nest is supposed to convince them that the place was solitary and inviolate. "We are only two," said the trembling Abubeker. "There is a third," replied the prophet; "it is God himself." No sooner was the pursuit abated than the two fugitives issued from the rock and mounted their camels: on the road to Medina they were overtaken by the emissaries of the Koreish; they redeemed themselves with prayers and promises from their hands. In this eventful moment the lance of an Arab might have changed the history of the world. The flight of the prophet from Mecca to Medina has fixed the memorable era of the *Hegira*, which, at the end of twelve centuries, still discriminates the lunar years of the Mahometan nations.

The religion of the Koran might have perished in its cradle had not Medina embraced with faith and reverence the holy outcasts of Mecca. Medina, or the *city*, known under the name of Yathreb before it was sanctified by the throne of the prophet, was divided between the tribes of the Charegites and the Awsites, whose hereditary feud was rekindled by the slightest provocations: two colonies of Jews, who boasted a sacerdotal race, were their humble allies, and, without converting the Arabs, they introduced the taste of science and religion, which distinguished Medina as the city of the Book. Some of her noblest citizens, in a pilgrimage to the Caaba, were converted by the preaching of Mahomet; on their return they diffused the belief of God and his prophet, and the new alliance was ratified by their deputies in two secret and nocturnal interviews on a hill in the suburbs of Mecca. In the first, ten Charegites and two Awsites, united in faith and love, protested, in the name of their wives, their children, and their absent brethren, that they would for ever profess the creed and observe the precepts of the Koran. The second was a political association, the first vital spark of the empire of the Saracens. Seventy-three men and two women of Medina held a solemn conference with Mahomet, his kinsmen, and his disciples, and pledged themselves to each other by a mutual oath of fidelity. They promised, in the name of the city, that if he should be banished they would receive him as a confederate, obey him as a leader, and defend him to the last extremity, like their wives and children. "But if you are recalled by your country," they asked with a flattering anxiety, "will you not abandon your new allies?" "All things," replied Mahomet, with a smile, "are now common between us; your blood is as my blood, your ruin as my ruin. We are bound to each other by the ties of honour and interest. I am your friend, and the enemy of your foes." "But if we are killed in your service, what," exclaimed the deputies of Medina, "will be our reward?" "Paradise," replied the prophet. "Stretch forth thy hand." He stretched it forth, and they reiterated the oath of allegiance and fidelity. Their treaty was ratified by the people, who unanimously embraced the profession of Islam; they rejoiced in the exile of the apostle, but they trembled for his safety, and impatiently expected his arrival. After a perilous and rapid journey along the sea-coast, he halted at Koba, two miles from the city, and made his public entry into Medina, sixteen days after his flight from Mecca. Five hundred of the citizens advanced to meet him; he was hailed with acclamations of loyalty and devotion; Mahomet was mounted on a she-camel, an umbrella shaded his head, and a turban was unfurled before him to supply the deficiency of a standard. His bravest disciples, who had been scattered by the storm, assembled round his person; and the equal, though various, merit of the Moslems was distinguished by the names of *Mohagerians* and *Ansars*, the fugitives of Mecca, and the auxiliaries of Medina. To eradicate the seeds of jealousy, Mahomet judiciously coupled his principal followers with the rights and obligations of brethren; and when Ali found himself without a peer, the prophet tenderly declared that *he* would be the companion and brother of the noble youth. The expedient was crowned with success; the holy fraternity was respected in peace and war, and the two parties vied with each other in a generous emulation of courage and fidelity. Once only the concord was slightly ruffled by an accidental quarrel: a patriot of Medina arraigned the insolence of the strangers, but the hint of their expulsion was heard with abhorrence; and his own son most eagerly offered to lay at the apostle's feet the head of his father.

From his establishment at Medina Mahomet assumed the exercise of the regal and sacerdotal office; and it was impious to appeal from a judge whose decrees were inspired by the divine wisdom. A small portion of ground, the patrimony of two orphans, was acquired by gift or purchase; on that chosen spot he built a house and a mosch, more venerable in their rude simplicity than the palaces and temples of the Assyrian caliphs. His seal of gold, or silver, was inscribed with the apostolic title; when he prayed and preached in the weekly assembly, he leaned against the trunk of a palm-tree; and it was long before he indulged himself in the use of a chair or pulpit of rough timber. After a reign of six years, fifteen hundred Moslems, in arms and in the field, renewed their oath of allegiance; and their chief repeated the assurance of protection till the death of the last member, or the final dissolution of the party. It was in the same camp that the deputy of Mecca was astonished by the attention of the faithful to the words and looks of the prophet, by the eagerness with which they collected his spittle, a hair that dropped on the ground, the refuse water of his lustrations, as if they participated in some degree of the prophetic virtue. "I have seen," said he, "the Chosroes of Persia and the Cæsar of Rome, but never did I

behold a king among his subjects like Mahomet among his companions."
The devout fervour of enthusiasm acts with more energy and truth than
the cold and formal servility of courts.

MAHOMET DECLARES WAR AGAINST THE INFIDEL

In the state of nature every man has a right to defend, by force of
arms, his person and his possessions; to repel, or even to prevent, the
violence of his enemies, and to extend his hostilities to a reasonable
measure of satisfaction and retaliation. In the free society of the Arabs,
the duties of subject and citizen imposed a feeble restraint; and Mahomet, in the exercise of a peaceful and benevolent mission, had been
despoiled and banished by the injustice of his countrymen. The choice
of an independent people had exalted the fugitive of Mecca to the rank
of a sovereign; and he was invested with the just prerogative of forming
alliances, and of waging offensive or defensive war. The imperfection
of human rights was supplied and armed by the plenitude of divine
power: the prophet of Medina assumed, in his new revelations, a fiercer
and more sanguinary tone, which proves that his former moderation
was the effect of weakness: the means of persuasion had been tried, the
season of forbearance was elapsed, and he was now commanded to
propagate his religion by the sword, to destroy the monuments of
idolatry, and, without regarding the sanctity of days or months, to
pursue the unbelieving nations of the earth. The same bloody precepts,
so repeatedly inculcated in the Koran, are ascribed by the author to the
Pentateuch and the Gospel. But the mild tenor of the evangelic style
may explain an ambiguous text, that Jesus did not bring peace on the
earth, but a sword: his patient and humble virtues should not be confounded with the intolerant zeal of princes and bishops, who have disgraced the name of his disciples. In the prosecution of religious war,
Mahomet might appeal with more propriety to the example of Moses,
of the Judges, and the kings of Israel. The military laws of the Hebrews
are still more rigid than those of the Arabian legislator.[1] The Lord of
hosts marched in person before the Jews: if a city resisted their summons,
the males, without distinction, were put to the sword: the seven nations
of Canaan were devoted to destruction; and neither repentance nor conversion could shield them from the inevitable doom, that no creature
within their precincts should be left alive. The fair option of friendship,
or submission, or battle, was proposed to the enemies of Mahomet. If
they professed the creed of Islam, they were admitted to all the temporal
and spiritual benefits of his primitive disciples, and marched under the

[1] The xth and xxth chapters of Deuteronomy, with the practical comments of
Joshua, David, &c., are read with more awe than satisfaction by the pious Christians
of the present age. But the bishops, as well as the rabbis of former times, have beat
the drum-ecclesiastic with pleasure and success.

same banner to extend the religion which they had embraced. The clemency of the prophet was decided by his interest: yet he seldom trampled on a prostrate enemy; and he seems to promise that on the payment of a tribute the least guilty of his unbelieving subjects might be indulged in their worship, or at least in their imperfect faith. In the first months of his reign he practised the lessons of holy warfare, and displayed his white banner before the gates of Medina: the martial apostle fought in person at nine battles or sieges; and fifty enterprises of war were achieved in ten years by himself or his lieutenants. The Arab continued to unite the professions of a merchant and a robber; and his petty excursions for the defence or the attack of a caravan insensibly prepared his troops for the conquest of Arabia. The distribution of the spoil was regulated by a divine law: the whole was faithfully collected in one common mass: a fifth of the gold and silver, the prisoners and cattle, the moveables and immoveables, was reserved by the prophet for pious and charitable uses; the remainder was shared in adequate portions by the soldiers who had obtained the victory or guarded the camp, the rewards of the slain devolved to their widows and orphans: and the increase of cavalry was encouraged by the allotment of a double share to the horse and to the man. From all sides the roving Arabs were allured to the standard of religion and plunder: the apostle sanctified the licence of embracing the female captives as their wives or concubines; and the enjoyment of wealth and beauty was a feeble type of the joys of paradise prepared for the valiant martyrs of the faith. "The sword," says Mahomet, "is the key of heaven and of hell: a drop of blood shed in the cause of God, a night spent in arms, is of more avail than two months of fasting or prayer: whosoever falls in battle, his sins are forgiven: at the day of judgment his wounds shall be resplendent as vermilion, and odoriferous as musk; and the loss of his limbs shall be supplied by the wings of angels and cherubim." The intrepid souls of the Arabs were fired with enthusiasm: the picture of the invisible world was strongly painted on their imagination; and the death which they had always despised became an object of hope and desire. The Koran inculcates, in the most absolute sense, the tenets of fate and predestination, which would extinguish both industry and virtue, if the actions of man were governed by his speculative belief. Yet their influence in every age has exalted the courage of the Saracens and Turks. The first companions of Mahomet advanced to battle with a fearless confidence: there is no danger where there is no chance: they were ordained to perish in their beds; or they were safe and invulnerable amidst the darts of the enemy.

Perhaps the Koreish would have been content with the flight of Mahomet, had they not been provoked and alarmed by the vengeance of an enemy who could intercept their Syrian trade as it passed and repassed through the territory of Medina. Abu Sophian himself, with only thirty or forty followers, conducted a wealthy caravan of a thousand camels; the fortune or dexterity of his march escaped the vigilance of Mahomet; but the chief of the Koreish was informed that the holy robbers were placed in ambush to await his return. He despatched a messenger to his brethren of Mecca, and they were roused, by the fear of losing their merchandise and their provisions, unless they hastened to his relief with the military force of the city. The sacred band of Mahomet was formed of three hundred and thirteen Moslems, of whom seventy-seven were fugitives, and the rest auxiliaries: they mounted by turns a train of seventy camels (the camels of Yathreb were formidable in war); but such was the poverty of his first disciples, that only two could appear on horseback in the field. In the fertile and famous vale of Beder, three stations from Medina, he was informed by his scouts of the caravan that approached on one side; of the Koreish, one hundred horse, eight hundred and fifty foot, who advanced on the other. After a short debate he sacrificed the prospect of wealth to the pursuit of glory and revenge; and a slight intrenchment was formed to cover his troops, and a stream of fresh water that glided through the valley. "O God," he exclaimed as the numbers of the Koreish descended from the hills, "O God, if these are destroyed, by whom wilt thou be worshipped on the earth?—Courage, my children; close your ranks; discharge your arrows, and the day is your own." At these words he placed himself, with Abubeker, on a throne or pulpit, and instantly demanded the succour of Gabriel and three thousand angels. His eye was fixed on the field of battle: the Musulmans fainted and were pressed: in that decisive moment the prophet started from his throne, mounted his horse, and cast a handful of sand into the air; "Let their faces be covered with confusion." Both armies heard the thunder of his voice: their fancy beheld the angelic warriors: the Koreish trembled and fled: seventy of the bravest were slain; and seventy captives adorned the first victory of the faithful. The dead bodies of the Koreish were despoiled and insulted: two of the most obnoxious prisoners were punished with death; and the ransom of the others, four thousand drachms of silver, compensated in some degree the escape of the caravan. But it was in vain that the camels of Abu Sophian explored a new road through the desert and along the Euphrates: they were overtaken by the diligence of the Musulmans; and wealthy must have been the prize, if twenty thousand drachms could be set apart for the fifth of the apostle. The resentment of the public and private loss stimulated Abu Sophian to collect a body of three thousand men, seven hundred of whom were armed with cuirasses, and two hundred were mounted on horseback; three thousand camels attended his march; and his wife Henda, with fifteen matrons of Mecca, incessantly sounded their timbrels to animate the troops, and to magnify the greatness of Hobal, the most popular deity of the Caaba. The standard of God and Mahomet was upheld by nine hundred and fifty believers: the disproportion of numbers was not more alarming than in the field of Beder; and their presumption of victory prevailed against the divine and human sense of the apostle. The second battle was fought on Mount Ohud, six miles to the north of Medina: the Koreish advanced in the form of a crescent; and the right wing of cavalry was led by Caled, the fiercest and most successful of the Arabian warriors. The troops of Mahomet were skilfully posted on the declivity of the hill; and their rear was guarded by a detachment of fifty archers. The weight of their charge impelled and broke the centre of the idolaters: but in the pursuit they lost the advantage of their ground: the archers deserted their station: the Musulmans were tempted by the spoil, disobeyed their general, and disordered their ranks. The intrepid Caled, wheeling his cavalry on their flank and rear, exclaimed, with a loud voice, that Mahomet was slain. He was indeed wounded in the face with a javelin: two of his teeth were shattered with a stone; yet, in the midst of tumult and dismay, he reproached the infidels with the murder of a prophet; and blessed the friendly hand that stanched his blood, and conveyed him to a place of safety. Seventy martyrs died for the sins of the people: they fell, said the apostle, in pairs, each brother embracing his lifeless companion; their bodies were mangled by the inhuman females of Mecca; and the wife of Abu Sophian tasted the entrails of Hamza, the uncle of Mahomet. They might applaud their superstition and satiate their fury; but the Musulmans soon rallied in the field, and the Koreish wanted strength or courage to undertake the siege of Medina. It was attacked the ensuing year by an army of ten thousand enemies; and this third expedition is variously named, from the *nations* which marched under the banner of Abu Sophian, from the *ditch* which was drawn before the city, and a camp of three thousand Musulmans. The prudence of Mahomet declined a general engagement: the valour of Ali was signalised in single combat; and the war was protracted twenty days, till the final separation of the confederates. A tempest of wind, rain, and hail overturned their tents: their private quarrels were fomented by an insidious adversary; and the Koreish, deserted by their allies, no longer hoped to subvert the throne, or to check the conquests, of their invincible exile.

The choice of Jerusalem for the first kebla of prayer discovers the early propensity of Mahomet in favour of the Jews; and happy would it have been for their temporal interest had they recognised in the Arabian prophet the hope of Israel and the promised Messiah. Their obstinacy converted his friendship into implacable hatred, with which he pursued that unfortunate people to the last moment of his life; and in the double character of an apostle and a conqueror, his persecution was extended to both worlds. The Kainoka dwelt at Medina under the protection of the city: he seized the occasion of an accidental tumult, and summoned them to embrace his religion, or contend with him in battle.

"Alas," replied the trembling Jews, "we are ignorant of the use of arms, but we persevere in the faith and worship of our fathers; why wilt thou reduce us to the necessity of a just defence?" The unequal conflict was terminated in fifteen days; and it was with extreme reluctance that Mahomet yielded to the importunity of his allies, and consented to spare the lives of the captives. But their riches were confiscated, their arms became more effectual in the hands of the Musulmans; and a wretched colony of seven hundred exiles was driven with their wives and children to implore a refuge on the confines of Syria. The Nadhirites were more guilty, since they conspired in a friendly interview to assassinate the prophet. He besieged their castle, three miles from Medina; but their resolute defence obtained an honourable capitulation; and the garrison, sounding their trumpets and beating their drums, was permitted to depart with the honours of war. The Jews had excited and joined the war of the Koreish: no sooner had the *nations* retired from the *ditch*, than Mahomet, without laying aside his armour, marched on the same day to extirpate the hostile race of the children of Koraidha. After a resistance of twenty-five days they surrendered at discretion. They trusted to the intercession of their old allies of Medina: they could not be ignorant that fanaticism obliterates the feelings of humanity. A venerable elder, to whose judgment they appealed, pronounced the sentence of their death: seven hundred Jews were dragged in chains to the market-place of the city; they descended alive into the grave prepared for their execution and burial; and the apostle beheld with an inflexible eye the slaughter of his helpless enemies. Their sheep and camels were inherited by the Musulmans: three hundred cuirasses, five hundred pikes, a thousand lances, composed the most useful portion of the spoil. Six days' journey to the north-east of Medina, the ancient and wealthy town of Chaibar was the seat of the Jewish power in Arabia: the territory, a fertile spot in the desert, was covered with plantations and cattle, and protected by eight castles, some of which were esteemed of impregnable strength. The forces of Mahomet consisted of two hundred horse and fourteen hundred foot: in the succession of eight regular and painful sieges they were exposed to danger, and fatigue, and hunger; and the most undaunted chiefs despaired of the event. The apostle revived their faith and courage by the example of Ali, on whom he bestowed the surname of the Lion of God: perhaps we may believe that an Hebrew champion of gigantic stature was cloven to the chest by his irresistible scimitar; but we cannot praise the modesty of romance, which represents him as tearing from its hinges the gate of a fortress and wielding the ponderous buckler in his left hand.[1] After the reduction of the castles the town of Chaibar submitted to the yoke.

---

[1] Abu Rafe, the servant of Mahomet, is said to affirm that he himself and seven other men afterwards tried, without success, to move the same gate from the ground. Abu Rafe was an eye-witness, but who will be witness for Abu Rafe?

The chief of the tribe was tortured, in the presence of Mahomet, to force a confession of his hidden treasure: the industry of the shepherds and husbandmen was rewarded with a precarious toleration: they were permitted, so long as it should please the conqueror, to improve their patrimony, in equal shares, for *his* emolument and their own. Under the reign of Omar, the Jews of Chaibar were transplanted to Syria; and the caliph alleged the injunction of his dying master, that one and the true religion should be professed in his native land of Arabia.

Five times each day the eyes of Mahomet were turned towards Mecca, and he was urged by the most sacred and powerful motives to revisit, as a conqueror, the city and the temple from whence he had been driven as an exile. The Caaba was present to his waking and sleeping fancy: an idle dream was translated into vision and prophecy; he unfurled the holy banner; and a rash promise of success too hastily dropped from the lips of the apostle. His march from Medina to Mecca displayed the peaceful and solemn pomp of a pilgrimage: seventy camels, chosen and bedecked for sacrifice, preceded the van; the sacred territory was respected; and the captives were dismissed without ransom to proclaim his clemency and devotion. But no sooner did Mahomet descend into the plain, within a day's journey of the city, than he exclaimed, "They have clothed themselves with the skins of tigers": the numbers and resolution of the Koreish opposed his progress; and the roving Arabs of the desert might desert or betray a leader whom they had followed for the hopes of spoil. The intrepid fanatic sunk into a cool and cautious politician: he waived in the treaty his title of apostle of God; concluded with the Koreish and their allies a truce of ten years; engaged to restore the fugitives of Mecca who should embrace his religion; and stipulated only, for the ensuing vear, the humble privilege of entering the city as a friend, and of remaining three days to accomplish the rites of the pilgrimage. A cloud of shame and sorrow hung on the retreat of the Musulmans, and their disappointment might justly accuse the failure of a prophet who had so often appealed to the evidence of success. The faith and hope of the pilgrims were rekindled by the prospect of Mecca: their swords were sheathed: seven times in the footsteps of the apostle they encompassed the Caaba: the Koreish had retired to the hills, and Mahomet, after the customary sacrifice, evacuated the city on the fourth day. The people was edified by his devotion; the hostile chiefs were awed, or divided, or seduced; and both Caled and Amrou, the future conquerors of Syria and Egypt, most seasonably deserted the sinking cause of idolatry. The power of Mahomet was increased by the submission of the Arabian tribes; ten thousand soldiers were assembled for the conquest of Mecca; and the idolaters, the weaker party, were easily convicted of violating the truce. Enthusiasm and discipline impelled the march, and preserved the secret, till the blaze of ten thousand fires proclaimed to the astonished Koreish the design, the approach, and the irresistible force of the enemy.

The haughty Abu Sophian presented the keys of the city; admired the variety of arms and ensigns that passed before him in review; observed that the son of Abdallah had acquired a mighty kingdom; and confessed, under the scimitar of Omar, that he was the apostle of the true God. The return of Marius and Sulla was stained with the blood of the Romans: the revenge of Mahomet was stimulated by religious zeal, and his injured followers were eager to execute or to prevent the order of a massacre. Instead of indulging their passions and his own,[1] the victorious exile forgave the guilt, and united the factions, of Mecca. His troops, in three divisions, marched into the city: eight-and-twenty of the inhabitants were slain by the sword of Caled; eleven men and six women were proscribed by the sentence of Mahomet; but he blamed the cruelty of his lieutenant; and several of the most obnoxious victims were indebted for their lives to his clemency or contempt. The chiefs of the Koreish were prostrate at his feet. "What mercy can you expect from the man whom you have wronged?" "We confide in the generosity of our kinsman." "And you shall not confide in vain: begone! you are safe, you are free." The people of Mecca deserved their pardon by the profession of Islam; and after an exile of seven years, the fugitive missionary was enthroned as the prince and prophet of his native country. But the three hundred and sixty idols of the Caaba were ignominiously broken: the house of God was purified and adorned: as an example to future times, the apostle again fulfilled the duties of a pilgrim; and a perpetual law was enacted that no unbeliever should dare to set his foot on the territory of the holy city.

The conquest of Mecca determined the faith and obedience of the Arabian tribes; who, according to the vicissitudes of fortune, had obeyed, or disregarded, the eloquence or the arms of the prophet. Indifference for rites and opinions still marks the character of the Bedoweens; and they might accept, as loosely as they hold, the doctrine of the Koran. Yet an obstinate remnant still adhered to the religion and liberty of their ancestors, and the war of Honain derived a proper appellation from the *idols*, whom Mahomet had vowed to destroy, and whom the confederates of Tayef had sworn to defend. Four thousand Pagans advanced with secrecy and speed to surprise the conqueror: they pitied and despised the supine negligence of the Koreish, but they depended on the wishes, and perhaps the aid, of a people who had so lately renounced their gods, and bowed beneath the yoke of their enemy. The banners of Medina and Mecca were displayed by the prophet; a crowd

[1] After the conquest of Mecca, the Mahomet of Voltaire imagines and perpetrates the most horrid crimes. The poet confesses that he is not supported by the truth of history, and can only allege, que celui qui fait la guerre à sa patrie au nom de Dieu est capable de tout. The maxim is neither charitable nor philosophic; and some reverence is surely due to the fame of heroes and the religion of nations. I am informed that a Turkish ambassador at Paris was much scandalised at the representation of this tragedy.

of Bedoweens increased the strength or numbers of the army, and twelve thousand Musulmans entertained a rash and sinful presumption of their invincible strength. They descended without precaution into the valley of Honain: the heights had been occupied by the archers and slingers of the confederates; their numbers were oppressed, their discipline was confounded, their courage was appalled, and the Koreish smiled at their impending destruction. The prophet, on his white mule, was encompassed by the enemies: he attempted to rush against their spears in search of a glorious death: ten of his faithful companions interposed their weapons and their breasts; three of these fell dead at his feet: "O my brethren," he repeatedly cried with sorrow and indignation, "I am the son of Abdallah, I am the apostle of truth! O man, stand fast in the faith! O God, send down thy succour!" His uncle Abbas, who, like the heroes of Homer, excelled in the loudness of his voice, made the valley resound with the recital of the gifts and promises of God: the flying Moslems returned from all sides to the holy standard; and Mahomet observed with pleasure that the furnace was again rekindled: his conduct and example restored the battle, and he animated his victorious troops to inflict a merciless revenge on the authors of their shame. From the field of Honain he marched without delay to the siege of Tayef, sixty miles to the south-east of Mecca, a fortress of strength, whose fertile lands produce the fruits of Syria in the midst of the Arabian desert. A friendly tribe, instructed (I know not how) in the art of sieges, supplied him with a train of battering-rams and military engines, with a body of five hundred artificers. But it was in vain that he offered freedom to the slaves of Tayef; that he violated his own laws by the extirpation of the fruit-trees; that the ground was opened by the miners; that the breach was assaulted by the troops. After a siege of twenty days the prophet sounded a retreat; but he retreated with a song of devout triumph, and affected to pray for the repentance and safety of the unbelieving city. The spoil of this fortunate expedition amounted to six thousand captives, twenty-four thousand camels, forty thousand sheep, and four thousand ounces of silver: a tribe who had fought at Honain redeemed their prisoners by the sacrifice of their idols: but Mahomet compensated the loss by resigning to the soldiers his fifth of the plunder, and wished, for their sake, that he possessed as many head of cattle as there were trees in the province of Tehama. Instead of chastising the disaffection of the Koreish, he endeavoured to cut out their tongues (his own expression), and to secure their attachment, by a superior measure of liberality: Abu Sophian alone was presented with three hundred camels and twenty ounces of silver; and Mecca was sincerely converted to the profitable religion of the Koran.

The *fugitives* and *auxiliaries* complained that they who had borne the burden were neglected in the season of victory. "Alas!" replied their artful leader, "suffer me to conciliate these recent enemies, these doubtful proselytes, by the gift of some perishable goods. To your guard I intrust my life and fortunes. You are the companions of my exile, of my kingdom, of my paradise." He was followed by the deputies of Tayef, who dreaded the repetition of a siege. "Grant us, O apostle of God! a truce of three years with the toleration of our ancient worship." "Not a month, not an hour." "Excuse us at least from the obligation of prayer." "Without prayer religion is of no avail." They submitted in silence: their temples were demolished, and the same sentence of destruction was executed on all the idols of Arabia. His lieutenants, on the shores of the Red Sea, the Ocean, and the Gulf of Persia, were saluted by the acclamations of a faithful people; and the ambassadors who knelt before the throne of Medina were as numerous (says the Arabian proverb) as the dates that fall from the maturity of a palm-tree. The nation submitted to the God and the sceptre of Mahomet: the opprobrious name of tribute was abolished: the spontaneous or reluctant oblations of alms and tithes were applied to the service of religion; and one hundred and fourteen thousand Moslems accompanied the last pilgrimage of the apostle.

When Heraclius returned in triumph from the Persian war, he entertained, at Emesa, one of the ambassadors of Mahomet, who invited the princes and nations of the earth to the profession of Islam. On this foundation the zeal of the Arabians has supposed the secret conversion of the Christian emperor: the vanity of the Greeks has feigned a personal visit of the prince of Medina, who accepted from the royal bounty a rich domain, and a secure retreat, in the province of Syria. But the friendship of Heraclius and Mahomet was of short continuance: the new religion had inflamed rather than assuaged the rapacious spirit of the Saracens; and the murder of an envoy afforded a decent pretence for invading, with three thousand soldiers, the territory of Palestine, that extends to the eastward of the Jordan. The holy banner was intrusted to Zeid; and such was the discipline or enthusiasm of the rising sect, that the noblest chiefs served without reluctance under the slave of the prophet. On the event of his decease, Jaafar and Abdallah were successively substituted to the command; and if the three should perish in the war, the troops were authorised to elect their general. The three leaders were slain in the battle of Muta, the first military action which tried the valour of the Moslems against a foreign enemy. Zeid fell, like a soldier, in the foremost ranks: the death of Jaafar was heroic and memorable: he lost his right hand: he shifted the standard to his left: the left was severed from his body: he embraced the standard with his bleeding stumps, till he was transfixed to the ground with fifty honourable wounds. "Advance," cried Abdallah, who stepped into the vacant place, "advance with confidence: either victory or paradise is our own." The lance of a Roman decided the alternative; but the falling standard was rescued by Caled, the proselyte of Mecca: nine swords were broken in his hand; and his valour withstood and repulsed the superior numbers of the Christians. In the nocturnal council of the camp he was chosen to command: his skilful evolutions of the ensuing day secured either the victory or the retreat of the Saracens; and Caled is renowned among his brethren and his enemies by the glorious appellation of the *Sword of God*. In the pulpit, Mahomet described, with prophetic rapture, the crowns of the blessed martyrs; but in private he betrayed the feelings of human nature: he was surprised as he wept over the daughter of Zeid: "What do I see?" said the astonished votary. "You see," replied the apostle, "a friend who is deploring the loss of his most faithful friend." After the conquest of Mecca the sovereign of Arabia affected to prevent the hostile preparations of Heraclius; and solemnly proclaimed war against the Romans, without attempting to disguise the hardships and dangers of the enterprise. The Moslems were discouraged: they alleged the want of money, or horses, or provisions; the season of harvest, and the intolerable heat of the summer: "Hell is much hotter," said the indignant prophet. He disdained to compel their service: but on his return he admonished the most guilty, by an excommunication of fifty days. Their desertion enhanced the merit of Abubeker, Othman, and the faithful companions who devoted their lives and fortunes; and Mahomet displayed his banner at the head of ten thousand horse and twenty thousand foot. Painful indeed was the distress of the march: lassitude and thirst were aggravated by the scorching and pestilential winds of the desert: ten men rode by turns on the same camel; and they were reduced to the shameful necessity of drinking the water from the belly of that useful animal. In the mid-way, ten days' journey from Medina and Damascus, they reposed near the grove and fountain of Tabuc. Beyond that place Mahomet declined the prosecution of the war: he declared himself satisfied with the peaceful intentions, he was more probably daunted by the martial array, of the emperor of the East. But the active and intrepid Caled spread around the terror of his name; and the prophet received the submission of the tribes and cities, from the Euphrates to Ailah, at the head of the Red Sea. To his Christian subjects Mahomet readily granted the security of their persons, the freedom of their trade, the property of their goods, and the toleration of their worship. The weakness of their Arabian brethren had restrained them from opposing his ambition; the disciples of Jesus were endeared to the enemy of the Jews; and it was the interest of a conqueror to propose a fair capitulation to the most powerful religion of the earth.

DEATH OF MAHOMET

Till the age of sixty-three years the strength of Mahomet was equal to the temporal and spiritual fatigues of his mission. His epileptic fits, an absurd calumny of the Greeks, would be an object of pity rather than abhorrence; but he seriously believed that he was poisoned at Chaibar by the revenge of a Jewish female. During four years the health of the prophet declined; his infirmities increased; but his mortal disease was a fever of fourteen days, which deprived him by intervals of the use of reason. As soon as he was conscious of his danger, he edified his brethren by the humility of his virtue or penitence. "If there be any man," said the apostle from the pulpit, "whom I have unjustly scourged, I submit my own back to the lash of retaliation. Have I aspersed the reputation of a Musulman? let him proclaim *my* faults in the face of the congregation. Has any one been despoiled of his goods? the little that I possess shall compensate the principal and the interest of the debt." "Yes," replied a voice from the crowd, "I am entitled to three drachms of silver." Mahomet heard the complaint, satisfied the demand, and thanked his creditor for accusing him in this world rather than at the day of judgment. He beheld with temperate firmness the approach of death; enfranchised his slaves (seventeen men, as they are named, and eleven women); minutely directed the order of his funeral; and moderated the lamentations of his weeping friends, on whom he bestowed the benediction of peace. Till the third day before his death he regularly performed the function of public prayer: the choice of Abubeker to supply his place appeared to mark that ancient and faithful friend as his successor in the sacerdotal and regal office; but he prudently declined the risk and envy of a more explicit nomination. At a moment when his faculties were visibly impaired, he called for pen and ink to write, or, more properly, to dictate, a divine book, the sum and accomplishment of all his revelations: a dispute arose in the chamber whether he should be allowed to supersede the authority of the Koran; and the prophet was forced to reprove the indecent vehemence of his disciples. If the slightest credit may be afforded to the traditions of his wives and companions, he maintained, in the bosom of his family, and to the last moments of his life, the dignity of an apostle, and the faith of an enthusiast; described the visits of Gabriel, who bid an everlasting farewell to the earth; and expressed his lively confidence, not only of the mercy, but of the favour, of the Supreme Being. In a familiar discourse he had mentioned his special prerogative, that the angel of death was not allowed to take his soul till he had respectfully asked the permission of the prophet. The request was granted; and Mahomet immediately fell into the agony of his dissolution: his head was reclined on the lap of Ayesha, the best beloved of all his wives; he fainted with the violence of pain; recovering his spirits, he raised his eyes towards the roof of the house, and, with a steady look, though a faltering voice, uttered the last broken, though articulate, words: "O God! . . . pardon my sins. . . . Yes, . . . I come, . . . among my fellow citizens on high;" and thus peaceably expired on a carpet spread upon the floor. An expedition for the conquest of Syria was stopped by this mournful event: the army halted at the gates of

Medina; the chiefs were assembled round their dying master. The city, more especially the house, of the prophet, was a scene of clamorous sorrow or silent despair: fanaticism alone could suggest a ray of hope and consolation. "How can he be dead, our witness, our intercessor, our mediator, with God? By God he is not dead: like Moses and Jesus, he is wrapt in a holy trance, and speedily will he return to his faithful people." The evidence of sense was disregarded; and Omar, unsheathing his scimitar, threatened to strike off the heads of the infidels who should dare to affirm that the prophet was no more. The tumult was appeased by the weight and moderation of Abubeker. "Is it Mahomet," said he to Omar and the multitude, "or the God of Mahomet, whom you worship? The God of Mahomet liveth for ever; but the apostle was a mortal like ourselves, and, according to his own prediction, he has experienced the common fate of mortality." He was piously interred, by the hands of his nearest kinsman, on the same spot on which he expired: Medina has been sanctified by the death and burial of Mahomet; and the innumerable pilgrims of Mecca often turn aside from the way, to bow, in voluntary devotion, before the simple tomb of the prophet.

THE CHARACTER AND PRIVATE LIFE OF MAHOMET

At the conclusion of the life of Mahomet it may perhaps be expected that I should balance his faults and virtues, that I should decide whether the title of enthusiast or impostor more properly belongs to that extraordinary man. Had I been intimately conversant with the son of Abdallah, the task would still be difficult, and the success uncertain: at the distance of twelve centuries I darkly contemplate his shade through a cloud of religious incense; and could I truly delineate the portrait of an hour, the fleeting resemblance would not equally apply to the solitary of Mount Hera, to the preacher of Mecca, and to the conqueror of Arabia. The author of a mighty revolution appears to have been endowed with a pious and contemplative disposition: so soon as marriage had raised him above the pressure of want, he avoided the paths of ambition and avarice; and till the age of forty he lived with innocence, and would have died without a name. The unity of God is an idea most congenial to nature and reason; and a slight conversation with the Jews and Christians would teach him to despise and detest the idolatry of Mecca. It was the duty of a man and a citizen to impart the doctrine of salvation, to rescue his country from the dominion of sin and error. The energy of a mind incessantly bent on the same object would convert a general obligation into a particular call; the warm suggestions of the understanding or the fancy would be felt as the inspirations of Heaven; the labour of thought would expire in rapture and vision; and the inward sensation, the invisible monitor, would be described with the form and attributes of an angel of God. From enthusiasm to imposture the step is perilous and slippery; the dæmon of Socrates affords a memorable instance how a wise man may deceive himself, how a good man may deceive others, how the conscience may slumber in a mixed and middle state between self-illusion and voluntary fraud. Charity may believe that the original motives of Mahomet were those of pure and genuine benevolence; but a human missionary is incapable of cherishing the obstinate unbelievers who reject his claims, despise his arguments, and persecute his life; he might forgive his personal adversaries, he may lawfully hate the enemies of God; the stern passions of pride and revenge were kindled in the bosom of Mahomet, and he sighed, like the prophet of Nineveh, for the destruction of the rebels whom he had condemned. The injustice of Mecca and the choice of Medina transformed the citizen into a prince, the humble preacher into the leader of armies; but his sword was consecrated by the example of the saints; and the same God who afflicts a sinful world with pestilence and earthquakes might inspire for their conversion or chastisement the valour of his servants. In the exercise of political government he was compelled to abate of the stern rigour of fanaticism, to comply in some measure with the prejudices and passions of his followers, and to employ even the vices of mankind as the instruments of their salvation. The use of fraud and perfidy, of cruelty and injustice, were often subservient to the propagation of the faith; and Mahomet commanded or approved the assassination of the Jews and idolaters who had escaped from the field of battle. By the repetition of such acts the character of Mahomet must have been gradually stained; and the influence of such pernicious habits would be poorly compensated by the practice of the personal and social virtues which are necessary to maintain the reputation of a prophet among his sectaries and friends. Of his last years ambition was the ruling passion; and a politician will suspect that he secretly smiled (the victorious impostor!) at the enthusiasm of his youth, and the credulity of his proselytes.[1] A philosopher will observe that *their* credulity and *his* success would tend more strongly to fortify the assurance of his divine mission, that his interest and religion were inseparably connected, and that his conscience would be soothed by the persuasion that he alone was absolved by the Deity from the obligation of positive and moral laws. If he retained any vestige of his native innocence, the sins of Mahomet may be allowed as an evidence of his sincerity. In the support of truth, the arts of fraud and fiction may be deemed less criminal; and he would have started at the foulness of the means, had he not been satisfied of the importance and justice of the end. Even in a conqueror or a priest I can surprise a word or action of unaffected humanity; and the decree of Mahomet, that, in the sale of captives, the mothers should

---

[1] In some passage of his voluminous writings, Voltaire compares the prophet, in his old age, to a fakir "qui détache la chaîne de son cou pour en donner sur les oreilles à ses confrères."

never be separated from their children, may suspend, or moderate, the censure of the historian.

The good sense of Mahomet despised the pomp of royalty; the apostle of God submitted to the menial offices of the family; he kindled the fire, swept the floor, milked the ewes, and mended with his own hands his shoes and his woollen garment. Disdaining the penance and merit of an hermit, he observed, without effort or vanity, the abstemious diet of an Arab and a soldier. On solemn occasions he feasted his companions with rustic and hospitable plenty; but in his domestic life many weeks would elapse without a fire being kindled on the hearth of the prophet. The interdiction of wine was confirmed by his example; his hunger was appeased with a sparing allowance of barley-bread: he delighted in the taste of milk and honey; but his ordinary food consisted of dates and water. Perfumes and women were the two sensual enjoyments which his nature required, and his religion did not forbid; and Mahomet affirmed that the fervour of his devotion was increased by these innocent pleasures. The heat of the climate inflames the blood of the Arabs, and their libidinous complexion has been noticed by the writers of antiquity. Their incontinence was regulated by the civil and religious laws of the Koran: their incestuous alliances were blamed: the boundless licence of polygamy was reduced to four legitimate wives or concubines; their rights both of bed and of dowry were equitably determined; the freedom of divorce was discouraged; adultery was condemned as a capital offence; and fornication, in either sex, was punished with an hundred stripes. Such were the calm and rational precepts of the legislator; but in his private conduct Mahomet indulged the appetites of a man, and abused the claims of a prophet. A special revelation dispensed him from the laws which he had imposed on his nation; the female sex, without reserve, was abandoned to his desires; and this singular prerogative excited the envy rather than the scandal, the veneration rather than the envy, of the devout Musulmans. If we remember the seven hundred wives and three hundred concubines of the wise Solomon, we shall applaud the modesty of the Arabian, who espoused no more than seventeen or fifteen wives; eleven are enumerated who occupied at Medina their separate apartments round the house of the apostle, and enjoyed in their turns the favour of his conjugal society. What is singular enough, they were all widows, excepting only Ayesha, the daughter of Abubeker. *She* was doubtless a virgin, since Mahomet consummated his nuptials (such is the premature ripeness of the climate) when she was only nine years of age. The youth, the beauty, the spirit of Ayesha gave her a superior ascendant: she was beloved and trusted by the prophet; and, after his death, the daughter of Abubeker was long revered as the mother of the faithful. Her behaviour had been ambiguous and indiscreet: in a nocturnal march she was accidentally left behind, and in the morning Ayesha returned to the camp with a man. The temper of

Mahomet was inclined to jealousy; but a divine revelation assured him of her innocence: he chastised her accusers, and published a law of domestic peace, that no woman should be condemned unless four male witnesses had seen her in the act of adultery. In his adventures with Zeineb, the wife of Zeid, and with Mary, an Egyptian captive, the amorous prophet forgot the interest of his reputation. At the house of Zeid, his freedman and adopted son, he beheld, in a loose undress, the beauty of Zeineb, and burst forth into an ejaculation of devotion and desire. The servile, or grateful, freedman understood the hint, and yielded without hesitation to the love of his benefactor. But as the filial relation had excited some doubt and scandal, the angel Gabriel descended from heaven to ratify the deed, to annul the adoption, and gently to reprove the apostle for distrusting the indulgence of his God. One of his wives, Hafna, the daughter of Omar, surprised him on her own bed in the embraces of his Egyptian captive: she promised secrecy and forgiveness: he swore that he would renounce the possession of Mary. Both parties forgot their engagements; and Gabriel again descended with a chapter of the Koran to absolve him from his oath, and to exhort him freely to enjoy his captives and concubines without listening to the clamours of his wives. In a solitary retreat of thirty days he laboured alone with Mary to fulfil the commands of the angel. When his love and revenge were satiated, he summoned to his presence his eleven wives, reproached their disobedience and indiscretion, and threatened them with a sentence of divorce, both in this world and in the next—a dreadful sentence, since those who had ascended the bed of the prophet were for ever excluded from the hope of a second marriage. Perhaps the incontinence of Mahomet may be palliated by the tradition of his natural or preternatural gifts:[1] he united the manly virtue of thirty of the children of Adam; and the apostle might rival the thirteenth labour of the Grecian Hercules. A more serious and decent excuse may be drawn from his fidelity to Cadijah. During the twenty-four years of their marriage her youthful husband abstained from the right of polygamy, and the pride or tenderness of the venerable matron was never insulted by the society of a rival. After her death he placed her in the rank of the four perfect women, with the sister of Moses, the mother of Jesus, and Fatima, the best beloved of his daughters. "Was she not old?" said Ayesha, with the insolence of a blooming beauty; "has not God given you a better in her place?" "No, by God," said Mahomet, with an effusion of honest gratitude, "there never can be a better! She

---

[1] Sibi robur ad generationem, quantum triginta viri habent, inesse jactaret: ita ut unicâ horâ posset undecim fœminis *satisfacere*, ut ex Arabum libris refert S^{tus.} Petrus Paschasius, c. 2 (Maracci). Al Jannabi records his own testimony, that he surpassed all men in conjugal vigour; and Abulfeda mentions the exclamation of Ali, who washed his body after his death, "O propheta, certe penis tuus cœlum versus erectus est."

believed in me when men despised me; she relieved my wants when I was poor and persecuted by the world."

In spite of his polygamy Mahomet left no heir. In 655 or 656 his son-in-law, Ali, became Commander of the Faithful, but his descendants did not retain power.

INFLUENCE OF MAHOMET

The talents of Mahomet are entitled to our applause; but his success has, perhaps, too strongly attracted our admiration. Are we surprised that a multitude of proselytes should embrace the doctrine and the passions of an eloquent fanatic? In the heresies of the church the same seduction has been tried and repeated from the time of the apostles to that of the reformers. Does it seem incredible that a private citizen should grasp the sword and the sceptre, subdue his native country, and erect a monarchy by his victorious arms? In the moving picture of the dynasties of the East, a hundred fortunate usurpers have arisen from a baser origin, surmounted more formidable obstacles, and filled a larger scope of empire and conquest. Mahomet was alike instructed to preach and to fight; and the union of these opposite qualities, while it enhanced his merit, contributed to his success: the operation of force and persuasion, of enthusiasm and fear, continually acted on each other, till every barrier yielded to their irresistible power. His voice invited the Arabs to freedom and victory, to arms and rapine, to the indulgence of their darling passions in this world and the other: the restraints which he imposed were requisite to establish the credit of the prophet, and to exercise the obedience of the people; and the only objection to his success was his rational creed of the unity and perfections of God. It is not the propagation, but the permanency of his religion, that deserves our wonder: the same pure and perfect impression which he engraved at Mecca and Medina is preserved, after the revolutions of twelve centuries, by the Indian, the African, and the Turkish proselytes of the Koran. If the Christian apostles, St. Peter or St. Paul, could return to the Vatican, they might possibly inquire the name of the Deity who is worshipped with such mysterious rites in that magnificent temple: at Oxford or Geneva they would experience less surprise; but it might still be incumbent on them to peruse the catechism of the church, and to study the orthodox commentators on their own writings and the words of their Master. But the Turkish dome of St. Sophia, with an increase of splendour and size, represents the humble tabernacle erected at Medina by the hands of Mahomet. The Mahometans have uniformly withstood the temptation of reducing the object of their faith and devotion to a level with the senses and imagination of man. "I believe in one God, and Mahomet the apostle of God," is the simple and invariable profession of Islam. The intellectual image of the Deity has never been degraded by any visible idol; the honours of the prophet have never transgressed the measure of human virtue; and his living precepts have restrained the gratitude of his disciples within the bounds of reason and religion. The votaries of Ali have, indeed, consecrated the memory of their hero, his wife, and his children; and some of the Persian doctors pretend that the divine essence was incarnate in the person of the Imams; but their superstition is universally condemned by the Sonnites; and their impiety has afforded a seasonable warning against the worship of saints and martyrs. The metaphysical questions on the attributes of God, and the liberty of man, have been agitated in the schools of the Mahometans as well as in those of the Christians; but among the former they have never engaged the passions of the people, or disturbed the tranquillity of the state. The cause of this important difference may be found in the separation or union of the regal and sacerdotal characters. It was the interest of the caliphs, the successors of the prophet and commanders of the faithful, to repress and discourage all religious innovations: the order, the discipline, the temporal and spiritual ambition of the clergy, are unknown to the Moslems; and the sages of the law are the guides of their conscience and the oracles of their faith. From the Atlantic to the Ganges the Koran is acknowledged as the fundamental code, not only of theology but of civil and criminal jurisprudence; and the laws which regulate the actions and the property of mankind are guarded by the infallible and immutable sanction of the will of God. This religious servitude is attended with some practical disadvantage; the illiterate legislator had been often misled by his own prejudices and those of his country; and the institutions of the Arabian desert may be ill adapted to the wealth and numbers of Ispahan and Constantinople. On these occasions the Cadhi respectfully places on his head the holy volume, and substitutes a dexterous interpretation more apposite to the principles of equity and the manners and policy of the times.

His beneficial or pernicious influence on the public happiness is the last consideration in the character of Mahomet. The most bitter or most bigoted of his Christian or Jewish foes will surely allow that he assumed a false commission to inculcate a salutary doctrine, less perfect only than their own. He piously supposed, as the basis of his religion, the truth and sanctity of *their* prior revelations, the virtues and miracles of their founders. The idols of Arabia were broken before the throne of God; the blood of human victims was expiated by prayer, and fasting, and alms, the laudable or innocent arts of devotion; and his rewards and punishments of a future life were painted by the images most congenial to an ignorant and carnal generation. Mahomet was, perhaps, incapable of dictating a moral and political system for the use of his countrymen: but he breathed among the faithful a spirit of charity and friendship; recommended the practice of the social virtues; and checked, by his laws and precepts, the thirst of revenge, and the oppression of widows and orphans. The hostile tribes were united in faith and obedience, and the valour which had been idly spent in domestic quarrels was vigorously directed against a foreign enemy. Had the impulse been less powerful, Arabia, free at home, and formidable abroad, might have flourished under a succession of her native monarchs. Her sovereignty was lost by the extent and rapidity of conquest. The colonies of the nation were scattered over the East and West, and their blood was mingled with the blood of their converts and captives. After the reign of three caliphs, the throne was transported from Medina to the valley of Damascus and the banks of the Tigris; the holy cities were violated by impious war; Arabia was ruled by the rod of a subject, perhaps of a stranger; and the Bedoweens of the desert, awakening from their dream of dominion, resumed their old and solitary independence.

Chapter 51

THE FATE OF THE ALEXANDRIAN LIBRARY

Chapters 51 and 52 are omitted. They contain the narrative of the Arab conquests and the extension of their power and civilisation to Africa and Spain. Their advance into France was checked in 732 by the victory of Charles Martel. After they spread to the West these invasions lie, strictly speaking, outside the Roman Empire. One passage only from Chapter 51 is printed here. It describes the destruction of the Library at Alexandria. This deed was at least a symbol of the eclipse of the ancient culture, and, as Gibbon says, cannot be passed over. The story allowed him to pay a last salute to that literature which was the standard of his life and thought and from which as much as from anything he traced the decline and fall of civilisation. Nevertheless he tells the story critically and his scepticism is supported by modern opinion.

THE ALEXANDRIAN LIBRARY

I SHOULD deceive the expectation of the reader if I passed in silence the fate of the Alexandrian library, as it is described by the learned Abulpharagius. The spirit of Amrou was more curious and liberal than that of his brethren, and in his leisure hours the Arabian chief was pleased with the conversation of John, the last disciple of Ammonius, and who derived the surname of *Philoponus* from his laborious studies of grammar and philosophy. Emboldened by this familiar intercourse, Philoponus presumed to solicit a gift, inestimable in *his* opinion, contemptible in that of the barbarians—the royal library, which alone, among the spoils of Alexandria, had not been appropriated by the visit and the seal of the conqueror. Amrou was inclined to gratify the wish of the grammarian, but his rigid integrity refused to alienate the minutest object without the consent of the caliph: and the well-known answer of Omar was inspired by the ignorance of a fanatic. "If these writings of the Greeks agree with the book of God, they are useless and need not be preserved: if they disagree, they are pernicious and ought to be destroyed." The sentence was executed with blind obedience: the volumes of paper or parchment were distributed to the four thousand baths of the city; and such was their incredible multitude, that six months were barely sufficient for the consumption of this precious fuel. Since the Dynasties of Abulpharagius have been given to the world in a Latin version, the tale has been repeatedly transcribed; and every scholar, with pious indignation, has deplored the irreparable shipwreck of the learning, the arts, and the genius of antiquity. For my own part, I am strongly tempted to deny both the fact and the consequences. The fact is indeed marvellous. "Read and wonder!" says the historian himself: and the solitary report of a stranger who wrote at the end of six hundred years on the confines of Media is overbalanced by the silence of two annalists of a more early date, both Christians, both natives of Egypt, and the most ancient of whom, the patriarch Eutychius, has amply described the conquest of Alexandria. The rigid sentence of Omar is repugnant to the sound and orthodox precept of the Mahometan casuists: they expressly declare that the religious books of the Jews and Christians, which are acquired by the right of war, should never be committed to the flames; and that the works of profane science, historians or poets, physicians or philosophers, may be lawfully applied to the faithful. A more destructive zeal may perhaps be attributed to the first successors of Mahomet; yet in this instance the conflagration would have speedily expired in the deficiency of materials. I shall not recapitulate the disasters of the Alexandrian library, the involuntary flame that was kindled by Cæsar in his own defence, or the mischievous bigotry of the Christians, who studied to destroy the monuments of idolatry. But if we gradually descend from the age of the Antonines to that of Theodosius, we shall learn from a chain of contemporary witnesses that the royal palace and the temple of Serapis no longer contained the four, or the seven, hundred thousand volumes which had been assembled by the curiosity and magnificence of the Ptolemies. Perhaps the church and seat of the patriarchs might be enriched with a repository of books; but if the ponderous mass of Arian and Monophysite controversy were indeed consumed in the public baths, a philosopher may allow, with a smile, that it was ultimately devoted to the benefit of mankind. I sincerely regret the more valuable libraries which have been involved in the ruin of the Roman empire; but when I seriously compute the lapse of ages, the waste of ignorance, and the calamities of war, our treasures, rather than our losses, are the object of my surprise. Many curious and interesting facts are buried in oblivion: the three great historians of Rome have been transmitted to our hands in a mutilated state; and we are deprived of many pleasing compositions of the lyric, iambic, and dramatic poetry of the Greeks. Yet we should gratefully remember that the mischances of time and accident have spared the classic works to which the suffrage of antiquity had adjudged the first place of genius and glory: the teachers of ancient knowledge, who are still extant, had perused and compared the writings of their predecessors; nor can it fairly be presumed that any important truth, any useful discovery in art or nature, has been snatched away from the curiosity of modern ages.

THE DECLINE OF THE
EMPIRE IN THE EAST

Chapter 53

A RAY of historic light seems to beam from the darkness of the tenth century. We open with curiosity and respect the royal volumes of Constantine Porphyrogenitus, which he composed at a mature age for the instruction of his son, and which promise to unfold the state of the Eastern empire, both in peace and war, both at home and abroad. In the first of these works he minutely describes the pompous ceremonies of the church and palace of Constantinople, according to his own practice and that of his predecessors. In the second he attempts an accurate survey of the provinces, the *themes*, as they were then denominated, both of Europe and Asia. The system of Roman tactics, the discipline and order of the troops, and the military operations by land and sea, are explained in the third of these didactic collections, which may be ascribed to Constantine or his father Leo. In the fourth, of the administration of the empire, he reveals the secrets of the Byzantine policy, in friendly or hostile intercourse with the nations of the earth. The literary labours of the age, the practical systems of law, agriculture, and history, might redound to the benefit of the subject, and the honour of the Macedonian princes. The sixty books of the *Basilics*, the code and pandects of civil jurisprudence, were gradually framed in the three first reigns of that prosperous dynasty. The art of agriculture had amused the leisure, and exercised the pens, of the best and wisest of the ancients; and their chosen precepts are comprised in the twenty books of the *Geoponics* of Constantine. At his command the historical examples of vice and virtue were methodised in fifty-three books, and every citizen might apply to his contemporaries or himself the lesson or the warning of past times. From the august character of a legislator, the sovereign of the East descends to the more humble office of a teacher and a scribe; and if his successors and subjects were regardless of his paternal cares, *we* may inherit and enjoy the everlasting legacy.

A closer survey will indeed reduce the value of the gift and the gratitude of posterity: in the possession of these Imperial treasures we may still deplore our poverty and ignorance; and the fading glories of

698

their authors will be obliterated by indifference or contempt. The *Basilics* will sink to a broken copy, a partial and mutilated version in the Greek language, of the laws of Justinian; but the sense of the old civilians is often superseded by the influence of bigotry: and the absolute prohibition of divorce, concubinage, and interest for money, enslaves the freedom of trade and the happiness of private life. In the historical book a subject of Constantine might admire the inimitable virtues of Greece and Rome: he might learn to what a pitch of energy and elevation the human character had formerly aspired. But a contrary effect must have been produced by a new edition of the lives of the saints, which the great logothete, or chancellor of the empire, was directed to prepare; and the dark fund of superstition was enriched by the fabulous and florid legends of Simon the *Metaphrast*. The merits and miracles of the whole calendar are of less account in the eyes of a sage than the toil of a single husbandman, who multiplies the gifts of the Creator and supplies the food of his brethren. Yet the royal authors of the *Geoponics* were more seriously employed in expounding the precepts of the destroying art, which has been taught since the days of Xenophon as the art of heroes and kings. But the *Tactics* of Leo and Constantine are mingled with the baser alloy of the age in which they lived. It was destitute of original genius; they implicitly transcribe the rules and maxims which had been confirmed by victories. It was unskilled in the propriety of style and method; they blindly confound the most distant and discordant institutions, the phalanx of Sparta and that of Macedon, the legions of Cato and Trajan, of Augustus and Theodosius. Even the use, or at least the importance, of these military rudiments may be fairly questioned: their general theory is dictated by reason; but the merit, as well as difficulty, consists in the application. The discipline of a soldier is formed by exercise rather than by study: the talents of a commander are appropriated to those calm, though rapid, minds, which nature produces to decide the fate of armies and nations: the former is the habit of a life, the latter the glance of a moment; and the battles won by lessons of tactics may be numbered with the epic poems created from the rules of criticism. The book of ceremonies is a recital, tedious yet imperfect, of the despicable pageantry which had infected the church and state since the gradual decay of the purity of the one and the power of the other. A review of the themes or provinces might promise such authentic and useful information as the curiosity of government only can obtain, instead of traditionary fables on the origin of the cities, and malicious epigrams on the vices of their inhabitants. Such information the historian would have been pleased to record; nor should his silence be condemned if the most interesting objects, the population of the capital and provinces, the amount of the taxes and revenues, the numbers of subjects and strangers who served under the Imperial standard, have been unnoticed by Leo the Philosopher and his son Constantine. His treatise of the public administration is stained with the same blemishes; yet it is discriminated by peculiar merit: the antiquities of the nations may be doubtful or fabulous; but the geography and manners of the barbaric world are delineated with curious accuracy. Of these nations the Franks alone were qualified to observe in their turn, and to describe, the metropolis of the East. The ambassador of the great Otho, a bishop of Cremona, has painted the state of Constantinople about the middle of the tenth century: his style is glowing, his narrative lively, his observation keen; and even the prejudices and passions of Liutprand are stamped with an original character of freedom and genius. From this scanty fund of foreign and domestic materials I shall investigate the form and substance of the Byzantine empire; the provinces and wealth, the civil government and military force, the character and literature, of the Greeks in a period of six hundred years, from the reign of Heraclius to the successful invasion of the Franks or Latins.

After the final division between the sons of Theodosius, the swarms of barbarians from Scythia and Germany overspread the provinces and extinguished the empire of ancient Rome. The weakness of Constantinople was concealed by extent of dominion; her limits were inviolate, or at least entire; and the kingdom of Justinian was enlarged by the splendid acquisition of Africa and Italy. But the possession of these new conquests was transient and precarious, and almost a moiety of the Eastern empire was torn away by the arms of the Saracens. Syria and Egypt were oppressed by the Arabian caliphs, and, after the reduction of Africa, their lieutenants invaded and subdued the Roman province which had been changed into the Gothic monarchy of Spain. The islands of the Mediterranean were not inaccessible to their naval powers; and it was from their extreme stations, the harbours of Crete and the fortresses of Cilicia, that the faithful or rebel emirs insulted the majesty of the throne and capital. The remaining provinces, under the obedience of the emperors, were cast into a new mould; and the jurisdiction of the presidents, the consulars, and the counts was superseded by the institution of the *themes*, or military governments, which prevailed under the successors of Heraclius, and are described by the pen of the royal author. Of the twenty-nine themes, twelve in Europe and seventeen in Asia, the origin is obscure, the etymology doubtful or capricious, the limits were arbitrary and fluctuating; but some particular names that sound the most strangely to our ear were derived from the character and attributes of the troops that were maintained at the expense and for the guard of the respective divisions. The vanity of the Greek princes most eagerly grasped the shadow of conquest and the memory of lost dominion. A new Mesopotamia was created on the western side of the Euphrates; the appellation and prætor of Sicily were transferred to a narrow slip of Calabria; and a fragment of the duchy of Beneventum was promoted to

the style and title of the theme of Lombardy. In the decline of the
Arabian empire the successors of Constantine might indulge their pride
in more solid advantages. The victories of Nicephorus, John Zimisces,
and Basil the Second, revived the fame, and enlarged the boundaries, of
the Roman name; the province of Cilicia, the metropolis of Antioch,
the islands of Crete and Cyprus were restored to the allegiance of Christ
and Cæsar; one-third of Italy was annexed to the throne of Constantinople, the kingdom of Bulgaria was destroyed, and the last sovereigns
of the Macedonian dynasty extended their sway from the sources of
the Tigris to the neighbourhood of Rome. In the eleventh century the
prospect was again clouded by new enemies and new misfortunes; the
relics of Italy were swept away by the Norman adventurers, and almost
all the Asiatic branches were dissevered from the Roman trunk by the
Turkish conquerors. After these losses the emperors of the Comnenian
family continued to reign from the Danube to Peloponnesus, and from
Belgrade to Nice, Trebizond, and the winding stream of the Meander.
The spacious provinces of Thrace, Macedonia, and Greece were obedient
to their sceptre; the possession of Cyprus, Rhodes, and Crete was
accompanied by the fifty islands of the Ægean or Holy Sea, and the
remnant of their empire transcends the measure of the largest of the
European kingdoms.

WEALTH, MANUFACTURES, AND REVENUE OF THE EMPIRE

The same princes might assert, with dignity and truth, that of all the
monarchs of Christendom they possessed the greatest city, the most
ample revenue, the most flourishing and populous state. With the
decline and fall of the empire the cities of the West had decayed and
fallen; nor could the ruins of Rome, or the mud walls, wooden hovels,
and narrow precincts of Paris and London, prepare the Latin stranger
to contemplate the situation and extent of Constantinople, her stately
palaces and churches, and the arts and luxury of an innumerable people.
Her treasures might attract, but her virgin strength had repelled, and
still promised to repel, the audacious invasion of the Persian and Bulgarian, the Arab and the Russian. The provinces were less fortunate
and impregnable, and few districts, few cities, could be discovered which
had not been violated by some fierce barbarian, impatient to despoil,
because he was hopeless to possess. From the age of Justinian the
Eastern empire was sinking below its former level; the powers of destruction were more active than those of improvement; and the calamities of
war were embittered by the more permanent evils of civil and ecclesiastical tyranny. The captive who had escaped from the barbarians was
often stripped and imprisoned by the ministers of his sovereign; the
Greek superstition relaxed the mind by prayer, and emaciated the body
by fasting; and the multitude of convents and festivals diverted many

hands and many days from the temporal service of mankind. Yet the subjects of the Byzantine empire were still the most dexterous and diligent of nations; their country was blessed by nature with every advantage of soil, climate, and situation; and, in the support and restoration of the arts, their patient and peaceful temper was more useful than the warlike spirit and feudal anarchy of Europe. The provinces that still adhered to the empire were repeopled and enriched by the misfortunes of those which were irrecoverably lost. From the yoke of the caliphs, the Catholics of Syria, Egypt, and Africa retired to the allegiance of their prince, to the society of their brethren; the moveable wealth, which eludes the search of oppression, accompanied and alleviated their exile, and Constantinople received into her bosom the fugitive trade of Alexandria and Tyre. The chiefs of Armenia and Scythia, who fled from hostile or religious persecution, were hospitably entertained; their followers were encouraged to build new cities and to cultivate waste lands; and many spots, both in Europe and Asia, preserved the name, the manners, or at least the memory, of these national colonies. Even the tribes of barbarians who had seated themselves in arms on the territory of the empire were gradually reclaimed to the laws of the church and state, and, as long as they were separated from the Greeks, their posterity supplied a race of faithful and obedient soldiers. Did we possess sufficient materials to survey the twenty-nine themes of the Byzantine monarchy, our curiosity might be satisfied with a chosen example: it is fortunate enough that the clearest light should be thrown on the most interesting province, and the name of PELOPONNESUS will awaken the attention of the classic reader.

As early as the eighth century, in the troubled reign of the Iconoclasts, Greece, and even Peloponnesus, were overrun by some Sclavonian bands who outstripped the royal standard of Bulgaria. The strangers of old, Cadmus, and Danaus, and Pelops, had planted in that fruitful soil the seeds of policy and learning; but the savages of the north eradicated what yet remained of their sickly and withered roots. In this irruption the country and the inhabitants were transformed; the Grecian blood was contaminated; and the proudest nobles of Peloponnesus were branded with the names of foreigners and *slaves*. By the diligence of succeeding princes, the land was in some measure purified from the barbarians; and the humble remnant was bound by an oath of obedience, tribute, and military service, which they often renewed and often violated. The siege of Patras was formed by a singular concurrence of the Sclavonians of Peloponnesus and the Saracens of Africa. In their last distress a pious fiction of the approach of the prætor of Corinth revived the courage of the citizens. Their sally was bold and successful; the strangers embarked, the rebels submitted, and the glory of the day was ascribed to a phantom or a stranger, who fought in the foremost ranks under the character of St. Andrew the Apostle. The shrine which contained his relics was decorated with the trophies of victory, and the captive race was for ever devoted to the service and vassalage of the metropolitan church of Patras. By the revolt of two Sclavonian tribes in the neighbourhood of Helos and Lacedæmon, the peace of the peninsula was often disturbed. They sometimes insulted the weakness, and sometimes resisted the oppression, of the Byzantine government, till at length the approach of their hostile brethren extorted a golden bull to define the rights and obligations of the Ezzerites and Milengi, whose annual tribute was defined at twelve hundred pieces of gold. From these strangers the Imperial geographer has accurately distinguished a domestic and perhaps original race, who, in some degree, might derive their blood from the much-injured Helots. The liberality of the Romans, and especially of Augustus, had enfranchised the maritime cities from the dominion of Sparta; and the continuance of the same benefit ennobled them with the title of *Eleuthero*, or Free-Laconians. In the time of Constantine Porphyrogenitus they had acquired the name of *Mainotes*, under which they dishonour the claim of liberty by the inhuman pillage of all that is shipwrecked on their rocky shores. Their territory, barren of corn but fruitful of olives, extended to the Cape of Malea: they accepted a chief or prince from the Byzantine prætor; and a light tribute of four hundred pieces of gold was the badge of their immunity rather than of their dependence. The freemen of Laconia assumed the character of Romans, and long adhered to the religion of the Greeks. By the zeal of the emperor Basil, they were baptized in the faith of Christ: but the altars of Venus and Neptune had been crowned by these rustic votaries five hundred years after they were proscribed in the Roman world. In the theme of Peloponnesus forty cities were still numbered, and the declining state of Sparta, Argos, and Corinth may be suspended in the tenth century, at an equal distance, perhaps, between their antique splendour and their present desolation. The duty of military service, either in person or by substitute, was imposed on the lands or benefices of the province; a sum of five pieces of gold was assessed on each of the substantial tenants; and the same capitation was shared among several heads of inferior value. On the proclamation of an Italian war, the Peloponnesians excused themselves by a voluntary oblation of one hundred pounds of gold (four thousand pounds sterling), and a thousand horses with their arms and trappings. The churches and monasteries furnished their contingent; a sacrilegious profit was extorted from the sale of ecclesiastical honours; and the indigent bishop of Leucadia was made responsible for a pension of one hundred pieces of gold.

But the wealth of the province, and the trust of the revenue, were founded on the fair and plentiful produce of trade and manufactures; and some symptoms of liberal policy may be traced in a law which exempts from all personal taxes the mariners of Peloponnesus, and the workmen in parchment and purple. This denomination may be fairly applied or extended to the manufactures of linen, woollen, and more especially of silk: the two former of which had flourished in Greece since the days of Homer; and the last was introduced perhaps as early as the reign of Justinian. These arts, which were exercised at Corinth, Thebes, and Argos, afforded food and occupation to a numerous people: the men, women, and children were distributed according to their age and strength; and if many of these were domestic slaves, their masters, who directed the work and enjoyed the profit, were of a free and honourable condition. The gifts which a rich and generous matron of Peloponnesus presented to the emperor Basil, her adopted son, were doubtless fabricated in the Grecian looms. Danielis bestowed a carpet of fine wool, of a pattern which imitated the spots of a peacock's tail, of a magnitude to overspread the floor of a new church, erected in the triple name of Christ, of Michael the archangel, and of the prophet Elijah. She gave six hundred pieces of silk and linen, of various use and denomination: the silk was painted with the Tyrian dye, and adorned by the labours of the needle; and the linen was so exquisitely fine, that an entire piece might be rolled in the hollow of a cane. In his description of the Greek manufactures, an historian of Sicily discriminates their price, according to the weight and quality of the silk, the closeness of the texture, the beauty of the colours, and the taste and materials of the embroidery. A single, or even a double or treble thread was thought sufficient for ordinary sale; but the union of six threads composed a piece of stronger and more costly workmanship. Among the colours, he celebrates, with affectation of eloquence, the fiery blaze of the scarlet, and the softer lustre of the green. The embroidery was raised either in silk or gold: the more simple ornament of stripes or circles was surpassed by the nicer imitation of flowers: the vestments that were fabricated for the palace or the altar often glittered with precious stones; and the figures were delineated in strings of Oriental pearls. Till the twelfth century, Greece alone, of all the countries of Christendom, was possessed of the insect who is taught by nature, and of the workmen who are instructed by art, to prepare this elegant luxury. But the secret had been stolen by the dexterity and diligence of the Arabs: the caliphs of the East and West scorned to borrow from the unbelievers their furniture and apparel; and two cities of Spain, Almeria and Lisbon, were famous for the manufacture, the use, and perhaps the exportation of silk. It was first introduced into Sicily by the Normans; and this emigration of trade distinguishes the victory of Roger from the uniform and fruitless hostilities of every age. After the sack of Corinth, Athens, and Thebes, his lieutenant embarked with a captive train of weavers and artificers of both sexes, a trophy glorious to their master and disgraceful to the Greek emperor. The king of Sicily was not insensible of the value of the present; and, in the restitution of the prisoners, he excepted only the male and female manufacturers of Thebes and Corinth, who labour, says the Byzantine historian, under a barbarous lord, like the old Eretrians in the service of Darius. A stately edifice, in the palace of Palermo, was erected for the use of this industrious colony; and the art was propagated by their children and disciples to satisfy the increasing demand of the western world. Tne decay of the looms of Sicily may be ascribed to the troubles of the island and the competition of the Italian cities. In the year thirteen hundred and fourteen, Lucca alone, among her sister republics, enjoyed the lucrative monopoly. A domestic revolution dispersed the manufacturers to Florence, Bologna, Venice, Milan, and even the countries beyond the Alps; and thirteen years after this event, the statutes of Modena enjoin the planting of mulberry-trees and regulate the duties on raw silk. The northern climates are less propitious to the education of the silkworm; but the industry of France and England is supplied and enriched by the productions of Italy and China.

I must repeat the complaint that the vague and scanty memorials of the times will not afford any just estimate of the taxes, the revenue, and the resources of the Greek empire. From every province of Europe and Asia the rivulets of gold and silver discharged into the Imperial reservoir a copious and perennial stream. The separation of the branches from the trunk increased the relative magnitude of Constantinople; and the maxims of despotism contracted the state to the capital, the capital to the palace, and the palace to the royal person. A Jewish traveller, who visited the East in the twelfth century, is lost in his admiration of the Byzantine riches. "It is here," says Benjamin of Tudela, "in the queen of cities, that the tributes of the Greek empire are annually deposited, and the lofty towers are filled with precious magazines of silk, purple, and gold. It is said that Constantinople pays each day to her sovereign twenty thousand pieces of gold, which are levied on the shops, taverns, and markets, on the merchants of Persia and Egypt, of Russia and Hungary, of Italy and Spain, who frequent the capital by sea and land." In all pecuniary matters the authority of a Jew is doubtless respectable; but as the three hundred and sixty-five days would produce a yearly income exceeding seven millions sterling, I am tempted to retrench at least the numerous festivals of the Greek calendar. The mass of treasure that was saved by Theodora and Basil the Second will suggest a splendid, though indefinite, idea of their supplies and resources. The mother of Michael, before she retired to a cloister, attempted to check or expose the prodigality of her ungrateful son by a free and faithful account of the wealth which he inherited; one hundred and nine thousand pounds of gold and three hundred thousand of silver, the fruits of her own economy and that of her deceased husband. The avarice of Basil is not less renowned than his valour and fortune: his victorious armies were paid and rewarded without breaking into the mass of two hundred thousand pounds of gold (about eight millions sterling), which he had buried in the subterraneous vaults of the palace. Such accumulation of treasure is rejected by the theory and practice of modern policy; and we are more apt to compute the national riches by the use and abuse of the public credit. Yet the maxims of antiquity are still embraced by a monarch formidable to his enemies; by a republic respectable to her allies; and both have attained their respective ends of military power and domestic tranquillity.

THE IMPERIAL PALACE

Whatever might be consumed for the present wants or reserved for the future use of the state, the first and most sacred demand was for the pomp and pleasure of the emperor; and his discretion only could define the measure of his private expense. The princes of Constantinople were far removed from the simplicity of nature; yet, with the revolving seasons, they were led by taste or fashion to withdraw to a purer air from the smoke and tumult of the capital. They enjoyed, or affected to enjoy, the rustic festival of the vintage: their leisure was amused by the exercise of the chase and the calmer occupation of fishing; and in the summer heats they were shaded from the sun, and refreshed by the cooling breezes from the sea. The coasts and islands of Asia and Europe were covered with their magnificent villas; but instead of the modest art which secretly strives to hide itself and to decorate the scenery of nature, the marble structure of their gardens served only to expose the riches of the lord and the labours of the architect. The successive casualties of inheritance and forfeiture had rendered the sovereign proprietor of many stately houses in the city and suburbs, of which twelve were appropriated to the ministers of state; but the great palace, the centre of the Imperial residence, was fixed during eleven centuries to the same position, between the hippodrome, the cathedral of St. Sophia, and the gardens, which descended by many a terrace to the shores of the Propontis. The primitive edifice of the first Constantine was a copy, or rival, of ancient Rome; the gradual improvements of his successors aspired to emulate the wonders of the old world, and in the tenth century the Byzantine palace excited the admiration, at least of the Latins, by an unquestionable pre-eminence of strength, size, and magnificence. But the toil and treasure of so many ages had produced a vast and irregular pile: each separate building was marked with the character of the times and of the founder; and the want of space might excuse the reigning monarch who demolished, perhaps with secret satisfaction, the works of his predecessors. The economy of the emperor Theophilus allowed a more free and ample scope for his domestic luxury and splendour. A favourite ambassador, who had astonished the Abbassides themselves by his pride and liberality, presented on his return the model of a palace which the caliph of Bagdad had recently constructed on the banks of the Tigris. The model was instantly copied and surpassed: the new buildings of Theophilus were accompanied with gardens and with five churches, one of which was conspicuous for size and beauty: it was crowned with three domes, the roof of gilt brass reposed on columns of Italian marble, and the walls were incrusted with marbles of various colours. In the face of the church a semicircular portico, of the figure and name of the Greek *sigma*, was supported by fifteen columns of Phrygian marble, and the subterraneous vaults were of a similar construction. The square before the sigma was decorated with a fountain, and the margin of the basin was lined and encompassed with plates of silver. In the beginning of each season the basin, instead of water, was replenished with the most exquisite fruits, which were abandoned to the populace for the entertainment of the prince. He enjoyed this tumultuous spectacle from a throne resplendent with gold and gems, which was raised by a marble staircase to the height of a lofty terrace. Below the throne were seated the officers of his guards, the magistrates, the chiefs of the factions of the circus; the inferior steps were occupied by the people, and the place below was covered with troops of dancers, singers, and pantomimes. The square was surrounded by the hall of justice, the arsenal, and the various offices of business and pleasure; and the *purple* chamber was named from the annual distribution of robes of scarlet and purple by the hand of the empress herself. The long series of the apartments was adapted to the seasons, and decorated with marble and porphyry, with painting, sculpture, and mosaics, with a profusion of gold, silver, and precious stones. His fanciful magnificence employed the skill and patience of such artists as the times could afford; but the taste of Athens would have despised their frivolous and costly labours; a golden tree, with its leaves and branches, which sheltered a multitude of birds warbling their artificial notes, and two lions of massy gold, and of the natural size, who looked and roared like their brethren of the forest. The successors of Theophilus, of the Basilian and Comnenian dynasties, were not less ambitious of leaving some memorial of their residence; and the portion of the palace most splendid and august was dignified with the title of the golden *triclinium*. With becoming modesty the rich and noble Greeks aspired to imitate their sovereign, and when they passed through the streets on horseback, in their robes of silk and embroidery, they were mistaken by the children for kings. A matron of Peloponnesus, who had cherished the infant fortunes of Basil the Macedonian, was excited by tenderness or vanity to visit the greatness of her adopted son. In a journey of five hundred miles from Patras to Constantinople, her age or indolence declined the fatigue of an horse or carriage; the soft litter or bed of Danielis was transported on the shoulders of ten robust slaves, and, as they were relieved at easy distances, a band of three hundred was selected for the performance of this service. She was entertained in the Byzantine palace with filial reverence and the honours of a queen; and whatever might be the origin of her wealth, her gifts were not unworthy of the regal dignity. I have already described the fine and curious manufactures of Peloponnesus, of linen, silk, and woollen; but the most acceptable of her presents consisted in three hundred beautiful youths, of whom one hundred were eunuchs; "for she was not ignorant," says the historian, "that the air of the palace is more congenial to such insects, than a shepherd's dairy to the flies of the summer." During her lifetime she bestowed the greater part of her estates in Peloponnesus, and her testament instituted Leo, the son of Basil, her universal heir. After the payment of the legacies, four-score villas or farms were added to the Imperial domain, and three thousand slaves of Danielis were enfranchised by their new lord, and transplanted as a colony to the Italian coast. From this example of a private matron we may estimate the wealth and magnificence of the emperors. Yet our enjoyments are confined by a narrow circle, and, whatsoever may be its value, the luxury of life is possessed with more innocence and safety by the master of his own, than by the steward of the public, fortune.

In an absolute government, which levels the distinctions of noble and plebeian birth, the sovereign is the sole fountain of honour; and the rank, both in the palace and the empire, depends on the titles and offices which are bestowed and resumed by his arbitrary will. Above a thousand years, from Vespasian to Alexius Comnenus, the *Cæsar* was the second person, or at least the second degree, after the supreme title of *Augustus* was more freely communicated to the sons and brothers of the reigning monarch. To elude without violating his promise to a powerful associate, the husband of his sister, and, without giving himself an equal, to reward the piety of his brother Isaac, the crafty Alexius interposed a new and supereminent dignity. The happy flexibility of the Greek tongue allowed him to compound the names of Augustus and Emperor (Sebastos and Autocrator), and the union produced the sonorous title of *Sebastocrator*. He was exalted above the Cæsar on the first step of the throne: the public acclamations repeated his name; and he was only distinguished from the sovereign by some peculiar orna-ments of the head and feet. The emperor alone could assume the purple or red buskins, and the close diadem or tiara, which imitated the fashion of the Persian kings. It was an high pyramidal cap of cloth or silk, almost concealed by a profusion of pearls and jewels: the crown was formed by an horizontal circle and two arches of gold: at the summit, the point of their intersection, was placed a globe or cross, and two strings or lappets of pearl depended on either cheek. Instead of red, the buskins of the Sebastocrator and Cæsar were green; and on their *open* coronets, or crowns, the precious gems were more sparingly distributed. Beside and below the Cæsar the fancy of Alexius created the *Panhyperse-bastos* and the *Protosebastos*, whose sound and signification will satisfy a Grecian ear. They imply a superiority and a priority above the simple name of Augustus; and this sacred and primitive title of the Roman prince was degraded to the kinsmen and servants of the Byzantine court. The daughter of Alexius applauds with fond complacency this artful gradation of hopes and honours; but the science of words is accessible to the meanest capacity; and this vain dictionary was easily enriched by the pride of his successors. To their favourite sons or brothers they imparted the more lofty appellation of Lord or *Despot*, which was illustrated with new ornaments and prerogatives, and placed immediately after the person of the emperor himself. The five titles of, 1. *Despot*; 2. *Sebastocrator*; 3. *Cæsar*; 4. *Panhypersebastos*; and, 5. *Protosebastos*; were usually confined to the princes of his blood: they were the emanations of his majesty; but as they exercised no regular functions, their existence was useless, and their authority precarious.

But in every monarchy the substantial powers of government must be divided and exercised by the ministers of the palace and treasury, the fleet and army. The titles alone can differ; and in the revolution of ages, the counts and prefects, the prætor and quæstor, insensibly descended, while their servants rose above their heads to the first honours of the state. 1. In a monarchy, which refers every object to the person of the prince, the care and ceremonies of the palace form the most respectable department. The *Curopalata*, so illustrious in the age of Justinian, was supplanted by the *Protovestiare*, whose primitive functions were limited to the custody of the wardrobe. From thence his jurisdiction was extended over the numerous menials of pomp and luxury; and he presided with his silver wand at the public and private audience. 2. In the ancient system of Constantine, the name of *Logothete*, or accountant, was applied to the receivers of the finances: the principal officers were distinguished as the Logothetes of the domain, of the posts, the army, the private and public treasure; and the *great Logothete*, the supreme guardian of the laws and revenues, is compared with the chancellor of the Latin monarchies. His discerning eye pervaded the civil administration; and he was assisted, in due subordination, by the eparch or prefect of the city, the first secretary, and the keepers of the privy seal, the archives, and the red or purple ink which was reserved for the sacred signature of the emperor alone. The introductor and interpreter of foreign ambassadors were the great *Chiauss* and the *Dragoman*, two names of Turkish origin, and which are still familiar to the Sublime Porte. 3. From the humble style and service of guards, the *Domestics* insensibly rose to the station of generals; the military themes of the East and West, the legions of Europe and Asia, were often divided, till the *great Domestic* was finally invested with the universal and absolute command of the land forces. The *Protostrator*, in his original functions, was the assistant of the emperor when he mounted on horseback: he gradually became the lieutenant of the great Domestic in the field; and his jurisdiction extended over the stables, the cavalry, and the royal train of hunting and hawking. The *Stratopedarch* was the great judge of the camp: the *Protospathaire* commanded the guards; the *Constable*, the great *Æteriarch*, and the *Acolyth*, were the separate chiefs of the Franks, the barbarians, and the Varangi, or English, the mercenary strangers, who, in the decay of the national spirit, formed the nerve of the Byzantine armies. 4. The naval powers were under the command of the *great Duke*; in his absence they obeyed the *great Drungaire* of the fleet; and, in *his* place, the *Emir*, or *Admiral*, a name of Saracen extraction, but which has been naturalised in all the modern languages of Europe. Of these officers, and of many more whom it would be useless to enumerate, the civil and military hierarchy was framed. Their honours and emoluments, their dress and titles, their mutual salutations, and respective pre-eminence, were balanced with more exquisite labour than would have fixed the constitution of a free people; and the code was almost perfect when this baseless fabric, the monument of pride and servitude, was for ever buried in the ruins of the empire.

The most lofty titles, and the most humble postures, which devotion has applied to the Supreme Being, have been prostituted by flattery and fear to creatures of the same nature with ourselves. The mode of *adoration*, of falling prostrate on the ground and kissing the feet of the emperor, was borrowed by Diocletian from Persian servitude; but it was continued and aggravated till the last age of the Greek monarchy. Excepting only on Sundays, when it was waived, from a motive of religious pride, this humiliating reverence was exacted from all who entered the royal presence, from the princes invested with the diadem and purple, and from the ambassadors who represented their independent sovereigns, the caliphs of Asia, Egypt, or Spain, the kings of France and Italy, and the Latin emperors of ancient Rome. In his transactions of business, Liutprand, bishop of Cremona, asserted the free sprit of a Frank and the dignity of his master Otho. Yet his sincerity cannot disguise the abasement of his first audience. When he approached the throne, the birds of the golden tree began to warble their notes, which were accompanied by the roarings of the two lions of gold. With his two companions Liutprand was compelled to bow and to fall prostrate; and thrice he touched the ground with his forehead. He arose; but in the short interval the throne had been hoisted by an engine from the floor to the ceiling, the Imperial figure appeared in new and more gorgeous apparel, and the interview was concluded in haughty and majestic silence. In this honest and curious narrative the bishop of Cremona represents the ceremonies of the Byzantine court, which are still practised in the Sublime Porte, and which were preserved in the last age by the dukes of Muscovy or Russia. After a long journey by the sea and land, from Venice to Constantinople, the ambassador halted at the golden gate, till he was conducted by the formal officers to the hospitable palace prepared for his reception; but this palace was a prison, and his jealous keepers prohibited all social intercourse either with strangers or natives. At his first audience he offered the gifts of his master—slaves, and golden vases, and costly armour. The ostentatious payment of the officers and troops displayed before his eyes the riches of the empire: he was entertained at a royal banquet, in which the ambassadors of the nations were marshalled by the esteem or contempt of the Greeks: from his own table, the emperor, as the most signal favour, sent the plates which he had tasted; and his favourites were dismissed with a robe of honour. In the morning and evening of each day his civil and military servants attended their duty in the palace; their labour was repaid by the sight, perhaps by the smile, of their lord; his commands were signified by a nod or a sign: but all earthly greatness *stood* silent and submissive in his presence. In his regular or extraordinary processions through the capital, he unveiled his person to the public view: the rites of policy were connected with those of religion, and his visits to the principal churches were regulated by the festivals of the Greek calendar. On the eve of these processions the gracious or devout intention of the monarch was proclaimed by the heralds. The streets were cleared and purified; the pavement was strewed with flowers; the most precious furniture, the gold and silver plate and silken hangings, were displayed from the windows and balconies; and a severe discipline restrained and silenced the tumult of the populace. The march was opened by the military officers at the head of their troops: they were followed in long order by the magistrates and ministers of the civil government: the person of the emperor was guarded by his eunuchs and domestics, and at the church door he was solemnly received by the patriarch and his clergy. The task of applause was not abandoned to the rude and spontaneous voices of the crowd. The most convenient stations were occupied by the bands of the blue and green factions of the circus; and their furious conflicts, which had shaken the capital, were insensibly sunk to an emulation of servitude. From either side they echoed in responsive melody the praises of the emperor; their poets and musicians directed the choir, and long life and victory were the burden of every song. The same acclamations were performed at the audience, the banquet, and the church; and as an evidence of boundless sway, they were repeated in the Latin, Gothic, Persian, French, and even English language, by the mercenaries who sustained the real or fictitious character of those nations. By the pen of Constantine Porphyrogenitus this science of form and flattery has been reduced into a pompous and trifling volume, which the vanity of succeeding times might enrich with an ample supplement. Yet the calmer reflection of a prince would surely suggest that the same acclamations were applied to every character and every reign: and if he had risen from a private rank, he might remember that his own voice had been the loudest and most eager in applause, at the very moment when he envied the fortune, or conspired against the life, of his predecessor.

The princes of the North, of the nations, says Constantine, without faith or fame, were ambitious of mingling their blood with the blood of the Cæsars, by their marriage with a royal virgin, or by the nuptials of their daughters with a Roman prince. The aged monarch, in his instructions to his son, reveals the secret maxims of policy and pride, and suggests the most decent reasons for refusing these insolent and unreasonable demands. Every animal, says the discreet emperor, is prompted by nature to seek a mate among the animals of his own species; and the human species is divided into various tribes, by the distinction of language, religion, and manners. A just regard to the purity of descent preserves the harmony of public and private life; but the mixture of foreign blood is the fruitful source of disorder and discord. Such had ever been the opinion and practice of the sage Romans: their jurisprudence proscribed the marriage of a citizen and a stranger: in the days of freedom and virtue a senator would have scorned to match his daughter with a king: the glory of Mark Antony was sullied by an Egyptian wife: and the emperor Titus was compelled, by popular censure, to dismiss with reluctance the reluctant Berenice.[1] This perpetual interdict was ratified by the fabulous sanction of the great Constantine. The ambassadors of the nations, more especially of the unbelieving nations, were solemnly admonished that such strange alliances had been condemned by the founder of the church and city. The irrevocable law was inscribed on the altar of St. Sophia; and the impious prince who should stain the majesty of the purple was excluded from the civil and ecclesiastical communion of the Romans. If the ambassadors were instructed by any false brethren in the Byzantine history, they might produce three memorable examples of the violation of this imaginary law: the marriage of Leo, or rather of his father Constantine the Fourth, with the daughter of the king of the Chazars, the nuptials of the grand-daughter of Romanus with a Bulgarian prince, and the union of Bertha of France or Italy with young Romanus, the son of Constantine Porphyrogenitus himself.

*   *   *   *   *

OBLIVION OF THE LATIN LANGUAGE

By the well-known edict of Caracalla, his subjects, from Britain to Egypt, were entitled to the name and privileges of Romans, and their national sovereign might fix his occasional or permanent residence in any province of their common country. In the division of the East and West an ideal unity was scrupulously preserved, and in their titles, laws,

---

[1] Berenicem invitus invitam dimisit (Suetonius in Tito, c. 7). Have I observed elsewhere that this Jewish beauty was at this time above fifty years of age? The judicious Racine has most discreetly suppressed both her age and her country.

and statutes the successors of Arcadius and Honorius announced themselves as the inseparable colleagues of the same office, as the joint sovereigns of the Roman world and city, which were bounded by the same limits. After the fall of the Western monarchy the majesty of the purple resided solely in the princes of Constantinople, and of these Justinian was the first who, after a divorce of sixty years, regained the dominion of ancient Rome, and asserted, by the right of conquest, the august title of Emperor of the Romans. A motive of vanity or discontent solicited one of his successors, Constans the Second, to abandon the Thracian Bosphorus and to restore the pristine honours of the Tiber: an extravagant project (exclaims the malicious Byzantine), as if he had despoiled a beautiful and blooming virgin, to enrich, or rather to expose, the deformity of a wrinkled and decrepit matron. But the sword of the Lombards opposed his settlement in Italy; he entered Rome not as a conqueror, but as a fugitive, and, after a visit of twelve days, he pillaged and for ever deserted the ancient capital of the world. The final revolt and separation of Italy was accomplished about two centuries after the conquests of Justinian, and from his reign we may date the gradual oblivion of the Latin tongue. That legislator had composed his Institutes, his Code, and his Pandects in a language which he celebrates as the proper and public style of the Roman government, the consecrated idiom of the palace and senate of Constantinople, of the camps and tribunals of the East. But this foreign dialect was unknown to the people and soldiers of the Asiatic provinces, it was imperfectly understood by the greater part of the interpreters of the laws and the ministers of the state. After a short conflict, nature and habit prevailed over the obsolete institutions of human power: for the general benefit of his subjects Justinian promulgated his Novels in the two languages, the several parts of his voluminous jurisprudence were successively translated, the original was forgotten, the version was studied, and the Greek, whose intrinsic merit deserved indeed the preference, obtained a legal as well as popular establishment in the Byzantine monarchy. The birth and residence of succeeding princes estranged them from the Roman idiom; Tiberius by the Arabs, and Maurice by the Italians, are distinguished as the first of the Greek Cæsars, as the founders of a new dynasty and empire; the silent revolution was accomplished before the death of Heraclius, and the ruins of the Latin speech were darkly preserved in the terms of jurisprudence and the acclamations of the palace. After the restoration of the Western empire by Charlemagne and the Othos, the names of Franks and Latins acquired an equal signification and extent, and these haughty barbarians asserted, with some justice, their superior claim to the language and dominion of Rome. They insulted the aliens of the East who had renounced the dress and idiom of Romans, and their reasonable practice will justify the frequent appellation of Greeks. But this contemptuous appellation was indignantly rejected by the prince and people to whom it is applied. Whatsoever changes had been introduced by the lapse of ages, they alleged a lineal and unbroken succession from Augustus and Constantine; and, in the lowest period of degeneracy and decay, the name of ROMANS adhered to the last fragments of the empire of Constantinople.

While the government of the East was transacted in Latin, the Greek was the language of literature and philosophy, nor could the masters of this rich and perfect idiom be tempted to envy the borrowed learning and imitative taste of their Roman disciples. After the fall of Paganism, the loss of Syria and Egypt, and the extinction of the schools of Alexandria and Athens, the studies of the Greeks insensibly retired to some regular monasteries, and, above all, to the royal college of Constantinople, which was burnt in the reign of Leo the Isaurian. In the pompous style of the age, the president of that foundation was named the Sun of Science; his twelve associates, the professors in the different arts and faculties, were the twelve signs of the zodiac; a library of thirty-six thousand five hundred volumes was open to their inquiries; and they could show an ancient manuscript of Homer, on a roll of parchment one hundred and twenty feet in length, the intestines, as it was fabled, of a prodigious serpent. But the seventh and eighth centuries were a period of discord and darkness; the library was burnt, the college was abolished, the Iconoclasts are represented as the foes of antiquity, and a savage ignorance and contempt of letters has disgraced the princes of the Heraclean and Isaurian dynasties.

REVIVAL OF GREEK LEARNING

In the ninth century we trace the first dawnings of the restoration of science. After the fanaticism of the Arabs had subsided, the caliphs aspired to conquer the arts, rather than the provinces, of the empire: their liberal curiosity rekindled the emulation of the Greeks, brushed away the dust from their ancient libraries, and taught them to know and reward the philosophers, whose labours had been hitherto repaid by the pleasure of study and the pursuit of truth. The Cæsar Bardas, the uncle of Michael the Third, was the generous protector of letters, a title which alone has preserved his memory and excused his ambition. A particle of the treasures of his nephew was sometimes diverted from the indulgence of vice and folly; a school was opened in the palace of Magnaura, and the presence of Bardas excited the emulation of the masters and students. At their head was the philosopher Leo, archbishop of Thessalonica; his profound skill in astronomy and the mathematics was admired by the strangers of the East, and this occult science was magnified by vulgar credulity, which modestly supposes that all knowledge superior to its own must be the effect of inspiration or magic. At the pressing entreaty of the Cæsar, his friend, the celebrated Photius, renounced the freedom of a secular and studious life, ascended the patriarchal throne, and was alternately excommunicated and absolved by the synods of the East and West. By the confession even of priestly hatred, no art or science, except poetry, was foreign to this universal scholar, who was deep in thought, indefatigable in reading, and eloquent in diction. Whilst he exercised the office of protospathaire, or captain of the guards, Photius was sent ambassador to the caliph of Bagdad. The tedious hours of exile, perhaps of confinement, were beguiled by the hasty composition of his *Library*, a living monument of erudition and criticism. Two hundred and fourscore writers, historians, orators, philosophers, theologians, are reviewed without any regular method; he abridges their narrative or doctrine, appreciates their style and character, and judges even the fathers of the church with a discreet freedom which often breaks through the superstition of the times. The emperor Basil, who lamented the defects of his own education, intrusted to the care of Photius his son and successor Leo the Philosopher, and the reign of that prince and of his son Constantine Porphyrogenitus forms one of the most prosperous eras of the Byzantine literature. By their munificence the treasures of antiquity were deposited in the Imperial library; by their pens, or those of their associates, they were imparted in such extracts and abridgments as might amuse the curiosity, without oppressing the indolence, of the public. Besides the *Basilics*, or code of laws, the arts of husbandry and war, of feeding or destroying the human species, were propagated with equal diligence; and the history of Greece and Rome was digested into fifty-three heads or titles, of which two only (of embassies, and of virtues and vices) have escaped the injuries of time. In every station the reader might contemplate the image of the past world, apply the lesson or warning of each page, and learn to admire, perhaps to imitate, the examples of a brighter period. I shall not expatiate on the works of the Byzantine Greeks, who, by the assiduous study of the ancients, have deserved, in some measure, the remembrance and gratitude of the moderns. The scholars of the present age may still enjoy the benefit of the philosophical commonplace-book of Stobæus, the grammatical and historic lexicon of Suidas, the Chiliads of Tzetzes, which comprise six hundred narratives in twelve thousand verses, and the commentaries on Homer of Eustathius archbishop of Thessalonica, who, from his horn of plenty, has poured the names and authorities of four hundred writers. From these originals, and from the numerous tribe of scholiasts and critics, some estimate may be formed of the literary wealth of the twelfth century. Constantinople was enlightened by the genius of Homer and Demosthenes, of Aristotle and Plato; and in the enjoyment or neglect of our present riches we must envy the generation that could still peruse the history of Theopompus, the orations of Hyperides, the comedies of Menander, and the odes of Alcæus and Sappho. The frequent labour of illustration attests not only the existence but the popularity of the Grecian classics; the general knowledge of the age may be deduced from the example of two learned females, the empress Eudocia and the princess Anna Comnena, who cultivated, in the purple, the arts of rhetoric and philosophy. The vulgar dialect of the city was gross and barbarous: a more correct and elaborate style distinguished the discourse, or at least the compositions, of the church and palace, which sometimes affected to copy the purity of the Attic models.

THE DECAY OF TASTE

In our modern education, the painful though necessary attainment of two languages which are no longer living may consume the time and damp the ardour of the youthful student. The poets and orators were long imprisoned in the barbarous dialects of our Western ancestors, devoid of harmony or grace; and their genius, without precept or example, was abandoned to the rude and native powers of their judgment and fancy. But the Greeks of Constantinople, after purging away the impurities of their vulgar speech, acquired the free use of their ancient language, the most happy composition of human art, and a familiar knowledge of the sublime masters who had pleased or instructed the first of nations. But these advantages only tend to aggravate the reproach and shame of a degenerate people. They held in their lifeless hands the riches of their fathers, without inheriting the spirit which had created and improved that sacred patrimony: they read, they praised, they compiled, but their languid souls seemed alike incapable of thought and action. In the revolution of ten centuries, not a single discovery was made to exalt the dignity or promote the happiness of mankind. Not a single idea has been added to the speculative systems of antiquity, and a succession of patient disciples became in their turn the dogmatic teachers of the next servile generation. Not a single composition of history, philosophy, or literature, has been saved from oblivion by the intrinsic beauties of style or sentiment, of original fancy, or even of successful imitation. In prose, the least offensive of the Byzantine writers are absolved from censure by their naked and unpresuming simplicity: but the orators, most eloquent in their own conceit, are the farthest removed from the models whom they affect to emulate. In every page our taste and reason are wounded by the choice of gigantic and obsolete words, a stiff and intricate phraseology, the discord of images, the childish play of false or unseasonable ornament, and the painful attempt to elevate themselves, to astonish the reader, and to involve a trivial meaning in the smoke of obscurity and exaggeration. Their prose is soaring to the vicious affectation of poetry: their poetry is sinking below the flatness and insipidity of prose. The tragic, epic, and lyric muses were silent and inglorious: the bards of Constantinople seldom rose above a riddle or epigram, a panegyric or tale; they forgot even the rules of prosody; and with the melody of Homer yet sounding in their ears, they confounded all measure of feet and syllables in the impotent strains which have received the name of *political* or city verses. The minds of the Greeks were bound in the fetters of a base and imperious superstition, which extends her dominion round the circle of profane science. Their understandings were bewildered in metaphysical controversy: in the belief of visions and miracles they had lost all principles of moral evidence, and their taste was vitiated by the homilies of the monks, an absurd medley of declamation and Scripture. Even these contemptible studies were no longer dignified by the abuse of superior talents: the leaders of the Greek church were humbly content to admire and copy the oracles of antiquity, nor did the schools or pulpit produce any rivals of the fame of Athanasius and Chrysostom.

In all the pursuits of active and speculative life, the emulation of states and individuals is the most powerful spring of the efforts and improvements of mankind. The cities of ancient Greece were cast in the happy mixture of union and independence, which is repeated on a larger scale, but in a looser form, by the nations of modern Europe: the union of language, religion, and manners, which renders them the spectators and judges of each other's merit: the independence of government and interest, which asserts their separate freedom, and excites them to strive for pre-eminence in the career of glory. The situation of the Romans was less favourable; yet in the early ages of the republic, which fixed the national character, a similar emulation was kindled among the states of Latium and Italy; and in the arts and sciences they aspired to equal or surpass their Grecian masters. The empire of the Cæsars undoubtedly checked the activity and progress of the human mind: its magnitude might indeed allow some scope for domestic competition; but when it was gradually reduced, at first to the East, and at last to Greece and Constantinople, the Byzantine subjects were degraded to an abject and languid temper, the natural effect of their solitary and insulated state. From the North they were oppressed by nameless tribes of barbarians, to whom they scarcely imparted the appellation of men. The language and religion of the more polished Arabs were an insurmountable bar to all social intercourse. The conquerors of Europe were their brethren in the Christian faith; but the speech of the Franks or Latins was unknown, their manners were rude, and they were rarely connected, in peace or war, with the successors of Heraclius. Alone in the universe, the self-satisfied pride of the Greeks was not disturbed by the comparison of foreign merit; and it is no wonder if they fainted in the race, since they had neither competitors to urge their speed, nor judges to crown their victory. The nations of Europe and Asia were mingled by the expeditions to the Holy Land; and it is under the Comnenian dynasty that a faint emulation of knowledge and military virtue was rekindled in the Byzantine empire.

In Chapter 54, Gibbon describes the rise and persecution of the Paulicians (A.D. 600–880), a Gnostic sect, and indicates that in some way they foreshadowed the ideas of the Reformation. In Chapter 55 he describes the establishment of the Bulgarians, Croats, and Hungarians in the old provinces of the Danube, the origin of the Russian monarchy and the conversion of the Russians and northern Europeans to Christianity.

Chapter 56

CONFLICT OF THE SARACENS, FRANKS AND GREEKS IN
ITALY. THE COMING OF THE NORMANS. CONQUESTS OF
ROBERT GUISCARD

THE three great nations of the world, the Greeks, the Saracens, and
the Franks, encountered each other on the theatre of Italy. The
southern provinces, which now compose the kingdom of Naples,
were subject, for the most part, to the Lombard dukes and princes of
Beneventum—so powerful in war, that they checked for a moment the
genius of Charlemagne—so liberal in peace, that they maintained in their
capital an academy of thirty-two philosophers and grammarians. The
division of this flourishing state produced the rival principalities of
Benevento, Salerno, and Capua; and the thoughtless ambition or revenge
of the competitors invited the Saracens to the ruin of their common inheritance. During a calamitous period of two hundred years Italy was
exposed to a repetition of wounds, which the invaders were not capable
of healing by the union and tranquillity of a perfect conquest. Their
frequent and almost annual squadrons issued from the port of Palermo,
and were entertained with too much indulgence by the Christians of
Naples: the more formidable fleets were prepared on the African coast;
and even the Arabs of Andalusia were sometimes tempted to assist or
oppose the Moslems of an adverse sect. In the revolution of human
events a new ambuscade was concealed in the Caudine forks, the fields
of Cannæ were bedewed a second time with the blood of the Africans,
and the sovereign of Rome again attacked or defended the walls of Capua
and Tarentum. A colony of Saracens had been planted at Bari, which
commands the entrance of the Adriatic Gulf; and their impartial depredations provoked the resentment and conciliated the union of the
two emperors. An offensive alliance was concluded between Basil the
Macedonian, the first of his race, and Lewis the great-grandson of
Charlemagne; and each party supplied the deficiencies of his associate.
It would have been imprudent in the Byzantine monarch to transport
his stationary troops of Asia to an Italian campaign; and the Latin arms
would have been insufficient if *his* superior navy had not occupied the
mouth of the Gulf. The fortress of Bari was invested by the infantry of
the Franks, and by the cavalry and galleys of the Greeks; and, after a
defence of four years, the Arabian emir submitted to the clemency of
Lewis, who commanded in person the operations of the siege. This important conquest had been achieved by the concord of the East and

719

West; but their recent amity was soon embittered by the mutual complaints of jealousy and pride. The Greeks assumed as their own the merit of the conquest and the pomp of the triumph, extolled the greatness of their powers, and affected to deride the intemperance and sloth of the handful of barbarians who appeared under the banners of the Carlovingian prince. His reply is expressed with the eloquence of indignation and truth: "We confess the magnitude of your preparations," says the great-grandson of Charlemagne. "Your armies were indeed as numerous as a cloud of summer locusts, who darken the day, flap their wings, and, after a short flight, tumble weary and breathless to the ground. Like them, ye sunk after a feeble effort; ye were vanquished by your own cowardice, and withdrew from the scene of action to injure and despoil our Christian subjects of the Sclavonian coast. We were few in number, and why were we few? because, after a tedious expectation of your arrival, I had dismissed my host, and retained only a chosen band of warriors to continue the blockade of the city. If they indulged their hospitable feasts in the face of danger and death, did these feasts abate the vigour of their enterprise? Is it by your fasting that the walls of Bari have been overturned? Did not these valiant Franks, diminished as they were by languor and fatigue, intercept and vanquish the three most powerful emirs of the Saracens? and did not their defeat precipitate the fall of the city? Bari is now fallen; Tarentum trembles; Calabria will be delivered; and, if we command the sea, the island of Sicily may be rescued from the hands of the infidels. My brother" (a name most offensive to the vanity of the Greek), "accelerate your naval succours, respect your allies, and distrust your flatterers."

These lofty hopes were soon extinguished by the death of Lewis, and the decay of the Carlovingian house; and whoever might deserve the honour, the Greek emperors, Basil and his son Leo, secured the advantage, of the reduction of Bari. The Italians of Apulia and Calabria were persuaded or compelled to acknowledge their supremacy, and an ideal line from Mount Garganus to the bay of Salerno leaves the far greater part of the kingdom of Naples under the dominion of the Eastern empire. Beyond that line the dukes or republics of Amalfi and Naples, who had never forfeited their voluntary allegiance, rejoiced in the neighbourhood of their lawful sovereign; and Amalfi was enriched by supplying Europe with the produce and manufactures of Asia. But the Lombard princes of Benevento, Salerno, and Capua were reluctantly torn from the communion of the Latin world, and too often violated their oaths of servitude and tribute. The city of Bari rose to dignity and wealth as the metropolis of the new theme or province of Lombardy; the title of patrician, and afterwards the singular name of *Catapan*, was assigned to the supreme governor; and the policy both of the church and state was modelled in exact subordination to the throne of Constantinople. As long as the sceptre was disputed by the princes of Italy, their efforts were feeble and adverse; and the Greeks resisted or eluded the forces of Germany which descended from the Alps under the Imperial standard of the Othos. The first and greatest of those Saxon princes was compelled to relinquish the siege of Bari: the second, after the loss of his stoutest bishops and barons, escaped with honour from the bloody field of Crotona. On that day the scale of war was turned against the Franks by the valour of the Saracens. These corsairs had indeed been driven by the Byzantine fleets from the fortresses and coasts of Italy; but a sense of interest was more prevalent than superstition or resentment, and the caliph of Egypt had transported forty thousand Moslems to the aid of his Christian ally. The successors of Basil amused themselves with the belief that the conquest of Lombardy had been achieved, and was still preserved, by the justice of their laws, the virtues of their ministers, and the gratitude of a people whom they had rescued from anarchy and oppression. A series of rebellions might dart a ray of truth into the palace of Constantinople; and the illusions of flattery were dispelled by the easy and rapid success of the Norman adventurers.

The revolution of human affairs had produced in Apulia and Calabria a melancholy contrast between the age of Pythagoras and the tenth century of the Christian era. At the former period the coast of Great Greece (as it was then styled) was planted with free and opulent cities: these cities were peopled with soldiers, artists, and philosophers; and the military strength of Tarentum, Sybaris, or Crotona was not inferior to that of a powerful kingdom. At the second era these once flourishing provinces were clouded with ignorance, impoverished by tyranny, and depopulated by barbarian war: nor can we severely accuse the exaggeration of a contemporary, that a fair and ample district was reduced to the same desolation which had covered the earth after the general deluge. Among the hostilities of the Arabs, the Franks, and the Greeks in the southern Italy, I shall select two or three anecdotes expressive of their national manners. 1. It was the amusement of the Saracens to profane, as well as to pillage, the monasteries and churches. At the siege of Salerno a Musulman chief spread his couch on the communion-table, and on that altar sacrificed each night the virginity of a Christian nun. As he wrestled with a reluctant maid, a beam in the roof was accidentally or dexterously thrown down on his head; and the death of the lustful emir was imputed to the wrath of Christ, which was at length awakened or the defence of his faithful spouse. 2. The Saracens besieged the cities of Beneventum and Capua: after a vain appeal to the successors of Charlemagne, the Lombards implored the clemency and aid of the Greek emperor. A fearless citizen dropped from the walls, passed the intrenchments, accomplished his commission, and fell into the hands of the barbarians as he was returning with the welcome news. They commanded him to assist their enterprise, and deceive his countrymen, with the assurance that wealth and honours should be the reward of his falsehood, and that his sincerity would be punished with immediate death. He affected to yield, but as soon as he was conducted within hearing of the Christians on the rampart, "Friends and brethren," he cried with a loud voice, "be bold and patient; maintain the city; your sovereign is informed of your distress, and your deliverers are at hand. I know my doom, and commit my wife and children to your gratitude." The rage of the Arabs confirmed his evidence; and the self-devoted patriot was transpierced with an hundred spears. He deserves to live in the memory of the virtuous, but the repetition of the same story in ancient and modern times may sprinkle some doubts on the reality of this generous deed.[1] 3. The recital of the third incident may provoke a smile amidst the horrors of war. Theobald, marquis of Camerino and Spoleto, supported the rebels of Beneventum; and his wanton cruelty was not incompatible in that age with the character of an hero. His captives of the Greek nation or party were castrated without mercy, and the outrage was aggravated by a cruel jest, that he wished to present the emperor with a supply of eunuchs, the most precious ornaments of the Byzantine court. The garrison of a castle had been defeated in a sally, and the prisoners were sentenced to the customary operation. But the sacrifice was disturbed by the intrusion of a frantic female, who, with bleeding cheeks, dishevelled hair, and importunate clamours, compelled the marquis to listen to her complaint. "Is it thus," she cried, "ye magnanimous heroes, that ye wage war against women, against women who have never injured ye, and whose only arms are the distaff and the loom?" Theobald denied the charge, and protested that, since the Amazons, he had never heard of a female war. "And how," she furiously exclaimed, "can you attack us more directly, how can you wound us in a more vital part, than by robbing our husbands of what we most dearly cherish, the source of our joys, and the hope of our posterity? The plunder of our flocks and herds I have endured without a murmur, but this fatal injury, this irreparable loss, subdues my patience, and calls aloud on the justice of heaven and earth." A general laugh applauded her eloquence; the savage Franks, inaccessible to pity, were moved by her ridiculous, yet rational, despair; and with the deliverance of the captives she obtained the restitution of her effects. As she returned in triumph to the castle she was overtaken by a messenger, to inquire, in the name of Theobald, what punishment should be inflicted on her husband, were he again taken in arms? "Should such," she answered without hesitation, "be his guilt and misfortune, he has eyes, and a nose, and hands, and feet.

[1] In the year 663 the same tragedy is described by Paul the Deacon under the walls of the same city of Beneventum. But the actors are different, and the guilt is imputed to the Greeks themselves, which in the Byzantine edition is applied to the Saracens. In the late war in Germany, M. d'Assas, a French officer of the regiment of Auvergne, *is said* to have devoted himself in a similar manner. His behaviour is the more heroic, as mere silence was required by the enemy who had made him prisoner (Voltaire, Siècle de Louis XV, c. 33).

These are his own, and these he may deserve to forfeit by his personal offences. But let my lord be pleased to spare what his little handmaid presumes to claim as her peculiar and lawful property." [1]

THE COMING OF THE NORMANS

The establishment of the Normans in the kingdoms of Naples and Sicily is an event most romantic in its origin, and in its consequences most important both to Italy and the Eastern empire. The broken provinces of the Greeks, Lombards, and Saracens were exposed to every invader, and every sea and land were invaded by the adventurous spirit of the Scandinavian pirates. After a long indulgence of rapine and slaughter, a fair and ample territory was accepted, occupied, and named, by the Normans of France: they renounced their gods for the God of the Christians; and the dukes of Normandy acknowledged themselves the vassals of the successors of Charlemagne and Capet. The savage fierceness which they had brought from the snowy mountains of Norway was refined, without being corrupted, in a warmer climate; the companions of Rollo insensibly mingled with the natives; they imbibed the manners, language, and gallantry of the French nation; and, in a martial age, the Normans might claim the palm of valour and glorious achievements. Of the fashionable superstitions, they embraced with ardour the pilgrimages of Rome, Italy, and the Holy Land. In this active devotion their minds and bodies were invigorated by exercise: danger was the incentive, novelty the recompense; and the prospect of the world was decorated by wonder, credulity, and ambitious hope. They confederated for their mutual defence; and the robbers of the Alps, who had been allured by the garb of a pilgrim, were often chastised by the arm of a warrior. In one of these pious visits to the cavern of Mount Garganus in Apulia, which had been sanctified by the apparition of the archangel Michael, they were accosted by a stranger in the Greek habit, but who soon revealed himself as a rebel, a fugitive, and a mortal foe of the Greek empire. His name was Melo; a noble citizen of Bari, who, after an unsuccessful revolt, was compelled to seek new allies and avengers of his country. The bold appearance of the Normans revived his hopes and solicited his confidence: they listened to the complaints, and still more to the promises, of the patriot. The assurance of wealth demonstrated the justice of his cause; and they viewed, as the inheritance of the brave, the fruitful land which was oppressed by effeminate tyrants. On their return to Normandy they kindled a spark of enterprise, and a small but intrepid band was freely associated for the deliverance of Apulia. They passed the Alps by separate roads, and in the disguise of

---

[1] Liutprand. Should the licentiousness of the tale be questioned, I may exclaim, with poor Sterne, that it is hard if I may not transcribe with caution what a bishop could write without scruple. What if I had translated, ut viris certetis testiculos amputare, in quibus nostri corporis refocillatio, &c.?

pilgrims; but in the neighbourhood of Rome they were saluted by the chief of Bari, who supplied the more indigent with arms and horses, and instantly led them to the field of action. In the first conflict their valour prevailed; but in the second engagement they were overwhelmed by the numbers and military engines of the Greeks, and indignantly retreated with their faces to the enemy. The unfortunate Melo ended his life a suppliant at the court of Germany: his Norman followers, excluded from their native and their promised land, wandered among the hills and valleys of Italy, and earned their daily subsistence by the sword. To that formidable sword the princes of Capua, Beneventum, Salerno, and Naples alternately appealed in their domestic quarrels; the superior spirit and discipline of the Normans gave victory to the side which they espoused; and their cautious policy observed the balance of power, lest the preponderance of any rival state should render their aid less important and their service less profitable. Their first asylum was a strong camp in the depth of the marshes of Campania; but they were soon endowed by the liberality of the duke of Naples with a more plentiful and permanent seat. Eight miles from his residence, as a bulwark against Capua, the town of Aversa was built and fortified for their use; and they enjoyed as their own the corn and fruits, the meadows and groves, of that fertile district. The report of their success attracted every year new swarms of pilgrims and soldiers: the poor were urged by necessity; the rich were excited by hope; and the brave and active spirits of Normandy were impatient of ease and ambitious of renown. The independent standard of Aversa afforded shelter and encouragement to the outlaws of the province, to every fugitive who had escaped from the injustice or justice of his superiors; and these foreign associates were quickly assimilated in manners and language to the Gallic colony. The first leader of the Normans was Count Rainulf; and, in the origin of society, pre-eminence of rank is the reward and the proof of superior merit.

Since the conquest of Sicily by the Arabs, the Grecian emperors had been anxious to regain that valuable possession; but their efforts, however strenuous, had been opposed by the distance and the sea. Their costly armaments, after a gleam of success, added new pages of calamity and disgrace to the Byzantine annals: twenty thousand of their best troops were lost in a single expedition; and the victorious Moslems derided the policy of a nation which entrusted eunuchs not only with the custody of their women, but with the command of their men. After a reign of two hundred years, the Saracens were ruined by their divisions. The emir disclaimed the authority of the king of Tunis; the people rose against the emir; the cities were usurped by the chiefs; each meaner rebel was independent in his village or castle; and the weaker of two rival brothers implored the friendship of the Christians. In every service of danger the Normans were prompt and useful; and five hundred *knights*, or warriors on horseback, were enrolled by Arduin, the agent and in-

terpreter of the Greeks, under the standard of Maniaces, governor of
Lombardy. Before their landing the brothers were reconciled; the union
of Sicily and Africa was restored; and the island was guarded to the
water's edge. The Normans led the van, and the Arabs of Messina felt
the valour of an untried foe. In a second action the emir of Syracuse
was unhorsed and transpierced by the *iron arm* of William of Hauteville.
In a third engagement his intrepid companions discomfited the host of
sixty thousand Saracens, and left the Greeks no more than the labour of
the pursuit: a splendid victory; but of which the pen of the historian
may divide the merit with the lance of the Normans. It is, however, true,
that they essentially promoted the success of Maniaces, who reduced
thirteen cities, and the greater part of Sicily, under the obedience of the
emperor. But his military fame was sullied by ingratitude and tyranny.
In the division of the spoil the deserts of his brave auxiliaries were forgotten; and neither their avarice nor their pride could brook this injurious treatment. They complained by the mouth of their interpreter:
their complaint was disregarded; their interpreter was scourged; the
sufferings were *his*; the insult and resentment belonged to *those* whose
sentiments he had delivered. Yet they dissembled till they had obtained,
or stolen, a safe passage to the Italian continent: their brethren of Aversa
sympathised in their indignation, and the province of Apulia was invaded
as the forfeit of the debt. Above twenty years after the first emigration,
the Normans took the field with no more than seven hundred horse and
five hundred foot; and after the recall of the Byzantine legions from the
Sicilian war, their numbers are magnified to the amount of three-score
thousand men. Their herald proposed the option of battle or retreat;
"Of battle," was the unanimous cry of the Normans; and one of their
stoutest warriors, with a stroke of his fist, felled to the ground the horse
of the Greek messenger. He was dismissed with a fresh horse; the insult
was concealed from the Imperial troops; but in two successive battles
they were more fatally instructed of the prowess of their adversaries. In
the plains of Cannæ the Asiatics fled before the adventurers of France;
the duke of Lombardy was made prisoner; the Apulians acquiesced in a
new dominion; and the four places of Bari, Otranto, Brundusium, and
Tarentum were alone saved in the shipwreck of the Grecian fortunes.
From this era we may date the establishment of the Norman power,
which soon eclipsed the infant colony of Aversa. Twelve counts were
chosen by the popular suffrage; and age, birth, and merit were the motives of their choice. The tributes of their peculiar districts were appropriated to their use; and each count erected a fortress in the midst of his
lands, and at the head of his vassals. In the centre of the province the
common habitation of Melphi was reserved as the metropolis and citadel
of the republic; a house and separate quarter was allotted to each of the
twelve counts; and the national concerns were regulated by this military
senate. The first of his peers, their president and general, was entitled

Count of Apulia; and this dignity was conferred on William of the iron arm, who, in the language of the age, is styled a lion in battle, a lamb in society, and an angel in council. The manners of his countrymen are fairly delineated by a contemporary and national historian. "The Normans," says Malaterra, "are a cunning and revengeful people; eloquence and dissimulation appear to be their hereditary qualities: they can stoop to flatter; but, unless they are curbed by the restraint of law, they indulge the licentiousness of nature and passion. Their princes affect the praise of popular munificence; the people observe the medium, or rather blend the extremes, of avarice and prodigality; and in their eager thirst of wealth and dominion, they despise whatever they possess, and hope whatever they desire. Arms and horses, the luxury of dress, the exercises of hunting and hawking are the delight of the Normans; but, on pressing occasions, they can endure with incredible patience the inclemency of every climate, and the toil of a military life."

The Normans of Apulia were seated on the verge of the two empires, and, according to the policy of the hour, they accepted the investiture of their lands from the sovereigns of Germany or Constantinople. But the firmest title of these adventurers was the right of conquest; they neither loved nor trusted; they were neither trusted nor beloved; the contempt of the princes was mixed with fear, and the fear of the natives was mingled with hatred and resentment. Every object of desire, a horse, a woman, a garden, tempted and gratified the rapaciousness of the strangers, and the avarice of their chiefs was only coloured by the more specious names of ambition and glory. The twelve counts were sometimes joined in a league of injustice; in their domestic quarrels they disputed the spoils of the people; the virtues of William were buried in his grave; and Drogo, his brother and successor, was better qualified to lead the valour, than to restrain the violence, of his peers. Under the reign of Constantine Monomachus, the policy, rather than benevolence, of the Byzantine court attempted to relieve Italy from this adherent mischief, more grievous than a flight of barbarians; and Argyrus, the son of Melo, was invested for this purpose with the most lofty titles and the most ample commission. The memory of his father might recommend him to the Normans, and he had already engaged their voluntary service to quell the revolt of Maniaces, and to avenge their own and the public injury. It was the design of Constantine to transplant this warlike colony from the Italian provinces to the Persian war, and the son of Melo distributed among the chiefs the gold and manufactures of Greece as the first-fruits of the Imperial bounty. But his arts were baffled by the sense and spirit of the conquerors of Apulia: his gifts, or at least his proposals, were rejected, and they unanimously refused to relinquish their possessions and their hopes for the distant prospect of Asiatic fortune. After the means of persuasion had failed, Argyrus resolved to compel or to destroy: the Latin powers were solicited against the common enemy, and an offensive alliance was formed of the pope and the two emperors of the East and West. The throne of St. Peter was occupied by Leo the Ninth, a simple saint, of a temper most apt to deceive himself and the world, and whose venerable character would consecrate with the name of piety the measures least compatible with the practice of religion. His humanity was affected by the complaints, perhaps the calumnies, of an injured people; the impious Normans had interrupted the payment of tithes, and the temporal sword might be lawfully unsheathed against the sacrilegious robbers who were deaf to the censures of the church. As a German of noble birth and royal kindred, Leo had free access to the court and confidence of the emperor Henry the Third, and in search of arms and allies his ardent zeal transported him from Apulia to Saxony, from the Elbe to the Tiber. During these hostile preparations, Argyrus indulged himself in the use of secret and guilty weapons: a crowd of Normans became the victims of public or private revenge, and the valiant Drogo was murdered in a church. But his spirit survived in his brother Humphrey, the third count of Apulia. The assassins were chastised, and the son of Melo, overthrown and wounded, was driven from the field to hide his shame behind the walls of Bari, and to await the tardy succour of his allies.

But the power of Constantine was distracted by a Turkish war, the mind of Henry was feeble and irresolute, and the pope, instead of repassing the Alps with a German army, was accompanied only by a guard of seven hundred Swabians and some volunteers of Lorraine. In his long progress from Mantua to Beneventum a vile and promiscuous multitude of Italians was enlisted under the holy standard; the priest and the robber slept in the same tent, the pikes and crosses were intermingled in the front, and the martial saint repeated the lessons of his youth in the order of march, of encampment, and of combat. The Normans of Apulia could muster in the field no more than three thousand horse, with a handful of infantry; the defection of the natives intercepted their provisions and retreat; and their spirit, incapable of fear, was chilled for a moment by superstitious awe. On the hostile approach of Leo, they knelt, without disgrace or reluctance, before their spiritual father. But the pope was inexorable; his lofty Germans affected to deride the diminutive stature of their adversaries; and the Normans were informed that death or exile was their only alternative. Flight they disdained, and, as many of them had been three days without tasting food, they embraced the assurance of a more easy and honourable death. They climbed the hill of Civitella, descended into the plain, and charged in three divisions the army of the pope. On the left, and in the centre, Richard count of Aversa, and Robert the famous Guiscard, attacked, broke, routed, and pursued the Italian multitudes, who fought without discipline and fled without shame. A harder trial was reserved for the valour of Count Humphrey, who led the cavalry of the right wing. The Germans have been described as unskilful in the management of the horse and lance, but on foot they formed a strong and impenetrable phalanx, and neither man, nor steed, nor armour could resist the weight of their long and two-handed swords. After a severe conflict they were encompassed by the squadrons returning from the pursuit, and died in their ranks with the esteem of their foes and the satisfaction of revenge. The gates of Civitella were shut against the flying pope, and he was overtaken by the pious conquerors, who kissed his feet to implore his blessing and the absolution of their sinful victory. The soldiers beheld in their enemy and captive the vicar of Christ; and, though we may suppose the policy of the chiefs, it is probable that they were infected by the popular superstition. In the calm of retirement the well-meaning pope deplored the effusion of Christian blood which must be imputed to his account; he felt that he had been the author of sin and scandal; and, as his undertaking had failed, the indecency of his military character was universally condemned. With these dispositions he listened to the offers of a beneficial treaty, deserted an alliance which he had preached as the cause of God, and ratified the past and future conquests of the Normans. By whatever hands they had been usurped, the provinces of Apulia and Calabria were a part of the donation of Constantine and the patrimony of St. Peter: the grant and the acceptance confirmed the mutual claims of the pontiff and the adventurers. They promised to support each other with spiritual and temporal arms; a tribute or quit-rent of twelve pence was afterwards stipulated for every plough-land, and since this memorable transaction the kingdom of Naples has remained above seven hundred years a fief of the Holy See.

CONQUESTS OF ROBERT GUISCARD

The pedigree of Robert Guiscard is variously deduced from the peasants and the dukes of Normandy: from the peasants, by the pride and ignorance of a Grecian princess; from the dukes, by the ignorance and flattery of the Italian subjects. His genuine descent may be ascribed to the second or middle order of private nobility. He sprang from a race of *valvassors* or *bannerets*, of the diocese of Coutances, in the Lower Normandy; the castle of Hauteville was their honourable seat; his father Tancred was conspicuous in the court and army of the duke, and his military service was furnished by ten soldiers or knights. Two marriages, of a rank not unworthy of his own, made him the father of twelve sons, who were educated at home by the impartial tenderness of his second wife. But a narrow patrimony was insufficient for this numerous and daring progeny; they saw around the neighbourhood the mischiefs of poverty and discord, and resolved to seek in foreign wars a more glorious inheritance. Two only remained to perpetuate the race and cherish their father's age; their ten brothers, as they successively attained the vigour of manhood, departed from the castle, passed the Alps, and joined the Apulian camp of the Normans. The elder were prompted by native spirit:

their success encouraged their younger brethren; and the three first in seniority, William, Drogo, and Humphrey, deserved to be the chiefs of their nation and the founders of the new republic. Robert was the eldest of the seven sons of the second marriage, and even the reluctant praise of his foes has endowed him with the heroic qualities of a soldier and a statesman. His lofty stature surpassed the tallest of his army; his limbs were cast in the true proportion of strength and gracefulness; and to the decline of life he maintained the patient vigour of health and the commanding dignity of his form. His complexion was ruddy, his shoulders were broad, his hair and beard were long and of a flaxen colour, his eyes sparkled with fire, and his voice, like that of Achilles, could impress obedience and terror amidst the tumult of battle. In the ruder ages of chivalry such qualifications are not below the notice of the poet or historian; they may observe that Robert, at once, and with equal dexterity, could wield in the right hand his sword, his lance in the left; that in the battle of Civitella he was thrice unhorsed, and that in the close of that memorable day he was adjudged to have borne away the prize of valour from the warriors of the two armies. His boundless ambition was founded on the consciousness of superior worth; in the pursuit of greatness he was never arrested by the scruples of justice, and seldom moved by the feelings of humanity; though not insensible of fame, the choice of open or clandestine means was determined only by his present advantage. The surname of *Guiscard* was applied to this master of political wisdom, which is too often confounded with the practice of dissimulation and deceit, and Robert is praised by the Apulian poet for excelling the cunning of Ulysses and the eloquence of Cicero. Yet these arts were disguised by an appearance of military frankness; in his highest fortune he was accessible and courteous to his fellow-soldiers; and while he indulged the prejudices of his new subjects, he affected in his dress and manners to maintain the ancient fashion of his country. He grasped with a rapacious, that he might distribute with a liberal, hand; his primitive indigence had taught the habits of frugality; the gain of a merchant was not below his attention; and his prisoners were tortured with slow and unfeeling cruelty to force a discovery of their secret treasure. According to the Greeks, he departed from Normandy with only five followers on horseback and thirty on foot; yet even this allowance appears too bountiful; the sixth son of Tancred of Hauteville passed the Alps as a pilgrim, and his first military band was levied among the adventurers of Italy. His brothers and countrymen had divided the fertile lands of Apulia, but they guarded their shares with the jealousy of avarice; the aspiring youth was driven forwards to the mountains of Calabria, and in his first exploits against the Greeks and the natives it is not easy to discriminate the hero from the robber. To surprise a castle or a convent, to ensnare a wealthy citizen, to plunder the adjacent villages for necessary food, were the obscure labours which formed and exercised the powers of his mind and body. The volunteers of Normandy adhered to his standard, and, under his command, the peasants of Calabria assumed the name and character of Normans.

As the genius of Robert expanded with his fortune, he awakened the jealousy of his elder brother, by whom, in a transient quarrel, his life was threatened and his liberty restrained. After the death of Humphrey the tender age of his sons excluded them from the command; they were reduced to a private estate by the ambition of their guardian and uncle; and Guiscard was exalted on a buckler, and saluted count of Apulia and general of the republic. With an increase of authority and of force, he resumed the conquest of Calabria, and soon aspired to a rank that should raise him for ever above the heads of his equals. By some acts of rapine or sacrilege he had incurred a papal excommunication: but Nicholas the Second was easily persuaded that the divisions of friends could terminate only in their mutual prejudice; that the Normans were the faithful champions of the Holy See; and it was safer to trust the alliance of a prince than the caprice of an aristocracy. A synod of one hundred bishops was convened at Melphi; and the count interrupted an important enterprise to guard the person and execute the decrees of the Roman pontiff. His gratitude and policy conferred on Robert and his posterity the ducal title, with the investiture of Apulia, Calabria, and all the lands, both in Italy and Sicily, which his sword could rescue from the schismatic Greeks and the unbelieving Saracens. This apostolic sanction might justify his arms: but the obedience of a free and victorious people could not be transferred without their consent; and Guiscard dissembled his elevation till the ensuing campaign had been illustrated by the conquest of Consenza and Reggio. In the hour of triumph he assembled his troops and solicited the Normans to confirm by their suffrage the judgment of the vicar of Christ: the soldiers hailed with joyful acclamations their valiant duke; and the counts, his former equals, pronounced the oath of fidelity with hollow smiles and secret indignation. After this inauguration, Robert styled himself, "By the grace of God and St. Peter, duke of Apulia, Calabria, and hereafter of Sicily;" and it was the labour of twenty years to deserve and realise these lofty appellations. Such tardy progress, in a narrow space, may seem unworthy of the abilities of the chief and the spirit of the nation: but the Normans were few in number; their resources were scanty; their service was voluntary and precarious. The bravest designs of the duke were sometimes opposed by the free voice of his parliament of barons: the twelve counts of popular election conspired against his authority; and against their perfidious uncle the sons of Humphrey demanded justice and revenge. By his policy and vigour Guiscard discovered their plots, suppressed their rebellions, and punished the guilty with death or exile; but in these domestic feuds his years, and the national strength, were unprofitably consumed. After the defeat of his foreign enemies, the Greeks, Lombards, and Saracens, their broken forces retreated to the strong and populous cities of the sea-coast. They excelled in the arts of fortification and defence; the Normans were accustomed to serve on horseback in the field, and their rude attempts could only succeed by the efforts of persevering courage. The resistance of Salerno was maintained above eight months: the siege or blockade of Bari lasted near four years. In these actions the Norman duke was the foremost in every danger, in every fatigue the last and most patient. As he pressed the citadel of Salerno an huge stone from the rampart shattered one of his military engines, and by a splinter he was wounded in the breast. Before the gates of Bari he lodged in a miserable hut or barrack, composed of dry branches, and thatched with straw—a perilous station, on all sides open to the inclemency of the winter and the spears of the enemy.

The Italian conquests of Robert correspond with the limits of the present kingdom of Naples; and the countries united by his arms have not been dissevered by the revolutions of seven hundred years. The monarchy has been composed of the Greek provinces of Calabria and Apulia, of the Lombard principality of Salerno, the republic of Amalphi, and the inland dependencies of the large and ancient duchy of Beneventum. Three districts only were exempted from the common law of subjection—the first for ever, and the two last till the middle of the succeeding century. The city and immediate territory of Benevento had been transferred, by gift or exchange, from the German emperor to the Roman pontiff; and although this holy land was sometimes invaded, the name of St. Peter was finally more potent than the sword of the Normans. Their first colony of Aversa subdued and held the state of Capua, and her princes were reduced to beg their bread before the palace of their fathers. The dukes of Naples, the present metropolis, maintained the popular freedom under the shadow of the Byzantine empire. Among the new acquisitions of Guiscard the science of Salerno and the trade of Amalphi may detain for a moment the curiosity of the reader. I. Of the learned faculties jurisprudence implies the previous establishment of laws and property; and theology may perhaps be superseded by the full light of religion and reason. But the savage and the sage must alike implore the assistance of physic; and if *our* diseases are inflamed by luxury, the mischiefs of blows and wounds would be more frequent in the ruder ages of society. The treasures of Grecian medicine had been communicated to the Arabian colonies of Africa, Spain, and Sicily; and in the intercourse of peace and war a spark of knowledge had been kindled and cherished at Salerno, an illustrious city, in which the men were honest and the women beautiful. A school, the first that arose in the darkness of Europe, was consecrated to the healing art: the conscience of monks and bishops was reconciled to that salutary and lucrative profession; and a crowd of patients of the most eminent rank and most distant climates invited or visited the physicians of Salerno. They were protected by the Norman conquerors; and Guiscard, though bred in arms, could discern the merit and value of a philosopher. After a pilgrimage of thirty-nine years, Constantine, an African Christian, returned from Bagdad, a master of the language and learning of the Arabians; and Salerno was enriched by the practice, the lessons, and the writings of the pupil of Avicenna. The school of medicine has long slept in the name of an university; but her precepts are abridged in a string of aphorisms, bound together in the Leonine verses, or Latin rhymes, of the twelfth century. II. Seven miles to the west of Salerno, and thirty to the south of Naples, the obscure town of Amalphi displayed the power and rewards of industry. The land, however fertile, was of narrow extent; but the sea was accessible and open: the inhabitants first assumed the office of supplying the western world with the manufactures and productions of the East; and this useful traffic was the source of their opulence and freedom. The government was popular, under the administration of a duke and the supremacy of the Greek emperor. Fifty thousand citizens were numbered in the walls of Amalphi; nor was any city more abundantly provided with gold, silver, and the objects of precious luxury. The mariners who swarmed in her port excelled in the theory and practice of navigation and astronomy; and the discovery of the compass, which has opened the globe, is due to their ingenuity or good fortune. Their trade was extended to the coasts, or at least to the commodities, of Africa, Arabia, and India; and their settlements in Constantinople, Antioch, Jerusalem, and Alexandria acquired the privileges of independent colonies. After three hundred years of prosperity Amalphi was oppressed by the arms of the Normans, and sacked by the jealousy of Pisa; but the poverty of one thousand fishermen is yet dignified by the remains of an arsenal, a cathedral, and the palaces of royal merchants.

Roger, the twelfth and last of the sons of Tancred, had been long detained in Normandy by his own and his father's age. He accepted the welcome summons; hastened to the Apulian camp; and deserved at first the esteem, and afterwards the envy, of his elder brother. Their valour and ambition were equal; but the youth, the beauty, the elegant manners, of Roger, engaged the disinterested love of the soldiers and people. So scanty was his allowance, for himself and forty followers, that he descended from conquest to robbery, and from robbery to domestic theft; and so loose were the notions of property, that, by his own historian, at his special command, he is accused of stealing horses from a stable at Melphi. His spirit emerged from poverty and disgrace: from these base practices he rose to the merit and glory of a holy war; and the invasion of Sicily was seconded by the zeal and policy of his brother Guiscard. After the retreat of the Greeks, the *idolaters*, a most audacious reproach of the Catholics, had retrieved their losses and possessions; but the deliverance of the island, so vainly undertaken by the forces of the Eastern empire, was achieved by a small and private band of adventurers. In the first attempt Roger braved, in an open boat, the real and fabulous dangers of Scylla and Charybdis; landed with only sixty soldiers on a hostile shore, drove the Saracens to the gates of Messina; and safely returned with the spoils of the adjacent country. In the fortress of Trani his active and patient courage were equally conspicuous. In his old age he related with pleasure, that, by the distress of the siege, himself, and the countess his wife, had been reduced to a single cloak or mantle, which they wore alternately: that in a sally his horse had been slain, and he was dragged away by the Saracens; but that he owed his rescue to his good sword, and had retreated with his saddle on his back, lest the meanest trophy might be left in the hands of the miscreants. In the siege of Trani, three hundred Normans withstood and repulsed the forces of the island. In the field of Ceramio fifty thousand horse and foot were overthrown by one hundred and thirty-six Christian soldiers, without reckoning St. George, who fought on horseback in the foremost ranks. The captive banners, with four camels, were reserved for the successor of St. Peter; and had these barbaric spoils been exposed not in the Vatican, but in the Capitol, they might have revived the memory of the Punic triumphs. These insufficient numbers of the Normans most probably denote their knights, the soldiers of honourable and equestrian rank, each of whom was attended by five or six followers in the field; yet, with the aid of this interpretation, and after every fair allowance on the side of valour, arms, and reputation, the discomfiture of so many myriads will reduce the prudent reader to the alternative of a miracle or a fable. The Arabs of Sicily derived a frequent and powerful succour from their countrymen of Africa: in the siege of Palermo the Norman cavalry was assisted by the galleys of Pisa; and, in the hour of action, the envy of the two brothers was sublimed to a generous and invincible emulation. After a war of thirty years, Roger, with the title of great count, obtained the sovereignty of the largest and most fruitful island of the Mediterranean; and his administration displays a liberal and enlightened mind above the limits of his age and education. The Moslems were maintained in the free enjoyment of their religion and property: a philosopher and physician of Mazara, of the race of Mahomet, harangued the conqueror, and was invited to court; his geography of the seven climates was translated into Latin; and Roger, after a diligent perusal, preferred the work of the Arabian to the writings of the Grecian Ptolemy. A remnant of Christian natives had promoted the success of the Normans: they were rewarded by the triumph of the cross. The island was restored to the jurisdiction of the Roman pontiff; new bishops were planted in the principal cities; and the clergy was satisfied by a liberal endowment of churches and monasteries. Yet the Catholic hero asserted the rights of the civil magistrate. Instead of resigning the investiture of benefices, he dexterously applied to his own profit the papal claims: the supremacy of the crown was secured and enlarged by the singular bull which declares the princes of Sicily hereditary and perpetual legates of the Holy See.

To Robert Guiscard the conquest of Sicily was more glorious than beneficial: the possession of Apulia and Calabria was inadequate to his ambition; and he resolved to embrace or create the first occasion of invading, perhaps of subduing, the Roman empire of the East. From his first wife, the partner of his humble fortunes, he had been divorced under the pretence of consanguinity; and her son Bohemond was destined to imitate, rather than to succeed, his illustrious father. The second wife of Guiscard was the daughter of the princes of Salerno; the Lombards acquiesced in the lineal succession of their son Roger; their five daughters were given in honourable nuptials, and one of them was betrothed, in a tender age, to Constantine, a beautiful youth, the son and heir of the emperor Michael. But the throne of Constantinople was shaken by a revolution: the Imperial family of Ducas was confined to the palace or the cloister; and Robert deplored and resented the disgrace of his daughter and the expulsion of his ally. A Greek, who styled himself the father of Constantine, soon appeared at Salerno, and related the adventures of his fall and flight. That unfortunate friend was acknowledged by the duke, and adorned with the pomp and titles of Imperial dignity: in his triumphal progress through Apulia and Calabria, Michael was saluted with the tears and acclamations of the people; and pope Gregory the Seventh exhorted the bishops to preach, and the Catholics to fight, in the pious work of his restoration. His conversations with Robert were frequent and familiar; and their mutual promises were justified by the valour of the Normans and the treasures of the East. Yet this Michael, by the confession of the Greeks and Latins, was a pageant and an impostor; a monk who had fled from his convent, or a domestic who had served in the palace. The fraud had been contrived by the subtle Guiscard; and he trusted that, after this pretender had given a decent colour to his arms, he would sink, at the nod of the conqueror, into his primitive obscurity. But victory was the only argument that could determine the belief of the Greeks; and the ardour of the Latins was much inferior to their credulity: the Norman veterans wished to enjoy the harvest of their toils, and the unwarlike Italians trembled at the known and unknown dangers of a transmarine expedition. In his new levies Robert exerted the influence of gifts and promises, the terrors of civil and ecclesiastical authority; and some acts of violence might justify the reproach that age and infancy were pressed without distinction into the service of their unrelenting prince. After two years' incessant preparations the land and naval forces were assembled at Otranto, at the heel, or extreme promontory, of Italy; and Robert was accompanied by his wife, who fought by his side, his son Bohemond, and the representative of the emperor Michael. Thirteen hundred knights of Norman race or discipline formed the sinews of the army, which might be swelled to thirty thousand followers of every denomination. The men, the horses, the arms, the engines, the wooden towers covered with raw hides, were embarked on board one hundred and fifty vessels: the transports had been built in the ports of Italy, and the galleys were supplied by the alliance of the republic of Ragusa.

At the mouth of the Adriatic Gulf the shores of Italy and Epirus incline towards each other. The space between Brundusium and Durazzo, the Roman passage, is no more than one hundred miles; at the last station of Otranto it is contracted to fifty; and this narrow distance had suggested to Pyrrhus and Pompey the sublime or extravagant idea of a bridge. Before the general embarkation the Norman duke despatched Bohemond with fifteen galleys to seize or threaten the isle of Corfu, to survey the opposite coast, and to secure an harbour in the neighbourhood of Vallona for the landing of the troops. They passed and landed without perceiving an enemy; and this successful experiment displayed the neglect and decay of the naval power of the Greeks. The islands of Epirus and the maritime towns were subdued by the arms or the name of Robert, who led his fleet and army from Corfu (I use the modern appellation) to the siege of Durazzo. That city, the western key of the empire, was guarded by ancient renown and recent fortifications, by George Palæologus, a patrician, victorious in the Oriental wars, and a numerous garrison of Albanians and Macedonians, who, in every age, have maintained the character of soldiers. In the prosecution of his enterprise the courage of Guiscard was assailed by every form of danger and mischance. In the most propitious season of the year, as his fleet passed along the coast, a storm of wind and snow unexpectedly arose: the Adriatic was swelled by the raging blast of the south, and a new shipwreck confirmed the old infamy of the Acroceraunian rocks. The sails, the masts, and the oars were shattered or torn away; the sea and shore were covered with the fragments of vessels, with arms and dead bodies; and the greatest part of the provisions were either drowned or damaged. The ducal galley was laboriously rescued from the waves, and Robert halted seven days on the adjacent cape to collect the relics of his loss and revive the drooping spirits of his soldiers. The Normans were no longer the bold and experienced mariners who had explored the ocean from Greenland to Mount Atlas, and who smiled at the petty dangers of the Mediterranean. They had wept during the tempest; they were alarmed by the hostile approach of the Venetians, who had been solicited by the prayers and promises of the Byzantine court. The first day's action was not disadvantageous to Bohemond, a beardless youth, who led the naval powers of his father. All night the galleys of the republic lay on their anchors in the form of a crescent; and the victory of the second day was decided by the dexterity of their evolutions, the station of their archers, the weight of their javelins, and the borrowed aid of the Greek fire. The Apulian and Ragusian vessels fled to the shore, several were cut from their cables and dragged away by the conqueror; and a sally from the town carried slaughter and dismay to the tents of the Norman duke. A seasonable relief was poured into Durazzo, and, as soon as the besiegers had lost the command of the sea, the islands and maritime towns withdrew from the camp the supply of tribute and provision. That camp was soon afflicted with a pestilential disease; five hundred knights perished by an inglorious death; and the list of burials (if all could obtain a decent burial) amounted to ten thousand persons. Under these calamities the mind of Guiscard alone was firm and invincible; and while he collected new forces from Apulia and Sicily, he battered, or scaled, or sapped, the walls of Durazzo. But his industry and valour were encountered by equal valour and more perfect industry. A moveable turret, of a size and capacity to contain five hundred soldiers, had been rolled forwards to the foot of the rampart: but the descent of the door or drawbridge was checked by an enormous beam, and the wooden structure was instantly consumed by artificial flames.

While the Roman empire was attacked by the Turks in the East, and the Normans in the West, the aged successor of Michael surrendered the sceptre to the hands of Alexius, an illustrious captain, and the founder of the Comnenian dynasty. The princess Anne, his daughter and historian, observes, in her affected style, that even Hercules was unequal to a double combat; and, on this principle, she approves an hasty peace with the Turks, which allowed her father to undertake in person the relief of Durazzo. On his accession, Alexius found the camp without soldiers, and the treasury without money; yet such were the vigour and activity of his measures, that in six months he assembled an army of seventy thousand men, and performed a march of five hundred miles. His troops were levied in Europe and Asia, from Peloponnesus to the Black Sea; his majesty was displayed in the silver arms and rich trappings of the companies of horseguards; and the emperor was attended by a train of nobles and princes, some of whom, in rapid succession, had been clothed with the purple, and were indulged by the lenity of the times in a life of affluence and dignity. Their youthful ardour might animate the multitude; but their love of pleasure and contempt of subordination were pregnant with disorder and mischief; and their importunate clamours for speedy and decisive action disconcerted the prudence of Alexius, who might have surrounded and starved the besieging army. The enumeration of provinces recalls a sad comparison of the past and present limits of the Roman world: the raw levies were drawn together in haste and terror; and the garrisons of Anatolia, or Asia Minor, had been purchased by the evacuation of the cities which were immediately occupied by the Turks. The strength of the Greek army consisted in the Varangians, the Scandinavian guards, whose numbers were recently augmented by a colony of exiles and volunteers from the British island of Thule. Under the yoke of the Norman conqueror, the Danes and English were oppressed and united: a band of adventurous youths resolved to desert a land of slavery; the sea was open to their escape; and, in their long pilgrimage, they visited every coast that afforded any hope of liberty and revenge. They were entertained in the service of the Greek emperor; and their first station was in a new city on the Asiatic shore: but Alexius soon recalled them to the defence of his person and palace; and bequeathed to his successors the inheritance of their faith and valour. The name of a Norman invader revived the memory of their wrongs: they marched with alacrity against the national foe, and panted to regain in Epirus the glory which they had lost in the battle of Hastings. The Varangians were supported by some companies of Franks or Latins; and the rebel who had fled to Constantinople from the tyranny of Guiscard were eager to signalize their zeal and gratify their revenge. In this emergency the emperor had not disdained the impure aid of the Paulicians or Manichæans of Thrace and Bulgaria; and these heretics united with the patience of martyrdom the spirit and discipline of active valour. The treaty with the sultan had procured a supply of some thousand Turks; and the arrows of the Scythian horse were opposed to the lances of the Norman cavalry. On the report and distant prospect of these formidable numbers, Robert assembled a council of his principal officers. "You behold," said he, "your danger: it is urgent and inevitable. The hills are covered with arms and standards; and the emperor of the Greeks is accustomed to wars and triumphs. Obedience and union are our only safety; and I am ready to yield the command to a more worthy leader." The vote and acclamation, even of his secret enemies, assured him, in that perilous moment, of their esteem and confidence; and the duke thus continued: "Let us trust in the rewards of victory, and deprive cowardice of the means of escape. Let us burn our vessels and our baggage, and give battle on this spot, as if it were the place of our nativity and our burial." The resolution was unanimously approved; and, without confining himself to his lines, Guiscard awaited in battle-array the nearer approach of the enemy. His rear was covered by a small river; his right wing extended to the sea; his left to the hills: nor was he conscious, perhaps, that on the same ground Cæsar and Pompey had formerly disputed the empire of the world.

Against the advice of his wisest captains, Alexius resolved to risk the event of a general action, and exhorted the garrison of Durazzo to assist their own deliverance by a well-timed sally from the town. He marched in two columns to surprise the Normans before daybreak on two different sides: his light cavalry was scattered over the plain; the archers formed the second line; and the Varangians claimed the honours of the vanguard. In the first onset the battle-axes of the strangers made a deep and bloody impression on the army of Guiscard, which was now reduced to fifteen thousand men. The Lombards and Calabrians ignominiously turned their backs; they fled towards the river and the sea; but the bridge had been broken down to check the sally of the garrison, and the coast was lined with the Venetian galleys, who played their engines among the disorderly throng. On the verge of ruin, they were saved by the spirit and conduct of their chiefs. Gaita, the wife of Robert, is painted by the Greeks as a warlike Amazon, a second Pallas; less skilful in arts, but not less terrible in arms, than the Athenian goddess: though wounded by an arrow, she stood her ground, and strove, by her exhortation and example, to rally the flying troops. Her female voice was seconded by the more powerful voice and arm of the Norman duke, as calm in action as he was magnanimous in council: "Whither," he cried aloud, "whither do ye fly? Your enemy is implacable; and death is less grievous than servitude." The moment was decisive: as the Varangians advanced before the line, they discovered the nakedness of their flanks: the main battle of the duke, of eight hundred knights, stood firm and entire; they couched their lances, and the Greeks deplore the furious and irresistible shock of the French cavalry. Alexius was not deficient in the duties of a soldier or a general; but he no sooner beheld the slaughter of the Varangians, and the flight of the Turks, than he despised his subjects, and despaired of his fortune. The princess Anne, who drops a tear on this melancholy event, is reduced to praise the strength and swiftness of her father's horse, and his vigorous struggle when he was almost overthrown by the stroke of a lance which had shivered the Imperial helmet. His desperate valour broke through a squadron of Franks who opposed his flight; and after wandering two days and as many nights in the mountains, he found some repose, of body, though not of mind, in the walls of Lychnidus. The victorious Robert reproached the tardy and feeble pursuit which had suffered the escape of so illustrious a prize: but he consoled his disappointment by the trophies and standards of the field, the wealth and luxury of the Byzantine camp, and the glory of defeating an army five times more numerous than his own. A multitude of Italians had been the victims of their own fears; but only thirty of his knights were slain in this memorable day. In the Roman host, the loss of Greeks, Turks, and English amounted to five or six thousand: the plain of Durazzo was stained with noble and royal blood; and the end of the impostor Michael was more honourable than his life.

It is more than probable that Guiscard was not afflicted by the loss of a costly pageant, which had merited only the contempt and derision of the Greeks. After their defeat they still persevered in the defence of Durazzo; and a Venetian commander supplied the place of George Palæologus, who had been imprudently called away from his station. The tents of the besiegers were converted into barracks, to sustain the inclemency of the winter; and in answer to the defiance of the garrison, Robert insinuated that his patience was at least equal to their obstinacy. Perhaps he already trusted to his secret correspondence with a Venetian noble, who sold the city for a rich and honourable marriage. At the dead of night several rope-ladders were dropped from the walls; the light Calabrians ascended in silence; and the Greeks were awakened by the name and trumpets of the conqueror. Yet they defended the streets three days against an enemy already master of the rampart; and near seven months elapsed between the first investment and the final surrender of the place. From Durazzo the Norman duke advanced into the heart of Epirus or Albania; traversed the first mountains of Thessaly; surprised three hundred English in the city of Castoria; approached Thessalonica; and made Constantinople tremble. A more pressing duty suspended the prosecution of his ambitious designs. By shipwreck, pestilence, and the sword, his army was reduced to a third of the original numbers; and instead of being recruited from Italy, he was informed, by plaintive epistles, of the mischiefs and dangers which had been produced by his absence: the revolt of the cities and barons of Apulia; the distress of the pope; and the approach or invasion of Henry king of Germany. Highly presuming that his person was sufficient for the public safety, he repassed the sea in a single brigantine, and left the remains of the army under the command of his son and the Norman counts, exhorting Bohemond to respect the freedom of his peers, and the counts to obey the authority of their leader. The son of Guiscard trod in the footsteps of his father; and the two destroyers are compared by the Greeks to the caterpillar and the locust, the last of whom devours whatever has escaped the teeth of the former. After winning two battles against the emperor, he descended into the plain of Thessaly, and besieged Larissa, the fabulous realm of Achilles, which contained the treasure and magazines of the Byzantine camp. Yet a just praise must not be refused to the fortitude and prudence of Alexius, who bravely struggled with the calamities of the times. In the poverty of the state, he presumed to borrow the superfluous ornaments of the churches: the desertion of the Manichæans was supplied by some tribes of Moldavia: a reinforcement of seven thousand Turks replaced and revenged the loss of their brethren; and the Greek soldiers were exercised to ride, to draw the bow, and to the daily practice of ambuscades and evolutions. Alexius had been taught by experience that the formidable cavalry of the Franks on foot was unfit for action, and almost incapable of motion; his archers were directed to aim their arrows at the horse rather than the man; and a variety of spikes and snares were scattered over the ground on which he might expect an attack. In the neighbourhood of Larissa the events of war were protracted and balanced. The courage of Bohemond was always conspicuous, and often successful; but his camp was pillaged by a stratagem of the Greeks; the city was impregnable; and the venal or discontented counts deserted his standard, betrayed their trusts, and enlisted in the service of the emperor. Alexius returned to Constantinople with the advantage, rather than the honour, of victory. After evacuating the conquests which he could no longer defend, the son of Guiscard embarked for Italy, and was embraced by a father who esteemed his merit, and sympathised in his misfortune.

Of the Latin princes, the allies of Alexius and enemies of Robert, the most prompt and powerful was Henry the Third or Fourth, king of Germany and Italy, and future emperor of the West. The epistle of the Greek monarch to his brother is filled with the warmest professions of friendship, and the most lively desire of strengthening their alliance by every public and private tie. He congratulates Henry on his success in a just and pious war, and complains that the prosperity of his own empire is disturbed by the audacious enterprises of the Norman Robert. The list of his presents expresses the manners of the age—a radiated crown of gold, a cross set with pearls to hang on the breast, a case of relics with the names and titles of the saints, a vase of crystal, a vase of sardonyx, some balm, most probably of Mecca, and one hundred pieces of purple. To these he added a more solid present, of one hundred and forty-four thousand Byzantines of gold, with a farther assurance of two hundred and sixteen thousand, so soon as Henry should have entered in arms the Apulian territories, and confirmed by an oath the league against the common enemy. The German, who was already in Lombardy at the head of an army and a faction, accepted these liberal offers, and marched towards the south: his speed was checked by the sound of the battle of Durazzo; but the influence of his arms, or name, in the hasty return of Robert, was a full equivalent for the Grecian bribe. Henry was the sincere adversary of the Normans, the allies and vassals of Gregory the Seventh, his implacable foe. The long quarrel of the throne and mitre had been recently kindled by the zeal and ambition of that haughty priest: the king and the pope had degraded each other; and each had seated a rival on the temporal or spiritual throne of his antagonist. After the defeat and death of his Swabian rebel, Henry descended into Italy, to assume the Imperial crown, and to drive from the Vatican the tyrant of the church. But the Roman people adhered to the cause of Gregory: their resolution was fortified by supplies of men and money from Apulia; and the city was thrice ineffectually besieged by the king of Germany. In the fourth year he corrupted, as it is said, with Byzantine gold, the nobles of Rome, whose estates and castles had been ruined by the war. The gates, the bridges, and fifty hostages were delivered into his hands: the anti-pope, Clement the Third, was consecrated in the Lateran: the grateful pontiff crowned his protector in the Vatican; and the emperor Henry fixed his residence in the Capitol, as the lawful successor of Augustus and Charlemagne. The ruins of the Septizonium were still defended by the nephew of Gregory: the pope himself was invested in the castle of St. Angelo; and his last hope was in the courage and fidelity of his Norman vassal. Their friendship had been interrupted by some reciprocal injuries and complaints; but, on this pressing occasion, Guiscard was urged by the obligation of his oath, by his interest, more potent than oaths, by the love of fame, and his enmity to the two emperors. Unfurling the holy banner, he resolved to fly to the relief of the prince of the apostles: the most numerous of his armies, six thousand horse and thirty thousand foot, was instantly assembled; and his march from Salerno to Rome was animated by the public applause and the promise of the divine favour. Henry, invincible in sixty-six battles, trembled at his approach; recollected some indispensable affairs that required his presence in Lombardy; exhorted the Romans to persevere in their allegiance; and hastily retreated three days before the entrance of the Normans. In less than three years the son of Tancred of Hauteville enjoyed the glory of delivering the pope, and of compelling the two emperors, of the East and West, to fly before his victorious arms. But the triumph of Robert was clouded by the calamities of Rome. By the aid of the friends of Gregory the walls had been perforated or scaled; but the Imperial faction was still powerful and active; on the third day the people rose in a furious tumult; and an hasty word of the conqueror, in his defence or revenge, was the signal of fire and pillage. The Saracens of Sicily, the subjects of Roger, and auxiliaries of his brother, embraced this fair occasion of rifling and profaning the holy city of the Christians; many thousands of the citizens, in the sight and by the allies of their spiritual father, were exposed to violation, captivity, or death; and a spacious quarter of the city, from the Lateran to the Coliseum, was consumed by the flames, and devoted to perpetual solitude. From a city where he was now hated, and might be no longer feared, Gregory retired to end his days in the palace of Salerno. The artful pontiff might flatter the vanity of Guiscard with the hope of a Roman or Imperial crown; but this dangerous measure, which would have inflamed the ambition of the Norman, must for ever have alienated the most faithful princes of Germany.

The remainder of this chapter summarises the further conflicts between the Normans and the East and West. Roger King of Sicily invaded Greece and rescued Louis VII of France in 1146. In return the Emperor Manuel repulsed the Normans and carried an offensive into Apulia and Calabria (1148–1155). His design of recovering the Empire in the West went no further. In 1194 the Emperor Henry VI conquered Sicily and by 1204 the power of the Normans in the Mediterranean area was at an end.

Chapter 57

THE KINGDOM OF ROUM.
THE TURKISH CONQUEST OF JERUSALEM

The Seljuk Turks were the first to appear of the nations destined to achieve the final overthrow of the Roman empire. After expeditions into Hindustan and the subjection of Persia, they invaded the Asiatic provinces. In 1071, under Alp Arslan, they defeated the Romans, capturing the emperor, Romanus Diogenes. Over the next twenty years the Seljukian empire reached its height of prosperity under Alp Arslan's son, Malek Shah. The Roman provinces of Asia Minor came under the power of Soliman, a direct descendant of Seljuk.

THE KINGDOM OF ROUM

SINCE the first conquests of the caliphs, the establishment of the Turks in Anatolia or Asia Minor was the most deplorable loss which the church and empire had sustained. By the propagation of the Moslem faith, Soliman deserved the name of *Gazi*, a holy champion; and his new kingdom of the Romans, or of *Roum*, was added to the tables of Oriental geography. It is described as extending from the Euphrates to Constantinople, from the Black Sea to the confines of Syria; pregnant with mines of silver and iron, of alum and copper, fruitful in corn and wine, and productive of cattle and excellent horses. The wealth of Lydia, the arts of the Greeks, the splendour of the Augustan age, existed only in books and ruins, which were equally obscure in the eyes of the Scythian conquerors. Yet in the present decay Anatolia still contains *some* wealthy and populous cities; and, under the Byzantine empire, they were far more flourishing in numbers, size, and opulence. By the choice of the sultan, Nice, the metropolis of Bithynia, was preferred for his palace and fortress: the seat of the Seljukian dynasty of Roum was planted one hundred miles from Constantinople; and the divinity of Christ was denied and derided in the same temple in which it had been pronounced by the first general synod of the Catholics. The unity of God, and the mission of Mahomet, were preached in the moschs; the Arabian learning was taught in the schools; the Cadhis judged according to the law of the Koran; the Turkish manners and language prevailed in the cities; and Turkman camps were scattered over the plains and mountains of Anatolia. On the hard conditions of tribute and servitude, the Greek Christians might enjoy the exercise of their religion; but their most holy churches were profaned, their priests and bishops were insulted, they were compelled to suffer the triumph of the *pagans* and the apostacy of their brethren, many thousand children were marked by the knife of circumcision, and many thousand captives were devoted to the service or the pleasures of their masters. After the loss of Asia, Antioch still maintained her primitive allegiance to Christ and Cæsar; but the solitary province was separated from all Roman aid, and surrounded on all sides by the Mahometan powers. The despair of Philaretus the governor prepared the sacrifice of his religion and loyalty, had not his guilt been prevented by his son, who hastened to the Nicene palace, and offered to deliver this valuable prize into the hands of Soliman. The ambitious sultan mounted on horseback, and in twelve nights (for he reposed in the day) performed a march of six hundred miles. Antioch was oppressed by the speed and secrecy of his enterprise; and the dependent cities, as far as Laodicea and the confines of Aleppo, obeyed the example of the metropolis. From Laodicea to the Thracian Bosphorus, or arm of St. George, the conquests and reign of Soliman extended thirty days' journey in length, and in breadth about ten or fifteen, between the rocks of Lycia and the Black Sea. The Turkish ignorance of navigation protected for a while the inglorious safety of the emperor; but no sooner had a fleet of two hundred ships been constructed by the hands of the captive Greeks, than Alexius trembled behind the walls of his capital. His plaintive epistles were dispersed over Europe to excite the compassion of the Latins, and to paint the danger, the weakness, and the riches of the city of Constantine.

TURKISH CONQUEST OF JERUSALEM

But the most interesting conquest of the Seljukian Turks was that of Jerusalem, which soon became the theatre of nations. In their capitulation with Omar, the inhabitants had stipulated the assurance of their religion and property, but the articles were interpreted by a master against whom it was dangerous to dispute; and in the four hundred years of the reign of the caliphs the political climate of Jerusalem was exposed to the vicissitudes of storms and sunshine. By the increase of proselytes and population the Mahometans might excuse their usurpation of three-fourths of the city: but a peculiar quarter was reserved for the patriarch with his clergy and people; a tribute of two pieces of gold was the price of protection; and the sepulchre of Christ, with the church of the Resurrection, was still left in the hands of his votaries. Of these votaries the most numerous and respectable portion were strangers to Jerusalem; the pilgrimages to the Holy Land had been stimulated, rather than suppressed, by the conquest of the Arabs; and the enthusiasm which had always prompted these perilous journeys was nourished by the congenial passions of grief and indignation. A crowd of pilgrims from the

East and West continued to visit the holy sepulchre and the adjacent sanctuaries, more especially at the festival of Easter; and the Greeks and Latins, the Nestorians and Jacobites, the Copts and Abyssinians, the Armenians and Georgians, maintained the chapels, the clergy, and the poor of their respective communions. The harmony of prayer in so many various tongues, the worship of so many nations in the common temple of their religion, might have afforded a spectacle of edification and peace; but the zeal of the Christian sects was embittered by hatred and revenge; and in the kingdom of a suffering Messiah, who had pardoned his enemies, they aspired to command and persecute their spiritual brethren. The pre-eminence was asserted by the spirit and numbers of the Franks, and the greatness of Charlemagne protected both the Latin pilgrims and the Catholics of the East. The poverty of Carthage, Alexandria, and Jerusalem was relieved by the alms of that pious emperor, and many monasteries of Palestine were founded or restored by his liberal devotion. Harun Alrashid, the greatest of the Abbassides, esteemed in his Christian brother a similar supremacy of genius and power: their friendship was cemented by a frequent intercourse of gifts and embassies; and the caliph, without resigning the substantial dominion, presented the emperor with the keys of the holy sepulchre, and perhaps of the city of Jerusalem. In the decline of the Carlovingian monarchy the republic of Amalphi promoted the interest of trade and religion in the East. Her vessels transported the Latin pilgrims to the coasts of Egypt and Palestine, and deserved, by their useful imports, the favour and alliance of the Fatimite caliphs: an annual fair was instituted on Mount Calvary; and the Italian merchants founded the convent and hospital of St. John of Jerusalem, the cradle of the monastic and military order which has since reigned in the isles of Rhodes and of Malta. Had the Christian pilgrims been content to revere the tomb of a prophet, the disciples of Mahomet, instead of blaming, would have imitated, their piety; but these rigid *Unitarians* were scandalized by a worship which represents the birth, death, and resurrection of a God; the Catholic images were branded with the name of idols; and the Moslems smiled with indignation at the miraculous flame which was kindled on the eve of Easter in the holy sepulchre. This pious fraud, first devised in the ninth century, was devoutly cherished by the Latin crusaders, and is annually repeated by the clergy of the Greek, Armenian, and Coptic sects, who impose on the credulous spectators for their own benefit and that of their tyrants. In every age a principle of toleration has been fortified by a sense of interest, and the revenue of the prince and his emir was increased each year by the expense and tribute of so many thousand strangers.

The revolution which transferred the sceptre from the Abbassides to the Fatimites was a benefit rather than an injury to the Holy Land. A sovereign resident in Egypt was more sensible of the importance of

Christian trade; and the emirs of Palestine were less remote from the justice and power of the throne. But the third of these Fatimite caliphs was the famous Hakem, a frantic youth, who was delivered by his impiety and despotism from the fear either of God or man, and whose reign was a wild mixture of vice and folly. Regardless of the most ancient customs of Egypt, he imposed on the women an absolute confinement; the restraint excited the clamours of both sexes; their clamours provoked his fury; a part of Old Cairo was delivered to the flames, and the guards and citizens were engaged many days in a bloody conflict. At first the caliph declared himself a zealous Musulman, the founder or benefactor of moschs and colleges: twelve hundred and ninety copies of the Koran were transcribed at his expense in letters of gold, and his edict extirpated the vineyards of the Upper Egypt. But his vanity was soon flattered by the hope of introducing a new religion; he aspired above the fame of a prophet, and styled himself the visible image of the Most High God, who, after nine apparitions on earth, was at length manifest in his royal person. At the name of Hakem, the lord of the living and the dead, every knee was bent in religious adoration; his mysteries were performed on a mountain near Cairo; sixteen thousand converts had signed his profession of faith; and at the present hour a free and warlike people, the Druses of Mount Libanus, are persuaded of the life and divinity of a madman and tyrant. In his divine character Hakem hated the Jews and Christians, as the servants of his rivals, while some remains of prejudice or prudence still pleaded in favour of the law of Mahomet. Both in Egypt and Palestine his cruel and wanton persecution made some martyrs and many apostates; the common rights and special privileges of the sectaries were equally disregarded, and a general interdict was laid on the devotion of strangers and natives. The temple of the Christian world, the church of the Resurrection, was demolished to its foundations; the luminous prodigy of Easter was interrupted; and much profane labour was exhausted to destroy the cave in the rock which properly constitutes the holy sepulchre. At the report of this sacrilege the nations of Europe were astonished and afflicted: but, instead of arming in the defence of the Holy Land, they contented themselves with burning or banishing the Jews, as the secret advisers of the impious barbarian. Yet the calamities of Jerusalem were in some measure alleviated by the inconstancy or repentance of Hakem himself; and the royal mandate was sealed for the restitution of the churches when the tyrant was assassinated by the emissaries of his sister. The succeeding caliphs resumed the maxims of religion and policy: a free toleration was again granted; with the pious aid of the emperor of Constantinople the holy sepulchre arose from its ruins; and, after a short abstinence, the pilgrims returned with an increase of appetite to the spiritual feast. In the sea-voyage of Palestine the dangers were frequent, and the opportunities rare; but the conversion of Hungary opened a safe communication between Germany and Greece. The charity of St. Stephen, the apostle of his kingdom, relieved and conducted his itinerant brethren; and from Belgrade to Antioch they traversed fifteen hundred miles of a Christian empire. Among the Franks the zeal of pilgrimage prevailed beyond the example of former times, and the roads were covered with multitudes of either sex and of every rank, who professed their contempt of life so soon as they should have kissed the tomb of their Redeemer. Princes and prelates abandoned the care of their dominions, and the numbers of these pious caravans were a prelude to the armies which marched in the ensuing age under the banner of the cross. About thirty years before the first crusade, the archbishop of Mentz, with the bishops of Utrecht, Bamberg, and Ratisbon, undertook this laborious journey from the Rhine to the Jordan, and the multitude of their followers amounted to seven thousand persons. At Constantinople they were hospitably entertained by the emperor, but the ostentation of their wealth provoked the assault of the wild Arabs; they drew their swords with scrupulous reluctance, and sustained a siege in the village of Capernaum till they were rescued by the venal protection of the Fatimite emir. After visiting the holy places they embarked for Italy, but only a remnant of two thousand arrived in safety in their native land. Ingulphus, a secretary of William the Conqueror, was a companion of this pilgrimage; he observes that they sallied from Normandy thirty stout and well-appointed horsemen; but that they repassed the Alps twenty miserable palmers, with the staff in their hand, and the wallet at their back.

After the defeat of the Romans the tranquillity of the Fatimite caliphs was invaded by the Turks. One of the lieutenants of Malek Shah, Atsiz the Carizmian, marched into Syria at the head of a powerful army, and reduced Damascus by famine and the sword. Hems, and the other cities of the province, acknowledged the caliph of Bagdad and the sultan of Persia; and the victorious emir advanced without resistance to the banks of the Nile: the Fatimite was preparing to fly into the heart of Africa; but the negroes of his guard and the inhabitants of Cairo made a desperate sally, and repulsed the Turk from the confines of Egypt. In his retreat he indulged the licence of slaughter and rapine: the judge and notaries of Jerusalem were invited to his camp; and their execution was followed by the massacre of three thousand citizens. The cruelty or the defeat of Atsiz was soon punished by the sultan Toucush, the brother of Malek Shah, who, with a higher title and more formidable powers, asserted the dominion of Syria and Palestine. The house of Seljuk reigned about twenty years in Jerusalem; but the hereditary command of the holy city and territory was intrusted or abandoned to the emir Ortok, the chief of a tribe of Turkmans, whose children, after their expulsion from Palestine, formed two dynasties on the borders of Armenia and Assyria. The Oriental Christians and the Latin pilgrims deplored a revolution which, instead of the regular government and old alliance of the caliphs, imposed on their necks the iron yoke of the strangers of the North. In his court and camp the great sultan had adopted in some degree the arts and manners of Persia; but the body of the Turkish nation, and more especially the pastoral tribes, still breathed the fierceness of the desert. From Nice to Jerusalem the western countries of Asia were a scene of foreign and domestic hostility; and the shepherds of Palestine, who held a precarious sway on a doubtful frontier, had neither leisure nor capacity to await the slow profits of commercial and religious freedom. The pilgrims, who, through innumerable perils, had reached the gates of Jerusalem, were the victims of private rapine or public oppression, and often sunk under the pressure of famine and disease, before they were permitted to salute the holy sepulchre. A spirit of native barbarism, or recent zeal, prompted the Turkmans to insult the clergy of every sect: the patriarch was dragged by the hair along the pavement and cast into a dungeon, to extort a ransom from the sympathy of his flock; and the divine worship in the church of the Resurrection was often disturbed by the savage rudeness of its masters. The pathetic tale excited the millions of the West to march under the standard of the cross to the relief of the Holy Land; and yet how trifling is the sum of these accumulated evils, if compared with the single act of the sacrilege of Hakem, which had been so patiently endured by the Latin Christians! A slighter provocation inflamed the more irascible temper of their descendants: a new spirit had arisen of religious chivalry and papal dominion; a nerve was touched of exquisite feeling; and the sensation vibrated to the heart of Europe.

THE CRUSADES

Chapter 59

ST. LOUIS AND THE SIXTH AND SEVENTH CRUSADES. THE LOSS OF ANTIOCH. THE LOSS OF ACRE AND THE HOLY LAND

The capture of Jerusalem by the Turks stimulated both the spiritual and temporal enthusiasm in Western Europe which led to the crusades. In 1099 Jerusalem was retaken by Godfrey de Bouillon and a kingdom established there. Saladin conquered Jerusalem in 1187 and brought the kingdom to an end. Subsequent efforts to re-capture the city were unsuccessful.

Gibbon begins his account of the crusades in Chapter 58. He reserves his description of the Fourth Crusade, which had a very direct bearing on the fate of the Roman Empire, for a subsequent chapter, (c. 60), which is included in full.

ST. LOUIS AND THE SIXTH AND SEVENTH CRUSADES

OF the seven crusades, the two last were undertaken by Louis the Ninth, king of France, who lost his liberty in Egypt, and his life on the coast of Africa. Twenty-eight years after his death he was canonised at Rome, and sixty-five miracles were readily found and solemnly attested to justify the claim of the royal saint. The voice of history renders a more honourable testimony, that he united the virtues of a king, an hero, and a man; that his martial spirit was tempered by the love of private and public justice; and that Louis was the father of his people, the friend of his neighbours, and the terror of the infidels. Superstition alone, in all the extent of her baleful influence, corrupted his understanding and his heart; his devotion stooped to admire and imitate the begging friars of Francis and Dominic; he pursued with blind and cruel zeal the enemies of the faith; and the best of kings twice descended from his throne to seek the adventures of a spiritual knight-errant. A monkish historian would have been content to applaud the most despicable part of his character; but the noble and gallant Joinville, who shared the friendship and captivity of Louis, has traced with the pencil of nature the free portrait of his virtues as well as of his failings. From this intimate knowledge we may learn to suspect the political views of depressing their great vassals, which are so often imputed to the royal authors of the crusades. Above all the princes of the middle ages Louis the Ninth successfully laboured to restore the prerogatives of the crown; but it was at home, and not in the East, that he acquired these for himself and his posterity; his vow was the result of enthusiasm and sickness; and if he were the promoter, he was likewise the victim, of this holy madness. For the invasion of Egypt, France was exhausted of her troops and treasures; he covered the sea of Cyprus with eighteen hundred sails; the most modest enumeration amounts to fifty thousand men; and, if we might trust his own confession, as it is reported by Oriental vanity, he disembarked nine thousand five hundred horse, and one hundred and thirty thousand foot, who performed their pilgrimage under the shadow of his power.

In complete armour, the oriflamme waving before him, Louis leaped foremost on the beach; and the strong city of Damietta, which had cost his predecessors a siege of sixteen months, was abandoned on the first assault by the trembling Moslems. But Damietta was the first and the last of his conquests; and in the fifth and sixth crusades the same causes, almost on the same ground, were productive of similar calamities. After a ruinous delay, which introduced into the camp the seeds of an epidemical disease, the Franks advanced from the sea-coast towards the capital of Egypt, and strove to surmount the unseasonable inundation of the Nile which opposed their progress. Under the eye of their intrepid monarch, the barons and knights of France displayed their invincible contempt of danger and discipline; his brother, the count of Artois, stormed with inconsiderate valour the town of Massoura; and the carrier pigeons announced to the inhabitants of Cairo that all was lost. But a soldier, who afterwards usurped the sceptre, rallied the flying troops: the main body of the Christians was far behind their vanguard, and Artois was overpowered and slain. A shower of Greek fire was incessantly poured on the invaders; the Nile was commanded by the Egyptian galleys, the open country by the Arabs; all provisions were intercepted; each day aggravated the sickness and famine; and about the same time a retreat was found to be necessary and impracticable. The Oriental writers confess that Louis might have escaped if he would have deserted his subjects: he was made prisoner, with the greatest part of his nobles; all who could not redeem their lives by service or ransom were inhumanly massacred, and the walls of Cairo were decorated with a circle of Christian heads. The king of France was loaded with chains, but the generous victor, a great-grandson of the brother of Saladin, sent a robe of honour to his royal captive, and his deliverance, with that of his soldiers, was obtained by the restitution of Damietta and the payment of four hundred thousand pieces of gold. In a soft and luxurious climate the degenerate children of the companions of Noureddin and Saladin were incapable of resisting the flower of European chivalry; they triumphed by the arms of their slaves or Mamalukes, the hardy natives of Tartary, who at a tender age had been purchased of the Syrian merchants, and were educated in the camp and palace of the sultan. But

Egypt soon afforded a new example of the danger of prætorian bands; and the rage of these ferocious animals, who had been let loose on the strangers, was provoked to devour their benefactor. In the pride of conquest, Touran Shaw, the last of his race, was murdered by his Mamalukes; and the most daring of the assassins entered the chamber of the captive king, with drawn scimitars, and their hands imbrued in the blood of their sultan. The firmness of Louis commanded their respect; their avarice prevailed over cruelty and zeal, the treaty was accomplished, and the king of France, with the relics of his army, was permitted to embark for Palestine. He wasted four years within the walls of Acre, unable to visit Jerusalem, and unwilling to return without glory to his native country.

The memory of his defeat excited Louis, after sixteen years of wisdom and repose, to undertake the seventh and last of the crusades. His finances were restored, his kingdom was enlarged; a new generation of warriors had arisen, and he embarked with fresh confidence at the head of six thousand horse and thirty thousand foot. The loss of Antioch had provoked the enterprise; a wild hope of baptizing the king of Tunis tempted him to steer for the African coast; and the report of an immense treasure reconciled his troops to the delay of their voyage to the Holy Land. Instead of a proselyte, he found a siege; the French panted and died on the burning sands; St. Louis expired in his tent; and no sooner had he closed his eyes than his son and successor gave the signal of the retreat. "It is thus," says a lively writer, "that a Christian king died near the ruins of Carthage, waging war against the sectaries of Mahomet, in a land to which Dido had introduced the deities of Syria."

THE LOSS OF ANTIOCH

A more unjust and absurd constitution cannot be devised than that which condemns the natives of a country to perpetual servitude under the arbitrary dominion of strangers and slaves. Yet such has been the state of Egypt above five hundred years. The most illustrious sultans of the Baharite and Borgite dynasties were themselves promoted from the Tartar and Circassian bands; and the four-and-twenty beys, or military chiefs, have ever been succeeded, not by their sons, but by their servants. They produce the great charter of their liberties, the treaty of Selim the First with the republic; and the Othman emperor still accepts from Egypt a slight acknowledgment of tribute and subjection. With some breathing intervals of peace and order, the two dynasties are marked as a period of rapine and bloodshed; but their throne, however shaken, reposed on the two pillars of discipline and valour; their sway extended over Egypt, Nubia, Arabia, and Syria; their Mamalukes were multiplied from eight hundred to twenty-five thousand horse; and their numbers were increased by a provincial militia of one hundred and seven thousand foot, and the occasional aid of sixty-six thousand Arabs. Princes of such power and spirit could not long endure on their coast an hostile and independent nation; and if the ruin of the Franks was postponed about forty years, they were indebted to the cares of an unsettled reign, to the invasion of the Mogols, and to the occasional aid of some warlike pilgrims. Among these the English reader will observe the name of our first Edward, who assumed the cross in the lifetime of his father Henry. At the head of a thousand soldiers the future conqueror of Wales and Scotland delivered Acre from a siege; marched as far as Nazareth with an army of nine thousand men; emulated the fame of his uncle Richard; extorted, by his valour, a ten years' truce; and escaped, with a dangerous wound, from the dagger of a fanatic *assassin*. Antioch, whose situation had been less exposed to the calamities of the holy war, was finally occupied and ruined by Bondocdar, or Bibars, sultan of Egypt and Syria; the Latin principality was extinguished; and the first seat of the Christian name was dispeopled by the slaughter of seventeen, and the captivity of one hundred, thousand of her inhabitants. The maritime towns of Laodicea, Gabala, Tripoli, Berytus, Sidon, Tyre, and Jaffa, and the stronger castles of the Hospitalers and Templars, successively fell; and the whole existence of the Franks was confined to the city and colony of St. John of Acre, which is sometimes described by the more classic title of Ptolemais.

THE LOSS OF ACRE AND THE HOLY LAND

After the loss of Jerusalem, Acre, which is distant about seventy miles, became the metropolis of the Latin Christians, and was adorned with strong and stately buildings, with aqueducts, an artificial port, and a double wall. The population was increased by the incessant streams of pilgrims and fugitives; in the pauses of hostility the trade of the East and West was attracted to this convenient station, and the market could offer the produce of every clime and the interpreters of every tongue. But in this conflux of nations every vice was propagated and practised: of all the disciples of Jesus and Mahomet, the male and female inhabitants of Acre were esteemed the most corrupt, nor could the abuse of religion be corrected by the discipline of law. The city had many sovereigns and no government. The kings of Jerusalem and Cyprus, of the house of Lusignan, the princes of Antioch, the counts of Tripoli and Sidon, the great masters of the hospital, the temple, and the Teutonic order, the republics of Venice, Genoa, and Pisa, the pope's legate, the kings of France and England, assumed an independent command; seventeen tribunals exercised the power of life and death; every criminal was protected in the adjacent quarter; and the perpetual jealousy of the nations often burst forth in acts of violence and blood. Some adventurers, who disgraced the ensign of the cross, compensated their want of pay by the plunder of the Mahometan villages; nineteen Syrian merchants, who traded under the public faith, were despoiled and hanged by the Christians, and the denial of satisfaction justified the arms of the sultan Khalil. He marched against Acre at the head of sixty thousand horse and one hundred and forty thousand foot; his train of artillery (if I may use the word) was numerous and weighty; the separate timbers of a single engine were transported in one hundred waggons; and the royal historian Abulfeda, who served with the troops of Hamah, was himself a spectator of the holy war. Whatever might be the vices of the Franks, their courage was rekindled by enthusiasm and despair; but they were torn by the discord of seventeen chiefs, and overwhelmed on all sides by the powers of the sultan. After a siege of thirty-three days the double wall was forced by the Moslems; the principal tower yielded to their engines; the Mamalukes made a general assault; the city was stormed, and death or slavery was the lot of sixty thousand Christians. The convent, or rather fortress, of the Templars resisted three days longer; but the great master was pierced with an arrow, and, of five hundred knights, only ten were left alive, less happy than the victims of the sword, if they lived to suffer on a scaffold in the unjust and cruel proscription of the whole order. The king of Jerusalem, the patriarch, and the great master of the hospital effected their retreat to the shore; but the sea was rough, the vessels were insufficient, and great numbers of the fugitives were drowned before they could reach the isle of Cyprus, which might comfort Lusignan for the loss of Palestine. By the command of the sultan the churches and fortifications of the Latin cities were demolished: a motive of avarice or fear still opened the holy sepulchre to some devout and defenceless pilgrims: and a mournful and solitary silence prevailed along the coast which had so long resounded with the WORLD'S DEBATE.

Chapter 60

SCHISM AND ENMITY OF THE GREEKS AND LATINS. THE
FOURTH CRUSADE. ALLIANCE OF THE FRENCH AND VENE-
TIANS AND THEIR VOYAGE TO CONSTANTINOPLE. CONQUEST
AND PILLAGE OF CONSTANTINOPLE BY THE LATINS

THE restoration of the Western empire by Charlemagne was
speedily followed by the separation of the Greek and Latin
churches. A religious and national animosity still divides the two
largest communions of the Christian world; and the schism of Constantinople, by alienating her most useful allies, and provoking her most
dangerous enemies, has precipitated the decline and fall of the Roman
empire in the East.

In the course of the present history the aversion of the Greeks for the
Latins has been often visible and conspicuous. It was originally derived
from the disdain of servitude, inflamed, after the time of Constantine, by
the pride of equality or dominion, and finally exasperated by the preference which their rebellious subjects had given to the alliance of the
Franks. In every age the Greeks were proud of their superiority in profane and religious knowledge: they had first received the light of
Christianity; they had pronounced the decrees of the seven general
councils; they alone possessed the language of Scripture and philosophy:
nor should the barbarians, immersed in the darkness of the West, presume to argue on the high and mysterious questions of theological
science. Those barbarians despised in their turn the restless and subtle
levity of the Orientals, the authors of every heresy, and blessed their
own simplicity, which was content to hold the tradition of the apostolic
church. Yet in the seventh century the synods of Spain, and afterwards
of France, improved or corrupted the Nicene creed, on the mysterious
subject of the third person of the Trinity. In the long controversies of
the East the nature and generation of the Christ had been scrupulously
defined; and the well-known relation of father and son seemed to convey a faint image to the human mind. The idea of birth was less
analogous to the Holy Spirit, who, instead of a divine gift or attribute,
was considered by the Catholics as a substance, a person, a god; he was
not begotten, but in the orthodox style he *proceeded*. Did he proceed
from the Father alone, perhaps *by* the Son? or from the Father *and* the
Son? The first of these opinions was asserted by the Greeks, the second
by the Latins; and the addition to the Nicene creed of the word *filioque*
kindled the flame of discord between the Oriental and the Gallic

churches. In the origin of the dispute the Roman pontiffs affected a character of neutrality and moderation: they condemned the innovation, but they acquiesced in the sentiment, of their Transalpine brethren: they seemed desirous of casting a veil of silence and charity over the superfluous research; and in the correspondence of Charlemagne and Leo the Third, the pope assumes the liberality of a statesman, and the prince descends to the passions and prejudices of a priest. But the orthodoxy of Rome spontaneously obeyed the impulse of her temporal policy; and the *filioque*, which Leo wished to erase, was transcribed in the symbol and chanted in the liturgy of the Vatican. The Nicene and Athanasian creeds are held as the Catholic faith, without which none can be saved; and both Papists and Protestants must now sustain and return the anathemas of the Greeks, who deny the procession of the Holy Ghost from the Son as well as from the Father. Such articles of faith are not susceptible of treaty; but the rules of discipline will vary in remote and independent churches; and the reason, even of divines, might allow that the difference is inevitable and harmless. The craft or superstition of Rome has imposed on her priests and deacons the rigid obligation of celibacy; among the Greeks it is confined to the bishops; the loss is compensated by dignity or annihilated by age; and the parochial clergy, the papas, enjoy the conjugal society of the wives whom they have married before their entrance into holy orders. A question concerning the *Azyms* was fiercely debated in the eleventh century, and the essence of the Eucharist was supposed in the East and West to depend on the use of leavened or unleavened bread. Shall I mention in a serious history the furious reproaches that were urged against the Latins, who for a long while remained on the defensive? They neglected to abstain, according to the apostolical decree, from things strangled, and from blood: they fasted, a Jewish observance! on the Saturday of each week: during the first week of Lent they permitted the use of milk and cheese; their infirm monks were indulged in the taste of flesh; and animal grease was substituted for the want of vegetable oil: the holy chrism or unction in baptism was reserved to the episcopal order; the bishops, as the bridegrooms of their churches, were decorated with rings; their priests shaved their faces, and baptized by a single immersion. Such were the crimes which provoked the zeal of the patriarchs of Constantinople, and which were justified with equal zeal by the doctors of the Latin church.

Bigotry and national aversion are powerful magnifiers of every object of dispute; but the immediate cause of the schism of the Greeks may be traced in the emulation of the leading prelates, who maintained the supremacy of the old metropolis, superior to all, and of the reigning capital, inferior to none, in the Christian world. About the middle of the ninth century, Photius, an ambitious layman, the captain of the guards and principal secretary, was promoted by merit and favour to the more desirable office of patriarch of Constantinople. In science, even ecclesiastical science, he surpassed the clergy of the age; and the purity of his morals has never been impeached: but his ordination was hasty, his rise was irregular; and Ignatius, his abdicated predecessor, was yet supported by the public compassion and the obstinacy of his adherents. They appealed to the tribunal of Nicholas the First, one of the proudest and most aspiring of the Roman pontiffs, who embraced the welcome opportunity of judging and condemning his rival of the East. Their quarrel was embittered by a conflict of jurisdiction over the king and nation of the Bulgarians; nor was their recent conversion to Christianity of much avail to either prelate, unless he could number the proselytes among the subjects of his power. With the aid of his court the Greek patriarch was victorious; but in the furious contest he deposed in his turn the successor of St. Peter, and involved the Latin church in the reproach of heresy and schism. Photius sacrificed the peace of the world to a short and precarious reign: he fell with his patron, the Cæsar Bardas; and Basil the Macedonian performed an act of justice in the restoration of Ignatius, whose age and dignity had not been sufficiently respected. From his monastery, or prison, Photius solicited the favour of the emperor by pathetic complaints and artful flattery; and the eyes of his rival were scarcely closed when he was again restored to the throne of Constantinople. After the death of Basil he experienced the vicissitudes of courts and the ingratitude of a royal pupil: the patriarch was again deposed, and in his last solitary hours he might regret the freedom of a secular and studious life. In each revolution the breath, the nod, of the sovereign had been accepted by a submissive clergy; and a synod of three hundred bishops was always prepared to hail the triumph, or to stigmatise the fall, of the holy, or the execrable, Photius. By a delusive promise of succour or reward, the popes were tempted to countenance these various proceedings; and the synods of Constantinople were ratified by their epistles or legates. But the court and the people, Ignatius and Photius, were equally adverse to their claims; their ministers were insulted or imprisoned; the procession of the Holy Ghost was forgotten; Bulgaria was for ever annexed to the Byzantine throne; and the schism was prolonged by their rigid censure of all the multiplied ordinations of an irregular patriarch. The darkness and corruption of the tenth century suspended the intercourse, without reconciling the minds, of the two nations. But when the Norman sword restored the churches of Apulia to the jurisdiction of Rome, the departing flock was warned, by a petulant epistle of the Greek patriarch, to avoid and abhor the errors of the Latins. The rising majesty of Rome could no longer brook the insolence of a rebel; and Michael Cerularius was excommunicated in the heart of Constantinople by the pope's legates. Shaking the dust from their feet, they deposited on the altar of St. Sophia a direful anathema, which enumerates the seven mortal heresies of the Greeks, and devotes the guilty teachers, and their unhappy sectaries, to the eternal society of the devil and his angels. According to the emergencies of the church and state, a friendly correspondence was sometimes resumed; the language of charity and concord was sometimes affected; but the Greeks have never recanted their errors, the popes have never repealed their sentence; and from this thunderbolt we may date the consummation of the schism. It was enlarged by each ambitous step of the Roman pontiffs: the emperors blushed and trembled at the ignominious fate of their royal brethren of Germany; and the people was scandalised by the temporal power and military life of the Latin clergy.

ENMITY OF THE GREEKS AND LATINS

The aversion of the Greeks and Latins was nourished and manifested in the three first expeditions to the Holy Land. Alexius Comnenus contrived the absence at least of the formidable pilgrims: his successors, Manuel and Isaac Angelus, conspired with the Moslems for the ruin of the greatest princes of the Franks; and their crooked and malignant policy was seconded by the active and voluntary obedience of every order of their subjects. Of this hostile temper a large portion may doubtless be ascribed to the difference of language, dress, and manners, which severs and alienates the nations of the globe. The pride as well as the prudence of the sovereign was deeply wounded by the intrusion of foreign armies that claimed a right of traversing his dominions, and passing under the walls of his capital: his subjects were insulted and plundered by the rude strangers of the West: and the hatred of the pusillanimous Greeks was sharpened by secret envy of the bold and pious enterprises of the Franks. But these profane causes of national enmity were fortified and inflamed by the venom of religious zeal. Instead of a kind embrace, an hospitable reception from their Christian brethren of the East, every tongue was taught to repeat the names of schismatic and heretic, more odious to an orthodox ear than those of pagan and infidel: instead of being loved for the general conformity of faith and worship, they were abhorred for some rules of discipline, some questions of theology, in which themselves or their teachers might differ from the Oriental church. In the crusade of Louis the Seventh the Greek clergy washed and purified the altars which had been defiled by the sacrifice of a French priest. The companions of Frederic Barbarossa deplore the injuries which they endured, both in word and deed, from the peculiar rancour of the bishops and monks. Their prayers and sermons excited the people against the impious barbarians; and the patriarch is accused of declaring that the faithful might obtain the redemption of all their sins by the extirpation of the schismatics. An enthusiast named Dorotheus alarmed the fears and restored the confidence of the emperor by a prophetic assurance that the German heretic, after assaulting the gate of Blachernæ, would be made a signal example of the divine vengeance. The passage of these mighty armies were rare and perilous events; but the crusades introduced a frequent and familiar intercourse between the two nations, which enlarged their knowledge without abating their prejudices. The wealth and luxury of Constantinople demanded the productions of every climate: these imports were balanced by the art and labour of her numerous inhabitants; her situation invites the commerce of the world; and, in every period of her existence, that commerce has been in the hands of foreigners. After the decline of Amalphi, the Venetians, Pisans, and Genoese introduced their factories and settlements into the capital of the empire: their services were rewarded with honours and immunities; they acquired the possession of lands and houses, their families were multiplied by marriages with the natives, and, after the toleration of a Mahometan mosque, it was impossible to interdict the churches of the Roman rite. The two wives of Manuel Comnenus were of the race of the Franks: the first, a sister-in-law of the emperor Conrad; the second, a daughter of the prince of Antioch: he obtained for his son Alexius a daughter of Philip Augustus king of France; and he bestowed his own daughter on a marquis of Montferrat, who was educated and dignified in the palace of Constantinople. The Greek encountered the arms, and aspired to the empire, of the West: he esteemed the valour, and trusted the fidelity, of the Franks; their military talents were unfitly recompensed by the lucrative offices of judges and treasurers; the policy of Manuel had solicited the alliance of the pope; and the popular voice accused him of a partial bias to the nation and religion of the Latins. During his reign and that of his successor Alexius, they were exposed at Constantinople to the reproach of foreigners, heretics, and favourites; and this triple guilt was severely expiated in the tumult which announced the return and elevation of Andronicus. The people rose in arms: from the Asiatic shore the tyrant despatched his troops and galleys to assist the national revenge; and the hopeless resistance of the strangers served only to justify the rage and sharpen the daggers of the assassins. Neither age, nor sex, nor the ties of friendship or kindred, could save the victims of national hatred, and avarice, and religious zeal: the Latins were slaughtered in their houses and in the streets; their quarter was reduced to ashes; the clergy were burnt in their churches, and the sick in their hospitals; and some estimate may be formed of the slain from the clemency which sold above four thousand Christians in perpetual slavery to the Turks. The priests and monks were the loudest and most active in the destruction of the schismatics; and they chanted a thanksgiving to the Lord when the head of a Roman cardinal, the pope's legate, was severed from his body, fastened to the tail of a dog, and dragged, with savage mockery, through the city. The more diligent of the strangers had retreated, on the first alarm, to their vessels, and escaped through the Hellespont from the scene of blood. In their flight they burnt and ravaged two hundred miles of the sea-coast, inflicted a severe revenge on the guiltless subjects of the empire, marked the priests and monks as their peculiar enemies, and compensated, by the accumulation of plunder, the loss of their property and friends. On their return they exposed to Italy and Europe the wealth and weakness, the perfidy and malice of the Greeks, whose vices were painted as the genuine characters of heresy and schism. The scruples of the first crusaders had neglected the fairest opportunities of securing, by the possession of Constantinople, the way to the Holy Land: a domestic revolution invited, and almost compelled, the French and Venetians to achieve the conquest of the Roman empire of the East.

In the series of the Byzantine princes I have exhibited the hypocrisy and ambition, the tyranny and fall, of Andronicus, the last male of the Comnenian family who reigned at Constantinople. The revolution which cast him headlong from the throne saved and exalted Isaac Angelus, who descended by the females from the same Imperial dynasty. The successor of a second Nero might have found it an easy task to deserve the esteem and affection of his subjects: they sometimes had reason to regret the administration of Andronicus. The sound and vigorous mind of the tyrant was capable of discerning the connection between his own and the public interest; and while he was feared by all who could inspire him with fear, the unsuspected people, and the remote provinces, might bless the inexorable justice of their master. But his successor was vain and jealous of the supreme power, which he wanted courage and abilities to exercise: his vices were pernicious, his virtues (if he possessed any virtues) were useless, to mankind; and the Greeks, who imputed their calamities to his negligence, denied him the merit of any transient or accidental benefits of the times. Isaac slept on the throne, and was awakened only by the sound of pleasure: his vacant hours were amused by comedians and buffoons, and even to these buffoons the emperor was an object of contempt: his feasts and buildings exceeded the examples of royal luxury: the number of his eunuchs and domestics amounted to twenty thousand; and a daily sum of four thousand pounds of silver would swell to four millions sterling the annual expense of his household and table. His poverty was relieved by oppression; and the public discontent was inflamed by equal abuses in the collection and the application of the revenue. While the Greeks numbered the days of their servitude, a flattering prophet, whom he rewarded with the dignity of patriarch, assured him of a long and victorious reign of thirty-two years, during which he should extend his sway to Mount Libanus, and his conquests beyond the Euphrates. But his only step towards the accomplishment of the prediction was a splendid and scandalous embassy to Saladin, to demand the restitution of the holy sepulchre, and to propose an offensive and defensive league with the enemy of the Christian name. In these unworthy hands, of Isaac and his brother, the remains of the Greek empire crumbled into dust.

The island of Cyprus, whose name excites the ideas of elegance and pleasure, was usurped by his namesake, a Comnenian prince; and by a strange concatenation of events, the sword of our English Richard bestowed that kingdom on the house of Lusignan, a rich compensation for the loss of Jerusalem.

The honour of the monarchy and the safety of the capital were deeply wounded by the revolt of the Bulgarians and Wallachians. Since the victory of the second Basil, they had supported, above an hundred and seventy years, the loose dominion of the Byzantine princes; but no effectual measures had been adopted to impose the yoke of laws and manners on these savage tribes. By the command of Isaac, their sole means of subsistence, their flocks and herds, were driven away to contribute towards the pomp of the royal nuptials; and their fierce warriors were exasperated by the denial of equal rank and pay in the military service. Peter and Asan, two powerful chiefs, of the race of the ancient kings, asserted their own rights and the national freedom: their demoniac imposters proclaimed to the crowd that their glorious patron St. Demetrius had for ever deserted the cause of the Greeks: and the conflagration spread from the banks of the Danube to the hills of Macedonia and Thrace. After some faint efforts, Isaac Angelus and his brother acquiesced in their independence; and the Imperial troops were soon discouraged by the bones of their fellow-soldiers that were scattered along the passes of Mount Hæmus. By the arms and policy of John, or Joannices, the second kingdom of Bulgaria was firmly established. The subtle barbarian sent an embassy to Innocent the Third to acknowledge himself a genuine son of Rome in descent and religion, and humbly received from the pope the licence of coining money, the royal title, and a Latin archbishop or patriarch. The Vatican exulted in the spiritual conquest of Bulgaria, the first object of the schism; and if the Greeks could have preserved the prerogatives of the church, they would gladly have resigned the rights of the monarchy.

The Bulgarians were malicious enough to pray for the long life of Isaac Angelus, the surest pledge of their freedom and prosperity. Yet their chiefs could involve in the same indiscriminate contempt the family and nation of the emperor. "In all the Greeks," said Asan to his troops, "the same climate, and character, and education, will be productive of the same fruits. Behold my lance," continued the warrior, "and the long streamers that float in the wind. They differ only in colour; they are formed of the same silk, and fashioned by the same workman; nor has the stripe that is stained in purple any superior price or value above its fellows." Several of these candidates for the purple successively rose and fell under the empire of Isaac: a general who had repelled the fleets of Sicily was driven to revolt and ruin by the ingratitude of the prince; and his luxurious repose was disturbed by secret conspiracies and popular insurrections. The emperor was saved by accident, or the merit of his servants: he was at length oppressed by an ambitious brother, who, for the hope of a precarious diadem, forgot the obligations of nature, of loyalty, and of friendship. While Isaac in the Thracian valleys pursued the idle and solitary pleasures of the chase, his brother, Alexius Angelus, was invested with the purple by the unanimous suffrage of the camp: the capital and the clergy subscribed to their choice; and the vanity of the new sovereign rejected the name of his fathers for the lofty and royal appellation of the Comnenian race. On the despicable character of Isaac I have exhausted the language of contempt, and can only add that in a reign of eight years the baser Alexius was supported by the masculine vices of his wife Euphrosyne. The first intelligence of his fall was conveyed to the late emperor by the hostile aspect and pursuit of the guards, no longer his own: he fled before them above fifty miles as far as Stagyra in Macedonia; but the fugitive, without an object or a follower, was arrested, brought back to Constantinople, deprived of his eyes, and confined in a lonesome tower, on a scanty allowance of bread and water. At the moment of the revolution, his son Alexius, whom he educated in the hope of empire, was twelve years of age. He was spared by the usurper, and reduced to attend his triumph both in peace and war; but as the army was encamped on the sea-shore, an Italian vessel facilitated the escape of the royal youth; and, in the disguise of a common sailor, he eluded the search of his enemies, passed the Hellespont, and found a secure refuge in the isle of Sicily. After saluting the threshold of the apostles, and imploring the protection of Pope Innocent the Third, Alexius accepted the kind invitation of his sister Irene, the wife of Philip of Swabia, king of the Romans. But in his passage through Italy he heard that the flower of Western chivalry was assembled at Venice for the deliverance of the Holy Land; and a ray of hope was kindled in his bosom that their invincible swords might be employed in his father's restoration.

THE FOURTH CRUSADE

About ten or twelve years after the loss of Jerusalem, the nobles of France were again summoned to the holy war by the voice of a third prophet, less extravagant, perhaps, than Peter the Hermit, but far below St. Bernard in the merit of an orator and a statesman. An illiterate priest of the neighbourhood of Paris, Fulk of Neuilly, forsook his parochial duty, to assume the more flattering character of a popular and itinerant missionary. The fame of his sanctity and miracles was spread over the land: he declaimed, with severity and vehemence, against the vices of the age; and his sermons, which he preached in the streets of Paris, converted the robbers, the usurers, the prostitutes, and even the doctors and scholars of the university. No sooner did Innocent the Third ascend the chair of St. Peter than he proclaimed in Italy, Germany, and France, the obligation of a new crusade. The eloquent pontiff described the ruin of Jerusalem, the triumph of the Pagans, and the shame of Christendom: his liberality proposed the redemption of sins, a plenary indulgence to all who should serve in Palestine, either a year in person, or two years by a substitute: and among his legates and orators who blew the sacred trumpet, Fulk of Neuilly was the loudest and most successful. The situation of the principal monarchs was averse to the pious summons. The emperor Frederic the Second was a child; and his kingdom of Germany was disputed by the rival houses of Brunswick and Swabia, the memorable factions of the Guelphs and Ghibelines. Philip Augustus of France had performed, and could not be persuaded to renew, the perilous vow; but as he was not less ambitious of praise than of power, he cheerfully instituted a perpetual fund for the defence of the Holy Land. Richard of England was satiated with the glory and misfortunes of his first adventure, and he presumed to deride the exhortations of Fulk of Neuilly, who was not abashed in the presence of kings. "You advise me," said Plantagenet, "to dismiss my three daughters, pride, avarice, and incontinence: I bequeath them to the most deserving; my pride to the knights-templars, my avarice to the monks of Cisteaux, and my incontinence to the prelates." But the preacher was heard and obeyed by the great vassals, the princes of the second order; and Theobald, or Thibaut, count of Champagne, was the foremost in the holy race. The valiant youth, at the age of twenty-two years, was encouraged by the domestic examples of his father, who marched in the second crusade, and of his elder brother, who had ended his days in Palestine with the title of King of Jerusalem: two thousand two hundred knights owed service and homage to his peerage: the nobles of Champagne excelled in all the exercises of war; and, by his marriage with the heiress of Navarre, Thibaut could draw a band of hardy Gascons from either side of the Pyrenæan mountains. His companion in arms was Louis, count of Blois and Chartres; like himself of regal lineage, for both the princes were nephews, at the same time, of the kings of France and England. In a crowd of prelates and barons, who imitated their zeal, I distinguish the birth and merit of Matthew of Montmorency; the famous Simon of Montfort, the scourge of the Albigeois; and a valiant noble, Jeffrey of Villehardouin, marshal of Champagne, who has condescended, in the rude idiom of his age and country, to write or dictate an original narrative of the councils and actions in which he bore a memorable part. At the same time, Baldwin count of Flanders, who had married the sister of Thibaut, assumed the cross at Bruges, with his brother Henry and the principal knights and citizens of that rich and industrious province. The vow which the chiefs had pronounced in churches, they ratified in tournaments: the operations of the war were debated in full and frequent assemblies: and it was resolved to seek the deliverance of Palestine in Egypt, a country, since Saladin's death, which was almost ruined by famine and civil war. But the fate of so many royal armies displayed the toils and perils of a land expedition; and if the Flemings dwelt along the ocean, the French barons were destitute of ships and ignorant of navigation. They embraced the wise resolution of choosing six deputies or representatives of whom Villehardouin was one, with a discretionary trust to direct the motions, and to pledge the faith, of the whole confederacy. The maritime states of Italy were alone possessed of the means of transporting the holy warriors with their arms and horses; and the six deputies proceeded to Venice to solicit, on motives of piety or interest, the aid of that powerful republic.

In the invasion of Italy by Attila, I have mentioned the flight of the Venetians from the fallen cities of the continent, and their obscure shelter in the chain of islands that line the extremity of the Adriatic Gulf. In the midst of the waters, free, indigent, laborious, and inaccessible, they gradually coalesced into a republic: the first foundations of Venice were laid in the island of Rialto; and the annual election of the twelve tribunes was superseded by the permanent office of a duke or doge. On the verge of the two empires, the Venetians exult in the belief of primitive and perpetual independence. Against the Latins their antique freedom has been asserted by the sword, and may be justified by the pen. Charlemagne himself resigned all claims of sovereignty to the islands of the Adriatic Gulf: his son Pepin was repulsed in the attacks of the *lagunas* or canals, too deep for the cavalry, and too shallow for the vessels; and in every age, under the German Cæsars, the lands of the republic have been clearly distinguished from the kingdom of Italy. But the inhabitants of Venice were considered by themselves, by strangers, and by their sovereigns, as an inalienable portion of the Greek empire: in the ninth and tenth centuries the proofs of their subjection are numerous and unquestionable; and the vain titles, the servile honours, of the Byzantine court, so ambitiously solicited by their dukes, would have degraded the magistrates of a free people. But the bands of this dependence, which was never absolute or rigid, were imperceptibly relaxed by the ambition of Venice and the weakness of Constantinople. Obedience was softened into respect, privilege ripened into prerogative, and the freedom of domestic government was fortified by the independence of foreign dominion. The maritime cities of Istria and Dalmatia bowed to the sovereigns of the Adriatic; and when they armed against the Normans in the cause of Alexius, the emperor applied, not to the duty of his subjects, but to the gratitude and generosity of his faithful allies. The sea was their patrimony: the western parts of the Mediterranean, from Tuscany to Gibraltar, were indeed abandoned to their rivals of Pisa and Genoa; but the Venetians acquired an early and lucrative share of the commerce of Greece and Egypt. Their riches increased with the increasing demand of Europe: their manufactures of silk and glass, perhaps the institution of their bank, are of high antiquity; and they enjoyed the fruits of their industry in the magnificence of public and private life. To assert her flag, to avenge her injuries, to protect the freedom of navigation, the republic could launch and man a fleet of an hundred galleys; and the Greeks, the Saracens, and the Normans were encountered by her naval arms. The Franks of Syria were assisted by the Venetians in the reduction of the sea-coast; but their zeal was neither blind nor disinterested; and in the conquest of Tyre they shared the sovereignty of a city, the first seat of the commerce of the world. The policy of Venice was marked by the avarice of a trading, and the insolence of a maritime power; yet her ambition was prudent: nor did she often forget that, if armed galleys were the effect and safeguard, merchant vessels were the cause and supply, of her greatness. In her religion she avoided the schism of the Greeks, without yielding a servile obedience to the Roman pontiff; and a free intercourse with the infidels of every clime appears to have allayed betimes the fever of superstition. Her primitive government was a loose mixture of democracy and monarchy: the doge was elected by the votes of the general assembly; as long as he was popular and successful, he reigned with the pomp and authority of a prince; but in the frequent revolutions of the state, he was deposed, or banished, or slain, by the justice or injustice of the multitude. The twelfth century produced the first rudiments of the wise and jealous aristocracy, which has reduced the doge to a pageant, and the people to a cipher.

ALLIANCE OF THE FRENCH AND VENETIANS

When the six ambassadors of the French pilgrims arrived at Venice, they were hospitably entertained in the palace of St. Mark, by the reigning duke: his name was Henry Dandolo; and he shone in the last period of human life as one of the most illustrious characters of the times. Under the weight of years, and after the loss of his eyes, Dandolo retained a sound understanding and a manly courage; the spirit of an hero, ambitious to signalise his reign by some memorable exploits; and the wisdom of a patriot, anxious to build his fame on the glory and advantage of his country. He praised the bold enthusiasm and liberal confidence of the barons and their deputies: in such a cause, and with such associates, he should aspire, were he a private man, to terminate his life; but he was the servant of the republic, and some delay was requisite to consult, on this arduous business, the judgment of his colleagues. The proposal of the French was first debated by the six *sages* who had been recently appointed to control the administration of the doge: it was next disclosed to the forty members of the council of state; and finally communicated to the legislative assembly of four hundred and fifty representatives, who were annualy chosen in the six quarters of the city. In peace and war the doge was still the chief of the republic; his legal authority was supported by the personal reputation of Dandolo; his arguments of public interest were balanced and approved; and he was authorised to inform the ambassadors of the following conditions of the treaty. It was proposed that the crusaders should assemble at Venice on the feast of St. John of the ensuing year; that flat-bottomed vessels should be prepared for four thousand five hundred horses and nine thousand squires, with a number of ships sufficient for the embarkation of four thousand five hundred knights and twenty thousand foot: that during a term of nine months they should be supplied with provisions, and transported to whatsoever coast the service of God and Christendom should require; and that the republic should join the armament with a squadron of fifty galleys. It was required that the pilgrims should pay, before their departure, a sum of eighty-five thousand marks of silver; and that all conquests, by sea and land, should be equally divided between the confederates. The terms were hard; but the emergency was pressing, and the French barons were not less profuse of money than of blood. A general assembly was convened to ratify the treaty: the stately chapel and place of St. Mark were filled with ten thousand citizens; and the noble deputies were taught a new lesson of humbling themselves before the majesty of the people. "Illustrious Venetians," said the marshal of Champagne, "we are sent by the greatest and most powerful barons of France to implore the aid of the masters of the sea for the deliverance of Jerusalem. They have enjoined us to fall prostrate at your feet; nor will we rise from the ground till you have promised to avenge with us the injuries of Christ." The eloquence of their words and tears, their martial aspect and suppliant attitude, were applauded by an universal shout; as it were, says Jeffrey, by the sound of an earthquake. The venerable doge ascended the pulpit to urge their request by those motives of honour and virtue which alone can be offered to a popular assembly: the treaty was transcribed on parchment, attested with oaths and seals, mutually accepted by the weeping and joyful representatives of France and Venice, and despatched to Rome for the approbation of Pope Innocent the Third. Two thousand marks were borrowed of the merchants for the first expenses of the armament. Of the six deputies, two repassed the Alps to announce their success, while their four companions made a fruitless trial of the zeal and emulation of the republics of Genoa and Pisa.

The execution of the treaty was still opposed by unforeseen difficulties and delays. The marshal, on his return to Troyes, was embraced and approved by Thibaut count of Champagne, who had been unanimously chosen general of the confederates. But the health of that valiant youth already declined, and soon became hopeless; and he deplored the untimely fate which condemned him to expire, not in a field of battle, but on a bed of sickness. To his brave and numerous vassals the dying prince distributed his treasures: they swore in his presence to accomplish his vow and their own; but some there were, says the marshal, who accepted his gifts and forfeited their word. The more resolute champions of the cross held a parliament at Soissons for the election of a new general but such was the incapacity, or jealousy, or reluctance, of the princes of France, that none could be found both able and willing to assume the conduct of the enterprise. They acquiesced in the choice of a stranger, of Boniface, marquis of Montferrat, descended of a race of heroes, and himself of conspicuous fame in the wars and negociations of the times; nor could the piety or ambition of the Italian chief decline this honourable invitation. After visiting the French court, where he was received as a friend and kinsman, the marquis, in the church of Soissons, was invested with the cross of a pilgrim and the staff of a general; and immediately repassed the Alps, to prepare for the distant expedition of the East. About the festival of the Pentecost he displayed his banner, and marched towards Venice at the head of the Italians: he was preceded or followed by the counts of Flanders and Blois and the most respectable barons of France; and their numbers were swelled by the pilgrims of Germany, whose object and motives were similar to their own. The Venetians had fulfilled, and even surpassed, their engagements: stables were constructed for the horses, and barracks for the troops; the magazines were abundantly replenished with forage and provisions; and the fleet of transports, ships, and galleys, was ready to hoist sail as soon as the republic had received the price of the freight and armament. But that price far exceeded the wealth of the crusaders who were assembled at Venice. The Flemings, whose obedience to their count was voluntary and precarious, had embarked in their vessels for the long navigation of the ocean and Mediterranean; and many of the French and Italians had preferred a cheaper and more convenient passage from Marseilles and Apulia to the Holy Land. Each pilgrim might complain that, after he had furnished his own contribution, he was made responsible for the deficiency of his absent brethren; the gold and silver plate of the chiefs, which they freely delivered to the treasury of St. Mark, was a generous but inadequate sacrifice; and after all their efforts, thirty-four thousand marks were still wanting to complete the stipulated sum. The obstacle was removed by the policy and patriotism of the doge, who proposed to the barons that, if they would join their arms in reducing some revolted cities of Dalmatia, he would expose his person in the holy war, and obtain from the republic a long indulgence, till some wealthy conquest should afford the means of satisfying the debt. After much scruple and hesitation, they chose rather to accept the offer than to relinquish the enterprise; and the first hostilities of the fleet and army were directed against Zara, a strong city of the Sclavonian coast, which had renounced its allegiance to Venice, and implored the protection of the king of Hungary. The crusaders burst the chain or boom of the harbour; landed their horses, troops, and military engines; and compelled the inhabitants, after a defence of five days, to surrender at discretion: their lives were spared, but the revolt was punished by the pillage of their houses and the demolition of their walls. The season was far advanced; the French and Venetians resolved to pass the winter in a secure harbour and plentiful country; but their repose was disturbed by national and tumultuous quarrels of the soldiers and mariners. The conquest of Zara had scattered the seeds of discord and scandal: the arms of the allies had been stained in their outset with the blood, not of infidels, but of Christians: the king of Hungary and his new subjects were themselves enlisted under the banner of the cross; and the scruples of the devout were magnified by the fear or lassitude of the reluctant pilgrims. The pope had excommunicated the false crusaders who had pillaged and massacred their brethren, and only the marquis Boniface and Simon of Montfort escaped these spiritual thunders; the one by his absence from the siege, the other by his final departure from the camp. Innocent might absolve the simple and submissive penitents of France; but he was provoked by the stubborn reason of the Venetians, who refused to confess their guilt, to accept their pardon, or to allow, in their temporal concerns, the interposition of a priest.

The assembly of such formidable powers by sea and land had revived the hopes of young Alexius, and both at Venice and Zara he solicited the arms of the crusaders for his own restoration and his father's deliverance. The royal youth was recommended by Philip, king of Germany; his prayers and presence excited the compassion of the camp, and his cause was embraced and pleaded by the marquis of Montferrat and the doge of Venice. A double alliance, and the dignity of Cæsar, had connected with the Imperial family the two elder brothers of Boniface; he expected to derive a kingdom from the important service; and the more generous ambition of Dandolo was eager to secure the inestimable benefits of trade and dominion that might accrue to his country. Their influence procured a favourable audience for the ambassadors of Alexius; and if the magnitude of his offers excited some suspicion, the motives and rewards which he displayed might justify the delay and diversion of those forces which had been consecrated to the deliverance of Jerusalem. He promised, in his own and his father's name, that, as soon as they should be seated on the throne of Constantinople, they would terminate the long schism of the Greeks, and submit themselves and their people to the lawful supremacy of the Roman church. He engaged to recompense the labours and merits of the crusaders by the immediate payment of two hundred thousand marks of silver; to accompany them in person to Egypt; or, if it should be judged more advantageous, to maintain, during a year, ten thousand men, and, during his life, five hundred knights, for the service of the Holy Land. These tempting conditions were accepted by the republic of Venice, and the eloquence of the doge and marquis persuaded the counts of Flanders, Blois, and St. Pol, with eight barons of France, to join in the glorious enterprise. A treaty of offensive and defensive alliance was confirmed by their oaths and seals;

and each individual, according to his situation and character, was swayed by the hope of public or private advantage; by the honour of restoring an exiled monarch; or by the sincere and probable opinion that their efforts in Palestine would be fruitless and unavailing, and that the acquisition of Constantinople must precede and prepare the recovery of Jerusalem. But they were the chiefs or equals of a valiant band of freemen and volunteers, who thought and acted for themselves: the soldiers and clergy were divided; and, if a large majority subscribed to the alliance, the numbers and arguments of the dissidents were strong and respectable. The boldest hearts were appalled by the report of the naval power and impregnable strength of Constantinople, and their apprehensions were disguised to the world, and perhaps to themselves, by the more decent objections of religion and duty. They alleged the sanctity of a vow which had drawn them from their families and homes to the rescue of the holy sepulchre; nor should the dark and crooked counsels of human policy divert them from a pursuit, the event of which was in the hands of the Almighty. Their first offence, the attack of Zara, had been severely punished by the reproach of their conscience and the censures of the pope, nor would they again imbrue their hands in the blood of their fellow Christians. The apostle of Rome had pronounced; nor would they usurp the right of avenging with the sword the schism of the Greeks and the doubtful usurpation of the Byzantine monarch. On these principles or pretences many pilgrims, the most distinguished for their valour and piety, withdrew from the camp; and their retreat was less pernicious than the open or secret opposition of a discontented party that laboured, on every occasion, to separate the army and disappoint the enterprise.

THE VOYAGE TO CONSTANTINOPLE

Notwithstanding this defection, the departure of the fleet and army was vigorously pressed by the Venetians, whose zeal for the service of the royal youth concealed a just resentment to his nation and family. They were mortified by the recent preference which had been given to Pisa, the rival of their trade; they had a long arrear of debt and injury to liquidate with the Byzantine court; and Dandolo might not discourage the popular tale that he had been deprived of his eyes by the emperor Manuel, who perfidiously violated the sanctity of an ambassador. A similar armament, for ages, had not rode the Adriatic: it was composed of one hundred and twenty flat-bottomed vessels or *palanders* for the horses, two hundred and forty transports filled with men and arms, seventy store-ships laden with provisions, and fifty stout galleys well prepared for the encounter of an enemy. While the wind was favourable, the sky serene, and the water smooth, every eye was fixed with wonder and delight on the scene of military and naval pomp which overspread the sea. The shields of the knights and squires, at once an ornament and a defence, were arranged on either side of the ships; the banners of the nations and families were displayed from the stern; our modern artillery was supplied by three hundred engines for casting stones and darts; the fatigues of the way were cheered with the sound of music; and the spirits of the adventurers were raised by the mutual assurance that forty thousand Christian heroes were equal to the conquest of the world. In the navigation from Venice and Zara the fleet was successfully steered by the skill and experience of the Venetian pilots: at Durazzo the confederates first landed on the territories of the Greek empire; the isle of Corfu afforded a station and repose; they doubled, without accident, the perilous cape of Malea, the southern point of Peloponnesus or the Morea; made a descent in the islands of Negropont and Andros; and cast anchor at Abydus on the Asiatic side of the Hellespont. These preludes of conquest were easy and bloodless; the Greeks of the provinces, without patriotism or courage, were crushed by an irresistible force; the presence of the lawful heir might justify their obedience, and it was rewarded by the modesty and discipline of the Latins. As they penetrated through the Hellespont, the magnitude of their navy was compressed in a narrow channel, and the face of the waters was darkened with innumerable sails. They again expanded in the basin of the Propontis, and traversed that placid sea, till they approached the European shore at the abbey of St. Stephen, three leagues to the west of Constantinople. The prudent doge dissuaded them from dispersing themselves in a populous and hostile land; and, as their stock of provisions was reduced, it was resolved, in the season of harvest, to replenish their storeships in the fertile islands of the Propontis. With this resolution they directed their course; but a strong gale and their own impatience drove them to the eastward, and so near did they run to the shore and the city, that some volleys of stones and darts were exchanged between the ships and the rampart. As they passed along, they gazed with admiration on the capital of the East, or, as it should seem, of the earth, rising from her seven hills, and towering over the continents of Europe and Asia. The swelling domes and lofty spires of five hundred palaces and churches were gilded by the sun and reflected in the waters; the walls were crowded with soldiers and spectators, whose numbers they beheld, of whose temper they were ignorant; and each heart was chilled by the reflection that, since the beginning of the world, such an enterprise had never been undertaken by such a handful of warriors. But the momentary apprehension was dispelled by hope and valour; and every man, says the marshal of Champagne, glanced his eye on the sword or lance which he must speedily use in the glorious conflict. The Latins cast anchor before Chalcedon; the mariners only were left in the vessels; the soldiers, horses, and arms were safely landed; and, in the luxury of an Imperial palace, the barons tasted the first fruits of their success. On the third day the fleet and army moved towards Scutari, the Asiatic suburb of Constantinople: a detachment of five hundred Greek horse was surprised and defeated by fourscore French knights; and in a halt of nine days the camp was plentifully supplied with forage and provisions.

In relating the invasion of a great empire, it may seem strange that I have not described the obstacles which should have checked the progress of the strangers. The Greeks, in truth, were an unwarlike people; but they were rich, industrious, and subject to the will of a single man: had that man been capable of fear when his enemies were at a distance, or of courage when they approached his person. The first rumour of his nephew's alliance with the French and Venetians was despised by the usurper Alexius: his flatterers persuaded him that in this contempt he was bold and sincere; and each evening, in the close of the banquet, he thrice discomfited the barbarians of the West. These barbarians had been justly terrified by the report of his naval power; and the sixteen hundred fishing-boats of Constantinople could have manned a fleet to sink them in the Adriatic, or stop their entrance in the mouth of the Hellespont. But all force may be annihilated by the negligence of the prince and the venality of his ministers. The great duke or admiral made a scandalous, almost a public, auction of the sails, the masts, and the rigging; the royal forests were reserved for the more important purpose of the chase; and the trees, says Nicetas, were guarded by the eunuchs like the groves of religious worship. From his dream of pride Alexius was awakened by the siege of Zara and the rapid advances of the Latins; as soon as he saw the danger was real, he thought it inevitable, and his vain presumption was lost in abject despondency and despair. He suffered these contemptible barbarians to pitch their camp in the sight of the palace, and his apprehensions were thinly disguised by the pomp and menace of a suppliant embassy. The sovereign of the Romans was astonished (his ambassadors were instructed to say) at the hostile appearance of the strangers. If these pilgrims were sincere in their vow for the deliverance of Jerusalem, his voice must applaud, and his treasures should assist, their pious design; but should they dare to invade the sanctuary of empire, their numbers, were they ten times more considerable, should not protect them from his just resentment. The answer of the doge and barons was simple and magnanimous. "In the cause of honour and justice," they said, "we despise the usurper of Greece, his threats, and his offers. *Our* friendship and *his* allegiance are due to the lawful heir, to the young prince who is seated among us, and to his father the emperor Isaac, who has been deprived of his sceptre, his freedom, and his eyes by the crime of an ungrateful brother. Let that brother confess his guilt and implore forgiveness, and we ourselves will intercede that he may be permitted to live in affluence and security. But let him not insult us by a second message: our reply will be made in arms, in the palace of Constantinople."

On the tenth day of their encampment at Scutari the crusaders prepared themselves, as soldiers and as Catholics, for the passage of the Bosphorus. Perilous indeed was the adventure: the stream was broad and rapid; in a calm the current of the Euxine might drive down the liquid and unextinguishable fires of the Greeks, and the opposite shores of Europe were defended by seventy thousand horse and foot in formidable array. On this memorable day, which happened to be bright and pleasant, the Latins were distributed in six battles or divisions; the first, or vanguard, was led by the count of Flanders, one of the most powerful of the Christian princes in the skill and number of his cross-bows. The four successive battles of the French were commanded by his brother Henry, the counts of St. Pol and Blois, and Matthew of Montmorency, the last of whom was honoured by the voluntary service of the marshal and nobles of Champagne. The sixth division, the rear-guard and reserve of the army, was conducted by the marquis of Montferrat, at the head of the Germans and Lombards. The chargers, saddled, with their long caparisons dragging on the ground, were embarked in the flat *palanders*, and the knights stood by the side of their horses, in complete armour, their helmets laced, and their lances in their hands. Their numerous train of *serjeants* and archers occupied the transports, and each transport was towed by the strength and swiftness of a galley. The six divisions traversed the Bosphorus without encountering an enemy or an obstacle; to land the foremost was the wish, to conquer or die was the resolution, of every division and of every soldier. Jealous of the pre-eminence of danger, the knights in their heavy armour leaped into the sea when it rose as high as their girdle; the serjeants and archers were animated by their valour; and the squires, letting down the drawbridges of the palanders, led the horses to the shore. Before the squadrons could mount, and form, and couch their lances, the seventy thousand Greeks had vanished from their sight; the timid Alexius gave the example to his troops, and it was only by the plunder of his rich pavilions that the Latins were informed that they had fought against an emperor. In the first consternation of the flying enemy, they resolved, by a double attack, to open the entrance of the harbour. The tower of Galata, in the suburb of Pera, was attacked and stormed by the French, while the Venetians assumed the more difficult task of forcing the boom or chain that was stretched from that tower to the Byzantine shore. After some fruitless attempts their intrepid perseverance prevailed; twenty ships of war, the relics of the Grecian navy, were either sunk or taken; the enormous and massy links of iron were cut asunder by the shears or broken by the weight of the galleys; and the Venetian fleet, safe and triumphant, rode at anchor in the port of Constantinople. By these daring achievements a remnant of twenty thousand Latins solicited the licence of besieging a capital which contained above four hundred thousand inhabitants, able, though not willing, to bear arms in the defence of their country. Such an account would indeed suppose a population of near two millions: but whatever abatement may be required in the numbers of the Greeks, the *belief* of those numbers will equally exalt the fearless spirit of their assailants.

THE CONQUEST OF CONSTANTINOPLE BY THE LATINS

In the choice of the attack the French and Venetians were divided by their habits of life and warfare. The former affirmed with truth that Constantinople was most accessible on the side of the sea and the harbour. The latter might assert with honour that they had long enough trusted their lives and fortunes to a frail bark and a precarious element, and loudly demanded a trial of knighthood, a firm ground, and a close onset, either on foot or horseback. After a prudent compromise of employing the two nations by sea and land in the service best suited to their character, the fleet covering the army, they both proceeded from the entrance to the extremity of the harbour: the stone bridge of the river was hastily repaired; and the six battles of the French formed their encampment against the front of the capital, the basis of the triangle which runs about four miles from the port to the Propontis. On the edge of a broad ditch, at the foot of a lofty rampart, they had leisure to contemplate the difficulties of their enterprise. The gates to the right and left of their narrow camp poured forth frequent sallies of cavalry and light infantry, which cut off their stragglers, swept the country of provisions, sounded the alarm five or six times in the course of each day, and compelled them to plant a palisade and sink an entrenchment for their immediate safety. In the supplies and convoys the Venetians had been too sparing, or the Franks too voracious: the usual complaints of hunger and scarcity were heard, and perhaps felt: their stock of flour would be exhausted in three weeks; and their disgust of salt meat tempted them to taste the flesh of their horses. The trembling usurper was supported by Theodore Lascaris, his son-in-law, a valiant youth, who aspired to save and to rule his country; the Greeks, regardless of that country, were awakened to the defence of their religion; but their firmest hope was in the strength and spirit of the Varangian guards, of the Danes and English, as they are named in the writers of the times. After ten days' incessant labour the ground was levelled, the ditch filled, the approaches of the besiegers were regularly made, and two hundred and fifty engines of assault exercised their various powers to clear the rampart, to batter the walls, and to sap the foundations. On the first appearance of a breach the scaling-ladders were applied: the numbers that defended the vantage-ground repulsed and oppressed the adventurous Latins: but they admired the resolution of fifteen knights and serjeants, who had gained the ascent, and maintained their perilous station till they were precipitated or made prisoners by the Imperial guards. On the side of the harbour the naval attack was more successfully conducted by the Venetians; and that industrious people employed every resource that was known and practised before the invention of gunpowder. A double line, three bow-shots in front, was formed by the galleys and ships; and the swift motion of the former was supported by the weight and loftiness of the latter, whose decks, and poops, and turret, were the platform of military engines, that discharged their shot over the heads of the first line. The soldiers, who leaped from the galleys on shore, immediately planted and ascended their scaling-ladders, while the large ships, advancing more slowly into the intervals, and lowering a drawbridge, opened a way through the air from their masts to the rampart. In the midst of the conflict the doge, a venerable and conspicuous form, stood aloft in complete armour on the prow of his galley. The great standard of St. Mark was displayed before him; his threats, promises, and exhortations urged the diligence of the rowers; his vessel was the first that struck; and Dandolo was the first warrior on the shore. The nations admired the magnanimity of the blind old man, without reflecting that his age and infirmities diminished the price of life and enhanced the value of immortal glory. On a sudden, by an invisible hand (for the standard-bearer was probably slain), the banner of the republic was fixed on the rampart: twenty-five towers were rapidly occupied; and, by the cruel expedient of fire, the Greeks were driven from the adjacent quarter. The doge had despatched the intelligence of his success, when he was checked by the danger of his confederates. Nobly declaring that he would rather die with the pilgrims than gain a victory by their destruction, Dandolo relinquished his advantage, recalled his troops and hastened to the scene of action. He found the six weary diminutive *battles* of the French encompassed by sixty squadrons of the Greek cavalry, the least of which was more numerous than the largest of their divisions. Shame and despair had provoked Alexius to the last effort of a general sally; but he was awed by the firm order and manly aspect of the Latins; and, after skirmishing at a distance, withdrew his troops in the close of the evening. The silence or tumult of the night exasperated his fears; and the timid usurper, collecting a treasure of ten thousand pounds of gold, basely deserted his wife, his people, and his fortune; threw himself into a bark; stole through the Bosphorus; and landed in shameful safety in an obscure harbour of Thrace. As soon as they were apprised of his flight, the Greek nobles sought pardon and peace in the dungeon where the blind Isaac expected each hour the visit of the executioner. Again saved and exalted by the vicissitudes of fortune, the captive in his Imperial robes was replaced on the throne, and surrounded with prostrate slaves, whose real terror and affected joy he was incapable of discerning. At the dawn of day hostilities were suspended, and the Latin chiefs were surprised by a message from the lawful and reigning emperor, who was impatient to embrace his son and to reward his generous deliverers.

But these generous deliverers were unwilling to release their hostage till they had obtained from his father the payment, or at least the promise, of their recompense. They chose four ambassadors, Matthew of Montmorency, our historian the marshal of Champagne, and two Venetians, to congratulate the emperor. The gates were thrown open on their approach, the streets on both sides were lined with the battle-axes of the Danish and English guard: the presence-chamber glittered with gold and jewels, the false substitutes of virtue and power: by the side of the blind Isaac his wife was seated, the sister of the king of Hungary: and, by her appearance, the noble matrons of Greece were drawn from their domestic retirement and mingled with the circle of senators and soldiers. The Latins, by the mouth of the marshal, spoke like men conscious of their merits, but who respected the work of their own hands; and the emperor clearly understood that his son's engagements with Venice and the pilgrims must be ratified without hesitation or delay. Withdrawing into a private chamber with the empress, a chamberlain, an interpreter, and the four ambassadors, the father of young Alexius inquired with some anxiety into the nature of his stipulations. The submission of the Eastern empire to the pope, the succour of the Holy Land, and a present contribution of two hundred thousand marks of silver.— "These conditions are weighty," was his prudent reply: "they are hard to accept, and difficult to perform. But no conditions can exceed the measure of your services and deserts." After this satisfactory assurance, the barons mounted on horseback and introduced the heir of Constantinople to the city and palace: his youth and marvellous adventures engaged every heart in his favour, and Alexius was solemnly crowned with his father in the dome of St. Sophia. In the first days of his reign, the people, already blessed with the restoration of plenty and peace, was delighted by the joyful catastrophe of the tragedy; and the discontent of the nobles, their regret, and their fears, were covered by the polished surface of pleasure and loyalty. The mixture of two discordant nations in the same capital might have been pregnant with mischief and danger; and the suburb of Galata, or Pera, was assigned for the quarters of the French and Venetians. But the liberty of trade and familiar intercourse was allowed between the friendly nations; and each day the pilgrims were tempted by devotion or curiosity to visit the churches and palaces of Constantinople. Their rude minds, insensible perhaps of the finer arts, were astonished by the magnificent scenery: and the poverty of their native towns enhanced the populousness and riches of the first metropolis of Christendom. Descending from his state, young Alexius was prompted by interest and gratitude to repeat his frequent and familiar visits to his Latin allies; and in the freedom of the table the gay petulance of the French sometimes forgot the emperor of the East. In their more serious conferences it was agreed that the re-union of the two churches must be the result of patience and time; but avarice was less tractable than zeal; and a large sum was instantly disbursed to appease the wants, and silence the importunity, of the crusaders. Alexius was alarmed by the approaching hour of their departure: their absence might have relieved him from the engagement which he was yet incapable of performing; but his friends would have left him, naked and alone, to the caprice and prejudices of a perfidious nation. He wished to bribe their stay, the delay of a year, by undertaking to defray their expense, and to satisfy, in their name, the freight of the Venetian vessels. The offer was agitated in the council of the barons; and, after a repetition of their debates and scruples, a majority of votes again acquiesced in the advice of the doge and the prayer of the young emperor. At the price of sixteen hundred pounds of gold, he prevailed on the marquis of Montferrat to lead him with an army round the provinces of Europe; to establish his authority, and pursue his uncle, while Constantinople was awed by the presence of Baldwin and his confederates of France and Flanders. The expedition was successful: the blind emperor exulted in the success of his arms, and listened to the predictions of his flatterers, that the same Providence which had raised him from the dungeon to the throne would heal his gout, restore his sight, and watch over the long prosperity of his reign. Yet the mind of the suspicious old man was tormented by the rising glories of his son; nor could his pride conceal from his envy, that, while his own name was pronounced in faint and reluctant acclamations, the royal youth was the theme of spontaneous and universal praise.

By the recent invasion the Greeks were awakened from a dream of nine centuries; from the vain presumption that the capital of the Roman empire was impregnable to foreign arms. The strangers of the West had violated the city, and bestowed the sceptre, of Constantine: their Imperial clients soon became as unpopular as themselves: the well-known vices of Isaac were rendered still more contemptible by his infirmities, and the young Alexius was hated as an apostate who had renounced the manners and religion of his country. His secret covenant with the Latins was divulged or suspected; the people, and especially the clergy, were devoutly attached to their faith and superstition; and every convent, and every shop, resounded with the danger of the church and the tyranny of the pope. An empty treasury could ill supply the demands of regal luxury and foreign extortion: the Greeks refused to avert, by a general tax, the impending evils of servitude and pillage; the oppression of the rich excited a more dangerous and personal resentment; and if the emperor melted the plate and despoiled the images of the sanctuary, he seemed to justify the complaints of heresy and sacrilege. During the absence of marquis Boniface and his Imperial pupil, Constantinople was visited with a calamity which might be justly imputed to the zeal and indiscretion of the Flemish pilgrims. In one of their visits to the city they were scandalised by the aspect of a mosch or synagogue, in which one God was worshipped, without a partner or a son. Their effectual mode of controversy was to attack the infidels with the sword, and their habitation with fire: but the infidels, and some Christian neighbours, presumed to defend their lives and properties; and the flames which bigotry had kindled consumed the most orthodox and innocent structures. During eight days and nights the conflagration spread above a league in front, from the harbour to the Propontis, over the thickest and most populous regions of the city. It is not easy to count the stately churches and palaces that were reduced to a smoking ruin, to value the merchandise that perished in the trading streets, or to number the families that were involved in the common destruction. By this outrage, which the doge and the barons in vain affected to disclaim, the name of the Latins became still more unpopular; and the colony of that nation, above fifteen thousand persons, consulted their safety in a hasty retreat from the city to the protection of their standard in the suburb of Pera. The emperor returned in triumph; but the firmest and most dexterous policy would have been insufficient to steer him through the tempest which overwhelmed the person and government of that unhappy youth. His own inclination, and his father's advice, attached him to his benefactors; but Alexius hesitated between gratitude and patriotism, between the fear of his subjects and of his allies. By his feeble and fluctuating conduct he lost the esteem and confidence of both; and, while he invited the marquis of Montferrat to occupy the palace, he suffered the nobles to conspire, and the people to arm, for the deliverance of their country. Regardless of his painful situation, the Latin chiefs repeated their demands, resented his delays, suspected his intentions, and exacted a decisive answer of peace or war. The haughty summons was delivered by three French knights and three Venetian deputies, who girded their swords, mounted their horses, pierced through the angry multitude, and entered, with a fearless countenance, the palace and presence of the Greek emperor. In a peremptory tone they recapitulated their services and his engagements; and boldly declared that, unless their just claims were fully and immediately satisfied, they should no longer hold him either as a sovereign or a friend. After this defiance, the first that had ever wounded an Imperial ear, they departed without betraying any symptoms of fear; but their escape from a servile palace and a furious city astonished the ambassadors themselves; and their return to the camp was the signal of mutual hostility.

Among the Greeks all authority and wisdom were overborne by the impetuous multitude, who mistook their rage for valour, their numbers for strength, and their fanaticism for the support and inspiration of Heaven. In the eyes of both nations Alexius was false and contemptible: the base and spurious race of the Angeli was rejected with clamorous disdain; and the people of Constantinople encompassed the senate to demand at their hands a more worthy emperor. To every senator, conspicuous by his birth or dignity, they successively presented the purple: by each senator the deadly garment was repulsed: the contest lasted three days; and we may learn from the historian Nicetas, one of the

members of the assembly, that fear and weakness were the guardians of
their loyalty. A phantom, who vanished in oblivion, was forcibly proclaimed by the crowd: but the author of the tumult, and the leader of
the war, was a prince of the house of Ducas; and his common appellation
of Alexius must be discriminated by the epithet of Mourzoufle, which in
the vulgar idiom expressed the close junction of his black and shaggy
eyebrows. At once a patriot and a courtier, the perfidious Mourzoufle,
who was not destitute of cunning and courage, opposed the Latins both
in speech and action, inflamed the passions and prejudices of the
Greeks, and insinuated himself into the favour and confidence of Alexius,
who trusted him with the office of great chamberlain, and tinged his
buskins with the colours of royalty. At the dead of night he rushed into
the bed-chamber with an affrighted aspect, exclaiming that the palace
was attacked by the people and betrayed by the guards. Starting from
his couch, the unsuspecting prince threw himself into the arms of his
enemy, who had contrived his escape by a private staircase. But that
staircase terminated in a prison: Alexius was seized, stripped, and
loaded with chains; and, after tasting some days the bitterness of death,
he was poisoned, or strangled, or beaten with clubs, at the command,
and in the presence, of the tyrant. The emperor Isaac Angelus soon
followed his son to the grave; and Mourzoufle, perhaps, might spare the
superfluous crime of hastening the extinction of impotence and blindness.

THE PILLAGE OF CONSTANTINOPLE

The death of the emperors, and the usurpation of Mourzoufle, had
changed the nature of the quarrel. It was no longer the disagreement of
allies who overvalued their services, or neglected their obligations: the
French and Venetians forgot their complaints against Alexius, dropped a
tear on the untimely fate of their companion, and swore revenge against
the perfidious nation who had crowned his assassin. Yet the prudent
doge was still inclined to negociate: he asked as a debt, a subsidy, or a
fine, fifty thousand pounds of gold, about two millions sterling; nor
would the conference have been abruptly broken if the zeal, or policy, of
Mourzoufle had not refused to sacrifice the Greek church to the safety
of the state. Amidst the invectives of his foreign and domestic enemies,
we may discern that he was not unworthy of the character which he had
assumed, of the public champion: the second siege of Constantinople
was far more laborious than the first; the treasury was replenished, and
discipline was restored, by a severe inquisition into the abuses of the
former reign; and Mourzoufle, an iron mace in his hand, visiting the
posts, and affecting the port and aspect of a warrior, was an object of
terror to his soldiers, at least, and to his kinsmen. Before and after the
death of Alexius, the Greeks made two vigorous and well-conducted
attempts to burn the navy in the harbour; but the skill and courage of

the Venetians repulsed the fire-ships; and the vagrant flames wasted themselves without injury in the sea. In a nocturnal sally the Greek emperor was vanquished by Henry, brother of the count of Flanders: the advantages of number and surprise aggravated the shame of his defeat: his buckler was found on the field of battle; and the Imperial standard, a divine image of the Virgin, was presented, as a trophy and a relic, to the Cistercian monks, the disciples of St. Bernard. Near three months, without excepting the holy season of Lent, were consumed in skirmishes and preparations, before the Latins were ready or resolved for a general assault. The land fortifications had been found impregnable; and the Venetian pilots represented, that, on the shore of the Propontis, the anchorage was unsafe, and the ships must be driven by the current far away to the straits of the Hellespont; a prospect not unpleasing to the reluctant pilgrims, who sought every opportunity of breaking the army. From the harbour, therefore, the assault was determined by the assailants and expected by the besieged; and the emperor had placed his scarlet pavilions on a neighbouring height, to direct and animate the efforts of his troops. A fearless spectator, whose mind could entertain the ideas of pomp and pleasure, might have admired the long array of two embattled armies, which extended above half a league, the one on the ships and galleys, the other on the walls and towers raised above the ordinary level by several stages of wooden turrets. Their first fury was spent in the discharge of darts, stones, and fire, from the engines; but the water was deep; the French were bold; the Venetians were skilful; they approached the walls; and a desperate conflict of swords, spears, and battle-axes, was fought on the trembling bridges that grappled the floating to the stable batteries. In more than a hundred places the assault was urged and the defence was sustained; till the superiority of ground and numbers finally prevailed, and the Latin trumpets sounded a retreat. On the ensuing days the attack was renewed with equal vigour and a similar event; and, in the night, the doge and the barons held a council, apprehensive only for the public danger: not a voice pronounced the words of escape or treaty; and each warrior, according to his temper, embraced the hope of victory or the assurance of a glorious death. By the experience of the former siege the Greeks were instructed, but the Latins were animated; and the knowledge that Constantinople *might* be taken was of more avail than the local precautions which that knowledge had inspired for its defence. In the third assault two ships were linked together to double their strength; a strong north wind drove them on the shore; the bishops of Troyes and Soissons led the van; and the auspicious names of the *Pilgrim* and the *Paradise* resounded along the line. The episcopal banners were displayed on the walls; a hundred marks of silver had been promised to the first adventurers; and if their reward was intercepted by death, their names have been immortalised by fame. Four towers were scaled; three gates were burst open; and the French knights, who might tremble on the waves, felt themselves invincible on horseback on the solid ground. Shall I relate that the thousands who guarded the emperor's person fled on the approach, and before the lance, of a single warrior? Their ignominious flight is attested by their countryman Nicetas: an army of phantoms marched with the French hero, and he was magnified to a giant in the eyes of the Greeks. While the fugitives deserted their posts and cast away their arms, the Latins entered the city under the banners of their leaders: the streets and gates opened for their passage; and either design or accident kindled a third conflagration, which consumed in a few hours the measure of three of the largest cities of France. In the close of evening the barons checked their troops and fortified their stations: they were awed by the extent and populousness of the capital, which might yet require the labour of a month, if the churches and palaces were conscious of their internal strength. But in the morning a suppliant procession, with crosses and images, announced the submission of the Greeks and deprecated the wrath of the conquerors: the usurper escaped through the golden gate: the palaces of Blachernæ and Boucoleon were occupied by the count of Flanders and the marquis of Montferrat; and the empire, which still bore the name of Constantine and the title of Roman, was subverted by the arms of the Latin pilgrims.

Constantinople had been taken by storm; and no restraints except those of religion and humanity were imposed on the conquerors by the laws of war. Boniface, marquis of Montferrat, still acted as their general; and the Greeks, who revered his name as that of their future sovereign, were heard to exclaim in a lamentable tone, "Holy marquis-king, have mercy upon us!" His prudence or compassion opened the gates of the city to the fugitives, and he exhorted the soldiers of the cross to spare the lives of their fellow-Christians. The streams of blood that flow down the pages of Nicetas may be reduced to the slaughter of two thousand of his unresisting countrymen; and the greater part was massacred, not by the strangers, but by the Latins who had been driven from the city, and who exercised the revenge of a triumphant faction. Yet of these exiles, some were less mindful of injuries than of benefits; and Nicetas himself was indebted for his safety to the generosity of a Venetian merchant. Pope Innocent the Third accuses the pilgrims of respecting, in their lust, neither age, nor sex, nor religious profession; and bitterly laments that the deeds of darkness, fornication, adultery, and incest, were perpetrated in open day; and that noble matrons and holy nuns were polluted by the grooms and peasants of the Catholic camp. It is indeed probable that the licence of victory prompted and covered a multitude of sins: but it is certain that the capital of the East contained a stock of venal or willing beauty sufficient to satiate the desires of twenty thousand pilgrims, and female prisoners were no longer subject to the right or abuse of domestic slavery. The marquis of Montferrat was the patron of discipline and decency: the count of Flanders was the mirror of chastity: they had forbidden, under pain of death, the rape of married women, or virgins, or nuns; and the proclamation was sometimes invoked by the vanquished and respected by the victors. Their cruelty and lust were moderated by the authority of the chiefs and feelings of the soldiers; for we are no longer describing an irruption of the northern savages; and however ferocious they might still appear, time, policy, and religion had civilised the manners of the French, and still more of the Italians. But a free scope was allowed to their avarice, which was glutted, even in the holy week, by the pillage of Constantinople. The right of victory, unshackled by any promise or treaty, had confiscated the public and private wealth of the Greeks; and every hand, according to its size and strength, might lawfully execute the sentence and seize the forfeiture. A portable and universal standard of exchange was found in the coined and uncoined metals of gold and silver, which each captor, at home or abroad, might convert into the possessions most suitable to his temper and situation. Of the treasures which trade and luxury had accumulated, the silks, velvets, furs, the gems, spices, and rich moveables, were the most precious, as they could not be procured for money in the ruder countries of Europe. An order of rapine was instituted; nor was the share of each individual abandoned to industry or chance. Under the tremendous penalties of perjury—excommunication and death—the Latins were bound to deliver their plunder into the common stock: three churches were selected for the deposit and distribution of the spoil: a single share was allotted to a foot soldier, two for a serjeant on horseback, four to a knight, and larger proportions according to the rank and merit of the barons and princes. For violatint this sacred engagement, a knight belonging to the count of St. Paul was hanged with his shield and coat of arms round his neck: his example might render similar offenders more artful and discreet, but avarice was more powerful than fear, and it is generally believed that the secret far exceeded the acknowledged plunder. Yet the magnitude of the prize surpassed the largest scale of experience or expectation. After the whole had been equally divided between the French and Venetians, fifty thousand marks were deducted to satisfy the debts of the former and the demands of the latter. The residue of the French amounted to four hundred thousand marks of silver, about eight hundred thousand pounds sterling; nor can I better appreciate the value of that sum in the public and private transactions of the age than by defining it as seven times the annual revenue of the kingdom of England.

In this great revolution we enjoy the singular felicity of comparing the narratives of Villehardouin and Nicetas, the opposite feelings of the marshal of Champagne and the Byzantine senator. At the first view it should seem that the wealth of Constantinople was only transferred from one nation to another, and that the loss and sorrow of the Greeks is exactly balanced by the joy and advantage of the Latins. But in the miserable account of war the gain is never equivalent to the loss, the pleasure to the pain; the smiles of the Latins were transient and fallacious; the Greeks for ever wept over the ruins of their country, and their real calamities were aggravated by sacrilege and mockery. What benefits accrued to the conquerors from the three fires which annihilated so vast a portion of the buildings and riches of the city? What a stock of such things as could neither be used nor transported was maliciously or wantonly destroyed! How much treasure was idly wasted in gaming, debauchery, and riot! And what precious objects were bartered for a vile price by the impatience or ignorance of the soldiers, whose reward was stolen by the base industry of the last of the Greeks! These alone who had nothing to lose might derive some profit from the revolution; but the misery of the upper ranks of society is strongly painted in the personal adventures of Nicetas himself. His stately palace had been reduced to ashes in the second conflagration; and the senator, with his family and friends, found an obscure shelter in another house which he possessed near the church of St. Sophia. It was the door of this mean habitation that his friend the Venetian merchant guarded, in the disguise of a soldier, till Nicetas could save by a precipitate flight the relics of his fortune and the chastity of his daughter. In a cold wintry season these fugitives, nursed in the lap of prosperity, departed on foot; his wife was with child; the desertion of their slaves compelled them to carry their baggage on their own shoulders; and their women, whom they placed in the centre, were exhorted to conceal their beauty with dirt, instead of adorning it with paint and jewels. Every step was exposed to insult and danger: the threats of the strangers were less painful than the taunts of the plebeians, with whom they were now levelled; nor did the exiles breathe in safety till their mournful pilgrimage was concluded at Selymbria, above forty miles from the capital. On the way they overtook the patriarch, without attendance and almost without apparel, riding on an ass, and reduced to a state of apostolical poverty, which, had it been voluntary, might perhaps have been meritorious. In the mean while his desolate churches were profaned by the licentiousness and party zeal of the Latins. After stripping the gems and pearls, they converted the chalices into drinking-cups; their tables, on which they gamed and feasted, were covered with the pictures of Christ and the saints; and they trampled under foot the most venerable objects of the Christian worship. In the cathedral of St. Sophia the ample veil of the sanctuary was rent asunder for the sake of the golden fringe; and the altar, a monument of art and riches, was broken in pieces and shared among the captors. Their mules and horses were laden with the wrought silver and gilt carvings which they tore down from the doors and pulpit;

and if the beasts stumbled under the burden, they were stabbed by their impatient drivers, and the holy pavement streamed with their impure blood. A prostitute was seated on the throne of the patriarch; and that daughter of Belial, as she is styled, sung and danced in the church to ridicule the hymns and processions of the Orientals. Nor were the repositories of the royal dead secure from violation: in the church of the Apostles the tombs of the emperors were rifled; and it is said that after six centuries the corpse of Justinian was found without any signs of decay or putrefaction. In the streets the French and Flemings clothed themselves and their horses in painted robes and flowing head-dresses of linen; and the coarse intemperance of their feasts insulted the splendid sobriety of the East. To expose the arms of a people of scribes and scholars, they affected to display a pen, an inkhorn, and a sheet of paper, without discerning that the instruments of science and valour were *alike* feeble and useless in the hands of the modern Greeks.

Their reputation and their language encouraged them, however, to despise the ignorance and to overlook the progress of the Latins. In the love of the arts the national difference was still more obvious and real; the Greeks preserved with reverence the works of their ancestors, which they could not imitate; and, in the destruction of the statues of Constantinople, we are provoked to join in the complaints and invectives of the Byzantine historian. We have seen how the rising city was adorned by the vanity and despotism of the Imperial founder: in the ruins of paganism some gods and heroes were saved from the axe of superstition; and the forum and hippodrome were dignified with the relics of a better age. Several of these are described by Nicetas in a florid and affected style; and from his descriptions I shall select some interesting particulars. 1. The victorious charioteers were cast in bronze, at their own, or the public, charge, and fitly placed in the hippodrome: they stood aloft in their chariots wheeling round the goal: the spectators could admire their attitude and judge of the resemblance; and of these figures, the most perfect might have been transported from the Olympic stadium. 2. The sphinx, river-horse, and crocodile, denote the climate and manufacture of Egypt and the spoils of that ancient province. 3. The she-wolf suckling Romulus and Remus, a subject alike pleasing to the *old* and the *new* Romans, but which could rarely be treated before the decline of the Greek sculpture. 4. An eagle holding and tearing a serpent in his talons—a domestic monument of the Byzantines, which they ascribed, not to a human artist, but to the magic power of the philosopher Apollonius, who, by this talisman, delivered the city from such venomous reptiles. 5. An ass and his driver, which were erected by Augustus in his colony of Nicopolis, to commemorate a verbal omen of the victory of Actium. 6. An equestrian statue, which passed in the vulgar opinion for Joshua, the Jewish conqueror, stretching out his hand to stop the course of the descending sun. A more classical tradition recognised the figures of Bellerophon and Pegasus; and the free attitude of the steed seemed to mark that he trod on air rather than on the earth. 7. A square and lofty obelisk of brass; the sides were embossed with a variety of picturesque and rural scenes: birds singing, rustics labouring or playing on their pipes, sheep bleating, lambs skipping, the sea, and a scene of fish and fishing, little naked Cupids laughing, playing, and pelting each other with apples, and on the summit a female figure turning with the slightest breath, and thence denominated *the wind's attendant*. 8. The Phrygian shepherd presenting to Venus the prize of beauty, the apple of discord. 9. The incomparable statue of Helen, which is delineated by Nicetas in the words of admiration and love: her well-turned feet, snowy arms, rosy lips, bewitching smiles, swimming eyes, arched eyebrows, the harmony of her shape, the lightness of her drapery, and her flowing locks that waved in the wind—a beauty that might have moved her barbarian destroyers to pity and remorse. 10. The manly, or divine, form of Hercules, as he was restored to life by the master-hand of Lysippus, of such magnitude that his thumb was equal to the waist, his leg to the stature, of a common man: his chest ample, his shoulders broad, his limbs strong and muscular, his hair curled, his aspect commanding. Without his bow, or quiver, or club, his lion's skin carelessly thrown over him, he was seated on an osier basket, his right leg and arm stretched to the utmost, his left knee bent and supporting his elbow, his head reclining on his left hand, his countenance indignant and pensive. 11. A colossal statue of Juno, which had once adorned her temple of Samos; the enormous head by four yoke of oxen was laboriously drawn to the palace. 12. Another colossus, of Pallas or Minerva, thirty feet in height, and representing with admirable spirit the attributes and character of the martial maid. Before we accuse the Latins, it is just to remark that this Pallas was destroyed after the first siege by the fear and superstition of the Greeks themselves. The other statues of brass which I have enumerated were broken and melted by the unfeeling avarice of the crusaders: the cost and labour were consumed in a moment; the soul of genius evaporated in smoke, and the remnant of base metal was coined into money for the payment of the troops. Bronze is not the most durable of monuments: from the marble forms of Phidias and Praxiteles the Latins might turn aside with stupid contempt; but unless they were crushed by some accidental injury, those useless stones stood secure on their pedestals. The most enlightened of the strangers, above the gross and sensual pursuits of their countrymen, more piously exercised the right of conquest in the search and seizure of the relics of the saints. Immense was the supply of heads and bones, crosses and images, that were scattered by this revolution over the churches of Europe; and such was the increase of pilgrimage and oblation, that no branch, perhaps, of more lucrative plunder was imported from the East. Of the writings of antiquity many that still existed in the twelfth century are now lost. But the pilgrims were not solicitous to save or transport the volumes of an unknown tongue: the perishable substance of paper or parchment can only be preserved by the multiplicity of copies; the literature of the Greeks had almost centred in the metropolis; and, without computing the extent of our loss, we may drop a tear over the libraries that have perished in the triple fire of Constantinople.

Chapter 61

BALDWIN II AND THE HOLY CROWN OF THORNS. RECOVERY OF CONSTANTINOPLE BY THE GREEKS. GENERAL CONSEQUENCES OF THE CRUSADES

The capture of Constantinople by the Latins in 1204 was followed by the establishment there of the so called Latin Emperors, Baldwin I and his four successors. At the same time Greek claimants to the empire were established at Nicæa and Trebizond. The rule of the Latin Emperors was incompetent and disastrous, and the last of them, Baldwin II, made a public appeal for help to the West.

BALDWIN II AND THE HOLY CROWN OF THORNS

IT was only in the age of chivalry that valour could ascend from a private station to the thrones of Jerusalem and Constantinople. The titular kingdom of Jerusalem had devolved to Mary, the daughter of Isabella and Conrad of Montferrat, and the grand-daughter of Almeric or Amaury. She was given to John of Brienne, of a noble family in Champagne, by the public voice, and the judgment of Philip Augustus, who named him as the most worthy champion of the Holy Land. In the fifth crusade he led an hundred thousand Latins to the conquest of Egypt: by him the siege of Damietta was achieved; and the subsequent failure was justly ascribed to the pride and avarice of the legate. After the marriage of his daughter with Frederic the Second he was provoked by the emperor's ingratitude to accept the command of the army of the church; and though advanced in life, and despoiled of royalty, the sword and spirit of John of Brienne were still ready for the service of Christendom. In the seven years of his brother's reign, Baldwin of Courtenay had not emerged from a state of childhood, and the barons of Romania felt the strong necessity of placing the sceptre in the hands of a man and an hero. The veteran king of Jerusalem might have disdained the name and office of regent; they agreed to invest him for his life with the title and prerogatives of emperor, on the sole condition that Baldwin should marry his second daughter, and succeed at a mature age to the throne of Constantinople. The expectation, both of the Greeks and Latins, was kindled by the renown, the choice, and the presence of John of Brienne; and they admired his martial aspect, his green and vigorous age of more than fourscore years, and his size and stature, which surpassed the common measure of mankind. But avarice, and the love of ease, appear to have chilled the ardour of enterprise: his troops were disbanded, and two years rolled away without action or honour, till he was awakened by the dangerous alliance of Vataces, emperor of Nice, and of Azan king of Bulgaria. They besieged Constantinople by sea and land, with an army of one hundred thousand men, and a fleet of three hundred ships of war; while the entire force of the Latin emperor was reduced to one hundred and sixty knights, and a small addition of serjeants and archers. I tremble to relate, that, instead of defending the city, the hero made a sally at the head of his cavalry; and that, of forty-eight squadrons of the enemy, no more than three escaped from the edge of his invincible sword. Fired by his example, the infantry and the citizens boarded the vessels that anchored close to the walls; and twenty-five were dragged in triumph into the harbour of Constantinople. At the summons of the emperor, the vassals and allies armed in her defence; broke through every obstacle that opposed their passage; and, in the succeeding year, obtained a second victory over the same enemies. By the rude poets of the age John of Brienne is compared to Hector, Roland, and Judas Maccabæus: but their credit, and his glory, receives some abatement from the silence of the Greeks. The empire was soon deprived of the last of her champions; and the dying monarch was ambitious to enter paradise in the habit of a Franciscan friar.

In the double victory of John of Brienne I cannot discover the name or exploits of his pupil Baldwin, who had attained the age of military service, and who succeeded to the imperial dignity on the decease of his adoptive father. The royal youth was employed on a commission more suitable to his temper; he was sent to visit the Western courts, of the pope more especially, and of the king of France; to excite their pity by the view of his innocence and distress; and to obtain some supplies of men or money for the relief of the sinking empire. He thrice repeated these mendicant visits, in which he seemed to prolong his stay, and postpone his return; of the five-and-twenty years of his reign, a greater number were spent abroad than at home; and in no place did the emperor deem himself less free and secure than in his native country and his capital. On some public occasions, his vanity might be soothed by the title of Augustus, and by the honours of the purple; and at the general council of Lyons, when Frederic the Second was excommunicated and deposed, his Oriental colleague was enthroned on the right hand of the pope. But how often was the exile, the vagrant, the Imperial beggar, humbled with scorn, insulted with pity, and degraded in his own eyes and those of the nations! In his first visit to England he was stopped at Dover by a severe reprimand, that he should presume, without leave, to enter an independent kingdom. After some delay, Baldwin, however, was permitted to pursue his journey, was entertained with cold civility, and thankfully departed with a present of seven hundred marks. From the avarice of Rome he could only obtain the proclamation of a crusade, and a treasure of indulgences: a coin whose currency was depreciated by too frequent and indiscriminate abuse. His birth and misfortunes recommended him to the generosity of his cousin Louis the Ninth; but the martial zeal of the saint was diverted from Constantinople to Egypt and Palestine; and the public and private poverty of Baldwin was alleviated, for a moment, by the alienation of the marquisate of Namur and the lordship of Courtenay, the last remains of his inheritance. By such shameful or ruinous expedients he once more returned to Romania, with an army of thirty thousand soldiers, whose numbers were doubled in the apprehension of the Greeks. His first despatches to France and England announced his victories and his hopes: he had reduced the country round the capital to the distance of three days' journey; and if he succeeded against an important, though nameless, city (most probably Chiorli), the frontier would be safe and the passage accessible. But these expectations (if Baldwin was sincere) quickly vanished like a dream: the troops and treasures of France melted away in his unskilful hands: and the throne of the Latin emperor was protected by a dishonourable alliance with the Turks and Comans. To secure the former, he consented to bestow his niece on the unbelieving sultan of Cogni; to please the latter, he complied with their pagan rites; a dog was sacrificed between the two armies; and the contracting parties tasted each other's blood, as a pledge of their fidelity. In the palace, or prison, of Constantinople, the successor of Augustus demolished the vacant houses for winter-fuel, and stripped the lead from the churches for the daily expense of his family. Some usurious loans were dealt with a scanty hand by the merchants of Italy; and Philip, his son and heir, was pawned at Venice as the security for a debt. Thirst, hunger, and nakedness are positive evils: but wealth is relative; and a prince, who would be rich in a private station, may be exposed by the increase of his wants to all the anxiety and bitterness of poverty.

But in this abject distress the emperor and empire were still possessed of an ideal treasure, which drew its fantastic value from the superstition of the Christian world. The merit of the true cross was somewhat impaired by its frequent division; and a long captivity among the infidels might shed some suspicion on the fragments that were produced in the East and West. But another relic of the Passion was preserved in the Imperial chapel of Constantinople; and the crown of thorns which had been placed on the head of Christ was equally precious and authentic. It had formerly been the practice of the Egyptian debtors to deposit, as a security, the mummies of their parents; and both their honour and religion were bound for the redemption of the pledge. In the same manner, and in the absence of the emperor, the barons of Romania borrowed the sum of thirteen thousand one hundred and thirty-four pieces of gold on the credit of the holy crown: they failed in the performance of their contract; and a rich Venetian, Nicholas Querini, undertook to satisfy their impatient creditors, on condition that the relic should be lodged at Venice, to become his absolute property if it were not redeemed within a short and definite term. The barons apprised their sovereign of the hard treaty and impending loss; and as the empire could not afford a ransom of seven thousand pounds sterling, Baldwin was anxious to snatch the prize from the Venetians, and to vest it with more honour and emolument in the hands of the most Christian king. Yet the negociation was attended with some delicacy. In the purchase of relics the saint would have started at the guilt of simony; but if the mode of expression were changed, he might lawfully repay the debt, accept the gift, and acknowledge the obligation. His ambassadors, two Dominicans, were despatched to Venice to redeem and receive the holy crown, which had escaped the dangers of the sea and the galleys of Vataces. On opening a wooden box they recognised the seals of the doge and barons, which were applied on a shrine of silver; and within this shrine the monument of the Passion was enclosed in a golden vase. The reluctant Venetians yielded to justice and power; the emperor Frederic granted a free and honourable passage; the court of France advanced as far as Troyes in Champagne to meet with devotion this inestimable relic: it was borne in triumph through Paris by the king himself, barefoot, and in his shirt; and a free gift of ten thousand marks of silver reconciled Baldwin to his loss. The success of this transaction tempted the Latin emperor to offer with the same generosity the remaining furniture of his chapel; a large and authentic portion of the true cross; the baby-linen of the Son of God; the lance, the sponge, and the chain of his Passion; the rod of Moses; and part of the skull of St. John the Baptist. For the reception of these spiritual treasures twenty thousand marks were expended by St. Louis on a stately foundation, the holy chapel of Paris, on which the muse of Boileau has bestowed a comic immortality. The truth of such remote and ancient relics, which cannot be proved by any human testimony, must be admitted by those who believe in the miracles which they have performed. About the middle of the last age, an inveterate ulcer was touched and cured by an holy prickle of the holy crown: the prodigy is attested by the most pious and enlightened Christians of France; nor will the fact be easily disproved, except by those who are armed with a general antidote against religious credulity.

RECOVERY OF CONSTANTINOPLE BY THE GREEKS

The Latins of Constantinople were on all sides encompassed and pressed: their sole hope, the last delay of their ruin, was in the division of their Greek and Bulgarian enemies; and of this hope they were deprived by the superior arms and policy of Vataces, emperor of Nice.

From the Propontis to the rocky coast of Pamphylia, Asia was peaceful and prosperous under his reign; and the events of every campaign extended his influence in Europe. The strong cities of the hills of Macedonia and Thrace were rescued from the Bulgarians, and their kingdom was circumscribed by its present and proper limits along the southern banks of the Danube. The sole emperor of the Romans could no longer brook that a lord of Epirus, a Comnenian prince of the West, should presume to dispute or share the honours of the purple; and the humble Demetrius changed the colour of his buskins, and accepted with gratitude the appellation of despot. His own subjects were exasperated by his baseness and incapacity; they implored the protection of their supreme lord. After some resistance, the kingdom of Thessalonica was united to the empire of Nice; and Vataces reigned without a competitor from the Turkish borders to the Adriatic gulf. The princes of Europe revered his merit and power; and had he subscribed an orthodox creed, it should seem that the pope would have abandoned without reluctance the Latin throne of Constantinople. But the death of Vataces, the short and busy reign of Theodore his son, and the helpless infancy of his grandson John, suspended the restoration of the Greeks. In the next chapter I shall explain their domestic revolutions; in this place it will be sufficient to observe that the young prince was oppressed by the ambition of his guardian and colleague Michael Palæologus, who displayed the virtues and vices that belong to the founder of a new dynasty. The emperor Baldwin had flattered himself that he might recover some provinces or cities by an impotent negociation. His ambassadors were dismissed from Nice with mockery and contempt. At every place which they named Palæologus alleged some special reason which rendered it dear and valuable in his eyes: in the one he was born; in another he had been first promoted to military command; and in a third he had enjoyed, and hoped long to enjoy, the pleasures of the chase. "And what then do you propose to give us?" said the astonished deputies. "Nothing," replied the Greek; "not a foot of land. If your master be desirous of peace, let him pay me, as an annual tribute, the sum which he receives from the trade and customs of Constantinople. On these terms I may allow him to reign. If he refuses, it is war. I am not ignorant of the art of war, and I trust the event to God and my sword." An expedition against the despot of Epirus was the first prelude of his arms. If a victory was followed by a defeat, if the race of the Comneni or Angeli survived in those mountains his efforts and his reign, the captivity of Villehardouin prince of Achaia deprived the Latins of the most active and powerful vassal of their expiring monarchy. The republics of Venice and Genoa disputed, in the first of their naval wars, the command of the sea and the commerce of the East. Pride and interest attached the Venetians to the defence of Constantinople; their rivals were tempted to promote the designs of her enemies, and the alliance of the Genoese with the schismatic conqueror provoked the indignation of the Latin church.

Intent on his great object, the emperor Michael visited in person and strengthened the troops and fortifications of Thrace. The remains of the Latins were driven from their last possessions: he assaulted without success the suburb of Galata, and corresponded with a perfidious baron, who proved unwilling, or unable, to open the gates of the metropolis. The next spring his favourite general, Alexius Strategopulus, whom he had decorated with the title of Cæsar, passed the Hellespont with eight hundred horse and some infantry on a secret expedition. His instructions enjoined him to approach, to listen, to watch, but not to risk any doubtful or dangerous enterprise against the city. The adjacent territory between the Propontis and the Black Sea was cultivated by an hardy race of peasants and outlaws, exercised in arms, uncertain in their allegiance, but inclined by language, religion, and present advantage, to the party of the Greeks. They were styled the *volunteers*, and by their free service the army of Alexius, with the regulars of Thrace and the Coman auxiliaries, was augmented to the number of five-and-twenty thousand men. By the ardour of the volunteers, and by his own ambition, the Cæsar was stimulated to disobey the precise orders of his master, in the just confidence that success would plead his pardon and reward. The weakness of Constantinople and the distress and terror of the Latins were familiar to the observation of the volunteers; and they represented the present moment as the most propitious to surprise and conquest. A rash youth, the new governor of the Venetian colony, had sailed away with thirty galleys and the best of the French knights on a wild expedition to Daphnusia, a town on the Black Sea, at the distance of forty leagues, and the remaining Latins were without strength or suspicion. They were informed that Alexius had passed the Hellespont; but their apprehensions were lulled by the smallness of his original numbers, and their imprudence had not watched the subsequent increase of his army. If he left his main body to second and support his operations, he might advance unperceived in the night with a chosen detachment. While some applied scaling-ladders to the lowest part of the walls, they were secure of an old Greek who would introduce their companions through a subterraneous passage into his house; they could soon on the inside break an entrance through the golden gate, which had been long obstructed: and the conqueror would be in the heart of the city before the Latins were conscious of their danger. After some debate, the Cæsar resigned himself to the faith of the volunteers; they were trusty, bold, and successful; and, in describing the plan, I have already related the execution and success. But no sooner had Alexius passed the threshold of the golden gate than he trembled at his own rashness; he paused, he deliberated, till the desperate volunteers urged him forwards by the assurance that in retreat lay the greatest and most inevitable danger. Whilst the Cæsar kept his regulars in firm array, the Comans dispersed themselves on all sides; an alarm was sounded, and the threats of fire and pillage compelled the citizens to a decisive resolution. The Greeks of Constantinople remembered their native sovereigns; the Genoese merchants their recent alliance and Venetian foes; every quarter was in arms; and the air resounded with a general acclamation of "Long life and victory to Michael and John, the august emperors of the Romans!" Their rival, Baldwin, was awakened by the sound; but the most pressing danger could not prompt him to draw his sword in the defence of a city which he deserted perhaps with more pleasure than regret: he fled from the palace to the sea-shore, where he descried the welcome sails of the fleet returning from the vain and fruitless attempt on Daphnusia. Constantinople was irrecoverably lost; but the Latin emperor and the principal families embarked on board the Venetian galleys, and steered for the isle of Eubœa, and afterwards for Italy, where the royal fugitive was entertained by the pope and Sicilian king with a mixture of contempt and pity. From the loss of Constantinople to his death he consumed thirteen years soliciting the Catholic powers to join in his restoration: the lesson had been familiar to his youth; nor was his last exile more indigent or shameful than his three former pilgrimages to the courts of Europe. His son Philip was the heir of an ideal empire; and the pretensions of *his* daughter Catherine were transported by her marriage to Charles of Valois, the brother of Philip the Fair, king of France. The house of Courtenay was represented in the female line by successive alliances, till the title of emperor of Constantinople, too bulky and sonorous for a private name, modestly expired in silence and oblivion.

GENERAL CONSEQUENCES OF THE CRUSADES

After this narrative of the expeditions of the Latins to Palestine and Constantinople, I cannot dismiss the subject without revolving the general consequences on the countries that were the scene, and on the nations that were the actors, of these memorable crusades. As soon as the arms of the Franks were withdrawn, the impression, though not the memory, was erased in the Mahometan realms of Egypt and Syria. The faithful disciples of the prophet were never tempted by a profane desire to study the laws or language of the idolaters; nor did the simplicity of their primitive manners receive the slightest alteration from their intercourse in peace and war with the unknown strangers of the West. The Greeks, who thought themselves proud, but who were only vain, showed a disposition somewhat less inflexible. In the efforts for the recovery of their empire they emulated the valour, discipline, and tactics of their antagonists. The modern literature of the West they might justly despise; but its free spirit would instruct them in the rights of man; and some institutions of public and private life were adopted from the French.

The correspondence of Constantinople and Italy diffused the knowledge of the Latin tongue; and several of the fathers and classics were at length honoured with a Greek version. But the national and religious prejudices of the Orientals were inflamed by persecution; and the reign of the Latins confirmed the separation of the two churches.

If we compare, at the era of the crusades, the Latins of Europe with the Greeks and Arabians, their respective degrees of knowledge, industry, and art, our rude ancestors must be content with the third rank in the scale of nations. Their successive improvement and present superiority may be ascribed to a peculiar energy of character, to an active and imitative spirit, unknown to their more polished rivals, who at that time were in a stationary or retrograde state. With such a disposition the Latins should have derived the most early and essential benefits from a series of events which opened to their eyes the prospect of the world, and introduced them to a long and frequent intercourse with the more cultivated regions of the East. The first and most obvious progress was in trade and manufactures, in the arts which are strongly prompted by the thirst of wealth, the calls of necessity, and the gratification of the sense or vanity. Among the crowd of unthinking fanatics a captive or a pilgrim might sometimes observe the superior refinements of Cairo and Constantinople: the first importer of windmills was the benefactor of nations; and if such blessings are enjoyed without any grateful remembrance, history has condescended to notice the more apparent luxuries of silk and sugar, which were transported into Italy from Greece and Egypt. But the intellectual wants of the Latins were more slowly felt and supplied; the ardour of studious curiosity was awakened in Europe by different causes and more recent events; and, in the age of the crusades, they viewed with careless indifference the literature of the Greeks and Arabians. Some rudiments of mathematical and medicinal knowledge might be imparted in practice and in figures; necessity might produce some interpreters for the grosser business of merchants and soldiers; but the commerce of the Orientals had not diffused the study and knowledge of their languages in the schools of Europe. If a similar principle of religion repulsed the idiom of the Koran, it should have excited their patience and curiosity to understand the original text of the Gospel; and the same grammar would have unfolded the sense of Plato and the beauties of Homer. Yet, in a reign of sixty years, the Latins of Constantinople disdained the speech and learning of their subjects; and the manuscripts were the only treasures which the natives might enjoy without rapine or envy. Aristotle was indeed the oracle of the Western universities, but it was a barbarous Aristotle; and, instead of ascending to the fountain head, his Latin votaries humbly accepted a corrupt and remote version from the Jews and Moors of Andalusia. The principle of the crusades was a savage fanaticism; and the most important effects were analogous to the cause. Each pilgrim was ambitious to return with his sacred spoils, the relics of Greece and Palestine; and each relic was preceded and followed by a train of miracles and visions. The belief of the Catholics was corrupted by new legends, their practice by new superstitions; and the establishment of the inquisition, the mendicant orders of monks and friars, the last abuse of indulgences, and the final progress of idolatry, flowed from the baleful fountain of the holy war. The active spirit of the Latins preyed on the vitals of their reason and religion; and if the ninth and tenth centuries were the times of darkness, the thirteenth and fourteenth were the age of absurdity and fable.

In the profession of Christianity, in the cultivation of a fertile land, the northern conquerors of the Roman empire insensibly mingled with the provincials and rekindled the embers of the arts of antiquity. Their settlements about the age of Charlemagne had acquired some degree of order and stability, when they were overwhelmed by new swarms of invaders, the Normans, Saracens, and Hungarians, who replunged the western countries of Europe into their former state of anarchy and barbarism. About the eleventh century the second tempest had subsided by the expulsion or conversion of the enemies of Christendom: the tide of civilisation, which had so long ebbed, began to flow with a steady and accelerated course; and a fairer prospect was opened to the hopes and efforts of the rising generations. Great was the increase, and rapid the progress, during the two hundred years of the crusades; and some philosophers have applauded the propitious influence of these holy wars, which appear to me to have checked rather than forwarded the maturity of Europe.[1] The lives and labours of millions which were buried in the East would have been more profitably employed in the improvement of their native country: the accumulated stock of industry and wealth would have overflowed in navigation and trade; and the Latins would have been enriched and enlightened by a pure and friendly correspondence with the climates of the East. In one respect I can indeed perceive the accidental operation of the crusades, not so much in producing a benefit as in removing an evil. The larger portion of the inhabitants of Europe was chained to the soil, without freedom, or property, or knowledge; and the two orders of ecclesiastics and nobles, whose numbers were comparatively small, alone deserved the name of citizens and men. This oppressive system was supported by the arts of the clergy and the swords of the barons. The authority of the priests operated in the darker ages as a salutary antidote: they prevented the total extinction of letters, mitigated the fierceness of the times, sheltered the poor and defenceless, and preserved or revived the peace and order of civil society. But the independence, rapine, and discord of the feudal lords were un-

---

[1] On this interesting subject, the progress of society in Europe, a strong ray of philosophic light has broke from Scotland in our own times; and it is with private, as well as public regard, that I repeat the names of Hume, Robertson, and Adam Smith.

mixed with any semblance of good; and every hope of industry and improvement was crushed by the iron weight of the martial aristocracy. Among the causes that undermined that Gothic edifice, a conspicuous place must be allowed to the crusades. The estates of the barons were dissipated, and their race was often extinguished, in these costly and perilous expeditions. Their poverty extorted from their pride those charters of freedom which unlocked the fetters of the slave, secured the farm of the peasant and the shop of the artificer, and gradually restored a substance and a soul to the most numerous and useful part of the community. The conflagration which destroyed the tall and barren trees of the forest gave air and scope to the vegetation of the smaller and nutritive plants of the soil.

In A.D. 1261 the Greeks recovered Constantinople and enthroned Michael Palæologus, the first Emperor of what was to be the last Byzantine dynasty. In the second half of the 13th century the city was beset by Mogul invaders under the successors of Genghis Khan. As the Mogul power waned, the Ottoman Turks established themselves in Asia Minor and gained a footing in Europe. Gibbon describes these developments in the following three chapters, cc. 62–64.

THE END OF THE ROMAN EMPIRE

Chapter 65

SIEGE OF CONSTANTINOPLE BY AMURATH II. DISCIPLINE OF THE TURKS. INVENTION OF GUNPOWDER

In 1402 imminent danger from the Ottoman Turks was relieved by Timour (or Tamerlaine), who captured the Ottoman ruler Bajazet II. The Ottoman power, however, revived under Amurath II and the doom of Constantinople was certain.

SIEGE OF CONSTANTINOPLE BY AMURATH II

IN these conflicts the wisest Turks, and indeed the body of the nation, were strongly attached to the unity of the empire; and Romania and Anatolia, so often torn asunder by private ambition, were animated by a strong and invincible tendency of cohesion. Their efforts might have instructed the Christian powers; and had they occupied, with a confederate fleet, the straits of Gallipoli, the Ottomans, at least in Europe, must have been speedily annihilated. But the schism of the West, and the factions and wars of France and England, diverted the Latins from this generous enterprise: they enjoyed the present respite, without a thought of futurity; and were often tempted by a momentary interest to serve the common enemy of their religion. A colony of Genoese, which had been planted at Phocæa on the Ionian coast, was enriched by the lucrative monopoly of alum; and their tranquillity, under the Turkish empire, was secured by the annual payment of tribute. In the last civil war of the Ottomans, the Genoese governor, Adorno, a bold and ambitious youth, embraced the party of Amurath; and undertook, with seven stout galleys, to transport him from Asia to Europe. The sultan and five hundred guards embarked on board the admiral's ship; which was manned by eight hundred of the bravest Franks. His life and liberty were in their hands; nor can we, without reluctance, applaud the fidelity of Adorno, who, in the midst of the passage, knelt before him, and gratefully accepted a discharge of his arrears of tribute. They landed in sight of Mustapha and Gallipoli; two thousand Italians, armed with lances and battle-axes, attended Amurath to the conquest of Adrianople; and this venal service was soon repaid by the ruin of the commerce and colony of Phocæa.

If Timour had generously marched at the request, and to the relief, of the Greek emperor, he might be entitled to the praise and gratitude of the Christians. But a Musulman who carried into Georgia the sword of persecution, and respected the holy warfare of Bajazet, was not disposed to pity or succour the *idolaters* of Europe. The Tartar followed the impulse of ambition; and the deliverance of Constantinople was the accidental consequence. When Manuel abdicated the government, it was his prayer, rather than his hope, that the ruin of the church and state might be delayed beyond his unhappy days; and after his return from a western pilgrimage, he expected every hour the news of the sad catastrophe. On a sudden he was astonished and rejoiced by the intelligence of the retreat, the overthrow, and the captivity of the Ottoman. Manuel immediately sailed from Modon in the Morea; ascended the throne of Constantinople, and dismissed his blind competitor to an easy exile in the isle of Lesbos. The ambassadors of the son of Bajazet were soon introduced to his presence; but their pride was fallen, their tone was modest: they were awed by the just apprehension lest the Greeks should open to the Moguls the gates of Europe. Soliman saluted the emperor by the name of father; solicited at his hands the government or gift of Romania; and promised to deserve his favour by inviolable friendship, and the restitution of Thessalonica, with the most important places along the Strymon, the Propontis, and the Black Sea. The alliance of Soliman exposed the emperor to the enmity and revenge of Mousa: the Turks appeared in arms before the gates of Constantinople; but they were repulsed by sea and land; and unless the city was guarded by some foreign mercenaries, the Greeks must have wondered at their own triumph. But, instead of prolonging the division of the Ottoman powers, the policy or passion of Manuel was tempted to assist the most formidable of the sons of Bajazet. He concluded a treaty with Mahomet, whose progress was checked by the insuperable barrier of Gallipoli: the sultan and his troops were transported over the Bosphorus; he was hospitably entertained in the capital; and his successful sally was the first step to the conquest of Romania. The ruin was suspended by the prudence and moderation of the conqueror: he faithfully discharged his own obligations and those of Soliman; respected the laws of gratitude and peace; and left the emperor guardian of his two younger sons, in the vain hope of saving them from the jealous cruelty of their brother Amurath. But the execution of his last testament would have offended the national honour and religion; and the divan unanimously pronounced that the royal youths should never be abandoned to the custody and education of a Christian dog. On this refusal the Byzantine councils were divided: but the age and caution of Manuel yielded to the presumption of his son John; and they unsheathed a dangerous weapon of revenge, by dismissing the true or false Mustapha, who had long been detained as a captive and hostage, and for whose maintenance they received an annual pension of three hundred thousand aspers. At the door of his prison, Mustapha subscribed to every proposal; and the keys of Gallipoli, or rather of Europe, were stipulated as the price of his deliverance. But no sooner was he seated on the throne of Romania than he dismissed the Greek ambassadors with a smile of contempt, declaring, in a pious tone, that, at the day of judgment, he would rather answer for the violation of an oath, than for the surrender of a Musulman city into the hands of the infidels. The emperor was at once the enemy of the two rivals, from whom he had sustained, and to whom he had offered, an injury; and the victory of Amurath was followed, in the ensuing spring, by the siege of Constantinople.

The religious merit of subduing the city of the Cæsars attracted from Asia a crowd of volunteers, who aspired to the crown of martyrdom; their military ardour was inflamed by the promise of rich spoils and beautiful females; and the sultan's ambition was consecrated by the presence and prediction of Seid Bechar, a descendant of the prophet, who arrived in the camp, on a mule, with a venerable train of five hundred disciples. But he might blush, if a fanatic could blush, at the failure of his assurances. The strength of the walls resisted an army of two hundred thousand Turks: their assaults were repelled by the sallies of the Greeks and their foreign mercenaries; the old resources of defence were opposed to the new engines of attack; and the enthusiasm of the dervish, who was snatched to heaven in visionary converse with Mahomet, was answered by the credulity of the Christians, who *beheld* the Virgin Mary, in a violet garment, walking on the rampart and animating their courage. After a siege of two months Amurath was recalled to Boursa by a domestic revolt, which had been kindled by Greek treachery, and was soon extinguished by the death of a guiltless brother. While he led his Janizaries to new conquests in Europe and Asia, the Byzantine empire was indulged in a servile and precarious respite of thirty years. Manuel sank into the grave; and John Palæologus was permitted to reign, for an annual tribute of three hundred thousand aspers, and the dereliction of almost all that he held beyond the suburbs of Constantinople.

DISCIPLINE OF THE TURKS

In the establishment and restoration of the Turkish empire the first merit must doubtless be assigned to the personal qualities of the sultans; since, in human life, the most important scenes will depend on the character of a single actor. By some shades of wisdom and virtue they may be discriminated from each other; but, except in a single instance, a period of nine reigns, and two hundred and sixty-five years, is occupied, from the elevation of Othman to the death of Soliman, by a rare series of warlike and active princes, who impressed their subjects with obedience and their enemies with terror. Instead of the slothful luxury of the seraglio, the heirs of royalty were educated in the council and the field: from early youth they were entrusted by their fathers with the command of provinces and armies; and this manly institution, which was often productive of civil war, must have essentially contributed to the discipline and vigour of the monarchy. The Ottomans cannot style themselves, like the Arabian caliphs, the descendants or successors of the apostle of God; and the kindred which they claim with the Tartar khans of the house of Zingis appears to be founded in flattery rather than in truth. Their origin is obscure; but their sacred and indefeasible right, which no time can erase, and no violence can infringe, was soon and unalterably implanted in the minds of their subjects. A weak or vicious sultan may be deposed and strangled; but his inheritance devolves to an infant or an idiot: nor has the most daring rebel presumed to ascend the throne of his lawful sovereign. While the transient dynasties of Asia have been continually subverted by a crafty vizir in the palace or a victorious general in the camp, the Ottoman succession has been confirmed by the practice of five centuries, and is now incorporated with the vital principle of the Turkish nation.

To the spirit and constitution of that nation a strong and singular influence may however be ascribed. The primitive subjects of Othman were the four hundred families of wandering Turkmans who had followed his ancestors from the Oxus to the Sangar; and the plains of Anatolia are still covered with the white and black tents of their rustic brethren. But this original drop was dissolved in the mass of voluntary and vanquished subjects, who, under the name of Turks, are united by the common ties of religion, language, and manners. In the cities from Erzeroum to Belgrade, that national appellation is common to all the Moslems, the first and most honourable inhabitants; but they have abandoned, at least in Romania, the villages and the cultivation of the land to the Christian peasants. In the vigorous age of the Ottoman government the Turks were themselves excluded from all civil and military honours; and a servile class, an artificial people, was raised by the discipline of education to obey, to conquer, and to command. From the time of Orchan and the first Amurath the sultans were persuaded that a government of the sword must be renewed in each generation with new soldiers; and that such soldiers must be sought, not in effeminate Asia, but among the hardy and warlike natives of Europe. The provinces of Thrace, Macedonia, Albania, Bulgaria, and Servia became the perpetual seminary of the Turkish army; and when the royal fifth of the captives was diminished by conquest, an inhuman tax of the fifth child, or of every fifth year, was rigorously levied on the Christian families. At the age of twelve or fourteen years the most robust youths were torn from their parents; their names were enrolled in a book; and from that moment they were clothed, taught, and maintained for the public service. According to the promise of their appearance, they were selected for the royal schools of Boursa, Pera, and Adrianople, entrusted to the care of the bashaws, or dispersed in the houses of the Anatolian peasantry. It was the first care of their masters to instruct them in the Turkish language: their bodies were exercised by every labour that could fortify their strength; they learned to wrestle, to leap, to run, to shoot with the bow, and afterwards with the musket; till they were drafted into the chambers and companies of the Janizaries, and severely trained in the military or monastic discipline of the order. The youths most conspicuous for birth, talents, and beauty, were admitted into the inferior class of *Agiamoglans*, or the more liberal rank of *Ichoglans*, of whom the former were attached to the palace, and the latter to the person of the prince. In four successive schools, under the rod of the white eunuchs, the arts of horsemanship and of darting the javelin were their daily exercise, while those of a more studious cast applied themselves to the study of the Koran, and the knowledge of the Arabic and Persian tongues. As they advanced in seniority and merit, they were gradually dismissed to military, civil, and even ecclesiastical employments: the longer their stay, the higher was their expectation; till, at a mature period, they were admitted into the number of the forty agas, who stood before the sultan, and were promoted by his choice to the government of provinces and the first honours of the empire. Such a mode of institution was admirably adapted to the form and spirit of a despotic monarchy. The ministers and generals were, in the strictest sense, the slaves of the emperor, to whose bounty they were indebted for their instruction and support. When they left the seraglio, and suffered their beards to grow as the symbol of enfranchisement, they found themselves in an important office, without faction or friendship, without parents and without heirs, dependent on the hand which had raised them from the dust, and which, on the slightest displeasure, could break in pieces these statues of glass, as they are aptly termed by the Turkish proverb. In the slow and painful steps of education, their characters and talents were unfolded to a discerning eye: the *man*, naked and alone, was reduced to the standard of his personal merit; and, if the sovereign had wisdom to choose, he possessed a pure and boundless liberty of choice. The Ottoman candidates were trained by the virtues of abstinence to those of action; by the habits of submission to those of command. A similar spirit was diffused among the troops; and their silence and sobriety, their patience and modesty, have extorted the reluctant praise of their Christian enemies. Nor can the victory appear doubtful, if we compare the discipline and exercise of the Janizaries with the pride of birth, the independence of chivalry, the ignorance of the new levies, the mutinous temper of the veterans, and the vices of intemperance and disorder which so long contaminated the armies of Europe.

INVENTION OF GUNPOWDER

The only hope of salvation for the Greek empire and the adjacent kingdoms would have been some more powerful weapon, some discovery in the art of war, that should give them a decisive superiority over their Turkish foes. Such a weapon was in their hands; such a discovery had been made in the critical moment of their fate. The chemists of China or Europe had found, by casual or elaborate experiments, that a mixture of saltpetre, sulphur, and charcoal produces, with a spark of fire, a tremendous explosion. It was soon observed that, if the expansive force were compressed in a strong tube, a ball of stone or iron might be expelled with irresistible and destructive velocity. The precise era of the invention and application of gunpowder is involved in doubtful traditions and equivocal language; yet we may clearly discern that it was known before the middle of the fourteenth century, and that before the end of the same the use of artillery in battles and sieges by sea and land was familiar to the states of Germany, Italy, Spain, France, and England. The priority of nations is of small account; none could derive any exclusive benefit from their previous or superior knowledge; and in the common improvement they stood on the same level of relative power and military science. Nor was it possible to circumscribe the secret within the pale of the church; it was disclosed to the Turks by the treachery of apostates and the selfish policy of rivals; and the sultans had sense to adopt, and wealth to reward, the talents of a Christian engineer. The Genoese, who transported Amurath into Europe, must be accused as his preceptors; and it was probably by their hands that his cannon was cast and directed at the siege of Constantinople. The first attempt was indeed unsuccessful; but in the general warfare of the age the advantage was on *their* side who were most commonly the assailants; for a while the proportion of the attack and defence was suspended, and this thundering artillery was pointed against the walls and towers which had been erected only to resist the less potent engines of antiquity. By the Venetians the use of gunpowder was communicated without reproach to the sultans of Egypt and Persia, their allies against the Ottoman power; the secret was soon propagated to the extremities of Asia; and the advantage of the European was confined to his easy victories over the savages of the new world. If we contrast the rapid progress of this mischievous discovery with the slow and laborious advances of reason, science, and the arts of peace, a philosopher, according to his temper, will laugh or weep at the folly of mankind.

Chapter 66

GREEK APPEALS TO THE WEST. VISIT OF JOHN PALÆOLOGUS
TO ROME. VISIT OF MANUEL TO ITALY, FRANCE, AND
ENGLAND. EXPEDITION OF JOHN PALÆOLOGUS II. TEM-
PORARY UNION OF THE GREEKS AND LATINS. REVIVAL OF
GREEK LEARNING IN ITALY. POPE NICHOLAS V. USE AND
ABUSE OF ANCIENT LEARNING

IN the four last centuries of the Greek emperors, their friendly or
hostile aspect towards the pope and the Latins may be observed as
the thermometer of their prosperity or distress—as the scale of the
rise and fall of the barbarian dynasties. When the Turks of the house
of Seljuk pervaded Asia, and threatened Constantinople, we have seen
at the council of Placentia the suppliant ambassadors of Alexius imploring the protection of the common father of the Christians. No
sooner had the arms of the French pilgrims removed the sultan from
Nice to Iconium than the Greek princes resumed, or avowed, their
genuine hatred and contempt for the schismatics of the West, which
precipitated the first downfall of their empire. The date of the Mogul
invasion is marked in the soft and charitable language of John Vataces.
After the recovery of Constantinople the throne of the first Palæologus
was encompassed by foreign and domestic enemies: as long as the
sword of Charles was suspended over his head he basely courted the
favour of the Roman pontiff, and sacrificed to the present danger his
faith, his virtue, and the affection of his subjects. On the decease of
Michael the prince and people asserted the independence of their church
and the purity of their creed: the elder Andronicus neither feared nor
loved the Latins; in his last distress pride was the safeguard of superstition; nor could he decently retract in his age the firm and orthodox declarations of his youth. His grandson, the younger Andronicus, was
less a slave in his temper and situation; and the conquest of Bithynia by
the Turks admonished him to seek a temporal and spiritual alliance with
the Western princes. After a separation and silence of fifty years a
secret agent, the monk Barlaam, was despatched to Pope Benedict the
Twelfth; and his artful instructions appear to have been drawn by the
master-hand of the great domestic. "Most holy father," was he commissioned to say, "the emperor is not less desirous than yourself of an
union between the two churches; but in this delicate transaction he is
obliged to respect his own dignity and the prejudices of his subjects.
The ways of union are twofold, force and persuasion. Of force, the

inefficacy has been already tried, since the Latins have subdued the empire without subduing the minds of the Greeks. The method of persuasion, though slow, is sure and permanent. A deputation of thirty or forty of our doctors would probably agree with those of the Vatican in the love of truth and the unity of belief; but on their return, what would be the use, the recompense, of such agreement? the scorn of their brethren, and the reproaches of a blind and obstinate nation. Yet that nation is accustomed to reverence the general councils which have fixed the articles of our faith; and if they reprobate the decrees of Lyons, it is because the Eastern churches were neither heard nor represented in that arbitrary meeting. For this salutary end it will be expedient, and even necessary, that a well-chosen legate should be sent into Greece to convene the patriarchs of Constantinople, Alexandria, Antioch, and Jerusalem, and with their aid to prepare a free and universal synod. But at this moment," continued the subtle agent, "the empire is assaulted and endangered by the Turks, who have occupied four of the greatest cities of Anatolia. The Christian inhabitants have expressed a wish of returning to their allegiance and religion; but the forces and revenues of the emperor are insufficient for their deliverance: and the Roman legate must be accompanied or preceded by an army of Franks to expel the infidels, and open a way to the holy sepulchre." If the suspicious Latins should require some pledge, some previous effect of the sincerity of the Greeks, the answers of Barlaam were perspicuous and rational. "1. A general synod can alone consummate the union of the churches; nor can such a synod be held till the three Oriental patriarchs and a great number of bishops are enfranchised from the Mahometan yoke. 2. The Greeks are alienated by a long series of oppression and injury: they must be reconciled by some act of brotherly love, some effectual succour, which may fortify the authority and arguments of the emperor and the friends of the union. 3. If some difference of faith or ceremonies should be found incurable, the Greeks however are the disciples of Christ, and the Turks are the common enemies of the Christian name. The Armenians, Cyprians, and Rhodians are equally attacked; and it will become the piety of the French princes to draw their swords in the general defence of religion. 4. Should the subjects of Andronicus be treated as the worst of schismatics, of heretics, of pagans, a judicious policy may yet instruct the powers of the West to embrace a useful ally, to uphold a sinking empire, to guard the confines of Europe, and rather to join the Greeks against the Turks than to expect the union of the Turkish arms with the troops and treasures of captive Greece." The reasons, the offers, and the demands of Andronicus were eluded with cold and stately indifference. The kings of France and Naples declined the dangers and glory of a crusade: the pope refused to call a new synod to determine old articles of faith; and his reward for the obsolete claims of the Latin emperor and clergy engaged him to use an offensive superscription,—"To the *moderator* of the Greeks, and the persons who style themselves the patriarchs of the Eastern churches." For such an embassy a time and character less propitious could not easily have been found. Benedict the Twelfth was a dull peasant, perplexed with scruples, and immersed in sloth and wine: his pride might enrich with a third crown the papal tiara, but he was alike unfit for the regal and the pastoral office.

After the decease of Andronicus, while the Greeks were distracted by intestine war, they could not presume to agitate a general union of the Christians. But as soon as Cantacuzene had subdued and pardoned his enemies, he was anxious to justify, or at least to extenuate, the introduction of the Turks into Europe and the nuptials of his daughter with a Musulman prince. Two officers of state, with a Latin interpreter, were sent in his name to the Roman court, which was transplanted to Avignon, on the banks of the Rhône, during a period of seventy years: they represented the hard necessity which had urged him to embrace the alliance of the miscreants, and pronounced by his command the specious and edifying sounds of union and crusade. Pope Clement the Sixth, the successor of Benedict, received them with hospitality and honour, acknowledged the innocence of their sovereign, excused his distress, applauded his magnanimity, and displayed a clear knowledge of the state and revolutions of the Greek empire, which he had imbibed from the honest accounts of a Savoyard lady, an attendant of the empress Anne. If Clement was ill endowed with the virtues of a priest, he possessed however the spirit and magnificence of a prince whose liberal hand distributed benefices and kingdoms with equal facility. Under his reign Avignon was the seat of pomp and pleasure: in his youth he had surpassed the licentiousness of a baron; and the palace, nay the bedchamber of the pope, was adorned, or polluted, by the visits of his female favourites. The wars of France and England were adverse to the holy enterprise; but his vanity was amused by the splendid idea; and the Greek ambassadors returned with two Latin bishops, the ministers of the pontiff. On their arrival at Constantinople the emperor and the nuncios admired each other's piety and eloquence; and their frequent conferences were filled with mutual praises and promises, by which both parties were amused, and neither could be deceived. "I am delighted," said the devout Cantacuzene, "with the project of our holy war, which must redound to my personal glory as well as to the public benefit of Christendom. My dominions will give a free passage to the armies of France: my troops, my galleys, my treasures, shall be consecrated to the common cause; and happy would be my fate could I deserve and obtain the crown of martyrdom. Words are insufficient to express the ardour with which I sigh for the reunion of the scattered members of Christ. If my death could avail, I would gladly present my sword and my neck: if the spiritual phœnix could arise from my ashes, I would erect the pile and kindle the flame with my own hands." Yet the Greek emperor presumed to observe that the articles of faith which divided the two churches had been introduced by the pride and precipitation of the Latins: he disclaimed the servile and arbitrary steps of the first Palæologus, and firmly declared that he would never submit his conscience unless to the decrees of a free and universal synod. "The situation of the times," continued he, "will not allow the pope and myself to meet either at Rome or Constantinople; but some maritime city may be chosen on the verge of the two empires, to unite the bishops, and to instruct the faithful of the East and West." The nuncios seemed content with the proposition; and Cantacuzene affects to deplore the failure of his hopes, which were soon overthrown by the death of Clement, and the different temper of his successor. His own life was prolonged, but it was prolonged in a cloister; and, except by his prayers, the humble monk was incapable of directing the counsels of his pupil or the state.

VISIT OF JOHN PALÆOLOGUS TO ROME

Yet of all the Byzantine princes, that pupil, John Palæologus, was the best disposed to embrace, to believe, and to obey the shepherd of the West. His mother, Anne of Savoy, was baptized in the bosom of the Latin church: her marriage with Andronicus imposed a change of name, of apparel, and of worship, but her heart was still faithful to her country and religion: she had formed the infancy of her son, and she governed the emperor after his mind, or at least his stature, was enlarged to the size of man. In the first year of his deliverance and restoration the Turks were still masters of the Hellespont; the son of Cantacuzene was in arms at Adrianople, and Palæologus could depend neither on himself nor on his people. By his mother's advice, and in the hope of foreign aid, he abjured the rights both of the church and state; and the act of slavery, subscribed in purple ink, and sealed with the *golden* bull, was privately intrusted to an Italian agent. The first article of the treaty is an oath of fidelity and obedience to Innocent the Sixth and his successors, the supreme pontiffs of the Roman and Catholic church. The emperor promises to entertain with due reverence their legates and nuncios, to assign a palace for their residence and a temple for their worship, and to deliver his second son Manuel as the hostage of his faith. For these condescensions he requires a prompt succour of fifteen galleys, with five hundred men-at-arms and a thousand archers, to serve against his Christian and Musulman enemies. Palæologus engages to impose on his clergy and people the same spiritual yoke; but as the resistance of the Greeks might be justly foreseen, he adopts the two effectual methods of corruption and education. The legate was empowered to distribute the vacant benefices among the ecclesiastics who should subscribe the creed of the Vatican: three schools were instituted to instruct the youth of Constantinople in the language and doctrine of the Latins; and the name of Andronicus, the heir of the empire, was enrolled as the first student. Should he fail in the measures of persuasion or force, Palæologus declares himself unworthy to reign, transfers to the pope all regal and paternal authority, and invests Innocent with full power to regulate the family, the government, and the marriage of his son and successor. But this treaty was neither executed nor published: the Roman galleys were as vain and imaginary as the submission of the Greeks; and it was only by the secrecy that their sovereign escaped the dishonour of this fruitless humiliation.

The tempest of the Turkish arms soon burst on his head; and after the loss of Adrianople and Romania he was enclosed in his capital, the vassal of the haughty Amurath, with the miserable hope of being the last devoured by the savage. In this abject state Palæologus embraced the resolution of embarking for Venice, and casting himself at the feet of the pope: he was the first of the Byzantine princes who had ever visited the unknown regions of the West, yet in them alone he could seek consolation or relief; and with less violation of his dignity he might appear in the sacred college than at the Ottoman *Porte*. After a long absence the Roman pontiffs were returning from Avignon to the banks of the Tiber: Urban the Fifth, of a mild and virtuous character, encouraged or allowed the pilgrimage of the Greek prince, and, within the same year, enjoyed the glory of receiving in the Vatican the two Imperial shadows who represented the majesty of Constantine and Charlemagne. In this suppliant visit the emperor of Constantinople, whose vanity was lost in his distress, gave more than could be expected of empty sounds and formal submissions. A previous trial was imposed; and in the presence of four cardinals he acknowledged, as a true Catholic, the supremacy of the pope, and the double procession of the Holy Ghost. After this purification he was introduced to a public audience in the church of St. Peter: Urban, in the midst of the cardinals, was seated on his throne; the Greek monarch, after three genuflexions, devoutly kissed the feet, the hands, and at length the mouth of the holy father, who celebrated high mass in his presence, allowed him to lead the bridle of his mule, and treated him with a sumptuous banquet in the Vatican. The entertainment of Palæologus was friendly and honourable, yet some difference was observed between the emperors of the East and West; nor could the former be entitled to the rare privilege of chanting the Gospel in the rank of a deacon. In favour of his proselyte, Urban strove to rekindle the zeal of the French king and the other powers of the West; but he found them cold in the general cause, and active only in their domestic quarrels. The last hope of the emperor was in an English mercenary, John Hawkwood, or Acuto, who, with a band of adventurers, the White Brotherhood, had ravaged Italy from the Alps to Calabria, sold his services to the hostile states, and incurred a just excommunication by shooting his arrows against the papal residence. A special licence was granted to negotiate with the outlaw, but the forces, or the spirit, of Hawkwood were unequal to the enterprise: and it was for the advantage perhaps of Palæologus to be disappointed of a succour that must have been costly, that could not be effectual, and which might have been dangerous. The disconsolate Greek prepared for his return, but even his return was impeded by a most ignominious obstacle. On his arrival at Venice he had borrowed large sums at exorbitant usury; but his coffers were empty, his creditors were impatient, and his person was detained as the best security for the payment. His eldest son Andronicus, the regent of Constantinople, was repeatedly urged to exhaust every resource, and even by stripping the churches, to extricate his father from captivity and disgrace. But the unnatural youth was insensible of the disgrace, and secretly pleased with the captivity of the emperor: the state was poor, the clergy was obstinate; nor could some religious scruple be wanting to excuse the guilt of his indifference and delay. Such undutiful neglect was severely reproved by the piety of his brother Manuel, who instantly sold or mortgaged all that he possessed, embarked for Venice, relieved his father, and pledged his own freedom to be responsible for the debt. On his return to Constantinople the parent and king distinguished his two sons with suitable rewards; but the faith and manners of the slothful Palæologus had not been improved by his Roman pilgrimage; and his apostasy or conversion, devoid of any spiritual or temporal effects, was speedily forgotten by the Greeks and Latins.

VISIT OF MANUEL TO ITALY, FRANCE, AND ENGLAND

Thirty years after the return of Palæologus, his son and successor Manuel, from a similar motive, but on a larger scale, again visited the countries of the West. In a preceding chapter I have related his treaty with Bajazet, the violation of that treaty, the siege or blockade of Constantinople, and the French succour under the command of the gallant Boucicault. By his ambassadors Manuel had solicited the Latin powers; but it was thought that the presence of a distressed monarch would draw tears and supplies from the hardest barbarians, and the marshal who advised the journey prepared the reception of the Byzantine prince. The land was occupied by the Turks; but the navigation of Venice was safe and open: Italy received him as the first, or at least as the second, of the Christian princes; Manuel was pitied as the champion and confessor of the faith, and the dignity of his behaviour prevented that pity from sinking into contempt. From Venice he proceeded to Padua and Pavia; and even the duke of Milan, a secret ally of Bajazet, gave him safe and honourable conduct to the verge of his dominions. On the confines of France the royal officers undertook the care of his person, journey, and expenses; and two thousand of the richest citizens, in arms and on

horseback, came forth to meet him as far as Charenton, in the neighbourhood of the capital. At the gates of Paris he was saluted by the chancellor and the parliament; and Charles the Sixth, attended by his princes
and nobles, welcomed his brother with a cordial embrace. The successor
of Constantine was clothed in a robe of white silk and mounted on a
milk-white steed, a circumstance, in the French ceremonial, of singular
importance: the white colour is considered as the symbol of sovereignty;
and in a late visit the German emperor, after an haughty demand and a
peevish refusal, had been reduced to content himself with a black
courser. Manuel was lodged in the Louvre: a succession of feasts and
balls, the pleasures of the banquet and the chase, were ingeniously varied
by the politeness of the French to display their magnificence and amuse
his grief; he was indulged in the liberty of his chapel, and the doctors of
the Sorbonne were astonished, and possibly scandalised, by the language,
the rites, and the vestments of his Greek clergy. But the slightest glance
on the state of the kingdom must teach him to despair of any effectual
assistance. The unfortunate Charles, though he enjoyed some lucid
intervals, continually relapsed into furious or stupid insanity; the reins
of government were alternately seized by his brother and uncle, the
dukes of Orleans and Burgundy, whose factious competition prepared
the miseries of civil war. The former was a gay youth, dissolved in
luxury and love: the latter was the father of John, count of Nevers, who
had so lately been ransomed from Turkish captivity; and, if the fearless
son was ardent to revenge his defeat, the more prudent Burgundy was
content with the cost and peril of the first experiment. When Manuel
had satiated the curiosity, and perhaps fatigued the patience of the
French, he resolved on a visit to the adjacent island. In his progress from
Dover he was entertained at Canterbury with due reverence by the prior
and monks of St. Austin, and, on Blackheath, king Henry the Fourth,
with the English court, saluted the Greek hero (I copy our old historian),
who, during many days, was lodged and treated in London as emperor
of the East. But the state of England was still more adverse to the
design of the holy war. In the same year the hereditary sovereign had
been deposed and murdered: the reigning prince was a successful usurper,
whose ambition was punished by jealousy and remorse; nor could
Henry of Lancaster withdraw his person or forces from the defence of a
throne incessantly shaken by conspiracy and rebellion. He pitied, he
praised, he feasted, the emperor of Constantinople; but if the English
monarch assumed the cross, it was only to appease his people, and perhaps his conscience, by the merit or semblance of this pious intention.
Satisfied, however, with gifts and honours, Manuel returned to Paris;
and, after a residence of two years in the West, shaped his course through
Germany and Italy, embarked at Venice, and patiently expected, in the
Morea, the moment of his ruin or deliverance. Yet he had escaped the
ignominious necessity of offering his religion to public or private sale.

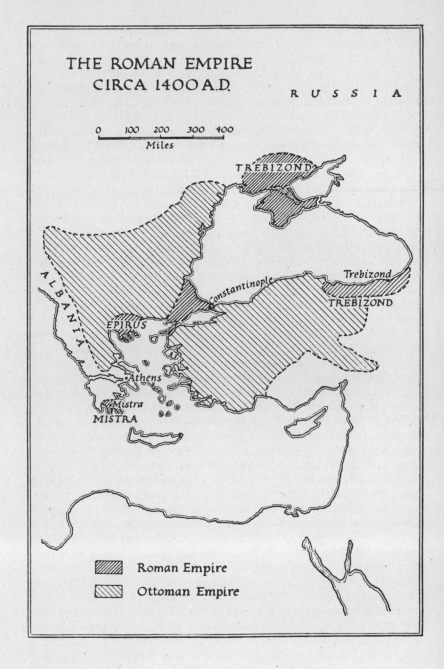

THE ROMAN EMPIRE
CIRCA 1400 A.D.

RUSSIA

0   100   200   300   400
            Miles

TREBIZOND

ALBANIA

EPIRUS

Constantinople

Trebizond

TREBIZOND

Athens

Mistra

MISTRA

Roman Empire
Ottoman Empire

The Latin church was distracted by the great schism: the kings, the nations, the universities of Europe, were divided in their obedience between the popes of Rome and Avignon; and the emperor, anxious to conciliate the friendship of both parties, abstained from any correspondence with the indigent and unpopular rivals. His journey coincided with the year of the jubilee; but he passed through Italy without desiring or deserving the plenary indulgence which abolished the guilt or penance of the sins of the faithful. The Roman pope was offended by this neglect, accused him of irreverence to an image of Christ, and exhorted the princes of Italy to reject and abandon the obstinate schismatic.

During the period of the crusades the Greeks beheld with astonishment and terror the perpetual stream of emigration that flowed, and continued to flow, from the unknown climates of the West. The visits of their last emperors removed the veil of separation, and they disclosed to their eyes the powerful nations of Europe, whom they no longer presumed to brand with the name of barbarians. The observations of Manuel and his more inquisitive followers have been preserved by a Byzantine historian of the times: his scattered ideas I shall collect and abridge; and it may be amusing enough, perhaps instructive, to contemplate the rude pictures of Germany, France, and England, whose ancient and modern state are so familiar to *our* minds. I. GERMANY (says the Greek Chalcondyles) is of ample latitude from Vienna to the Ocean, and it stretches (a strange geography) from Prague, in Bohemia, to the river Tartessus and the Pyrenæan mountains. The soil, except in figs and olives, is sufficiently fruitful; the air is salubrious, the bodies of the natives are robust and healthy, and these cold regions are seldom visited with the calamities of pestilence or earthquakes. After the Scythians or Tartars, the Germans are the most numerous of nations: they are brave and patient, and, were they united under a single head, their force would be irresistible. By the gift of the pope, they have acquired the privilege of choosing the Roman emperor; nor is any people more devoutly attached to the faith and obedience of the Latin patriarch. The greatest part of the country is divided among the princes and prelates; but Strasburg, Cologne, Hamburg, and more than two hundred free cities, are governed by sage and equal laws, according to the will and for the advantage of the whole community. The use of duels, or single combats on foot, prevails among them in peace and war; their industry excells in all the mechanic arts; and the Germans may boast of the invention of gunpowder and cannon, which is now diffused over the greatest part of the world. II. The kingdom of FRANCE is spread above fifteen or twenty days' journey from Germany to Spain, and from the Alps to the British Ocean, containing many flourishing cities, and among these Paris, the seat of the king, which surpasses the rest in riches and luxury. Many princes and lords alternately wait in his palace and acknowledge him as their sovereign: the most powerful are the dukes of Bretagne and Burgundy, of whom the latter possesses the wealthy province of Flanders, whose harbours are frequented by the ships and merchants of our own and the more remote seas. The French are an ancient and opulent people, and their language and manners, though somewhat different, are not dissimilar from those of the Italians. Vain of the Imperial dignity of Charlemagne, of their victories over the Saracens, and of the exploits of their heroes Oliver and Rowland, they esteem themselves the first of the western nations; but this foolish arrogance has been recently humbled by the unfortunate events of their wars against the English, the inhabitants of the British island. III. BRITAIN, in the ocean and opposite to the shores of Flanders, may be considered either as one or as three islands; but the whole is united by a common interest, by the same manners, and by a similar government. The measure of its circumference is five thousand stadia: the land is overspread with towns and villages; though destitute of wine, and not abounding in fruit-trees, it is fertile in wheat and barley, in honey and wool, and much cloth is manufactured by the inhabitants. In populousness and power, in riches and luxury, London, the metropolis of the isle, may claim a pre-eminence over all the cities of the West. It is situate on the Thames, a broad and rapid river, which at the distance of thirty miles falls into the Gallic Sea; and the daily flow and ebb of the tide affords a safe entrance and departure to the vessels of commerce. The king is the head of a powerful and turbulent aristocracy: his principal vassals hold their estates by a free and unalterable tenure, and the laws define the limits of his authority and their obedience. The kingdom has been often afflicted by foreign conquest and domestic sedition; but the natives are bold and hardy, renowned in arms and victorious in war. The form of their shields or targets is derived from the Italians, that of their swords from the Greeks; the use of the long bow is the peculiar and decisive advantage of the English. Their language bears no affinity to the idioms of the continent: in the habits of domestic life they are not easily distinguished from their neighbours of France; but the most singular circumstance of their manners is their disregard of conjugal honour and of female chastity. In their mutual visits, as the first act of hospitality, the guest is welcomed in the embraces of their wives and daughters: among friends they are lent and borrowed without shame; nor are the islanders offended at this strange commerce and its inevitable consequences. Informed as we are of the customs of old England, and assured of the virtue of our mothers, we may smile at the credulity, or resent the injustice, of the Greek, who must have confounded a modest salute [1] with a criminal embrace. But his credulity and injustice may teach an important lesson, to distrust the accounts of foreign and remote nations,

[1] Erasmus has a pretty passage on the English fashion of kissing strangers on their arrival and departure, from whence, however, he draws no scandalous inferences.

and to suspend our belief of every tale that deviates from the laws of nature and the character of man.

After his return, and the victory of Timour, Manuel reigned many years in prosperity and peace. As long as the sons of Bajazet solicited his friendship and spared his dominions, he was satisfied with the national religion; and his leisure was employed in composing twenty theological dialogues for its defence. The appearance of the Byzantine ambassadors at the council of Constance announces the restoration of the Turkish power, as well as of the Latin church: the conquest of the sultans, Mahomet and Amurath, reconciled the emperor to the Vatican; and the siege of Constantinople almost tempted him to acquiesce in the double procession of the Holy Ghost. When Martin the Fifth ascended without a rival the chair of St. Peter, a friendly intercourse of letters and embassies was revived between the East and West. Ambition on one side, and distress on the other, dictated the same decent language of charity and peace: the artful Greek expressed a desire of marrying his six sons to Italian princesses; and the Roman, not less artful, despatched the daughter of the marquis of Montferrat, with a company of noble virgins, to soften, by their charms, the obstinacy of the schismatics. Yet under this mask of zeal a discerning eye will perceive that all was hollow and insincere in the court and church of Constantinople. According to the vicissitudes of danger and repose, the emperor advanced or retreated; alternately instructed and disavowed his ministers; and escaped from an importunate pressure by urging the duty of inquiry, the obligation of collecting the sense of his patriarchs and bishops, and the impossibility of convening them at a time when the Turkish arms were at the gates of his capital. From a review of the public transactions it will appear that the Greeks insisted on three successive measures, a succour, a council, and a final reunion, while the Latins eluded the second, and only promised the first as a consequential and voluntary reward of the third. But we have an opportunity of unfolding the most secret intentions of Manuel, as he explained them in a private conversation without artifice or disguise. In his declining age the emperor had associated John Palæologus, the second of the name, and the eldest of his sons, on whom he devolved the greatest part of the authority and weight of government. One day, in the presence only of the historian Phranza, his favourite chamberlain, he opened to his colleague and successor the true principle of his negociations with the pope. "Our last resource," said Manuel, "against the Turks is their fear of our union with the Latins, of the warlike nations of the West, who may arm for our relief and for their destruction. As often as you are threatened by the miscreants, present this danger before their eyes. Propose a council; consult on the means; but ever delay and avoid the convocation of an assembly, which cannot tend either to our spiritual or temporal emolument. The Latins are proud; the Greeks are obstinate; neither party will recede or retract; and the attempt of a perfect union will confirm the schism, alienate the churches, and leave us, without hope or defence, at the mercy of the barbarians." Impatient of this salutary lesson, the royal youth arose from his seat and departed in silence; and the wise monarch (continues Phranza), casting his eyes on me, thus resumed his discourse: "My son deems himself a great and heroic prince; but, alas! our miserable age does not afford scope for heroism or greatness. His daring spirit might have suited the happier times of our ancestors; but the present state requires not an emperor, but a cautious steward of the last relics of our fortunes. Well do I remember the lofty expectations which he built on our alliance with Mustapha; and much do I fear that his rash courage will urge the ruin of our house, and that even religion may precipitate our downfall." Yet the experience and authority of Manuel preserved the peace and eluded the council; till, in the seventy-eighth year of his age, and in the habit of a monk, he terminated his career, dividing his precious moveables among his children and the poor, his physicians and his favourite servants. Of his six sons, Andronicus the Second was invested with the principality of Thessalonica, and died of a leprosy soon after the sale of that city to the Venetians and its final conquest by the Turks. Some fortunate incidents had restored Peloponnesus, or the Morea, to the empire; and in his more prosperous days, Manuel had fortified the narrow isthmus of six miles with a stone wall and one hundred and fifty-three towers. The wall was overthrown by the first blast of the Ottomans; the fertile peninsula might have been sufficient for the four younger brothers, Theodore and Constantine, Demetrius and Thomas; but they wasted in domestic contests the remains of their strength; and the least successful of the rivals were reduced to a life of dependence in the Byzantine palace.

EXPEDITION OF JOHN PALÆOLOGUS II

The eldest of the sons of Manuel, John Palæologus the Second, was acknowledged, after his father's death, as the sole emperor of the Greeks. He immediately proceeded to repudiate his wife, and to contract a new marriage with the princess of Trebizond: beauty was in his eyes the first qualification of an empress; and the clergy had yielded to his firm assurance, that, unless he might be indulged in a divorce, he would retire to a cloister and leave the throne to his brother Constantine. The first, and in truth the only victory of Palæologus, was over a Jew, whom, after a long and learned dispute, he converted to the Christian faith; and this momentous conquest is carefully recorded in the history of the times. But he soon resumed the design of uniting the East and West; and, regardless of his father's advice, listened, as it should seem with sincerity, to the proposal of meeting the pope in a general council beyond the Adriatic. This dangerous project was encouraged by Martin the Fifth, and coldly entertained by his successor Eugenius,

till, after a tedious negotiation, the emperor received a summons from
a Latin assembly of a new character, the independent prelates of Basil,
who styled themselves the representatives and judges of the Catholic
church.

The Roman pontiff had fought and conquered in the cause of ecclesiastical freedom; but the victorious clergy were soon exposed to the
tyranny of their deliverer; and his sacred character was invulnerable to
those arms which they found so keen and effectual against the civil
magistrate. Their great charter, the right of election, was annihilated by
appeals, evaded by trusts or commendams, disappointed by reversionary
grants, and superseded by previous and arbitrary reservations. A public
auction was instituted in the court of Rome: the cardinals and favourites
were enriched with the spoils of nations; and every country might complain that the most important and valuable benefices were accumulated
on the heads of aliens and absentees. During their residence at Avignon,
the ambition of the popes subsided in the meaner passions of avarice [1]
and luxury: they rigorously imposed on the clergy the tributes of first-
fruits and tenths; but they freely tolerated the impunity of vice, disorder,
and corruption. These manifold scandals were aggravated by the great
schism of the West, which continued above fifty years. In the furious
conflicts of Rome and Avignon, the vices of the rivals were mutually
exposed; and their precarious situation degraded their authority, relaxed their discipline, and multiplied their wants and exactions. To heal
the wounds, and restore the monarchy, of the church, the synods of
Pisa and Constance were successively convened; but these great assemblies, conscious of their strength, resolved to vindicate the privileges of
the Christian aristocracy. From a personal sentence against two pontiffs
whom they rejected, and a third, their acknowledged sovereign, whom
they deposed, the fathers of Constance proceeded to examine the nature
and limits of the Roman supremacy; nor did they separate till they had
established the authority, above the pope, of a general council. It was
enacted, that, for the government and reformation of the church, such
assemblies should be held at regular intervals; and that each synod,
before its dissolution, should appoint the time and place of the subsequent meeting. By the influence of the court of Rome, the next convocation at Sienna was easily eluded; but the bold and vigorous proceedings of the council of Basel had almost been fatal to the reigning
pontiff, Eugenius the Fourth. A just suspicion of his design prompted
the fathers to hasten the promulgation of their first decree, that the
representatives of the church-militant on earth were invested with a

[1] Pope John XXII (in 1334) left behind him, at Avignon, eighteen millions of gold
florins, and the value of seven millions more in plate and jewels. See the Chronicle of
John Villani, whose brother received the account from the papal treasurers. A
treasure of six or eight millions sterling in the xivth century is enormous, and almost
incredible.

divine and spiritual jurisdiction over all Christians, without excepting the pope; and that a general council could not be dissolved, prorogued, or transferred, unless by their free deliberation and consent. On the notice that Eugenius had fulminated a bull for that purpose, they ventured to summon, to admonish, to threaten, to censure, the contumacious successor of St. Peter. After many delays, to allow time for repentance, they finally declared, that, unless he submitted within the term of sixty days, he was suspended from the exercise of all temporal and ecclesiastical authority. And to mark their jurisdiction over the prince as well as the priest, they assumed the government of Avignon, annulled the alienation of the sacred patrimony, and protected Rome from the imposition of new taxes. Their boldness was justified, not only by the general opinion of the clergy, but by the support and power of the first monarchs of Christendom: the emperor Sigismond declared himself the servant and protector of the synod; Germany and France adhered to their cause; the duke of Milan was the enemy of Eugenius; and he was driven from the Vatican by an insurrection of the Roman people. Rejected at the same time by his temporal and spiritual subjects, submission was his only choice: by a most humiliating bull, the pope repealed his own acts, and ratified those of the council; incorporated his legates and cardinals with that venerable body; and *seemed* to resign himself to the decrees of the supreme legislature. Their fame pervaded the countries of the East: and it was in their presence that Sigismond received the ambassadors of the Turkish sultan, who laid at his feet twelve large vases filled with robes of silk and pieces of gold. The fathers of Basel aspired to the glory of reducing the Greeks, as well as the Bohemians, within the pale of the church; and their deputies invited the emperor and patriarch of Constantinople to unite with an assembly which possessed the confidence of the Western nations. Palæologus was not averse to the proposal; and his ambassadors were introduced with due honours into the Catholic senate. But the choice of the place appeared to be an insuperable obstacle, since he refused to pass the Alps, or the sea of Sicily, and positively required that the synod should be adjourned to some convenient city in Italy, or at least on the Danube. The other articles of this treaty were more readily stipulated: it was agreed to defray the travelling expenses of the emperor, with a train of seven hundred persons, to remit an immediate sum of eight thousand ducats for the accommodation of the Greek clergy; and in his absence to grant a supply of ten thousand ducats, with three hundred archers and some galleys, for the protection of Constantinople. The city of Avignon advanced the funds for the preliminary expenses; and the embarkation was prepared at Marseilles with some difficulty and delay.

In his distress the friendship of Palæologus was disputed by the ecclesiastical powers of the West; but the dexterous activity of a monarch prevailed over the slow debates and inflexible temper of a republic. The decrees of Basel continually tended to circumscribe the despotism of the pope, and to erect a supreme and perpetual tribunal in the church. Eugenius was impatient of the yoke; and the union of the Greeks might afford a decent pretence for translating a rebellious synod from the Rhine to the Po. The independence of the fathers was lost if they passed the Alps: Savoy or Avignon, to which they acceded with reluctance, were described at Constantinople as situate far beyond the Pillars of Hercules; the emperor and his clergy were apprehensive of the dangers of a long navigation; they were offended by an haughty declaration, that, after suppressing the *new* heresy of the Bohemians, the council would soon eradicate the *old* heresy of the Greeks. On the side of Eugenius all was smooth, and yielding, and respectful; and he invited the Byzantine monarch to heal by his presence the schism of the Latin, as well as of the Eastern, church. Ferrara, near the coast of the Adriatic, was proposed for their amicable interview: and with some indulgence of forgery and theft, a surreptitious decree was procured, which transferred the synod, with its own consent, to that Italian city. Nine galleys were equipped for this service at Venice and in the isle of Candia; their diligence anticipated the slower vessels of Basel: the Roman admiral was commissioned to burn, sink, and destroy; and these priestly squadrons might have encountered each other in the same seas where Athens and Sparta had formerly contended for the pre-eminence of glory. Assaulted by the importunity of the factions, who were ready to fight for the possession of his person, Palæologus hesitated before he left his palace and country on a perilous experiment. His father's advice still dwelt on his memory; and reason must suggest, that, since the Latins were divided among themselves, they could never unite in a foreign cause. Sigismond dissuaded the unseasonable adventure; his advice was impartial, since he adhered to the council; and it was enforced by the strange belief that the German Cæsar would nominate a Greek his heir and successor in the empire of the West. Even the Turkish sultan was a counsellor whom it might be unsafe to trust, but whom it was dangerous to offend. Amurath was unskilled in the disputes, but he was apprehensive of the union, of the Christians. From his own treasures he offered to relieve the wants of the Byzantine court; yet he declared with seeming magnanimity that Constantinople should be secure and inviolate in the absence of her sovereign. The resolution of Palæologus was decided by the most splendid gifts and the most specious promises: he wished to escape for a while from a scene of danger and distress; and after dismissing with an ambiguous answer the messengers of the council, he declared his intention of embarking in the Roman galleys. The age of the patriarch Joseph was more susceptible of fear than of hope; he trembled at the perils of the sea, and expressed his apprehension that his feeble voice, with thirty perhaps of his orthodox brethren, would be oppressed in a foreign land by the power and numbers of a Latin synod. He yielded to the royal mandate, to the flattering assurance that he would be heard as the oracle of nations, and to the secret wish of learning from his brother of the West to deliver the church from the yoke of kings. The five *crossbearers*, or dignitaries, of St. Sophia, were bound to attend his person; and one of these, the great ecclesiarch or preacher, Sylvester Syropulus, has composed a free and curious history of the *false* union. Of the clergy that reluctantly obeyed the summons of the emperor and the patriarch, submission was the first duty, and patience the most useful virtue. In a chosen list of twenty bishops we discover the metropolitan titles of Heraclea and Cyzicus, Nice and Nicomedia, Ephesus and Trebizond, and the personal merit of Mark and Bessarion, who, in the confidence of their learning and eloquence, were promoted to the episcopal rank. Some monks and philosophers were named to display the science and sanctity of the Greek church; and the service of the choir was performed by a select band of singers and musicians. The patriarchs of Alexandria, Antioch, and Jerusalem, appeared by their genuine or fictitious deputies; the primate of Russia represented a national church, and the Greeks might contend with the Latins in the extent of their spiritual empire. The precious vases of St. Sophia were exposed to the winds and waves, that the patriarch might officiate with becoming splendour: whatever gold the emperor could procure was expended in the massy ornaments of his bed and chariot; and while they affected to maintain the prosperity of their ancient fortune, they quarrelled for the division of fifteen thousand ducats, the first alms of the Roman pontiff. After the necessary preparations, John Palæologus, with a numerous train, accompanied by his brother Demetrius and the most respectable persons of the church and state, embarked in eight vessels with sails and oars, which steered through the Turkish straits of Gallipoli to the Archipelago, the Morea, and the Adriatic Gulf.

TEMPORARY UNION OF THE GREEKS AND LATINS

After a tedious and troublesome navigation of seventy-seven days, this religious squadron cast anchor before Venice; and their reception proclaimed the joy and magnificence of that powerful republic. In the command of the world the modest Augustus had never claimed such honours from his subjects as were paid to his feeble successor by an independent state. Seated on the poop, on a lofty throne, he received the visit, or, in the Greek style, the *adoration*, of the doge and senators. They sailed in the Bucentaur, which was accompanied by twelve stately galleys: the sea was overspread with innumerable gondolas of pomp and pleasure; the air resounded with music and acclamations; the mariners, and even the vessels, were dressed in silk and gold; and in all the emblems and pageants the Roman eagles were blended with the lions of St. Mark. The triumphal procession, ascending the great canal, passed under the bridge of the Rialto; and the Eastern strangers gazed with admiration on the palaces, the churches, and the populousness of a city that seems to float on the bosom of the waves. They sighed to behold the spoils and trophies with which it had been decorated after the sack of Constantinople. After an hospitable entertainment of fifteen days, Palæologus pursued his journey by land and water from Venice to Ferrara; and on this occasion the pride of the Vatican was tempered by policy to indulge the ancient dignity of the emperor of the East. He made his entry on a *black* horse; but a milk-white steed, whose trappings were embroidered with golden eagles, was led before him; and the canopy was borne over his head by the princes of Este, the sons or kinsmen of Nicholas, marquis of the city, and a sovereign more powerful than himself. Palæologus did not alight till he reached the bottom of the staircase: the pope advanced to the door of the apartment; refused his proffered genuflexion; and, after a paternal embrace, conducted the emperor to a seat on his left hand. Nor would the patriarch descend from his galley till a ceremony, almost equal, had been stipulated between the bishops of Rome and Constantinople. The latter was saluted by his brother with a kiss of union and charity; nor would any of the Greek ecclesiastics submit to kiss the feet of the Western primate. On the opening of the synod, the place of honour in the centre was claimed by the temporal and ecclesiastical chiefs; and it was only by alleging that his predecessors had not assisted in person at Nice or Chalcedon that Eugenius could evade the ancient precedents of Constantine and Marcian. After much debate it was agreed that the right and left sides of the church should be occupied by the two nations; that the solitary chair of St. Peter should be raised the first of the Latin line; and that the throne of the Greek emperor, at the head of his clergy, should be equal and opposite to the second place, the vacant seat of the emperor of the West.[1]

But as soon as festivity and form had given place to a more serious treaty, the Greeks were dissatisfied with their journey, with themselves, and with the pope. The artful pencil of his emissaries had painted him in a prosperous state, at the head of the princes and prelates of Europe, obedient at his voice to believe and to arm. The thin appearance of the universal synod of Ferrara betrayed his weakness; and the Latins opened the first session with only five archbishops, eighteen bishops, and ten abbots, the greatest part of whom were the subjects or countrymen of the Italian pontiff. Except the duke of Burgundy, none of the potentates of the West condescended to appear in person, or by their ambassadors; nor was it possible to suppress the judicial acts of Basel

---

[1] The Latin vulgar was provoked to laughter at the strange dresses of the Greeks, and especially the length of their garments, their sleeves, and their beards; nor was the emperor distinguished, except by the purple colour, and his diadem or tiara with a jewel on the top. Yet another spectator confesses that the Greek fashion was più grave e più degna than the Italian.

against the dignity and person of Eugenius, which were finally concluded by a new election. Under these circumstances a truce or delay was asked and granted, till Palæologus could expect from the consent of the Latins some temporal reward for an unpopular union; and, after the first session, the public proceedings were adjourned above six months. The emperor, with a chosen band of his favourites and *Janizaries*, fixed his summer residence at a pleasant spacious monastery, six miles from Ferrara; forgot, in the pleasures of the chase, the distress of the church and state; and persisted in destroying the game, without listening to the just complaints of the marquis or the husbandman. In the mean while his unfortunate Greeks were exposed to all the miseries of exile and poverty; for the support of each stranger a monthly allowance was assigned of three or four gold florins, and, although the entire sum did not amount to seven hundred florins, a long arrear was repeatedly incurred by the indigence or policy of the Roman court.[1] They sighed for a speedy deliverance, but their escape was prevented by a triple chain; a passport from their superiors was required at the gates of Ferrara; the government of Venice had engaged to arrest and send back the fugitives, and inevitable punishment awaited them at Constantinople; excommunication, fines, and a sentence, which did not respect the sacerdotal dignity, that they should be stripped naked and publicly whipped. It was only by the alternative of hunger or dispute that the Greeks could be persuaded to open the first conference, and they yielded with extreme reluctance to attend from Ferrara to Florence the rear of a flying synod. This new translation was urged by inevitable necessity: the city was visited by the plague; the fidelity of the marquis might be suspected; the mercenary troops of the duke of Milan were at the gates, and, as they occupied Romagna, it was not without difficulty and danger that the pope, the emperor, and the bishops explored their way through the unfrequented paths of the Apennine.

Yet all these obstacles were surmounted by time and policy. The violence of the fathers of Basel rather promoted than injured the cause of Eugenius: the nations of Europe abhorred the schism, and disowned the election, of Felix the Fifth, who was successively a duke of Savoy, an hermit, and a pope; and the great princes were gradually reclaimed by his competitor to a favourable neutrality and a firm attachment. The legates, with some respectable members, deserted to the Roman army, which insensibly rose in numbers and reputation; the council of

---

[1] The Greeks obtained, with much difficulty, that, instead of provisions, money should be distributed, four florins *per* month to the persons of honourable rank, and three florins to their servants, with an addition of thirty more to the emperor, twenty-five to the patriarch, and twenty to the prince, or despot, Demetrius. The payment of the first month amounted to 691 florins, a sum which will not allow us to reckon above 200 Greeks of every condition. On the 20th October, 1438, there was an arrear of four months; in April, 1439, of three; and of five and a half in July, at the time of the union.

Basel was reduced to thirty-nine bishops and three hundred of the inferior clergy; while the Latins of Florence could produce the subscriptions of the pope himself, eight cardinals, two patriarchs, eight archbishops, fifty-two bishops, and forty-five abbots or chiefs of religious orders. After the labour of nine months and the debates of twenty-five sessions, they attained the advantage and glory of the reunion of the Greeks. Four principal questions had been agitated between the two churches: 1. The use of unleavened bread in the communion of Christ's body. 2. The nature of purgatory. 3. The supremacy of the pope. And, 4. The single or double procession of the Holy Ghost. The cause of either nation was managed by ten theological champions: the Latins were supported by the inexhaustible eloquence of Cardinal Julian, and Mark of Ephesus and Bessarion of Nice were the bold and able leaders of the Greek forces. We may bestow some praise on the progress of human reason, by observing that the first of these questions was *now* treated as an immaterial rite, which might innocently vary with the fashion of the age and country. With regard to the second, both parties were agreed in the belief of an intermediate state of purgation for the venial sins of the faithful; and whether their souls were purified by elemental fire was a doubtful point, which in a few years might be conveniently settled on the spot by the disputants. The claims of supremacy appeared of a more weighty and substantial kind, yet by the Orientals the Roman bishop had ever been respected as the first of the five patriarchs; nor did they scruple to admit that his jurisdiction should be exercised agreeably to the holy canons: a vague allowance, which might be defined or eluded by occasional convenience. The procession of the Holy Ghost from the Father alone, or from the Father and the Son, was an article of faith which had sunk much deeper into the minds of men; and in the sessions of Ferrara and Florence the Latin addition of *filioque* was subdivided into two questions, whether it were legal, and whether it were orthodox. Perhaps it may not be necessary to boast on this subject of my own impartial indifference: but I must think that the Greeks were strongly supported by the prohibition of the council of Chalcedon against adding any article whatsoever to the creed of Nice, or rather of Constantinople.[1] In earthly affairs it is not easy to conceive how an assembly of legislators can bind their successors invested with powers equal to their own. But the dictates of inspiration must be true and unchangeable; nor should a private bishop or a provincial synod have presumed to innovate against the judgment of the Catholic church. On the substance of the doctrine the controversy was equal and endless; reason is confounded by the procession of a deity; the Gospel, which lay on the altar, was silent; the various texts of the fathers might be cor-

---

[1] The Greeks, who disliked the union, were unwilling to sally from this strong fortress. The shame of the Latins was aggravated by their producing an old MS. of the second council of Nice, with *filioque* in the Nicene creed. A palpable forgery!

rupted by fraud or entangled by sophistry; and the Greeks were ignorant of the characters and writings of the Latin saints.[1] Of this at least we may be sure, that neither side could be convinced by the arguments of their opponents. Prejudice may be enlightened by reason, and a superficial glance may be rectified by a clear and more perfect view of an object adopted to our faculties. But the bishops and monks had been taught from their infancy to repeat a form of mysterious words: their national and personal honour depended on the repetition of the same sounds, and their narrow minds were hardened and inflamed by the acrimony of a public dispute.

While they were lost in a cloud of dust and darkness, the pope and emperor were desirous of a seeming union, which could alone accomplish the purposes of their interview; and the obstinacy of public dispute was softened by the arts of private and personal negotiation. The patriarch Joseph had sunk under the weight of age and infirmities; his dying voice breathed the counsels of charity and concord, and his vacant benefice might tempt the hopes of the ambitious clergy. The ready and active obedience of the archbishops of Russia and Nice, of Isidore and Bessarion, was prompted and recompensed by their speedy promotion to the dignity of cardinals. Bessarion, in the first debates, had stood forth the most strenuous and eloquent champion of the Greek church; and if the apostate, the bastard, was reprobated by his country, he appears in ecclesiastical story a rare example of a patriot who was recommended to court favour by loud opposition and well-timed compliance. With the aid of his two spiritual coadjutors, the emperor applied his arguments to the general situation and personal characters of the bishops, and each was successively moved by authority and example. Their revenues were in the hands of the Turks, their persons in those of the Latins; an episcopal treasure, three robes and forty ducats, was soon exhausted; the hopes of their return still depended on the ships of Venice and the alms of Rome; and such was their indigence, that their arrears, the payment of a debt, would be accepted as a favour, and might operate as a bribe. The danger and relief of Constantinople might excuse some prudent and pious dissimulation; and it was insinuated that the obstinate heretics who should resist the consent of the East and West would be abandoned in a hostile land to the revenge or justice of the Roman pontiff. In the first private assembly of the Greeks the formulary of union was approved by twenty four, and rejected by twelve, members; but the five *crossbearers* of St. Sophia, who aspired to represent the patriarch, were disqualified by ancient discipline, and their right of voting was transferred to an obsequious train of monks, grammarians, and profane laymen. The will of the monarch produced a

[1] "When I go into a Latin church, I do not bow to the saints there because I do not know any of them." [Translation of a remark by Syropulus quoted by Gibbon in Greek.]

false and servile unanimity, and no more than two patriots had courage
to speak their own sentiments and those of their country. Demetrius,
the emperor's brother, retired to Venice, that he might not be witness
of the union; and Mark of Ephesus, mistaking perhaps his pride for his
conscience, disclaimed all communion with the Latin heretics, and
avowed himself the champion and confessor of the orthodox creed.[1] In
the treaty between the two nations several forms of consent were proposed, such as might satisfy the Latins without dishonouring the
Greeks; and they weighed the scruples of words and syllables till the
theological balance trembled with a slight preponderance in favour of
the Vatican. It was agreed (I must entreat the attention of the reader)
that the Holy Ghost proceeds from the Father *and* the Son, as from one
principle and one substance; that he proceeds *by* the Son, being of the
same nature and substance; and that he proceeds from the Father *and*
the Son, by one *spiration* and production. It is less difficult to understand the articles of the preliminary treaty: that the pope should defray
all the expenses of the Greeks in their return home; that he should
annually maintain two galleys and three hundred soldiers for the
defence of Constantinople; that all the ships which transported pilgrims
to Jerusalem should be obliged to touch at that port; that as often as
they were required, the pope should furnish ten galleys for a year, or
twenty for six months; and that he should powerfully solicit the princes
of Europe, if the emperor had occasion for land-forces.

The same year, and almost the same day, were marked by the deposition of Eugenius at Basel, and, at Florence, by his reunion of the Greeks
and Latins. In the former synod (which he styled indeed an assembly of
dæmons) the pope was branded with the guilt of simony, perjury,
tyranny, heresy, and schism; and declared to be incorrigible in his vices,
unworthy of any title, and incapable of holding any ecclesiastical office.
In the latter he was revered as the true and holy vicar of Christ, who,
after a separation of six hundred years, had reconciled the Catholics of
the East and West in one fold, and under one shepherd. The act of
union was subscribed by the pope, the emperor, and the principal members of both churches; even by those who, like Syropulus, had been
deprived of the right of voting. Two copies might have sufficed for the
East and West; but Eugenius was not satisfied unless four authentic and
similar transcripts were signed and attested as the monuments of his
victory. On a memorable day, the sixth of July, the successors of St.
Peter and Constantine ascended their thrones; the two nations assembled in the cathedral of Florence; their representatives, Cardinal
Julian, and Bessarion archbishop of Nice, appeared in the pulpit, and,

---

[1] I had forgot another popular and orthodox protester: a favourite hound, who
usually lay quiet on the foot-cloth of the emperor's throne, but who barked most
furiously while the act of union was reading, without being silenced by the soothing
or the lashes of the royal attendants.

after reading in their respective tongues the act of union, they mutually embraced in the name and the presence of their applauding brethren. The pope and his ministers then officiated according to the Roman liturgy; the creed was chanted with the addition of *filioque*; the acquiescence of the Greeks was poorly excused by their ignorance of the harmonious but inarticulate sounds; and the more scrupulous Latins refused any public celebration of the Byzantine rite. Yet the emperor and his clergy were not totally unmindful of national honour. The treaty was ratified by their consent: it was tacitly agreed that no innovation should be attempted in their creed or ceremonies; they spared and secretly respected the generous firmness of Mark of Ephesus, and, on the decease of the patriarch, they refused to elect his successor, except in the cathedral of St. Sophia. In the distribution of public and private rewards the liberal pontiff exceeded their hopes and his promises: the Greeks, with less pomp and pride, returned by the same road of Ferrara and Venice; and their reception at Constantinople was such as will be described in the following chapter. The success of the first trial encouraged Eugenius to repeat the same edifying scenes, and the deputies of the Armenians, the Maronites, the Jacobites of Syria and Egypt, the Nestorians, and the Ethiopians, were successively introduced to kiss the feet of the Roman pontiff, and to announce the obedience and the orthodoxy of the East. These Oriental embassies, unknown in the countries which they presumed to represent, diffused over the West the fame of Eugenius; and a clamour was artfully propagated against the remnant of a schism in Switzerland and Savoy which alone impeded the harmony of the Christian world. The vigour of opposition was succeeded by the lassitude of despair; the council of Basel was silently dissolved; and Felix, renouncing the tiara, again withdrew to the devout or delicious hermitage of Ripaille. A general peace was secured by mutual acts of oblivion and indemnity: all ideas of reformation subsided; the popes continued to exercise and abuse their ecclesiastical despotism; nor has Rome been since disturbed by the mischiefs of a contested election.

REVIVAL OF GREEK LEARNING IN ITALY

The journeys of three emperors were unavailing for their temporal, or perhaps their spiritual, salvation; but they were productive of a beneficial consequence, the revival of the Greek learning in Italy, from whence it was propagated to the last nations of the West and North. In their lowest servitude and depression, the subjects of the Byzantine throne were still possessed of a golden key that could unlock the treasures of antiquity, of a musical and prolific language that gives a soul to the objects of sense, and a body to the abstractions of philosophy. Since the barriers of the monarchy, and even of the capital, had been trampled under foot, the various barbarians had doubtless corrupted the form and substance of the national dialect; and ample glossaries have been composed, to interpret a multitude of words, of Arabic, Turkish, Sclavonian, Latin, or French origin. But a purer idiom was spoken in the court and taught in the college, and the flourishing state of the language is described, and perhaps embellished, by a learned Italian, who, by a long residence and noble marriage, was naturalised at Constantinople about thirty years before the Turkish conquest. "The vulgar speech," said Philelphus, "has been depraved by the people, and infected by the multitude of strangers and merchants, who every day flock to the city and mingle with the inhabitants. It is from the disciples of such a school that the Latin language received the versions of Aristotle and Plato, so obscure in sense, and in spirit so poor. But the Greeks, who have escaped the contagion, are those whom *we* follow, and they alone are worthy of our imitation. In familiar discourse they still speak the tongue of Aristophanes and Euripides, of the historians and philosophers of Athens; and the style of their writings is still more elaborate and correct. The persons who, by their birth and offices, are attached to the Byzantine court, are those who maintain, with the least alloy, the ancient standard of elegance and purity; and the native graces of language most conspicuously shine among the noble matrons, who are excluded from all intercourse with foreigners. With foreigners do I say? They live retired and sequestered from the eyes of their fellow-citizens. Seldom are they seen in the streets; and when they leave their houses, it is in the dusk of evening, on visits to the churches and their nearest kindred. On these occasions they are on horseback, covered with a veil, and encompassed by their parents, their husbands, or their servants."

Among the Greeks a numerous and opulent clergy was dedicated to the service of religion; their monks and bishops have ever been distinguished by the gravity and austerity of their manners, nor were they diverted, like the Latin priests, by the pursuits and pleasures of a secular and even military life. After a large deduction for the time and talents that were lost in the devotion, the laziness, and the discord of the church and cloister, the more inquisitive and ambitious minds would explore the sacred and profane erudition of their native language. The ecclesiastics presided over the education of youth: the schools of philosophy and eloquence were perpetuated till the fall of the empire; and it may be affirmed that more books and more knowledge were included within the walls of Constantinople than could be dispersed over the extensive countries of the West. But an important distinction has been already noticed: the Greeks were stationary or retrograde, while the Latins were advancing with a rapid and progressive motion. The nations were excited by the spirit of independence and emulation; and even the little world of the Italian states contained more people and industry than the decreasing circle of the Byzantine empire. In Europe the lower ranks of society were relieved from the yoke of feudal servitude; and freedom is the first step to curiosity and knowledge. The use, however rude and corrupt, of the Latin tongue had been preserved by superstition; the universities, from Bologna to Oxford,[1] were peopled with thousands of scholars; and their misguided ardour might be directed to more liberal and manly studies. In the resurrection of science Italy was the first that cast away her shroud; and the eloquent Petrarch, by his lessons and his example, may justly be applauded as the first harbinger of day. A purer style of composition, a more generous and rational strain of sentiment, flowed from the study and imitation of the writers of ancient Rome; and the disciples of Cicero and Virgil approached, with reverence and love, the sanctuary of their Grecian masters. In the sack of Constantinople the French, and even the Venetians, had despised and destroyed the works of Lysippus and Homer; the monuments of art may be annihilated by a single blow, but the immortal mind is renewed and multiplied by the copies of the pen, and such copies it was the ambition of Petrarch and his friends to possess and understand. The arms of the Turks undoubtedly pressed the flight of the Muses: yet we may tremble at the thought that Greece might have been overwhelmed, with her schools and libraries, before Europe had emerged from the deluge of barbarism; that the seeds of science might have been scattered by the winds before the Italian soil was prepared for their cultivation.

The most learned Italians of the fifteenth century have confessed and applauded the restoration of Greek literature, after a long oblivion of many hundred years. Yet in that country, and beyond the Alps, some names are quoted; some profound scholars who, in the darker ages, were honourably distinguished by their knowledge of the Greek tongue; and national vanity has been loud in the praise of such rare examples of erudition. Without scrutinising the merit of individuals, truth must observe that their science is without a cause and without an effect; that it was easy for them to satisfy themselves and their more ignorant contemporaries; and that the idiom, which they had so marvellously acquired, was transcribed in few manuscripts, and was not taught in any university of the West. In a corner of Italy it faintly existed as the popular, or at least as the ecclesiastical, dialect. The first impression of the Doric and Ionic colonies has never been completely erased; the Calabrian churches were long attached to the throne of Constantinople; and the monks of St. Basil pursued their studies in Mount Athos and the schools of the East. Calabria was the native country of Barlaam,

---

[1] At the end of the xvth century there existed in Europe about fifty universities, and of these the foundation of ten or twelve is prior to the year 1300. They were crowded in proportion to their scarcity. Bologna contained 10,000 students, chiefly of the civil law. In the year 1357 the number at Oxford had decreased from 30,000 to 6000 scholars. Yet even this decrease is much superior to the present list of the members of the university.

who has already appeared as a sectary and an ambassador; and Barlaam was the first who revived, beyond the Alps, the memory, or at least the writings, of Homer. He is described, by Petrarch and Boccace, as a man of a diminutive stature, though truly great in the measure of learning and genius: of a piercing discernment, though of a slow and painful elocution. For many ages (as they affirm) Greece had not produced his equal in the knowledge of history, grammar, and philosophy; and his merit was celebrated in the attestations of the princes and doctors of Constantinople. One of these attestations is still extant; and the emperor Cantacuzene, the protector of his adversaries, is forced to allow that Euclid, Aristotle, and Plato were familiar to that profound and subtle logician. In the court of Avignon he formed an intimate connection with Petrarch, the first of the Latin scholars; and the desire of mutual instruction was the principle of their literary commerce. The Tuscan applied himself with eager curiosity and assiduous diligence to the study of the Greek language, and in a laborious struggle with the dryness and difficulty of the first rudiments he began to reach the sense, and to feel the spirit, of poets and philosophers whose minds were congenial to his own. But he was soon deprived of the society and lessons of this useful assistant; Barlaam relinquished his fruitless embassy, and, on his return to Greece, he rashly provoked the swarms of fanatic monks, by attempting to substitute the light of reason to that of their navel. After a separation of three years the two friends again met in the court of Naples; but the generous pupil renounced the fairest occasion of improvement; and by his recommendation Barlaam was finally settled in a small bishopric of his native Calabria. The manifold avocations of Petrarch, love and friendship, his various correspondence and frequent journeys, the Roman laurel, and his elaborate compositions in prose and verse, in Latin and Italian, diverted him from a foreign idiom; and as he advanced in life the attainment of the Greek language was the object of his wishes rather than of his hopes. When he was about fifty years of age, a Byzantine ambassador, his friend and a master of both tongues, presented him with a copy of Homer, and the answer of Petrarch is at once expressive of his eloquence, gratitude, and regret. After celebrating the generosity of the donor, and the value of a gift more precious in his estimation than gold or rubies, he thus proceeds:—"Your present of the genuine and original text of the divine poet, the fountain of all invention, is worthy of yourself and of me; you have fulfilled your promise, and satisfied my desires. Yet your liberality is still imperfect: with Homer you should have given me yourself; a guide who could lead me into the fields of light, and disclose to my wondering eyes the specious miracles of the Iliad and Odyssey. But, alas! Homer is dumb, or I am deaf; nor is it in my power to enjoy the beauty which I possess. I have seated him by the side of Plato, the prince of poets near the prince of philosophers, and I glory in the sight of my

illustrious guests. Of their immortal writings, whatever had been translated into the Latin idiom I had already acquired; but if there be no
profit, there is some pleasure, in beholding these venerable Greeks in
their proper and national habit. I am delighted with the aspect of
Homer; and as often as I embrace the silent volume, I exclaim with a
sigh, Illustrious bard! with what pleasure should I listen to thy song, if
my sense of hearing were not obstructed and lost by the death of one
friend, and in the much lamented absence of another! Nor do I yet
despair, and the example of Cato suggests some comfort and hope, since
it was in the last period of age that he attained the knowledge of the
Greek letters."

The prize which eluded the efforts of Petrarch was obtained by the fortune and industry of his friend Boccace, the father of the Tuscan prose.
That popular writer, who derives his reputation from the Decameron,
an hundred novels of pleasantry and love, may aspire to the more
serious praise of restoring in Italy the study of the Greek language. In
the year one thousand three hundred and sixty a disciple of Barlaam,
whose name was Leo or Leontius Pilatus, was detained in his way to
Avignon by the advice and hospitality of Boccace, who lodged the
stranger in his house, prevailed on the republic of Florence to allow him
an annual stipend, and devoted his leisure to the first Greek professor,
who taught that language in the Western countries of Europe. The
appearance of Leo might disgust the most eager disciple: he was clothed
in the mantle of a philosopher or a mendicant; his countenance was
hideous; his face was overshadowed with black hair; his beard long and
uncombed; his deportment rustic; his temper gloomy and inconstant;
nor could he grace his discourse with the ornaments or even the perspicuity of Latin elocution. But his mind was stored with a treasure of
Greek learning: history and fable, philosophy and grammar, were alike
at his command; and he read the poems of Homer in the schools of
Florence. It was from his explanation that Boccace composed and
transcribed a literal prose version of the Iliad and Odyssey, which satisfied the thirst of his friend Petrarch, and which, perhaps in the succeeding century, was clandestinely used by Laurentius Valla, the Latin
interpreter. It was from his narratives that the same Boccace collected
the materials for his treatise on the genealogy of the heathen gods, a
work, in that age, of stupendous erudition, and which he ostentatiously
sprinkled with Greek characters and passages, to excite the wonder and
applause of his more ignorant readers. The first steps of learning are
slow and laborious; no more than ten votaries of Homer could be
enumerated in all Italy, and neither Rome, nor Venice, nor Naples,
could add a single name to this studious catalogue. But their numbers
would have multiplied, their progress would have been accelerated, if
the inconstant Leo, at the end of three years, had not relinquished an
honourable and beneficial station. In his passage Petrarch entertained

him at Padua a short time: he enjoyed the scholar, but was justly offended with the gloomy and unsocial temper of the man. Discontented with the world and with himself, Leo depreciated his present enjoyments, while absent persons and objects were dear to his imagination. In Italy he was a Thessalian, in Greece a native of Calabria; in the company of the Latins he disdained their language, religion, and manners: no sooner was he landed at Constantinople than he again sighed for the wealth of Venice and the elegance of Florence. His Italian friends were deaf to his importunity: he depended on their curiosity and indulgence, and embarked on a second voyage; but on his entrance into the Adriatic the ship was assailed by a tempest, and the unfortunate teacher, who like Ulysses had fastened himself to the mast, was struck dead by a flash of lightning. The humane Petrarch dropped a tear on his disaster; but he was most anxious to learn whether some copy of Euripides or Sophocles might not be saved from the hands of the mariners.

But the faint rudiments of Greek learning, which Petrarch had encouraged and Boccace had planted, soon withered and expired. The succeeding generation was content for a while with the improvement of Latin eloquence; nor was it before the end of the fourteenth century that a new and perpetual flame was rekindled in Italy. Previous to his own journey, the emperor Manuel despatched his envoys and orators to implore the compassion of the Western princes. Of these envoys the most conspicuous, or the most learned, was Manuel Chrysoloras, of noble birth, and whose Roman ancestors are supposed to have migrated with the great Constantine. After visiting the courts of France and England, where he obtained some contributions and more promises, the envoy was invited to assume the office of a professor; and Florence had again the honour of this second invitation. By his knowledge, not only of the Greek but of the Latin tongue, Chrysoloras deserved the stipend and surpassed the expectation of the republic. His school was frequented by a crowd of disciples of every rank and age; and one of these, in a general history, has described his motives and his success. "At that time," said Leonard Aretin, "I was a student of the civil law; but my soul was inflamed with the love of letters, and I bestowed some application on the sciences of logic and rhetoric. On the arrival of Manuel I hesitated whether I should desert my legal studies or relinquish this golden opportunity; and thus, in the ardour of youth, I communed with my own mind—Wilt thou be wanting to thyself and thy fortune? Wilt thou refuse to be introduced to a familiar converse with Homer, Plato, and Demosthenes? with those poets, philosophers, and orators, of whom such wonders are related, and who are celebrated by every age as the great masters of human science? Of professors and scholars in civil law, a sufficient supply will always be found in our universities; but a teacher, and such a teacher of the Greek language, if he once be suffered to escape, may never afterwards be retrieved. Convinced by these reasons, I gave myself to Chrysoloras, and so strong was my passion, that the lessons which I had imbibed in the day were the constant subject of my nightly dreams." At the same time and place the Latin classics were explained by John of Ravenna, the domestic pupil of Petrarch: the Italians, who illustrated their age and country, were formed in this double school, and Florence became the fruitful seminary of Greek and Roman erudition. The presence of the emperor recalled Chrysoloras from the college to the court; but he afterwards taught at Pavia and Rome with equal industry and applause. The remainder of his life, about fifteen years, was divided between Italy and Constantinople, between embassies and lessons. In the noble office of enlightening a foreign nation, the grammarian was not unmindful of a more sacred duty to his prince and country; and Emanuel Chrysoloras died at Constance on a public mission from the emperor to the council.

After his example, the restoration of the Greek letters in Italy was prosecuted by a series of emigrants, who were destitute of fortune and endowed with learning, or at least with language. From the terror or oppression of the Turkish arms, the natives of Thessalonica and Constantinople escaped to a land of freedom, curiosity, and wealth. The synod introduced into Florence the lights of the Greek church and the oracles of the Platonic philosophy; and the fugitives who adhered to the union had the double merit of renouncing their country, not only for the Christian but for the Catholic cause. A patriot, who sacrifices his party and conscience to the allurements of favour, may be possessed however of the private and social virtues: he no longer hears the reproachful epithets of slave and apostate, and the consideration which he acquires among his new associates will restore in his own eyes the dignity of his character. The prudent conformity of Bessarion was rewarded with the Roman purple: he fixed his residence in Italy, and the Greek cardinal, the titular patriarch of Constantinople, was respected as the chief and protector of his nation: his abilities were exercised in the legations of Bologna, Venice, Germany, and France; and his election to the chair of St. Peter floated for a moment on the uncertain breath of a conclave.[1] His ecclesiastical honours diffused a splendour and pre-eminence over his literary merit and service: his palace was a school; as often as the cardinal visited the Vatican he was attended by a learned train of both nations; of men applauded by themselves and the public, and whose writings, now overspread with dust, were popular and useful in their own times. I shall not attempt to enumerate the restorers of Grecian literature in the fifteenth century; and it may be sufficient to mention with gratitude the names of Theodore Gaza, of

---

[1] The cardinals knocked at his door, but his conclavist refused to interrupt the studies of Bessarion; "Nicholas," said he, "thy respect has cost thee an hat, and me the tiara."

George of Trebizond, of John Argyropulus, and Demetrius Chalcondyles, who taught their native language in the schools of Florence and Rome. Their labours were not inferior to those of Bessarion, whose purple they revered, and whose fortune was the secret object of their envy. But the lives of these grammarians were humble and obscure: they had declined the lucrative paths of the church; their dress and manners secluded them from the commerce of the world; and since they were confined to the merit, they might be content with the rewards of learning. From this character Janus Lascaris will deserve an exception. His eloquence, politeness, and Imperial descent, recommended him to the French monarchs; and in the same cities he was alternately employed to teach and to negociate. Duty and interest prompted them to cultivate the study of the Latin language, and the most successful attained the faculty of writing and speaking with fluency and elegance in a foreign idiom. But they ever retained the inveterate vanity of their country: their praise, or at least their esteem, was reserved for the national writers to whom they owed their fame and subsistence; and they sometimes betrayed their contempt in licentious criticism or satire on Virgil's poetry and the oratory of Tully. The superiority of these masters arose from the familiar use of a living language; and their first disciples were incapable of discerning how far they had degenerated from the knowledge and even the practice of their ancestors. A vicious pronunciation,[1] which they introduced, was banished from the schools by the reason of the succeeding age. Of the power of the Greek accents they were ignorant; and those musical notes, which, from an Attic tongue and to an Attic ear, must have been the secret soul of harmony, were to their eyes, as to our own, no more than mute and unmeaning marks, in prose superfluous and troublesome in verse. The art of grammar they truly possessed; the valuable fragments of Apollonius and Herodian were transfused into their lessons; and their treatises of syntax and etymology, though devoid of philosophic spirit, are still useful to the Greek student. In the shipwreck of the Byzantine libraries each fugitive seized a fragment of treasure, a copy of some author, who, without his industry, might have perished: the transcripts were multiplied by an assiduous and sometimes an elegant pen, and the text was corrected and explained

---

[1] Manuel Chrysoloras and his colleagues are accused of ignorance, envy, or avarice. The modern Greeks pronounce the β as a V consonant, and confound three vowels ($\eta\ \iota\ \upsilon$) and several diphthongs. Such was the vulgar pronunciation which the stern Gardiner maintained by penal statutes in the university of Cambridge; but the monosyllable $\beta\eta$ represented to an Attic ear the bleating of sheep, and a bellwether is better evidence than a bishop or a chancellor. The treatises of those scholars, particularly Erasmus, who asserted a more classical pronunciation, are collected in the Sylloge of Havercamp; but it is difficult to paint sounds by words; and, in their reference to modern use, they can be understood only by their respective countrymen. We may observe that our peculiar pronunciation of the θ, *th*, is approved by Erasmus.

by their own comments or those of the elder scholiasts. The sense, though not the spirit, of the Greek classics was interpreted to the Latin world: the beauties of style evaporate in a version; but the judgment of Theodore Gaza selected the more solid works of Aristotle and Theophrastus, and their natural histories of animals and plants opened a rich fund of genuine and experimental science.

Yet the fleeting shadows of metaphysics were pursued with more curiosity and ardour. After a long oblivion, Plato was revived in Italy by a venerable Greek,[1] who taught in the house of Cosmo of Medicis. While the synod of Florence was involved in theological debate, some beneficial consequences might flow from the study of his elegant philosophy: his style is the purest standard of the Attic dialect, and his sublime thoughts are sometimes adapted to familiar conversation, and sometimes adorned with the richest colours of poetry and eloquence. The dialogues of Plato are a dramatic picture of the life and death of a sage; and, as often as he descends from the clouds, his moral system inculcates the love of truth, of our country, and of mankind. The precept and example of Socrates recommended a modest doubt and liberal inquiry; and if the Platonists, with blind devotion, adored the visions and errors of their divine master, their enthusiasm might correct the dry, dogmatic method of the Peripatetic school. So equal, yet so opposite, are the merits of Plato and Aristotle, that they may be balanced in endless controversy; but some spark of freedom may be produced by the collision of adverse servitude. The modern Greeks were divided between the two sects: with more fury than skill they fought under the banner of their leaders, and the field of battle was removed in their flight from Constantinople to Rome. But this philosophical debate soon degenerated into an angry and personal quarrel of grammarians; and Bessarion, though an advocate for Plato, protected the national honour by interposing the advice and authority of a mediator. In the gardens of the Medici the academical doctrine was enjoyed by the polite and learned; but their philosophic society was quickly dissolved; and if the writings of the Attic sage were perused in the closet, the more powerful Stagyrite continued to reign the oracle of the church and school.

POPE NICHOLAS V

I have fairly represented the literary merits of the Greeks; yet it must be confessed that they were seconded and surpassed by the ardour of the Latins. Italy was divided into many independent states; and at that time it was the ambition of princes and republics to vie with each other in the encouragement and reward of literature. The fame of Nicholas

---

[1] George Gemistus Pletho, a various and voluminous writer, the master of Bessarion, and all the Platonists of the times. He visited Italy in his old age, and soon returned to end his days in Peloponnesus.

the Fifth has not been adequate to his merits. From a plebeian origin he raised himself by his virtue and learning: the character of the man prevailed over the interest of the pope, and he sharpened those weapons which were soon pointed against the Roman church. He had been the friend of the most eminent scholars of the age: he became their patron; and such was the humility of his manners, that the change was scarcely discernible either to them or to himself. If he pressed the acceptance of a liberal gift, it was not as the measure of desert, but as the proof of benevolence; and when modest merit declined his bounty, "Accept it," would he say, with a consciousness of his own worth: "you will not always have a Nicholas among ye." The influence of the holy see pervaded Christendom; and he exerted that influence in the search, not of benefices, but of books. From the ruins of the Byzantine libraries, from the darkest monasteries of Germany and Britain, he collected the dusty manuscripts of the writers of antiquity; and wherever the original could not be removed, a faithful copy was transcribed and transmitted for his use. The Vatican, the old repository for bulls and legends, for superstition and forgery, was daily replenished with more precious furniture; and such was the industry of Nicholas, that in a reign of eight years he formed a library of five thousand volumes. To his munificence the Latin world was indebted for the versions of Xenophon, Diodorus, Polybius, Thucydides, Herodotus, and Appian; of Strabo's Geography, of the Iliad, of the most valuable works of Plato and Aristotle, of Ptolemy and Theophrastus, and of the fathers of the Greek church. The example of the Roman pontiff was preceded or imitated by a Florentine merchant, who governed the republic without arms and without a title. Cosmo of Medicis was the father of a line of princes whose name and age are almost synonymous with the restoration of learning: his credit was ennobled into fame; his riches were dedicated to the service of mankind; he corresponded at once with Cairo and London; and a cargo of Indian spices and Greek books was often imported in the same vessel. The genius and education of his grandson Lorenzo rendered him not only a patron but a judge and candidate in the literary race. In his palace, distress was entitled to relief, and merit to reward: his leisure hours were delightfully spent in the Platonic academy; he encouraged the emulation of Demetrius Chalcondyles and Angelo Politian; and his active missionary Janus Lascaris returned from the East with a treasure of two hundred manuscripts, fourscore of which were as yet unknown in the libraries of Europe. The rest of Italy was animated by a similar spirit, and the progress of the nation repaid the liberality of her princes. The Latins held the exclusive property of their own literature; and these disciples of Greece were soon capable of transmitting and improving the lessons which they had imbibed. After a short succession of foreign teachers, the tide of emigration subsided; but the language of Constantinople was spread beyond the Alps, and the natives of France, Germany, and England [1] imparted to their country the sacred fire which they had kindled in the schools of Florence and Rome. In the productions of the mind, as in those of the soil, the gifts of nature are excelled by industry and skill: the Greek authors, forgotten on the banks of the Ilissus, have been illustrated on those of the Elbe and the Thames; and Bessarion or Gaza might have envied the superior science of the barbarians, the accuracy of Budæus, the taste of Erasmus, the copiousness of Stephens, the erudition of Scaliger, the discernment of Reiske or of Bentley. On the side of the Latins the discovery of printing was a casual advantage; but this useful art has been applied by Aldus and his innumerable successors to perpetuate and multiply the works of antiquity.[2] A single manuscript imported from Greece is revived in ten thousand copies, and each copy is fairer than the original. In this form Homer and Plato would peruse with more satisfaction their own writings; and their scholiasts must resign the prize to the labours of our Western editors.

USE AND ABUSE OF ANCIENT LEARNING

Before the revival of classic literature the barbarians in Europe were immersed in ignorance; and their vulgar tongues were marked with the rudeness and poverty of their manners. The students of the more perfect idioms of Rome and Greece were introduced to a new world of light and science; to the society of the free and polished nations of antiquity; and to a familiar converse with those immortal men who spoke the sublime language of eloquence and reason. Such an intercourse must tend to refine the taste and to elevate the genius of the moderns; and yet, from the first experiment, it might appear that the study of the ancients had given fetters, rather than wings, to the human mind. However laudable, the spirit of imitation is of a servile cast; and the first disciples of the Greeks and Romans were a colony of strangers in the midst of their age and country. The minute and laborious diligence which explored the antiquities of remote times might have improved or adorned the present state of society; the critic and metaphysician were the slaves of Aristotle; the poets, historians, and orators

---

[1] The Greek language was introduced into the university of Oxford in the last years of the xvth century by Grocyn, Linacer, and Latimer, who had all studied at Florence under Demetrius Chalcondyles. See Dr. Knight's curious Life of Erasmus. Although a stout academical patriot, he is forced to acknowledge that Erasmus learned Greek at Oxford, and taught it at Cambridge.

[2] The press of Aldus Manutius, a Roman, was established at Venice about the year 1494: he printed above sixty considerable works of Greek literature, almost all for the first time; several containing different treatises and authors, and of several authors two, three, or four editions. Yet his glory must not tempt us to forget that the first Greek book, the Grammar of Constantine Lascaris, was printed at Milan in 1476, and that the Florence Homer of 1488 displays all the luxury of the typographical art. See the Annales Typographici of Maittaire, and the Bibliographie Instructive of De Bure, a knowing bookseller of Paris.

were proud to repeat the thoughts and words of the Augustan age: the works of nature were observed with the eyes of Pliny and Theophrastus; and some Pagan votaries professed a secret devotion to the gods of Homer and Plato.[1] The Italians were oppressed by the strength and number of their ancient auxiliaries: the century after the deaths of Petrarch and Boccace was filled with a crowd of Latin imitators, who decently repose on our shelves; but in that era of learning it will not be easy to discern a real discovery of science, a work of invention or eloquence, in the popular language of the country. But as soon as it had been deeply saturated with the celestial dew, the soil was quickened into vegetation and life; the modern idioms were refined; the classics of Athens and Rome inspired a pure taste and a generous emulation; and in Italy, as afterwards in France and England, the pleasing reign of poetry and fiction was succeeded by the light of speculative and experimental philosophy. Genius may anticipate the season of maturity; but in the education of a people, as in that of an individual, memory must be exercised before the powers of reason and fancy can be expanded: nor may the artist hope to equal or surpass, till he has learned to imitate, the works of his predecessors.

[1] I will select three singular examples of this classic enthusiasm. 1. At the synod of Florence, Gemistus Pletho said, in familiar conversation, to George of Trebizond, that in a short time mankind would unanimously renounce the Gospel and the Koran for a religion similar to that of the Gentiles. 2. Paul II. persecuted the Roman academy, which had been founded by Pomponius Lætus; and the principal members were accused of heresy, impiety, and *paganism*. 3. In the next century some scholars and poets in France celebrated the success of Jodelle's tragedy of Cleopatra by a festival of Bacchus, and, as it is said, by the sacrifice of a goat. Yet the spirit of bigotry might often discern a serious impiety in the sportive play of fancy and learning.

The Union of the churches achieved at the Council of Florence was soon followed by the final schism of the Greek church (1440–1448). The operations of Ladislaus king of Poland and Hungary and the revolts of John Huniades and Scanderbeg hampered the Turks but could not hold off the final issue. Constantine Palæologus became, as it proved, the last Roman emperor in Constantinople, from 1448–1453. These events are described by Gibbon in Chapter 67.

Chapter 68

CHARACTER AND REIGN OF MAHOMET II. HIS SIEGE AND
CAPTURE OF CONSTANTINOPLE. HIS ENTRY INTO THE CITY.
GRIEF AND TERROR OF EUROPE

THE siege of Constantinople by the Turks attracts our first attention to the person and character of the great destroyer. Mahomet the Second was the son of the second Amurath; and though his mother has been decorated with the titles of Christian and princess, she is more probably confounded with the numerous concubines who peopled from every climate the harem of the sultan. His first education and sentiments were those of a devout Musulman; and as often as he conversed with an infidel he purified his hands and face by the legal rites of ablution. Age and empire appear to have relaxed this narrow bigotry: his aspiring genius disdained to acknowledge a power above his own; and in his looser hours he presumed (it is said) to brand the prophet of Mecca as a robber and impostor. Yet the sultan persevered in a decent reverence for the doctrine and discipline of the Koran: his private indiscretion must have been sacred from the vulgar ear; and we should suspect the credulity of strangers and sectaries, so prone to believe that a mind which is hardened against truth must be armed with superior contempt for absurdity and error. Under the tuition of the most skilful masters Mahomet advanced with an early and rapid progress in the paths of knowledge; and besides his native tongue it is affirmed that he spoke or understood five languages, the Arabic, the Persian, the Chaldæan or Hebrew, the Latin, and the Greek. The Persian might indeed contribute to his amusement, and the Arabic to his edification; and such studies are familiar to the Oriental youth. In the intercourse of the Greeks and Turks a conqueror might wish to converse with the people over whom he was ambitious to reign: his own praises in Latin poetry or prose might find a passage to the royal ear; but what use or merit could recommend to the statesman or the scholar the uncouth dialect of his Hebrew slaves? The history and geography of the world were familiar to his memory: the lives of the heroes of the East, perhaps of the West, excited his emulation: his skill in astrology is excused by the folly of the times, and supposes some rudiments of mathematical science; and a profane taste for the arts is betrayed in his liberal invitation and reward of the painters of Italy.[1] But the influence

[1] The famous Gentile Bellino, whom he had invited from Venice, was dismissed with a chain and collar of gold and a purse of 300 ducats. With Voltaire I laugh at the foolish story of a slave purposely beheaded to instruct the painter in the action of the muscles.

833

of religion and learning were employed without effect on his savage and
licentious nature. I will not transcribe, nor do I firmly believe, the
stories of his fourteen pages whose bellies were ripped open in search
of a stolen melon, or of the beauteous slave whose head he severed from
her body to convince the Janizaries that their master was not the votary
of love.[1] His sobriety is attested by the silence of the Turkish annals,
which accuse three, and three only, of the Ottoman line of the vice of
drunkenness.[2] But it cannot be denied that his passions were at once
furious and inexorable; that in the palace, as in the field, a torrent of
blood was spilt on the slightest provocation; and that the noblest of the
captive youth were often dishonoured by his unnatural lust. In the
Albanian war he studied the lessons, and soon surpassed the example,
of his father; and the conquest of two empires, twelve kingdoms, and
two hundred cities, a vain and flattering account, is ascribed to his
invincible sword. He was doubtless a soldier, and possibly a general;
Constantinople has sealed his glory; but if we compare the means, the
obstacles, and the achievements, Mahomet the Second must blush to
sustain a parallel with Alexander or Timour. Under his command the
Ottoman forces were always more numerous than their enemies, yet
their progress was bounded by the Euphrates and the Adriatic, and his
arms were checked by Huniades and Scanderbeg, by the Rhodian
knights, and by the Persian king.

In the reign of Amurath he twice tasted of royalty, and twice descended from the throne: his tender age was incapable of opposing his
father's restoration, but never could he forgive the vizirs who had
recommended that salutary measure. His nuptials were celebrated with
the daughter of a Turkman emir; and, after a festival of two months, he
departed from Adrianople with his bride to reside in the government of
Magnesia. Before the end of six weeks he was recalled by a sudden
message from the divan which announced the decease of Amurath and
the mutinous spirit of the Janizaries. His speed and vigour commanded
their obedience: he passed the Hellespont with a chosen guard: and at
the distance of a mile from Adrianople the vizirs and emirs, the imams
and cadhis, the soldiers and the people, fell prostrate before the new
sultan. They affected to weep, they affected to rejoice: he ascended the
throne at the age of twenty-one years, and removed the cause of sedition
by the death, the inevitable death, of his infant brothers. The ambassadors of Europe and Asia soon appeared to congratulate his accession
and solicit his friendship, and to all he spoke the language of moderation
and peace. The confidence of the Greek emperor was revived by the

[1] Dr. Johnson's *Irene* is founded on this story. Gibbon's doubts have been
confirmed by later writers. Bury points out the story is found in Seneca's (b. 55 B.C.)
Controversiæ, x. 5.—D.M.L.

[2] These Imperial drunkards were Soliman I., Selim II., and Amurath IV. The
sophis of Persia can produce a more regular succession; and in the last age our
European travellers were the witnesses and companions of their revels.

solemn oaths and fair assurances with which he sealed the ratification of the treaty: and a rich domain on the banks of the Strymon was assigned for the annual payment of three hundred thousand aspers, the pension of an Ottoman prince who was detained at his request in the Byzantine court. Yet the neighbours of Mahomet might tremble at the severity with which a youthful monarch reformed the pomp of his father's household: the expenses of luxury were applied to those of ambition, and an useless train of seven thousand falconers was either dismissed from his service or enlisted in his troops. In the first summer of his reign he visited with an army the Asiatic provinces; but after humbling the pride Mahomet accepted the submission of the Caramanian, that he might not be diverted by the smallest obstacle from the execution of his great design.

Mahomet built a fortress at Asomaton on the Bosphorus and made preparations for the siege of Constantinople. A cannon was constructed of tremendous power. Meanwhile the emperor Constantine Palæologus tried unsuccessfully to attract help from the West.

THE SIEGE OF CONSTANTINOPLE

Of the triangle which composes the figure of Constantinople the two sides along the sea were made inaccessible to an enemy; the Propontis by nature, and the harbour by art. Between the two waters, the basis of the triangle, the land side was protected by a double wall and a deep ditch of the depth of one hundred feet. Against this line of fortification, which Phranza, an eye-witness, prolongs to the measure of six miles, the Ottomans directed their principal attack; and the emperor, after distributing the service and command of the most perilous stations, undertook the defence of the external wall. In the first days of the siege the Greek soldiers descended into the ditch, or sallied into the field; but they soon discovered that, in the proportion of their numbers, one Christian was of more value than twenty Turks: and, after these bold preludes, they were prudently content to maintain the rampart with their missile weapons. Nor should this prudence be accused of pusillanimity. The nation was indeed pusillanimous and base; but the last Constantine deserves the name of an hero: his noble band of volunteers was inspired with Roman virtue; and the foreign auxiliaries supported the honour of the Western chivalry. The incessant volleys of lances and arrows were accompanied with the smoke, the sound, and the fire of their musketry and cannon. Their small arms discharged at the same time either five, or even ten, balls of lead, of the size of a walnut; and, according to the closeness of the ranks and the force of the powder, several breastplates and bodies were transpierced by the same shot. But the Turkish approaches were soon sunk in trenches or covered with ruins. Each day added to the science of the Christians; but their inadequate stock of gunpowder was wasted in the operations of each day. Their ordnance was not powerful either in size or number; and if they possessed some heavy cannon, they feared to plant them on the walls, lest the aged structure should be shaken and overthrown by the explosion. The same destructive secret had been revealed to the Moslems; by whom it was employed with the superior energy of zeal, riches, and despotism. The great cannon of Mahomet has been separately noticed; an important and visible object in the history of the times: but that enormous engine was flanked by two fellows almost of equal magnitude: the long order of the Turkish artillery was pointed against the walls; fourteen batteries thundered at once on the most accessible places; and of one of these it is ambiguously expressed that it was mounted with one hundred and thirty guns, or that it discharged one hundred and thirty bullets. Yet in the power and activity of the sultan we may discern the infancy of the new science. Under a master who counted the moments the great cannon could be loaded and fired no more than seven times in one day. The heated metal unfortunately burst; several workmen were destroyed; and the skill of an artist was admired who bethought himself of preventing the danger and the accident, by pouring oil, after each explosion, into the mouth of the cannon.

The first random shots were productive of more sound than effect; and it was by the advice of a Christian that the engineers were taught to level their aim against the two opposite sides of the salient angles of a bastion. However imperfect, the weight and repetition of the fire made some impression on the walls; and the Turks, pushing their approaches to the edge of the ditch, attempted to fill the enormous chasm and to build a road to the assault. Innumerable fascines, and hogsheads, and trunks of trees, were heaped on each other; and such was the impetuosity of the throng, that the foremost and the weakest were pushed headlong down the precipice and instantly buried under the accumulated mass. To fill the ditch was the toil of the besiegers; to clear away the rubbish was the safety of the besieged; and, after a long and bloody conflict, the web that had been woven in the day was still unravelled in the night. The next resource of Mahomet was the practice of mines; but the soil was rocky; in every attempt he was stopped and undermined by the Christian engineers; nor had the art been yet invented of replenishing those subterraneous passages with gunpowder and blowing whole towers and cities into the air. A circumstance that distinguishes the siege of Constantinople is the re-union of the ancient and modern artillery. The cannon were intermingled with the mechanical engines for casting stones and darts; the bullet and the battering-ram were directed against the same walls; nor had the discovery of gunpowder superseded the use of the liquid and unextinguishable fire. A wooden turret of the largest size was advanced on rollers: this portable magazine of ammunition and fascines was protected by a threefold covering of bulls' hides; incessant volleys were securely discharged from the loopholes; in the front three doors were contrived for the alternate sally and retreat of the soldiers and workmen. They ascended by a staircase to the upper platform, and, as high as the level of that platform, a scaling-ladder could be raised by pulleys to form a bridge and grapple with the adverse rampart. By these various arts of annoyance, some as new as they were pernicious to the Greeks, the tower of St. Romanus was at length overturned: after a severe struggle the Turks were repulsed from the breach and interrupted by darkness; but they trusted that with the return of light they should renew the attack with fresh vigour and decisive success. Of this pause of action, this interval of hope, each moment was improved by the activity of the emperor and Justiniani, who passed the night on the spot, and urged the labours which involved the safety of the church and city. At the dawn of day the impatient sultan perceived, with astonishment and grief, that his wooden turret had been reduced to ashes: the ditch was cleared and restored, and the tower of St. Romanus was again strong and entire. He deplored the failure of his design, and uttered a profane exclamation, that the word of the thirty-seven thousand prophets should not have compelled him to believe that such a work, in so short a time, could have been accomplished by the infidels.

The generosity of the Christian princes was cold and tardy; but in the first apprehension of a siege Constantine had negotiated, in the isles of the Archipelago, the Morea, and Sicily, the most indispensable supplies. As early as the beginning of April, five great ships, equipped for merchandise and war, would have sailed from the harbour of Chios, had not the wind blown obstinately from the north. One of these ships bore the Imperial flag; the remaining four belonged to the Genoese; and they were laden with wheat and barley, with wine, oil, and vegetables, and, above all, with soldiers and mariners, for the service of the capital. After a tedious delay a gentle breeze, and on the second day a strong gale from the south, carried them through the Hellespont and the Propontis; but the city was already invested by sea and land, and the Turkish fleet, at the entrance of the Bosphorus, was stretched from shore to shore, in the form of a crescent, to intercept, or at least to repel, these bold auxiliaries. The reader who has present to his mind the geographical picture of Constantinople will conceive and admire the greatness of the spectacle. The five Christian ships continued to advance with joyful shouts, and a full press both of sails and oars, against an hostile fleet of three hundred vessels; and the rampart, the camp, the coasts of Europe and Asia, were lined with innumerable spectators, who anxiously awaited the event of this momentous succour. At the first view that event could not appear doubtful; the superiority of the Moslems was beyond all measure or account, and, in a calm, their numbers and valour must inevitably have prevailed. But their hasty and imperfect navy had been created, not by the genius of the people, but by the will of the sultan: in the height of their prosperity the Turks have acknowledged that, if God had given them the earth, he had left the sea to the infidels; and a series of defeats, a rapid progress of decay, has established the truth of their modest confession. Except eighteen galleys of some force, the rest of their fleet consisted of open boats, rudely constructed and awkwardly managed, crowded with troops, and destitute of cannon; and since courage arises in a great measure from the consciousness of strength, the bravest of the Janizaries might tremble on a new element. In the Christian squadron five stout and lofty ships were guided by skilful pilots, and manned with the veterans of Italy and Greece, long practised in the arts and perils of the sea. Their weight was directed to sink or scatter the weak obstacles that impeded their passage: their artillery swept the waters; their liquid fire was poured on the heads of the adversaries, who, with the design of boarding, presumed to approach them; and the winds and waves are always on the side of the ablest navigators. In this conflict the Imperial vessel, which had been almost overpowered, was rescued by the Genoese; but the Turks, in a distant and a closer attack, were twice repulsed with considerable loss. Mahomet himself sat on horseback on the beach, to encourage their valour by his voice and presence, by the promise of reward, and by fear more potent than the fear of the enemy. The passions of his soul, and even the gestures of his body, seemed to imitate the actions of the combatants; and, as if he had been the lord of nature, he spurred his horse with a fearless and impotent effort into the sea. His loud reproaches, and the clamours of the camp, urged the Ottomans to a third attack, more fatal and bloody than the two former; and I must repeat, though I cannot credit, the evidence of Phranza, who affirms, from their own mouth, that they lost above twelve thousand men in the slaughter of the day. They fled in disorder to the shores of Europe and Asia, while the Christian squadron, triumphant and unhurt, steered along the Bosphorus, and securely anchored within the chain of the harbour. In the confidence of victory, they boasted that the whole Turkish power must have yielded to their arms; but the admiral, or captain bashaw, found some consolation for a painful wound in his eye, by representing that accident as the cause of his defeat. Baltha Ogli was a renegade of the race of the Bulgarian princes: his military character was tainted with the unpopular vice of avarice; and under the despotism of the prince or people, misfortune is a sufficient evidence of guilt. His rank and services were annihilated by the displeasure of Mahomet. In the royal presence, the captain bashaw was extended on the ground by four slaves, and received one hundred strokes with a golden rod: his death had been pronounced, and he adored the clemency of the sultan, who was satisfied with the milder punishment of confiscation and exile. The introduction of this supply revived the hopes of the Greeks, and accused the supineness of their Western allies. Amidst the deserts of Anatolia and the rocks of Palestine, the millions of the crusades had buried themselves in a voluntary and inevitable grave; but the situation of the Imperial city was strong against her enemies, and accessible to her friends; and a rational and moderate armament of the maritime states might have saved the relics of the Roman name, and maintained a Christian fortress in the heart of the Ottoman empire. Yet this was the sole and feeble attempt for the deliverance of Constantinople: the more distant powers were insensible of its danger; and the ambassador of Hungary, or at least of Huniades, resided in the Turkish camp, to remove the fears and to direct the operations of the sultan.

It was difficult for the Greeks to penetrate the secret of the divan; yet the Greeks are persuaded that a resistance so obstinate and surprising had fatigued the perseverance of Mahomet. He began to meditate a retreat; and the siege would have been speedily raised, if the ambition and jealousy of the second vizir had not opposed the perfidious advice of Calil Bashaw, who still maintained a secret correspondence with the Byzantine court. The reduction of the city appeared to be hopeless, unless a double attack could be made from the harbour as well as from the land; but the harbour was inaccessible: an impenetrable chain was now defended by eight large ships, more than twenty of a smaller size, with several galleys and sloops; and, instead of forcing this barrier, the Turks might apprehend a naval sally and a second encounter in the open sea. In this perplexity the genius of Mahomet conceived and executed a plan of a bold and marvellous cast, of transporting by land his lighter vessels and military stores from the Bosphorus into the higher part of the harbour. The distance is about ten miles; the ground is uneven, and was overspread with thickets; and, as the road must be opened behind the suburb of Galata, their free passage or total destruction must depend on the option of the Genoese. But these selfish merchants were ambitious of the favour of being the last devoured, and the deficiency of art was supplied by the strength of obedient myriads. A level way was covered with a broad platform of strong and solid planks; and to render them more slippery and smooth, they were anointed with the fat of sheep and oxen. Fourscore light galleys and brigantines of fifty and thirty oars were disembarked on the Bosphorus shore, arranged successively on rollers, and drawn forwards by the power of men and pulleys. Two guides or pilots were stationed at the helm and the prow of each vessel: the sails were unfurled to the winds, and the labour was cheered by song and acclamation. In the course of a single night this Turkish fleet painfully climbed the hill, steered over the plain, and was launched from the declivity into the shallow waters of the harbour, far above the molestation of the deeper vessels of the Greeks. The real importance of this operation was magnified by the consternation and confidence which it inspired; but the notorious, unquestionable fact was displayed before the eyes, and is recorded by the pens, of the two nations. A similar stratagem had been repeatedly practised by the ancients; the Ottoman galleys (I must again repeat) should be considered as large boats; and, if we compare the magnitude and the distance, the obstacles and the means, the boasted miracle has perhaps been equalled by the industry of our own times. As soon as Mahomet had occupied the upper harbour with a fleet and army, he constructed in the narrowest part a bridge, or rather mole, of fifty cubits in breadth and one hundred in length: it was formed of casks and hogsheads, joined with rafters, linked with iron, and covered with a solid floor. On this floating battery he planted one of his largest cannon, while the fourscore galleys, with troops and scaling-ladders, approached the most accessible side, which had formerly been stormed by the Latin conquerors. The indolence of the Christians has been accused for not destroying these unfinished works; but their fire, by a superior fire, was controlled and silenced; nor were they wanting in a nocturnal attempt to burn the vessels as well as the bridge of the sultan. His vigilance prevented their approach: their foremost galliots were sunk or taken; forty youths, the bravest of Italy and Greece, were inhumanly massacred at his command; nor could the emperor's grief be assuaged by the just though cruel retaliation of exposing from the walls the heads of two hundred and sixty Musulman captives. After a siege of forty days the fate of Constantinople could no longer be averted. The diminutive garrison was exhausted by a double attack: the fortifications, which had stood for ages against hostile violence, were dismantled on all sides by the Ottoman cannon; many breaches were opened, and near the gate of St. Romanus four towers had been levelled with the ground. For the payment of his feeble and mutinous troops, Constantine was compelled to despoil the churches with the promise of a fourfold restitution; and his sacrilege offered a new reproach to the enemies of the union. A spirit of discord impaired the remnant of the Christian strength: the Genoese and Venetian auxiliaries asserted the pre-eminence of their respective service; and Justiniani and the great duke, whose ambition was not extinguished by the common danger, accused each other of treachery and cowardice.

During the siege of Constantinople the words of peace and capitulation had been sometimes pronounced; and several embassies had passed between the camp and the city. The Greek emperor was humbled by adversity; and would have yielded to any terms compatible with religion and royalty. The Turkish sultan was desirous of sparing the blood of his soldiers; still more desirous of securing for his own use the Byzantine treasures; and he accomplished a sacred duty in presenting to the Gabours the choice of circumcision, of tribute, or of death. The avarice of Mahomet might have been satisfied with an annual sum of one hundred thousand ducats; but his ambition grasped the capital of the East: to the prince he offered a rich equivalent, to the people a free toleration, or a safe departure: but after some fruitless treaty, he declared his resolution of finding either a throne or a grave under the walls of Constantinople. A sense of honour, and the fear of universal reproach, forbade Palæologus to resign the city into the hands of the Ottomans; and he determined to abide the last extremities of war. Several days were employed by the sultan in the preparations of the assault; and a respite was granted by his favourite science of astrology, which had fixed on the twenty-ninth of May as the fortunate and fatal hour. On the evening of the twenty-seventh he issued his final orders; assembled in his presence the military chiefs; and dispersed his heralds through the camp to proclaim the duty and the motives of the perilous enterprise. Fear is the first principle of a despotic government; and his menaces were expressed in the Oriental style, that the fugitives and deserters, had they the wings of a bird, should not escape from his inexorable justice. The greatest part of his bashaws and Janizaries were the offspring of Christian parents: but the glories of the Turkish name were perpetuated by successive adoption; and in the gradual change of individuals, the spirit of a legion, a regiment, or an *oda*, is kept alive by imitation and discipline. In this holy warfare the Moslems were exhorted to purify their minds with prayer, their bodies with seven ablutions; and to abstain from food till the close of the ensuing day. A crowd of dervishes visited the tents, to instil the desire of martyrdom, and the assurance of spending an immortal youth amidst the rivers and gardens of paradise, and in the embraces of the black-eyed virgins. Yet Mahomet principally trusted to the efficacy of temporal and visible rewards. A double pay was promised to the victorious troops; "The city and the buildings," said Mahomet, "are mine; but I resign to your valour the captives and the spoil, the treasures of gold and beauty; be rich and be happy. Many are the provinces of my empire: the intrepid soldier who first ascends the walls of Constantinople shall be rewarded with the government of the fairest and most wealthy; and my gratitude shall accumulate his honours and fortunes above the measure of his own hopes." Such various and potent motives diffused among the Turks a general ardour, regardless of life and impatient for action: the camp re-echoed with the Moslem shouts of "God is God: there is but one God, and "Mahomet is the apostle of God," and the sea and land, from Galata to the seven towers, were illuminated by the blaze of their nocturnal fires.

Far different was the state of the Christians; who, with loud and impotent complaints, deplored the guilt, or the punishment, of their sins. The celestial image of the Virgin had been exposed in solemn procession; but their divine patroness was deaf to their entreaties: they accused the obstinacy of the emperor for refusing a timely surrender; anticipated the horrors of their fate; and sighed for the repose and security of Turkish servitude. The noblest of the Greeks, and the bravest of the allies, were summoned to the palace, to prepare them, on the evening of the twenty-eighth, for the duties and dangers of the general assault. The last speech of Palæologus was the funeral oration of the Roman empire: he promised, he conjured, and he vainly attempted to infuse the hope which was extinguished in his own mind. In this world all was comfortless and gloomy; and neither the Gospel nor the church have proposed any conspicuous recompense to the heroes who fall in the service of their country. But the example of their prince, and the confinement of a siege, had armed these warriors with the courage of despair; and the pathetic scene is described by the feelings of the historian Phranza, who was himself present at this mournful assembly. They wept, they embraced: regardless of their families and fortunes, they devoted their lives; and each commander, departing to his station, maintained all night a vigilant and anxious watch on the rampart. The emperor, and some faithful companions, entered the dome of St. Sophia, which in a few hours was to be converted into a mosch; and devoutly received, with tears and prayers, the sacrament of the holy communion. He reposed some moments in the palace, which resounded with cries and lamentations; solicited the pardon of all whom he might have injured; and mounted on horseback to visit the guards, and explore the motions of the enemy. The distress and fall of the last Constantine are more glorious than the long prosperity of the Byzantine Cæsars.

THE CAPTURE OF CONSTANTINOPLE

In the confusion of darkness an assailant may sometimes succeed; but in this great and general attack, the military judgment and astrological knowledge of Mahomet advised him to expect the morning, the memorable twenty-ninth of May, in the fourteen hundred and fifty-third year of the Christian era. The preceding night had been strenuously employed: the troops, the cannon, and the fascines were advanced to the edge of the ditch, which in many parts presented a smooth and level passage to the breach; and his fourscore galleys almost touched, with the prows and their scaling ladders, the less defensible walls of the harbour. Under pain of death, silence was enjoined; but the physical laws of motion and sound are not obedient to discipline or fear: each individual might suppress his voice and measure his footsteps; but the march and labour of thousands must inevitably produce a strange confusion of dissonant clamours, which reached the ears of the watchmen of the towers. At daybreak, without the customary signal of the morning gun, the Turks assaulted the city by sea and land; and the similitude of a twined or twisted thread has been applied to the closeness and continuity of their line of attack. The foremost ranks consisted of the refuse of the host, a voluntary crowd who fought without order or command; of the feebleness of age or childhood, of peasants and vagrants, and of all who had joined the camp in the blind hope of plunder and martyrdom. The common impulse drove them onwards to the wall; the most audacious to climb were instantly precipitated; and not a dart, not a bullet, of the Christians, was idly wasted on the accumulated throng. But their strength and ammunition were exhausted in this laborious defence: the ditch was filled with the bodies of the slain; they supported the footsteps of their companions; and of this devoted vanguard the death was more serviceable than the life. Under their respective bashaws and sanjaks, the troops of Anatolia and Romania were successively led to the charge: their progress was various and doubtful; but, after a conflict of two hours, the Greeks still maintained and improved their advantage; and the voice of the emperor was heard, encouraging his soldiers to achieve, by a last effort, the deliverance of their country. In that fatal moment the Janizaries arose, fresh, vigorous, and invincible. The sultan himself on horseback, with an iron mace in his hand, was the spectator and judge of their valour; he was surrounded by ten thousand of his domestic troops, whom he reserved for the decisive occasion; and the tide of battle was directed and impelled by his voice and eye. His numerous ministers of justice were posted behind the line, to urge, to restrain, and to punish; and if danger was in the front, shame and inevitable death were in the rear, of the fugitives. The cries of fear and of pain were drowned in the martial music of drums, trumpets, and attaballs; and experience has proved that the mechanical operation of sounds, by quickening the circulation of the blood and spirits, will act on the human machine more forcibly than the eloquence of reason and honour. From the lines, the galleys, and the bridge, the Ottoman artillery thundered on all sides; and the camp and city, the Greeks and the Turks, were involved in a cloud of smoke, which could only be dispelled by the final deliverance or destruction of the Roman empire. The single combats of the heroes of history or fable amuse our fancy and engage our affections: the skilful evolutions of war may inform the mind, and improve a necessary, though pernicious, science. But in the uniform and odious pictures of a general assault, all is blood, and horror, and confusion; nor shall I strive, at the distance of three centuries and a thousand miles, to delineate a scene of which there could be no spectators, and of which the actors themselves were incapable of forming any just or adequate idea.

The immediate loss of Constantinople may be ascribed to the bullet or arrow, which pierced the gauntlet of John Justiniani. The sight of his blood, and the exquisite pain, appalled the courage of the chief, whose arms and counsels were the firmest rampart of the city. As he withdrew from his station in quest of a surgeon, his flight was perceived and stopped by the indefatigable emperor. "Your wound," exclaimed

Palæologus, "is slight; the danger is pressing: your presence is necessary; and whither will you retire?"—"I will retire," said the trembling Genoese, "by the same road which God has opened to the Turks;" and at these words he hastily passed through one of the breaches of the inner wall. By this pusillanimous act he stained the honours of a military life and the few days which he survived in Galata, or the isle of Chios, were embittered by his own and the public reproach. His example was imitated by the greatest part of the Latin auxiliaries, and the defence began to slacken when the attack was pressed with redoubled vigour. The number of the Ottomans was fifty, perhaps a hundred, times superior to that of the Christians; the double walls were reduced by the cannon to a heap of ruins: in a circuit of several miles some places must be found more easy of access, or more feebly guarded; and if the besiegers could penetrate in a single point, the whole city was irrecoverably lost. The first who deserved the sultan's reward was Hassan the Janizary, of gigantic stature and strength. With his scimitar in one hand and his buckler in the other, he ascended the outward fortification: of the thirty Janizaries who were emulous of his valour, eighteen perished in the bold adventure. Hassan and his twelve companions had reached the summit: the giant was precipitated from the rampart: he rose on one knee, and was again oppressed by a shower of darts and stones. But his success had proved that the achievement was possible: the walls and towers were instantly covered with a swarm of Turks; and the Greeks, now driven from the vantage ground, were overwhelmed by increasing multitudes. Amidst these multitudes, the emperor,[1] who accomplished all the duties of a general and a soldier, was long seen and finally lost. The nobles, who fought round his person, sustained, till their last breath, the honourable names of Palæologus and Cantacuzene: his mournful exclamation was heard, "Cannot there be found a Christian to cut off my head?" and his last fear was that of falling alive into the hands of the infidels. The prudent despair of Constantine cast away the purple: amidst the tumult he fell by an unknown hand, and his body was buried under a mountain of the slain. After his death resistance and order were no more: the Greeks fled towards the city; and many were pressed and stifled in the narrow pass of the gate of St. Romanus. The victorious Turks rushed through the breaches of the inner wall; and as they

[1] Ducas kills him with two blows of Turkish soldiers; Chalcondyles wounds him in the shoulder, and then tramples him in the gate. The grief of Phranza, carrying him among the enemy, escapes from the precise image of his death; but we may, without flattery, apply these noble lines of Dryden:—

As to Sebastian, let them search the field;
And, where they find a mountain of the slain,
Send one to climb, and, looking down beneath,
There they will find him at his manly length,
With his face up to heaven, in that red monument
Which his good sword had digg'd.

advanced into the streets, they were soon joined by their brethren, who had forced the gate Phenar on the side of the harbour. In the first heat of the pursuit about two thousand Christians were put to the sword; but avarice soon prevailed over cruelty; and the victors acknowledged that they should immediately have given quarter, if the valour of the emperor and his chosen bands had not prepared them for a similar opposition in every part of the capital. It was thus, after a siege of fifty-three days, that Constantinople, which had defied the power of Chosroes, the Chagan, and the caliphs, was irretrievably subdued by the arms of Mahomet the Second. Her empire only had been subverted by the Latins: her religion was trampled in the dust by the Moslem conquerors.

The tidings of misfortune fly with a rapid wing; yet such was the extent of Constantinople, that the more distant quarters might prolong, some moments, the happy ignorance of their ruin. But in the general consternation, in the feelings of selfish or social anxiety, in the tumult and thunder of the assault, a *sleepless* night and morning must have elapsed; nor can I believe that many Grecian ladies were awakened by the Janizaries from a sound and tranquil slumber. On the assurance of the public calamity, the houses and convents were instantly deserted; and the trembling inhabitants flocked together in the streets, like a herd of timid animals, as if accumulated weakness could be productive of strength, or in the vain hope that amid the crowd each individual might be safe and invisible. From every part of the capital they flowed into the church of St. Sophia: in the space of an hour, the sanctuary, the choir, the nave, the upper and lower galleries, were filled with the multitudes of fathers and husbands, of women and children, of priests, monks, and religious virgins: the doors were barred on the inside, and they sought protection from the sacred dome which they had so lately abhorred as a profane and polluted edifice. Their confidence was founded on the prophecy of an enthusiast or impostor, that one day the Turks would enter Constantinople, and pursue the Romans as far as the column of Constantine in the square before St. Sophia: but that this would be the term of their calamities; that an angel would descend from heaven with a sword in his hand, and would deliver the empire, with that celestial weapon, to a poor man seated at the foot of the column. "Take this sword," would he say, "and avenge the people of the Lord." At these animating words the Turks would instantly fly, and the victorious Romans would drive them from the West, and from all Anatolia, as far as the frontiers of Persia. It is on this occasion that Ducas, with some fancy and much truth, upbraids the discord and obstinacy of the Greeks. "Had that angel appeared," exclaims the historian, "had he offered to exterminate your foes if you would consent to the union of the church, even then, in that fatal moment, you would have rejected your safety, or have deceived your God."

While they expected the descent of the tardy angel, the doors were broken with axes; and as the Turks encountered no resistance, their bloodless hands were employed in selecting and securing the multitude of their prisoners. Youth, beauty, and the appearance of wealth, attracted their choice; and the right of property was decided among themselves by a prior seizure, by personal strength, and by the authority of command. In the space of an hour the male captives were bound with cords, the females with their veils and girdles. The senators were linked with their slaves; the prelates with the porters of the church; and young men of a plebeian class with noble maids whose faces had been invisible to the sun and their nearest kindred. In this common captivity the ranks of society were confounded; the ties of nature were cut asunder; and the inexorable soldier was careless of the father's groans, the tears of the mother, and the lamentations of the children. The loudest in their wailings were the nuns, who were torn from the altar with naked bosoms, outstretched hands, and dishevelled hair; and we should piously believe that few could be tempted to prefer the vigils of the harem to those of the monastery. Of these unfortunate Greeks, of these domestic animals, whole strings were rudely driven through the streets; and as the conquerors were eager to return for more prey, their trembling pace was quickened with menaces and blows. At the same hour a similar rapine was exercised in all the churches and monasteries, in all the palaces and habitations, of the capital; nor could any place, however sacred or sequestered, protect the persons or the property of the Greeks. Above sixty thousand of this devoted people were transported from the city to the camp and fleet; exchanged or sold according to the caprice or interest of their masters, and dispersed in remote servitude through the provinces of the Ottoman empire. Among these we may notice some remarkable characters. The historian Phranza, first chamberlain and principal secretary, was involved with his family in the common lot. After suffering four months the hardships of slavery, he recovered his freedom: in the ensuing winter he ventured to Adrianople, and ransomed his wife from the *mir bashi*, or master of the horse; but his two children, in the flower of youth and beauty, had been seized for the use of Mahomet himself. The daughter of Phranza died in the seraglio, perhaps a virgin: his son, in the fifteenth year of his age, preferred death to infamy, and was stabbed by the hand of the royal lover. A deed thus inhuman cannot surely be expiated by the taste and liberality with which he released a Grecian matron and her two daughters, on receiving a Latin ode from Philelphus, who had chosen a wife in that noble family. The pride or cruelty of Mahomet would have been most sensibly gratified by the capture of a Roman legate; but the dexterity of Cardinal Isidore eluded the search, and he escaped from Galata in a plebeian habit. The chain and entrance of the outward harbour was still occupied by the Italian ships of merchandise and war. They had signalised their

valour in the siege: they embraced the moment of retreat, while the Turkish mariners were dissipated in the pillage of the city. When they hoisted sail, the beach was covered with a suppliant and lamentable crowd; but the means of transportation were scanty; the Venetians and Genoese selected their countrymen; and, notwithstanding the fairest promises of the sultan, the inhabitants of Galata evacuated their houses, and embarked with their most precious effects.

In the fall and the sack of great cities an historian is condemned to repeat the tale of uniform calamity: the same effects must be produced by the same passions; and when those passions may be indulged without control, small, alas! is the difference between civilised and savage man. Amidst the vague exclamations of bigotry and hatred, the Turks are not accused of a wanton or immoderate effusion of Christian blood: but according to their maxims (the maxims of antiquity), the lives of the vanquished were forfeited; and the legitimate reward of the conqueror was derived from the service, the sale, or the ransom of his captives of both sexes. The wealth of Constantinople had been granted by the sultan to his victorious troops; and the rapine of an hour is more productive than the industry of years. But as no regular division was attempted of the spoil, the respective shares were not determined by merit; and the rewards of valour were stolen away by the followers of the camp, who had declined the toil and danger of the battle. The narrative of their depredations could not afford either amusement or instruction: the total amount, in the last poverty of the empire, has been valued at four millions of ducats; and of this sum a small part was the property of the Venetians, the Genoese, the Florentines, and the merchants of Ancona. Of these foreigners the stock was improved in quick and perpetual circulation: but the riches of the Greeks were displayed in the idle ostentation of palaces and wardrobes, or deeply buried in treasures of ingots and old coin, lest it should be demanded at their hands for the defence of their country. The profanation and plunder of the monasteries and churches excited the most tragic complaints. The dome of St. Sophia itself, the earthly heaven, the second firmament, the vehicle of the cherubim, the throne of the glory of God, was despoiled of the oblations of ages; and the gold and silver, the pearls and jewels, the vases and sacerdotal ornaments, were most wickedly converted to the service of mankind. After the divine images had been stripped of all that could be valuable to a profane eye, the canvas, or the wood, was torn, or broken, or burnt, or trod under foot, or applied, in the stables or the kitchen, to the vilest uses. The example of sacrilege was imitated, however, from the Latin conquerors of Constantinople; and the treatment which Christ, the Virgin, and the saints had sustained from the guilty Catholic, might be inflicted by the zealous Musulman on the monuments of idolatry. Perhaps, instead of joining the public clamour, a philosopher will observe that in the decline of the arts the workmanship could not be more valuable than the work, and that a fresh supply of visions and miracles would speedily be renewed by the craft of the priest and the credulity of the people. He will more seriously deplore the loss of the Byzantine libraries, which were destroyed or scattered in the general confusion: one hundred and twenty thousand manuscripts are said to have disappeared; ten volumes might be purchased for a single ducat; and the same ignominious price, too high perhaps for a shelf of theology, included the whole works of Aristotle and Homer, the noblest productions of the science and literature of ancient Greece. We may reflect with pleasure that an inestimable portion of our classic treasures was safely deposited in Italy; and that the mechanics of a German town had invented an art which derides the havoc of time and barbarism.

THE ENTRY OF MAHOMET II

From the first hour of the memorable twenty-ninth of May, disorder and rapine prevailed in Constantinople till the eighth hour of the same day, when the sultan himself passed in triumph through the gate of St. Romanus. He was attended by his vizirs, bashaws, and guards, each of whom (says a Byzantine historian) was robust as Hercules, dexterous as Apollo, and equal in battle to any ten of the race of ordinary mortals. The conqueror gazed with satisfaction and wonder on the strange though splendid appearance of the domes and palaces, so dissimilar from the style of Oriental architecture. In the hippodrome, or *atmeidan*, his eye was attracted by the twisted column of the three serpents; and, as a trial of his strength, he shattered with his iron mace or battle-axe the under jaw of one of these monsters, which in the eyes of the Turks were the idols or talismans of the city. At the principal door of St. Sophia he alighted from his horse and entered the dome; and such was his jealous regard for that monument of his glory, that, on observing a zealous Musulman in the act of breaking the marble pavement, he admonished him with his scimitar that, if the spoil and captives were granted to the soldiers, the public and private buildings had been reserved for the prince. By his command the metropolis of the Eastern church was transformed into a mosch: the rich and portable instruments of superstition had been removed; the crosses were thrown down; and the walls, which were covered with images and mosaics, were washed and purified, and restored to a state of naked simplicity. On the same day, or on the ensuing Friday, the *muezin*, or crier, ascended the most lofty turret, and proclaimed the *ezan*, or public invitation, in the name of God and his prophet; the imam preached; and Mahomet the Second performed the *namaz* of prayer and thanksgiving on the great altar, where the Christian mysteries had so lately been celebrated before the last of the Cæsars. From St. Sophia he proceeded to the august but desolate mansion of an hundred successors of the great Constantine, but which in a few hours had been stripped of the pomp of royalty. A melancholy reflection on the vicissitudes of human greatness forced itself on his mind, and he repeated an elegant distich of Persian poetry: "The spider has wove his web in the Imperial palace, and the owl hath sung her watch-song on the towers of Afrasiab."

Yet his mind was not satisfied, nor did the victory seem complete, till he was informed of the fate of Constantine—whether he had escaped, or been made prisoner, or had fallen in the battle. Two Janizaries claimed the honour and reward of his death: the body, under a heap of slain, was discovered by the golden eagles embroidered on his shoes; the Greeks acknowledged with tears the head of their late emperor; and, after exposing the bloody trophy, Mahomet bestowed on his rival the honours of a decent funeral. After his decease Lucas Notaras, great duke and first minister of the empire, was the most important prisoner. When he offered his person and his treasures at the foot of the throne, "And why," said the indignant sultan, "did you not employ these treasures in the defence of your prince and country?"—"They were yours," answered the slave; "God had reserved them for your hands." —"If he reserved them for me," replied the despot, "how have you presumed to withhold them so long by a fruitless and fatal resistance?" The great duke alleged the obstinacy of the strangers, and some secret encouragement from the Turkish vizir; and from this perilous interview he was at length dismissed with the assurance of pardon and protection. Mahomet condescended to visit his wife, a venerable princess oppressed with sickness and grief; and his consolation for her misfortunes was in the most tender strain of humanity and filial reverence. A similar clemency was extended to the principal officers of state, of whom several were ransomed at his expense; and during some days he declared himself the friend and father of the vanquished people. But the scene was soon changed, and before his departure the hippodrome streamed with the blood of his noblest captives. His perfidious cruelty is execrated by the Christians: they adorn with the colours of heroic martyrdom the execution of the great duke and his two sons, and his death is ascribed to the generous refusal of delivering his children to the tyrant's lust. Yet a Byzantine historian has dropped an unguarded word of conspiracy, deliverance, and Italian succour: such treason may be glorious; but the rebel who bravely ventures, has justly forfeited his life; nor should we blame a conqueror for destroying the enemies whom he can no longer trust. On the eighteenth of June the victorious sultan returned to Adrianople, and smiled at the base and hollow embassies of the Christian princes, who viewed their approaching ruin in the fall of the Eastern empire.

Constantinople had been left naked and desolate, without a prince or a people. But she could not be despoiled of the incomparable situation which marks her for the metropolis of a great empire; and the genius of the place will ever triumph over the accidents of time and fortune. Boursa and Adrianople, the ancient seats of the Ottomans, sunk into provincial towns; and Mahomet the Second established his own residence and that of his successors on the same commanding spot which had been chosen by Constantine. The fortifications of Galata, which might afford a shelter to the Latins, were prudently destroyed; but the damage of the Turkish cannon was soon repaired, and before the month of August great quantities of lime had been burnt for the restoration of the walls of the capital. As the entire property of the soil and buildings, whether public or private, or profane or sacred, was now transferred to the conqueror, he first separated a space of eight furlongs from the point of the triangle for the establishment of his seraglio or palace. It is here, in the bosom of luxury, that the *Grand Signor* (as he has been emphatically named by the Italians) appears to reign over Europe and Asia; but his person on the shores of the Bosphorus may not always be secure from the insults of an hostile navy. In the new character of a mosch, the cathedral of St. Sophia was endowed with an ample revenue, crowned with lofty minarets, and surrounded with groves and fountains for the devotion and refreshment of the Moslems. The same model was imitated in the *jami*, or royal moschs; and the first of these was built by Mahomet himself, on the ruins of the church of the holy apostles and the tombs of the Greek emperors. On the third day after the conquest the grave of Abou Ayub, or Job, who had fallen in the first siege of the Arabs, was revealed in a vision; and it is before the sepulchre of the martyr that the new sultans are girded with the sword of empire. Constantinople no longer appertains to the Roman historian; nor shall I enumerate the civil and religious edifices that were profaned or erected by its Turkish masters: the population was speedily renewed, and before the end of September five thousand families of Anatolia and Romania had obeyed the royal mandate, which enjoined them, under pain of death, to occupy their new habitations in the capital. The throne of Mahomet was guarded by the numbers and fidelity of his Moslem subjects; but his rational policy aspired to collect the remnant of the Greeks, and they returned in crowds as soon as they were assured of their lives, their liberties, and the free exercise of their religion. In the election and investiture of a patriarch the ceremonial of the Byzantine court was revived and imitated. With a mixture of satisfaction and horror, they beheld the sultan on his throne, who delivered into the hands of Gennadius the crosier or pastoral staff, the symbol of his ecclesiastical office; who conducted the patriarch to the gate of the seraglio, presented him with a horse richly caparisoned, and directed the vizirs and bashaws to lead him to the palace which had been allotted for his residence. The churches of Constantinople were shared between the two religions: their limits were marked; and, till it was infringed by Selim, the grandson of Mahomet, the Greeks enjoyed above sixty years the benefit of this equal partition. Encouraged by the ministers of the divan, who wished to elude the fanaticism of the sultan, the Christian advocates presumed to allege that this division had been an act, not of generosity, but of justice; not a concession, but a compact; and that, if one-half of the city had been taken by storm, the other moiety had surrendered on the faith of a sacred capitulation. The original grant had indeed been consumed by fire; but the loss was supplied by the testimony of three aged Janizaries who remembered the transaction, and their venal oaths are of more weight in the opinion of Cantemir than the positive and unanimous consent of the history of the times.

The remaining fragments of the Greek kingdom in Europe and Asia I shall abandon to the Turkish arms; but the final extinction of the two last dynasties which have reigned in Constantinople should terminate the decline and fall of the Roman empire in the East. The despots of the Morea, Demetrius and Thomas, the two surviving brothers of the name of PALÆOLOGUS, were astonished by the death of the emperor Constantine and the ruin of the monarchy. Hopeless of defence, they prepared, with the noble Greeks who adhered to their fortune, to seek a refuge in Italy, beyond the reach of the Ottoman thunder. Their first apprehensions were dispelled by the victorious sultan, who contented himself with a tribute of twelve thousand ducats; and while his ambition explored the continent and the islands in search of prey, he indulged the Morea in a respite of seven years. But this respite was a period of grief, discord, and misery. The *hexamilion*, the rampart of the isthmus, so often raised and so often subverted, could not long be defended by three hundred Italian archers: the keys of Corinth were seized by the Turks; they returned from their summer excursions with a train of captives and spoil, and the complaints of the injured Greeks were heard with indifference and disdain. The Albanians, a vagrant tribe of shepherds and robbers, filled the peninsula with rapine and murder: the two despots implored the dangerous and humiliating aid of a neighbouring bashaw; and when he had quelled the revolt, his lessons inculcated the rule of their future conduct. Neither the ties of blood, nor the oaths which they repeatedly pledged in the communion and before the altar, nor the stronger pressure of necessity, could reconcile or suspend their domestic quarrels. They ravaged each other's patrimony with fire and sword; the alms and succours of the West were consumed in civil hostility, and their power was only exerted in savage and arbitrary executions. The distress and revenge of the weaker rival invoked their supreme lord; and, in the season of maturity and revenge, Mahomet declared himself the friend of Demetrius, and marched into the Morea with an irresistible force. When he had taken possession of Sparta, "You are too weak," said the sultan, "to control this turbulent province; I will take your daughter to my bed, and you shall pass the remainder of your life in security and honour." Demetrius sighed and obeyed; surrendered his daughter and his castles, followed to Adrianople his sovereign and son, and received for his own maintenance and that of his followers a city in Thrace, and the adjacent isles of Imbros, Lemnos, and Samothrace. He was joined the next year by a companion of misfortune, the last of the Comnenian race, who, after the taking of Constantinople by the Latins, had founded a new empire on the coast of the Black Sea. In the progress of his Anatolian conquests, Mahomet invested with a fleet and army the capital of David, who presumed to style himself emperor of Trebizond; and the negotiation was comprised in a short and peremptory question, "Will you secure your life and treasures by resigning your kingdom? or had you rather forfeit your kingdom, your treasures, and your life?" The feeble Comnenus was subdued by his own fears, and the example of a Musulman neighbour, the prince of Sinope, who, on a similar summons, had yielded a fortified city with four hundred cannon and ten or twelve thousand soldiers. The capitulation of Trebizond was faithfully performed, and the emperor, with his family, was transported to a castle in Romania; but on a slight suspicion of corresponding with the Persian king, David, and the whole Comnenian race, were sacrificed to the jealousy or avarice of the conqueror. Nor could the name of father long protect the unfortunate Demetrius from exile and confiscation: his abject submission moved the pity and contempt of the sultan; his followers were transplanted to Constantinople, and his poverty was alleviated by a pension of fifty thousand aspers, till a monastic habit and a hardy death released Palæologus from an earthly master. It is not easy to pronounce whether the servitude of Demetrius, or the exile of his brother Thomas, be the most inglorious. On the conquest of the Morea the despot escaped to Corfu, and from thence to Italy, with some naked adherents: his name, his sufferings, and the head of the apostle St. Andrew, entitled him to the hospitality of the Vatican; and his misery was prolonged by a pension of six thousand ducats from the pope and cardinals. His two sons, Andrew and Manuel, were educated in Italy; but the eldest, contemptible to his enemies and burdensome to his friends, was degraded by the baseness of his life and marriage. A title was his sole inheritance; and that inheritance he successively sold to the kings of France and Arragon. During his transient prosperity, Charles the Eighth was ambitious of joining the empire of the East with the kingdom of Naples: in a public festival he assumed the appellation and the purple of *Augustus*; the Greeks rejoiced, and the Ottoman already trembled, at the approach of the French chivalry. Manuel Palæologus, the second son, was tempted to revisit his native country: his return might be grateful, and could not be dangerous, to the Porte; he was maintained at Constantinople in safety and ease, and an honourable train of Christians and Moslems attended him to the grave. If there be some animals of so generous a nature that they refuse to propagate in a domestic state, the last of the

Imperial race must be ascribed to an inferior kind: he accepted from the sultan's liberality two beautiful females, and his surviving son was lost in the habit and religion of a Turkish slave.

GRIEF AND TERROR OF EUROPE

The importance of Constantinople was felt and magnified in its loss: the pontificate of Nicholas the Fifth, however peaceful and prosperous, was dishonoured by the fall of the Eastern empire; and the grief and terror of the Latins revived, or seemed to revive, the old enthusiasm of the crusades. In one of the most distant countries of the West, Philip duke of Burgundy entertained, at Lisle in Flanders, an assembly of his nobles; and the pompous pageants of the feast were skilfully adapted to their fancy and feelings. In the midst of the banquet a gigantic Saracen entered the hall, leading a fictitious elephant with a castle on his back: a matron in a mourning robe, the symbol of religion, was seen to issue from her castle: she deplored her oppression, and accused the slowness of her champions: the principal herald of the golden fleece advanced, bearing on his fist a live pheasant, which, according to the rites of chivalry, he presented to the duke. At this extraordinary summons, Philip, a wise and aged prince, engaged his person and powers in the holy war against the Turks: his example was imitated by the barons and knights of the assembly: they swore to God, the Virgin, the ladies, and the *pheasant*; and their particular vows were not less extravagant than the general sanction of their oath. But the performance was made to depend on some future and foreign contingency; and during twelve years, till the last hour of his life, the duke of Burgundy might be scrupulously, and perhaps sincerely, on the eve of his departure. Had every breast glowed with the same ardour; had the union of the Christians corresponded with their bravery; had every country from Sweden to Naples supplied a just proportion of cavalry and infantry, of men and money, it is indeed probable that Constantinople would have been delivered, and that the Turks might have been chased beyond the Hellespont or the Euphrates. But the secretary of the emperor, who composed every epistle, and attended every meeting, Æneas Sylvius, a statesman and orator, describes from his own experience the repugnant state and spirit of Christendom. "It is a body," says he, "without a head; a republic without laws or magistrates. The pope and the emperor may shine as lofty titles, as splendid images; but *they* are unable to command, and none are willing to obey; every state has a separate prince, and every prince has a separate interest. What eloquence could unite so many discordant and hostile powers under the same standard? Could they be assembled in arms, who would dare to assume the office of general? What order could be maintained?—what military discipline? Who would undertake to feed such an enormous multitude? Who would understand their various languages, or direct their stranger and incompatible manners? What mortal could reconcile the English with the French, Genoa with Arragon, the Germans with the natives of Hungary and Bohemia? If a small number enlisted in the holy war, they must be overthrown by the infidels: if many, by their own weight and confusion." Yet the same Æneas, when he was raised to the papal throne, under the name of Pius the Second, devoted his life to the prosecution of the Turkish war. In the council of Mantua he excited some sparks of a false or feeble enthusiasm; but when the pontiff appeared at Ancona, to embark in person with the troops, engagements vanished in excuses; a precise day was adjourned to an indefinite term; and his effective army consisted of some German pilgrims, whom he was obliged to disband with indulgences and alms. Regardless of futurity, his successors and the powers of Italy were involved in the schemes of present and domestic ambition; and the distance or proximity of each object determined in their eyes its apparent magnitude. A more enlarged view of their interest would have taught them to maintain a defensive and naval war against the common enemy; and the support of Scanderbeg and his brave Albanians might have prevented the subsequent invasion of the kingdom of Naples. The siege and sack of Otranto by the Turks diffused a general consternation; and Pope Sixtus was preparing to fly beyond the Alps, when the storm was instantly dispelled by the death of Mahomet the Second, in the fifty-first year of his age. His lofty genius aspired to the conquest of Italy: he was possessed of a strong city and a capacious harbour; and the same reign might have been decorated with the trophies of the New and the Ancient Rome.

Two results of the appeal for help to the West (see summary, p. 835) require a mention here. One was the despatch of two thousand Genoese soldiers led by Justiniani (Giustiniani); the other was a mission with Cardinal Isidore, as papal legate. The account of Justiniani's conduct on p. 843 is neither historical nor fair. The immediate cause of the city's capture was the entry of some Turks through a postern which Justiniani had opened for a sally. Isidore's mission served only to increase the Greeks' enmity towards the Latins. Someone remarked that he would rather see a Mahomet's turban in the city than a cardinal's hat. After the Latin rites had been used in St. Sophia, the church was deserted, and "a vast and gloomy silence prevailed in that venerable dome". This explains the reference to pollution on p. 845.

THE EPILOGUE:
MEDIEVAL ROME AND THE DAWN
OF THE RENAISSANCE

Chapter 69

AUTHORITY OF THE POPES IN ROME. METHODS OF PAPAL
ELECTION. MIGRATION OF THE POPES TO AVIGNON.
INSTITUTION OF THE JUBILEE, OR HOLY YEAR. THE ROMAN
NOBILITY

IN the first ages of the decline and fall of the Roman empire our eye
is invariably fixed on the royal city, which had given laws to the
fairest portion of the globe. We contemplate her fortunes, at first
with admiration, at length with pity, always with attention; and when
that attention is diverted from the Capitol to the provinces, they are
considered as so many branches which have been successively severed
from the Imperial trunk. The foundation of a second Rome, on the
shores of the Bosphorus, has compelled the historian to follow the successors of Constantine; and our curiosity has been tempted to visit the
most remote countries of Europe and Asia, to explore the causes and
the authors of the long decay of the Byzantine monarchy. By the conquests of Justinian we have been recalled to the banks of the Tiber, to
the deliverance of the ancient metropolis; but that deliverance was a
change, or perhaps an aggravation, of servitude. Rome had been
already stripped of her trophies, her gods, and her Cæsars; nor was the
Gothic dominion more inglorious and oppressive than the tyranny of
the Greeks. In the eighth century of the Christian era a religious
quarrel, the worship of images, provoked the Romans to assert their
independence: their bishop became the temporal, as well as the spiritual,
father of a free people; and of the Western empire, which was restored
by Charlemagne, the title and image still decorate the singular constitution of modern Germany. The name of Rome must yet command our
involuntary respect: the climate (whatsoever may be its influence) was
no longer the same: the purity of blood had been contaminated through
a thousand channels; but the venerable aspect of her ruins, and the
memory of past greatness, rekindled a spark of the national character.
The darkness of the middle ages exhibits some scenes not unworthy of
our notice. Nor shall I dismiss the present work till I have reviewed the
state and revolutions of the ROMAN CITY, which acquiesced under the

absolute dominion of the popes about the same time that Constantinople was enslaved by the Turkish arms.

In the beginning of the twelfth century,[1] the era of the first crusade, Rome was revered by the Latins as the metropolis of the world, as the throne of the pope and the emperor, who, from the eternal city, derived their title, their honours, and the right or exercise of temporal dominion. After so long an interruption it may not be useless to repeat that the successors of Charlemagne and the Othos were chosen beyond the Rhine in a national diet; but that these princes were content with the humble names of kings of Germany and Italy till they had passed the Alps and the Apennine, to seek their Imperial crown on the banks of the Tiber. At some distance from the city their approach was saluted by a long procession of the clergy and people with palms and crosses; and the terrific emblems of wolves and lions, of dragons and eagles, that floated in the military banners, represented the departed legions and cohorts of the republic. The royal oath to maintain the liberties of Rome was thrice reiterated, at the bridge, the gate, and on the stairs of the Vatican; and the distribution of a customary donative feebly imitated the magnificence of the first Cæsars. In the church of St. Peter the coronation was performed by his successor: the voice of God was confounded with that of the people; and the public consent was declared in the acclamations of "Long life and victory to our lord the pope! long life and victory to our lord the emperor! long life and victory to the Roman and Teutonic armies!" The names of Cæsar and Augustus, the laws of Constantine and Justinian, the example of Charlemagne and Otho, established the supreme dominion of the emperors: their title and image was engraved on the papal coins; and their jurisdiction was marked by the sword of justice, which they delivered to the prefect of the city. But every Roman prejudice was awakened by the name, the language, and the manners of a barbarian lord. The Cæsars of Saxony or Franconia were the chiefs of a feudal aristocracy; nor could they exercise the discipline of civil and military power, which alone secures the obedience of a distant people, impatient of servitude, though perhaps incapable of freedom. Once, and once only, in his life, each emperor, with an army of Teutonic vassals, descended from the Alps. I have described the peaceful order of his entry and coronation; but that order was commonly disturbed by the clamour and sedition of the Romans, who encountered their sovereign as a foreign invader: his departure was always speedy, and often shameful; and, in the absence of a long reign, his authority was insulted and his name was forgotten. The progress of independence in Germany and Italy undermined the foundations of the Imperial sovereignty, and the triumph of the popes was the deliverance of Rome.

---

[1] The reader has been so long absent from Rome that I would advise him to recollect or review the 49th chapter of this History.

Of her two sovereigns, the emperor had precariously reigned by the right of conquest; but the authority of the pope was founded on the soft though more solid basis of opinion and habit. The removal of a foreign influence restored and endeared the shepherd to his flock. Instead of the arbitrary or venal nomination of a German court, the vicar of Christ was freely chosen by the college of cardinals, most of whom were either natives or inhabitants of the city. The applause of the magistrates and people confirmed his election; and the ecclesiastical power that was obeyed in Sweden and Britain had been ultimately derived from the suffrage of the Romans. The same suffrage gave a prince, as well as a pontiff, to the capital. It was universally believed that Constantine had invested the popes with the temporal dominion of Rome; and the boldest civilians, the most profane sceptics, were satisfied with disputing the right of the emperor and the validity of his gift. The truth of the fact, the authenticity of his donation, was deeply rooted in the ignorance and tradition of four centuries; and the fabulous origin was lost in the real and permanent effects. The name of *Dominus*, or Lord, was inscribed on the coin of the bishops: their title was acknowledged by acclamations and oaths of allegiance, and, with the free or reluctant consent of the German Cæsars, they had long exercised a supreme or subordinate jurisdiction over the city and patrimony of St. Peter. The reign of the popes, which gratified the prejudices, was not incompatible with the liberties of Rome; and a more critical inquiry would have revealed a still nobler source of their power—the gratitude of a nation whom they had rescued from the heresy and oppression of the Greek tyrant. In an age of superstition it should seem that the union of the royal and sacerdotal characters would mutually fortify each other, and that the keys of Paradise would be the surest pledge of earthly obedience. The sanctity of the office might indeed be degraded by the personal vices of the man. But the scandals of the tenth century were obliterated by the austere and more dangerous virtues of Gregory the Seventh and his successors; and in the ambitious contests which they maintained for the rights of the church, their sufferings or their success must equally tend to increase the popular veneration. They sometimes wandered in poverty and exile, the victims of persecution; and the apostolic zeal with which they offered themselves to martyrdom must engage the favour and sympathy of every Catholic breast. And sometimes, thundering from the Vatican, they created, judged, and deposed the kings of the world; nor could the proudest Roman be disgraced by submitting to a priest whose feet were kissed and whose stirrup was held by the successors of Charlemagne. Even the temporal interest of the city should have protected in peace and honour the residence of the popes, from whence a vain and lazy people derived the greatest part of their subsistence and riches. The fixed revenue of the popes was probably impaired: many of the old patrimonial estates, both in Italy and the provinces, had been invaded by sacrilegious hands; nor could the loss be compensated by the claim, rather than the possession, of the more ample gifts of Pepin and his descendants. But the Vatican and Capitol were nourished by the incessant and increasing swarms of pilgrims and suppliants: the pale of Christianity was enlarged, and the pope and cardinals were overwhelmed by the judgment of ecclesiastical and secular causes. A new jurisprudence had established in the Latin church the right and practice of appeals; and from the North and West the bishops and abbots were invited or summoned to solicit, to complain, to accuse, or to justify, before the threshold of the apostles. A rare prodigy is once recorded, that two horses, belonging to the archbishops of Maintz and Cologne, repassed the Alps, yet laden with gold and silver; but it was soon understood that the success, both of the pilgrims and clients, depended much less on the justice of their cause than on the value of their offering. The wealth and piety of these strangers were ostentatiously displayed, and their expenses, sacred or profane, circulated in various channels for the emolument of the Romans.

Such powerful motives should have firmly attached the voluntary and pious obedience of the Roman people to their spiritual and temporal father. But the operation of prejudice and interest is often disturbed by the sallies of ungovernable passion. The Indian who fells the tree that he may gather the fruit, and the Arab who plunders the caravans of commerce, are actuated by the same impulse of savage nature, which overlooks the future in the present, and relinquishes for momentary rapine the long and secure possession of the most important blessings. And it was thus that the shrine of St. Peter was profaned by the thoughtless Romans, who pillaged the offerings and wounded the pilgrims, without computing the number and value of similar visits, which they prevented by their inhospitable sacrilege. Even the influence of superstition is fluctuating and precarious; and the slave, whose reason is subdued, will often be delivered by his avarice or pride. A credulous devotion for the fables and oracles of the priesthood most powerfully acts on the mind of a barbarian; yet such a mind is the least capable of preferring imagination to sense, of sacrificing to a distant motive, to an invisible, perhaps an ideal object, the appetites and interests of the present world. In the vigour of health and youth, his practice will perpetually contradict his belief, till the pressure of age, or sickness, or calamity, awakens his terrors, and compels him to satisfy the double debt of piety and remorse. I have already observed that the modern times of religious indifference are the most favourable to the peace and security of the clergy. Under the reign of superstition they had much to hope from the ignorance, and much to fear from the violence, of mankind. The wealth, whose constant increase must have rendered them the sole proprietors of the earth, was alternately bestowed by the repentant father and plundered by the rapacious son: their persons were adored or violated; and the same idol, by the hands of the same votaries, was placed on the altar or trampled in the dust. In the feudal system of Europe, arms were the title of distinction and the measure of allegiance; and amidst their tumult the still voice of law and reason was seldom heard or obeyed. The turbulent Romans disdained the yoke and insulted the impotence of their bishop; nor would his education or character allow him to exercise, with decency or effect, the power of the sword. The motives of his election and the frailties of his life were exposed to their familiar observation; and proximity must diminish the reverence which his name and his decrees impressed on a barbarous world. This difference has not escaped the notice of our philosophic historian: "Though the name and authority of the court of Rome were so terrible in the remote countries of Europe, which were sunk in profound ignorance and were entirely unacquainted with its character and conduct, the pope was so little revered at home, that his inveterate enemies surrounded the gates of Rome itself, and even controlled his government in that city; and the ambassadors, who from a distant extremity of Europe carried to him the humble, or rather abject, submissions of the greatest potentate of the age, found the utmost difficulty to make their way to him and to throw themselves at his feet." [1]

Since primitive times the popes had had to contend with opposition, insult, and violence. In the middle of the twelfth century a movement to restore the republic was started by Arnold of Brescia. Arnold was expelled from Rome by Adrian IV (the English pope) and the emperor Frederic Barbarossa, and subsequently burnt alive. But a form of republican government, which included the office of Senator, was established.

METHODS OF PAPAL ELECTION

Ambition is a weed of quick and early vegetation in the vineyard of Christ. Under the first Christian princes the chair of St. Peter was disputed by the votes, the venality, the violence, of a popular election: the sanctuaries of Rome were polluted with blood; and, from the third to the twelfth century, the church was distracted by the mischief of frequent schisms. As long as the final appeal was determined by the civil magistrate, these mischiefs were transient and local: the merits were tried by equity or favour; nor could the unsuccessful competitor long disturb the triumph of his rival. But after the emperors had been

---

[1] Hume's History of England, vol. i. p. 419. The same writer has given us from Fitz-Stephen a singular act of cruelty perpetrated on the clergy by Geoffrey, the father of Henry II. "When he was master of Normandy the chapter of Seez presumed, without his consent, to proceed to the election of a bishop: upon which he ordered all of them, with the bishop elect, to be castrated, and made all their testicles be brought him in a platter." Of the pain and danger they might justly complain; yet, since they had vowed chastity, he deprived them of a superfluous treasure.

divested of their prerogatives, after a maxim had been established that
the vicar of Christ is amenable to no earthly tribunal, each vacancy of
the holy see might involve Christendom in controversy and war. The
claims of the cardinals and inferior clergy, of the nobles and people,
were vague and litigious: the freedom of choice was overruled by the
tumults of a city that no longer owned or obeyed a superior. On the
decease of a pope, two factions proceeded in different churches to a
double election: the number and weight of votes, the priority of time,
the merit of the candidates, might balance each other: the most respectable of the clergy were divided; and the distant princes, who bowed
before the spiritual throne, could not distinguish the spurious from the
legitimate idol. The emperors were often the authors of the schism,
from the political motive of opposing a friendly to an hostile pontiff;
and each of the competitors was reduced to suffer the insults of his
enemies, who were not awed by conscience, and to purchase the support
of his adherents, who were instigated by avarice or ambition. A peaceful
and perpetual succession was ascertained by Alexander the Third, who
finally abolished the tumultuary votes of the clergy and people, and
defined the right of election in the sole college of cardinals. The three
orders of bishops, priests, and deacons, were assimilated to each other
by this important privilege; the parochial clergy of Rome obtained the
first rank in the hierarchy: they were indifferently chosen among the
nations of Christendom; and the possession of the richest benefices, of
the most important bishoprics, was not incompatible with their title and
office. The senators of the Catholic church, the coadjutors and legates
of the supreme pontiff, were robed in purple, the symbol of martyrdom
or royalty; they claimed a proud equality with kings; and their dignity
was enhanced by the smallness of their number, which, till the reign of
Leo the Tenth, seldom exceeded twenty or twenty-five persons. By this
wise regulation all doubt and scandal were removed, and the root of
schism was so effectually destroyed, that in a period of six hundred
years a double choice has only once divided the unity of the sacred college. But as the concurrence of two-thirds of the votes had been made
necessary, the election was often delayed by the private interest and
passions of the cardinals; and while they prolonged their independent
reign, the Christian world was left destitute of a head. A vacancy of
almost three years had preceded the elevation of Gregory the Tenth,
who resolved to prevent the future abuse; and his bull, after some
opposition, has been consecrated in the code of the canon law. Nine
days are allowed for the obsequies of the deceased pope, and the arrival
of the absent cardinals; on the tenth, they are imprisoned, each with
one domestic, in a common apartment or *conclave*, without any separation of walls or curtains; a small window is reserved for the introduction
of necessaries; but the door is locked on both sides, and guarded by the
magistrates of the city, to seclude them from all correspondence with

the world. If the election be not consummated in three days, the luxury of their table is contracted to a single dish at dinner and supper; and after the eighth day they are reduced to a scanty allowance of bread, water, and wine. During the vacancy of the holy see the cardinals are prohibited from touching the revenues, or assuming, unless in some rare emergency, the government of the church: all agreements and promises among the electors are formally annulled; and their integrity is fortified by their solemn oath and the prayers of the Catholics. Some articles of inconvenient or superfluous rigour have been gradually relaxed, but the principle of confinement is vigorous and entire: they are still urged, by the personal motives of health and freedom, to accelerate the moment of their deliverance; and the improvement of ballot or secret votes has wrapped the struggles of the conclave in the silky veil of charity and politeness. By these institutions the Romans were excluded from the election of their prince and bishop; and in the fever of wild and precarious liberty, they seemed insensible of the loss of this inestimable privilege. The emperor Lewis of Bavaria revived the example of the great Otho. After some negotiation with the magistrates, the Roman people was assembled in the square before St. Peter's: the pope of Avignon, John the Twenty-second, was deposed: the choice of his successor was ratified by their consent and applause. They freely voted for a new law, that their bishop should never be absent more than three months in the year, and two days' journey from the city; and that, if he neglected to return on the third summons, the public servant should be degraded and dismissed. But Lewis forgot his own debility and the prejudices of the times: beyond the precincts of a German camp, his useless phantom was rejected; the Romans despised their own workmanship; the antipope implored the mercy of his lawful sovereign; and the exclusive right of the cardinals was more firmly established by this unseasonable attack.

MIGRATION OF THE POPES TO AVIGNON

Had the election been always held in the Vatican, the rights of the senate and people would not have been violated with impunity. But the Romans forgot, and were forgotten, in the absence of the successors of Gregory the Seventh, who did not keep as a divine precept their ordinary residence in the city and diocese. The care of that diocese was less important than the government of the universal church; nor could the popes delight in a city in which their authority was always opposed, and their person was often endangered. From the persecution of the emperors, and the wars of Italy, they escaped beyond the Alps into the hospitable bosom of France; from the tumults of Rome they prudently withdrew to live and die in the more tranquil stations of Anagni, Perugia, Viterbo, and the adjacent cities. When the flock was offended or impoverished by the absence of the shepherd, they were recalled by a stern admonition, that St. Peter had fixed his chair, not in an obscure village, but in the capital of the world; by a ferocious menace that the Romans would march in arms to destroy the place and people that should dare to afford them a retreat. They returned with timorous obedience, and were saluted with the account of a heavy debt, of all the losses which their desertion had occasioned, the hire of lodgings, the sale of provisions, and the various expenses of servants and strangers who attended the court. After a short interval of peace, and perhaps of authority, they were again banished by new tumults, and again summoned by the imperious or respectful invitation of the senate. In these occasional retreats the exiles and fugitives of the Vatican were seldom long, or far, distant from the metropolis; but in the beginning of the fourteenth century the apostolic throne was transported, as it might seem for ever, from the Tiber to the Rhône; and the cause of the transmigration may be deduced from the furious contest between Boniface the Eighth and the king of France. The spiritual arms of excommunication and interdict were repulsed by the union of the three estates, and the privileges of the Gallican church; but the pope was not prepared against the carnal weapons which Philip the Fair had courage to employ. As the pope resided at Anagni, without the suspicion of danger, his palace and person were assaulted by three hundred horse, who had been secretly levied by William of Nogaret, a French minister, and Sciarra Colonna, of a noble but hostile family of Rome. The cardinals fled; the inhabitants of Anagni were seduced from their allegiance and gratitude; but the dauntless Boniface, unarmed and alone, seated himself in his chair, and awaited, like the conscript fathers of old, the swords of the Gauls. Nogaret, a foreign adversary, was content to execute the orders of his master: by the domestic enmity of Colonna, he was insulted with words and blows; and during a confinement of three days his life was threatened by the hardships which they inflicted on the obstinacy which they provoked. Their strange delay gave time and courage to the adherents of the church, who rescued him from sacrilegious violence; but his imperious soul was wounded in a vital part; and Boniface expired at Rome in a frenzy of rage and revenge. His memory is stained with the glaring vices of avarice and pride; nor has the courage of a martyr promoted this ecclesiastical champion to the honours of a saint; a magnanimous sinner (say the chronicles of the times), who entered like a fox, reigned like a lion, and died like a dog. He was succeeded by Benedict the Eleventh, the mildest of mankind. Yet he excommunicated the impious emissaries of Philip, and devoted the city and people of Anagni by a tremendous curse, whose effects are still visible to the eyes of superstition.

After his decease, the tedious and equal suspense of the conclave was fixed by the dexterity of the French faction. A specious offer was made and accepted, that, in the term of forty days, they would elect one of the three candidates who should be named by their opponents. The archbishop of Bordeaux, a furious enemy of his king and country, was the first on the list; but his ambition was known; and his conscience obeyed the calls of fortune and the commands of a benefactor, who had been informed by a swift messenger that the choice of a pope was now in his hands. The terms were regulated in a private interview; and with such speed and secrecy was the business transacted, that the unanimous conclave applauded the elevation of Clement the Fifth. The cardinals of both parties were soon astonished by a summons to attend him beyond the Alps; from whence, as they soon discovered, they must never hope to return. He was engaged by promise and affection to prefer the residence of France; and, after dragging his court through Poitou and Gascony, and devouring, by his expense, the cities and convents on the road, he finally reposed at Avignon, which flourished above seventy years the seat of the Roman pontiff and the metropolis of Christendom. By land, by sea, by the Rhône, the position of Avignon was on all sides accessible; the southern provinces of France do not yield to Italy itself; new palaces arose for the accommodation of the pope and cardinals; and the arts of luxury were soon attracted by the treasures of the church. They were already possessed of the adjacent territory, the Venaissin county, a populous and fertile spot; and the sovereignty of Avignon was afterwards purchased from the youth and distress of Jane, the first queen of Naples and countess of Provence, for the inadequate price of fourscore thousand florins. Under the shadow of the French monarchy, amidst an obedient people, the popes enjoyed an honourable and tranquil state, to which they long had been strangers: but Italy deplored their absence; and Rome, in solitude and poverty, might repent of the ungovernable freedom which had driven from the Vatican the successor of St. Peter. Her repentance was tardy and fruitless: after the death of the old members, the sacred college was filled with French cardinals, who beheld Rome and Italy with abhorrence and contempt, and perpetuated a series of national, and even provincial, popes, attached by the most indissoluble ties to their native country.

INSTITUTION OF THE JUBILEE, OR HOLY YEAR

The progress of industry had produced and enriched the Italian republics: the era of their liberty is the most flourishing period of population and agriculture, of manufactures and commerce; and their mechanic labours were gradually refined into the arts of elegance and genius But the position of Rome was less favourable, the territory less fruitful: the character of the inhabitants was debased by indolence and elated by pride; and they fondly conceived that the tribute of subjects must for ever nourish the metropolis of the church and empire. This prejudice was encouraged in some degree by the resort of pilgrims to the shrines of the apostles; and the last legacy of the popes, the institution of the HOLY YEAR, was not less beneficial to the people than to the clergy. Since the loss of Palestine, the gift of plenary indulgences, which had been applied to the crusades, remained without an object; and the most valuable treasure of the church was sequestered above eight years from public circulation. A new channel was opened by the diligence of Boniface the Eighth, who reconciled the vices of ambition and avarice; and the pope had sufficient learning to recollect and revive the secular games which were celebrated in Rome at the conclusion of every century. To sound without danger the depth of popular credulity, a sermon was seasonably pronounced, a report was artfully scattered, some aged witnesses were produced; and on the first of January of the year thirteen hundred the church of St. Peter was crowded with the faithful, who demanded the *customary* indulgence of the holy time. The pontiff, who watched and irritated their devout impatience, was soon persuaded by ancient testimony of the justice of their claim; and he proclaimed a plenary absolution to all Catholics who, in the course of that year, and at every similar period, should respectfully visit the apostolic churches of St. Peter and St. Paul. The welcome sound was propagated through Christendom; and at first from the nearest provinces of Italy, and at length from the remote kingdoms of Hungary and Britain, the highways were thronged with a swarm of pilgrims who sought to expiate their sins in a journey, however costly or laborious, which was exempt from the perils of military service. All exceptions of rank or sex, of age or infirmity, were forgotten in the common transport; and in the streets and churches many persons were trampled to death by the eagerness of devotion. The calculation of their numbers could not be easy nor accurate; and they have probably been magnified by a dexterous clergy, well apprised of the contagion of example: yet we are assured by a judicious historian, who assisted at the ceremony, that Rome was never replenished with less than two hundred thousand strangers; and another spectator has fixed at two millions the total concourse of the year. A trifling oblation from each individual would accumulate a royal treasure; and two priests stood night and day, with rakes in their hands, to collect, without counting, the heaps of gold and silver that were poured on the altar of St. Paul. It was fortunately a season of peace and plenty; and if forage was scarce, if inns and lodgings were extravagantly dear, an inexhaustible supply of bread and wine, of meat and fish, was provided by the policy of Boniface and the venal hospitality of the Romans. From a city without trade or industry all casual riches will speedily evaporate: but the avarice and envy of the next generation solicited Clement the Sixth to anticipate the distant period of the century. The gracious pontiff complied with their wishes; afforded Rome this poor consolation for his loss; and justified the change by the name and practice of the Mosaic Jubilee. His summons was obeyed; and the number, zeal, and liberality of the pilgrims did not yield to the primitive festival. But they encountered the triple scourge of war, pestilence, and famine: many wives and virgins were violated in the castles of Italy; and many strangers were pillaged or murdered by the savage Romans, no longer moderated by the presence of their bishop. To the impatience of the popes we may ascribe the successive reduction to fifty, thirty-three, and twenty-five years; although the second of these terms is commensurate with the life of Christ. The profusion of indulgences, the revolt of the Protestants, and the decline of superstition, have much diminished the value of the jubilee; yet even the nineteenth and last festival was a year of pleasure and profit to the Romans; and a philosophic smile will not disturb the triumph of the priest or the happiness of the people.

THE ROMAN NOBILITY

In the beginning of the eleventh century Italy was exposed to the feudal tyranny, alike oppressive to the sovereign and the people. The rights of human nature were vindicated by her numerous republics, who soon extended their liberty and dominion from the city to the adjacent country. The sword of the nobles was broken; their slaves were enfranchised; their castles were demolished; they assumed the habits of society and obedience; their ambition was confined to municipal honours; and in the proudest aristocracy of Venice or Genoa, each patrician was subject to the laws. But the feeble and disorderly government of Rome was unequal to the task of curbing her rebellious sons, who scorned the authority of the magistrate within and without the walls. It was no longer a civil contention between the nobles and plebeians for the government of the state: the barons asserted in arms their personal independence; their palaces and castles were fortified against a siege; and their private quarrels were maintained by the numbers of their vassals and retainers. In origin and affection they were aliens to their country: and a genuine Roman, could such have been produced, might have renounced these haughty strangers, who disdained the appellation of citizens, and proudly styled themselves the princes of Rome. After a dark series of revolutions all records of pedigree were lost; the distinction of surnames was abolished; the blood of the nations was mingled in a thousand channels; and the Goths and Lombards, the Greeks and Franks, the Germans and Normans, had obtained the fairest possessions by royal bounty, or the prerogative of valour. These examples might be readily presumed; but the elevation of a Hebrew race to the rank of senators and consuls is an event without a parallel in the long captivity of these miserable exiles. In the time of Leo the Ninth a wealthy and learned Jew was converted to Christianity; and honoured at his baptism with the name of his godfather, the reigning pope. The zeal and courage of Peter the son of Leo were signalised in the cause of Gregory the Seventh, who entrusted his faithful adherent with the government of Hadrian's mole, the tower of Crescentius, or, as it is now called, the castle of St. Angelo. Both the father and the son were the parents of a numerous progeny: their riches, the fruits of usury, were shared with the noblest families of the city; and so extensive was their alliance, that the grandson of the proselyte was exalted by the weight of his kindred to the throne of St. Peter. A majority of the clergy and people supported his cause: he reigned several years in the Vatican; and it is only the eloquence of St. Bernard, and the final triumph of Innocent the Second, that has branded Anacletus with the epithet of antipope. After his defeat and death the posterity of Leo is no longer conspicuous; and none will be found of the modern nobles ambitious of descending from a Jewish stock. It is not my design to enumerate the Roman families which have failed at different periods, or those which are continued in different degrees of splendour to the present time. The old consular line of the *Frangipani* discover their name in the generous act of *breaking* or dividing bread in a time of famine; and such benevolence is more truly glorious than to have enclosed, with their allies the *Corsi*, a spacious quarter of the city in the chains of their fortifications; the *Savelli*, as it should seem a Sabine race, have maintained their original dignity; the obsolete surname of the *Capizucchi* is inscribed on the coins of the first senators; the *Conti* preserve the honour, without the estate, of the counts of Signia; and the *Annibaldi* must have been very ignorant, or very modest, if they had not descended from the Carthaginian hero.

But among, perhaps above, the peers and princes of the city, I distinguish the rival houses of COLONNA and URSINI, whose private story is an essential part of the annals of modern Rome. I. The name and arms of Colonna have been the theme of much doubtful etymology; nor have the orators and antiquarians overlooked either Trajan's pillar, or the columns of Hercules, or the pillar of Christ's flagellation, or the luminous column that guided the Israelites in the desert. Their first historical appearance in the year eleven hundred and four attests the power and antiquity, while it explains the simple meaning, of the name. By the usurpation of Cavæ the Colonna provoked the arms of Paschal the Second; but they lawfully held in the Campagna of Rome the hereditary fiefs of Zagarola and *Colonna*; and the latter of these towns was probably adorned with some lofty pillar, the relic of a villa or temple. They likewise possessed one moiety of the neighbouring city of Tusculum; a strong presumption of their descent from the counts of Tusculum, who in the tenth century were the tyrants of the apostolic see. According to their own and the public opinion, the primitive and remote source was derived from the banks of the Rhine; and the sovereigns of Germany were not ashamed of a real or fabulous affinity with a noble race, which in the revolutions of seven hundred years has been often illustrated by merit and always by fortune. About the end of the thirteenth century the most powerful branch was composed of an uncle and six brothers, all conspicuous in arms or in the honours of the church. Of these, Peter was elected senator of Rome, introduced to the Capitol in a triumphant car, and hailed in some vain acclamations with the title of Cæsar; while John and Stephen were declared marquis of Ancona and count of Romagna, by Nicholas the Fourth, a patron so partial to their family, that he has been delineated in satirical portraits, imprisoned as it were in a hollow pillar. After his decease their haughty behaviour provoked the displeasure of the most implacable of mankind. The two cardinals, the uncle and the nephew, denied the election of Boniface the Eighth; and the Colonna were oppressed for a moment by his temporal and spiritual arms. He proclaimed a crusade against his personal enemies; their estates were confiscated; their fortresses on either side of the Tiber were besieged by the troops of St. Peter and those of the rival nobles; and after the ruin of Palestrina or Præneste, their principal seat, the ground was marked with a ploughshare, the emblem of perpetual desolation. Degraded, banished, proscribed, the six brothers, in disguise and danger, wandered over Europe without renouncing the hope of deliverance and revenge. In this double hope the French court was their surest asylum: they prompted and directed the enterprise of Philip; and I should praise their magnanimity had they respected the misfortune and courage of the captive tyrant. His civil acts were annulled by the Roman people, who restored the honours and possessions of the Colonna; and some estimate may be formed of their wealth by their losses, of their losses by the damages of one hundred thousand gold florins which were granted them against the accomplices and heirs of the deceased pope. All the spiritual censures and disqualifications were abolished by his prudent successors; and the fortune of the house was more firmly established by this transient hurricane. The boldness of Sciarra Colonna was signalised in the captivity of Boniface, and long afterwards in the coronation of Lewis of Bavaria; and by the gratitude of the emperor the pillar in their arms was encircled with a royal crown. But the first of the family in fame and merit was the elder Stephen, whom Petrarch loved and esteemed as a hero superior to his own times and not unworthy of ancient Rome. Persecution and exile displayed to the nations his abilities in peace and war; in his distress he was an object, not of pity but of reverence; the aspect of danger provoked him to avow his name and country; and when he was asked, "Where is now your fortress?" he laid his hand on his heart, and answered, "Here." He supported with the same virtue the return of prosperity; and, till the ruin of his declining age, the ancestors, the character, and the children of Stephen Colonna exalted his dignity in the Roman republic and at the court of Avignon. II. The Ursini migrated from Spoleto; the sons of Ursus, as they are styled in the twelfth century, from some eminent person who is only known as the father of their race. But they were soon distinguished among the nobles of Rome by the number and bravery of their kinsmen, the strength of their towers, the honours of the senate and sacred college, and the elevation of two popes, Celestin the Third and Nicholas the Third, of their name and lineage. Their riches may be accused as an early abuse of nepotism: the estates of St. Peter were alienated in their favour by the liberal Celestin; and Nicholas was ambitious for their sake to solicit the alliance of monarchs; to found new kingdoms in Lombardy and Tuscany; and to invest them with the perpetual office of senators of Rome. All that has been observed of the greatness of the Colonna will likewise redound to the glory of the Ursini, their constant and equal antagonists in the long hereditary feud which distracted above two hundred and fifty years the ecclesiastical state. The jealousy of pre-eminence and power was the true ground of their quarrel; but as a specious badge of distinction, the Colonna embraced the name of Ghibelines and the party of the empire; the Ursini espoused the title of Guelphs and the cause of the church. The eagle and the keys were displayed in their adverse banners; and the two factions of Italy most furiously raged when the origin and nature of the dispute were long since forgotten. After the retreat of the popes to Avignon they disputed in arms the vacant republic; and the mischiefs of discord were perpetuated by the wretched compromise of electing each year two rival senators. By their private hostilities the city and country were desolated, and the fluctuating balance inclined with their alternate success. But none of either family had fallen by the sword till the most renowned champion of the Ursini was surprised and slain by the younger Stephen Colonna. His triumph is stained with the reproach of violating the truce; their defeat was basely avenged by the assassination, before the church door, of an innocent boy and his two servants. Yet the victorious Colonna, with an annual colleague, was declared senator of Rome during the term of five years. And the muse of Petrarch inspired a wish, a hope, a prediction, that the generous youth, the son of his venerable hero, would restore Rome and Italy to their pristine glory; that his justice would extirpate the wolves and lions, the serpents and bears, who laboured to subvert the eternal basis of the marble COLUMN.

Chapter 70

PETRARCH. RIENZI AND THE RESTORATION OF THE *GOOD ESTATE*. PROSPERITY OF THE ROMAN REPUBLIC. KNIGHT-HOOD, CORONATION, AND FOLLIES OF RIENZI. RETURN OF THE POPES TO ROME. GREAT SCHISM OF THE WEST. GOVERNMENT OF ROME IN THE FIFTEENTH CENTURY. ECCLESIASTICAL GOVERNMENT

IN the apprehension of modern times Petrarch is the Italian songster of Laura and love. In the harmony of his Tuscan rhymes Italy applauds, or rather adores, the father of her lyric poetry; and his verse, or at least his name, is repeated by the enthusiasm or affection of amorous sensibility. Whatever may be the private taste of a stranger, his slight and superficial knowledge should humbly acquiesce in the taste of a learned nation; yet I may hope or presume that the Italians do not compare the tedious uniformity of sonnets and elegies with the sublime compositions of their epic muse, the original wildness of Dante, the regular beauties of Tasso, and the boundless variety of the incomparable Ariosto. The merits of the lover I am still less qualified to appreciate: nor am I deeply interested in a metaphysical passion for a nymph so shadowy, that her existence has been questioned; for a matron so prolific, that she was delivered of eleven legitimate children, while her amorous swain sighed and sung at the fountain of Vaucluse. But in the eyes of Petrarch and those of his graver contemporaries his love was a sin, and Italian verse a frivolous amusement. His Latin works of philosophy, poetry, and eloquence established his serious reputation which was soon diffused from Avignon over France and Italy: his friends and disciples were multiplied in every city; and if the ponderous volume of his writings be now abandoned to a long repose, our gratitude must applaud the man who, by precept and example, revived the spirit and study of the Augustan age. From his earliest youth Petrarch aspired to the poetic crown. The academical honours of the three faculties had introduced a royal degree of master or doctor in the art of poetry; and the title of poet-laureat, which custom, rather than vanity, perpetuates in the English court, was first invented by the Cæsars of Germany. In the musical games of antiquity a prize was bestowed on the victor: the belief that Virgil and Horace had been crowned in the Capitol inflamed the emulation of a Latin bard; and the laurel was endeared to the lover by a verbal resemblance with the name of his mistress. The value of either object was enhanced by the difficulties of the pursuit; and if the virtue or prudence of Laura was inexorable, he enjoyed, and might boast of enjoying, the nymph of poetry. His vanity was not of the most delicate kind, since he applauds the success of his own *labours*; his name was popular; his friends were active; the open or secret opposition of envy and prejudice was surmounted by the dexterity of patient merit. In the thirty-sixth year of his age he was solicited to accept the object of his wishes; and on the same day, in the solitude of Vaucluse, he received a similar and solemn invitation from the senate of Rome and the university of Paris. The learning of a theological school, and the ignorance of a lawless city, were alike unqualified to bestow the ideal though immortal wreath which genius may obtain from the free applause of the public and of posterity: but the candidate dismissed this troublesome reflection; and, after some moments of complacency and suspense, preferred the summons of the metropolis of the world.

The ceremony of his coronation was performed in the Capitol, by his friend and patron the supreme magistrate of the republic. Twelve patrician youths were arrayed in scarlet; six representatives of the most illustrious families, in green robes, with garlands of flowers, accompanied the procession; in the midst of the princes and nobles, the senator, count of Anguillara, a kinsman of the Colonna, assumed his throne; and at the voice of a herald Petrarch arose. After discoursing on a text of Virgil, and thrice repeating his vows for the prosperity of Rome, he knelt before the throne and received from the senator a laurel crown, with a more precious declaration, "This is the reward of merit." The people shouted, "Long life to the Capitol and the poet!" A sonnet in praise of Rome was accepted as the effusion of genius and gratitude; and after the whole procession had visited the Vatican the profane wreath was suspended before the shrine of St. Peter. In the act or diploma which was presented to Petrarch, the title and prerogatives of poet-laureat are revived in the Capitol after the lapse of thirteen hundred years; and he receives the perpetual privilege of wearing, at his choice, a crown of laurel, ivy, or myrtle, of assuming the poetic habit, and of teaching, disputing, interpreting, and composing, in all places whatsoever, and on all subjects of literature. The grant was ratified by the authority of the senate and people; and the character of citizen was the recompense of his affection for the Roman name. They did him honour, but they did him justice. In the familiar society of Cicero and Livy he had imbibed the ideas of an ancient patriot; and his ardent fancy kindled every idea to a sentiment, and every sentiment to a passion. The aspect of the seven hills and their majestic ruins confirmed these lively impressions; and he loved a country by whose liberal spirit he had been crowned and adopted. The poverty and debasement of Rome excited the indignation and pity of her grateful son: he dissembled the faults of his fellow-citizens; applauded with partial fondness the last of their heroes and matrons; and in the remembrance of the past, in the hope of the future, was pleased to forget the miseries of the present time. Rome was still the lawful mistress of the world; the pope and the emperor, her bishop and general, had abdicated their station by an inglorious retreat to the Rhône and the Danube; but if she could resume her virtue, the republic might again vindicate her liberty and dominion. Amidst the indulgence of enthusiasm and eloquence, Petrarch, Italy, and Europe were astonished by a revolution which realised for a moment his most splendid visions. The rise and fall of the tribune Rienzi will occupy the following pages: the subject is interesting, the materials are rich, and the glance of a patriot bard will sometimes vivify the copious, but simple, narrative of the Florentine, and more especially of the Roman, historian.

RIENZI AND THE RESTORATION OF THE *GOOD ESTATE*

In a quarter of the city which was inhabited only by mechanics and Jews, the marriage of an innkeeper and a washerwoman produced the future deliverer of Rome. From such parents Nicholas Rienzi Gabrini could inherit neither dignity nor fortune; and the gift of a liberal education, which they painfully bestowed, was the cause of his glory and untimely end. The study of history and eloquence, the writings of Cicero, Seneca, Livy, Cæsar, and Valerius Maximus, elevated above his equals and contemporaries the genius of the young plebeian: he perused with indefatigable diligence the manuscripts and marbles of antiquity; loved to dispense his knowledge in familiar language, and was often provoked to exclaim, "Where are now these Romans? their virtue, their justice, their power? why was I not born in those happy times?" When the republic addressed to the throne of Avignon an embassy of the three orders, the spirit and eloquence of Rienzi recommended him to a place among the thirteen deputies of the commons. The orator had the honour of haranguing Pope Clement the Sixth, and the satisfaction of conversing with Petrarch, a congenial mind; but his aspiring hopes were chilled by disgrace and poverty, and the patriot was reduced to a single garment and the charity of the hospital. From this misery he was relieved by the sense of merit or the smile of favour; and the employment of apostolic notary afforded him a daily stipend of five gold florins, a more honourable and extensive connection, and the right of contrasting, both in words and actions, his own integrity with the vices of the state. The eloquence of Rienzi was prompt and persuasive: the multitude is always prone to envy and censure: he was stimulated by the loss of a brother and the impunity of the assassins; nor was it possible to excuse or exaggerate the public calamities. The blessings of peace and justice, for which civil society has been instituted, were banished from Rome: the jealous citizens, who might have endured every personal or pecuniary injury, were most deeply wounded in the dishonour of their wives and daughters; they were equally oppressed by the arrogance of

the nobles and the corruption of the magistrates; and the abuse of arms
or of laws was the only circumstance that distinguished the lions from
the dogs and serpents of the Capitol. These allegorical emblems were
variously repeated in the pictures which Rienzi exhibited in the streets
and churches; and while the spectators gazed with curious wonder, the
bold and ready orator unfolded the meaning, applied the satire, inflamed their passions, and announced a distant hope of comfort and
deliverance. The privileges of Rome, her eternal sovereignty over her
princes and provinces, was the theme of his public and private discourse;
and a monument of servitude became in his hands a title and incentive
of liberty. The decree of the senate, which granted the most ample prerogatives to the emperor Vespasian, had been inscribed on a copper-
plate still extant in the choir of the church of St. John Lateran. A
numerous assembly of nobles and plebeians was invited to this political
lecture, and a convenient theatre was erected for their reception. The
notary appeared in a magnificent and mysterious habit, explained the
inscription by a version and commentary, and descanted with eloquence
and zeal on the ancient glories of the senate and people, from whom all
legal authority was derived. The supine ignorance of the nobles was
incapable of discerning the serious tendency of such representations:
they might sometimes chastise with words and blows the plebeian
reformer; but he was often suffered in the Colonna palace to amuse the
company with his threats and predictions; and the modern Brutus was
concealed under the mask of folly and the character of a buffoon. While
they indulged their contempt, the restoration of the *good estate*, his
favourite expression, was entertained among the people as a desirable,
a possible, and at length as an approaching, event; and while all had
the disposition to applaud, some had the courage to assist, their promised deliverer.

A prophecy, or rather a summons, affixed on the church door of St.
George, was the first public evidence of his designs; a nocturnal assembly of an hundred citizens on Mount Aventine, the first step to their
execution. After an oath of secrecy and aid, he represented to the
conspirators the importance and facility of their enterprise; that the
nobles, without union or resources, were strong only in the fear of their
imaginary strength; that all power, as well as right, was in the hands of
the people; that the revenues of the apostolical chamber might relieve
the public distress; and that the pope himself would approve their victory over the common enemies of government and freedom. After
securing a faithful band to protect his first declaration, he proclaimed
through the city, by sound of trumpet, that on the evening of the following day all persons should assemble without arms before the church of
St. Angelo, to provide for the re-establishment of the good estate. The
whole night was employed in the celebration of thirty masses of the
Holy Ghost; and in the morning Rienzi, bareheaded, but in complete

armour, issued from the church, encompassed by the hundred conspirtors. The pope's vicar, the simple bishop of Orvieto, who had been persuaded to sustain a part in this singular ceremony, marched on his right hand, and three great standards were borne aloft as the emblems of their design. In the first, the banner of *liberty*, Rome was seated on two lions, with a palm in one hand and a globe in the other; St. Paul, with a drawn sword, was delineated in the banner of *justice*; and in the third, St. Peter held the keys of *concord* and *peace*. Rienzi was encouraged by the presence and applause of an innumerable crowd, who understood little and hoped much; and the procession slowly rolled forwards from the castle of St. Angelo to the Capitol. His triumph was disturbed by some secret emotions which he laboured to suppress: he ascended without opposition, and with seeming confidence, the citadel of the republic; harangued the people from the balcony, and received the most flattering confirmation of his acts and laws. The nobles, as if destitute of arms and counsels, beheld in silent consternation this strange revolution; and the moment had been prudently chosen when the most formidable, Stephen Colonna, was absent from the city. On the first rumour he returned to his palace, affected to despise this plebeian tumult, and declared to the messenger of Rienzi that at his leisure he would cast the madman from the windows of the Capitol. The great bell instantly rang an alarm, and so rapid was the tide, so urgent was the danger, that Colonna escaped with precipitation to the suburb of St. Laurence: from thence, after a moment's refreshment, he continued the same speedy career till he reached in safety his castle of Palestrina, lamenting his own imprudence, which had not trampled the spark of this mighty conflagration. A general and peremptory order was issued from the Capitol to all the nobles that they should peaceably retire to their estates: they obeyed, and their departure secured the tranquillity of the free and obedient citizens of Rome.

But such voluntary obedience evaporates with the first transports of zeal; and Rienzi felt the importance of justifying his usurpation by a regular form and a legal title. At his own choice, the Roman people would have displayed their attachment and authority by lavishing on his head the names of senator or consul, of king or emperor: he preferred the ancient and modest appellation of tribune; the protection of the commons was the essence of that sacred office, and they were ignorant that it had never been invested with any share in the legislative or executive powers of the republic. In this character, and with the consent of the Romans, the tribune enacted the most salutary laws for the restoration and maintenance of the good estate. By the first he fulfils the wish of honesty and inexperience, that no civil suit should be protracted beyond the term of fifteen days. The danger of frequent perjury might justify the pronouncing against a false accuser the same penalty which his evidence would have inflicted: the disorders of the times might compel the legislator to punish every homicide with death and every injury with equal retaliation. But the execution of justice was hopeless till he had previously abolished the tyranny of the nobles. It was formally provided that none, except the supreme magistrate, should possess or command the gates, bridges, or towers of the state; that no private garrisons should be introduced into the towns or castles of the Roman territory; that none should bear arms or presume to fortify their houses in the city or country; that the barons should be responsible for the safety of the highways and the free passage of provisions; and that the protection of malefactors and robbers should be expiated by a fine of a thousand marks of silver. But these regulations would have been impotent and nugatory, had not the licentious nobles been awed by the sword of the civil power. A sudden alarm from the bell of the Capitol could still summon to the standard above twenty thousand volunteers: the support of the tribune and the laws required a more regular and permanent force. In each harbour of the coast a vessel was stationed for the assurance of commerce: a standing militia of three hundred and sixty horse and thirteen hundred foot was levied, clothed, and paid in the thirteen quarters of the city; and the spirit of a commonwealth may be traced in the grateful allowance of one hundred florins, or pounds, to the heirs of every soldier who lost his life in the service of his country. For the maintenance of the public defence, for the establishment of granaries, for the relief of widows, orphans, and indigent convents, Rienzi applied, without fear of sacrilege, the revenues of the apostolic chamber: the three branches of hearth-money, the salt-duty, and the customs, were each of the annual produce of one hundred thousand florins; and scandalous were the abuses, if in four or five months the amount of the salt-duty could be trebled by his judicious economy. After thus restoring the forces and finances of the republic, the tribune recalled the nobles from their solitary independence, required their personal appearance in the Capitol, and imposed an oath of allegiance to the new government, and of submission to the laws of the good estate. Apprehensive for their safety, but still more apprehensive of the danger of a refusal, the princes and barons returned to their houses at Rome in the garb of simple and peaceful citizens: the Colonna and Ursini, the Savelli and Frangipani, were confounded before the tribunal of a plebeian, of the vile buffoon whom they had so often derided, and their disgrace was aggravated by the indignation which they vainly struggled to disguise. The same oath was successively pronounced by the several orders of society, the clergy and gentlemen, the judges and notaries, the merchants and artisans, and the gradual descent was marked by the increase of sincerity and zeal. They swore to live and die with the republic and the church, whose interest was artfully united by the nominal association of the bishop of Orvieto, the pope's vicar, to the office of tribune. It was the boast of Rienzi that he had delivered the throne and patrimony of St. Peter from a rebellious aristocracy; and Clement the Sixth, who rejoiced in its fall, affected to believe the professions, to applaud the merits, and to confirm the title of his trusty servant. The speech, perhaps the mind, of the tribune, was inspired with a lively regard for the purity of the faith: he insinuated his claim to a supernatural mission from the Holy Ghost; enforced by a heavy forfeiture the annual duty of confession and communion; and strictly guarded the spiritual as well as temporal welfare of his faithful people.

PROSPERITY OF THE ROMAN REPUBLIC

Never perhaps has the energy and effect of a single mind been more remarkably felt than in the sudden, though transient, reformation of Rome by the tribune Rienzi. A den of robbers was converted to the discipline of a camp or convent: patient to hear, swift to redress, inexorable to punish, his tribunal was always accessible to the poor and stranger; nor could birth, or dignity, or the immunities of the church, protect the offender or his accomplices. The privileged houses, the private sanctuaries in Rome, on which no officer of justice would presume to trespass, were abolished; and he applied the timber and iron of their barricades in the fortifications of the Capitol. The venerable father of the Colonna was exposed in his own palace to the double shame of being desirous and of being unable to protect a criminal. A mule, with a jar of oil, had been stolen near Capranica; and the lord of the Ursini family was condemned to restore the damage and to discharge a fine of four hundred florins for his negligence in guarding the highways. Nor were the persons of the barons more inviolate than their lands or houses; and, either from accident or design, the same impartial rigour was exercised against the heads of the adverse factions. Peter Agapet Colonna, who had himself been senator of Rome, was arrested in the street for injury or debt; and justice was appeased by the tardy execution of Martin Ursini, who, among his various acts of violence and rapine, had pillaged a shipwrecked vessel at the mouth of the Tiber. His name, the purple of two cardinals, his uncles, a recent marriage, and a mortal disease, were disregarded by the inflexible tribune, who had chosen his victim. The public officers dragged him from his palace and nuptial bed: his trial was short and satisfactory; the bell of the Capitol convened the people: stripped of his mantle, on his knees, with his hands bound behind his back, he heard the sentence of death, and, after a brief confession, Ursini was led away to the gallows. After such an example, none who were conscious of guilt could hope for impunity, and the flight of the wicked, the licentious, and the idle, soon purified the city and territory of Rome. In this time (says the historian) the woods began to rejoice that they were no longer infested with robbers; the oxen began to plough; the pilgrims visited the sanctuaries; the roads and inns were replenished with travellers; trade, plenty, and good faith were restored in the markets; and a purse of gold might be exposed without danger in the midst of the highway. As soon as the life and property of the subject are secure, the labours and rewards of industry spontaneously revive: Rome was still the metropolis of the Christian world, and the fame and fortunes of the tribune were diffused in every country by the strangers who had enjoyed the blessings of his government.

The deliverance of his country inspired Rienzi with a vast and perhaps visionary idea of uniting Italy in a great federative republic, of which Rome should be the ancient and lawful head, and the free cities and princes the members and associates. His pen was not less eloquent than his tongue, and his numerous epistles were delivered to swift and trusty messengers. On foot, with a white wand in their hand, they traversed the forests and mountains; enjoyed, in the most hostile states, the sacred security of ambassadors; and reported, in the style of flattery or truth, that the highways along their passage were lined with kneeling multitudes, who implored Heaven for the success of their undertaking. Could passion have listened to reason, could private interest have yielded to the public welfare, the supreme tribunal and confederate union of the Italian republic might have healed their intestine discord, and closed the Alps against the barbarians of the North. But the propitious season had elapsed; and if Venice, Florence, Sienna, Perugia, and many inferior cities, offered their lives and fortunes to the good estate, the tyrants of Lombardy and Tuscany must despise or hate the plebeian author of a free constitution. From them, however, and from every part of Italy, the tribune received the most friendly and respectful answers: they were followed by the ambassadors of the princes and republics; and in this foreign conflux, on all the occasions of pleasure or business, the low-born notary could assume the familiar or majestic courtesy of a sovereign.[1] The most glorious circumstance of his reign was an appeal to his justice from Lewis king of Hungary, who complained that his brother and her husband had been perfidiously strangled by Jane queen of Naples: her guilt or innocence was pleaded in a solemn trial at Rome; but after hearing the advocates, the tribune adjourned this weighty and invidious cause, which was soon determined by the sword of the Hungarian. Beyond the Alps, more especially at Avignon, the revolution was the theme of curiosity, wonder, and applause. Petrarch had been the private friend, perhaps the secret counsellor, of Rienzi: his writings breathe the most ardent spirit of patriotism and joy; and all respect for the pope, all gratitude for the Colonna, was lost in the superior duties of a Roman citizen. The poet-laureat of the Capi-

[1] It was thus that Oliver Cromwell's old acquaintance, who remembered his vulgar and ungracious entrance into the House of Commons, were astonished at the ease and majesty of the Protector on his throne. The consciousness of merit and power will sometimes elevate the manners to the station.

tol maintains the act, applauds the hero, and mingles with some apprehension and advice the most lofty hopes of the permanent and rising greatness of the republic.

KNIGHTHOOD, CORONATION, AND FOLLIES OF RIENZI

While Petrarch indulged these prophetic visions, the Roman hero was fast declining from the meridian of fame and power; and the people, who had gazed with astonishment on the ascending meteor, began to mark the irregularity of its course, and the vicissitudes of light and obscurity. More eloquent than judicious, more enterprising than resolute, the faculties of Rienzi were not balanced by cool and commanding reason; he magnified in a tenfold proportion the objects of hope and fear; and prudence, which could not have erected, did not presume to fortify, his throne. In the blaze of prosperity, his virtues were insensibly tinctured with the adjacent vices; justice with cruelty, liberality with profusion, and the desire of fame with puerile and ostentatious vanity. He might have learned that the ancient tribunes, so strong and sacred in the public opinion, were not distinguished in style, habit, or appearance, from an ordinary plebeian; and that, as often as they visited the city on foot, a single viator, or beadle, attended the exercise of their office. The Gracchi would have frowned or smiled, could they have read the sonorous titles and epithets of their successor,—"NICHOLAS, SEVERE AND MERCIFUL; DELIVERER OF ROME; DEFENDER OF ITALY; FRIEND OF MANKIND, AND OF LIBERTY, PEACE, AND JUSTICE; TRIBUNE AUGUST:" his theatrical pageants had prepared the revolution; but Rienzi abused, in luxury and pride, the political maxim of speaking to the eyes, as well as the understanding, of the multitude. From nature he had received the gift of a handsome person, till it was swelled and disfigured by intemperance: and his propensity to laughter was corrected in the magistrate by the affectation of gravity and sternness. He was clothed, at least on public occasions, in a parti-coloured robe of velvet or satin, lined with fur, and embroidered with gold: the rod of justice, which he carried in his hand, was a sceptre of polished steel, crowned with a globe and cross of gold, and enclosing a small fragment of the true and holy wood. In his civil and religious processions through the city, he rode on a white steed, the symbol of royalty: the great banner of the republic, a sun with a circle of stars, a dove with an olive-branch, was displayed over his head; a shower of gold and silver was scattered among the populace; fifty guards with halberds encompassed his person; a troop of horse preceded his march; and their tymbals and trumpets were of massy silver.

The ambition of the honours of chivalry betrayed the meanness of his birth and degraded the importance of his office; and the equestrian tribune was not less odious to the nobles, whom he adopted, than to the plebeians, whom he deserted. All that yet remained of treasure, or luxury, or art, was exhausted on that solemn day. Rienzi led the procession from the Capitol to the Lateran; the tediousness of the way was relieved with decorations and games; the ecclesiastical, civil, and military orders marched under their various banners; the Roman ladies attended his wife; and the ambassadors of Italy might loudly applaud or secretly deride the novelty of the pomp. In the evening, when they had reached the church and palace of Constantine, he thanked and dismissed the numerous assembly, with an invitation to the festival of the ensuing day. From the hands of a venerable knight he received the order of the Holy Ghost; the purification of the bath was a previous ceremony; but in no step of his life did Rienzi excite such scandal and censure as by the profane use of the porphyry vase in which Constantine (a foolish legend) had been healed of his leprosy by Pope Sylvester. With equal presumption the tribune watched or reposed within the consecrated precincts of the baptistery; and the failure of his state-bed was interpreted as an omen of his approaching downfall. At the hour of worship he showed himself to the returning crowds in a majestic attitude, with a robe of purple, his sword, and gilt spurs; but the holy rites were soon interrupted by his levity and insolence. Rising from his throne, and advancing towards the congregation, he proclaimed in a loud voice, "We summon to our tribunal Pope Clement, and command him to reside in his diocese of Rome: we also summon the sacred college of cardinals. We again summon the two pretenders, Charles of Bohemia and Lewis of Bavaria, who style themselves emperors: we likewise summon all the electors of Germany to inform us on what pretence they have usurped the inalienable right of the Roman people, the ancient and lawful sovereigns of the empire." Unsheathing his maiden sword, he thrice brandished it to the three parts of the world, and thrice repeated the extravagant declaration, "And this too is mine!" The pope's vicar, the bishop of Orvieto, attempted to check this career of folly; but his feeble protest was silenced by martial music; and instead of withdrawing from the assembly, he consented to dine with his brother tribune at a table which had hitherto been reserved for the supreme pontiff. A banquet, such as the Cæsars had given, was prepared for the Romans. The apartments, porticoes, and courts of the Lateran were spread with innumerable tables for either sex and every condition; a stream of wine flowed from the nostrils of Constantine's brazen horse; no complaint, except of the scarcity of water, could be heard; and the licentiousness of the multitude was curbed by discipline and fear. A subsequent day was appointed for the coronation of Rienzi; seven crowns of different leaves or metals were successively placed on his head by the most eminent of the Roman clergy; they represented the seven gifts of the Holy Ghost; and he still professed to imitate the example of the ancient tribunes. These extraordinary spectacles might deceive or flatter the people; and their own vanity was gratified in the vanity of their leader. But in his private life he soon deviated from the strict rule of frugality and abstinence; and the plebeians, who were awed by the splendour of the nobles, were provoked by the luxury of their equal. His wife, his son, his uncle (a barber in name and profession) exposed the contrast of vulgar manners and princely expense; and without acquiring the majesty, Rienzi degenerated into the vices, of a king.

In 1347 Rienzi was degraded from office and forced into exile. After seven years he returned to Rome with the title of Senator but was murdered four months later, September, 1354.

RETURN OF THE POPES TO ROME

The first and most generous wish of Petrarch was the restoration of a free republic; but after the exile and death of his plebeian hero, he turned his eyes from the tribune to the king of the Romans. The Capitol was yet stained with the blood of Rienzi when Charles the Fourth descended from the Alps to obtain the Italian and Imperial crowns. In his passage through Milan he received the visit, and repaid the flattery, of the poet-laureat; accepted a medal of Augustus; and promised, without a smile, to imitate the founder of the Roman monarchy. A false application of the names and maxims of antiquity was the source of the hopes and disappointments of Petrarch; yet he could not overlook the difference of times and characters; the immeasurable distance between the first Cæsars and a Bohemian prince, who by the favour of the clergy had been elected the titular head of the German aristocracy. Instead of restoring to Rome her glory and her provinces, he had bound himself by a secret treaty with the pope to evacuate the city on the day of his coronation; and his shameful retreat was pursued by the reproaches of the patriot bard.

After the loss of liberty and empire, his third and more humble wish was to reconcile the shepherd with his flock; to recall the Roman bishop to his ancient and peculiar diocese. In the fervour of youth, with the authority of age, Petrarch addressed his exhortations to five successive popes, and his eloquence was always inspired by the enthusiasm of sentiment and the freedom of language. The son of a citizen of Florence invariably preferred the country of his birth to that of his education; and Italy, in his eyes, was the queen and garden of the world. Amidst her domestic factions she was doubtless superior to France both in art and science, in wealth and politeness; but the difference could scarcely support the epithet of barbarous, which he promiscuously bestows on the countries beyond the Alps. Avignon, the mystic Babylon, the sink of vice and corruption, was the object of his hatred and contempt; but he forgets that her scandalous vices were not the growth of the soil, and that in every residence they would adhere to the power and luxury of the papal court. He confesses that the successor of St. Peter is the bishop of the universal church; yet it was not on the banks of the Rhône, but of the Tiber, that the apostle had fixed his everlasting throne: and while every city in the Christian world was blessed with a bishop, the metropolis alone was desolate and forlorn. Since the removal of the Holy See the sacred buildings of the Lateran and the Vatican, their altars and their saints, were left in a state of poverty and decay; and Rome was often painted under the image of a disconsolate matron, as if the wandering husband could be reclaimed by the homely portrait of the age and infirmities of his weeping spouse. But the cloud which hung over the seven hills would be dispelled by the presence of their lawful sovereign: eternal fame, the prosperity of Rome, and the peace of Italy, would be the recompense of the pope who should dare to embrace this generous resolution. Of the five whom Petrarch exhorted, the three first, John the Twenty-second, Benedict the Twelfth, and Clement the Sixth, were importuned or amused by the boldness of the orator; but the memorable change which had been attempted by Urban the Fifth was finally accomplished by Gregory the Eleventh. The execution of their design was opposed by weighty and almost insuperable obstacles. A king of France, who has deserved the epithet of wise, was unwilling to release them from a local dependence: the cardinals, for the most part his subjects, were attached to the language, manners, and climate of Avignon; to their stately palaces; above all, to the wines of Burgundy. In their eyes Italy was foreign or hostile; and they reluctantly embarked at Marseilles, as if they had been sold or banished into the land of the Saracens. Urban the Fifth resided three years in the Vatican with safety and honour; his sanctity was protected by a guard of two thousand horse; and the king of Cyprus, the queen of Naples, and the emperors of the East and West, devoutly saluted their common father in the chair of St. Peter. But the joy of Petrarch and the Italians was soon turned into grief and indignation. Some reasons of public or private moment, his own impatience or the prayers of the cardinals, recalled Urban to France; and the approaching election was saved from the tyrannic patriotism of the Romans. The powers of heaven were interested in their cause: Bridget of Sweden, a saint and pilgrim, disapproved the return, and foretold the death, of Urban the Fifth; the migration of Gregory the Eleventh was encouraged by St. Catherine of Sienna, the spouse of Christ and ambassadress of the Florentines; and the popes themselves, the great masters of human credulity, appear to have listened to these visionary females. Yet those celestial admonitions were supported by some arguments of temporal policy. The residence of Avignon had been invaded by hostile violence: at the head of thirty thousand robbers an hero had extorted ransom and absolution from the vicar of Christ and the sacred college; and the maxim of the French warriors, to spare the people and plunder the church, was a new heresy of the most dangerous import. While the pope was driven from Avignon, he was strenuously invited to Rome. The senate and people acknowledged him as their lawful sovereign, and laid at his feet the keys of the gates, the bridges, and the fortresses; of the quarter at least beyond the Tiber. But this loyal offer was accompanied by a declaration that they could no longer suffer the scandal and calamity of his absence; and that his obstinacy would finally provoke them to revive and assert the primitive right of election. The abbot of Mount Cassino had been consulted whether he would accept the triple crown from the clergy and people: "I am a citizen of Rome," replied that venerable ecclesiastic, "and my first law is the voice of my country."

If superstition will interpret an untimely death; if the merit of counsels be judged from the event; the heavens may seem to frown on a measure of such apparent reason and propriety. Gregory the Eleventh did not survive above fourteen months his return to the Vatican; and his decease was followed by the great schism of the West, which distracted the Latin church above forty years. The sacred college was then composed of twenty-two cardinals: six of these had remained at Avignon; eleven Frenchmen, one Spaniard, and four Italians, entered the conclave in the usual form. Their choice was not yet limited to the purple; and their unanimous votes acquiesced in the archbishop of Bari, a subject of Naples, conspicuous for his zeal and learning, who ascended the throne of St. Peter under the name of Urban the Sixth. The epistle of the sacred college affirms his free and regular election, which had been inspired as usual by the Holy Ghost; he was adored, invested, and crowned, with the customary rites; his temporal authority was obeyed at Rome and Avignon, and his ecclesiastical supremacy was acknowledged in the Latin world. During several weeks the cardinals attended their new master with the fairest professions of attachment and loyalty, till the summer heats permitted a decent escape from the city. But as soon as they were united at Anagni and Fundi, in a place of security, they cast aside the mask, accused their own falsehood and hypocrisy, excommunicated the apostate and antichrist of Rome, and proceeded to a new election of Robert of Geneva, Clement the Seventh, whom they announced to the nations as the true and rightful vicar of Christ. Their first choice, an involuntary and illegal act, was annulled by the fear of death and the menaces of the Romans; and their complaint is justified by the strong evidence of probability and fact. The twelve French cardinals, above two-thirds of the votes, were masters of the election; and whatever might be their provincial jealousies, it cannot fairly be presumed that they would have sacrificed their right and interest to a foreign candidate, who would never restore them to their native country. In the various, and often inconsistent, narratives, the shades of popular violence are more darkly or faintly coloured: but the licentiousness of the seditious Romans was inflamed by a sense of their privileges, and the danger of a second emigration. The conclave was intimidated by the shouts, and encompassed by the arms, of thirty thousand rebels; the bells of the Capitol and St. Peter's rang an alarm; "Death, or an Italian pope!" was the universal cry; the same threat was repeated by the twelve bannerets or chiefs of the quarters, in the form of charitable advice; some preparations were made for burning the obstinate cardinals; and had they chosen a Transalpine subject, it is probable that they would never have departed alive from the Vatican. The same constraint imposed the necessity of dissembling in the eyes of Rome and of the world; the pride and cruelty of Urban presented a more inevitable danger; and they soon discovered the features of the tyrant, who could walk in his garden and recite his breviary while he heard from an adjacent chamber six cardinals groaning on the rack. His inflexible zeal, which loudly censured their luxury and vice, would have attached them to the stations and duties of their parishes at Rome; and had he not fatally delayed a new promotion, the French cardinals would have been reduced to a helpless minority in the sacred college. For these reasons, and in the hope of repassing the Alps, they rashly violated the peace and unity of the church; and the merits of their double choice are yet agitated in the Catholic schools. The vanity, rather than the interest of the nation, determined the court and clergy of France. The states of Savoy, Sicily, Cyprus, Arragon, Castile, Navarre, and Scotland, were inclined by their example and authority to the obedience of Clement the Seventh, and, after his decease, of Benedict the Thirteenth. Rome and the principal states of Italy, Germany, Portugal, England, the Low Countries, and the kingdoms of the North, adhered to the prior election of Urban the Sixth, who was succeeded by Boniface the Ninth, Innocent the Seventh, and Gregory the Twelfth.

GREAT SCHISM OF THE WEST

From the banks of the Tiber and the Rhône the hostile pontiffs encountered each other with the pen and the sword: the civil and ecclesiastical order of society was disturbed; and the Romans had their full share of the mischiefs of which they may be arraigned as the primary authors. They had vainly flattered themselves with the hope of restoring the seat of the ecclesiastical monarchy, and of relieving their poverty with the tributes and offerings of the nations; but the separation of France and Spain diverted the stream of lucrative devotion; nor could the loss be compensated by the two jubilees which were crowded into the space of ten years. By the avocations of the schism, by foreign arms, and popular tumults, Urban the Sixth and his three successors were often compelled to interrupt their residence in the Vatican. The Colonna and Ursini still exercised their deadly feuds: the bannerets of Rome asserted and abused the privileges of a republic: the vicars of Christ, who had levied a military force, chastised their rebellion with the gibbet, the sword, and the dagger; and, in a friendly conference, eleven deputies of the people were perfidiously murdered and cast into the street. Since the invasion of Robert the Norman, the Romans had pursued their domestic quarrels without the dangerous interposition of a stranger. But in the disorders of the schism, an aspiring neighbour, Ladislaus king of Naples, alternately supported and betrayed the pope and the people; by the former he was declared *gonfalonier*, or general of the church, while the latter submitted to his choice the nomination of their magistrates. Besieging Rome by land and water, he thrice entered the gates as a barbarian conqueror; profaned the altars, violated the virgins, pillaged the merchants, performed his devotions at St. Peter's, and left a garrison in the castle of St. Angelo. His arms were sometimes unfortunate, and to a delay of three days he was indebted for his life and crown: but Ladislaus triumphed in his turn; and it was only his premature death that could save the metropolis and the ecclesiastical state from the ambitious conqueror, who had assumed the title, or at least the powers, of King of Rome.

I have not undertaken the ecclesiastical history of the schism; but Rome, the object of these last chapters, is deeply interested in the disputed succession of her sovereigns. The first counsels for the peace and union of Christendom arose from the university of Paris, from the faculty of the Sorbonne, whose doctors were esteemed, at least in the Gallican church, as the most consummate masters of theological science. Prudently waiving all invidious inquiry into the origin and merits of the dispute, they proposed, as a healing measure, that the two pretenders of Rome and Avignon should abdicate at the same time, after qualifying the cardinals of the adverse factions to join in a legitimate election; and that the nations should *subtract* their obedience, if either of the competitors preferred his own interest to that of the public. At each vacancy these physicians of the church deprecated the mischiefs of a hasty choice; but the policy of the conclave and the ambition of its members were deaf to reason and entreaties; and whatsoever promises were made, the pope could never be bound by the oaths of the cardinal. During fifteen years the pacific designs of the university were eluded by the arts of the rival pontiffs, the scruples or passions of their adherents, and the vicissitudes of French factions, that ruled the insanity of Charles the Sixth. At length a vigorous resolution was embraced; and a solemn embassy, of the titular patriarch of Alexandria, two archbishops, five bishops, five abbots, three knights, and twenty doctors, was sent to the courts of Avignon and Rome, to require, in the name of the church and king, the abdication of the two pretenders, of Peter de Luna, who styled himself Benedict the Thirteenth, and of Angelo Corrario, who assumed the name of Gregory the Twelfth. For the ancient honour of Rome, and the success of their commission, the ambassadors solicited a conference with the magistrates of the city, whom they gratified by a positive declaration that the most Christian king did not entertain a wish of transporting the holy see from the Vatican, which he considered as the genuine and proper seat of the successor of St. Peter. In the name of the senate and people, an eloquent Roman asserted their desire to co-oper-ate in the union of the church, deplored the temporal and spiritual calamities of the long schism, and requested the protection of France against the arms of the king of Naples. The answers of Benedict and Gregory were alike edifying and alike deceitful; and, in evading the demand of their abdication, the two rivals were animated by a common spirit. They agreed on the necessity of a previous interview; but the time, the place, and the manner, could never be ascertained by mutual consent. "If the one advances," says a servant of Gregory, "the other retreats; one appears an animal fearful of the land, the other a creature apprehensive of the water. And thus, for a short remnant of life and power, will these aged priests endanger the peace and salvation of the Christian world."

The Christian world was at length provoked by their obstinacy and fraud: they were deserted by their cardinals, who embraced each other as friends and colleagues; and their revolt was supported by a numerous assembly of prelates and ambassadors. With equal justice, the council of Pisa deposed the popes of Rome and Avignon; the conclave was unanimous in the choice of Alexander the Fifth, and his vacant seat was soon filled by a similar election of John the Twenty-third, the most profligate of mankind. But instead of extinguishing the schism, the rashness of the French and Italians had given a third pretender to the chair of St. Peter. Such new claims of the synod and conclave were dis-puted; three kings, of Germany, Hungary, and Naples, adhered to the cause of Gregory the Twelfth: and Benedict the Thirteenth, himself a Spaniard, was acknowledged by the devotion and patriotism of that powerful nation. The rash proceedings of Pisa were corrected by the council of Constance; the emperor Sigismond acted a conspicuous part as the advocate or protector of the Catholic church; and the number and weight of civil and ecclesiastical members might seem to constitute the states-general of Europe. Of the three popes, John the Twenty-third was the first victim: he fled and was brought back a prisoner: the most scandalous charges were suppressed; the vicar of Christ was only accused of piracy, murder, rape, sodomy, and incest; and after subscrib-ing his own condemnation, he expiated in prison the imprudence of trusting his person to a free city beyond the Alps. Gregory the Twelfth, whose obedience was reduced to the narrow precincts of Rimini, descended with more honour from the throne; and his ambassador con-vened the session in which he renounced the title and authority of lawful pope. To vanquish the obstinacy of Benedict the Thirteenth or his adherents, the emperor in person undertook a journey from Constance to Perpignan. The kings of Castile, Arragon, Navarre, and Scotland,

obtained an equal and honourable treaty: with the concurrence of the
Spaniards, Benedict was deposed by the council; but the harmless old
man was left in a solitary castle to excommunicate twice each day the
rebel kingdoms which had deserted his cause. After thus eradicating
the remains of the schism, the synod of Constance proceeded with slow
and cautious steps to elect the sovereign of Rome and the head of the
church. On this momentous occasion the college of twenty-three cardinals was fortified with thirty deputies; six of whom were chosen in
each of the five great nations of Christendom,—the Italian, the German,
the French, the Spanish, and the *English*: the interference of strangers
was softened by their generous preference of an Italian and a Roman;
and the hereditary, as well as personal, merit of Otho Colonna recommended him to the conclave. Rome accepted with joy and obedience
the noblest of her sons; the ecclesiastical state was defended by his
powerful family; and the elevation of Martin the Fifth is the era of the
restoration and establishment of the popes in the Vatican.

THE GOVERNMENT OF ROME IN THE FIFTEENTH CENTURY

A citizen has remarked, with pride and pleasure, that the king of the
Romans, after passing with a slight salute the cardinals and prelates who
met him at the gate, distinguished the dress and person of the senator of
Rome; and in this last farewell, the pageants of the empire and the republic were clasped in a friendly embrace. According to the laws of Rome
her first magistrate was required to be a doctor of laws, an alien, of a
place at least forty miles from the city, with whose inhabitants he must
not be connected in the third canonical degree of blood or alliance.
The election was annual: a severe scrutiny was instituted into the conduct of the departing senator; nor could he be recalled to the same office
till after the expiration of two years. A liberal salary of three thousand
florins was assigned for his expense and reward; and his public appearance represented the majesty of the republic. His robes were of gold
brocade or crimson velvet, or in the summer season of a lighter silk: he
bore in his hand an ivory sceptre; the sound of trumpets announced his
approach; and his solemn steps were preceded at least by four lictors or
attendants, whose red wands were enveloped with bands or streamers of
the golden colour or livery of the city. His oath in the Capitol proclaims his right and duty, to observe and assert the laws, to control the
proud, to protect the poor, and to exercise justice and mercy within the
extent of his jurisdiction. In these useful functions he was assisted by
three learned strangers; the two *collaterals* and the judge of criminal
appeals: their frequent trials of robberies, rapes, and murders are attested
by the laws; and the weakness of these laws connives at the licentiousness of private feuds and armed associations for mutual defence. But
the senator was confined to the administration of justice: the Capitol,
the treasury, and the government of the city and its territory were

entrusted to the three *conservators*, who were changed four times in each year: the militia of the thirteen regions assembled under the banners of their respective chiefs, or *caporioni*; and the first of these was distinguished by the name and dignity of the *prior*. The popular legislature consisted of the secret and the common councils of the Romans. The former was composed of the magistrates and their immediate predecessors, with some fiscal and legal officers, and three classes of thirteen, twenty-six, and forty counsellors; amounting in the whole to about one hundred and twenty persons. In the common council all male citizens had a right to vote; and the value of their privilege was enhanced by the care with which any foreigners were prevented from usurping the title and character of Romans. The tumult of a democracy was checked by wise and jealous precautions: except the magistrates, none could propose a question; none were permitted to speak, except from an open pulpit or tribunal; all disorderly acclamations were suppressed; the sense of the majority was decided by a secret ballot; and their decrees were promulgated in the venerable name of the Roman senate and people. It would not be easy to assign a period in which this theory of government has been reduced to accurate and constant practice, since the establishment of order has been gradually connected with the decay of liberty. But in the year one thousand five hundred and eighty the ancient statutes were collected, methodised in three books, and adapted to present use, under the pontificate, and with the approbation, of Gregory the Thirteenth: this civil and criminal code is the modern law of the city; and, if the popular assemblies have been abolished, a foreign senator, with the three conservators, still resides in the palace of the Capitol. The policy of the Cæsars has been repeated by the popes; and the bishop of Rome affected to maintain the form of a republic, while he reigned with the absolute powers of a temporal, as well as spiritual, monarch.

ECCLESIASTICAL GOVERNMENT

The spiritual thunders of the Vatican depend on the force of opinion; and if that opinion be supplanted by reason or passion, the sound may idly waste itself in the air; and the helpless priest is exposed to the brutal violence of a noble or a plebeian adversary. But after their return from Avignon, the keys of St. Peter were guarded by the sword of St. Paul. Rome was commanded by an impregnable citadel: the use of cannon is a powerful engine against popular seditions: a regular force of cavalry and infantry was enlisted under the banners of the pope: his ample revenues supplied the resources of war; and, from the extent of his domain, he could bring down on a rebellious city an army of hostile neighbours and loyal subjects. Since the union of the duchies of Ferrara and Urbino, the ecclesiastical state extends from the Mediterranean to the Adriatic, and from the confines of Naples to the banks of the Po;

and as early as the sixteenth century the greater part of that spacious and fruitful country acknowledged the lawful claims and temporal sovereignty of the Roman pontiffs. Their claims were readily deduced from the genuine or fabulous donations of the darker ages: the successive steps of their final settlement would engage us too far in the transactions of Italy, and even of Europe; the crimes of Alexander the Sixth, the martial operations of Julius the Second, and the liberal policy of Leo the Tenth, a theme which has been adorned by the pens of the noblest historians of the times. In the first period of their conquests, till the expedition of Charles the Eighth, the popes might successfully wrestle with the adjacent princes and states, whose military force was equal or inferior to their own. But as soon as the monarchs of France, Germany, and Spain contended with gigantic arms for the dominion of Italy, they supplied with art the deficiency of strength, and concealed, in a labyrinth of wars and treaties, their aspiring views and the immortal hope of chasing the barbarians beyond the Alps. The nice balance of the Vatican was often subverted by the soldiers of the North and West, who were united under the standard of Charles the Fifth: the feeble and fluctuating policy of Clement the Seventh exposed his person and dominions to the conqueror; and Rome was abandoned seven months to a lawless army, more cruel and rapacious than the Goths and Vandals. After this severe lesson the popes contracted their ambition, which was almost satisfied, resumed the character of a common parent, and abstained from all offensive hostilities, except in an hasty quarrel, when the vicar of Christ and the Turkish sultan were armed at the same time against the kingdom of Naples. The French and Germans at length withdrew from the field of battle: Milan, Naples, Sicily, Sardinia, and the sea-coast of Tuscany, were firmly possessed by the Spaniards; and it became their interest to maintain the peace and dependence of Italy, which continued almost without disturbance from the middle of the sixteenth to the opening of the eighteenth century. The Vatican was swayed and protected by the religious policy of the Catholic king: his prejudice and interest disposed him in every dispute to support the prince against the people; and instead of the encouragement, the aid, and the asylum which they obtained from the adjacent states, the friends of liberty or the enemies of law were enclosed on all sides within the iron circle of despotism. The long habits of obedience and education subdued the turbulent spirit of the nobles and commons of Rome. The barons forgot the arms and factions of their ancestors, and insensibly became the servants of luxury and government. Instead of maintaining a crowd of tenants and followers, the produce of their estates was consumed in the private expenses which multiply the pleasures and diminish the power of the lord. The Colonna and Ursini vied with each other in the decoration of their palaces and chapels; and their antique splendour was rivalled or surpassed by the sudden opulence of the papal families.

In Rome the voice of freedom and discord is no longer heard; and, instead of the foaming torrent, a smooth and stagnant lake reflects the image of idleness and servitude.

A Christian, a philosopher, and a patriot, will be equally scandalised by the temporal kingdom of the clergy; and the local majesty of Rome, the remembrance of her consuls and triumphs, may seem to embitter the sense and aggravate the shame of her slavery. If we calmly weigh the merits and defects of the ecclesiastical government, it may be praised in its present state as a mild, decent, and tranquil system, exempt from the dangers of a minority, the sallies of youth, the expenses of luxury, and the calamities of war. But these advantages are overbalanced by a frequent, perhaps a septennial, election of a sovereign, who is seldom a native of the country: the reign of a *young* statesman of threescore, in the decline of his life and abilities, without hope to accomplish, and without children to inherit, the labours of his transitory reign. The successful candidate is drawn from the church, and even the convent; from the mode of education and life the most adverse to reason, humanity, and freedom. In the trammels of servile faith he has learned to believe because it is absurd, to revere all that is contemptible, and to despise whatever might deserve the esteem of a rational being; to punish error as a crime, to reward mortification and celibacy as the first of virtues; to place the saints of the calendar above the heroes of Rome and the sages of Athens; and to consider the missal, or the crucifix, as more useful instruments than the plough or the loom. In the office of nuncio, or the rank of cardinal, he may acquire some knowledge of the world; but the primitive stain will adhere to his mind and manners: from study and experience he may suspect the mystery of his profession; but the sacerdotal artist will imbibe some portion of the bigotry which he inculcates. The genius of Sixtus the Fifth burst from the gloom of a Franciscan cloister. In a reign of five years he exterminated the outlaws and banditti, abolished the *profane* sanctuaries of Rome, formed a naval and military force, restored and emulated the monuments of antiquity, and, after a liberal use and large increase of the revenue, left five millions of crowns in the castle of St. Angelo. But his justice was sullied with cruelty, his activity was prompted by the ambition of conquest: after his decease the abuses revived; the treasure was dissipated; he entailed on posterity thirty-five new taxes and the venality of offices; and, after his death, his statue was demolished by an ungrateful or an injured people. The wild and original character of Sixtus the Fifth stands alone in the series of the pontiffs: the maxims and effects of their temporal government may be collected from the positive and comparative view of the arts and philosophy, the agriculture and trade, the wealth and population, of the ecclesiastical state. For myself, it is my wish to depart in charity with all mankind, nor am I willing, in these last moments, to offend even the pope and clergy of Rome.

Chapter 71

POGGIO'S DISCOURSE ON THE RUINS OF ROME IN THE
FIFTEENTH CENTURY. FOUR CAUSES OF RUIN. THE COLI-
SEUM. RESTORATION OF THE CITY. FINAL REFLECTIONS
ON THE DECLINE AND FALL OF THE ROMAN EMPIRE

IN the last days of Pope Eugenius the Fourth,[1] two of his servants,
the learned Poggius and a friend, ascended the Capitoline hill,
reposed themselves among the ruins of columns and temples, and
viewed from that commanding spot the wide and various prospect of
desolation. The place and the object gave ample scope for moralising
on the vicissitudes of fortune, which spares neither man nor the proudest
of his works, which buries empires and cities in a common grave; and it
was agreed that, in proportion to her former greatness, the fall of Rome
was the more awful and deplorable. "Her primæval state, such as she
might appear in a remote age, when Evander entertained the stranger
of Troy, has been delineated by the fancy of Virgil. This Tarpeian rock
was then a savage and solitary thicket: in the time of the poet it was
crowned with the golden roofs of a temple; the temple is overthrown,
the gold has been pillaged, the wheel of fortune has accomplished her
revolution, and the sacred ground is again disfigured with thorns and
brambles. The hill of the Capitol, on which we sit, was formerly the
head of the Roman empire, the citadel of the earth, the terror of kings;
illustrated by the footsteps of so many triumphs, enriched with the
spoils and tributes of so many nations. This spectacle of the world,
how is it fallen! how changed! how defaced! the path of victory is
obliterated by vines, and the benches of the senators are concealed by a
dunghill. Cast your eyes on the Palatine hill, and seek among the shapeless and enormous fragments the marble theatre, the obelisks, the
colossal statues, the porticoes of Nero's palace: survey the other hills of
the city, the vacant space is interrupted only by ruins and gardens. The
forum of the Roman people, where they assembled to enact their laws
and elect their magistrates, is now enclosed for the cultivation of pot-
herbs, or thrown open for the reception of swine and buffaloes. The
public and private edifices, that were founded for eternity, lie prostrate,
naked, and broken, like the limbs of a mighty giant; and the ruin is the

[1] This seems to be a slip for Pope Martin the Fifth. In note 51 to chapter 65
Gibbon points out that Poggio's dialogue *De Varietate Fortunæ* was composed
shortly before Martin's death about the end of 1430. Milman comments on this; Bury
passes it over.—D.M.L.

more visible, from the stupendous relics that have survived the injuries of time and fortune."

These relics are minutely described by Poggius, one of the first who raised his eyes from the monuments of legendary to those of classic superstition. 1. Besides a bridge, an arch, a sepulchre, and the pyramid of Cestius, he could discern, of the age of the republic, a double row of vaults in the salt-office of the Capitol, which were inscribed with the name and munificence of Catulus. 2. Eleven temples were visible in some degree, from the perfect form of the Pantheon to the three arches and a marble column of the temple of Peace, which Vespasian erected after the civil wars and the Jewish triumph. 3. Of the number, which he rashly defines, of seven *thermæ*, or public baths, none were sufficiently entire to represent the use and distribution of the several parts; but those of Diocletian and Antoninus Caracalla still retained the titles of the founders, and astonished the curious spectator, who, in observing their solidity and extent, the variety of marbles, the size and multitude of the columns, compared the labour and expense with the use and importance. Of the baths of Constantine, of Alexander, of Domitian, or rather of Titus, some vestige might yet be found. 4. The triumphal arches of Titus, Severus, and Constantine, were entire, both the structure and the inscriptions: a falling fragment was honoured with the name of Trajan; and two arches, then extant, in the Flaminian way, have been ascribed to the baser memory of Faustina and Gallienus. 5. After the wonder of the Coliseum, Poggius might have overlooked a small amphitheatre of brick, most probably for the use of the prætorian camp: the theatres of Marcellus and Pompey were occupied in a great measure by public and private buildings; and in the Circus, Agonalis and Maximus, little more than the situation and the form could be investigated. 6. The columns of Trajan and Antonine were still erect; but the Egyptian obelisks were broken or buried. A people of gods and heroes, the workmanship of art, was reduced to one equestrian figure of gilt brass and to five marble statues, of which the most conspicuous were the two horses of Phidias and Praxiteles. 7. The two mausoleums or sepulchres of Augustus and Hadrian could not totally be lost; but the former was only visible as a mound of earth, and the latter, the castle of St. Angelo, had acquired the name and appearance of a modern fortress. With the addition of some separate and nameless columns, such were the remains of the ancient city; for the marks of a more recent structure might be detected in the walls, which formed a circumference of ten miles, included three hundred and seventy-nine turrets, and opened into the country by thirteen gates.

This melancholy picture was drawn above nine hundred years after the fall of the Western empire, and even of the Gothic kingdom of Italy. A long period of distress and anarchy, in which empire, and arts, and riches had migrated from the banks of the Tiber, was incapable of restoring or adorning the city; and, as all that is human must retrograde if it do not advance, every successive age must have hastened the ruin of the works of antiquity. To measure the progress of decay, and to ascertain, at each era, the state of each edifice, would be an endless and a useless labour; and I shall content myself with two observations, which will introduce a short inquiry into the general causes and effects. 1. Two hundred years before the eloquent complaint of Poggius, an anonymous writer composed a description of Rome. His ignorance may repeat the same objects under strange and fabulous names. Yet this barbarous topographer had eyes and ears; he could observe the visible remains; he could listen to the tradition of the people; and he distinctly enumerates seven theatres, eleven baths, twelve arches, and eighteen palaces, of which many had disappeared before the time of Poggius. It is apparent that many stately monuments of antiquity survived till a late period, and that the principles of destruction acted with vigorous and increasing energy in the thirteenth and fourteenth centuries. 2. The same reflection must be applied to the three last ages; and we should vainly seek the Septizonium of Severus, which is celebrated by Petrarch and the antiquarians of the sixteenth century. While the Roman edifices were still entire, the first blows, however weighty and impetuous, were resisted by the solidity of the mass and the harmony of the parts; but the slightest touch would precipitate the fragments of arches and columns, that already nodded to their fall.

FOUR CAUSES OF DESTRUCTION

After a diligent inquiry I can discern four principal causes of the ruin of Rome, which continued to operate in a period of more than a thousand years. I. The injuries of time and nature. II. The hostile attacks of the barbarians and Christians. III. The use and abuse of the materials. And, IV. The domestic quarrels of the Romans.

I. The art of man is able to construct monuments far more permanent than the narrow span of his own existence: yet these monuments, like himself, are perishable and frail; and in the boundless annals of time his life and his labours must equally be measured as a fleeting moment. Of a simple and solid edifice it is not easy however to circumscribe the duration. As the wonders of ancient days, the pyramids attracted the curiosity of the ancients: a hundred generations, the leaves of autumn, have dropped into the grave; and after the fall of the Pharaohs and Ptolemies, the Cæsars and Caliphs, the same pyramids stand erect and unshaken above the floods of the Nile. A complex figure of various and minute parts is more accessible to injury and decay; and the silent lapse of time is often accelerated by hurricanes and earthquakes, by fires and inundations. The air and earth have doubtless been shaken; and the lofty turrets of Rome have tottered from their foundations; but the seven hills do not appear to be placed on the great cavities of the globe;

nor has the city, in any age, been exposed to the convulsions of nature, which, in the climate of Antioch, Lisbon, or Lima, have crumbled in a few moments the works of ages into dust. Fire is the most powerful agent of life and death: the rapid mischief may be kindled and propagated by the industry or negligence of mankind; and every period of the Roman annals is marked by the repetition of similar calamities. A memorable conflagration, the guilt or misfortune of Nero's reign, continued, though with unequal fury, either six or nine days. Innumerable buildings, crowded in close and crooked streets, supplied perpetual fuel for the flames; and when they ceased, four only of the fourteen regions were left entire; three were totally destroyed, and seven were deformed by the relics of smoking and lacerated edifices. In the full meridian of empire the metropolis arose with fresh beauty from her ashes; yet the memory of the old deplored their irreparable losses, the arts of Greece, the trophies of victory, the monuments of primitive or fabulous antiquity. In the days of distress and anarchy every wound is mortal, every fall irretrievable; nor can the damage be restored either by the public care of government, or the activity of private interest. Yet two causes may be alleged which render the calamity of fire more destructive to a flourishing than a decayed city. 1. The more combustible materials of brick, timber, and metals, are first melted or consumed; but the flames may play without injury or effect on the naked walls and massy arches that have been despoiled of their ornaments. 2. It is among the common and plebeian habitations that a mischievous spark is most easily blown to a conflagration; but as soon as they are devoured, the greater edifices which have resisted or escaped are left as so many islands in a state of solitude and safety. From her situation, Rome is exposed to the danger of frequent inundations. Without excepting the Tiber, the rivers that descend from either side of the Apennine have a short and irregular course; a shallow stream in the summer heats; an impetuous torrent when it is swelled in the spring or winter, by the fall of rain and the melting of the snows. When the current is repelled from the sea by adverse winds, when the ordinary bed is inadequate to the weight of waters, they rise above the banks, and overspread, without limits or control, the plains and cities of the adjacent country. Soon after the triumph of the first Punic war the Tiber was increased by unusual rains; and the inundation, surpassing all former measure of time and place, destroyed all the buildings that were situate below the hills of Rome. According to the variety of ground, the same mischief was produced by different means; and the edifices were either swept away by the sudden impulse, or dissolved and undermined by the long continuance, of the flood. Under the reign of Augustus the same calamity was renewed: the lawless river overturned the palaces and temples on its banks; and, after the labours of the emperor in cleansing and widening the bed that was encumbered with ruins, the vigilance of his successors was exercised by similar dangers and designs. The project of diverting into new channels the Tiber itself, or some of the dependent streams, was long opposed by superstition and local interests; nor did the use compensate the toil and cost of the tardy and imperfect execution. The servitude of rivers is the noblest and most important victory which man has obtained over the licentiousness of nature; and if such were the ravages of the Tiber under a firm and active government, what could oppose, or who can enumerate, the injuries of the city after the fall of the Western empire? A remedy was at length produced by the evil itself: the accumulation of rubbish and the earth that has been washed down from the hills is supposed to have elevated the plain of Rome fourteen or fifteen feet, perhaps, above the ancient level; and the modern city is less accessible to the attacks of the river.

II. The crowd of writers of every nation, who impute the destruction of the Roman monuments to the Goths and the Christians, have neglected to inquire how far they were animated by an hostile principle, and how far they possessed the means and the leisure to satiate their enmity. In the preceding volumes of this History I have described the triumph of barbarism and religion; and I can only resume, in a few words, their real or imaginary connection with the ruin of ancient Rome. Our fancy may create, or adopt, a pleasing romance, that the Goths and Vandals sallied from Scandinavia, ardent to avenge the flight of Odin; [1] to break the chains, and to chastise the oppressors, of mankind; that they wished to burn the records of classic literature, and to found their national architecture on the broken members of the Tuscan and Corinthian orders. But in simple truth, the northern conquerors were neither sufficiently savage, nor sufficiently refined, to entertain such aspiring ideas of destruction and revenge. The shepherds of Scythia and Germany had been educated in the armies of the empire, whose discipline they acquired, and whose weakness they invaded: with the familiar use of the Latin tongue they had learned to reverence the name and titles of Rome; and, though incapable of emulating, they were more inclined to admire than to abolish the arts and studies of a brighter period. In the transient possession of a rich and unresisting capital, the soldiers of Alaric and Genseric were stimulated by the passions of a victorious army; amidst the wanton indulgence of lust or cruelty, portable wealth was the object of their search: nor could they derive either pride or pleasure from the unprofitable reflection that they had battered to the ground the works of the consuls and Cæsars. Their moments were indeed precious: the Goths evacuated Rome on the sixth, the Vandals on the fifteenth day; and, though it be far more difficult to build than to destroy, their hasty

[1] I take this opportunity of declaring that, in the course of twelve years, I have forgotten, or renounced, the flight of Odin from Azoph to Sweden, which I never very seriously believed. The Goths are apparently Germans; but all beyond Cæsar and Tacitus is darkness or fable in the antiquities of Germany.

assault would have made a slight impression on the solid piles of antiquity. We may remember that both Alaric and Genseric affected to spare the buildings of the city; that they subsisted in strength and beauty under the auspicious government of Theodoric; and that the momentary resentment of Totila was disarmed by his own temper and the advice of his friends and enemies. From these innocent barbarians the reproach may be transferred to the Catholics of Rome. The statues, altars, and houses of the dæmons were an abomination in their eyes; and in the absolute command of the city, they might labour with zeal and perseverance to erase the idolatry of their ancestors. The demolition of the temples in the East affords to *them* an example of conduct, and to us an argument of belief; and it is probable that a portion of guilt or merit may be imputed with justice to the Roman proselytes. Yet their abhorrence was confined to the monuments of heathen superstition; and the civil structures that were dedicated to the business or pleasure of society might be preserved without injury or scandal. The change of religion was accomplished, not by a popular tumult, but by the decrees of the emperors, of the senate, and of time. Of the Christian hierarchy, the bishops of Rome were commonly the most prudent and least fanatic; nor can any positive charge be opposed to the meritorious act of saving and converting the majestic structure of the Pantheon.

III. The value of any object that supplies the wants or pleasures of mankind is compounded of its substance and its form, of the materials and the manufacture. Its price must depend on the number of persons by whom it may be acquired and used; on the extent of the market; and consequently on the ease or difficulty of remote exportation, according to the nature of the commodity, its local situation, and the temporary circumstances of the world. The barbarian conquerors of Rome usurped in a moment the toil and treasure of successive ages; but, except the luxuries of immediate consumption, they must view without desire all that could not be removed from the city in the Gothic waggons or the fleet of the Vandals. Gold and silver were the first objects of their avarice; as in every country, and in the smallest compass, they represent the most ample command of the industry and possessions of mankind. A vase or a statue of those precious metals might tempt the vanity of some barbarian chief; but the grosser multitude, regardless of the form, was tenacious only of the substance; and the melted ingots might be readily divided and stamped into the current coin of the empire. The less active or less fortunate robbers were reduced to the baser plunder of brass, lead, iron, and copper: whatever had escaped the Goths and Vandals was pillaged by the Greek tyrants; and the emperor Constans, in his rapacious visit, stripped the bronze tiles from the roof of the Pantheon. The edifices of Rome might be considered as a vast and various mine: the first labour of extracting the materials was already performed; the metals were purified and cast; the marbles were hewn and polished; and after foreign and domestic rapine had been satiated, the remains of the city, could a purchaser have been found, were still venal. The monuments of antiquity had been left naked of their precious ornaments; but the Romans would demolish with their own hands the arches and walls, if the hope of profit could surpass the cost of the labour and exportation. If Charlemagne had fixed in Italy the seat of the Western empire, his genius would have aspired to restore, rather than to violate, the works of the Cæsars; but policy confined the French monarch to the forests of Germany; his taste could be gratified only by destruction; and the new palace of Aix la Chapelle was decorated with the marbles of Ravenna and Rome. Five hundred years after Charlemagne, a king of Sicily, Robert, the wisest and most liberal sovereign of the age, was supplied with the same materials by the easy navigation of the Tiber and the sea; and Petrarch sighs an indignant complaint, that the ancient capital of the world should adorn from her own bowels the slothful luxury of Naples. But these examples of plunder or purchase were rare in the darker ages; and the Romans, alone and unenvied, might have applied to their private or public use the remaining structures of antiquity, if in their present form and situation they had not been useless in a great measure to the city and its inhabitants. The walls still described the old circumference, but the city had descended from the seven hills into the Campus Martius; and some of the noblest monuments which had braved the injuries of time were left in a desert far remote from the habitations of mankind. The palaces of the senators were no longer adapted to the manners or fortunes of their indigent successors: the use of baths and porticoes was forgotten: in the sixth century the games of the theatre, amphitheatre, and circus had been interrupted: some temples were devoted to the prevailing worship; but the Christian churches preferred the holy figure of the cross; and fashion, or reason, had distributed after a peculiar model the cells and offices of the cloister. Under the ecclesiastical reign the number of these pious foundations was enormously multiplied; and the city was crowded with forty monasteries of men, twenty of women, and sixty chapters and colleges of canons and priests, who aggravated, instead of relieving, the depopulation of the tenth century. But if the forms of ancient architecture were disregarded by a people insensible of their use and beauty, the plentiful materials were applied to every call of necessity or super otition; till the fairest columns of the Ionic and Corinthian orders, the richest marbles of Paros and Numidia, were degraded, perhaps to the support of a convent or a stable. The daily havoc which is perpetrated by the Turks in the cities of Greece and Asia may afford a melancholy example; and in the gradual destruction of the monuments of Rome, Sixtus the Fifth may alone be excused for employing the stones of the Septizonium in the glorious edifice of St. Peter's. A fragment, a ruin, howsoever mangled or profaned, may be viewed with pleasure and regret; but the greater part of the marble was deprived of substance, as well as of place and proportion; it was burnt to lime for the purpose of cement. Since the arrival of Poggius the temple of Concord and many capital structures had vanished from his eyes; and an epigram of the same age expresses a just and pious fear that the continuance of this practice would finally annihilate all the monuments of antiquity. The smallness of their numbers was the sole check on the demands and depredations of the Romans. The imagination of Petrarch might create the presence of a mighty people; and I hesitate to believe that, even in the fourteenth century, they could be reduced to a contemptible list of thirty-three thousand inhabitants. From that period to the reign of Leo the Tenth, if they multiplied to the amount of eighty-five thousand, the increase of citizens was in some degree pernicious to the ancient city.

IV. I have reserved for the last the most potent and forcible cause of destruction, the domestic hostilities of the Romans themselves. Under the dominion of the Greek and French emperors the peace of the city was disturbed by accidental, though frequent, seditions: it is from the decline of the latter, from the beginning of the tenth century, that we may date the licentiousness of private war, which violated with impunity the laws of the Code and the Gospel, without respecting the majesty of the absent sovereign, or the presence and person of the vicar of Christ. In a dark period of five hundred years Rome was perpetually afflicted by the sanguinary quarrels of the nobles and the people, the Guelphs and Ghibelines, the Colonna and Ursini; and if much has escaped the knowledge, and much is unworthy of the notice, of history, I have exposed in the two preceding chapters the causes and effects of the public disorders. At such a time, when every quarrel was decided by the sword, and none could trust their lives or properties to the impotence of law, the powerful citizens were armed for safety, or offence, against the domestic enemies whom they feared or hated. Except Venice alone, the same dangers and designs were common to all the free republics of Italy; and the nobles usurped the prerogative of fortifying their houses, and erecting strong towers that were capable of resisting a sudden attack. The cities were filled with these hostile edifices; and the example of Lucca, which contained three hundred towers; her law, which confined their height to the measure of fourscore feet, may be extended with suitable latitude to the more opulent and populous states. The first step of the senator Brancaleone in the establishment of peace and justice was to demolish (as we have already seen) one hundred and forty of the towers of Rome; and, in the last days of anarchy and discord, as late as the reign of Martin the Fifth, forty-four still stood in one of the thirteen or fourteen regions of the city. To this mischievous purpose the remains of antiquity were most readily adapted: the temples and arches afforded a broad and solid basis for the new structures of

brick and stone; and we can name the modern turrets that were raised
on the triumphal monuments of Julius Cæsar, Titus, and the Antonines.
With some slight alterations, a theatre, an amphitheatre, a mausoleum,
was transformed into a strong and spacious citadel. I need not repeat
that the mole of Hadrian has assumed the title and form of the castle of
St. Angelo; the Septizonium of Severus was capable of standing against
a royal army; the sepulchre of Metella has sunk under its outworks; the
theatres of Pompey and Marcellus were occupied by the Savelli and
Ursini families; and the rough fortress has been gradually softened to
the splendour and elegance of an Italian palace. Even the churches
were encompassed with arms and bulwarks, and the military engines
on the roof of St. Peter's were the terror of the Vatican and the scandal
of the Christian world. Whatever is fortified will be attacked; and whatever is attacked may be destroyed. Could the Romans have wrested
from the popes the castle of St. Angelo, they had resolved by a public
decree to annihilate that monument of servitude. Every building of
defence was exposed to a siege; and in every siege the arts and engines
of destruction were laboriously employed. After the death of Nicholas
the Fourth, Rome, without a sovereign or a senate, was abandoned six
months to the fury of civil war. "The houses," says a cardinal and poet
of the times, were crushed by the weight and velocity of enormous
stones; the walls were perforated by the strokes of the battering-ram;
the towers were involved in fire and smoke; and the assailants were
stimulated by rapine and revenge." The work was consummated by
the tyranny of the laws; and the factions of Italy alternately exercised a
blind and thoughtless vengeance on their adversaries, whose houses and
castles they razed to the ground. In comparing the *days* of foreign with
the *ages* of domestic hostility, we must pronounce that the latter have
been far more ruinous to the city; and our opinion is confirmed by the
evidence of Petrarch. "Behold," says the laureat, "the relics of Rome,
the image of her pristine greatness! neither time nor the barbarian can
boast the merit of this stupendous destruction: it was perpetrated by her
own citizens, by the most illustrious of her sons; and your ancestors (he
writes to a noble Annibaldi) have done with the battering-ram what the
Punic hero could not accomplish with the sword." The influence of the
two last principles of decay must in some degree be multiplied by each
other; since the houses and towers which were subverted by civil war
required a new and perpetual supply from the monuments of antiquity.

THE COLISEUM

These general observations may be separately applied to the amphitheatre of Titus, which has obtained the name of the COLISEUM, either
from its magnitude, or from Nero's colossal statue: an edifice, had it
been left to time and nature, which might perhaps have claimed an
eternal duration. The curious antiquaries, who have computed the

numbers and seats, are disposed to believe that above the upper row of
stone steps the amphitheatre was encircled and elevated with several
stages of wooden galleries, which were repeatedly consumed by fire, and
restored by the emperors. Whatever was precious, or portable, or profane, the statues of gods and heroes, and the costly ornaments of sculpture, which were cast in brass, or overspread with leaves of silver and
gold, became the first prey of conquest or fanaticism, of the avarice of
the barbarians or the Christians. In the massy stones of the Coliseum
many holes are discerned; and the two most probable conjectures represent the various accidents of its decay. These stones were connected
by solid links of brass or iron, nor had the eye of rapine overlooked the
value of the baser metals; the vacant space was converted into a fair or
market; the artisans of the Coliseum are mentioned in an ancient survey;
and the chasms were perforated or enlarged to receive the poles that
supported the shops or tents of the mechanic trades. Reduced to its
naked majesty, the Flavian amphitheatre was contemplated with awe
and admiration by the pilgrims of the North; and their rude enthusiasm
broke forth in a sublime proverbial expression, which is recorded in the
eighth century, in the fragments of the venerable Bede: "As long as the
Coliseum stands, Rome shall stand; when the Coliseum falls, Rome will
fall; when Rome falls, the world will fall." In the modern system of
war, a situation commanded by three hills would not be chosen for a
fortress; but the strength of the walls and arches could resist the engines
of assault; a numerous garrison might be lodged in the enclosure; and
while one faction occupied the Vatican and the Capitol, the other was
entrenched in the Lateran and the Coliseum.

The abolition at Rome of the ancient games must be understood with
some latitude; and the carnival sports, of the Testacean mount and the
Circus Agonalis, were regulated by the law or custom of the city. The
senator presided with dignity and pomp to adjudge and distribute the
prizes, the gold ring, or the *pallium*, as it was styled, of cloth or silk. A
tribute on the Jews supplied the annual expense; and the races, on foot,
on horseback, or in chariots, were ennobled by a tilt and tournament of
seventy-two of the Roman youth. In the year one thousand three
hundred and thirty-two, a bull-feast, after the fashion of the Moors and
Spaniards, was celebrated in the Coliseum itself; and the living manners
are painted in a diary of the times. A convenient order of benches was
restored; and a general proclamation, as far as Rimini and Ravenna,
invited the nobles to exercise their skill and courage in this perilous
adventure. The Roman ladies were marshalled in three squadrons, and
seated in three balconies, which on this day, the third of September,
were lined with scarlet cloth. The fair Jacova di Rovere led the matrons
from beyond the Tiber, a pure and native race, who still represent the
features and character of antiquity. The remainder of the city was
divided as usual between the Colonna and Ursini: the two factions were

proud of the number and beauty of their female bands: the charms of
Savella Ursini are mentioned with praise; and the Colonna regretted
the absence of the youngest of their house, who had sprained her ankle
in the garden of Nero's tower. The lots of the champions were drawn
by an old and respectable citizen; and they descended into the arena,
or pit, to encounter the wild bulls, on foot as it should seem, with a
single spear. Amidst the crowd, our annalist has selected the names,
colours, and devices of twenty of the most conspicuous knights. Several
of the names are the most illustrious of Rome and the ecclesiastical
state: Malatesta, Polenta, della Valle, Cafarello, Savelli, Capoccio,
Conti, Annibaldi, Altieri, Corsi: the colours were adapted to their taste
and situation; the devices are expressive of hope or despair, and breathe
the spirit of gallantry and arms. "I am alone, like the youngest of the
Horatii," the confidence of an intrepid stranger: "I live disconsolate," a
weeping widower: "I burn under the ashes," a discreet lover: "I adore
Lavinia, or Lucretia," the ambiguous declaration of a modern passion:
"My faith is as pure," the motto of a white livery: "Who is stronger
than myself?" of a lion's hide: "If I am drowned in blood, what a
pleasant death!" the wish of ferocious courage. The pride or prudence
of the Ursini restrained them from the field, which was occupied by
three of their hereditary rivals, whose inscriptions denoted the lofty
greatness of the Colonna name: "Though sad, I am strong:" "Strong
as I am great:" "If I fall," addressing himself to the spectators, "you
fall with me:" intimating (says the contemporary writer) that, while
the other families were the subjects of the Vatican, they alone were the
supporters of the Capitol. The combats of the amphitheatre were
dangerous and bloody. Every champion successively encountered a
wild bull; and the victory may be ascribed to the quadrupeds, since no
more than eleven were left on the field, with the loss of nine wounded
and eighteen killed on the side of their adversaries. Some of the noblest
families might mourn, but the pomp of the funerals, in the churches of
St. John Lateran and Sta. Maria Maggiore, afforded a second holiday
to the people. Doubtless it was not in such conflicts that the blood of
the Romans should have been shed; yet, in blaming their rashness, we
are compelled to applaud their gallantry; and the noble volunteers,
who display their magnificence, and risk their lives, under the balconies
of the fair, excite a more generous sympathy than the thousands of
captives and malefactors who were reluctantly dragged to the scene of
slaughter.

This use of the amphitheatre was a rare, perhaps a singular, festival:
the demand for the materials was a daily and continual want, which
the citizens could gratify without restraint or remorse. In the fourteenth
century a scandalous act of concord secured to both factions the privilege of extracting stones from the free and common quarry of the
Coliseum; and Poggius laments that the greater part of these stones had

been burnt to lime by the folly of the Romans. To check this abuse, and to prevent the nocturnal crimes that might be perpetrated in the vast and gloomy recess, Eugenius the Fourth surrounded it with a wall; and, by a charter, long extant, granted both the ground and edifice to the monks of an adjacent convent. After his death the wall was overthrown in a tumult of the people; and had they themselves respected the noblest monument of their fathers, they might have justified the resolve that it should never be degraded to private property. The inside was damaged: but in the middle of the sixteenth century, an era of taste and learning, the exterior circumference of one thousand six hundred and twelve feet was still entire and inviolate; a triple elevation of fourscore arches, which rose to the height of one hundred and eight feet. Of the present ruin the nephews of Paul the Third are the guilty agents; and every traveller who views the Farnese palace may curse the sacrilege and luxury of these upstart princes. A similar reproach is applied to the Barberini; and the repetition of injury might be dreaded from every reign, till the Coliseum was placed under the safeguard of religion by the most liberal of the pontiffs, Benedict the Fourteenth, who consecrated a spot which persecution and fable had stained with the blood of so many Christian martyrs.

RESTORATION OF THE CITY

When Petrarch first gratified his eyes with a view of those monuments whose scattered fragments so far surpass the most eloquent descriptions, he was astonished at the supine indifference of the Romans themselves; he was humbled rather than elated by the discovery that, except his friend Rienzi, and one of the Colonna, a stranger of the Rhône was more conversant with these antiquities than the nobles and natives of the metropolis. The ignorance and credulity of the Romans are elaborately displayed in the old survey of the city which was composed about the beginning of the thirteenth century; and, without dwelling on the manifold errors of name and place, the legend of the Capitol may provoke a smile of contempt and indignation. "The Capitol," says the anonymous writer, "is so named as being the head of the world; where the consuls and senators formerly resided for the government of the city and the globe. The strong and lofty walls were covered with glass and gold, and crowned with a roof of the richest and most curious carving. Below the citadel stood a palace, of gold for the greatest part, decorated with precious stones, and whose value might be esteemed at one third of the world itself. The statues of all the provinces were arranged in order; each with a small bell suspended from its neck; and such was the contrivance of art magic, that, if the province rebelled against Rome, the statue turned round to that quarter of the heavens, the bell rang, the prophet of the Capitol reported the prodigy, and the senate was admonished of the impending danger." A second example, of less importance, though of equal absurdity, may be drawn from the two marble horses, led by two naked youths, which have since been transported from the baths of Constantine to the Quirinal hill. The groundless application of the names of Phidias and Praxiteles may perhaps be excused; but these Grecian sculptors should not have been removed above four hundred years from the age of Pericles to that of Tiberius; they should not have been transformed into two philosophers or magicians, whose nakedness was the symbol of truth and knowledge, who revealed to the emperor his most secret actions; and, after refusing all pecuniary recompense, solicited the honour of leaving this eternal monument of themselves. Thus awake to the power of magic, the Romans were insensible to the beauties of art: no more than five statues were visible to the eyes of Poggius; and of the multitudes which chance or design had buried under the ruins, the resurrection was fortunately delayed till a safer and more enlightened age. The Nile, which now adorns the Vatican, had been explored by some labourers, in digging a vineyard near the temple, or convent, of the Minerva; but the impatient proprietor, who was tormented by some visits of curiosity, restored the unprofitable marble to its former grave. The discovery of a statue of Pompey, ten feet in length, was the occasion of a lawsuit. It had been found under a partition wall: the equitable judge had pronounced that the head should be separated from the body to satisfy the claims of the contiguous owners; and the sentence would have been executed if the intercession of a cardinal, and the liberality of a pope, had not rescued the Roman hero from the hands of his barbarous countrymen.

But the clouds of barbarism were gradually dispelled; and the peaceful authority of Martin the Fifth and his successors restored the ornaments of the city as well as the order of the ecclesiastical state. The improvements of Rome, since the fifteenth century, have not been the spontaneous produce of freedom and industry. The first and most natural root of a great city is the labour and populousness of the adjacent country, which supplies the materials of subsistence, of manufactures, and of foreign trade. But the greater part of the Campagna of Rome is reduced to a dreary and desolate wilderness: the overgrown estates of the princes and the clergy are cultivated by the lazy hands of indigent and hopeless vassals; and the scanty harvests are confined or exported for the benefit of a monopoly. A second and more artificial cause of the growth of a metropolis is the residence of a monarch, the expense of a luxurious court, and the tributes of dependent provinces. Those provinces and tributes had been lost in the fall of the empire; and if some streams of the silver of Peru and the gold of Brazil have been attracted by the Vatican, the revenues of the cardinals, the fees of office, the oblations of pilgrims and clients, and the remnant of ecclesiastical taxes, afford a poor and precarious supply, which maintains, however,

the idleness of the court and city. The population of Rome, far below
the measure of the great capitals of Europe, does not exceed one hundred
and seventy thousand inhabitants; and within the spacious enclosure
of the walls, the largest portion of the seven hills is overspread with
vineyards and ruins. The beauty and splendour of the modern city may
be ascribed to the abuses of the government, to the influence of superstition. Each reign (the exceptions are rare) has been marked by the
rapid elevation of a new family, enriched by the childless pontiff at the
expense of the church and country. The palaces of these fortunate
nephews are the most costly monuments of elegance and servitude: the
perfect arts of architecture, painting, and sculpture, have been prostituted in their service; and their galleries and gardens are decorated with
the most precious works of antiquity, which taste or vanity has
prompted them to collect. The ecclesiastical revenues were more decently employed by the popes themselves in the pomp of the Catholic
worship; but it is superfluous to enumerate their pious foundations of
altars, chapels, and churches, since these lesser stars are eclipsed by the
sun of the Vatican, by the dome of St. Peter, the most glorious structure
that ever has been applied to the use of religion. The fame of Julius
the Second, Leo the Tenth, and Sixtus the Fifth, is accompanied by the
superior merit of Bramante and Fontana, of Raphael and Michael
Angelo; and the same munificence which had been displayed in palaces
and temples was directed with equal zeal to revive and emulate the labours of antiquity. Prostrate obelisks were raised from the ground, and
erected in the most conspicuous places; of the eleven aqueducts of the
Cæsars and consuls, three were restored; the artificial rivers were conducted over a long series of old or of new arches, to discharge into
marble basins a flood of salubrious and refreshing waters: and the
spectator, impatient to ascend the steps of St. Peter's, is detained by a
column of Egyptian granite, which rises between two lofty and perpetual
fountains to the height of one hundred and twenty feet. The map, the
description, the monuments of ancient Rome, have been elucidated by
the diligence of the antiquarian and the student; and the footsteps of
heroes, the relics, not of superstition, but of empire, are devoutly visited
by a new race of pilgrims from the remote and once savage countries of
the North.

FINAL REFLECTIONS ON THE DECLINE AND FALL OF THE ROMAN EMPIRE

Of these pilgrims, and of every reader, the attention will be excited by
an History of the Decline and Fall of the Roman Empire; the greatest,
perhaps, and most awful scene in the history of mankind. The various
causes and progressive effects are connected with many of the events
most interesting in human annals: the artful policy of the Cæsars, who
long maintained the name and image of a free republic; the disorders of

military despotism; the rise, establishment, and sects of Christianity; the foundation of Constantinople; the division of the monarchy; the invasion and settlements of the barbarians of Germany and Scythia; the institutions of the civil law; the character and religion of Mahomet; the temporal sovereignty of the popes; the restoration and decay of the Western empire of Charlemagne; the crusades of the Latins in the East; the conquests of the Saracens and Turks; the ruin of the Greek empire; the state and revolutions of Rome in the middle age. The historian may applaud the importance and variety of his subject; but, while he is conscious of his own imperfections, he must often accuse the deficiency of his materials. It was among the ruins of the Capitol that I first conceived the idea of a work which has amused and exercised near twenty years of my life, and which, however inadequate to my own wishes, I finally deliver to the curiosity and candour of the public.

LAUSANNE,
June 27, 1787

Bibliographical Note

The Decline and Fall was originally published in 6 volumes quarto. The first appeared in 1776, the second and third in 1783, and the last three in 1788. An edition in 12 volumes octavo appeared during the author's lifetime. Allowing for some obvious errors, the text presented may be taken to be what Gibbon wrote with his own typographical arrangements of capitals, italics, etc., and with his very individual spelling.

Of the numerous later editions the most pre-eminent for scholarship is that of J. B. Bury in 7 volumes, which appeared in various issues from 1896 onwards; the best of these is the illustrated one (1900 14). Dr. William Smith's edition of Dean Milman's edition (1853–54) can still be consulted with profit, and is in several ways easier to use than Bury's.

It is no part of a work such as this to compile a bibliography. The reader who desires to study the Roman Empire in the light of modern research can be referred to the relevant volumes of the *Cambridge Ancient History* and the *Cambridge Medieval History*, in all of which also full bibliographies are to be found. The following works, some of which have appeared since the histories mentioned above, will be found useful. Most of them also contain bibliographies.

A. Stuart Jones, *The Roman Empire 29 B.C.–A.D. 476* (1908). (This is still one of the best short accounts of the period.)

Methuen's History of the Roman World. Vol. VI, by R. P. Longden. Vol. VII, by H. M. D. Parker.

A. A. Vasiliev, *History of the Byzantine Empire A.D. 324–1453* (1952).

N. H. Baynes, *The Byzantine Empire* (1925).

N. H. Baynes and H. St. L. B. Moss, *Byzantium* (1948).

Christopher Dawson, *The Making of Europe* (1932).

H. Mattingly, *Roman Imperial Civilisation* (1957).

Steven Runciman, *Byzantine Civilisation* (1935).

Steven Runciman, *A History of the Crusades* (1951–54).

J. B. Bury, *The Invasion of Europe by the Barbarians* (1928).

E. A. Thompson, *A History of Attila and the Huns* (1948).

F. W. Walbank, *The Decline of the Roman Empire in the West* (1946).

A Chronological List of the Roman Emperors

The English forms of names are given where they are in general use

I. FROM AUGUSTUS TO THE FALL OF THE EMPIRE IN THE WEST

B.C. A.D.

27–14	AUGUSTUS
14–37	TIBERIUS
37–41	GAIUS (CALIGULA)
41–54	CLAUDIUS
54–68	NERO
68–69	GALBA
69	OTHO
69	VITELLIUS
69–79	VESPASIAN
79–81	TITUS
81–96	DOMITIAN
96–98	NERVA
98–117	TRAJAN
117–138	HADRIAN
138–161	ANTONINUS PIUS
161–180	MARCUS AURELIUS with LUCIUS VERUS 161–169 and COMMODUS from 177
180–192	COMMODUS
193	PERTINAX followed by DIDIUS JULIANUS
193–211	SEPTIMIUS SEVERUS with CARACALLA from 198 and GETA from 209
211–217	ANTONINUS (CARACALLA) with GETA (211–212)
217–218	MACRINUS with DIADUMENIANUS in 218
218–222	ANTONINUS (ELAGABALUS)
222–235	SEVERUS ALEXANDER
233–238	MAXIMINUS THRAX
238	GORDIAN I, GORDIAN II, PUPIENUS (MAXIMUS) and BALBINUS
238–244	GORDIAN III
244–249	PHILIP THE ARAB with his son PHILIP 247–249
249–251	DECIUS
251–253	TREBONIANUS GALLUS and VOLUSIANUS
253–260	VALERIAN with GALLIENUS

A.D.

260–268	GALLIENUS
268–270	CLAUDIUS II GOTHICUS
270–275	AURELIAN
275–276	TACITUS (and FLORIANUS 276)
276–282	PROBUS
282–283	CARUS
283–284	CARINUS and NUMERIAN
284–305	DIOCLETIAN ⎫
286–305	MAXIMIAN ⎬ Both abdicated in 305

305–311   GALERIUS, associated with him over various periods CONSTANTIUS I CHLORUS, SEVERUS II, LICINIUS, CONSTANTINE I, and MAXIMINUS DAZA. In 309 there were six Augusti

311–324	CONSTANTINE I and LICINIUS
324–337	CONSTANTINE I
337–340	CONSTANTINE II, CONSTANTIUS II, and CONSTANS
340–350	CONSTANTIUS II and CONSTANS
350–361	CONSTANTIUS II
361–363	JULIAN
363–364	JOVIAN
364–375	VALENTINIAN I and VALENS with GRATIAN from 367
375–378	VALENS, GRATIAN and VALENTINIAN II

378–395   THEODOSIUS I (the Great) reigned with GRATIAN and VALENTINIAN II from 378 to 383, with VALENTINIAN II and ARCADIUS 383 to 392, and with ARCADIUS and HONORIUS 392 until his death in 395

395   Partition of the Roman Empire between the West and the East. The following Emperors from HONORIUS to ROMULUS AUGUSTULUS reigned in the West only

395–423	HONORIUS
425–455	VALENTINIAN III
455	PETRONIUS MAXIMUS
455–456	AVITUS
457–461	MAJORIAN
461–465	LIBIUS SEVERUS
467–472	ANTHEMIUS
472	OLYBRIUS
473–474	GLYCERIUS
474–475	JULIUS NEPOS
475–476	ROMULUS AUGUSTULUS (deposed)

END OF THE ROMAN EMPIRE IN THE WEST

II. THE ROMAN EMPERORS IN THE EAST FROM THE PARTITION OF THE EMPIRE UNTIL THE FINAL FALL OF CONSTANTINOPLE

A.D.

DYNASTY OF THEODOSIUS

395–408   ARCADIUS
408–450   THEODOSIUS II
450–457   MARCIAN (m. PULCHERIA, daughter of THEODOSIUS I)

DYNASTY OF LEO

457–474   LEO I
474   LEO II
474–491   ZENO
491–518   ANASTASIUS

DYNASTY OF JUSTINIAN

518–527   JUSTIN I
527–565   JUSTINIAN I
565–578   JUSTIN II
578–582   TIBERIUS II
582–602   MAURICE
602–610   PHOCAS

DYNASTY OF HERACLIUS

610–641   HERACLIUS
641–668   CONSTANS II
668 685   CONSTANTINE IV
685–695   JUSTINIAN II (banished)
695–698   LEONTIUS
698–705   TIBERIUS III
705–711   JUSTINIAN II (restored)
711–713   BARDANES
713–716   ANASTASIUS II
716–717   THEODOSIUS III

These three Emperors belong to no dynasty and obtained brief power in a disturbed period.

ISAURIAN DYNASTY (THE ICONOCLASTS)

717–741   LEO III
741–775   CONSTANTINE V COPRONYMUS
775–780   LEO IV
780–797   CONSTANTINE VI (blinded and murdered by his mother IRENE)
797–802   IRENE

A.D.

END OF THE ISAURIAN DYNASTY

802–811	NICEPHORUS I
811	STRAURACIUS
811–813	MICHAEL I
813–820	LEO V

PHRYGIAN DYNASTY

820–829	MICHAEL II
829–842	THEOPHILUS
842–867	MICHAEL III

MACEDONIAN DYNASTY

867–886	BASIL I
886–912 and 913	LEO VI and ALEXANDER
912–959	CONSTANTINE VII PORPHYROGENITUS
919–944	ROMANUS I LECAPENUS (co-emperor with CONSTANTINE VII until 944. His son CONSTANTINE (VIII) attempted usurpation in 924)
959–963	ROMANUS II
963	Regency of THEOPHANO widow of ROMANUS II for her infant sons BASIL II and CONSTANTINE VIII (IX). THEOPHANO married NICEPHORUS PHOCAS, who reigned as
963–969	NICEPHORUS II and was murdered by
969–976	JOHN I ZIMISKES
1025	Death of BASIL II BULGAROCTONUS
1028	Death of CONSTANTINE VIII (IX)
1028–1034	ROMANUS III ARGYRUS
1034–1041	MICHAEL IV THE PAPHLAGONIAN
1041–1042	MICHAEL V CALAPHATES
1042	ZOE and THEODORA, joint Empresses
	ZOE married and conferred the diadem on
1042–1055	CONSTANTINE IX (X) MONOMACHUS
1050	Death of ZOE
1055–1056	THEODORA, sole Empress
1056–1057	MICHAEL VI STRATIOTICUS

END OF THE MACEDONIAN DYNASTY

PRELUDE TO THE COMNENIAN DYNASTY

1057–1059	ISAAC I COMNENUS (abdicated)
1059–1067	CONSTANTINE X (XI) DUCAS
1067–1071	ROMANUS IV DIOGENES (CONSTANTINE (XII) 1071)
1071–1078	MICHAEL VII DUCAS
1078–1081	NICEPHORUS III BOTANIATES (revolt of NICEPHORUS BRYENNIUS)

A.D.
DYNASTY OF THE COMNENI
1081–1118 ALEXIUS I COMNENUS
1118–1143 JOHN II CALOJOHANNES
1143–1180 MANUEL I
1180–1183 ALEXIUS II
1183–1185 ANDRONICUS I

DYNASTY OF THE ANGELI
1185–1195 ISAAC II (dethroned)
1195–1203 ALEXIUS III
1203–1204 ISAAC II (restored) with ALEXIUS IV
1204 ALEXIUS V DUCAS MURTZUPHIUS
1204 Capture of Constantinople by the Fourth Crusade, and establishment of Latin Emperors in the City

EASTERN ROMAN EMPERORS IN NICÆA
1204–1222 THEODORUS I LASCARIS
1222–1254 JOHN III DUCAS VATATZES
1254–1258 THEODORUS II LASCARIS
1258–1261 JOHN IV LASCARIS
1259–1282 MICHAEL VIII PALÆOLOGUS
1261 Recapture of Constantinople and re-establishment of the Eastern Emperors there

DYNASTY OF THE PALÆOLOGI
1261–1282 MICHAEL VIII PALÆOLOGUS
1282–1328 ANDRONICUS II
(1293–1320) MICHAEL IX
Period of anarchy followed by
1328–1341 ANDRONICUS III
1341–1376 JOHN V CANTACUZENUS
1341–1354 JOHN VI
1376–1379 ANDRONICUS IV
1379–1391 JOHN V (restored)
1390 JOHN VII
1391–1425 MANUEL II
1425–1448 JOHN VIII
1449–1453 CONSTANTINE XI (XIII) DRAGASES
1453 Capture of Constantinople by MAHOMET II and end of the Roman Empire

Note. The enumeration of the Constantines in this list follows modern usage, making the last emperor of that name Constantine XI. The older notation made the rebel son of Romanus I Constantine VIII with a consequent advance in the series for subsequent bearers of the name down to Constantine Ducas (1059–1067). Another transitory claimant to power obtained the title of Constantine XII in 1071, so that the last Constantine was known as the XIIIth.

INDEX

life, 342; vegetable diet, *ib.*; chastity, 343; works, *ib.*; an orator and judge, *ib.*; merits and faults as judge and legislator, 344; character, *ib.*; his religion examined, 346; cause of his apostasy, 347; Christian education, *ib.*; officiates in church, *ib.*; opinion on the Trinity, *ib.*; admiration for Homer and his mythology, 348; embraces paganism, *ib.*; adopts allegorical mythology of Platonists, 349; his theological system, 350; initiated in Eleusinian mysteries, 351; dissembles his religion, 352–3; work against Christianity, 354; edict of universal toleration, 355; recalls Christian exiles, *ib.*; secret motives for tolerating them, *ib.*; becomes Pontifex Maximus, *ib.*; zealous in restoring paganism, 356; his extravagant superstition, *ib.*; directions for reformation of pagan priests, 357; abhorrence of Epicureans and Sceptics, *ib.*; his proselytizing zeal, 358–9; success with soldiery, 359–60; favours Jews, 360 ff.; names the Christians Galilaeans, 365; his unjust prejudices against them, *ib.*; transfers revenues of church to pontiffs, *ib.*; prohibits Christians from teaching schools, *ib.*; excludes them from offices of trust and profit, 366; condemns them to restore pagan temples, 367; his visit to the Apollo of Daphne, 369; shuts cathedral of Antioch, 370; confiscates property of church of Edessa, 372; epistle to Alexandrians, 373; expels Athanasius, 374; his mortal hatred of that prelate, *ib.*; funeral, 384–5; rumours respecting his assassination, 385

JULIAN, cardinal, at council of Florence, 818
JULIANUS, DIDIUS, purchases the empire, 58
JUSTIN the Elder, commander of the guards, seizes empire on death of Anastasius, 545; character and reign, 546; death, 548
JUSTIN MARTYR, his opinion respecting Judaising Christians, 149; exaggerated account of progress of Christianity, 186; his education and conversion, 188
JUSTINA, an Arian, 390; her disputes with St. Ambrose, *ib.* ff.; death, 401
JUSTINIAN, emperor, his Institutes, to whom addressed, 258; birth and education of, 545; his artful ambition, 547; orthodoxy, *ib.*; splendour, *ib.*; invested with diadem, *ib.*; abolishes law prohibiting marriage of a senator with a slave or actress, 551; marriage with Theodora, *ib.*; associates her in the empire, *ib.*; patron of the blue faction, 555; *Nika* sedition, 556–7; extent, agriculture, and manufactures of his dominions, 559 ff.; edifices and architects, 564; founds St. Sophia, 566; churches and palaces, 568; suppresses schools of Athens, 569 ff.; and Roman consulship, 574; rumoured death and consequent riots, 578; conspiracy against, *ib.*; disgraces Belisarius, *ib.*; death and character, 579–80; physical phenomena during his reign, 580 ff.; his religious character and government, 615; affected name of Pius, *ib.*; his persecution, 616; his orthodoxy, 619; heresy, *ib.*; translation of Code and Pandects into Greek, 713; discovery of his corpse by crusaders, 781

LÆTA, widow of Gratian, relieves indigent Romans during the siege of Alaric, 443
LASCARIS, THEODORE, defends Constantinople against Latins, 771
LASCARIS, JANUS, Greek grammarian, 828, 830
LEO III, the Isaurian, his proceedings for the abolition of images, 627; insolent epistles of Gregory II to, 630 ff.; revolt of Italy from, 632
LEO VI, the Philosopher, education and reign of, 715
LEO the Great, bishop of Rome, embassy to Attila, 491; assisted by apparition of St. Peter and St. Paul, 492; calls council of Chalcedon, 609; his epistle on the incarnation subscribed by Oriental bishops, 610; approved by council of Chalcedon, 611
LEO III, pope, attempted assassination of, 643; miraculous restoration of his eyes and tongue, *ib.*; visits Charlemagne, *ib.*; crowns him, *ib.*; his conduct in dispute respecting procession of Holy Ghost, 754